SAS® User's Guide: Statistics, Version 5 Edition

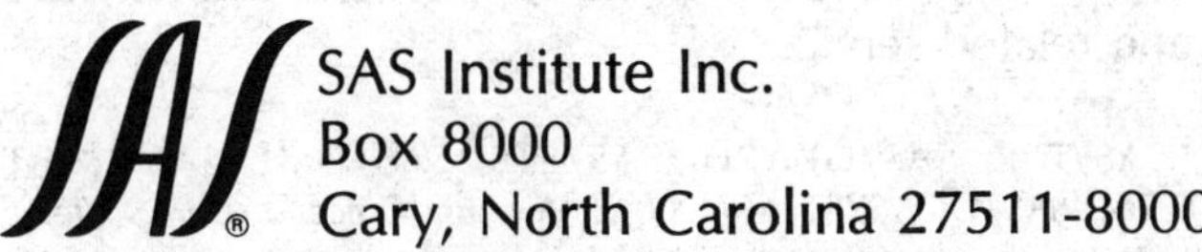

SAS Institute Inc.
Box 8000
Cary, North Carolina 27511-8000

The correct bibliographic citation for this manual is as follows: SAS Institute Inc. *SAS® User's Guide: Statistics, Version 5 Edition*. Cary, NC: SAS Institute Inc., 1985. 956 pp.

SAS® User's Guide: Statistics, Version 5 Edition

ISBN 0-917382-66-8

87 86 5 4 3

Base SAS® software, the foundation of the SAS System, provides data retrieval and management, programming, statistical, and reporting capabilities. Also in the SAS System are SAS/GRAPH,® SAS/FSP,® SAS/ETS,® SAS/IMS-DL/I,® SAS/OR,® SAS/AF,® SAS/DMI,® SAS/QC,® SAS/IML,™ SAS/STAT,™ SAS/SHARE,™ and SAS/DB2™software. These products, SYSTEM 2000® Data Base Management System, including basic SYSTEM 2000,® QueX,™ Multi-User,™ Screen Writer,™ CREATE,™ DISKMGR,™ SAS/RTERM,® SAS/C™ and SAS/CX™ compilers, and CICS interface software, are available from SAS Institute Inc. *SAS Communications,® SAS Training,® SAS Views,®* SASware Ballot® are published by SAS Institute Inc. The Institute is a private company devoted to the support and further development of the software and related services.

Contents

Illustrations

Figures

Screens

Tables

Acknowledgments

Program authorship includes design, programming, debugging, support, and preliminary documentation. The SAS Institute staff member listed first currently has primary responsibility for the procedure; others give specific assistance.

ACECLUS	W.S. Sarle
ANOVA	P.C. Spector, J.H. Goodnight
CANCORR	W.S. Sarle
CANDISC	W.S. Sarle
CATMOD	W.M. Stanish, J.P. Sall
CLUSTER	W.S. Sarle
DISCRIM	W.S. Sarle, J.H. Goodnight
FACTOR	W.S. Sarle
FASTCLUS	W.S. Sarle
FREQ	W.M. Stanish, J.P. Sall
GLM	P.C. Spector, J.H. Goodnight, J.P. Sall, W.S. Sarle
LIFEREG	D.M. DeLong
LIFETEST	D.M. DeLong
NEIGHBOR	W.S. Sarle, J.H. Goodnight
NESTED	L.A. Ihnen
NLIN	L.A. Ihnen, J.H. Goodnight
NPAR1WAY	J.P. Sall
PLAN	L.A. Ihnen
PRINCOMP	W.S. Sarle
PROBIT	D.M. DeLong, J.H. Goodnight
RANK	K.D. Kumar, J.P. Sall
REG	L.A. Ihnen, J.P. Sall
RSQUARE	W.S. Sarle, J.H. Goodnight
RSREG	J.P. Sall
SCORE	J.P. Sall
STANDARD	G.K. Howell
STEPDISC	W.S. Sarle
STEPWISE	P.C. Spector, J.H. Goodnight
TREE	G.K. Howell, W.S. Sarle
TTEST	W.M. Stanish, J.H. Goodnight
VARCLUS	W.S. Sarle
VARCOMP	P.C. Spector, J.H. Goodnight
Probability Routines	D.M. DeLong, J.H. Goodnight
Multiple Comparisons Routines	W.S. Sarle, D.M. DeLong
Multivariate Routines	W.S. Sarle
Other Numerical Routines	W.S. Sarle, D.M. DeLong, J.P. Sall, J.H. Goodnight
Other Library Routines	W.S. Sarle, R.D. Langston, J.P. Sall
Consulting Statisticians	D.M. DeLong, J.H. Goodnight, W.S. Sarle, J.P. Sall, H.J. Kirk, F. W. Young

(If you have questions or encounter problems, call SAS Institute and ask for the Technical Support Department rather than an individual staff member.)

Hundreds of people have helped the SAS System in many ways since its inception. The individuals that we remember here have been especially helpful in the development of statistical procedures. An acknowledgment for the SAS System generally is in *SAS User's Guide: Basics, Version 5 Edition.*

Anthony James Barr	Barr Systems
Wilbert P. Byrd	Clemson University
George Chao	Arnar-Stone Laboratories
Daniel Chilko	West Virginia University
Richard Cooper	USDA
Sandra Donaghy	North Carolina State University
David B. Duncan	Johns Hopkins University
R.J. Freund	Texas A & M University
Wayne Fuller	Iowa State University
A. Ronald Gallant	North Carolina State University
Charles Gates	Texas A & M University
Thomas M. Gerig	North Carolina State University
Francis Giesbrecht	North Carolina State University
Harvey J. Gold	North Carolina State University
Harold Gugel	General Motors Corporation
Donald Guthrie	University of California at Los Angeles
Gerald Hajian	Burroughs Wellcome Company
Frank Harrell	Duke University
Walter Harvey	Ohio State University
Ronald Helms	University of North Carolina at Chapel Hill
Jane T. Helwig	Seasoned Systems Inc., Chapel Hill
Don Henderson	ORI
Harold Huddleston	Data Collection & Analysis, Inc., Falls Church, Virginia
David Hurst	University of Alabama at Birmingham
Emilio A. Icaza	Louisiana State University
William Kennedy	Iowa State University
Gary Koch	University of North Carolina at Chapel Hill
Kenneth Koonce	Louisiana State University
Clyde Y. Kramer (deceased)	Virginia Polytechnic Institute and State University of Kentucky and Upjohn
Ardell C. Linnerud	North Carolina State University
Ramon Littell	University of Florida
H.L. Lucas (deceased)	North Carolina State University
David D. Mason	North Carolina State University
J. Philip Miller	Washington University
Robert J. Monroe	North Carolina State University
Robert D. Morrison	Oklahoma State University
Kenneth Offord	Mayo Clinic
Robert Parks	Washington University
Richard M. Patterson	Auburn University
Virginia Patterson	University of Tennessee
C.H. Proctor	North Carolina State University

Dana Quade	University of North Carolina at Chapel Hill
William L. Sanders	University of Tennessee
Robert Schechter	Scott Paper Company
Shayle Searle	Cornell University
Jolayne Service	University of California at Irvine
Roger Smith	USDA
Michael Speed	formerly of Louisiana State University
Robert Teichman	ICI Americas Inc.
Glenn Ware	University of Georgia
Love Casanova Webb	Santa Fe International
Edward W. Whitehorne	Family Health International
William Wigton	USDA
Forrest W. Young	University of North Carolina at Chapel Hill

The final responsibility for the SAS System lies with SAS Institute alone. We hope that you will always let us know your feelings about the SAS System and its documentation. It is through such communications that the progress of SAS software has been accomplished.

The Staff of SAS Institute Inc.

Preface

This volume, the *SAS User's Guide: Statistics, Version 5 Edition*, contains the primary description of the advanced statistical procedures in base SAS software. The SAS language and base SAS procedures for data processing, summarizing, and reporting are documented in the *SAS User's Guide: Basics, Version 5 Edition*.

As you begin, select a chapter in the OVERVIEW section of the manual that describes the type of statistical analysis you need. This chapter directs you to the specific SAS procedures you can use to perform your analyses. Next, read the appendix "Operating System Notes." This information will help you use your operating system's capabilities to get your data into and out of the SAS System.

To start learning more about writing SAS programs, go to the *SAS User's Guide: Basics* chapter entitled "Introduction to the SAS Language." If you are using OS batch or TSO, you can also refer to the *SAS Introductory Guide*.

The *SAS User's Guide: Statistics* documents a collection of advanced SAS procedures for analyzing statistical data. The statistical procedures in base SAS software are designed for new users and statisticians who want to perform the following types of analysis:

- regression
- analysis of variance
- categorical data
- multivariate
- discriminant
- clustering
- survival.

The procedures documented in this manual are part of the SAS System and behave like other SAS procedures. To begin using the procedures in this manual you need two things:

- a statistical application or an analysis need
- an understanding of the SAS System as documented in the *SAS User's Guide: Basics* and elementary statistics.

The procedure descriptions in the *SAS User's Guide: Statistics* provide references to statistical texts for more detailed treatments of statistical theory and applications.

What is the SAS System?

The SAS System is a software system for data analysis. The goal of SAS Institute is to provide data analysts one system to meet all their computing needs. When your computing needs are met, you are free to concentrate on results rather than on the mechanics of getting them. Instead of learning programming languages, several statistical packages, and utility programs, you only need to learn the SAS System.

To the all-purpose base SAS software, you can add tools for graphics, forecasting, data entry, and interfaces to other data bases to provide one total system. SAS software runs on IBM 370/30xx/43xx and compatible machines in batch and interactively under OS and TSO, CMS, VSE, and SSX; on Digital Equipment Corporation VAX™ 11/7xx series under VMS;™ Data General ECLIPSE® MV series under AOS/VS; Prime Series 50 under PRIMOS;® and IBM PC AT/370 and XT/370 under VM/PC; and on the IBM PC XT and PC AT under PC DOS. Note: not all products are available for all operating systems.

Base SAS software provides tools for:

- information storage and retrieval
- data modification and programming
- report writing
- statistical analysis
- file handling.

Information storage and retrieval The SAS System reads data values in virtually any form from cards, disk, or tape and then organizes the values into a SAS data set. The data can be combined with other SAS data sets using the file-handling operations described below. The data can be analyzed statistically and can be used to produce reports. SAS data sets are automatically self-documenting since they contain both the data values and their descriptions. The special structure of a SAS data library minimizes maintenance.

Data modification and programming A complete set of SAS statements and functions is available for modifying data. Some program statements perform standard operations such as creating new variables, accumulating totals, and checking for errors; others are powerful programming tools such as DO/END and IF-THEN/ELSE statements. The data-handling features are so valuable that base SAS software is used by many as a data base management system.

Report writing Just as base SAS software reads data in almost any form, it can write data in almost any form. In addition to the preformatted reports that SAS procedures produce, SAS software users can design and produce printed reports in any form, as well as punched cards and output files.

Statistical analysis The statistical analysis procedures in the SAS System are among the finest available. They range from simple descriptive statistics to complex multivariate techniques. Their designs are based on our belief that you should never need to tell the SAS System anything it can figure out by itself. Statistical integrity is thus accompanied by ease of use. Especially noteworthy statistical features are the linear model procedures, of which GLM (**G**eneral **L**inear **M**odels) is the flagship.

File handling Combining values and observations from several data sets is often necessary for data analysis. SAS software has tools for editing, subsetting, concatenating, merging, and updating data sets. Multiple input files can be processed simultaneously, and several reports can be produced in one pass of the data.

Other SAS System Products

With base SAS software, you can integrate SAS software products for graphics, data entry, operations research, and interfaces to other data bases to provide one total system:

- SAS/FSP software—interactive, menu-driven facilities for data entry, editing, retrieval of SAS files, letter writing, and spreadsheet analysis

---

- SAS/GRAPH software—device-intelligent color graphics for business and research applications
- SAS/REPLAY-CICS software—interface that allows users of CICS/OS/VS and CICS/DOS/VS to store, manage, and replay SAS/GRAPH displays
- SAS/OR software—decision support tools for operations research and project management
- SAS/AF software—a full-screen, interactive applications facility
- SAS/ETS software—expanded tools for business analysis, forecasting, and financial planning
- SAS/IMS-DL/I software—interface for reading, updating, and writing IMS/VS or CICS DL/I data bases
- SAS/IML software—multi-level, interactive programming language whose data elements are matrices.

SAS Institute Documentation

Using this manual Chapters 1 through 9 of this manual provide an overview and describe the capabilities of the statistical procedures in base SAS software. In planning your analyses, you should refer to these general discussions for examples that may be similar to yours that you can adapt.

Procedure descriptions follow alphabetically in the next chapters. Each procedure description is self-contained; you need to be familiar with only the most basic features of the SAS System and SAS terminology to use most procedures. The statements and syntax necessary to run each procedure are presented in a uniform format throughout the manual.

Each procedure description is divided into the following major parts:

ABSTRACT: a short paragraph describing what the procedure does.
INTRODUCTION: introductory and background material, including definitions and occasional introductory examples.
SPECIFICATIONS: reference section for the syntax of the control language for the procedure.
DETAILS: expanded descriptions of features, internal operations, output, treatment of missing values, computational methods, required computational resources, and usage notes.
EXAMPLES: examples using the procedure, including data, SAS statements, and printed output. You can reproduce these examples by copying the statements and data and running the job.
REFERENCES: a selected bibliography.
NOTES: a listing of operating system differences.

There are five appendices, including a discussion of special SAS data sets; a summary of Version 5 changes and enhancements to the statistical procedures in base SAS software; operating system notes; a discussion of full-screen editing capabilities with the SAS System; and a guide to the SAS Display Manager System for full-screen terminals.

If you have any problems with this manual, please take time to complete the review page at the end of this book and send it to SAS Institute. We will consider your suggestions for future editions. In the meantime, ask your installation's SAS Software Consultant for help.

New features in Version 5 statistical procedures Version 5 of base SAS software statistical procedures contains many new features, including three new procedures, enhancements to existing procedures, and other new system features. The FUNCAT procedure has been replaced by the CATMOD procedure; the FREQ procedure has been added to this manual; and the chapters on the MATRIX language are now documented in "The MATRIX Procedure," SAS Institute Technical Report P-135. The MATRIX procedure will be replaced by SAS/IML software in future releases of the SAS System. See the appendix "Version 5 Changes and Enhancements to Base SAS Software" for a complete description of new features.

SAS release? To find out which release of SAS software you are using, run any SAS job and look at the release number in the notes at the beginning of the SAS log. This user's guide documents Version 5 base SAS software. If you have an earlier release (for example, the 82.4 release), you should use the 1982 edition of the *SAS User's Guide: Statistics.*

Other SAS Institute manuals and technical reports Below is a list of other manuals that document Version 5 SAS System software:

SAS User's Guide: Basics, Version 5 Edition
SAS/GRAPH User's Guide, Version 5 Edition
SAS/FSP User's Guide, Version 5 Edition
SAS/OR User's Guide, Version 5 Edition
SAS/AF User's Guide, Version 5 Edition
SAS/ETS User's Guide, Version 5 Edition
SAS/IML User's Guide, Version 5 Edition

The SAS Technical Report Series documents work in progress, describes new supplemental procedures and covers a variety of applications areas. Some of the features described in these reports are still in experimental form and are not yet available as SAS procedures.

Write to SAS Institute for a current publications catalog, which describes the manuals as well as technical reports and lists their prices.

SAS Services to Users

Technical support SAS Institute supports users through the Technical Support Department. If you have a problem running a SAS job, you should contact your site's SAS Software Consultant. If the problem cannot be resolved locally, your local support personnel should call the Institute's Technical Support Department at (919) 467-8000 on weekdays between 9:00 a.m. and 5:00 p.m. Eastern Standard Time. A brochure describing the services provided by the Technical Support Department is available from SAS Institute.

Training SAS Institute sponsors a comprehensive training program, including programs of study for novice data processors, statisticians, applications programmers, systems programmers, and local support personnel. *SAS Training,* a semiannual training publication, describes the total training program and each course currently being offered by SAS Institute.

News magazine *SAS Communications* is the quarterly news magazine of SAS Institute. Each issue contains ideas for more effective use of the SAS System, information about research and development underway at SAS Institute, the current training schedule, new publications, and news of the SAS Users Group International (SUGI).

To receive a copy of *SAS Communications* regularly, send your name and complete address to:

SAS Institute Mailing List
SAS Institute Inc.
Box 8000
Cary, NC 27511-8000

Sample library One of the data sets included on the base SAS software installation tape is called SAS.SAMPLE. This data set contains sample SAS applications to illustrate features of SAS procedures and creative SAS programming techniques that can help you gain an in-depth knowledge of SAS capabilities.

Here are a few examples of programs included:

ANOVA	analyzing a Latin-square split-plot design
ARIMA5	fitting an intervention model to an ozone time series
CENSUS	reading hierarchical files of the U.S. Census Bureau Public Use Sample tapes
HARRIS	reading Harris Poll tapes coded in column-binary format
PDL	fitting a polynomial distributed lag regression model
TEACH	teaching arithmetic to your child.

Check with your SAS Software Consultant to find out how to access the library since it may have been put on disk at your site.

SUGI

The SAS Users Group International (SUGI) is a nonprofit association of professionals who are interested in how others are using the SAS System. Although SAS Institute provides administrative support, SUGI is independent from the Institute. Membership is open to all users at SAS sites, and there is no membership fee.

Annual conferences are structured to allow many avenues of discussion. Users present invited and contributed papers on various topics, for example:

- computer performance evaluation and systems software
- econometrics and time series
- graphics
- information systems
- interactive techniques
- statistics
- tutorials in SAS System software.

Proceedings of the annual conferences are distributed free to SUGI registrants. Extra copies may be purchased from SAS Institute.

SASware Ballot SAS users provide valuable input toward the direction of future SAS development by ranking their priorities on the annual SASware Ballot. The top vote-getters are announced at the SUGI conference. Complete results of the SASware Ballot are also printed in the *SUGI Proceedings*.

Supplemental library SAS users at many installations have written their own SAS procedures for a wide variety of specialized applications. Some of these user-written procedures are available through the SUGI supplemental library and are documented in the *SUGI Supplemental Library User's Guide*. The procedures in the supplemental library are sent to each installation that licenses base SAS software, although only a few procedures are supported by SAS Institute staff.

Licensing the SAS System

The SAS System is licensed to customers in the Western Hemisphere from the Institute's headquarters in Cary, NC. To serve the needs of our international customers, the Institute maintains subsidiaries in the United Kingdom, New Zealand, Australia, Singapore, Germany, and France. In addition, agents in other countries are licensed distributors for the SAS System. For a complete list of offices, write or call:

SAS Institute Inc.
SAS Circle
Box 8000
Cary, NC 27511-8000
(919) 467-8000

OVERVIEW

SAS® Regression Procedures

SAS® Analysis-of-Variance Procedures

SAS® Categorical Data Procedures

SAS® Multivariate Procedures

SAS® Discriminant Procedures

SAS® Clustering Procedures

SAS® Survival Analysis Procedures

SAS® Scoring Procedures

The Four Types of Estimable Functions

Chapter 1

SAS® Regression Procedures

Introduction

This chapter reviews the base SAS software procedures that are used for regression analysis: REG, RSQUARE, STEPWISE, NLIN, and RSREG.

Many SAS procedures, each with special features, perform regression analysis. The following procedures have similar specifications and computations:

REG — performs general-purpose regression with many diagnostic and input/output capabilities.

RSQUARE — builds models and shows measures of fit for all possible models.

STEPWISE — implements several stepping methods for selecting models.

NLIN — builds nonlinear regression models.

RSREG — builds quadratic response-surface regression models.

Several other procedures also perform regression:

GLM — performs an analysis of general linear models including models containing categorical terms and polynomials (documented with other analysis-of-variance procedures).

AUTOREG implements regression models using time-series data where the errors are autocorrelated (documented in the *SAS/ETS User's Guide*).

SYSLIN handles linear simultaneous systems of equations, such as econometric models (documented in the *SAS/ETS User's Guide*).

SYSNLIN handles nonlinear simultaneous systems of equations, such as econometric models (documented in the *SAS/ETS User's Guide*).

PDLREG performs regression analysis with polynomial distributed lags (documented in the *SAS/ETS User's Guide*).

Other regression procedures contributed by SAS users are documented in the *SUGI Supplemental Library User's Guide*.

These procedures perform regression analysis, which is the fitting of an equation to a set of values. The equation predicts a *response variable* from a function of *regressor variables* and *parameters*, adjusting the parameters such that a measure of fit is optimized. For example, the equation for the *i*th observation might be:

$$y_i = \beta_0 + \beta_1 x_i + \varepsilon_i$$

where y_i is the response variable, x_i is a regressor variable, β_0 and β_1 are unknown parameters to be estimated, and ε_i is an error term.

For example, you might use regression analysis to find out how well you can predict a person's weight if you know his height. Suppose you collect your data by measuring heights and weights of twenty school children. You need to estimate the intercept β_0 and the slope β_1 of a line of fit described by the equation:

$$\text{WEIGHT} = \beta_0 + \beta_1 \text{ HEIGHT} + \varepsilon$$

where

WEIGHT is the response variable (also called the *dependent variable*)

β_0, β_1 are the unknown parameters

HEIGHT is the regressor variable (also called the *independent variable, predictor, explanatory variable, factor, carrier*)

ε is the unknown error.

A plot of your data is given in **Output 1.1**.

Regression estimates for these data are $b_0 = -125.6$ and $b_1 = 3.7$, so the line of fit is described by the equation

$$\text{WEIGHT} = -125.6 + 3.7{*}\text{HEIGHT} \quad .$$

Regression is often used in an exploratory fashion to look for empirical relationships, such as the relationship between HEIGHT and WEIGHT. In this example HEIGHT is not the cause of WEIGHT. We do not even have evidence that the two variables change together over time since these data are across subjects (cross-sectional) rather than across time (longitudinal). (We would need a controlled experiment to confirm the relationship scientifically.)

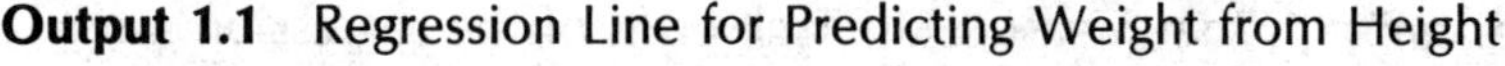

Output 1.1 Regression Line for Predicting Weight from Height

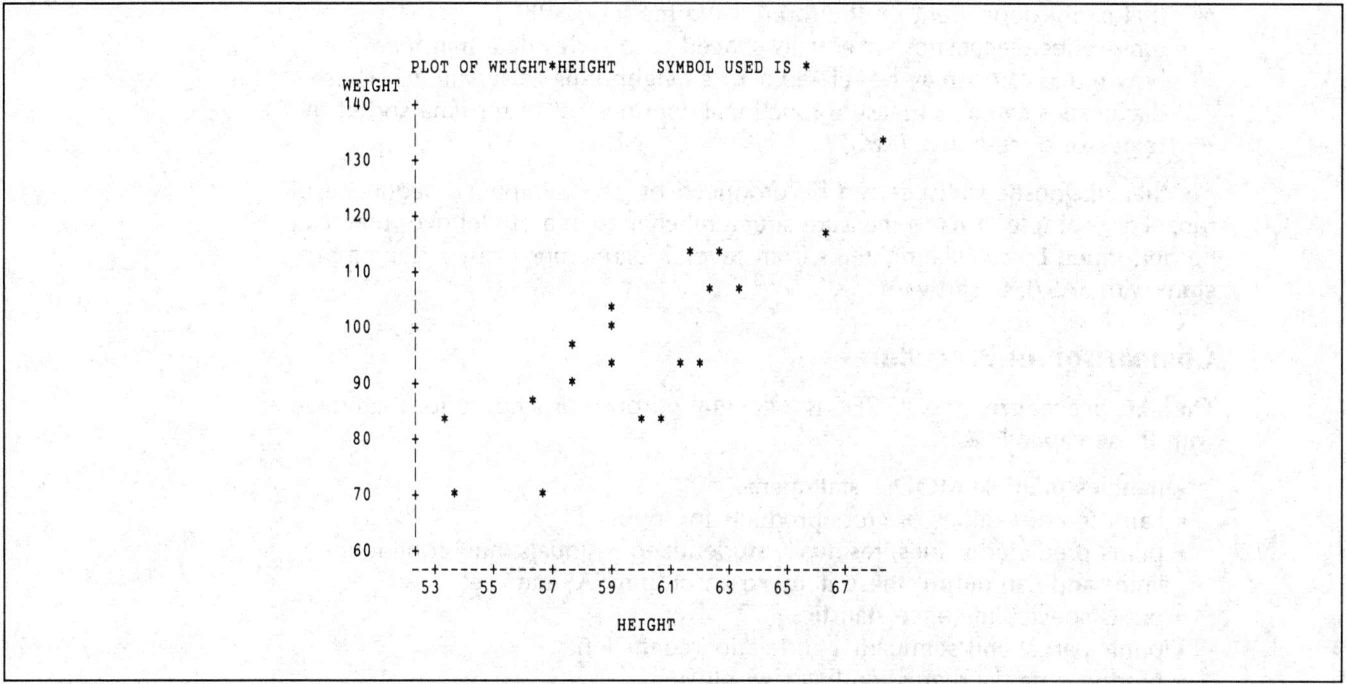

The method used to estimate the parameters is to minimize the sum of squares of the differences between the actual response value and the value predicted by the equation. The estimates are called *least-squares estimates*, and the criterion value is called the *error sum of squares*:

$$SSE = \Sigma \, (y_i - b_0 - b_1 x_i)^2$$

where b_0 and b_1 are the values for β_0 and β_1 that minimize SSE.

For a general discussion of the theory of least-squares estimation of linear models and its application to regression and analysis of variance, see one of the applied regression texts including Draper and Smith (1981), Daniel and Wood (1980), and Johnston (1972).

SAS regression procedures produce the following information for a typical regression analysis:

- parameter estimates using the least-squares criterion
- estimates of the variance of the error term
- estimates of the variance or standard deviation of the parameter estimates
- tests of hypotheses about the parameters
- predicted values and residuals using the estimates
- statistics for evaluating the fit or lack of fit.

Besides the usual statistics of fit produced for a regression, SAS regression procedures can produce many other specialized diagnostic statistics, including:

- collinearity diagnostics to measure how much regressors are related to other regressors and how this affects the stability and variance of the estimates (REG)
- influence diagnostics to measure how each individual observation contributes to determining the parameter estimates, the SSE, and the fitted values (REG, RSREG)

- lack-of-fit diagnostics that measure the lack of fit of the regression model by comparing the error variance estimate to another pure error variance that is not dependent on the form of the model (RSREG)
- time-series diagnostics for equally spaced time-series data that measure how much errors may be related across neighboring observations. These diagnostics can also measure functional goodness of fit for data sorted by regressor or response (REG).

Other diagnostic statistics can be produced by programming a sequence of runs. For example, tests to measure structural change in a model over time can be performed by calculating items from several regressions or by writing a program with SAS/IML software.

Comparison of Procedures

The REG procedure PROC REG is a general-purpose procedure for regression with these capabilities:

- handles multiple MODEL statements
- can use correlations or cross products for input
- prints predicted values, residuals, studentized residuals, and confidence limits and can output these items to an output SAS data set
- prints special influence statistics
- prints partial and semipartial correlation coefficients
- produces partial regression leverage plots
- estimates parameters subject to linear restrictions
- tests linear hypotheses
- tests multivariate hypotheses
- writes estimates to an output SAS data set
- writes the cross-products matrix to an output SAS data set
- computes special collinearity diagnostics.

The RSQUARE procedure PROC RSQUARE fits all possible combinations of a list of variables specified in a MODEL statement. The procedure prints parameter estimates and several statistics for evaluating fit. PROC RSQUARE is useful when you want to look at alternative models. Since the number of possible models (2^n) gets large quickly, you should use the RSQUARE procedure only when you have fewer than 20 regressors to consider.

The STEPWISE procedure PROC STEPWISE selects regressors for a model by various stepping strategies; you can request five different methods to search for good models. The FORWARD method starts with an empty model and at each step selects the variable that would maximize the fit. The BACKWARD method starts with a full model and at each step removes the variable that contributes least to the fit. There are three other variations: STEPWISE, MAXR, and MINR. If the FORWARD, BACKWARD, or STEPWISE method is used, the procedure produces a table of statistics for entry or removal for each step in the model-building process. PROC STEPWISE also produces an analysis of variance and parameter estimates but cannot give predicted and residual values.

The NLIN procedure PROC NLIN implements iterative methods that attempt to find least-squares estimates for nonlinear models. The default method is Gauss-Newton, although several other methods are available. You must specify parameter names and starting values, expressions for the model, and expressions for derivatives of the model with respect to the parameters (except for METHOD= DUD). A grid search is also available to select starting values for the parameters.

Since nonlinear models are often difficult to estimate, NLIN may not always find the least-squares estimates.

The RSREG procedure PROC RSREG fits a quadratic response-surface model, which is useful in searching for factor values that optimize a response. The following features in RSREG make it preferable to other regression procedures for analyzing response surfaces:

- automatic generation of quadratic effects
- a lack-of-fit test
- solutions for critical values of the surface
- eigenvalues of the associated quadratic form.

The GLM procedure PROC GLM for linear models can handle regression, analysis-of-variance, and analysis of covariance. Certain of its features for regression distinguish GLM from other regression procedures:

- ease of specifying categorical effects (GLM automatically generates dummy variables for class variables)
- direct specification of polynomial effects.

Statistical Background

The rest of this chapter outlines the way many SAS regression procedures calculate various regression quantities. Exceptions and further details are documented with individual procedures.

In matrix algebra notation, a linear model is written as:

$$\mathbf{y} = \mathbf{X}\beta + \varepsilon$$

where **X** is the *n*x*k* design matrix (rows are observations and columns are the regressors), β is the *k*x1 vector of unknown parameters, and ε is the *n*x1 vector of unknown errors. The first column of **X** is usually a vector of 1s used in estimating the intercept term.

The statistical theory of linear models is based on some strict classical assumptions. Ideally, the response is measured with all the factors controlled in an experimentally determined environment. Or, if you cannot control the factors experimentally, you must assume that the factors are fixed with respect to the response variable.

Other assumptions are that:

- the form of the model is correct
- regressor variables are measured without error
- the expected value of the errors is zero
- the variance of the errors (and thus the dependent variable) is a constant across observations and is called σ^2
- the errors are uncorrelated across observations.

When hypotheses are tested, the additional assumption is made that:

- the errors are normally distributed.

Statistical model If the model satisfies all the necessary assumptions, the least-squares estimates are the best linear unbiased estimates (BLUE); in other words, the estimates have minimum variance among the class of estimators that are a linear function of the responses. If the additional assumption that the error term is normally distributed is also satisfied, then:

- the statistics that are computed have the proper sampling distributions for hypothesis testing
- parameter estimates will be normally distributed
- various sums of squares are distributed proportional to chi-square, at least under proper hypotheses
- ratios of estimates to standard errors are distributed as Student's *t* under certain hypotheses
- appropriate ratios of sums of squares are distributed as *F* under certain hypotheses.

When regression analysis is used to model data that do not meet the assumptions, the results should be interpreted in a cautious, exploratory fashion, with discounted credence in the significance probabilities.

Box (1966) and Tukey and Mosteller (1977, chapters 12-13) discuss the problems that are encountered with regression data, especially when the data are not under experimental control.

Parameter Estimates and Associated Statistics

Parameter estimates are formed using least-squares criteria by solving the normal equations:

$$(\mathbf{X'X})\ \mathbf{b} = \mathbf{X'y}$$

yielding

$$\mathbf{b} = (\mathbf{X'X})^{-1}\mathbf{X'y} \quad .$$

Assume for the present that $(\mathbf{X'X})$ is full rank (this is relaxed later). The variance of the error σ^2 is estimated by the mean square error

$$s^2 = \text{MSE} = \text{SSE}/(n\text{-}k) = \Sigma(y_i\text{-}\mathbf{x}_i\mathbf{b})^2/(n\text{-}k)$$

where x_i is the *i*th row of regressors.

The parameter estimates are unbiased:

$$\text{E}(\mathbf{b}) = \beta$$

$$\text{E}(s^2) = \sigma^2 \quad .$$

The estimates have the variance-covariance matrix:

$$\text{Var}(\mathbf{b}) = (\mathbf{X'X})^{-1}\sigma^2 \quad .$$

The estimate of the variance matrix replaces σ^2 with s^2 in the formula above:

$$\text{COVB} = (\mathbf{X'X})^{-1}s^2 \quad .$$

The correlations of the estimates are derived by scaling to 1s on the diagonal. Let:

$$\mathbf{S} = \text{diag}((\mathbf{X'X})^{-1})^{-.5}$$

$$\text{CORRB} = \mathbf{S}(\mathbf{X'X})^{-1}\mathbf{S} \quad .$$

Standard errors of the estimates are computed using the equation:

$$\text{STDERR}(b_i) = \sqrt{(\mathbf{X'X})^{ii}s^2}$$

where $(\mathbf{X'X})^{ii}$ is the ith diagonal element of $(\mathbf{X'X})^{-1}$. The ratio

$$t = b_i/\text{stderr}(b_i)$$

is distributed as Student's t under the hypothesis that β_i is zero. Regression procedures print the t ratio and the significance probability, the probability under the hypothesis $\beta_i=0$ of a larger absolute t value than was actually obtained. When the probability is less than some small level, the event is considered so unlikely that the hypothesis is rejected.

Type I SS and Type II SS measure the contribution of a variable to the reduction in SSE. Type I SS measure the reduction in SSE as that variable is entered into the model in sequence. Type II SS are the increment in SSE that results from removing the variable from the full model. Type II SS are equivalent to the Type III and Type IV SS reported in the GLM procedure. If Type II SS are used in the numerator of an F test, the test is equivalent to the t test for the hypothesis that the parameter is zero. In polynomial models, Type I SS measure the contribution of each polynomial term after it is orthogonalized to the previous terms in the model. The four types of SS are described in a more general context for the GLM procedure and in "The Four Types of Estimable Functions," elsewhere in this manual.

Standardized estimates are defined as the estimates that result when all variables are standardized to a mean of 0 and a variance of 1. Standardized estimates are computed by multiplying the original estimates by the standard deviation of the regressor variable and dividing by the sample standard deviation of the dependent variable.

Tolerances and variance inflation factors measure the strength of interrelationships among the regressor variables in the model. If all variables are orthogonal to each other, both tolerance and variance inflation are 1. If a variable is very closely related to other variables, the tolerance goes to 0 and the variance inflation gets very large. Tolerance (TOL) is 1 minus the R^2 that results from the regression of the other variables in the model on that regressor. Variance inflation (VIF) is the diagonal of $(\mathbf{X'X})^{-1}$ if $(\mathbf{X'X})$ is scaled to correlation form. The statistics are related as shown below:

$$\text{VIF} = 1/\text{TOL} \quad .$$

Models not of full rank If the model is not full rank, then a generalized inverse can be used to solve the normal equations to minimize the SSE:

$$\mathbf{b} = (\mathbf{X'X})^{-}\mathbf{X'y} \quad .$$

However, these estimates are not unique since there are an infinite number of solutions using different generalized inverses. REG and other regression procedures choose a nonzero solution for all variables that are linearly independent of previous variables and a zero solution for other variables. This corresponds to using a generalized inverse in the normal equations, and the expected values of the "estimates" are the Hermite normal form of $\mathbf{X'X}$ times the true parameters:

$$E(\mathbf{b}) = (\mathbf{X'X})^{-}(\mathbf{X'X})\beta \quad .$$

Degrees of freedom for the zeroed estimates are reported as zero. The hypotheses that are not testable have t tests printed as missing. The message that the model is not full rank includes a printout of the relations that exist in the matrix.

Predicted Values and Residuals

After the model has been fit, predicted values and residuals are usually calculated and output. The predicted values are calculated from the estimated regression equation; the residuals are calculated as actual minus predicted. Some procedures can calculate standard errors.

Consider the *i*th observation where $\mathbf{x}_i$ is the row of regressors, **b** is the vector of parameter estimates, and s^2 is the mean squared error.

Let:

$$h_i = \mathbf{x}_i(\mathbf{X'X})^{-1}\mathbf{x}_i' \text{(the leverage)} \quad .$$

Then

$$\hat{y}_i = \mathbf{x}_i\mathbf{b} \text{ (the predicted value)}$$

$$\text{STDERR}(\hat{y}_i) = \sqrt{(h_i s^2)} \text{ (the standard error of the predicted value)}$$

$$\text{resid}_i = \mathbf{y}_i - \mathbf{x}_i\mathbf{b} \text{ (the residual)}$$

$$\text{STDERR}(\text{resid}_i) = \sqrt{((1-h_i)s^2)} \text{ (the standard error of the residual).}$$

The ratio of the residual to its standard error, called the *studentized residual*, is sometimes shown as:

$$\text{Student} = \text{resid} \; / \; \text{STDERR(resid)} \quad .$$

There are two kinds of confidence intervals for predicted values. One type of confidence interval is an interval for the the expected value of the response. The other type of confidence interval is an interval for the actual value of a response, which is the expected value plus error.

For example, you can construct for the *i*th observation a confidence interval that contains the true expected value of the response with probability 1-α. The upper and lower limits of the confidence interval for the expected value are

$$\text{LowerM} = \mathbf{x}_i\mathbf{b} - t_{\alpha/2}\sqrt{(h_i s^2)}$$

$$\text{UpperM} = \mathbf{x}_i\mathbf{b} + t_{\alpha/2}\sqrt{(h_i s^2)} \quad .$$

The limits for the confidence interval for an actual individual response (forecasting interval) are

$$\text{LowerI} = \mathbf{x}_i\mathbf{b} - t_{\alpha/2}\sqrt{(h_i s^2 + s^2)}$$

$$\text{UpperI} = \mathbf{x}_i\mathbf{b} + t_{\alpha/2}\sqrt{(h_i s^2 + s^2)} \quad .$$

One measure of influence, Cook's *D*, measures the change to the estimates that results from deleting each observation:

$$\text{COOKD} = \text{Student}^2 \, (\text{STDERR}(\hat{y})/\text{STDERR(resid)})^2/k \quad .$$

For more information, see Cook (1977, 1979).

The *predicted residual* for observation *i* is defined as the residual for the *i*th observation that results from dropping the *i*th observation from the parameter estimates. The sum of squares of predicted residual errors is called the *press* statistic:

$$\text{presid}_i = \text{resid}_i/(1-h_i)$$

$$\text{press} = \Sigma\ \text{presid}_i^2 \quad .$$

Testing Linear Hypotheses

The general form of a linear hypothesis for the parameters is

$$\mathbf{H_0}{:}\mathbf{L}\beta = \mathbf{c}$$

where **L** is *q*x*k*, β is *k*x1, and **c** is *q*x1. To test this hypothesis, the linear function is taken with respect to the parameters:

$$(\mathbf{Lb}-\mathbf{c}) \quad .$$

This has variance:

$$\text{Var}(\mathbf{Lb}-\mathbf{c}) = \mathbf{L}\ \text{Var}(\mathbf{b})\mathbf{L}' = \mathbf{L}(\mathbf{X}'\mathbf{X})^{-}\mathbf{L}'\sigma^2$$

where **b** is the estimate of β.

A quadratic form called the *sum of squares due to the hypothesis* is calculated:

$$\text{SS}(\mathbf{Lb}-\mathbf{c}) = (\mathbf{Lb}-\mathbf{c})'(\mathbf{L}(\mathbf{X}'\mathbf{X})^{-}\mathbf{L}')^{-1}(\mathbf{Lb}-\mathbf{c}) \quad .$$

Assuming that this is testable, the SS can be used as a numerator of the *F* test:

$$F = \text{SS}(\mathbf{Lb}-\mathbf{c})/q\ /s^2 \quad .$$

This is referred to an *F* distribution with *q* and *dfe* degrees of freedom, where *dfe* is the degrees of freedom for residual error.

Multivariate Tests

Multivariate hypotheses involve several dependent variables in the form:

$$\mathbf{H_0}{:}\mathbf{L}\beta\mathbf{M} = \mathbf{d}$$

where **L** is a linear function on the regressor side, β is a matrix of parameters, **M** is a linear function on the dependent side, and **d** is a matrix of constants.

The special case (handled by REG) where the constants are the same for each dependent variable is written:

$$(\mathbf{L}\beta-\mathbf{cj})\mathbf{M} = 0$$

where **c** is a column vector of constants and **j** is a row vector of 1s. The special case where the constants are 0 is

$$\mathbf{L}\beta\mathbf{M} = 0 \quad .$$

These multivariate tests are covered in detail in Morrison (1976); Timm (1975); Mardia, Kent, and Bibby (1979); Bock (1975); and other works cited in "SAS Multivariate Procedures."

To test this hypothesis, construct two matrices, **H** and **E**, that correspond to the numerator and denominator of a univariate *F* test:

$$\mathbf{H} = \mathbf{M}'(\mathbf{LB}-\mathbf{cj})'(\mathbf{L}(\mathbf{X}'\mathbf{X})^{-1}\mathbf{L}')^{-1}(\mathbf{LB}-\mathbf{cj})\mathbf{M}$$

$$\mathbf{E} = \mathbf{M}'(\mathbf{Y}'\mathbf{Y}-\mathbf{B}'(\mathbf{X}'\mathbf{X})\mathbf{B})\mathbf{M} \quad .$$

Four test statistics, based on the eigenvalues of $\mathbf{E}^{-1}\mathbf{H}$ or $(\mathbf{E}+\mathbf{H})^{-1}\mathbf{H}$, are formed. Let λ_i be the ordered eigenvalues of $\mathbf{E}^{-1}\mathbf{H}$ (if the inverse exists), and let ξ_i be the ordered eigenvalues of $(\mathbf{E}+\mathbf{H})^{-1}\mathbf{H}$. It happens that $\xi_i=\lambda_i/(1+\lambda_i)$ and $\lambda_i=\xi_i/(1-\xi_i)$, and it turns out that $\rho_i=\sqrt{\xi_i}$ is the ith canonical correlation.

Let p be the rank of $(\mathbf{H}+\mathbf{E})$, which is less than or equal to the number of columns of $\mathbf{M}$. Let q be the rank of $\mathbf{L}(\mathbf{X}'\mathbf{X})^{-1}\mathbf{L}'$. Let v be the degrees of freedom for error. Let $s=\min(p,q)$. Let $m=.5(|p-q|-1)$, and let $n=.5(v-p-1)$. Then the statistics below have the approximate F statistics as shown:

Wilks' lambda

$$\Lambda = \det(\mathbf{E})/\det(\mathbf{H}+\mathbf{E}) = \Pi\ 1/(1+\lambda_i) = \Pi(1-\xi_i) \quad .$$

$F=(1-\Lambda^{1/t})/(\Lambda^{1/t})\ (rt-2u)/pq$ is approximately F, where $r=v-(p-q+1)/2$ and $u=(pq-2)/4$, and $t=\sqrt{(p^2q^2-4)/(p^2+q^2-5)}$ if $(p^2+q^2-5)>0$ or 1 otherwise. The degrees of freedom are pq and $rt-2u$. This approximation is exact if $\min(p, q)\leq 2$. (See Rao 1973, 556.)

Pillai's trace

$$\mathbf{V} = \text{trace}(\mathbf{H}(\mathbf{H}+\mathbf{E})^{-1}) = \Sigma\lambda_i/(1+\lambda_i) = \Sigma\ \xi_i \quad .$$

$F=(2n+s+1)/(2m+s+1)\ \mathbf{V}/(s-\mathbf{V})$ is approximately F with $s(2m+s+1)$ and $s(2n+s+1)$ degrees of freedom.

Hotelling-Lawley trace

$$\mathbf{U} = \text{trace}(\mathbf{E}^{-1}\mathbf{H}) = \Sigma\ \lambda_i = \Sigma\ \xi_i/(1-\xi_i) \quad .$$

$F=2(sn+1)\ \mathbf{U}/(s^2(2m+s+1))$ is approximately F with $s(2m+s+1)$ and $2(sn+1)$ degrees of freedom.

Roy's maximum root

$$\Theta=\lambda_1 \quad .$$

$F=\Theta(v-r-1)/r$ where $r=\max(p,q)$ is an upper bound on F that yields a lower bound on the significance level.

Tables of critical values for these statistics are found in Pillai (1960).

References

Allen, D.M. (1971), "Mean Square Error of Prediction as a Criterion for Selecting Variables," *Technometrics*, 13, 469-475.

Allen, D.M. and Cady, F.B. (1982), *Analyzing Experimental Data by Regression*, Belmont, CA: Lifetime Learning Publications.

Belsley, D.A., Kuh, E., and Welsch, R.E. (1980), *Regression Diagnostics*, New York: John Wiley & Sons.

Bock, R.D. (1975), *Multivariate Statistical Methods in Behavioral Research*, New York: McGraw-Hill.

Box, G.E.P. (1966), "The Use and Abuse of Regression," *Technometrics*, 8, 625-629.

Cook, R.D. (1977), "Detection of Influential Observations in Linear Regression," *Technometrics*, 19, 15-18.

Cook, R.D. (1979), "Influential Observations in Linear Regression," *Journal of the American Statistical Association*, 74, 169-174.

Daniel, C. and Wood, F. (1980), *Fitting Equations to Data*, Revised Edition, New York: John Wiley & Sons.

Draper, N. and Smith, H. (1981), *Applied Regression Analysis*, Second Edition, New York: John Wiley & Sons.

Durbin, J. and Watson, G.S. (1951), "Testing for Serial Correlation in Least Squares Regression," *Biometrika*, 37, 409-428.

Freund, R.J. and Littell, R.C. (1981), *SAS for Linear Models*, Cary, NC: SAS Institute.

Goodnight, J.H. (1979), "A Tutorial on the SWEEP Operator," *The American Statistician*, 33, 149-158.

Johnston, J. (1972), *Econometric Methods*, New York: McGraw-Hill.

Kennedy, W.J. and Gentle, J.E. (1980), *Statistical Computing*, New York: Marcel Dekker.

Mallows, C.L. (1973), "Some Comments on Cp," *Technometrics*, 15, 661-675.

Mardia, K.V., Kent, J.T., and Bibby, J.M. (1979), *Multivariate Analysis*, London: Academic Press.

Morrison, D.F. (1976), *Multivariate Statistical Methods*, Second Edition, New York: McGraw-Hill.

Mosteller, F. and Tukey, J.W. (1977), *Data Analysis and Regression*, Reading, MA: Addison-Wesley.

Neter, J. and Wasserman, W. (1974), *Applied Linear Statistical Models*, Homewood, IL: Irwin.

Pillai, K.C.S. (1960), *Statistical Table for Tests of Multivariate Hypotheses*, Manila: The Statistical Center, University of Philippines.

Pindyck, R.S. and Rubinfeld, D.L. (1981), *Econometric Models and Econometric Forecasts*, Second Edition, New York: McGraw-Hill.

Rao, C.R. (1973), *Linear Statistical Inference and Its Applications*, Second Edition, New York: John Wiley & Sons.

Sall, J.P. (1981), "SAS Regression Application," Revised Edition, SAS Technical Report A-102, Cary, NC: SAS Institute.

Timm, N.H. (1975), *Multivariate Analysis with Applications in Education and Psychology*, Monterey, CA: Brooks/Cole.

Weisberg, S. (1980), *Applied Linear Regression*, New York: John Wiley & Sons.

Chapter 2

SAS® Analysis-of-Variance Procedures

This chapter reviews the SAS procedures that are used for analysis of variance: GLM, ANOVA, NESTED, VARCOMP, NPAR1WAY, TTEST, and PLAN.

The most general analysis-of-variance procedure is GLM, which can handle most problems. Other procedures are used for special cases as described below:

GLM	performs analysis of variance, regression, analysis of covariance, and multivariate analysis of variance.
ANOVA	handles analysis of variance for balanced designs.
NESTED	performs analysis of variance for purely nested random models.
VARCOMP	estimates variance components.
NPAR1WAY	performs nonparametric one-way analysis of rank scores.
TTEST	compares the means of two groups of observations.
PLAN	generates random permutations for experimental plans.

Introduction

These procedures perform analysis of variance, which is a technique for analyzing experimental data. A continuous response variable is measured under various experimental conditions identified by classification variables. The variation in the response is explained as due to effects in the classification with random error accounting for the remaining variation.

For each observation, the ANOVA model predicts the response, often by a sample mean. The difference between the actual and the predicted response is the residual error. Analysis-of-variance procedures fit parameters to minimize the sum of squares of residual errors. Thus, the method is called *least squares*. The variance of the random error, σ^2, is estimated by the mean squared error (MSE or s^2).

Analysis of variance was pioneered by R.A. Fisher (1925). For a general introduction to analysis of variance, see an intermediate statistical methods textbook such as Steel and Torrie (1980), Snedecor and Cochran (1980), Mendenhall (1968), John (1971), Ott (1977), or Kirk (1968). A classic source is Scheffe (1959). Freund and Littell (1981) bring together a treatment of these statistical methods and SAS procedures. Linear models texts include Searle (1971), Graybill (1961), and Bock (1975). Kennedy and Gentle (1980) survey the computing aspects.

ANOVA for Balanced Designs

One of the factors that determines which procedure to use is whether your data are balanced or unbalanced. When you design an experiment, you choose how many experimental units to assign to each combination of levels (or cells) in the classification. In order to achieve good statistical properties and simplify the statistical arithmetic, you typically attempt to assign the same number of units to every cell in the design. These designs are called *balanced*.

If you have balanced data, the arithmetic for calculating sums of squares can be greatly simplified. In SAS, you can use the ANOVA procedure rather than the more expensive GLM procedure for balanced data. Generalizations of the balanced concept can be made to use the arithmetic for balanced designs even though the design does not contain an equal number of observations per cell. You can use balanced arithmetic for all one-way models regardless of how unbalanced the cell counts are. You can even use the balanced arithmetic for Latin squares that do not always have data in all cells.

However, if you use the ANOVA procedure to analyze a design that is not balanced, you may get incorrect results, including negative values reported for the sums of squares.

Analysis-of-variance procedures construct ANOVA tests by comparing mean squares relative to their expected values under the null hypothesis. Each mean square in a fixed analysis-of-variance model has an expected value that is composed of two components: quadratic functions of fixed parameters and random variation. For a fixed effect called A, the expected value of its mean square is written

$$E(MS(A)) = Q(\beta) + \sigma^2_e \quad .$$

The mean square is constructed so that under the hypothesis to be tested (null hypothesis) the fixed portion $Q(\beta)$ of the expected value is zero. This mean square is then compared to another mean square, say MS(E), that is independent of the first, yet has the expected value σ^2_e. The ratio of the two mean squares is an F statistic that has the F distribution under the null hypothesis:

$$F = MS(A)/MS(E) \quad .$$

When the null hypothesis is false, the numerator term has a larger expected value, but the expected value of the denominator remains the same. Thus, large F values lead to rejection of the null hypothesis. The test decides an outcome by controlling for the Type 1 error rate, the probability of rejecting a true null hypothesis. You look at the significance probability, the probability of getting an even larger F value if the null hypothesis is true. If this probability is small, say below .05 or .01, you are wrong in rejecting less than .05 or .01 of the time respectively. If you are unable to reject the hypothesis, you conclude that either the null hypothesis was true or that you do not have enough data to detect the small differences to be tested.

General Linear Models

If your data do not fit into a balanced design, then you probably need the framework of linear models in the GLM procedure.

An analysis-of-variance model can be written as a linear model, an equation to predict the response as a linear function of parameters and design variables. In general we write:

$$y_i = \beta_0 x_{0i} + \beta_1 x_{1i} + \dots + \beta_k x_{ki} + \varepsilon_i \, , \; i = 1 \dots n$$

where y_i is the response for the ith observation, β_k are unknown parameters to be estimated, and x_{ij} are design variables. Design variables for analysis of variance are indicator variables, that is, they are always either 0 or 1.

The simplest model is to fit a single mean to all observations. In this case there is only one parameter, β_0, and one design variable, x_{0i}, which always has the value 1:

$$\begin{aligned} y_i &= \beta_0 x_{0i} + \varepsilon_i \\ &= \beta_0 + \varepsilon_i \quad . \end{aligned}$$

The least-squares estimator of β_0 is the mean of the y_i. This simple model underlies all more complex models, and all larger models are compared to this simple mean model.

A one-way model is written by introducing an indicator variable for each level of the classification variable. Suppose that a variable A has four levels, with two observations per level. The indicators are created as shown below:

intercept	a1	a2	a3	a4
1	1	0	0	0
1	1	0	0	0
1	0	1	0	0
1	0	1	0	0
1	0	0	1	0
1	0	0	1	0
1	0	0	0	1
1	0	0	0	1

The linear model can be written

$$y_i = \beta_0 + a1_i\beta_1 + a2_i\beta_2 + a3_i\beta_3 + a4_i\beta_4 \quad .$$

To construct crossed and nested effects, you can simply multiply out all combinations of the main-effect columns. This is described in detail in the section **Parameterization** in the GLM procedure.

Linear hypotheses When models are expressed in the framework of linear models, hypothesis tests are expressed in terms of a linear function of the parameters. For example, you may want to test that $\beta_2 - \beta_3 = 0$. In general, the coefficients for linear hypotheses are some set of Ls:

$$H_0: \; L_0\beta_0 + L_1\beta_1 + \dots + L_k\beta_k = 0 \quad .$$

Several of these linear functions can be combined to make one joint test. Tests can also be expressed in one matrix equation:

$$H_0: \; L\beta=0 \quad .$$

For each linear hypothesis, a sum of squares due to that hypothesis can be constructed. These sums of squares can be calculated either as a quadratic form of the estimates:

$$SS(L\beta = 0) = (Lb)'(L(X'X)^{-}L')^{-1}(Lb)$$

or as the increase in SSE for the model constrained by the hypothesis

$$SS(L\beta = 0) = SSE(\text{constrained}) - SSE(\text{full}) \quad .$$

This SS is then divided by degrees of freedom and used as a numerator of an F statistic.

Random effects To estimate the variances of random effects, use the VARCOMP or NESTED procedures; PROC GLM does not estimate variance components but can produce expected mean squares.

A *random effect* is an effect whose parameters are drawn from a normally distributed random process with mean zero and common variance. Effects are declared random when the levels are randomly selected from a large population of possible levels. The inferences concern fixed effects but can be generalized across the whole population of random effects levels rather than only those levels in your sample.

In agricultural experiments, it is common to declare location or plot as random since these levels are chosen randomly from a large population and you assume fertility to vary normally across locations. In repeated-measures experiments with people or animals as subjects, subjects are declared random since they are selected from the larger population to which you want to generalize.

When effects are declared random in GLM, the expected mean square of each effect is calculated. Each expected mean square is a function of variances of random effects and quadratic functions of parameters of fixed effects. To test a given effect, you must search for a term that has the same expectation as your numerator term, except for the portion of the expectation that you want to test to be zero. If the two mean squares are independent, then the F test is valid. Sometimes, however, you will not be able to find a proper denominator term.

Comparison of means When you have more than two means to compare, an *ANOVA F* test tells you if the means are significantly different from each other, but it does not tell you which means differ from which other means.

If you have specific comparisons in mind, you can use the CONTRAST statement in GLM to make these comparisons. However, if you make many comparisons using some alpha level to judge significance, you are more likely to make a Type 1 error (rejecting incorrectly a hypothesis that means are equal) simply because you have more chances to make the error.

Multiple comparison methods give you more detailed information about the differences among the means and allow you to control error rates for a multitude of comparisons. A variety of multiple comparison methods are available with the MEANS statement in the ANOVA and GLM procedures. These are described in detail in the section **Comparison of Means** in GLM.

Nonparametric analysis Analysis of variance is sensitive to the distribution of the error term. If the error term is not normally distributed, the statistics based on normality can be misleading. The traditional test statistics are called *parametric tests* because they depend on the specification of a certain probability distribution up to a set of free parameters. Nonparametric methods make the tests without making distributional assumptions. If the data are distributed normally, often nonparametric methods are almost as powerful as parametric methods.

Most nonparametric methods are based on taking the ranks of a variable and analyzing these ranks (or transformations of them) instead of the original values. The NPAR1WAY procedure is available to perform a nonparametric one-way analysis of variance. Other nonparametric tests can be performed by taking ranks of the data (using PROC RANK) and using a regular parametric procedure to perform the analysis. Some of these techniques are outlined in the description of PROC RANK and in Conover and Iman (1981) cited below.

References

Bock, M.E. (1975), "Minimax Estimators of the Mean of a Multivariate Normal Distribution," *Annals of Statistics*, 3, 209-218.

Conover, W.J. and Iman, R.L. (1981), "Rank Transformations as a Bridge Between Parametric and Nonparametric Statistics," *The American Statistician*, 35, 124-129.

Fisher, R.A. (1925), *Statistical Methods for Research Workers*, Edinburgh: Oliver & Boyd.

Freund, R.J. and Littell, R.C. (1981), *SAS for Linear Models*, Cary, NC: SAS Institute Inc.

Graybill, F.A. (1961), *An Introduction to Linear Statistical Models*, New York: McGraw-Hill.

John, P. (1971), *Statistical Design and Analysis of Experiments*, New York: Macmillan.

Kennedy, W.J., Jr. and Gentle, J.E. (1980), *Statistical Computing*, New York: Marcel Dekker.

Kirk, R.E. (1968), *Experimental Design: Procedures for the Behavioral Sciences*, Monterey, CA: Brooks/Cole.

Mendenhall, W. (1968), *Introduction to Linear Models and the Design and Analysis of Experiments*, Belmont, CA: Duxbury.

Ott, L. (1977), *An Introduction of Statistical Methods and Data Analysis*, Belmont, CA: Duxbury.

Scheffe, H. (1959), *The Analysis of Variance*, New York: John Wiley & Sons.

Searle, S.R. (1971), *Linear Models*, New York: John Wiley & Sons.

Snedecor, G.W. and Cochran, W.G. (1980), *Statistical Methods*, Seventh Edition, Ames, Iowa: The Iowa State University Press.

Steel R.G.D. and Torrie, J.H. (1980), *Principles and Procedures of Statistics*, Second Edition, New York: McGraw-Hill.

Chapter 3

SAS® Categorical Data Procedures

There are two procedures in the SAS System that are designed for the analysis of categorical data:

FREQ builds frequency tables or contingency tables, and produces a number of tests and measures of association such as chi-square (χ^2) statistics, Fisher's exact test, correlation statistics, and odds ratios. In addition, it does stratified analysis, computing Cochran-Mantel-Haenszel statistics and estimates of the common relative risk.

CATMOD fits linear models to functions of categorical data, facilitating such analyses as regression, analysis of variance, linear modeling, log-linear modeling, logistic regression, and repeated measurement analysis.

Introduction

A *categorical variable* is defined as one that can assume only a limited number of discrete values. The measurement scale for such a variable is unrestricted. It can be *nominal*, which means that the observed levels are not ordered. It can be *ordinal*, which means that the observed levels are ordered in some way. Or it can be *interval*, which means that the observed levels are ordered and numeric, and that any interval of one unit on the scale of measurement represents the same amount, regardless of its location on the scale. One example of such a categorical variable is litter size; another is the number of times a subject has been married. A variable that lies on a nominal scale is sometimes called a *qualitative* or *classification* variable.

Categorical data result from observations on multiple subjects, where one or more categorical variables are observed for each subject. If there is only one categorical variable, then the data are generally represented by a *frequency table*, which lists each observed value of the variable and its frequency of occurrence.

If there are two or more categorical variables, then a subject's *profile* is defined to be the subject's observed values for each of the variables. Such categorical data can be represented by a frequency table that lists each observed profile and its frequency of occurrence.

If there are exactly two categorical variables, then the data are often represented by a two-dimensional *contingency table*, which has one row for each level of Variable 1, and one column for each level of Variable 2. The intersections of rows and columns, called *cells*, correspond to variable profiles, and each cell contains the frequency of occurrence of the corresponding profile.

If there are more than two categorical variables, then the data can be represented by a *multi-dimensional* contingency table. There are two commonly used methods for displaying such tables, and both require that the variables be divided into two sets.

In the first method, one set contains a row variable and a column variable for a two-dimensional contingency table, and the second set contains all of the other variables. The variables in the second set are used to form a set of profiles. The data are then represented as a series of two-dimensional contingency tables, one for each profile. This is the data representation used by PROC FREQ.

In the second method, one set contains the independent variables, and the other set contains the dependent variables. Profiles based on the independent variables are called *population profiles*, while those based on the dependent variables are called *response profiles*. A two-dimensional contingency table is then formed, with one row for each population profile, and one column for each response profile. Since any subject can have only one population profile and one response profile, the contingency table is uniquely defined. This is the data representation used by PROC CATMOD.

Simple Random Sampling—One Population

Suppose you take a simple random sample of 100 people and ask each person the following question: Of the three colors, red, blue, and green, which is your favorite? You then tabulate the results in a frequency table:

Table 3.1 One-Way Frequency Table

	Favorite Color			
	Red	Blue	Green	Total
Frequency	52	31	17	100
Proportion	.52	.31	.17	1.00

In the population you are sampling, there is an unknown probability that a population member, selected at random, would choose any given color. In order to estimate that probability, you use the sample proportion:

$$p_j = n_j/n$$

where n_j is the frequency of the jth response, and n is the total frequency.

Because of the random variation inherent in any random sample, the frequencies have a probability distribution representing their relative frequency of occurrence in a hypothetical series of samples. For a simple random sample, the distribution of frequencies for a frequency table with three levels is as follows. The probability that the first frequency is n_1, the second frequency is n_2, and the third is $n_3=n-n_1-n_2$, is

$$\text{Prob}(n_1, n_2, n_3) = n!\pi_1^{n_1}\pi_2^{n_2}\pi_3^{n_3} \;/\; (n_1!\; n_2!\;\; n_3!)$$

where π_j is the true probability of observing the jth response level in the population. This distribution, called the *multinomial distribution,* can be generalized to any number of response levels. The special case of two response levels is called the *binomial distribution.*

Simple random sampling is the type of sampling required by PROC CATMOD when there is one population. CATMOD uses the multinomial distribution to estimate a probability vector and its covariance matrix. If the sample size is sufficiently large, then the probability vector is approximately normally distributed as a result of central limit theory, and CATMOD uses this result to compute appropriate test statistics for the specified statistical model.

Stratified Simple Random Sampling—Multiple Populations

Suppose you take two simple random samples, fifty men and fifty women, and ask the same question as above. You are now sampling two different populations that may have different response probabilities. The data can be tabulated as follows:

Table 3.2 Two-Way Contingency Table: Sex by Color

	Favorite Color			
Sex	Red	Blue	Green	Total
Male	30	10	10	50
Female	20	10	20	50
Total	50	20	30	100

It may be noted that the row marginal totals (50, 50) of the contingency table are fixed by the sampling design, but the column marginal totals (50, 20, 30) are random. There are six probabilities of interest for this table, and they are estimated by the sample proportions:

$$p_{ij} = n_{ij}/n_i$$

where n_{ij} denotes the frequency for the ith population and the jth response, and n_i is the total frequency for the ith population. For this contingency table, the sample proportions are

Table 3.3 Table of Sample of Proportions, by Sex

Sex	Favorite Color			
	Red	Blue	Green	Total
Male	.60	.20	.20	1.00
Female	.40	.20	.40	1.00

The probability distribution of the six frequencies is the *product multinomial distribution*:

$$\text{Prob}(n_{11}, n_{12}, n_{13}, n_{21}, n_{22}, n_{23}) =$$

$$n_1!\ n_2!\pi_{11}{}^{n_{11}}\pi_{12}{}^{n_{12}}\pi_{13}{}^{n_{13}}\pi_{21}{}^{n_{21}}\pi_{22}{}^{n_{22}}\pi_{23}{}^{n_{23}}/$$

$$(n_{11}!\ n_{12}!\ n_{13}!\ \ n_{21}!\ n_{22}!\ \ n_{23}!)$$

where π_{ij} is the true probability of observing the *j*th response level in the *i*th population. The product multinomial distribution is simply the product of two or more individual multinomial distributions since the populations are independent. This distribution can be generalized to any number of populations and response levels.

Stratified simple random sampling is the type of sampling required by PROC CATMOD when there is more than one population. CATMOD uses the product multinomial distribution to estimate a probability vector and its covariance matrix. If the sample sizes are sufficiently large, then the probability vector is approximately normally distributed as a result of central limit theory, and CATMOD uses this result to compute appropriate test statistics for the specified statistical model. The statistics are known as Wald statistics, and they are approximately distributed as chi-square when the null hypothesis is true.

Observational Data—Analyzing the Entire Population

Sometimes the observed data do not come from a random sample, but instead represent a complete set of observations on some population. For example, suppose a class of 100 students is classified according to sex and favorite color, and the results are as follows:

Table 3.4 Two-Way Contingency Table: Sex by Color

Sex	Favorite Color			
	Red	Blue	Green	Total
Male	16	21	20	57
Female	12	20	11	43
Total	28	41	31	100

In this case, one could argue that all of the frequencies are fixed since the entire population is observed, and therefore, there is no sampling error. On the other hand, one could hypothesize that the observed table has only fixed marginals and that the cell frequencies represent one realization of a conceptual process of assigning color preferences to individuals. The assignment process is open to hypothesis, which means that one can hypothesize restrictions on the joint probabilities.

The usual hypothesis (sometimes called *randomness*) is that the distribution of the column variable (favorite color) does not depend on the row variable (sex). This implies that, for each row of the table, the assignment process corresponds to a simple random sample (without replacement) from the finite population represented by the column marginal totals (or by the column marginal subtotals that remain after sampling other rows). The hypothesis of randomness induces a probability distribution on the frequencies in the table; it is called the *hypergeometric distribution*.

If the same row and column variables are observed for each of several populations, then the probability distribution of all the frequencies can be called the *multiple hypergeometric distribution*. Each population is called a *stratum*, and an analysis that draws information from each stratum and then summarizes across them is called a *stratified analysis* (or a *blocked analysis*, or a *matched analysis*). PROC FREQ does such a stratified analysis, computing test statistics and measures of association. In general, the populations are formed on the basis of cross-classifications of independent variables. Stratified analysis is a method of adjusting for the effect of these variables without being forced to estimate parameters for them.

The multiple hypergeometric distribution is the one used by PROC FREQ for the computation of Cochran-Mantel-Haenszel statistics. These statistics are in the class of *randomization model test statistics*, which require minimal assumptions for their validity. PROC FREQ uses the multiple hypergeometric distribution to compute the mean and the covariance matrix of a function vector in order to measure the deviation between the observed and expected frequencies with respect to a particular type of alternative hypothesis. If the cell frequencies are sufficiently large, then the function vector is approximately normally distributed as a result of central limit theory, and FREQ uses this result to compute a quadratic form that has a chi-square distribution when the null hypothesis is true.

Randomized Experiments

Consider a *randomized experiment* in which patients are assigned to one of two treatment groups according to a randomization process that allocates fifty patients to each group. After a specified period of time, the patients' status (cured or uncured) is recorded. Suppose the resulting data are shown in **Table 3.5**. The null hypothesis is that the two treatments are equally effective. Under this hypothesis, treatment is a randomly assigned label that has no effect on the cure rate of the patients. But this implies that each row of the table represents a simple random sample from the finite population whose cure rate is described by the column marginal totals. Therefore, the column marginals (58, 42) are fixed under the hypothesis. Since the row marginals (50, 50) are fixed by the allocation process, the hypergeometric distribution is induced on the cell frequencies. Randomized experiments can also be specified in a stratified framework, and Cochran-Mantel-Haenszel statistics can be computed relative to the corresponding multiple hypergeometric distribution.

Table 3.5 Two-Way Contingency Table: Treatment by Status

Treatment	Status		Total
	Cured	Uncured	
1	36	14	50
2	22	28	50
Total	58	42	100

Relaxation of Sampling Assumptions

As indicated above, the CATMOD procedure assumes that the data are from a stratified simple random sample, and so it uses the product multinomial distribution. If the data are not from such a sample, then in many cases it is still possible to use CATMOD by arguing that each row of the contingency table *does* represent a simple random sample from some hypothetical population. The extent to which the inferences are generalizable depends on the extent to which the hypothetical population is perceived to resemble the target population.

Similarly, the Cochran-Mantel-Haenszel statistics use the multiple hypergeometric distribution, which requires fixed row and column marginal totals in each contingency table. If the sampling process does not yield a table with fixed margins, then it is usually possible to fix the margins through conditioning arguments similar to the ones used by Fisher when he developed the Exact Test for 2 by 2 tables. In other words, if you want fixed marginal totals, you can generally make your analysis conditional on those observed totals.

For more information on sampling models for categorical data, see Chapter 13 of Bishop, Fienberg, and Holland (1975).

Tests of Homogeneity—One Independent Variable

With multiple populations, it is natural to test the hypothesis that the true response probabilities are the same for all populations. For the data on favorite color, obtained from the stratified simple random sample described above, the hypothesis is that males and females have the same response probabilities for the three colors.

This hypothesis (called *homogeneity*) can be tested by using the Pearson chi-square statistic (labeled CHI-SQUARE) or the LIKELIHOOD RATIO CHI-SQUARE statistic computed by PROC FREQ when the CHISQ option is specified. The statements to read the data and invoke PROC FREQ are

```
DATA A1;
   INPUT SEX $ COLOR $ COUNT @@;
   CARDS;
MALE   RED 30    MALE   BLUE 10    MALE   GREEN 10
FEMALE RED 20    FEMALE BLUE 10    FEMALE GREEN 20
;
PROC FREQ;
   WEIGHT COUNT;
   TABLES SEX*COLOR / CHISQ NOCOL NOPERCENT;
```

Output 3.1 Tests of Homogeneity: PROC FREQ

```
                                                                        1

                   TABLE OF SEX BY COLOR

         SEX         COLOR

         FREQUENCY|
          ROW PCT |BLUE    |GREEN   |RED     |  TOTAL
         ---------+--------+--------+--------+
         FEMALE   |     10 |     20 |     20 |      50
                  |  20.00 |  40.00 |  40.00 |
         ---------+--------+--------+--------+
         MALE     |     10 |     10 |     30 |      50
                  |  20.00 |  20.00 |  60.00 |
         ---------+--------+--------+--------+
         TOTAL          20       30       50      100

              STATISTICS FOR TABLE OF SEX BY COLOR

      STATISTIC                        DF     VALUE       PROB
      ------------------------------------------------------
      CHI-SQUARE                        2     5.333      0.069
      LIKELIHOOD RATIO CHI-SQUARE       2     5.412      0.067
      MANTEL-HAENSZEL CHI-SQUARE        1     1.623      0.203
      PHI                                     0.231
      CONTINGENCY COEFFICIENT                 0.225
      CRAMER'S V                              0.231

      SAMPLE SIZE = 100
```

The FREQ procedure yields a Pearson χ^2 value of 5.33 and a likelihood ratio χ^2 value of 5.41, both of which indicate a marginally significant ($p=.07$) difference in response probabilities between the two populations.

Alternatively, you can use the Wald statistic from the CATMOD procedure to test the hypothesis of homogeneity. For these data, COLOR is the dependent variable; SEX is the independent variable. The Wald statistic of interest is the one corresponding to the SEX effect, and it has a chi-square distribution when the hypothesis of homogeneity is true. The CATMOD statements required to fit a linear model to the joint probabilities and to test the hypothesis are as follows:

```
PROC CATMOD;
   WEIGHT COUNT;
   RESPONSE JOINT;
   MODEL COLOR=SEX/NOPARM;
```

The printed output is

Output 3.2 Test of Homogeneity: PROC CATMOD

```
                                                                              1

                         CATMOD PROCEDURE

RESPONSE: COLOR                         RESPONSE LEVELS (R)=      3
WEIGHT VARIABLE: COUNT                  POPULATIONS     (S)=      2
DATA SET: A1                            TOTAL FREQUENCY (N)=    100
                                        OBSERVATIONS  (OBS)=      6


                       POPULATION PROFILES
                                        SAMPLE
                    SAMPLE      SEX      SIZE
                    -------------------------
                       1      FEMALE      50
                       2      MALE        50


                        RESPONSE PROFILES

                        RESPONSE    COLOR
                        -----------------
                            1       BLUE
                            2       GREEN
                            3       RED


                   RESPONSE FUNCTIONS            DESIGN MATRIX
       SAMPLE          1              2               1       2
       ---------------------------------------------------------
          1           0.2            0.4              1       1
          2           0.2            0.2              1      -1


                    ANALYSIS OF VARIANCE TABLE

       SOURCE                  DF    CHI-SQUARE       PROB
       ---------------------------------------------------
       INTERCEPT                2        104.23     0.0001
       SEX                      2          5.63     0.0598

       RESIDUAL                 0         -0.00     1.0000
```

CATMOD reports a χ^2 value of 5.63 for the SEX effect, which is close to the values of the other types of chi-square statistics computed by PROC FREQ.

Tests of Homogeneity—Multiple Independent Variables

Suppose the respondents in a simple random sample give their age group, their sex, and their favorite color. You can tabulate the frequencies in six populations corresponding to three age groups by two sex levels:

Table 3.6 Two-Way Contingency Table: Age by Sex

			Favorite Color			
Population	Age	Sex	Red	Blue	Green	Total
1	Young	Female	50	40	100	190
2	Young	Male	55	10	30	95
3	Middle	Female	50	30	100	180
4	Middle	Male	95	20	50	165
5	Old	Female	50	30	100	180
6	Old	Male	50	20	20	90

The initial question remains the same: Are the response probabilities the same in each population? If the response probabilities are not the same, there are several possible explanations. The differences may be due to

- SEX alone
- AGE alone
- SEX and AGE (additively)
- SEX and AGE with interaction.

For the CATMOD procedure, the MODEL statements corresponding to these four models are

1. MODEL COLOR = SEX;
2. MODEL COLOR = AGE;
3. MODEL COLOR = SEX AGE;
4. MODEL COLOR = SEX AGE SEX*AGE;

The last model is sometimes called a *complete* or *saturated* model because all of the variation among populations (with respect to the response probabilities) is explained by the effects on the right-hand side of the MODEL statement. You can use the following statements to generate the data set and fit the saturated model:

```
DATA A;
   INPUT AGE $ SEX $ RED BLUE GREEN;
   CARDS;
YOUNG  FEMALE     50    40    100
YOUNG  MALE       55    10     30
MIDDLE FEMALE     50    30    100
MIDDLE MALE       95    20     50
OLD    FEMALE     50    30    100
OLD    MALE       50    20     20
;
DATA B;
   SET A;
   COLOR='RED  ';    COUNT=RED;      OUTPUT;
   COLOR='BLUE ';    COUNT=BLUE;     OUTPUT;
   COLOR='GREEN';    COUNT=GREEN;    OUTPUT;
```

```
      KEEP COLOR AGE SEX COUNT;
   PROC CATMOD DATA=B;
      WEIGHT COUNT;
      RESPONSE JOINT;
      MODEL COLOR = SEX AGE SEX*AGE / NOPARM;
      CONTRAST 'AGE & SEX*AGE'
         @1 AGE 1 0, @1 AGE 0 1, @1 SEX*AGE 1 0, @1 SEX*AGE 0 1,
         @2 AGE 1 0, @2 AGE 0 1, @2 SEX*AGE 1 0, @2 SEX*AGE 0 1;
```

The printed output is

Output 3.3 A Saturated Model: PROC CATMOD

```
                                                                              1

                             CATMOD PROCEDURE

           RESPONSE: COLOR                       RESPONSE LEVELS (R)=     3
           WEIGHT VARIABLE: COUNT                POPULATIONS     (S)=     6
           DATA SET: B                           TOTAL FREQUENCY (N)=   900
                                                 OBSERVATIONS  (OBS)=    18


                            POPULATION PROFILES
                                                       SAMPLE
                 SAMPLE       SEX           AGE         SIZE
                 ---------------------------------------------
                     1      FEMALE        MIDDLE         180
                     2      FEMALE        OLD            180
                     3      FEMALE        YOUNG          190
                     4      MALE          MIDDLE         165
                     5      MALE          OLD             90
                     6      MALE          YOUNG           95


                             RESPONSE PROFILES

                             RESPONSE    COLOR
                             -----------------
                                 1       BLUE
                                 2       GREEN
                                 3       RED


           RESPONSE FUNCTIONS                          DESIGN MATRIX
  SAMPLE        1              2            1     2      3      4      5      6
  ------------------------------------------------------------------------------
     1      0.166667       0.555556         1     1      1      0      1      0
     2      0.166667       0.555556         1     1      0      1      0      1
     3      0.210526       0.526316         1     1     -1     -1     -1     -1
     4      0.121212        0.30303         1    -1      1      0     -1      0
     5      0.222222       0.222222         1    -1      0      1      0     -1
     6      0.105263       0.315789         1    -1     -1     -1      1      1


                          ANALYSIS OF VARIANCE TABLE

               SOURCE                   DF    CHI-SQUARE      PROB
               ----------------------------------------------------
               INTERCEPT                 2       1203.41    0.0001
               SEX                       2         86.71    0.0001
               AGE                       4          2.81    0.5900
               SEX*AGE                   4          6.21    0.1839

               RESIDUAL                  0         -0.00    1.0000
```

```
                                                                    2

                         CATMOD PROCEDURE

                       ANALYSIS OF CONTRASTS

    CONTRAST                        DF    CHI-SQUARE       PROB
    ---------------------------------------------------------
    AGE & SEX*AGE                    8          7.82     0.4515
```

The ANALYSIS OF VARIANCE TABLE shows that the effects AGE and SEX*AGE are not significant ($p>.10$), and the ANALYSIS OF CONTRASTS indicates that their joint effect is similarly nonsignificant ($p>.10$). Thus, you can try fitting a reduced linear model that contains only the SEX main effect:

```
PROC CATMOD DATA=B;
   WEIGHT COUNT;
   POPULATION SEX AGE;
   RESPONSE JOINT;
   MODEL COLOR = SEX / NOPROFILE NODESIGN;
```

The printed output for the main-effect model is

Output 3.4 A Reduced Main-Effect Model: PROC CATMOD

```
                                                                         1

                           CATMOD PROCEDURE

RESPONSE: COLOR                              RESPONSE LEVELS (R)=      3
WEIGHT VARIABLE: COUNT                       POPULATIONS      (S)=      6
DATA SET: B                                  TOTAL FREQUENCY (N)=    900
                                             OBSERVATIONS   (OBS)=     18


                      ANALYSIS OF VARIANCE TABLE

       SOURCE                         DF    CHI-SQUARE      PROB
       ---------------------------------------------------------
       INTERCEPT                       2       1258.29    0.0001
       SEX                             2         94.97    0.0001

       RESIDUAL                        8          7.82    0.4515


                 ANALYSIS OF INDIVIDUAL PARAMETERS

                                              STANDARD      CHI-
EFFECT                 PARAMETER  ESTIMATE     ERROR      SQUARE   PROB
------------------------------------------------------------------------
INTERCEPT                      1  0.156797   .0121697     166.00  0.0001
                               2  0.415782   .0159784     677.12  0.0001
SEX                            3  .0232927   .0121697       3.66  0.0556
                               4  0.130825   .0159784      67.04  0.0001
```

The goodness-of-fit statistic (residual chi-square) for the reduced model tests the joint significance of all the effects deleted from the original saturated model (AGE and SEX*AGE). Since this statistic ($Q=7.82$, $df=8$) is nonsignificant ($p=.45$), the model is said to fit the data. For more information about this type of analysis, see Grizzle, Starmer, and Koch (1969).

Tests of Independence

In a previous section, the Pearson chi-square statistic was used to test the hypothesis that the true response probabilities are the same for two populations. You can also use the Pearson chi-square test for a two-dimensional contingency table to test the independence of two dependent variables.

Suppose you ask 200 people the favorite-color question given above, as well as the following one: Of the three desserts, ice cream, pie, and cake, which is your favorite? The results may be represented as in the following contingency table:

Table 3.7 Two-Way Contingency Table: Dessert by Color

	Favorite Color			
Favorite Dessert	Blue	Green	Red	Total
Ice Cream	16	11	50	77
Pie	21	19	22	62
Cake	21	32	8	61
Total	58	62	80	200

The hypothesis of independence is that the true cell probabilities are the product of the corresponding marginal probabilities. In other words,

$$\pi_{jk} = \pi_{j.}\pi_{.k}$$

where π_{jk} is the probability of observing the jth level of DESSERT and the kth level of COLOR in the population. Similarly, $\pi_{j.}$ is the probability of observing the jth level of DESSERT in the population, and $\pi_{.k}$ is the probability of observing the kth level of COLOR in the population.

This is a one-population problem since both variables are dependent variables. To test the hypothesis of independence, you can use the Pearson chi-square statistic (labeled CHI_SQUARE) or the LIKELIHOOD RATIO CHI-SQUARE statistic computed by PROC FREQ when the CHISQ option is specified. The statements to read the data and invoke PROC FREQ are

```
DATA IND;
   INPUT DESSERT $ COLOR $ COUNT @@;
   CARDS;
ICE  BLUE 16      ICE  GREEN 11     ICE  RED 50
PIE  BLUE 21      PIE  GREEN 19     PIE  RED 22
CAKE BLUE 21      CAKE GREEN 32     CAKE RED  8
;
PROC FREQ;
   WEIGHT COUNT;
   TABLES DESSERT*COLOR / CHISQ;
```

The following output shows the results:

Output 3.5 Tests of Independence: PROC FREQ

```
                TABLE OF DESSERT BY COLOR

DESSERT     COLOR

FREQUENCY|
 PERCENT |
 ROW PCT |
 COL PCT |BLUE    |GREEN   |RED     |  TOTAL
---------+--------+--------+--------+
CAKE     |     21 |     32 |      8 |     61
         |  10.50 |  16.00 |   4.00 |  30.50
         |  34.43 |  52.46 |  13.11 |
         |  36.21 |  51.61 |  10.00 |
---------+--------+--------+--------+
ICE      |     16 |     11 |     50 |     77
         |   8.00 |   5.50 |  25.00 |  38.50
         |  20.78 |  14.29 |  64.94 |
         |  27.59 |  17.74 |  62.50 |
---------+--------+--------+--------+
PIE      |     21 |     19 |     22 |     62
         |  10.50 |   9.50 |  11.00 |  31.00
         |  33.87 |  30.65 |  35.48 |
         |  36.21 |  30.65 |  27.50 |
---------+--------+--------+--------+
TOTAL          58       62       80      200
            29.00    31.00    40.00   100.00


            STATISTICS FOR TABLE OF DESSERT BY COLOR

STATISTIC                     DF      VALUE       PROB
------------------------------------------------------
CHI-SQUARE                     4     42.232      0.000
LIKELIHOOD RATIO CHI-SQUARE    4     44.581      0.000
MANTEL-HAENSZEL CHI-SQUARE     1      2.302      0.129
PHI                                   0.460
CONTINGENCY COEFFICIENT               0.418
CRAMER'S V                            0.325

SAMPLE SIZE = 200
```

The FREQ procedure yields a Pearson χ^2 value of 42.2 and a likelihood ratio χ^2 value of 44.6, both of which indicate a highly significant ($p<.01$) departure from independence.

CATMOD also produces tests of independence quite easily. For this example, specify

```
PROC CATMOD;
   WEIGHT COUNT;
   MODEL DESSERT*COLOR = _RESPONSE_ / ML NOGLS NOPARM;
   REPEATED / _RESPONSE_ = DESSERT COLOR;
```

The printed output is

Output 3.6 Test of Independence: PROC CATMOD

```
                                                                                                   1

                                      CATMOD PROCEDURE

                  RESPONSE: DESSERT*COLOR                 RESPONSE LEVELS (R)=     9
                  WEIGHT VARIABLE: COUNT                  POPULATIONS     (S)=     1
                  DATA SET: IND                           TOTAL FREQUENCY (N)=   200
                                                          OBSERVATIONS  (OBS)=     9


                                                SAMPLE
                                     SAMPLE      SIZE
                                     ------------------
                                         1        200


                                      RESPONSE PROFILES

                                 RESPONSE    DESSERT        COLOR
                                 -------------------------------
                                     1        CAKE          BLUE
                                     2        CAKE          GREEN
                                     3        CAKE          RED
                                     4        ICE           BLUE
                                     5        ICE           GREEN
                                     6        ICE           RED
                                     7        PIE           BLUE
                                     8        PIE           GREEN
                                     9        PIE           RED


                                 MAXIMUM LIKELIHOOD ANALYSIS

              SUB         -2 LOG     CONVERGENCE                     PARAMETER ESTIMATES
ITERATION  ITERATION   LIKELIHOOD     CRITERION          1             2             3             4
------------------------------------------------------------------------------------------------------
    0          0          878.89             1           0             0             0             0
    1          0         872.527     .00723935      -0.085         0.155         -0.13         -0.07
    2          0         872.516      1.26E-05   -.0830681      0.149872     -0.129444     -.0627209
    3          0         872.516      4.00E-11   -0.083064      0.149868     -0.129425     -.0627336


                                  ANALYSIS OF VARIANCE TABLE

                     SOURCE                    DF    CHI-SQUARE      PROB
                     -----------------------------------------------------
                     DESSERT                    2          2.40    0.3012
                     COLOR                      2          4.09    0.1293

                     LIKELIHOOD RATIO           4         44.58    0.0001
```

The goodness-of-fit statistic for this model is the test of independence. Using maximum likelihood estimation, CATMOD reports a likelihood ratio test of 44.6, which is identical to the one computed by PROC FREQ. Thus, the model of independence does not fit the data. For further information on independence and generalized independence when there are more than two variables, see Bishop, Fienberg, and Holland (1975).

Parameter Estimation

The CATMOD procedure has two methods of parameter estimation available for general specifications of linear models. Weighted least squares estimation is available for all types of response functions, and maximum likelihood estimation is available when the response functions are generalized logits (see the CATMOD documentation for details). The latter functions are used for log-linear model analysis, logistic regression, and tests of independence. Both types of estimators are *BAN* (best asymptotic normal) estimators, and therefore the difference between them goes to zero as the sample size goes to infinity.

Repeated Measures

Suppose you take a stratified simple random sample of two groups of workers, and at each of two time points (10 a.m. and 4 p.m. on a Friday), you ask every worker: Are you tired? The first group contains 100 male employees who work under incandescent lights; the second contains 100 male employees who work under fluorescent lights. The results could be tabulated as follows:

Table 3.8 Three-Way Frequency Table

Tired	Tired	Frequency	
at 10 a.m.	at 4 p.m.	Incandescent	Fluorescent
Yes	Yes	19	14
Yes	No	7	11
No	Yes	60	53
No	No	14	22

For these data, LIGHTING is the independent variable, and there are two dependent variables (for example, TIRED10 and TIRED4). You want to know about the main effects of lighting and time and their interaction. You can analyze the data with the following statements:

```
DATA REP;
   INPUT LIGHTING $ TIRED10 $ TIRED4 $ WT @@;
   CARDS;
INCAN YES YES 19       FLUOR YES YES 14
INCAN YES  NO  7       FLUOR YES  NO 11
INCAN  NO YES 60       FLUOR  NO YES 53
INCAN  NO  NO 14       FLUOR  NO  NO 22
;
PROC CATMOD;
   WEIGHT WT;
   RESPONSE MARGINALS;
   MODEL TIRED10*TIRED4 = LIGHTING _RESPONSE_ LIGHTING*_RESPONSE_ ;
   REPEATED TIME 2 / _RESPONSE_ = TIME;
```

These statements yield an analysis of the marginal probabilities of being tired at the two time points. The printed output is

Output 3.7 Repeated Measures Analysis: PROC CATMOD

```
                                                                                1

                              CATMOD PROCEDURE

RESPONSE: TIRED10*TIRED4                   RESPONSE LEVELS (R)=     4
WEIGHT VARIABLE: WT                        POPULATIONS     (S)=     2
DATA SET: REP                              TOTAL FREQUENCY (N)=   200
                                           OBSERVATIONS  (OBS)=     8


                           POPULATION PROFILES
                                             SAMPLE
                       SAMPLE    LIGHTING     SIZE
                       ---------------------------
                          1      FLUOR        100
                          2      INCAN        100


                            RESPONSE PROFILES

                   RESPONSE     TIRED10          TIRED4
                   ----------------------------------
                       1        NO               NO
                       2        NO               YES
                       3        YES              NO
                       4        YES              YES


           FUNCTION    RESPONSE               DESIGN MATRIX
   SAMPLE   NUMBER     FUNCTION          1        2        3        4
   ------------------------------------------------------------------
      1        1         0.75            1        1        1        1
               2         0.33            1        1       -1       -1

      2        1         0.74            1       -1        1       -1
               2         0.21            1       -1       -1        1


                       ANALYSIS OF VARIANCE TABLE

        SOURCE                     DF    CHI-SQUARE      PROB
        --------------------------------------------------
        INTERCEPT                   1        605.04    0.0001
        LIGHTING                    1          2.48    0.1152
        TIME                        1        105.84    0.0001
        LIGHTING*_RESPONSE_         1          1.42    0.2336

        RESIDUAL                    0          0.00    1.0000

        NOTE: _RESPONSE_ = TIME
```

```
                                                                                2

                              CATMOD PROCEDURE

                     ANALYSIS OF INDIVIDUAL PARAMETERS

                                                   STANDARD       CHI-
EFFECT                  PARAMETER   ESTIMATE        ERROR        SQUARE     PROB
--------------------------------------------------------------------------------
INTERCEPT                       1     0.5075     .0206322       605.04   0.0001
LIGHTING                        2     0.0325     .0206322         2.48   0.1152
TIME                            3     0.2375     .0230854       105.84   0.0001
LIGHTING*_RESPONSE_             4    -0.0275     .0230854         1.42   0.2336

NOTE: _RESPONSE_ = TIME
```

For further information on repeated measures analysis of categorical data, see Stanish and Koch (1984) and Koch et al. (1977).

References

Bishop, Y., Fienberg, S.E., and Holland, P.W. (1975), *Discrete Multivariate Analysis: Theory and Practice*, Cambridge: The MIT Press.

Grizzle, J.E., Starmer, C.F., and Koch, G.G. (1969), "Analysis of Categorical Data by Linear Models," *Biometrics 25*, 489-504.

Koch, G.G., Landis, J.R., Freeman, J.L., Freeman, D.H., and Lehnen, R.G. (1977), "A General Methodology for the Analysis of Experiments with Repeated Measurement of Categorical Data," *Biometrics 33*, 133-158.

Stanish, W.M. and Koch, G.G. (1984), "The Use of CATMOD for Repeated Measurement Analysis of Categorical Data," *Proceedings of the Ninth Annual SAS Users Group International Conference*.

Chapter 4
SAS® Multivariate Procedures

Introduction

The procedures discussed in this chapter investigate relationships among variables without designating some as independent and others as dependent. Principal component and common factor analysis examine relationships within a single set of variables, whereas canonical correlation looks at the relationship between two sets of variables. The following is a brief description of the procedures:

PRINCOMP performs a principal component analysis and outputs standardized or unstandardized principal component scores.

FACTOR performs principal component and common factor analyses with rotations and outputs standardized component scores or estimates of common factor scores.

CANCORR performs a canonical correlation analysis and outputs canonical variable scores.

Many other SAS procedures can also analyze multivariate data, for example, CATMOD, GLM, REG, and the clustering and discriminant procedures.

The purpose of principal component analysis is to derive a small number of linear combinations (principal components) of a set of variables that retain as much of the information in the original variables as possible. Often a small number of principal components can be used in place of the original variables for plotting, regression, clustering, and so on. Principal component analysis can also be viewed as an attempt to uncover approximate linear dependencies among variables.

The purpose of common factor analysis is to explain the correlations or covariances among a set of variables in terms of a limited number of unobservable, latent variables. The latent variables are not generally computable as linear combinations of the original variables. In common factor analysis it is assumed that the variables would be linearly related were it not for uncorrelated random error or unique variation in each variable; both the linear relations and the amount of unique variation can be estimated.

Principal component and common factor analysis are often followed by rotation of the components or factors. Rotation is the application of a non-singular linear transformation to components or common factors to aid interpretation.

The purpose of canonical correlation analysis is to explain or summarize the relationship between two sets of variables by finding a small number of linear combinations from each set of variables that have the highest possible between-set correlations. Plots of the canonical variables can be useful in examining multivariate dependencies. With appropriate input, the CANCORR procedure can be used for maximum redundancy analysis (van den Wollenberg 1977) or principal components of instrumental variables (Rao 1964); contingency table analysis and optimal scaling (Mardia, Kent, and Bibby 1979, pp. 290-295; Kshirsagar 1972; Nishisato 1980); orthogonal Procrustes rotation (Mulaik 1972; Hanson and Norris 1981); and finding a polynomial transformation of the dependent variable to minimize interaction in an analysis of variance.

Comparison of the PRINCOMP and FACTOR Procedures

Although PROC FACTOR performs common factor analysis, the default method for FACTOR is principal component analysis. FACTOR produces the same results as PRINCOMP except that the scoring coefficients from FACTOR are normalized to give principal component scores with unit variance, while PRINCOMP by default produces scores with variance equal to the corresponding eigenvalue. Optionally, PRINCOMP can compute standardized scores.

PRINCOMP has the following advantages over FACTOR:

- PRINCOMP is faster if a small number of components are requested.
- PRINCOMP is simpler to use.

FACTOR has the following advantages over PRINCOMP for principal component analysis:

- FACTOR has more output than PRINCOMP, including the scree plot, pattern matrix, and residual correlations.
- FACTOR has options for printing matrices in more easily interpretable forms than does PRINCOMP.
- FACTOR does rotations.

If you want to do a common factor analysis, you must use FACTOR instead of PRINCOMP. Principal component analysis should never be used if a common factor solution is desired (Dziuban and Harris 1973; Lee and Comrey 1979).

References

Dziuban, C.D. and Harris, C.W. (1973), "On the Extraction of Components and the Applicability of the Factor Model," *American Educational Research Journal*, 10, 93-99.

Hanson, R.J. and Norris, M.J. (1981), "Analysis of Measurements Based on the Singular Value Decomposition," *SIAM Journal on Scientific and Statistical Computing*, 2, 363-373.

Kshirsagar, A.M. (1972), *Multivariate Analysis*, New York: Marcel Dekker.

Lee, H.B. and Comrey, A.L. (1979), "Distortions in a Commonly Used Factor Analytic Procedure," *Multivariate Behavioral Research*, 14, 301-321.

Mardia, K.V., Kent, J.T., and Bibby, J.M. (1979), *Multivariate Analysis*, London: Academic Press.

Mulaik, S.A. (1972), *The Foundations of Factor Analysis*, New York: McGraw-Hill Book Co.

Nishisato, S. (1980), *Analysis of Categorical Data: Dual Scaling and Its Applications*, Toronto: University of Toronto Press.

Rao, C.R. (1964), "The Use and Interpretation of Principal Component Analysis in Applied Research," *Sankhya A*, 26, 329-358.

Van den Wollenberg, A.L. (1977), "Redundancy Analysis—An Alternative to Canonical Correlation Analysis," *Psychometrika*, 42, 207-219.

Chapter 5
SAS® Discriminant Procedures

Introduction

The SAS procedures for discriminant analysis treat data with one classification variable and several quantitative variables. The purpose of discriminant analysis can be to find

- a mathematical rule, or *discriminant function,* for guessing which class an observation belongs to based on knowledge of the quantitative variables only
- a set of linear combinations of the quantitative variables that best reveals the differences among the classes; or
- a subset of the quantitative variables that best reveals the differences among the classes.

The SAS discriminant procedures are as follows:

DISCRIM	classifies observations assuming a multivariate normal distribution within each class. The within-class covariance matrices may be assumed equal or unequal.
NEIGHBOR	classifies observations using a nonparametric nearest-neighbor method.
CANDISC	performs a canonical analysis to find linear combinations of the variables that best summarize the differences among the classes.
STEPDISC	uses forward selection, backward elimination, or stepwise selection to try to find a subset of variables that best reveals differences among the classes.

The term *discriminant analysis* (Fisher 1936; Cooley and Lohnes 1971; Tatsuoka 1971; Kshirsagar 1972; Lachenbruch 1975, 1979; Gnanadesikan 1977; Klecka 1980; Hand 1981) refers to several different types of analysis. *Classificatory discriminant analysis* is used to classify observations into two or more known groups on the basis of one or more numeric variables. Classification can be done by the DISCRIM and NEIGHBOR procedures. Use NEIGHBOR when the classes have radically non-normal distributions. DISCRIM is appropriate for approximately normal within-class distributions. *Canonical discriminant analysis* is a dimension-reduction technique related to principal components and canonical correlation and is performed by the CANDISC procedure. *Stepwise discriminant analysis* is a variable-selection technique implemented by the STEPDISC procedure. After selecting a subset of variables with STEPDISC, you can use any of the other discriminant procedures to obtain more detailed analyses. CANDISC and STEPDISC perform hypothesis tests that require the within-class distributions to be approximately normal, but these procedures can be used descriptively with non-normal data.

Discriminant analysis should not be confused with *cluster analysis*. All varieties of discriminant analysis require prior knowledge of the classes, usually in the form of a sample from each class. In cluster analysis the data do not include information on class membership; the purpose is to construct a classification. See "SAS Clustering Procedures."

If your quantitative variables are not normally distributed or if you wish to classify observations on the basis of categorical variables, you should consider using the CATMOD procedure to fit a categorical linear model with the classification variable as the dependent variable. Press and Wilson (1978) compare logistic regression and discriminant analysis and conclude that logistic regression is preferable to discriminant methods based on normality assumptions when the variables do not have multivariate normal distributions within classes.

Another alternative to discriminant analysis is to perform a series of univariate one-way *ANOVA*s. Both CANDISC and STEPDISC provide summaries of the univariate *ANOVA*s. The advantage of the multivariate approach is that two or more classes that overlap considerably when each variable is viewed separately may be more distinct when examined from a multivariate point of view. Consider the two classes indicated by H and O in the following example:

```
DATA RANDOM;
   DROP N;
   GROUP='H';
   DO N=1 TO 20;
      X=4.5+2*RANNOR(57391);
      Y=X+.5+RANNOR(57391);
      OUTPUT;
      END;
   GROUP='O';
   DO N=1 TO 20;
      X=6.25+2*RANNOR(57391);
      Y=X-1.+RANNOR(57391);
      OUTPUT;
      END;

PROC PLOT; PLOT Y*X=GROUP;

PROC CANDISC UNI;
   CLASS GROUP;
   VAR X Y;
```

Output 5.1 Contrasting Univariate and Multivariate Analyses

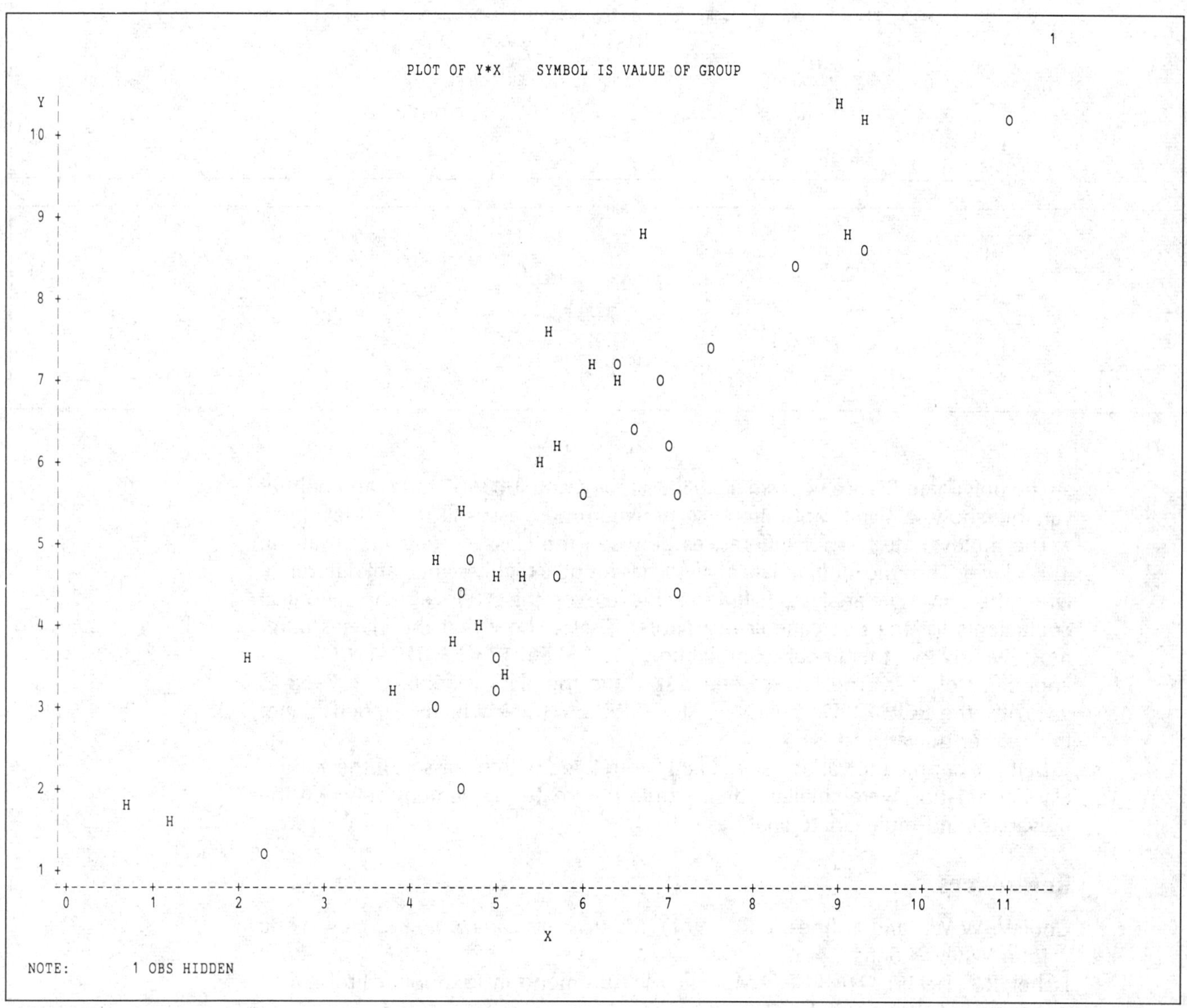

2

UNIVARIATE STATISTICS

VARIABLE	MEAN	TOTAL STD	WITHIN STD	BETWEEN STD	R-SQUARED	RSQ/(1-RSQ)	F	PROB > F
X	5.73427912	2.17755199	2.14981269	0.68202567	0.050307	0.053	2.013	0.1641
Y	5.51010980	2.42146553	2.44861869	0.20474923	0.003667	0.004	0.140	0.7105

	CANONICAL CORRELATION	ADJUSTED CANONICAL CORRELATION	APPROX STANDARD ERROR	SQUARED CANONICAL CORRELATION	EIGENVALUES OF INV(E)*H = CANRSQ/(1-CANRSQ) EIGENVALUE	DIFFERENCE	PROPORTION	CUMULATIVE
1	0.598300	0.589467	0.102808	0.357963	0.5575	.	1.0000	1.0000

(continued on next page)

(continued from previous page)

```
TESTS OF H0: THE CANONICAL CORRELATION IN THE CURRENT ROW AND ALL THAT FOLLOW ARE ZERO

                    LIKELIHOOD
                      RATIO          F          NUM DF     DEN DF   PR > F

                 1  0.64203704     10.3145          2          37   0.0003
```

```
                                                                                   3

                              RAW CANONICAL COEFFICIENTS

                                                 CAN1

                                X          -1.205756217
                                Y           1.010412967
```

The univariate R^2s are very small, .050307 for X and .003667 for Y, and neither variable shows a significant difference between the classes at the .10 level.

The multivariate test for differences between the classes is significant at the .0003 level. Thus the multivariate analysis has found a highly significant difference when the univariate analyses failed to achieve even the .10 level. The canonical coefficients for the first canonical variable, CAN1, show that the classes differ most widely on the linear combination -1.205756217X+1.010412967Y, or approximately Y-X. The R^2 between CAN1 and the class variable is .357963 as given by the SQUARED CANONICAL CORRELATION, which is much higher than either univariate R^2.

In this example the variables are highly correlated within classes. If the within-class correlation were smaller, there would be greater agreement between the univariate and multivariate analyses.

References

Cooley, W.W., and Lohnes, P.R. (1971), *Multivariate Data Analysis*, New York: John Wiley & Sons.

Fisher, R.A. (1936), "The Use of Multiple Measurements in Taxonomic Problems," *Annals of Eugenics*, 7, 179-188.

Gnanadesikan, R. (1977), *Methods for Statistical Data Analysis of Multivariate Observations*, New York: Wiley.

Hand, D.J. (1981), *Discrimination and Classification*, New York: John Wiley & Sons.

Klecka, W.R. (1980), *Discriminant Analysis*, Sage University Paper Series on Quantitative Applications in the Social Sciences, 07-019. Beverly Hills: Sage Publications.

Kshirsagar, A.M. (1972), *Multivariate Analysis*, New York: Marcel Dekker.

Lachenbruch, P.A. (1975), *Discriminant Analysis*, New York: Hafner.

Lachenbruch, P.A. (1979), "Discriminant Analysis," *Biometrics*, 35, 69-85.

Press, S.J. and Wilson, S. (1978), "Choosing Between Logistic Regression and Discriminant Analysis," *Journal of the American Statistical Association*, 73, 699-705.

Tatsuoka, M.M. (1971), *Multivariate Analysis*, New York: John Wiley & Sons.

Chapter 6

SAS® Clustering Procedures

Introduction

SAS clustering procedures can be used to cluster the observations or the variables in a SAS data set. Both hierarchical and disjoint clusters can be obtained. Only numeric variables are permitted.

The purpose of cluster analysis is to place objects into groups or clusters suggested by the data, not defined a priori, such that objects in a given cluster tend to be similar to each other in some sense, and objects in different clusters tend to be dissimilar. Cluster analysis can also be used for summarizing data rather than for finding "natural" or "real" clusters; this use of clustering is sometimes called *dissection* (Everitt 1980).

Any generalization about cluster analysis must be vague because a vast number of clustering methods have been developed in several different fields, with different definitions of clusters and similarity among objects. The variety of clustering techniques is reflected by the variety of terms used for cluster analysis: botryology, classification, clumping, morphometrics, nosography, nosology, numerical taxonomy, partitioning, Q-analysis, systematics, taximetrics, taxonorics, typology, and unsupervised pattern recognition. Good (1977) has also suggested aciniformics and agminatics.

Several types of clusters are possible:

- Disjoint clusters place each object in one and only one cluster.
- Hierarchical clusters are organized so that one cluster may be entirely contained within another cluster, but no other kind of overlap between clusters is allowed.
- Overlapping clusters can be constrained to limit the number of objects that belong simultaneously to two clusters, or they can be unconstrained, allowing any degree of overlap in cluster membership.
- Fuzzy clusters are defined by a probability or grade of membership of each object in each cluster. Fuzzy clusters can be disjoint, hierarchical, or overlapping.

The data representations of objects to be clustered also take many forms. The most common are

- a square distance or similarity matrix, in which both rows and columns correspond to the objects to be clustered. A correlation matrix is an example of a similarity matrix.

- a coordinate matrix, in which the rows are observations and the columns are variables, as in the usual SAS multivariate data set. The observations, or the variables, or both may be clustered.

The SAS procedures for clustering are oriented toward disjoint or hierarchical clusters from coordinate data, distance data, or a correlation or covariance matrix. The following procedures are used for clustering:

CLUSTER	does hierarchical clustering of observations using eleven agglomerative methods applied to coordinate data or distance data.
FASTCLUS	finds disjoint clusters of observations using a *k*-means method applied to coordinate data. PROC FASTCLUS is especially suitable for large data sets containing as many as 100,000 observations.
VARCLUS	is for both hierarchical and disjoint clustering of variables by oblique multiple-group component analysis.
TREE	draws tree diagrams, also called *dendrograms* or *phenograms*, using output from the CLUSTER or VARCLUS procedures. PROC TREE can also create a data set indicating cluster membership at any specified level of the cluster tree.

In addition, these procedures are described in the *SUGI Supplemental Library User's Guide*:

HIER	draws hierarchical diagrams and can be used instead of TREE with the output data sets from CLUSTER and VARCLUS.
IPFPHC	hierarchically clusters the units of a transaction flow table (an asymmetric similarity matrix) and can be used for single linkage clustering.
OVERCLUS	finds overlapping clusters from similarity data.

The following procedures are useful for processing data prior to the actual cluster analysis:

ACECLUS	attempts to estimate the pooled within-cluster covariance matrix from coordinate data without knowledge of the number or the membership of the clusters (Art, Gnanadesikan, and Kettenring 1982). PROC ACECLUS outputs a data set containing canonical variable scores to be used in the cluster analysis proper.
PRINCOMP	performs a principal component analysis and outputs principal component scores.
STANDARD	standardizes variables to a specified mean and variance.

The best introductions to cluster analysis are Everitt (1980) and Massart and Kaufman (1983). Other important texts are Anderberg (1973), Sneath and Sokal (1973), Duran and Odell (1974), and Hartigan (1975). Hartigan (1975) and Spath (1980) give numerous FORTRAN programs for clustering. Any prospective user of cluster analysis should study the Monte Carlo results of Milligan (1980), Milligan and Cooper (1983), and Cooper and Milligan (1984). Essential references on the statistical aspects of clustering include MacQueen (1967), Wolfe (1970), Scott and Symons (1971), Hartigan (1977; 1978; 1981), Binder (1978; 1981), Symons (1981), Wong and Schaack (1982), and Wong and Lane (1983). See Blashfield and Aldenderfer (1978) for a discussion of the fragmented state of the literature on cluster analysis.

Clustering Variables

Factor rotation is often used to cluster variables, but the resulting clusters are fuzzy. It is preferable to use PROC VARCLUS if you want hard (non-fuzzy), disjoint clusters. Factor rotation is better if you want to be able to find overlapping clusters. It is often a good idea to try both VARCLUS and FACTOR with an oblique rotation, compare the amount of variance explained by each, and see how fuzzy the factor loadings are and whether there seem to be overlapping clusters.

You can use PROC VARCLUS to harden a fuzzy factor rotation; use PROC FACTOR to create an output data set containing scoring coefficients and initialize VARCLUS with this data set:

```
PROC FACTOR ROTATE=PROMAX SCORE OUTSTAT=FACT;
PROC VARCLUS INITIAL=INPUT PROPORTION=0;
```

Any rotation method could be used instead of PROMAX. Only the SCORE and OUTSTAT= options are necessary in the PROC FACTOR statement. VARCLUS reads the correlation matrix from the data set created by FACTOR. The INITIAL=INPUT option tells VARCLUS to read initial scoring coefficients from the data set. PROPORTION=0 keeps VARCLUS from splitting any of the clusters.

Clustering Observations

CLUSTER is easier to use than FASTCLUS because one run produces results from one cluster up to as many as you like. You must run FASTCLUS once for each number of clusters.

The time required by FASTCLUS is roughly proportional to the number of observations, whereas the time required by CLUSTER with most methods varies with the square or cube of the number of observations. FASTCLUS can therefore be used with much larger data sets than CLUSTER.

If you want to cluster hierarchically a data set that is too large to use with CLUSTER directly, you can have FASTCLUS produce, for example, fifty clusters, and let CLUSTER analyze these fifty clusters instead of the entire data set. The MEAN= data set produced by FASTCLUS contains two special variables:

- _FREQ_ gives the number of observations in the cluster.
- _RMSSTD_ gives the root-mean-square across variables of the cluster standard deviations.

These variables are automatically used by CLUSTER to give the correct results when clustering clusters. For example, you could use Ward's minimum variance method (Ward 1963):

```
PROC FASTCLUS MAXCLUSTERS=50 MEAN=TEMP;
   VAR X Y Z;
PROC CLUSTER METHOD=WARD OUTTREE=TREE;
   VAR X Y Z;
```

or Wong's hybrid method (Wong 1982):

```
PROC FASTCLUS MAXCLUSTERS=50 MEAN=TEMP;
   VAR X Y Z;
PROC CLUSTER METHOD=DENSITY HYBRID OUTTREE=TREE;
   VAR X Y Z;
```

More detailed examples are given with the CLUSTER procedure documentation.

Characteristics of Methods for Clustering Observations

Many simulation studies comparing various methods of cluster analysis have been performed. In these studies, artificial data sets containing known clusters are produced using pseudo-random number generators. The data sets are analyzed by a variety of clustering methods and the degree to which each clustering method recovers the known cluster structure is evaluated. See Milligan (1981) for a review of such studies. In most of these studies, the clustering method with the best overall performance has been either average linkage or Ward's minimum variance method. The method with the poorest overall performance has almost invariably been single linkage. However, in many respects, the results of simulation studies have been inconsistent and confusing.

In attempting to evaluate clustering methods, it is essential to realize that most methods are biased toward finding clusters possessing certain characteristics related to size (number of members), shape, or dispersion. Methods based on the least-squares criterion (Sarle 1982), such as *k*-means and Ward's minimum variance method, tend to find clusters with roughly the same number of observations in each cluster. Average linkage is somewhat biased toward finding clusters of equal variance. Many clustering methods tend to produce compact, roughly hyperspherical clusters, and are incapable of detecting clusters with highly elongated or irregular shapes. The methods with the least bias are those based on nonparametric density estimation such as single linkage and density linkage.

Most simulation studies have generated compact (often multivariate-normal) clusters of roughly equal size or dispersion. Such studies naturally favor average linkage and Ward's method over most other hierarchical methods, especially single linkage. It would be easy, however, to design a study using elongated or irregular clusters in which single linkage would perform much better than average linkage or Ward's method (see some of the examples below). Even studies that compare clustering methods using "realistic" data may unfairly favor particular methods. For example, in all the data sets used by Mezzich and Solomon (1980), the clusters established by field experts are of equal size. In interpreting simulation or other comparative studies, you must therefore decide whether the artificially generated clusters in the study resemble the clusters you suspect may exist in your data in terms of size, shape, and dispersion. If, like many people doing exploratory cluster analysis, you have no idea what kinds of clusters to expect, you should include at least one of the relatively unbiased methods, such as density linkage, in your analysis.

If the population clusters are sufficiently well-separated, almost any clustering method will perform well, as in the following example using single linkage. In this and subsequent examples, the output from the clustering procedures is not shown, but cluster membership is displayed in scatter plots.

```
DATA COMPACT;
   KEEP X Y;
   N=50; SCALE=1;
   MX=0; MY=0; LINK GENERATE;
   MX=8; MY=0; LINK GENERATE;
   MX=4; MY=8; LINK GENERATE;
   STOP;
GENERATE:
   DO I=1 TO N;
      X=RANNOR(1)*SCALE+MX;
      Y=RANNOR(1)*SCALE+MY;
      OUTPUT;
```

```
      END;
   RETURN;

PROC CLUSTER DATA=COMPACT OUTTREE=TREE METHOD=SINGLE NOPRINT;
PROC TREE NOPRINT OUT=OUT N=3;
   COPY X Y;
PROC PLOT; PLOT Y*X=CLUSTER;
   TITLE 'SINGLE LINKAGE CLUSTER ANALYSIS';
   TITLE2 'OF DATA CONTAINING WELL-SEPARATED, COMPACT CLUSTERS';
```

Output 6.1 Data Containing Well-Separated Compact Clusters: PROC PLOT

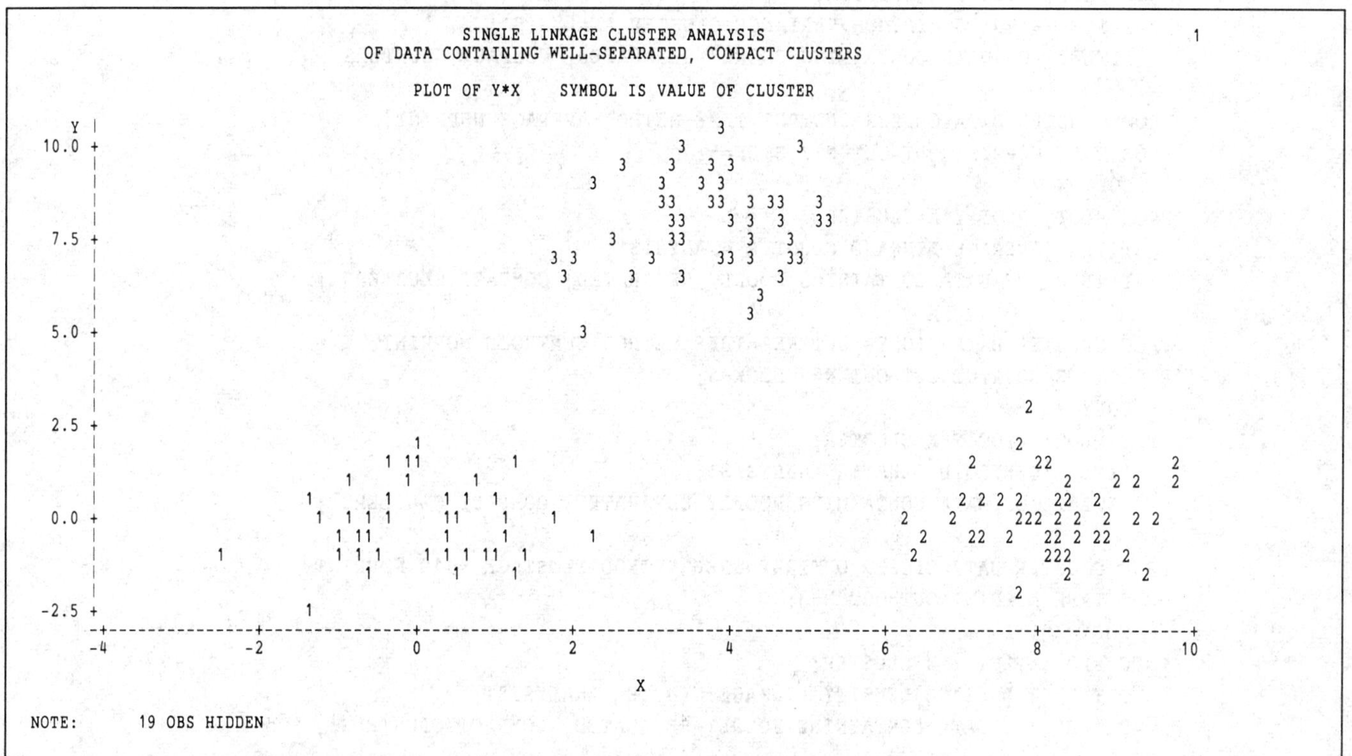

To see how various clustering methods differ, it is necessary to pose a more difficult problem. The following data set is similar to the first except that the three clusters are much closer together. FASTCLUS and five hierarchical methods described in "The CLUSTER Procedure" are used.

```
DATA CLOSER;
   KEEP X Y;
   N=50; SCALE=1;
   MX=0; MY=0; LINK GENERATE;
   MX=3; MY=0; LINK GENERATE;
   MX=1; MY=2; LINK GENERATE;
   STOP;
GENERATE:
   DO I=1 TO N;
      X=RANNOR(9)*SCALE+MX;
```

```
      Y=RANNOR(9)*SCALE+MY;
      OUTPUT;
      END;
   RETURN;

PROC FASTCLUS DATA=CLOSER OUT=OUT MAXC=3 NOPRINT;
PROC PLOT; PLOT Y*X=CLUSTER;
   TITLE 'FASTCLUS ANALYSIS';
   TITLE2 'OF DATA CONTAINING POORLY-SEPARATED, COMPACT CLUSTERS';

PROC CLUSTER DATA=CLOSER OUTTREE=TREE METHOD=WARD NOPRINT;
PROC TREE NOPRINT OUT=OUT N=3;
   COPY X Y;
PROC PLOT; PLOT Y*X=CLUSTER;
   TITLE 'WARD''S MINIMUM VARIANCE CLUSTER ANALYSIS';
   TITLE2 'OF DATA CONTAINING POORLY-SEPARATED, COMPACT CLUSTERS';

PROC CLUSTER DATA=CLOSER OUTTREE=TREE METHOD=AVERAGE NOPRINT;
PROC TREE NOPRINT OUT=OUT N=3 DOCK=5;
   COPY X Y;
PROC PLOT; PLOT Y*X=CLUSTER;
   TITLE 'AVERAGE LINKAGE CLUSTER ANALYSIS';
   TITLE2 'OF DATA CONTAINING POORLY-SEPARATED, COMPACT CLUSTERS';

PROC CLUSTER DATA=CLOSER OUTTREE=TREE METHOD=CENTROID NOPRINT;
PROC TREE NOPRINT OUT=OUT N=3 DOCK=5;
   COPY X Y;
PROC PLOT; PLOT Y*X=CLUSTER;
   TITLE 'CENTROID CLUSTER ANALYSIS';
   TITLE2 'OF DATA CONTAINING POORLY-SEPARATED, COMPACT CLUSTERS';

PROC CLUSTER DATA=CLOSER OUTTREE=TREE METHOD=TWOSTAGE K=10 NOPRINT;
PROC TREE NOPRINT OUT=OUT N=3;
   COPY X Y;
PROC PLOT; PLOT Y*X=CLUSTER;
   TITLE 'TWO-STAGE DENSITY LINKAGE CLUSTER ANALYSIS';
   TITLE2 'OF DATA CONTAINING POORLY-SEPARATED, COMPACT CLUSTERS';

PROC CLUSTER DATA=CLOSER OUTTREE=TREE METHOD=SINGLE NOPRINT;
PROC TREE DATA=TREE NOPRINT OUT=OUT N=3 DOCK=5;
   COPY X Y;
PROC PLOT; PLOT Y*X=CLUSTER;
   TITLE 'SINGLE LINKAGE CLUSTER ANALYSIS';
   TITLE2 'OF DATA CONTAINING POORLY-SEPARATED, COMPACT CLUSTERS';
```

Output 6.2 Data Containing Poorly Separated, Compact Clusters: PROC PLOT

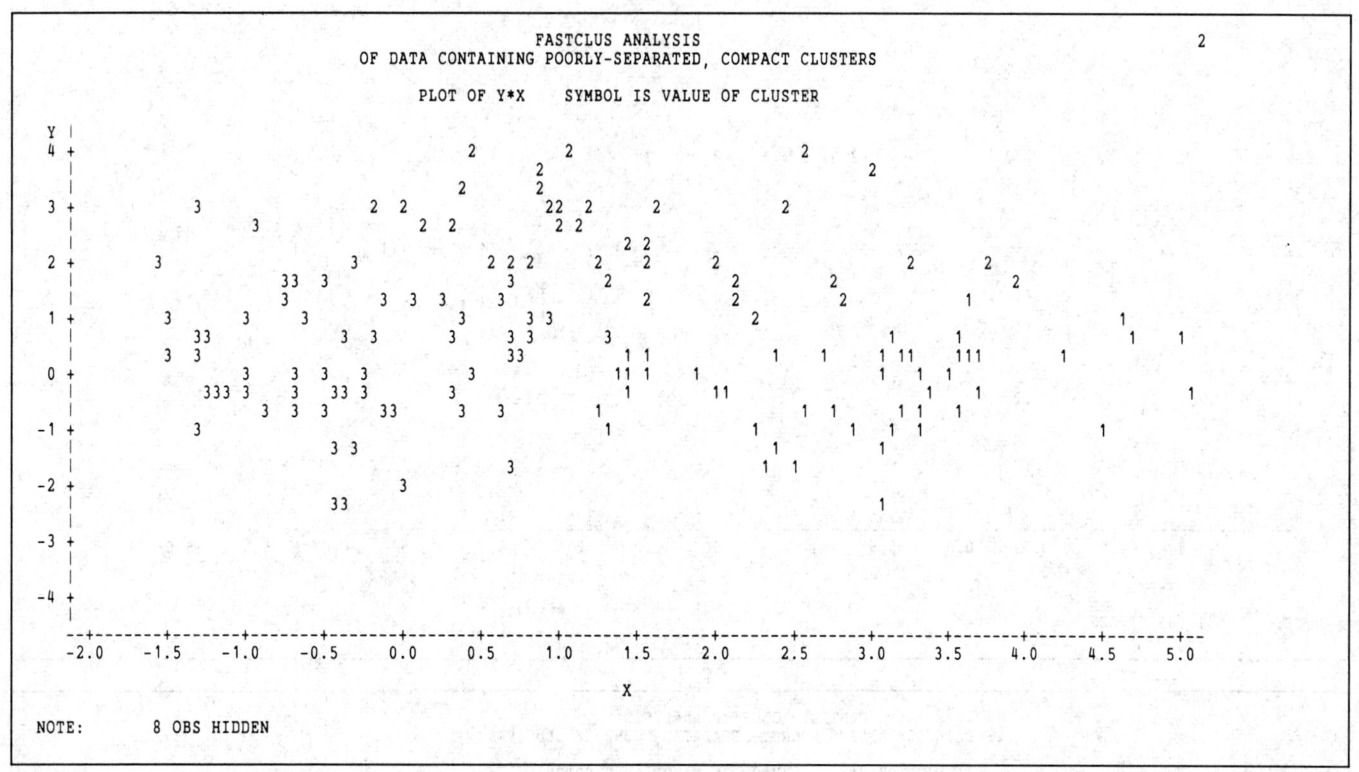

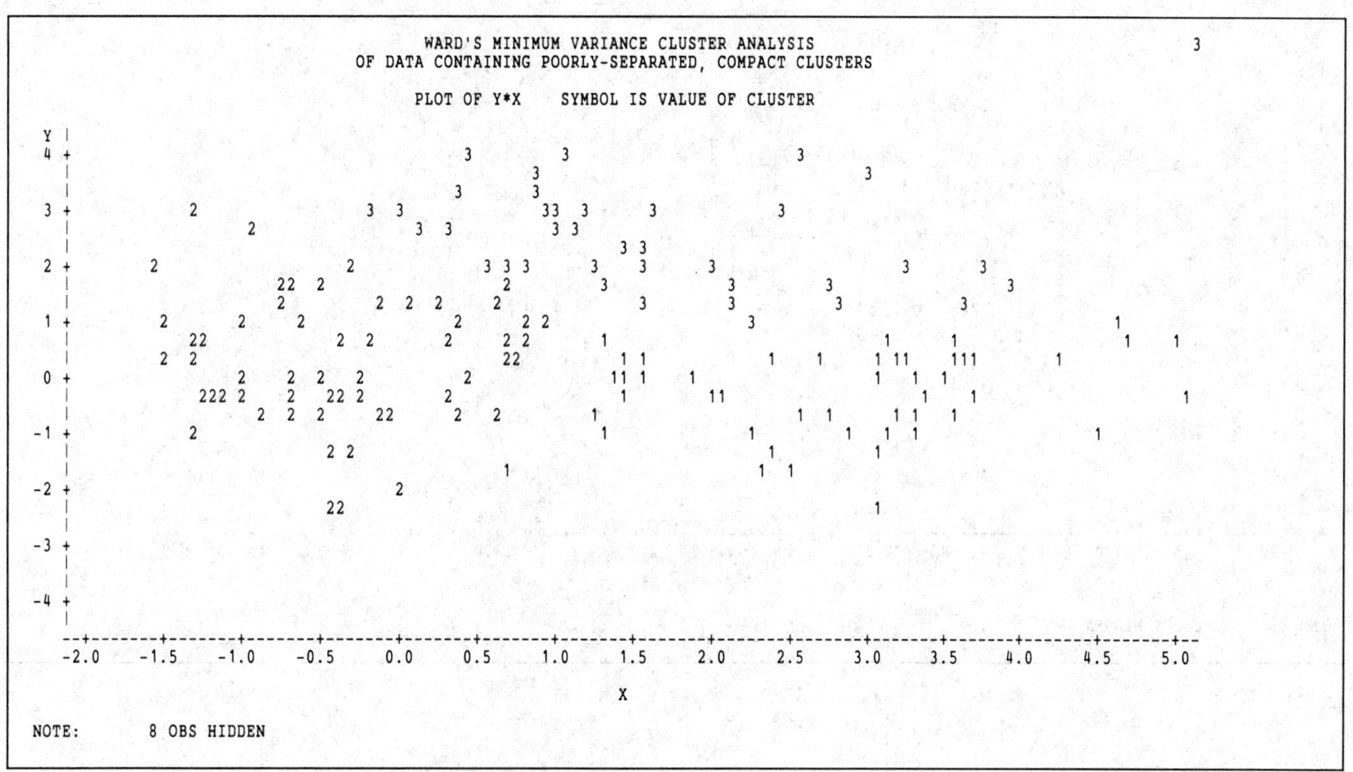

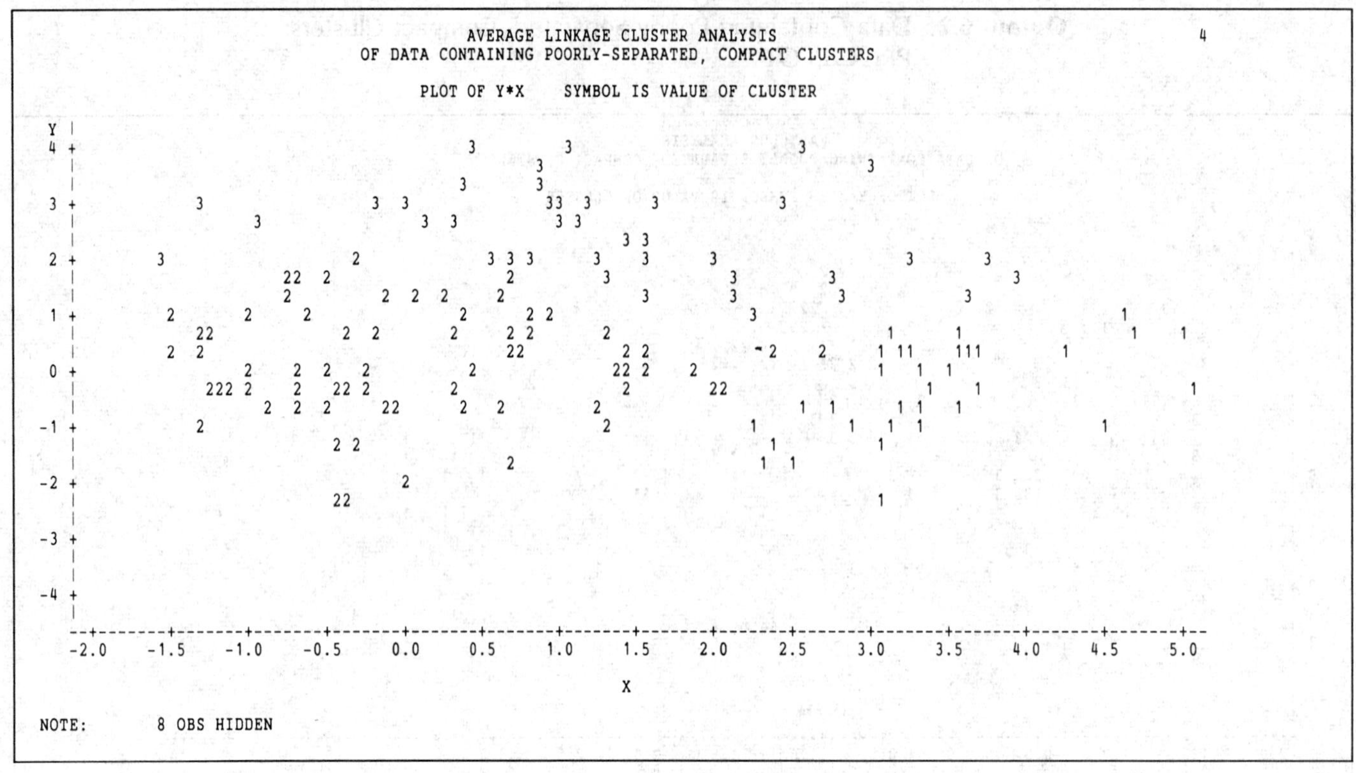
AVERAGE LINKAGE CLUSTER ANALYSIS
OF DATA CONTAINING POORLY-SEPARATED, COMPACT CLUSTERS
4
PLOT OF Y*X SYMBOL IS VALUE OF CLUSTER
Y
4
3
2
1
0
-1
-2
-3
-4
-2.0 -1.5 -1.0 -0.5 0.0 0.5 1.0 1.5 2.0 2.5 3.0 3.5 4.0 4.5 5.0
X
NOTE: 8 OBS HIDDEN

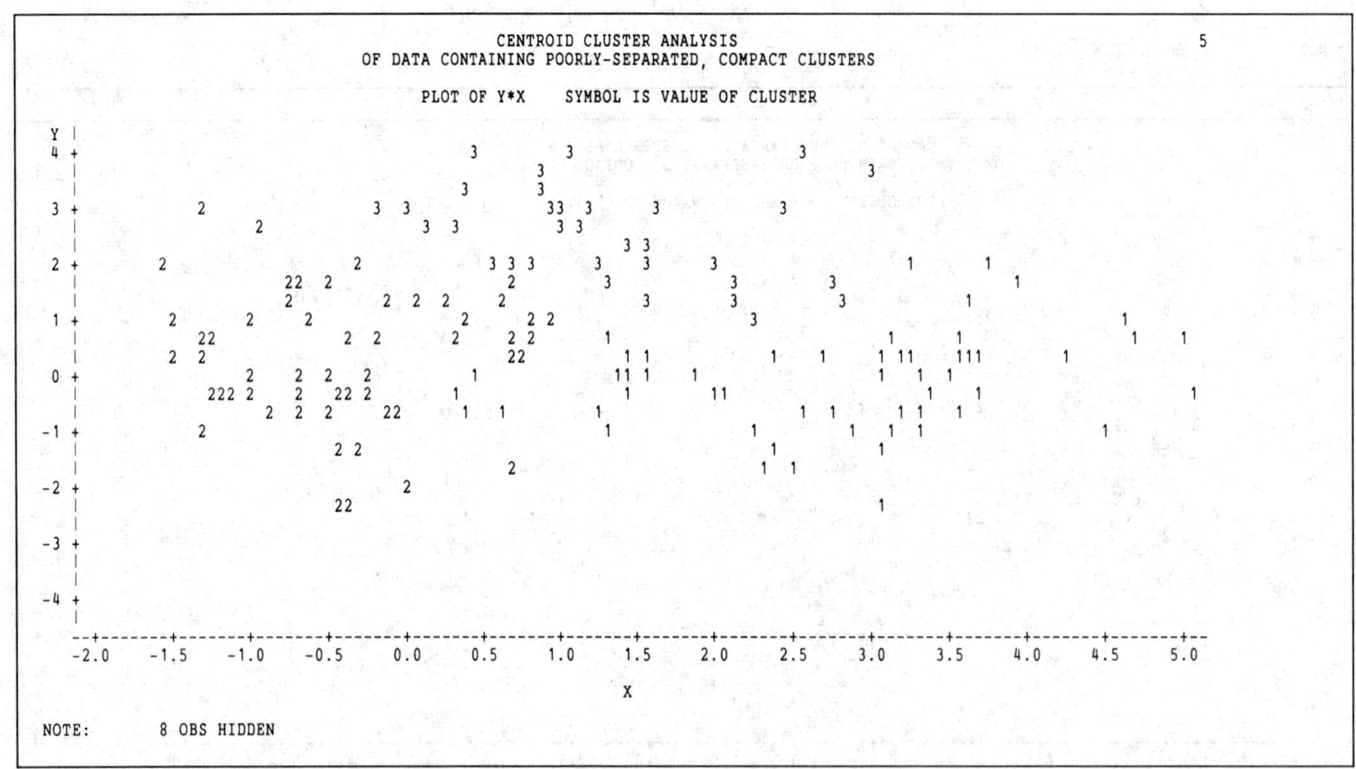
CENTROID CLUSTER ANALYSIS
OF DATA CONTAINING POORLY-SEPARATED, COMPACT CLUSTERS
5
PLOT OF Y*X SYMBOL IS VALUE OF CLUSTER
Y
4
3
2
1
0
-1
-2
-3
-4
-2.0 -1.5 -1.0 -0.5 0.0 0.5 1.0 1.5 2.0 2.5 3.0 3.5 4.0 4.5 5.0
X
NOTE: 8 OBS HIDDEN

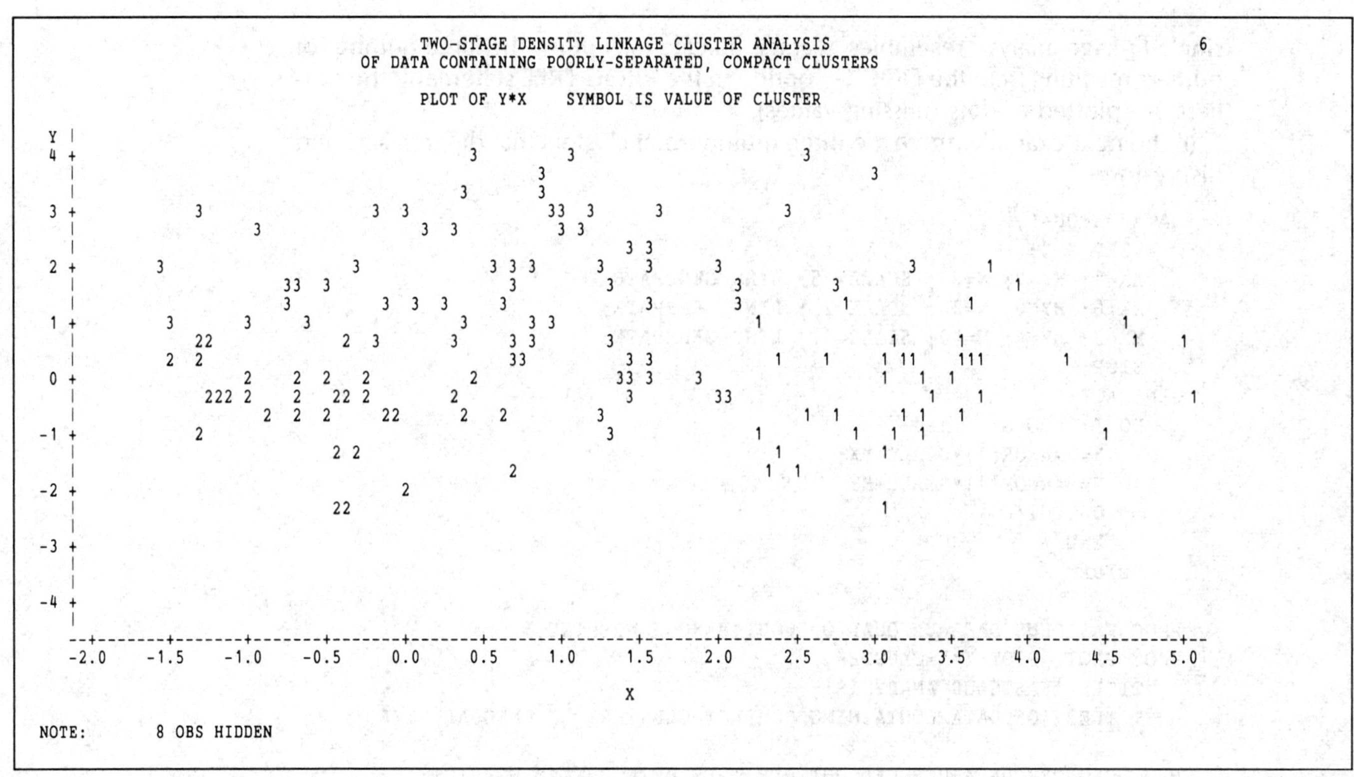

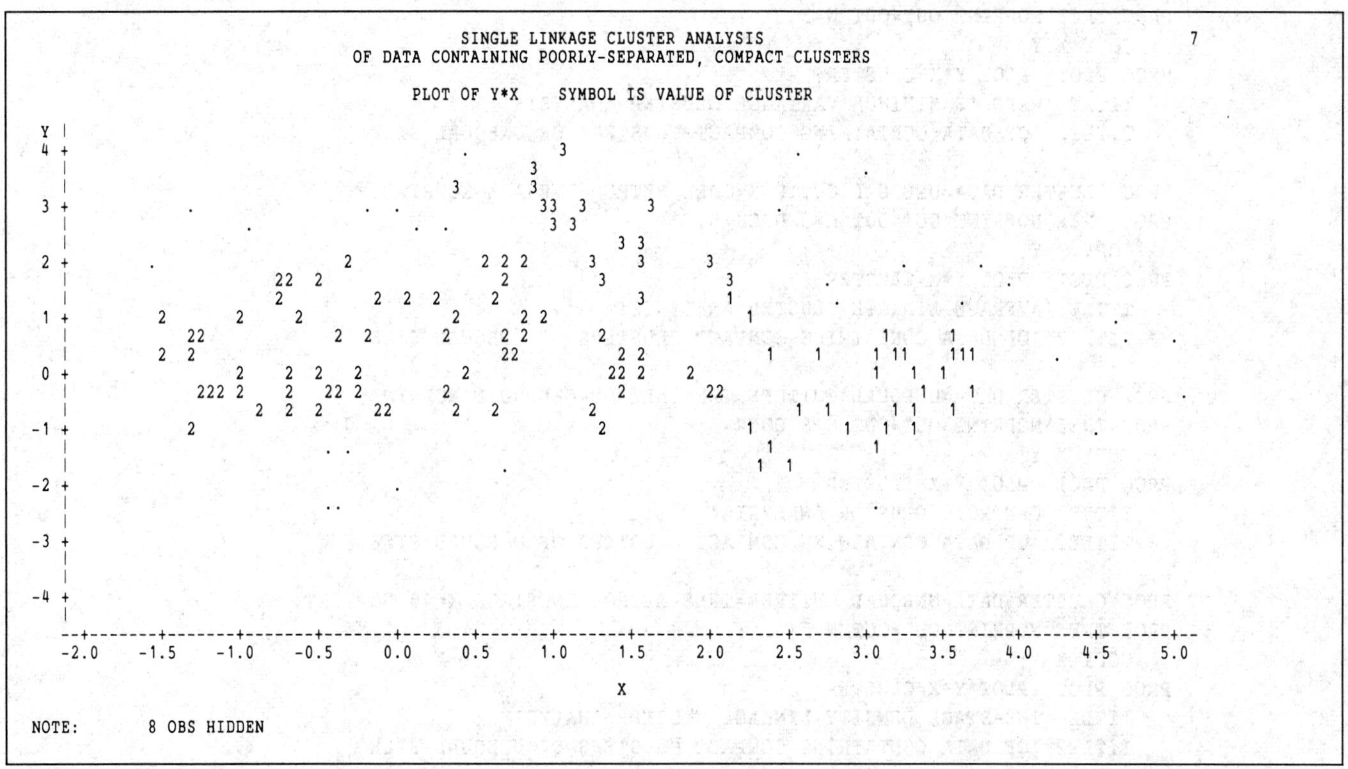

The two least-squares methods, FASTCLUS and Ward's, yield the most uniform cluster sizes and the best recovery of the true clusters. With average linkage, the lower left cluster is too large; with the centroid method, the lower right cluster is too large; and with two-stage density linkage, the top cluster is too large. The single linkage analysis resembles average linkage except for the large number of outliers resulting from the DOCK= option in the PROC TREE statement; the outliers are plotted as dots (missing values).

In the next example, there are three multinormal clusters that differ in size and dispersion:

```
DATA UNEQUAL;
   KEEP X Y;
   MX=1; MY=0; N=20; SCALE=.5; LINK GENERATE;
   MX=6; MY=0; N=80; SCALE=2.; LINK GENERATE;
   MX=3; MY=4; N=40; SCALE=1.; LINK GENERATE;
   STOP;
GENERATE:
   DO I=1 TO N;
      X=RANNOR(1)*SCALE+MX;
      Y=RANNOR(1)*SCALE+MY;
      OUTPUT;
      END;
   RETURN;

PROC FASTCLUS DATA=UNEQUAL OUT=OUT MAXC=3 NOPRINT;
PROC PLOT; PLOT Y*X=CLUSTER;
   TITLE 'FASTCLUS ANALYSIS';
   TITLE2 'OF DATA CONTAINING COMPACT CLUSTERS OF UNEQUAL SIZE';

PROC CLUSTER DATA=UNEQUAL OUTTREE=TREE METHOD=WARD NOPRINT;
PROC TREE NOPRINT OUT=OUT N=3;
   COPY X Y;
PROC PLOT; PLOT Y*X=CLUSTER;
   TITLE 'WARD''S MINIMUM VARIANCE CLUSTER ANALYSIS';
   TITLE2 'OF DATA CONTAINING COMPACT CLUSTERS OF UNEQUAL SIZE';

PROC CLUSTER DATA=UNEQUAL OUTTREE=TREE METHOD=AVERAGE NOPRINT;
PROC TREE NOPRINT OUT=OUT N=3 DOCK=5;
   COPY X Y;
PROC PLOT; PLOT Y*X=CLUSTER;
   TITLE 'AVERAGE LINKAGE CLUSTER ANALYSIS';
   TITLE2 'OF DATA CONTAINING COMPACT CLUSTERS OF UNEQUAL SIZE';

PROC CLUSTER DATA=UNEQUAL OUTTREE=TREE METHOD=CENTROID NOPRINT;
PROC TREE NOPRINT OUT=OUT N=3 DOCK=5;
   COPY X Y;
PROC PLOT; PLOT Y*X=CLUSTER;
   TITLE 'CENTROID CLUSTER ANALYSIS';
   TITLE2 'OF DATA CONTAINING COMPACT CLUSTERS OF UNEQUAL SIZE';

PROC CLUSTER DATA=UNEQUAL OUTTREE=TREE METHOD=TWOSTAGE K=10 NOPRINT;
PROC TREE NOPRINT OUT=OUT N=3;
   COPY X Y;
PROC PLOT; PLOT Y*X=CLUSTER;
   TITLE 'TWO-STAGE DENSITY LINKAGE CLUSTER ANALYSIS';
   TITLE2 'OF DATA CONTAINING COMPACT CLUSTERS OF UNEQUAL SIZE';

PROC CLUSTER DATA=UNEQUAL OUTTREE=TREE METHOD=SINGLE NOPRINT;
PROC TREE DATA=TREE NOPRINT OUT=OUT N=3 DOCK=5;
   COPY X Y;
PROC PLOT; PLOT Y*X=CLUSTER;
   TITLE 'SINGLE LINKAGE CLUSTER ANALYSIS';
   TITLE2 'OF DATA CONTAINING COMPACT CLUSTERS OF UNEQUAL SIZE';
```

Output 6.3 Data Containing Compact Clusters of Unequal Size: PROC PLOT

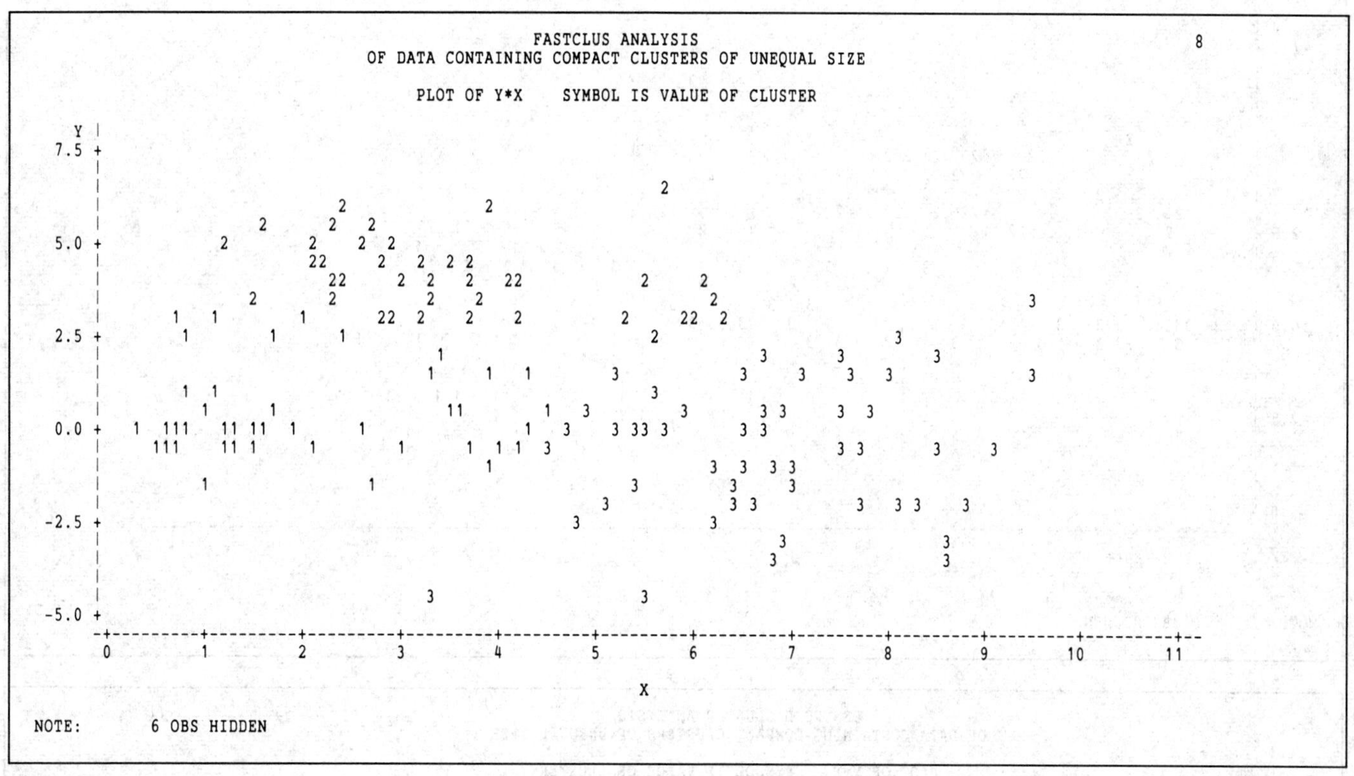

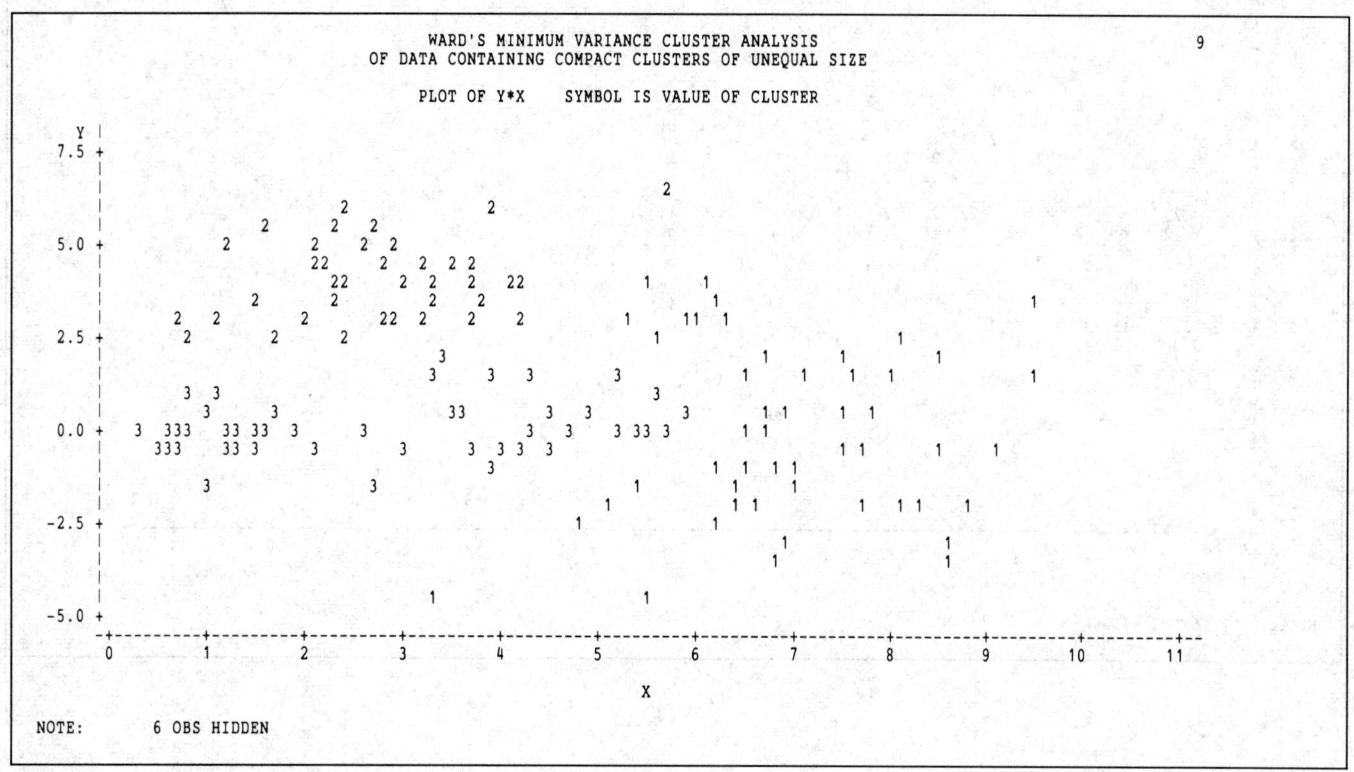

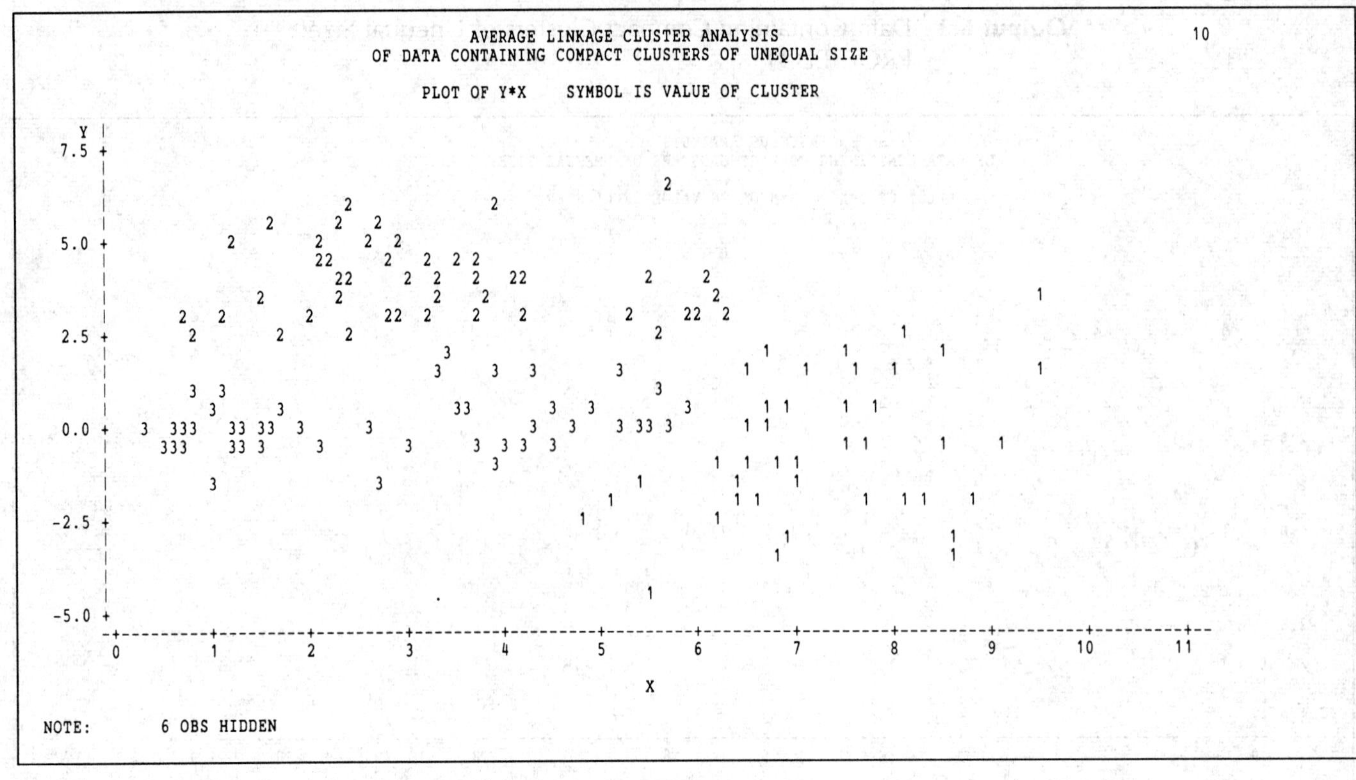
AVERAGE LINKAGE CLUSTER ANALYSIS
OF DATA CONTAINING COMPACT CLUSTERS OF UNEQUAL SIZE
10
PLOT OF Y*X SYMBOL IS VALUE OF CLUSTER
Y
7.5
5.0
2.5
0.0
-2.5
-5.0
0 1 2 3 4 5 6 7 8 9 10 11
X
NOTE: 6 OBS HIDDEN

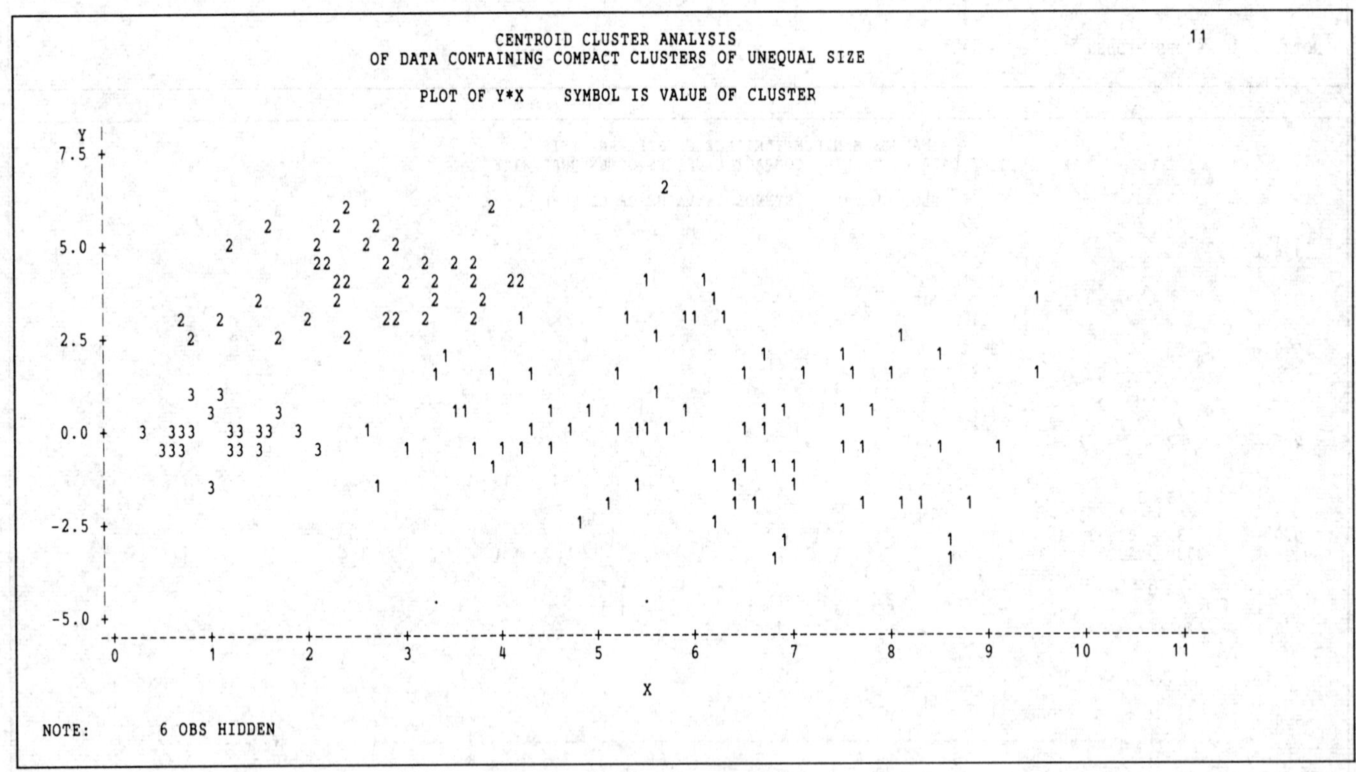
CENTROID CLUSTER ANALYSIS
OF DATA CONTAINING COMPACT CLUSTERS OF UNEQUAL SIZE
11
PLOT OF Y*X SYMBOL IS VALUE OF CLUSTER
Y
7.5
5.0
2.5
0.0
-2.5
-5.0
0 1 2 3 4 5 6 7 8 9 10 11
X
NOTE: 6 OBS HIDDEN

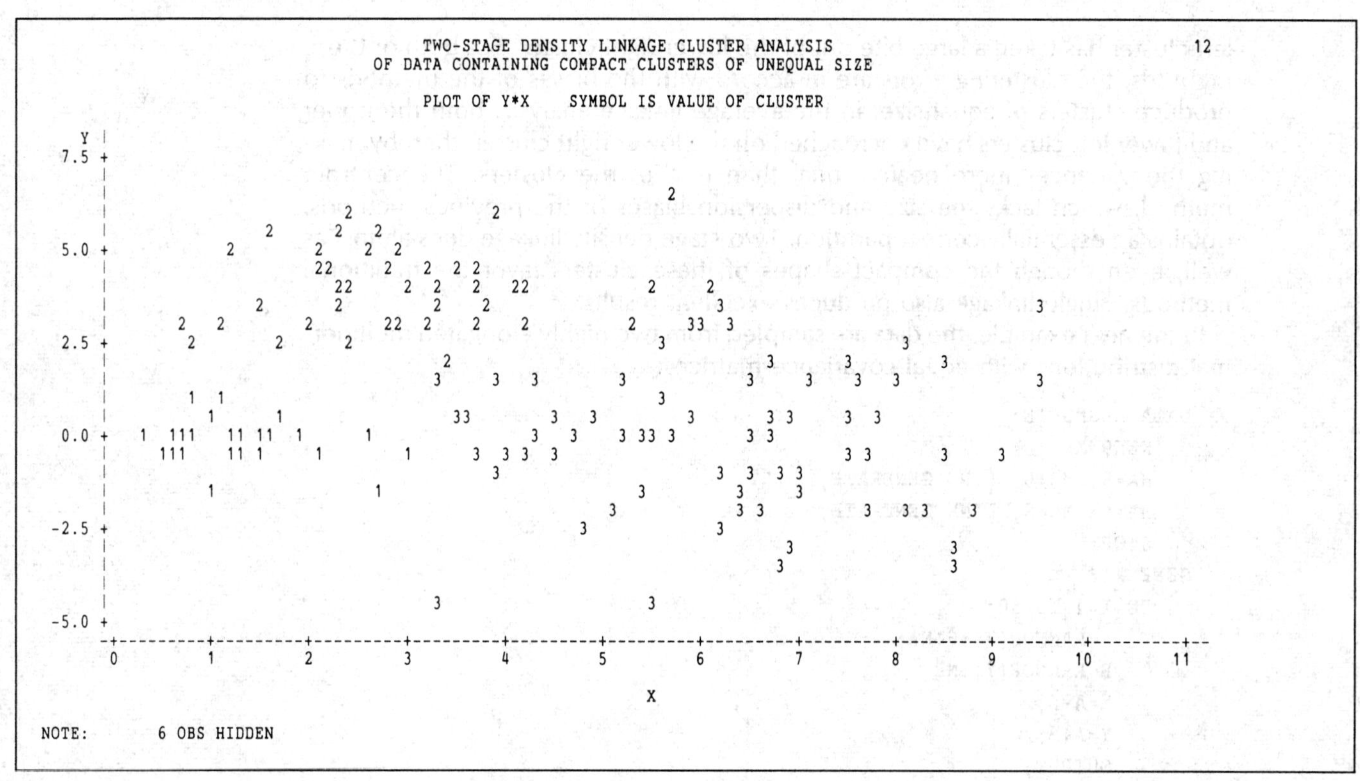

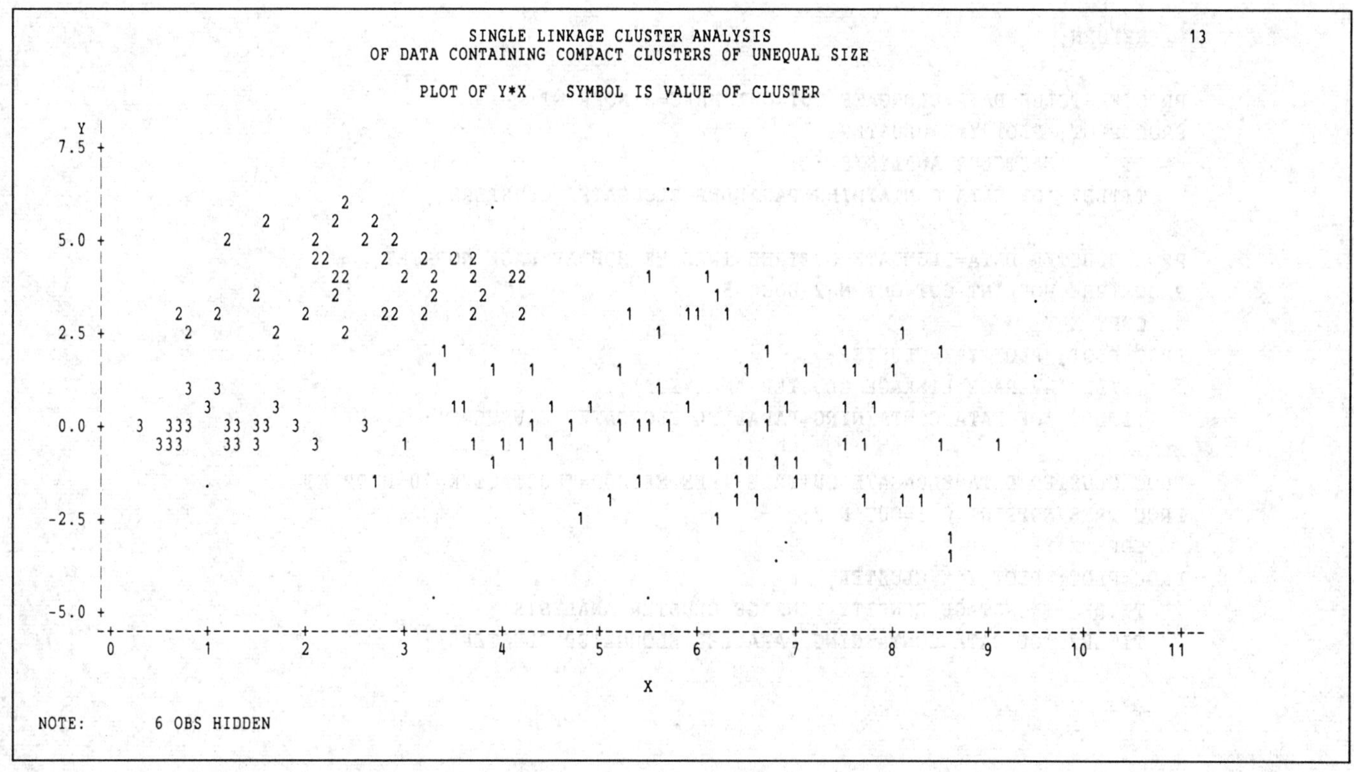

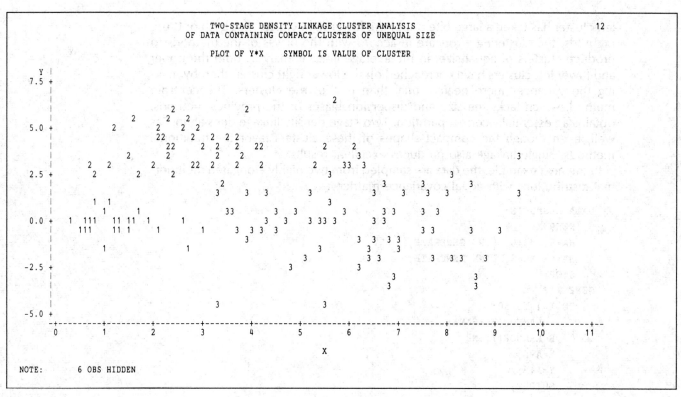

In the FASTCLUS analysis, the smallest cluster, in the bottom left of the plot, has stolen members from the other two clusters, and the upper left cluster has also acquired some observations that rightfully belong to the lower right cluster. With Ward's method, the upper left cluster is separated correctly, but the lower left cluster has taken a large bite out of the lower right cluster. For both of these methods, the clustering errors are in accord with the biases of the methods to produce clusters of equal size. In the average linkage analysis, both the upper and lower left clusters have encroached on the lower right cluster, thereby making the variances more nearly equal than in the true clusters. The centroid method, which lacks the size and dispersion biases of the previous methods, obtains an essentially correct partition. Two-stage density linkage does almost as well, even though the compact shapes of these clusters favor the traditional methods. Single linkage also produces excellent results.

In the next example, the data are sampled from two highly elongated multinormal distributions with equal covariance matrices:

```
DATA ELONGATE;
   KEEP X Y;
   MA=8; MB=0; LINK GENERATE;
   MA=6; MB=8; LINK GENERATE;
   STOP;
GENERATE:
   DO I=1 TO 50;
      A=RANNOR(7)*6+MA;
      B=RANNOR(7)+MB;
      X=A-B;
      Y=A+B;
      OUTPUT;
      END;
   RETURN;

PROC FASTCLUS DATA=ELONGATE OUT=OUT MAXC=2 NOPRINT;
PROC PLOT; PLOT Y*X=CLUSTER;
   TITLE 'FASTCLUS ANALYSIS';
   TITLE2 'OF DATA CONTAINING PARALLEL ELONGATED CLUSTERS';

PROC CLUSTER DATA=ELONGATE OUTTREE=TREE METHOD=AVERAGE NOPRINT;
PROC TREE NOPRINT OUT=OUT N=2 DOCK=5;
   COPY X Y;
PROC PLOT; PLOT Y*X=CLUSTER;
   TITLE 'AVERAGE LINKAGE CLUSTER ANALYSIS';
   TITLE2 'OF DATA CONTAINING PARALLEL ELONGATED CLUSTERS';

PROC CLUSTER DATA=ELONGATE OUTTREE=TREE METHOD=TWOSTAGE K=10 NOPRINT;
PROC TREE NOPRINT OUT=OUT N=2;
   COPY X Y;
PROC PLOT; PLOT Y*X=CLUSTER;
   TITLE 'TWO-STAGE DENSITY LINKAGE CLUSTER ANALYSIS';
   TITLE2 'OF DATA CONTAINING PARALLEL ELONGATED CLUSTERS';
```

Output 6.4 Data Containing Parallel Elongated Clusters: PROC PLOT

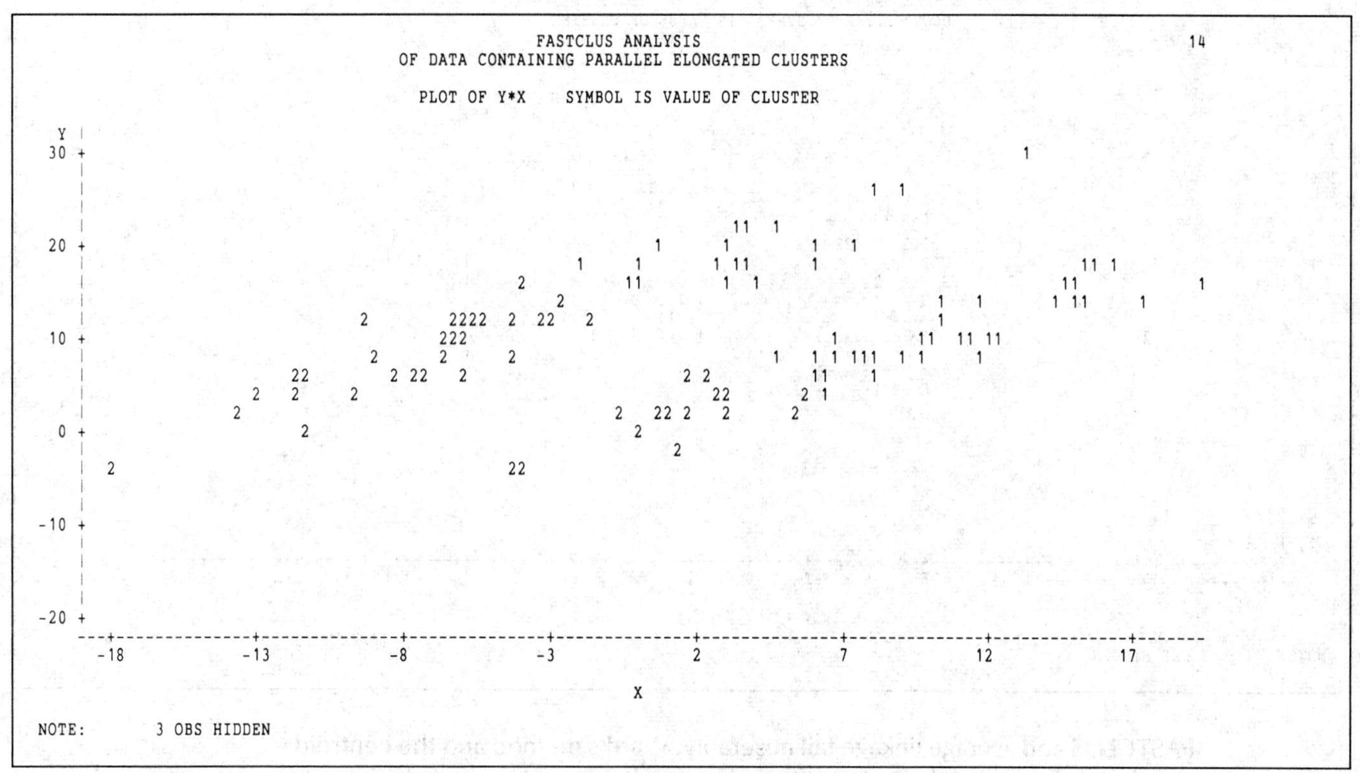

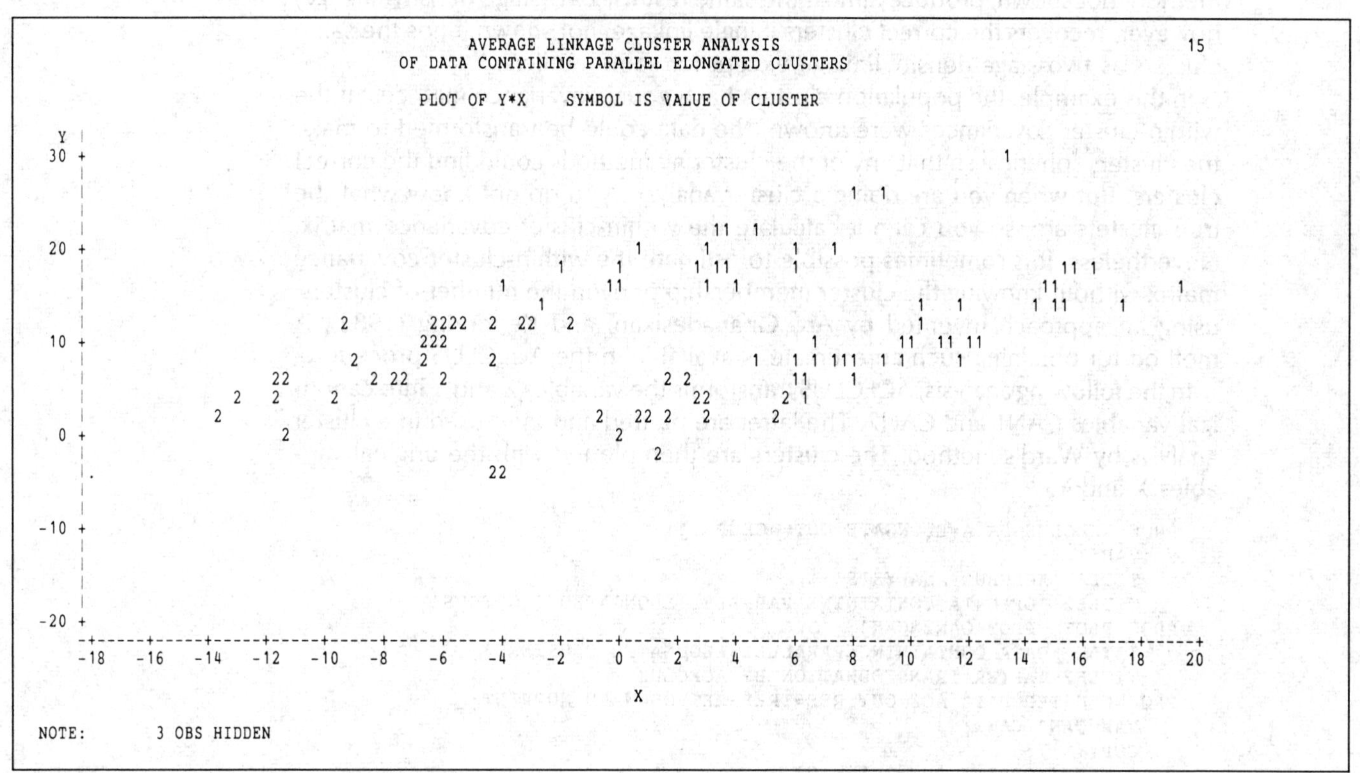

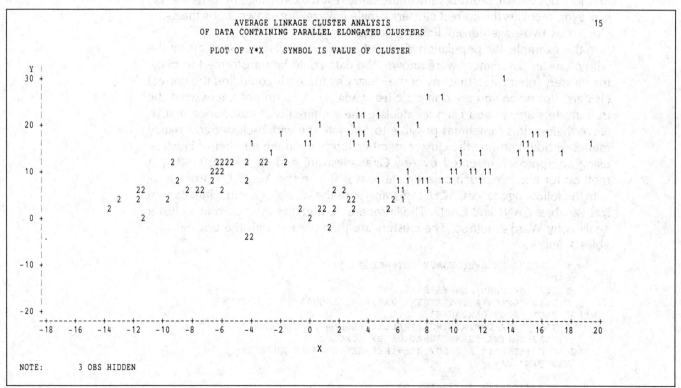

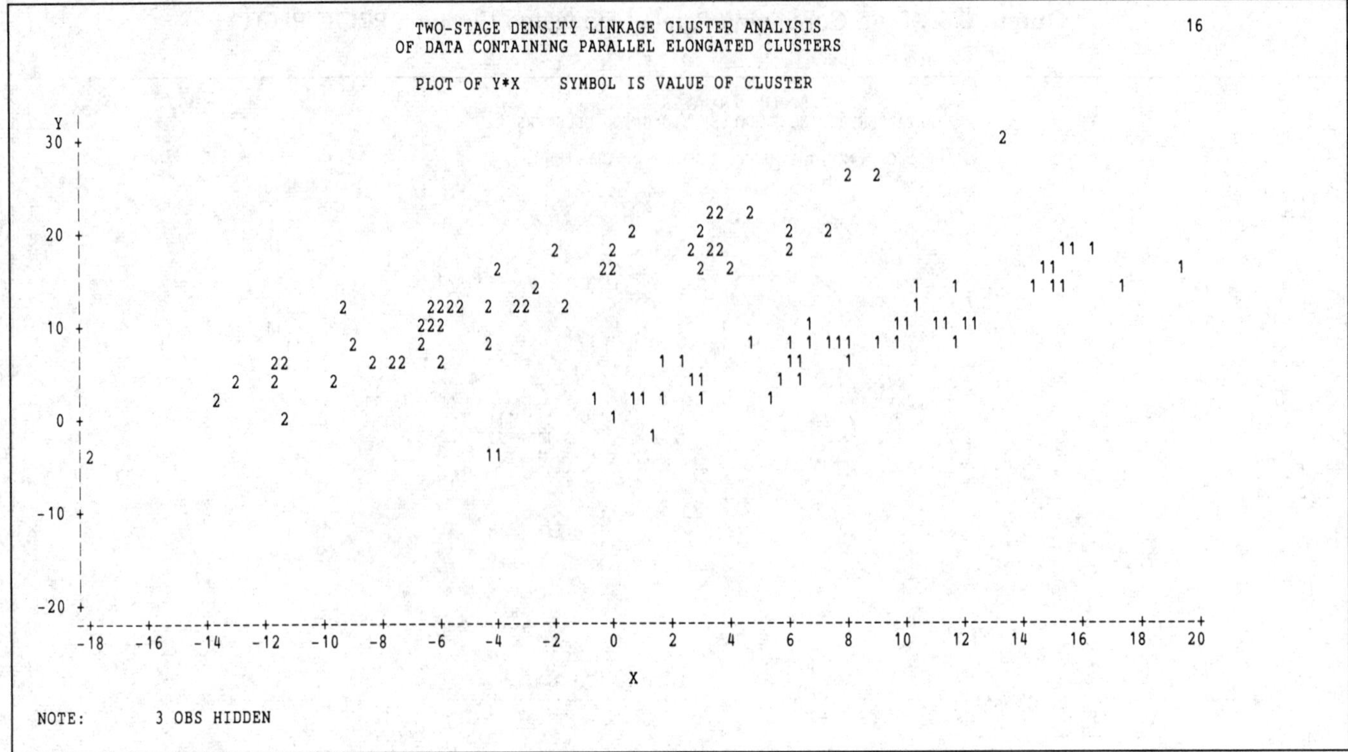

FASTCLUS and average linkage fail miserably. Ward's method and the centroid method, not shown, produce almost the same results. Two-stage density linkage, however, recovers the correct clusters. Single linkage, not shown, finds the same clusters as two-stage density linkage except for some outliers.

In this example, the population clusters have equal covariance matrices. If the within-cluster covariances were known, the data could be transformed to make the clusters spherical so that any of the clustering methods could find the correct clusters. But when you are doing a cluster analysis, you do not know what the true clusters are, so you cannot calculate the within-cluster covariance matrix. Nevertheless, it is sometimes possible to estimate the within-cluster covariance matrix without knowing the cluster membership or even the number of clusters, using an approach invented by Art, Gnanadesikan, and Kettenring (1982). A method for obtaining such an estimate is available in the ACECLUS procedure.

In the following analysis, ACECLUS transforms the variables X and Y into canonical variables CAN1 and CAN2. The latter are plotted and then used in a cluster analysis by Ward's method. The clusters are then plotted with the original variables X and Y.

```
PROC ACECLUS DATA=ELONGATE OUT=ACE P=.1;
   VAR X Y;
   TITLE 'ACECLUS ANALYSIS';
   TITLE2 'OF DATA CONTAINING PARALLEL ELONGATED CLUSTERS';
PROC PLOT; PLOT CAN2*CAN1;
   TITLE 'DATA CONTAINING PARALLEL ELONGATED CLUSTERS';
   TITLE2 'AFTER TRANSFORMATION BY ACECLUS';
PROC CLUSTER DATA=ACE OUTTREE=TREE METHOD=WARD NOPRINT;
   VAR CAN1 CAN2;
   COPY X Y;
PROC TREE NOPRINT OUT=OUT N=2;
   COPY X Y;
PROC PLOT; PLOT Y*X=CLUSTER;
   TITLE 'WARD''S MINIMUM VARIANCE CLUSTER ANALYSIS';
   TITLE2 'OF DATA CONTAINING PARALLEL ELONGATED CLUSTERS';
   TITLE3 'AFTER TRANSFORMATION BY ACECLUS';
```

Output 6.5 Data Containing Parallel Elongated Clusters: PROC FASTCLUS and PROC PLOT

```
                          ACECLUS ANALYSIS                                      17
                OF DATA CONTAINING PARALLEL ELONGATED CLUSTERS

             APPROXIMATE COVARIANCE ESTIMATION FOR CLUSTER ANALYSIS

                  100 OBSERVATIONS     PROPORTION=     0.1
                    2 VARIABLES        CONVERGE=      0.01


                         SIMPLE STATISTICS

                                    X                 Y

               MEAN         2.640587782       10.64882190
               ST DEV       8.349439993        6.84202080


                   COV: TOTAL SAMPLE COVARIANCES

                                 X                 Y

               X            69.71315          24.24269
               Y            24.24269          46.81325

      INITIAL WITHIN-CLUSTER COVARIANCE ESTIMATE=FULL COVARIANCE MATRIX

                          THRESHOLD=0.3284778
```

```
                          ACECLUS ANALYSIS                                      18
                OF DATA CONTAINING PARALLEL ELONGATED CLUSTERS

             APPROXIMATE COVARIANCE ESTIMATION FOR CLUSTER ANALYSIS

                                                 PAIRS
                     RMS      DISTANCE          WITHIN       CONVERGENCE
        ITERATION   DISTANCE     CUTOFF          CUTOFF          MEASURE

                1     2.000       0.657             672         0.673685
                2     9.382       3.082             716         0.006963


             ACE: APPROXIMATE COVARIANCE ESTIMATE WITHIN CLUSTERS

                                 X                 Y

               X            4.075078          2.287634
               Y            2.287634          2.852458


                 EIGENVALUES OF INV(ACE)*(COV-ACE)

             EIGENVALUE       DIFFERENCE       PROPORTION       CUMULATIVE

    CAN1         28.3405          15.0701         0.681084          0.68108
    CAN2         13.2704           .              0.318916          1.00000


                          EIGENVECTORS

                            CAN1          CAN2

                   X      -.618811      0.251827
                   Y      0.719460      0.346458
```

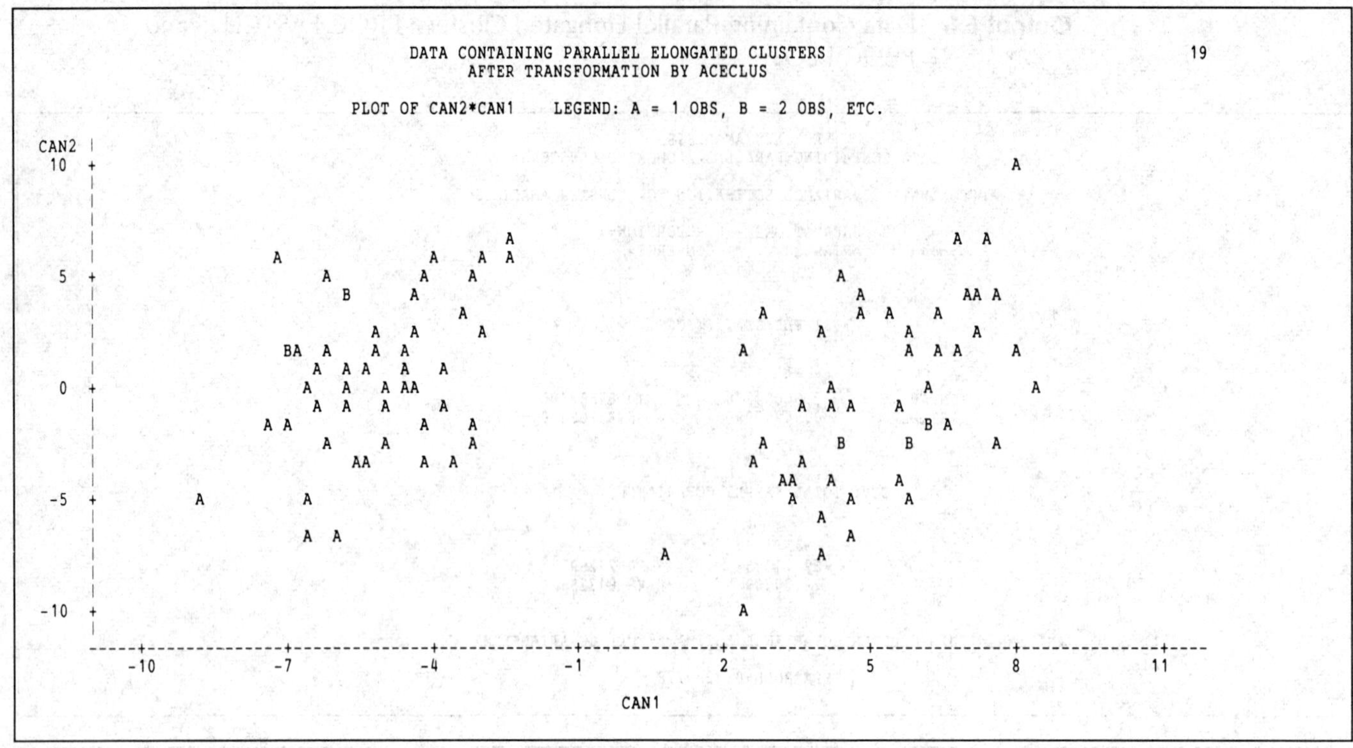
DATA CONTAINING PARALLEL ELONGATED CLUSTERS
AFTER TRANSFORMATION BY ACECLUS
19
PLOT OF CAN2*CAN1 LEGEND: A = 1 OBS, B = 2 OBS, ETC.
CAN2
CAN1

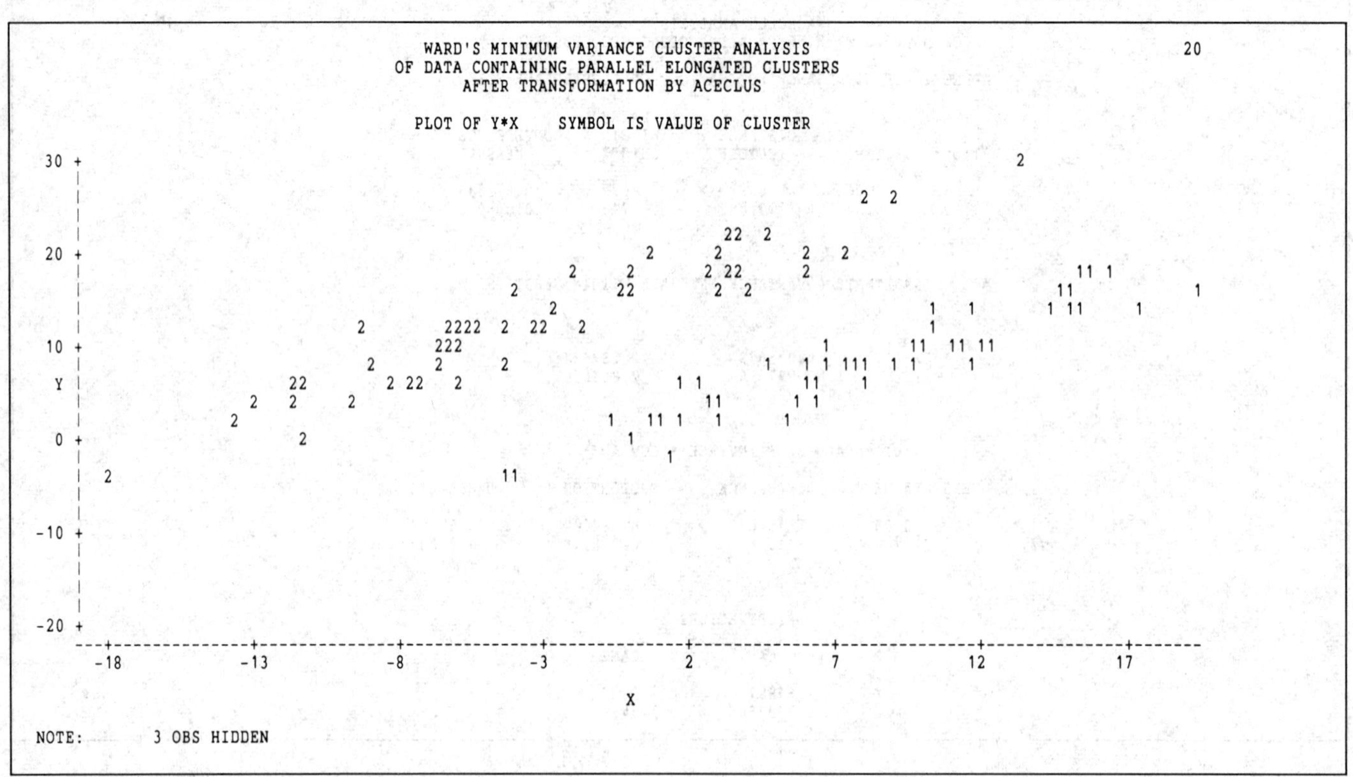
WARD'S MINIMUM VARIANCE CLUSTER ANALYSIS
OF DATA CONTAINING PARALLEL ELONGATED CLUSTERS
AFTER TRANSFORMATION BY ACECLUS
20
PLOT OF Y*X SYMBOL IS VALUE OF CLUSTER
Y
X
NOTE: 3 OBS HIDDEN

If the population clusters have very different covariance matrices, ACECLUS is of no avail. Although methods exist for estimating multinormal clusters with unequal covariance matrices (Wolfe 1970; Symons 1981; Everitt and Hand 1981), these methods tend to have serious problems with initialization and may converge to degenerate solutions. For unequal covariance matrices or radically nonnormal distributions, the best approach to cluster analysis is through nonparametric density estimation, as in density linkage. The following example illustrates population clusters with nonconvex density contours:

```
DATA IRREG;
   KEEP X Y;
   DO I=1 TO 100;
      A=I*.0628319;
      X=COS(A)+(I>50)+RANNOR(7)*.1;
      Y=SIN(A)+(I>50)*.3+RANNOR(7)*.1;
      OUTPUT;
      END;

PROC FASTCLUS DATA=IRREG OUT=OUT MAXC=2 NOPRINT;
PROC PLOT; PLOT Y*X=CLUSTER;
   TITLE 'FASTCLUS ANALYSIS';
   TITLE2 'OF DATA CONTAINING IRREGULAR CLUSTERS';

PROC CLUSTER DATA=IRREG OUTTREE=TREE METHOD=CENTROID NOPRINT;
PROC TREE NOPRINT OUT=OUT N=2 DOCK=5;
   COPY X Y;
PROC PLOT; PLOT Y*X=CLUSTER;
   TITLE 'CENTROID CLUSTER ANALYSIS';
   TITLE2 'OF DATA CONTAINING IRREGULAR CLUSTERS';

PROC CLUSTER DATA=IRREG OUTTREE=TREE METHOD=TWOSTAGE K=10 NOPRINT;
PROC TREE NOPRINT OUT=OUT N=2;
   COPY X Y;
PROC PLOT; PLOT Y*X=CLUSTER;
   TITLE 'TWO-STAGE DENSITY LINKAGE CLUSTER ANALYSIS';
   TITLE2 'OF DATA CONTAINING IRREGULAR CLUSTERS';
```

Output 6.6 Data Containing Irregular Clusters: PROC PLOT

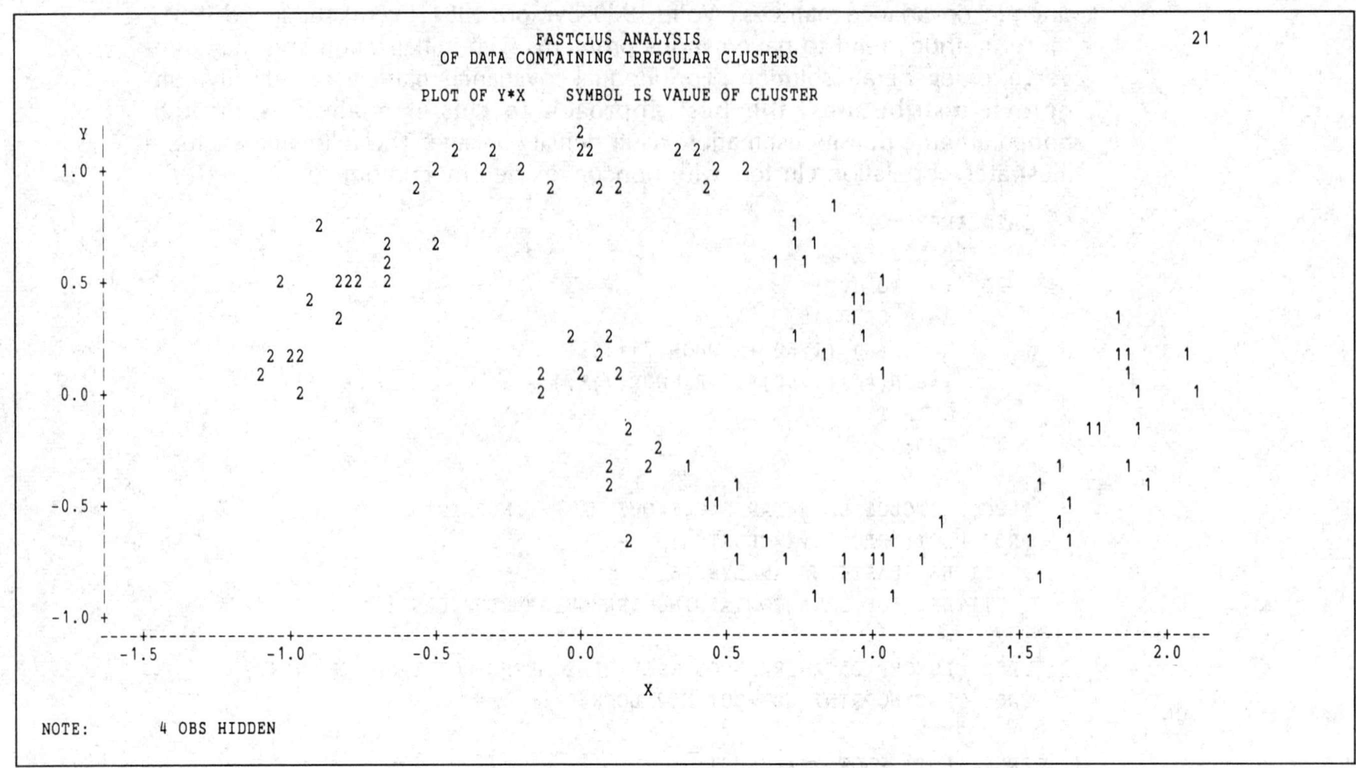

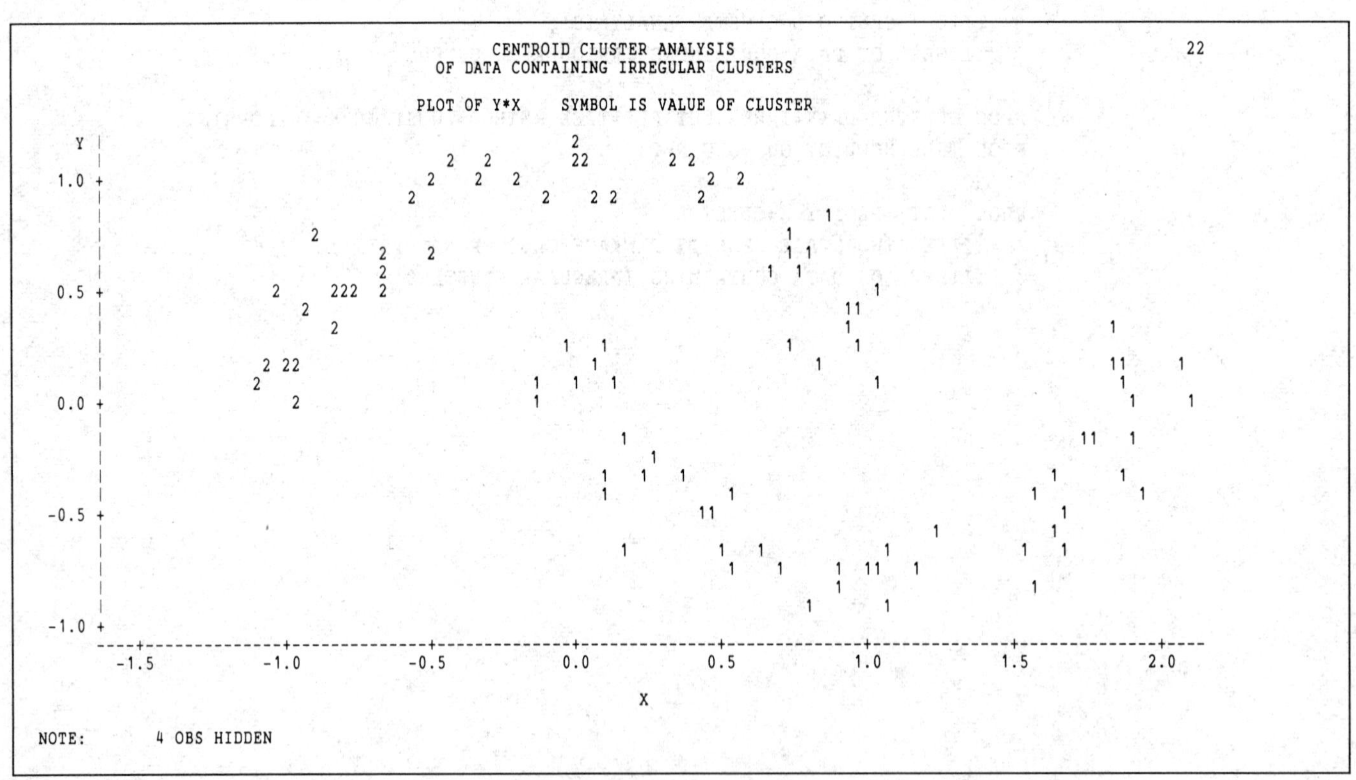

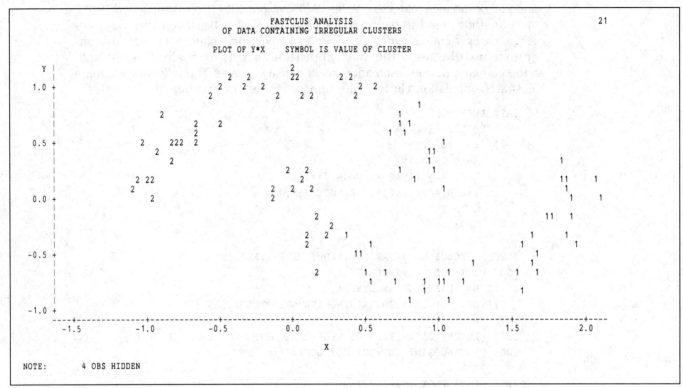

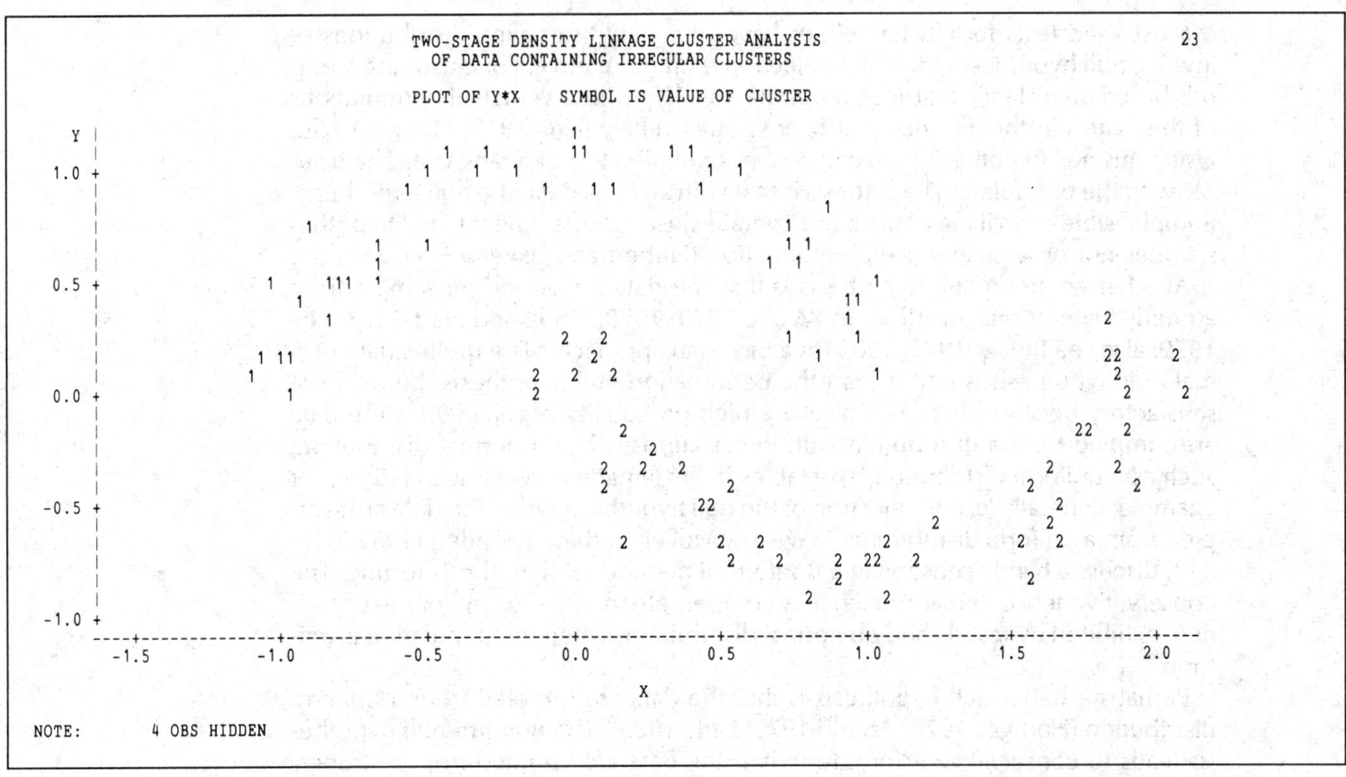

Ward's method and average linkage, not shown, do better than FASTCLUS but not as well as the centroid method. Two-stage density linkage recovers the correct clusters, as does single linkage, which is not shown.

The above examples are intended merely to illustrate some of the properties of clustering methods in common use. If you intend to perform a cluster analysis, you must consult more systematic and rigorous studies of the properties of clustering methods, such as Milligan (1980).

The Number of Clusters

There are no satisfactory methods for determining the number of population clusters for any type of cluster analysis (Everitt 1979, 1980). The number-of-clusters problem is, if anything, more difficult than the number-of-factors problem.

If your purpose in clustering is dissection, that is, to summarize the data without trying to uncover "real" clusters, it may suffice to look at R^2 for each variable and pooled over all variables. Plots of R^2 against the number of clusters are useful.

It is always a good idea to look at your data graphically. If you have only two or three variables, use PLOT to make scatterplots identifying the clusters. With more variables, use PROC CANDISC to compute canonical variables for plotting.

Ordinary significance tests, such as analysis of variance *F* tests, are not valid for testing differences between clusters. Since clustering methods attempt to maximize the separation between clusters, the assumptions of the usual significance tests, parametric or nonparametric, are drastically violated. For example, if you take a sample of 100 observations from a single univariate normal distribution, have FASTCLUS divide it into two clusters, and run a *t* test between the clusters, you will usually obtain a probability level of less than .0001. For the same reason, methods that purport to test for clusters against the null hypothesis that objects are assigned randomly to clusters (McClain and Rao 1975; Klastorin 1983) are useless.

Most valid tests for clusters either have intractable sampling distributions or involve null hypotheses for which rejection is uninformative. For clustering methods based on distance matrices, a popular null hypothesis is that all permutations of the values in the distance matrix are equally likely (Ling 1973; Hubert 1974). Using this null hypothesis, you can do a permutation test or a rank test. The trouble with the permutation hypothesis is that with any real data, the null hypothesis, is implausible even if the data do not contain clusters. Rejecting the null hypothesis does not provide any useful information (Hubert and Baker 1977).

Another common null hypothesis is that the data are a random sample from a multivariate normal distribution (Wolfe 1970, 1978; Duda and Hart 1973; Lee 1979; also see Binder 1978, 1981 for a Bayesian approach). The multivariate normal null hypothesis is better than the permutation null hypothesis, but it is not satisfactory because there is typically a high probability of rejection if the data are sampled from a distribution with lower kurtosis than a normal distribution, such as a uniform distribution. The tables in Englemann and Hartigan (1969), for example, generally lead to rejection of the null hypothesis when the data are sampled from a uniform distribution. Hawkins, Muller, and ten Krooden (1982, 337-340) discuss a highly conservative Bonferroni method for hypothesis testing. The conservativeness of this approach may compensate to some extent for the liberalness exhibited by tests based on normal distributions when the population is uniform.

Perhaps a better null hypothesis is that the data are sampled from a uniform distribution (Hartigan 1978; Arnold 1979; Sarle 1983). The uniform null hypothesis leads to conservative error rates when the data are sampled from a strongly unimodal distribution such as the normal. However, in two or more dimensions and depending on the test statistic, the results can be very sensitive to the shape of the region of support of the uniform distribution. Sarle (1983) suggests using a hyper-box with sides proportional in length to the singular values of the centered coordinate matrix.

Given that the uniform distribution provides an appropriate null hypothesis, there are still serious difficulties in obtaining sampling distributions. Hartigan (1978) has obtained asymptotic distributions for the within-cluster sum of squares, the criterion that FASTCLUS and Ward's minimum variance method attempt to optimize, but only in one dimension. Hartigan's results are very liberal when applied to small samples. No distributional theory for finite sample sizes has yet appeared. At present, the only practical way to obtain sampling distributions for realistic sample sizes is by computer simulation.

Arnold (1979) used simulation to derive tables of the distribution of a criterion based on the determinant of the within-cluster sum of squares matrix $|\mathbf{W}|$. Both normal and uniform null distributions were used. Having obtained clusters with either FASTCLUS or CLUSTER, you can compute Arnold's criterion with the ANOVA or CANDISC procedure. Arnold's tables provide a conservative test because FASTCLUS and CLUSTER attempt to minimize the trace of **W** rather than the determinant. Marriott (1971, 1975) also gives useful information on $|\mathbf{W}|$ as a criterion for the number of clusters.

Sarle (1983) used extensive simulations to develop the cubic clustering criterion (CCC), which can be used for crude hypothesis testing and estimating the number of population clusters. The CCC is based on the assumption that a uniform distribution on a hyperrectangle will be divided into clusters shaped roughly like hypercubes. In large samples that can be divided into the appropriate number of hypercubes, this assumption gives very accurate results. In other cases the approximation is generally conservative. For details about the interpretation of the CCC, consult Sarle (1983).

Milligan and Cooper (1983) and Cooper and Milligan (1984) compared thirty methods for estimating the number of population clusters using four hierarchical clustering methods. The three criteria that performed best in these simulation studies with a high degree of error in the data are a pseudo *F* statistic due to Calinski and Harabasz (1974), a statistic referred to as $J_e(2)/J_e(1)$ by Duda and Hart (1973) that can be transformed into a pseudo t^2 statistic, and the cubic clustering criterion. The pseudo *F* statistic and the CCC are printed by FASTCLUS; these two statistics and the pseudo t^2 statistic, which can be applied only to hierarchical methods, are printed by CLUSTER. It may be advisable to look for a consensus among the three statistics, that is, local peaks of the CCC and pseudo *F* statistics combined with a small value of the pseudo t^2 statistic and a larger pseudo t^2 for the next cluster fusion. It must be emphasized that these criteria are appropriate only for compact or slightly elongated clusters, preferably clusters that are roughly multivariate normal.

Perhaps the best approach to the number-of-clusters problem that has yet appeared is provided by Wong and Schaack (1982). The *k*th-nearest-neighbor clustering method developed by Wong and Lane (1983) is applied with varying values of *k*. Each value of *k* yields an estimate of the number of modal clusters. If the estimated number of modal clusters is constant for a wide range of *k* values, there is strong evidence of at least that many modes in the population. A plot of the estimated number of modes against *k* can be highly informative. Hypothesis testing requires bootstrapping or simulation. This method requires much weaker assumptions than any of the other approaches discussed above, namely, that the observations are sampled independently and that each cluster corresponds to a mode of the population density. The *k*th-nearest-neighbor clustering method is implemented in the CLUSTER procedure as METHOD=DENSITY with the K= option. The SAS macro language provides a convenient way to run CLUSTER with a range of K= values.

References

Anderberg, M.R. (1973), *Cluster Analysis for Applications*, New York: Academic Press.

Arnold, S.J. (1979), "A Test for Clusters," *Journal of Marketing Research*, 16, 545-551.

Art, D., Gnanadesikan, R., and Kettenring, R. (1982), "Data-based Metrics for Cluster Analysis," *Utilitas Mathematica*, 21A, 75-99.

Binder, D.A. (1978), "Bayesian Cluster Analysis," *Biometrika*, 65, 31-38.

Binder, D.A. (1981), "Approximations to Bayesian Clustering Rules," *Biometrika*, 68, 275-285.

Blashfield, R.K. and Aldenderfer, M.S. (1978), "The Literature on Cluster Analysis," *Multivariate Behavioral Research*, 13, 271-295.

Calinski, T. and Harabasz, J. (1974), "A Dendrite Method for Cluster Analysis," *Communications in Statistics*, 3, 1-27.

Cooper, M.C. and Milligan, G.W. (1984), "The Effect of Error on Determining the Number of Clusters," *College of Administrative Science Working Paper Series 84-2*, Columbus: The Ohio State University.

Duda, R.O. and Hart, P.E. (1973), *Pattern Classification and Scene Analysis*, New York: John Wiley & Sons.

Duran, B.S. and Odell, P.L. (1974), *Cluster Analysis*, New York: Springer-Verlag.

Englemann, L. and Hartigan, J.A. (1969), "Percentage Points of a Test for Clusters," *Journal of the American Statistical Association*, 64, 1647-1648.

Everitt, B.S. (1979), "Unresolved Problems in Cluster Analysis," *Biometrics*, 35, 169-181.

Everitt, B.S. (1980), *Cluster Analysis*, Second Edition, London: Heineman Educational Books Ltd.

Everitt, B.S. and Hand, D.J. (1981), *Finite Mixture Distributions*, New York: Chapman and Hall.

Good, I.J. (1977), "The Botryology of Botryology," in *Classification and Clustering*, ed. J. Van Ryzin, New York: Academic Press.

Harman, H.H. (1976), *Modern Factor Analysis*, Third Edition, Chicago: University of Chicago Press.

Hartigan, J.A. (1975), *Clustering Algorithms*, New York: John Wiley & Sons.

Hartigan, J.A. (1977), "Distribution Problems in Clustering," in *Classification and Clustering*, ed. J. Van Ryzin, New York: Academic Press.

Hartigan, J.A. (1978), "Asymptotic Distributions for Clustering Criteria," *Annals of Statistics*, 6, 117-131.

Hartigan, J.A. (1981), "Consistency of Single Linkage for High-Density Clusters," *Journal of the American Statistical Association*, 76, 388-394.

Hawkins, D.M., Muller, M.W., and ten Krooden, J.A. (1982), "Cluster Analysis," in *Topics in Applied Multivariate Analysis*, ed. D.M. Hawkins, Cambridge: Cambridge University Press.

Hubert, L. (1974), "Approximate Evaluation Techniques for the Single-Link and Complete-Link Hierarchical Clustering Procedures," *Journal of the American Statistical Association*, 69, 698-704.

Hubert, L.J. and Baker, F.B. (1977), "An Empirical Comparison of Baseline Models for Goodness-of-Fit in r-Diameter Hierarchical Clustering," in *Classification and Clustering*, ed. J. Van Ryzin, New York: Academic Press.

Klastorin, T.D. (1983), "Assessing Cluster Analysis Results," *Journal of Marketing Research*, 20, 92-98.

Lee, K.L. (1979), "Multivariate Tests for Clusters," *Journal of the American Statistical Association*, 74, 708-714.

Ling, R.F (1973), "A Probability Theory of Cluster Analysis," *Journal of the American Statistical Association*, 68, 159-169.

MacQueen, J.B. (1967), "Some Methods for Classification and Analysis of Multivariate Observations," *Proceedings of the Fifth Berkeley Symposium on Mathematical Statistics and Probability*, 1, 281-297.

McClain, J.O. and Rao, V.R. (1975), "CLUSTISZ: A Program to Test for the Quality of Clustering of a Set of Objects," *Journal of Marketing Research*, 12, 456-460.

Marriott, F.H.C. (1971), "Practical Problems in a Method of Cluster Analysis," *Biometrics*, 27, 501-514.

Marriott, F.H.C. (1975), "Separating Mixtures of Normal Distributions," *Biometrics*, 31, 767-769.

Massart, D.L. and Kaufman, L. (1983), *The Interpretation of Analytical Chemical Data by the Use of Cluster Analysis*, New York: John Wiley & Sons.

Mezzich, J.E and Solomon, H. (1980), *Taxonomy and Behavioral Science*, New York: Academic Press.

Milligan, G.W. (1980), "An Examination of the Effect of Six Types of Error Perturbation on Fifteen Clustering Algorithms," *Psychometrika*, 45, 325-342.

Milligan, G.W. (1981), "A Review of Monte Carlo Tests of Cluster Analysis," *Multivariate Behavioral Research*, 16, 379-407.

Milligan, G.W. and Cooper, M.C. (1983), "An Examination of Procedures for Determining the Number of Clusters in a Data Set," *College of Administrative Science Working Paper Series 83-51*, Columbus: The Ohio State University. To appear in *Psychometrika*, 1985.

Sarle, W.S. (1982), "Cluster Analysis by Least Squares," Proceedings of the Seventh Annual SAS Users Group International Conference, 651-653.

Sarle, W.S. (1983), "The Cubic Clustering Criterion," SAS Technical Report A-108, Cary, NC: SAS Institute Inc.

Scott, A.J. and Symons, M.J. (1971), "Clustering Methods Based on Likelihood Ratio Criteria," *Biometrics*, 27, 387-397.

Sneath, P.H.A. and Sokal, R.R. (1973), *Numerical Taxonomy*, San Francisco: Freeman.

Spath, H. (1980), *Cluster Analysis Algorithms*, Chichester, England: Ellis Horwood.

Symons, M.J. (1981), "Clustering Criteria and Multivariate Normal Mixtures," *Biometrics*, 37, 35-43.

Ward, J.H. (1963), "Hierarchical Grouping to Optimize an Objective Function," *Journal of the American Statistical Association*, 58, 236-244.

Wolfe, J.H. (1970), "Pattern Clustering by Multivariate Mixture Analysis," *Multivariate Behavioral Research*, 5, 329-350.

Wolfe, J.H. (1978), "Comparative Cluster Analysis of Patterns of Vocational Interest," *Multivariate Behavioral Research*, 13, 33-44.

Wong, M.A. (1982), "A Hybrid Clustering Method for Identifying High-Density Clusters," *Journal of the American Statistical Association*, 77, 841-847.

Wong, M.A. and Lane, T. (1983), "A *k*th Nearest Neighbor Clustering Procedure," *Journal of the Royal Statistical Society*, Series B, 45, 362-368.

Wong, M.A. and Schaack, C. (1982), "Using the *k*th Nearest Neighbor Clustering Procedure to Determine the Number of Subpopulations," *American Statistical Association 1982 Proceedings of the Statistical Computing Section*, 40-48.

Chapter 7

SAS® Survival Analysis Procedures

Introduction

An essential feature of lifetime or survival data is the presence of right-censored observations due either to withdrawal of experimental units or termination of the experiment. For such observations it is only known that the lifetime exceeded a given value. The exact lifetime remains unknown. Such data cannot be analyzed by ignoring the censored observations because, among other considerations, the longer-lived units are generally more likely to be censored. The analysis methodology must correctly utilize the censored observations as well as the noncensored observations.

Survival data consist of a response variable that measures the duration of time until a specified event occurs, often a type of system failure, and possibly other variables that are thought to be associated with the event-time variable. The system may be biological, as with most medical data, or it may be a physical system, as with engineering data. The primary purpose of survival analysis is to describe the distribution of the event-time variable and its relation to the other variables. The other variables may be either discrete classification variables, such as race and sex, or continuous variables, such as temperature and age.

Two features of survival data distinguish these data from other types of data. First, the response variable cannot be negative. This suggests that a transformation such as a *log* transformation may be necessary before standard statistical methods can be applied or that specialized methods may be more appropriate. Second, because the response is usually a specified time, some of the possible events may not have occurred when the data collection is terminated. Also, some of the possible responses may be lost to observation before the event occurs. In either case, only a lower bound for the event time is known for some of the observations, and these observations are said to be right censored. Thus, an additional censoring variable is incorporated into the analysis indicating which observations are event times and which are censored event times.

The following SAS procedures perform survival analysis:

LIFETEST computes nonparametric estimates of the survival distribution and rank tests for the association of the response variable with other variables. Either product-limit or life-table estimates of the distribution function may be requested. The distribution function estimates and the test statistics are available in output data sets for additional processing.

LIFEREG fits parametric models to event-time data that may be right censored. The baseline distribution can be specified as one of several possibilities including the log normal, log logistic, and Weibull distributions. The parameter estimates and their estimated covariance matrix are available in an output data set if no class variables appear in the model.

The initial stage in the analysis of a set of survival data is generally to compute and plot estimates of the distribution of the event time. The two most common methods of estimation are the product limit or Kaplan-Meier estimate and the life table or actuarial estimates. The texts by Cox and Oakes (1984) and Kalbfleisch and Prentice (1980) provide good discussions of the product limit estimator, and the text by Elandt-Johnson and Johnson (1980) includes a detailed discussion of the life table estimators.

Comparison of Procedures

The LIFETEST procedure can compute either product-limit or life-table estimates within strata defined by other variables. The relation of covariables can be investigated by computing estimates of the survival distribution within strata defined by the values of the covariables. In particular, if the proportional hazards model (Cox and Oakes 1984; Kalbfleisch and Prentice 1980) is appropriate, the estimates of the *log(-log*(SURVIVAL)) plotted against the *log*(TIME) variable should give approximately parallel lines where SURVIVAL is the survival distribution estimate and TIME is the event-time variable. Additionally, these lines should be approximately straight if the Weibull distribution is appropriate.

Statistics that test for a relation between covariables and failure time can be used to select covariables for further investigation. The LIFETEST procedure computes linear rank statistics using either Wilcoxon or log rank scores. These statistics and their covariance matrix can be used with the RSQUARE procedure to find the subsets of variables that produce the largest joint test statistic for association. An example of this method of variable selection is given in the **Examples** section of the PROC LIFETEST chapter.

If appropriate, the effects of the covariates on the response time can be modeled. One class of parametric models is of the form

$$y = \mathbf{x}'\beta + \varepsilon$$

where y is usually the log of the event time, $\mathbf{x}$ is the vector of covariate values, β is a vector of unknown parameters to be fit, and ε is an observation from some baseline distribution. The LIFEREG procedure fits this type of model allowing some of the more common distributions for ε. After the model is fit, the predicted values, residuals, and other computed values should be used to assess the model adequacy. Cox and Oakes (1984) and Lawless (1982) suggest some plots and other methods to examine the quality of fit for these and other types of models.

References

Cox, D.R. and Oakes, D. (1984), *Analysis of Survival Data*, London: Chapman and Hall.

Elandt-Johnson, R.C. and Johnson, N.L. (1980), *Survival Models and Data Analysis*, New York: John Wiley & Sons.

Gross, A.J. and Clark, V.A. (1975), *Survival Distributions: Reliability Applications in the Biomedical Sciences*, New York: John Wiley & Sons.

Kalbfleisch, J.D. and Prentice, R.L. (1980), *The Statistical Analysis of Failure Time Data*, New York: John Wiley & Sons.

Lawless, J.E. (1982), *Statistical Models and Methods for Lifetime Data*, New York: John Wiley & Sons.

Lee, E.T. (1980), *Statistical Methods for Survival Data Analysis*, Belmont, CA: Lifetime Learning Publications.

Chapter 8

SAS® Scoring Procedures

Scoring procedures are utilities that produce an output data set with new variables that are transformations of data in the old data set. PROC STANDARD transforms each variable individually. PROC SCORE constructs functions across the variables. PROC RANK produces rank scores across observations. All three procedures produce an output data set, but no printed output.

STANDARD	standardizes variables to a given mean and standard deviation.
RANK	ranks the observations of each numeric variable from low to high and outputs ranks or rank scores.
SCORE	constructs new variables that are a linear combination of old variables according to a scoring data set. This procedure is used with PROC FACTOR and other procedures that output scoring coefficients.

Chapter 9

The Four Types of Estimable Functions

INTRODUCTION

GLM, VARCOMP, and other SAS procedures label the sums of squares associated with the various effects in the model as TYPE I, TYPE II, TYPE III, and TYPE IV. The four types of hypotheses available in GLM may not always be sufficient for a statistician to perform all desired hypothesis tests, but they should suffice for the vast majority of analyses. The purpose of this chapter is to explain the hypotheses tested by each of the four types of SS (sums of squares). For additional discussion, see *SAS for Linear Models* (Freund and Littell 1981).

ESTIMABILITY

For linear models, such as

$$\mathbf{Y} = \mathbf{X}\boldsymbol{\beta} + \varepsilon$$

which have $E(\mathbf{Y}) = \mathbf{X}\boldsymbol{\beta}$, a primary analytical goal is to estimate or test (where possible) the elements of β or certain linear combinations of the elements of β. This is accomplished by computing linear combinations of the observed **Y**s. To estimate a specific linear function of the βs, say $\mathbf{L}\boldsymbol{\beta}$, you must be able to find a linear combination of the Ys that has an expected value of **L**β. Hence the following definition:

Lβ is estimable if and only if a linear combination of the **Ys** exists that has an expected value of **L**β.

Any linear combination of the **Y**s that is computed, say K**Y**, will have E(K**Y**)= K**X**β. Thus the expected value of any linear combination of the **Y**s is equal to that same linear combination of the rows of **X** multiplied by β. Therefore, **L**β is estimable if and only if we can find a linear combination of the rows of **X** that is equal to **L**.

Thus, the rows of **X** form a generating set from which an **L**, such that **L**β is estimable, can be constructed. Since **X** can be reconstructed from the rows of **X′X** (that is, **X**=[**X**(**X′X**)$^{-}$(**X′X**)], the rows of **X′X** also form a generating set from which all **L**s, such that **L**β is estimable, can be constructed. Similarly, the rows of (**X′X**)$^{-}$**X′X** also form a generating set for **L**.

Therefore, if **L** is generated as a linear combination of the rows of **X**, **X′X**, or (**X′X**)$^{-}$**X′X**, **L**β is estimable. Furthermore, any number of row operations that do not destroy the row rank can be performed on **X**, **X′X**, or (**X′X**)$^{-}$**X′X**. The rows of the resulting matrices also form a generating set for **L**.

Once an **L** of full row rank has been formed from a generating set, we can estimate **L**β by computing **Lb**, where **b**=(**X′X**)$^{-}$**X′Y**. From the general theory of linear models, **Lb** will be the best linear unbiased estimator of **L**β. To test the hypothesis that **L**β=0, compute SS(H0: **L**β=0) = (**Lb**)′(**L**(**X′X**)$^{-}$**L′**)$^{-1}$**Lb** and form an *F* test using the appropriate error term.

General Form of an Estimable Function

Although any generating set for **L**, such as **X**, **X′X**, or (**X′X**)$^{-}$**X′X**, could be printed to inform the user of what could be estimated, the volume of output would usually defeat the purpose. A rather simple shorthand technique for printing any generating set is demonstrated below.

Suppose

$$\mathbf{X} = \begin{bmatrix} 1 & 1 & 0 & 0 \\ 1 & 1 & 0 & 0 \\ 1 & 0 & 1 & 0 \\ 1 & 0 & 1 & 0 \\ 1 & 0 & 0 & 1 \\ 1 & 0 & 0 & 1 \end{bmatrix} \quad \text{and} \quad \beta = \begin{bmatrix} \mu \\ A1 \\ A2 \\ A3 \end{bmatrix} .$$

Although **X** is a generating set for **L**, so also is

$$\mathbf{X^*} = \begin{bmatrix} 1 & 1 & 0 & 0 \\ 1 & 0 & 1 & 0 \\ 1 & 0 & 0 & 1 \end{bmatrix}$$

X* is formed from **X** by deleting duplicate rows.

Since all **L**s must be linear functions of the rows of **X***, an **L** for a single-degree-of-freedom estimate can be represented symbolically as:

L1*(1 1 0 0) + L2*(1 0 1 0) +L3*(1 0 0 1)

or

L = (L1 + L2 + L3, L1, L2, L3) .

For this example, **L**β is estimable if and only if the first element of **L** is equal to the sum of the other elements of **L**, or

(L1 + L2 + L3)*μ + L1*A1 + L2*A2 + L3*A3

is estimable for any values of L1, L2, and L3.

If other generating sets for **L** are represented symbolically, the symbolic notation will look different. However, the inherent nature of the rules will be the same. For example, if row operations are performed on **X*** to produce an identity matrix in the first 3x3,

$$\mathbf{X^{**}} = \begin{bmatrix} 1 & 0 & 0 & 1 \\ 0 & 1 & 0 & -1 \\ 0 & 0 & 1 & -1 \end{bmatrix}$$

then **X**** is also a generating set for **L**. An **L** generated from **X**** can be represented symbolically as:

L = (L1,L2,L3,L1 − L2 − L3)

although, again, the first element of **L** is equal to the sum of the other elements.

With the thousands of generating sets available, the question arises as to which one is the best to represent **L** symbolically. Clearly, a generating set containing a minimum of rows (of full row rank) and a maximum of zero elements is desirable. Since the GLM procedure computes a g2 inverse of **X'X**, such that $\mathbf{(X'X)^{-}X'X}$ usually contains numerous zeros and such that the nonzero rows are linearly independent, GLM uses the nonzero rows of $\mathbf{(X'X)^{-}X'X}$ to represent **L** symbolically.

If the generating set represented symbolically is of full row rank, the number of symbols (L1, L2, ...) represents the maximum rank of any testable hypothesis (in other words, the maximum number of linearly independent rows for any **L** matrix that can be constructed). By letting each symbol in turn take on the value of 1 while the others are set to 0, the original generating set can be reconstructed.

A One-Way Classification Model

For the model

$$Y = \mu + A_i + \varepsilon\,,\ i = 1,2,3$$

the general form of estimable functions **Lb** is (from the previous example):

$$\mathbf{L}\beta = L1{*}\mu + L2{*}A_1 + L3{*}A_2 + (L1 - L2 - L3){*}A_3$$

Thus, **L**=(L1,L2,L3,L1 − L2 − L3) .

Tests involving only the parameters A1, A2, and A3 must have an **L** of the form

$$\mathbf{L} = (0, L2, L3, -L2 - L3) \quad .$$

Since the above **L** involves only two symbols, at most a two-degrées-of-freedom hypothesis can be constructed. For example, let L2=1 and L3=0; then let L2=0 and L3=1:

$$\mathbf{L} = \begin{bmatrix} 0 & 1 & 0 & -1 \\ 0 & 0 & 1 & -1 \end{bmatrix}$$

The above **L** can be used to test the hypothesis that A1=A2=A3. For this example, any **L** with two linearly independent rows with column 1 equal to zero will produce the same SS. For example, a pooled linear quadratic

$$\mathbf{L} = \begin{bmatrix} 0 & 1 & 0 & -1 \\ 0 & 1 & -2 & 1 \end{bmatrix}$$

gives the same SS. In fact, for any **L** of full row rank and any non-singular matrix **K** of conformable dimensions:

$$SS(H0: \mathbf{L}\beta = 0) = SS(H0: \mathbf{KL}\beta = 0) \quad .$$

A Three-Factor Main-Effects Model

Consider a three-factor main-effects model involving the CLASS variables A, B, and C, as shown in **Table 9.1**.

Table 9.1 Three-Factor Main-Effects Model

Obs	A	B	C
1	1	2	1
2	1	1	2
3	2	1	3
4	2	2	2
5	2	2	2

The general form of an estimable function is shown in **Table 9.2**.

Table 9.2 General Form of an Estimable Function for Three-Factor Main-Effects Model

Parameter	*Coefficient*
μ	L1
A1	L2
A2	L1−L2
B1	L4
B2	L1−L4
C1	L6
C2	L1+L2−L4−2*L6
C3	−L2+L4+L6

Since only four symbols (L1, L2, L4, and L6) are involved, the maximum rank hypothesis possible will have four degrees-of-freedom. If an **L** matrix with four linearly independent rows is formed, with each row being generated using the above rules, then

$$SS(H0: \mathbf{L}\beta = 0) = R(\mu, A, B, C) \quad .$$

In a main-effects model, the usual hypothesis desired for a main effect is the equality of all the parameters. In this example, it is not possible to test such a hypothesis because of confounding caused by inadequate design points. The best that can be done is to construct a maximum rank hypothesis (MRH) involving only the parameters of the main effect in question. This can be done using the general form of estimable functions. For example:

- To get an MRH involving only the parameters of A, the coefficients of **L** associated with μ, B1, B2, C1, C2, and C3 must be equated to zero. Starting at the top of the general form, let L1=0, then L4=0, then L6=0. If C2 and C3 are not to be involved, then L2 must also be zero. Thus, A1−A2 is not estimable; that is, the MRH involving only the A parameters has zero rank and R(A | μ,B,C)=0.
- To obtain the MRH involving only the B parameters, let L1=L2=L6=0. But then to remove C2 and C3 from the comparison, L4 must also be set to 0. Thus, B1−B2 is not estimable and R(B | μ,A,C,)=0.
- To obtain the MRH involving only the C parameters, let L1=L2=L4=0. Thus, the MRH involving only C parameters is

  $$C1 - 2*C2 + C3 = K \text{ (for any K)}$$

  or any multiple of the left-hand side equal to K. Furthermore,

  $$SS(H0: C1 = 2*C2 - C3 = 0) = R(C \mid \mu,A,B) \quad .$$

A Multiple Regression Model

Let

E(Y) = β0 + β1*X1 + β2*X2 + β3*X3 .

If the **X'X** matrix is of full rank, the general form of estimable functions is as shown in **Table 9.3**.

Table 9.3 General Form of Estimable Functions for a Multiple Regression Model When X'X Matrix is of Full Rank

Parameter	*Coefficient*
β0	L1
β1	L2
β2	L3
β3	L4

To test, for example, the hypothesis that β2=0, let L1=L2=L4=0 and let L3=1. Then SS(**L**β=0)=R(β2 | β0,β1,β3). In the full-rank case, all parameters, as well as any linear combination of parameters, are estimable.

Suppose, however, that X3=2*X1+3*X2. The general form of estimable functions is shown in **Table 9.4**.

Table 9.4 General Form of Estimable Functions for a Multiple Regression Model When X'X Matrix Is Not of Full Rank

Parameter	*Coefficient*
β0	L1
β1	L2
β2	L3
β3	2*L2 + 3*L3

For this example it is possible to test H0:β0=0. However, β1, β2, and β3 are not estimable; that is,

R(β1 | β0,β2,β3) = 0
R(β2 | β0,β1,β3) = 0
R(β3 | β0,β1,β2) = 0

Note on Symbolic Notation

The preceding examples demonstrate the ability to manipulate the symbolic representation of a generating set. It should be noted that any operations performed on the symbolic notation have corresponding row operations that are performed on the generating set itself.

ESTIMABLE FUNCTIONS

Type I SS and Estimable Functions

The Type I SS and the associated hypotheses they test are by-products of the modified sweep operator used to compute a g2 inverse of **X'X** and a solution to the normal equations. For the model E(Y) = X1*B1+X2*B2+X3*B3 where B1, B2 and B3 are vectors, the Type I SS for each effect correspond to:

Effect	*Type I SS*
B1	R(B1)
B2	R(B2 | B1)
B3	R(B3 | B1,B2)

The Type I SS are model-order-dependent; each effect is adjusted only for the preceding effects in the model.

There are numerous ways to obtain a Type I hypothesis matrix **L** for each effect. One way is to form the **X'X** matrix and then do a Forward-Doolittle on **X'X**, skipping over any rows with a zero diagonal. The nonzero rows of the resulting matrix associated with X1 provide an **L** such that

$$\text{SS(H0: } \mathbf{L}\beta = 0) = \text{R(B1)} \quad .$$

The nonzero rows of the Doolittle matrix associated with X2 provide an **L** such that SS(H0: $\mathbf{L}\beta=0$) = R(B1 | B2). The last set of nonzero rows (associated with X3) provide an **L** such that

$$\text{SS(H0: } \mathbf{L}\beta = 0) = \text{R(B3 | B1,B2)} \quad .$$

Another more formalized representation of Type I generating sets for B1, B2, and B3, respectively, is

G1 = (X1'X1 | X1'X2 | X1'X3)
G2 = (0 | **X2'M1X2 | X2'M1X3)**
G3 = (0 | 0 | **X3'M2X3)**

where

$$\mathbf{M1 = I - X1(X1'X1)^{-}X1'}$$

and

$$\mathbf{M2 = M1 - M1X2(X2'M1X2)^{-}X2'M1} \quad .$$

Using the Type I generating set **G2** (for example), if an **L** is formed from linear combinations of the rows of **G2** such that **L** is of full row rank and of the same row rank as **G2**, then SS(H0: $\mathbf{L}\beta=0$) = R(B2 | B1).

In the GLM procedure, the Type I estimable functions printed symbolically when the E1 option is requested are

$$\mathbf{G1^*} = (\mathbf{X1'X1})^- \mathbf{G1}$$
$$\mathbf{G2^*} = (\mathbf{X2'M1X2})^- \mathbf{G2}$$
$$\mathbf{G3^*} = (\mathbf{X3'M2X3})^- \mathbf{G3} \quad .$$

As can be seen from the nature of the generating sets **G1 G2** and **G3** only the Type I estimable functions for B3 are guaranteed not to involve the B1 and B2 parameters. The Type I hypothesis for B2 can (and usually does for unbalanced data) involve B3 parameters. The Type I hypothesis for B1 usually involves B2 and B3 parameters.

There are, however, a number of models for which the Type I hypotheses are considered appropriate. These are

1. balanced ANOVA models specified in proper sequence (that is, interactions do not precede main effects in the MODEL statement and so forth)
2. purely nested models (specified in the proper sequence)
3. polynomial regression models (in the proper sequence).

Type II SS and Estimable Functions

For main-effects models and regression models, the general form of estimable functions can be manipulated to provide tests of hypotheses involving only the parameters of the effect in question. The same result can also be obtained by entering each effect in turn as the last effect in the model and obtaining the Type I SS for that effect. Using a modified reversible sweep operator, it is possible to obtain the same results without actually re-running the model.

Thus, the Type II SS correspond to the R notation in which each effect is adjusted for all other effects possible. For a regression model such as

E(Y) = X1*B1 + X2*B2 + X3*B3

the Type II SS correspond to:

Effect	*SS*
B1	R(B1 | B2, B3)
B2	R(B2 | B1, B3)
B3	R(B3 | B1, B2)

For a main-effects model (A, B, and C as classification variables), the Type II SS correspond to:

Effect	*SS*
A	R(A | B, C)
B	R(B | A, C)
C	R(C | A, B)

From an earlier discussion, you know that the Type II SS provide (for regression and main-effects models) an MRH for each effect that does not involve the parameters of the other effects.

For models involving interactions and nested effects, it is not possible to obtain a test of a hypothesis for a main effect free of parameters of higher-level effects with which the main effect is involved (unless *a priori* parametric restrictions are assumed).

It is reasonable to assume, then, that any test of a hypothesis concerning an effect should involve the parameters of that effect and only those other parameters with which that effect is involved.

Definition: Given an effect E1 and another effect E2, E1 is contained in E2 provided that:

1. both effects involve the same continuous variables if any.
2. E2 has more CLASS variables than does E1; and if E1 has CLASS variables, they all appear in E2.
   Note: the effect μ is contained in all pure CLASS effects, but it is not contained in any effect involving a continuous variable. No effect is contained by μ.
   Type II, Type III, and Type IV estimable functions rely on this definition, and all have one thing in common: the estimable functions involving an effect E1 also involve the parameters of all effects that contain E1, and they do not involve the parameters of effects that do not contain E1 (other than E1).

Definition: The Type II estimable functions for an effect E1 have an **L** (before reduction to full row rank) of the following form:

1. All columns of **L** associated with effects not containing E1 (except E1) should be zero.
2. The submatrix of **L** associated with effect E1 should be $(\mathbf{X1'MX1})^{-}(\mathbf{X1'MX1})$.
3. Each of the remaining submatrices of **L** associated with an effect E2 that contains E1 should be $(\mathbf{X1'MX1})^{-}(\mathbf{X1'MX2})$, where

   X0 = the columns of **X** whose associated effects do not contain E1.

   X1 = the columns of **X** associated with E1.

   X2 = the columns of **X** associated with an effect E2 that contains E1.

   $\mathbf{M} = \mathbf{I} - \mathbf{X0}(\mathbf{X0'X0})^{-}\mathbf{X0'}$.

For the model Y = A B A*B, the Type II SS correspond to

$$R(A \mid \mu,B),\ R(B \mid \mu,A),\ R(A{*}B \mid \mu,A,B)\ .$$

For the model Y = A B(A) C(A B), the Type II SS correspond to

$$R(A \mid ,\mu),\ R(B(A) \mid \mu,A),\ R(C(A\ B) \mid \mu,A,B(A))\ .$$

For the model Y = **X X*X**, the Type II SS correspond to

$$R(X \mid \mu,\mathbf{X{*}X}) \text{ and } R(\mathbf{X{*}X} \mid \mu,X)\ .$$

Example of Type II Estimable Functions

For a 2x2 factorial with *w* observations per cell, the general form of estimable functions is shown in **Table 9.5**.

Any nonzero values for L2, L4, and L6 can be used to construct **L** vectors for computing the Type II SS for A, B, and A*B, respectively.

For an unbalanced 2x2 factorial (with 2 observations in every cell except the AB22 cell, which contains only 1 observation), the general form of estimable functions is the same as if it were balanced since the same effects are still estimable. However, the Type II estimable functions for A and B are not the same as they were for the balanced design.

Table 9.5 General Form of Estimable Functions for 2x2 Factorial

Effect	*Coefficient*
μ	L1
A1	L2
A2	L1− L2
B1	L4
B2	L1− L4
AB11	L6
AB12	L2− L6
AB21	L4− L6
AB22	L1− L2− L4 + L6

The Type II estimable functions are shown in **Table 9.6**.

Table 9.6 Type II Estimable Functions for Balanced 2x2 Factorial

	Coefficients for Effect		
Effect	A	B	A*B
μ	0	0	0
A1	L2	0	0
A2	− L2	0	0
B1	0	L4	0
B2	0	−L4	0
AB11	.5*L2	.5*L4	L6
AB12	.5*L2	−.5*L4	−L6
AB21	−.5*L2	.5*L4	−L6
AB22	−.5*L2	−.5*L4	L6

The Type II estimable functions for this unbalanced 2x2 are shown in **Table 9.7**.

Table 9.7 Type II Estimable Functions for Unbalanced 2x2 Factorial

	Coefficients for Effect		
Effect	A	B	A*B
μ	0	0	0
A1	L2	0	0
A2	−L2	0	0
B1	0	L4	0
B2	0	−L4	0
AB11	.6*L2	.6*L4	L6
AB12	.4*L2	−.6*L4	−L6
AB21	−.6*L2	.4*L4	−L6
AB22	−.4*L2	−.4*L4	L6

By comparing the hypothesis being tested in the balanced case to the hypothesis being tested in the unbalanced case for effects A and B, you can note that the Type II hypotheses for A and B are dependent on the cell frequencies in the design. For unbalanced designs in which the cell frequencies are not proportional to the background population, the Type II hypotheses for effects that are contained in other effects are of questionable merit.

However, if an effect is not contained in any other effect, the Type II hypothesis for that effect is an MRH that does not involve any parameters except those associated with the effect in question.

Thus, Type II SS are appropriate for:

1. any balanced model
2. any main-effects model
3. any pure regression model
4. an effect not contained in any other effect (regardless of the model).

In addition to the above, the Type II SS is generally accepted by most statisticians for purely nested models.

Type III SS and Estimable Functions

You have seen that when an effect is contained in another effect, the Type II hypotheses for that effect are dependent on the cell frequencies. The philosophy behind both the Type III and Type IV hypotheses is that the tests of hypotheses made for any given effect should be the same for all designs with the same general form of estimable functions.

To demonstrate this concept, recall the hypothesis being tested by the Type II SS in the balanced 2x2 factorial shown earlier. Those hypotheses are precisely the ones that the Type III and Type IV employ for all 2x2 factorials that have at least one observation per cell. The Type II and Type IV hypotheses for a design without missing cells usually differ from the hypothesis employed for the same design with missing cells since the general form of estimable functions usually differ.

Construction of Type III Hypotheses

Type III hypotheses are constructed by working directly with the general form of estimable functions. The following steps are used to construct a hypothesis for an effect E1:

1. For every effect in the model except E1 and those effects that contain E1, equate the coefficients in the general form of estimable functions to zero.
   Note: if E1 is not contained in any other effect, this step defines the Type III hypothesis (as well as the Type II and Type IV hypotheses). If E1 is contained in other effects, go on to step 2.
2. If necessary, equate new symbols to compound expressions in the E1 block in order to obtain the simplest form for the E1 coefficients.
3. Equate all symbolic coefficients outside of the E1 block to a linear function of the symbols in the E1 block in order to make the E1 hypothesis orthogonal to hypotheses associated with effects that contain E1.

By once again observing the Type II hypotheses being tested in the balanced 2x2 factorial, it is possible to verify that the A and A*B hypotheses are orthogonal and also that the B and A*B hypotheses are orthogonal. This principle of orthogonality between an effect and any effect that contains it holds for all balanced designs. Thus, construction of Type III hypotheses for any design is a logical extension of a process that is used for balanced designs.

The Type III hypotheses are precisely the hypotheses being tested by programs that reparameterize using the "usual assumptions." When no missing cells exist in a factorial model, Type III SS coincide with Yate's weighted squares-of-means technique. When cells are missing in factorial models, the Type III SS coincide with those produced by Walter Harvey's fixed-effects linear models program. See the HARVEY procedure in the *SUGI Supplemental Library User's Guide*.

The following steps illustrate the construction of Type III estimable functions for a 2x2 factorial with no missing cells.

To obtain the A*B interaction hypothesis, start with the general form and equate the coefficients for effects μ, A, and B to zero, as shown in **Table 9.8**.

Table 9.8 Type III Hypothesis for A*B Interaction

Effect	*General Form*	L1=L2= L4=0
μ	L1	0
A1	L2	0
A2	L1−L2	0
B1	L4	0
B2	L1−L4	0
AB11	L6	L6
AB12	L2−L6	−L6
AB21	L4−L6	−L6
AB22	L1−L2−L4+L6	L6

The last column in **Table 9.8** represents the form of the MRH for A*B.

To obtain the Type III hypothesis for A, first start with the general form and equate the coefficients for effects μ and B to zero (let L1=L4=0). Next let L6=K*L2, and find the value of K that makes the A hypothesis orthogonal to the A*B hypothesis. In this case, K=0.5. Each of these steps is shown in **Table 9.9**.

In **Table 9.9**, the fourth column (under L6=K*L2) represents the form of all estimable functions not involving μ, B1, or B2. The prime difference between the Type II and Type III hypotheses for A is the way K is determined. Type II chooses K as a function of the cell frequencies, whereas Type III chooses K such that the estimable functions for A are orthogonal to the estimable functions for A*B.

Table 9.9 Type III Hypothesis for A

Effect	*General Form*	L1=L4=0	L6=K*L2	K=0.5
μ	L1	0	0	0
A1	L2	L2	L2	L2
A2	L1−L2	−L2	−L2	−L2
B1	L4	0	0	0
B2	L1−L4	0	0	0
AB11	L6	L6	K*L2	.5*L2
AB12	L2−L6	L2−L6	(1−K)*L2	.5*L2
AB21	L4−L6	−L6	−K*L2	−.5*L2
AB22	L1−L2-L4+L6	−L2+L6	(K−1)*L2	−.5*L2

An example of Type III estimable functions in a 3x3 factorial with unequal cell frequencies and missing diagonals is given in **Table 9.10** (N1-N6 represent the nonzero cell frequencies).

Table 9.10 A 3x3 Factorial Design with Unequal Cell Frequencies and Missing Diagonals

		B 1	B 2	B 3
A	1		N1	N2
A	2	N3		N4
A	3	N5	N6	

For any nonzero values of N1-N6, the Type III estimable functions for each effect are shown in **Table 9.11**.

Table 9.11 Type III Estimable Functions for 3x3 Factorial Design with Unequal Cell Frequencies and Missing Diagonals

Effect	A	B	A*B
μ	0	0	0
A1	L2	0	0
A2	L3	0	0
A3	−L2−L3	0	0
B1	0	L5	0
B2	0	L6	0
B3	0	−L5-L6	0
AB12	.667*L2+.333*L3	.333*L5+.667*L6	L8
AB13	.333*L2−.333*L3	−.333*L5−.667*L6	−L8
AB21	.333*L2+.667*L3	.667*L5+.333*L6	−L8
AB23	−.333*L2+.333*L3	−.667*L5−.333*L6	L8
AB31	−.333*L2−.667*L3	.333*L5−.333*L6	L8
AB32	−.667*L2−.333*L3	−.333*L5+.333*L6	−L8

Type IV Estimable Functions

By once again looking at the Type II hypotheses being tested in the balanced 2x2 factorial, you can see another characteristic of the hypotheses employed for balanced designs: the coefficients of lower-order effects are averaged across each higher-level effect involving the same subscripts. For example, in the A hypothesis, the coefficients of AB11 and AB12 are equal to one-half the coefficient of A1; and the coefficients of AB21 and AB22 are equal to one-half the coefficient of A2. With this in mind then, the basic concept used to construct Type IV hypotheses is that the coefficients of any effect, say E1, are distributed equitably across higher-level effects that "contain" E1. When missing cells occur, this same general philosophy is adhered to, but care must be taken in the way the distributive concept is applied.

Construction of Type IV hypotheses begins as does the construction of the Type III hypotheses. That is, for an effect E1, equate to zero all coefficients in the general form that do not belong to E1 or to any other effect containing E1. If E1 is not contained in any other effect, then the Type IV hypothesis (and Type II and III) has been found. If E1 is contained in other effects, then simplify, if necessary, the coefficients associated with E1, such that they are all free coefficients or functions of other free coefficients in the E1 block.

To illustrate the method of resolving the free coefficients outside of the E1 block, suppose that you are interested in the estimable functions for an effect A and that A is contained in AB, AC, AD, and ABC.

With missing cells, the coefficients of intermediate effects (here they are AB and AC) do not always have an equal distribution of the lower-order coefficients, so the coefficients of the highest-order effects are determined first (here they are ABC and AD). Once the highest-order coefficients are determined, the coefficients of intermediate effects are automatically determined.

The following process is performed for each free coefficient of A in turn. The resulting symbolic vectors are then added together to give the Type IV estimable functions for A.

1. Select a free coefficient of A, and set all other free coefficients of A to zero.
2. If any of the levels of A have zero as a coefficient, equate all of the coefficients of higher-level effects involving that level of A to zero. This step alone usually resolves most of the free coefficients remaining.
3. Check to see if any higher-level coefficients are now zero, when the coefficient of the associated level of A is not zero. If this situation occurs, the Type IV estimable functions for A are not unique.
4. For each level of A in turn, if the A coefficient for that level is nonzero, count the number of times that level occurs in the higher-level effect. Then equate each of the higher-level coefficients to the coefficient of that level of A divided by the count.

An example of a 3x3 factorial with four missing cells (N1-N5 represent positive cell frequencies) is shown in **Table 9.12**.

Table 9.12 3x3 Factorial Design with Four Missing Cells

		B		
		1	2	3
	1	N1	N2	
A	2	N3	N4	
	3			N6

The Type IV estimable functions are shown in **Table 9.13**.

A Comparison of Type III and Type IV Hypotheses

For the vast majority of designs, Type III and Type IV hypotheses for a given effect are the same. Specifically, they are the same for any effect E1 that is not contained in other effects for any design (with or without missing cells). For factorial designs with no missing cells, the Type III and Type IV hypotheses coincide for all effects. When there are missing cells, the hypotheses can differ. By using the GLM procedure, you can study the differences in the hypotheses. Each user must decide on the appropriateness of the hypotheses for a particular model.

The Type III hypotheses for three-factor and higher completely nested designs with unequal Ns in the bottommost level differ from the Type II hypotheses; however, the Type IV hypotheses do correspond to the Type II hypotheses in this case.

When missing cells occur in a design, the Type IV hypotheses may not be unique. If this occurs in PROC GLM, you are notified, and you may need to consider defining your own specific comparisons.

Table 9.13 Type IV Estimable Functions for 3x3 Factorial Design with Four Missing Cells

Effect	A	B	A*B
μ	0	0	0
A1	−L3	0	0
A2	L3	0	0
A3	0	0	0
B1	0	L5	0
B2	0	−L5	0
B3	0	0	0
AB11	−0.5*L3	0.5*L5	L8
AB12	−0.5*L3	−0.5*L5	L8
AB11	0.5*L3	0.5*L5	L8
AB11	0.5*L3	−0.5*L5	L8
AB33	0	0	0

REFERENCES

Freund, Rudolf J. and Littell, Ramon C. (1981), *SAS for Linear Models*. Cary, N.C.: SAS Institute Inc.

Goodnight, J.H. (1978), "Tests of Hypotheses in Fixed Effects Linear Models," *SAS Technical Report R-101*, Cary, N.C.: SAS Institute Inc.

SAS PROCEDURES

The ACECLUS Procedure
The ANOVA Procedure
The CANCORR Procedure
The CANDISC Procedure
The CATMOD Procedure
The CLUSTER Procedure
The DISCRIM Procedure
The FACTOR Procedure
The FASTCLUS Procedure
The FREQ Procedure
The GLM Procedure
The LIFEREG Procedure
The LIFETEST Procedure
The NEIGHBOR Procedure
The NESTED Procedure
The NLIN Procedure
The NPAR1WAY Procedure
The PLAN Procedure
The PRINCOMP Procedure
The PROBIT Procedure
The RANK Procedure
The REG Procedure
The RSQUARE Procedure
The RSREG Procedure
The SCORE Procedure
The STANDARD Procedure
The STEPDISC Procedure
The STEPWISE Procedure
The TREE Procedure
The TTEST Procedure
The VARCLUS Procedure
The VARCOMP Procedure

Chapter 10
The ACECLUS Procedure

Operating systems: All

ABSTRACT

The ACECLUS (Approximate Covariance Estimation for CLUStering) procedure obtains approximate estimates of the pooled within-cluster covariance matrix when the clusters can be assumed multivariate normal with equal covariance matrices. Neither cluster membership nor the number of clusters need be known. ACECLUS is useful for preprocessing data to be subsequently clustered by CLUSTER or FASTCLUS. ACECLUS can produce output data sets containing the approximate within-cluster covariance estimate, eigenvalues and eigenvectors from a canonical analysis, and canonical variable scores. The method is a variation on an algorithm developed by Art, Gnanadesikan, and Kettenring (1982).

INTRODUCTION

Many clustering methods perform well with spherical clusters but poorly with elongated elliptical clusters (Everitt 1980). If the elliptical clusters have roughly the same orientation and eccentricity, you can apply a linear transformation to the data to yield a spherical within-cluster covariance matrix, that is, a covariance matrix proportional to the identity. Equivalently, the distance between observations can be measured in the metric of the inverse of the pooled within-cluster covariance matrix. The remedy is difficult to apply, however, because you need to know what the clusters are in order to compute the sample within-cluster covariance matrix. One approach is to estimate iteratively both cluster membership and within-cluster covariance (Wolfe 1970; Hartigan 1975). Another approach is provided by Art, Gnanadesikan, and Kettenring (1982), referred to hereafter as AGK, who have devised an ingenious method for estimating the within- cluster covariance matrix without knowledge of the clusters. The method can be applied prior to any of the usual clustering techniques, including hierarchical clustering methods.

AGK obtain a decomposition of the total-sample sum-of-squares-and-cross-products (SSCP) matrix into within-cluster and between-cluster SSCP matrices computed from pairwise differences between observations, rather than differences between observations and means. AGK then show how the within-cluster SSCP matrix based on pairwise differences can be approximated without knowing the number or the membership of the clusters. The approximate within-cluster SSCP matrix can be used to compute distances for cluster analysis or it can be used in a canonical analysis similar to canonical discriminant analysis (see the CANDISC procedure). AGK demonstrate by Monte Carlo calculations that their method can produce better clusters than the Euclidean metric even when the approximation to the within-cluster SSCP matrix is poor or the within-cluster covariances are moderately heterogeneous.

ACECLUS differs slightly from the AGK algorithm. The ACECLUS algorithm is described first; then differences between ACECLUS and the AGK method are summarized.

Background

It is well-known from the literature on nonparametric statistics that variances and, hence, covariances can be computed from pairwise differences instead of deviations from means. (For example, Puri and Sen (1971, 51-52) show that the variance is a *U* statistic of degree 2.) Let $\mathbf{X}=(x_{ij})$ be the data matrix with *n* observations (rows) and *v* variables (columns) and let $\bar{x}_j$ be the mean of the *j*th variable. The sample covariance matrix $\mathbf{S}=(s_{jk})$ is usually defined as

$$s_{jk} = \Sigma_{i=1}^{n}(x_{ij} - \bar{x}_j)(x_{ik} - \bar{x}_k)/(n\text{-}1) \quad .$$

S can also be computed as

$$s_{jk} = \Sigma_{i=2}^{n}\Sigma_{h=1}^{i-1}(x_{ij} - x_{hj})(x_{ik} - x_{hk})/(n(n-1)) \quad .$$

Let $\mathbf{W} = (w_{jk})$ be the pooled within-cluster covariance matrix, *q* be the number of clusters, n_c be the number of observations in the cth cluster, and

$$d''_{ic} = 1 \text{ if observation } i \text{ is in cluster c,}$$
$$= 0 \text{ otherwise.}$$

W is normally defined as

$$w_{jk} = \Sigma_{c=1}^{q}\Sigma_{i=1}^{n}d''_{ic}(x_{ij} - \bar{x}_{cj})(x_{ik} - \bar{x}_{ck})/(n-q) \quad .$$

where $\bar{x}_{cj}$ is the mean of the *j*th variable in cluster c. Let

$$d'_{ih} = 1/n_c \text{ if observations } i \text{ and } h \text{ are in cluster c,}$$

$$= 0 \text{ otherwise.}$$

W can also be computed as

$$w_{jk} = \Sigma_{i=2}^{n} \Sigma_{h=1}^{i-1} d'_{ih} \, (x_{ij} - x_{hj})(x_{ik} - x_{hk})/(n\text{-}q) \quad .$$

If the clusters are not known, d'_{ih} cannot be determined. However, an approximation to **W** can be obtained by using instead

$$d_{ih} = 1 \text{ if } \Sigma_{j=1}^{v} \Sigma_{k=1}^{v} m_{jk}(x_{ij} - x_{hj})(x_{ik} - x_{hk}) \leq u^2 \quad .$$

$$= 0 \text{ otherwise}$$

where u is an appropriately chosen value and $\mathbf{M} = (m_{jk})$ is an appropriate metric. Let $\mathbf{A} = (a_{jk})$ be defined as

$$a_{jk} = \Sigma_{i=2}^{n} \Sigma_{h=1}^{i-1} d_{ih} \, (x_{ij} - x_{hj})(x_{ik} - x_{hk}) \, / 2(\Sigma_{i=2}^{n} \Sigma_{h=1}^{i-1} d_{ih}) \quad .$$

A equals **W** if all of the following conditions hold:

- all within-cluster distances in the metric **M** are less than or equal to u
- all between-cluster distances in the metric **M** are greater than u
- all clusters have the same number of members n_c.

If the clusters are of unequal size, **A** gives more weight to large clusters than **W** does, but this discrepancy should be of little importance if the population within-cluster covariance matrices are equal. There may be large differences between **A** and **W** if the cutoff u does not discriminate between pairs in the same cluster and pairs in different clusters. Lack of discrimination may occur because

- the clusters are not well separated, or
- **M** or u is not chosen appropriately.

In the former case, little can be done to remedy the problem. The question remains of how to choose **M** and u. Let us consider **M** first. The best choice for **M** is $\mathbf{W}^{-1}$, but **W** is not known. The solution is to use an iterative algorithm:

1. Obtain an initial estimate of **A**, such as the identity or the total-sample covariance matrix.
2. Let **M** equal $\mathbf{A}^{-1}$.
3. Recompute **A** using the formula above.
4. Repeat steps 2 and 3 until the estimate stabilizes.

Convergence is assessed by comparing values of **A** on successive iterations. Let $\mathbf{A}_i$ be the value of **A** on the *i*th iteration, and $\mathbf{A}_0$ be the initial estimate of **A**. Let **Z** be a user-specified v by v matrix. The convergence measure is

$$e_i = \| \mathbf{Z}'(\mathbf{A}_i - \mathbf{A}_{i-1})\mathbf{Z} \| / v$$

where $\|...\|$ indicates the Euclidean norm, that is, the square root of the sum of the squares of the elements of the matrix. In ACECLUS, **Z** can be the identity or an inverse factor of **S** or diag(**S**). Iteration stops when e_i falls below a user-specified value.

The remaining question of how to choose u has no simple answer. In practice, it is necessary to try several different values. ACECLUS provides four different ways of specifying u:

1. You can specify a constant value for u. This method is useful if the initial estimate of **A** is quite good.
2. You can specify a value $t>0$ that is multiplied by the root-mean-square

distance between observations in the current metric on each iteration to give u. Thus the value of u changes from iteration to iteration. This method is appropriate if the initial estimate of **A** is poor.

3. You can specify a value p, $0<p<1$, to be transformed into a distance u such that approximately a proportion p of the pairwise Mahalanobis distances between observations in a random sample from a multivariate normal distribution will be less than u in repeated sampling. The transformation can be computed only if the number of observations exceeds the number of variables, preferably by at least 10%. This method also requires a good initial estimate of **A**.
4. You can specify a value p, $0<p<1$, to be transformed as above into a value t that is then multiplied by $1/\sqrt{(2v)}$ times the root-mean-square distance between observations in the current metric on each iteration to yield u. The value of u changes from iteration to iteration. This method can be used with a poor initial estimate of **A**.

In most cases the analysis should begin with the fourth method using values of p between 0.5 and 0.01 and using the full covariance matrix as the initial estimate of **A**.

Proportions p are transformed to distances t using the formula

$$t^2 = 2v\{[F^{-1}_{v,n-v}(p)]^{((n-v)/(n-1))}\}$$

where $F^{-1}_{v,n-v}$ is the quantile (inverse cumulative distribution) function of an F random variable with v and $n-v$ degrees of freedom. The squared Mahalanobis distance between a single pair of observations sampled from a multivariate normal distribution is distributed as $2v$ times an F random variable with degrees of freedom as above. The distances between two pairs of observations are correlated if the pairs have an observation in common. The quantile function is raised to the power given in the above formula to compensate approximately for the correlations among distances between pairs of observations that share a member. Monte Carlo studies indicate that the approximation is acceptable if the number of observations exceeds the number of variables by at least 10%.

If **A** becomes singular, step 2 in the iterative algorithm cannot be performed because **A** cannot be inverted. Let **Z** be the matrix defined above in discussing the convergence measure and let $\mathbf{Z'AZ} = \mathbf{R'\Lambda R}$ where $\mathbf{R'R} = \mathbf{RR'} = \mathbf{I}$ and $\mathbf{\Lambda} = (\lambda_{jk})$ is diagonal. Let $\mathbf{\Lambda}^* = (\lambda_{jk}^*)$ where $\lambda_{jk}^* = \lambda_{jk}$ for $j \neq k$, $\lambda_{jj}^* = \max(\lambda_{jj}, g\ \mathrm{trace}(\mathbf{\Lambda}))$, and $0<g<<1$ is a user-specified singularity criterion. Then **M** is computed as $\mathbf{ZR'(\Lambda^*)^{-1}RZ'}$.

ACECLUS differs from the AGK method in several respects. The AGK method:

- uses the identity matrix as the initial estimate, whereas ACECLUS allows you to specify any symmetric matrix as the initial estimate and defaults to the total-sample covariance matrix. The ACECLUS default was chosen to yield invariance under nonsingular linear transformations of the data, but may sometimes obscure clusters that would be apparent if the identity matrix were used.
- carries out all computations with SSCP matrices, whereas ACECLUS uses estimated covariance matrices because covariances are easier to interpret than cross products are.
- uses the m pairs with the smallest distances to form the new estimate at each iteration, where m is specified by the user, whereas ACECLUS uses all pairs closer than a given cutoff value. Kettenring (1984, personal communication) says that the m-closest-pairs method seems to give the user more direct control. ACECLUS uses a distance cutoff because it yields a slight decrease in the CPU time and because in some cases, such

as widely separated spherical clusters, the results are less sensitive to the choice of distance cutoff than to the choice of m. Much research remains to be done on this issue.

- uses a different convergence measure. Let $\mathbf{A}_i$ be computed on each iteration using the m-closest-pairs method and let $\mathbf{B}_i = \mathbf{A}_{i-1}^{-1}\mathbf{A}_i - \mathbf{I}$, where $\mathbf{I}$ is the identity matrix. The AGK convergence measure is equivalent to trace($\mathbf{B}_i^2$).

Analyses of Fisher's (1936) iris data, consisting of measurements of petal and sepal length and width for fifty specimens from each of three iris species, are summarized in **Table 10.1**. The number of misclassified observations out of 150 is given for four clustering methods:

- *k*-means as implemented in FASTCLUS with MAXC=3, MAXITER=99, and CONV=0
- Ward's minimum variance method as implemented in CLUSTER
- average linkage on Euclidean distances as implemented in CLUSTER
- the centroid method as implemented in CLUSTER.

Each hierarchical analysis was followed by PROC TREE with NCL=3 to determine cluster assignments at the three-cluster level. Clusters with twenty or fewer observations were discarded by using the DOCK=20 option. The observations in a discarded cluster were considered unclassified.

Each method was applied to:

- the raw data
- the data standardized to unit variance by the STANDARD procedure
- two standardized principal components accounting for 95% of the standardized variance and having an identity total-sample covariance matrix, computed by PRINCOMP with the STD option
- four standardized principal components having an identity total-sample covariance matrix, computed by PRINCOMP with the STD option
- the data transformed by ACECLUS using seven different settings of the PROPORTION= (P=) option
- four canonical variables having an identity pooled within-species covariance matrix, computed by CANDISC.

Theoretically, the best results should be obtained by using the canonical variables from CANDISC. ACECLUS yielded results comparable to CANDISC for values of the PROPORTION= option ranging from .005 to .02. At PROPORTION=.04 average linkage and the centroid method showed some deterioration, but *k*-means and Ward's method continued to produce excellent classifications. At larger values of PROPORTION=, all methods did poorly, although no worse than with four standardized principal components.

Table 10.1 Number of Misclassified and Unclassified Observations Using Fisher's (1936) Iris Data

Data	Clustering Method			
	k-means	Ward's	average linkage	centroid
raw data	16*	16*	25+12**	14*
standardized data	25	26	33+4	33+4
two standardized principal components	29	31	30+9	27+32
four standardized principal components	39	27	32+7	45+11
transformed by ACECLUS P=.32	39	10+9	7+25	.
transformed by ACECLUS P=.16	39	18+9	9+12	7+26
transformed by ACECLUS P=.08	19	9	3+12	8+13
transformed by ACECLUS P=.04	3	3	5+12	3+12
transformed by ACECLUS P=.02	4	3	3	3
transformed BY ACECLUS P=.01	4	4	3	4
transformed by ACECLUS P=.005	4	4	4	4
canonical variables	3	5	4	4+1

* A single number represents misclassified observations with no unclassified observations.

** Where two numbers are separated by a plus sign, the first is the number of misclassified observations; the second is the number of unclassified observations.

This example shows that:

- ACECLUS can produce results as good as those from the optimal transformation
- ACECLUS can be useful even when the within-cluster covariance matrices are moderately heterogeneous
- the choice of the distance cutoff as specified by the PROPORTION= or THRESHOLD= options is important and several values should be tried
- commonly used transformations such as standardization and principal components can produce poor classifications.

Although experience with the AGK and ACECLUS methods is limited, the results so far suggest that these methods help considerably more often than they hinder the subsequent cluster analysis, especially with normal-mixture techniques such as *k*-means and Ward's minimum variance method.

SPECIFICATIONS

The following statements invoke the ACECLUS procedure:

PROC ACECLUS *options*;
  VAR *variables*;
  FREQ *variable*;
  WEIGHT *variable*;
  BY *variables*;

Usually, only the VAR statement is used in addition to the PROC ACECLUS statement.

PROC ACECLUS Statement

PROC ACECLUS *options*;

The options listed below can be used in the PROC ACECLUS statement. You must specify either PROPORTION= or THRESHOLD= but not both.

The following options pertain to data sets used or created by ACECLUS:

DATA=*SASdataset*
: names the SAS data set to be analyzed. If DATA= is omitted, the most recently created SAS data set is used.

OUT=*SASdataset*
: names an output SAS data set that contains all the original data as well as the canonical variables having an identity estimated within-cluster covariance matrix. If you want to create a permanent SAS data set, you must specify a two-level name. See "SAS Files" in the *SAS User's Guide: Basics* for information on permanent SAS data sets.

OUTSTAT=*SASdataset*
: names a TYPE=ACE output SAS data set that contains means, standard deviations, number of observations, covariances, estimated within-cluster covariances, eigenvalues, and canonical coefficients. If you want to create a permanent SAS data set, you must specify a two-level name. See "SAS Files" in the *SAS User's Guide: Basics* for information on permanent SAS data sets.

The following option tells how to initialize the iterative algorithm and can also specify an input data set:

INITIAL=FULL | F
INITIAL=DIAGONAL | D
INITIAL=IDENTITY | I
INITIAL=INPUT=*SASdataset*

specifies the matrix to use for the initial estimate of the within-cluster covariance matrix. INITIAL=FULL uses the total-sample covariance matrix as the initial estimate of the within-cluster covariance matrix. INITIAL=DIAGONAL uses the diagonal matrix of sample variances as the initial estimate of the within-cluster covariance matrix. INITIAL=IDENTITY uses the identity matrix as the initial estimate of the within-cluster covariance matrix. INITIAL=INPUT=*SASdataset* names a SAS data set from which to obtain the initial estimate of the within-cluster covariance matrix. The data set can be TYPE=CORR, COV, SSCP, or ACE, or it can be an ordinary SAS data set. If INITIAL= is not specified, the default is the matrix specified by the METRIC= option. If neither INITIAL= nor METRIC= is specified, INITIAL=FULL is used if there are enough observations to obtain a non-singular total-sample covariance matrix; otherwise, INITIAL=DIAGONAL is used.

The following options control the iterative process:

THRESHOLD=*t*
T=*t*

specifies the threshold for including pairs of observations in the estimation of the within-cluster covariance matrix. A pair of observations is included if the Euclidean distance between them is less than or equal to *t* times the root-mean-square distance computed over all pairs of observations.

PROPORTION=*p*
PERCENT=*p*
P=*p*

specifies the approximate proportion of pairs to be included in the estimation of the within-cluster covariance matrix. A threshold value is computed from the PROPORTION= value under the assumption that the observations are sampled from a multivariate normal distribution.

ABSOLUTE

causes the THRESHOLD= value or the threshold computed from the PROPORTION= option to be treated absolutely rather than relative to the root-mean-square distance between observations. Use ABSOLUTE only when you are confident that the initial estimate of the within-cluster covariance matrix is close to the final estimate, such as when INITIAL= specifies a data set created by a previous execution of ACECLUS using the OUTSTAT= option.

MAXITER=*n*

specifies the maximum number of iterations. The default is 10.

CONVERGE=*c*

specifies the convergence criterion. The default is .01. Iteration stops when the convergence measure falls below the value specified by CONVERGE= or when the iteration limit as specified by MAXITER= is exceeded, whichever happens first.

SINGULAR=*g*

specifies a singularity criterion $0<g<1$ for the total-sample covariance matrix **S** and the approximate within-cluster covariance estimate **A**. The default is SINGULAR=1E-4.

The following options relate to the canonical analysis:

N=*n*

specifies the number of canonical variables to be computed. The default is the number of variables analyzed. N=0 suppresses the canonical analysis.

PREFIX=*name*

specifies a prefix for naming the canonical variables. By default the names are CAN1, CAN2,...,CAN*n*. If PREFIX=ABC is specified, the variables are named ABC1, ABC2, ABC3, and so on. The number of characters in the prefix plus the number of digits required to designate the variables should not exceed eight.

The following options control the printout:

PP

requests a PP probability plot of distances between pairs of observations computed in the last iteration.

QQ

requests a QQ probability plot of a power transformation of the distances between pairs of observations computed in the last iteration. **Warning:** the QQ plot may require an enormous amount of CPU time.

SHORT

omits all items from the standard printout except for the iteration history and the eigenvalue table.

NOPRINT

suppresses the printout.

The last option, METRIC=, is rather technical. It affects the computations in a variety of ways, but for well-conditioned data the effects are subtle. For most data sets, the METRIC= option is not needed.

METRIC=FULL | F
METRIC=DIAGONAL | D
METRIC=IDENTITY | I

specifies the metric in which the computations are performed, implies the default value for INITIAL=, and specifies the matrix **Z** used in the formula for the convergence measure e_i and for checking singularity of the **A** matrix. METRIC=FULL uses the total-sample covariance matrix **S** and sets $\mathbf{Z} = \mathbf{S}^{-1/2}$, where the superscript -1/2 indicates an inverse factor. METRIC=DIAGONAL uses the diagonal matrix of sample variances diag(**S**) and sets $\mathbf{Z} = \text{diag}(\mathbf{S})^{-1/2}$. METRIC=IDENTITY uses the identity matrix **I** and sets $\mathbf{Z} = \mathbf{I}$. If METRIC= is not specified, METRIC=FULL is used if there are enough observations to obtain a non-singular total-sample covariance matrix; otherwise, METRIC=DIAGONAL is used.

VAR Statement

VAR *variables;*

The VAR statement lists the numeric variables to be analyzed. If the VAR statement is omitted, all numeric variables not specified in other statements are analyzed.

FREQ Statement

FREQ *variable;*

If a variable in your data set represents the frequency of occurrence for the other values in the observation, include the name of that variable in a FREQ statement. The procedure then treats the data set as if each observation appears *n* times, where *n* is the value of the FREQ variable for the observation. If a value of the FREQ variable is not integral, it is truncated to the largest integer not exceeding the given value. The total number of observations is considered equal to the sum of the FREQ variable.

WEIGHT Statement

WEIGHT *variable;*

If you want to use relative weights for each observation in the input data set, place the weights in a variable in the data set and specify the name in a WEIGHT statement. This is often done when the variance associated with each observation is different and the values of the weight variable are proportional to the reciprocals of the variances. The values of the WEIGHT variable can be nonintegral and are not truncated.

The WEIGHT and FREQ statements have a similar effect, except in calculating the divisor of the **A** matrix.

BY Statement

BY *variables;*

A BY statement can be used with PROC ACECLUS to obtain separate analyses on observations in groups defined by the BY variables. When a BY statement appears, the procedure expects the input data set to be sorted in the order of the BY variables. If your input data set is not sorted in ascending order, use the SORT procedure with a similar BY statement to sort the data, or, if appropriate, use the BY statement options NOTSORTED or DESCENDING. For more information, see the discussion of the BY statement in the "Statements Used in the PROC Step" in *SAS User's Guide: Basics.*

If you specify INITIAL=INPUT= and the INITIAL=INPUT= data set does not contain any of the BY variables, the entire INITIAL=INPUT= data set provides the initial value for **A** for each BY group in the DATA= data set.

If the INITIAL=INPUT= data set contains some but not all of the BY variables, or if some BY variables do not have the same type or length in the INITIAL=INPUT= data set as in the DATA= data set, then ACECLUS prints an error message and stops.

If all the BY variables appear in the INITIAL=INPUT= data set with the same type and length as in the DATA= data set, then each BY group in the INITIAL=INPUT= data set provides the initial value for **A** for the corresponding BY group in the DATA= data set. The BY groups in the INITIAL=INPUT= data set must be in the same order as in the DATA= data set. If you specify NOTSORTED in the BY statement, exactly the same BY groups must occur and in the same order in both data sets. If you do not specify NOTSORTED it is permissible for some BY groups to appear in one data set but not in the other.

DETAILS

Missing Values

Observations with missing values are omitted from the analysis and are given missing values for canonical variable scores in the OUT= data set.

Output Data Sets

OUT= data set The OUT= data set contains all the variables in the original data set plus new variables containing the canonical variable scores. The N= option determines the number of new variables. The names of the new variables are formed by concatenating the value given by the PREFIX= option (or the prefix CAN if PREFIX= is not specified) and the numbers 1, 2, 3, and so on.

The OUT= data set can be used as input to CLUSTER or FASTCLUS. The cluster analysis should be performed on the canonical variables, not on the original variables.

OUTSTAT= data set The OUTSTAT= data set is a TYPE=ACE data set containing the following variables:

- the BY variables, if any
- the two new character variables, _TYPE_ and _NAME_
- the variables analyzed, that is, those in the VAR statement, or, if there is no VAR statement, all numeric variables not listed in any other statement.

Each observation in the new data set contains some type of statistic as indicated by the _TYPE_ variable. The values of the _TYPE_ variable are as follows:

TYPE	**Contents**
MEAN	mean of each variable.
N	number of observations on which the analysis is based. This value is the same for each variable.
SUMWGT	sum of the weights if a WEIGHT statement is used. This value is the same for each variable.
COV	covariances between each variable and the variable named by the _NAME_ variable. The number of observations with _TYPE_=COV is equal to the number of variables being analyzed.
ACE	estimated within-cluster covariances between each variable and the variable named by the _NAME_ variable. The number of observations with _TYPE_= ACE is equal to the number of variables being analyzed.
EIGENVAL	eigenvalues of INV(ACE)*(COV−ACE). If the N= option requests fewer than the maximum number of canonical variables, only the specified number of eigenvalues are produced, with missing values filling out the observation.
SCORE	eigenvectors. The _NAME_ variable contains the name of the corresponding canonical variable as constructed from the PREFIX= option. The number of observations with _TYPE_=SCORE equals the number of canonical variables computed.

The OUTSTAT= data set can be used

- to initialize another execution of ACECLUS
- to compute canonical variable scores with the SCORE procedure
- as input to the FACTOR procedure, specifying METHOD=SCORE, to rotate the canonical variables.

Computer Resources

Let:

n = number of observations
v = number of variables
i = number of iterations.

The time required by ACECLUS is roughly proportional to

$$2nv^2 + 10v^3 + i(n^2v/2 + nv^2 + 5v^3) \quad .$$

The array storage required is roughly $8(2n(v + 1) + 4v^2)$ bytes.

Printed Output

Unless the SHORT option is specified, the ACECLUS procedure prints the following items:

1. SIMPLE STATISTICS, including the MEAN and ST DEV (standard deviation) for each variable
2. the **S** matrix, labeled COV: TOTAL SAMPLE COVARIANCES
3. the name or value of the matrix used for the INITIAL WITHIN-CLUSTER COVARIANCE ESTIMATE
4. the THRESHOLD value if PROPORTION= is specified.

For each iteration, ACECLUS prints:

5. the ITERATION number
6. RMS DISTANCE, the root-mean-square distance between all pairs of observations
7. the DISTANCE CUTOFF (u) for including pairs of observations in the estimate of the within-cluster covariances, which equals the RMS distance times the threshold
8. the number of PAIRS WITHIN the CUTOFF
9. the CONVERGENCE MEASURE (e_i) as specified by the METRIC= option.

If SHORT is not specified, ACECLUS also prints:

10. the **A** matrix, labeled ACE: APPROXIMATE COVARIANCE ESTIMATE WITHIN CLUSTERS.

ACECLUS prints a table of eigenvalues from the canonical analysis containing the following items:

11. EIGENVALUES OF INV(ACE)*(COV−ACE)
12. the DIFFERENCE between successive eigenvalues
13. the PROPORTION of variance explained by each eigenvalue
14. the CUMULATIVE proportion of variance explained.

If SHORT is not specified, ACECLUS prints:

15. the EIGENVECTORS or raw canonical coefficients.

EXAMPLE

Transformation and Cluster Analysis of Fisher Iris Data

The iris data published by Fisher (1936) have been widely used for examples in discriminant analysis and cluster analysis. The sepal length, sepal width, petal length, and petal width were measured in millimeters on fifty iris specimens from each of three species, *Iris setosa, I. versicolor,* and *I. virginica*. Mezzich and Solomon (1980) discuss a variety of cluster analyses of the iris data.

In this example ACECLUS is used to transform the data, and the clustering is performed by FASTCLUS. Compare this with the example in the documentation for FASTCLUS.

```
DATA IRIS;
   TITLE 'FISHER (1936) IRIS DATA';
   INPUT SEPALLEN SEPALWID PETALLEN PETALWID SPEC_NO @@;
   IF SPEC_NO=1 THEN SPECIES='SETOSA    ';
   ELSE IF SPEC_NO=2 THEN SPECIES='VERSICOLOR';
   ELSE SPECIES='VIRGINICA ';
   LABEL SEPALLEN='SEPAL LENGTH IN MM.'
         SEPALWID='SEPAL WIDTH  IN MM.'
         PETALLEN='PETAL LENGTH IN MM.'
         PETALWID='PETAL WIDTH  IN MM.';
   CARDS;
50 33 14 02 1 64 28 56 22 3 65 28 46 15 2 67 31 56 24 3
63 28 51 15 3 46 34 14 03 1 69 31 51 23 3 62 22 45 15 2
59 32 48 18 2 46 36 10 02 1 61 30 46 14 2 60 27 51 16 2
65 30 52 20 3 56 25 39 11 2 65 30 55 18 3 58 27 51 19 3
68 32 59 23 3 51 33 17 05 1 57 28 45 13 2 62 34 54 23 3
77 38 67 22 3 63 33 47 16 2 67 33 57 25 3 76 30 66 21 3
49 25 45 17 3 55 35 13 02 1 67 30 52 23 3 70 32 47 14 2
64 32 45 15 2 61 28 40 13 2 48 31 16 02 1 59 30 51 18 3
55 24 38 11 2 63 25 50 19 3 64 32 53 23 3 52 34 14 02 1
49 36 14 01 1 54 30 45 15 2 79 38 64 20 3 44 32 13 02 1
67 33 57 21 3 50 35 16 06 1 58 26 40 12 2 44 30 13 02 1
77 28 67 20 3 63 27 49 18 3 47 32 16 02 1 55 26 44 12 2
50 23 33 10 2 72 32 60 18 3 48 30 14 03 1 51 38 16 02 1
61 30 49 18 3 48 34 19 02 1 50 30 16 02 1 50 32 12 02 1
61 26 56 14 3 64 28 56 21 3 43 30 11 01 1 58 40 12 02 1
51 38 19 04 1 67 31 44 14 2 62 28 48 18 3 49 30 14 02 1
51 35 14 02 1 56 30 45 15 2 58 27 41 10 2 50 34 16 04 1
46 32 14 02 1 60 29 45 15 2 57 26 35 10 2 57 44 15 04 1
50 36 14 02 1 77 30 61 23 3 63 34 56 24 3 58 27 51 19 3
57 29 42 13 2 72 30 58 16 3 54 34 15 04 1 52 41 15 01 1
71 30 59 21 3 64 31 55 18 3 60 30 48 18 3 63 29 56 18 3
49 24 33 10 2 56 27 42 13 2 57 30 42 12 2 55 42 14 02 1
49 31 15 02 1 77 26 69 23 3 60 22 50 15 3 54 39 17 04 1
66 29 46 13 2 52 27 39 14 2 60 34 45 16 2 50 34 15 02 1
44 29 14 02 1 50 20 35 10 2 55 24 37 10 2 58 27 39 12 2
47 32 13 02 1 46 31 15 02 1 69 32 57 23 3 62 29 43 13 2
74 28 61 19 3 59 30 42 15 2 51 34 15 02 1 50 35 13 03 1
56 28 49 20 3 60 22 40 10 2 73 29 63 18 3 67 25 58 18 3
49 31 15 01 1 67 31 47 15 2 63 23 44 13 2 54 37 15 02 1
56 30 41 13 2 63 25 49 15 2 61 28 47 12 2 64 29 43 13 2
```

```
51 25 30 11 2 57 28 41 13 2 65 30 58 22 3 69 31 54 21 3
54 39 13 04 1 51 35 14 03 1 72 36 61 25 3 65 32 51 20 3
61 29 47 14 2 56 29 36 13 2 69 31 49 15 2 64 27 53 19 3
68 30 55 21 3 55 25 40 13 2 48 34 16 02 1 48 30 14 01 1
45 23 13 03 1 57 25 50 20 3 57 38 17 03 1 51 38 15 03 1
55 23 40 13 2 66 30 44 14 2 68 28 48 14 2 54 34 17 02 1
51 37 15 04 1 52 35 15 02 1 58 28 51 24 3 67 30 50 17 2
63 33 60 25 3 53 37 15 02 1
;
PROC ACECLUS DATA=IRIS OUT=ACE P=.02;
   VAR SEPALLEN SEPALWID PETALLEN PETALWID;
PROC PLOT;
   PLOT CAN2*CAN1=SPEC_NO;
PROC FASTCLUS DATA=ACE MAXC=3 MAXITER=10 CONV=0 OUT=CLUS;
   VAR CAN:;
PROC FREQ;
   TABLES CLUSTER*SPECIES;
```

Output 10.1 Using PROC ACECLUS to Transform Fisher's Iris Data

```
                              FISHER (1936) IRIS DATA                                        1

                 APPROXIMATE COVARIANCE ESTIMATION FOR CLUSTER ANALYSIS

                        150 OBSERVATIONS     PROPORTION=     0.02
                          4 VARIABLES        CONVERGE=       0.01

                     ❶              SIMPLE STATISTICS

                      SEPALLEN           SEPALWID           PETALLEN           PETALWID

   MEAN            58.43333333        30.57333333        37.58000000        11.99333333
   ST DEV           8.28066128         4.35866285        17.65298233         7.62237669

                    ❷         COV: TOTAL SAMPLE COVARIANCES

                       SEPALLEN           SEPALWID           PETALLEN           PETALWID

   SEPALLEN            68.56935            -4.2434           127.4315           51.62707
   SEPALWID             -4.2434           18.99794           -32.9656           -12.1639
   PETALLEN            127.4315           -32.9656           311.6278           129.5609
   PETALWID            51.62707           -12.1639           129.5609           58.10063

           INITIAL WITHIN-CLUSTER COVARIANCE ESTIMATE=FULL COVARIANCE MATRIX

                        ❹          THRESHOLD=0.3342111
                                                          ❽            ❾
                          ❻          ❼                  PAIRS
                               RMS       DISTANCE        WITHIN      CONVERGENCE
   ❺          ITERATION      DISTANCE      CUTOFF         CUTOFF         MEASURE

                      1         2.828       0.945            408        0.465775
                      2        11.905       3.979            559        0.013487
                      3        13.152       4.396            940        0.029499
                      4        13.439       4.491           1506        0.046846
                      5        13.271       4.435           2036        0.046859
                      6        12.591       4.208           2285        0.025027
                      7        12.199       4.077           2366        0.009559

          ❿          ACE: APPROXIMATE COVARIANCE ESTIMATE WITHIN CLUSTERS

                       SEPALLEN           SEPALWID           PETALLEN           PETALWID

   SEPALLEN            11.59721           5.420118           4.853973           1.917794
   SEPALWID            5.420118           6.861158           2.312342           1.637997
   PETALLEN            4.853973           2.312342           6.410609           2.249789
   PETALWID            1.917794           1.637997           2.249789           1.911454
```

FISHER (1936) IRIS DATA 2

APPROXIMATE COVARIANCE ESTIMATION FOR CLUSTER ANALYSIS

(11) EIGENVALUES OF INV(ACE)*(COV-ACE)

	EIGENVALUE	(12) DIFFERENCE	(13) PROPORTION	(14) CUMULATIVE
CAN1	64.8910	62.0849	0.934284	0.93428
CAN2	2.8061	1.7287	0.040401	0.97469
CAN3	1.0774	0.3965	0.015512	0.99020
CAN4	0.6808	.	0.009802	1.00000

(15) EIGENVECTORS

	CAN1	CAN2	CAN3	CAN4
SEPALLEN	-.011557	-.086010	-.063420	0.408471
SEPALWID	-.207476	0.003865	0.407261	-.224872
PETALLEN	0.317869	-.347164	0.120527	-.317899
PETALWID	0.292458	0.902892	-.105137	0.307159

Output 10.2 Plot of Transformed Iris Data: PROC PLOT

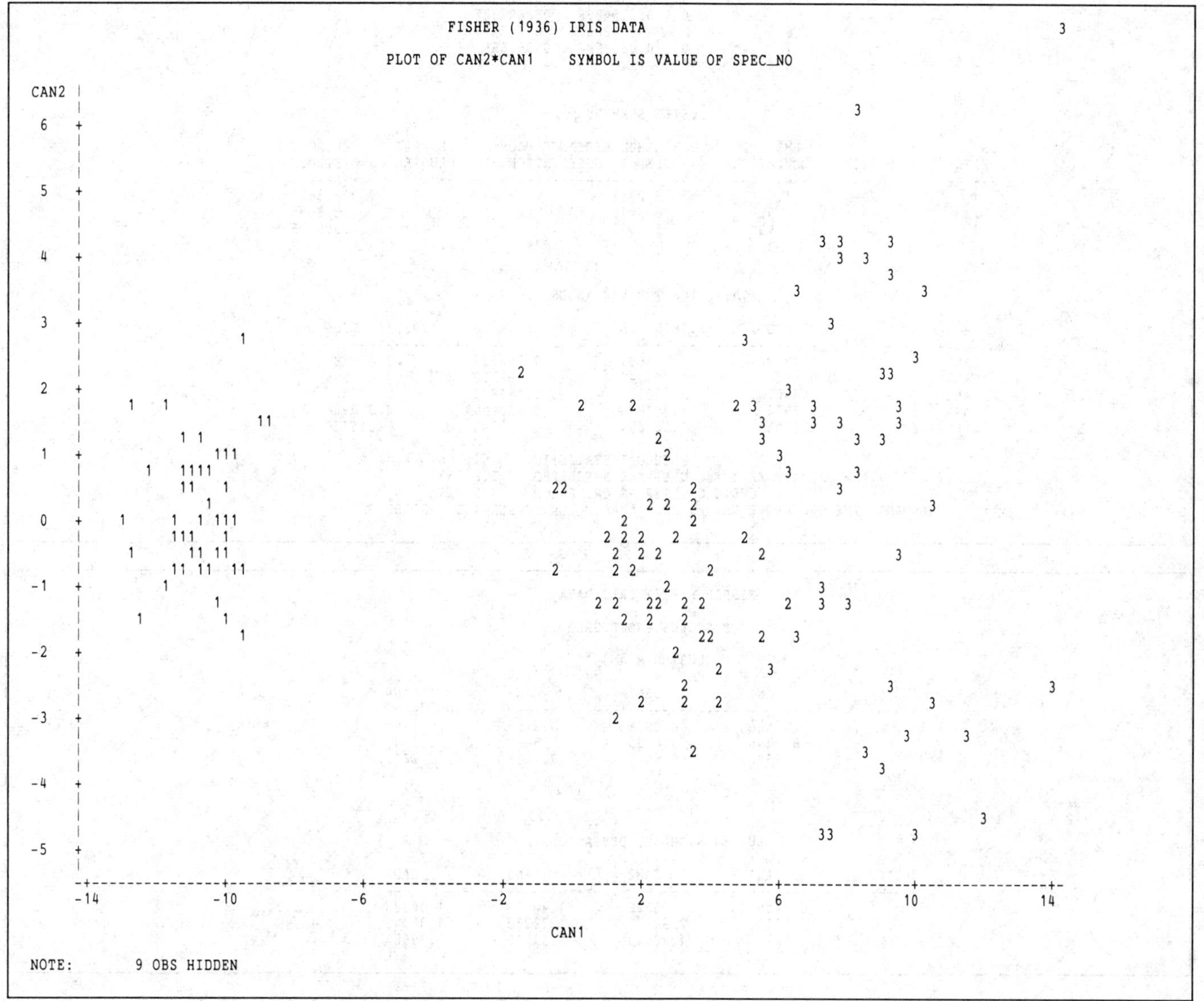

Output 10.3 Clustering of Transformed Iris Data: PROC FASTCLUS

FISHER (1936) IRIS DATA 4

FASTCLUS PROCEDURE

REPLACE=FULL RADIUS=0 MAXCLUSTERS=3 MAXITER=10 CONVERGE=0

INITIAL SEEDS

CLUSTER	CAN1	CAN2	CAN3	CAN4
1	-13.0045	-0.0687	1.8342	2.7655
2	13.9407	-2.5847	-0.4103	2.0048
3	0.8881	-0.2196	-3.8727	-0.8592

MINIMUM DISTANCE BETWEEN INITIAL SEEDS = 14.00551

ITERATION	CHANGE IN CLUSTER SEEDS 1	2	3
1	3.80996	5.89534	4.19485
2	0	0.723887	0.630225
3	0	0.215038	0.212079
4	0	0.140975	0.123366
5	0	0.0754898	0.0697387
6	0	0.12847	0.127277
7	0	0.0652247	0.0666345
8	0	0	0

CLUSTER SUMMARY

CLUSTER NUMBER	FREQUENCY	RMS STD DEVIATION	MAXIMUM DISTANCE FROM SEED TO OBSERVATION	NEAREST CLUSTER	CENTROID DISTANCE
1	50	1.1108	5.2959	3	13.3607
2	50	1.9206	6.8410	3	5.9695
3	50	1.4297	5.3490	2	5.9695

STATISTICS FOR VARIABLES

VARIABLE	TOTAL STD	WITHIN STD	R-SQUARED	RSQ/(1-RSQ)
CAN1	8.117329	1.491601	0.966687	29.018584
CAN2	1.950921	1.899748	0.064500	0.068948
CAN3	1.441307	1.336338	0.151893	0.179097
CAN4	1.296470	1.291825	0.020480	0.020908
OVER-ALL	4.285304	1.523854	0.875246	7.015774

PSEUDO F STATISTIC = 515.66
APPROXIMATE EXPECTED OVER-ALL R-SQUARED = 0.80253
CUBIC CLUSTERING CRITERION = 5.171
WARNING: THE TWO ABOVE VALUES ARE INVALID FOR CORRELATED VARIABLES

FISHER (1936) IRIS DATA 5

FASTCLUS PROCEDURE

CLUSTER MEANS

CLUSTER	CAN1	CAN2	CAN3	CAN4
1	-10.7586	0.0978	0.2756	0.1169
2	8.2246	0.5499	0.5050	0.1441
3	2.5340	-0.6478	-0.7806	-0.2610

CLUSTER STANDARD DEVIATIONS

CLUSTER	CAN1	CAN2	CAN3	CAN4
1	0.94562	0.95629	1.40905	1.06833
2	1.80580	2.81676	1.28262	1.38343
3	1.58729	1.40659	1.31410	1.39686

Output 10.4 Crosstabulation of Cluster by Species for Fisher's Iris Data: PROC FREQ

```
                FISHER (1936) IRIS DATA                                   6

              TABLE OF CLUSTER BY SPECIES

     CLUSTER     SPECIES

     FREQUENCY|
      PERCENT |
      ROW PCT |
      COL PCT |SETOSA  |VERSICOL|VIRGINIC|
              |        |OR      |A       |  TOTAL
     ---------+--------+--------+--------+
     1        |     50 |      0 |      0 |     50
              |  33.33 |   0.00 |   0.00 |  33.33
              | 100.00 |   0.00 |   0.00 |
              | 100.00 |   0.00 |   0.00 |
     ---------+--------+--------+--------+
     2        |      0 |      2 |     48 |     50
              |   0.00 |   1.33 |  32.00 |  33.33
              |   0.00 |   4.00 |  96.00 |
              |   0.00 |   4.00 |  96.00 |
     ---------+--------+--------+--------+
     3        |      0 |     48 |      2 |     50
              |   0.00 |  32.00 |   1.33 |  33.33
              |   0.00 |  96.00 |   4.00 |
              |   0.00 |  96.00 |   4.00 |
     ---------+--------+--------+--------+
     TOTAL          50       50       50      150
                 33.33    33.33    33.33   100.00
```

REFERENCES

Art, D., Gnanadesikan, R., and Kettenring, R. (1982), "Data-based Metrics for Cluster Analysis," *Utilitas Mathematica*, 21A, 75-99.

Everitt, B.S. (1980), *Cluster Analysis*, Second Edition, London: Heineman Educational Books Ltd.

Fisher, R.A. (1936), "The Use of Multiple Measurements in Taxonomic Problems," *Annals of Eugenics*, 7, 179-188.

Hartigan, J.A. (1975), *Clustering Algorithms*, New York: John Wiley & Sons.

Mezzich, J.E and Solomon, H. (1980), *Taxonomy and Behavioral Science*, New York: Academic Press.

Puri, M.L. and Sen, P.K. (1971), *Nonparametric Methods in Multivariate Analysis*, New York: John Wiley & Sons.

Wolfe, J.H. (1970), "Pattern Clustering by Multivariate Mixture Analysis," *Multivariate Behavioral Research*, 5, 329-350.

Chapter 11
The ANOVA Procedure

Operating systems: All

ABSTRACT

The ANOVA procedure performs analysis of variance for balanced data from a wide variety of experimental designs.

INTRODUCTION

ANOVA is one of several procedures available in the SAS System for *analysis of variance*, which is a technique for analyzing experimental data. A continuous response variable, known as a *dependent* variable, is measured under experimental conditions identified by classification variables, known as *independent* variables. The variation in the response is explained as being due to effects in the classification with random error accounting for the remaining variation. Fisher (1942) is the pioneering work.

The ANOVA procedure is designed to handle balanced data (that is, data with equal numbers of observations for every combination of the classification factors), whereas the GLM procedure can analyze both balanced and unbalanced data. Because ANOVA takes into account the special structure of a balanced design, it is faster and uses less storage than GLM for balanced data.

Use ANOVA for the analysis of balanced data only, with the exception of Latin-square designs, certain balanced incomplete blocks designs, completely nested (hierarchical) designs, and designs whose cell frequencies are proportional to each other and are also proportional to the background population. For further discussion, see Searle (1971, 138).

ANOVA does not check to see if your design is balanced or is one of the special cases described above. If you use ANOVA for analysis of unbalanced data, you must assume responsibility for the validity of the output.

Specification of Effects

In SAS analysis-of-variance procedures, the variables that identify levels of the classifications are called *classification variables* and are declared in the CLASS statement. Classification variables may also be called *categorical, qualitative, discrete,* or *nominal* variables. The values of a class variable are called *levels*. Class variables can be either numeric or character. This is in contrast to the *response* (or *dependent*) variables, which are continuous; response variables must be numeric.

The analysis-of-variance model specifies *effects*, which are combinations of classification variables used to explain the variability of the dependent variables in the following manner:

- Main effects are specified by writing the variables by themselves: A B C . Main effects used as independent variables test the hypothesis that the mean of the dependent variable is the same for each level of the factor in question, ignoring the other independent variables in the model.
- Crossed effects (interactions) are specified by joining the class variables with asterisks: A*B A*C A*B*C . Interaction terms in a model test the hypothesis that the effect of a factor does not depend on the levels of the other factors in the interaction.
- Nested effects are specified by placing a parenthetical field after a class variable or interaction indicating the variables within which the effect is nested: B(A) C*D(A B). Nested effects test hypotheses similar to interactions, but the levels of the nested variables are not the same for every combination within which they are nested.

The general form of an effect can be illustrated using the class variables A,B,C, D,E, and F:

A*B*C(D E F) .

The crossed list should come first, followed by the nested list in parentheses. Note that the nested list does not contain an asterisk between class variable names or before the first parenthesis.

Main-effects models For a three-factor main-effects model with A, B, and C as the factors and Y as the dependent variable, the necessary statements are

```
PROC ANOVA;
   CLASS A B C;
   MODEL Y=A B C;
```

Models with crossed factors To specify interactions in a factorial model, join effects with asterisks as described above. For example, these statements specify a complete factorial model, which includes all the interactions:

```
PROC ANOVA;
   CLASS A B C;
   MODEL Y=A B C A*B A*C B*C A*B*C;
```

Bar notation You can shorten the specifications of a full factorial model by using bar notation. For example, the statements above can also be written:

```
PROC ANOVA;
   CLASS A B C;
   MODEL Y=A|B|C;
```

When the bar (|) is used, the expression on the right side of the equal sign is expanded from left to right using the equivalents of rules 2-4 given in Searle (1971, 390). Other examples of the bar notation:

A | C(B)	is equivalent to A C(B) A*C(B)
A(B) | C(B)	is equivalent to A(B) C(B) A*C(B)
A(B) | B(DE)	is equivalent to A(B) B(D E)
A | B(A) | C	is equivalent to A B(A) C A*C B*C(A) .

Consult the description of the GLM procedure for further details on the bar notation.

Nested models Write the effect that is nested within another effect first, followed by the other effect in parentheses. For example, if A and B are main effects and C is nested within A and B (that is, the levels of C which were observed were not the same for each combination of A and B), the statements for PROC ANOVA are

```
PROC ANOVA;
   CLASS A B C;
   MODEL Y=A B C(A B);
```

The identity of a level is viewed within the context of the level of the containing effects. For example, CITY is nested within STATE.

The distinguishing feature of a nested specification is that nested effects never also appear as main effects. Another way of viewing nested effects is that they are effects that pool the main effect with the interaction of the nesting variable. See **Automatic Pooling** below.

Models involving nested, crossed, and main effects Asterisks and parentheses can be combined in the MODEL statement for models involving nested and crossed effects:

```
PROC ANOVA;
   CLASS A B C;
   MODEL Y=A B(A) C(A) B*C(A);
```

Automatic pooling In line with the general philosophy of the GLM procedure, there is no difference between the statements

```
MODEL Y=A B(A);
```

and

```
MODEL Y=A A*B;
```

The effect B becomes a nested effect by virtue of the fact that it does not occur as a main effect. If B is not written as a main effect in addition to participating in A*B, then the sum of squares that would be associated with B is pooled into A*B.

This feature allows the automatic pooling of sums of squares. If an effect is omitted from the model, it is automatically pooled with all the higher-level effects containing the class variables in the omitted effect (or within-error). This feature is most useful in split-plot designs.

SPECIFICATIONS

These statements are available in ANOVA:

PROC ANOVA *option;*
  CLASS *variables;*
  MODEL *dependents=effects / options;*
  MEANS *effects / options;*
  ABSORB *variables;*
  FREQ *variable;*
  TEST H=*effects* **E=***effect;*
  MANOVA H=*effects* **E=** *effects*
    M=*equations / options;*
  REPEATED *factornames / options;*
  BY *variables;*

The CLASS statement must precede the MODEL statement. TEST and MANOVA statements, if used, should follow the MODEL statement. More than one MEANS, TEST, or MANOVA statement can appear; the other statements can be used only once with a PROC ANOVA statement.

PROC ANOVA Statement

PROC ANOVA DATA=*SASdataset;*

DATA=*SASdataset*
: names the SAS data set to be analyzed by PROC ANOVA. If no DATA= option is specified, ANOVA uses the most recently created SAS data set.

CLASS Statement

CLASS *variables;*

Any variables used as classification variables in ANOVA must be declared first in the CLASS (or CLASSES) statement to identify the groups for the analysis. Typical classification variables are TRT, SEX, RACE, GROUP, and REP. They may be either numeric or character, but a character variable used in a CLASS statement cannot have a length greater than sixteen characters.

MODEL Statement

MODEL *dependents=effects / options;*

The MODEL statement names the dependent variables and independent effects. The syntax of effects is described in the introductory section **Specification of Effects**. If no effects are specified, ANOVA fits only the intercept, which tests the hypothesis that the mean of the dependent variable is zero.

The options listed below can be specified in the MODEL statement and must be separated from the list of independent effects by a slash (/):

NOUNI
: requests that ANOVA not print the univariate analyses that are produced by default. Use NOUNI when you want only the multivariate statistics produced by a MANOVA statement or when you are using the REPEATED statement and are not interested in the original dependent variables in the MODEL statement.

INT
INTERCEPT
: requests that ANOVA print the hypothesis tests associated with the intercept as an effect in the model. PROC ANOVA always includes the intercept in the model but by default prints no associated tests of hypotheses.

MEANS Statement

MEANS *effects / options;*

Means can be computed for any effect involving class variables, whether or not the effect is specified in the MODEL statement. Any number of MEANS statements can be used either before or after the MODEL statement.

For example,

```
PROC ANOVA;
   CLASS A B C;
   MODEL Y=A B C;
   MEANS A B C A*B;
```

Means are printed for each level of the variables A, B, and C and for the combined levels of A and B.

The options below can appear in the MEANS statement after a slash (/). For a further discussion of these options, see **Comparison of Means** in the GLM procedure description.

BON
: performs Bonferroni *t* tests of differences between means for all main-effect means in the MEANS statement.

DUNCAN
: performs Duncan's multiple-range test on all main-effect means given in the MEANS statement.

GABRIEL
: performs Gabriel's multiple-comparison procedure on all main-effect means in the MEANS statement.

REGWF
: performs the Ryan-Einot-Gabriel-Welsch multiple *F* test on all main-effect means in the MEANS statement.

REGWQ performs the Ryan-Einot-Gabriel-Welsch multiple range test on all main-effect means in the MEANS statement.

SCHEFFE performs Scheffe's multiple-comparison procedure on all main-effect means in the MEANS statement.

SIDAK performs pairwise *t* tests on differences between means with levels adjusted according to Sidak's inequality for all main-effect means in the MEANS statement.

SMM
GT2 performs pairwise comparisons based on the studentized maximum modulus and Sidak's uncorrelated-*t* inequality, yielding Hochberg's GT2 method when sample sizes are unequal, for all main-effect means in the MEANS statement.

SNK performs the Student-Newman-Keuls multiple range test on all main-effect means in the MEANS statement.

T
LSD performs pairwise *t* tests, equivalent to Fisher's least-significant-difference test in the case of equal cell sizes, for all main-effect means in the MEANS statement.

TUKEY performs Tukey's studentized range test (HSD) on all main-effects means in the MEANS statement.

ALPHA=*p* gives the level of significance for comparisons among the means. The default ALPHA value is .05. With the DUNCAN option, you can specify only values of .01, .05, or .1.

WALLER requests that the Waller-Duncan k-ratio *t* test be performed on all main-effect means in the MEANS statement.

KRATIO= *value* gives the type1/type2 error seriousness ratio for the Waller-Duncan test. Reasonable values for KRATIO are 50, 100, 500, which roughly correspond for the two-level case to ALPHA levels of .1, .05, and .01. If KRATIO is omitted, the procedure uses the default value of 100.

LINES requests that the results of the BON, DUNCAN, GABRIEL, REGWF, REGWQ, SCHEFFE, SIDAK, SMM, GT2, SNK, T, LSD, TUKEY, and WALLER options be presented by listing the means in descending order and indicating nonsignificant subsets by line segments beside the corresponding means. LINES is appropriate for equal cell sizes, for which it is the default. LINES is also the default if DUNCAN, REGWF, REGWQ, SNK, or WALLER is specified. If the cell sizes are unequal, the harmonic mean is used, which may lead to somewhat liberal tests if the cell sizes are highly disparate.

CLDIFF requests that the results of the BON, GABRIEL, SCHEFFE, SIDAK, SMM, GT2, T, LSD, and TUKEY options be presented as confidence intervals for all pairwise differences between means. CLDIFF is the default for unequal cell sizes unless DUNCAN, REGWF, REGWQ, SNK, or WALLER is specified.

E=*effect* specifies the error mean square to use in the multiple comparisons. If E= is omitted, the residual MS is used. The effect specified with the E= option must be a term in the model; otherwise, the residual MS is used. See **Comparison of Means** in the GLM procedure description for details on multiple comparison methods.

ABSORB Statement

ABSORB *variables;*

The technique of absorption, requested by the ABSORB statement, saves time and reduces storage requirements for certain types of models. The analysis of variance is adjusted for the absorbed effects. See **Absorption** in the GLM procedure description for more information.

Restrictions: with the ABSORB statement, the data set (or each BY group, if a BY statement appears) must be sorted by the variables in the ABSORB statement. Including an absorbed variable in the CLASS list or in the MODEL statement produces erroneous sums of squares.

FREQ Statement

FREQ *variable;*

When a FREQ (or FREQUENCY) statement appears, each observation in the input data set is assumed to represent *n* observations in the experiment, where *n* is the value of the FREQ variable. If the value of the FREQ variable is less than 1, the observation is not used in the analysis. If the value is not an integer, only the integer portion is used.

The analysis produced using a FREQ statement is identical to an analysis produced using a data set that contains *n* observations (where *n* is the value of the FREQ variable) in place of each observation of the input data set. Therefore, means and total degrees of freedom reflect the expanded number of observations.

TEST Statement

TEST H=*effects* E=*effect;*

Although an F value is computed for all SS in the analysis using the residual MS as an error term, you may request additional *F* tests using other effects as error terms. You need this feature when a non-Iσ^2 error structure (as in a split plot) exists.

These terms are specified on the TEST statement:

H=*effects* specifies the effects in the preceding model to be used as hypothesis (numerator) effects.

E=*effect* specifies one, and only one, effect to be used as the error (denominator) term. If you use a TEST statement, you must specify an error term with E=.

For example,

```
PROC ANOVA;
   CLASS A B C;
   MODEL Y=A | B(A) | C;
   TEST H=A E=B(A);
   TEST H=C A*C E=B*C(A);
```

MANOVA Statement

MANOVA H=*effects* E=*effect* M=*equation1,equation2,...*
MNAMES=*list of names* PREFIX=*name* / *options;*

If the MODEL statement includes more than one dependent variable, additional multivariate statistics can be requested with the MANOVA statement.

When a MANOVA statement appears, ANOVA enters a multivariate mode with respect to the handling of missing values: observations with missing independent or dependent variables are excluded from the analysis. Even when you do not want multivariate statistics, you can use the statement

```
MANOVA;
```

to request this method of treating missing values. See **Missing Values** below for more information.

The terms below are specified on the MANOVA statement:

H=*effects* specifies effects in the preceding model to use as hypothesis matrices. For each **H** matrix (the SSCP matrix associated with that effect), the H= option prints the characteristic roots and vectors of $\mathbf{E}^{-1}\mathbf{H}$ (where **E** is the matrix associated with the error effect), Hotelling-Lawley trace, Pillai's trace, Wilks' criterion, and Roy's maximum root criterion with approximate *F* statistics. To print tests for all effects listed in the MODEL statement, use the keyword _ALL_ in place of a list of effects. For background and further details, see the detail section **Multivariate Analysis of Variance** in the GLM procedure.

E=*effect* specifies the error effect. If E= is omitted, the error SSCP (residual) matrix from the analysis is used.

M=*equation1, equation2,...* specifies a transformation matrix for the dependent variables listed in the MODEL statement. The equations in the M= specification are of the form

$$\pm term\{\pm term...\}$$

where *term* is either *dependentvariable* or *number*dependentvariable* and brackets { } mean zero or more occurrences of the term in brackets. Although these combinations actually represent the columns of the **M** matrix, they are printed by rows.

When an M= specification is included, the analysis requested on the MANOVA statement is carried out for the variables defined by the equations in the specification, not the original dependent variables. Without an M= specification, the analysis is performed for the original dependent variables in the MODEL statement. Examples of the use of the M= specification are given below. For further information, see the detail section **Multivariate Analysis of Variance** in the GLM procedure.

If an M= specification is included without either MNAMES= or PREFIX= options, the variables are labeled MVAR1, MVAR2, and so forth by default.

The following two options allow specification of labels for the transformed variables defined by the M= statement:

MNAMES= *listofnames* provides names for the variables defined by the equations in the M= specification. Names in the list correspond to the M= equations.

PREFIX=*name* is an alternative means of identifying the transformed variables defined by the M= specification. For example, if PREFIX=DIFF is specified, the transformed variables are labeled DIFF1, DIFF2, and so forth.

The options below can appear in the MANOVA statement after a slash (/):

PRINTH requests that the **H** matrix (the SSCP matrix) associated with each effect specified by the H parameter be printed.

PRINTE requests printing of the **E** matrix. If the **E** matrix is the error SSCP (residual) matrix from the analysis, the partial correlations of the dependent variables given the independent variables are also printed.

For example, the statement

```
MANOVA / PRINTE;
```

prints the error SSCP matrix and the partial correlation matrix computed from the error SSCP matrix.

ORTH requests that the transformation matrix in the M= specification of the MANOVA statement be orthonormalized by rows prior to the analysis.

SHORT prints the multivariate test statistics and associated *F* statistics in a condensed form.

CANONICAL requests that a canonical analysis of the **H** and **E** matrices (transformed by the **M** matrix if specified) be printed instead of the usual printout of characteristic roots and vectors. This analysis is similar to that produced by PROC CANDISC.

SUMMARY produces analysis-of-variance tables for each dependent variable. When no **M** matrix is specified, a table is printed for each original dependent variable from the MODEL statement; with an **M** matrix other than the identity, a table is printed for each transformed variable defined by the **M** matrix.

Here is an example of the MANOVA statement:

```
PROC ANOVA;
   CLASS A B;
   MODEL Y1-Y5=A B(A);
   MANOVA H=A E=B(A) / PRINTH PRINTE ;
```

```
MANOVA H=B(A) / PRINTE;
MANOVA H=A E=B(A) M=Y1-Y2,Y2-Y3,Y3-Y4,Y4-Y5
 PREFIX=DIFF;
```

The first MANOVA statement specifies A as the hypothesis effect and B(A) as the error effect. The PRINTH option requests that the **H** matrix associated with the A effect be printed, and the PRINTE option requests that the **E** matrix associated with the B(A) effect be printed.

The second MANOVA statement specifies B(A) as the hypothesis effect. Since no error effect is specified, ANOVA uses the error SSCP matrix from the analysis as the **E** matrix. The PRINTE option requests that this **E** matrix be printed. Since the **E** matrix is the error SSCP matrix from the analysis, the partial correlation matrix computed from this matrix is also printed.

The third MANOVA statement requests the same analysis as the first MANOVA statement, but the analysis is carried out for variables transformed to be successive differences between the original dependent variables. The PREFIX=DIFF option specifies that the transformed variables be labeled as DIFF1, DIFF2, DIFF3, and DIFF4.

As a second example of the use of the M= specification, consider the following:

```
PROC ANOVA;
   CLASS GROUP;
   MODEL DOSE1-DOSE4=GROUP;
   MANOVA H=GROUP M=-3*DOSE1-DOSE2+DOSE3+3*DOSE4,
                  DOSE1-DOSE2-DOSE3+DOSE4,
                  -DOSE1+3*DOSE2-3*DOSE3+DOSE4
    MNAMES=LINEAR QUADRTIC CUBIC/ PRINTE;
```

The M= specification gives a transformation of the dependent variables DOSE1 through DOSE4 into orthogonal polynomial components, and the MNAMES= option labels the transformed variables as LINEAR, QUADRTIC, and CUBIC, respectively. Since the analysis uses the PRINTE option and uses the default residual matrix as an error term, the partial correlation matrix of the orthogonal polynomial components is also printed.

REPEATED Statement

REPEATED *factorname levels (levelvalues) transformation* [,...] / *options;*

When values of the dependent variables in the MODEL statement represent repeated measurements on the same experimental unit, REPEATED allows you to test hypotheses about the measurement factors (often called *within-subject factors*) as well as the interactions of within-subject factors with independent variables in the MODEL statement (often called *between-subject factors*). The REPEATED statement provides both multivariate and univariate tests as well as hypothesis tests for a variety of single-degree-of-freedom contrasts. When more than one within-subject factor is specified, the *factornames* (and associated level and transformation information) must be separated by a comma on the REPEATED statement. There is no limit to the number of within-subject factors that can be specified. For more information, see PROC GLM **Details**.

When a REPEATED statement appears, ANOVA enters a multivariate mode of handling missing values, so dependent variables corresponding to each combination of the within subject factors **must** be present for an observation, or that observation will be excluded from the analysis.

factorname names a factor to be associated with the dependent variables. The name should **not** be the same as any variable name that already exists in the data set being analyzed and should conform to the usual conventions of SAS variable names.

levels gives the number of levels associated with the factor being defined. When there is only one within-subjects factor, the number of levels is equal to the number of dependent variables. In this case, *levels* need not be specified. When more than one within-subject factor is defined, however, *levels* must be specified, and the product of the number of levels of all the factors **must** equal the number of dependent variables in the MODEL statement.

(levelvalues) gives values that correspond to levels of a repeated-measures factor. These values are used to label output and as spacings for constructing orthogonal polynomial contrasts. The number of level values specified must correspond to the number of levels for that factor in the REPEATED statement. Note that the level values appear in parentheses.

The following *transformation* keywords define single-degree-of-freedom contrasts for factors specified on the REPEATED statement. Since the number of contrasts generated is always one less than the number of levels of the factor, you have some control over which contrast is omitted from the analysis by which transformation you select.

CONTRAST {(*ordinalreferencelevel*)}
generates contrasts between levels of the factor and, optionally, a reference level which must appear in parentheses. The reference level corresponds to the ordinal value of the level rather than the level value specified. Without a reference level, the last level is used by default.

POLYNOMIAL
generates orthogonal polynomial contrasts. Level values, if provided are used as spacings in the construction of the polynomials; otherwise, equal spacing is assumed.

HELMERT
generates contrasts between each level of the factor and the mean of subsequent levels.

MEAN {(*ordinalreferencelevel*)}
generates contrasts between levels of the factor and the mean of all other levels of the factor. Specifying a reference level eliminates the contrast between that level and the mean. Without a reference level, the contrast involving the last level is omitted. Reference level specification must appear in parentheses.

PROFILE
generates contrasts between adjacent levels of the factor.

When specifying more than one factor, list the dependent variables in the MODEL statement so that the within-subject factors defined in the REPEATED statement are nested; that is, the first factor defined on the REPEATED statement **should be the one with values that change least frequently.** For example, assume three treatments are administered at each of four times, for a total of twelve dependent variables on each experimental unit. If the variables are listed on the MODEL statement as Y1-Y12, then the statement

```
REPEATED TRT 3, TIME 4;
```

implies the following structure:

DEP VARIABLE	Y1	Y2	Y3	Y4	Y5	Y6	Y7	Y8	Y9	Y10	Y11	Y12
value of TRT	1	1	1	1	2	2	2	2	3	3	3	3
value of TIME	1	2	3	4	1	2	3	4	1	2	3	4

REPEATED always produces a table like the one above.

The following options can appear in the REPEATED statement after a slash (/):

NOM prints only the results of the univariate analyses.

NOU prints only the results of the multivariate analyses.

PRINTM prints the transformation matrices that define the contrasts in the analysis.

PRINTH prints the **H** (SSCP) matrix associated with each multivariate test.

PRINTE prints the **E** matrix for each combination of within-subject factors, as well as partial correlation matrices for both the original dependent variables and the variables defined by the transformations specified in the REPEATED statement. In addition, the PRINTE option provides sphericity tests for each set of transformed variables. If the requested transformations are not orthogonal, the PRINTE option also provides a sphericity test for a set of orthogonal contrasts.

PRINTRV prints the characteristic roots and vectors for each multivariate test.

SHORT prints the multivariate test criteria and associated F statistics in a condensed form.

SUMMARY produces analysis-of-variance tables for each contrast defined by the within-subjects factors. Along with tests for the effects of the independent variables specified in the MODEL statement, a term labeled MEAN tests the hypothesis that the overall mean of the contrast is zero.

CANONICAL requests a canonical analysis of the **H** and **E** matrices corresponding to the transformed variables specified in the REPEATED statement. This analysis is similar to that produced by PROC CANDISC.

BY Statement

BY *variables;*

A BY statement can be used with PROC ANOVA to obtain separate analyses on observations in groups defined by the BY variables. When a BY statement appears, the procedure expects the input data set to be sorted in order of the BY variables. If your input data set is not sorted in ascending order, use the SORT procedure with a similar BY statement to sort the data, or, if appropriate, use the

BY statement options NOTSORTED or DESCENDING. For more information, see the discussion of the BY statement in "Statements Used in the PROC Step" in the *SAS User's Guide: Basics*.

DETAILS

Missing Values

The dependent variables are grouped based on the similarity of their patterns of missing values among the dependent variables. This feature is the same as the way GLM treats missing values.

When a MANOVA or REPEATED statement appears, the ANOVA procedure enters a multivariate mode for handling missing values. If any values for dependent variables are missing, the observation is excluded from the analysis.

Computational Method

Let **X** represent the *nxp* design matrix. The columns of **X** contain only 0s and 1s. Let **Y** represent the *n*x1 vector of dependent variables.

In the GLM procedure, **X'X**, **X'Y**, and **Y'Y** are formed in main storage. However, in the ANOVA procedure only the diagonals of **X'X** are computed, along with **X'Y** and **Y'Y**. Thus, ANOVA saves a considerable amount of storage as well as time.

The elements of **X'Y** are cell totals, and the diagonal elements of **X'X** are cell frequencies. Since ANOVA automatically pools omitted effects into the next higher-level effect containing the names of the omitted effect (or within-error), a slight modification to the rules given by Searle (1971, 389) is used.

Step 1: The sum of squares for each effect is computed as if it were a main effect. In other words, for each effect, square each cell total and divide by its cell frequency. Add these quantities together, and then subtract the correction factor for the mean (total squared over N).

Step 2: For each effect involving two class names, subtract the SS for any main effect whose name is contained in the two-factor effect.

Step 3: For each effect involving three class names, subtract the SS for all main effects and two-factor effects whose names are contained in the three-factor effect. If effects involving four or more class names are present, continue this process.

Printed Output

ANOVA first prints a table that includes:

1. the name of each variable in the CLASS statement
2. the number of different values or LEVELS of the CLASS variables
3. the VALUES of the CLASS variables
4. the number of observations in the data set and the number of observations excluded from the analysis because of missing values, if any.

ANOVA then prints an analysis-of-variance table for each dependent variable in the MODEL statement. This table breaks down:

5. the CORRECTED TOTAL sum of squares for the dependent variable
6. into the portion attributed to the MODEL
7. and the portion attributed to ERROR.
8. the MEAN SQUARE term is the

9. SUM OF SQUARES divided by the
10. DEGREES OF FREEDOM (DF).
11. the MEAN SQUARE for ERROR is an estimate of σ^2, the variance of the true errors.
12. the F VALUE is the ratio produced by dividing MS(MODEL), the mean square for the model, by the MS(ERROR), the mean square for error. It tests how well the model as a whole (adjusted for the mean) accounts for the dependent variable's behavior. This *F* test is a test that all parameters except the intercept are zero.
13. the significance probability associated with the *F* statistic, labeled PR>F.
14. R-SQUARE, R^2, measures how much variation in the dependent variable can be accounted for by the model. R^2, which can range from 0 to 1, is the ratio of the sum of squares for the model divided by the sum of squares for the corrected total. In general, the larger the R^2 value, the better the model fits the data.
15. C.V., the coefficient of variation, is often used to describe the amount of variation in the population. The C.V. is 100 times the standard deviation of the dependent variable, STD DEV, divided by the MEAN. The coefficient of variation is often a preferred measure because it is unitless.
16. ROOT MSE estimates the standard deviation of the dependent variable and is computed as the square root of MS(ERROR), the mean square of the error term
17. the MEAN of the dependent variable.

For each effect (or source of variation) in the model, ANOVA then prints:

18. DF, degrees of freedom
19. ANOVA SS, the sum of squares
20. the F VALUE for testing the hypothesis that the group means for that effect are equal
21. PR>F, the significance probability value associated with the F VALUE.

When a TEST statement is used, ANOVA prints the results of the tests requested in the TEST statement. When a MANOVA statement is used and the model includes more than one dependent variable, ANOVA prints these additional statistics (not shown in example output):

22. for each **H** matrix, the characteristic roots and vectors of $\mathbf{E}^{-1}\mathbf{H}$
23. the Hotelling-Lawley trace
24. Pillai's trace
25. Wilks' criterion
26. Roy's maximum root criterion.

These MANOVA tests are discussed in "SAS Regression Procedures" and in the GLM procedure description.

EXAMPLES

One-Way Layout with Means Comparisons: Example 1

The following data are derived from an experiment by Erdman (1946) and analyzed in Chapters 7 and 8 of Steel and Torrie (1980). The measurements are the nitrogen content of red clover plants inoculated with cultures of Rhizobium trifolii strains of bacteria and a composite of five Rhizobium meliloti strains. Several different means comparisons methods are requested.

```
DATA CLOVER;
   INPUT STRAIN $ NITROGEN @@;
   CARDS;
3DOK1  19.4  3DOK1  32.6  3DOK1  27.0  3DOK1  32.1  3DOK1  33.0
3DOK5  17.7  3DOK5  24.8  3DOK5  27.9  3DOK5  25.2  3DOK5  24.3
3DOK4  17.0  3DOK4  19.4  3DOK4   9.1  3DOK4  11.9  3DOK4  15.8
3DOK7  20.7  3DOK7  21.0  3DOK7  20.5  3DOK7  18.8  3DOK7  18.6
3DOK13 14.3  3DOK13 14.4  3DOK13 11.8  3DOK13 11.6  3DOK13 14.2
COMPOS 17.3  COMPOS 19.4  COMPOS 19.1  COMPOS 16.9  COMPOS 20.8
;
PROC ANOVA;
   CLASS STRAIN;
   MODEL NITROGEN=STRAIN;
   MEANS STRAIN / DUNCAN WALLER;
   MEANS STRAIN / LSD TUKEY CLDIFF;
```

Output 11.1 One-Way Layout with Means Comparisons: PROC ANOVA

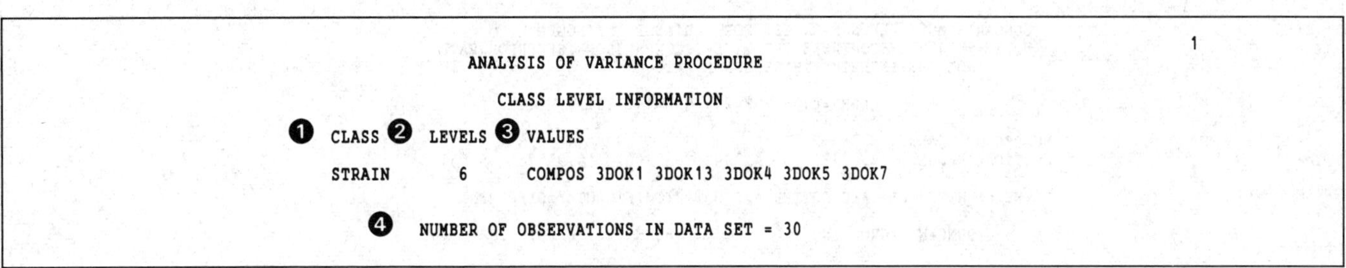

```
                                                                          1
                        ANALYSIS OF VARIANCE PROCEDURE

                           CLASS LEVEL INFORMATION

       ❶ CLASS ❷ LEVELS ❸ VALUES

         STRAIN      6      COMPOS 3DOK1 3DOK13 3DOK4 3DOK5 3DOK7

            ❹  NUMBER OF OBSERVATIONS IN DATA SET = 30
```

```
                                                                                          2
                             ANALYSIS OF VARIANCE PROCEDURE

DEPENDENT VARIABLE: NITROGEN
                                 ❾                  ❽             ⓬           ⓭           ⓮          ⓯
SOURCE             ❿  DF     SUM OF SQUARES      MEAN SQUARE     F VALUE     PR > F     R-SQUARE        C.V.

MODEL ❻                5       847.04666667     169.40933333       14.37     0.0001     0.749616     17.2651

ERROR ❼               24       282.92800000  ⓫   11.78866667             ⓰ ROOT MSE          ⓱ NITROGEN MEAN

CORRECTED TOTAL ❺     29      1129.97466667                               3.43346278           19.88666667
                                                 ⓴        ㉑
SOURCE             ⓲  DF      ⓳  ANOVA SS     F VALUE    PR > F

STRAIN                 5       847.04666667      14.37    0.0001
```

```
                                                                    3

                ANALYSIS OF VARIANCE PROCEDURE

      WALLER-DUNCAN K-RATIO T TEST FOR VARIABLE: NITROGEN
      NOTE: THIS TEST MINIMIZES THE BAYES RISK UNDER ADDITIVE LOSS
            AND CERTAIN OTHER ASSUMPTIONS

               KRATIO=100  DF=24  MSE=11.7887  F=14.3705
               CRITICAL VALUE OF T=1.92
               MINIMUM SIGNIFICANT DIFFERENCE=4.1661

      MEANS WITH THE SAME LETTER ARE NOT SIGNIFICANTLY DIFFERENT.

           WALLER  GROUPING            MEAN       N  STRAIN

                         A           28.820       5  3DOK1

                         B           23.980       5  3DOK5
                         B
                   C     B           19.920       5  3DOK7
                   C
                   C     D           18.700       5  COMPOS
                         D
                   E     D           14.640       5  3DOK4
                   E
                   E                 13.260       5  3DOK13
```

```
                                                                    4

                ANALYSIS OF VARIANCE PROCEDURE

     DUNCAN'S MULTIPLE RANGE TEST FOR VARIABLE: NITROGEN
     NOTE: THIS TEST CONTROLS THE TYPE I COMPARISONWISE ERROR RATE,
           NOT THE EXPERIMENTWISE ERROR RATE

                ALPHA=0.05  DF=24  MSE=11.7887

   NUMBER OF MEANS         2         3         4         5        6
   CRITICAL RANGE    4.47735     4.704    4.8602   4.95526  5.03172

      MEANS WITH THE SAME LETTER ARE NOT SIGNIFICANTLY DIFFERENT.

           DUNCAN  GROUPING            MEAN       N  STRAIN

                         A           28.820       5  3DOK1

                         B           23.980       5  3DOK5
                         B
                   C     B           19.920       5  3DOK7
                   C
                   C     D           18.700       5  COMPOS
                         D
                   E     D           14.640       5  3DOK4
                   E
                   E                 13.260       5  3DOK13
```

```
                                                                    5

                ANALYSIS OF VARIANCE PROCEDURE

     T TESTS (LSD) FOR VARIABLE: NITROGEN
     NOTE: THIS TEST CONTROLS THE TYPE I COMPARISONWISE ERROR RATE,
           NOT THE EXPERIMENTWISE ERROR RATE.

          ALPHA=0.05  CONFIDENCE=0.95  DF=24  MSE=11.7887
          CRITICAL VALUE OF T=2.06390
          LEAST SIGNIFICANT DIFFERENCE=4.4818

    COMPARISONS SIGNIFICANT AT THE 0.05 LEVEL ARE INDICATED BY '***'

                            LOWER    DIFFERENCE     UPPER
         STRAIN          CONFIDENCE    BETWEEN    CONFIDENCE
       COMPARISON           LIMIT       MEANS        LIMIT

      3DOK1   - 3DOK5       0.358       4.840        9.322    ***
      3DOK1   - 3DOK7       4.418       8.900       13.382    ***
      3DOK1   - COMPOS      5.638      10.120       14.602    ***
      3DOK1   - 3DOK4       9.698      14.180       18.662    ***
      3DOK1   - 3DOK13     11.078      15.560       20.042    ***
```

(continued on next page)

(continued from previous page)

```
 3DOK5  - 3DOK1       -9.322      -4.840      -0.358   ***
 3DOK5  - 3DOK7       -0.422       4.060       8.542
 3DOK5  - COMPOS       0.798       5.280       9.762   ***
 3DOK5  - 3DOK4        4.858       9.340      13.822   ***
 3DOK5  - 3DOK13       6.238      10.720      15.202   ***

 3DOK7  - 3DOK1      -13.382      -8.900      -4.418   ***
 3DOK7  - 3DOK5       -8.542      -4.060       0.422
 3DOK7  - COMPOS      -3.262       1.220       5.702
 3DOK7  - 3DOK4        0.798       5.280       9.762   ***
 3DOK7  - 3DOK13       2.178       6.660      11.142   ***

 COMPOS - 3DOK1      -14.602     -10.120      -5.638   ***
 COMPOS - 3DOK5       -9.762      -5.280      -0.798   ***
 COMPOS - 3DOK7       -5.702      -1.220       3.262
 COMPOS - 3DOK4       -0.422       4.060       8.542
 COMPOS - 3DOK13       0.958       5.440       9.922   ***

 3DOK4  - 3DOK1      -18.662     -14.180      -9.698   ***
 3DOK4  - 3DOK5      -13.822      -9.340      -4.858   ***
 3DOK4  - 3DOK7       -9.762      -5.280      -0.798   ***
 3DOK4  - COMPOS      -8.542      -4.060       0.422
 3DOK4  - 3DOK13      -3.102       1.380       5.862

 3DOK13 - 3DOK1      -20.042     -15.560     -11.078   ***
 3DOK13 - 3DOK5      -15.202     -10.720      -6.238   ***
 3DOK13 - 3DOK7      -11.142      -6.660      -2.178   ***
 3DOK13 - COMPOS      -9.922      -5.440      -0.958   ***
 3DOK13 - 3DOK4       -5.862      -1.380       3.102
```

```
                                                                          6

                        ANALYSIS OF VARIANCE PROCEDURE

              TUKEY'S STUDENTIZED RANGE (HSD) TEST FOR VARIABLE: NITROGEN
              NOTE: THIS TEST CONTROLS THE TYPE I EXPERIMENTWISE ERROR RATE

                   ALPHA=0.05  CONFIDENCE=0.95  DF=24  MSE=11.7887
                   CRITICAL VALUE OF STUDENTIZED RANGE=4.373
                   MINIMUM SIGNIFICANT DIFFERENCE=6.7142

         COMPARISONS SIGNIFICANT AT THE 0.05 LEVEL ARE INDICATED BY '***'

                           SIMULTANEOUS                SIMULTANEOUS
                               LOWER     DIFFERENCE       UPPER
               STRAIN       CONFIDENCE     BETWEEN      CONFIDENCE
             COMPARISON        LIMIT        MEANS          LIMIT

            3DOK1  - 3DOK5       -1.874       4.840      11.554
            3DOK1  - 3DOK7        2.186       8.900      15.614   ***
            3DOK1  - COMPOS       3.406      10.120      16.834   ***
            3DOK1  - 3DOK4        7.466      14.180      20.894   ***
            3DOK1  - 3DOK13       8.846      15.560      22.274   ***

            3DOK5  - 3DOK1      -11.554      -4.840       1.874
            3DOK5  - 3DOK7       -2.654       4.060      10.774
            3DOK5  - COMPOS      -1.434       5.280      11.994
            3DOK5  - 3DOK4        2.626       9.340      16.054   ***
            3DOK5  - 3DOK13       4.006      10.720      17.434   ***

            3DOK7  - 3DOK1      -15.614      -8.900      -2.186   ***
            3DOK7  - 3DOK5      -10.774      -4.060       2.654
            3DOK7  - COMPOS      -5.494       1.220       7.934
            3DOK7  - 3DOK4       -1.434       5.280      11.994
            3DOK7  - 3DOK13      -0.054       6.660      13.374

            COMPOS - 3DOK1      -16.834     -10.120      -3.406   ***
            COMPOS - 3DOK5      -11.994      -5.280       1.434
            COMPOS - 3DOK7       -7.934      -1.220       5.494
            COMPOS - 3DOK4       -2.654       4.060      10.774
            COMPOS - 3DOK13      -1.274       5.440      12.154

            3DOK4  - 3DOK1      -20.894     -14.180      -7.466   ***
            3DOK4  - 3DOK5      -16.054      -9.340      -2.626   ***
            3DOK4  - 3DOK7      -11.994      -5.280       1.434
            3DOK4  - COMPOS     -10.774      -4.060       2.654
            3DOK4  - 3DOK13      -5.334       1.380       8.094

            3DOK13 - 3DOK1      -22.274     -15.560      -8.846   ***
            3DOK13 - 3DOK5      -17.434     -10.720      -4.006   ***
            3DOK13 - 3DOK7      -13.374      -6.660       0.054
            3DOK13 - COMPOS     -12.154      -5.440       1.274
            3DOK13 - 3DOK4       -8.094      -1.380       5.334
```

Randomized Complete Block: Example 2

This example shows statements for the analysis of a randomized block. Since the data for the analysis are balanced, PROC ANOVA is used. The blocking variable BLOCK and the treatment variable TRTMENT appear in the CLASS statement, and the MODEL statement requests an analysis for each of the two dependent variables YIELD and WORTH.

```
TITLE 'RANDOMIZED COMPLETE BLOCK';
DATA RCB;
   INPUT BLOCK TRTMENT $ YIELD WORTH;
   CARDS;
1 A 32.6 112
1 B 36.4 130
1 C 29.5 106
2 A 42.7 139
2 B 47.1 143
2 C 32.9 112
3 A 35.3 124
3 B 40.1 134
3 C 33.6 116
PROC ANOVA;
   CLASS BLOCK TRTMENT;
   MODEL YIELD WORTH = BLOCK TRTMENT;
```

Output 11.2 Randomized Complete Block: PROC ANOVA

```
                              RANDOMIZED COMPLETE BLOCK                              1

                             ANALYSIS OF VARIANCE PROCEDURE

                                CLASS LEVEL INFORMATION

                              CLASS       LEVELS     VALUES

                              BLOCK            3     1 2 3

                              TRTMENT          3     A B C

                        NUMBER OF OBSERVATIONS IN DATA SET = 9
```

```
                              RANDOMIZED COMPLETE BLOCK                                                  2

                             ANALYSIS OF VARIANCE PROCEDURE

DEPENDENT VARIABLE: YIELD

SOURCE                   DF      SUM OF SQUARES        MEAN SQUARE      F VALUE        PR > F      R-SQUARE          C.V.

MODEL                     4        225.27777778        56.31944444         8.94        0.0283      0.899424        6.8400

ERROR                     4         25.19111111         6.29777778                   ROOT MSE                  YIELD MEAN

CORRECTED TOTAL           8        250.46888889                                    2.50953736                36.68888889

SOURCE                   DF            ANOVA SS    F VALUE     PR > F

BLOCK                     2         98.17555556       7.79     0.0417
TRTMENT                   2        127.10222222      10.09     0.0274
```

```
                              RANDOMIZED COMPLETE BLOCK                                                   3

                            ANALYSIS OF VARIANCE PROCEDURE

DEPENDENT VARIABLE: WORTH

SOURCE                   DF        SUM OF SQUARES           MEAN SQUARE        F VALUE          PR > F        R-SQUARE           C.V.

MODEL                     4        1247.33333333          311.83333333           8.28           0.0323        0.892227         4.9494

ERROR                     4         150.66666667           37.66666667                        ROOT MSE                     WORTH MEAN

CORRECTED TOTAL           8        1398.00000000                                            6.13731755                   124.00000000

SOURCE                   DF             ANOVA SS      F VALUE      PR > F

BLOCK                     2         354.66666667         4.71      0.0889
TRTMENT                   2         892.66666667        11.85      0.0209
```

Split Plot: Example 3

The statements below produce an analysis for a split-plot design. The CLASS statement includes the variables BLOCK, A, and B. The MODEL statement includes the independent effects BLOCK, A, BLOCK*A, B, and A*B. The TEST statement asks for an *F* test using the BLOCK*A effect as the error term and the A effect as the hypothesis effect.

```
*-----------------SPLIT PLOT--------------------*
| B DEFINES SUBPLOTS WITHIN A*BLOCK WHOLE PLOTS.|
| THE WHOLE PLOT EFFECTS MUST BE TESTED WITH A  |
| TEST STATEMENT AGAINST BLOCK*A. THE SUBPLOT   |
| EFFECTS CAN BE TESTED AGAINST THE RESIDUAL.   |
*-----------------------------------------------* ;
DATA SPLIT;
   INPUT BLOCK 1 A 2 B 3 RESPONSE ;
   CARDS;
142 40.0
141 39.5
112 37.9
111 35.4
121 36.7
122 38.2
132 36.4
131 34.8
221 42.7
222 41.6
212 40.3
211 41.6
241 44.5
242 47.6
231 43.6
232 42.8
PROC ANOVA;
   CLASS BLOCK A B;
   MODEL RESPONSE = BLOCK A BLOCK*A B A*B ;
   TEST H=A E=BLOCK*A;
   TITLE 'SPLIT PLOT DESIGN';
```

Output 11.3 Split Plot: PROC ANOVA

```
                                   SPLIT PLOT DESIGN                                              1

                              ANALYSIS OF VARIANCE PROCEDURE

                                 CLASS LEVEL INFORMATION

                               CLASS      LEVELS     VALUES

                               BLOCK           2     1 2

                               A               4     1 2 3 4

                               B               2     1 2

                         NUMBER OF OBSERVATIONS IN DATA SET = 16
```

```
                                   SPLIT PLOT DESIGN                                              2

                              ANALYSIS OF VARIANCE PROCEDURE

DEPENDENT VARIABLE: RESPONSE

SOURCE                  DF      SUM OF SQUARES       MEAN SQUARE      F VALUE       PR > F      R-SQUARE          C.V.

MODEL                   11        182.02000000       16.54727273         7.85       0.0306      0.955736        3.6090

ERROR                    4          8.43000000        2.10750000                  ROOT MSE                 RESPONSE MEAN

CORRECTED TOTAL         15        190.45000000                                  1.45172311                   40.22500000


SOURCE                  DF            ANOVA SS     F VALUE    PR > F

BLOCK                    1        131.10250000       62.21    0.0014
A                        3         40.19000000        6.36    0.0530
BLOCK*A                  3          6.92750000        1.10    0.4476
B                        1          2.25000000        1.07    0.3599
A*B                      3          1.55000000        0.25    0.8612


TESTS OF HYPOTHESES USING THE ANOVA MS FOR BLOCK*A AS AN ERROR TERM

SOURCE                  DF            ANOVA SS     F VALUE    PR > F

A                        3         40.19000000        5.80    0.0914
```

Latin-Square Split Plot: Example 4

The Latin-square design below using data from W.G. Smith (1951) is used to evaluate 6 different sugar beet varieties arranged in a 6-row (REP) by 6-column (COL) square. Then the data are recollected for a second harvest. Then HARVEST becomes a split plot on the original Latin-square design for whole plots.

```
DATA BEETS;
   DO HARVEST=1 TO 2;
      DO REP=1 TO 6;
         DO COL=1 TO 6;
            INPUT VARIETY Y @; OUTPUT;
            END;
         END;
      END;
CARDS;
3 19.1 6 18.3 5 19.6 1 18.6 2 18.2 4 18.5
6 18.1 2 19.5 4 17.6 3 18.7 1 18.7 5 19.9
1 18.1 5 20.2 6 18.5 4 20.1 3 18.6 2 19.2
2 19.1 3 18.8 1 18.7 5 20.2 4 18.6 6 18.5
```

```
4 17.5 1 18.1 2 18.7 6 18.2 5 20.4 3 18.5
5 17.7 4 17.8 3 17.4 2 17.0 6 17.6 1 17.6
3 16.2 6 17.0 5 18.1 1 16.6 2 17.7 4 16.3
6 16.0 2 15.3 4 16.0 3 17.1 1 16.5 5 17.6
1 16.5 5 18.1 6 16.7 4 16.2 3 16.7 2 17.3
2 17.5 3 16.0 1 16.4 5 18.0 4 16.6 6 16.1
4 15.7 1 16.1 2 16.7 6 16.3 5 17.8 3 16.2
5 18.3 4 16.6 3 16.4 2 17.6 6 17.1 1 16.5
;
PROC ANOVA;
   CLASS COL REP VARIETY HARVEST;
   MODEL Y= REP COL VARIETY REP*COL*VARIETY
            HARVEST HARVEST*REP
            HARVEST*VARIETY;

   TEST H=REP COL VARIETY E=REP*COL*VARIETY;
   TEST H=HARVEST E=HARVEST*REP;
```

Output 11.4 Latin-Square Split Plot: PROC ANOVA

```
                                                                                         1

                        ANALYSIS OF VARIANCE PROCEDURE
                           CLASS LEVEL INFORMATION

                       CLASS      LEVELS    VALUES

                       COL             6     1 2 3 4 5 6

                       REP             6     1 2 3 4 5 6

                       VARIETY         6     1 2 3 4 5 6

                       HARVEST         2     1 2

                   NUMBER OF OBSERVATIONS IN DATA SET = 72
```

```
                                                                                                   2

                                   ANALYSIS OF VARIANCE PROCEDURE

DEPENDENT VARIABLE: Y

SOURCE                   DF      SUM OF SQUARES        MEAN SQUARE      F VALUE       PR > F      R-SQUARE          C.V.

MODEL                    46         98.91472222         2.15032005         7.22       0.0001      0.929971        3.0855

ERROR                    25          7.44847222         0.29793889                  ROOT MSE                      Y MEAN

CORRECTED TOTAL          71        106.36319444                                   0.54583779                 17.69027778


SOURCE                   DF             ANOVA SS    F VALUE     PR > F

REP                       5           4.32069444       2.90     0.0337
COL                       5           1.57402778       1.06     0.4075
VARIETY                   5          20.61902778      13.84     0.0001
COL*REP*VARIETY          20           3.25444444       0.55     0.9144
HARVEST                   1          60.68347222     203.68     0.0001
REP*HARVEST               5           7.71736111       5.18     0.0021
VARIETY*HARVEST           5           0.74569444       0.50     0.7729

TESTS OF HYPOTHESES USING THE ANOVA MS FOR COL*REP*VARIETY AS AN ERROR TERM

SOURCE                   DF             ANOVA SS    F VALUE     PR > F

REP                       5           4.32069444       5.31     0.0029
```

(continued on next page)

(continued from previous page)

```
COL                       5         1.57402778        1.93    0.1333
VARIETY                   5        20.61902778       25.34    0.0001


TESTS OF HYPOTHESES USING THE ANOVA MS FOR REP*HARVEST AS AN ERROR TERM

SOURCE                   DF            ANOVA SS     F VALUE     PR > F

HARVEST                   1        60.68347222       39.32    0.0015
```

Strip-Split Plot: Example 5

In this example, the fertilizer treatments are laid out in vertical strips, which are then split into calcium-effect subplots. Soil type is stripped across the split-plot experiment, and the entire experiment is then replicated three times.

The input data are the 96 values of Y, arranged so that the calcium value (CA) changes most rapidly, then the fertilizer value (FERTIL), then the SOIL value, and finally the REP value. Values are shown for CA (0 and 1); FERTIL (0,1,2,3); SOIL (1,2,3); and REP (1,2,3,4).

```
*------------STRIP-SPLIT PLOT DESIGN: WINTER BARLEY--------------*
|                                                                 |
| FERTILIZER TREATMENTS ARE LAID OUT IN VERTICAL STRIPS WHICH ARE|
| THEN SPLIT INTO CALCIUM EFFECT SUB-PLOTS. SOIL TYPE IS THEN     |
| STRIPPED ACROSS THE SPLIT PLOT EXPERIMENT. THE WHOLE EXPERIMENT|
| IS REPLICATED THREE TIMES.                                      |
|                                                                 |
| DATA FROM THE NOTES OF G. COX AND A. ROTTI                      |
*-----------------------------------------------------------------*;

DATA BARLEY;
   DO REP=1 TO 4;
      DO SOIL=1 TO 3;                    * 1=D 2=H 3=P;
         DO FERTIL=0 TO 3;
            DO CA=0,1;
               INPUT Y @; OUTPUT;
               END;
            END;
         END;
      END;
   CARDS;
4.91 4.63 4.76 5.04 5.38 6.21 5.60 5.08
4.94 3.98 4.64 5.26 5.28 5.01 5.45 5.62
5.20 4.45 5.05 5.03 5.01 4.63 5.80 5.90
6.00 5.39 4.95 5.39 6.18 5.94 6.58 6.25
5.86 5.41 5.54 5.41 5.28 6.67 6.65 5.94
5.45 5.12 4.73 4.62 5.06 5.75 6.39 5.62
4.96 5.63 5.47 5.31 6.18 6.31 5.95 6.14
5.71 5.37 6.21 5.83 6.28 6.55 6.39 5.57
4.60 4.90 4.88 4.73 5.89 6.20 5.68 5.72
5.79 5.33 5.13 5.18 5.86 5.98 5.55 4.32
5.61 5.15 4.82 5.06 5.67 5.54 5.19 4.46
5.13 4.90 4.88 5.18 5.45 5.80 5.12 4.42
;
* NOTE THAT SINCE THE MODEL IS COMPLETELY SPECIFIED AND SEVERAL
```

```
* ERROR TERMS ARE PRESENT, THE TEST STATEMENT MUST BE USED TO
* OBTAIN THE PROPER TEST STATISTICS. THE TOP PORTION OF THE OUTPUT
* SHOULD BE IGNORED, SINCE THE RESIDUAL ERROR TERM IS NOT
* MEANINGFUL HERE;

PROC ANOVA;
   CLASS REP SOIL CA FERTIL;
   MEANS FERTIL CA SOIL CA*FERTIL;
   MODEL Y=REP
           FERTIL FERTIL*REP
           CA CA*FERTIL CA*REP(FERTIL)
           SOIL SOIL*REP
           SOIL*FERTIL SOIL*REP*FERTIL
           SOIL*CA SOIL*FERTIL*CA
           SOIL*CA*REP(FERTIL);
   TEST H=FERTIL         E=FERTIL*REP;
   TEST H=CA CA*FERTIL   E=CA*REP(FERTIL);
   TEST H=SOIL           E=SOIL*REP;
   TEST H=SOIL*FERTIL    E=SOIL*REP*FERTIL;
   TEST H=SOIL*CA
          SOIL*FERTIL*CA E=SOIL*CA*REP(FERTIL);
   TITLE 'STRIP-SPLIT PLOT';
```

Output 11.5 Strip-Split Plot: PROC ANOVA

```
                              STRIP-SPLIT PLOT                                 1

                        ANALYSIS OF VARIANCE PROCEDURE

                           CLASS LEVEL INFORMATION

                         CLASS      LEVELS    VALUES

                         REP             4    1 2 3 4

                         SOIL            3    1 2 3

                         CA              2    0 1

                         FERTIL          4    0 1 2 3

                    NUMBER OF OBSERVATIONS IN DATA SET = 96
```

```
                              STRIP-SPLIT PLOT                                 2

                        ANALYSIS OF VARIANCE PROCEDURE

DEPENDENT VARIABLE: Y

SOURCE                  DF       SUM OF SQUARES        MEAN SQUARE      F VALUE         PR > F      R-SQUARE             C.V.

MODEL                   95          31.89149583         0.33569996     99999.99         0.0001      1.000000           0.0000

ERROR                    0           0.00000000         0.00000000                    ROOT MSE                         Y MEAN

CORRECTED TOTAL         95          31.89149583                                     0.00000000                     5.42729167

SOURCE                  DF             ANOVA SS    F VALUE    PR > F

REP                      3           6.27974583          .         .
FERTIL                   3           7.22127083          .         .
REP*FERTIL               9           6.08211250          .         .
```

(continued on next page)

(continued from previous page)

```
CA                        1       0.27735000        .       .
CA*FERTIL                 3       1.96395833        .       .
REP*CA(FERTIL)           12       1.76705833        .       .
SOIL                      2       1.92658958        .       .
REP*SOIL                  6       1.66761042        .       .
SOIL*FERTIL               6       0.68828542        .       .
REP*SOIL*FERTIL          18       1.58698125        .       .
SOIL*CA                   2       0.04493125        .       .
SOIL*CA*FERTIL            6       0.18936042        .       .
REP*SOIL*CA(FERTIL)      24       2.19624167        .       .


TESTS OF HYPOTHESES USING THE ANOVA MS FOR REP*FERTIL AS AN ERROR TERM

SOURCE                   DF          ANOVA SS    F VALUE    PR > F

FERTIL                    3       7.22127083       3.56    0.0604


TESTS OF HYPOTHESES USING THE ANOVA MS FOR REP*CA(FERTIL) AS AN ERROR TERM

SOURCE                   DF          ANOVA SS    F VALUE    PR > F

CA                        1       0.27735000       1.88    0.1950
CA*FERTIL                 3       1.96395833       4.45    0.0255


TESTS OF HYPOTHESES USING THE ANOVA MS FOR REP*SOIL AS AN ERROR TERM

SOURCE                   DF          ANOVA SS    F VALUE    PR > F

SOIL                      2       1.92658958       3.47    0.0999
```

```
                                   STRIP-SPLIT PLOT                                  3

                             ANALYSIS OF VARIANCE PROCEDURE

DEPENDENT VARIABLE: Y

TESTS OF HYPOTHESES USING THE ANOVA MS FOR REP*SOIL*FERTIL AS AN ERROR TERM

SOURCE                   DF          ANOVA SS    F VALUE    PR > F

SOIL*FERTIL               6       0.68828542       1.30    0.3063


TESTS OF HYPOTHESES USING THE ANOVA MS FOR REP*SOIL*CA(FERTIL) AS AN ERROR TERM

SOURCE                   DF          ANOVA SS    F VALUE    PR > F

SOIL*CA                   2       0.04493125       0.25    0.7843
SOIL*CA*FERTIL            6       0.18936042       0.34    0.9059
```

```
                                   STRIP-SPLIT PLOT                                  4

                             ANALYSIS OF VARIANCE PROCEDURE

                                         MEANS

                             FERTIL          N              Y

                             0              24     5.18416667
                             1              24     5.12916667
                             2              24     5.75458333
                             3              24     5.64125000

                               CA          N              Y

                               0          48     5.48104167
                               1          48     5.37354167
```

(continued on next page)

(continued from previous page)

SOIL	N	Y
1	32	5.54312500
2	32	5.51093750
3	32	5.22781250

CA	FERTIL	N	Y
0	0	12	5.34666667
0	1	12	5.08833333
0	2	12	5.62666667
0	3	12	5.86250000
1	0	12	5.02166667
1	1	12	5.17000000
1	2	12	5.88250000
1	3	12	5.42000000

REFERENCES

Erdman, L.W. (1946), "Studies to Determine if Antibiosis Occurs among Rhizobia," *Journal of the American Society of Agronomy*, 38, 251-258.

Fisher, R.A. (1942), *The Design of Experiments,* Third Edition, Edinburgh: Oliver & Boyd.

Freund, R.J. and Littell, R.C. (1981), *SAS for Linear Models: A Guide to the ANOVA and GLM Procedures*, Cary, NC: SAS Institute, Inc.

Graybill, F.A. (1961), *An Introduction to Linear Statistical Models,* Vol. I, New York: McGraw-Hill.

Henderson, C.R. (1953), "Estimation of Variance and Covariance Components," *Biometrics*, 9, 226-252.

Remington, R.D. and Schork, M.A. (1970), *Statistics with Applications to the Biological and Health Sciences*, Englewood Cliffs, New Jersey: Prentice-Hall, Inc.

Scheffe, H. (1959), *The Analysis of Variance*, New York: John Wiley & Sons.

Searle, S.R. (1971), *Linear Models*, New York: John Wiley & Sons.

Smith, W.G. (1951), Dissertation Notes on Canadian Sugar Factories, Ltd., Alberta, Canada: Taber.

Snedecor, G.W. and Cochran, W.G. (1967), *Statistical Methods,* Sixth Edition, Ames, Iowa: The Iowa State University Press.

Steel, R.G.D. and Torrie, J.H. (1980), *Principles and Procedures of Statistics*, New York: McGraw-Hill.

REFERENCES

Chapter 12

The CANCORR Procedure

Operating systems: All

ABSTRACT

The CANCORR procedure performs canonical correlation, partial canonical correlation, and canonical redundancy analysis. CANCORR can create output data sets containing canonical coefficients and scores on canonical variables.

INTRODUCTION

Canonical correlation is a technique for analyzing the relationship between two sets of variables. Each set can contain several variables. Simple and multiple correlation are special cases of canonical correlation in which one or both sets contain a single variable.

CANCORR tests a series of hypotheses that each canonical correlation and all smaller canonical correlations are zero in the population. CANCORR uses an *F* approximation (Rao 1973; Kshirsagar 1972) that gives better small sample results than the usual χ^2 approximation. At least one of the two sets of variables should have an approximate multivariate normal distribution for the probability levels to be valid.

Both standardized and unstandardized canonical coefficients are produced, as well as all correlations between canonical variables and the original variables. A canonical redundancy analysis (Stewart and Love 1968; Cooley and Lohnes 1971) can also be performed.

CANCORR can produce a data set containing the scores on each canonical variable. You can use the PRINT procedure to list these values. A plot of each canonical variable against its counterpart in the other group is often useful, and PROC PLOT can be used with the output data set to produce these plots.

A second output data set contains the canonical coefficients, which can be rotated by the FACTOR procedure.

Background

Canonical correlation was developed by Hotelling (1935, 1936). The application of canonical correlation is discussed by Cooley and Lohnes (1971), Tatsuoka (1971), and Mardia, Kent and Bibby (1979). One of the best theoretical treatments is given by Kshirsagar (1972).

Given two sets of variables, CANCORR finds a linear combination from each set, called a canonical variable, such that the correlation between the two canonical variables is maximized. This correlation between the two canonical variables is the first canonical correlation. The coefficients of the linear combinations are canonical coefficients or canonical weights. It is customary to normalize the canonical coefficients so that each canonical variable has a variance of one.

CANCORR continues by finding a second set of canonical variables, uncorrelated with the first pair, that produces the second highest correlation coefficient. The process of constructing canonical variables continues until the number of pairs of canonical variables equals the number of variables in the smaller group.

Each canonical variable is uncorrelated with all the other canonical variables of either set except for the one corresponding canonical variable in the opposite set. The canonical coefficients are not generally orthogonal, however, so the canonical variables do not represent jointly perpendicular directions through the space of the original variables.

The first canonical correlation is at least as large as the multiple correlation between any variable and the opposite set of variables. It is possible for the first canonical correlation to be very high even if all the multiple correlations are low. It is also possible for the first canonical correlation to be very large while all the multiple correlations for predicting one of the original variables from the opposite set of canonical variables are small. Canonical redundancy analysis (Stewart and Love 1968; Cooley and Lohnes 1971; van den Wollenberg 1977), available with the CANCORR procedure, examines how well the original variables can be predicted from the canonical variables.

CANCORR can also perform partial canonical correlation, a multivariate generalization of ordinary partial correlation (Cooley and Lohnes 1971; Timm 1975). Most commonly used parametric statistical methods, ranging from *t* tests to multivariate analysis of covariance, are special cases of partial canonical correlation.

SPECIFICATIONS

The CANCORR procedure is invoked by the following statements:

PROC CANCORR *options;*
VAR *variables;*
WITH *variables;*
PARTIAL *variables;*
FREQ *variable;*

WEIGHT *variable;*
BY *variables;*

Usually only the VAR and WITH statements are needed in addition to the PROC CANCORR statement. The WITH statement is required.

PROC CANCORR Statement

PROC CANCORR *options;*

The options that can appear in the PROC CANCORR statement are listed below:

DATA=*SASdataset*
: names the SAS data set to be analyzed by CANCORR. It can be an ordinary SAS data set or a TYPE=CORR or TYPE=COV data set. If DATA= is omitted, the most recently created SAS data set is used.

OUT=*SASdataset*
: names an output SAS data set to contain all the original data plus scores on the canonical variables. If you want to create a permanent SAS data set, you must specify a two-level name. OUT= cannot be used when the DATA= data set is TYPE=CORR or TYPE=COV. See "SAS Files" in the *SAS User's Guide: Basics* for more information on permanent SAS data sets.

OUTSTAT=*SASdataset*
: produces a SAS data set containing various statistics including the canonical correlations and coefficients. If you want to create a permanent SAS data set, you must specify a two-level name. See "SAS Files" in the *SAS User's Guide: Basics* for more information on permanent SAS data sets.

SIMPLE
S
: prints means and standard deviations.

CORR
C
: prints correlations among the original variables.

REDUNDANCY
RED
: prints canonical redundancy statistics.

ALL
: prints all optional output.

SHORT
: suppresses all default output except the tables of canonical correlations and multivariate statistics.

NOPRINT
: suppresses the printout.

NCAN=*n*
: specifies the number of canonical variables for which full output is desired.

EDF=*errordf*
: specifies the error degrees of freedom from the regression analysis if the input observations are residuals from a regression. The effective number of observations is the EDF= value plus one. If you have 100 observations, then EDF=99 has the same effect as omitting EDF=.

RDF=*regressiondf*
specifies the regression degrees of freedom if the input observations are residuals from a regression analysis. The effective number of observations is the actual number minus the RDF= value. The degree of freedom for the intercept should not be included in RDF=.

NOINT
indicates that the model should not contain the intercept.

SINGULAR=*p*
SING=*p*
specifies the singularity criterion, where $0<p<1$. If a variable in the VAR or WITH statement has an R^2 as large as $1-p$ when predicted from the variables listed before it in the statement, it is omitted from the canonical analysis and assigned canonical coefficients of zero. The default is SINGULAR=1E-8.

VPREFIX=*name*
VP=*name*
specifies a prefix for naming canonical variables from the VAR statement. By default, these canonical variables are given the names V1, V2, and so on. If VPREFIX=ABC is specified, the names are ABC1, ABC2, and so forth.

WPREFIX=*name*
WP=*name*
specifies a prefix for naming canonical variables from the WITH statement. By default, these canonical variables are given the names W1, W2, and so on. If WPREFIX=XYZ is specified, then the names are XYZ1, XYZ2, and so forth.

VNAME=*'label'*
VN=*'label'*
specifies a character constant up to 40 characters long to refer to variables from the VAR statement on the printout. The constant should be enclosed in single quotes. If VNAME= is omitted, these variables are referred to as the 'VAR' VARIABLES.

WNAME=*'label'*
WN=*'label'*
specifies a character constant up to 40 characters long to refer to variables from the WITH statement on the printout. The constant should be enclosed in quotes. If WNAME= is omitted, these variables are referred to as the 'WITH' VARIABLES.

VAR Statement

VAR *variables;*

The VAR statement lists the variables in the first of the two sets of variables to be analyzed. The variables must be numeric. If the VAR statement is omitted, all numeric variables not mentioned in other statements make up the first set of variables.

WITH Statement

WITH *variables;*

The WITH statement lists the variables in the second set of variables to be analyzed. The variables must be numeric. The WITH statement must be present.

PARTIAL Statement

PARTIAL *variables;*

The PARTIAL statement can be used to base the canonical analysis on partial correlations. The variables in the PARTIAL statement are partialled out of the VAR and WITH variables.

FREQ Statement

FREQ *variable;*

If one variable in your input data set represents the frequency of occurrence for other values in the observation, specify the variable's name in a FREQ statement. CANCORR then treats the data set as if each observation appeared *n* times, where *n* is the value of the FREQ variable for the observation. The total number of observations is considered equal to the sum of the FREQ variable when CANCORR calculates significance probabilities.

WEIGHT Statement

WEIGHT *variable;*

If you want to compute weighted product-moment correlation coefficients, give the name of the weighting variable in a WEIGHT statement.

WEIGHT and FREQ statements have a similar effect except in calculating degrees of freedom.

BY Statement

BY *variables;*

A BY statement can be used with PROC CANCORR to obtain separate analyses on observations in groups defined by the BY variables. When a BY statement appears, the procedure expects the input data set to be sorted in order of the BY variables. If your input data set is not sorted in ascending order, use the SORT procedure with a similar BY statement to sort the data, or, if appropriate, use the BY statement options NOTSORTED or DESCENDING. For more information, see the discussion of the BY statement in "Statements Used in the PROC Step," in the *SAS User's Guide: Basics.*

DETAILS

Missing Values

If an observation has a missing value for any of the variables in the analysis, that observation is omitted from the analysis.

Output Data Sets

OUT= data set The OUT= data set contains all the variables in the original data set plus new variables containing the canonical variable scores. The number of new variables is twice that specified by the NCAN= option. The names of the new variables are formed by concatenating the values given by the VPREFIX= and WPREFIX= options (the defaults are V and W) with the numbers 1, 2, 3, and so on. The new variables have mean 0 and variance equal to 1. An OUT= data set cannot be created if the DATA= data set is TYPE=CORR or TYPE=COV or if a PARTIAL statement is used.

OUTSTAT= data set The OUTSTAT= data set is similar to the TYPE=CORR data set produced by the CORR procedure but contains several results in addition to those produced by CORR.

The new data set contains the following variables:

- the BY variables, if any
- two new character variables, _TYPE_ and _NAME_
- the variables analyzed (those in the VAR statement and WITH statement).

Each observation in the new data set contains some type of statistic as indicated by the _TYPE_ variable. The values of the _TYPE_ variable are as follows:

TYPE	Contents
MEAN	means.
STD	standard deviations.
N	number of observations.
CORR	correlations.
CANCORR	canonical correlations.
SCORE	standardized canonical coefficients.
RAWSCORE	raw canonical coefficients.
STRUCTUR	canonical structure.

Computational Resources

Let:

n = number of observations

v = number of VAR variables

w = number of WITH variables

p = max(v,w)

q = min(v,w).

The time required to compute the correlation matrix is roughly proportional to:

$$n(p+q)^2 \quad .$$

The time required for the canonical analysis is roughly proportional to:

$$p^3/6+p^2q+3pq^2/2+5q^3$$

but the coefficient for q^3 varies depending on the number of QR iterations in the singular value decomposition.

Printed Output

If SIMPLE is specified, CANCORR prints:

1. MEANs and STandard DEViations of the input variables.

If CORR is specified, CANCORR prints:

2. CORRELATIONS AMONG THE input variables.

Unless NOPRINT is specified, CANCORR prints a table of canonical correlations containing the following:

3. CANONICAL CORRELATIONs
4. ADJUSTED CANONICAL CORRELATIONs (Lawley 1959), which are asymptotically less biased than the raw correlations, and may be negative. The adjusted canonical correlations may not be computable and are printed as missing values if two canonical correlations are nearly equal or if some are close to zero. A missing value is also printed if an adjusted canonical correlation is larger than a previous adjusted canonical correlation.
5. APPROX STANDARD ERROR, the approximate standard error of the canonical correlations
6. SQUARED CANONICAL CORRELATION, the squared canonical correlations
7. EIGENVALUES OF INV(E)*H, which are equal to CANRSQ/(1-CANRSQ), where CANRSQ is the corresponding squared canonical correlation. Also printed for each eigenvalue is the DIFFERENCE from the next eigenvalue, the PROPORTION of the sum of the eigenvalues, and the CUMULATIVE proportion.
8. LIKELIHOOD RATIO for the hypothesis that the current canonical correlation and all smaller ones are 0 in the population. The likelihood ratio for all canonical correlations equals Wilks' lambda.
9. APPROX F based on Rao's approximation to the distribution of the likelihood ratio (Rao 1973, 556; Kshirsagar 1972, 326)
10. NUM DF and DEN DF (numerator and denominator degrees of freedom) and PROB>F (probability level) associated with the F statistic

Unless NOPRINT is specified, CANCORR prints a table of multivariate statistics for the null hypothesis that all canonical correlations are zero in the population. These statistics are described in **Multivariate Tests** in "SAS Regression Procedures." The statistics are as follows:

11. WILKS' LAMBDA
12. PILLAI'S TRACE
13. HOTELLING-LAWLEY TRACE
14. ROY'S GREATEST ROOT

For each of the above statistics, CANCORR prints:

15. an *F* approximation or upper bound
16. NUM DF, the numerator degrees of freedom
17. DEN DF, the denominator degrees of freedom
18. PROB>F, the probability level

Unless SHORT or NOPRINT is specified, CANCORR prints the following:

19. both STANDARDIZED and RAW (unstandardized) CANONICAL COEFFICIENTS normalized to give canonical variables with unit variance. Standardized coefficients can be used to compute canonical variable scores from the standardized (zero mean and unit variance) input variables. Raw coefficients can be used to compute canonical variable scores from the input variables without standardizing them.
20. all four CANONICAL STRUCTURE matrices, giving CORRELATIONS BETWEEN THE canonical variables AND THE original variables

If REDUNDANCY is specified, CANCORR prints:

21. the CANONICAL REDUNDANCY ANALYSIS (Stewart and Love 1968; Cooley and Lohnes 1971), including RAW (unstandardized) and STANDARDIZED PROPORTION and CUMULATIVE PROPORTION of

the VARIANCE OF each set of variables EXPLAINED BY THEIR OWN CANONICAL VARIABLES and the OPPOSITE CANONICAL VARIABLES

22. the SQUARED MULTIPLE CORRELATIONS of each variable with the first *m* canonical variables of the opposite set, where *m* varies from 1 to the number of canonical correlations.

EXAMPLE

Canonical Correlation Analysis of Fitness Club Data

Three physiological and three exercise variables were measured on twenty middle-aged men in a fitness club. CANCORR can be used to determine if the physiological variables are related in any way to the exercise variables.

```
DATA FIT;
   INPUT WEIGHT WAIST PULSE CHINS SITUPS JUMPS;
   CARDS;
191  36  50   5  162   60
189  37  52   2  110   60
193  38  58  12  101  101
162  35  62  12  105   37
189  35  46  13  155   58
182  36  56   4  101   42
211  38  56   8  101   38
167  34  60   6  125   40
176  31  74  15  200   40
154  33  56  17  251  250
169  34  50  17  120   38
166  33  52  13  210  115
154  34  64  14  215  105
247  46  50   1   50   50
193  36  46   6   70   31
202  37  62  12  210  120
176  37  54   4   60   25
157  32  52  11  230   80
156  33  54  15  225   73
138  33  68   2  110   43
;
PROC CANCORR DATA=FIT ALL
    VPREFIX=PHYS VNAME='PHYSIOLOGICAL MEASUREMENTS'
    WPREFIX=EXER WNAME='EXERCISES';
    VAR WEIGHT WAIST PULSE;
    WITH CHINS SITUPS JUMPS;
    TITLE 'MIDDLE-AGE MEN IN A HEALTH FITNESS CLUB';
    TITLE2 'DATA COURTESY OF DR. A. C. LINNERUD, NC STATE UNIV';
```

Output 12.1 Fitness Club Data: PROC CANCORR

```
                      MIDDLE-AGE MEN IN A HEALTH FITNESS CLUB                             1
                 DATA COURTESY OF DR. A. C. LINNERUD, NC STATE UNIV

                            SIMPLE UNIVARIATE STATISTICS

20 OBSERVATIONS
 3 PHYSIOLOGICAL MEASUREMENTS
 3 EXERCISES

                                            ❶
                   VARIABLE                MEAN             ST DEV

                   WEIGHT            178.6000000        24.69050531
                   WAIST              35.4000000         3.20197308
                   PULSE              56.1000000         7.21037265
                   CHINS               9.4500000         5.28627817
                   SITUPS            145.5500000        62.56657507
                   JUMPS              70.3000000        51.27747017


          ❷    CORRELATIONS AMONG THE PHYSIOLOGICAL MEASUREMENTS

                               WEIGHT           WAIST            PULSE

                 WEIGHT        1.0000          0.8702          -0.3658
                 WAIST         0.8702          1.0000          -0.3529
                 PULSE        -0.3658         -0.3529           1.0000


                          CORRELATIONS AMONG THE EXERCISES

                                CHINS          SITUPS            JUMPS

                 CHINS         1.0000          0.6957           0.4958
                 SITUPS        0.6957          1.0000           0.6692
                 JUMPS         0.4958          0.6692           1.0000


       CORRELATIONS BETWEEN THE PHYSIOLOGICAL MEASUREMENTS AND THE EXERCISES

                                CHINS          SITUPS            JUMPS

                 WEIGHT       -0.3897         -0.4931          -0.2263
                 WAIST        -0.5522         -0.6456          -0.1915
                 PULSE         0.1506          0.2250           0.0349
```

```
                      MIDDLE-AGE MEN IN A HEALTH FITNESS CLUB                             2
                 DATA COURTESY OF DR. A. C. LINNERUD, NC STATE UNIV

                           CANONICAL CORRELATION ANALYSIS
                                                                    ❼
       ❸            ❹           ❺           ❻                EIGENVALUES OF INV(E)*H
                ADJUSTED      APPROX       SQUARED                  = CANRSQ/(1-CANRSQ)
  CANONICAL     CANONICAL    STANDARD     CANONICAL
  CORRELATION  CORRELATION     ERROR     CORRELATION  EIGENVALUE  DIFFERENCE  PROPORTION  CUMULATIVE

1   0.795608     0.754056     0.084197     0.632992      1.7247      1.6828      0.9734      0.9734
2   0.200556     -.076399     0.220188     0.040223      0.0419      0.0366      0.0237      0.9970
3   0.072570         .        0.228208     0.005266      0.0053         .        0.0030      1.0000

  TESTS OF H0: THE CANONICAL CORRELATION IN THE CURRENT ROW AND ALL THAT FOLLOW ARE ZERO

                        ❽                ❾               ❿
                   LIKELIHOOD
                      RATIO       APPROX F    NUM DF    DEN DF   PR > F

                 1  0.35039053     2.0482        9     34.2229   0.0635
                 2  0.95472266     0.1758        4          30   0.9491
                 3  0.99473355     0.0847        1          16   0.7748
```

(continued on next page)

(continued from previous page)

MULTIVARIATE TEST STATISTICS AND F APPROXIMATIONS

S=3 M=-0.5 N=6.5

STATISTIC	VALUE	F	NUM DF	DEN DF	PR > F
WILKS' LAMBDA	0.3503905	2.048	9	34.2229	0.0635
PILLAI'S TRACE	0.6784815	1.559	9	48	0.1551
HOTELLING-LAWLEY TRACE	1.771941	2.494	9	38	0.0238
ROY'S GREATEST ROOT	1.724739	9.199	3	16	0.0009

NOTE: F STATISTIC FOR ROY'S GREATEST ROOT IS AN UPPER BOUND

⓳ RAW CANONICAL COEFFICIENTS FOR THE PHYSIOLOGICAL MEASUREMENTS

	PHYS1	PHYS2	PHYS3
WEIGHT	-.0314046879	-.0763195063	-.0077350467
WAIST	0.4932416756	0.3687229894	0.1580336471
PULSE	-.0081993154	-.0320519942	0.1457322421

RAW CANONICAL COEFFICIENTS FOR THE EXERCISES

	EXER1	EXER2	EXER3
CHINS	-.0661139864	-.0710412111	-.2452753473
SITUPS	-.0168462308	0.0019737454	0.0197676373
JUMPS	0.0139715689	0.0207141063	-.0081674724

MIDDLE-AGE MEN IN A HEALTH FITNESS CLUB 3

DATA COURTESY OF DR. A. C. LINNERUD, NC STATE UNIV

CANONICAL CORRELATION ANALYSIS

⓳ STANDARDIZED CANONICAL COEFFICIENTS FOR THE PHYSIOLOGICAL MEASUREMENTS

	PHYS1	PHYS2	PHYS3
WEIGHT	-0.7754	-1.8844	-0.1910
WAIST	1.5793	1.1806	0.5060
PULSE	-0.0591	-0.2311	1.0508

STANDARDIZED CANONICAL COEFFICIENTS FOR THE EXERCISES

	EXER1	EXER2	EXER3
CHINS	-0.3495	-0.3755	-1.2966
SITUPS	-1.0540	0.1235	1.2368
JUMPS	0.7164	1.0622	-0.4188

MIDDLE-AGE MEN IN A HEALTH FITNESS CLUB 4

DATA COURTESY OF DR. A. C. LINNERUD, NC STATE UNIV

⓴ CANONICAL STRUCTURE

CORRELATIONS BETWEEN THE PHYSIOLOGICAL MEASUREMENTS AND THEIR CANONICAL VARIABLES

	PHYS1	PHYS2	PHYS3
WEIGHT	0.6206	-0.7724	-0.1350
WAIST	0.9254	-0.3777	-0.0310
PULSE	-0.3328	0.0415	0.9421

CORRELATIONS BETWEEN THE EXERCISES AND THEIR CANONICAL VARIABLES

	EXER1	EXER2	EXER3
CHINS	-0.7276	0.2370	-0.6438
SITUPS	-0.8177	0.5730	0.0544
JUMPS	-0.1622	0.9586	-0.2339

(continued on next page)

(continued from previous page)

```
CORRELATIONS BETWEEN THE PHYSIOLOGICAL MEASUREMENTS AND THE CANONICAL VARIABLES OF THE EXERCISES

                              EXER1          EXER2          EXER3

              WEIGHT         0.4938        -0.1549        -0.0098
              WAIST          0.7363        -0.0757        -0.0022
              PULSE         -0.2648         0.0083         0.0684


CORRELATIONS BETWEEN THE EXERCISES AND THE CANONICAL VARIABLES OF THE PHYSIOLOGICAL MEASUREMENTS

                              PHYS1          PHYS2          PHYS3

              CHINS         -0.5789         0.0475        -0.0467
              SITUPS        -0.6506         0.1149         0.0040
              JUMPS         -0.1290         0.1923        -0.0170
```

```
                MIDDLE-AGE MEN IN A HEALTH FITNESS CLUB                              5
           DATA COURTESY OF DR. A. C. LINNERUD, NC STATE UNIV

       (21)         CANONICAL REDUNDANCY ANALYSIS

              RAW VARIANCE OF THE PHYSIOLOGICAL MEASUREMENTS
                                EXPLAINED BY

               THEIR OWN                            THE OPPOSITE
          CANONICAL VARIABLES                   CANONICAL VARIABLES

                    CUMULATIVE   CANONICAL               CUMULATIVE
         PROPORTION PROPORTION   R-SQUARED   PROPORTION  PROPORTION

     1      0.3712     0.3712      0.6330      0.2349      0.2349
     2      0.5436     0.9148      0.0402      0.0219      0.2568
     3      0.0852     1.0000      0.0053      0.0004      0.2573

                      RAW VARIANCE OF THE EXERCISES
                                EXPLAINED BY

               THEIR OWN                            THE OPPOSITE
          CANONICAL VARIABLES                   CANONICAL VARIABLES

                    CUMULATIVE   CANONICAL               CUMULATIVE
         PROPORTION PROPORTION   R-SQUARED   PROPORTION  PROPORTION

     1      0.4111     0.4111      0.6330      0.2602      0.2602
     2      0.5635     0.9746      0.0402      0.0227      0.2829
     3      0.0254     1.0000      0.0053      0.0001      0.2830


         STANDARDIZED VARIANCE OF THE PHYSIOLOGICAL MEASUREMENTS
                                EXPLAINED BY

               THEIR OWN                            THE OPPOSITE
          CANONICAL VARIABLES                   CANONICAL VARIABLES

                    CUMULATIVE   CANONICAL               CUMULATIVE
         PROPORTION PROPORTION   R-SQUARED   PROPORTION  PROPORTION

     1      0.4508     0.4508      0.6330      0.2854      0.2854
     2      0.2470     0.6978      0.0402      0.0099      0.2953
     3      0.3022     1.0000      0.0053      0.0016      0.2969

                 STANDARDIZED VARIANCE OF THE EXERCISES
                                EXPLAINED BY

               THEIR OWN                            THE OPPOSITE
          CANONICAL VARIABLES                   CANONICAL VARIABLES

                    CUMULATIVE   CANONICAL               CUMULATIVE
         PROPORTION PROPORTION   R-SQUARED   PROPORTION  PROPORTION

     1      0.4081     0.4081      0.6330      0.2584      0.2584
     2      0.4345     0.8426      0.0402      0.0175      0.2758
     3      0.1574     1.0000      0.0053      0.0008      0.2767
```

MIDDLE-AGE MEN IN A HEALTH FITNESS CLUB 6
DATA COURTESY OF DR. A. C. LINNERUD, NC STATE UNIV

CANONICAL REDUNDANCY ANALYSIS

SQUARED MULTIPLE CORRELATIONS BETWEEN THE PHYSIOLOGICAL MEASUREMENTS AND THE FIRST 'M' CANONICAL VARIABLES OF THE EXERCISES

M	1	2	3
WEIGHT	0.2438	0.2678	0.2679
WAIST	0.5421	0.5478	0.5478
PULSE	0.0701	0.0702	0.0749

22 SQUARED MULTIPLE CORRELATIONS BETWEEN THE EXERCISES AND THE FIRST 'M' CANONICAL VARIABLES OF THE PHYSIOLOGICAL MEASUREMENTS

M	1	2	3
CHINS	0.3351	0.3374	0.3396
SITUPS	0.4233	0.4365	0.4365
JUMPS	0.0167	0.0536	0.0539

MIDDLE-AGE MEN IN A HEALTH FITNESS CLUB 7
DATA COURTESY OF DR. A. C. LINNERUD, NC STATE UNIV

CANONICAL CORRELATION ANALYSIS

	CANONICAL CORRELATION	ADJUSTED CANONICAL CORRELATION	APPROX STANDARD ERROR	SQUARED CANONICAL CORRELATION	EIGENVALUES OF INV(E)*H = CANRSQ/(1-CANRSQ) EIGENVALUE	DIFFERENCE	PROPORTION	CUMULATIVE
1	0.795608	0.754056	0.084197	0.632992	1.7247	1.6828	0.9734	0.9734
2	0.200556	-.076399	0.220188	0.040223	0.0419	0.0366	0.0237	0.9970
3	0.072570	.	0.228208	0.005266	0.0053	.	0.0030	1.0000

TESTS OF H0: THE CANONICAL CORRELATION IN THE CURRENT ROW AND ALL THAT FOLLOW ARE ZERO

	LIKELIHOOD RATIO	APPROX F	NUM DF	DEN DF	PR > F
1	0.35039053	2.0482	9	34.2229	0.0635
2	0.95472266	0.1758	4	30	0.9491
3	0.99473355	0.0847	1	16	0.7748

MULTIVARIATE TEST STATISTICS AND F APPROXIMATIONS
S=3 M=-0.5 N=6.5

STATISTIC	VALUE	F	NUM DF	DEN DF	PR > F
WILKS' LAMBDA	0.3503905	2.048	9	34.2229	0.0635
PILLAI'S TRACE	0.6784815	1.559	9	48	0.1551
HOTELLING-LAWLEY TRACE	1.771941	2.494	9	38	0.0238
ROY'S GREATEST ROOT	1.724739	9.199	3	16	0.0009

NOTE: F STATISTIC FOR ROY'S GREATEST ROOT IS AN UPPER BOUND

RAW CANONICAL COEFFICIENTS FOR THE PHYSIOLOGICAL MEASUREMENTS

	PHYS1	PHYS2	PHYS3
WEIGHT	-.0314046879	-.0763195063	-.0077350467
WAIST	0.4932416756	0.3687229894	0.1580336471
PULSE	-.0081993154	-.0320519942	0.1457322421

RAW CANONICAL COEFFICIENTS FOR THE EXERCISES

	EXER1	EXER2	EXER3
CHINS	-.0661139864	-.0710412111	-.2452753473
SITUPS	-.0168462308	0.0019737454	0.0197676373
JUMPS	0.0139715689	0.0207141063	-.0081674724

```
                    MIDDLE-AGE MEN IN A HEALTH FITNESS CLUB                              8
                 DATA COURTESY OF DR. A. C. LINNERUD, NC STATE UNIV

                          CANONICAL CORRELATION ANALYSIS

     STANDARDIZED CANONICAL COEFFICIENTS FOR THE PHYSIOLOGICAL MEASUREMENTS

                          PHYS1          PHYS2          PHYS3

          WEIGHT        -0.7754        -1.8844        -0.1910
          WAIST          1.5793         1.1806         0.5060
          PULSE         -0.0591        -0.2311         1.0508


          STANDARDIZED CANONICAL COEFFICIENTS FOR THE EXERCISES

                          EXER1          EXER2          EXER3

          CHINS         -0.3495        -0.3755        -1.2966
          SITUPS        -1.0540         0.1235         1.2368
          JUMPS          0.7164         1.0622        -0.4188
```

```
                    MIDDLE-AGE MEN IN A HEALTH FITNESS CLUB                              9
                 DATA COURTESY OF DR. A. C. LINNERUD, NC STATE UNIV

                               CANONICAL STRUCTURE

   CORRELATIONS BETWEEN THE PHYSIOLOGICAL MEASUREMENTS AND THEIR CANONICAL VARIABLES

                          PHYS1          PHYS2          PHYS3

          WEIGHT         0.6206        -0.7724        -0.1350
          WAIST          0.9254        -0.3777        -0.0310
          PULSE         -0.3328         0.0415         0.9421


        CORRELATIONS BETWEEN THE EXERCISES AND THEIR CANONICAL VARIABLES

                          EXER1          EXER2          EXER3

          CHINS         -0.7276         0.2370        -0.6438
          SITUPS        -0.8177         0.5730         0.0544
          JUMPS         -0.1622         0.9586        -0.2339


CORRELATIONS BETWEEN THE PHYSIOLOGICAL MEASUREMENTS AND THE CANONICAL VARIABLES OF THE EXERCISES

                          EXER1          EXER2          EXER3

          WEIGHT         0.4938        -0.1549        -0.0098
          WAIST          0.7363        -0.0757        -0.0022
          PULSE         -0.2648         0.0083         0.0684


CORRELATIONS BETWEEN THE EXERCISES AND THE CANONICAL VARIABLES OF THE PHYSIOLOGICAL MEASUREMENTS

                          PHYS1          PHYS2          PHYS3

          CHINS         -0.5789         0.0475        -0.0467
          SITUPS        -0.6506         0.1149         0.0040
          JUMPS         -0.1290         0.1923        -0.0170
```

```
                    MIDDLE-AGE MEN IN A HEALTH FITNESS CLUB                             10
                 DATA COURTESY OF DR. A. C. LINNERUD, NC STATE UNIV

                          CANONICAL REDUNDANCY ANALYSIS

                 RAW VARIANCE OF THE PHYSIOLOGICAL MEASUREMENTS
                                  EXPLAINED BY

              THEIR OWN                             THE OPPOSITE
         CANONICAL VARIABLES                    CANONICAL VARIABLES

                      CUMULATIVE   CANONICAL               CUMULATIVE
          PROPORTION  PROPORTION   R-SQUARED  PROPORTION   PROPORTION

      1     0.3712      0.3712       0.6330     0.2349       0.2349
      2     0.5436      0.9148       0.0402     0.0219       0.2568
```

(continued on next page)

(continued from previous page)

3	0.0852	1.0000	0.0053	0.0004	0.2573

RAW VARIANCE OF THE EXERCISES
EXPLAINED BY

	THEIR OWN CANONICAL VARIABLES			THE OPPOSITE CANONICAL VARIABLES	
	PROPORTION	CUMULATIVE PROPORTION	CANONICAL R-SQUARED	PROPORTION	CUMULATIVE PROPORTION
1	0.4111	0.4111	0.6330	0.2602	0.2602
2	0.5635	0.9746	0.0402	0.0227	0.2829
3	0.0254	1.0000	0.0053	0.0001	0.2830

STANDARDIZED VARIANCE OF THE PHYSIOLOGICAL MEASUREMENTS
EXPLAINED BY

	THEIR OWN CANONICAL VARIABLES			THE OPPOSITE CANONICAL VARIABLES	
	PROPORTION	CUMULATIVE PROPORTION	CANONICAL R-SQUARED	PROPORTION	CUMULATIVE PROPORTION
1	0.4508	0.4508	0.6330	0.2854	0.2854
2	0.2470	0.6978	0.0402	0.0099	0.2953
3	0.3022	1.0000	0.0053	0.0016	0.2969

STANDARDIZED VARIANCE OF THE EXERCISES
EXPLAINED BY

	THEIR OWN CANONICAL VARIABLES			THE OPPOSITE CANONICAL VARIABLES	
	PROPORTION	CUMULATIVE PROPORTION	CANONICAL R-SQUARED	PROPORTION	CUMULATIVE PROPORTION
1	0.4081	0.4081	0.6330	0.2584	0.2584
2	0.4345	0.8426	0.0402	0.0175	0.2758
3	0.1574	1.0000	0.0053	0.0008	0.2767

MIDDLE-AGE MEN IN A HEALTH FITNESS CLUB 11
DATA COURTESY OF DR. A. C. LINNERUD, NC STATE UNIV

CANONICAL REDUNDANCY ANALYSIS

SQUARED MULTIPLE CORRELATIONS BETWEEN THE PHYSIOLOGICAL MEASUREMENTS
AND THE FIRST 'M' CANONICAL VARIABLES OF THE EXERCISES

M	1	2	3
WEIGHT	0.2438	0.2678	0.2679
WAIST	0.5421	0.5478	0.5478
PULSE	0.0701	0.0702	0.0749

SQUARED MULTIPLE CORRELATIONS BETWEEN THE EXERCISES AND THE FIRST
'M' CANONICAL VARIABLES OF THE PHYSIOLOGICAL MEASUREMENTS

M	1	2	3
CHINS	0.3351	0.3374	0.3396
SITUPS	0.4233	0.4365	0.4365
JUMPS	0.0167	0.0536	0.0539

Interpretation

The correlations between the physiological and exercise variables are moderate, the largest being −.6456 between WAIST and SITUPS. There are larger within-set correlations: 0.8702 between WEIGHT and WAIST, 0.6957 between CHINS and SITUPS, and 0.6692 between SITUPS and JUMPS.

The first canonical correlation is 0.7956, which would appear to be substantially larger than any of the between-set correlations. The probability level for the null hypothesis that all the canonical correlations are 0 in the population is only .0635, so no firm conclusions can be drawn. The remaining canonical correlations are not worthy of consideration, as can be seen from the probability levels and especially from the negative adjusted canonical correlations.

Because the variables are not measured in the same units, the standardized coefficients rather than the raw coefficients should be interpreted. The correlations given in the canonical structure matrices should also be examined.

The first canonical variable for the physiological variables is a weighted difference of WAIST (1.5793) and WEIGHT (-.07754), with more emphasis on WAIST. The coefficient for PULSE is near 0. The correlations between WAIST and WEIGHT and the first canonical variable are both positive, 0.9254 for WAIST and 0.6206 for WEIGHT. WEIGHT is therefore a suppressor variable, meaning that its coefficient and its correlation have opposite signs.

The first canonical variable for the exercise variables also shows a mixture of signs, subtracting SITUPS (-1.0540) and CHINS (-0.3495) from JUMPS (0.7164), with the most weight on SITUPS. All the correlations are negative, indicating that JUMPS is also a suppressor variable.

It may seem contradictory that a variable should have a coefficient of opposite sign from that of its correlation with the canonical variable. In order to explain how this can happen, consider a simplified situation: predicting SITUPS from WAIST and WEIGHT by multiple regression. In informal terms, it seems plausible that fat people should do fewer situps than skinny people. Assume that the men in the sample do not vary much in height, so there is a strong correlation between WAIST and WEIGHT (0.8702). Examine the relationships between fatness and the independent variables:

- People with large WAISTs tend to be fatter than people with small WAISTs. Hence the correlation between WAIST and SITUPS should be negative.
- People with high WEIGHTs tend to be fatter than people with low WEIGHTs. Therefore WEIGHT should correlate negatively with SITUPS.
- For a fixed value of WEIGHT, people with large WAISTs tend to be shorter and fatter. Thus the multiple regression coefficient for WAIST should be negative.
- For a fixed value of WAIST, people with higher WEIGHTS tend to be taller and skinnier. The multiple regression coefficient for WEIGHT should therefore be positive, of opposite sign from the correlation between WEIGHT and SITUPS.

The general interpretation of the first canonical correlation is therefore that WEIGHT and JUMPS act as suppressor variables to enhance the correlation between WAIST and SITUPS. This canonical correlation may be strong enough to be of practical interest, but the sample size is not large enough to draw definite conclusions.

The canonical redundancy analysis shows that neither of the first pair of canonical variables is a good overall predictor of the opposite set of variables, the proportions of variance explained being 0.2854 and 0.2584. The second and third canonical variables add virtually nothing, with cumulative proportions for all three canonical variables being 0.2969 and 0.2767. The squared multiple correlations indicate that the first canonical variable of the physiological measurements has some predictive power for CHINS (0.3351) and SITUPS (0.4233) but almost none for JUMPS (0.0167). The first canonical variable of the exercises is a fairly good predictor of WAIST (0.5421), a poorer predictor of WEIGHT (0.2438), and nearly useless for predicting PULSE (0.0701).

REFERENCES

Cooley, W.W. and Lohnes, P.R. (1971), *Multivariate Data Analysis*, New York: John Wiley & Sons.

Fisher, R.A. (1938), *Statistical Methods for Research Workers*, Tenth Edition, Edinburgh: Oliver & Boyd.

Hanson, R.J. and Norris, M.J. (1981), "Analysis of Measurements Based on the Singular Value Decomposition," *SIAM Journal of Scientific and Statistical Computing*, 2, 363-373.

Hotelling, H. (1936), "Relations Between Two Sets of Variables," *Biometrika*, 28, 321-377.

Kshirsagar, A.M. (1972), *Multivariate Analysis*, New York: Marcel Dekker.

Lawley, D.N. (1959), "Tests of Significance in Canonical Analysis," *Biometrika*, 46, 59-66.

Mardia, K.V., Kent, J.T., and Bibby, J.M. (1979), *Multivariate Analysis*, London: Academic Press.

Mulaik, S.A. (1972), *The Foundations of Factor Analysis*, New York: McGraw-Hill Book Co.

Rao, C.R. (1964), "The Use and Interpretation of Principal Component Analysis in Applied Research," *Sankhya A*, 26, 329-358.

Rao, C.R. (1973), *Linear Statistical Inference*, New York: John Wiley & Sons.

Stewart, D.K. and Love, W.A. (1968), "A General Canonical Correlation Index," *Psychological Bulletin*, 70, 160-163.

Tatsuoka, M.M. (1971), *Multivariate Analysis*, New York: John Wiley & Sons.

Timm, N.H. (1975), *Multivariate Analysis*, Monterey, California: Brooks/Cole Publishing Co.

van den Wollenberg, A.L. (1977), "Redundancy Analysis—An Alternative to Canonical Correlation Analysis," *Psychometrika*, 42, 207-219.

Chapter 13
The CANDISC Procedure

Operating systems: All

ABSTRACT

The CANDISC procedure performs a canonical discriminant analysis, computes Mahalanobis distances, and does both univariate and multivariate one-way analyses of variance. Output data sets containing canonical coefficients and scores on the canonical variables can be created.

INTRODUCTION

Canonical discriminant analysis is a dimension-reduction technique related to principal component analysis and canonical correlation. Given a classification variable and several quantitative variables, CANDISC derives *canonical variables* (linear combinations of the quantitative variables) that summarize between-class variation in much the same way that principal components summarize total variation.

For each canonical correlation CANDISC tests the hypothesis that it and all smaller canonical correlations are zero in the population. An F approximation (Rao 1973; Kshirsagar 1972) is used that gives better small sample results than the usual chi-squared approximation. The variables should have an approximate multivariate normal distribution within each class with a common covariance matrix in order for the probability levels to be valid.

Both standardized and unstandardized canonical coefficients are printed, as well as the correlations between canonical variables and the original variables, and the means of each class on the canonical variables.

CANDISC performs univariate and multivariate one-way analyses of variance and computes and tests Mahalanobis distances for pairwise comparisons of the classes.

The procedure can produce an output data set containing the scores on each canonical variable. You can use the PRINT procedure to list these values and the PLOT procedure to plot pairs of canonical variables to aid visual interpretation of group differences. A second output data set contains canonical coefficients that can be rotated by the FACTOR procedure.

Background

Given two or more groups of observations with measurements on several quantitative variables, canonical discriminant analysis derives a linear combination of the variables that has the highest possible multiple correlation with the groups. This maximal multiple correlation is called the *first canonical correlation*. The coefficients of the linear combination are the *canonical coefficients* or *canonical weights*. The variable defined by the linear combination is the *first canonical variable* or *canonical component*. It is customary to normalize the canonical coefficients so that the pooled within-group variance of the canonical variable is one. Canonical variables are sometimes called *discriminant functions*, but this usage is ambiguous since DISCRIM produces very different functions for classification that are also called discriminant functions.

The second canonical correlation is obtained by finding the linear combination uncorrelated with the first canonical variable that has the highest possible multiple correlation with the groups. The process of extracting canonical variables can be repeated until the number of canonical variables equals the number of original variables or the number of classes minus one, whichever is smaller.

The first canonical correlation is at least as large as the multiple correlation between the groups and any of the original variables. If the original variables have low within-group correlations, then the first canonical correlation is not much greater than the largest multiple correlation. If the original variables have high within-group correlations, the first canonical correlation can be large even if all the multiple correlations are small. In other words, the first canonical variable can show substantial differences among the classes even if none of the original variables do.

Canonical discriminant analysis is equivalent to canonical correlation analysis between the quantitative variables and a set of dummy variables coded from the class variable. Canonical discriminant analysis is also equivalent to performing the following steps:

- Transform the variables so that the pooled within-class covariance matrix is an identity matrix.
- Compute class means on the transformed variables.
- Do a principal component analysis on the means, weighting each mean by the number of observations in the class. The eigenvalues are equal to the ratio of between-class variation to within-class variation in the direction of each principal component.
- Back-transform the principal components into the space of the original variables, obtaining the canonical variables.

An interesting property of the canonical variables is that they are uncorrelated whether the correlation is calculated from the total sample or from the pooled within-class correlations. The canonical coefficients are not orthogonal, however, so the canonical variables do not represent perpendicular directions through the space of the original variables.

SPECIFICATIONS

The CANDISC procedure is invoked by the following statements:

PROC CANDISC *options;*
VAR *variables;*
CLASS *variable;*
PROB *variables;*
FREQ *variable;*
WEIGHT *variable;*
BY *variables;*

Either the CLASS statement or the PROB statement must be specified, but not both.

PROC CANDISC Statement

PROC CANDISC *options;*

The following options can appear in the PROC statement:

DATA=*SASdataset*
names the data set to be analyzed. The data set can be an ordinary SAS data set, or a TYPE=CORR or TYPE=COV data set produced by either the CORR procedure using a BY statement, or a previous run of CANDISC using the OUTSTAT= option. If DATA= is omitted, the most recently created SAS data set is used.

OUT=*SASdataset*
names an output SAS data set containing the original data and the canonical variable scores. If you want to create a permanent SAS data set, you must specify a two-level name (see "SAS Files" in *SAS User's Guide: Basics* for more information on permanent SAS data sets).

OUTSTAT=*SASdataset*
names an output SAS data set that contains various statistics including class means, pooled standard deviations, correlation and covariance matrices for both the total sample and pooled within-classes, and canonical correlations, coefficients, and means. Use a two-level name if you want to create a permanent data set (see "SAS Files" in the *SAS User's Guide: Basics* for more information on permanent SAS data sets).

NCAN=*n*
specifies the number of canonical variables to be computed. The default is the number of variables. If NCAN=0 is specified, the procedure prints the canonical correlations, but not the canonical coefficients, structures, or means. A negative value suppresses the canonical analysis entirely.

PREFIX=*name*
specifies a prefix for naming the canonical variables. By default the names are CAN1, CAN2,...,CAN*n*. If PREFIX=ABC is specified, the components are named ABC1, ABC2, ABC3, and so on. The number

of characters in the prefix plus the number of digits required to designate the canonical variables should not exceed eight. The prefix will be truncated if the combined length exceeds eight.

UNIVARIATE
UNI

prints univariate statistics including means, standard deviations, R^2s, and F statistics and probability levels for analyses of variance.

STDMEAN

prints standardized means.

TCORR

prints total-sample correlations.

WCORR

prints pooled within-class correlations.

BCORR

prints between-class correlations.

TCOV

prints total-sample covariances.

WCOV

prints pooled within-class covariances.

BCOV

prints between-class covariances.

TSSCP

prints the total-sample SSCP matrix.

WSSCP

prints the pooled within-class SSCP matrix.

BSSCP

prints the between-class SSCP matrix.

MAHALANOBIS
MAH

prints Mahalanobis distances between classes.

ALL

prints everything.

SHORT

suppresses all default output except the tables of canonical correlations and multivariate test statistics.

NOPRINT

suppresses the printout.

SINGULAR=*p*
SING=*p*

specifies the criterion for determining the singularity of the total correlation matrix, where $0<p<1$. If the R^2 for predicting a quantitative variable from the variables preceding it in the VAR statement exceeds $1-p$, that variable is dropped from the canonical analysis. The default is SINGULAR=1E−8.

EDF=*n*

specifies the error degrees of freedom from the regression analysis if your input observations are residuals from a regression analysis. The effective number of observations is the EDF= value plus one. Thus, if you have 100 observations, specifying EDF=99 has the same effect as omitting EDF=.

RDF=*n*

specifies the regression degrees of freedom if your input observations are residuals from a regression analysis. The effective number of observations is the actual number minus the RDF= value. The degree of freedom for the intercept should not be included in RDF=.

VAR Statement

VAR *variables;*

The VAR statement lists the numeric variables to be analyzed. If the VAR statement is omitted, all numeric variables not specified in any other statements are used.

CLASS Statement

CLASS *variable;*

The CLASS statement specifies the name of a variable, either character or numeric, that defines the classes to be analyzed. Class levels are determined by the formatted values of the class variable. You **must** include either a CLASS statement or a PROB statement.

PROB Statement

PROB *variables;*

A PROB statement can be used instead of a CLASS statement. Each variable in the PROB statement defines a class. The variables must be numeric, with values summing to one for each observation. There are at least two situations in which the PROB statement can be used:

- when some observations are repeated many times. The FREQ variable (see below) gives the total number of times each observation occurs, while the PROB statement gives the proportion belonging to each class.
- when you do not know with certainty the class to which each observation belongs. The PROB variables give the probabilities of the observations coming from each class. The standard errors and significance levels printed by CANDISC are not valid in this case.

FREQ Statement

FREQ *variable;*

If a variable in your data set represents the frequency of occurrence for the other values in the observation, include the variable's name in a FREQ statement. The procedure then treats the data set as if each observation appears *n* times, where *n* is the value of the FREQ variable for the observation. The total number of observations is considered to be equal to the sum of the FREQ variable when the procedure determines degrees of freedom for significance probabilities.

The WEIGHT and FREQ statements have a similar effect, except in the calculation of degrees of freedom.

WEIGHT Statement

WEIGHT *variable;*

If you want to use relative weights for each observation in the input data set, place the weights in a variable in the data set and specify the name in a WEIGHT statement. This is often done when the variance associated with each observation is different and the values of the weight variable are proportional to the reciprocals of the variances.

BY Statement

BY *variables;*

A BY statement can be used with PROC CANDISC to obtain separate analyses on observations in groups defined by the BY variables. When a BY statement appears, the procedure expects the input data set to be sorted in order of the BY variables. If your input data set is not sorted in ascending order, use the SORT procedure with a similar BY statement to sort the data, or, if appropriate, use the BY statement options NOTSORTED or DESCENDING. For more information, see the discussion of the BY statement in "Statements Used in the PROC Step" in the *SAS User's Guide: Basics.*

DETAILS

Missing Values

If an observation has a missing value for any of the continuous variables, it is omitted from the analysis. If an observation has a missing CLASS value but is otherwise complete, it is not used in computing the canonical correlations and coefficients; but canonical variable scores are computed for the OUT= data set.

Output Data Sets

OUT= data set The OUT= data set contains all the variables in the original data set plus new variables containing the canonical variable scores. The NCAN= option determines the number of new variables. The names of the new variables are formed as described in the PREFIX= option. The new variables have mean 0 and pooled within-class variance equal to 1.

An OUT= data set cannot be created if the DATA= data set is TYPE=CORR or TYPE=COV.

OUTSTAT= data set The OUTSTAT= data set is similar to the TYPE=CORR data set produced by the CORR procedure but contains many results in addition to those produced by CORR.

The OUTSTAT= data set contains the following variables:

- the BY variables, if any
- the CLASS variable if a CLASS statement was used, or a new variable called _CLASS_ if a PROB statement was used
- two new character variables, _TYPE_ and _NAME_
- the quantitative variables, that is, those in the VAR statement, or, if there is no VAR statement, all numeric variables not listed in any other statement.

Each observation in the new data set contains some type of statistic as indicated by the _TYPE_ variable. The values of the _TYPE_ variable are as follows:

TYPE	**Contents**
SSCP	total-sample SSCP matrix
BSSCP	between-class SSCP matrix
WSSCP	pooled within-class SSCP matrix

COV	total-sample covariance matrix
BCOV	between-class covariance matrix
WCOV	pooled within-class covariance matrix
CORR	total-sample correlation matrix
BCORR	between-class correlation matrix
WCORR	pooled within-class correlation matrix
MEAN	means for both the total sample (CLASS variable missing) and each class (CLASS variable present)
STD	total-sample standard deviations
BSTD	between-class standard deviations
WSTD	pooled within-class standard deviations
RSQUARED	univariate R^2s
N	number of observations in the total sample (CLASS variable missing) and within each class (CLASS variable present)
TSTDMEAN	total-standardized class means
WSTDMEAN	within-standardized class means
CANCORR	canonical correlations
STRUCTUR	canonical structure
SCORE	standardized canonical coefficients
RAWSCORE	raw canonical coefficients
CANMEAN	means of the canonical variables for each class.

Computational Resources

Let:

n = number of observations
v = number of variables
c = number of classes.

The time required to compute correlation/covariance matrices is roughly proportional to $(n+c)v^2$.

The time required to compute Mahalanobis distances is roughly proportional to cv^2.

The time required for the canonical analysis is roughly proportional to v^3.

Printed Output

If the UNIVARIATE option is specified, the following statistics are printed:

1. MEANS for the total sample
2. TOTAL STD, total-sample standard deviations
3. WITHIN STD, pooled within-class standard deviations
4. BETWEEN STD, between-class standard deviations
5. R-SQUARED, univariate R^2s
6. RSQ/(1-RSQ), $R^2/(1-R^2)$
7. univariate F values and PROB GT F, probability levels, for one-way analyses of variance
8. CLASS MEANS.

If requested, the following statistics are printed:

9. TOTAL-STANDARDIZED CLASS MEANS.
10. WITHIN-STANDARDIZED CLASS MEANS.
11. TOTAL-SAMPLE SSCP MATRIX.
12. BETWEEN-CLASS SSCP MATRIX.
13. POOLED WITHIN-CLASS SSCP MATRIX.
14. TOTAL SAMPLE COVARIANCE MATRIX, equal to the total-sample SSCP matrix divided by the corrected total degrees of freedom.
15. BETWEEN-CLASS COVARIANCE MATRIX, equal to the between-class SSCP matrix divided by *n*(c-1)/c, where *n* is the number of observations and c is the number of classes. The between-class covariances should be interpreted descriptively in comparison with the total-sample and within-class covariances, not as formal estimates of population parameters, which would depend on the sampling method.
16. POOLED WITHIN-CLASS COVARIANCE MATRIX, equal to the within-class SSCP matrix divided by the within-class degrees of freedom.
17. TOTAL-SAMPLE CORRELATION MATRIX.
18. BETWEEN-CLASS CORRELATION MATRIX.
19. POOLED WITHIN-CLASS CORRELATION MATRIX.
20. MAHALANOBIS DISTANCES BETWEEN CLASSES and PROB > MAHALANOBIS DISTANCE. If the ALL option is specified, a matrix of F statistics, based on Mahalanobis distance between classes, is printed.

By default, the printout contains these statistics:

21. CANONICAL CORRELATIONS.
22. ADJUSTED CANCORR, adjusted canonical correlations (Lawley 1959). These are asymptotically less biased than the raw correlations and can be negative. The adjusted canonical correlations may not be computable and are printed as missing values if two canonical correlations are nearly equal or if some are close to zero. A missing value is also printed if an adjusted canonical correlation is larger than a previous adjusted canonical correlation.
23. APPROX STD ERROR, approximate standard error of the canonical correlations.
24. a table of EIGENVALUES OF INV(E)*H. Each eigenvalue is equal to CANRSQ/(1-CANRSQ), where CANRSQ represents the corresponding squared canonical correlation, and can be interpreted as the ratio of between-class variation to within-class variation for the corresponding canonical variable. The table includes EIGENVALUES, DIFFERENCEs between successive eigenvalues, the PROPORTION of the sum of the eigenvalues, and the CUMULATIVE proportion.
25. CANONICAL R-SQUARED, the squared canonical correlations.
26. LIKELIHOOD RATIO for the hypothesis that the current canonical correlation and all smaller ones are zero in the population. The likelihood ratio for all canonical correlations equals Wilks' lambda.
27. F STATISTIC based on Rao's approximation to the distribution of the likelihood ratio (Rao 1973, p. 556; Kshirsagar 1972, p. 326).
28. NUM DF (numerator degrees of freedom), DEN DF (denominator degrees of freedom), and PROB>F, the probability level associated with the F statistic.
29. WILKS' LAMBDA, PILLAI'S TRACE, HOTELLING-LAWLEY TRACE, and ROY'S GREATEST ROOT with F approximations, degrees of freedom (NUM DF and DEN DF), and probability values (PROB>F). Each of

these four multivariate statistics tests the hypothesis that the class means are equal in the population. See **Multivariate Tests** in "SAS Regression Procedures" for more information.

The following statistics can be suppressed by the SHORT option:

30. TOTAL CANONICAL STRUCTURE giving total-sample correlations between the canonical variables and the original variables
31. BETWEEN CANONICAL STRUCTURE giving between-class correlations between the canonical variables and the original variables
32. WITHIN CANONICAL STRUCTURE giving within-class correlations between the canonical variables and the original variables
33. STANDARDIZED CANONICAL COEFFICIENTS normalized to give canonical variables with unit within-class variance when applied to the standardized variables
34. RAW (unstandardized) CANONICAL COEFFICIENTS normalized to give canonical variables with unit within-class variance when applied to the raw variables
35. CLASS MEANS ON CANONICAL VARIABLES.

EXAMPLE

Analysis of Iris Data Using PROC CANDISC

The iris data published by Fisher (1936) have been widely used for examples in discriminant analysis and cluster analysis. The sepal length, sepal width, petal length, and petal width were measured in millimeters on 50 iris specimens from each of three species, *Iris setosa, I. versicolor,* and *I. virginica*. The following example is a canonical discriminant analysis, creating an output data set containing scores on the canonical variables, and plotting the canonical variables.

```
DATA IRIS;
   TITLE 'FISHER (1936) IRIS DATA';
   INPUT SEPALLEN SEPALWID PETALLEN PETALWID SPEC_NO @@;
   IF SPEC_NO=1 THEN SPECIES='SETOSA    ';
   IF SPEC_NO=2 THEN SPECIES='VERSICOLOR';
   IF SPEC_NO=3 THEN SPECIES='VIRGINICA ';
   LABEL SEPALLEN='SEPAL LENGTH IN MM.'
         SEPALWID='SEPAL WIDTH  IN MM.'
         PETALLEN='PETAL LENGTH IN MM.'
         PETALWID='PETAL WIDTH  IN MM.';
   CARDS;
50 33 14 02 1 64 28 56 22 3 65 28 46 15 2
67 31 56 24 3 63 28 51 15 3 46 34 14 03 1
69 31 51 23 3 62 22 45 15 2 59 32 48 18 2
46 36 10 02 1 61 30 46 14 2 60 27 51 16 2
65 30 52 20 3 56 25 39 11 2 65 30 55 18 3
58 27 51 19 3 68 32 59 23 3 51 33 17 05 1
57 28 45 13 2 62 34 54 23 3 77 38 67 22 3
63 33 47 16 2 67 33 57 25 3 76 30 66 21 3
49 25 45 17 3 55 35 13 02 1 67 30 52 23 3
70 32 47 14 2 64 32 45 15 2 61 28 40 13 2
48 31 16 02 1 59 30 51 18 3 55 24 38 11 2
63 25 50 19 3 64 32 53 23 3 52 34 14 02 1
```

```
 49 36 14 01 1 54 30 45 15 2 79 38 64 20 3
 44 32 13 02 1 67 33 57 21 3 50 35 16 06 1
 58 26 40 12 2 44 30 13 02 1 77 28 67 20 3
 63 27 49 18 3 47 32 16 02 1 55 26 44 12 2
 50 23 33 10 2 72 32 60 18 3 48 30 14 03 1
 51 38 16 02 1 61 30 49 18 3 48 34 19 02 1
 50 30 16 02 1 50 32 12 02 1 61 26 56 14 3
 64 28 56 21 3 43 30 11 01 1 58 40 12 02 1
 51 38 19 04 1 67 31 44 14 2 62 28 48 18 3
 49 30 14 02 1 51 35 14 02 1 56 30 45 15 2
 58 27 41 10 2 50 34 16 04 1 46 32 14 02 1
 60 29 45 15 2 57 26 35 10 2 57 44 15 04 1
 50 36 14 02 1 77 30 61 23 3 63 34 56 24 3
 58 27 51 19 3 57 29 42 13 2 72 30 58 16 3
 54 34 15 04 1 52 41 15 01 1 71 30 59 21 3
 64 31 55 18 3 60 30 48 18 3 63 29 56 18 3
 49 24 33 10 2 56 27 42 13 2 57 30 42 12 2
 55 42 14 02 1 49 31 15 02 1 77 26 69 23 3
 60 22 50 15 3 54 39 17 04 1 66 29 46 13 2
 52 27 39 14 2 60 34 45 16 2 50 34 15 02 1
 44 29 14 02 1 50 20 35 10 2 55 24 37 10 2
 58 27 39 12 2 47 32 13 02 1 46 31 15 02 1
 69 32 57 23 3 62 29 43 13 2 74 28 61 19 3
 59 30 42 15 2 51 34 15 02 1 50 35 13 03 1
 56 28 49 20 3 60 22 40 10 2 73 29 63 18 3
 67 25 58 18 3 49 31 15 01 1 67 31 47 15 2
 63 23 44 13 2 54 37 15 02 1 56 30 41 13 2
 63 25 49 15 2 61 28 47 12 2 64 29 43 13 2
 51 25 30 11 2 57 28 41 13 2 65 30 58 22 3
 69 31 54 21 3 54 39 13 04 1 51 35 14 03 1
 72 36 61 25 3 65 32 51 20 3 61 29 47 14 2
 56 29 36 13 2 69 31 49 15 2 64 27 53 19 3
 68 30 55 21 3 55 25 40 13 2 48 34 16 02 1
 48 30 14 01 1 45 23 13 03 1 57 25 50 20 3
 57 38 17 03 1 51 38 15 03 1 55 23 40 13 2
 66 30 44 14 2 68 28 48 14 2 54 34 17 02 1
 51 37 15 04 1 52 35 15 02 1 58 28 51 24 3
 67 30 50 17 2 63 33 60 25 3 53 37 15 02 1
;
PROC CANDISC ALL OUT=DISC;
   CLASSES SPECIES;
   VAR SEPALLEN SEPALWID PETALLEN PETALWID;
PROC PLOT;
   PLOT CAN2*CAN1=SPEC_NO;
   TITLE2 'PLOT OF CANONICAL DISCRIMINANT FUNCTIONS';
```

Output 13.1 Iris Data: PROC CANDISC

FISHER (1936) IRIS DATA 1

CANONICAL DISCRIMINANT ANALYSIS

150 OBSERVATIONS	149 DF TOTAL
4 VARIABLES	147 DF WITHIN CLASSES
3 CLASSES	2 DF BETWEEN CLASSES

SPECIES	FREQUENCY	WEIGHT	PROPORTION
SETOSA	50	50	0.333333
VERSICOLOR	50	50	0.333333
VIRGINICA	50	50	0.333333

[11] TOTAL-SAMPLE SSCP MATRIX

VARIABLE	SEPALLEN	SEPALWID	PETALLEN	PETALWID
SEPALLEN	10216.83	-632.267	18987.3	7692.433
SEPALWID	-632.267	2830.693	-4911.88	-1812.43
PETALLEN	18987.3	-4911.88	46432.54	19304.58
PETALWID	7692.433	-1812.43	19304.58	8656.993

[12] BETWEEN-CLASS SSCP MATRIX

VARIABLE	SEPALLEN	SEPALWID	PETALLEN	PETALWID
SEPALLEN	6321.213	-1995.27	16524.84	7127.933
SEPALWID	-1995.27	1134.493	-5723.96	-2293.27
PETALLEN	16524.84	-5723.96	43710.28	18677.4
PETALWID	7127.933	-2293.27	18677.4	8041.333

[13] POOLED WITHIN-CLASS SSCP MATRIX

VARIABLE	SEPALLEN	SEPALWID	PETALLEN	PETALWID
SEPALLEN	3895.62	1363	2462.46	564.5
SEPALWID	1363	1696.2	812.08	480.84
PETALLEN	2462.46	812.08	2722.26	627.18
PETALWID	564.5	480.84	627.18	615.66

UNIVARIATE STATISTICS

VARIABLE	[1] MEAN	[2] TOTAL STD	[3] WITHIN STD	[4] BETWEEN STD	[5] R-SQUARED	[6] RSQ/(1-RSQ)	F	[7] PROB > F
SEPALLEN	58.43333333	8.28066128	5.14789436	7.95060585	0.618706	1.623	119.265	0.0001
SEPALWID	30.57333333	4.35866285	3.39687732	3.36822406	0.400783	0.669	49.160	0.0001
PETALLEN	37.58000000	17.65298233	4.30334469	20.90700361	0.941372	16.057	1180.161	0.0
PETALWID	11.99333333	7.62237669	2.04650025	8.96734818	0.928883	13.061	960.007	0.0

AVERAGE R-SQUARED: UNWEIGHTED = 0.7224358 WEIGHTED BY VARIANCE = 0.8689444

FISHER (1936) IRIS DATA 2

CANONICAL DISCRIMINANT ANALYSIS

[8] CLASS MEANS

SPECIES	SEPALLEN	SEPALWID	PETALLEN	PETALWID
SETOSA	50.06000000	34.28000000	14.62000000	2.46000000
VERSICOLOR	59.36000000	27.70000000	42.60000000	13.26000000
VIRGINICA	65.88000000	29.74000000	55.52000000	20.26000000

[9] TOTAL-STANDARDIZED CLASS MEANS

SPECIES	SEPALLEN	SEPALWID	PETALLEN	PETALWID
SETOSA	-1.0112	0.8504	-1.3006	-1.2507
VERSICOLOR	0.1119	-0.6592	0.2844	0.1662
VIRGINICA	0.8993	-0.1912	1.0163	1.0845

(continued on next page)

(continued from previous page)

⑩ WITHIN-STANDARDIZED CLASS MEANS

SPECIES	SEPALLEN	SEPALWID	PETALLEN	PETALWID
SETOSA	-1.6266	1.0912	-5.3354	-4.6584
VERSICOLOR	0.1800	-0.8459	1.1665	0.6189
VIRGINICA	1.4465	-0.2453	4.1689	4.0394

⑭ TOTAL-SAMPLE COVARIANCE MATRIX

VARIABLE	SEPALLEN	SEPALWID	PETALLEN	PETALWID
SEPALLEN	68.5693512	-4.2434004	127.4315436	51.6270694
SEPALWID	-4.2434004	18.9979418	-32.9656376	-12.1639374
PETALLEN	127.4315436	-32.9656376	311.6277852	129.5609396
PETALWID	51.6270694	-12.1639374	129.5609396	58.1006264

⑮ BETWEEN-CLASS COVARIANCE MATRIX

VARIABLE	SEPALLEN	SEPALWID	PETALLEN	PETALWID
SEPALLEN	63.2121333	-19.9526667	165.2484000	71.2793333
SEPALWID	-19.9526667	11.3449333	-57.2396000	-22.9326667
PETALLEN	165.2484000	-57.2396000	437.1028000	186.7740000
PETALWID	71.2793333	-22.9326667	186.7740000	80.4133333

FISHER (1936) IRIS DATA 3

CANONICAL DISCRIMINANT ANALYSIS

⑯ POOLED WITHIN-CLASS COVARIANCE MATRIX

VARIABLE	SEPALLEN	SEPALWID	PETALLEN	PETALWID
SEPALLEN	26.50081633	9.27210884	16.75142857	3.84013605
SEPALWID	9.27210884	11.53877551	5.52435374	3.27102041
PETALLEN	16.75142857	5.52435374	18.51877551	4.26653061
PETALWID	3.84013605	3.27102041	4.26653061	4.18816327

⑰ TOTAL-SAMPLE CORRELATION MATRIX

VARIABLE	SEPALLEN	SEPALWID	PETALLEN	PETALWID
SEPALLEN	1.0000	-0.1176	0.8718	0.8179
SEPALWID	-0.1176	1.0000	-0.4284	-0.3661
PETALLEN	0.8718	-0.4284	1.0000	0.9629
PETALWID	0.8179	-0.3661	0.9629	1.0000

⑱ BETWEEN-CLASS CORRELATION MATRIX

VARIABLE	SEPALLEN	SEPALWID	PETALLEN	PETALWID
SEPALLEN	1.0000	-0.7451	0.9941	0.9998
SEPALWID	-0.7451	1.0000	-0.8128	-0.7593
PETALLEN	0.9941	-0.8128	1.0000	0.9962
PETALWID	0.9998	-0.7593	0.9962	1.0000

⑲ POOLED WITHIN-CLASS CORRELATION MATRIX

VARIABLE	SEPALLEN	SEPALWID	PETALLEN	PETALWID
SEPALLEN	1.0000	0.5302	0.7562	0.3645
SEPALWID	0.5302	1.0000	0.3779	0.4705
PETALLEN	0.7562	0.3779	1.0000	0.4845
PETALWID	0.3645	0.4705	0.4845	1.0000

```
      (20)     MAHALANOBIS DISTANCES BETWEEN CLASSES

     SPECIES              SETOSA      VERSICOLOR        VIRGINICA

     SETOSA                  .           9.4797          13.3935
     VERSICOLOR           9.4797           .              4.1474
     VIRGINICA           13.3935         4.1474             .
```

```
                         FISHER (1936) IRIS DATA                                   4

                     CANONICAL DISCRIMINANT ANALYSIS

                       F STATISTICS, NDF=4 DDF=144

     SPECIES              SETOSA      VERSICOLOR        VIRGINICA

     SETOSA                  .          550.19           1098.27
     VERSICOLOR           550.19          .               105.31
     VIRGINICA           1098.27        105.31              .


                       PROB > MAHALANOBIS DISTANCE

     SPECIES              SETOSA      VERSICOLOR        VIRGINICA

     SETOSA                  .           0.0              0.0
     VERSICOLOR           0.0             .               0.0001
     VIRGINICA            0.0            0.0001             .
                 (22)          (23)        (25)           (24)       EIGENVALUES OF INV(E)*H
               ADJUSTED        APPROX      SQUARED                     = CANRSQ/(1-CANRSQ)
  (21) CANONICAL  CANONICAL   STANDARD    CANONICAL
   CORRELATION  CORRELATION    ERROR    CORRELATION  EIGENVALUE  DIFFERENCE  PROPORTION  CUMULATIVE

 1   0.984821     0.984508    0.002468    0.969872      32.1919     31.9065     0.9912      0.9912
 2   0.471197     0.461445    0.063734    0.222027       0.2854        .        0.0088      1.0000

   TESTS OF H0: THE CANONICAL CORRELATION IN THE CURRENT ROW AND ALL THAT FOLLOW ARE ZERO

               (26)   LIKELIHOOD       (27)                  (28)
                        RATIO            F        NUM DF     DEN DF  PR > F

                    1 0.02343863     199.1453        8         288  0.0
                    2 0.77797337      13.7939        3         145  0.0001

              (29)    MULTIVARIATE TEST STATISTICS AND F APPROXIMATIONS
                                  S=2    M=0.5    N=71.5

 STATISTIC                         VALUE             F          NUM DF        DEN DF      PR > F

 WILKS' LAMBDA                  0.02343863        199.145          8            288       0.0
 PILLAI'S TRACE                   1.191899         53.466          8            290       0.0001
 HOTELLING-LAWLEY TRACE           32.47732        580.532          8            286       0.0
 ROY'S GREATEST ROOT              32.19193       1166.957          4            145       0.0

           NOTE: F STATISTIC FOR ROY'S GREATEST ROOT IS AN UPPER BOUND
                     F STATISTIC FOR WILKS' LAMBDA IS EXACT
```

```
                         FISHER (1936) IRIS DATA                                   5

                     CANONICAL DISCRIMINANT ANALYSIS

                  (30)    TOTAL CANONICAL STRUCTURE

                                  CAN1          CAN2

                SEPALLEN         0.7919        0.2176
                SEPALWID        -0.5308        0.7580
                PETALLEN         0.9850        0.0460
                PETALWID         0.9728        0.2229


                 (31)    BETWEEN CANONICAL STRUCTURE

                                  CAN1          CAN2
```

(continued on next page)

(continued from previous page)

	CAN1	CAN2
SEPALLEN	0.9915	0.1303
SEPALWID	-0.8257	0.5642
PETALLEN	0.9998	0.0224
PETALWID	0.9940	0.1090

32 WITHIN CANONICAL STRUCTURE

	CAN1	CAN2
SEPALLEN	0.2226	0.3108
SEPALWID	-0.1190	0.8637
PETALLEN	0.7061	0.1677
PETALWID	0.6332	0.7372

33 STANDARDIZED CANONICAL COEFFICIENTS

	CAN1	CAN2
SEPALLEN	-0.6868	0.0200
SEPALWID	-0.6688	0.9434
PETALLEN	3.8858	-1.6451
PETALWID	2.1422	2.1641

34 RAW CANONICAL COEFFICIENTS

	CAN1	CAN2
SEPALLEN	-.0829377642	0.0024102149
SEPALWID	-.1534473068	0.2164521235
PETALLEN	0.2201211656	-.0931921210
PETALWID	0.2810460309	0.2839187853

FISHER (1936) IRIS DATA 6

35 CANONICAL DISCRIMINANT ANALYSIS

CLASS MEANS ON CANONICAL VARIABLES

SPECIES	CAN1	CAN2
SETOSA	-7.6076	0.2151
VERSICOLOR	1.8250	-0.7279
VIRGINICA	5.7826	0.5128

Output 13.2 Iris Data: PROC PLOT

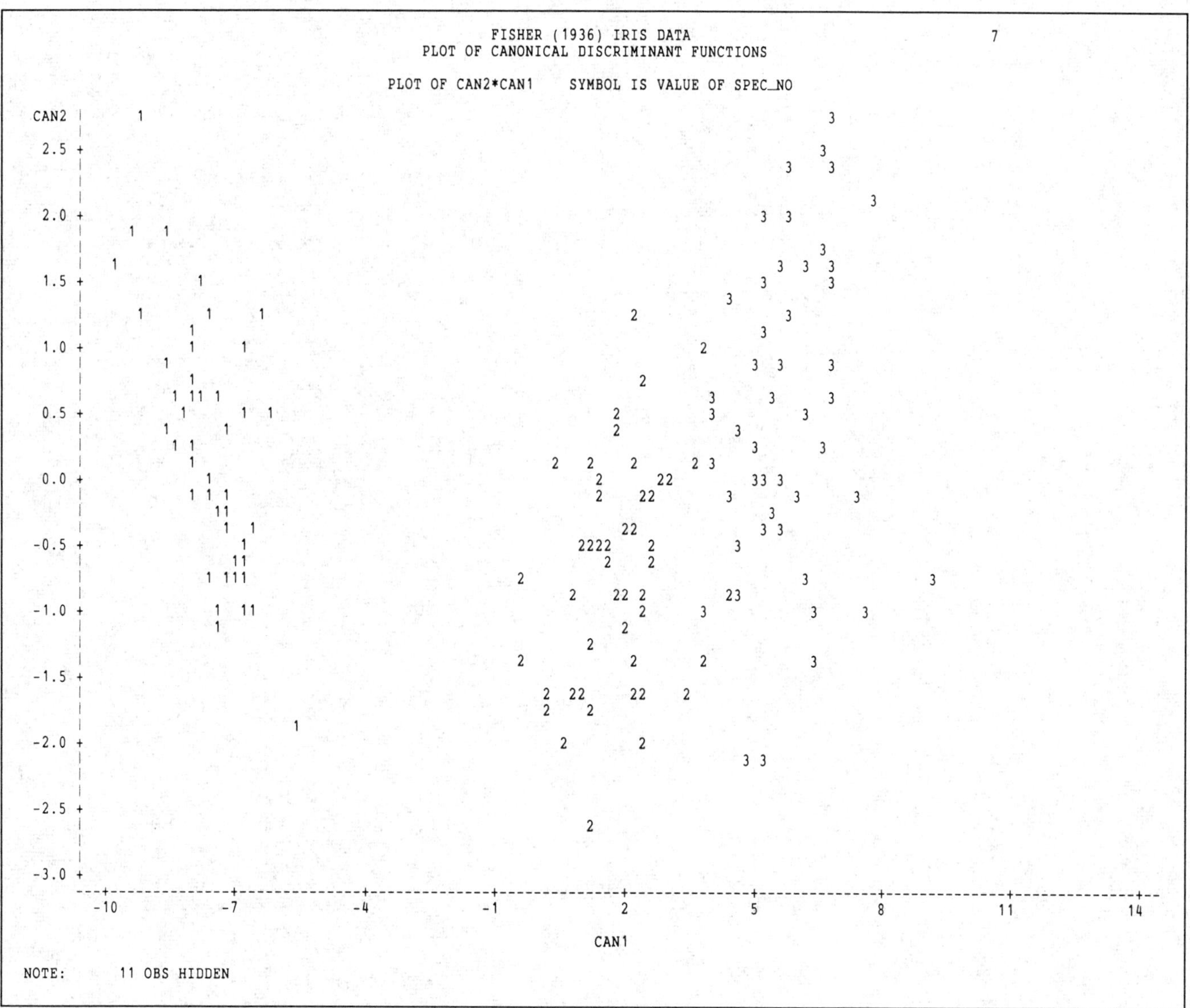

REFERENCES

Fisher, R.A. (1936), "The Use of Multiple Measurements in Taxonomic Problems," *Annals of Eugenics*, 7, 179-188.

Kshirsagar, A.M. (1972), *Multivariate Analysis*, New York: Marcel Dekker.

Lawley, D.N. (1959), "Tests of Significance in Canonical Analysis," *Biometrika*, 46, 59-66.

Rao, C.R. (1973), *Linear Statistical Inference*, New York: John Wiley & Sons.

Chapter 14
The CATMOD Procedure

Operating systems: All

ABSTRACT

CATMOD is a procedure for **CAT**egorical data **MOD**eling. It fits linear models to functions of response frequencies and can be used for linear modeling, log-linear modeling, logistic regression, and repeated measurement analysis. CATMOD uses

- maximum-likelihood estimation of parameters for log-linear models and the analysis of generalized logits
- weighted-least-squares estimation of parameters for a wide range of general linear models.

INTRODUCTION

CATMOD analyzes data that can be represented by a two-dimensional contingency table. The rows of the table correspond to populations (or samples) formed on the basis of one or more independent variables. The columns of the table correspond to observed responses formed on the basis of one or more dependent variables. The frequency in the (i,j)th cell is the number of subjects in the ith population that have the jth response. The frequencies in the table are assumed to follow a product multinomial distribution, corresponding to a sampling design in which a simple random sample is taken for each population. The contingency table can be represented as shown in **Table 14.1.**

Table 14.1 Contingency Table Representation

Sample	Response 1	2	...	r	
1	n_{11}	n_{12}	...	n_{1r}	n_1
2	n_{21}	n_{22}	...	n_{2r}	n_2
...	...	...	...	...	..
s	n_{s1}	n_{s2}	...	n_{sr}	n_s

For each sample *i*, the probability of the *j*th response (π_{ij}) is estimated by the sample proportion, $p_{ij}=n_{ij}/n_i$. The vector(**p**) of all such proportions is then transformed into a vector of functions, denoted by **F**=**F(p)**. If $\boldsymbol{\pi}$ denotes the vector of true probabilities for the entire table, then the functions of the true probabilities, denoted by **F(π)**, are assumed to follow a linear model:

$$\mathbf{E_A(F)} = \mathbf{F}(\boldsymbol{\pi}) = \mathbf{X}\boldsymbol{\beta}$$

where $\mathbf{E_A}$ denotes asymptotic expectation, **X** is the design matrix containing fixed constants, and $\boldsymbol{\beta}$ is a vector of parameters to be estimated.

CATMOD provides two estimation methods:

1. The maximum-likelihood method estimates the parameters of the linear model so as to maximize the value of the joint multinomial likelihood function of the responses. Maximum-likelihood estimation is available only for the standard log-linear response functions, which are used for logistic regression analysis and log-linear model analysis. For details of the theory, see Bishop, Fienberg, and Holland (1975).
2. The weighted-least-squares method minimizes the weighted residual sum of squares for the model. The weights are contained in the inverse covariance matrix of the functions **F(p)**. According to central limit theory, if the sample sizes are sufficiently large, the elements of **F** and **b** (the estimate of $\boldsymbol{\beta}$) are approximately distributed as multivariate normal. This allows the computation of statistics for testing the goodness of fit of the model and the significance of other sources of variation. For details of the theory, see Grizzle, Starmer, and Koch (1969), or Appendix 1 of Koch et al. (1977). Weighted-least-squares estimation is available for all types of response functions.

Following parameter estimation, hypotheses about linear combinations of the parameters can be tested. For that purpose, CATMOD computes generalized Wald (1943) statistics, which are approximately distributed as chi-square if the sample sizes are sufficiently large.

Linear Models Contrasted with Log-Linear Models

Linear model methods (as typified by the Grizzle, Starmer, Koch approach) make a very clear distinction between independent and dependent variables. The emphasis of these methods is estimation and hypothesis testing of the model parameters. Therefore, it is easy to test for differences among probabilities, perform repeated measurement analysis, and test for marginal homogeneity, but it is awkward to test independence and generalized independence. These methods are a natural extension of the usual ANOVA approach for continuous data.

In contrast, log-linear model methods (as typified by the Bishop, Fienberg, Holland approach) do not make an a priori distinction between independent and dependent variables, although model specifications that allow for the distinction can be made. The emphasis of these methods is on model building, goodness-of-fit tests, and estimation of cell frequencies or probabilities for the underlying contingency table. With these methods, it is easy to test independence and generalized independence, but it is awkward to test for differences among probabilities, do repeated measurement analysis, and test for marginal homogeneity.

Acknowledgments

CATMOD is similar in capabilities to the GENCAT program by Landis, Stanish, Freeman, and Koch (1976), but has been adapted to match the design syntax of ANOVA and GLM in the SAS System. CATMOD replaces the FUNCAT procedure that appeared in previous versions of the SAS System. The major enhancements contained in CATMOD are features that facilitate repeated measurement analysis and log-linear modeling. Moreover, there are numerous design features that make the CATMOD procedure more flexible and more informative.

SPECIFICATIONS

The following statements can be used with the CATMOD procedure:

PROC CATMOD *options;*
BY *variables;*
CONTRAST *'label' row_description, row_description, ...;*
DIRECT *variables;*
MODEL *response_effect = design_effects / options;*
POPULATION *variables;*
REPEATED *factor_description, ... / _RESPONSE_ = effects;*
RESPONSE *function options;*
WEIGHT *variable;*

The PROC and MODEL statements are required. If used, the DIRECT statement must precede the MODEL statement. Any number of RESPONSE and CONTRAST statements can be used. The CONTRAST statements, if any, must be preceded by the MODEL statement. The purpose of each statement, other than the PROC statement, can be summarized as follows:

BY	determines groups in which data are to be processed separately.
CONTRAST	specifies a hypothesis to test.
DIRECT	specifies independent variables containing design matrix values.
MODEL	determines the design matrix and the columns of the contingency table
POPULATION	determines the rows of the contingency table.
REPEATED	specifies the repeated measurement factors and helps to determine the design matrix.
RESPONSE	determines the functions that are to be modeled.
WEIGHT	specifies a variable containing frequency counts.

PROC CATMOD Statement

PROC CATMOD *options;*

This statement invokes the procedure. Two options are available:

DATA=*SASdataset* names the SAS data set containing the data to be analyzed. If DATA= is not given, CATMOD uses the most recently created SAS data set.

ORDER=DATA specifies that variable levels are to be ordered according to the sequence in which they appear in the input stream. This, in turn, affects the ordering of the populations, the responses, and the parameters, as well as the definitions of the parameters. If ORDER=DATA is not specified, then the variable levels are ordered according to their internal sorting sequence (for example, numeric order or alphabetical order). See the section **Ordering of Populations and Responses** for more information and examples.

BY Statement

BY *variables;*

A BY statement can be used with PROC CATMOD to obtain separate analyses of groups determined by the BY variables. When a BY statement appears, the procedure expects the input data set to be sorted in order of the BY variables. If your input data set is not sorted in ascending order, use the SORT procedure with a similar BY statement to sort the data, or, if appropriate, use the BY statement options NOTSORTED or DESCENDING. For more information, see the discussion of the BY statement in "SAS Statements Used in the PROC Step," in the *SAS User's Guide: Basics.*

CONTRAST Statement

CONTRAST *'label'* row_description, row_description, ...;

where

row_description = *@n effect values* ... *@n effect values*

The CONTRAST statement allows you to construct and test linear functions of the parameters. Each row_description specifies one row of the matrix **C**, which CATMOD uses to test the hypothesis $\mathbf{C\beta}=\mathbf{0}$. Row_descriptions are separated by a comma. The CONTRAST statements, if any, must be preceded by the MODEL statement. The following terms are specified with the CONTRAST statement:

'label' specifies up to twenty characters of identifying information printed with the test. *'label'* is required.

@n If the model type is not AVERAGED, (see the section **Generation of the Design Matrix**), then there is one set of parameters for each of the *q* response functions. The *@n* points to the parameters in the *n*th set. If *@n* is not given, @1 is assumed. If the model type is AVERAGED, then the *@n* notation is invalid.

effect is one of the effects listed in the MODEL statement. The effect labeled INTERCEPT can be specified for the intercept parameter. The effect labeled ALL_PARMS can be specified for the complete set of parameters.

values are numbers that form the coefficients of the parameters associated with the given effect. If there are fewer values than parameters for an effect, the remaining coefficients become zero.

CATMOD is parameterized differently than GLM, so you must be careful not to use the same contrasts that you would with GLM. Since CATMOD uses a full-rank parameterization, all estimable parameters are *directly* estimable without involving other parameters.

For example, suppose a class variable A has four levels. Then there are four parameters (α_1, α_2, α_3, α_4), of which CATMOD uses only the first three. The fourth parameter is related to the others by the equation

$$\alpha_4 = - \alpha_1 - \alpha_2 - \alpha_3$$

To test the first versus the fourth level of A, you would test $\alpha_1 = \alpha_4$, which is

$$\alpha_1 = - \alpha_1 - \alpha_2 - \alpha_3$$

or, equivalently,

$$2\alpha_1 + \alpha_2 + \alpha_3 = 0$$

Therefore, you would use the CONTRAST statement:

```
CONTRAST '1 VS. 4'  A  2  1  1;
```

To contrast the first 2 levels with the third, you would test

$$(\alpha_1 + \alpha_2)/2 = \alpha_3$$

or, equivalently,

$$\alpha_1 + \alpha_2 - 2\alpha_3 = 0$$

Therefore, you would use the CONTRAST statement:

```
CONTRAST '1&2 VS. 3'  A  1  1 -2;
```

Other contrast statements are constructed similarly, for example:

```
CONTRAST '1 VS. 2    '  A  1 -1  0 ;
CONTRAST '1&2 VS. 4  '  A  3  3  2 ;
CONTRAST '1&2 VS. 3&4'  A  2  2  0 ;

CONTRAST 'MAIN EFFECT'  A  1  0  0 ,
                        A  0  1  0 ,
                        A  0  0  1 ;
```

The actual form of the **C** matrix depends on the effects in the model. For example, if you specify

```
PROC CATMOD;
   MODEL Y = A;
   CONTRAST '1 VS. 4'  A  2  1  1;
```

then the **C** matrix is

$$C= \begin{bmatrix} 0 & 2 & 1 & 1 \end{bmatrix}$$

since the first parameter corresponds to the intercept. But if there is a variable B with three levels, and the MODEL statement is

```
MODEL Y = B A;
```

then the same CONTRAST statement induces the **C** matrix:

$$C= \begin{bmatrix} 0\,0\,0\,2\,1\,1 \end{bmatrix}$$

since the first parameter corresponds to the intercept, and the next two correspond to the B main effect.

The CONTRAST statement can also be used to test the joint effect of two or more effects in the MODEL statement. For example, the joint effect of A and B in the model given above has five degrees of freedom and is obtained by specifying:

```
CONTRAST 'JOINT EFFECT OF A&B'     A 1 0 0  ,
                                   A 0 1 0  ,
                                   A 0 0 1  ,
                                   B 1 0    ,
                                   B 0 1    ;
```

The ordering of variable levels is determined by the ORDER= option in the PROC CATMOD statement. Whenever you specify a contrast that depends on the order of the variable levels, you should verify the order from the POPULATION PROFILES, the RESPONSE PROFILES, or the ONEWAY table.

The *effect* in the CONTRAST statement can be replaced by the keyword ALL_PARMS, which is then regarded as an effect with the same number of parameters as the number of columns in the design matrix. This is particularly useful when the design matrix is input directly, as in the following example:

```
MODEL Y = ( 1 0 0 0 ,
            1 0 1 0 ,
            1 1 0 0 ,
            1 1 1 1 ) ;
CONTRAST 'MAIN EFFECT OF B' ALL_PARMS 0 1 0 0 ;
CONTRAST 'MAIN EFFECT OF C' ALL_PARMS 0 0 1 0 ;
CONTRAST 'B*C INTERACTION ' ALL_PARMS 0 0 0 1 ;
```

The @*n* notation is seldom needed. It allows you to test the variation that is due to differences among the levels of dependent variables or repeated measurement factors. However, it is usually easier to model and test such variation by using the _RESPONSE_ effect in the MODEL statement.

DIRECT Statement

DIRECT *variables*;

You can use the DIRECT statement to declare numeric variables to be treated in a quantitative, rather than qualitative, way. For example, if the variable X has five levels, and you specify

```
PROC CATMOD;
   DIRECT X;
   MODEL Y = X;
```

then the main effect X induces only one column in the design matrix, rather than four. The values inserted into the design matrix are the actual values of X.

The DIRECT statement is useful for logistic regression, which is described in the **Details** section. If used, the DIRECT statement must precede the MODEL statement.

MODEL Statement

MODEL *response_effect* = *design_effects* / *options*;

CATMOD requires one (and only one) MODEL statement.

The *response_effect* indicates the dependent variables that determine the response categories (the columns of the underlying contingency table). The *response_effect* is either a single variable or a crossed effect having two or more variables joined by asterisks (*).

The *design_effects* specify potential sources of variation (such as main effects and interactions) to be included in the model. Thus, they determine the number of model parameters, as well as the interpretation of such parameters. In addition, if there is no POPULATION statement, any variables contained in the specification of the *design_effects* are used by CATMOD to determine the populations (the rows of the underlying contingency table).

Design_effects can be any of those described in the section **Specification of Effects**, or they can be defined by specifying the actual design matrix, enclosed in parentheses. Also, the keyword _RESPONSE_ can be used in place of a variable name in the specification of *design_effects*, except that an effect cannot be nested within _RESPONSE_. For more information on the _RESPONSE_ effect, see the section **The _RESPONSE_ EFFECT**.

Some examples of MODEL statements are

`MODEL R = A B;`	main effects only
`MODEL R = A B A*B;`	main effects with interaction
`MODEL R = A B(A);`	nested effect
`MODEL R = A|B;`	complete factorial
`MODEL R = A B(A=1) B(A=2);`	nested-by-value effects
`MODEL R*S = _RESPONSE_;`	log-linear model
`MODEL R*S = A _RESPONSE_(A);`	nested repeated measurement factor

The relationship between these specifications and the structure of the design matrix **X** is described in the section **Generation of the Design Matrix**.

If you specify the design matrix directly, adjacent rows of the matrix must be separated by a comma, and the matrix must have *q**s* rows, where *s* is the number of populations, and *q* is the number of response functions per population. The first *q* rows correspond to the response functions for the first population, the second set of *q* rows corresponds to the functions for the second population, and so forth. An example of a MODEL statement using direct specification of the design matrix is

```
MODEL R = ( 1 0 ,
            1 1 ,
            1 2 ,
            1 3 ) ;
```

When you input the design matrix directly, you also have the option of specifying that any subsets of the parameters be tested for equality to zero. You indicate each subset by specifying the appropriate column numbers of the design matrix, followed by an equal sign and a label (24 characters or less, in single quotes) that describes the subset. Adjacent subsets are separated by a comma, and the entire specification is enclosed in parentheses and placed after the design matrix. An example of a MODEL statement using this option is

```
MODEL R = ( 1    1  0  0  ,
            1    1  0  1  ,
            1    1  0  2  ,
            1    0  1  0  ,
            1    0  1  1  ,
            1    0  1  2  ,
            1   -1 -1  0  ,
            1   -1 -1  1  ,
            1   -1 -1  2  ) (  1='INTERCEPT',
                             2 3='GROUP MAIN EFFECT',
                               4='LINEAR EFFECT OF TIME' );
```

If you input the design matrix directly, but do not specify any subsets of the parameters to be tested, then CATMOD tests the effect of MODEL|MEAN, which represents the significance of the model beyond what is explained by an overall mean. For the previous example, the MODEL|MEAN effect would be the same as that obtained by specifying

(2 3 4 = 'MODEL|MEAN')

at the end of the MODEL statement.

The options below can be specified in the MODEL statement after a slash (/).

Options to request additional computation and printing

ONEWAY produces a one-way table of frequencies for each variable used in the analysis. This table is useful in determining the order of the observed levels for each variable.

FREQ prints the two-way frequency table for the cross-classification of populations by responses.

PROB prints the two-way table of probability estimates for the cross-classification of populations by responses. These estimates add to 1 across the response categories for each population.

XPX prints $\mathbf{X'S^{-1}X}$, the cross-products matrix for the normal equations.

COV prints $\mathbf{S}_i$, the covariance matrix of the response functions for each population.

COVB prints the estimated covariance matrix of the parameter estimates.

CORRB prints the estimated correlation matrix of the parameter estimates.

ML requests maximum-likelihood estimates. This option is available only when the standard response functions are used.

PRED
PREDICT
PRED=FREQ
PRED=PROB prints the observed and predicted values of the response functions for each population, together with their standard errors and the residual (observed — predicted). In addition, if the response functions are the standard ones (generalized logits), then PRED=FREQ specifies the computation and printing of predicted cell frequencies, while PRED=PROB (or PREDICT) specifies the computation and printing of predicted cell probabilities.

Options to suppress computation and printing

NODESIGN suppresses printing of the design matrix **X**.

NOPARM suppresses printing of the estimated parameters and the statistics for testing that each parameter is zero.

NOPROFILE suppresses printing of the population profiles and the response profiles.

NOINT suppresses the intercept term in the model.

NOGLS suppresses the computation of the generalized (weighted) least-squares estimates. This is useful when only the maximum-likelihood estimates are needed. In that case, you must specify the ML option, and the ML parameter estimates start out at zero in the iterative estimation procedure. This option is particularly useful for logistic regression and for log-linear models in which random zeros have been replaced by some very small frequency (such as 1E-10).

Options to specify details of computation and printing

ADDCELL=*number* specifies that *number* be added to the frequency count in each cell, where *number* is any positive number. This option has no effect on maximum likelihood analysis; it is only used for weighted least-squares analysis.

AVERAGED specifies that dependent variable effects can be modeled, and that independent variable main effects are averaged across the response functions in a population. For further information on the effect of using (or not using) the AVERAGED option, see the section: **Generation of the Design Matrix**. Direct input of the design matrix or specification of _RESPONSE_ in the MODEL statement automatically induces an AVERAGED model type.

MAXITER=*number* specifies the maximum number of iterations to be used for the maximum likelihood estimation of the parameters. If MAXITER= is omitted, then MAXITER=20.

EPSILON=*number* specifies the convergence criterion for the maximum likelihood estimation of the parameters. The iterative estimation process stops when the proportional change in the log likelihood is less than EPSILON, or after MAXITER iterations, whichever comes first. If EPSILON= is omitted, then EPSILON=1E-8.

POPULATION Statement

POPULATION *variables;*

The POPULATION statement specifies that populations are to be formed on the basis of cross-classifications of the specified variables. If you do not specify the POPULATION statement, then populations are formed on the basis of cross-classifications of the independent variables in the MODEL statement. The statement has two major uses:

1. When the design matrix is input directly, there are no independent variables in the MODEL statement; therefore the POPULATION statement is the only way of inducing more than one population.
2. When you fit a reduced model, the POPULATION statement may be necessary if you want to induce the same number of populations as there were for the saturated model.

To illustrate the first use, suppose you specify the following statements:

```
DATA ONE;
   INPUT A $ B $ WT @@;
   CARDS;
YES YES 23   YES NO 31   NO YES 47   NO NO 50
PROC CATMOD;
   WEIGHT WT;
   POPULATION B;
   MODEL A = ( 1 0 ,
               1 1 ) ;
```

Since the dependent variable A has two levels, there is one response function per population. Since the variable B has two levels, there are two populations. Thus, the MODEL statement is valid since the number of rows in the design matrix (2) is the same as the total number of response functions. If the POPULATION statement had been omitted, there would have been only one population and one response function, and the MODEL statement would have been invalid.

To illustrate the second use, suppose you specify:

```
DATA TWO;
   INPUT A $ B $ Y WT @@;
   CARDS;
YES  YES  1  23      YES  YES  2  63
YES  NO   1  31      YES  NO   2  70
NO   YES  1  47      NO   YES  2  80
NO   NO   1  50      NO   NO   2  84
PROC CATMOD;
   WEIGHT WT;
   MODEL Y = A B A*B;
```

These statements induce four populations and the following design matrix and analysis-of-variance table.

$$X=\begin{bmatrix}1 & 1 & 1 & 1\\ 1 & 1 & -1 & -1\\ 1 & -1 & 1 & -1\\ 1 & -1 & -1 & 1\end{bmatrix}$$

EFFECT	DF	CHI-SQ	PROB
INTERCEPT	1	48.10	.0001
A	1	3.47	.0625
B	1	0.25	.6186
A*B	1	0.19	.6638
RESIDUAL	0	0.00	1.000

Since the B and A*B effects are nonsignificant (p>.10), you may want to fit the reduced model that contains only the A effect. If your new statements are

```
PROC CATMOD;
   WEIGHT WT;
   MODEL Y = A;
```

then only two populations are induced, and the design matrix and the analysis-of-variance table are as follows:

$$X=\begin{bmatrix}1 & 1\\ 1 & -1\end{bmatrix}$$

EFFECT	DF	CHI-SQ	PROB
INTERCEPT	1	47.94	.0001
A	1	3.33	.0678
RESIDUAL	0	0.00	1.000

However, if the new statements are

```
PROC CATMOD;
   WEIGHT WT;
   POPULATION A B;
   MODEL Y = A;
```

then four populations are induced, and the design matrix and the analysis-of-variance table are as follows:

$$X=\begin{bmatrix}1 & 1\\ 1 & 1\\ 1 & -1\\ 1 & -1\end{bmatrix}$$

EFFECT	DF	CHI-SQ	PROB
INTERCEPT	1	47.76	.0001
A	1	3.30	.0694
RESIDUAL	2	0.35	.8374

The resulting differences are due to the fact that the latter analysis uses pure weighted-least-squares estimates with respect to the four populations that were actually sampled. The former analysis pools populations and therefore uses parameter estimates that can be regarded as weighted-least-squares estimates of maximum-likelihood-predicted cell frequencies. In any case, the estimation methods are asymptotically equivalent; therefore, the results are very similar. If the ML option had been specified in the MODEL statement, then the parameter estimates would have been identical for the two analyses.

The advantage of the latter analysis is that it retains four populations for the reduced model, thereby creating a built-in goodness-of-fit test: the residual chi-square. Such a test is important because the cumulative (or joint) effect of deleting two or more effects from the model may be significant, even if the individual effects are not.

REPEATED Statement

REPEATED *factor_description, ...* / _RESPONSE_ = *effects* ;

where

factor_description = *factor_name* . *levels*

and *factor_descriptions* are separated from each other by a comma. *Factor_descriptions* are not allowed in the REPEATED statement if the response functions are the standard ones (generalized logits).

The REPEATED statement can be used whenever there is more than one dependent variable, and the keyword _RESPONSE_ is used in the MODEL statement. If the dependent variables correspond to one or more repeated measurement factors, you can use the REPEATED statement to specify the names of any such factors, as well as the number of levels in each factor. Furthermore, you can use the REPEATED statement to define _RESPONSE_ as one or more effects that are based on the dependent variables or on the repeated measurement factors.

factor_name
: gives the name of a repeated measurement factor that corresponds to two or more response functions. The *factor_name* should conform to naming conventions of SAS variables, and it should not be the same as the name of a variable that already exists in the data set being analyzed.

levels
: specifies the number of levels of the corresponding repeated measurement factor. If there is only one such factor, and the number is omitted, then CATMOD assumes that the number of levels is equal to the number of response functions per population *(q)*. The product of the number of levels of all the factors must either equal *q* or be a multiple of *q*.

RESPONSE = *effects*
: specifies crossed design effects (for example, A, A*B*C). If the response functions are the standard ones (generalized logits), then the variables named in the design effects must be dependent variables in the MODEL statement. For any other response functions, the variables named in the effects must be *factor_names* that appear in the REPEATED statement. If _RESPONSE_= is omitted, then CATMOD builds a full factorial _RESPONSE_ effect with respect to the dependent variables (for the standard response functions) or the repeated measurement factors (for other response functions).

For example, consider an experiment in which each subject is measured at three time points, and you specify RESPONSE MARGINALS. If the dependent variables each had *k* levels, then CATMOD would compute *k-1* response functions for each time point. Differences among the response functions with respect to these time points could be attributed to the repeated measurement factor TIME. To incorporate TIME variation into the model, specify

```
PROC CATMOD;
   RESPONSE MARGINALS;
   MODEL T1*T2*T3 = _RESPONSE_ ;
   REPEATED TIME 3 / _RESPONSE_ = TIME;
```

These statements would induce a TIME effect that would have 2*(*k-1*) degrees of freedom since there are *k-1* response functions at each time point.

Now suppose that at each time point, each subject has x-rays taken, and the x-rays are read by two different radiologists. This would create six dependent variables that represent the 3 x 2 cross-classification of the repeated measurement factors TIME and READER. A saturated model with respect to these factors could be obtained by specifying

```
PROC CATMOD;
   RESPONSE MARGINALS;
   MODEL T1R1*T1R2*T2R1*T2R2*T3R1*T3R2 = _RESPONSE_ ;
   REPEATED TIME 3, READER 2 / _RESPONSE_ = TIME READER TIME*READER;
```

If you want to fit a main-effects model with respect to TIME and READER, then change the REPEATED statement to

```
   REPEATED TIME 3, READER 2 / _RESPONSE_ = TIME READER;
```

When two or more repeated measurement factors are specified, CATMOD presumes that the response functions are ordered so that the levels of the rightmost factor change most rapidly. If the RESPONSE statement specifies MEANS or MARGINALS, then the dependent variables should be specified in the same order. For this example, the order implied by the REPEATED statement is

Response Function	Dependent Variable	TIME	READER
1	T1R1	1	1
2	T1R2	1	2
3	T2R1	2	1
4	T2R2	2	2
5	T3R1	3	1
6	T3R2	3	2

where T*i*R*j* corresponds to Time *i* and Reader *j*. Thus, the order of dependent variables in the MODEL statement must agree with the order implied by the REPEATED statement.

For log-linear model analysis, the effects in the REPEATED statement are written in terms of the dependent variables. For example,

```
PROC CATMOD;
   MODEL A*B*C = _RESPONSE_ ;
   REPEATED /_RESPONSE_ = A|B B|C A|C;
```

yields a log-linear model analysis that contains all main effects and two-variable interactions.

RESPONSE Statement

RESPONSE *function options;*

You can use the RESPONSE statement to specify functions of the response probabilities. It is these response functions that are modeled as linear combinations of the parameters. If no RESPONSE statement is specified, CATMOD uses the default standard response functions: generalized logits (explained in detail below). More than one RESPONSE statement can be specified, in which case each RESPONSE statement produces a separate analysis. The *function* specification is one of the following:

transformation

specified by any combinations of the four operations **LOG**, **EXP**, matrix literal, or + matrix literal. The operations are described in detail below.

MARGINAL
MARGINALS

specifies that the response functions are marginal probabilities for each of the dependent variables in the MODEL statement. For each dependent variable, the response functions are a set of linearly independent marginals, obtained by deleting the marginal probability corresponding to the last level.

MEAN
MEANS

specifies that the response functions are the means of the dependent variables in the MODEL statement. This specification requires that all of the dependent variables be numeric.

LOGIT
LOGITS

specifies that the response functions are generalized logits of the marginal probabilities for each of the dependent variables. For each dependent variable, the response functions are a set of linearly independent generalized logits, obtained by taking the logarithms of the ratios of two probabilities. The denominator of each ratio is the marginal probability corresponding to the last observed level of the variable, and the numerators are the marginal probabilities corresponding to each of the other levels. If there is one dependent variable, then specifying LOGIT is equivalent to using the standard response functions.

JOINT

specifies that the response functions are the joint response probabilities. A linearly independent set is created by deleting the last response probability.

If the computed response functions for any population are linearly dependent (yielding a singular covariance matrix), then CATMOD prints an error message and stops processing. See the **Cautions** section for methods of dealing with this.

Two *options* can be specified in a RESPONSE statement:

OUT=*SASdataset*

produces a SAS data set that contains, for each population, the observed and predicted values of the response functions, their standard errors, and the residuals. Moreover, if the standard response functions are used, the data set also includes observed and predicted values of the cell frequencies or the cell probabilities.

OUTEST=*SASdataset*

produces a SAS data set that contains the estimated parameter vector and its estimated covariance matrix.

If you want an output data set to be a permanent SAS data set, you must specify a two-level name. See "SAS Files," in the *SAS User's Guide: Basics* for more information on permanent SAS data sets.

The *transformation*, if specified, is applied to the vector that contains the sample proportions in each population. It can be any combination of the following four operations:

Operation	Specification
linear combination	matrix literal
logarithm	**LOG**
exponential	**EXP**
adding constant	**+** matrix literal

The **LOG** of a vector transforms each element of the vector into its natural logarithm; the **EXP** of a vector transforms each element into its exponential function (anti-logarithm). If more than one operation is specified, then CATMOD applies the operations consecutively from right to left. If two matrix literals appear next to each other, they should be separated by an asterisk (*), in which case CATMOD multiplies the two matrices.

A matrix literal is a series of numbers with each row of the matrix separated from the next by a comma. For example:

```
RESPONSE 1 0 0 , 0 1 0 ;
```

specifies a linear response function for data that have *r=3* response categories. The matrix literal specifies a 2 x 3 matrix, which is applied to each population as follows:

$$\begin{bmatrix} F1 \\ F2 \end{bmatrix} = \begin{bmatrix} 1 & 0 & 0 \\ 0 & 1 & 0 \end{bmatrix} * \begin{bmatrix} P1 \\ P2 \\ P3 \end{bmatrix}$$

where P1, P2, and P3 are sample proportions for the three response categories in a population, and F1 and F2 are the two response functions computed for that population. This response function therefore sets F1=P1 and F2=P2 in each population.

As another example of the linear response function, suppose you have two dependent variables corresponding to two observers who evaluate the same subjects. If the observers grade on the same 3-point scale, and if all nine possible responses are observed, then the following RESPONSE statement would compute the probability that the observers agree on their assessments:

```
RESPONSE  1 0 0  0 1 0  0 0 1 ;
```

Another way of writing this response function is

$$F = P11 + P22 + P33 = \begin{bmatrix} 1\,0\,0 & 0\,1\,0 & 0\,0\,1 \end{bmatrix} * \begin{bmatrix} P11 \\ P12 \\ P13 \\ P21 \\ P22 \\ P23 \\ P31 \\ P32 \\ P33 \end{bmatrix}$$

where P*ij* denotes the probability that a subject gets a grade of *i* from the first observer and *j* from the second observer.

If the function is a compound function, requiring more than one operation to specify it, then the operations should be listed in order, so that the first operation to be applied is on the right, and the last operation to be applied is on the left. For example, if there are two response levels, the response function

```
RESPONSE 1 -1 LOG;
```

is equivalent to the matrix expression:

$$F = \begin{bmatrix} 1 & -1 \end{bmatrix} * \begin{bmatrix} \log(P1) \\ \log(P2) \end{bmatrix}$$

As a programming statement, this would appear as:

```
F1 = LOG(P1) - LOG(P2);
```

which is the logit function:

```
F1 = LOG( P1/(1-P1) );
```

since P2=1-P1 when there are only two response levels.

Another example of a compound response function is:

```
RESPONSE 1 -1 EXP 1 0 0 1 , 0 1 1 0 LOG;
```

which is equivalent to the matrix expression

F = A*EXP(B*LOG(P));

where **P** is the vector of sample proportions for some population,

$$\mathbf{A} = \begin{bmatrix} 1 & -1 \end{bmatrix} \quad \text{and} \quad \mathbf{B} = \begin{bmatrix} 1\,0\,0\,1 \\ 0\,1\,1\,0 \end{bmatrix}$$

If the four responses are based on two dependent variables, each with the same two levels, then the function can also be written as

```
F = P11*P22 - P12*P21;
```

which is the cross-product ratio for a 2 x 2 table.

If no RESPONSE statement is specified, CATMOD computes the standard response functions, which contrast the log of each response probability with the log of the probability for the last response category. If there are *r* response categories, then there are *r-1* standard response functions. For example, if there are four response categories, using no RESPONSE statement is equivalent to specifying:

```
RESPONSE  1 0 0 -1,
          0 1 0 -1,
          0 0 1 -1  LOG;
```

This results in three response functions:

$$\mathbf{F} = \begin{bmatrix} F1 \\ F2 \\ F3 \end{bmatrix} = \begin{bmatrix} \log(P1/P4) \\ \log(P2/P4) \\ \log(P3/P4) \end{bmatrix}$$

If there were only two response levels, the resulting response function would be a logit. Thus, the standard response functions are called generalized logits. They are useful in dealing with the log-linear model:

$$\pi = \mathbf{EXP(X\beta)}$$

If **C** denotes the matrix in the RESPONSE statement given above, then because of the restriction that the probabilities sum to 1, it follows that an equivalent model is

$$\mathbf{C\ LOG(\pi)} = \mathbf{(CX)\beta}$$

But **C LOG(P)** is simply the vector of standard response functions. Thus, the equation means that fitting a log-linear model on the cell probabilities is equivalent to fitting a linear model on the generalized logits.

EXAMPLES OF RESPONSE STATEMENTS

Example	Result
`RESPONSE MARGINALS;`	marginals for each dependent variable
`RESPONSE MEANS;`	the mean of each dependent variable
`RESPONSE LOGITS;`	generalized logits of the marginal probabilities
`RESPONSE JOINT;`	the joint probabilities
`RESPONSE 1 -1 LOG;`	the logit
`RESPONSE OUT=PRED1;`	generalized logits and an output data set
`RESPONSE 1 2 3;`	the mean score, with scores of 1, 2, and 3 corresponding to the three response levels

WEIGHT Statement

WEIGHT *variable;*

A WEIGHT statement can be used to refer to a variable containing the cell frequencies, which need not be integers. The WEIGHT statement lets you use summary data sets containing a count variable. See **Input Data Set** in the **Details** section for further information concerning the WEIGHT statement.

DETAILS

Missing Values

Observations with missing values for any variable listed in the MODEL and WEIGHT statements are omitted from the analysis.

Input Data Set

Data to be analyzed by CATMOD must be a SAS data set containing either

- raw data values (data values for every subject)
- frequency counts and the corresponding data values.

CATMOD assumes the SAS data set contains raw data values unless a WEIGHT statement is included.

If raw data are used, CATMOD first counts the number of observations having each combination of values for all variables used in the MODEL and POPULATION statements. For example, suppose the variables A and B each take on the values 1 and 2, and their frequencies can be represented as follows:

	A=1	A=2
B=1	2	1
B=2	3	0

The SAS data set containing the raw data might be as follows:

data set RAW:

OBS	A	B
1	1	1
2	1	1
3	1	2
4	1	2
5	1	2
6	2	1

and the statements for CATMOD would be:

```
PROC CATMOD DATA=RAW;
   MODEL A = B;
```

If your data set contains frequency counts, then use the WEIGHT statement in CATMOD to specify the variable containing the frequencies. For example, you could create the following data set:

```
data set SUMMARY:          OBS    A    B    COUNT
                             1    1    1      2
                             2    1    2      3
                             3    2    1      1
```

in which case the corresponding CATMOD statements would be

```
PROC CATMOD DATA=SUMMARY;
   WEIGHT COUNT;
   MODEL A = B;
```

The data set SUMMARY can be created directly, or it can be created from data set RAW by using PROC FREQ:

```
PROC FREQ DATA=RAW;
   TABLES A*B / OUT=SUMMARY;
```

Output Data Sets

OUT= data set This output data set contains, for each population, observed and predicted values of the response functions, their standard errors, and the residuals. In addition, if the standard response functions are used, the data set includes observed and predicted values for the cell frequencies or the cell probabilities, together with their standard errors and residuals. For the standard response functions, there are $s^*(2q+1)$ observations in the data set for each BY group, where s is the number of populations, and q is the number of response functions per population. Otherwise, there are s^*q observations in the data set for each BY group. The new data set contains the BY variables (if any) and the following new variables:

SAMPLE specifies the population number.

TYPE specifies a character variable with three possible values. When _TYPE_=FUNCTION, the observed and predicted values are values of the response functions. When _TYPE_=PROB, they are values of the cell probabilities. When _TYPE_ =FREQ, they are values of the cell frequencies.

NUMBER specifies the sequence number of the response function or the cell probability or the cell frequency.

OBS specifies the observed value.

SEOBS specifies the standard error of the observed value.

PRED specifies the predicted value.

SEPRED specifies the standard error of the predicted value.

RESID specifies the residual (observed-predicted).

OUTEST= data set This output data set, which contains the estimated parameter vector and its estimated covariance matrix, has TYPE=EST. See the *SAS User's Guide: Basics,* for more information on special SAS data sets. For each BY group, there are $p+1$ observations in the data set, where p is the number of estimated parameters. The data set contains the following variables:

- the BY variables, if any.
- the new character variable _TYPE_, with 2 possible values. When _TYPE_=EST, the variables B1, B2, etc. contain parameter estimates; when _TYPE_=COV, they contain covariance estimates.
- the new character variable _NAME_. When _TYPE_=EST, _NAME_ is blank, but when _TYPE_=COV, _NAME_ has one of the values B1, B2, and so on, corresponding to the parameter names.
- one variable for each estimated parameter: B1, B2, and so on.

Logistic Regression

If you have continuous effect variables, then each observation represents a separate sample. At this extreme of sparseness, the weighted-least-squares method is unworkable since there are too many zero frequencies. Therefore, the maximum-likelihood method should be used. CATMOD was not designed specifically for logistic regression, and is less efficient than more specialized procedures, but one advantage of CATMOD is that it works for nominally-scaled responses with more than two levels.

To use CATMOD for logistic regression, specify the continuous predictors in a DIRECT statement, as well as in the MODEL statement. Then use the ML and NOGLS options:

```
PROC CATMOD;
   DIRECT X1 X2 X3;
   MODEL RESPONSE = X1 X2 X3 / ML NOGLS;
```

The parameter estimates from CATMOD are the same as those from a logistic regression program such as LOGIST, except that the signs are reversed. This is because CATMOD normalizes on the lowest response value of 0 while LOGIST normalizes on the 1 response. (The LOGIST procedure, contributed by Frank Harrell, is described in the *SUGI Supplemental Library User's Guide, 1983 Edition.*)

Ordering of Populations and Responses

Suppose you specify the following statements:

```
DATA ONE;
   INPUT A $ B $ WT @@;
   CARDS;
YES YES 23   YES NO 31   NO YES 47   NO NO 50
PROC CATMOD;
   WEIGHT WT;
   MODEL A = B;
```

Then the ordering of populations and responses corresponds to the alphabetical order of the levels of the character variables:

POPULATION PROFILES

SAMPLE	B
1	NO
2	YES

RESPONSE PROFILES

RESPONSE	A
1	NO
2	YES

and the parameter for the main effect of B corresponds to the first level of B, which is NO. However, if you specify the ORDER=DATA option:

```
PROC CATMOD ORDER=DATA;
```

then the ordering of populations and responses is as follows:

POPULATION PROFILES

SAMPLE	B
1	YES
2	NO

RESPONSE PROFILES

RESPONSE	A
1	YES
2	NO

and the parameter for the main effect of B corresponds to the first level of B, which is YES. Thus, you can use the ORDER=DATA option to ensure that populations and responses are ordered in a specific way. But since this also affects the definitions and the ordering of the parameters, you must exercise caution when using the _RESPONSE_ effect, the CONTRAST statement, or direct input of the design matrix. See the **Cautions** section for additional examples.

An alternative method of ensuring that populations and responses are ordered in a specific way is to replace any character variables by numeric variables, and to assign formatted values such as 'yes' and 'no' to the numeric levels.

GENERATION OF THE DESIGN MATRIX

Each row of the design matrix (corresponding to a population) is generated by a unique combination of independent variable values. The columns of the design matrix are produced from the effect specifications in the MODEL and REPEATED statements. To facilitate the presentation, this section is divided into four parts:

- Specification of Effects
- One Response Function Per Population
- Two or More Response Functions Per Population, Excluding Log-Linear Models
- Log-Linear Models

Specification of Effects

The parameters of a linear model are generally divided into subsets that correspond to meaningful sources of variation in the response functions. These sources, called effects, can be specified in the MODEL, REPEATED, and CONTRAST statements. Effects can be specified in any of the following ways:

- Crossed effects are one or more variables joined by asterisks (*). The variables are presumed to be class variables (that is, they induce classification levels): A A*B A*B*C.
- Nested effects are effects followed by a crossed effect in parentheses: B(A) C(A*B) A*B(C*D).
- Direct effects are effects specified in a DIRECT statement: X Y.
- Nested-by-value effects are the same as nested effects, except that any variable in the parentheses can be followed by an equal sign and a value: B(A=1) C(A*B=1) C*D(A=1*B=1).
- Direct effects can be crossed with other direct effects or with crossed effects: X*Y X*X*X X*A*B(C*D=1).

The variables for crossed and nested effects remain in the order in which they are first encountered. For example, in the model

```
MODEL R = B A A*B C(A B);
```

the effect A*B is reported as B*A, since B appeared before A in the statement. Also, C(A B) is interpreted as C(A*B), and is therefore reported as C(B*A). You can shorten the specification of effects by using bar notation. For example, two methods of writing a full three-way factorial model are

```
PROC CATMOD;
   MODEL Y = A B C A*B A*C B*C A*B*C;

PROC CATMOD;
   MODEL Y = A|B|C;
```

When the bar (|) is used, the right and left sides become effects, and the cross of them becomes an effect. Multiple bars are permitted. The expressions are expanded from left to right, using rules 1-4 given in Searle (1971, p. 390):

- multiple bars are evaluated left to right. For instance, A | B | C is [A | B] | C, which is [A B A*B] | C, which is
  A B A*B C A*C B*C A*B*C.
- crossed and nested groups of variables are combined. For example, A(B) | C(D) generates A*C(B D), among other terms.
- duplicate variables are removed. For example, A(C) | B(C) generates A*B(C), among other terms, and the extra C is removed.
- effects are discarded if a variable occurs on both the crossed and nested sides of an effect. For instance, A(B) | B(D E) generates A*B(B D E), but this effect is eliminated immediately.

Other examples of the bar notation:

A | C(B)	is equivalent to A C(B) A*C(B)
A(B) | C(B)	is equivalent to A(B) C(B) A*C(B)
A(B) | B(D E)	is equivalent to A(B) B(D E)
A | B(A) | C	is equivalent to A B(A) C A*C B*C(A).

One Response Function Per Population

Intercept When there is one response function per population, all design matrices start with a column of 1s for the intercept unless the NOINT option is specified or the design matrix is input directly.

Main effects If a class variable A has *k* levels, then its main effect has *k*-1 degrees of freedom, and the design matrix has *k*-1 columns that correspond to the first *k*-1 levels of A. The *i*th column contains a 1 in the *i*th row, a -1 in the last row, and zeros everywhere else. If α_i denotes the parameter that corresponds to the *i*th level of variable A, then the *k*-1 columns yield estimates of the independent parameters, α_1, α_2, ..., α_{k-1}. The last parameter is not needed because CATMOD constrains the *k* parameters to sum to zero. In other words, CATMOD uses a full-rank center-point parameterization to build design matrices. Two examples:

Data Levels	Design Columns	
A	A	
1	1	0
2	0	1
3	−1	−1

Data Levels	Design Columns
B	B
1	1
2	−1

Crossed effects (interactions) Crossed effects (such as A*B) are formed by the horizontal direct products of main effects. For example:

Data Levels		Design Matrix Columns				
A	B	A		B	A*B	
1	1	1	0	1	1	0
1	2	1	0	−1	−1	0
2	1	0	1	1	0	1
2	2	0	1	−1	0	−1
3	1	−1	−1	1	−1	−1
3	2	−1	−1	−1	1	1

The number of degrees of freedom for a crossed effect (that is, the number of design matrix columns) is equal to the product of the numbers of degrees of freedom for the separate effects.

Nested effects The effect A(B) is read "A within B" and is like specifying an A main effect for every value of B. If n_a and n_b are the number of levels in A and B, respectively, then the number of columns for A(B) is $(n_a\text{-}1)n_b$ if every combination of levels exists in the data. For example:

Data Levels		Design Matrix Columns			
B	A	A(B)			
1	1	1	0	0	0
1	2	0	1	0	0
1	3	−1	−1	0	0
2	1	0	0	1	0
2	2	0	0	0	1
2	3	0	0	−1	−1

CATMOD actually allocates a column for all possible combinations of values even though some combinations may not be present in the data.

Nested-by-value effects Instead of nesting an effect within all values of the main effect, you can nest an effect within specified values of the nested variable (A(B=1), for example). The four degrees of freedom for the A(B) effect shown above can also be obtained by specifying the two separate nested effects with values:

Data Levels		Design Matrix Columns			
B	A	A(B=1)		A(B=2)	
1	1	1	0	0	0
1	2	0	1	0	0
1	3	−1	−1	0	0
2	1	0	0	1	0
2	2	0	0	0	1
2	3	0	0	−1	−1

Each effect has $n_a - 1$ degrees of freedom, assuming a complete combination. Thus, for the example, each effect has two degrees of freedom.

Direct effects To request that the actual values of a variable be inserted into the design matrix, declare the variable in a DIRECT statement, and specify the effect by the variable name. For example, specifying the effects X1 and X2 in the MODEL statement results in:

Data Levels		Design Columns	
X1	X2	X1	X2
1	1	1	1
2	4	2	4
3	9	3	9

provided that X1 and X2 are declared in a DIRECT statement.

Unless there is a POPULATION statement that excludes the direct variables, those variables help induce the classification for the sample populations to be defined. In general, the variables should not be continuous in the sense that every subject has a different value, because this would induce a separate population for each subject (note, however, that such a strategy is used purposely for logistic regression).

If there *is* a POPULATION statement that omits mention of the direct variables, then the values of the direct variables must be identical for all subjects in a given population since there can only be one independent variable profile for each population.

Two or More Response Functions Per Population, Excluding Log-Linear Models

When there is more than one response function per population, the structure of the design matrix depends on whether or not the model type is AVERAGED. The following subsections illustrate the effect of specifying (or not specifying) an AVERAGED model type.

Model type not AVERAGED Suppose the variable A has two levels, and you specify

```
PROC CATMOD;
   MODEL Y = A;
```

If the variable Y has two levels, then there is only one response function per population, and the design matrix is

Sample	Design Matrix INTERCEPT	A
1	1	1
2	1	−1

But if the variable Y has three levels, then there are two response functions per population, and the above design matrix is assumed to hold for each of the two response functions. The response functions are always ordered so that the multiple response functions within a population are grouped together. For this example, the design matrix would be:

Sample	Response Function Number	Design Matrix INTERCEPT		A	
1	1	1	0	1	0
1	2	0	1	0	1
2	1	1	0	−1	0
2	2	0	1	0	−1

Since the same submatrix applies to each of the multiple response functions, CATMOD prints only the submatrix (that is, the one it would print if there were only one response function per population), rather than the entire design matrix.

Model type AVERAGED When the model type is AVERAGED (for example, when the AVERAGED option is specified in the MODEL statement), CATMOD does not assume that the same submatrix applies to each of the *q* response functions per population. Rather, it averages any independent variable effects across the functions, and it allows you to study variation among the *q* functions. The first column of the design matrix is always a column of 1s corresponding to the intercept, unless the NOINT option is specified in the MODEL statement or the design matrix is input directly. Also, since the design matrix does not have any special submatrix structure, CATMOD prints the entire matrix.

For example, suppose the dependent variable Y has three levels, the independent variable A has two levels, and you specify

```
PROC CATMOD;
   RESPONSE 1 0 0 / 0 1 0;
   MODEL Y = A / AVERAGED;
```

Then there are two response functions per population, and the response functions are always ordered so that the multiple response functions within a population are grouped together. For this example, the design matrix would be:

Sample	Response Function Number	Design Matrix INTERCEPT	A
1	1	1	1
1	2	1	1
2	1	1	−1
2	2	1	−1

It should be noted that the model now has only two degrees of freedom. The remaining two degrees of freedom in the residual correspond to variation among the three levels of the dependent variable. Generally, that variation tends to be statistically significant, and therefore should not be left out of the model. You can include it in the model by including the two effects, _RESPONSE_ and _RESPONSE_*A, but if the study is not a repeated measurement study, those sources of variation tend to be uninteresting. Thus, the usual solution for this type of study (one dependent variable) is to exclude the AVERAGED option from the MODEL statement.

An AVERAGED model type is automatically induced whenever the _RESPONSE_ keyword is used in the MODEL statement. The _RESPONSE_ effect models variation among the *q* response functions per population. If there is no REPEATED statement, then CATMOD builds a main effect with q-1 degrees of freedom. For example, three response functions would induce the following design columns:

Response Function Number	Design Columns _RESPONSE_	
1	1	0
2	0	1
3	−1	−1

If there is more than one population, then the _RESPONSE_ effect is averaged over the populations. Also, the _RESPONSE_ effect can be crossed with any other effect, or it can be nested within an effect.

If there is a REPEATED statement that contains only one repeated measurement factor, then CATMOD builds the design columns for _RESPONSE_ in the same way, except that the printed output labels the main effect with the factor name, rather than with the word _RESPONSE_. For example, suppose an independent variable A has two levels, and the input statements are

```
PROC CATMOD;
   RESPONSE MARGINALS;
   MODEL TIME1*TIME2 = A _RESPONSE_ A*_RESPONSE_;
   REPEATED TIME 2 / _RESPONSE_ = TIME;
```

If TIME1 and TIME2 each have two levels (so that they each have one independent marginal probability), then the RESPONSE statement causes CATMOD to compute two response functions per population. Thus, the design matrix would be:

Sample	Response Function Number	Design Matrix INTERCEPT	A	TIME	A*TIME
1	1	1	1	1	1
1	2	1	1	−1	−1
2	1	1	−1	1	−1
2	2	1	−1	−1	1

However, if TIME1 and TIME2 each have three levels (so that they each have two independent marginal probabilities) then the RESPONSE statement causes CATMOD to compute four response functions per population. In that case, since TIME has two levels, CATMOD groups the functions into sets of 2(=4/2), and constructs the above submatrix for each function in the set. This results in the following design matrix, which is obtained from the previous one by multiplying each element by an identity matrix of order two:

Sample	Response Function	Design Matrix INTERCEPT		A		TIME		A*TIME	
1	P(TIME1=1)	1	0	1	0	1	0	1	0
1	P(TIME1=2)	0	1	0	1	0	1	0	1
1	P(TIME2=1)	1	0	1	0	−1	0	−1	0
1	P(TIME2=2)	0	1	0	1	0	−1	0	−1
2	P(TIME1=1)	1	0	−1	0	1	0	−1	0
2	P(TIME1=2)	0	1	0	−1	0	1	0	−1
2	P(TIME2=1)	1	0	−1	0	−1	0	1	0
2	P(TIME2=2)	0	1	0	−1	0	−1	0	1

If there is a REPEATED statement that contains two or more repeated measurement factors, then CATMOD builds the design columns for _RESPONSE_ according to the definition of _RESPONSE_ in the REPEATED statement. For example, suppose you specify

```
PROC CATMOD;
   RESPONSE MARGINALS;
   MODEL R11*R12*R21*R22 = _RESPONSE_ ;
   REPEATED TIME 2, PLACE 2 / _RESPONSE_ = TIME PLACE;
```

If each of the dependent variables had two levels, then CATMOD would build four response functions. The _RESPONSE_ effect would generate a main-effects model with respect to TIME and PLACE:

Response Function Number	Variable	TIME	PLACE	Design Matrix INTERCEPT	_RESPONSE_	
1	R11	1	1	1	1	1
2	R12	1	2	1	1	−1
2	R21	2	1	1	−1	1
2	R22	2	2	1	−1	−1

Log-Linear Models

When the response functions are the standard ones (generalized logits), then inclusion of the keyword _RESPONSE_ in any design effect induces a log-linear model. The design matrix for a log-linear model looks different from a standard design matrix because the standard one is transformed by the same linear transformation that converts the *r* response probabilities to *r*-1 generalized logits. For example, suppose the dependent variables X and Y each have two levels, and you specify a saturated log-linear model analysis:

```
PROC CATMOD;
   MODEL X*Y = _RESPONSE_ ;
   REPEATED / _RESPONSE_ = X Y X*Y;
```

Then the cross-classification of X and Y yields four response probabilities, P11, P12, P21, and P22, which are then reduced to three generalized logit response functions, F1=log(P11/P22), F2=log(P12/P22), and F3=log(P21/P22).

Since the saturated log-linear model implies that

$$\begin{bmatrix} \log P11 \\ \log P12 \\ \log P21 \\ \log P22 \end{bmatrix} = \begin{bmatrix} 1 & 1 & 1 & 1 \\ 1 & 1 & -1 & -1 \\ 1 & -1 & 1 & -1 \\ 1 & -1 & -1 & 1 \end{bmatrix} \boldsymbol{\gamma} - \lambda \begin{bmatrix} 1 \\ 1 \\ 1 \\ 1 \end{bmatrix}$$

$$= \begin{bmatrix} 1 & 1 & 1 \\ 1 & -1 & -1 \\ -1 & 1 & -1 \\ -1 & -1 & 1 \end{bmatrix} \boldsymbol{\beta} - \delta \begin{bmatrix} 1 \\ 1 \\ 1 \\ 1 \end{bmatrix}$$

where $\boldsymbol{\gamma}$ and $\boldsymbol{\beta}$ are parameter vectors, and λ and δ are normalizing constants required by the restriction that the probabilities sum to 1, it follows that the MODEL statement yields

$$\begin{bmatrix} F1 \\ F2 \\ F3 \end{bmatrix} = \begin{bmatrix} 1 & 0 & 0 & -1 \\ 0 & 1 & 0 & -1 \\ 0 & 0 & 1 & -1 \end{bmatrix} \begin{bmatrix} \log P11 \\ \log P12 \\ \log P21 \\ \log P22 \end{bmatrix}$$

$$= \begin{bmatrix} 1 & 0 & 0 & -1 \\ 0 & 1 & 0 & -1 \\ 0 & 0 & 1 & -1 \end{bmatrix} \begin{bmatrix} 1 & 1 & 1 \\ 1 & -1 & -1 \\ -1 & 1 & -1 \\ -1 & -1 & 1 \end{bmatrix} \boldsymbol{\beta}$$

$$= \begin{bmatrix} 2 & 2 & 0 \\ 2 & 0 & -2 \\ 0 & 2 & -2 \end{bmatrix} \boldsymbol{\beta}$$

Thus, the design matrix is

Sample	Response Function Number	Design Matrix X	Y	X*Y
1	1	2	2	0
1	2	2	0	−2
1	3	0	2	−2

Design matrices for reduced models are constructed similarly. For example, suppose you request a main-effects log-linear model analysis of the factors X and Y:

```
PROC CATMOD;
   MODEL X*Y = _RESPONSE_ ;
   REPEATED / _RESPONSE_ = X Y;
```

Since the main-effects log-linear model implies that

$$\begin{bmatrix} \log P11 \\ \log P12 \\ \log P21 \\ \log P22 \end{bmatrix} = \begin{bmatrix} 1 & 1 & 1 \\ 1 & 1 & -1 \\ 1 & -1 & 1 \\ 1 & -1 & -1 \end{bmatrix} \gamma - \lambda \begin{bmatrix} 1 \\ 1 \\ 1 \\ 1 \end{bmatrix}$$

$$= \begin{bmatrix} 1 & 1 \\ 1 & -1 \\ -1 & 1 \\ -1 & -1 \end{bmatrix} \beta - \delta \begin{bmatrix} 1 \\ 1 \\ 1 \\ 1 \end{bmatrix}$$

it follows that the MODEL statement yields

$$\begin{bmatrix} F1 \\ F2 \\ F3 \end{bmatrix} = \begin{bmatrix} 1 & 0 & 0 & -1 \\ 0 & 1 & 0 & -1 \\ 0 & 0 & 1 & -1 \end{bmatrix} \begin{bmatrix} \log P11 \\ \log P12 \\ \log P21 \\ \log P22 \end{bmatrix}$$

$$= \begin{bmatrix} 1 & 0 & 0 & -1 \\ 0 & 1 & 0 & -1 \\ 0 & 0 & 1 & -1 \end{bmatrix} \begin{bmatrix} 1 & 1 \\ 1 & -1 \\ -1 & 1 \\ -1 & -1 \end{bmatrix} \beta$$

$$= \begin{bmatrix} 2 & 2 \\ 2 & 0 \\ 0 & 2 \end{bmatrix} \beta$$

Therefore, the corresponding design matrix is

Sample	Response Function Number	Design Matrix X	Y
1	1	2	2
1	2	2	0
1	3	0	2

THE _RESPONSE_ EFFECT

If there is only one response function per population, then all of the variation among the functions must be due to variation among the levels of the independent variables that define the populations. Therefore, the design effects in the right-hand side of the MODEL statement contain only independent variables.

If, on the other hand, there is more than one response function per population, then some of the variation among the functions is due to variation among the dependent variables or to variation among the levels of each dependent variable. In this case, it makes sense to allow specification of dependent variables in the right-hand side of the MODEL statement so that this kind of variation can be included in the statistical model.

For this purpose, CATMOD allows the keyword _RESPONSE_ in any effect in the right-hand side of the MODEL statement (except that *effect* nested within _RESPONSE_ is not allowed). Specification of _RESPONSE_ in a design effect tells CATMOD that the effect is to include variation due to one or more dependent variables. The way in which CATMOD builds the effect depends on the structure of the response functions and on the information contained in the REPEATED statement.

Throughout this section, df is used as an abbreviation for degrees of freedom. The section is divided into two parts:

- Log-Linear Model Analysis (Default Response Functions)
- Repeated Measurement Analysis (Other Response Functions)

Log-Linear Model Analysis (Default Response Functions)

When the response functions are the standard ones (generalized logits), then inclusion of the keyword _RESPONSE_ in any design effect induces a log-linear model. Furthermore, if _RESPONSE_ is in any effect, then it must be in **all** of the effects.

Suppose the dependent variables X and Y each have two levels. Then the statements

```
PROC CATMOD;
   MODEL X*Y = _RESPONSE_;
   REPEATED / _RESPONSE_ = X Y X*Y;
```

yield a saturated log-linear model analysis of the factors X and Y.

If you want to fit a reduced model with respect to the dependent variables (for example, a model of independence or conditional independence), specify the reduced model in the REPEATED statement. For example, the following statements

```
PROC CATMOD;
   MODEL X*Y = _RESPONSE_ / PRED=PROB;
   REPEATED / _RESPONSE_ = X Y;
```

yield a main-effects log-linear model analysis of the factors X and Y. The output includes test statistics for the individual effects X and Y, as well as predicted cell probabilities. Moreover, the goodness-of-fit statistic tests the hypothesis of independence between X and Y. The specified MODEL statement results in weighted-least-squares estimation of the model parameters. However, changing the MODEL statement to:

```
MODEL X*Y = _RESPONSE_ / ML NOGLS PRED=FREQ;
```

results in maximum-likelihood estimation of the model parameters, and the goodness-of-fit statistic is the likelihood ratio test for the hypothesis of independence between X and Y. Predicted cell frequencies are also computed and printed.

If there are any independent variables, then you can also specify interactions between the independent and the dependent variables. Continuing with the example given above, suppose there are three populations formed by the independent variable GROUP. Then there are a total of nine response functions, and

```
MODEL X*Y = _RESPONSE_    _RESPONSE_*GROUP;
REPEATED / _RESPONSE_ = X Y X*Y;
```

specifies a saturated model (3 df for _RESPONSE_ AND 6 df for the interaction between _RESPONSE_ and GROUP). From another point of view, _RESPONSE_*GROUP can be regarded as a main effect for GROUP with respect to the 3 response functions, while _RESPONSE_ can be regarded as an intercept effect with respect to the functions. In other words, these statements give essentially the same results as

```
MODEL X*Y = GROUP;
```

The ability to model the interaction between the independent and the dependent variables becomes particularly useful when a reduced model is specified for the dependent variables. For example,

```
MODEL X*Y = _RESPONSE_  _RESPONSE_*GROUP;
REPEATED / _RESPONSE_ = X Y;
```

specifies a model with 2 df for _RESPONSE_ (1 for X and 1 for Y) and 4 df for the interaction of _RESPONSE_*GROUP, and the goodness-of-fit statistic (3 df) tests the hypothesis that X and Y are independent in each of the 3 groups.

One word of caution about log-linear model analyses is that sampling zeros in the input data set should be replaced by some positive number close to zero (such as 1E-20) by adding one line to the data step, and that such data containing sampling zeros should be analyzed with maximum likelihood estimation. See the **Cautions** section and **Example 6** for further information.

Repeated Measurement Analysis (Other Response Functions)

Suppose each subject in a study is measured at three different time points, and the corresponding dependent variables are labeled T1, T2, and T3. Suppose further that one response function is computed for each of these dependent variables. If there is no REPEATED statement, or if the REPEATED statement is

```
REPEATED TIME / _RESPONSE_ = TIME;
```

then CATMOD regards _RESPONSE_ as a variable with three levels corresponding to the three response functions in each population, and forms an effect with 2 df. The advantage of using a REPEATED statement for this situation is that CATMOD labels _RESPONSE_ as TIME in the printed output.

If, in addition, GROUP is an independent variable that has five levels, and you specify

```
POPULATION GROUP;
```

then there are five populations and a total of 15 response functions, and the following statements result in the indicated analyses:

`MODEL T1*T2*T3 = GROUP / AVERAGED;`	specifies the GROUP main effect (with 4 df).
`MODEL T1*T2*T3 = _RESPONSE_;`	specifies the TIME main effect (with 2 df).
`MODEL T1*T2*T3 = _RESPONSE_*GROUP;`	specifies the interaction between TIME and GROUP (with 8 df).
`MODEL T1*T2*T3 = _RESPONSE_|GROUP;`	specifies both main effects, and the interaction between TIME and GROUP (with 14 df).
`MODEL T1*T2*T3 = _RESPONSE_(GROUP);`	specifies a TIME main effect within each GROUP (with 10 df).

But

`MODEL T1*T2*T3 = GROUP(_RESPONSE_);`	is invalid.

If CATMOD computes *k* response functions for each time point, rather than just one (for example, if the dependent variables each have three levels, and you specify RESPONSE MARGINALS), then the _RESPONSE_ effect has 2**k* df (rather than 2 df), and all other effects containing _RESPONSE_ also have a greater number of degrees of freedom.

Now suppose there is more than one repeated measurement factor. For example, consider an experiment in which subjects are measured under each of two lighting conditions at each of two time points. The four dependent variables may be labeled:

R11 = Measurement at Time 1 in Bright Light
R12 = Measurement at Time 1 in Dim Light
R21 = Measurement at Time 2 in Bright Light
R22 = Measurement at Time 2 in Dim Light

If one response function were computed for each of these variables, and if the REPEATED statement were

```
REPEATED TIME 2, LIGHT 2 / _RESPONSE_ = TIME LIGHT TIME*LIGHT;
```

then CATMOD would build the _RESPONSE_ effect as a full factorial with respect to the repeated measurement factors TIME and LIGHT.

If you wish to fit a model that contains only a main effect for LIGHT, then you would use the statement

```
REPEATED TIME 2, LIGHT 2 / _RESPONSE_ = LIGHT;
```

and the _RESPONSE_ effect would then have only 1 df corresponding to the main effect for LIGHT.

As before, independent variables can be combined with the _RESPONSE_ effect in the MODEL statement. For example, let GROUP be an independent variable with five levels. Then there are a total of 20 response functions, and for the previous REPEATED statement, the following MODEL statements would result in the indicated analyses:

`MODEL R11*R12*R21*R22 = GROUP / AVERAGED;`	specifies the GROUP main effect (with 4 df).
`MODEL R11*R12*R21*R22 = _RESPONSE_;`	specifies the LIGHT main effect (with 1 df).
`MODEL R11*R12*R21*R22 = _RESPONSE_*GROUP;`	specifies the interaction between LIGHT and GROUP (with 4 df).
`MODEL R11*R12*R21*R22 = _RESPONSE_|GROUP;`	specifies main effects and the interaction between LIGHT and GROUP (9 df).
`MODEL R11*R12*R21*R22 = _RESPONSE_(GROUP);`	specifies the LIGHT main effect within each GROUP (with 5 df).

CAUTIONS

Since the method depends on asymptotic approximations, you need to be careful that the sample sizes are sufficiently large to support the asymptotic normal distributions of the response functions. A general guideline is that you would like to have an *effective* sample size of at least 25 to 30 for each response function that is being analyzed. For example, if you have one dependent variable and $r=4$ response levels, and you use the standard response functions to compute three generalized logits for each population, then you would like the sample size of each population to be at least 75. Moreover, the subjects should be dispersed throughout the table so that less than 20% of the response functions have an *effective* sample size less than 5. For example, if each population had less than 5 subjects in the first response category, then it would be wiser to pool this category with another, rather than to assume the asymptotic normality of the first response function. Or, if the dependent variable is ordinally scaled, an alternative is to request the mean score response function, rather than three generalized logits.

If there is more than one dependent variable, and you specify RESPONSE MEANS, then the *effective* sample size for each response function is the same as the actual sample size. Thus, a sample size of 30 could be sufficient to support four response functions, provided that the functions were the means of four dependent variables.

If there is a singular (non-invertible) covariance matrix for the response functions in any population, then CATMOD prints an error message and stops processing. You have several options available to correct this situation:

- You can reduce the number of response functions according to how many can be supported by the populations with the smallest sample sizes.
- If there are three or more levels for any independent variable, you can pool the levels into a fewer number of categories, thereby reducing the number of populations. However, your interpretation of results must be done more cautiously since such pooling implies a different sampling scheme and masks any differences that existed among the pooled categories.
- If there are two or more independent variables, you can delete at least one of them from the model. However, this is just another form of pooling, and therefore, the same cautions that apply to the previous option also apply here.
- If there is one independent variable, then in some situations, you might simply eliminate the populations that are causing the covariance matrices to be singular.
- You can use the ADDCELL option to add a small amount (say, 0.5) to every cell frequency, but this can seriously bias the results if the cell frequencies are small.

If you use the standard response functions, and there are zero frequencies, you should use maximum-likelihood estimation rather than weighted least squares to analyze the data. For weighted-least-squares analysis, CATMOD always computes the observed response functions. If CATMOD needs to take the logarithm of a zero proportion, it prints a warning and then proceeds to take the log of a small value ($.5/n_i$ for the probability) in order to continue. This can produce invalid results if the cells contain too few observations. The ML analysis, on the other hand, does not require computation of the observed response functions, and therefore yields valid results for the parameter estimates and all of the predicted values. The only ML results that would be inexact are the observed values and the residuals that appear in the table of predicted values, since the .5 correction would be used to compute the observed logits whenever there was a zero frequency.

For any log-linear model analysis, it is important to remember that CATMOD treats zero frequencies as structural zeros. If you want them to be interpreted as sampling zeros, simply insert a one-line statement into the data step that changes each zero to a very small number (such as 1E-20). See Bishop, Fienberg, and Holland (1975) for a discussion of the issues, and **Example 6** for an illustration of a log-linear model analysis of data that contain both structural and random zeros.

If weighted-least-squares analysis is used for a contingency table that contains zero cell frequencies, then avoid using the LOG transformation as the first transformation on the observed proportions. In general, it may be better to change the response functions or to pool some of the response categories than to settle for the .5 correction or to use the ADDCELL option.

If you use the keyword _RESPONSE_ in the MODEL statement, and you specify MARGINALS or LOGITS in your RESPONSE statement, you may receive the following warning message printed by CATMOD:

```
WARNING: THE _RESPONSE_ EFFECT MAY BE TESTING THE WRONG
         HYPOTHESIS SINCE THE MARGINAL LEVELS OF THE
         DEPENDENT VARIABLES DO NOT COINCIDE. CONSULT THE
         RESPONSE PROFILES AND THE CATMOD DOCUMENTATION.
```

The following examples illustrate situations in which the _RESPONSE_ effect tests the wrong hypothesis.

Example 1: Zeros in the Marginal Frequencies Suppose you specify the following statements:

```
DATA A1;
   INPUT TIME1 TIME2 @@;
   CARDS;
1 2    2 3    1 3
PROC CATMOD;
   RESPONSE MARGINALS;
   MODEL TIME1*TIME2 = _RESPONSE_ ;
   REPEATED TIME 2 / _RESPONSE_ = TIME;
```

One marginal probability is computed for each dependent variable, resulting in two response functions. The model is a saturated one: one degree of freedom for the intercept, and one for the main effect of TIME. Except for the warning message, CATMOD produces an analysis with no apparent errors, but the RESPONSE PROFILES printed by CATMOD are

RESPONSE PROFILES

RESPONSE	TIME1	TIME2
1	1	2
2	1	3
3	2	3

Since RESPONSE MARGINALS yields marginal probabilities for every level but the last, the two response functions being analyzed are Prob(TIME1=1) and Prob(TIME2=2). Thus, the TIME effect is testing the hypothesis that Prob(TIME1=1)=Prob(TIME2=2). What it *should* be testing is the hypothesis

Prob(TIME1=1) = Prob(TIME2=1)
Prob(TIME1=2) = Prob(TIME2=2)
Prob(TIME1=3) = Prob(TIME2=3)

but there are not enough data to support the test (assuming that none of the probabilities are structural zeros by the design of the study).

Example 2: The ORDER=DATA Option Suppose you specify

```
DATA A1;
   INPUT TIME1 TIME2 @@;
   CARDS;
2 1   2 2   1 1   1 2   2 1
PROC CATMOD ORDER=DATA;
   RESPONSE MARGINALS;
   MODEL TIME1*TIME2 = _RESPONSE_ ;
   REPEATED TIME 2 / _RESPONSE_ = TIME;
```

As in the first example, one marginal probability is computed for each dependent variable, resulting in two response functions. The model is also the same: one degree of freedom for the intercept, and one for the main effect of TIME. CATMOD issues the warning message and prints the following RESPONSE PROFILES:

RESPONSE PROFILES

RESPONSE	TIME1	TIME2
1	2	1
2	2	2
3	1	1
4	1	2

Although the marginal levels are the same for the two dependent variables, they are not in the same order because the ORDER=DATA option specified that they be ordered according to their appearance in the input stream. Since RESPONSE MARGINALS yields marginal probabilities for every level except the last, the two response functions being analyzed are Prob(TIME1=2) and Prob(TIME2=1). Thus, the TIME effect is testing the hypothesis that Prob(TIME1=2)=Prob(TIME2=1). What it *should* be testing is the hypothesis

Prob(TIME1=1) = Prob(TIME2=1)
Prob(TIME1=2) = Prob(TIME2=2)

Whenever the above warning message appears, look at the RESPONSE PROFILES or the ONEWAY table to determine what hypothesis is actually being tested. For the latter example, a correct analysis can be obtained by deleting the ORDER=DATA option, or by reordering the data so that the (1,1) observation is first.

COMPUTATIONAL METHOD

The notation used in CATMOD differs slightly from that used in other literature. A complete description of the computational method follows.

Summary of Basic Dimensions

s = number of populations or samples (= number of rows in the underlying contingency table)

r = number of response categories (= number of columns in the underlying contingency table)

q = number of response functions computed for each population

d = number of parameters

Notation

A column vector of 1s is denoted by **j**. A square matrix of 1s is denoted by **J**. Σ_k is the sum over all the possible values of k. $\mathbf{DIAG}_n(\mathbf{p})$ is the diagonal matrix formed from the first n elements of the vector **p**. The inverse is $\mathbf{DIAG}_n^{-1}(\mathbf{p})$. $\mathbf{DIAG}(\mathbf{A}_1, \mathbf{A}_2, \ldots \mathbf{A}_k)$ denotes a block diagonal matrix with the **A** matrices on the main diagonal. Input data can be represented by a contingency table, as shown in **Table 14.2**.

Table 14.2 Input Data Represented by a Contingency Table

	Response				
Population	1	2	...	r	
1	n_{11}	n_{12}	...	n_{1r}	n_1
2	n_{21}	n_{22}	...	n_{2r}	n_2
...	...	...	...	...	..
s	n_{s1}	n_{s2}	...	n_{sr}	n_s

Let n_i denote the row sum $\Sigma_j n_{ij}$.

Computational Formulas

The following calculations are shown for each population, then for all populations combined.

Probability Estimates

Dimension

*j*th response $\quad p_{ij} = n_{ij}/n_i \quad$ 1x1

*i*th population $\quad \mathbf{p}_i = \begin{bmatrix} p_{i1} \\ p_{i2} \\ \ldots \\ p_{ir} \end{bmatrix} \quad$ rx1

		Dimension
all populations	$\mathbf{p} = \begin{bmatrix} \mathbf{p}_1 \\ \mathbf{p}_2 \\ \cdots \\ \mathbf{p}_r \end{bmatrix}$	*srx*1

Variance of Probability Estimates

*i*th population	$\mathbf{V}_i = (\mathbf{DIAG}(\mathbf{p}_i) - \mathbf{p}_i\mathbf{p}_i')/n_i$	*rxr*
all populations	$\mathbf{V} = \mathbf{DIAG}(\mathbf{V}_1, \mathbf{V}_2, \ldots, \mathbf{V}_s)$	*srxsr*

Response Functions

*i*th population	$\mathbf{F}_i = \mathbf{F}(\mathbf{p}_i)$	*qx*1
all populations	$\mathbf{F} = \begin{bmatrix} \mathbf{F}_1 \\ \mathbf{F}_2 \\ \cdots \\ \mathbf{F}_s \end{bmatrix}$	*sqx*1

Derivative of Function with Respect to Probability Estimates

*i*th population	$\mathbf{H}_i = \partial\mathbf{F}(\mathbf{p}_i)/\partial\mathbf{p}_i$	*qxr*
all populations	$\mathbf{H} = \mathbf{DIAG}(\mathbf{H}_1, \mathbf{H}_2, \ldots, \mathbf{H}_s)$	*sqxsr*

Variance of Functions

*i*th population	$\mathbf{S}_i = \mathbf{H}_i\mathbf{V}_i\mathbf{H}_i'$	*qxq*
all populations	$\mathbf{S} = \mathbf{DIAG}(\mathbf{S}_1, \mathbf{S}_2, \ldots, \mathbf{S}_s)$	*sqxsq*

Inverse Variance of Functions

*i*th population	$\mathbf{S}^i = (\mathbf{S}_i)^{-1}$	*qxq*
all populations	$\mathbf{S}^{-1} = \mathbf{DIAG}(\mathbf{S}^1, \mathbf{S}^2, \ldots, \mathbf{S}^s)$	*sqxsq*

Design Matrix		Dimension
*i*th population	$\mathbf{X}_i$	*qxd*
all populations	$\mathbf{X} = \begin{bmatrix} \mathbf{X}_1 \\ \mathbf{X}_2 \\ \cdots \\ \mathbf{X}_s \end{bmatrix}$	*sqxd*

Crossproduct of Design Matrix

*i*th population	$\mathbf{C}_i = \mathbf{X}_i{'}\mathbf{S}^i\mathbf{X}_i$	*dxd*
all populations	$\mathbf{C} = \mathbf{X'S}^{-1}\mathbf{X} = \Sigma_i\mathbf{C}_i$	*dxd*

Crossproduct of Design Matrix with Function

$$\mathbf{R} = \mathbf{X'S}^{-1}\mathbf{F} = \Sigma_i\mathbf{X}_i{'}\ \mathbf{S}^i\mathbf{F}_i \qquad dx1$$

Parameter Estimates

$$\mathbf{b} = \mathbf{C}^{-1}\mathbf{R} = (\mathbf{X'S}^{-1}\mathbf{X})^{-1}(\mathbf{X'S}^{-1}\mathbf{F}) \qquad dx1$$

Covariance of Parameter Estimates

$$\mathbf{COV(b)} = \mathbf{C}^{-1} \qquad dxd$$

Predicted Response Functions

$$\hat{\mathbf{F}} = \mathbf{Xb} \qquad sqx1$$

Residual Chi-Square

$$\text{RSS} = \mathbf{F'S}^{-1}\mathbf{F} - \hat{\mathbf{F}}'\mathbf{S}^{-1}\hat{\mathbf{F}} \qquad 1x1$$

Chi-Square for H_0: $\mathbf{L\beta}=0$

$$\text{Q} = (\mathbf{Lb})'(\mathbf{LC}^{-1}\mathbf{L}')^{-1}(\mathbf{Lb}) \qquad 1x1$$

In the following section, let **G**(**p**) be a vector of functions of **p**, and let **D** denote ∂**G**/∂**p**, the first derivative matrix of **G** with respect to **p**.

Derivative Table for Compound Functions: Y=F(G(p))

Function	Y = F(G)	Derivative(∂Y/∂p)
Multiply matrix	Y = A*G	A * D
Logarithm	Y = LOG(G)	DIAG^{-1}(G) * D
Exponential	Y = EXP(G)	DIAG(Y) * D
Add constant	Y = G+A	D

Default Response Functions: Every Response vs. Last Response

In this section, subscripts *i* for the population are suppressed.

$f_j = \log(p_j/p_r)$ for $j = 1,..,r-1$

for each population $i = 1,...,s$

Inverse of response functions for a population

$p_j = \exp(f_j)/(1 + \Sigma_k \exp(f_k))$, for $j = 1,...,r-1$

$p_r = 1/(1 + \Sigma_k \exp(f_k))$

Form of F and derivative for a population

$\mathbf{F} = \mathbf{K}\ \mathbf{LOG(p)} = (\mathbf{I}_{r-1}, -\mathbf{j})\mathbf{LOG(p)}$

$\mathbf{H} = \partial\mathbf{F}/\partial\mathbf{p} = (\mathbf{DIAG}_{r-1}{}^{-1}(\mathbf{p})\ ,\ (\text{-}1/p_r)\mathbf{j})$

Covariance results for a population

$\mathbf{S} = \mathbf{H\ V\ H'} = (\mathbf{DIAG}_{r-1}{}^{-1}(\mathbf{p})\ + (1/p_r)\mathbf{J}_{r-1})/n$

$\mathbf{S}^{-1} = n(\mathbf{DIAG}_{r-1}(\mathbf{p}) - \mathbf{qq}')$, where $\mathbf{q} = \mathbf{DIAG}_{r-1}(\mathbf{p})\ \mathbf{j}$

$\mathbf{S}^{-1}\mathbf{F} = n\ \mathbf{DIAG}_{r-1}(\mathbf{p})\ \mathbf{F} - (n\Sigma_j p_j f_j)\mathbf{q}$

$\mathbf{F'S}^{-1}\mathbf{F} = n\Sigma_j p_j f_j^2 - n(\Sigma_j p_j f_j)^2$

Maximum-Likelihood Method

Let **C** be the Hessian matrix and **G** be the gradient of the log-likelihood function (both functions of $\boldsymbol{\pi}$ and the parameters $\boldsymbol{\beta}$). Let $\mathbf{p}_i^*$ denote the vector containing the first *r*-1 sample proportions from population *i*, and let $\boldsymbol{\pi}_i^*$ denote the corresponding vector of probability estimates from the current iteration. Starting with the least-squares estimates $\mathbf{b}_0$ of $\boldsymbol{\beta}$, the probabilities $\boldsymbol{\pi}(\mathbf{b})$ are computed, and **b** is calculated iteratively by the Newton-Raphson method until it converges. λ is a step-halving factor that equals 1 at the start of each iteration. For any iteration in which the likelihood decreases, CATMOD uses a series of subiterations in which λ is iteratively divided by 2. The subiterations continue until the likelihood is greater than that of the previous iteration. If the likelihood has not reached that point after 10 subiterations, then convergence is assumed, but a warning message is printed. The following equations summarize the method:

$$\mathbf{b}_{k+1} = \mathbf{b}_k - \lambda \mathbf{C}^{-1}\mathbf{G}$$

where

$$\mathbf{C} = \mathbf{X'S}(\pi)^{-1}\mathbf{X}$$

$$\mathbf{N} = \begin{bmatrix} n_1(\mathbf{p}_1^* - \pi_1^*) \\ \cdots \\ n_s(\mathbf{p}_s^* - \pi_s^*) \end{bmatrix}$$

$$\mathbf{G} = \mathbf{X'N} \ .$$

PRINTED OUTPUT

CATMOD prints the following information in a header section:

1. the RESPONSE effect
2. the WEIGHT variable, if one is specified
3. the DATA SET name
4. the number of RESPONSE LEVELS (R)
5. the number of samples or POPULATIONS (S)
6. the TOTAL FREQUENCY (N), which is the total sample size
7. the number of OBSERVATIONS (OBS) from the data set (the number of data records).

Except for the analysis-of-variance table, all of the following items can be printed or suppressed, depending on your specification of statements and options:

8. The ONEWAY option induces printing of the ONE-WAY FREQUENCIES for each variable used in the analysis.
9. The populations (or samples) are defined in a section labeled POPULATION PROFILES. The SAMPLE SIZE and the values of the defining variables are printed for each SAMPLE. Printing is suppressed if the NOPROFILE option is specified.
10. The observed responses are defined in a section labeled RESPONSE PROFILES. The values of the defining variables are printed for each SAMPLE, unless the NOPROFILE option is specified.
11. If the FREQ option is specified, then the RESPONSE FREQUENCIES are printed for each population.
12. If the PROB option is specified, then the RESPONSE PROBABILITIES are printed for each population.
13. If the COV option is specified, the COVARIANCE MATRIX of the response functions is printed for each SAMPLE.
14. The RESPONSE FUNCTIONS are printed next to the DESIGN MATRIX, unless the COV option is specified, in which case they are printed next to the COVARIANCE MATRIX of the functions.
15. The DESIGN MATRIX is printed for weighted-least-squares analyses unless the NODESIGN option is specified. If the model type is AVERAGED, then the design matrix is printed with *q**s* rows, assuming *q*

response functions for each of s populations. Otherwise, the design matrix is printed with only s rows since the model is the same for each of the q response functions.

16. The X'*INV(S)*X MATRIX is printed for weighted-least-squares analyses if the XPX option is specified.
17. The ANALYSIS OF VARIANCE TABLE for the weighted-least-squares analysis gives the results of significance tests for each of the *design_effects* in the right-hand side of the MODEL statement. If _RESPONSE_ is a *design_effect* and is defined explicitly in the REPEATED statement, then the table contains test statistics for the individual effects comprised by the composite _RESPONSE_ effect. If the design matrix is input directly, then the content of the printed output depends on whether you specify any subsets of the parameters to be tested. If you specify one or more subsets, then the table contains one test for each subset. Otherwise, the table contains one test for the effect MODEL | MEAN. In every case, the table also contains the RESIDUAL goodness-of-fit test. Printed for each test of significance are the SOURCE of variation, the number of degrees of freedom (DF), the CHI-SQUARE value (which is a Wald statistic), and the significance probability (PROB).
18. The ANALYSIS OF INDIVIDUAL PARAMETERS for the weighted-least-squares analysis gives the EFFECT in the model for which parameters are formed, the PARAMETER number, the least-squares ESTIMATE, the estimated STANDARD ERROR of the parameter estimate, the CHI-SQUARE value (a Wald statistic) for testing that the parameter is zero, and the significance probability (PROB) of the test.
19. The COVARIANCE OF ESTIMATES for the weighted-least-squares analysis gives the estimated covariance matrix of the least-squares estimates of the parameters, provided the COVB option is specified.
20. The CORRELATION OF ESTIMATES for the weighted-least-squares analysis gives the estimated correlation matrix of the least-squares estimates of the parameters, provided that the CORRB option is specified.
21. The MAXIMUM LIKELIHOOD ANALYSIS is printed when the ML option is specified for the standard response functions (generalized logits). It gives the ITERATION number, the number of step-halving SUB-ITERATIONs, -2 LOG LIKELIHOOD for that iteration, the CONVERGENCE CRITERION, and the PARAMETER ESTIMATES for each iteration.
22. The ANALYSIS OF VARIANCE TABLE for the maximum-likelihood analysis, printed when the ML option is specified for the standard response functions, is similar to the table produced for the least-squares analysis. The CHI-SQUARE test for each effect is a Wald test based on the information matrix from the likelihood calculations. The LIKELIHOOD RATIO statistic compares the specified model with the unrestricted model, and is an appropriate goodness-of-fit test for the model.
23. The ANALYSIS OF INDIVIDUAL PARAMETERS for the maximum-likelihood analysis, printed when the ML option is specified for the standard response functions, is similar to the one produced for the least-squares analysis. The table includes the maximum-likelihood estimates, the estimated STANDARD ERRORS based on the information matrix, and the Wald Statistics (CHI-SQUARE) based on the estimated standard errors.
24. The COVARIANCE OF ESTIMATES for the maximum-likelihood analysis

gives the estimated covariance matrix of the maximum likelihood estimates of the parameters, provided that the COVB and ML options are specified for the standard response functions.

25. The CORRELATION OF ESTIMATES for the maximum-likelihood analysis gives the estimated correlation matrix of the maximum likelihood estimates of the parameters, provided that the CORRB and ML options are specified for the standard response functions.
26. For each source of variation specified in a CONTRAST statement, the ANALYSIS OF CONTRASTS gives the label for the source, the number of degrees of freedom (DF), the CHI-SQUARE value (which is a Wald statistic), and the significance probability (PROB).
27. Specification of the PREDICT option in the MODEL statement has the following effect. Printed for each response function within each population are the observed and predicted function values, their standard errors, and the residual (observed-predicted). If the linesize is large enough, the printed output also includes the values of the variables that define the populations. If the response functions are the default ones (generalized logits), additional information printed for each response within each population includes the observed and predicted cell probabilities, their standard errors, and the residual. The first cell probability is labeled P1, the second P2, and so forth. However, specifying PRED=FREQ in the MODEL statement results in printing of the predicted cell frequencies, rather than the predicted cell probabilities. The first cell frequency is labeled F1, the second F2, and so forth.
28. When there are multiple response statements, the output for each statement starts on a new page. For each response statement beyond the first, the number of the response statement is identified at the top of each page.
29. If the ADDCELL= option is specified in the MODEL statement, the adjusted sample size for each population (with number added to each cell) is labeled ADJ. SAMPLE SIZE. Similarly, the adjusted frequencies and probabilities are labeled ADJUSTED RESPONSE FREQUENCIES and ADJUSTED RESPONSE PROBABILITIES, respectively.
30. If _RESPONSE_ is defined explicitly in the REPEATED statement, then the definition is printed as a footnote whenever _RESPONSE_ appears in the printed output.

EXAMPLES

The examples in this section illustrate the following twelve types of analysis:

1. Linear response function, $r=2$ responses
2. Mean score response function, $r=3$ responses
3. Logistic regression, standard response function
4. Log-linear model, one dependent variable
5. Log-linear model, no zero frequencies
6. Log-linear model, structural zeros and random zeros
7. Repeated measures, two levels of response, one population
8. Repeated measures, two levels of response, two populations
9. Repeated measures, four levels of response, one population
10. Repeated measures, four levels of response, two populations
11. Repeated measures, logistic analysis of growth curve
12. Repeated measures, two repeated measurement factors.

Linear Response Function, r=2 Responses: Example 1

The choice of detergent brand is related to three other categorical variables. The linear response function yields one probability, Pr(brand preference = M), as the response function to be analyzed. The first model is a saturated one, containing all of the main effects and interactions. The second is a reduced model containing only the main effects. See **Example 4** for a log-linear model analysis of these data.

```
*----------------------CATMOD EXAMPLE 1--------------------------------*
|                                                                      |
|                 DETERGENT PREFERENCE STUDY                           |
|                 --------------------------                           |
| THE DATA ARE FROM A CONSUMER BLIND TRIAL OF DETERGENT PREFERENCE.    |
| THE VARIABLES MEASURED IN THE STUDY WERE:                            |
|    SOFTNESS=SOFTNESS OF LAUNDRY WATER (SOFT, MED, HARD)              |
|    PREV=PREVIOUS USER OF BRAND M? (YES, NO)                          |
|    TEMP=TEMPERATURE OF LAUNDRY WATER (HIGH, LOW)                     |
|    BRAND=BRAND PREFERRED (M, X)                                      |
|                                                                      |
| FROM: RIES AND SMITH (1963), CHEMICAL ENGINEERING PROGRESS 59, 39-43|
|        ALSO SEE COX (1970), 38                                       |
|                                                                      |
| ILLUSTRATE: LINEAR RESPONSE FUNCTION, R=2 RESPONSES                  |
|                                                                      |
*----------------------------------------------------------------------*;

TITLE 'DETERGENT PREFERENCE STUDY';
DATA DETERG;
   INPUT SOFTNESS $ BRAND $ PREV $ TEMP $ COUNT @@;
   CARDS;
SOFT X YES HIGH 19 SOFT X YES LOW 57 SOFT X NO HIGH 29 SOFT X NO LOW 63
SOFT M YES HIGH 29 SOFT M YES LOW 49 SOFT M NO HIGH 27 SOFT M NO LOW 53
MED  X YES HIGH 23 MED  X YES LOW 47 MED  X NO HIGH 33 MED  X NO LOW 66
MED  M YES HIGH 47 MED  M YES LOW 55 MED  M NO HIGH 23 MED  M NO LOW 50
HARD X YES HIGH 24 HARD X YES LOW 37 HARD X NO HIGH 42 HARD X NO LOW 68
HARD M YES HIGH 43 HARD M YES LOW 52 HARD M NO HIGH 30 HARD M NO LOW 42
;
PROC CATMOD;
   RESPONSE 1 0;
   WEIGHT COUNT;
   MODEL BRAND = SOFTNESS|PREV|TEMP / FREQ PROB NODESIGN;
   TITLE2 'SATURATED MODEL';

PROC CATMOD;
   RESPONSE 1 0;
   WEIGHT COUNT;
   MODEL BRAND = SOFTNESS PREV TEMP / NOPROFILE;
   TITLE2 'MAIN-EFFECTS MODEL';
```

Output 14.1 Detergent Preference Study: Linear Model Analysis

```
                    DETERGENT PREFERENCE STUDY                                    1
                          SATURATED MODEL

                         CATMOD PROCEDURE

RESPONSE: BRAND                                  RESPONSE LEVELS (R)=      2
WEIGHT VARIABLE: COUNT                           POPULATIONS     (S)=     12
DATA SET: DETERG                                 TOTAL FREQUENCY (N)=   1008
                                                 OBSERVATIONS  (OBS)=     24


                       POPULATION PROFILES
                                                       SAMPLE
        SAMPLE    SOFTNESS       PREV         TEMP      SIZE
        ----------------------------------------------------
            1     HARD           NO           HIGH        72
            2     HARD           NO           LOW        110
            3     HARD           YES          HIGH        67
            4     HARD           YES          LOW         89
            5     MED            NO           HIGH        56
            6     MED            NO           LOW        116
            7     MED            YES          HIGH        70
            8     MED            YES          LOW        102
            9     SOFT           NO           HIGH        56
           10     SOFT           NO           LOW        116
           11     SOFT           YES          HIGH        48
           12     SOFT           YES          LOW        106


                         RESPONSE PROFILES

                         RESPONSE   BRAND
                         ----------------
                             1        M
                             2        X
```

```
                    DETERGENT PREFERENCE STUDY                                    2
                          SATURATED MODEL

                         CATMOD PROCEDURE

                       RESPONSE FREQUENCIES

                            RESPONSE NUMBER
                    SAMPLE        1           2
                    -------------------------
                        1        30          42
                        2        42          68
                        3        43          24
                        4        52          37
                        5        23          33
                        6        50          66
                        7        47          23
                        8        55          47
                        9        27          29
                       10        53          63
                       11        29          19
                       12        49          57
```

(continued on next page)

(continued from previous page)

RESPONSE PROBABILITIES

SAMPLE	RESPONSE NUMBER 1	2
1	.416667	.583333
2	.381818	.618182
3	.641791	.358209
4	0.58427	0.41573
5	.410714	.589286
6	.431034	.568966
7	.671429	.328571
8	.539216	.460784
9	.482143	.517857
10	.456897	.543103
11	.604167	.395833
12	.462264	.537736

DETERGENT PREFERENCE STUDY
SATURATED MODEL 3

CATMOD PROCEDURE

ANALYSIS OF VARIANCE TABLE

SOURCE	DF	CHI-SQUARE	PROB
INTERCEPT	1	983.13	0.0001
SOFTNESS	2	0.09	0.9575
PREV	1	22.68	0.0001
SOFTNESS*PREV	2	3.85	0.1457
TEMP	1	3.67	0.0555
SOFTNESS*TEMP	2	0.23	0.8914
PREV*TEMP	1	2.26	0.1324
SOFTNESS*PREV*TEMP	2	0.76	0.6850
RESIDUAL	0	-0.00	1.0000

ANALYSIS OF INDIVIDUAL PARAMETERS

EFFECT	PARAMETER	ESTIMATE	STANDARD ERROR	CHI-SQUARE	PROB
INTERCEPT	1	0.506867	.0161655	983.13	0.0001
SOFTNESS	2	-7.3E-04	.0224655	0.00	0.9740
	3	.0062309	.0226234	0.08	0.7830
PREV	4	-.076989	.0161655	22.68	0.0001
SOFTNESS*PREV	5	-.029905	.0224655	1.77	0.1831
	6	-.015235	.0226234	0.45	0.5007
TEMP	7	.0309509	.0161655	3.67	0.0555
SOFTNESS*TEMP	8	-.007858	.0224655	0.12	0.7265
	9	-.002978	.0226234	0.02	0.8953
PREV*TEMP	10	-.024322	.0161655	2.26	0.1324
SOFTNESS*PREV*TEMP	11	.0186536	.0224655	0.69	0.4064
	12	-.013811	.0226234	0.37	0.5415

DETERGENT PREFERENCE STUDY
MAIN-EFFECTS MODEL 4

CATMOD PROCEDURE

```
RESPONSE: BRAND                  RESPONSE LEVELS (R)=     2
WEIGHT VARIABLE: COUNT           POPULATIONS     (S)=    12
DATA SET: DETERG                 TOTAL FREQUENCY (N)=  1008
                                 OBSERVATIONS  (OBS)=    24
```

(continued on next page)

(continued from previous page)

SAMPLE	RESPONSE FUNCTIONS	DESIGN MATRIX 1	2	3	4	5
1	0.416667	1	1	0	1	1
2	0.381818	1	1	0	1	-1
3	0.641791	1	1	0	-1	1
4	0.58427	1	1	0	-1	-1
5	0.410714	1	0	1	1	1
6	0.431034	1	0	1	1	-1
7	0.671429	1	0	1	-1	1
8	0.539216	1	0	1	-1	-1
9	0.482143	1	-1	-1	1	1
10	0.456897	1	-1	-1	1	-1
11	0.604167	1	-1	-1	-1	1
12	0.462264	1	-1	-1	-1	-1

ANALYSIS OF VARIANCE TABLE

SOURCE	DF	CHI-SQUARE	PROB
INTERCEPT	1	1004.93	0.0001
SOFTNESS	2	0.24	0.8859
PREV	1	20.96	0.0001
TEMP	1	3.95	0.0468
RESIDUAL	7	8.26	0.3100

ANALYSIS OF INDIVIDUAL PARAMETERS

EFFECT	PARAMETER	ESTIMATE	STANDARD ERROR	CHI-SQUARE	PROB
INTERCEPT	1	0.50797	0.016024	1004.93	0.0001
SOFTNESS	2	-.002562	.0218391	0.01	0.9066
	3	.0103542	.0217608	0.23	0.6342
PREV	4	-.071088	.0155288	20.96	0.0001
TEMP	5	.0319446	0.016071	3.95	0.0468

Mean Score Response Function, r=3 Responses: Example 2

The response variable is ordinally scaled with three levels, so that assignment of scores is appropriate (0=none, .5=slight, 1=moderate). For these scores, the response function yields the mean score. The ORDER= option is used so that the levels of the response variable remain in the correct order. A main-effects model is fitted.

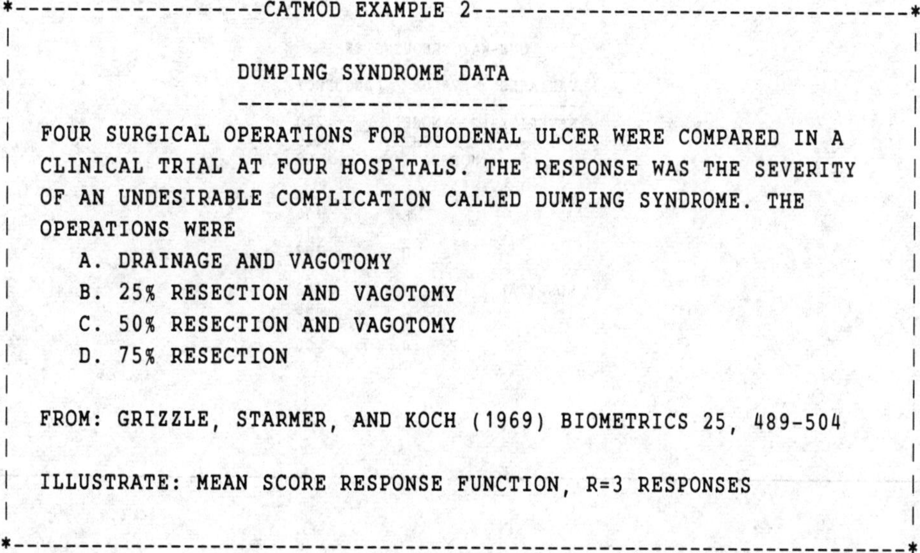

```
*-------------------CATMOD EXAMPLE 2----------------------------------*
|                                                                      |
|                     DUMPING SYNDROME DATA                            |
|                     ---------------------                            |
| FOUR SURGICAL OPERATIONS FOR DUODENAL ULCER WERE COMPARED IN A      |
| CLINICAL TRIAL AT FOUR HOSPITALS. THE RESPONSE WAS THE SEVERITY     |
| OF AN UNDESIRABLE COMPLICATION CALLED DUMPING SYNDROME. THE         |
| OPERATIONS WERE                                                      |
|    A. DRAINAGE AND VAGOTOMY                                          |
|    B. 25% RESECTION AND VAGOTOMY                                     |
|    C. 50% RESECTION AND VAGOTOMY                                     |
|    D. 75% RESECTION                                                  |
|                                                                      |
| FROM: GRIZZLE, STARMER, AND KOCH (1969) BIOMETRICS 25, 489-504      |
|                                                                      |
| ILLUSTRATE: MEAN SCORE RESPONSE FUNCTION, R=3 RESPONSES             |
|                                                                      |
*----------------------------------------------------------------------*;
```

```
TITLE 'DUMPING SYNDROME DATA';
DATA OPERATE;
   INPUT HOSPITAL TRT $ SEVERITY $ WT @@;
   CARDS;
1 A NONE 23    1 A SLIGHT  7    1 A MODERATE 2
1 B NONE 23    1 B SLIGHT 10    1 B MODERATE 5
1 C NONE 20    1 C SLIGHT 13    1 C MODERATE 5
1 D NONE 24    1 D SLIGHT 10    1 D MODERATE 6
2 A NONE 18    2 A SLIGHT  6    2 A MODERATE 1
2 B NONE 18    2 B SLIGHT  6    2 B MODERATE 2
2 C NONE 13    2 C SLIGHT 13    2 C MODERATE 2
2 D NONE  9    2 D SLIGHT 15    2 D MODERATE 2
3 A NONE  8    3 A SLIGHT  6    3 A MODERATE 3
3 B NONE 12    3 B SLIGHT  4    3 B MODERATE 4
3 C NONE 11    3 C SLIGHT  6    3 C MODERATE 2
3 D NONE  7    3 D SLIGHT  7    3 D MODERATE 4
4 A NONE 12    4 A SLIGHT  9    4 A MODERATE 1
4 B NONE 15    4 B SLIGHT  3    4 B MODERATE 2
4 C NONE 14    4 C SLIGHT  8    4 C MODERATE 3
4 D NONE 13    4 D SLIGHT  6    4 D MODERATE 4
;
PROC CATMOD ORDER=DATA;
   WEIGHT WT;
   RESPONSE 0  0.5  1;
   MODEL SEVERITY = TRT HOSPITAL / FREQ ONEWAY;
   TITLE2 'MAIN-EFFECTS MODEL';
```

Output 14.2 Surgical Data: Analysis of Mean Scores

```
                           DUMPING SYNDROME DATA                               1
                            MAIN-EFFECTS MODEL

                             CATMOD PROCEDURE

RESPONSE: SEVERITY                         RESPONSE LEVELS (R)=      3
WEIGHT VARIABLE: WT                        POPULATIONS     (S)=     16
DATA SET: OPERATE                          TOTAL FREQUENCY (N)=    417
                                           OBSERVATIONS  (OBS)=     48


                           ONE-WAY FREQUENCIES

                      VARIABLE     VALUE   FREQUENCY
                      ------------------------------
                      SEVERITY      NONE        240
                                  SLIGHT        129
                                MODERATE         48

                      TRT              A         96
                                       B        104
                                       C        110
                                       D        107

                      HOSPITAL         1        148
                                       2        105
                                       3         74
                                       4         90
```

(continued on next page)

(continued from previous page)

POPULATION PROFILES

SAMPLE	TRT	HOSPITAL	SAMPLE SIZE
1	A	1	32
2	A	2	25
3	A	3	17
4	A	4	22
5	B	1	38
6	B	2	26
7	B	3	20
8	B	4	20
9	C	1	38
10	C	2	28
11	C	3	19
12	C	4	25
13	D	1	40
14	D	2	26
15	D	3	18
16	D	4	23

DUMPING SYNDROME DATA
MAIN-EFFECTS MODEL 2

CATMOD PROCEDURE

RESPONSE PROFILES

RESPONSE	SEVERITY
1	NONE
2	SLIGHT
3	MODERATE

RESPONSE FREQUENCIES

SAMPLE	RESPONSE NUMBER 1	2	3
1	23	7	2
2	18	6	1
3	8	6	3
4	12	9	1
5	23	10	5
6	18	6	2
7	12	4	4
8	15	3	2
9	20	13	5
10	13	13	2
11	11	6	2
12	14	8	3
13	24	10	6
14	9	15	2
15	7	7	4
16	13	6	4

DUMPING SYNDROME DATA
MAIN-EFFECTS MODEL 3

CATMOD PROCEDURE

SAMPLE	RESPONSE FUNCTIONS	DESIGN MATRIX 1	2	3	4	5	6	7
1	0.171875	1	1	0	0	1	0	0
2	0.16	1	1	0	0	0	1	0
3	0.352941	1	1	0	0	0	0	1
4	0.25	1	1	0	0	-1	-1	-1
5	0.263158	1	0	1	0	1	0	0
6	0.192308	1	0	1	0	0	1	0
7	0.3	1	0	1	0	0	0	1

(continued on next page)

(continued from previous page)

```
  8      0.175       1     0     1     0    -1    -1    -1
  9   0.302632       1     0     0     1     1     0     0
 10   0.303571       1     0     0     1     0     1     0
 11   0.263158       1     0     0     1     0     0     1
 12       0.28       1     0     0     1    -1    -1    -1
 13      0.275       1    -1    -1    -1     1     0     0
 14   0.365385       1    -1    -1    -1     0     1     0
 15   0.416667       1    -1    -1    -1     0     0     1
 16   0.304348       1    -1    -1    -1    -1    -1    -1


                ANALYSIS OF VARIANCE TABLE

        SOURCE                 DF   CHI-SQUARE      PROB
        ------------------------------------------------
        INTERCEPT               1       248.77    0.0001
        TRT                     3         8.90    0.0307
        HOSPITAL                3         2.33    0.5065

        RESIDUAL                9         6.33    0.7069


              ANALYSIS OF INDIVIDUAL PARAMETERS

                                            STANDARD     CHI-
EFFECT                  PARAMETER ESTIMATE    ERROR    SQUARE   PROB
---------------------------------------------------------------------
INTERCEPT                       1 0.272431  .0172726   248.77 0.0001
TRT                             2 -.055236  .0270395     4.17 0.0411
                                3 -.036493  .0289366     1.59 0.2073
                                4 .0248148  .0280114     0.78 0.3757
HOSPITAL                        5 -.020408  .0263603     0.60 0.4388
                                6 -.017822  .0267672     0.44 0.5055
                                7 .0530541  .0351529     2.28 0.1312
```

Logistic Regression, Standard Response Function: Example 3

For logistic regression, the *design_effects* are declared in a DIRECT statement, and the NOGLS and ML options are specified.

```
*-------------------CATMOD EXAMPLE 3-----------------------------*
|                                                                |
|         MAXIMUM LIKELIHOOD LOGISTIC REGRESSION                 |
|         --------------------------------------                 |
|  INGOTS PREPARED WITH DIFFERENT HEATING AND SOAKING TIMES ARE  |
|  TESTED FOR READINESS TO ROLL.                                 |
|                                                                |
|  FROM: COX (1970), 67-68                                       |
|                                                                |
|  ILLUSTRATE: LOGISTIC REGRESSION, STANDARD RESPONSE FUNCTION   |
|                                                                |
*----------------------------------------------------------------*;

TITLE 'MAXIMUM LIKELIHOOD LOGISTIC REGRESSION';
DATA INGOTS;
   INPUT HEAT SOAK NREADY NTOTAL @@;
   COUNT=NREADY; Y=1; OUTPUT;
   COUNT=NTOTAL-NREADY; Y=0; OUTPUT;
   DROP NREADY NTOTAL;
   CARDS;
 7  1.0  0  10    7  1.7  0  17    7  2.2  0  7     7  2.8  0  12
 7  4.0  0   9   14  1.0  0  31   14  1.7  0 43    14  2.2  2  33
14  2.8  0  31   14  4.0  0  19   27  1.0  1 56    27  1.7  4  44
27  2.2  0  21   27  2.8  1  22   27  4.0  1 16    51  1.0  3  13
51  1.7  0   1   51  2.2  0   1   51  4.0  0  1
```

```
PROC CATMOD;
   WEIGHT COUNT;
   DIRECT HEAT SOAK;
   MODEL Y = HEAT SOAK / FREQ ML NOGLS COVB CORRB;
```

Output 14.3 Maximum Likelihood Logistic Regession

```
                    MAXIMUM LIKELIHOOD LOGISTIC REGRESSION                          1

                               CATMOD PROCEDURE

RESPONSE: Y                            RESPONSE LEVELS (R)=     2
WEIGHT VARIABLE: COUNT                 POPULATIONS     (S)=    19
DATA SET: INGOTS                       TOTAL FREQUENCY (N)=   387
                                       OBSERVATIONS  (OBS)=    25


                             POPULATION PROFILES
                                                   SAMPLE
                   SAMPLE    HEAT          SOAK     SIZE
                   ------------------------------------
                      1         7             1       10
                      2         7           1.7       17
                      3         7           2.2        7
                      4         7           2.8       12
                      5         7             4        9
                      6        14             1       31
                      7        14           1.7       43
                      8        14           2.2       33
                      9        14           2.8       31
                     10        14             4       19
                     11        27             1       56
                     12        27           1.7       44
                     13        27           2.2       21
                     14        27           2.8       22
                     15        27             4       16
                     16        51             1       13
                     17        51           1.7        1
                     18        51           2.2        1
                     19        51             4        1


                              RESPONSE PROFILES

                              RESPONSE     Y
                              -------------
                                  1        0
                                  2        1
```

```
                    MAXIMUM LIKELIHOOD LOGISTIC REGRESSION                          2

                               CATMOD PROCEDURE

                             RESPONSE FREQUENCIES

                                  RESPONSE NUMBER
                      SAMPLE          1        2
                      ---------------------------
                         1           10        0
                         2           17        0
                         3            7        0
                         4           12        0
                         5            9        0
                         6           31        0
                         7           43        0
                         8           31        2
                         9           31        0
                        10           19        0
                        11           55        1
```

(continued on next page)

(continued from previous page)

12	40	4
13	21	0
14	21	1
15	15	1
16	10	3
17	1	0
18	1	0
19	1	0

MAXIMUM LIKELIHOOD ANALYSIS

ITERATION	SUB ITERATION	-2 LOG LIKELIHOOD	CONVERGENCE CRITERION	PARAMETER ESTIMATES 1	2	3
0	0	536.496	1	0	0	0
1	0	152.59	0.715581	2.15941	-.0138784	-.0037327
2	0	106.761	0.300341	3.53344	-.0363154	-.0119734
3	0	96.6922	0.094309	4.7489	-.0640013	-.0299201
4	0	95.3838	0.013531	5.41382	-.0790272	-0.04982
5	0	95.3457	.00040013	5.55393	-.0819276	-.0564395
6	0	95.3456	4.83E-07	5.55916	-.0820307	-.0567708
7	0	95.3456	7.73E-13	5.55917	-.0820308	-.0567713

ANALYSIS OF VARIANCE TABLE

SOURCE	DF	CHI-SQUARE	PROB
INTERCEPT	1	24.65	0.0001
HEAT	1	11.95	0.0005
SOAK	1	0.03	0.8639
LIKELIHOOD RATIO	16	13.75	0.6171

MAXIMUM LIKELIHOOD LOGISTIC REGRESSION 3

CATMOD PROCEDURE

ANALYSIS OF INDIVIDUAL PARAMETERS

EFFECT	PARAMETER	ESTIMATE	STANDARD ERROR	CHI-SQUARE	PROB
INTERCEPT	1	5.55917	1.11969	24.65	0.0001
HEAT	2	-.082031	.0237345	11.95	0.0005
SOAK	3	-.056771	0.331213	0.03	0.8639

COVARIANCE OF ESTIMATES

	1	2	3
1	1.25371	-0.0215664	-0.281765
2	-0.0215664	.000563325	0.00262426
3	-0.281765	0.00262426	0.109702

CORRELATION OF ESTIMATES

	1	2	3
1	1	-0.811521	-0.759767
2	-0.811521	1	0.333826
3	-0.759767	0.333826	1

Log-Linear Model, One Dependent Variable: Example 4

The choice of detergent brand is related to three other categorical variables. The linear response function yields one probability, Pr(brand preference = M), as the response function to be analyzed. The first model is a saturated one, containing all of the main effects and interactions. The second is a reduced model containing only the main effects. See **Example 1** for a linear model analysis of these data.

```
*----------------------CATMOD EXAMPLE 4-------------------------------*
|                                                                     |
|                  DETERGENT PREFERENCE STUDY                         |
|                  --------------------------                         |
| THE DATA ARE FROM A CONSUMER BLIND TRIAL OF DETERGENT PREFERENCE.   |
| THE VARIABLES MEASURED IN THE STUDY WERE:                           |
|    SOFTNESS=SOFTNESS OF LAUNDRY WATER (SOFT, MED, HARD)             |
|    PREV=PREVIOUS USER OF BRAND M? (YES, NO)                         |
|    TEMP=TEMPERATURE OF LAUNDRY WATER (HIGH, LOW)                    |
|    BRAND=BRAND PREFERRED (M, X)                                     |
|                                                                     |
| FROM: RIES AND SMITH (1963), CHEMICAL ENGINEERING PROGRESS 59, 39-43|
|       ALSO SEE COX (1970), 38                                       |
|                                                                     |
| ILLUSTRATE: LOG-LINEAR MODEL, ONE DEPENDENT VARIABLE                |
|                                                                     |
*---------------------------------------------------------------------*;

TITLE 'DETERGENT PREFERENCE STUDY';
DATA DETERG;
   INPUT SOFTNESS $ BRAND $ PREV $ TEMP $ COUNT @@;
   CARDS;
SOFT X YES HIGH 19 SOFT X YES LOW 57 SOFT X NO HIGH 29 SOFT X NO LOW 63
SOFT M YES HIGH 29 SOFT M YES LOW 49 SOFT M NO HIGH 27 SOFT M NO LOW 53
MED  X YES HIGH 23 MED  X YES LOW 47 MED  X NO HIGH 33 MED  X NO LOW 66
MED  M YES HIGH 47 MED  M YES LOW 55 MED  M NO HIGH 23 MED  M NO LOW 50
HARD X YES HIGH 24 HARD X YES LOW 37 HARD X NO HIGH 42 HARD X NO LOW 68
HARD M YES HIGH 43 HARD M YES LOW 52 HARD M NO HIGH 30 HARD M NO LOW 42
;
PROC CATMOD;
   WEIGHT COUNT;
   MODEL BRAND = SOFTNESS|PREV|TEMP / FREQ PROB NODESIGN;
   TITLE2 'SATURATED MODEL';

PROC CATMOD;
   WEIGHT COUNT;
   MODEL BRAND = SOFTNESS PREV TEMP / NOPROFILE;
   TITLE2 'MAIN-EFFECTS MODEL';
```

Output 14.4 Detergent Preference Study: Log-Linear Model Analysis

```
                    DETERGENT PREFERENCE STUDY                                       1
                          SATURATED MODEL

                          CATMOD PROCEDURE

RESPONSE: BRAND                          RESPONSE LEVELS (R)=     2
WEIGHT VARIABLE: COUNT                   POPULATIONS     (S)=    12
DATA SET: DETERG                         TOTAL FREQUENCY (N)=  1008
                                         OBSERVATIONS  (OBS)=    24



                        POPULATION PROFILES
                                                        SAMPLE
        SAMPLE    SOFTNESS        PREV         TEMP      SIZE
        ---------------------------------------------------------
           1      HARD            NO           HIGH        72
           2      HARD            NO           LOW        110
           3      HARD            YES          HIGH        67
           4      HARD            YES          LOW         89
           5      MED             NO           HIGH        56
           6      MED             NO           LOW        116
           7      MED             YES          HIGH        70
           8      MED             YES          LOW        102
           9      SOFT            NO           HIGH        56
          10      SOFT            NO           LOW        116
          11      SOFT            YES          HIGH        48
          12      SOFT            YES          LOW        106


                        RESPONSE PROFILES

                        RESPONSE    BRAND
                        ----------------
                            1         M
                            2         X
```

```
                    DETERGENT PREFERENCE STUDY                                       2
                          SATURATED MODEL

                          CATMOD PROCEDURE

                        RESPONSE FREQUENCIES

                             RESPONSE NUMBER
                    SAMPLE          1          2
                    --------------------------
                       1           30         42
                       2           42         68
                       3           43         24
                       4           52         37
                       5           23         33
                       6           50         66
                       7           47         23
                       8           55         47
                       9           27         29
                      10           53         63
                      11           29         19
                      12           49         57


                      RESPONSE PROBABILITIES

                             RESPONSE NUMBER
                    SAMPLE          1          2
                    --------------------------
                       1      .416667    .583333
                       2      .381818    .618182
                       3      .641791    .358209
                       4      0.58427    0.41573
                       5      .410714    .589286
                       6      .431034    .568966
                       7      .671429    .328571
                       8      .539216    .460784
                       9      .482143    .517857
```

(continued on next page)

(continued from previous page)

10	.456897	.543103
11	.604167	.395833
12	.462264	.537736

DETERGENT PREFERENCE STUDY 3
SATURATED MODEL

CATMOD PROCEDURE

ANALYSIS OF VARIANCE TABLE

SOURCE	DF	CHI-SQUARE	PROB
INTERCEPT	1	0.21	0.6505
SOFTNESS	2	0.10	0.9522
PREV	1	21.80	0.0001
SOFTNESS*PREV	2	3.80	0.1493
TEMP	1	3.63	0.0567
SOFTNESS*TEMP	2	0.20	0.9066
PREV*TEMP	1	2.25	0.1335
SOFTNESS*PREV*TEMP	2	0.74	0.6916
RESIDUAL	0	0.00	1.0000

ANALYSIS OF INDIVIDUAL PARAMETERS

EFFECT	PARAMETER	ESTIMATE	STANDARD ERROR	CHI-SQUARE	PROB
INTERCEPT	1	.0304733	.0672532	0.21	0.6505
SOFTNESS	2	-.004183	.0939794	0.00	0.9645
	3	.0278252	0.094676	0.09	0.7688
PREV	4	-.314016	.0672532	21.80	0.0001
SOFTNESS*PREV	5	-.121429	.0939794	1.67	0.1963
	6	-.063605	0.094676	0.45	0.5017
TEMP	7	0.128145	.0672532	3.63	0.0567
SOFTNESS*TEMP	8	-.031099	.0939794	0.11	0.7407
	9	-.009624	0.094676	0.01	0.9190
PREV*TEMP	10	-.100917	.0672532	2.25	0.1335
SOFTNESS*PREV*TEMP	11	.0765537	.0939794	0.66	0.4153
	12	-.059295	0.094676	0.39	0.5311

DETERGENT PREFERENCE STUDY 4
MAIN-EFFECTS MODEL

CATMOD PROCEDURE

```
RESPONSE: BRAND                    RESPONSE LEVELS (R)=     2
WEIGHT VARIABLE: COUNT             POPULATIONS     (S)=    12
DATA SET: DETERG                   TOTAL FREQUENCY (N)=  1008
                                   OBSERVATIONS  (OBS)=    24
```

SAMPLE	RESPONSE FUNCTIONS	DESIGN MATRIX 1	2	3	4	5
1	-0.336472	1	1	0	1	1
2	-0.481838	1	1	0	1	-1
3	0.583146	1	1	0	-1	1
4	0.340326	1	1	0	-1	-1
5	-0.361013	1	0	1	1	1
6	-0.277632	1	0	1	1	-1
7	0.714653	1	0	1	-1	1
8	0.157186	1	0	1	-1	-1
9	-0.071459	1	-1	-1	1	1
10	-0.172843	1	-1	-1	1	-1
11	0.422857	1	-1	-1	-1	1
12	-0.151231	1	-1	-1	-1	-1

(continued on next page)

(continued from previous page)

```
                    ANALYSIS OF VARIANCE TABLE

        SOURCE                    DF   CHI-SQUARE      PROB
        --------------------------------------------------
        INTERCEPT                  1         0.20    0.6519
        SOFTNESS                   2         0.20    0.9033
        PREV                       1        19.28    0.0001
        TEMP                       1         3.63    0.0566

        RESIDUAL                   7         8.18    0.3169


                ANALYSIS OF INDIVIDUAL PARAMETERS

                                              STANDARD     CHI-
EFFECT              PARAMETER  ESTIMATE        ERROR     SQUARE    PROB
-------------------------------------------------------------------------
INTERCEPT                   1  .0301634     .0668634       0.20  0.6519
SOFTNESS                    2  -0.00991     .0910619       0.01  0.9133
                            3  .0391404     .0901922       0.19  0.6643
PREV                        4  -.281692     .0641546      19.28  0.0001
TEMP                        5    0.1277     0.066998       3.63  0.0566
```

Log-Linear Model, Three Dependent Variables: Example 5

This analysis reproduces the predicted cell frequencies for Bartlett's data using a log-linear model of no three-variable interaction (Bishop, Fienberg, and Holland 1975, p. 89). As in the text, the variable levels are simply labeled 1 and 2.

```
*-------------------CATMOD EXAMPLE 5----------------------------------*
|                                                                     |
|                    BARTLETT'S DATA                                  |
|                    ---------------                                  |
|  CUTTINGS OF TWO DIFFERENT LENGTHS WERE PLANTED AT ONE OF TWO TIME  |
|  POINTS, AND THEIR SURVIVAL STATUS WAS RECORDED. THE VARIABLES ARE  |
|     V1=SURVIVAL STATUS (DEAD OR ALIVE)                              |
|     V2=TIME OF PLANTING (SPRING OR AT_ONCE)                         |
|     V3=LENGTH OF CUTTING (LONG OR SHORT)                            |
|                                                                     |
|  FROM: BISHOP, FIENBERG, AND HOLLAND (1975), 89                     |
|                                                                     |
|  ILLUSTRATE: LOG-LINEAR MODEL, THREE DEPENDENT VARIABLES            |
|                                                                     |
*---------------------------------------------------------------------*;

TITLE 'BARTLETT''S DATA';
DATA B;
   INPUT V3 V2 V1 WT @@;
   CARDS;
1 1 1 156     1 1 2  84     1 2 1 84     1 2 2 156
2 1 1 107     2 1 2 133     2 2 1 31     2 2 2 209
;
PROC CATMOD;
   WEIGHT WT;
   MODEL V3*V2*V1 = _RESPONSE_ / NOGLS NOPARM PRED=FREQ ML;
   REPEATED / _RESPONSE_ = V3|V2  V3|V1  V2|V1;
   TITLE2 'MODEL WITH NO 3-VARIABLE INTERACTION';
```

Output 14.5 Analysis of Bartlett's Data: Log-Linear Model

```
                                    BARTLETT'S DATA                                                   1
                           MODEL WITH NO 3-VARIABLE INTERACTION

                                    CATMOD PROCEDURE

                  RESPONSE: V3*V2*V1                   RESPONSE LEVELS (R)=     8
                  WEIGHT VARIABLE: WT                  POPULATIONS     (S)=     1
                  DATA SET: B                          TOTAL FREQUENCY (N)=   960
                                                       OBSERVATIONS  (OBS)=     8


                                                 SAMPLE
                                    SAMPLE        SIZE
                                    ------------------
                                       1          960


                                    RESPONSE PROFILES

                          RESPONSE    V3         V2         V1
                          ------------------------------------
                              1        1          1          1
                              2        1          1          2
                              3        1          2          1
                              4        1          2          2
                              5        2          1          1
                              6        2          1          2
                              7        2          2          1
                              8        2          2          2


                               MAXIMUM LIKELIHOOD ANALYSIS

                SUB        -2 LOG     CONVERGENCE                          PARAMETER ESTIMATES
ITERATION   ITERATION   LIKELIHOOD     CRITERION         1            2            3            4            5            6
-------------------------------------------------------------------------------------------------------------------------------
    0           0         3992.53             1            0            0            0            0            0            0
    1           0         3812.51     0.0450897   -5.92E-17    -5.92E-17     5.92E-17      -0.2125       0.2125     0.308333
    2           0         3800.22     .00322336   0.0493803     0.075214    -0.075214    -0.248607     0.248607     0.350164
    3           0         3800.12      2.55E-05    0.055527    0.0809486    -.0809486    -0.254341     0.254341     0.356803
    4           0         3800.12      3.69E-09   0.0555811    0.0810182    -.0810182    -0.254423     0.254423     0.356886
```

```
                                    BARTLETT'S DATA                                                   2
                           MODEL WITH NO 3-VARIABLE INTERACTION

                                    CATMOD PROCEDURE

                              ANALYSIS OF VARIANCE TABLE

                       SOURCE                    DF   CHI-SQUARE      PROB
                       -----------------------------------------------------
                       V3                         1         2.64    0.1041
                       V2                         1         5.25    0.0220
                       V3*V2                      1         5.25    0.0220
                       V1                         1        48.94    0.0001
                       V3*V1                      1        48.94    0.0001
                       V2*V1                      1        95.01    0.0001

                       LIKELIHOOD RATIO           1         2.29    0.1299
```

(continued on next page)

(continued from previous page)

PREDICTED VALUES FOR RESPONSE FUNCTIONS AND FREQUENCIES

SAMPLE	V3	V2	V1	FUNCTION NUMBER	OBSERVED FUNCTION	OBSERVED STANDARD ERROR	PREDICTED FUNCTION	PREDICTED STANDARD ERROR	RESIDUAL
1				1	-0.292478	0.105806	-0.235647	0.0984862	-0.056831
				2	-0.911517	0.129188	-0.949418	0.129948	0.037901
				3	-0.911517	0.129188	-0.949418	0.129948	0.037901
				4	-0.292478	0.105806	-0.235647	0.0984862	-0.056831
				5	-0.669505	0.118872	-0.693619	0.120172	0.0241134
				6	-0.451985	0.110921	-0.389699	0.102267	-0.0622866
				7	-1.90835	0.192465	-1.73146	0.142969	-0.176884
	1	1	1	F1	156	11.4302	161.096	11.0738	-5.09614
	1	1	2	F2	84	8.755	78.9039	7.80861	5.09614
	1	2	1	F3	84	8.755	78.9039	7.80861	5.09614
	1	2	2	F4	156	11.4302	161.096	11.0738	-5.09614
	2	1	1	F5	107	9.75059	101.904	8.9243	5.09614
	2	1	2	F6	133	10.7039	138.096	10.3343	-5.09614
	2	2	1	F7	31	5.47713	36.0961	4.82631	-5.09614
	2	2	2	F8	209	12.7867	203.904	12.2128	5.09614

Log-Linear Model, Structural Zeros and Random Zeros: Example 6

This example illustrates a log-linear model of independence, using data that contain structural zero frequencies, as well as random (sampling) zero frequencies. The structural zeros are automatically deleted by CATMOD. The sampling zeros should be replaced in the DATA step by some positive number close to zero (such as 1E-20). Also, the row for Monkey T is deleted since it contains all zeros, and therefore the cell frequencies predicted by a model of independence are also zero.

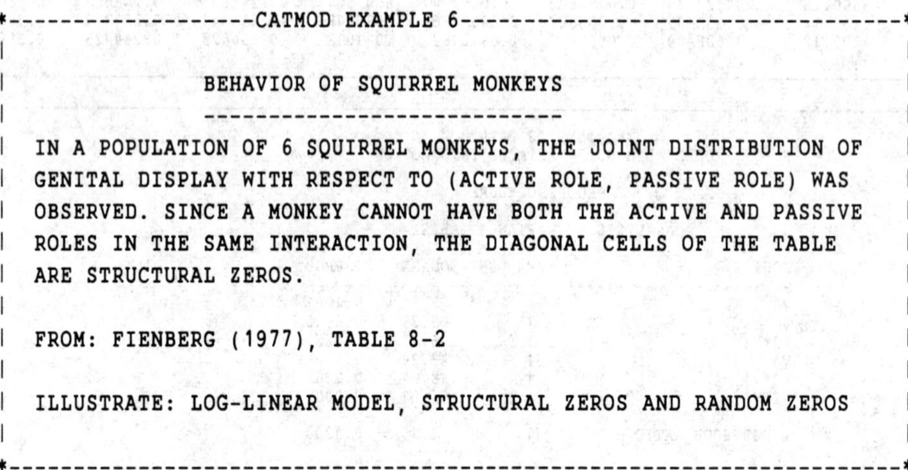

```
*-------------------CATMOD EXAMPLE 6---------------------------------*
|                                                                    |
|                  BEHAVIOR OF SQUIRREL MONKEYS                      |
|                  ----------------------------                      |
| IN A POPULATION OF 6 SQUIRREL MONKEYS, THE JOINT DISTRIBUTION OF   |
| GENITAL DISPLAY WITH RESPECT TO (ACTIVE ROLE, PASSIVE ROLE) WAS    |
| OBSERVED. SINCE A MONKEY CANNOT HAVE BOTH THE ACTIVE AND PASSIVE   |
| ROLES IN THE SAME INTERACTION, THE DIAGONAL CELLS OF THE TABLE     |
| ARE STRUCTURAL ZEROS.                                              |
|                                                                    |
| FROM: FIENBERG (1977), TABLE 8-2                                   |
|                                                                    |
| ILLUSTRATE: LOG-LINEAR MODEL, STRUCTURAL ZEROS AND RANDOM ZEROS    |
|                                                                    |
*--------------------------------------------------------------------*;
```

```
TITLE 'BEHAVIOR OF SQUIRREL MONKEYS';
DATA DISPLAY;
   INPUT ACTIVE $ PASSIVE $ WT @@;
   IF ACTIVE ¬= 'T';
   IF ACTIVE ¬= PASSIVE THEN IF WT=0 THEN WT=1E-20;
   CARDS;
R R  0    R S  1    R T  5    R U  8    R V  9    R W  0
S R 29    S S  0    S T 14    S U 46    S V  4    S W  0
T R  0    T S  0    T T  0    T U  0    T V  0    T W  0
U R  2    U S  3    U T  1    U U  0    U V 38    U W  2
V R  0    V S  0    V T  0    V U  0    V V  0    V W  1
W R  9    W S 25    W T  4    W U  6    W V 13    W W  0
;
PROC CATMOD;
   WEIGHT WT;
   MODEL ACTIVE*PASSIVE = _RESPONSE_ / ML NOGLS FREQ PRED=FREQ NOPARM;
   REPEATED / _RESPONSE_ = ACTIVE PASSIVE;
   TITLE2 'TEST QUASI-INDEPENDENCE FOR THE INCOMPLETE TABLE';
```

Output 14.6 Log-Linear Model Analysis with Zero Frequencies

```
                         BEHAVIOR OF SQUIRREL MONKEYS                                1
               TEST QUASI-INDEPENDENCE FOR THE INCOMPLETE TABLE

                               CATMOD PROCEDURE

RESPONSE: ACTIVE*PASSIVE              RESPONSE LEVELS (R)=    25
WEIGHT VARIABLE: WT                   POPULATIONS     (S)=     1
DATA SET: DISPLAY                     TOTAL FREQUENCY (N)=   220
                                      OBSERVATIONS  (OBS)=    25


                                        SAMPLE
                              SAMPLE     SIZE
                              ------------------
                                  1      220


                              RESPONSE PROFILES

                          RESPONSE    ACTIVE       PASSIVE
                          ---------------------------------
                                 1      R            S
                                 2      R            T
                                 3      R            U
                                 4      R            V
                                 5      R            W
                                 6      S            R
                                 7      S            T
                                 8      S            U
                                 9      S            V
                                10      S            W
                                11      U            R
                                12      U            S
                                13      U            T
                                14      U            V
                                15      U            W
                                16      V            R
                                17      V            S
                                18      V            T
                                19      V            U
                                20      V            W
                                21      W            R
                                22      W            S
                                23      W            T
                                24      W            U
                                25      W            V
```

BEHAVIOR OF SQUIRREL MONKEYS
TEST QUASI-INDEPENDENCE FOR THE INCOMPLETE TABLE

CATMOD PROCEDURE

RESPONSE FREQUENCIES

SAMPLE	RESPONSE NUMBER 1	2	3	4	5	6	7	8	9
1	1	5	8	9	10E-21	29	14	46	4

RESPONSE FREQUENCIES

SAMPLE	RESPONSE NUMBER 10	11	12	13	14	15	16	17	18
1	10E-21	2	3	1	38	2	10E-21	10E-21	10E-21

RESPONSE FREQUENCIES

SAMPLE	RESPONSE NUMBER 19	20	21	22	23	24	25
1	10E-21	1	9	25	4	6	13

MAXIMUM LIKELIHOOD ANALYSIS

ITERATION	SUB ITERATION	-2 LOG LIKELIHOOD	CONVERGENCE CRITERION
0	0	1416.31	1
1	0	1238.24	0.125724
2	0	1205.13	0.0267439
3	0	1199.51	.00466302
4	0	1198.63	.00073344
5	0	1198.56	5.51E-05
6	0	1198.56	6.54E-07
7	0	1198.56	1.22E-10

BEHAVIOR OF SQUIRREL MONKEYS
TEST QUASI-INDEPENDENCE FOR THE INCOMPLETE TABLE

CATMOD PROCEDURE

PARAMETER ESTIMATES

ITERATION	1	2	3	4	5	6	7	8	9
0	0	0	0	0	0	0	0	0	0
1	-0.497608	1.11124	0.172249	-0.880383	-.0069777	0.0827352	-0.473485	0.728668	0.579147
2	-0.342037	1.09619	0.561197	-1.75493	0.223326	0.389929	-0.40862	0.787467	0.572797
3	-0.156991	1.26871	0.705794	-2.39919	0.303445	0.436033	-0.316231	0.881153	0.67035
4	-.0466114	1.37908	0.816998	-2.84216	0.330948	0.462488	-0.288981	0.908534	0.696808
5	-0.002748	1.42295	0.860866	-3.01759	0.333372	0.464928	-0.286558	0.910968	0.699214
6	.00276007	1.42846	0.866375	-3.03962	0.333391	0.464947	-0.28654	0.910986	0.699232
7	0.0028366	1.42854	0.866451	-3.03993	0.333391	0.464947	-0.28654	0.910986	0.699232

ANALYSIS OF VARIANCE TABLE

SOURCE	DF	CHI-SQUARE	PROB
ACTIVE	4	56.58	0.0001
PASSIVE	5	47.94	0.0001
LIKELIHOOD RATIO	15	135.17	0.0001

BEHAVIOR OF SQUIRREL MONKEYS 4
TEST QUASI-INDEPENDENCE FOR THE INCOMPLETE TABLE

CATMOD PROCEDURE

PREDICTED VALUES FOR RESPONSE FUNCTIONS AND FREQUENCIES

				OBSERVED		PREDICTED		
SAMPLE	ACTIVE	PASSIVE	FUNCTION NUMBER	FUNCTION	STANDARD ERROR	FUNCTION	STANDARD ERROR	RESIDUAL
1			1	-2.56495	1.03775	-0.973554	0.339019	-1.5914
			2	-0.955511	0.526235	-1.72504	0.345438	0.769529
			3	-0.485508	0.449359	-0.527514	0.309254	0.0420066
			4	-0.367725	0.433629	-0.739268	0.249006	0.371543
			5	-48.6167	1.000E+10	-3.56052	0.634104	-45.0561
			6	0.802346	0.333775	0.320589	0.26629	0.481758
			7	0.074108	0.385164	-0.299342	0.295634	0.37345
			8	1.26369	0.314105	0.898184	0.250857	0.365508
			9	-1.17865	0.571772	0.686431	0.173396	-1.86509
			10	-48.6167	1.000E+10	-2.13482	0.608071	-46.4818
			11	-1.8718	0.759555	-0.241495	0.287218	-1.63031
			12	-1.46634	0.640513	-0.109939	0.303568	-1.3564
			13	-2.56495	1.03775	-0.861426	0.314794	-1.70352
			14	1.07264	0.321308	0.124346	0.204345	0.94829
			15	-1.8718	0.759555	-2.6969	0.617433	0.8251
			16	-48.6167	1.000E+10	-4.14787	1.02451	-44.4688
			17	-48.6167	1.000E+10	-4.01632	1.03006	-44.6003
			18	-48.6167	1.000E+10	-4.76781	1.03246	-43.8488
			19	-48.6167	1.000E+10	-3.57028	1.02079	-45.0464
			20	-2.56495	1.03775	-6.60328	1.16129	4.03833
			21	-0.367725	0.433629	-0.365842	0.202959	-.00188305
			22	0.653926	0.34194	-0.234286	0.232794	0.888212
			23	-1.17865	0.571772	-0.985772	0.239408	-0.192883
			24	-0.77319	0.493548	0.211754	0.185007	-0.984944
	R	S	F1	1	0.997725	5.25951	1.36156	-4.25951
	R	T	F2	5	2.21051	2.48073	0.691066	2.51927
	R	U	F3	8	2.77652	8.21595	1.85515	-0.215948
	R	V	F4	9	2.938	6.64805	1.50932	2.35195
	R	W	F5	1.000E-20	1.000E-10	0.395769	0.240268	-0.395769
	S	R	F6	29	5.0177	19.186	3.14791	9.81401
	S	T	F7	14	3.62065	10.3217	2.1696	3.67828
	S	U	F8	46	6.03173	34.1846	4.42871	11.8154
	S	V	F9	4	1.98173	27.661	3.72279	-23.661
	S	W	F10	1.000E-20	1.000E-10	1.6467	0.952712	-1.6467
	U	R	F11	2	1.40777	10.9364	2.12322	-8.9364
	U	S	F12	3	1.7202	12.4741	2.55434	-9.47407
	U	T	F13	1	0.997725	5.88358	1.38066	-4.88358
	U	V	F14	38	5.60681	15.7673	2.68469	22.2327
	U	W	F15	2	1.40777	0.938652	0.551645	1.06135
	V	R	F16	1.000E-20	1.000E-10	0.219966	0.221779	-0.219966
	V	S	F17	1.000E-20	1.000E-10	0.250893	0.253706	-0.250893
	V	T	F18	1.000E-20	1.000E-10	0.118338	0.120314	-0.118338
	V	U	F19	1.000E-20	1.000E-10	0.391924	0.393255	-0.391924
	V	W	F20	1	0.997725	0.0188793	0.0217276	0.981121
	W	R	F21	9	2.938	9.65765	1.80866	-0.657645
	W	S	F22	25	4.70734	11.0155	2.27502	13.9845
	W	T	F23	4	1.98173	5.19564	1.18445	-1.19564

BEHAVIOR OF SQUIRREL MONKEYS 5
TEST QUASI-INDEPENDENCE FOR THE INCOMPLETE TABLE

CATMOD PROCEDURE

				OBSERVED		PREDICTED		
SAMPLE	ACTIVE	PASSIVE	FUNCTION NUMBER	FUNCTION	STANDARD ERROR	FUNCTION	STANDARD ERROR	RESIDUAL
1	W	U	F24	6	2.41586	17.2075	2.7721	-11.2075
	W	V	F25	13	3.4974	13.9237	2.24158	-0.923689

Repeated Measures, Two Levels of Response, One Population: Example 7

The repeated measurement factor in this example is DRUG since every subject receives each of the drugs and therefore has a response for each one. The hypothesis of marginal homogeneity is tested by the DRUG effect in the first model. Since that hypothesis is rejected, the second model equates only the A and B marginal probability estimates.

```
*-------------------CATMOD EXAMPLE 7----------------------------------*
|                                                                    |
|                    ONE-POPULATION DRUG STUDY                       |
|                    -------------------------                       |
|  EACH SUBJECT IS GIVEN THREE DIFFERENT DRUGS, AND THEIR RESPONSE   |
|  TO EACH (F=FAVORABLE OR U=UNFAVORABLE) IS RECORDED.               |
|                                                                    |
|  FROM: KOCH ET AL.(1977), BIOMETRICS 33, 133-158                   |
|                                                                    |
|  ILLUSTRATE: REPEATED MEASURES, 2 LEVELS OF RESPONSE, 1 POPULATION |
|                                                                    |
*--------------------------------------------------------------------*;

TITLE 'ONE-POPULATION DRUG STUDY';
DATA DRUGS;
   INPUT DRUGA $ DRUGB $ DRUGC $ COUNT @@;
   CARDS;
F F F 6 F F U 16 F U F 2 F U U 4 U F F 2 U F U 4 U U F 6 U U U 6
;
PROC CATMOD;
   WEIGHT COUNT;
   RESPONSE MARGINALS;
   MODEL DRUGA*DRUGB*DRUGC = _RESPONSE_ ;
   REPEATED DRUG 3;
   TITLE2 'TEST MARGINAL HOMOGENEITY';
PROC CATMOD;
   WEIGHT COUNT;
   RESPONSE MARGINALS;
   TITLE2 'MODEL FOR EQUALITY OF A AND B MARGINAL PROBABILITIES';
   MODEL DRUGA*DRUGB*DRUGC = ( 1 0 ,
                               1 0 ,
                               0 1 ) / NOPROFILE;
```

Output 14.7 Analysis of One-Population Drug Study

```
                    ONE-POPULATION DRUG STUDY                                    1
                    TEST MARGINAL HOMOGENEITY

                        CATMOD PROCEDURE

RESPONSE: DRUGA*DRUGB*DRUGC          RESPONSE LEVELS (R)=      8
WEIGHT VARIABLE: COUNT               POPULATIONS     (S)=      1
DATA SET: DRUGS                      TOTAL FREQUENCY (N)=     46
                                     OBSERVATIONS  (OBS)=      8


                              SAMPLE
                      SAMPLE    SIZE
                      ----------------
                         1        46


                      RESPONSE PROFILES

            RESPONSE    DRUGA        DRUGB        DRUGC
            ------------------------------------------
                1         F            F            F
                2         F            F            U
                3         F            U            F
                4         F            U            U
                5         U            F            F
                6         U            F            U
                7         U            U            F
                8         U            U            U


                 FUNCTION   RESPONSE          DESIGN MATRIX
        SAMPLE    NUMBER    FUNCTION           1      2      3
        ------------------------------------------------------
           1         1      0.608696           1      1      0
                     2      0.608696           1      0      1
                     3      0.347826           1     -1     -1


                    ANALYSIS OF VARIANCE TABLE

        SOURCE                   DF   CHI-SQUARE      PROB
        ---------------------------------------------------
        INTERCEPT                 1       146.84    0.0001
        DRUG                      2         6.58    0.0372

        RESIDUAL                  0         0.00    1.0000
```

```
                    ONE-POPULATION DRUG STUDY                                    2
                    TEST MARGINAL HOMOGENEITY

                        CATMOD PROCEDURE
                ANALYSIS OF INDIVIDUAL PARAMETERS

                                                STANDARD     CHI-
EFFECT                 PARAMETER  ESTIMATE       ERROR     SQUARE    PROB
--------------------------------------------------------------------------
INTERCEPT                      1  0.521739    .0430561     146.84  0.0001
DRUG                           2   .0869565   .0506571       2.95  0.0861
                               3   .0869565   .0506571       2.95  0.0861
```

```
                ONE-POPULATION DRUG STUDY                                        3
      MODEL FOR EQUALITY OF A AND B MARGINAL PROBABILITIES

                       CATMOD PROCEDURE

RESPONSE: DRUGA*DRUGB*DRUGC             RESPONSE LEVELS (R)=     8
WEIGHT VARIABLE: COUNT                  POPULATIONS      (S)=     1
DATA SET: DRUGS                         TOTAL FREQUENCY (N)=    46
                                        OBSERVATIONS   (OBS)=     8


              FUNCTION    RESPONSE        DESIGN MATRIX
         SAMPLE  NUMBER    FUNCTION           1      2
         ---------------------------------------------
           1       1      0.608696           1      0
                   2      0.608696           1      0
                   3      0.347826           0      1


                 ANALYSIS OF VARIANCE TABLE

       SOURCE                  DF   CHI-SQUARE      PROB
       ---------------------------------------------
       MODEL|MEAN               1         6.58    0.0103

       RESIDUAL                 1        -0.00    1.0000


               ANALYSIS OF INDIVIDUAL PARAMETERS

                                           STANDARD     CHI-
EFFECT                 PARAMETER ESTIMATE    ERROR     SQUARE   PROB
----------------------------------------------------------------------
MODEL                          1 0.608696  .0613202     98.54  0.0001
                               2 0.347826  .0702237     24.53  0.0001
```

Repeated Measures, Two Levels of Response, Two Populations: Example 8

The analysis of the marginal probabilities is directed at assessing the main effects of the repeated measurement factor (TRIAL) and the independent variable (GROUP), as well as their interaction. Since the interaction is significant, a reduced model is fitted in which the only trial effect is that within group 3. The residual goodness-of-fit statistic tests the joint effect of TRIAL(GROUP=1) and TRIAL(GROUP=2). Although the contingency table is incomplete (only 13 of the 16 possible responses are observed), this poses no problem in the computation of the marginal probabilities.

```
*---------------------------CATMOD EXAMPLE 8----------------------------*
|                                                                       |
|                  TWO-POPULATION REPEATED MEASURES                     |
|                  --------------------------------                     |
|  SUBJECTS FROM 3 GROUPS HAVE THEIR RESPONSE (0 OR 1) RECORDED AT      |
|  EACH OF FOUR TRIALS.                                                 |
|                                                                       |
|  FROM: GUTHRIE(1981) PSYCHOLOGICAL BULLETIN 90, 189-195               |
|                                                                       |
|  ILLUSTRATE: REPEATED MEASURES, 2 LEVELS OF RESPONSE, 3 POPULATIONS   |
|                                                                       |
*-----------------------------------------------------------------------*;
```

```
TITLE 'TWO-POPULATION REPEATED MEASURES';
DATA GROUP;
   INPUT A B C D GROUP WT @@;
   CARDS;
1 1 1 1 2 2     0 0 0 0 2 2     0 0 1 0 1 2     0 0 1 0 2 2
0 0 0 1 1 4     0 0 0 1 2 1     0 0 0 1 3 3     1 0 0 1 2 1
0 0 1 1 1 1     0 0 1 1 2 2     0 0 1 1 3 5     0 1 0 0 1 4
0 1 0 0 2 1     0 1 0 1 2 1     0 1 0 1 3 2     0 1 1 0 3 1
1 0 0 0 1 3     1 0 0 0 2 1     0 1 1 1 2 1     0 1 1 1 3 2
1 0 1 0 1 1     1 0 1 1 2 1     1 0 1 1 3 2
;
PROC CATMOD;
   WEIGHT WT;
   RESPONSE MARGINALS;
   MODEL A*B*C*D = GROUP _RESPONSE_ GROUP*_RESPONSE_/ FREQ NODESIGN;
   REPEATED TRIAL 4;
   TITLE2 'SATURATED MODEL';
PROC CATMOD;
   WEIGHT WT;
   RESPONSE MARGINALS;
   MODEL A*B*C*D = GROUP _RESPONSE_(GROUP=3) / NOPROFILE NOPARM;
   REPEATED TRIAL 4;
   TITLE2 'TRIAL NESTED WITHIN GROUP 3';
```

Output 14.8 Analysis of Two-Population Repeated Measures

```
                    TWO-POPULATION REPEATED MEASURES                          1
                             SATURATED MODEL

                             CATMOD PROCEDURE

RESPONSE: A*B*C*D                      RESPONSE LEVELS (R)=     13
WEIGHT VARIABLE: WT                    POPULATIONS     (S)=      3
DATA SET: GROUP                        TOTAL FREQUENCY (N)=     45
                                       OBSERVATIONS  (OBS)=     23


                           POPULATION PROFILES
                                            SAMPLE
                        SAMPLE    GROUP      SIZE
                        ------------------------
                           1          1       15
                           2          2       15
                           3          3       15


                             RESPONSE PROFILES

                  RESPONSE    A         B         C         D
                  -------------------------------------------
                         1    0         0         0         0
                         2    0         0         0         1
                         3    0         0         1         0
                         4    0         0         1         1
                         5    0         1         0         0
                         6    0         1         0         1
                         7    0         1         1         0
                         8    0         1         1         1
                         9    1         0         0         0
                        10    1         0         0         1
                        11    1         0         1         0
                        12    1         0         1         1
                        13    1         1         1         1
```

(continued on next page)

(continued from previous page)

RESPONSE FREQUENCIES

	RESPONSE NUMBER						
SAMPLE	1	2	3	4	5	6	7
1	0	4	2	1	4	0	0
2	2	1	2	2	1	1	0
3	0	3	0	5	0	2	1

TWO-POPULATION REPEATED MEASURES 2
SATURATED MODEL

CATMOD PROCEDURE

RESPONSE FREQUENCIES

	RESPONSE NUMBER					
SAMPLE	8	9	10	11	12	13
1	0	3	0	1	0	0
2	1	1	1	0	1	2
3	2	0	0	0	2	0

ANALYSIS OF VARIANCE TABLE

SOURCE	DF	CHI-SQUARE	PROB
INTERCEPT	1	354.88	0.0001
GROUP	2	24.79	0.0001
TRIAL	3	21.45	0.0001
GROUP*_RESPONSE_	6	18.71	0.0047
RESIDUAL	0	0.00	1.0000

NOTE: _RESPONSE_ = TRIAL

ANALYSIS OF INDIVIDUAL PARAMETERS

EFFECT	PARAMETER	ESTIMATE	STANDARD ERROR	CHI-SQUARE	PROB
INTERCEPT	1	0.583333	.0309653	354.88	0.0001
GROUP	2	0.133333	.0334566	15.88	0.0001
	3	-.033333	0.055072	0.37	0.5450
TRIAL	4	0.172222	.0556666	9.57	0.0020
	5	0.105556	0.064693	2.66	0.1028
	6	-.072222	.0576994	1.57	0.2107
GROUP*_RESPONSE_	7	-.155556	.0852013	3.33	0.0679
	8	-.088889	.0953227	0.87	0.3511
	9	.0888889	.0821521	1.17	0.2793
	10	-.055556	.0800463	0.48	0.4877
	11	.0111111	.0865669	0.02	0.8979
	12	-.011111	.0823772	0.02	0.8927

NOTE: _RESPONSE_ = TRIAL

TWO-POPULATION REPEATED MEASURES 3
TRIAL NESTED WITHIN GROUP 3

CATMOD PROCEDURE

```
RESPONSE: A*B*C*D                  RESPONSE LEVELS (R)=    13
WEIGHT VARIABLE: WT                POPULATIONS     (S)=     3
DATA SET: GROUP                    TOTAL FREQUENCY (N)=    45
                                   OBSERVATIONS  (OBS)=    23
```

(continued on next page)

(continued from previous page)

```
           FUNCTION   RESPONSE                   DESIGN MATRIX
SAMPLE      NUMBER    FUNCTION       1      2      3      4      5      6
---------------------------------------------------------------------------
    1          1      0.733333       1      1      0      0      0      0
               2      0.733333       1      1      0      0      0      0
               3      0.733333       1      1      0      0      0      0
               4      0.666667       1      1      0      0      0      0

    2          1      0.666667       1      0      1      0      0      0
               2      0.666667       1      0      1      0      0      0
               3      0.466667       1      0      1      0      0      0
               4           0.4       1      0      1      0      0      0

    3          1      0.866667       1     -1     -1      1      0      0
               2      0.666667       1     -1     -1      0      1      0
               3      0.333333       1     -1     -1      0      0      1
               4     0.0666667       1     -1     -1     -1     -1     -1


                    ANALYSIS OF VARIANCE TABLE

             SOURCE                   DF   CHI-SQUARE      PROB
             --------------------------------------------------
             INTERCEPT                 1       386.94    0.0001
             GROUP                     2        25.42    0.0001
             _RESPONSE_(GROUP=3)       3        75.07    0.0001

             RESIDUAL                  6         5.09    0.5319

             NOTE: _RESPONSE_ = TRIAL
```

Repeated Measures, Four Levels of Response, One Population: Example 9

This example illustrates a repeated measurement analysis in which there are more than two levels of response. Since there are four levels, the RESPONSE statement induces the computation of three marginal probabilities for each dependent variable, resulting in six response functions for analysis. Since the model contains a repeated measurement factor (SIDE) with two levels (RIGHT, LEFT), CATMOD groups the functions into sets of three (=6/2). Therefore, the SIDE effect has three degrees of freedom (one for each marginal probability), and it is the appropriate test of marginal homogeneity.

```
*-------------------------CATMOD EXAMPLE 9----------------------------*
|                                                                     |
|                   TESTING VISION: RIGHT EYE VS LEFT                 |
|                   ---------------------------------                 |
| 7477 WOMEN AGED 30-39 WERE TESTED FOR VISION ON BOTH RIGHT AND      |
| LEFT EYES. MARGINAL HOMOGENEITY IS TESTED BY THE MAIN EFFECT OF     |
| THE REPEATED MEASUREMENT FACTOR, SIDE.                              |
|                                                                     |
| FROM: GRIZZLE, STARMER AND KOCH (1969), BIOMETRICS, 25,  493.       |
|                                                                     |
| ILLUSTRATE: REPEATED MEASURES, 4 LEVELS OF RESPONSE, 1 POPULATION   |
|                                                                     |
*---------------------------------------------------------------------*;

TITLE 'VISION SYMMETRY';
DATA VISION;
INPUT RIGHT LEFT COUNT @@;
CARDS;
```

```
1 1 1520     1 2  266     1 3  124     1 4  66
2 1  234     2 2 1512     2 3  432     2 4  78
3 1  117     3 2  362     3 3 1772     3 4 205
4 1   36     4 2   82     4 3  179     4 4 492
;
PROC CATMOD;
   WEIGHT COUNT;
   RESPONSE MARGINALS;
   MODEL RIGHT*LEFT =  _RESPONSE_ / FREQ;
   REPEATED SIDE 2;
   TITLE2 'TEST OF MARGINAL HOMOGENEITY';
```

Output 14.9 Vision Study: Analysis of Marginal Homogeneity

```
                              VISION SYMMETRY                                              1
                        TEST OF MARGINAL HOMOGENEITY

                              CATMOD PROCEDURE

        RESPONSE: RIGHT*LEFT                     RESPONSE LEVELS (R)=    16
        WEIGHT VARIABLE: COUNT                   POPULATIONS      (S)=     1
        DATA SET: VISION                         TOTAL FREQUENCY (N)=  7477
                                                 OBSERVATIONS   (OBS)=   16


                                         SAMPLE
                              SAMPLE      SIZE
                              -----------------
                                  1       7477


                             RESPONSE PROFILES

                         RESPONSE   RIGHT     LEFT
                         -------------------------
                             1        1        1
                             2        1        2
                             3        1        3
                             4        1        4
                             5        2        1
                             6        2        2
                             7        2        3
                             8        2        4
                             9        3        1
                            10        3        2
                            11        3        3
                            12        3        4
                            13        4        1
                            14        4        2
                            15        4        3
                            16        4        4


                            RESPONSE FREQUENCIES

                                     RESPONSE NUMBER
   SAMPLE          1         2         3         4         5         6         7         8
   ----------------------------------------------------------------------------------------
       1        1520       266       124        66       234      1512       432        78
```

```
                              VISION SYMMETRY                                       2
                        TEST OF MARGINAL HOMOGENEITY

                              CATMOD PROCEDURE

                            RESPONSE FREQUENCIES

                                RESPONSE NUMBER
SAMPLE        9        10       11        12        13        14        15        16
--------------------------------------------------------------------------------------
   1        117       362     1772       205        36        82       179       492


       FUNCTION    RESPONSE                        DESIGN MATRIX
SAMPLE  NUMBER     FUNCTION        1      2        3        4        5      6
------------------------------------------------------------------------------
   1       1       0.264277        1      0        0        1        0      0
           2       0.301725        0      1        0        0        1      0
           3       0.328474        0      0        1        0        0      1
           4       0.255049        1      0        0       -1        0      0
           5       0.297178        0      1        0        0       -1      0
           6       0.335295        0      0        1        0        0     -1


                      ANALYSIS OF VARIANCE TABLE

             SOURCE                 DF    CHI-SQUARE      PROB
             ----------------------------------------------------
             INTERCEPT               3      78744.17     0.0001
             SIDE                    3         11.98     0.0075

             RESIDUAL                0         -0.00     1.0000


                  ANALYSIS OF INDIVIDUAL PARAMETERS

                                                 STANDARD     CHI-
        EFFECT            PARAMETER  ESTIMATE     ERROR      SQUARE    PROB
        ---------------------------------------------------------------------
        INTERCEPT                 1  0.259663   .0046841    3073.03  0.0001
                                  2  0.299452   .0046427    4160.17  0.0001
                                  3  0.331884   .0048281    4725.25  0.0001
        SIDE                      4  .0046142   .0019409       5.65  0.0174
                                  5  .0022736   .0025498       0.80  0.3726
                                  6  -0.00341   .0025187       1.83  0.1757
```

Repeated Measures, Four Levels of Response, Two Populations: Example 10

This example illustrates a repeated measurement analysis in which there is a multi-leveled response and two populations. As in **Example 9**, CATMOD groups the response functions into sets of three (one for each marginal probability). Thus, the OBSERVER effect, which is averaged over the populations, has three degrees of freedom. The hypothesis of marginal homogeneity is tested by the OBSERVER(GROUP) effect in the second model.

```
*------------------------CATMOD EXAMPLE 10----------------------------*
|                                                                    |
|                MULTIPLE SCLEROSIS DATA ANALYSIS                    |
|                --------------------------------                    |
| PATIENTS FROM EACH OF TWO GROUPS ARE EVALUATED BY TWO NEUROLOGISTS |
| (OBSERVERS) WITH RESPECT TO THE FOLLOWING RESPONSE:                |
|    1. CERTAIN MULTIPLE SCLEROSIS;                                  |
|    2. PROBABLE MULTIPLE SCLEROSIS;                                 |
|    3. POSSIBLE MULTIPLE SCLEROSIS (ODDS 50:50);                    |
|    4. DOUBTFUL, UNLIKELY, OR DEFINITELY NOT MULTIPLE SCLEROSIS.    |
|                                                                    |
| FROM: LANDIS AND KOCH (1977), BIOMETRICS 33, 159-174               |
|                                                                    |
| ILLUSTRATE: REPEATED MEASURES, 4 LEVELS OF RESPONSE, 2 POPULATIONS |
|                                                                    |
*--------------------------------------------------------------------*;

TITLE 'MULTIPLE SCLEROSIS DATA ANALYSIS';
DATA ONE;
   INPUT GROUP OBS1 OBS2  WT @@;
   CARDS;
1 4 4 10    1 4 1  3   1 4 2  7    1 4 3  3
1 1 4  1    1 1 1 38   1 1 2  5    1 1 3  0
1 2 4  0    1 2 1 33   1 2 2 11    1 2 3  3
1 3 4  6    1 3 1 10   1 3 2 14    1 3 3  5
2 4 1  1    2 4 2  2   2 4 3  4    2 4 4 14
2 3 1  2    2 3 2 13   2 3 3  3    2 3 4  4
2 2 1  3    2 2 2 11   2 2 3  4    2 2 4  0
2 1 1  5    2 1 2  3   2 1 3  0    2 1 4  0
;
PROC CATMOD;
   TITLE2 'SATURATED MODEL';
   WEIGHT WT;
   RESPONSE MARGINALS;
   MODEL OBS1*OBS2 = GROUP _RESPONSE_  GROUP*_RESPONSE_ / FREQ NODESIGN;
   REPEATED OBSERVER 2;
PROC CATMOD;
   TITLE2 'TEST MARGINAL HOMOGENEITY BY OBSERVER NESTED WITHIN GROUP';
   WEIGHT WT;
   RESPONSE MARGINALS;
   MODEL OBS1*OBS2 = GROUP _RESPONSE_(GROUP) / NOPROFILE NODESIGN;
   REPEATED OBSERVER 2;
```

Output 14.10 Multiple Sclerosis Data: Repeated Measures Analysis

```
                    MULTIPLE SCLEROSIS DATA ANALYSIS                                1
                            SATURATED MODEL

                            CATMOD PROCEDURE

 RESPONSE: OBS1*OBS2                     RESPONSE LEVELS (R)=    14
 WEIGHT VARIABLE: WT                     POPULATIONS     (S)=     2
 DATA SET: ONE                           TOTAL FREQUENCY (N)=   218
                                         OBSERVATIONS  (OBS)=    27


                          POPULATION PROFILES
                                          SAMPLE
                       SAMPLE    GROUP     SIZE
                       -------------------------
                          1        1       149
                          2        2        69


                           RESPONSE PROFILES

                     RESPONSE    OBS1         OBS2
                     ----------------------------
                         1         1            1
                         2         1            2
                         3         1            4
                         4         2            1
                         5         2            2
                         6         2            3
                         7         3            1
                         8         3            2
                         9         3            3
                        10         3            4
                        11         4            1
                        12         4            2
                        13         4            3
                        14         4            4


                         RESPONSE FREQUENCIES

                                RESPONSE NUMBER
SAMPLE          1         2         3         4         5         6         7
-----------------------------------------------------------------------------
   1           38         5         1        33        11         3        10
   2            5         3         0         3        11         4         2
```

```
                    MULTIPLE SCLEROSIS DATA ANALYSIS                                2
                            SATURATED MODEL

                            CATMOD PROCEDURE

                         RESPONSE FREQUENCIES

                                RESPONSE NUMBER
SAMPLE          8         9        10        11        12        13        14
-----------------------------------------------------------------------------
   1           14         5         6         3         7         3        10
   2           13         3         4         1         2         4        14
```

(continued on next page)

(continued from previous page)

ANALYSIS OF VARIANCE TABLE

SOURCE	DF	CHI-SQUARE	PROB
INTERCEPT	3	875.79	0.0001
GROUP	3	37.62	0.0001
OBSERVER	3	47.90	0.0001
GROUP*_RESPONSE_	3	14.09	0.0028
RESIDUAL	0	0.00	1.0000

NOTE: _RESPONSE_ = OBSERVER

ANALYSIS OF INDIVIDUAL PARAMETERS

EFFECT	PARAMETER	ESTIMATE	STANDARD ERROR	CHI-SQUARE	PROB
INTERCEPT	1	0.283606	.0240158	139.46	0.0001
	2	0.311229	.0255073	148.88	0.0001
	3	0.196746	.0205538	91.63	0.0001
GROUP	4	0.145925	.0240158	36.92	0.0001
	5	-0.02935	.0255073	1.32	0.2499
	6	-.042384	.0205538	4.25	0.0392
OBSERVER	7	-.077984	.0152511	26.15	0.0001
	8	-.023077	.0218591	1.11	0.2911
	9	.0801235	.0205399	15.22	0.0001
GROUP*_RESPONSE_	10	-.056245	.0152511	13.60	0.0002
	11	.0566336	.0218591	6.71	0.0096
	12	4.1E-04	.0205399	0.00	0.9839

NOTE: _RESPONSE_ = OBSERVER

MULTIPLE SCLEROSIS DATA ANALYSIS 3
TEST MARGINAL HOMOGENEITY BY OBSERVER NESTED WITHIN GROUP

CATMOD PROCEDURE

RESPONSE: OBS1*OBS2	RESPONSE LEVELS (R)=	14
WEIGHT VARIABLE: WT	POPULATIONS (S)=	2
DATA SET: ONE	TOTAL FREQUENCY (N)=	218
	OBSERVATIONS (OBS)=	27

ANALYSIS OF VARIANCE TABLE

SOURCE	DF	CHI-SQUARE	PROB
INTERCEPT	3	875.79	0.0001
GROUP	3	37.62	0.0001
RESPONSE(GROUP)	6	69.01	0.0001
RESIDUAL	0	-0.00	1.0000

NOTE: _RESPONSE_ = OBSERVER

ANALYSIS OF INDIVIDUAL PARAMETERS

EFFECT	PARAMETER	ESTIMATE	STANDARD ERROR	CHI-SQUARE	PROB
INTERCEPT	1	0.283606	.0240158	139.46	0.0001
	2	0.311229	.0255073	148.88	0.0001
	3	0.196746	.0205538	91.63	0.0001
GROUP	4	0.145925	.0240158	36.92	0.0001
	5	-0.02935	.0255073	1.32	0.2499
	6	-.042384	.0205538	4.25	0.0392
RESPONSE(GROUP)	7	-.134228	.0215555	38.78	0.0001
	8	0.033557	.0262794	1.63	0.2016
	9	.0805369	.0190225	17.92	0.0001
	10	-.021739	0.021581	1.01	0.3138
	11	-0.07971	0.034938	5.21	0.0225
	12	.0797101	0.03641	4.79	0.0286

NOTE: _RESPONSE_ = OBSERVER

Repeated Measures, Logistic Analysis of Growth Curve: Example 11

The data are from a longitudinal study in which patients from four populations (2 diagnoses x 2 treatments) were measured at three time points to assess their response (N=Normal or A=Abnormal) to treatment. The analysis is directed at assessing the effect of the repeated measurement factor, TIME, as well as the independent variables, DIAG and TRTMENT. The RESPONSE statement is used to compute the logits of the marginal probabilities. The timepoints used in the design matrix (0, 1, 2) correspond to the logarithms (base 2) of the actual timepoints (1, 2, 4).

```
*-------------------------CATMOD EXAMPLE 11----------------------------*
|                                                                      |
|                     GROWTH CURVE ANALYSIS                            |
|                     ---------------------                            |
|  SUBJECTS FROM 2 DIAGNOSTIC GROUPS (MILD OR SEVERE) ARE GIVEN ONE    |
|  OF 2 TREATMENTS (STANDARD OR NEW), AND THEIR RESPONSE TO TREATMENT  |
|  (N=NORMAL OR A=ABNORMAL) IS RECORDED AT EACH OF 3 TIME POINTS       |
|  (WEEKS 1, 2, AND 4).                                                |
|                                                                      |
|  FROM: KOCH ET AL.(1977), BIOMETRICS 33, 133-158                     |
|                                                                      |
|  ILLUSTRATE: REPEATED MEASURES, LOGISTIC ANALYSIS OF GROWTH CURVE    |
|                                                                      |
*----------------------------------------------------------------------*;

TITLE 'GROWTH CURVE ANALYSIS';
DATA GROWTH2;
   INPUT DIAG $ TRT $ WEEK1 $ WEEK2 $ WEEK4 $ COUNT @@;
   CARDS;
MILD STANDARD N N N 16    SEVERE STANDARD N N N  2
MILD STANDARD N N A 13    SEVERE STANDARD N N A  2
MILD STANDARD N A N  9    SEVERE STANDARD N A N  8
MILD STANDARD N A A  3    SEVERE STANDARD N A A  9
MILD STANDARD A N N 14    SEVERE STANDARD A N N  9
MILD STANDARD A N A  4    SEVERE STANDARD A N A 15
MILD STANDARD A A N 15    SEVERE STANDARD A A N 27
MILD STANDARD A A A  6    SEVERE STANDARD A A A 28
MILD       NEW N N N 31   SEVERE      NEW N N N  7
MILD       NEW N N A  0   SEVERE      NEW N N A  2
MILD       NEW N A N  6   SEVERE      NEW N A N  5
MILD       NEW N A A  0   SEVERE      NEW N A A  2
MILD       NEW A N N 22   SEVERE      NEW A N N 31
MILD       NEW A N A  2   SEVERE      NEW A N A  5
MILD       NEW A A N  9   SEVERE      NEW A A N 32
MILD       NEW A A A  0   SEVERE      NEW A A A  6
;

PROC CATMOD ORDER=DATA;
   TITLE2 'LINEAR LOGISTIC MODEL';
   WEIGHT COUNT;
   POPULATION DIAG TRT;
   RESPONSE LOGIT;
   MODEL WEEK1*WEEK2*WEEK4 = ( 1 0 0 0 0 0 0 0 ,
                               1 1 0 0 0 0 0 0 ,
```

```
                                          1 2 0 0 0 0 0 0 ,
                                          0 0 1 0 0 0 0 0 ,
                                          0 0 1 1 0 0 0 0 ,
                                          0 0 1 2 0 0 0 0 ,
                                          0 0 0 0 1 0 0 0 ,
                                          0 0 0 0 1 1 0 0 ,
                                          0 0 0 0 1 2 0 0 ,
                                          0 0 0 0 0 0 1 0 ,
                                          0 0 0 0 0 0 1 1 ,
                                          0 0 0 0 0 0 1 2 ) / FREQ;
PROC CATMOD ORDER=DATA;
   TITLE2 'REDUCED MODEL';
   WEIGHT COUNT;
   POPULATION DIAG TRT;
   RESPONSE LOGIT;
   MODEL WEEK1*WEEK2*WEEK4 = ( 1 0 0 0 ,
                               1 0 1 0 ,
                               1 0 2 0 ,
                               1 0 0 0 ,
                               1 0 0 1 ,
                               1 0 0 2 ,
                               0 1 0 0 ,
                               0 1 1 0 ,
                               0 1 2 0 ,
                               0 1 0 0 ,
                               0 1 0 1 ,
                               0 1 0 2 )  (3='SLOPE FOR STD TRT',
                                           4='SLOPE FOR NEW TRT') /
                                           NOPROFILE;
   CONTRAST 'EQUAL INTERCEPTS'
            ALL_PARMS 1 -1  0  0;
   CONTRAST 'EQUAL SLOPES'
            ALL_PARMS 0  0  1 -1;
```

Output 14.11 Logistic Analysis of Growth Curve

```
                          GROWTH CURVE ANALYSIS                                  1
                          LINEAR LOGISTIC MODEL

                             CATMOD PROCEDURE

RESPONSE: WEEK1*WEEK2*WEEK4         RESPONSE LEVELS (R)=      8
WEIGHT VARIABLE: COUNT              POPULATIONS     (S)=      4
DATA SET: GROWTH2                   TOTAL FREQUENCY (N)=    340
                                    OBSERVATIONS  (OBS)=     29
```

(continued on next page)

(continued from previous page)

POPULATION PROFILES

SAMPLE	DIAG	TRT	SAMPLE SIZE
1	MILD	STANDARD	80
2	MILD	NEW	70
3	SEVERE	STANDARD	100
4	SEVERE	NEW	90

RESPONSE PROFILES

RESPONSE	WEEK1	WEEK2	WEEK4
1	N	N	N
2	N	N	A
3	N	A	N
4	N	A	A
5	A	N	N
6	A	N	A
7	A	A	N
8	A	A	A

RESPONSE FREQUENCIES

	RESPONSE NUMBER							
SAMPLE	1	2	3	4	5	6	7	8
1	16	13	9	3	14	4	15	6
2	31	0	6	0	22	2	9	0
3	2	2	8	9	9	15	27	28
4	7	2	5	2	31	5	32	6

GROWTH CURVE ANALYSIS 2
LINEAR LOGISTIC MODEL

CATMOD PROCEDURE

SAMPLE	FUNCTION NUMBER	RESPONSE FUNCTION	DESIGN MATRIX 1	2	3	4	5	6	7	8
1	1	0.0500104	1	0	0	0	0	0	0	0
	2	0.35364	1	1	0	0	0	0	0	0
	3	0.730888	1	2	0	0	0	0	0	0
2	1	0.11441	0	0	1	0	0	0	0	0
	2	1.29928	0	0	1	1	0	0	0	0
	3	3.52636	0	0	1	2	0	0	0	0
3	1	-1.32493	0	0	0	0	1	0	0	0
	2	-0.944462	0	0	0	0	1	1	0	0
	3	-0.160343	0	0	0	0	1	2	0	0
4	1	-1.53148	0	0	0	0	0	0	1	0
	2	-4.163E-17	0	0	0	0	0	0	1	1
	3	1.60944	0	0	0	0	0	0	1	2

ANALYSIS OF VARIANCE TABLE

SOURCE	DF	CHI-SQUARE	PROB
MODEL|MEAN	7	171.63	0.0001
RESIDUAL	4	1.60	0.8094

(continued on next page)

(continued from previous page)

ANALYSIS OF INDIVIDUAL PARAMETERS

EFFECT	PARAMETER	ESTIMATE	STANDARD ERROR	CHI-SQUARE	PROB
MODEL	1	.0453205	0.221235	0.04	0.8377
	2	0.334602	0.16995	3.88	0.0490
	3	.0425067	0.229166	0.03	0.8528
	4	1.44131	0.249401	33.40	0.0001
	5	-1.4113	0.211654	44.46	0.0001
	6	0.596471	0.155897	14.64	0.0001
	7	-1.54753	0.251837	37.76	0.0001
	8	1.56951	0.207398	57.27	0.0001

GROWTH CURVE ANALYSIS 3
REDUCED MODEL

CATMOD PROCEDURE

```
RESPONSE: WEEK1*WEEK2*WEEK4          RESPONSE LEVELS (R)=    8
WEIGHT VARIABLE: COUNT               POPULATIONS     (S)=    4
DATA SET: GROWTH2                    TOTAL FREQUENCY (N)=  340
                                     OBSERVATIONS  (OBS)=   29
```

SAMPLE	FUNCTION NUMBER	RESPONSE FUNCTION	DESIGN MATRIX 1	2	3	4
1	1	0.0500104	1	0	0	0
	2	0.35364	1	0	1	0
	3	0.730888	1	0	2	0
2	1	0.11441	1	0	0	0
	2	1.29928	1	0	0	1
	3	3.52636	1	0	0	2
3	1	-1.32493	0	1	0	0
	2	-0.944462	0	1	1	0
	3	-0.160343	0	1	2	0
4	1	-1.53148	0	1	0	0
	2	-4.163E-17	0	1	0	1
	3	1.60944	0	1	0	2

ANALYSIS OF VARIANCE TABLE

SOURCE	DF	CHI-SQUARE	PROB
SLOPE FOR STD TRT	1	26.35	0.0001
SLOPE FOR NEW TRT	1	125.09	0.0001
RESIDUAL	8	4.20	0.8387

ANALYSIS OF INDIVIDUAL PARAMETERS

EFFECT	PARAMETER	ESTIMATE	STANDARD ERROR	CHI-SQUARE	PROB
MODEL	1	-.071582	0.13484	0.28	0.5955
	2	-1.35294	0.134968	100.48	0.0001
	3	0.4944	.0963077	26.35	0.0001
	4	1.45516	0.130109	125.09	0.0001

```
                    GROWTH CURVE ANALYSIS                                   4
                        REDUCED MODEL

                      CATMOD PROCEDURE

                    ANALYSIS OF CONTRASTS

CONTRAST                  DF    CHI-SQUARE       PROB
-----------------------------------------------------
EQUAL INTERCEPTS           1         77.02     0.0001
EQUAL SLOPES               1         59.12     0.0001
```

Repeated Measures, Two Repeated Measurement Factors: Example 12

This example illustrates a repeated measurement analysis in which there are two repeated measurement factors. For the first two models, the response functions are marginal probabilities, and the repeated measurement factors are TIME and TRTMENT. The first model is a saturated one, containing effects for TIME, TRTMENT, and TIME*TRTMENT. The second fits a main-effect model with respect to TRTMENT.

The third CATMOD procedure illustrates a response statement that computes sensitivity and specificity at each of the two time points. Since these are measures of the relative accuracy of the two diagnostic procedures, the repeated measurement factors in this case are labeled TIME and ACCURACY. Only fifteen of the sixteen possible responses are observed, so that additional care must be taken in formulating the RESPONSE statement for computation of sensitivity and specificity.

```
*------------------------CATMOD EXAMPLE 12---------------------------*
|                                                                   |
|               DIAGNOSTIC PROCEDURE COMPARISON                     |
|               -------------------------------                     |
|  TWO DIAGNOSTIC PROCEDURES (STANDARD AND TEST) ARE DONE ON EACH   |
|  SUBJECT, AND THE RESULTS OF BOTH ARE EVALUATED AT EACH OF TWO TIME |
|  POINTS AS BEING POSITIVE OR NEGATIVE.                            |
|                                                                   |
|  FROM: MACMILLAN ET AL.(1981)                                     |
|                                                                   |
|  ILLUSTRATE: REPEATED MEASURES, 2 REPEATED MEASUREMENT FACTORS    |
|                                                                   |
*-------------------------------------------------------------------*;

TITLE 'DIAGNOSTIC PROCEDURE COMPARISON';
DATA A;
   INPUT STD1 $ TEST1 $ STD2 $ TEST2 $ WT @@;
   CARDS;
NEG NEG NEG NEG 509    NEG NEG NEG POS  4    NEG NEG POS NEG  17
NEG NEG POS POS   3    NEG POS NEG NEG 13    NEG POS NEG POS   8
NEG POS POS POS   8    POS NEG NEG NEG 14    POS NEG NEG POS   1
POS NEG POS NEG  17    POS NEG POS POS  9    POS POS NEG NEG   7
POS POS NEG POS   4    POS POS POS NEG  9    POS POS POS POS 170
;
```

```
PROC CATMOD;
   TITLE2 'MARGINAL SYMMETRY, SATURATED MODEL';
   WEIGHT WT;
   RESPONSE MARGINALS;
   MODEL STD1*TEST1*STD2*TEST2 = _RESPONSE_ / FREQ NOPARM;
   REPEATED TIME 2, TRTMENT 2 / _RESPONSE_ = TIME TRTMENT TIME*TRTMENT;
PROC CATMOD;
   TITLE2 'MARGINAL SYMMETRY, REDUCED MODEL';
   WEIGHT WT;
   RESPONSE MARGINALS;
   MODEL STD1*TEST1*STD2*TEST2 = _RESPONSE_ / NOPROFILE CORRB;
   REPEATED TIME 2, TRTMENT 2 / _RESPONSE_ = TRTMENT;
PROC CATMOD;
   TITLE2 'SENSITIVITY AND SPECIFICITY ANALYSIS, MAIN-EFFECTS MODEL';
   MODEL STD1*TEST1*STD2*TEST2 = _RESPONSE_ / COVB NOPROFILE;
   REPEATED TIME 2, ACCURACY 2 / _RESPONSE_ = TIME ACCURACY;
   WEIGHT WT;
   RESPONSE EXP 1 -1 0 0  0 0 0 0 ,
                0  0 1 -1 0 0 0 0 ,
                0  0 0 0  1 -1 0 0 ,
                0  0 0 0  0 0 1 -1
            LOG
                0 0 0 0  0 0 0  0 0 0 0  1 1 1 1 ,
                0 0 0 0  0 0 0  1 1 1 1  1 1 1 1 ,
                1 1 1 1  0 0 0  0 0 0 0  0 0 0 0 ,
                1 1 1 1  1 1 1  0 0 0 0  0 0 0 0 ,
                0 0 0 1  0 0 1  0 0 0 1  0 0 0 1 ,
                0 0 1 1  0 0 1  0 0 1 1  0 0 1 1 ,
                1 0 0 0  1 0 0  1 0 0 0  1 0 0 0 ,
                1 1 0 0  1 1 0  1 1 0 0  1 1 0 0 ;
```

Output 14.12 Diagnosis Data: Two Repeated Measurement Factors

```
                         DIAGNOSTIC PROCEDURE COMPARISON                                  1
                        MARGINAL SYMMETRY, SATURATED MODEL

                               CATMOD PROCEDURE

    RESPONSE: STD1*TEST1*STD2*TEST2          RESPONSE LEVELS (R)=     15
    WEIGHT VARIABLE: WT                      POPULATIONS     (S)=      1
    DATA SET: A                              TOTAL FREQUENCY (N)=    793
                                             OBSERVATIONS  (OBS)=     15


                                        SAMPLE
                              SAMPLE     SIZE
                              -----------------
                                 1        793
```

(continued on next page)

(continued from previous page)

RESPONSE PROFILES

RESPONSE	STD1	TEST1	STD2	TEST2
1	NEG	NEG	NEG	NEG
2	NEG	NEG	NEG	POS
3	NEG	NEG	POS	NEG
4	NEG	NEG	POS	POS
5	NEG	POS	NEG	NEG
6	NEG	POS	NEG	POS
7	NEG	POS	POS	POS
8	POS	NEG	NEG	NEG
9	POS	NEG	NEG	POS
10	POS	NEG	POS	NEG
11	POS	NEG	POS	POS
12	POS	POS	NEG	NEG
13	POS	POS	NEG	POS
14	POS	POS	POS	NEG
15	POS	POS	POS	POS

RESPONSE FREQUENCIES

SAMPLE	RESPONSE NUMBER 1	2	3	4	5	6	7	8
1	509	4	17	3	13	8	8	14

RESPONSE FREQUENCIES

SAMPLE	RESPONSE NUMBER 9	10	11	12	13	14	15
1	1	17	9	7	4	9	170

DIAGNOSTIC PROCEDURE COMPARISON
MARGINAL SYMMETRY, SATURATED MODEL 2

CATMOD PROCEDURE

SAMPLE	FUNCTION NUMBER	RESPONSE FUNCTION	DESIGN MATRIX 1	2	3	4
1	1	0.708701	1	1	1	1
	2	0.723834	1	1	-1	-1
	3	0.706179	1	-1	1	-1
	4	0.738966	1	-1	-1	1

ANALYSIS OF VARIANCE TABLE

SOURCE	DF	CHI-SQUARE	PROB
INTERCEPT	1	2385.34	0.0001
TIME	1	0.85	0.3570
TRTMENT	1	8.20	0.0042
TIME*TRTMENT	1	2.40	0.1215
RESIDUAL	0	0.00	1.0000

DIAGNOSTIC PROCEDURE COMPARISON
MARGINAL SYMMETRY, REDUCED MODEL 3

CATMOD PROCEDURE

```
RESPONSE: STD1*TEST1*STD2*TEST2      RESPONSE LEVELS (R)=    15
WEIGHT VARIABLE: WT                  POPULATIONS     (S)=     1
DATA SET: A                          TOTAL FREQUENCY (N)=   793
                                     OBSERVATIONS  (OBS)=    15
```

(continued on next page)

(continued from previous page)

SAMPLE	FUNCTION NUMBER	RESPONSE FUNCTION	DESIGN MATRIX 1	2
1	1	0.708701	1	1
	2	0.723834	1	-1
	3	0.706179	1	1
	4	0.738966	1	-1

ANALYSIS OF VARIANCE TABLE

SOURCE	DF	CHI-SQUARE	PROB
INTERCEPT	1	2386.97	0.0001
TRTMENT	1	9.55	0.0020
RESIDUAL	2	3.51	0.1731

ANALYSIS OF INDIVIDUAL PARAMETERS

EFFECT	PARAMETER	ESTIMATE	STANDARD ERROR	CHI-SQUARE	PROB
INTERCEPT	1	0.719627	.0147294	2386.97	0.0001
TRTMENT	2	-.012849	.0041586	9.55	0.0020

CORRELATION OF ESTIMATES

	1	2
1	1	0.0419376
2	0.0419376	1

DIAGNOSTIC PROCEDURE COMPARISON 4
SENSITIVITY AND SPECIFICITY ANALYSIS, MAIN-EFFECTS MODEL

CATMOD PROCEDURE

```
RESPONSE: STD1*TEST1*STD2*TEST2       RESPONSE LEVELS (R)=    15
WEIGHT VARIABLE: WT                   POPULATIONS     (S)=     1
DATA SET: A                           TOTAL FREQUENCY (N)=   793
                                      OBSERVATIONS  (OBS)=    15
```

SAMPLE	FUNCTION NUMBER	RESPONSE FUNCTION	DESIGN MATRIX 1	2	3
1	1	0.822511	1	1	1
	2	0.948399	1	1	-1
	3	0.815451	1	-1	1
	4	0.969643	1	-1	-1

ANALYSIS OF VARIANCE TABLE

SOURCE	DF	CHI-SQUARE	PROB
INTERCEPT	1	6448.79	0.0001
TIME	1	4.10	0.0428
ACCURACY	1	38.81	0.0001
RESIDUAL	1	1.00	0.3178

(continued on next page)

(continued from previous page)

ANALYSIS OF INDIVIDUAL PARAMETERS

EFFECT	PARAMETER	ESTIMATE	STANDARD ERROR	CHI-SQUARE	PROB
INTERCEPT	1	0.889174	.0110725	6448.79	0.0001
RESPONSE	2	-.009318	.0046005	4.10	0.0428
	3	-.070202	.0112683	38.81	0.0001

NOTE: _RESPONSE_ = TIME ACCURACY

DIAGNOSTIC PROCEDURE COMPARISON
SENSITIVITY AND SPECIFICITY ANALYSIS, MAIN-EFFECTS MODEL 5

CATMOD PROCEDURE

COVARIANCE OF ESTIMATES

	1	2	3
1	.000122601	2.292E-06	.000101375
2	2.292E-06	.000021165	-5.873E-06
3	.000101375	-5.873E-06	.000126975

REFERENCES

Bishop, Y.M.M., Fienberg, S.E., and Holland, P.W. (1975), *Discrete Multivariate Analysis: Theory and Practice*, Cambridge, Massachusetts: The MIT Press.

Bock, R.D. (1975), *Multivariate Statistical Methods in Behavioral Research*, Chapter 8, New York: McGraw-Hill.

Cox, D.R. (1970), *The Analysis of Binary Data*, New York: Halsted Press.

Fienberg, S.E. (1980), *The Analysis of Cross-Classified Categorical Data*, Second Edition, Cambridge, Massachusetts: The MIT Press.

Forthofer, R.N. and Koch, G.G. (1973), "An Analysis of Compounded Functions of Categorical Data," *Biometrics* 29, 143-157.

Forthofer, R.N. and Lehnen R.G. (1981), *Public Program Analysis: A New Categorical Data Approach*, Belmont, CA: Wadsworth.

Grizzle, J.E., Starmer, C.F., and Koch, G.G. (1969), "Analysis of Categorical Data by Linear Models," *Biometrics* 25, 489-504.

Koch, G.G., Landis, J.R., Freeman, J.L., Freeman, D.H., and Lehnen, R.G. (1977), "A General Methodology for the Analysis of Experiments with Repeated Measurement of Categorical Data," *Biometrics* 33, 133-158.

Kritzer, Herbert (1979), "Approaches to the Analysis of Complex Contingency Tables: A Guide for the Perplexed," *Sociological Methods and Research* 7, 305-329.

Landis, J.R. and Koch, G.G. (1977), "The Measurement of Observer Agreement for Categorical Data," *Biometrics* 33, 159-174.

Landis, J.R., Stanish, W.M., Freeman, J.L. and Koch, G.G. (1976), "A Computer Program for the Generalized Chi-Square Analysis of Categorical Data Using Weighted Least Squares, (GENCAT)," *Computer Programs in Biomedicine* 6, 196-231.

Searle, S.R. (1971), *Linear Models*, New York: John Wiley & Sons, Inc.

Wald, A. (1943), "Tests of Statistical Hypotheses Concerning General Parameters When the Number of Observations Is Large," *Transactions of the American Mathematical Society* 54, 426-482.

Chapter 15

The CLUSTER Procedure

Operating systems: All

ABSTRACT

The CLUSTER procedure hierarchically clusters the observations in a SAS data set using one of eleven methods. The data can be numeric coordinates or distances. CLUSTER creates an output data set from which the TREE procedure can draw a tree diagram or output clusters at a specified level of the tree.

INTRODUCTION

The CLUSTER procedure finds hierarchical clusters of the observations in a SAS data set. The data can be coordinates or distances. If the data are coordinates, CLUSTER computes (possibly squared) Euclidean distances. The clustering methods available are average linkage, the centroid method, complete linkage, density linkage (including Wong's hybrid and *k*th-nearest-neighbor methods), maximum-likelihood for mixtures of spherical multivariate normal distributions with equal variances but possibly unequal mixing proportions, the flexible-beta method, McQuitty's similarity analysis, the median method, single linkage, two-stage density linkage, and Ward's minimum variance method.

All methods are based on the usual agglomerative hierarchical clustering procedure. Each observation begins in a cluster by itself. The two closest clusters are merged to form a new cluster replacing the two old clusters. Merging of the two closest clusters is repeated until only one cluster is left. The various clustering methods differ in how the distance between two clusters is computed. Each method is described below in **Clustering Methods**.

CLUSTER prints a history of the clustering process, giving statistics useful for estimating the number of clusters in the population from which the data were sampled. CLUSTER also creates an output data set that can be used by the TREE procedure to draw a tree diagram of the cluster hierarchy or to output a partition at any desired level.

Agglomerative hierarchical clustering is discussed in all standard references on cluster analysis, for example, Anderberg (1973), Sneath and Sokal (1973), Hartigan (1975), Everitt (1980), and Spath (1980). An especially good introduction is given by Massart and Kaufman (1983). Anyone considering doing a hierarchical cluster analysis should study the Monte Carlo results of Milligan (1980), Milligan and Cooper (1983), and Cooper and Milligan (1984). Other essential, though more advanced, references on hierarchical clustering include Hartigan (1977, 60-68; 1981), Wong (1982), Wong and Schaak (1982), and Wong and Lane (1983). See Blashfield and Aldenderfer (1978) for a discussion of the confusing terminology in hierarchical cluster analysis.

SPECIFICATIONS

Use the following statements to invoke the CLUSTER procedure:

PROC CLUSTER *options;*
  VAR *variables;*
  ID *variables;*
  COPY *variables;*
  FREQ *variable;*
  RMSSTD *variable;*
  BY *variables;*

Usually, only the VAR statement is needed in addition to the PROC CLUSTER statement.

PROC CLUSTER Statement

PROC CLUSTER *options;*

The METHOD= option must be specified.

The following data set options can appear in the PROC statement:

DATA=*SASdataset*

names the input data set containing observations to be clustered. If DATA= is omitted, the most recently created SAS data set is used. If the data set is TYPE=DISTANCE, the data are interpreted as a distance matrix; the number of variables must equal the number of observations in the data set or in each BY group. The distances are assumed to be Euclidean, but the procedure accepts other types of distances or dissimilarities. If the data set is not TYPE=DISTANCE, the data are interpreted as coordinates in a Euclidean space, and Euclidean distances are computed.

All methods produce the same results when used with coordinate data as when used with Euclidean distances computed from the coordinates. However, the DIM= option must be used with distance data if METHOD=TWOSTAGE or METHOD=DENSITY is specified or if the TRIM= option is used.

Certain methods that are most naturally defined in terms of coordinates require *squared* Euclidean distances to be used in the combinatorial distance formulas (Lance and Williams 1967). For this reason, distance data are automatically squared when used with METHOD=AVERAGE, CENTROID, MEDIAN, or WARD. If you want the combinatorial formulas to be applied to the (unsquared) distances with these methods, use the NOSQUARE option.

OUTTREE=*SASdataset*

names an output data set that can be used by the TREE procedure to draw a tree diagram. The data set must be given a two-level name if it is to be saved. See "SAS Files" in *SAS User's Guide: Basics* for a discussion of permanent data sets. If OUTTREE= is omitted, the data set is named using the DATA*n* convention and is not permanently saved. If you do not want to create an output data set, use OUTTREE=_NULL_.

The following options concern the printout and data processing before the actual clustering:

SIMPLE

S

prints means, standard deviations, skewness, kurtosis, and a coefficient of bimodality. The SIMPLE option applies only to coordinate data.

NOEIGEN

suppresses computation of eigenvalues for the cubic clustering criterion. Specifying NOEIGEN saves time if the number of variables is large but should only be used if the variables are nearly uncorrelated or if you are not interested in the cubic clustering criterion. If you specify NOEIGEN and the variables are highly correlated, the cubic clustering criterion may be very liberal. NOEIGEN applies only to coordinate data.

STANDARD

STD

standardizes the variables to mean 0 and standard deviation 1. The STANDARD option applies only to coordinate data.

NOSQUARE

prevents input distances from being squared with METHOD= AVERAGE, CENTROID, MEDIAN, or WARD.

TRIM=*p*

requests that points with low estimated probability densities be omitted from the analysis. If $p<1$, then *p* is the proportion of observations omitted. If $p\geq 1$, then *p* is interpreted as a percentage. The specification TRIM=10, trimming 10% of the points, is a reasonable value for many data sets. Densities are estimated by the *k*th-nearest-neighbor or uniform-kernel methods. You must use either K= or R= when specifying TRIM=. See also the DIM= option, below. Trimmed points are indicated by _FREQ_=0 in the OUTTREE= data set.

If the STANDARD option is specified in combination with TRIM=, the variables are standardized both before and after trimming.

TRIM= is useful for removing outliers and reducing chaining. Trimming is highly recommended with METHOD=WARD or METHOD=COMPLETE because clusters from these methods can be severely distorted by outliers. Trimming is also valuable with METHOD=SINGLE, since single linkage is the method most susceptible to chaining. Most other methods also benefit from trimming. However, trimming is unnecessary with METHOD=TWOSTAGE or DENSITY when *k*th-nearest-neighbor density estimation is used.

DIM=*n*

specifies the dimensionality to be used when computing density estimates. The default is the number of variables if the data are coordinates; the default is 1 if the data are distances.

If you request an analysis that requires density estimation (TRIM=, METHOD= DENSITY, or METHOD=TWOSTAGE) you must specify one and only one of the following three options:

K=*n*

specifies the number of neighbors to use for *k*th-nearest-neighbor density estimation. The number of neighbors must be at least two but less than the number of observations.

R=*n*

specifies the radius of the sphere of support for uniform-kernel density estimation.

HYBRID

requests Wong's (1982) hybrid clustering method in which density estimates are computed from a preliminary cluster analysis using the *k*-means method. The DATA= data set must contain means, frequencies, and root-mean-square standard deviations of the preliminary clusters (see the FREQ and RMSSTD statements). The MEAN= data set produced by the FASTCLUS procedure is suitable for input to the CLUSTER procedure for hybrid clustering. You must specify either METHOD=DENSITY or METHOD=TWOSTAGE with the HYBRID option. HYBRID cannot be used with the TRIM= option.

The following options determine the type of cluster analysis:

METHOD=*name*
M=*name*
specifies what clustering method to use. The METHOD= option is required. Any one of the eleven methods listed below can be specified for *name*.

METHOD=AVERAGE | AVE
requests average linkage (group average, unweighted pair-group method using arithmetic averages, UPGMA). Distance data are squared unless you specify the NOSQUARE option.

METHOD=CENTROID | CEN
requests the centroid method (unweighted pair-group method using centroids, UPGMC, centroid sorting, weighted-group method). Distance data are squared unless you specify the NOSQUARE option.

METHOD=COMPLETE | COM
requests complete linkage (furthest neighbor, maximum method, diameter method, rank order typal analysis).

METHOD=DENSITY | DEN
requests density linkage, a class of clustering methods using nonparametric probability density estimation. You must also specify K=, R=, or HYBRID to indicate the type of density estimation to be used. See also the MODE= and DIM= options.

METHOD=EML
requests maximum-likelihood hierarchical clustering for mixtures of spherical multivariate normal distributions with equal variances but possibly unequal mixing proportions. Use METHOD=EML only with coordinate data.

METHOD=FLEXIBLE | FLE
requests the Lance-Williams flexible-beta method. See the BETA= option.

METHOD=MCQUITTY | MCQ
requests McQuitty's similarity analysis (weighted average linkage, weighted pair-group method using arithmetic averages, WPGMA).

METHOD=MEDIAN | MED
requests Gower's median method (weighted pair-group method using centroids, WPGMC). Distance data are squared unless the NOSQUARE option is specified.

METHOD=SINGLE | SIN
requests single linkage (nearest neighbor, minimum method, connectedness method, elementary linkage analysis, or dendritic method). To reduce chaining, you should use the TRIM= option with METHOD=SINGLE.

METHOD=TWOSTAGE | TWO
requests two-stage density linkage. You must also specify K=, R=, or HYBRID to indicate the type of density estimation to be used. See also the MODE= and DIM= options.

METHOD=WARD | WAR
requests Ward's minimum variance method (error sum of squares, trace W). Distance data are squared unless you specify the NOSQUARE option.

BETA=*n*

specifies the beta parameter for METHOD=FLEXIBLE. The value should be less than 1, usually between 0 and −1. The default is BETA=−.25.

PENALTY=*p*

specifies the penalty coefficient used with METHOD=EML. See **Clustering Methods** below. The default is PENALTY=2.

MODE=*n*

specifies that when two clusters are joined, each must have at least *n* members for either cluster to be designated a modal cluster. If MODE=1 is specified, each cluster must also have a maximum density greater than the fusion density for either cluster to be designated a modal cluster. Use the MODE= option only with METHOD=DENSITY or TWOSTAGE. With METHOD=TWOSTAGE, the MODE= option affects the number of modal clusters formed. With METHOD=DENSITY, MODE= does not affect the clustering process but does determine the number of modal clusters reported on the printout and identified by the _MODE_ variable in the output data set. If you specify the K= option, the default value of MODE= is the same as the value of K= because the use of *k*th-nearest-neighbor density estimation limits the resolution that can be obtained for clusters with fewer than *k* members. If K= is not specified, the default is MODE=2. If MODE=0 is specified, the default value is used instead of 0. If a FREQ statement is used or the _FREQ_ variable exists in the input data set, the MODE= value is compared to the number of observations in each cluster, not to the sum of the frequencies.

The following options affect the printing of the cluster history:

PRINT=*n*
P=*n*

specifies the number of generations of the cluster history to print. The default is to print all generations. PRINT=0 suppresses the cluster history.

RMSSTD

prints the root-mean-square standard deviation of each cluster. This option is effective only when the data are coordinates or METHOD=AVERAGE, CENTROID, or WARD. See **Miscellaneous Formulas** below.

RSQUARE
RSQ

prints R^2 and semipartial R^2. This option is effective only when the data are coordinates or METHOD=AVERAGE or CENTROID. The R^2 and semipartial R^2 statistics are always printed with METHOD=WARD. See **Miscellaneous Formulas** below.

CCC

prints the cubic clustering criterion and approximate expected R^2 under the uniform null hypothesis (Sarle 1983). The statistics associated with the RSQUARE option, R^2 and semipartial R^2, are also printed. The CCC option applies only to coordinate data.

PSEUDO
prints pseudo F and t^2 statistics. This option is effective only when the data are coordinates or METHOD=AVERAGE, CENTROID, or WARD. See **Miscellaneous Formulas** below.

NOID
suppresses printing the ID values of the clusters joined at each generation of the cluster history.

NONORM
prevents the distances from being normalized to unit mean or unit root mean square with most methods. With METHOD=WARD, NONORM prevents the between-cluster sum of squares from being normalized by the total sum of squares to yield a squared semipartial correlation. The NONORM option has no effect with METHOD=DENSITY, EML, or TWOSTAGE.

Miscellaneous options:

NOPRINT
suppresses the printout.

VAR Statement

VAR *variables;*

The VAR statement lists numeric variables to be used in the cluster analysis. If the VAR statement is omitted, all numeric variables not listed in other statements are used.

ID Statement

ID *variables;*

The values of the ID variable identify observations in the printed cluster history and in the OUTTREE= data set. If the ID statement is omitted, each observation is denoted by OB*n*, where *n* is the observation number.

COPY Statement

COPY *variables;*

The variables in the COPY statement are copied from the input data set to the OUTTREE= data set. Observations in the OUTTREE= data set that represent clusters of more than one observation from the input data set have missing values for the COPY variables.

FREQ Statement

FREQ *variable;*

If one variable in the input data set represents the frequency of occurrence for other values in the observation, specify the variable's name in a FREQ statement. CLUSTER then treats the data set as if each observation appeared *n* times, where *n* is the value of the FREQ variable for the observation. Nonintegral values of the FREQ variable are truncated to the largest integer less than the FREQ value.

If the FREQ statement is omitted but the DATA= data set contains a variable called _FREQ_, then frequencies are obtained from the _FREQ_ variable. If neither a FREQ statement nor a _FREQ_ variable is present, each observation is assumed to have a frequency of 1.

If each observation in the DATA= data set represents a cluster (for example, clusters formed by PROC FASTCLUS), the variable specified in the FREQ statement should give the number of original observations in each cluster.

A FREQ statement or _FREQ_ variable is required when the HYBRID option is used.

With most clustering methods, the same clusters are obtained from a data set with a FREQ variable as from a similar data set without a FREQ variable, if each observation is repeated as many times as the value of the FREQ variable in the first data set. The DENSITY and TWOSTAGE methods are exceptions, however, because two identical observations can be absorbed one at a time by a cluster with a higher density.

RMSSTD Statement

RMSSTD *variable;*

If the coordinates in the DATA= data set represent cluster means (for example, formed by the FASTCLUS procedure), you can obtain accurate statistics in the cluster histories for METHOD=AVERAGE, CENTROID, or WARD if the data set contains:

- a variable giving the number of original observations in each cluster (see the FREQ statement, above)
- a variable giving the root-mean-square standard deviation of each cluster.

Specify the name of the variable containing root-mean-square standard deviations in the RMSSTD statement. If the RMSSTD statement is used, the FREQ statement must also be specified.

If the RMSSTD statement is omitted but the DATA= data set contains a variable called _RMSSTD_, then root-mean-square standard deviations are obtained from the _RMSSTD_ variable.

An RMSSTD statement or _RMSSTD_ variable is required when the HYBRID option is used.

A data set created by FASTCLUS using the MEAN= option contains _FREQ_ and _RMSSTD_ variables, so you do not have to use FREQ and WEIGHT statements with such a data set as input to the CLUSTER procedure.

BY Statement

BY *variables;*

A BY statement can be used with PROC CLUSTER to obtain separate analyses on observations in groups defined by the BY variables. When a BY statement appears, the procedure expects the input data set to be sorted in order of the BY variables. If your input data set is not sorted in ascending order, use the SORT procedure with a similar BY statement to sort the data, or, if appropriate, use the BY statement options NOTSORTED or DESCENDING. For more information, see the discussion of the BY statement in "Statements Used in the PROC Step" in the *SAS User's Guide: Basics.*

DETAILS

Clustering Methods

The following notation is used, with lowercase symbols generally pertaining to observations, uppercase symbols to clusters:

n	number of observations
v	number of variables if data are coordinates
G	number of clusters at any given level of the hierarchy
x_i or $\mathbf{x}_i$	*i*th observation (row vector if coordinate data)
C_K	*K*th cluster, subset of {1, 2, ..., n}
N_K	number of observations in C_K
$\bar{\mathbf{x}}$	sample mean vector
$\bar{\mathbf{x}}_K$	mean vector for cluster C_K
$\|\mathbf{x}\|$	Euclidean length of the vector **x**, that is, the square root of the sum of the squares of the elements of **x**
T	$\Sigma_{i=1}^{n} \|\mathbf{x}_i - \bar{\mathbf{x}}\|^2$
W_K	$\Sigma_{i \in C_k} \|\mathbf{x}_i - \bar{\mathbf{x}}_K\|^2$
P_G	ΣW_J, where summation is over the G clusters at the Gth level of the hierarchy.
B_{KL}	$W_M - W_K - W_L$ if $C_M = C_K \cup C_L$
$d(\mathbf{x},\mathbf{y})$	any distance or dissimilarity measure between observations or vectors **x** and **y**
D_{KL}	any distance or dissimilarity measure between clusters C_K and C_L

The distance between two clusters can be defined either directly or combinatorially (Lance and Williams 1967), that is, by an equation for updating a distance matrix when two clusters are joined. In all combinatorial formulas below, it is assumed that clusters C_K and C_L are merged to form C_M, and the formula gives the distance between the new cluster C_M and any other cluster C_J.

For an introduction to most of the methods used in the CLUSTER procedure, see Massart and Kaufman (1983).

Average linkage The distance between two clusters is defined by

$$D_{KL} = \Sigma_{i \in C_K} \Sigma_{j \in C_L} d(x_i, x_j) \ / \ (N_K N_L) \ .$$

If $d(\mathbf{x},\mathbf{y}) = \|\mathbf{x}\text{-}\mathbf{y}\|^2$ then

$$D_{KL} = \|\bar{\mathbf{x}}_K - \bar{\mathbf{x}}_L\|^2 + W_K/N_K + W_L/N_L \ .$$

The combinatorial formula is

$$D_{JM} = (N_K D_{JK} + N_L D_{JL})/N_M \ .$$

In average linkage the distance between two clusters is the average distance between pairs of observations, one in each cluster. Average linkage tends to join clusters with small variances and is slightly biased toward producing clusters with the same variance.

Average linkage was originated by Sokal and Michener (1958).

Centroid method The distance between two clusters is defined by

$$D_{KL} = \|\bar{\mathbf{x}}_K - \bar{\mathbf{x}}_L\|^2 \ .$$

If $d(\mathbf{x},\mathbf{y}) = \|\mathbf{x}\text{-}\mathbf{y}\|^2$ then the combinatorial formula is

$$D_{JM} = (N_K D_{JK} + N_L D_{JL})/N_M - N_K N_L D_{KL}/N_M^2 \quad .$$

In the centroid method the distance between two clusters is defined as the (squared) Euclidean distance between their centroids or means. The centroid method is more robust to outliers than most other hierarchical methods but in other respects may not perform as well as Ward's method or average linkage (Milligan 1980).

The centroid method was originated by Sokal and Michener (1958).

Complete linkage The distance between two clusters is defined by

$$D_{KL} = max_{i \varepsilon C_K} max_{j \varepsilon C_L} d(x_i,x_j) \quad .$$

The combinatorial formula is

$$D_{JM} = max(D_{JK}, D_{JL}) \quad .$$

In complete linkage the distance between two clusters is the maximum distance between an observation in one cluster and an observation in the other cluster. Complete linkage is strongly biased toward producing clusters with roughly equal diameters and can be severely distorted by moderate outliers (Milligan 1980).

Complete linkage was originated by Sorensen (1948).

Density linkage The phrase *density linkage* is used here to refer to a class of clustering methods using nonparametric probability density estimates (for example, Hartigan 1975, 205-212; Wong 1982; Wong and Lane 1983). Density linkage consists of two steps:

- a new dissimilarity measure d^* based on density estimates and adjacencies is computed. If x_i and x_j are adjacent (the definition of *adjacency* depends on the method of density estimation), then $d^*(x_i,x_j)$ is the reciprocal of an estimate of the density midway between x_i and x_j; otherwise, $d^*(x_i,x_j)$ is infinite.
- a single linkage cluster analysis is performed using d^*.

The CLUSTER procedure supports three types of density linkage: the *k*th-nearest-neighbor method, the uniform kernel method, and Wong's hybrid method.

The *k*th-nearest-neighbor method (Wong and Lane 1983) uses *k*th-nearest neighbor density estimates. Let $r_k(x)$ be the distance from a point x to the *k*th-nearest observation, where k is the value specified for the K= option. Consider a closed sphere centered at x with radius $r_k(x)$. The estimated density at x, $f(x)$, is the number of observations within the sphere divided by the volume of the sphere. The new dissimilarity measure is computed as

$$d^*(x_i,x_j) = (1/2)(1/f(x_i) + 1/f(x_j)) \text{ if } d(x_i,x_j) \leq max\ (r_k(x_i),\ r_k(x_j))$$

$$= \infty \text{ otherwise} \quad .$$

Wong and Lane (1983) show that *k*th-nearest-neighbor density linkage is strongly set consistent for high-density (density-contour) clusters if k is chosen such that $k/n \rightarrow 0$ and $k/\ln(n) \rightarrow \infty$ as $n \rightarrow \infty$. Wong and Schaak (1982) discuss methods for estimating the number of population clusters using *k*th-nearest-neighbor clustering.

The uniform-kernel method uses uniform-kernel density estimates. Let r be the value specified for the R= option. Consider a closed sphere centered at a point x with radius *r*. The estimated density at x, *f*(x), is the number of observations within the sphere divided by the volume of the sphere. The new dissimilarity measure is computed as

$$d^*(x_i,x_j) = (1/2)(1/f(x_i) + 1/f(x_j)) \text{ if } d(x_i,x_j) \leq r$$

$$= \infty \text{ otherwise} \quad .$$

Wong's (1982) hybrid clustering method uses density estimates based on a preliminary cluster analysis by the *k*-means method. The preliminary clustering can be done by the FASTCLUS procedure, using the MEAN= option to create a data set containing cluster means, frequencies, and root-mean-square standard deviations. This data set is used as input to the CLUSTER procedure, and the HYBRID option is specified together with METHOD=DENSITY to request the hybrid analysis. The hybrid method is appropriate for very large data sets but should not be used with small data sets, say fewer than 100 observations in the original data. In the following discussion, the term *cluster* refers to a *preliminary cluster*, that is, an observation in the DATA= data set.

For cluster C_K, N_K and W_K are obtained from the input data set, as are the cluster means or the distances between the cluster means. Clusters C_K and C_L are considered adjacent if the midpoint between $\bar{x}_K$ and $\bar{x}_L$ is closer to either $\bar{x}_K$ or $\bar{x}_L$ than to any other cluster mean or, equivalently, if $d^2(\bar{x}_K,\bar{x}_L) < d^2(\bar{x}_K,\bar{x}_M) + d^2(\bar{x}_L,\bar{x}_M)$ for all other clusters C_M, $M \neq K$ or L. The new dissimilarity measure is computed as

$$d^*(\bar{x}_K,\bar{x}_L) = (W_K+W_L+(N_K+N_L)d^2(\bar{x}_K,\bar{x}_L)/4)^{v/2}/(N_K+N_L)^{1+v/2}$$

if C_K and C_L are adjacent,

$$= \infty \text{ otherwise} \quad .$$

The values of K= and R= are called *smoothing parameters*. Small values of K= or R= produce jagged density estimates and, as a consequence, many modes. Large values of K= or R= produce smoother density estimates and fewer modes. In the hybrid method, the smoothing parameter is the number of clusters in the preliminary cluster analysis. The number of modes in the final analysis tends to increase as the number of clusters in the preliminary analysis increases. Wong (1982) suggests using $n^{0.3}$ preliminary clusters, where *n* is the number of observations in the original data set. There is no general rule-of-thumb for selecting K= or R= values. For all types of density linkage, you should repeat the analysis with several different values of the smoothing parameter (Wong and Schaack 1982).

Since infinite d^* values occur in density linkage, the final number of clusters may exceed one when there are wide gaps between the clusters or when the smoothing parameter results in little smoothing.

Density linkage applies no constraints to the shapes of the clusters and, unlike most other hierarchical clustering methods, is capable of recovering clusters with elongated or irregular shapes. Since density linkage employs less prior knowledge about the shape of the clusters than do methods restricted to compact clusters, density linkage is less effective at recovering compact clusters from small samples than are methods that always recover compact clusters regardless of the data.

EML The distance between two clusters is given by

$$D_{KL} = nv \ln(1 + B_{KL}/P_G) - 2(n_M \ln(n_M) - n_K \ln(n_K) - n_L \ln(n_L)) \quad .$$

EML joins clusters to maximize the likelihood at each level of the hierarchy under the following assumptions:

- multivariate normal mixture
- equal spherical covariance matrices
- unequal sampling probabilities.

EML is similar to Ward's minimum variance method but removes the bias toward equal-sized clusters. Practical experience has indicated that EML is somewhat biased toward unequal-sized clusters. The PENALTY= option can be used to adjust the degree of bias. If PENALTY=p is specified, the formula is modified to

$$D_{KL} = nv\ \ln(1 + B_{KL}/P_G) - p(n_M \ln(n_M) - n_K \ln(n_K) - n_L \ln(n_L)) \quad .$$

The EML method was derived by W.S. Sarle of SAS Institute Inc., from the maximum likelihood formula obtained by Symons (1981, 37, eq. [8]) for disjoint clustering. There are currently no other published references on the EML method.

Flexible-beta method The combinatorial formula is

$$D_{JM} = (D_{JK} + D_{JL})(1-b)/2 + D_{KL}b$$

where b is the value of the BETA= option, or -0.25 by default.

The flexible-beta method was developed by Lance and Williams (1967).

McQuitty's similarity analysis The combinatorial formula is

$$D_{JM} = (D_{JK} + D_{JL})/2 \quad .$$

The method was independently developed by Sokal and Michener (1958) and McQuitty (1966).

Median method If $d(\mathbf{x},\mathbf{y}) = \|\mathbf{x}-\mathbf{y}\|^2$ then the combinatorial formula is

$$D_{JM} = (D_{JK} + D_{JL})/2 - D_{KL}/4 \quad .$$

The median method is due to Gower (1967).

Single linkage The distance between two clusters is defined by

$$D_{KL} = min_{i \varepsilon C_K} min_{j \varepsilon C_L}\ d(x_i, x_j) \quad .$$

The combinatorial formula is

$$D_{JM} = min(D_{JK}, D_{JL}) \quad .$$

In single linkage the distance between two clusters is the minimum distance between an observation in one cluster and an observation in the other cluster. Single linkage has many desirable theoretical properties (Jardine and Sibson 1971; Fisher and Van Ness 1971; Hartigan 1981) but has fared poorly in Monte Carlo studies (for example, Milligan 1980). By imposing no constraints on the shape of clusters, single linkage sacrifices performance in the recovery of compact clusters in return for the ability to detect elongated and irregular clusters. You must also recognize that single linkage tends to chop off the tails of distributions before separating the main clusters (Hartigan 1981). The notorious "chaining" tendency of single linkage can be alleviated by the TRIM= option (Wishart 1969).

Density linkage and two-stage density linkage retain most of the virtues of single linkage while performing better with compact clusters and possessing better asymptotic properties (Wong and Lane 1983).

Single linkage was originated by Florek et al. (1951a,b) and later reinvented by McQuitty (1957) and Sneath (1957).

Two-stage density linkage If you specify METHOD=DENSITY, the modal clusters often merge before all the points in the tails have clustered. METHOD=TWOSTAGE is a modification of density linkage that ensures that all points are assigned to modal clusters before the modal clusters are allowed to join. The CLUSTER procedure supports the same three varieties of two-stage density linkage as of ordinary density linkage: *k*th nearest neighbor, uniform kernel, and hybrid.

In the first stage, disjoint modal clusters are formed. The algorithm is the same as the single linkage algorithm ordinarily used with density linkage, with one exception: two clusters are joined only if at least one has fewer members than the number specified by the MODE= option. At the end of the first stage, each point belongs to one modal cluster.

In the second stage, the modal clusters are hierarchically joined by single linkage. The final number of clusters may exceed one when there are wide gaps between the clusters or the smoothing parameter is small.

Each stage forms a tree that can be printed by the TREE procedure. By default, the TREE procedure prints the tree from the first stage. To obtain the tree for the second stage, use the option HEIGHT=MODE in the PROC TREE statement. You can also produce a single tree diagram containing both stages, with the number of clusters as the height axis, by using HEIGHT=N in the PROC TREE statement. To produce an output data set from TREE containing the modal clusters, use _HEIGHT_ for the HEIGHT variable (the default) and specify LEVEL=0.

Two-stage density linkage was developed by W.S. Sarle of SAS Institute Inc. There are currently no other published references on two-stage density linkage.

Ward's minimum variance method The distance between two clusters is defined by

$$D_{KL} = B_{KL} = \|\bar{\mathbf{x}}_K - \bar{\mathbf{x}}_L\|^2 / (1/n_K + 1/n_L) \quad .$$

If $d(\mathbf{x},\mathbf{y}) = \|x\text{-}y\|^2/2$ then the combinatorial formula is

$$D_{JM} = ((N_J + N_K)D_{JK} + (N_J + N_L)D_{JL} - N_J D_{KL})/(N_J + N_M) \quad .$$

In Ward's minimum variance method the distance between two clusters is the ANOVA sum of squares between the two clusters added up over all the variables. At each generation, the within-cluster sum of squares is minimized over all partitions obtainable by merging two clusters from the previous generation. The sums of squares are easier to interpret when divided by the total sum of squares to give proportions of variance.

Ward's method joins clusters to maximize the likelihood at each level of the hierarchy under the following assumptions:

- multivariate normal mixture
- equal spherical covariance matrices
- equal sampling probabilities.

Ward's method tends to join clusters with a small number of observations and is strongly biased toward producing clusters with roughly the same number of observations. It is also very sensitive to outliers (Milligan 1980).

See Ward (1963).

Miscellaneous Formulas

The root-mean-square standard deviation of a cluster C_K is

$$\mathrm{RMSSTD} = \sqrt{W_K/(v(N_K-1))} \quad .$$

The R^2 statistic for a given level of the hierarchy is

$$R^2 = 1 - (P_G/T) \quad .$$

The squared semipartial correlation for joining clusters C_K and C_L is

$$\text{semipartial } R^2 = B_{KL}/T \quad .$$

Formulas for the cubic clustering criterion and approximate expected R^2 are given in Sarle (1983).

The pseudo *F* statistic for a given level is

$$\text{pseudo } F = ((T - P_G)/(G-1)) \;/\; (P_G/(n - G)) \quad .$$

The pseudo t^2 statistic for joining C_K and C_L is

$$\text{pseudo } t^2 = B_{KL} \;/\; ((W_K + W_L)/(N_K + N_L - 2)) \quad .$$

The pseudo *F* and t^2 statistics may be useful indicators of the number of clusters but are **not** distributed as *F* and t^2 random variables. If the data were independently sampled from a multivariate normal distribution with a scalar covariance matrix, and if the clustering method allocated observations to clusters randomly (which no clustering method actually does), then the pseudo *F* statistic would be distributed as an *F* random variable with $v(G\text{-}1)$ and $v(n\text{-}G)$ degrees of freedom. Under the same assumptions, the pseudo t^2 statistic would be distributed as an *F* random variable with *v* and $v(N_K+N_L\text{-}2)$ degrees of freedom. The pseudo t^2 statistic differs computationally from Hotelling's T^2 in that the latter uses a general symmetric covariance matrix instead of a scalar covariance matrix. The pseudo *F* statistic was suggested by Calinski and Harabasz (1974). The pseudo t^2 statistic is related to the $J_e(2)/J_e(1)$ statistic of Duda and Hart (1973) by

$$J_e(2)/J_e(1) = (W_K + W_L) \;/\; W_M = 1/(1 + ((t^2/(N_K + N_L - 2))) \quad .$$

See Milligan and Cooper (1983) and Cooper and Milligan (1984) regarding the performance of the above statistics in estimating the number of population clusters. Conservative tests for the number of clusters using the pseudo *F* and t^2 statistics can be obtained by the Bonferroni approach (Hawkins, Muller, and ten Krooden 1982, 337-340).

Ultrametrics

A dissimilarity measure d(x,y) is called an *ultrametric* if it satisfies the following conditions:

- $d(x,x) = 0$ for all x
- $d(x,y) \geq 0$ for all x,y
- $d(x,y) = d(y,x)$ for all x,y
- $d(x,y) \leq \max(d(x,z), d(y,z))$ for all x, y, and z.

Any hierarchical clustering method induces a dissimilarity measure on the observations, say $h(x_i,x_j)$. Let C_M be the cluster with the fewest members that contains both x_i and x_j. Assume C_M was formed by joining C_K and C_L. Then define $h(x_i,x_j) = D_{KL}$.

If the fusion of C_K and C_L reduced the number of clusters from g to g-1, then define $D_{(g)} = D_{KL}$. Johnson (1967) showed that if

$$0 \leq D_{(n)} \leq D_{(n-1)} \leq \ldots \leq D_{(2)}$$

then $h(.,.)$ is an ultrametric. A method that always satisfies the above condition is said to be a monotonic or ultrametric clustering method. All methods implemented in CLUSTER except CENTROID, EML, and MEDIAN are ultrametric (Milligan 1979; Batagelj 1981).

Algorithms

Anderberg (1973) describes three algorithms for implementing agglomerative hierarchical clustering: stored data, stored distance, and sorted distance. The algorithms used by CLUSTER for each method are indicated in **Table 15.1**. For METHOD=AVERAGE, CENTROID, or WARD, either the stored data or the stored distance algorithm can be used. For these methods, if the data are distances or the NOSQUARE option is specified, the stored distance algorithm is used; otherwise the stored data algorithm is used.

Table 15.1 Three Algorithms for Implementing Agglomerative Hierarchical Clustering

	Algorithm		
Method	Stored Data	Stored Distance	Sorted Distance
AVERAGE	x	x	
CENTROID	x	x	
COMPLETE		x	
DENSITY			x
EML	x		
FLEXIBLE		x	
MCQUITTY		x	
MEDIAN		x	
SINGLE		x	
TWOSTAGE			x
WARD	x	x	

Computational Resources

CLUSTER stores the data in core. If eigenvalues are computed, the covariance matrix is stored in core. If the stored distance or sorted distance algorithm is used, the distances are stored in core.

With coordinate data, the increase in CPU time is roughly proportionate to the number of variables. The VAR statement should list the variables in order of decreasing variance for greatest efficiency.

For both coordinate and distance data, the dominant factor determining CPU time is the number of observations. For density methods with coordinate data, the asymptotic time requirements are somewhere between $n\ln(n)$ and n^2, depending on how the smoothing parameter increases. For other ultrametric methods, time is roughly proportional to n^2. For non-ultrametric methods, time is roughly proportional to n^3. The EML method is much slower than the CENTROID or MEDIAN methods.

Missing Values

If the data are coordinates, observations with missing values are excluded from the analysis. If the data are distances, missing values are not allowed in the lower triangle of the distance matrix. The upper triangle is ignored.

Ties

Each cluster is identified by the smallest observation number among its members. For each pair of clusters there is a smaller identification number and a larger identification number. If two or more pairs of clusters are tied for minimum distance between clusters, the pair that has the maximum larger identification number is merged. If there is a tie for maximum larger identification number, the pair that has the maximum smaller identification number is merged.

Output Data Set

The OUTTREE= data set contains one observation for each observation in the input data set, plus one observation for each cluster of two or more observations, that is, one observation for each node of the cluster tree. The total number of output observations is usually 2*n*-1, where *n* is the number of input observations. The density methods may produce fewer output observations when the number of clusters cannot be reduced to one.

The label of the OUTTREE= data set identifies the type of cluster analysis performed and is automatically printed when the TREE procedure is invoked.

The variables in the OUTTREE= data set are as follows:

- the BY variables, if any.
- _NAME_, a character variable giving the name of the node. If the node is a cluster, the name will be CL*n* where *n* is the number of the cluster. If the node is an observation, the name will be OB*n* where *n* is the observation number, unless the ID statement is used, in which case the name is the formatted value of the first ID variable.
- _PARENT_, a character variable giving the value of _NAME_ of the parent of the node.
- _NCL_, the number of clusters.
- _FREQ_, the number of observations in the current cluster.
- _HEIGHT_, the distance or similarity between the last clusters joined, D_{KL} as defined above in **Clustering Methods**. _HEIGHT_ is used by the TREE procedure as the default height axis. The label of the _HEIGHT_ variable identifies the between-cluster distance measure. For METHOD= TWOSTAGE, _HEIGHT_ contains the densities at which clusters joined in the first stage; for clusters formed in the second stage, _HEIGHT_ is a very small negative number.
- the ID variable, if any.

- the COPY variables, if any.

If the input data set contains coordinates and METHOD=AVERAGE, CENTROID, or WARD, then the following variables appear in the output data set:

- _DIST_, the Euclidean distance between the means of the last clusters joined
- _AVLINK_, the average linkage between the last clusters joined.

If the input data set contains coordinates or METHOD=AVERAGE, CENTROID, or WARD, then the following variables appear in the output data set:

- _RMSSTD_, the root-mean-square standard deviation of the current cluster
- _SPRSQ_, the semipartial squared multiple correlation, or the decrease in the proportion of variance accounted for due to joining two clusters to form the current cluster
- _RSQ_, the squared multiple correlation
- _PSF_, the pseudo F statistic
- _PST2_, the pseudo t^2 statistic.

If METHOD=EML is used, then the following variable appears in the output data set:

- _LNLR_, the log likelihood ratio.

If the input data set contains coordinates, the following variables appear in the output data set:

- the variables containing the coordinates used in the cluster analysis. For output observations that correspond to input observations, the values of the coordinates are the same in both data sets except for some slight numeric error possibly introduced by standardizing and unstandardizing if the STANDARD option is used. For output observations that correspond to clusters of more than one input observation, the values of the coordinates are the cluster means.
- _ERSQ_, the approximate expected value of R^2 under the uniform null hypothesis.
- _RATIO_, equal to (1−_ERSQ_)/(1−_RSQ_).
- _LOGR_, natural logarithm of _RATIO_.
- _CCC_, the cubic clustering criterion.

The variables _ERSQ_, _RATIO_, _LOGR_, and _CCC_ have missing values when the number of clusters is greater than one-fifth the number of observations.

If METHOD=TWOSTAGE or METHOD=DENSITY is used, the following variables appear in the output data set:

- _DENS_, the maximum density in the current cluster.
- _MODE_, pertaining to the modal clusters. With METHOD=DENSITY, _MODE_ indicates the number of modal clusters contained by the current cluster. With METHOD=TWOSTAGE, _MODE_ gives the maximum density in each modal cluster and the fusion density, d^*, for clusters containing two or more modal clusters; for clusters containing no modal clusters, _MODE_ is missing.

Printed Output

If you specify the SIMPLE option and the data are coordinates, CLUSTER prints simple descriptive statistics for each variable:

1. the MEAN
2. the standard deviation, STD DEV
3. the SKEWNESS
4. the KURTOSIS
5. a coefficient of BIMODALITY

$$b = (m_3^2 + 1)/(m_4+3)$$

where m_3 is skewness and m_4 is kurtosis. Values of b greater than 0.555 may indicate bimodal or multimodal marginal distributions.

If the data are coordinates and NOEIGEN is not specified, CLUSTER prints:

6. the EIGENVALUEs OF THE CORRELATION or COVARIANCE MATRIX
7. the DIFFERENCE between successive eigenvalues
8. the PROPORTION of variance explained by each eigenvalue
9. the CUMULATIVE proportion of variance explained.

If the data are coordinates, CLUSTER prints

10. the ROOT-MEAN-SQUARE TOTAL-SAMPLE STANDARD DEVIATION of the variables.

If the distances are normalized, CLUSTER prints either

11. the ROOT-MEAN-SQUARE DISTANCE BETWEEN OBSERVATIONS
or
12. the MEAN DISTANCE BETWEEN OBSERVATIONS
depending on whether squared or unsquared distances are used.

For the generations in the clustering process specified by the PRINT= option, CLUSTER prints:

13. the NUMBER OF CLUSTERS or NCL.
14. the names of the CLUSTERS JOINED. The observations are identified by the formatted value of the ID variable if any, otherwise by OB*n*, where *n* is the observation number. Clusters of two or more observations are identified as CL*n*, where *n* is the number of clusters existing after the cluster in question is formed.
15. the number of observations in the new cluster, FREQUENCY OF NEW CLUSTER or FREQ.

If you specify the RMSSTD option, and if the data are coordinates or you specify METHOD=AVERAGE, CENTROID, or WARD, the CLUSTER procedure prints:

16. the root-mean-square standard deviation of the new cluster, RMS STD OF NEW CLUSTER or RMS STD.

The procedure prints the following items if you specify METHOD=WARD. It also prints them if you specify RSQUARE and either the data are coordinates or you specify METHOD=AVERAGE or CENTROID.

17. the decrease in the proportion of variance accounted for resulting from joining the two clusters, SEMIPARTIAL R-SQUARED or SPRSQ. This equals the between-cluster sum of squares divided by the corrected total sum of squares.
18. the squared multiple correlation, R-SQUARED or RSQ. R^2 is the proportion of variance accounted for by the clusters.

If you specify the CCC option and the data are coordinates, the procedure prints the following:

19. APPROXIMATE EXPECTED R-SQUARED or ERSQ, the approximate expected value of R^2 under the uniform null hypothesis
20. the CUBIC CLUSTERING CRITERION or CCC.
    The cubic clustering criterion and approximate expected R^2 are given missing values when the number of clusters is greater than one-fifth the number of observations.

If you specify the PSEUDO option, and if the data are coordinates or METHOD=AVERAGE, CENTROID, or WARD, then the following are printed:

21. PSEUDO F or PSF, the pseudo F statistic measuring the separation among all the clusters at the current level
22. PSEUDO T**2 or PST2, the pseudo t^2 statistic measuring the separation between the two clusters most recently joined.

If you specify the NOSQUARE option along with METHOD=AVERAGE, CLUSTER prints:

23. (NORMALIZED) AVERAGE DISTANCE or AVER DIST, the average distance between pairs of objects in the two clusters joined, one object in each cluster.

If you specify METHOD=AVERAGE but do not specify the NOSQUARE option, CLUSTER prints:

24. (NORMALIZED) RMS DISTANCE or RMS DIST, the root-mean-square distance between pairs of objects in the two clusters joined, one object in each cluster.

If you specify METHOD=CENTROID, CLUSTER prints:

25. (NORMALIZED) CENTROID DISTANCE or CENT DIST, the distance between the two cluster centroids.

If METHOD=COMPLETE, CLUSTER prints:

26. (NORMALIZED) MAXIMUM DISTANCE or MAX DIST, the maximum distance between the two clusters.

If METHOD=DENSITY or METHOD=TWOSTAGE, CLUSTER prints:

27. FUSION DENSITY or FUSION DENS, the value of d^* as defined in **Clustering Methods**
28. the MAXIMUM DENSITY IN EACH CLUSTER joined, including the LESSER or MIN, and the GREATER or MAX, of the two maximum density values.

If METHOD=EML, CLUSTER prints:

29. LOG LIKELIHOOD RATIO or LNLR
30. LOG LIKELIHOOD or LNLIKE.

If METHOD=FLEXIBLE, CLUSTER prints:

31. (NORMALIZED) FLEXIBLE DISTANCE or FLEX DIST, the distance between the two clusters based on the Lance-Williams flexible formula.

If METHOD=MEDIAN, CLUSTER prints:

32. (NORMALIZED) MEDIAN DISTANCE or MED DIST, the distance between the two clusters based on the median method.

If METHOD=MCQUITTY, CLUSTER prints:

33. (NORMALIZED) MCQUITTY'S SIMILARITY or MCQ, the distance between the two clusters based on McQuitty's similarity method.

If METHOD=SINGLE, CLUSTER prints:

34. (NORMALIZED) MINIMUM DISTANCE or MIN DIST, the minimum distance between the two clusters.

If you specify the NONORM option along with METHOD=WARD, CLUSTER prints:

35. BETWEEN_CLUSTER SUM OF SQUARES or BSS, the ANOVA sum of squares between the two clusters joined.

If METHOD=TWOSTAGE or DENSITY, CLUSTER prints:

36. the number of MODAL CLUSTERS.

EXAMPLES

Cluster Analysis of Flying Mileages between Ten American Cities: Example 1

The first example clusters ten American cities based on the flying mileages between them. Six clustering methods are shown with corresponding tree diagrams produced by the TREE procedure. The EML method cannot be used because it requires coordinate data. The other omitted methods produce the same clusters, although not the same distances between clusters, as one of the illustrated methods: complete linkage and the flexible-beta method yield the same clusters as Ward's method, McQuitty's similarity analysis produces the same clusters as average linkage, and the median method corresponds to the centroid method.

All of the methods suggest a division of the cities into two clusters along the east-west dimension. There is disagreement, however, about which cluster Denver should belong to. Some of the methods indicate a possible third cluster containing Denver and Houston.

```
TITLE 'CLUSTER ANALYSIS OF FLYING MILEAGES BETWEEN 10 AMERICAN CITIES';

DATA   MILEAGES(TYPE=DISTANCE);
   INPUT  (ATLANTA CHICAGO DENVER HOUSTON LOSANGEL
          MIAMI NEWYORK SANFRAN SEATTLE WASHDC) (5.)
          @56 CITY $15.;
   CARDS;
   0                                                   ATLANTA
 587    0                                              CHICAGO
1212  920    0                                         DENVER
 701  940  879    0                                    HOUSTON
1936 1745  831 1374    0                               LOS ANGELES
 604 1188 1726  968 2339    0                          MIAMI
 748  713 1631 1420 2451 1092    0                     NEW YORK
2139 1858  949 1645  347 2594 2571    0                SAN FRANCISCO
2182 1737 1021 1891  959 2734 2408  678    0           SEATTLE
 543  597 1494 1220 2300  923  205 2442 2329    0      WASHINGTON
                                                         D.C.
   ;
```

```
PROC CLUSTER DATA=MILEAGES METHOD=AVERAGE PSEUDO;
   ID CITY;
PROC TREE;

PROC CLUSTER DATA=MILEAGES METHOD=CENTROID PSEUDO;
   ID CITY;
PROC TREE;
PROC CLUSTER DATA=MILEAGES METHOD=DENSITY K=3;
   ID CITY;
PROC TREE;

PROC CLUSTER DATA=MILEAGES METHOD=SINGLE;
   ID CITY;
PROC TREE;

PROC CLUSTER DATA=MILEAGES METHOD=TWOSTAGE K=3;
   ID CITY;
PROC TREE;

PROC CLUSTER DATA=MILEAGES METHOD=WARD PSEUDO;
   ID CITY;
PROC TREE;
```

Output 15.1 Six Different Clustering Methods: PROC CLUSTER and PROC TREE

CLUSTER ANALYSIS OF FLYING MILEAGES BETWEEN 10 AMERICAN CITIES 1

AVERAGE LINKAGE CLUSTER ANALYSIS

(11) ROOT-MEAN-SQUARE DISTANCE BETWEEN OBSERVATIONS = 1580.24

(13) NUMBER OF CLUSTERS	(14) CLUSTERS JOINED		(16) FREQUENCY OF NEW CLUSTER	(21) PSEUDO F	(22) PSEUDO T**2	NORMALIZED RMS DISTANCE (24)
9	NEW YORK	WASHINGTON D	2	66.72	.	0.129727
8	LOS ANGELES	SAN FRANCISC	2	39.25	.	0.219587
7	ATLANTA	CHICAGO	2	21.66	.	0.371462
6	CL7	CL9	4	14.52	3.45	0.414859
5	CL8	SEATTLE	3	12.44	7.30	0.525534
4	DENVER	HOUSTON	2	13.91	.	0.556244
3	CL6	MIAMI	5	15.49	3.75	0.618457
2	CL3	CL4	7	16.02	5.32	0.800540
1	CL2	CL5	10	.	16.02	1.296665

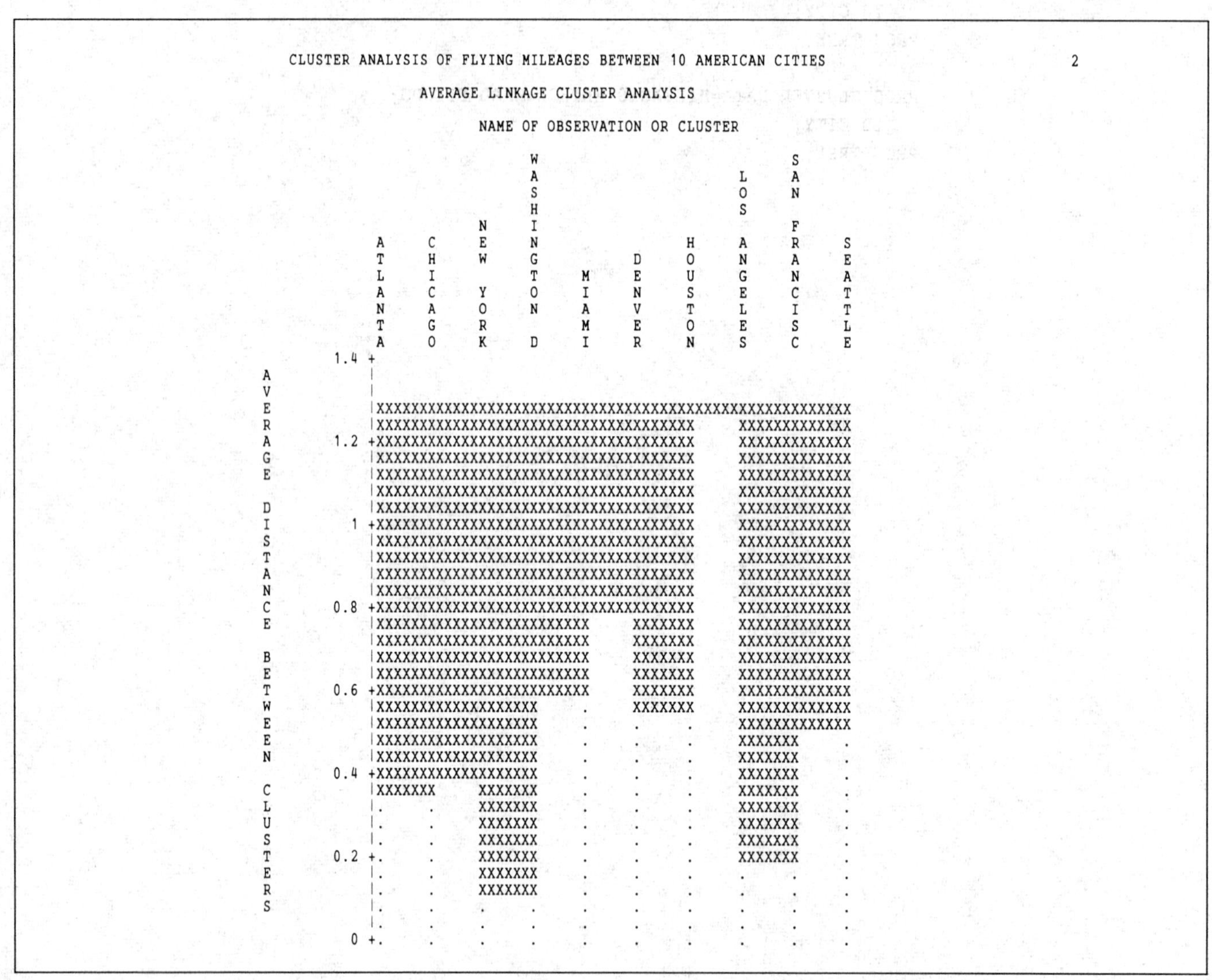

```
CLUSTER ANALYSIS OF FLYING MILEAGES BETWEEN 10 AMERICAN CITIES                        3

CENTROID HIERARCHICAL CLUSTER ANALYSIS

ROOT-MEAN-SQUARE DISTANCE BETWEEN OBSERVATIONS   =  1580.24
```

NUMBER OF CLUSTERS	CLUSTERS JOINED		FREQUENCY OF NEW CLUSTER	PSEUDO F	PSEUDO T**2	(25) NORMALIZED CENTROID DISTANCE
9	NEW YORK	WASHINGTON D	2	66.72	.	0.129727
8	LOS ANGELES	SAN FRANCISC	2	39.25	.	0.219587
7	ATLANTA	CHICAGO	2	21.66	.	0.371462
6	CL7	CL9	4	14.52	3.45	0.365246
5	CL8	SEATTLE	3	12.44	7.30	0.513937
4	DENVER	CL5	4	12.41	2.13	0.533679
3	CL6	MIAMI	5	14.23	3.75	0.574270
2	CL3	HOUSTON	6	22.06	2.61	0.609053
1	CL2	CL4	10	.	22.06	1.173036

```
CLUSTER ANALYSIS OF FLYING MILEAGES BETWEEN 10 AMERICAN CITIES                        4

CENTROID HIERARCHICAL CLUSTER ANALYSIS

NAME OF OBSERVATION OR CLUSTER

                                 W                             S
                                 A                       L     A
                                 S                       O     N
                                 H                       S
                           N     I                             F
               A     C     E     N           H           A     R     S
               T     H     W     G           O     D     N     A     E
               L     I           T     M     U     E     G     N     A
               A     C     Y     O     I     S     N     E     C     T
               N     A     O     N     A     T     V     L     I     T
               T     G     R           M     O     E     E     S     L
               A     O     K     D     I     N     R     S     C     E
          1.2 +
D             |XXXXXXXXXXXXXXXXXXXXXXXXXXXXXXXXXXXXXXXXXXXXXXXXXXXXXXX
I             |XXXXXXXXXXXXXXXXXXXXXXXXXXXXXXX     XXXXXXXXXXXXXXXXXXX
S             |XXXXXXXXXXXXXXXXXXXXXXXXXXXXXXX     XXXXXXXXXXXXXXXXXXX
T             |XXXXXXXXXXXXXXXXXXXXXXXXXXXXXXX     XXXXXXXXXXXXXXXXXXX
A             |XXXXXXXXXXXXXXXXXXXXXXXXXXXXXXX     XXXXXXXXXXXXXXXXXXX
N           1 +XXXXXXXXXXXXXXXXXXXXXXXXXXXXXXX     XXXXXXXXXXXXXXXXXXX
C             |XXXXXXXXXXXXXXXXXXXXXXXXXXXXXXX     XXXXXXXXXXXXXXXXXXX
E             |XXXXXXXXXXXXXXXXXXXXXXXXXXXXXXX     XXXXXXXXXXXXXXXXXXX
              |XXXXXXXXXXXXXXXXXXXXXXXXXXXXXXX     XXXXXXXXXXXXXXXXXXX
B             |XXXXXXXXXXXXXXXXXXXXXXXXXXXXXXX     XXXXXXXXXXXXXXXXXXX
E             |XXXXXXXXXXXXXXXXXXXXXXXXXXXXXXX     XXXXXXXXXXXXXXXXXXX
T         0.8 +XXXXXXXXXXXXXXXXXXXXXXXXXXXXXXX     XXXXXXXXXXXXXXXXXXX
W             |XXXXXXXXXXXXXXXXXXXXXXXXXXXXXXX     XXXXXXXXXXXXXXXXXXX
E             |XXXXXXXXXXXXXXXXXXXXXXXXXXXXXXX     XXXXXXXXXXXXXXXXXXX
E             |XXXXXXXXXXXXXXXXXXXXXXXXXXXXXXX     XXXXXXXXXXXXXXXXXXX
N             |XXXXXXXXXXXXXXXXXXXXXXXXXXXXXXX     XXXXXXXXXXXXXXXXXXX
              |XXXXXXXXXXXXXXXXXXXXXXXXXXXXXXX     XXXXXXXXXXXXXXXXXXX
C         0.6 +XXXXXXXXXXXXXXXXXXXXXXXXXXXXXXX     XXXXXXXXXXXXXXXXXXX
L             |XXXXXXXXXXXXXXXXXXXXXXXXX     .     XXXXXXXXXXXXXXXXXXX
U             |XXXXXXXXXXXXXXXXXXX     .     .     XXXXXXXXXXXXXXXXXXX
S             |XXXXXXXXXXXXXXXXXXX     .     .     .     XXXXXXXXXXXXX
T             |XXXXXXXXXXXXXXXXXXX     .     .     .     XXXXXXX     .
E             |XXXXXXXXXXXXXXXXXXX     .     .     .     XXXXXXX     .
R         0.4 +XXXXXXXXXXXXXXXXXXX     .     .     .     XXXXXXX     .
              |XXXXXXXXXXXXXXXXXXX     .     .     .     XXXXXXX     .
C             |.     .     XXXXXXX     .     .     .     XXXXXXX     .
E             |.     .     XXXXXXX     .     .     .     XXXXXXX     .
N             |.     .     XXXXXXX     .     .     .     XXXXXXX     .
T             |.     .     XXXXXXX     .     .     .     XXXXXXX     .
R         0.2 +.     .     XXXXXXX     .     .     .     .     .     .
O             |.     .     XXXXXXX     .     .     .     .     .     .
I             |.     .     XXXXXXX     .     .     .     .     .     .
D             |.     .     .     .     .     .     .     .     .     .
S             |.     .     .     .     .     .     .     .     .     .
              |.     .     .     .     .     .     .     .     .     .
            0 +.     .     .     .     .     .     .     .     .     .
```

CLUSTER ANALYSIS OF FLYING MILEAGES BETWEEN 10 AMERICAN CITIES 5

DENSITY LINKAGE CLUSTER ANALYSIS

K = 3

NUMBER OF CLUSTERS	CLUSTERS JOINED		FREQUENCY OF NEW CLUSTER	(27) FUSION DENSITY	(28) MAXIMUM DENSITY IN EACH CLUSTER		
					LESSER	GREATER	
9	ATLANTA	WASHINGTON D	2	.0026549	.0025554	.0027624	
8	CL9	CHICAGO	3	.0026316	.0025126	.0027624	
7	CL8	NEW YORK	4	.0023885	.0021038	.0027624	
6	CL7	MIAMI	5	.0020464	.0016251	.0027624	
5	CL6	HOUSTON	6	.0020464	.0017065	.0027624	
4	LOS ANGELES	SAN FRANCISC	2	.0019881	.0018051	.0022124	
3	CL4	SEATTLE	3	.0018326	.0015641	.0022124	
2	CL3	DENVER	4	.0017544	.0017065	.0022124	
1	CL5	CL2	10	.0017065	.0022124	.0027624	*

* INDICATES FUSION OF TWO MODAL CLUSTERS

(36) 2 MODAL CLUSTERS WERE FORMED

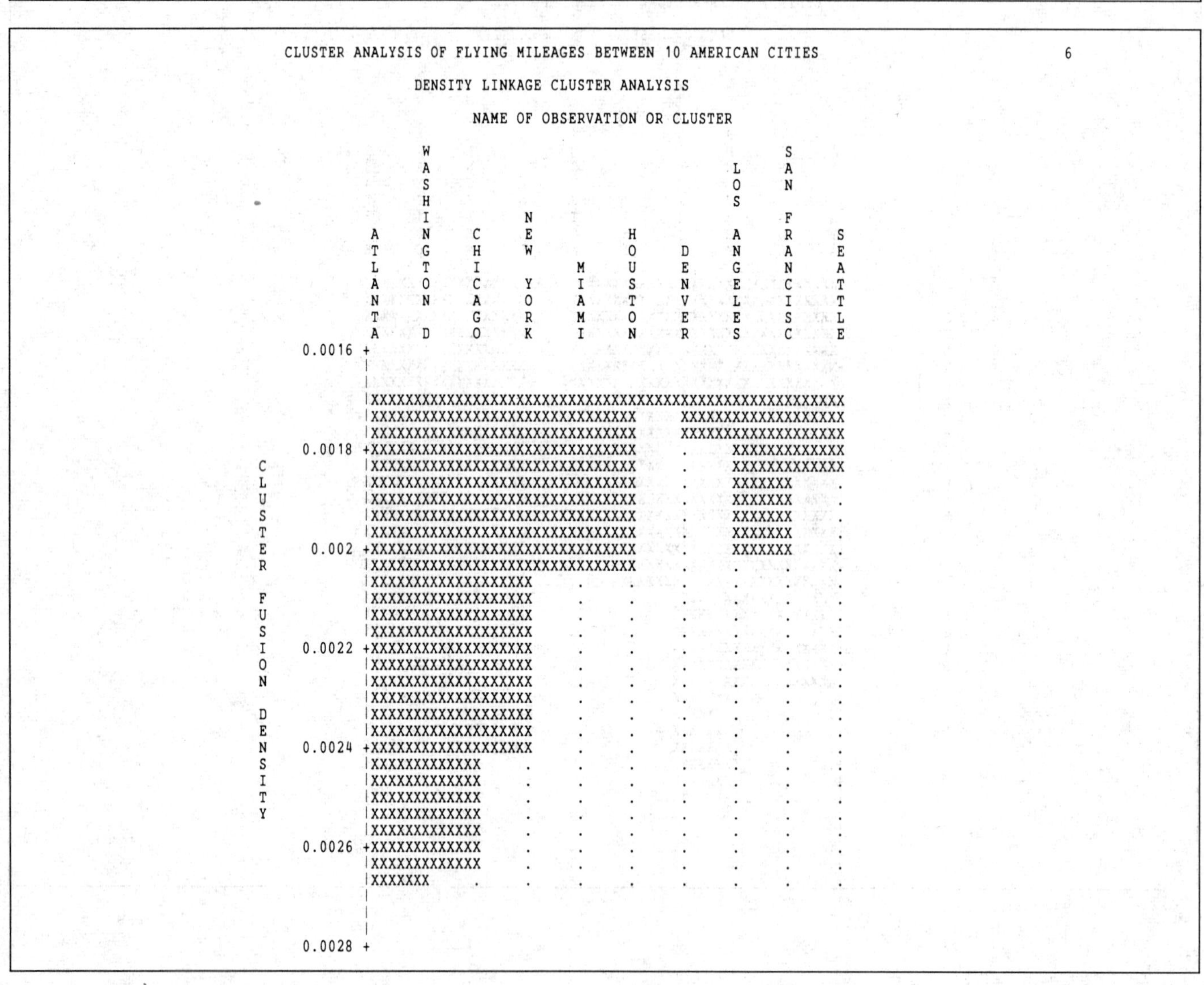

```
        CLUSTER ANALYSIS OF FLYING MILEAGES BETWEEN 10 AMERICAN CITIES                    7

                      SINGLE LINKAGE CLUSTER ANALYSIS

❿12     MEAN DISTANCE BETWEEN OBSERVATIONS                       =  1417.13

  NUMBER                                           FREQUENCY    NORMALIZED     ❸34
    OF                                               OF NEW       MINIMUM
  CLUSTERS    CLUSTERS JOINED                       CLUSTER      DISTANCE

      9       NEW YORK        WASHINGTON D              2        0.144658
      8       LOS ANGELES     SAN FRANCISC              2        0.244861
      7       ATLANTA         CL9                       3        0.383168
      6       CL7             CHICAGO                   4        0.414216
      5       CL6             MIAMI                     5        0.426213
      4       CL8             SEATTLE                   3        0.478431
      3       CL5             HOUSTON                   6        0.494661
      2       DENVER          CL4                       4        0.586395
      1       CL3             CL2                      10        0.620266
```

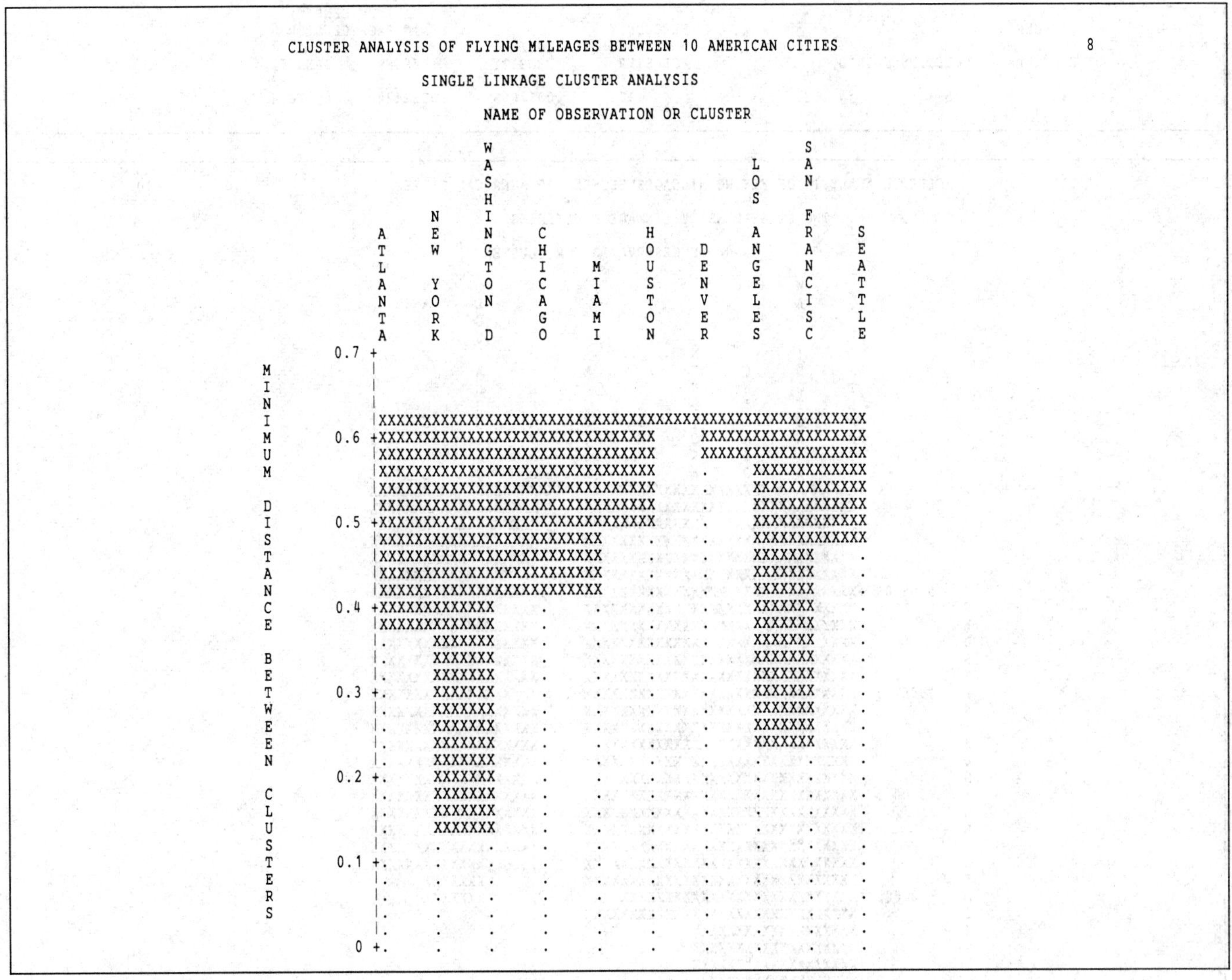

```
                 CLUSTER ANALYSIS OF FLYING MILEAGES BETWEEN 10 AMERICAN CITIES                               9

                                   TWO STAGE DENSITY LINKAGE CLUSTERING

                                                  K = 3

                                                                          MAXIMUM DENSITY    28
 NUMBER                                      FREQUENCY                    IN EACH CLUSTER
   OF                                         OF NEW        FUSION
CLUSTERS  CLUSTERS JOINED                     CLUSTER       DENSITY       LESSER       GREATER

    9     ATLANTA          WASHINGTON D           2        .0026549      .0025554     .0027624
    8     CL9              CHICAGO                3        .0026316      .0025126     .0027624
    7     CL8              NEW YORK               4        .0023885      .0021038     .0027624
    6     CL7              MIAMI                  5        .0020464      .0016251     .0027624
    5     CL6              HOUSTON                6        .0020464      .0017065     .0027624
    4     LOS ANGELES      SAN FRANCISC           2        .0019881      .0018051     .0022124
    3     CL4              SEATTLE                3        .0018326      .0015641     .0022124
    2     CL3              DENVER                 4        .0017544      .0017065     .0022124

                                   2 MODAL CLUSTERS HAVE BEEN FORMED

                                                                          MAXIMUM DENSITY
 NUMBER                                      FREQUENCY                    IN EACH CLUSTER
   OF                                         OF NEW        FUSION
CLUSTERS  CLUSTERS JOINED                     CLUSTER       DENSITY       LESSER       GREATER

    1     CL5              CL2                   10        .0017065      .0022124     .0027624
```

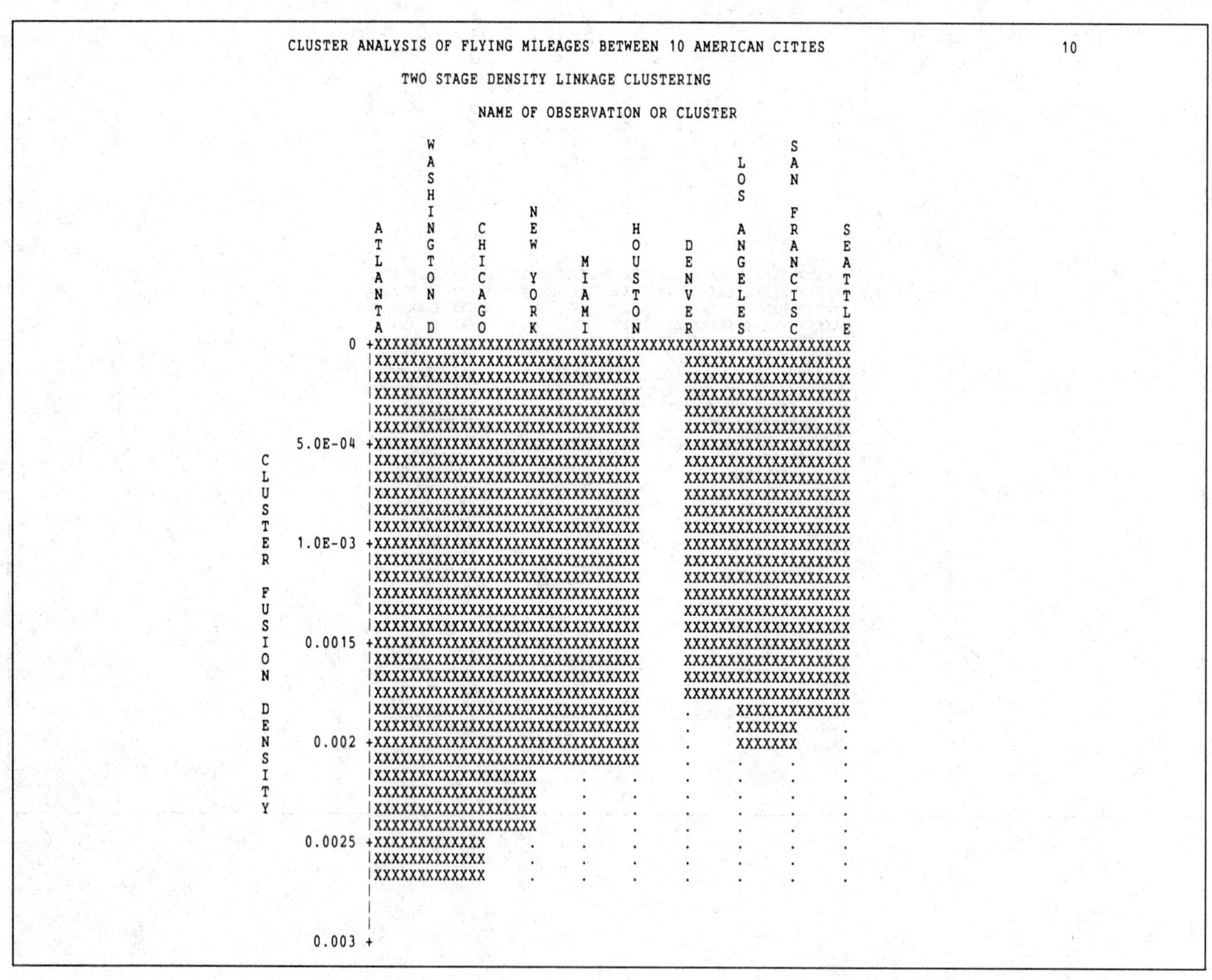

CLUSTER ANALYSIS OF FLYING MILEAGES BETWEEN 10 AMERICAN CITIES 11

WARD'S MINIMUM VARIANCE CLUSTER ANALYSIS

ROOT-MEAN-SQUARE DISTANCE BETWEEN OBSERVATIONS = 1580.24

NUMBER OF CLUSTERS	CLUSTERS JOINED		FREQUENCY OF NEW CLUSTER	(17) SEMIPARTIAL R-SQUARED	(18) R-SQUARED	PSEUDO F	PSEUDO T**2
9	NEW YORK	WASHINGTON D	2	0.001870	0.998130	66.72	.
8	LOS ANGELES	SAN FRANCISC	2	0.005358	0.992773	39.25	.
7	ATLANTA	CHICAGO	2	0.015332	0.977441	21.66	.
6	CL7	CL9	4	0.029646	0.947795	14.52	3.45
5	DENVER	HOUSTON	2	0.034379	0.913417	13.19	.
4	CL8	SEATTLE	3	0.039131	0.874286	13.91	7.30
3	CL6	MIAMI	5	0.058629	0.815658	15.49	3.75
2	CL3	CL5	7	0.148757	0.666901	16.02	5.32
1	CL2	CL4	10	0.666901	0.000000	.	16.02

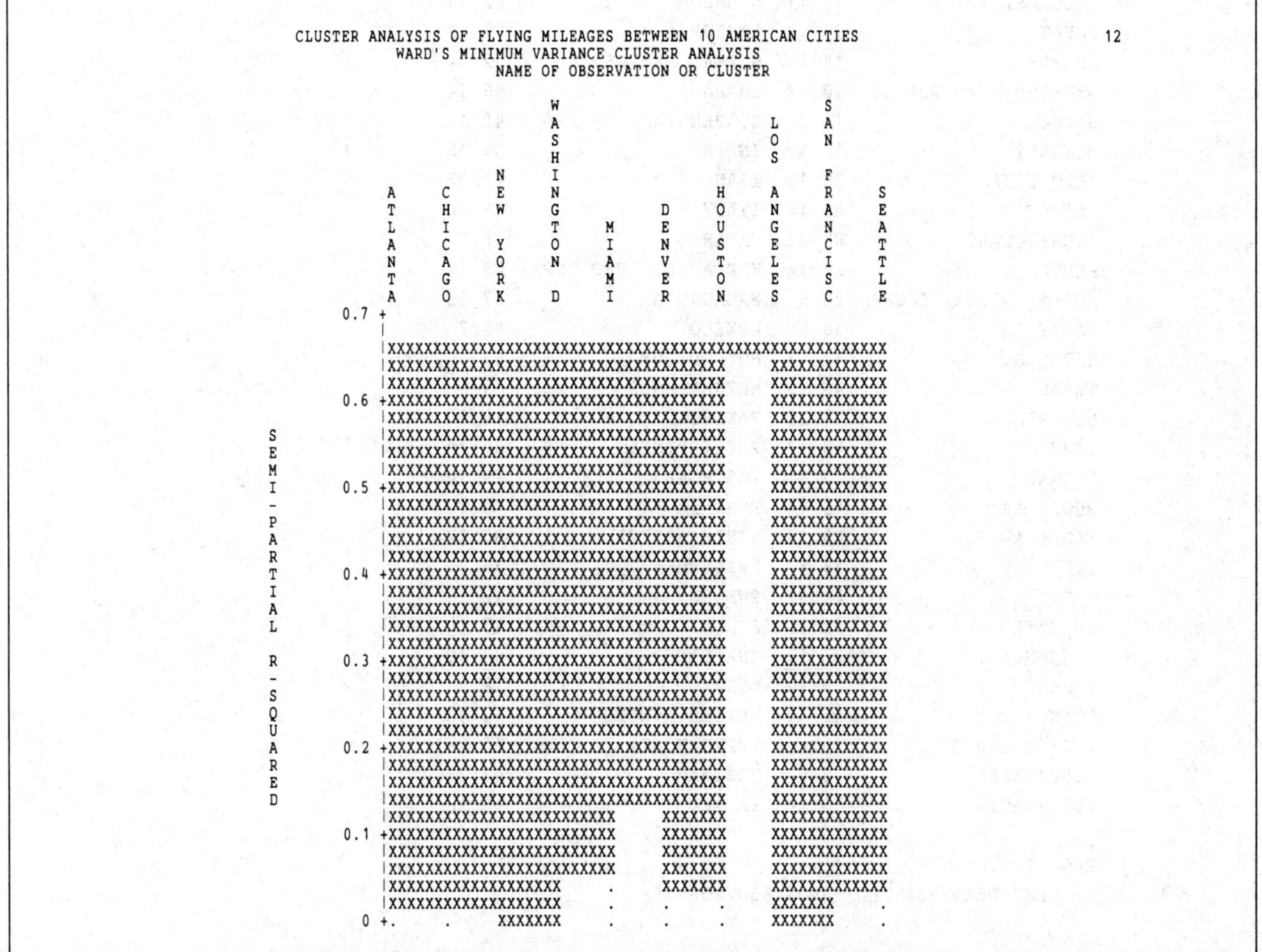

Crude Birth and Death Rates in 1976: Example 2

The data for the next example are crude birth and death rates per 100,000 population in 1976 for 74 countries. Twelve cluster analyses are performed with ten methods. Scatter plots showing cluster membership at selected levels are produced instead of tree diagrams.

```
DATA VITAL;
   TITLE 'CRUDE BIRTH AND DEATH RATES IN 1976';
   INPUT COUNTRY & $20. BIRTH DEATH @@;
   CARDS;
AFGHANISTAN          52 30  ALGERIA              50 16
ANGOLA               47 23  ARGENTINA            22 10
AUSTRALIA            16 8   AUSTRIA              12 13
BANGLADESH           47 19  BELGIUM              12 12
BRAZIL               36 10  BULGARIA             17 10
BURMA                38 15  CAMEROON             42 22
CANADA               16 7   CHILE                22 7
CHINA                31 11  TAIWAN               26 5
COLOMBIA             34 10  CUBA                 20 6
CZECHOSLOVAKIA       19 11  ECUADOR              42 11
EGYPT                39 13  ETHIOPIA             48 23
FRANCE               14 11  GERMAN DEM REP       12 14
GERMANY, FED REP OF  10 12  GHANA                46 14
GREECE               16 9   GUATEMALA            40 14
HUNGARY              18 12  INDIA                36 15
INDONESIA            38 16  IRAN                 42 12
IRAQ                 48 14  ITALY                14 10
IVORY COAST          48 23  JAPAN                16 6
KENYA                50 14  KOREA, DEM PEO REP   43 12
KOREA, REPUBLIC OF   26 6   MADAGASCAR           47 22
MALAYSIA             30 6   MEXICO               40 7
MOROCCO              47 16  MOZAMBIQUE           45 18
NEPAL                46 20  NETHERLANDS          13 8
NIGERIA              49 22  PAKISTAN             44 14
PERU                 40 13  PHILIPPINES          34 10
POLAND               20 9   PORTUGAL             19 10
RHODESIA             48 14  ROMANIA              19 10
SAUDI ARABIA         49 19  SOUTH AFRICA         36 12
SPAIN                18 8   SRI LANKA            26 9
SUDAN                49 17  SWEDEN               12 11
SWITZERLAND          12 9   SYRIA                47 14
TANZANIA             47 17  THAILAND             34 10
TURKEY               34 12  USSR                 18 9
UGANDA               48 17  UNITED KINGDOM       12 12
UNITED STATES        15 9   UPPER VOLTA          50 28
VENEZUELA            36 6   VIETNAM              42 17
YUGOSLAVIA           18 8   ZAIRE                45 18
;
PROC PLOT;
   PLOT DEATH*BIRTH / HPOS=86 VPOS=26;
```

Output 15.2 Plot of Raw Data for 1976 Birth and Death Rates: PROC PLOT

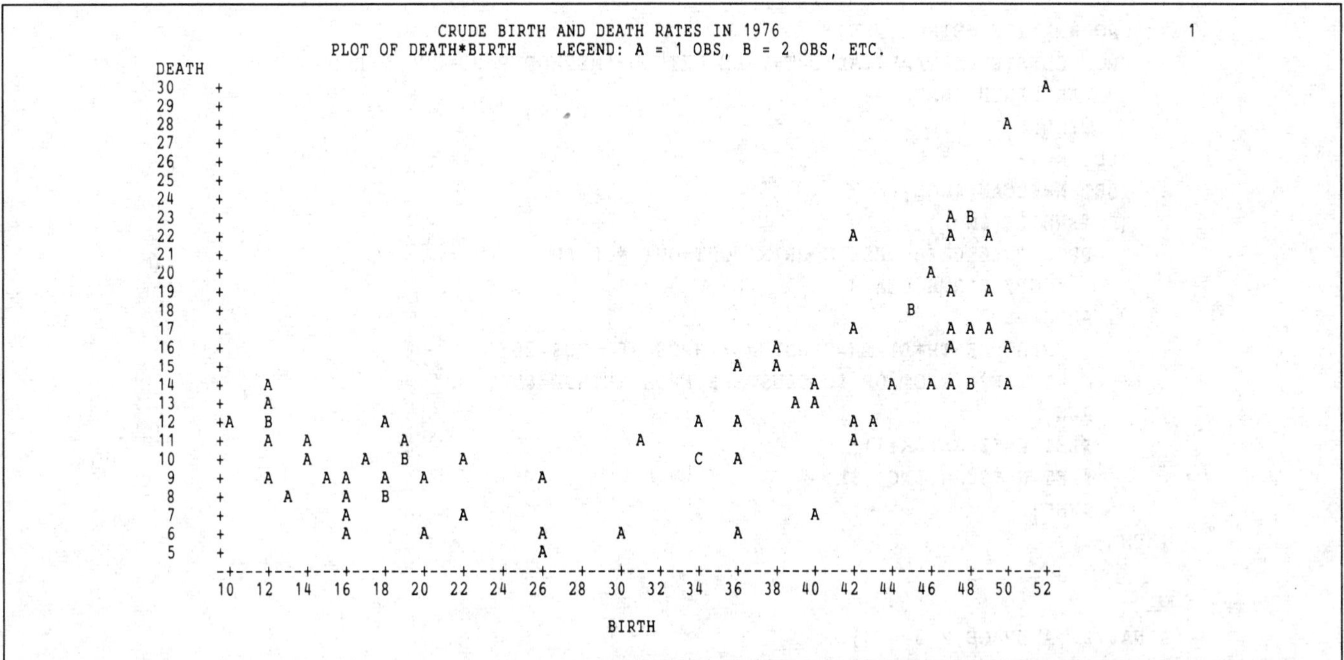

Each cluster analysis is peformed by a macro called %ANALYZE. The macro takes two arguments. The first, &METHOD, specifies the value of the METHOD= option to be used in the PROC CLUSTER statement. The second, &NCL, must be specified as a list of integers, separated by blanks, indicating the number of clusters desired in each scatter plot. For example, the first invocation of %ANALYZE specifies the AVERAGE method and requests plots of 2, 3, 4, and 8 clusters. When two-stage density linkage is used, the K= and R= options are specified as part of the first argument.

The %ANALYZE macro first invokes the CLUSTER procedure with METHOD= &METHOD, where &METHOD represents the value of the first argument to %ANALYZE. There follows a %DO loop that processes &NCL, the list of numbers of clusters to plot. The macro variable &K is a counter that indexes the numbers within &NCL. The %SCAN function picks out the &Kth number in &NCL, which is then assigned to the macro variable &N. When &K exceeds the number of numbers in &NCL, %SCAN returns a null string. Thus, the %DO loop executes while &N is not equal to a null string. In the %WHILE condition, a null string is indicated by the absence of any characters between the comparison operator ¬= and the right parenthesis that terminates the condition.

Within the %DO loop, the TREE procedure creates an output data set containing &N clusters. The PLOT procedure then produces a scatter plot in which each observation is identified by the number of the cluster to which it belongs. The TITLE2 statement uses double quotes so that &N and &METHOD can be used within the title. At the end of the loop, &K is incremented by 1, and the next number is extracted from &NCL by %SCAN.

```
   TITLE 'CLUSTER ANALYSIS OF BIRTH AND DEATH RATES IN 74 COUNTRIES';

%MACRO ANALYZE(METHOD,NCL);
   PROC CLUSTER DATA=VITAL OUT=TREE METHOD=&METHOD P=20 CCC PSEUDO;
      VAR BIRTH DEATH;
      TITLE2;
   %LET K=1;
   %LET N=%SCAN(&NCL,&K);
   %DO %WHILE(&N¬=);
      PROC TREE DATA=TREE NOPRINT OUT=OUT NCL=&N;
         COPY BIRTH DEATH;
      PROC PLOT;
         PLOT DEATH*BIRTH=CLUSTER / HPOS=86 VPOS=26;
         TITLE2 "PLOT OF &N CLUSTERS FROM METHOD=&METHOD";
      RUN;
      %LET K=%EVAL(&K+1);
      %LET N=%SCAN(&NCL,&K);
      %END;
%MEND;


%ANALYZE(AVERAGE,2 3 4 8)
%ANALYZE(CENTROID,8)
%ANALYZE(COMPLETE,3 8)
%ANALYZE(EML,8)
%ANALYZE(FLEXIBLE,3 4 9)
%ANALYZE(MCQUITTY,)
%ANALYZE(MEDIAN,)
%ANALYZE(SINGLE,3 5)
%ANALYZE(TWO K=6,3)
%ANALYZE(TWO K=10,2)
%ANALYZE(TWO R=5,3)
%ANALYZE(WARD,4)
```

Output 15.3 Ten Different Clustering Methods: Using a Macro to Invoke PROC CLUSTER and PROC PLOT

CLUSTER ANALYSIS OF BIRTH AND DEATH RATES IN 74 COUNTRIES 2

AVERAGE LINKAGE CLUSTER ANALYSIS

EIGENVALUES OF THE COVARIANCE MATRIX

(6)	EIGENVALUE (7)	DIFFERENCE (8)	PROPORTION	CUMULATIVE (9)
1	205.619	191.684	0.936528	0.93653
2	13.936	.	0.063472	1.00000

(10) ROOT-MEAN-SQUARE TOTAL-SAMPLE STANDARD DEVIATION = 10.4775
ROOT-MEAN-SQUARE DISTANCE BETWEEN OBSERVATIONS = 20.955

NUMBER OF CLUSTERS	CLUSTERS JOINED		FREQUENCY OF NEW CLUSTER	SEMIPARTIAL R-SQUARED	R-SQUARED	(19) APPROXIMATE EXPECTED R-SQUARED	(20) CUBIC CLUSTERING CRITERION	PSEUDO F	PSEUDO T**2	NORMALIZED RMS DISTANCE (24)
20	CL26	CL25	11	0.001580	0.990259	.	.	288.93	10.30	0.173818
19	CL28	CL23	14	0.001929	0.988330	.	.	258.78	12.13	0.174526
18	CL33	CL29	10	0.001577	0.986753	.	.	245.37	12.32	0.178025
17	OB4	CL34	3	0.000551	0.986202	.	.	254.62	3.53	0.181718
16	CL30	OB15	7	0.000725	0.985477	.	.	262.37	5.45	0.186867
15	OB42	OB71	2	0.000530	0.984946	.	.	275.74	.	0.196760
14	CL35	OB72	5	0.000855	0.984092	0.977256	3.1571	285.51	7.47	0.205258
13	CL21	OB41	4	0.000770	0.983322	0.974631	3.7165	299.71	2.85	0.209829
12	CL17	CL19	17	0.002539	0.980783	0.971547	3.4905	287.66	8.38	0.236897
11	CL20	CL14	16	0.003687	0.977096	0.967879	3.0216	268.76	12.41	0.240250
10	CL22	CL24	10	0.003355	0.973741	0.963450	2.9707	263.70	16.33	0.249874
9	CL41	OB12	6	0.001768	0.971973	0.958006	3.6577	281.78	28.33	0.281516
8	CL16	CL15	9	0.003168	0.968806	0.951163	4.0897	292.82	11.54	0.302086
7	CL11	CL9	22	0.009824	0.958981	0.942319	3.1453	261.07	19.92	0.335184
6	CL12	CL18	27	0.015896	0.943085	0.930469	1.8755	225.35	41.03	0.341839
5	CL8	CL10	19	0.012086	0.930999	0.913803	2.1300	232.75	20.37	0.363331
4	CL27	CL7	24	0.015289	0.915711	0.888695	2.7517	253.49	16.87	0.584465
3	CL6	CL13	31	0.028481	0.887229	0.842018	2.5170	279.30	30.71	0.587309
2	CL4	CL5	43	0.096770	0.790460	0.709627	2.9901	271.61	69.12	0.655162
1	CL2	CL3	74	0.790460	0.000000	0.000000	0.0000	.	271.61	1.340796

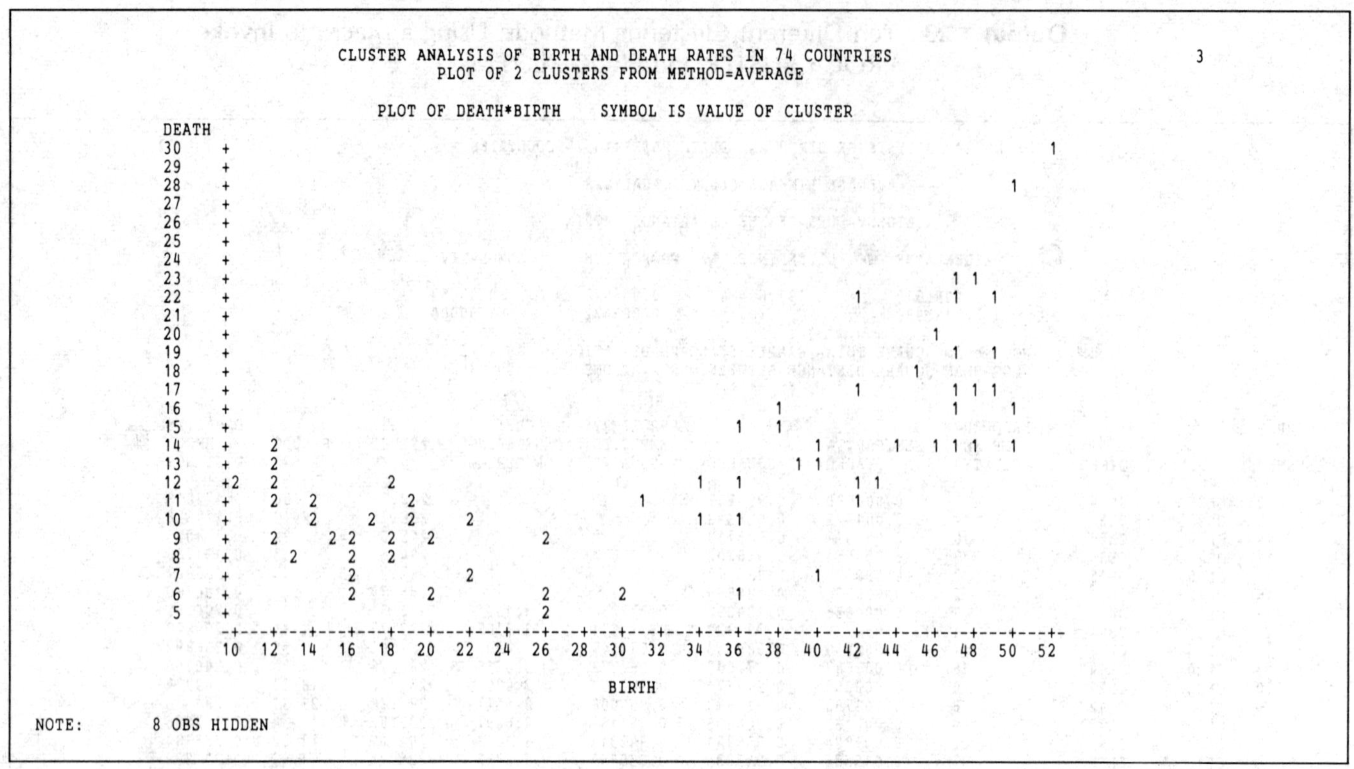
CLUSTER ANALYSIS OF BIRTH AND DEATH RATES IN 74 COUNTRIES
3
PLOT OF 2 CLUSTERS FROM METHOD=AVERAGE
PLOT OF DEATH*BIRTH   SYMBOL IS VALUE OF CLUSTER
DEATH
30
29
28
27
26
25
24
23
22
21
20
19
18
17
16
15
14
13
12
11
10
9
8
7
6
5
10 12 14 16 18 20 22 24 26 28 30 32 34 36 38 40 42 44 46 48 50 52
BIRTH
NOTE: 8 OBS HIDDEN

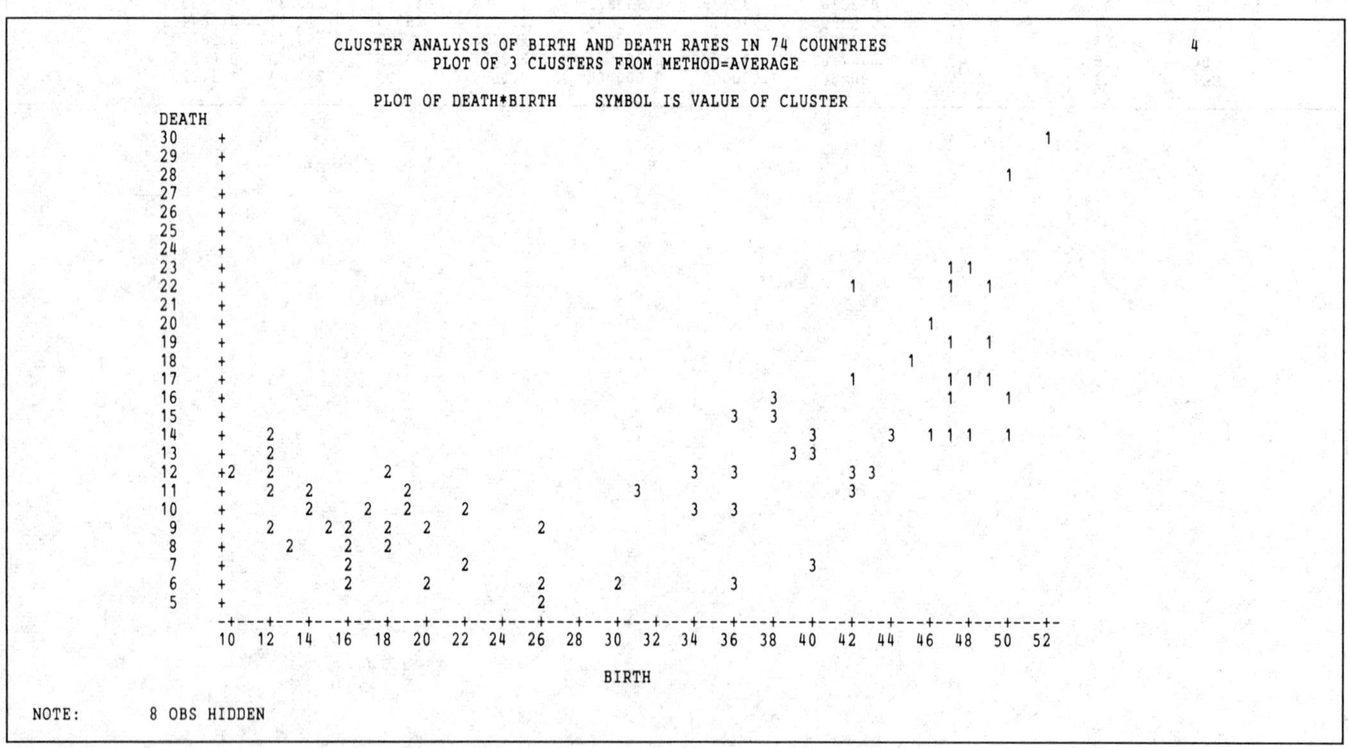
CLUSTER ANALYSIS OF BIRTH AND DEATH RATES IN 74 COUNTRIES
4
PLOT OF 3 CLUSTERS FROM METHOD=AVERAGE
PLOT OF DEATH*BIRTH   SYMBOL IS VALUE OF CLUSTER
DEATH
30
29
28
27
26
25
24
23
22
21
20
19
18
17
16
15
14
13
12
11
10
9
8
7
6
5
10 12 14 16 18 20 22 24 26 28 30 32 34 36 38 40 42 44 46 48 50 52
BIRTH
NOTE: 8 OBS HIDDEN

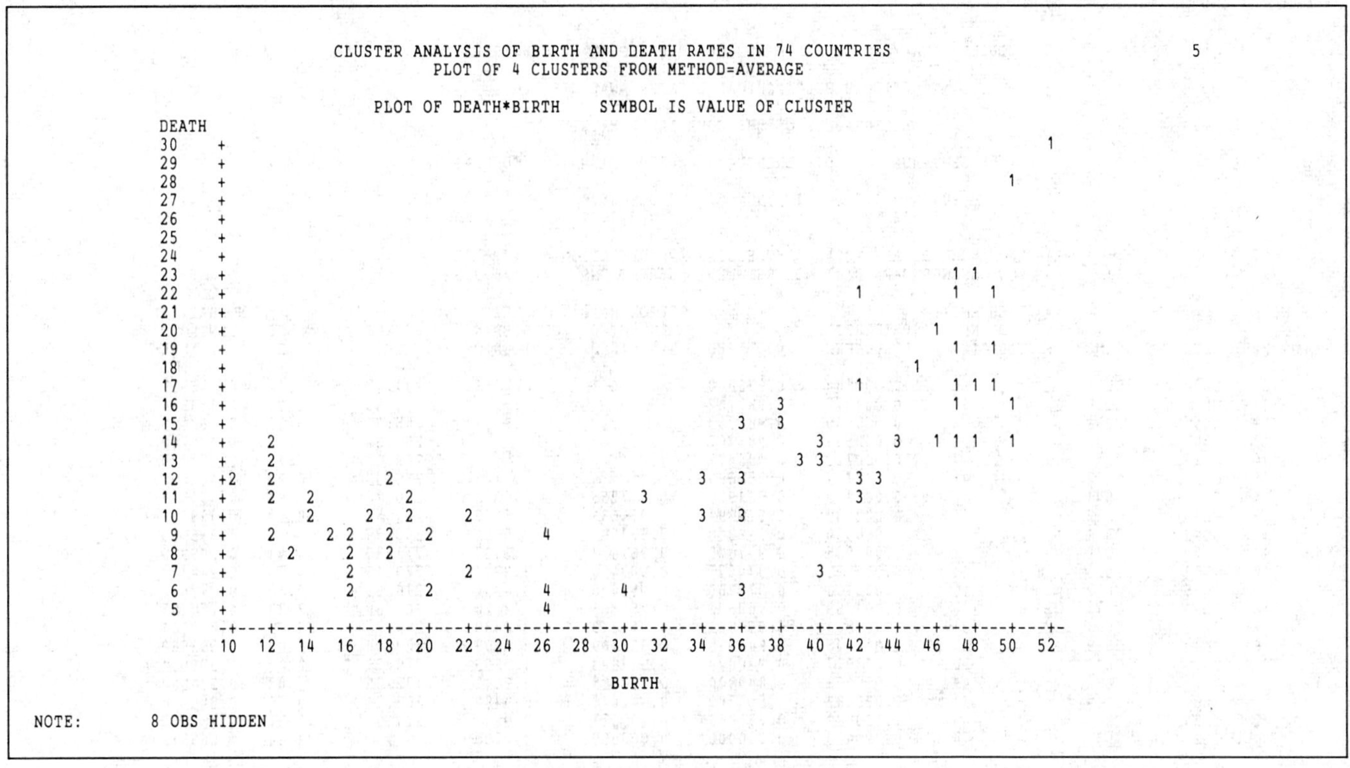
CLUSTER ANALYSIS OF BIRTH AND DEATH RATES IN 74 COUNTRIES
5
PLOT OF 4 CLUSTERS FROM METHOD=AVERAGE
PLOT OF DEATH*BIRTH SYMBOL IS VALUE OF CLUSTER
DEATH
BIRTH
NOTE: 8 OBS HIDDEN

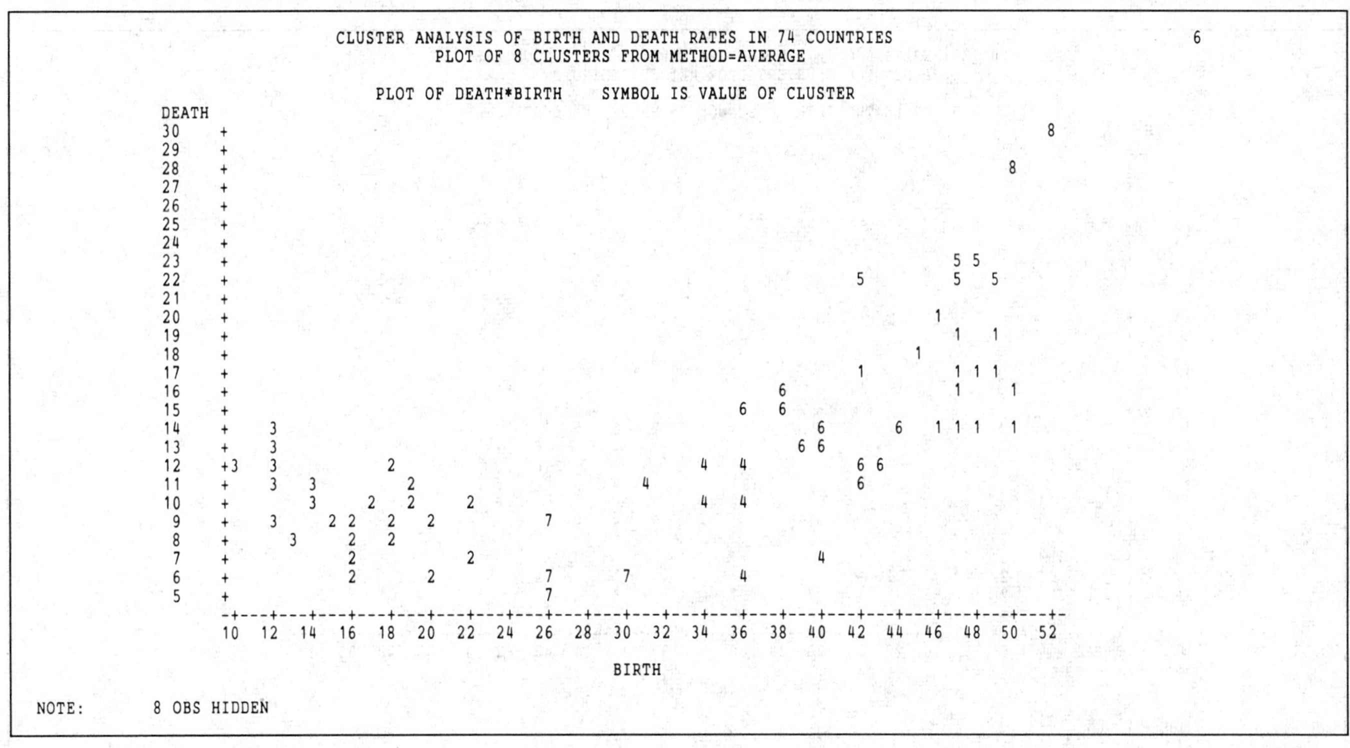
CLUSTER ANALYSIS OF BIRTH AND DEATH RATES IN 74 COUNTRIES
6
PLOT OF 8 CLUSTERS FROM METHOD=AVERAGE
PLOT OF DEATH*BIRTH SYMBOL IS VALUE OF CLUSTER
DEATH
BIRTH
NOTE: 8 OBS HIDDEN

CLUSTER ANALYSIS OF BIRTH AND DEATH RATES IN 74 COUNTRIES 7

CENTROID HIERARCHICAL CLUSTER ANALYSIS

EIGENVALUES OF THE COVARIANCE MATRIX

	EIGENVALUE	DIFFERENCE	PROPORTION	CUMULATIVE
1	205.619	191.684	0.936528	0.93653
2	13.936	.	0.063472	1.00000

ROOT-MEAN-SQUARE TOTAL-SAMPLE STANDARD DEVIATION = 10.4775
ROOT-MEAN-SQUARE DISTANCE BETWEEN OBSERVATIONS = 20.955

NUMBER OF CLUSTERS	CLUSTERS JOINED		FREQUENCY OF NEW CLUSTER	SEMIPARTIAL R-SQUARED	R-SQUARED	APPROXIMATE EXPECTED R-SQUARED	CUBIC CLUSTERING CRITERION	PSEUDO F	PSEUDO T**2	(25) NORMALIZED CENTROID DISTANCE
20	CL34	CL49	6	0.000884	0.988840	.	.	251.82	12.14	0.146657
19	CL36	CL29	10	0.001577	0.987262	.	.	236.83	12.32	0.154890
18	CL57	OB58	3	0.000510	0.986753	.	.	245.37	16.33	0.167025
17	OB4	CL30	3	0.000551	0.986202	.	.	254.62	3.53	0.173709
16	CL35	OB15	7	0.000725	0.985477	.	.	262.37	5.45	0.175700
15	CL21	CL32	15	0.002777	0.982699	.	.	239.38	10.93	0.185897
14	CL18	OB41	4	0.000770	0.981930	0.977256	2.0318	250.80	2.85	0.193519
13	CL17	CL22	17	0.002539	0.979391	0.974631	1.8412	241.57	8.38	0.193682
12	OB42	OB71	2	0.000530	0.978860	0.971547	2.6425	260.99	.	0.196760
11	CL20	OB72	7	0.001035	0.977825	0.967879	3.3107	277.80	4.41	0.209980
10	CL11	CL23	11	0.003198	0.974627	0.963450	3.2791	273.15	10.75	0.214137
9	CL16	CL12	9	0.003168	0.971460	0.958006	3.4934	276.56	11.54	0.272630
8	CL41	OB12	6	0.001768	0.969692	0.951163	4.3526	301.66	28.33	0.278261
7	CL15	CL8	21	0.009841	0.959851	0.942319	3.3430	266.96	23.09	0.289501
6	CL13	CL19	27	0.015896	0.943955	0.930469	2.0198	229.06	41.03	0.303560
5	CL9	CL10	20	0.013927	0.930028	0.913803	1.9963	229.28	22.86	0.320457
4	CL7	CL5	41	0.080198	0.849830	0.888695	-2.9642	132.05	73.03	0.534560
3	CL6	CL14	31	0.028481	0.821349	0.842018	-0.9180	163.21	30.71	0.546254
2	CL24	CL4	43	0.030889	0.790460	0.709627	2.9901	271.61	10.27	0.768912
1	CL2	CL3	74	0.790460	0.000000	0.000000	0.0000	.	271.61	1.265573

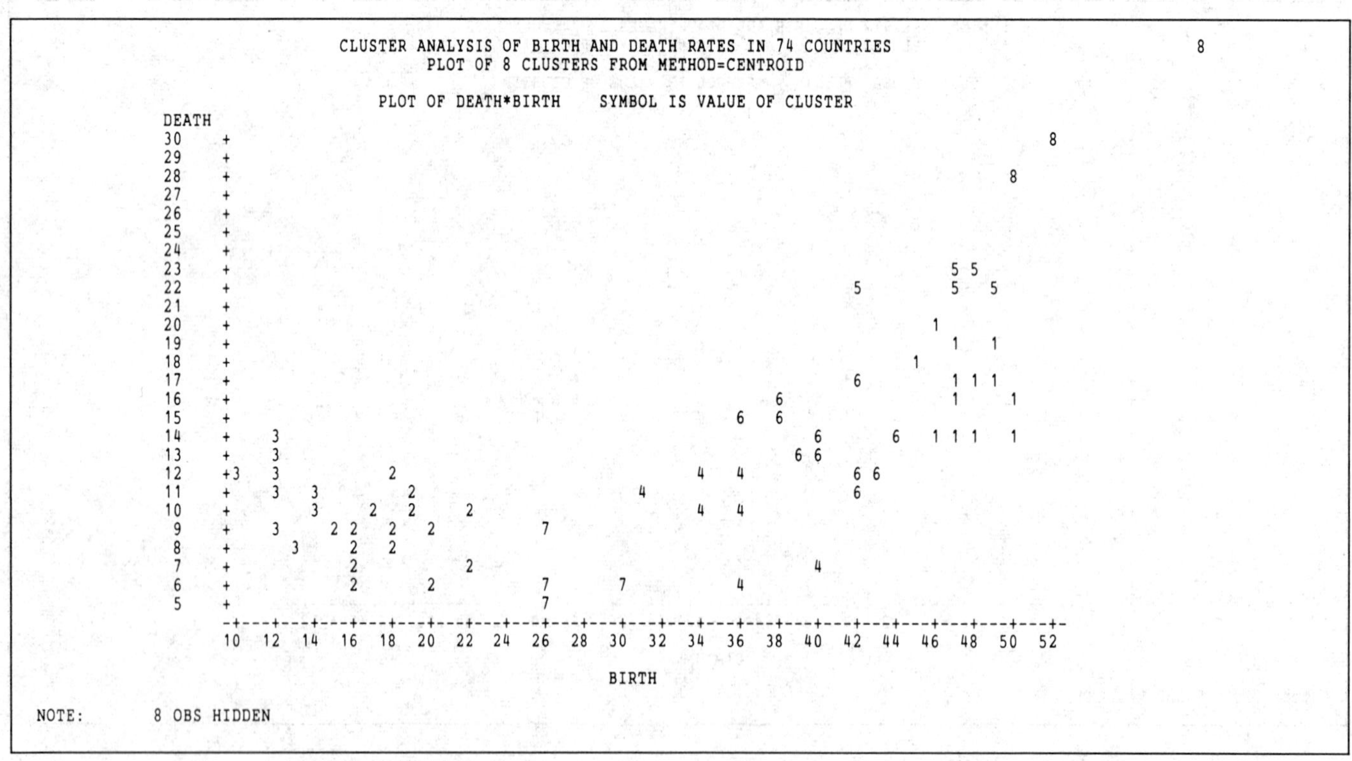

CLUSTER ANALYSIS OF BIRTH AND DEATH RATES IN 74 COUNTRIES 9

COMPLETE LINKAGE CLUSTER ANALYSIS

EIGENVALUES OF THE COVARIANCE MATRIX

	EIGENVALUE	DIFFERENCE	PROPORTION	CUMULATIVE
1	205.619	191.684	0.936528	0.93653
2	13.936	.	0.063472	1.00000

ROOT-MEAN-SQUARE TOTAL-SAMPLE STANDARD DEVIATION = 10.4775
MEAN DISTANCE BETWEEN OBSERVATIONS = 17.5961

NUMBER OF CLUSTERS	CLUSTERS JOINED		FREQUENCY OF NEW CLUSTER	SEMIPARTIAL R-SQUARED	R-SQUARED	APPROXIMATE EXPECTED R-SQUARED	CUBIC CLUSTERING CRITERION	PSEUDO F	PSEUDO T**2	(26) NORMALIZED MAXIMUM DISTANCE
20	OB4	CL33	3	0.000551	0.991401	.	.	327.67	3.53	0.254155
19	CL42	OB72	3	0.000749	0.990652	.	.	323.82	6.00	0.284154
18	CL24	OB41	4	0.000770	0.989883	.	.	322.30	2.85	0.284154
17	CL31	OB15	7	0.000725	0.989158	.	.	325.01	5.45	0.289782
16	CL25	CL30	10	0.001349	0.987809	.	.	313.31	9.56	0.306044
15	CL26	CL27	9	0.001302	0.986507	.	.	308.11	9.52	0.306044
14	CL39	OB12	5	0.001229	0.985278	0.977256	3.8414	308.88	10.75	0.331378
13	CL20	CL23	12	0.001733	0.983544	0.974631	3.8355	303.83	8.80	0.363895
12	CL35	CL14	10	0.002820	0.980724	0.971547	3.4635	286.77	12.38	0.397816
11	CL21	CL19	9	0.001903	0.978821	0.967879	3.7215	291.17	6.78	0.401855
10	CL17	CL38	10	0.004129	0.974692	0.963450	3.3022	273.87	20.67	0.488878
9	CL15	CL29	15	0.005227	0.969465	0.958006	2.8824	257.96	24.26	0.508311
8	CL10	CL22	12	0.004136	0.965329	0.951163	3.1258	262.52	6.61	0.579564
7	CL16	CL12	20	0.009562	0.955768	0.942319	2.4494	241.29	24.18	0.642968
6	CL13	CL9	27	0.013851	0.941917	0.930469	1.6851	220.55	29.52	0.738802
5	CL7	CL11	29	0.021026	0.920891	0.913803	0.8213	200.80	27.63	0.764581
4	CL8	CL18	16	0.017866	0.903024	0.888695	1.3640	217.28	21.37	0.925140
3	CL32	CL5	31	0.020588	0.882436	0.842018	2.2062	266.46	14.28	1.220211
2	CL6	CL4	43	0.190667	0.691769	0.709627	-0.5470	161.59	141.74	1.728444
1	CL3	CL2	74	0.691769	0.000000	0.000000	0.0000	.	161.59	2.596867

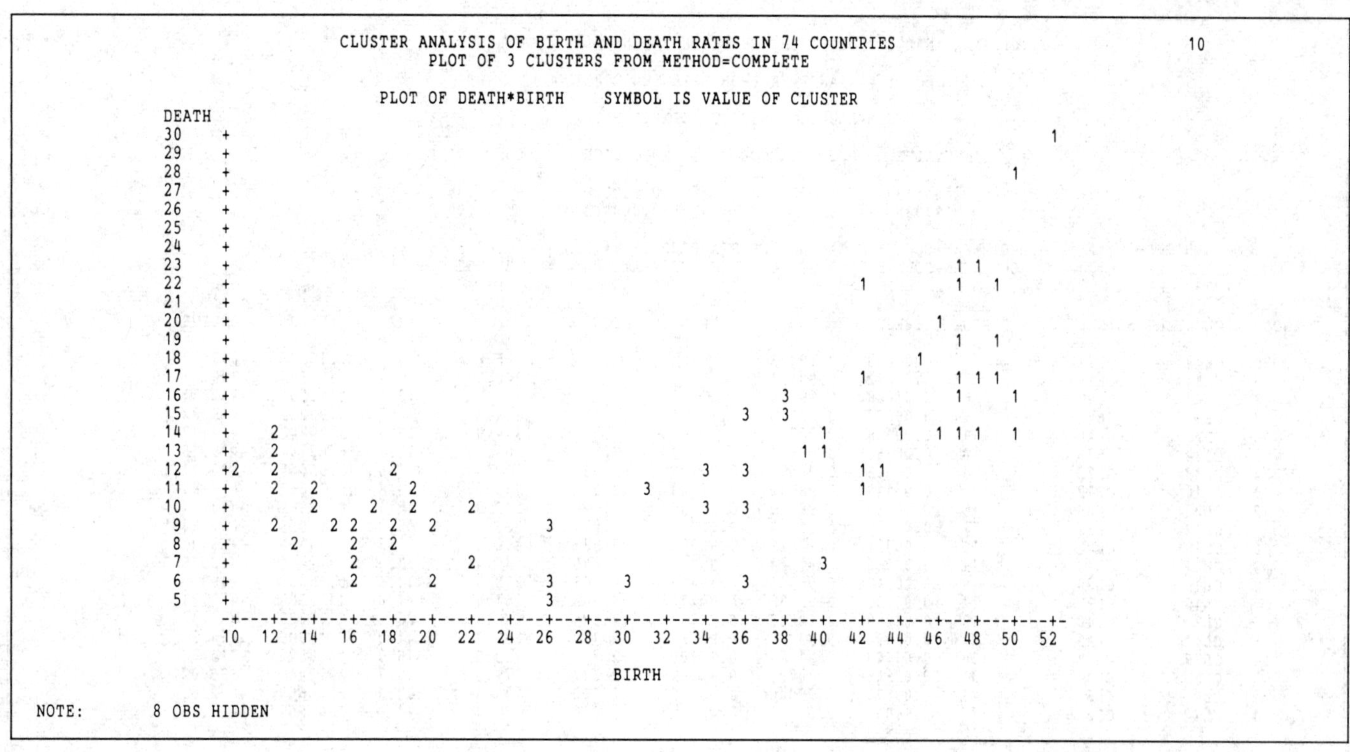

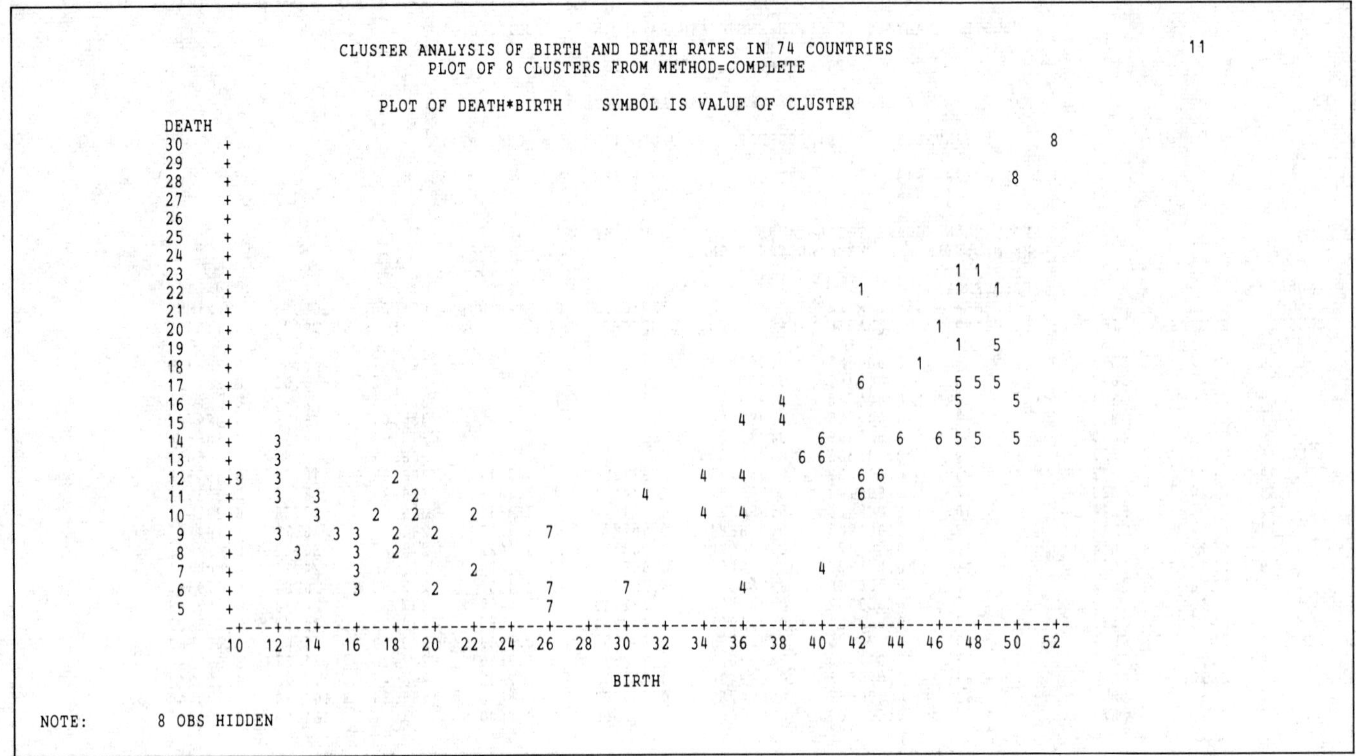

CLUSTER ANALYSIS OF BIRTH AND DEATH RATES IN 74 COUNTRIES 12

EQUAL VARIANCE MAXIMUM LIKELIHOOD METHOD

EIGENVALUES OF THE COVARIANCE MATRIX

	EIGENVALUE	DIFFERENCE	PROPORTION	CUMULATIVE
1	205.619	191.684	0.936528	0.93653
2	13.936	.	0.063472	1.00000

ROOT-MEAN-SQUARE TOTAL-SAMPLE STANDARD DEVIATION = 10.4775
ROOT-MEAN-SQUARE DISTANCE BETWEEN OBSERVATIONS = 20.955

NCL	CLUSTERS JOINED		FREQ	SPRSQ	RSQ	ERSQ	CCC	PSEUDO F	PSEUDO T**2	(29) LNLR	(30) LNLIKE
20	OB42	OB71	2	0.00053	0.99183	.	.	345.0	.	7.16098	-399.77
19	CL31	OB15	7	0.00072	0.99111	.	.	340.5	5.4	6.841	-406.61
18	CL37	CL49	6	0.00088	0.99022	.	.	333.6	12.1	5.704	-412.31
17	CL21	OB41	4	0.00077	0.98945	.	.	334.2	2.8	6.71252	-419.02
16	CL28	CL24	11	0.00158	0.98787	.	.	315.0	10.3	5.49803	-424.52
15	CL34	CL26	10	0.00158	0.98629	.	.	303.3	12.3	4.63744	-429.16
14	CL33	OB72	5	0.00085	0.98544	0.97726	3.939	312.4	7.5	3.95009	-433.11
13	CL14	OB12	6	0.00114	0.98430	0.97463	4.251	318.7	3.8	5.76665	-438.88
12	CL22	CL25	15	0.00280	0.98149	0.97155	3.826	298.9	16.1	4.12885	-443.01
11	CL12	CL38	17	0.00185	0.97964	0.96788	4.074	303.1	5.3	1.8068	-444.81
10	CL18	CL23	10	0.00335	0.97629	0.96345	3.887	292.8	16.3	9.11394	-453.93
9	CL41	CL13	11	0.00406	0.97223	0.95801	3.740	284.4	14.1	8.2226	-462.15
8	CL19	CL20	9	0.00317	0.96906	0.95116	4.165	295.3	11.5	6.45092	-468.6
7	CL16	CL9	22	0.01008	0.95898	0.94232	3.145	261.1	21.0	11.2368	-479.84
6	CL8	CL10	19	0.01209	0.94689	0.93047	2.524	242.5	20.4	11.9328	-491.77
5	CL11	CL15	27	0.01590	0.93100	0.91380	2.130	232.7	41.0	3.15909	-494.93
4	CL29	CL7	24	0.01529	0.91571	0.88870	2.752	253.5	16.9	15.8522	-510.78
3	CL5	CL17	31	0.02848	0.88723	0.84202	2.517	279.3	30.7	19.2411	-530.02
2	CL4	CL6	43	0.09677	0.79046	0.70963	2.990	271.6	69.1	32.6669	-562.69
1	CL2	CL3	74	0.79046	0.00000	0.00000	0.000	.	271.6	130.669	-693.36

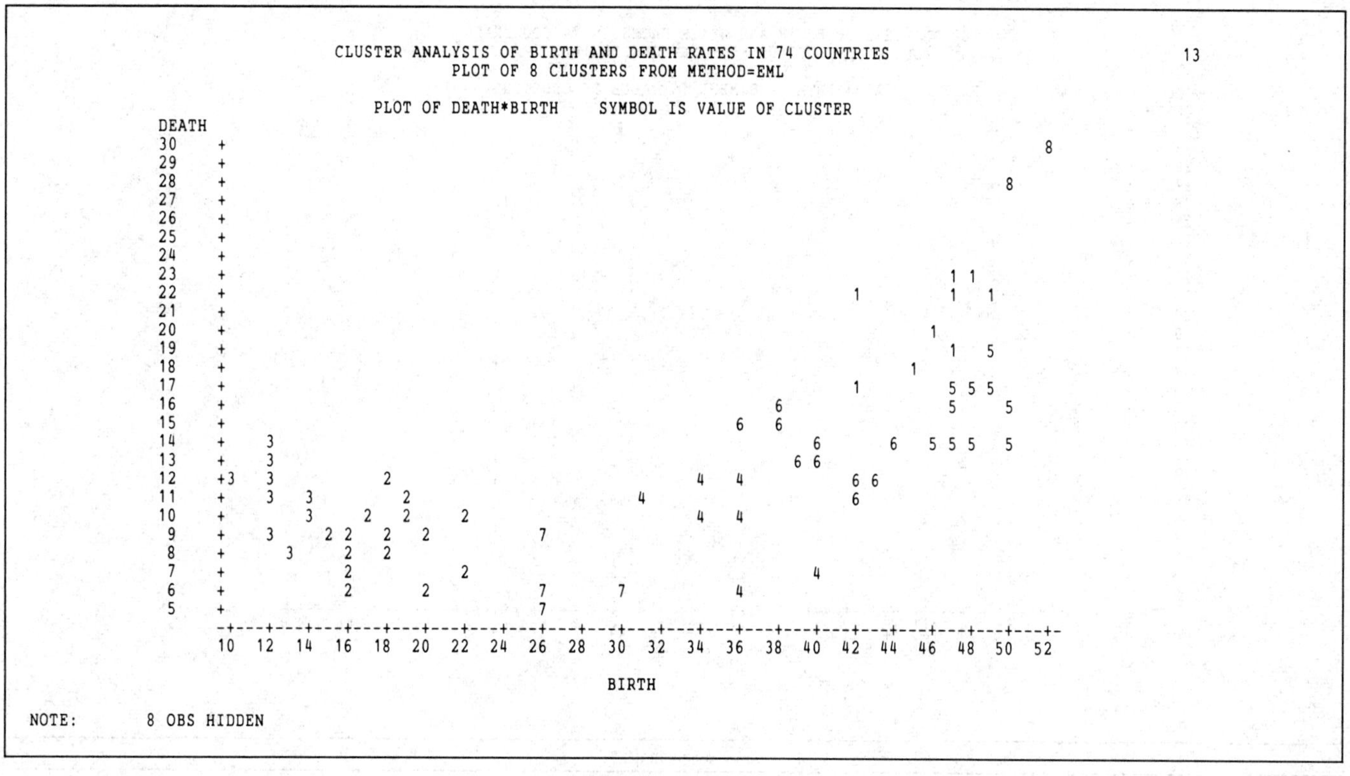

CLUSTER ANALYSIS OF BIRTH AND DEATH RATES IN 74 COUNTRIES 14

FLEXIBLE-BETA CLUSTER ANALYSIS

EIGENVALUES OF THE COVARIANCE MATRIX

	EIGENVALUE	DIFFERENCE	PROPORTION	CUMULATIVE
1	205.619	191.684	0.936528	0.93653
2	13.936	.	0.063472	1.00000

BETA=-0.25

ROOT-MEAN-SQUARE TOTAL-SAMPLE STANDARD DEVIATION = 10.4775
MEAN DISTANCE BETWEEN OBSERVATIONS = 17.5961

NUMBER OF CLUSTERS	CLUSTERS JOINED		FREQUENCY OF NEW CLUSTER	SEMIPARTIAL R-SQUARED	R-SQUARED	APPROXIMATE EXPECTED R-SQUARED	CUBIC CLUSTERING CRITERION	PSEUDO F	PSEUDO T**2	(31) NORMALIZED FLEXIBLE DISTANCE
20	CL33	CL73	5	0.000541	0.991453	.	.	329.68	4.87	0.253787
19	CL21	CL42	10	0.000937	0.990516	.	.	319.12	6.30	0.284509
18	OB15	OB41	2	0.000811	0.989705	.	.	316.67	.	0.289782
17	CL37	CL49	6	0.000884	0.988821	.	.	315.11	12.14	0.293902
16	CL50	CL26	5	0.001133	0.987688	.	.	310.18	6.96	0.338945
15	CL31	CL28	9	0.001302	0.986385	.	.	305.32	9.52	0.362002
14	CL24	CL25	12	0.001733	0.984652	0.977256	3.4739	296.10	8.80	0.402146
13	CL18	CL22	5	0.001768	0.982884	0.974631	3.4870	291.92	3.92	0.392922
12	CL20	OB12	6	0.001539	0.981345	0.971547	3.7547	296.51	7.05	0.437209
11	CL40	CL12	11	0.002590	0.978755	0.967879	3.6935	290.24	8.76	0.522513
10	CL17	CL16	11	0.003079	0.975676	0.963450	3.6584	285.24	9.91	0.535916
9	CL27	CL23	8	0.002665	0.973011	0.958006	3.9991	292.93	13.37	0.542036
8	CL15	CL30	15	0.005227	0.967784	0.951163	3.7958	283.24	24.26	0.721224
7	CL34	CL11	13	0.009079	0.958705	0.942319	3.0835	259.25	18.15	1.015918
6	CL9	CL13	13	0.012333	0.946373	0.930469	2.4328	240.00	19.44	1.033372
5	CL14	CL8	27	0.013851	0.932522	0.913803	2.3436	238.39	29.52	1.248735
4	CL19	CL10	21	0.019776	0.912746	0.888695	2.4095	244.08	46.94	1.412327
3	CL7	CL4	34	0.034062	0.878684	0.842018	1.9717	257.12	25.73	2.143336
2	CL5	CL6	40	0.150192	0.728492	0.709627	0.6157	193.19	127.13	4.142826
1	CL3	CL2	74	0.728492	0.000000	0.000000	0.0000	.	193.19	9.083011

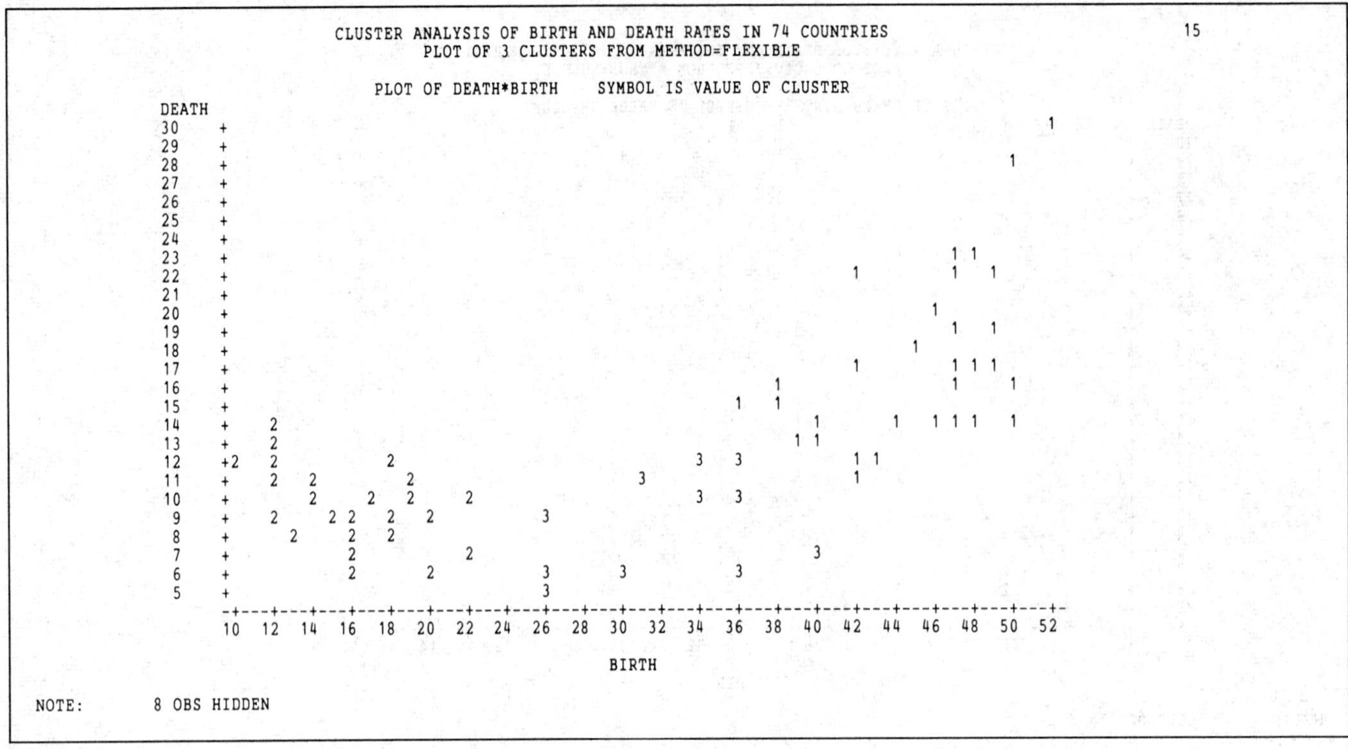
CLUSTER ANALYSIS OF BIRTH AND DEATH RATES IN 74 COUNTRIES
PLOT OF 3 CLUSTERS FROM METHOD=FLEXIBLE
15
PLOT OF DEATH*BIRTH SYMBOL IS VALUE OF CLUSTER
DEATH
BIRTH
NOTE: 8 OBS HIDDEN

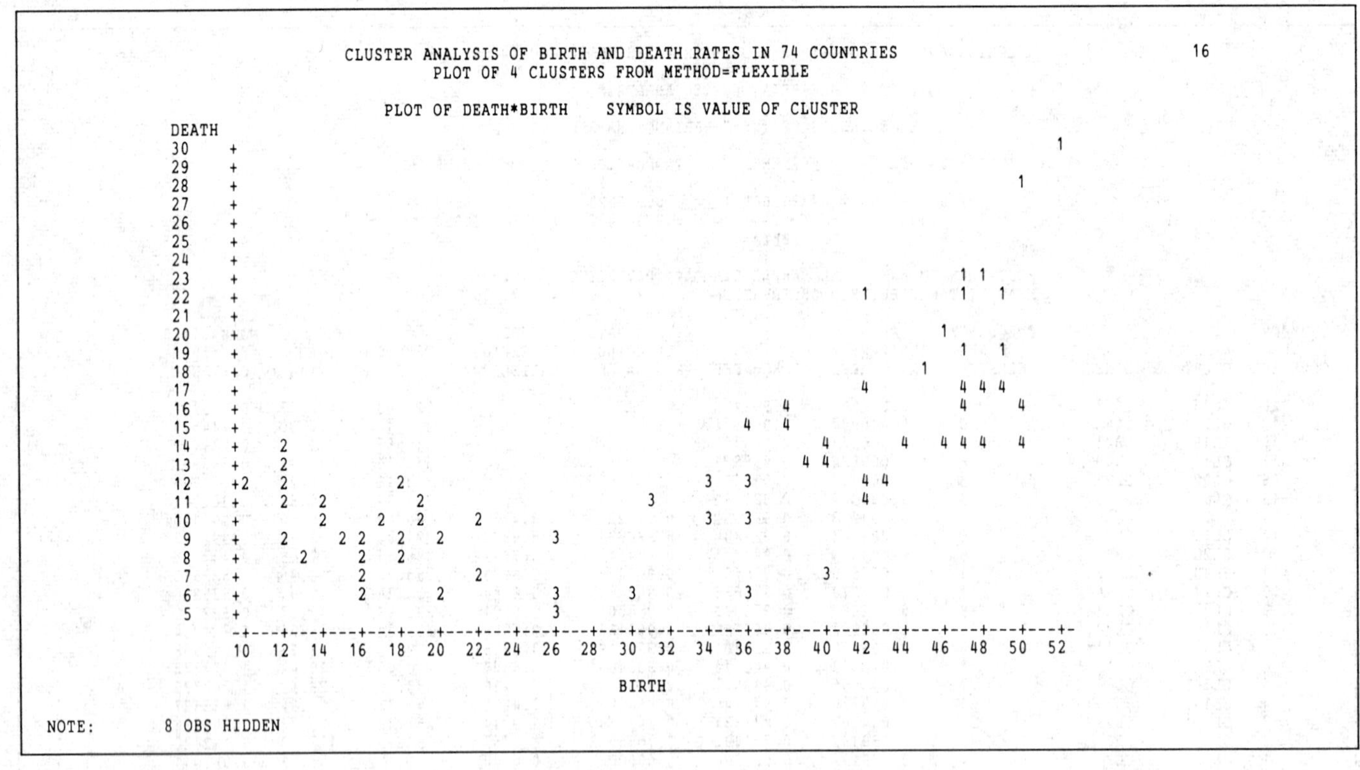
CLUSTER ANALYSIS OF BIRTH AND DEATH RATES IN 74 COUNTRIES
PLOT OF 4 CLUSTERS FROM METHOD=FLEXIBLE
16
PLOT OF DEATH*BIRTH SYMBOL IS VALUE OF CLUSTER
DEATH
BIRTH
NOTE: 8 OBS HIDDEN

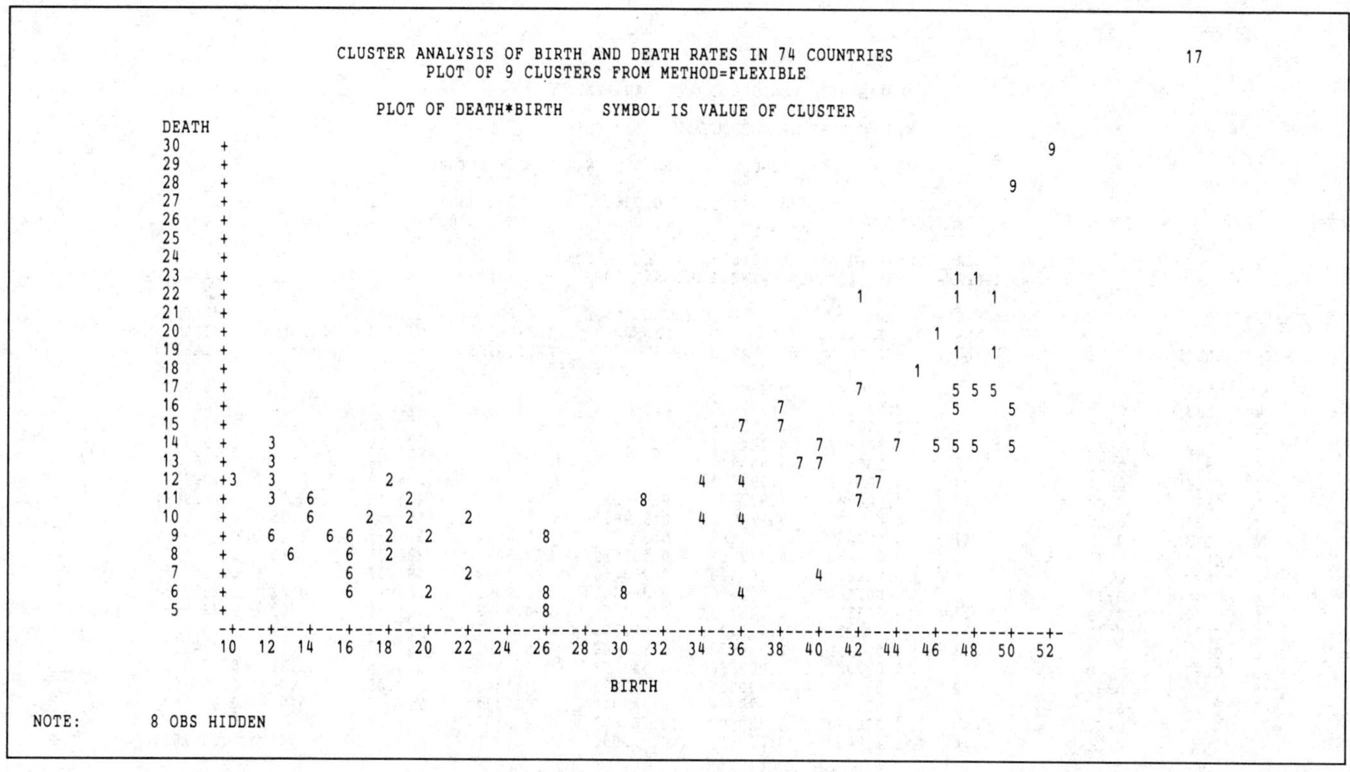

CLUSTER ANALYSIS OF BIRTH AND DEATH RATES IN 74 COUNTRIES 18

MCQUITTY'S SIMILARITY ANALYSIS

EIGENVALUES OF THE COVARIANCE MATRIX

	EIGENVALUE	DIFFERENCE	PROPORTION	CUMULATIVE
1	205.619	191.684	0.936528	0.93653
2	13.936	.	0.063472	1.00000

ROOT-MEAN-SQUARE TOTAL-SAMPLE STANDARD DEVIATION = 10.4775
MEAN DISTANCE BETWEEN OBSERVATIONS = 17.5961

NUMBER OF CLUSTERS	CLUSTERS JOINED		FREQUENCY OF NEW CLUSTER	SEMIPARTIAL R-SQUARED	R-SQUARED	APPROXIMATE EXPECTED R-SQUARED	CUBIC CLUSTERING CRITERION	PSEUDO F	PSEUDO T**2	㉝ NORMALIZED MCQUITTY'S SIMILARITY
20	CL36	CL28	9	0.001302	0.989445	.	.	266.41	9.52	0.207037
19	OB4	CL33	3	0.000551	0.988893	.	.	272.06	3.53	0.212324
18	OB42	OB71	2	0.000530	0.988363	.	.	279.78	.	0.234320
17	CL30	OB15	7	0.000725	0.987638	.	.	284.62	5.45	0.234748
16	CL22	OB41	4	0.000770	0.986869	.	.	290.59	2.85	0.257488
15	CL27	OB72	6	0.001568	0.985300	.	.	282.48	8.98	0.262568
14	CL21	CL42	15	0.005045	0.980255	0.977256	1.2489	229.13	22.75	0.265043
13	CL19	CL26	12	0.001733	0.978522	0.974631	1.4752	231.59	8.80	0.265194
12	CL35	CL23	9	0.002679	0.975842	0.971547	1.4555	227.68	14.43	0.281333
11	CL20	CL32	15	0.005227	0.970615	0.967879	0.7954	208.10	24.26	0.307702
10	CL12	CL15	15	0.008487	0.962129	0.963450	-0.3192	180.66	17.66	0.338901
9	CL14	OB12	16	0.002164	0.959965	0.958006	0.4321	194.82	3.82	0.364875
8	CL17	CL16	11	0.010924	0.949041	0.951163	-0.3880	175.59	36.40	0.406224
7	CL13	CL11	27	0.013851	0.935190	0.942319	-1.0751	161.13	29.52	0.443745
6	CL9	CL10	31	0.027045	0.908144	0.930469	-2.6083	134.46	31.59	0.488722
5	CL8	CL18	13	0.005158	0.902986	0.913803	-1.1317	160.56	4.01	0.490149
4	CL6	OB37	32	0.002136	0.900850	0.888695	1.1445	212.00	1.24	0.512183
3	CL24	CL4	34	0.022166	0.878684	0.842018	1.9717	257.12	13.07	0.825323
2	CL7	CL5	40	0.150192	0.728492	0.709627	0.6157	193.19	127.13	1.042364
1	CL3	CL2	74	0.728492	0.000000	0.000000	0.0000	.	193.19	1.621562

CLUSTER ANALYSIS OF BIRTH AND DEATH RATES IN 74 COUNTRIES 19

MEDIAN HIERARCHICAL CLUSTER ANALYSIS

EIGENVALUES OF THE COVARIANCE MATRIX

	EIGENVALUE	DIFFERENCE	PROPORTION	CUMULATIVE
1	205.619	191.684	0.936528	0.93653
2	13.936	.	0.063472	1.00000

ROOT-MEAN-SQUARE TOTAL-SAMPLE STANDARD DEVIATION = 10.4775
ROOT-MEAN-SQUARE DISTANCE BETWEEN OBSERVATIONS = 20.955

32

NUMBER OF CLUSTERS	CLUSTERS JOINED		FREQUENCY OF NEW CLUSTER	SEMIPARTIAL R-SQUARED	R-SQUARED	APPROXIMATE EXPECTED R-SQUARED	CUBIC CLUSTERING CRITERION	PSEUDO F	PSEUDO T**2	NORMALIZED MEDIAN DISTANCE
20	CL57	OB58	3	0.000510	0.989410	.	.	265.54	16.33	0.167025
19	CL33	CL28	10	0.001577	0.987833	.	.	248.07	12.32	0.169562
18	CL36	OB15	7	0.000725	0.987108	.	.	252.22	5.45	0.190886
17	CL50	CL25	8	0.002767	0.984341	.	.	223.94	21.23	0.190979
16	OB42	OB71	2	0.000530	0.983811	.	.	234.98	.	0.196760
15	CL20	OB41	4	0.000770	0.983041	.	.	244.29	2.85	0.199989
14	CL23	CL42	15	0.005045	0.977996	0.977256	0.2920	205.13	22.75	0.202909
13	CL21	CL29	16	0.003117	0.974878	0.974631	0.0869	197.27	13.35	0.219032
12	CL13	OB29	17	0.000696	0.974183	0.971547	0.8644	212.68	1.63	0.195928
11	CL17	OB72	9	0.001332	0.972851	0.967879	1.5024	225.75	2.63	0.220490
10	CL22	CL11	15	0.008677	0.964173	0.963450	0.1794	191.37	18.63	0.224196
9	CL14	OB12	16	0.002164	0.962009	0.958006	0.9062	205.74	3.82	0.285255
8	CL12	CL19	27	0.015896	0.946113	0.951163	-0.8976	165.54	41.03	0.297689
7	CL18	CL15	11	0.010924	0.935190	0.942319	-1.0751	161.13	36.40	0.317053
6	CL7	CL16	13	0.005158	0.930032	0.930469	-0.0588	180.77	4.01	0.374537
5	CL9	CL10	31	0.027045	0.902986	0.913803	-1.1317	160.56	31.59	0.375375
4	CL5	OB37	32	0.002136	0.900850	0.888695	1.1445	212.00	1.24	0.393100
3	CL24	CL4	34	0.022166	0.878684	0.842018	1.9717	257.12	13.07	0.661850
2	CL8	CL6	40	0.150192	0.728492	0.709627	0.6157	193.19	127.13	0.918106
1	CL3	CL2	74	0.728492	0.000000	0.000000	0.0000	.	193.19	1.310266

CLUSTER ANALYSIS OF BIRTH AND DEATH RATES IN 74 COUNTRIES 20

SINGLE LINKAGE CLUSTER ANALYSIS

EIGENVALUES OF THE COVARIANCE MATRIX

	EIGENVALUE	DIFFERENCE	PROPORTION	CUMULATIVE
1	205.619	191.684	0.936528	0.93653
2	13.936	.	0.063472	1.00000

ROOT-MEAN-SQUARE TOTAL-SAMPLE STANDARD DEVIATION = 10.4775
MEAN DISTANCE BETWEEN OBSERVATIONS = 17.5961

NUMBER OF CLUSTERS	CLUSTERS JOINED		FREQUENCY OF NEW CLUSTER	SEMIPARTIAL R-SQUARED	R-SQUARED	APPROXIMATE EXPECTED R-SQUARED	CUBIC CLUSTERING CRITERION	PSEUDO F	PSEUDO T**2	NORMALIZED MINIMUM DISTANCE
20	CL22	CL73	16	0.001128	0.973497	.	.	104.40	2.63	0.127078
19	CL50	CL48	6	0.000925	0.972572	.	.	108.35	22.25	0.127078
18	CL26	CL19	9	0.002679	0.969893	.	.	106.12	14.43	0.127078
17	OB14	OB18	2	0.000156	0.969737	.	.	114.15	.	0.127078
16	CL20	CL18	25	0.023022	0.946715	.	.	68.70	47.62	0.127078
15	OB4	CL21	25	0.002663	0.944052	.	.	71.11	3.39	0.127078
14	CL16	CL39	30	0.016659	0.927393	0.977256	-10.2521	58.95	13.56	0.127078
13	OB1	OB70	2	0.000250	0.927144	0.974631	-9.3478	64.69	.	0.160742
12	CL15	CL17	27	0.004721	0.922423	0.971547	-8.9215	67.02	5.66	0.160742
11	CL55	OB58	3	0.000510	0.921914	0.967879	-7.9371	74.38	16.33	0.170493
10	CL14	CL23	36	0.044574	0.877340	0.963450	-10.8777	50.86	29.31	0.170493
9	CL10	OB72	37	0.000244	0.877095	0.958006	-9.7137	57.98	0.09	0.179715
8	CL9	OB15	38	0.010495	0.866601	0.951163	-9.1678	61.25	3.91	0.179715
7	CL8	OB71	39	0.008405	0.858196	0.942319	-8.2991	67.58	2.91	0.227324
6	CL11	OB41	4	0.000770	0.857426	0.930469	-6.7265	81.79	2.85	0.227324
5	CL7	OB42	40	0.004579	0.852847	0.913803	-5.1197	99.97	1.51	0.234320
4	CL12	CL6	31	0.028481	0.824366	0.888695	-4.5146	109.52	30.71	0.234320
3	CL5	OB12	41	0.003017	0.821349	0.842018	-0.9180	163.21	0.98	0.254155
2	CL3	CL4	72	0.744191	0.077158	0.709627	-10.5974	6.02	292.00	0.289782
1	CL13	CL2	74	0.077158	0.000000	0.000000	0.0000	.	6.02	0.306044

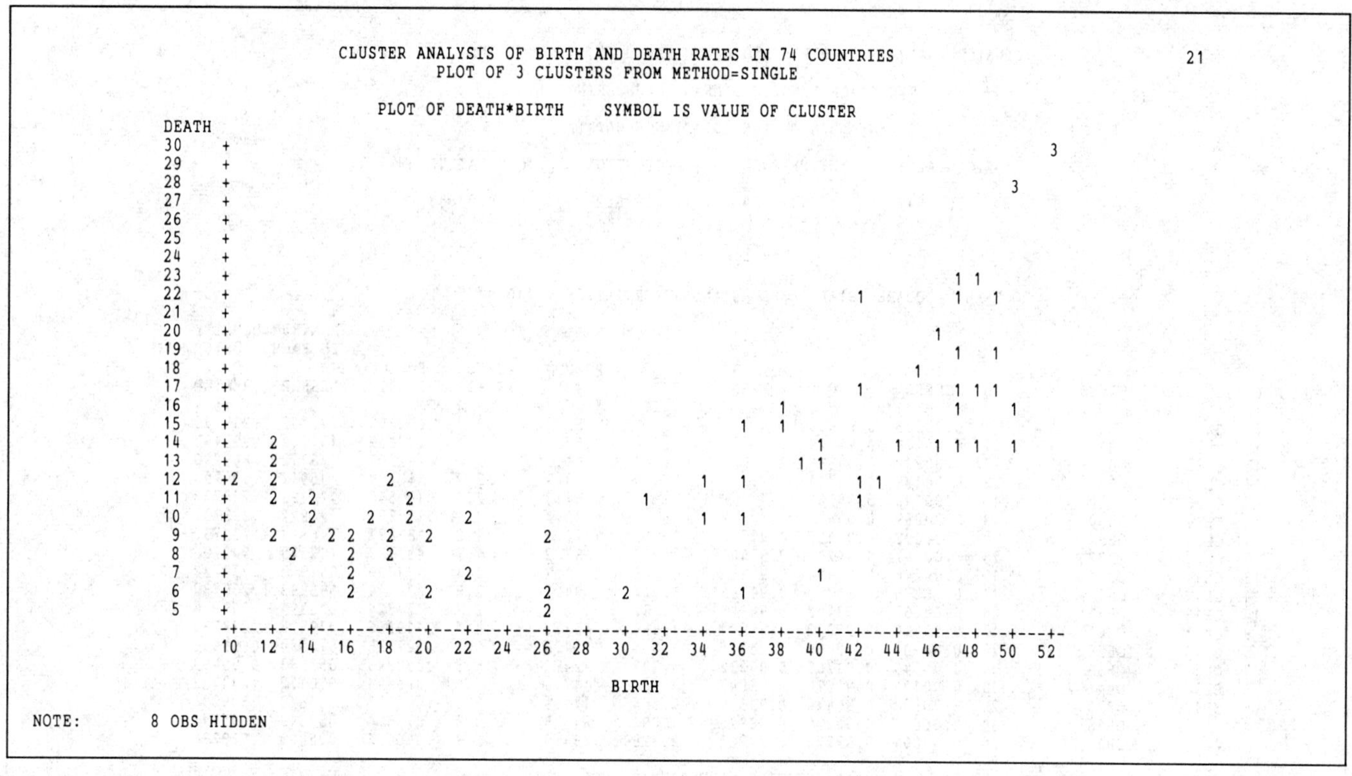
CLUSTER ANALYSIS OF BIRTH AND DEATH RATES IN 74 COUNTRIES
21
PLOT OF 3 CLUSTERS FROM METHOD=SINGLE
PLOT OF DEATH*BIRTH SYMBOL IS VALUE OF CLUSTER
DEATH
BIRTH
NOTE: 8 OBS HIDDEN

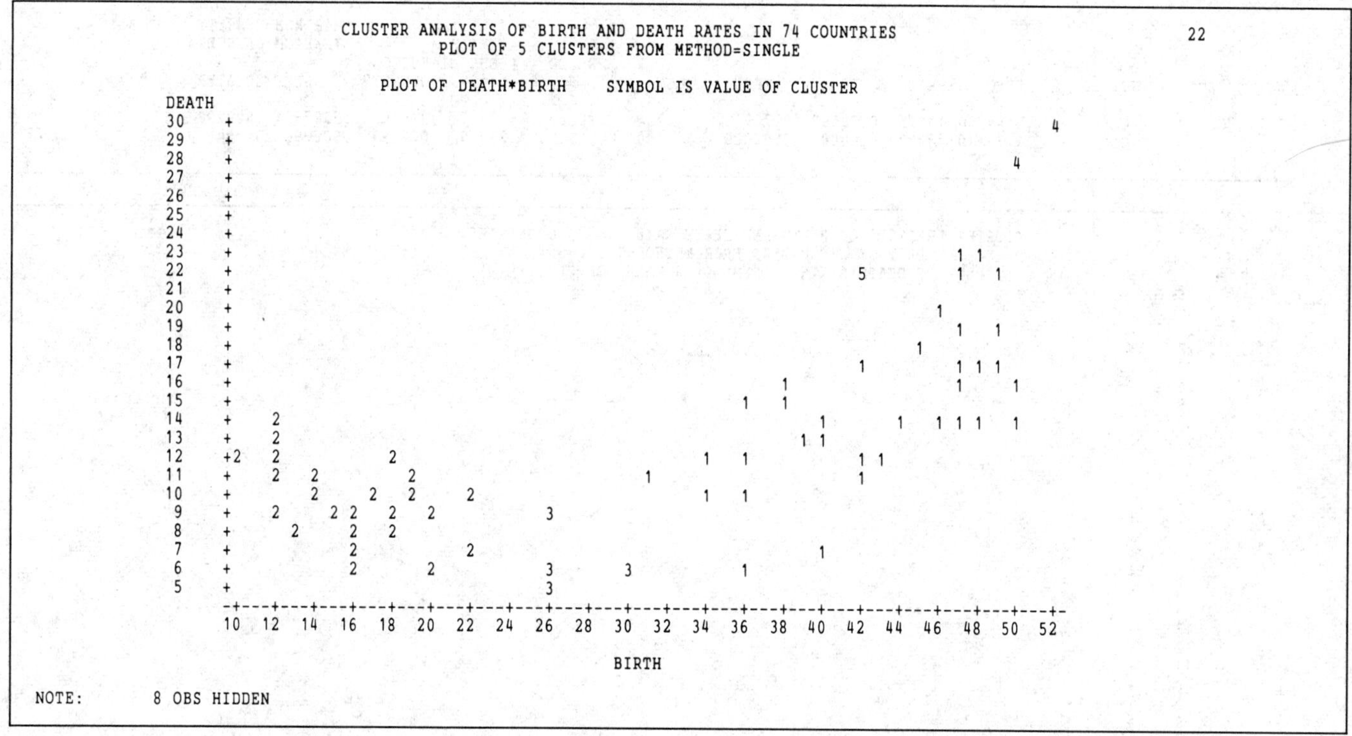
CLUSTER ANALYSIS OF BIRTH AND DEATH RATES IN 74 COUNTRIES
22
PLOT OF 5 CLUSTERS FROM METHOD=SINGLE
PLOT OF DEATH*BIRTH SYMBOL IS VALUE OF CLUSTER
DEATH
BIRTH
NOTE: 8 OBS HIDDEN

CLUSTER ANALYSIS OF BIRTH AND DEATH RATES IN 74 COUNTRIES 23

TWO STAGE DENSITY LINKAGE CLUSTERING

EIGENVALUES OF THE COVARIANCE MATRIX

	EIGENVALUE	DIFFERENCE	PROPORTION	CUMULATIVE
1	205.619	191.684	0.936528	0.93653
2	13.936	.	0.063472	1.00000

K = 6

ROOT-MEAN-SQUARE TOTAL-SAMPLE STANDARD DEVIATION = 10.4775

NCL	CLUSTERS JOINED		FREQ	SPRSQ	RSQ	ERSQ	CCC	PSEUDO F	PSEUDO T**2	FUSION DENSITY	MAXIMUM DENSITY IN EACH CLUSTER LESSER	GREATER
20	CL26	CL21	11	0.00576	0.95408	.	.	59.1	33.7	0.2305	.238732	.238732
19	CL33	OB14	27	0.00279	0.95129	.	.	59.7	3.1	.217382	.131069	0.95493
18	CL22	OB22	21	0.00219	0.94910	.	.	61.4	2.6	.212207	.146912	.509296
17	CL18	OB35	22	0.00199	0.94711	.	.	63.8	2.2	.212207	.146912	.509296
16	CL20	OB20	12	0.00148	0.94564	.	.	67.3	2.0	.199538	.171398	.238732
15	CL16	OB30	13	0.00069	0.94494	.	.	72.3	0.9	.181891	.146912	.238732
14	CL15	OB31	14	0.00092	0.94402	0.97726	-7.955	77.8	1.2	.181891	.146912	.238732
13	CL17	OB72	23	0.00162	0.94240	0.97463	-7.265	83.2	1.7	.152789	.112345	.509296
12	CL14	OB15	15	0.00246	0.93994	0.97155	-6.645	88.2	3.1	.138899	.097942	.238732
11	CL12	OB71	16	0.00235	0.93760	0.96788	-5.934	94.7	2.6	.136419	.095493	.238732
10	CL13	OB12	24	0.00267	0.93493	0.96345	-5.182	102.2	2.7	.127324	.076394	.509296
9	CL11	OB41	17	0.00480	0.93012	0.95801	-4.606	108.2	4.7	.119366	.079577	.238732
8	CL19	OB58	28	0.00604	0.92408	0.95116	-4.025	114.8	6.1	.109135	.076394	0.95493
7	CL8	OB39	29	0.00640	0.91768	0.94232	-3.282	124.5	5.5	.090946	.059683	0.95493
6	CL9	OB42	18	0.00194	0.91574	0.93047	-1.800	147.8	1.6	.090946	.056172	.238732
5	CL10	OB70	25	0.00698	0.90876	0.91380	-0.544	171.8	6.6	.083037	.051618	.509296
4	CL7	OB16	30	0.00646	0.90230	0.88870	1.291	215.5	4.8	.076394	.051618	0.95493
3	CL5	OB1	26	0.01004	0.89226	0.84202	2.858	294.0	7.7	.046021	.025809	.509296

3 MODAL CLUSTERS HAVE BEEN FORMED

NCL	CLUSTERS JOINED		FREQ	SPRSQ	RSQ	ERSQ	CCC	PSEUDO F	PSEUDO T**2	FUSION DENSITY	MAXIMUM DENSITY IN EACH CLUSTER LESSER	GREATER
2	CL3	CL6	44	0.10728	0.78499	0.70963	2.754	262.9	71.2	.215195	.238732	.509296
1	CL2	CL4	74	0.78499	0.00000	0.00000	0.000	.	262.9	.077953	.509296	0.95493

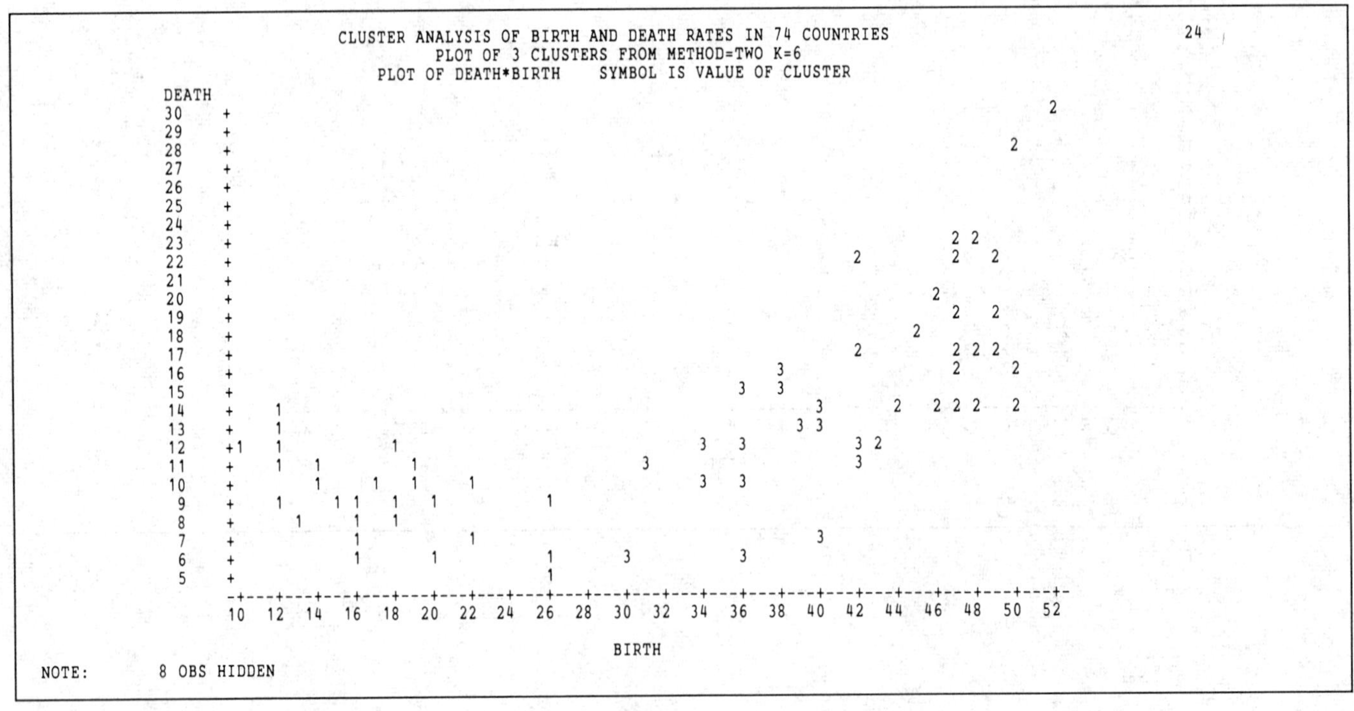

CLUSTER ANALYSIS OF BIRTH AND DEATH RATES IN 74 COUNTRIES 25

TWO STAGE DENSITY LINKAGE CLUSTERING

EIGENVALUES OF THE COVARIANCE MATRIX

	EIGENVALUE	DIFFERENCE	PROPORTION	CUMULATIVE
1	205.619	191.684	0.936528	0.93653
2	13.936	.	0.063472	1.00000

K = 10

ROOT-MEAN-SQUARE TOTAL-SAMPLE STANDARD DEVIATION = 10.4775

NCL	CLUSTERS JOINED		FREQ	SPRSQ	RSQ	ERSQ	CCC	PSEUDO F	PSEUDO T**2	FUSION DENSITY	MAXIMUM DENSITY IN EACH CLUSTER LESSER	GREATER
20	CL21	OB30	30	0.00532	0.91976	.	.	32.6	2.9	.158495	.131714	.445634
19	CL20	OB11	31	0.00305	0.91671	.	.	33.6	1.6	.155273	.127324	.445634
18	CL29	OB24	27	0.00225	0.91446	.	.	35.2	2.4	.151576	.093621	.700282
17	CL19	OB65	32	0.00812	0.90634	.	.	34.5	4.1	.148051	.122427	.445634
16	CL17	OB12	33	0.00237	0.90396	.	.	36.4	1.1	.138396	0.08603	.445634
15	CL16	OB20	34	0.00209	0.90187	.	.	38.7	0.9	.136774	.099472	.445634
14	CL15	OB31	35	0.00238	0.89949	0.97726	-13.124	41.3	1.1	.132629	.099472	.445634
13	CL14	OB17	36	0.00852	0.89097	0.97463	-12.920	41.5	3.9	.129922	.099472	.445634
12	CL13	OB50	37	0.00806	0.88290	0.97155	-12.584	42.5	3.4	.129922	.099472	.445634
11	CL12	OB64	38	0.00764	0.87527	0.96788	-12.122	44.2	3.0	.129922	.099472	.445634
10	CL18	OB58	28	0.00604	0.86922	0.96345	-11.453	47.3	6.1	.116908	.070028	.700282
9	CL11	OB42	39	0.00530	0.86392	0.95801	-10.635	51.6	2.0	.116811	.084883	.445634
8	CL9	OB15	40	0.01030	0.85362	0.95116	-10.015	55.0	3.7	.109762	.077637	.445634
7	CL8	OB71	41	0.00828	0.84535	0.94232	-9.099	61.0	2.8	.095018	.063662	.445634
6	CL10	OB39	29	0.00640	0.83895	0.93047	-7.868	70.8	5.5	.093496	.053868	.700282
5	CL7	OB41	42	0.01500	0.82395	0.91380	-6.836	80.7	4.9	.090946	.067335	.445634
4	CL6	OB16	30	0.00646	0.81749	0.88870	-4.895	104.5	4.8	.089208	.047965	.700282
3	CL5	OB70	43	0.01387	0.80362	0.84202	-1.624	145.3	4.1	.064305	.035368	.445634
2	CL3	OB1	44	0.01864	0.78499	0.70963	2.754	262.9	5.2	.041072	.021802	.445634

2 MODAL CLUSTERS HAVE BEEN FORMED

NCL	CLUSTERS JOINED		FREQ	SPRSQ	RSQ	ERSQ	CCC	PSEUDO F	PSEUDO T**2	FUSION DENSITY	MAXIMUM DENSITY IN EACH CLUSTER LESSER	GREATER
1	CL2	CL4	74	0.78499	0.00000	0.00000	0.000	.	262.9	.073636	.445634	.700282

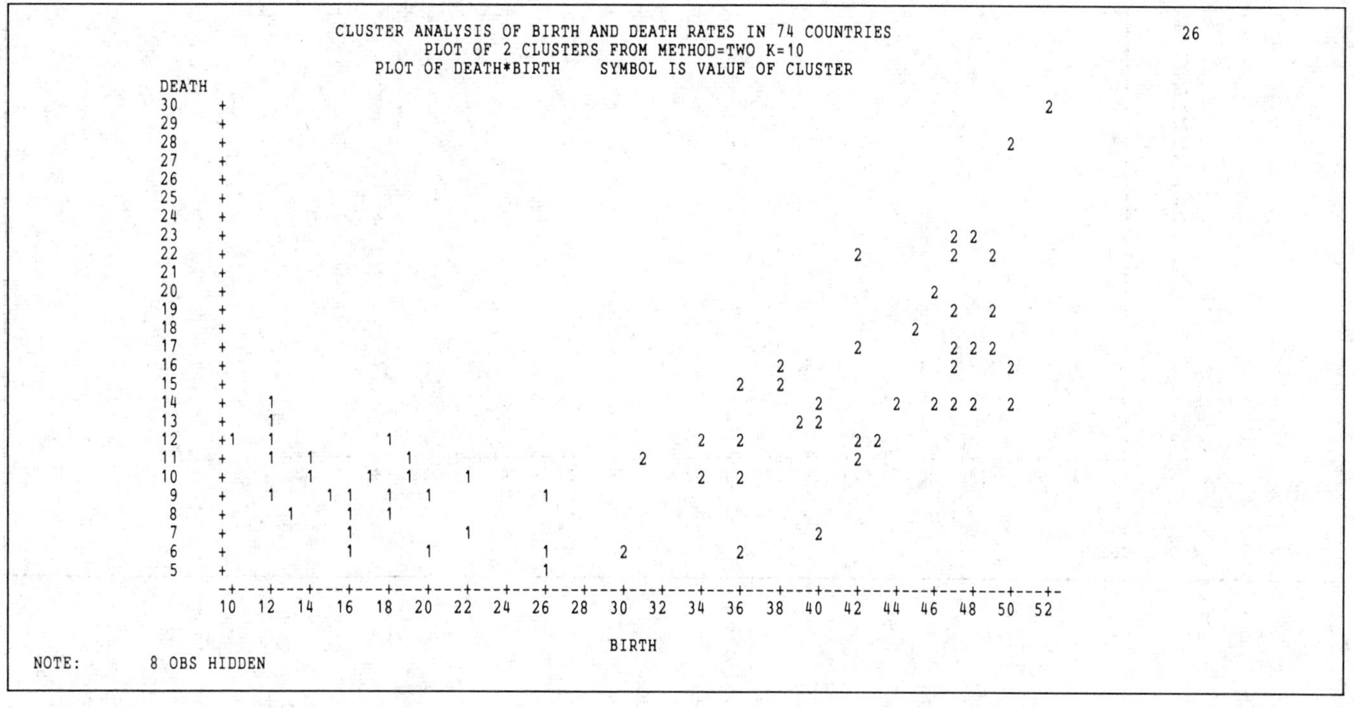

CLUSTER ANALYSIS OF BIRTH AND DEATH RATES IN 74 COUNTRIES 27

TWO STAGE DENSITY LINKAGE CLUSTERING

EIGENVALUES OF THE COVARIANCE MATRIX

	EIGENVALUE	DIFFERENCE	PROPORTION	CUMULATIVE
1	205.619	191.684	0.936528	0.93653
2	13.936	.	0.063472	1.00000

R = 5

ROOT-MEAN-SQUARE TOTAL-SAMPLE STANDARD DEVIATION = 10.4775

NCL	CLUSTERS JOINED		FREQ	SPRSQ	RSQ	ERSQ	CCC	PSEUDO F	PSEUDO T**2	FUSION DENSITY	MAXIMUM DENSITY IN EACH CLUSTER LESSER	GREATER
20	CL21	OB3	29	0.00372	0.92456	.	.	34.8	2.2	.135812	.101859	.229183
19	CL20	OB35	30	0.00381	0.92075	.	.	35.5	2.1	.135812	.101859	.229183
18	CL19	OB22	31	0.00356	0.91719	.	.	36.5	1.9	.135812	.101859	.229183
17	CL18	OB30	32	0.00492	0.91227	.	.	37.0	2.6	.135426	.114592	.229183
16	CL17	OB65	33	0.00793	0.90434	.	.	36.6	4.0	.130962	.114592	.229183
15	CL16	OB31	34	0.00243	0.90191	.	.	38.7	1.1	.129639	.101859	.229183
14	CL15	OB17	35	0.00847	0.89344	0.97726	-13.640	38.7	3.9	.122231	.101859	.229183
13	CL14	OB50	36	0.00800	0.88545	0.97463	-13.358	39.3	3.4	.122231	.101859	.229183
12	CL13	OB64	37	0.00756	0.87789	0.97155	-12.957	40.5	3.0	.122231	.101859	.229183
11	CL12	OB12	38	0.00262	0.87527	0.96788	-12.122	44.2	1.0	.112931	.076394	.229183
10	CL28	OB58	28	0.00604	0.86922	0.96345	-11.453	47.3	6.1	0.10454	.076394	.280113
9	CL11	OB71	39	0.00899	0.86023	0.95801	-10.877	50.0	3.4	.098863	.076394	.229183
8	CL10	OB39	29	0.00640	0.85383	0.95116	-10.002	55.1	5.5	.091956	.063662	.280113
7	CL8	OB16	30	0.00646	0.84737	0.94232	-8.978	62.0	4.8	.091956	.063662	.280113
6	CL9	OB15	40	0.01014	0.83723	0.93047	-7.967	70.0	3.6	.081851	.063662	.229183
5	CL6	OB42	41	0.00475	0.83249	0.91380	-6.360	85.7	1.6	.074697	0.05093	.229183
4	CL7	OB41	31	0.01089	0.82160	0.88870	-4.669	107.5	7.1	.061115	0.05093	.280113
3	OB1	OB70	2	0.00025	0.82135	0.84202	-0.918	163.2	.	.025465	.025465	.025465

3 MODAL CLUSTERS HAVE BEEN FORMED

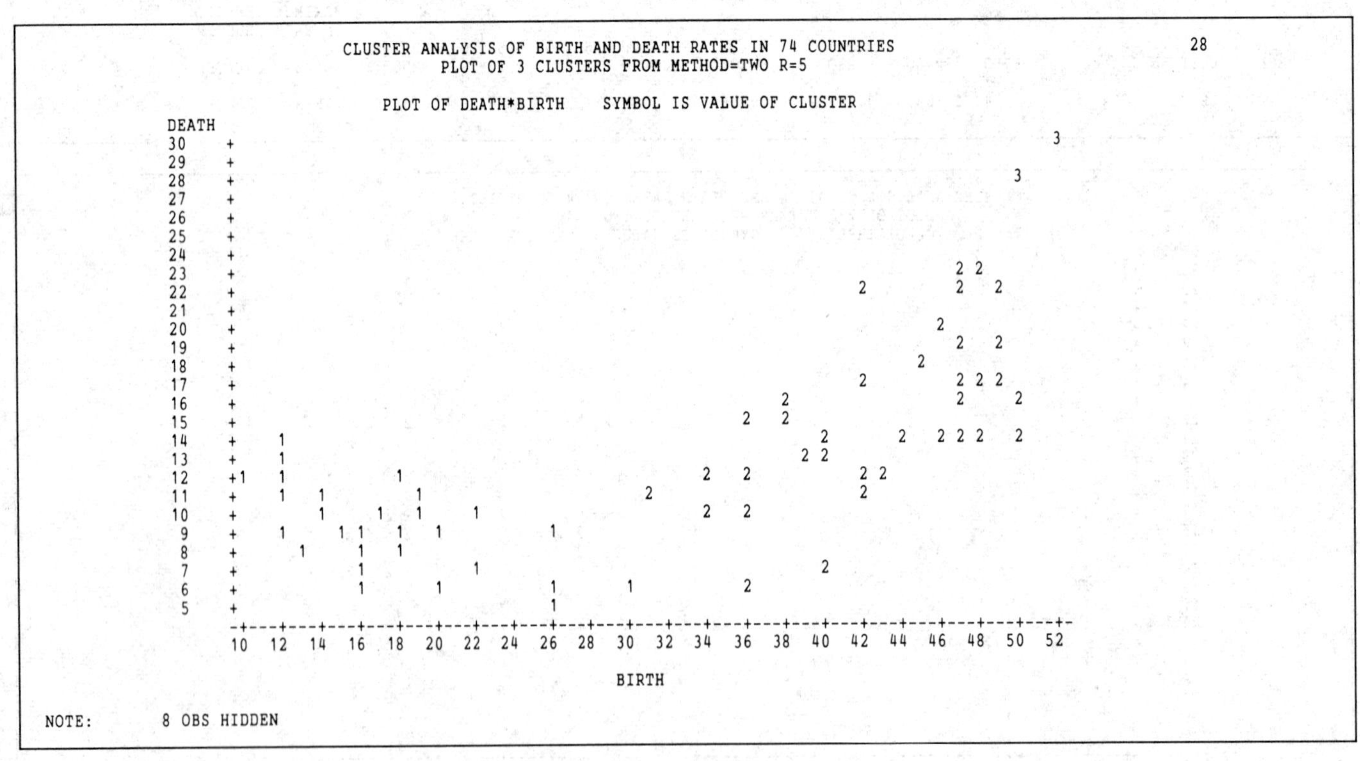

CLUSTER ANALYSIS OF BIRTH AND DEATH RATES IN 74 COUNTRIES 29

WARD'S MINIMUM VARIANCE CLUSTER ANALYSIS

EIGENVALUES OF THE COVARIANCE MATRIX

	EIGENVALUE	DIFFERENCE	PROPORTION	CUMULATIVE
1	205.619	191.684	0.936528	0.93653
2	13.936	.	0.063472	1.00000

ROOT-MEAN-SQUARE TOTAL-SAMPLE STANDARD DEVIATION = 10.4775
ROOT-MEAN-SQUARE DISTANCE BETWEEN OBSERVATIONS = 20.955

NUMBER OF CLUSTERS	CLUSTERS JOINED		FREQUENCY OF NEW CLUSTER	SEMIPARTIAL R-SQUARED	R-SQUARED	APPROXIMATE EXPECTED R-SQUARED	CUBIC CLUSTERING CRITERION	PSEUDO F	PSEUDO T**2
20	CL32	CL51	6	0.000603	0.991598	.	.	335.44	5.80
19	CL29	OB15	7	0.000725	0.990874	.	.	331.75	5.45
18	CL24	OB41	4	0.000770	0.990104	.	.	329.58	2.85
17	CL37	CL49	6	0.000884	0.989220	.	.	326.91	12.14
16	CL20	CL40	10	0.000937	0.988283	.	.	326.14	6.30
15	OB12	CL25	4	0.001066	0.987217	.	.	325.47	5.12
14	CL41	CL33	8	0.001274	0.985943	0.977256	4.2502	323.73	13.13
13	CL28	CL26	9	0.001302	0.984641	0.974631	4.4467	325.89	9.52
12	CL22	CL21	12	0.001733	0.982908	0.971547	4.5329	324.13	8.80
11	CL19	CL23	9	0.003168	0.979740	0.967879	4.1179	304.66	11.54
10	CL17	CL27	10	0.003355	0.976386	0.963450	3.9245	294.03	16.33
9	CL14	CL15	12	0.003978	0.972408	0.958006	3.7992	286.35	11.92
8	CL13	CL31	15	0.005227	0.967181	0.951163	3.6265	277.86	24.26
7	CL34	CL9	14	0.010141	0.957040	0.942319	2.7187	248.77	16.09
6	CL11	CL10	19	0.012086	0.944954	0.930469	2.1882	233.47	20.37
5	CL12	CL18	16	0.012816	0.932137	0.913803	2.2892	236.94	35.80
4	CL7	CL16	24	0.015392	0.916745	0.888695	2.8739	256.93	17.07
3	CL5	CL8	31	0.029516	0.887229	0.842018	2.5170	279.30	33.10
2	CL4	CL6	43	0.096770	0.790460	0.709627	2.9901	271.61	69.12
1	CL2	CL3	74	0.790460	0.000000	0.000000	0.0000	.	271.61

CLUSTER ANALYSIS OF BIRTH AND DEATH RATES IN 74 COUNTRIES 30
PLOT OF 4 CLUSTERS FROM METHOD=WARD

PLOT OF DEATH*BIRTH SYMBOL IS VALUE OF CLUSTER

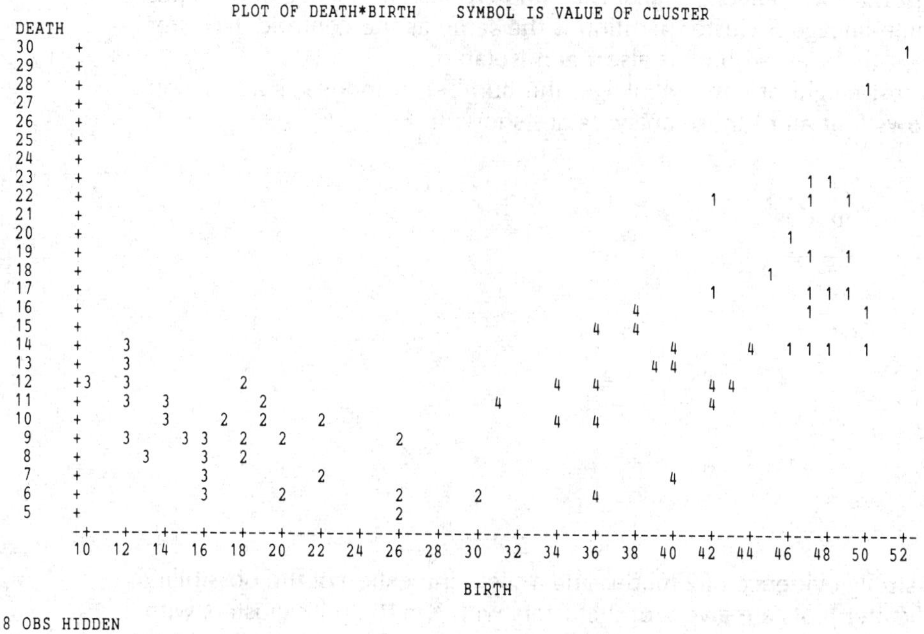

NOTE: 8 OBS HIDDEN

For average linkage, the CCC has peaks at 2, 4, and 8 clusters, but the 4-cluster peak is lower and less sharp than the 2-cluster peak. The pseudo *F* statistic has peaks at 3 and 8 clusters. The pseudo t^2 statistic drops sharply at 2 clusters, continues to fall as far as 4 clusters, and has a particularly low value at 8 clusters. Scatter plots are given for 2, 3, 4, and 8 clusters.

For the centroid method, the CCC has a sharp peak at 2 clusters and a higher but less sharp peak at 8 clusters. The pseudo *F* statistic also has peaks at 2 and 8 clusters. The pseudo t^2 statistic plummets dramatically at 2 clusters but provides no corroboration for 8 clusters. The 2-cluster partition is the same as for average linkage, while the 8-cluster partition differs at only one point, Vietnam, which is assigned to cluster 6 instead of cluster 1. Only the 8-cluster partition is plotted.

Complete linkage shows CCC peaks at 3 and 8 clusters. The pseudo *F* statistic also peaks at 3 and 8 clusters. The further increase of the pseudo *F* statistic at 10 clusters and beyond does not appear to represent real clusters. The pseudo t^2 statistic strongly indicates 3 clusters. The 3- and 8-cluster partitions are plotted but neither is visually appealing.

The EML method yields the same clusters as average linkage for 5 or fewer clusters and gives very similar clusters at the 8-cluster level. Only the 8-cluster partition is plotted.

For the flexible-beta method, the CCC suggests 4 or 9 clusters while the pseudo *F* statistic indicates 3 or 9. The pseudo t^2 statistic supports 3 clusters. Partitions for 3, 4, and 9 clusters are plotted.

For McQuitty's similarity analysis and the median method, all three statistics indicate 3 clusters. Both methods produce the same 3 clusters as flexible-beta.

The CCC and pseudo *F* statistics are not appropriate for use with single linkage because of the method's tendency to chop off tails of distributions. The pseudo t^2 statistic can be used by looking for *large* values and taking the number of clusters to be one greater than the level at which the large pseudo t^2 value is printed. For these data there are large values at levels 2 and 4, suggesting 3 or 5 clusters. The 3-cluster partition is the same as the 2-cluster partition from the centroid method except that two outliers, Afghanistan and Upper Volta, have been separated. The single-linkage 5-cluster partition is the same as the centroid 3-cluster partition except that Cameroon has also been isolated.

For *k*th-nearest-neighbor density linkage, the number of modes as a function of *k* is as follows (not all of these analyses are shown):

k	modes
3	12
4	7
5	5
6-7	3
8-26	2
28+	1

Thus there is strong evidence of 2 modes and a slight indication of the possibility of 3 modes. Scatter plots are given for 2 clusters with K=10 and 3 clusters with K=6. Uniform-kernel density linkage gives similar results except that Afghanistan and Upper Volta are considered a separate mode. The 3-cluster scatter plot with R=5 is shown.

For Ward's method, the CCC indicates 2 or 4 clusters while the pseudo *F* statistic suggests 3 clusters. Both statistics have local peaks with higher values for 12 or more clusters, but there are not enough observations to seriously consider that many clusters. The 2- and 3-cluster partitions are the same as for average linkage. The 4-cluster partition is plotted.

In summary, most of the clustering methods indicate 2 or 3 clusters. There is also a possibility of 8 clusters as suggested by average linkage, the centroid method, and EML. However, at the 2- and 3-cluster levels there is considerable disagreement about the composition of the clusters.

Cluster Analysis of Fisher Iris Data: Example 3

The iris data published by Fisher (1936) have been widely used for examples in discriminant analysis and cluster analysis. The sepal length, sepal width, petal length, and petal width were measured in millimeters on 50 iris specimens from each of three species, *Iris setosa, I. versicolor,* and *I. virginica*. Mezzich and Solomon (1980) discuss a variety of cluster analyses of the iris data.

This example analyzes the iris data by Ward's method and two-stage density linkage, and then illustrates how the FASTCLUS procedure can be used in combination with CLUSTER to analyze large data sets.

```
DATA IRIS;
   TITLE 'CLUSTER ANALYSIS OF FISHER (1936) IRIS DATA';
   INPUT SEPALLEN SEPALWID PETALLEN PETALWID SPEC_NO @@;
   IF SPEC_NO=1 THEN SPECIES='SETOSA     ';
   IF SPEC_NO=2 THEN SPECIES='VERSICOLOR';
   IF SPEC_NO=3 THEN SPECIES='VIRGINICA  ';
   LABEL SEPALLEN='SEPAL LENGTH IN MM.'
         SEPALWID='SEPAL WIDTH  IN MM.'
         PETALLEN='PETAL LENGTH IN MM.'
         PETALWID='PETAL WIDTH  IN MM.';
   CARDS;
50 33 14 02 1 64 28 56 22 3 65 28 46 15 2 67 31 56 24 3
63 28 51 15 3 46 34 14 03 1 69 31 51 23 3 62 22 45 15 2
59 32 48 18 2 46 36 10 02 1 61 30 46 14 2 60 27 51 16 2
65 30 52 20 3 56 25 39 11 2 65 30 55 18 3 58 27 51 19 3
68 32 59 23 3 51 33 17 05 1 57 28 45 13 2 62 34 54 23 3
77 38 67 22 3 63 33 47 16 2 67 33 57 25 3 76 30 66 21 3
49 25 45 17 3 55 35 13 02 1 67 30 52 23 3 70 32 47 14 2
64 32 45 15 2 61 28 40 13 2 48 31 16 02 1 59 30 51 18 3
55 24 38 11 2 63 25 50 19 3 64 32 53 23 3 52 34 14 02 1
49 36 14 01 1 54 30 45 15 2 79 38 64 20 3 44 32 13 02 1
67 33 57 21 3 50 35 16 06 1 58 26 40 12 2 44 30 13 02 1
77 28 67 20 3 63 27 49 18 3 47 32 16 02 1 55 26 44 12 2
50 23 33 10 2 72 32 60 18 3 48 30 14 03 1 51 38 16 02 1
61 30 49 18 3 48 34 19 02 1 50 30 16 02 1 50 32 12 02 1
61 26 56 14 3 64 28 56 21 3 43 30 11 01 1 58 40 12 02 1
51 38 19 04 1 67 31 44 14 2 62 28 48 18 3 49 30 14 02 1
51 35 14 02 1 56 30 45 15 2 58 27 41 10 2 50 34 16 04 1
46 32 14 02 1 60 29 45 15 2 57 26 35 10 2 57 44 15 04 1
50 36 14 02 1 77 30 61 23 3 63 34 56 24 3 58 27 51 19 3
57 29 42 13 2 72 30 58 16 3 54 34 15 04 1 52 41 15 01 1
71 30 59 21 3 64 31 55 18 3 60 30 48 18 3 63 29 56 18 3
49 24 33 10 2 56 27 42 13 2 57 30 42 12 2 55 42 14 02 1
49 31 15 02 1 77 26 69 23 3 60 22 50 15 3 54 39 17 04 1
66 29 46 13 2 52 27 39 14 2 60 34 45 16 2 50 34 15 02 1
44 29 14 02 1 50 20 35 10 2 55 24 37 10 2 58 27 39 12 2
47 32 13 02 1 46 31 15 02 1 69 32 57 23 3 62 29 43 13 2
74 28 61 19 3 59 30 42 15 2 51 34 15 02 1 50 35 13 03 1
```

```
56 28 49 20 3 60 22 40 10 2 73 29 63 18 3 67 25 58 18 3
49 31 15 01 1 67 31 47 15 2 63 23 44 13 2 54 37 15 02 1
56 30 41 13 2 63 25 49 15 2 61 28 47 12 2 64 29 43 13 2
51 25 30 11 2 57 28 41 13 2 65 30 58 22 3 69 31 54 21 3
54 39 13 04 1 51 35 14 03 1 72 36 61 25 3 65 32 51 20 3
61 29 47 14 2 56 29 36 13 2 69 31 49 15 2 64 27 53 19 3
68 30 55 21 3 55 25 40 13 2 48 34 16 02 1 48 30 14 01 1
45 23 13 03 1 57 25 50 20 3 57 38 17 03 1 51 38 15 03 1
55 23 40 13 2 66 30 44 14 2 68 28 48 14 2 54 34 17 02 1
51 37 15 04 1 52 35 15 02 1 58 28 51 24 3 67 30 50 17 2
63 33 60 25 3 53 37 15 02 1
;
```

The following macro %SHOW is used in the subsequent analyses to display cluster results. It invokes the FREQ procedure to crosstabulate clusters and species. The CANDISC procedure is used to compute canonical variables for discriminating among the clusters, and the first two canonical variables are plotted to show cluster membership. See the chapter "The CANDISC Procedure" for a canonical discriminant analysis of the iris species.

```
%MACRO SHOW;
   PROC FREQ;
      TABLES CLUSTER*SPECIES;
   PROC CANDISC NOPRINT OUT=CAN;
      CLASS CLUSTER;
      VAR PETAL: SEPAL:;
   PROC PLOT;
      PLOT CAN2*CAN1=CLUSTER;
   %MEND;
```

The first analysis clusters the iris data by Ward's method and plots the CCC and pseudo F and t^2 statistics. The CCC has a local peak at 3 clusters but a higher peak at 6 clusters. The pseudo F statistic indicates 3 clusters, while the pseudo t^2 statistic suggests 3 or 6 clusters.

The TREE procedure creates an output data set containing the 3-cluster partition for use by the %SHOW macro. The FREQ procedure reveals 16 misclassifications.

```
TITLE2 'BY WARD''S METHOD';
PROC CLUSTER DATA=IRIS METHOD=WARD PRINT=20 CCC PSEUDO;
   VAR PETAL: SEPAL:;
   COPY SPECIES;
PROC PLOT;
   PLOT _CCC_*_NCL_ /
      HAXIS=1 TO 30 BY 1;
   PLOT _PSF_*_NCL_='F'  _PST2_*_NCL_='T' /
      OVERLAY HAXIS=1 TO 30 BY 1 VAXIS=0 TO 600 BY 100;
PROC TREE NOPRINT NCL=3 OUT=OUT;
   COPY PETAL: SEPAL: SPECIES;
%SHOW
```

The second analysis uses two-stage density linkage. The raw data suggest 2 or 6 modes instead of 3:

k	modes
3	12
4-6	6
7	4
8	3
9-50	2
51+	1

However, the ACECLUS procedure can be used to reveal 3 modes. This analysis uses K=8 to produce 3 clusters for comparison with other analyses. There are only 6 misclassifications.

```
TITLE2 'BY TWO-STAGE DENSITY LINKAGE';
PROC CLUSTER DATA=IRIS METHOD=TWOSTAGE K=8 PRINT=20 CCC PSEUDO;
   VAR PETAL: SEPAL:;
   COPY SPECIES;
PROC TREE NOPRINT NCL=3 OUT=OUT;
   COPY PETAL: SEPAL: SPECIES;
%SHOW
```

The CLUSTER procedure is not practical for very large data sets because with most methods the CPU time varies as the square or cube of the number of observations. The FASTCLUS procedure requires time proportional to the number of observations and can therefore be used with much larger data sets than CLUSTER. If you want to hierarchically cluster a very large data set, you can use FASTCLUS for a preliminary cluster analysis producing a large number of clusters, then use CLUSTER to hierarchically cluster the preliminary clusters.

FASTCLUS automatically creates variables _FREQ_ and _RMSSTD_ in the MEAN= output data set. These variables are then automatically used by CLUSTER in the computation of various statistics.

The iris data are used to illustrate the process of clustering clusters. In the preliminary analysis, FASTCLUS produces ten clusters which are then crosstabulated with species. The data set containing the preliminary clusters is sorted in preparation for later merges.

```
PROC FASTCLUS DATA=IRIS SUMMARY MAXC=10 MAXITER=99 CONVERGE=0
      MEAN=MEAN OUT=PRELIM CLUSTER=PRECLUS;
   VAR PETAL: SEPAL:;
PROC FREQ;
   TABLES PRECLUS*SPECIES;
PROC SORT DATA=PRELIM;
   BY PRECLUS;
```

The following macro %CLUS clusters the preliminary clusters. There is one argument to choose the METHOD= specification to be used by CLUSTER. The TREE procedure creates an output data set containing the 3-cluster partition, which is sorted and merged with the OUT= data set from FASTCLUS to determine which cluster each of the original 150 observations belongs to. The %SHOW macro is then used to display the results.

```
%MACRO CLUS(METHOD);
   PROC CLUSTER DATA=MEAN METHOD=&METHOD CCC PSEUDO;
      VAR PETAL: SEPAL:;
      COPY PRECLUS;
   PROC TREE NOPRINT NCL=3 OUT=OUT;
      COPY PETAL: SEPAL: PRECLUS;
   PROC SORT DATA=OUT;
      BY PRECLUS;
   DATA CLUS;
      MERGE PRELIM OUT;
      BY PRECLUS;
   %SHOW
   %MEND;
```

The %CLUS macro is now invoked using Ward's method, which produces sixteen misclassifications, and Wong's hybrid method, which produces twenty-two misclassifications.

```
TITLE2 'CLUSTERING CLUSTERS BY WARD''S METHOD';
%CLUS(WARD);
TITLE2 'CLUSTERING CLUSTERS BY WONG''S HYBRID METHOD';
%CLUS(TWOSTAGE HYBRID);
```

Output 15.4 Cluster Analysis of Fisher Iris Data: PROC CLUSTER with Ward's Method

CLUSTER ANALYSIS OF FISHER (1936) IRIS DATA 1
BY WARD'S METHOD

WARD'S MINIMUM VARIANCE CLUSTER ANALYSIS

EIGENVALUES OF THE COVARIANCE MATRIX

	EIGENVALUE	DIFFERENCE	PROPORTION	CUMULATIVE
1	422.824	398.557	0.924619	0.92462
2	24.267	16.446	0.053066	0.97769
3	7.821	5.437	0.017103	0.99479
4	2.384	.	0.005212	1.00000

ROOT-MEAN-SQUARE TOTAL-SAMPLE STANDARD DEVIATION = 10.6922
ROOT-MEAN-SQUARE DISTANCE BETWEEN OBSERVATIONS = 30.2422

NUMBER OF CLUSTERS	CLUSTERS JOINED		FREQUENCY OF NEW CLUSTER	SEMIPARTIAL R-SQUARED	R-SQUARED	APPROXIMATE EXPECTED R-SQUARED	CUBIC CLUSTERING CRITERION	PSEUDO F	PSEUDO T**2
20	CL37	OB25	10	0.001087	0.977819	0.967119	6.1385	301.62	9.80
19	CL41	CL46	12	0.001154	0.976665	0.965579	6.0734	304.60	7.37
18	CL25	CL40	10	0.001249	0.975415	0.963906	6.0124	308.07	6.15
17	CL32	CL22	21	0.001380	0.974035	0.962081	5.9431	311.83	8.72
16	CL35	CL31	15	0.001462	0.972574	0.960079	5.9055	316.79	9.01
15	CL24	CL28	15	0.001641	0.970932	0.957871	5.8544	322.10	9.83
14	CL21	CL53	7	0.001873	0.969059	0.955418	5.7798	327.65	5.09
13	CL18	CL48	15	0.002271	0.966788	0.952670	5.6247	332.34	8.92
12	CL16	CL23	24	0.002274	0.964514	0.949541	4.5819	340.99	9.63
11	CL14	CL43	12	0.002500	0.962014	0.945886	4.6274	352.02	5.77
10	CL26	CL20	22	0.002694	0.959320	0.941547	4.7662	366.83	12.87
9	CL27	CL19	29	0.002702	0.956618	0.936296	5.0858	388.65	16.60
8	CL36	CL15	23	0.003095	0.953523	0.929791	5.5064	416.18	13.81
7	CL10	CL47	26	0.005811	0.947713	0.921496	5.4832	431.98	19.07
6	CL8	CL13	38	0.006042	0.941671	0.910514	5.8580	464.95	16.26
5	CL9	CL17	50	0.010753	0.930917	0.895232	5.8170	488.48	44.95
4	CL12	CL11	36	0.017245	0.913673	0.872331	3.9867	515.08	41.00
3	CL6	CL7	64	0.030051	0.883621	0.826664	4.3292	558.06	57.25
2	CL4	CL3	100	0.111026	0.772595	0.696871	3.8329	502.82	115.57
1	CL5	CL2	150	0.772595	0.000000	0.000000	0.0000	.	502.82

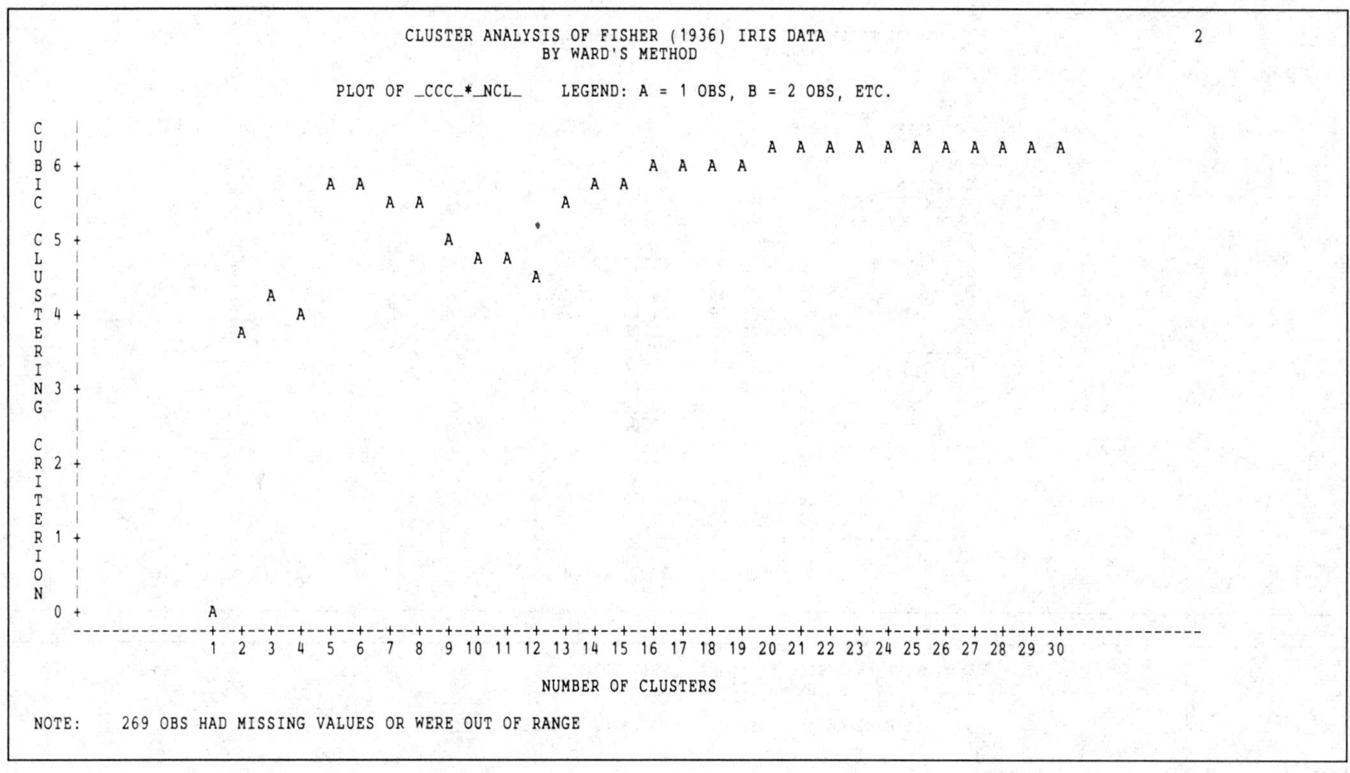
CLUSTER ANALYSIS OF FISHER (1936) IRIS DATA
BY WARD'S METHOD
2
PLOT OF _CCC_*_NCL_ LEGEND: A = 1 OBS, B = 2 OBS, ETC.
CUBIC CLUSTERING CRITERION
NUMBER OF CLUSTERS
NOTE: 269 OBS HAD MISSING VALUES OR WERE OUT OF RANGE

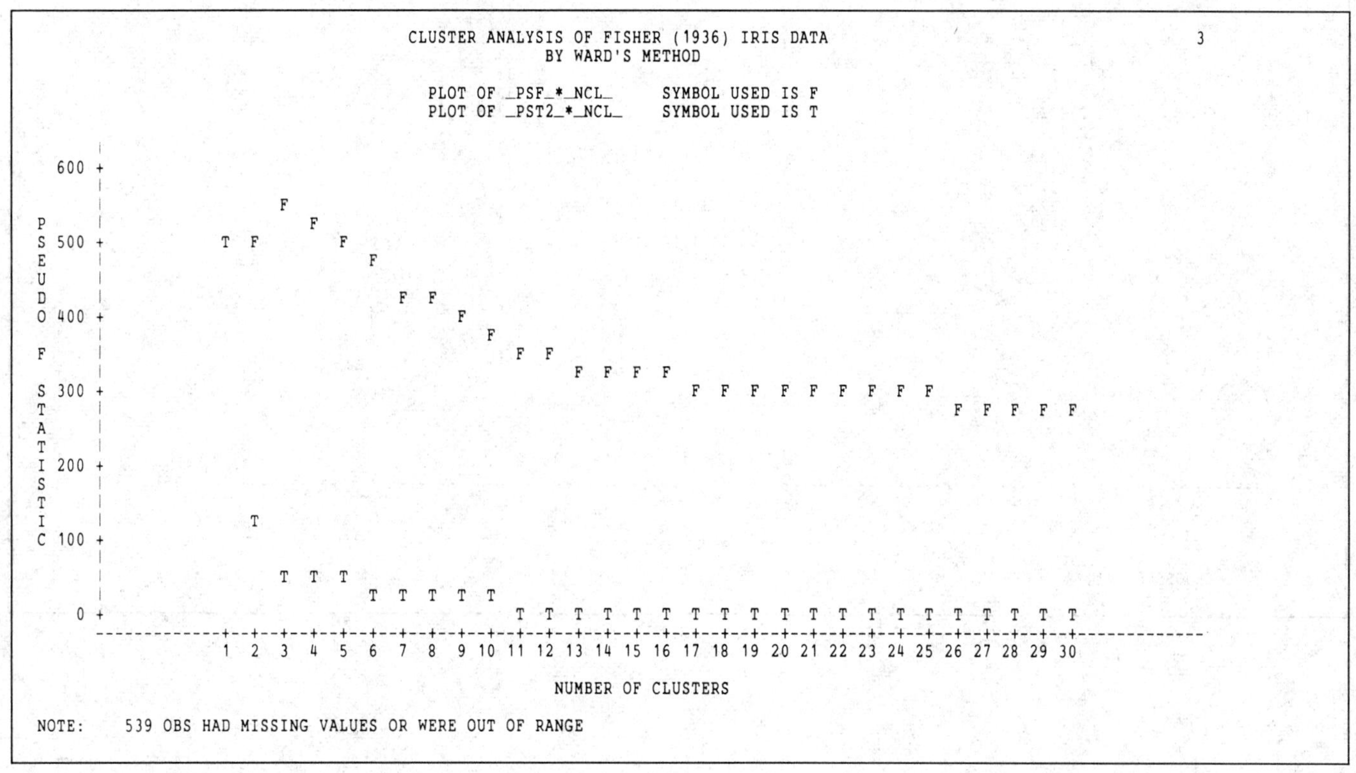
CLUSTER ANALYSIS OF FISHER (1936) IRIS DATA
BY WARD'S METHOD
3
PLOT OF _PSF_*_NCL_ SYMBOL USED IS F
PLOT OF _PST2_*_NCL_ SYMBOL USED IS T
PSEUDO F STATISTIC
NUMBER OF CLUSTERS
NOTE: 539 OBS HAD MISSING VALUES OR WERE OUT OF RANGE

CLUSTER ANALYSIS OF FISHER (1936) IRIS DATA
BY WARD'S METHOD

4

TABLE OF CLUSTER BY SPECIES

CLUSTER / FREQUENCY PERCENT ROW PCT COL PCT	SPECIES: SETOSA	VERSICOLOR	VIRGINICA	TOTAL
1	0 0.00 0.00 0.00	49 32.67 76.56 98.00	15 10.00 23.44 30.00	64 42.67
2	50 33.33 100.00 100.00	0 0.00 0.00 0.00	0 0.00 0.00 0.00	50 33.33
3	0 0.00 0.00 0.00	1 0.67 2.78 2.00	35 23.33 97.22 70.00	36 24.00
TOTAL	50 33.33	50 33.33	50 33.33	150 100.00

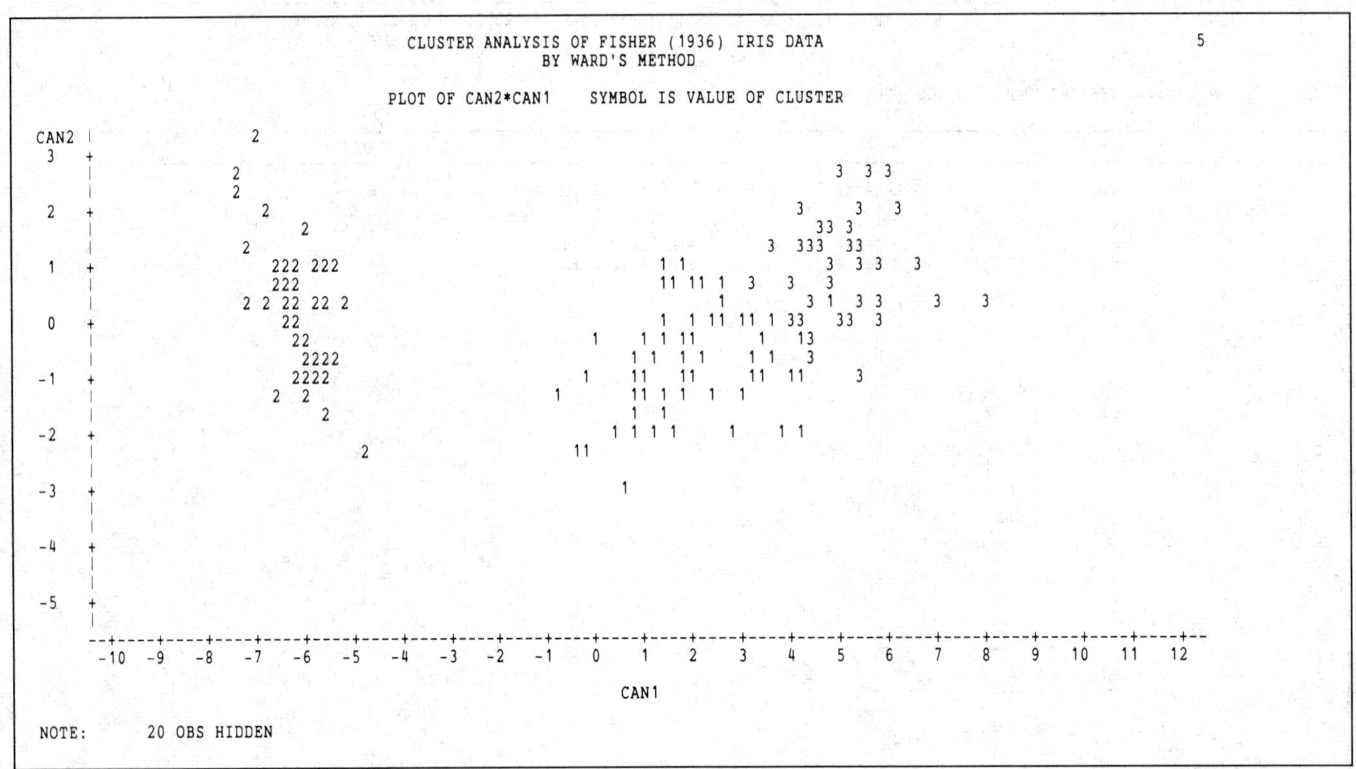

Output 15.5 Cluster Analysis of Fisher Iris Data: PROC CLUSTER with Two-Stage Density Linkage Method

CLUSTER ANALYSIS OF FISHER (1936) IRIS DATA
BY TWO-STAGE DENSITY LINKAGE

6

TWO STAGE DENSITY LINKAGE CLUSTERING

EIGENVALUES OF THE COVARIANCE MATRIX

	EIGENVALUE	DIFFERENCE	PROPORTION	CUMULATIVE
1	422.824	398.557	0.924619	0.92462
2	24.267	16.446	0.053066	0.97769
3	7.821	5.437	0.017103	0.99479
4	2.384	.	0.005212	1.00000

K = 8

ROOT-MEAN-SQUARE TOTAL-SAMPLE STANDARD DEVIATION = 10.6922

NCL	CLUSTERS JOINED		FREQ	SPRSQ	RSQ	ERSQ	CCC	PSEUDO F	PSEUDO T**2	FUSION DENSITY	MAXIMUM DENSITY IN EACH CLUSTER LESSER	GREATER
20	CL21	OB111	40	0.00232	0.92337	0.96712	-13.195	82.4	3.4	.001096	8E-04	.006333
19	CL20	OB147	41	0.00103	0.92234	0.96558	-12.714	86.4	1.4	.001025	6E-04	.006333
18	CL19	OB57	42	0.00090	0.92144	0.96391	-12.178	91.1	1.2	.001012	6E-04	.006333
17	CL18	OB78	43	0.00128	0.92016	0.96208	-11.685	95.8	1.7	.001002	6E-04	.006333
16	CL27	OB72	49	0.00209	0.91807	0.96008	-11.311	100.1	5.5	8E-04	4E-04	.180127
15	CL17	OB127	44	0.00255	0.91553	0.95787	-10.975	104.5	3.4	7E-04	4E-04	.006333
14	CL16	OB137	50	0.00233	0.91319	0.95542	-10.544	110.1	5.6	7E-04	3E-04	.180127
13	CL15	OB74	45	0.00295	0.91025	0.95267	-10.161	115.8	3.7	6E-04	4E-04	.006333
12	CL28	OB49	46	0.00357	0.90667	0.94954	-8.004	121.9	5.2	6E-04	3E-04	.015073
11	CL12	OB85	47	0.00358	0.90309	0.94589	-7.619	129.5	4.8	6E-04	3E-04	.015073
10	CL11	OB98	48	0.00334	0.89975	0.94155	-7.093	139.6	4.1	5E-04	3E-04	.015073
9	CL13	OB24	46	0.00369	0.89606	0.93630	-6.480	152.0	4.4	5E-04	4E-04	.006333
8	CL10	OB25	49	0.00192	0.89414	0.92979	-5.481	171.3	2.2	5E-04	2E-04	.015073
7	CL8	OB121	50	0.00352	0.89063	0.92150	-4.474	194.1	4.0	5E-04	2E-04	.015073
6	CL9	OB45	47	0.00419	0.88643	0.91051	-3.262	224.8	4.6	3E-04	1E-04	.006333
5	CL6	OB39	48	0.00489	0.88154	0.89523	-1.716	269.8	5.0	2E-04	1E-04	.006333
4	CL5	OB21	49	0.00495	0.87659	0.87233	0.346	345.7	4.7	2E-04	10E-05	.006333
3	CL4	OB90	50	0.00474	0.87186	0.82666	3.283	500.1	4.1	1E-04	7E-05	.006333

3 MODAL CLUSTERS HAVE BEEN FORMED

NCL	CLUSTERS JOINED		FREQ	SPRSQ	RSQ	ERSQ	CCC	PSEUDO F	PSEUDO T**2	FUSION DENS	MAXIMUM DENSITY IN EACH CLUSTER LESSER	GREATER
2	CL7	CL3	100	0.09926	0.77260	0.69687	3.833	502.8	91.9	.004733	.006333	.015073

CLUSTER ANALYSIS OF FISHER (1936) IRIS DATA
BY TWO-STAGE DENSITY LINKAGE 7

TABLE OF CLUSTER BY SPECIES

CLUSTER (FREQUENCY / PERCENT / ROW PCT / COL PCT)	SPECIES: SETOSA	VERSICOLOR	VIRGINICA	TOTAL
1	50	0	0	50
	33.33	0.00	0.00	33.33
	100.00	0.00	0.00	
	100.00	0.00	0.00	
2	0	47	3	50
	0.00	31.33	2.00	33.33
	0.00	94.00	6.00	
	0.00	94.00	6.00	
3	0	3	47	50
	0.00	2.00	31.33	33.33
	0.00	6.00	94.00	
	0.00	6.00	94.00	
TOTAL	50	50	50	150
	33.33	33.33	33.33	100.00

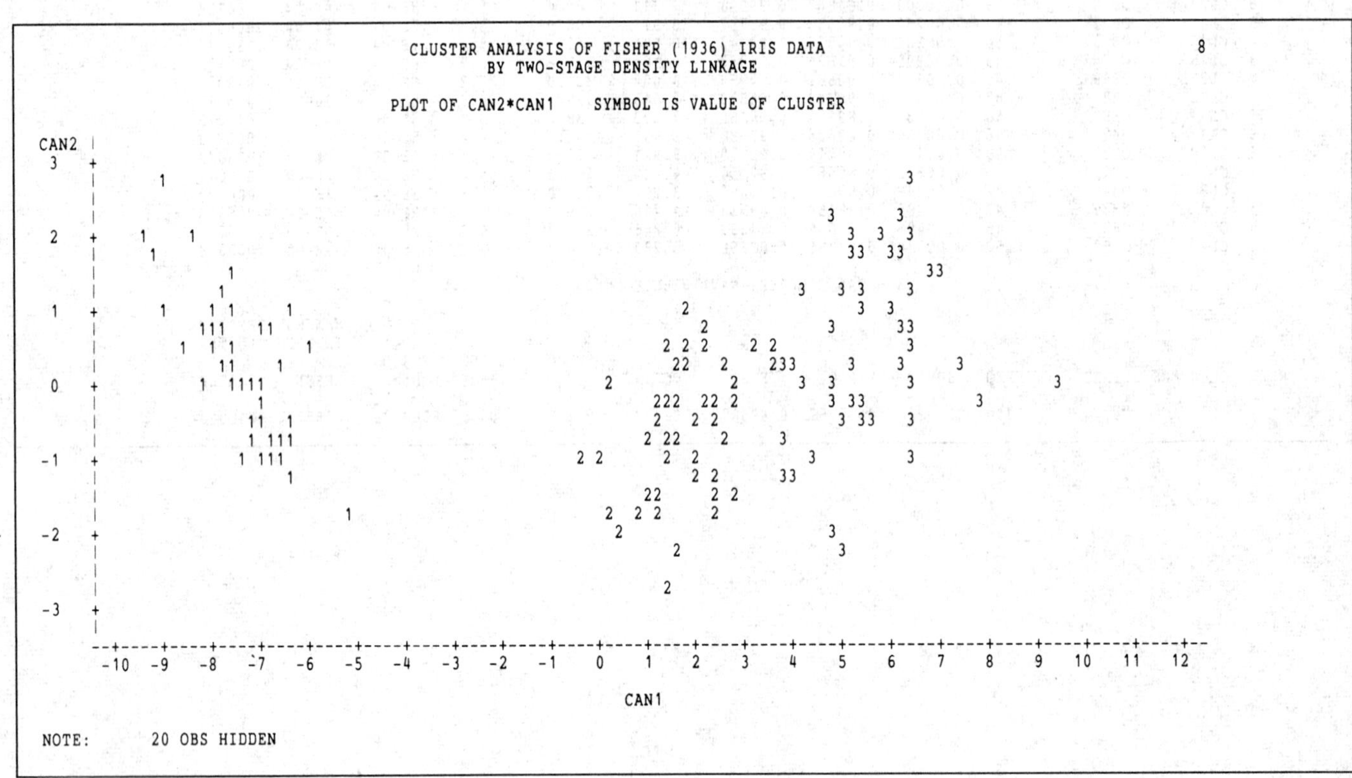

Output 15.6 Preliminary Analysis of Fisher Iris Data: PROC FASTCLUS

```
                    CLUSTER ANALYSIS OF FISHER (1936) IRIS DATA                                9
                          PRELIMINARY ANALYSIS BY FASTCLUS

                                 FASTCLUS PROCEDURE

            REPLACE=FULL  RADIUS=0  MAXCLUSTERS=10  MAXITER=99  CONVERGE=0

                                  CLUSTER SUMMARY

CLUSTER                  RMS STD        MAXIMUM DISTANCE FROM      NEAREST    CENTROID
 NUMBER    FREQUENCY    DEVIATION        SEED TO OBSERVATION       CLUSTER    DISTANCE
--------------------------------------------------------------------------------------
    1           9         2.7067            8.2027                     5        8.7362
    2          19         2.2001            7.7340                     4        6.2243
    3          18         2.1496            6.2173                     8        7.5049
    4           4         2.5249            5.3268                     2        6.2243
    5           3         2.7234            5.8214                     1        8.7362
    6           7         2.2939            5.1508                     2        9.3318
    7          17         2.0274            6.9576                    10        7.9503
    8          18         2.2628            7.1135                     3        7.5049
    9          22         2.2666            7.5029                     8        9.0090
   10          33         2.0594           10.0033                     7        7.9503

                                  PSEUDO F STATISTIC =    370.58
                           OBSERVED OVER-ALL R-SQUARED =  0.95971
                 APPROXIMATE EXPECTED OVER-ALL R-SQUARED =  0.82928
                           CUBIC CLUSTERING CRITERION =   27.077
          WARNING: THE TWO ABOVE VALUES ARE INVALID FOR CORRELATED VARIABLES
```

```
                    CLUSTER ANALYSIS OF FISHER (1936) IRIS DATA                               10
                          PRELIMINARY ANALYSIS BY FASTCLUS

                            TABLE OF PRECLUS BY SPECIES

                    PRECLUS      SPECIES

                    FREQUENCY|
                     PERCENT |
                     ROW PCT |
                     COL PCT |SETOSA   |VERSICOL|VIRGINIC|
                             |         |OR      |A       |  TOTAL
                    ---------+---------+--------+--------+
                           1 |       0 |      0 |      9 |      9
                             |    0.00 |   0.00 |   6.00 |   6.00
                             |    0.00 |   0.00 | 100.00 |
                             |    0.00 |   0.00 |  18.00 |
                    ---------+---------+--------+--------+
                           2 |       0 |     19 |      0 |     19
                             |    0.00 |  12.67 |   0.00 |  12.67
                             |    0.00 | 100.00 |   0.00 |
                             |    0.00 |  38.00 |   0.00 |
                    ---------+---------+--------+--------+
                           3 |       0 |     18 |      0 |     18
                             |    0.00 |  12.00 |   0.00 |  12.00
                             |    0.00 | 100.00 |   0.00 |
                             |    0.00 |  36.00 |   0.00 |
                    ---------+---------+--------+--------+
                           4 |       0 |      3 |      1 |      4
                             |    0.00 |   2.00 |   0.67 |   2.67
                             |    0.00 |  75.00 |  25.00 |
                             |    0.00 |   6.00 |   2.00 |
                    ---------+---------+--------+--------+
                           5 |       0 |      0 |      3 |      3
                             |    0.00 |   0.00 |   2.00 |   2.00
                             |    0.00 |   0.00 | 100.00 |
                             |    0.00 |   0.00 |   6.00 |
                    ---------+---------+--------+--------+
                    TOTAL          50        50       50      150
                                33.33     33.33    33.33   100.00

                    (CONTINUED)
```

```
                    CLUSTER ANALYSIS OF FISHER (1936) IRIS DATA                    11
                         PRELIMINARY ANALYSIS BY FASTCLUS

                              TABLE OF PRECLUS BY SPECIES

                   PRECLUS      SPECIES

                   FREQUENCY|
                    PERCENT |
                    ROW PCT |
                    COL PCT |SETOSA  |VERSICOL|VIRGINIC|
                            |        |OR      |A       |  TOTAL
                   ---------+--------+--------+--------+
                          6 |      0 |      7 |      0 |      7
                            |   0.00 |   4.67 |   0.00 |   4.67
                            |   0.00 | 100.00 |   0.00 |
                            |   0.00 |  14.00 |   0.00 |
                   ---------+--------+--------+--------+
                          7 |     17 |      0 |      0 |     17
                            |  11.33 |   0.00 |   0.00 |  11.33
                            | 100.00 |   0.00 |   0.00 |
                            |  34.00 |   0.00 |   0.00 |
                   ---------+--------+--------+--------+
                          8 |      0 |      3 |     15 |     18
                            |   0.00 |   2.00 |  10.00 |  12.00
                            |   0.00 |  16.67 |  83.33 |
                            |   0.00 |   6.00 |  30.00 |
                   ---------+--------+--------+--------+
                          9 |      0 |      0 |     22 |     22
                            |   0.00 |   0.00 |  14.67 |  14.67
                            |   0.00 |   0.00 | 100.00 |
                            |   0.00 |   0.00 |  44.00 |
                   ---------+--------+--------+--------+
                         10 |     33 |      0 |      0 |     33
                            |  22.00 |   0.00 |   0.00 |  22.00
                            | 100.00 |   0.00 |   0.00 |
                            |  66.00 |   0.00 |   0.00 |
                   ---------+--------+--------+--------+
                   TOTAL          50       50       50      150
                               33.33    33.33    33.33   100.00
```

Output 15.7 Cluster Analysis of Fisher Iris Data: Using Various Macros to Invoke Procedures

```
                        CLUSTER ANALYSIS OF FISHER (1936) IRIS DATA                            12
                            CLUSTERING CLUSTERS BY WARD'S METHOD

                          WARD'S MINIMUM VARIANCE CLUSTER ANALYSIS

                            EIGENVALUES OF THE COVARIANCE MATRIX

                     EIGENVALUE      DIFFERENCE      PROPORTION      CUMULATIVE

               1      416.976         398.666        0.950106         0.95011
               2       18.310          14.953        0.041720         0.99183
               3        3.357           3.127        0.007649         0.99948
               4        0.230            .           0.000524         1.00000

            ROOT-MEAN-SQUARE TOTAL-SAMPLE STANDARD DEVIATION =  10.6922
            ROOT-MEAN-SQUARE DISTANCE BETWEEN OBSERVATIONS    =  30.2422

 NUMBER                       FREQUENCY                           APPROXIMATE     CUBIC
   OF                          OF NEW   SEMIPARTIAL                 EXPECTED    CLUSTERING    PSEUDO      PSEUDO
CLUSTERS  CLUSTERS JOINED      CLUSTER   R-SQUARED     R-SQUARED    R-SQUARED    CRITERION       F          T**2

     9    OB2        OB4          23     0.001879      0.957836     0.932483       6.2627      400.38        6.33
     8    OB1        OB5          12     0.002520      0.955315     0.926089       6.7495      433.69        5.85
     7    CL9        OB6          30     0.006945      0.948370     0.917957       6.2778      437.79       19.51
     6    OB3        OB8          36     0.007440      0.940930     0.907217       6.2076      458.76       26.02
     5    OB7        OB10         50     0.010408      0.930522     0.892304       6.1465      485.50       42.24
     4    CL8        OB9          34     0.016180      0.914342     0.869844       4.2772      519.48       39.33
     3    CL7        CL6          66     0.031800      0.882542     0.824273       4.3930      552.26       59.72
     2    CL4        CL3         100     0.109947      0.772595     0.694823       3.9366      502.82      113.15
     1    CL2        CL5         150     0.772595      0.000000     0.000000       0.0000         .        502.82
```

CLUSTER ANALYSIS OF FISHER (1936) IRIS DATA
CLUSTERING CLUSTERS BY WARD'S METHOD

13

TABLE OF CLUSTER BY SPECIES

CLUSTER / SPECIES FREQUENCY PERCENT ROW PCT COL PCT	SETOSA	VERSICOLOR	VIRGINICA	TOTAL
1	0 0.00 0.00 0.00	50 33.33 75.76 100.00	16 10.67 24.24 32.00	66 44.00
2	0 0.00 0.00 0.00	0 0.00 0.00 0.00	34 22.67 100.00 68.00	34 22.67
3	50 33.33 100.00 100.00	0 0.00 0.00 0.00	0 0.00 0.00 0.00	50 33.33
TOTAL	50 33.33	50 33.33	50 33.33	150 100.00

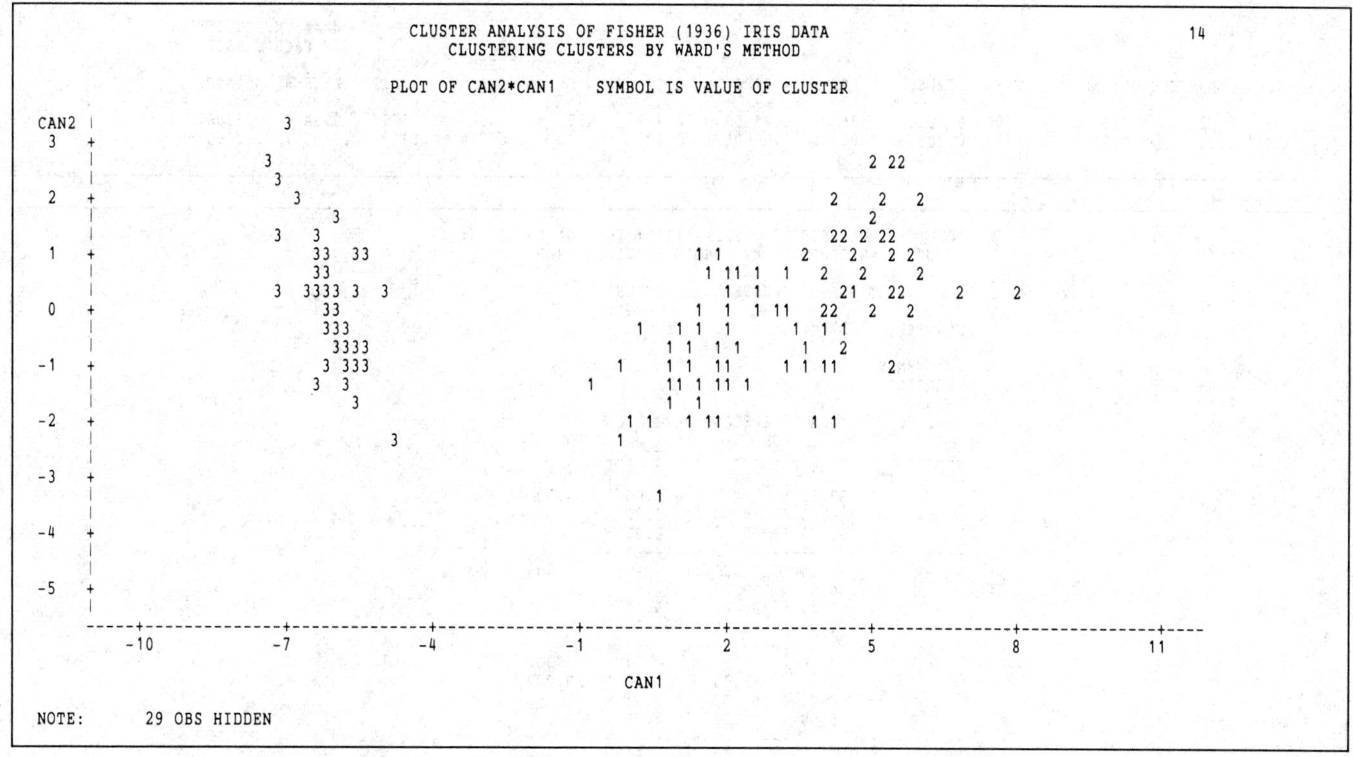

CLUSTER ANALYSIS OF FISHER (1936) IRIS DATA 15
CLUSTERING CLUSTERS BY WONG'S HYBRID METHOD

TWO STAGE DENSITY LINKAGE CLUSTERING

EIGENVALUES OF THE COVARIANCE MATRIX

	EIGENVALUE	DIFFERENCE	PROPORTION	CUMULATIVE
1	416.976	398.666	0.950106	0.95011
2	18.310	14.953	0.041720	0.99183
3	3.357	3.127	0.007649	0.99948
4	0.230	.	0.000524	1.00000

HYBRID METHOD

ROOT-MEAN-SQUARE TOTAL-SAMPLE STANDARD DEVIATION = 10.4747

NCL	CLUSTERS JOINED		FREQ	SPRSQ	RSQ	ERSQ	CCC	PSEUDO F	PSEUDO T**2	FUSION DENSITY	MAXIMUM DENSITY IN EACH CLUSTER LESSER	GREATER
9	OB10	OB7	50	0.01085	0.94718	0.95350	-1.651	316.0	42.2	.049073	.070997	.121951
8	OB8	OB3	36	0.00775	0.93943	0.94781	-1.944	314.6	26.0	.034123	.048111	.059067
7	OB4	OB2	23	0.00196	0.93747	0.94052	-0.658	357.3	6.3	.028994	.010936	.056466
6	CL8	OB9	58	0.02026	0.91721	0.93081	-2.393	319.1	46.3	.025273	.057176	.059067
5	CL7	OB6	30	0.00724	0.90997	0.91724	-1.143	366.4	19.5	.016224	.021507	.056466
4	CL6	OB1	67	0.03047	0.87950	0.89546	-1.403	355.2	41.0	.010261	.013263	.059067
3	CL4	OB5	70	0.01442	0.86508	0.84894	1.190	471.3	12.3	.006324	.007669	.059067

3 MODAL CLUSTERS HAVE BEEN FORMED

NCL	CLUSTERS JOINED		FREQ	SPRSQ	RSQ	ERSQ	CCC	PSEUDO F	PSEUDO T**2	FUSION DENSITY	MAXIMUM DENSITY IN EACH CLUSTER LESSER	GREATER
2	CL3	CL5	100	0.10203	0.76305	0.71598	2.339	476.6	89.5	.023797	.056466	.059067
1	CL2	CL9	150	0.80503	0.00000	0.00000	0.000	.	502.8	.001626	.059067	.121951

CLUSTER ANALYSIS OF FISHER (1936) IRIS DATA 16
CLUSTERING CLUSTERS BY WONG'S HYBRID METHOD

TABLE OF CLUSTER BY SPECIES

CLUSTER SPECIES

FREQUENCY / PERCENT / ROW PCT / COL PCT	SETOSA	VERSICOLOR	VIRGINICA	TOTAL
1	50	0	0	50
	33.33	0.00	0.00	33.33
	100.00	0.00	0.00	
	100.00	0.00	0.00	
2	0	21	49	70
	0.00	14.00	32.67	46.67
	0.00	30.00	70.00	
	0.00	42.00	98.00	
3	0	29	1	30
	0.00	19.33	0.67	20.00
	0.00	96.67	3.33	
	0.00	58.00	2.00	
TOTAL	50	50	50	150
	33.33	33.33	33.33	100.00

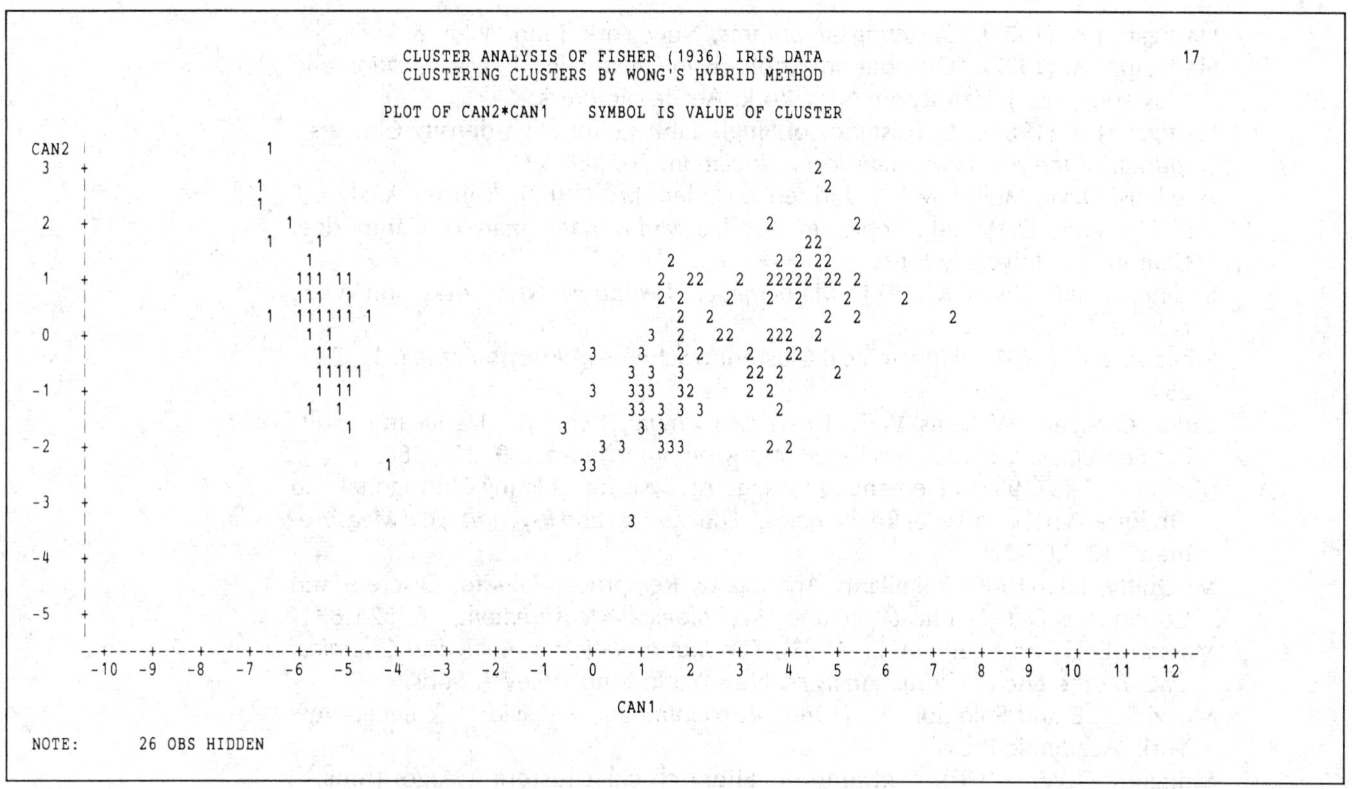

REFERENCES

Anderberg, M.R. (1973), *Cluster Analysis for Applications*, New York: Academic Press.

Batagelj, V. (1981), "Note on Ultrametric Hierarchical Clustering Algorithms," *Psychometrika*, 46, 351-352.

Blashfield, R.K. and Aldenderfer, M.S. (1978), "The Literature on Cluster Analysis," *Multivariate Behavioral Research*, 13, 271-295.

Calinski, T. and Harabasz, J. (1974), "A Dendrite Method for Cluster Analysis," *Communications in Statistics*, 3, 1-27.

Cooper, M.C. and Milligan, G.W. (1984), "The Effect of Error on Determining the Number of Clusters," *College of Administrative Science Working Paper Series 84-2*, Columbus: The Ohio State University.

Duda, R.O. and Hart, P.E. (1973), *Pattern Classification and Scene Analysis*, New York: John Wiley & Sons.

Everitt, B.S. (1980), *Cluster Analysis*, Second Edition, London: Heineman Educational Books Ltd.

Fisher, L. and Van Ness, J.W. (1971), "Admissible Clustering Procedures," *Biometrika*, 58, 91-104.

Fisher, R.A. (1936), "The Use of Multiple Measurements in Taxonomic Problems," *Annals of Eugenics*, 7, 179-188.

Florek, K., Lukaszewicz, J., Perkal, J., and Zubrzycki, S. (1951a), "Sur la Liaison et la Division des Points d'un Ensemble Fini," *Colloquium Mathematicae*, 2, 282-285.

Florek, K., Lukaszewicz, J., Perkal, J., and Zubrzycki, S. (1951b), "Taksonomia Wroclawska," *Przeglad Antropol.*, 17, 193-211.

Gower, J.C. (1967), "A Comparison of Some Methods of Cluster Analysis," *Biometrics*, 23, 623-637.

Hartigan, J.A. (1975), *Clustering Algorithms*, New York: John Wiley & Sons.

Hartigan, J.A. (1977), "Distribution Problems in Clustering," in *Classification and Clustering*, ed. J. Van Ryzin, New York: Academic Press.

Hartigan, J.A. (1981), "Consistency of Single Linkage for High-density Clusters," *Journal of the American Statistical Association*, 76, 388-394.

Hawkins, D.M., Muller, M.W., and ten Krooden, J.A. (1982), "Cluster Analysis," in Hawkins, D.M., ed., *Topics in Applied Multivariate Analysis*, Cambridge: Cambridge University Press.

Jardine, N. and Sibson, R. (1971), *Mathematical Taxonomy*, New York: John Wiley & Sons.

Johnson, S.C. (1967), "Hierarchical Clustering Schemes," *Psychometrika*, 32, 241-254.

Lance, G.N., and Williams, W.T. (1967), "A General Theory of Classificatory Sorting Strategies. I. Hierarchical systems," *Computer Journal*, 9, 373-380.

McQuitty, L.L. (1957), "Elementary Linkage Analysis for Isolating Orthogonal and Oblique Types and Typal Relevancies," *Educational and Psychological Measurement*, 17, 207-229.

McQuitty, L.L. (1966), "Similarity Analysis by Reciprocal Pairs for Discrete and Continuous Data," *Educational and Psychological Measurement*, 26, 825-831.

Massart, D.L. and Kaufman, L. (1983), *The Interpretation of Analytical Chemical Data by the Use of Cluster Analysis*, New York: John Wiley & Sons.

Mezzich, J.E and Solomon, H. (1980), *Taxonomy and Behavioral Science*, New York: Academic Press.

Milligan, G.W. (1979), "Ultrametric Hierarchical Clustering Algorithms," *Psychometrika*, 44, 343-346.

Milligan, G.W. (1980), "An Examination of the Effect of Six Types of Error Perturbation on Fifteen Clustering Algorithms," *Psychometrika*, 45, 325-342.

Milligan, G.W. and Cooper, M.C. (1983), "An Examination of Procedures for Determining the Number of Clusters in a Data Set," *College of Administrative Science Working Paper Series 83-51*, Columbus: The Ohio State University. To appear in *Psychometrika*, 1985.

Sarle, W.S. (1983), "The Cubic Clustering Criterion," SAS Technical Report A-108, Cary, NC: SAS Institute Inc.

Sneath, P.H.A. (1957), "The Application of Computers to Taxonomy," *Journal of General Microbiology*, 17,201-226.

Sneath, P.H.A. and Sokal, R.R. (1973), *Numerical Taxonomy*, San Francisco: Freeman.

Sokal, R.R. and Michener, C.D. (1958), "A Statistical Method for Evaluating Systematic Relationships," *University of Kansas Science Bulletin*, 38, 1409-1438.

Sorensen, T. (1948), "A Method of Establishing Groups of Equal Amplitude in Plant Sociology Based on Similarity of Species Content and Its Application to Analyses of the Vegetation on Danish Commons," *Biologiske Skrifter*, 5, 1-34.

Spath, H. (1980), *Cluster Analysis Algorithms*, Chichester, England: Ellis Horwood.

Symons, M.J. (1981), "Clustering Criteria and Multivariate Normal Mixtures," *Biometrics*, 37, 35-43.

Ward, J.H. (1963), "Hierarchical Grouping to Optimize an Objective Function," *Journal of the American Statistical Association*, 58, 236-244.

Wishart, D. (1969), "Mode Analysis: A Generalisation of Nearest Neighbour Which Reduces Chaining Effects," in *Numerical Taxonomy*, A.J. Cole, ed., London: Academic Press.

Wong, M.A. (1982), "A Hybrid Clustering Method for Identifying High-Density Clusters," *Journal of the American Statistical Association*, 77, 841-847.

Wong, M.A. and Lane, T. (1983), "A *k*th Nearest Neighbor Clustering Procedure," *Journal of the Royal Statistical Society*, Series B, 45, 362-368.

Wong, M.A. and Schaack, C. (1982), "Using the *k*th Nearest Neighbor Clustering Procedure to Determine the Number of Subpopulations," *American Statistical Association 1982 Proceedings of the Statistical Computing Section*, 40-48.

Chapter 16

The DISCRIM Procedure

Operating systems: All

ABSTRACT

The DISCRIM procedure computes linear or quadratic discriminant functions for classifying observations into two or more groups on the basis of one or more numeric variables. The discriminant functions can be stored in an output data set for future use.

INTRODUCTION

For a set of observations containing one or more quantitative variables and a classification variable defining groups of observations, PROC DISCRIM develops a discriminant function to classify each observation into one of the groups. The distribution within each group should be approximately multivariate normal.

The discriminant function, also known as a classification criterion, is determined by a measure of generalized squared distance (Rao 1973). The classification criterion can be based on either the individual within-group covariance matrices or the pooled covariance matrix; it also takes into account the prior probabilities of the groups.

Optionally, DISCRIM tests the homogeneity of the within-group covariance matrices. The results of the test determine whether the classification criterion is based on the within-group covariance matrices or the pooled covariance matrix. This test is not robust against non-normality.

The classification criterion can be applied to a second data set during the same execution of DISCRIM. DISCRIM can also store calibration information in a special SAS data set and apply it to other data sets.

Background

DISCRIM develops a discriminant function or classification criterion using a measure of generalized squared distance assuming that each class has a multivariate normal distribution. The classification criterion is based on either the individual within-group covariance matrices or the pooled covariance matrix; it also takes into account the prior probabilities of the groups. Each observation is placed in the class from which it has the smallest generalized squared distance. DISCRIM can also compute the posterior probability of an observation belonging to each class.

The notation below is used to describe the generalized squared distance:

t	a subscript to distinguish the groups
$\mathbf{S}_t$	the covariance matrix within group t
$\lvert\mathbf{S}_t\rvert$	the determinant of $\mathbf{S}_t$
$\mathbf{S}$	the pooled covariance matrix
$\mathbf{x}$	a vector containing the variables of an observation
$\mathbf{m}_t$	the vector containing means of the variables in the group t
q_t	the prior probability for group t.

The generalized squared distance from $\mathbf{x}$ to group t is

$$D_t^2(\mathbf{x}) = g_1(\mathbf{x}, t) + g_2(t)$$

where

$$g_1(\mathbf{x}, t) = (\mathbf{x} - \mathbf{m}_t)'\mathbf{S}_t^{-1}(\mathbf{x} - \mathbf{m}_t) + \log_e \lvert\mathbf{S}_t\rvert$$

if the within-group covariance matrices are used, or

$$g_1(\mathbf{x}, t) = (\mathbf{x} - \mathbf{m}_t)'\mathbf{S}^{-1}(\mathbf{x} - \mathbf{m}_t)$$

if the pooled covariance matrix is used; and

$$g_2(t) = -2\log_e(q_t)$$

if the prior probabilities are not all equal, or

$$g_2(t) = 0$$

if the prior probabilities are all equal.

The posterior probability of an observation $\mathbf{x}$ belonging to group t is

$$p_t(\mathbf{x}) = \frac{\exp(-0.5D_t^2(\mathbf{x}))}{\Sigma_u(\exp(-0.5D_u^2(\mathbf{x})))} \quad .$$

An observation is classified into group u if setting $t=u$ produces the smallest value of $D_t^2(\mathbf{x})$ or the largest value of $p_t(\mathbf{x})$.

SPECIFICATIONS

The following statements are used with DISCRIM:

PROC DISCRIM *options;*
CLASS *variable;*
VAR *variables;*
ID *variable;*
PRIORS *probabilities;*
TESTCLASS *variable;*
TESTID *variable;*
BY *variables;*

PROC DISCRIM Statement

PROC DISCRIM *options;*

The options below can appear in the PROC DISCRIM statement:

SIMPLE
S

prints simple descriptive statistics for all variables.

POOL=YES
POOL=NO
POOL=TEST

determines whether the pooled or within-group covariance matrix is the basis of the measure of generalized squared distance.

When POOL=YES appears or when the POOL= option is omitted, the measure of generalized squared distance is based on the pooled covariance matrix.

When you specify POOL=NO, the measure is based on the individual within-group covariance matrices.

When you specify POOL=TEST, a likelihood ratio test (Morrison 1976; Kendall and Stuart 1961; Anderson 1958) of the homogeneity of the within-group covariance matrices is made and the result is printed. If the test statistic is significant at the level specified by the SLPOOL= option (below), the within-group matrices are used. Otherwise, the pooled covariance matrix is used.

The discriminant function coefficients are printed only when the pooled covariance matrix is used.

SLPOOL=*n*

specifies the significance level for the test of homogeneity. SLPOOL= is used only when POOL=TEST is also specified.

If POOL=TEST appears but SLPOOL= is omitted, .10 is used as the significance level for the test.

WCOV

prints the within-group covariance matrices.

WCORR

prints the within-group correlation matrices.

PCOV
: prints the pooled covariance matrix.

PCORR
: prints the partial correlation matrix based on the pooled covariance matrix.

LIST
: prints the classification results for each observation.

LISTERR
: prints only misclassified observations.

THRESHOLD=*n*
: specifies the minimum acceptable posterior probability for classification. If the posterior probability associated with the smallest distance is less than the THRESHOLD value, the observation is classified into group OTHER.

DATA=*SASdataset*
: names the data set to be used by DISCRIM. If DATA= is omitted, DISCRIM uses the last SAS data set created.

NOSUMMARY
: produces a classification summary of the discriminant model unless NOSUMMARY is specified.

OUT=*SASdataset*
: names the output SAS data set. If you want to create a permanent SAS data set with PROC DISCRIM, you must specify a two-level name (see "SAS Files" in the *SAS User's Guide: Basics* for more information on permanent SAS data sets).

TESTDATA=*SASdataset*
: names a second data set whose observations are to be classified. The variable names in this data set must match those in the DATA= data set.

  When TESTDATA= is specified, TESTCLASS and TESTID statements can also be used (see below).

TESTLIST
: lists all observations in the TESTDATA= data set.

TESTLISTERR
: lists only misclassified observations in the TESTDATA= data set.

CLASS Statement

CLASS *variable*;

The classification *variable* values define the groups for analysis. Class levels are determined by the unformatted values of the class variable. The specified variable can be numeric or character. A CLASS statement must accompany the PROC DISCRIM statement.

VAR Statement

VAR *variables;*

The VAR statement specifies the quantitative variables to be included in the analysis. If you do not use a VAR statement, the analysis includes all numeric variables not listed in other statements.

ID Statement

ID *variable;*

The ID statement is effective only when LIST or LISTERR appears in the PROC DISCRIM statement. When DISCRIM prints the classification results, the ID *variable* is printed for each observation, rather than the observation number.

PRIORS Statement

PRIORS *probabilities;*

You need a PRIORS statement whenever you do not want DISCRIM to assume that the prior probabilities are equal.

If you want to set the prior probabilities proportional to the sample sizes, use:

```
PRIORS PROPORTIONAL;
```

The keyword PROPORTIONAL can be abbreviated PROP.

If you want other than equal or proportional priors, give the prior probability you want for each level of the classification variable. Each class level can be written as a numeric constant, a SAS name, or a quoted string, and it must be followed by an equal sign and a numeric constant between zero and one. For example, to define prior probabilities for each level of GRADE, where GRADE's values are A, B, C, and D, you can use the statement:

```
PRIORS A=.1  B=.3  C=.5  D=.1;
```

If GRADE were numeric, with values of 1, 2, and 3, the PRIORS statement can be:

```
PRIORS 1=.3  2=.6  3=.1;
```

The prior probabilities specified should sum to one.

TESTCLASS Statement

TESTCLASS *variable;*

The TESTCLASS statement names the *variable* in the TESTDATA= data set to use in determining whether an observation in the TESTDATA= data set is misclassified. The TESTCLASS variable should have the same type (character or numeric) and length as the variable given in the CLASS statement. DISCRIM considers an observation misclassified when the TESTCLASS variable's value does not match the group into which the TESTDATA= observation is classified.

TESTID Statement

TESTID *variable;*

When the TESTID statement appears and the TESTLIST or TESTLISTERR options also appear, DISCRIM uses the value of the TESTID variable, instead of the observation number, to identify each observation in the classification results for the TESTDATA= data set. The variable given in the TESTID statement must be in the TESTDATA= data set.

BY Statement

BY *variables;*

A BY statement can be used with PROC DISCRIM to obtain separate analyses on observations in groups defined by the BY variables. When a BY statement appears, the procedure expects the DATA= data set to be sorted in order of the BY variables. If your DATA= data set is not sorted in ascending order, use the SORT procedure with a similar BY statement to sort the data, or, if appropriate, use the BY statement options NOTSORTED or DESCENDING. For more information, see the discussion of the BY statement in "Statements Used in the PROC Step" in the *SAS User's Guide: Basics*.

If TESTDATA= is specified and the TESTDATA= data set does not contain any of the BY variables, then the entire TESTDATA= data set is classified according to the discriminant functions computed in each BY group in the DATA= data set.

If the TESTDATA= data set contains some but not all of the BY variables, or if some BY variables do not have the same type or length in the TESTDATA= data set as in the DATA= data set, then DISCRIM prints an error message and stops.

If all the BY variables appear in the TESTDATA= data set with the same type and length as in the DATA= data set, then each BY group in the TESTDATA= data set is classified by the discriminant function from the corresponding BY group in the DATA= data set. The BY groups in the TESTDATA= data set must be in the same order as in the DATA= data set. If NOTSORTED is specified on the BY statement, there must be exactly the same BY groups in the same order in both data sets. If NOTSORTED is not specified, it is permissible for some BY groups to appear in one data set but not in the other.

DETAILS

Missing Values

Observations with missing values for variables in the analysis are excluded from the development of the classification criterion. When the classification variable's values are missing, the observation is excluded from the development of the classification criterion, but if no other variables in the analysis have missing values for that observation, it is classified and printed with the classification results.

Saving and Using Calibration Information

Calibration information developed by DISCRIM can be saved in a SAS data set by specifying OUT= followed by the data set name in the PROC DISCRIM statement. DISCRIM then creates a specially structured SAS data set of TYPE=DISCAL that contains the calibration information.

To use this calibration information to classify observations in another data set:

- give the calibration data set after DATA= in the PROC DISCRIM statement, and
- give the data set to be classified after TESTDATA= in the PROC DISCRIM statement.

Only the TESTLIST, TESTLISTERR, and THRESHOLD options and the TESTCLASS and TESTID statements are effective in this case.

Here is an example:

```
DATA ORIGINAL;
   INPUT POSITION X1 X2;
   CARDS;
   data lines
PROC DISCRIM OUT=INFO;
   CLASS POSITION;
```

```
DATA CHECK;
   INPUT POSITION X1 X2;
   CARDS;
   second set of data lines
PROC DISCRIM DATA=INFO TESTDATA=CHECK TESTLIST;
   TESTCLASS POSITION;
```

The first DATA step creates the SAS data set ORIGINAL, which DISCRIM uses to develop a classification criterion. Specifying OUT=INFO in the PROC DISCRIM statement causes DISCRIM to store the calibration information in a new data set called INFO. The next DATA step creates the data set CHECK. The second PROC DISCRIM specifies DATA=INFO and TESTDATA=CHECK so that the classification criterion developed earlier is applied to the CHECK data set.

Machine Resources

Core requirements In the following discussion, let *n* equal the number of observations, *c* equal the number of class levels, and *v* equal the number of variables. If POOL=YES, DISCRIM needs core for one covariance matrix. If POOL=NO, DISCRIM needs core for one covariance matrix for each class plus the pooled covariance matrix. Each covariance matrix requires $4v(v + 1)$ bytes. Additional array storage is about $48v + 124c + 4c^2+2cv$ bytes.

Time requirements There are three stages in the time requirements of discriminant analysis.

1. Time needed for reading the data and computing covariance matrices is proportional to nv^2. DISCRIM must also look up each class level in the list; the time for this is proportional to c (this is faster if the data are sorted by the CLASS variable). Time for this step is proportional to a value ranging from *n* to *nc*.
2. Time for inverting covariance matrices is proportional to v^3 for each covariance matrix.
3. Time for classifying observations is proportional to *ncv*.

Each stage has a different constant of proportionality.

Printed Output

The printed output from PROC DISCRIM includes:

1. values of the classification variable, FREQUENCY (frequencies), and the PRIOR PROBABILITIES for each group.
2. optionally, SIMPLE descriptive STATISTICS including N (the number of observations), SUM, MEAN, VARIANCE, and STANDARD DEVIATION for each group.
3. optionally, the WITHIN COVARIANCE MATRICES, $\mathbf{S}_t$ for each group.
4. optionally, WITHIN CORRELATION COEFFICIENTS (the within-group correlation matrix for each group) and PROB>|R| to test the hypothesis that the population correlation coefficients are zero.
5. optionally, the POOLED COVARIANCE MATRIX, **S**.
6. optionally, PARTIAL CORRELATION COEFFICIENTS COMPUTED FROM POOLED COVARIANCE MATRIX (the partial correlation matrix based on the pooled covariance matrix) and PROB > |R| to test the hypothesis that the population correlation coefficients are zero.
7. WITHIN COVARIANCE MATRIX INFORMATION including COVARIANCE MATRIX RANK and NATURAL LOG OF DETERMINANT

OF THE COVARIANCE MATRIX for each group (the rank of $\mathbf{S}_t$ and $\log_e |\mathbf{S}_t|$ and pooled (the rank of $\mathbf{S}$ and $\log_e |\mathbf{S}|$).

8. optionally, TEST OF HOMOGENEITY OF WITHIN COVARIANCE MATRICES (the results of a chi-square test of homogeneity of the within-group covariance matrices) (Morrison 1976; Kendall and Stuart 1961; Anderson 1958).
9. the PAIRWISE SQUARED GENERALIZED DISTANCES BETWEEN GROUPS.
10. if the pooled covariance matrix is used, the LINEAR DISCRIMINANT FUNCTION
11. optionally, the CLASSIFICATION RESULTS FOR CALIBRATION DATA including OBS, the observation number (if an ID statement is included, the values of the identification variable are printed instead of the observation number), the actual group for the observation, the group into which the developed criterion would classify it, and the POSTERIOR PROBABILITY of its MEMBERSHIP in each group.
12. a CLASSIFICATION SUMMARY FOR CALIBRATION DATA, summary of the performance of the classification criterion.

EXAMPLES

Iris Data: Example 1

The iris data published by Fisher (1936) have been widely used for examples in discriminant analysis and cluster analysis. The sepal length, sepal width, petal length, and petal width were measured in millimeters on fifty iris specimens from each of three species, *Iris setosa, I. versicolor,* and *I. virginica*. DISCRIM is used to classify the irises using a quadratic classification function.

```
DATA IRIS;
   TITLE 'FISHER (1936) IRIS DATA';
   INPUT SEPALLEN SEPALWID PETALLEN PETALWID SPEC_NO @@;
   IF SPEC_NO=1 THEN SPECIES='SETOSA    ';
   IF SPEC_NO=2 THEN SPECIES='VERSICOLOR';
   IF SPEC_NO=3 THEN SPECIES='VIRGINICA ';
   DROP SPEC_NO;
   LABEL SEPALLEN=SEPAL LENGTH IN MM.
         SEPALWID=SEPAL WIDTH  IN MM.
         PETALLEN=PETAL LENGTH IN MM.
         PETALWID=PETAL WIDTH  IN MM.;
   CARDS;
50 33 14 02 1 64 28 56 22 3 65 28 46 15 2
67 31 56 24 3 63 28 51 15 3 46 34 14 03 1
69 31 51 23 3 62 22 45 15 2 59 32 48 18 2
46 36 10 02 1 61 30 46 14 2 60 27 51 16 2
65 30 52 20 3 56 25 39 11 2 65 30 55 18 3
58 27 51 19 3 68 32 59 23 3 51 33 17 05 1
57 28 45 13 2 62 34 54 23 3 77 38 67 22 3
63 33 47 16 2 67 33 57 25 3 76 30 66 21 3
49 25 45 17 3 55 35 13 02 1 67 30 52 23 3
70 32 47 14 2 64 32 45 15 2 61 28 40 13 2
48 31 16 02 1 59 30 51 18 3 55 24 38 11 2
63 25 50 19 3 64 32 53 23 3 52 34 14 02 1
49 36 14 01 1 54 30 45 15 2 79 38 64 20 3
44 32 13 02 1 67 33 57 21 3 50 35 16 06 1
58 26 40 12 2 44 30 13 02 1 77 28 67 20 3
63 27 49 18 3 47 32 16 02 1 55 26 44 12 2
50 23 33 10 2 72 32 60 18 3 48 30 14 03 1
51 38 16 02 1 61 30 49 18 3 48 34 19 02 1
```

```
50 30 16 02 1 50 32 12 02 1 61 26 56 14 3
64 28 56 21 3 43 30 11 01 1 58 40 12 02 1
51 38 19 04 1 67 31 44 14 2 62 28 48 18 3
49 30 14 02 1 51 35 14 02 1 56 30 45 15 2
58 27 41 10 2 50 34 16 04 1 46 32 14 02 1
60 29 45 15 2 57 26 35 10 2 57 44 15 04 1
50 36 14 02 1 77 30 61 23 3 63 34 56 24 3
58 27 51 19 3 57 29 42 13 2 72 30 58 16 3
54 34 15 04 1 52 41 15 01 1 71 30 59 21 3
64 31 55 18 3 60 30 48 18 3 63 29 56 18 3
49 24 33 10 2 56 27 42 13 2 57 30 42 12 2
55 42 14 02 1 49 31 15 02 1 77 26 69 23 3
60 22 50 15 3 54 39 17 04 1 66 29 46 13 2
52 27 39 14 2 60 34 45 16 2 50 34 15 02 1
44 29 14 02 1 50 20 35 10 2 55 24 37 10 2
58 27 39 12 2 47 32 13 02 1 46 31 15 02 1
69 32 57 23 3 62 29 43 13 2 74 28 61 19 3
59 30 42 15 2 51 34 15 02 1 50 35 13 03 1
56 28 49 20 3 60 22 40 10 2 73 29 63 18 3
67 25 58 18 3 49 31 15 01 1 67 31 47 15 2
63 23 44 13 2 54 37 15 02 1 56 30 41 13 2
63 25 49 15 2 61 28 47 12 2 64 29 43 13 2
51 25 30 11 2 57 28 41 13 2 65 30 58 22 3
69 31 54 21 3 54 39 13 04 1 51 35 14 03 1
72 36 61 25 3 65 32 51 20 3 61 29 47 14 2
56 29 36 13 2 69 31 49 15 2 64 27 53 19 3
68 30 55 21 3 55 25 40 13 2 48 34 16 02 1
48 30 14 01 1 45 23 13 03 1 57 25 50 20 3
57 38 17 03 1 51 38 15 03 1 55 23 40 13 2
66 30 44 14 2 68 28 48 14 2 54 34 17 02 1
51 37 15 04 1 52 35 15 02 1 58 28 51 24 3
67 30 50 17 2 63 33 60 25 3 53 37 15 02 1
;
PROC DISCRIM SIMPLE WCOV WCORR PCOV PCORR LISTERR POOL=TEST;
   CLASS SPECIES;
```

Output 16.1 Analysis of Iris Data Using PROC DISCRIM

FISHER (1936) IRIS DATA 1

❶ DISCRIMINANT ANALYSIS

SPECIES	FREQUENCY	PRIOR PROBABILITY
SETOSA	50	0.33333333
VERSICOLOR	50	0.33333333
VIRGINICA	50	0.33333333
TOTAL	150	1.00000000

FISHER (1936) IRIS DATA 2

❷ DISCRIMINANT ANALYSIS SIMPLE STATISTICS

SPECIES = SETOSA

VARIABLE	N	SUM	MEAN	VARIANCE	STANDARD DEVIATION
SEPALLEN	50	2503.00000000	50.06000000	12.42489796	3.52489687
SEPALWID	50	1714.00000000	34.28000000	14.36897959	3.79064369
PETALLEN	50	731.00000000	14.62000000	3.01591837	1.73663996
PETALWID	50	123.00000000	2.46000000	1.11061224	1.05385589

(continued on next page)

(continued from previous page)

```
                                         SPECIES = VERSICOLOR

SEPALLEN        50         2968.00000000          59.36000000           26.64326531           5.16171147
SEPALWID        50         1385.00000000          27.70000000            9.84693878           3.13798323
PETALLEN        50         2130.00000000          42.60000000           22.08163265           4.69910977
PETALWID        50          663.00000000          13.26000000            3.91061224           1.97752680
--------------------------------------------------------------------------------------------------------

                                         SPECIES = VIRGINICA

SEPALLEN        50         3294.00000000          65.88000000           40.43428571           6.35879593
SEPALWID        50         1487.00000000          29.74000000           10.40040816           3.22496638
PETALLEN        50         2776.00000000          55.52000000           30.45877551           5.51894696
PETALWID        50         1013.00000000          20.26000000            7.54326531           2.74650056
```

❸

```
                                        FISHER (1936) IRIS DATA                                     3

                               DISCRIMINANT ANALYSIS     WITHIN COVARIANCE MATRICES

                                   SPECIES = SETOSA            DF =     49

                 VARIABLE            SEPALLEN            SEPALWID            PETALLEN            PETALWID

                 SEPALLEN         12.42489796          9.92163265          1.63551020          1.03306122
                 SEPALWID          9.92163265         14.36897959          1.16979592          0.92979592
                 PETALLEN          1.63551020          1.16979592          3.01591837          0.60693878
                 PETALWID          1.03306122          0.92979592          0.60693878          1.11061224

                 ---------------------------------------------------------------------------------------

                                   SPECIES = VERSICOLOR        DF =     49

                 VARIABLE            SEPALLEN            SEPALWID            PETALLEN            PETALWID

                 SEPALLEN         26.64326531          8.51836735         18.28979592          5.57795918
                 SEPALWID          8.51836735          9.84693878          8.26530612          4.12040816
                 PETALLEN         18.28979592          8.26530612         22.08163265          7.31020408
                 PETALWID          5.57795918          4.12040816          7.31020408          3.91061224

                 ---------------------------------------------------------------------------------------

                                   SPECIES = VIRGINICA         DF =     49

                 VARIABLE            SEPALLEN            SEPALWID            PETALLEN            PETALWID

                 SEPALLEN         40.43428571          9.37632653         30.32897959          4.90938776
                 SEPALWID          9.37632653         10.40040816          7.13795918          4.76285714
                 PETALLEN         30.32897959          7.13795918         30.45877551          4.88244898
                 PETALWID          4.90938776          4.76285714          4.88244898          7.54326531
```

❹

```
                                        FISHER (1936) IRIS DATA                                     4

                    DISCRIMINANT ANALYSIS     WITHIN CORRELATION COEFFICIENTS    /    PROBABILITY > |R|

                                              SPECIES = SETOSA

                              VARIABLE    SEPALLEN    SEPALWID    PETALLEN    PETALWID

                              SEPALLEN    1.000000    0.742547    0.267176    0.278098
                                            0.0000      0.0001      0.0607      0.0505

                              SEPALWID    0.742547    1.000000    0.177700    0.232752
                                            0.0001      0.0000      0.2170      0.1038

                              PETALLEN    0.267176    0.177700    1.000000    0.331630
                                            0.0607      0.2170      0.0000      0.0186

                              PETALWID    0.278098    0.232752    0.331630    1.000000
                                            0.0505      0.1038      0.0186      0.0000

                              ------------------------------------------------------

                                              SPECIES = VERSICOLOR

                              VARIABLE    SEPALLEN    SEPALWID    PETALLEN    PETALWID

                              SEPALLEN    1.000000    0.525911    0.754049    0.546461
                                            0.0000      0.0001      0.0001      0.0001
```

(continued on next page)

(continued from previous page)

VARIABLE	SEPALLEN	SEPALWID	PETALLEN	PETALWID
SEPALWID	0.525911 0.0001	1.000000 0.0000	0.560522 0.0001	0.663999 0.0001
PETALLEN	0.754049 0.0001	0.560522 0.0001	1.000000 0.0000	0.786668 0.0001
PETALWID	0.546461 0.0001	0.663999 0.0001	0.786668 0.0001	1.000000 0.0000

SPECIES = VIRGINICA

VARIABLE	SEPALLEN	SEPALWID	PETALLEN	PETALWID
SEPALLEN	1.000000 0.0000	0.457228 0.0008	0.864225 0.0001	0.281108 0.0480
SEPALWID	0.457228 0.0008	1.000000 0.0000	0.401045 0.0039	0.537728 0.0001
PETALLEN	0.864225 0.0001	0.401045 0.0039	1.000000 0.0000	0.322108 0.0225
PETALWID	0.281108 0.0480	0.537728 0.0001	0.322108 0.0225	1.000000 0.0000

FISHER (1936) IRIS DATA 5

❺

DISCRIMINANT ANALYSIS POOLED COVARIANCE MATRIX DF = 147

VARIABLE	SEPALLEN	SEPALWID	PETALLEN	PETALWID
SEPALLEN	26.50081633	9.27210884	16.75142857	3.84013605
SEPALWID	9.27210884	11.53877551	5.52435374	3.27102041
PETALLEN	16.75142857	5.52435374	18.51877551	4.26653061
PETALWID	3.84013605	3.27102041	4.26653061	4.18816327

FISHER (1936) IRIS DATA 6

❻

DISCRIMINANT ANALYSIS PARTIAL CORRELATION COEFFICIENTS COMPUTED FROM POOLED COVARIANCE MATRIX / PROB > |R|

VARIABLE	SEPALLEN	SEPALWID	PETALLEN	PETALWID
SEPALLEN	1.000000 0.0000	0.530236 0.0001	0.756164 0.0001	0.364506 0.0001
SEPALWID	0.530236 0.0001	1.000000 0.0000	0.377916 0.0001	0.470535 0.0001
PETALLEN	0.756164 0.0001	0.377916 0.0001	1.000000 0.0000	0.484459 0.0001
PETALWID	0.364506 0.0001	0.470535 0.0001	0.484459 0.0001	1.000000 0.0000

FISHER (1936) IRIS DATA 7

❼

DISCRIMINANT ANALYSIS WITHIN COVARIANCE MATRIX INFORMATION

SPECIES	COVARIANCE MATRIX RANK	NATURAL LOG OF DETERMINANT OF THE COVARIANCE MATRIX
SETOSA	4	5.35332042
VERSICOLOR	4	7.54635570
VIRGINICA	4	9.49362227
POOLED	4	8.46214197

❽

```
                              FISHER (1936) IRIS DATA                                      8

        DISCRIMINANT ANALYSIS     TEST OF HOMOGENEITY OF WITHIN COVARIANCE MATRICES

              NOTATION:  K     =    NUMBER OF GROUPS

                         P     =    NUMBER OF VARIABLES

                         N     =    TOTAL NUMBER OF OBSERVATIONS

                         N(I) =     NUMBER OF OBSERVATIONS IN THE I'TH GROUP

                                     __                      N(I)/2
                                     ||   |WITHIN SS MATRIX(I)|
                         V     =    ----------------------------------
                                                          N/2
                                          |POOLED SS MATRIX|

                                          _            _     2
                                          |      1        1   |  2P + 3P - 1
                         RHO   =    1.0 - | SUM ------  -  ---  |  ------------
                                          |_     N(I)-1    N-K _|  6(P+1)(K-1)

                         DF    =    .5(K-1)P(P+1)

                        _                  _
                        |     PN/2          |
                        |    N        V     |
UNDER NULL HYPOTHESIS:  -2 RHO LN | ------------------ |  IS DISTRIBUTED APPROXIMATELY AS CHI-SQUARE(DF)
                        |    __      PN(I)/2 |
                        |_   ||  N(I)       _|

TEST CHI-SQUARE VALUE =          143.81943870     WITH        20 DF    PROB > CHI-SQ = 0.0001

SINCE THE CHI-SQUARE VALUE IS SIGNIFICANT AT THE 0.1000 LEVEL, THE WITHIN COVARIANCE MATRICES WILL BE USED IN
THE DISCRIMINANT FUNCTION.

REFERENCE: KENDALL,M.G. AND A.STUART  THE ADVANCED THEORY OF STATISTICS VOL.3 P266 & 282.
```

❾

```
                              FISHER (1936) IRIS DATA                                      9

        DISCRIMINANT ANALYSIS     PAIRWISE SQUARED GENERALIZED DISTANCES BETWEEN GROUPS

                    2            _    _          -1  _    _
                   D (I|J) = (X - X )' COV    (X - X ) + LN |COV |
                                I   J      J     I   J          J

                            GENERALIZED SQUARED DISTANCE TO SPECIES

        FROM SPECIES                 SETOSA          VERSICOLOR          VIRGINICA

            SETOSA               5.35332042        110.74017480       178.26120901
            VERSICOLOR         328.41534800          7.54635570        23.33237667
            VIRGINICA          711.43825544         25.41305990         9.49362227
```

⓫

```
                              FISHER (1936) IRIS DATA                                     10

        DISCRIMINANT ANALYSIS     CLASSIFICATION RESULTS FOR CALIBRATION DATA: WORK.IRIS

     GENERALIZED SQUARED DISTANCE FUNCTION:        POSTERIOR PROBABILITY OF MEMBERSHIP IN EACH SPECIES:

      2           _      -1   _                                     2                     2
     D (X) = (X-X )' COV   (X-X ) + LN |COV |       PR(J|X) = EXP(-.5 D (X)) / SUM EXP(-.5 D (X))
      J           J      J     J           J                        J          K          K

                                                        POSTERIOR PROBABILITY OF MEMBERSHIP IN SPECIES:

              OBS   FROM          CLASSIFIED              SETOSA  VERSICOLOR   VIRGINICA
                    SPECIES       INTO SPECIES

                5   VIRGINICA     VERSICOLOR   *          0.0000     0.6050       0.3950
                9   VERSICOLOR    VIRGINICA    *          0.0000     0.3359       0.6641
               12   VERSICOLOR    VIRGINICA    *          0.0000     0.1543       0.8457

                              * MISCLASSIFIED OBSERVATION
```

```
                                   FISHER (1936) IRIS DATA                                          11
                         ⓬
          DISCRIMINANT ANALYSIS     CLASSIFICATION SUMMARY FOR CALIBRATION DATA: WORK.IRIS

GENERALIZED SQUARED DISTANCE FUNCTION:          POSTERIOR PROBABILITY OF MEMBERSHIP IN EACH SPECIES:

 2         _         -1   _                                         2                   2
D (X) = (X-X )' COV   (X-X ) + LN |COV |         PR(J|X) = EXP(-.5 D (X)) / SUM EXP(-.5 D (X))
 J          J      J     J            J                             J         K         K

                                   NUMBER OF OBSERVATIONS AND PERCENTS CLASSIFIED INTO SPECIES:
                   FROM
                   SPECIES           SETOSA  VERSICOLOR   VIRGINICA      TOTAL

                   SETOSA                50           0           0         50
                                     100.00        0.00        0.00     100.00

                   VERSICOLOR             0          48           2         50
                                       0.00       96.00        4.00     100.00

                   VIRGINICA              0           1          49         50
                                       0.00        2.00       98.00     100.00

                   TOTAL                 50          49          51        150
                   PERCENT            33.33       32.67       34.00     100.00

                   PRIORS            0.3333      0.3333      0.3333
```

In the PROC DISCRIM statement, the WCOV, WCORR, PCOV, and PCORR options ask DISCRIM to print the within-group covariance and correlation matrices, the pooled covariance matrix, and the partial correlation matrix based on the pooled covariance matrix. The LISTERR option requests the classification results for misclassified observations. POOL=TEST asks DISCRIM to test the homogeneity of the within-group covariance matrices. The test is significant at the .10 level, so the covariance matrices are not pooled and the quadratic classification criterion is used.

Remote-Sensing Data on Crops: Example 2

In the example below, the observations are grouped into five crops: clover, corn, cotton, soybeans, and sugar beets. Four measures called X1-X4 make up the descriptive variables. The first PROC DISCRIM statement creates a calibration data set using the OUT= option. The second DISCRIM statement uses the information in the calibration data set to classify a test data set. Note that the values of the identification variable, XVALUES, are obtained by rereading the X1-X4 fields in the data lines as one character variable.

```
DATA CROPS;
   TITLE 'REMOTE SENSING DATA ON FIVE CROPS';
   INPUT CROP $ 1-10 X1-X4 XVALUES $ 11-21;
   CARDS;
CORN      16 27 31 33
CORN      15 23 30 30
CORN      16 27 27 26
CORN      18 20 25 23
CORN      15 15 31 32
CORN      15 32 32 15
CORN      12 15 16 73
SOYBEANS  20 23 23 25
SOYBEANS  24 24 25 32
SOYBEANS  21 25 23 24
SOYBEANS  27 45 24 12
SOYBEANS  12 13 15 42
SOYBEANS  22 32 31 43
```

```
COTTON    31 32 33 34
COTTON    29 24 26 28
COTTON    34 32 28 45
COTTON    26 25 23 24
COTTON    53 48 75 26
COTTON    34 35 25 78
SUGARBEETS22 23 25 42
SUGARBEETS25 25 24 26
SUGARBEETS34 25 16 52
SUGARBEETS54 23 21 54
SUGARBEETS25 43 32 15
SUGARBEETS26 54  2 54
CLOVER    12 45 32 54
CLOVER    24 58 25 34
CLOVER    87 54 61 21
CLOVER    51 31 31 16
CLOVER    96 48 54 62
CLOVER    31 31 11 11
CLOVER    56 13 13 71
CLOVER    32 13 27 32
CLOVER    36 26 54 32
CLOVER    53 08 06 54
CLOVER    32 32 62 16
;
PROC DISCRIM DATA=CROPS POOL=YES LIST OUT=CROPCAL;
  CLASS CROP;
  ID XVALUES;
  VAR X1-X4;
  TITLE2 'CLASSIFICATION OF CROP DATA';

DATA TEST;
   INPUT CROP $ 1-10 X1-X4 XVALUES $ 11-21;
   CARDS;
CORN      16 27 31 33
SOYBEANS  21 25 23 24
COTTON    29 24 26 28
SUGARBEETS54 23 21 54
CLOVER    32 32 62 16
;
PROC DISCRIM DATA=CROPCAL TESTDATA=TEST TESTLIST;
  CLASS CROP;
  TESTCLASS CROP;
  TESTID XVALUES;
  VAR X1-X4;
  TITLE2 'CLASSIFICATION OF TEST DATA';
```

Output 16.2 Remote Sensing Data on Five Crops: PROC DISCRIM

REMOTE SENSING DATA ON FIVE CROPS 1
CLASSIFICATION OF CROP DATA

DISCRIMINANT ANALYSIS

CROP	FREQUENCY	PRIOR PROBABILITY
CLOVER	11	0.20000000
CORN	7	0.20000000
COTTON	6	0.20000000
SOYBEANS	6	0.20000000
SUGARBEETS	6	0.20000000
-----	--	----------
TOTAL	36	1.00000000

REMOTE SENSING DATA ON FIVE CROPS 2
CLASSIFICATION OF CROP DATA

DISCRIMINANT ANALYSIS POOLED COVARIANCE MATRIX INFORMATION

COVARIANCE MATRIX RANK	NATURAL LOG OF DETERMINANT OF THE COVARIANCE MATRIX
4	21.30189392

REMOTE SENSING DATA ON FIVE CROPS 3
CLASSIFICATION OF CROP DATA

DISCRIMINANT ANALYSIS PAIRWISE SQUARED GENERALIZED DISTANCES BETWEEN GROUPS

$$D^2(I|J) = (\bar{X}_I - \bar{X}_J)' \, COV^{-1} \, (\bar{X}_I - \bar{X}_J)$$

GENERALIZED SQUARED DISTANCE TO CROP

FROM CROP	CLOVER	CORN	COTTON	SOYBEANS	SUGARBEETS
CLOVER	0.00000000	4.25308108	0.86616669	2.58313162	1.48909745
CORN	4.25308108	0.00000000	1.88446483	0.73030740	2.89042690
COTTON	0.86616669	1.88446483	0.00000000	1.43466961	1.29555784
SOYBEANS	2.58313162	0.73030740	1.43466961	0.00000000	1.07646391
SUGARBEETS	1.48909745	2.89042690	1.29555784	1.07646391	0.00000000

⑩ REMOTE SENSING DATA ON FIVE CROPS 4
CLASSIFICATION OF CROP DATA

DISCRIMINANT ANALYSIS LINEAR DISCRIMINANT FUNCTION

$$CONSTANT = -.5 \, \bar{X}_J' \, COV^{-1} \, \bar{X}_J \qquad COEFFICIENT\ VECTOR = COV^{-1} \, \bar{X}_J$$

CROP

	CLOVER	CORN	COTTON	SOYBEANS	SUGARBEETS
CONSTANT	-9.79894962	-6.08308779	-9.67360774	-5.49083759	-8.01003003
X1	0.08907263	-0.04180494	0.02462407	0.00003693	0.04244951
X2	0.17378658	0.11970448	0.17595574	0.15896277	0.20987506
X3	0.11899303	0.16510688	0.15880134	0.10622011	0.06540371
X4	0.15637491	0.16768459	0.18361917	0.14132806	0.16407580

REMOTE SENSING DATA ON FIVE CROPS
CLASSIFICATION OF CROP DATA
5

DISCRIMINANT ANALYSIS CLASSIFICATION RESULTS FOR CALIBRATION DATA: WORK.CROPS

GENERALIZED SQUARED DISTANCE FUNCTION:

$$D_J^2(X) = (X-\bar{X}_J)'\ COV^{-1}\ (X-\bar{X}_J)$$

POSTERIOR PROBABILITY OF MEMBERSHIP IN EACH CROP:

$$PR(J|X) = EXP(-.5\ D_J^2(X))\ /\ SUM_K\ EXP(-.5\ D_K^2(X))$$

POSTERIOR PROBABILITY OF MEMBERSHIP IN CROP:

XVALUES	FROM CROP	CLASSIFIED INTO CROP	CLOVER	CORN	COTTON	SOYBEANS	SUGARBEETS
16 27 31 33	CORN	CORN	0.0541	0.3855	0.1956	0.2653	0.0995
15 23 30 30	CORN	CORN	0.0466	0.4341	0.1579	0.2811	0.0802
16 27 27 26	CORN	SOYBEANS *	0.0591	0.3236	0.1506	0.3390	0.1277
18 20 25 23	CORN	SOYBEANS *	0.0637	0.3460	0.1198	0.3645	0.1060
15 15 31 32	CORN	CORN	0.0360	0.5535	0.1317	0.2342	0.0447
15 32 32 15	CORN	SOYBEANS *	0.0583	0.3091	0.1450	0.3762	0.1112
12 15 16 73	CORN	CORN	0.0274	0.4964	0.2044	0.1521	0.1197
20 23 23 25	SOYBEANS	SOYBEANS	0.0807	0.2672	0.1307	0.3675	0.1539
24 24 25 32	SOYBEANS	SOYBEANS	0.1091	0.2407	0.1794	0.3009	0.1698
21 25 23 24	SOYBEANS	SOYBEANS	0.0900	0.2320	0.1336	0.3696	0.1748
27 45 24 12	SOYBEANS	SUGARBEETS *	0.1452	0.0530	0.1148	0.3075	0.3795
12 13 15 42	SOYBEANS	CORN *	0.0330	0.4487	0.1014	0.3052	0.1117
22 32 31 43	SOYBEANS	COTTON *	0.0898	0.2494	0.2929	0.2063	0.1616
31 32 33 34	COTTON	COTTON	0.1806	0.1530	0.2795	0.2078	0.1791
29 24 26 28	COTTON	SOYBEANS *	0.1601	0.1838	0.1780	0.2967	0.1814
34 32 28 45	COTTON	COTTON	0.2021	0.1040	0.2851	0.1609	0.2480
26 25 23 24	COTTON	SOYBEANS *	0.1318	0.1767	0.1418	0.3469	0.2028
53 48 75 26	COTTON	COTTON	0.3407	0.0432	0.5660	0.0288	0.0214
34 35 25 78	COTTON	COTTON	0.1389	0.0768	0.4300	0.0669	0.2875
22 23 25 42	SUGARBEETS	CORN *	0.0870	0.2947	0.2132	0.2503	0.1548
25 25 24 26	SUGARBEETS	SOYBEANS *	0.1219	0.1994	0.1537	0.3359	0.1891
34 25 16 52	SUGARBEETS	SUGARBEETS	0.1869	0.0874	0.1949	0.1731	0.3576
54 23 21 54	SUGARBEETS	CLOVER *	0.4743	0.0232	0.1749	0.0694	0.2582
25 43 32 15	SUGARBEETS	SOYBEANS *	0.1398	0.1104	0.1868	0.3144	0.2486
26 54 2 54	SUGARBEETS	SUGARBEETS	0.0483	0.0072	0.0543	0.0688	0.8214
12 45 32 54	CLOVER	COTTON *	0.0406	0.2453	0.3648	0.1570	0.1923
24 58 25 34	CLOVER	SUGARBEETS *	0.0977	0.0351	0.1826	0.1579	0.5267
87 54 61 21	CLOVER	CLOVER	0.8835	0.0005	0.0831	0.0043	0.0287
51 31 31 16	CLOVER	CLOVER	0.5211	0.0253	0.1254	0.1380	0.1902
96 48 54 62	CLOVER	CLOVER	0.8649	0.0002	0.1039	0.0012	0.0297
31 31 11 11	CLOVER	SUGARBEETS *	0.1566	0.0392	0.0538	0.3424	0.4080
56 13 13 71	CLOVER	CLOVER	0.4657	0.0253	0.1707	0.0567	0.2817
32 13 27 32	CLOVER	SOYBEANS *	0.1731	0.2665	0.1797	0.2687	0.1121
36 26 54 32	CLOVER	COTTON *	0.1717	0.2693	0.4152	0.1091	0.0347
53 08 06 54	CLOVER	CLOVER	0.4433	0.0279	0.0929	0.1073	0.3287
32 32 62 16	CLOVER	COTTON *	0.1378	0.3183	0.3885	0.1313	0.0240

* MISCLASSIFIED OBSERVATION

REMOTE SENSING DATA ON FIVE CROPS
CLASSIFICATION OF CROP DATA
6

DISCRIMINANT ANALYSIS CLASSIFICATION SUMMARY FOR CALIBRATION DATA: WORK.CROPS

GENERALIZED SQUARED DISTANCE FUNCTION:

$$D_J^2(X) = (X-\bar{X}_J)'\ COV^{-1}\ (X-\bar{X}_J)$$

POSTERIOR PROBABILITY OF MEMBERSHIP IN EACH CROP:

$$PR(J|X) = EXP(-.5\ D_J^2(X))\ /\ SUM_K\ EXP(-.5\ D_K^2(X))$$

NUMBER OF OBSERVATIONS AND PERCENTS CLASSIFIED INTO CROP:

FROM CROP	CLOVER	CORN	COTTON	SOYBEANS	SUGARBEETS	TOTAL
CLOVER	5	0	3	1	2	11
	45.45	0.00	27.27	9.09	18.18	100.00
CORN	0	4	0	3	0	7
	0.00	57.14	0.00	42.86	0.00	100.00
COTTON	0	0	4	2	0	6
	0.00	0.00	66.67	33.33	0.00	100.00
SOYBEANS	0	1	1	3	1	6
	0.00	16.67	16.67	50.00	16.67	100.00
SUGARBEETS	1	1	0	2	2	6
	16.67	16.67	0.00	33.33	33.33	100.00

(continued on next page)

(continued from previous page)

```
          TOTAL                   6           6           8          11           5          36
          PERCENT             16.67       16.67       22.22       30.56       13.89      100.00

          PRIORS             0.2000      0.2000      0.2000      0.2000      0.2000
```

```
                                   REMOTE SENSING DATA ON FIVE CROPS                                   7
                                      CLASSIFICATION OF TEST DATA

                  DISCRIMINANT ANALYSIS     CLASSIFICATION RESULTS FOR TEST DATA: WORK.TEST

         GENERALIZED SQUARED DISTANCE FUNCTION:         POSTERIOR PROBABILITY OF MEMBERSHIP IN EACH CROP:

          2          _        -1  _                                     2                   2
         D (X) = (X-X )' COV   (X-X )                   PR(J|X) = EXP(-.5 D (X)) / SUM EXP(-.5 D (X))
          J          J            J                                     J        K          K

                                                        POSTERIOR PROBABILITY OF MEMBERSHIP IN CROP:

   XVALUES                FROM          CLASSIFIED      CLOVER       CORN        COTTON     SOYBEANS   SUGARBEETS
                          CROP          INTO CROP

   16 27 31 33            CORN          CORN            0.0541      0.3855      0.1956      0.2653      0.0995
   21 25 23 24            SOYBEANS      SOYBEANS        0.0900      0.2320      0.1336      0.3696      0.1748
   29 24 26 28            COTTON        SOYBEANS    *   0.1601      0.1838      0.1780      0.2967      0.1814
   54 23 21 54            SUGARBEETS    CLOVER      *   0.4743      0.0232      0.1749      0.0694      0.2582
   32 32 62 16            CLOVER        COTTON      *   0.1378      0.3183      0.3885      0.1313      0.0240

                                        * MISCLASSIFIED OBSERVATION
```

```
                                   REMOTE SENSING DATA ON FIVE CROPS                                   8
                                      CLASSIFICATION OF TEST DATA

                  DISCRIMINANT ANALYSIS     CLASSIFICATION SUMMARY FOR TEST DATA: WORK.TEST

         GENERALIZED SQUARED DISTANCE FUNCTION:         POSTERIOR PROBABILITY OF MEMBERSHIP IN EACH CROP:

          2          _        -1  _                                     2                   2
         D (X) = (X-X )' COV   (X-X )                   PR(J|X) = EXP(-.5 D (X)) / SUM EXP(-.5 D (X))
          J          J            J                                     J        K          K

                              NUMBER OF OBSERVATIONS AND PERCENTS CLASSIFIED INTO CROP:
           FROM
           CROP               CLOVER        CORN      COTTON    SOYBEANS  SUGARBEETS       TOTAL

           CLOVER                  0           0           1           0           0           1
                                0.00        0.00      100.00        0.00        0.00      100.00

           CORN                    0           1           0           0           0           1
                                0.00      100.00        0.00        0.00        0.00      100.00

           COTTON                  0           0           0           1           0           1
                                0.00        0.00        0.00      100.00        0.00      100.00

           SOYBEANS                0           0           0           1           0           1
                                0.00        0.00        0.00      100.00        0.00      100.00

           SUGARBEETS              1           0           0           0           0           1
                              100.00        0.00        0.00        0.00        0.00      100.00

           TOTAL                   1           1           1           2           0           5
           PERCENT             20.00       20.00       20.00       40.00        0.00      100.00

           PRIORS             0.2000      0.2000      0.2000      0.2000      0.2000
```

REFERENCES

Anderson, T.W. (1958), *An Introduction to Multivariate Statistical Analysis*, New York: John Wiley & Sons.

Kendall, M.G. and Stuart, A. (1961), *The Advanced Theory of Statistics*, Vol. 3. London: Charles Griffin and Company, Ltd.

Morrison, D.F. (1976), *Multivariate Statistical Methods*, New York: McGraw-Hill.

Rao, C. Radhakrishna (1973), *Linear Statistical Inference and Its Applications*, New York: John Wiley & Sons.

REFERENCES

[illegible]

Chapter 17

The FACTOR Procedure

Operating systems: All

ABSTRACT

The FACTOR procedure performs several types of common factor and component analysis. Both orthogonal and oblique rotations are available. Scoring coefficients can be computed by the regression method, and estimated factor scores can be written to an output data set. All major statistics computed by the procedure can also be saved in an output data set.

INTRODUCTION

The FACTOR procedure performs a variety of common factor and component analyses and rotations. Input can be multivariate data, a correlation matrix, a covariance matrix, a factor pattern, or a matrix of scoring coefficients. Either the correlation or covariance matrix can be factored. Most results can be saved in an output data set.

FACTOR can process output from other procedures. For example, the canonical coefficients from the CANDISC procedure can be rotated with FACTOR.

The methods for factor extraction are principal component analysis, principal factor analysis, iterated principal factor analysis, unweighted least-squares factor analysis, maximum-likelihood (canonical) factor analysis, alpha factor analysis, image component analysis, and Harris component analysis. A variety of methods for prior communality estimation are also available.

The methods for rotation are varimax, quartimax, equamax, orthomax with user-specified gamma, promax with user-specified exponent, Harris-Kaiser case II with user-specified exponent, and oblique Procrustean with a user-specified target pattern.

Output includes means, standard deviations, correlations, Kaiser's measure of sampling adequacy, eigenvalues, a scree plot, eigenvectors, prior and final communality estimates, the unrotated factor pattern, residual and partial correlations, the rotated primary factor pattern, the primary factor structure, inter-factor correlations, the reference structure, reference axis correlations, the variance explained by each factor both ignoring and eliminating other factors, plots of both rotated and unrotated factors, squared multiple correlation of each factor with the variables, and scoring coefficients.

Any topics that are not given explicit references are discussed in Mulaik (1972) or Harman (1976).

Background

See the PRINCOMP procedure for a discussion of principal component analysis.

Common factor analysis was invented by Spearman (1904). Gould (1981) gives an interesting nontechnical history of factor analysis. Kim and Mueller (1978) provide a very elementary discussion of the common factor model. Gorsuch (1974) contains a broad survey of factor analysis, and Gorsuch (1974) and Cattell (1978) are useful as guides to practical research methodology. Harman (1976) gives a lucid discussion of many of the more technical aspects of factor analysis, especially oblique rotation. Morrison (1976) and Mardia, Kent, and Bibby (1979) provide excellent statistical treatments of common factor analysis. Mulaik (1972) is the most thorough and authoritative general reference on factor analysis and is highly recommended to anyone comfortable with matrix algebra.

A frequent source of confusion in the field of factor analysis is the term *factor*. It sometimes refers to a hypothetical, unobservable variable, as in the phrase *common factor*. In this sense, *factor analysis* must be distinguished from component analysis, since a component is an observable linear combination. *Factor* is also used in the sense of *matrix factor*, in that one matrix is a factor of a second matrix if the first matrix multiplied by its transpose equals the second matrix. In this sense, *factor analysis* refers to all methods of data analysis using matrix factors, including component analysis and common factor analysis.

A *common factor* is an unobservable, hypothetical variable that contributes to the variance of at least two of the observed variables. The unqualified term "factor" often refers to a common factor. A *unique factor* is an unobservable, hypothetical variable that contributes to the variance of only one of the observed variables. The model for common factor analysis posits one unique factor for each observed variable.

The equation for the common factor model is

$$y_{ij} = x_{i1}b_{1j} + x_{i2}b_{2j} + \ldots + x_{iq}b_{qj} + e_{ij}$$

where

y_{ij} is the value of the ith observation on the jth variable,

x_{ik} is the value of the ith observation on the kth common factor,

b_{kj} is the regression coefficient of the kth common factor for predicting the jth variable,

e_{ij} is the value of the ith observation on the jth unique factor,

q is the number of common factors,

and it is assumed for convenience that all variables have a mean of 0. In matrix terms these equations reduce to

$$\mathbf{Y} = \mathbf{XB} + \mathbf{E} \ .$$

In the preceding equation **X** is the matrix of factor scores, and **B**′ is the factor pattern.

There are two critical assumptions:

- the unique factors are uncorrelated with each other
- the unique factors are uncorrelated with the common factors.

In principal component analysis, the residuals are generally correlated with each other. In common factor analysis, the unique factors play the role of residuals and are defined to be uncorrelated both with each other and with the common factors. Each common factor is assumed to contribute to at least two variables; otherwise, it would be a unique factor.

When the factors are initially extracted, it is also assumed for convenience that the common factors are uncorrelated with each other and have unit variance. In this case, the common factor model implies that the covariance s_{jk} between the jth and kth variables, $j \neq k$, is given by

$$s_{jk} = b_{1j}b_{1k} + b_{2j}b_{2k} + \ldots + b_{qj}b_{qk}$$

or

$$\mathbf{S} = \mathbf{B'B} + \mathbf{U}^2$$

where **S** is the covariance matrix of the observed variables and $\mathbf{U}^2$ is the diagonal covariance matrix of the unique factors.

If the original variables were standardized to unit variance, the above formula would yield correlations instead of covariances. It is in this sense that common factors explain the correlations among the observed variables. The difference between the correlation predicted by the common factor model and the actual correlation is the *residual correlation*. A good way to assess the goodness-of-fit of the common factor model is to examine the residual correlations.

The common factor model implies that the partial correlations among the variables, removing the effects of the common factors, must all be 0. When the common factors are removed, only unique factors, which are by definition uncorrelated, remain.

The assumptions of common factor analysis imply that the common factors are, in general, not linear combinations of the observed variables. In fact, even if the data contain measurements on the entire population of observations, you cannot compute the scores of the observations on the common factors. Although the common factor scores cannot be computed directly, they can be estimated in a variety of ways.

The problem of factor score indeterminacy has led several factor analysts to propose methods yielding components that can be considered approximations to common factors. Since these components are defined as linear combinations, they are computable. The methods include Harris component analysis and image component analysis. The advantage of producing determinate component scores is offset by the fact that, even if the data fit the common factor model perfectly, component methods do not generally recover the correct factor solution. You should not use any type of component analysis if you really want a common factor analysis (Dziuban and Harris 1973; Lee and Comrey 1979).

After the factors have been estimated, it is necessary to interpret them. Interpretation usually means assigning to each common factor a name that reflects the importance of the factor in predicting each of the observed variables, that is, the coefficients in the pattern matrix corresponding to the factor. Factor interpretation is a subjective process. It can sometimes be made less subjective by *rotating* the common factors, that is, by applying a nonsingular linear transformation. A rotated pattern matrix in which all the coefficients are close to 0 or ± 1 is easier to interpret than a pattern with many intermediate elements. Therefore, most rotation methods attempt to optimize a function of the pattern matrix that measures, in some sense, how close the elements are to 0 or ± 1.

After the initial factor extraction, the common factors are uncorrelated with each other. If the factors are rotated by an *orthogonal* transformation, the rotated factors are also uncorrelated. If the factors are rotated by an *oblique* transformation, the rotated factors become correlated. Oblique rotations often produce more pleasing patterns than do orthogonal rotations. However, a consequence of correlated factors is that there is no single unambiguous measure of the importance of a factor in explaining a variable. Thus, for oblique rotations, the pattern matrix does not provide all the necessary information for interpreting the factors; you must also examine the *factor structure* and the *reference structure*.

Rotating a set of factors does not change the statistical explanatory power of the factors. One cannot say that any rotation is better than any other rotation from a statistical point of view; all rotations are equally good statistically. Therefore, the choice among different rotations must be based on nonstatistical grounds. For most applications, the preferred rotation is that which is most easily interpretable.

If two rotations give rise to different interpretations, those two interpretations must not be regarded as conflicting. Rather, they are two different ways of looking at the same thing, two different points of view in the common-factor space. Any conclusion that depends on one and only one rotation being correct is invalid.

Outline of Use

Principal components The most important type of analysis performed by the FACTOR procedure is principal component analysis. The statement

```
PROC FACTOR;
```

results in a principal component analysis. The output includes all the eigenvalues and the pattern matrix for eigenvalues greater than one.

Most applications require additional output. You may, for example, want to compute principal component scores for use in subsequent analyses or obtain a graphical aid to help decide how many components to keep. It is recommended that you save the results of the analysis in a permanent SAS data library by using the OUTSTAT= option. Assuming your SAS data library has the libref SAVE and the data are in a SAS data set called RAW, you could do a principal component analysis as follows:

```
PROC FACTOR DATA=RAW SCREE MINEIGEN=0 SCORE
   OUTSTAT=SAVE.FACT_ALL;
```

The SCREE option produces a plot of the eigenvalues that is helpful in deciding how many components to use. The MINEIGEN=0 option causes all components with variance greater than zero to be retained. The SCORE option requests that scoring coefficients be computed. The OUTSTAT= option saves the results in a specially structured SAS data set. The name of the data set, in this case FACT_ALL, is arbitrary. To compute principal component scores, use the SCORE procedure:

```
PROC SCORE DATA=RAW SCORE=SAVE.FACT_ALL OUT=SAVE.SCORES;
```

The SCORE procedure uses the data and the scoring coefficients that were saved in SAVE.FACT_ALL to compute principal component scores. The component scores are placed in variables named FACTOR1, FACTOR2, ..., and saved in the data set SAVE.SCORES. If you know ahead of time how many principal components you want to use, you can obtain the scores directly from FACTOR by specifying the NFACTORS= and OUT= options. To get scores from three principal components, specify:

```
PROC FACTOR DATA=RAW NFACTORS=3 OUT=SAVE.SCORES;
```

To plot the scores for the first three components use the PLOT procedure:

```
PROC PLOT;
   PLOT FACTOR2*FACTOR1 FACTOR3*FACTOR1 FACTOR3*FACTOR2;
```

Principal factor analysis The simplest and computationally most efficient method of common factor analysis is principal factor analysis, which is obtained the same way as principal component analysis except for the use of the PRIORS= option. The usual form of the initial analysis is

```
PROC FACTOR DATA=RAW SCREE MINEIGEN=0 PRIORS=SMC
   OUTSTAT=SAVE.FACT_ALL;
```

The squared multiple correlations (SMC) of each variable with all the other variables are used as the prior communality estimates. If your correlation matrix is singular, you should specify PRIORS=MAX instead of PRIORS=SMC. The SCREE and MINEIGEN= options serve the same purpose as in the principal component analysis above. Saving the results with the OUTSTAT= option allows you to examine the eigenvalues and scree plot before deciding how many factors to rotate and to try several different rotations without re-extracting the factors. The OUTSTAT= data set is automatically marked TYPE=FACTOR so the FACTOR procedure realizes that it contains statistics from a previous analysis instead of data.

After looking at the eigenvalues to estimate the number of factors, you can try some rotations. Two and three factors can be rotated with the statements:

```
PROC FACTOR DATA=SAVE.FACT_ALL N=2 ROTATE=PROMAX
```

```
          ROUND REORDER SCORE OUTSTAT=SAVE.FACT_2;
    PROC FACTOR DATA=SAVE.FACT_ALL N=3 ROTATE=PROMAX
          ROUND REORDER SCORE OUTSTAT=SAVE.FACT_3;
```

The output data set from the previous run is used as input for these analyses. The options N=2 and N=3 specify the number of factors to be rotated. The specification ROTATE=PROMAX requests a promax rotation, which has the advantage of providing both orthogonal and oblique rotations with only one invocation of FACTOR. The ROUND option causes the various factor matrices to be printed in an easily-interpretable format, and the REORDER option causes the variables to be reordered on the printout so that variables associated with the same factor appear next to each other.

You can now compute and plot factor scores for the two-factor promax-rotated solution as follows:

```
    PROC SCORE DATA=RAW SCORE=SAVE.FACT_2 OUT=SAVE.SCORES;
    PROC PLOT;
       PLOT FACTOR2*FACTOR1;
```

Maximum-likelihood factor analysis Although principal factor analysis is perhaps the most commonly used method of common factor analysis, most statisticians prefer maximum-likelihood (ML) factor analysis (Lawley and Maxwell 1971). ML estimation has desirable asymptotic properties (Bickel and Doksum 1977) and gives better estimates than principal factor analysis in large samples. You can test hypotheses about the number of common factors using the ML method.

The ML solution is equivalent to Rao's (1955) canonical factor solution and Howe's solution maximizing the determinant of the partial correlation matrix (Morrison 1976). Thus, as a descriptive method, ML factor analysis does not require a multivariate normal distribution. The validity of the χ^2 test for the number of factors does require approximate normality plus additional regularity conditions that are usually satisfied in practice (Geweke and Singleton 1980).

The ML method is more expensive than principal factor analysis for two reasons. First, the communalities are estimated iteratively, and each iteration takes about as much computer time as principal factor analysis. The number of iterations typically ranges from about five to twenty. Second, if you want to extract different numbers of factors, as is often the case, you must run the FACTOR procedure once for each number of factors. Therefore, an ML analysis may well take 100 times as long as a principal factor analysis.

It is a good idea to use principal factor analysis to get a rough idea of the number of factors before doing an ML analysis. If you think that there are between one and three factors, you can use the following statements for the ML analysis:

```
    PROC FACTOR DATA=RAW METHOD=ML N=1
          OUTSTAT=SAVE.FACT1;
    PROC FACTOR DATA=RAW METHOD=ML N=2 ROTATE=PROMAX
          OUTSTAT=SAVE.FACT2;
    PROC FACTOR DATA=RAW METHOD=ML N=3 ROTATE=PROMAX
          OUTSTAT=SAVE.FACT3;
```

The output data sets can be used for trying different rotations, computing scoring coefficients, or restarting the procedure in case it does not converge within the allotted number of iterations.

The ML method cannot be used with a singular correlation matrix and is especially prone to Heywood cases. If you have problems with ML, the best alternative is METHOD=ULS for unweighted least-squares factor analysis.

SPECIFICATIONS

The FACTOR procedure is invoked by the following statements:

PROC FACTOR *options;*
  PRIORS *communalities;*
  VAR *variables;*
  PARTIAL *variables;*
  FREQ *variable;*
  WEIGHT *variable;*
  BY *variables;*

Usually only the VAR statement is needed in addition to the PROC FACTOR statement.

PROC FACTOR Statement

PROC FACTOR *options;*

The options available with the PROC FACTOR statement are discussed in the following sections:

- Data set options
- Factor extraction options
- Rotation options
- Output options
- Miscellaneous options.

Data set options

DATA=*SASdataset*
: names the input data set, which can be an ordinary SAS data set or a specially structured SAS data set as described in **Input Data Set**. If DATA= is omitted, the most recently created SAS data set is used.

TARGET=*SASdataset*
: names a data set containing the target pattern for Procrustes rotation. See the ROTATE= option below. The TARGET= data set must contain variables with the same names as those being factored. Each observation in the TARGET= data set becomes one column of the target factor pattern. Missing values are treated as zeros. _NAME_ and _TYPE_ variables are not required and are ignored if present.

OUT=*SASdataset*
: creates a data set containing all the data from the DATA= data set plus variables called FACTOR1, FACTOR2, and so on, containing estimated factor scores. The DATA= data set must contain multivariate data, not correlations or covariances. The NFACTORS= option must also be specified to determine the number of factor score variables. If you want to create a permanent SAS data set, you must specify a two-level name. See "SAS Files" in the *SAS User's Guide: Basics* for more information on permanent data sets.

OUTSTAT=*SASdataset*
: names an output data set containing most of the results of the analysis. The output data set is described in detail in **Output Data Set**. If you want to create a permanent SAS data set, you must specify a two-level name. See "SAS Files" in the *SAS User's Guide: Basics* for more information on permanent data sets.

Factor extraction options

METHOD=*name*
M=*name*

specifies the method for extracting factors. The default is METHOD=PRINCIPAL unless the DATA= data set is TYPE=FACTOR, in which case the default is METHOD=PATTERN.

METHOD=PRINCIPAL | PRIN | P

yields principal component analysis if no PRIORS option or statement is used or if PRIORS=ONE is specified; if a PRIORS statement or a PRIORS= value other than PRIORS=ONE is specified, a principal factor analysis is performed.

METHOD=PRINIT

yields iterated principal factor analysis.

METHOD=ULS | U

produces unweighted least squares factor analysis.

METHOD=ALPHA | A

produces alpha factor analysis.

METHOD=ML | M

performs maximum-likelihood factor analysis with an algorithm due, except for minor details, to Wayne A. Fuller (personal communication). METHOD=ML requires a nonsingular correlation matrix.

METHOD=HARRIS | H

yields Harris component analysis of $\mathbf{S}^{-1}\mathbf{R}\mathbf{S}^{-1}$ (Harris 1962), a noniterative approximation to canonical component analysis. This method is equivalent to METHOD=IMAGE in SAS release 79.5, and requires a nonsingular correlation matrix.

METHOD=IMAGE | I

yields principal component analysis of the image covariance matrix, not Kaiser's (1963, 1970, 1974) image analysis. A nonsingular correlation matrix is required.

METHOD=PATTERN

reads a factor pattern from a TYPE=FACTOR, CORR, or COV data set. If you create a TYPE=FACTOR data set in a DATA step, only observations containing the factor pattern (_TYPE_='PATTERN') and, if the factors are correlated, the inter-factor correlations (_TYPE_='FCORR') are required.

METHOD=SCORE

reads scoring coefficients (_TYPE_='SCORE') from a TYPE=FACTOR, CORR, or COV data set. The data set must also contain either a correlation or a covariance matrix.

PRIORS=*name*

specifies a method for computing prior communality estimates. You can specify numeric values for the prior communality estimates by using the PRIORS statement.

PRIORS=ONE | O

sets all prior communalities to 1.0.

PRIORS=MAX | M

sets the prior communality estimate for each variable to its maximum absolute correlation with any other variable.

PRIORS=SMC | S
sets the prior communality estimate for each variable to its squared multiple correlation with all other variables.

PRIORS=ASMC | A
sets the prior communality estimates proportional to the squared multiple correlations but adjusted so that their sum is equal to that of the maximum absolute correlations (Cureton 1968).

PRIORS=INPUT | I
reads the prior communality estimates from the first observation with either _TYPE_='PRIORS' or _TYPE_= 'COMMUNAL' in the DATA= data set (which must be TYPE=FACTOR).

PRIORS=RANDOM | R
sets the prior communality estimates to random numbers uniformly distributed between 0 and 1.

The default prior communality estimates are as follows:

METHOD=	**PRIORS=**
PRINCIPAL	ONE
PRINIT	ONE
ALPHA	SMC
ULS	SMC
ML	SMC
HARRIS	(not applicable)
IMAGE	(not applicable)
PATTERN	(not applicable)
SCORE	(not applicable)

COVARIANCE
COV
requests factoring of the covariance matrix instead of the correlation matrix. The COV option can be used only with METHOD= PRINCIPAL, PRINIT, ULS, or IMAGE.

WEIGHT
requests that a weighted correlation or covariance matrix be factored. The WEIGHT option can be used only with METHOD=PRINCIPAL, PRINIT, ULS, or IMAGE. The input data set must be TYPE=CORR, COV, or FACTOR, and the variable weights are obtained from an observation with _TYPE_='WEIGHT'.

MAXITER=*n*
specifies the maximum number of iterations with METHOD=PRINIT, ULS, ALPHA, or ML. The default is 30.

CONVERGE=*n*
CONV=*n*
specifies the convergence criterion for METHOD=PRINIT, ULS, ALPHA, or ML. Iteration stops when the maximum change in the communalities is less than the CONVERGE= value. The default value is .001.

The following options jointly control the number of factors extracted. If two or more of the NFACTORS=, MINEIGEN=, and PROPORTION= options are specified, the number of factors retained is the minimum number satisfying any of the criteria.

NFACTORS=*n*
NFACT=*n*
N=*n*

specifies the maximum number of factors to be extracted and determines the amount of core storage to be allocated for factor matrices. The default is the number of variables. Specifying a number that is small relative to the number of variables can substantially decrease the region required to run FACTOR, especially with oblique rotations. If NFACTORS=0 is specified, eigenvalues are computed but no factors are extracted. If NFACTORS=−1 is specified, neither eigenvalues nor factors are computed. This option can be used with METHOD=PATTERN or METHOD=SCORE to specify a smaller number of factors than are present in the data set.

PROPORTION=*n*
PERCENT=*n*
P=*n*

specifies the proportion of common variance to be accounted for by the retained factors using the prior communality estimates. If the value is greater than one, it is interpreted as a percentage and divided by 100. PROPORTION=0.75 and PERCENT=75 are equivalent. The default is 1.0 or 100%. You cannot specify PROPORTION= with METHOD=PATTERN or METHOD=SCORE.

MINEIGEN=*n*
MIN=*n*

specifies the smallest eigenvalue for which a factor is retained. This option cannot be used with METHOD=PATTERN or METHOD=SCORE. The default is 0 unless neither NFACTORS= nor PROPORTION= is specified and one of the following conditions holds:

If METHOD=ALPHA or METHOD=HARRIS, then MINEIGEN=1.
If METHOD=IMAGE, then

$$\text{MINEIGEN} = \frac{\text{total image variance}}{\text{number of variables}} .$$

For any other METHOD= value, if prior communality estimates of 1.0 are used, then

$$\text{MINEIGEN} = \frac{\text{total weighted variance}}{\text{number of variables}} .$$

When factoring an unweighted correlation matrix, this value is 1.

By default, METHOD=PRINIT, ULS, ALPHA, and ML stop iterating and set the number of factors to zero if an estimated communality exceeds one. The following options allow processing to continue:

HEYWOOD
HEY

sets to 1 any communality greater than 1, allowing iterations to proceed.

ULTRAHEYWOOD
ULTRA

allows communalities to exceed 1. The ULTRAHEYWOOD option may cause convergence problems because communalities may become extremely large, and ill-conditioned Hessians may occur.

Rotation options

ROTATE=*name*
R=*name*

gives the rotation method. The default is ROTATE=NONE.

ROTATE=VARIMAX | V
specifies varimax rotation.

ROTATE=QUARTIMAX | Q
specifies quartimax rotation.

ROTATE=EQUAMAX | E
specifies equamax rotation.

ROTATE=ORTHOMAX
specifies general orthomax rotation with the weight specified by the GAMMA= option.

ROTATE=HK
specifies Harris-Kaiser case II orthoblique rotation. The HKPOWER= option can be used to set the power of the square roots of the eigenvalues by which the eigenvectors are scaled.

ROTATE=PROMAX | P
specifies promax rotation. The PREROTATE= and POWER= options can be used with ROTATE=PROMAX.

ROTATE=PROCRUSTES
specifies oblique Procrustes rotation with target pattern given by the TARGET= data set. The unrestricted least squares method is used with factors scaled to unit length after rotation.

ROTATE=NONE | N
specifies that no rotation be performed.

GAMMA=*n*

specifies the orthomax weight. This option can be used only with ROTATE=ORTHOMAX or PREROTATE=ORTHOMAX.

HKPOWER=*n*
HKP=*n*

specifies the power of the square roots of the eigenvalues used to rescale the eigenvectors for Harris-Kaiser (ROTATE=HK) rotation. Values between 0.0 and 1.0 are reasonable. The default value is 0.0, yielding the independent cluster solution. A value of 1.0 is equivalent to a varimax rotation. The HKPOWER= option can also be specified with ROTATE=QUARTIMAX, VARIMAX, EQUAMAX, or ORTHOMAX, in which case the Harris-Kaiser rotation uses the specified orthogonal rotation method.

POWER=*n*

specifies the power to be used in computing the target pattern for ROTATE=PROMAX. The default value is 3.

PRERETOTATE=*name*
PRE=*name*

specifies the prerotation method for ROTATE=PROMAX. Any rotation method other than PROMAX or PROCRUSTES can be used. The default is VARIMAX. If a previously rotated pattern is read using METHOD=PATTERN, PREROTATE=NONE should be specified.

NORM=*name*

specifies the method for normalizing the rows of the factor pattern for rotation. If NORM=KAISER is specified, Kaiser's normalization is used. If NORM=WEIGHT is used, the rows are weighted by the Cureton-Mulaik technique (Cureton and Mulaik 1975). If NORM=COV is specified, the rows of the pattern matrix are rescaled to represent covariances instead of correlations. If NORM=NONE or NORM=RAW is specified, normalization is not performed. The default is NORM=KAISER.

Output options

SIMPLE
S

prints means and standard deviations.

CORR
C

prints the correlation matrix.

MSA

prints the partial correlations between each pair of variables controlling for all other variables (the negative anti-image correlations) and Kaiser's measure of sampling adequacy (Kaiser 1970; Kaiser and Rice 1974; Cerny and Kaiser 1977).

SCREE

prints a scree plot of the eigenvalues (Cattell 1966; Cattell 1978; Cattell and Vogelman 1977; Horn and Engstrom 1979).

EIGENVECTORS
EV

prints the eigenvectors.

PRINT

prints input factor pattern or scoring coefficients and related statistics. In oblique cases, the reference and factor structures are computed and printed. The PRINT option is effective only with METHOD=PATTERN or METHOD=SCORE.

RESIDUALS
RES

prints the residual correlation matrix and the associated partial correlation matrix.

PREPLOT

plots the factor pattern before rotation.

PLOT

plots the factor pattern after rotation.

NPLOT=*n*

specifies the number of factors to be plotted. The default is all the factors. The smallest allowable value is 2. If NPLOT=*n* is specified, all pairs of the first *n* factors are plotted, giving a total of $n(n-1)/2$ plots.

SCORE

prints the factor scoring coefficients. The squared multiple correlation of each factor with the variables is also printed except in the case of unrotated principal components.

ALL

prints all optional output except plots. When the input data set is TYPE=CORR, COV, or FACTOR, simple statistics, correlations, and MSA are not printed.

REORDER
RE

causes the rows (variables) of various factor matrices to be reordered on the printout. Variables with their highest absolute loading (reference structure loading for oblique rotations) on the first factor are printed first, from largest to smallest loading, followed by variables with their highest absolute loading on the second factor, and so on. The order of the variables in the output data set is not affected. The factors are not reordered.

ROUND

prints correlation and loading matrices with entries multiplied by 100 and rounded to the nearest integer. The exact values can be obtained from the output data set. (See also the FLAG= option.)

FLAG=*n*

causes absolute values larger than *n* to be flagged by an asterisk when used with the ROUND option. The default value is the root mean square of all the values in the matrix being printed.

FUZZ=*n*

causes correlations and factor loadings with absolute values less than the specified number to print as missing values. For partial correlations the FUZZ= value is divided by 2. For residual correlations the FUZZ= value is divided by 4. The exact values in any matrix can be obtained from the output data set.

Miscellaneous options

NOINT

requests that no intercept be used; covariances or correlations are not corrected for the mean.

NOCORR

prevents the correlation matrix from being transferred to the OUTSTAT= data set when METHOD=PATTERN or METHOD=SCORE is specified. NOCORR greatly reduces core requirements when there are many variables but few factors.

SINGULAR=*p*
SING=*p*

specifies the singularity criterion, where $0<p<1$. The default value is 1E-8.

PRIORS Statement

PRIORS *communalities;*

The PRIORS statement specifies numeric values between 0.0 and 1.0 for the prior communality estimates for each variable. The first numeric value corresponds to the first variable in the VAR statement, the second value to the second variable, and so on. The number of numeric values must equal the number of variables, for example:

```
PROC FACTOR;
   VAR    X  Y  Z;
   PRIORS .7 .8 .9;
```

Various methods for computing prior communality estimates can be specified by the PRIORS= option of the PROC FACTOR statement. Refer to that option for a description of the default prior communality estimates.

VAR Statement

VAR *variables;*

The VAR statement lists the numeric variables to be analyzed. If the VAR statement is omitted, all numeric variables not given in other statements are analyzed.

PARTIAL Statement

PARTIAL *variables;*

If you want the analysis to be based on a partial correlation or covariance matrix, use the PARTIAL statement to list the variables to be partialled out.

FREQ Statement

FREQ *variable;*

If a variable in your data set represents the frequency of occurrence for the other values in the observation, include the variable's name in a FREQ statement. The procedure then treats the data set as if each observation appears *n* times, where *n* is the value of the FREQ variable for the observation. The total number of observations is considered equal to the sum of the FREQ variable when the procedure computes significance probabilities.

The WEIGHT and FREQ statements have a similar effect, except in determining the number of observations.

WEIGHT Statement

WEIGHT *variable;*

If you want to use relative weights for each observation in the input data set, specify a variable containing weights in a WEIGHT statement. This is often done when the variance associated with each observation is different and the values of the weight variable are proportional to the reciprocals of the variances.

BY Statement

BY *variables;*

A BY statement can be used with PROC FACTOR to obtain separate analyses on observations in groups defined by the BY variables. When a BY statement appears, the procedure expects the DATA= data set to be sorted in order of the BY variables. If your DATA= data set is not sorted in ascending order, use the SORT procedure with a similar BY statement to sort the data, or, if appropriate, use the BY statement options NOTSORTED or DESCENDING. For more information, see the discussion of the BY statement in "Statements Used in the PROC Step" in the *SAS User's Guide: Basics.*

If TARGET= is specified and the TARGET= data set does not contain any of the BY variables, then the entire TARGET= data set is used as a Procrustean target for each BY group in the DATA= data set.

If the TARGET= data set contains some but not all of the BY variables, or if some BY variables do not have the same type or length in the TARGET= data set as in the DATA= data set, then FACTOR prints an error message and stops.

If all the BY variables appear in the TARGET= data set with the same type and length as in the DATA= data set, then each BY group in the TARGET= data set is used as a Procrustean target for the corresponding BY group in the DATA= data set. The BY groups in the TARGET= data set must be in the same order as in the DATA= data set. If NOTSORTED is specified in the BY statement, there must be exactly the same BY groups in the same order in both data sets. If NOTSORTED is not specified, it is permissible for some BY groups to appear in one data set but not in the other.

DETAILS

Input Data Set

The FACTOR procedure can read an ordinary SAS data set containing raw data or a special TYPE=CORR, TYPE=COV, or TYPE=FACTOR data set containing previously computed statistics. A TYPE=CORR data set can be created by the CORR procedure or various other procedures such as PRINCOMP. It contains means, standard deviations, the sample size, the correlation matrix, and possibly other statistics if created by some procedure other than CORR. A TYPE=COV data set is similar to a TYPE=CORR data set but contains a covariance matrix. A TYPE=FACTOR data set can be created by the FACTOR procedure and is described in **Output Data Set**.

If your data set has many observations and you plan to run FACTOR several times, you can save computer time by first creating a TYPE=CORR data set and using it as input to FACTOR:

```
PROC CORR   DATA=RAW OUTP=CORREL;  * create TYPE=CORR data set;
PROC FACTOR DATA=CORREL METHOD=ML; * maximum likelihood;
PROC FACTOR DATA=CORREL;           * principal components;
```

The data set created by the CORR procedure is automatically given the TYPE=CORR attribute, so you do not have to specify TYPE=CORR. However, if you use a DATA step with a SET statement to modify the correlation data set, you must use the TYPE=CORR attribute in the new data set. You can use a VAR statement with FACTOR when reading a TYPE=CORR data set to select a subset of the variables or change the order of the variables.

Problems can arise from using the CORR procedure when there are missing data. By default, CORR computes each correlation from all observations that have values present for the pair of variables involved (pairwise deletion). The resulting correlation matrix may have negative eigenvalues. If the NOMISS option is used with CORR, observations with any missing values are completely omitted from the calculations (listwise deletion), and there is no possibility of negative eigenvalues.

You can also have FACTOR create a TYPE=FACTOR data set, which includes all the information in a TYPE=CORR data set, and use it for repeated analyses. For a TYPE=FACTOR data set, the default value of the METHOD= option is PATTERN. The following statements give the same FACTOR results as the previous example:

```
PROC FACTOR DATA=RAW METHOD=ML OUTSTAT=FACT; * maximum likelihood;
PROC FACTOR DATA=FACT METHOD=PRIN;           * principal components;
```

A TYPE=FACTOR data set can be used to try several different rotation methods on the same data without repeatedly extracting the factors. In the following example, the second and third PROC FACTOR statements use the data set FACT created by the first PROC FACTOR statement:

```
PROC FACTOR DATA=RAW OUTSTAT=FACT; * principal components;
PROC FACTOR ROTATE=VARIMAX;        * varimax rotation;
PROC FACTOR ROTATE=QUARTIMAX;      * quartimax rotation;
```

You can create a TYPE=CORR or TYPE=FACTOR data set in a DATA step. Be sure to specify the TYPE= option in parentheses after the data set name in the DATA statement, and include the _TYPE_ and _NAME_ variables. In a TYPE=CORR data set only the correlation matrix (_TYPE_='CORR') is necessary. It can contain missing values as long as every pair of variables has at least one nonmissing value:

```
DATA CORREL(TYPE=CORR);
   _TYPE_='CORR';
   INPUT _NAME_ $ X Y Z;
   CARDS;
X  1.0  .   .
Y   .7 1.0  .
Z   .5  .4 1.0
;
PROC FACTOR;
```

You can create a TYPE=FACTOR data set containing only a factor pattern (_TYPE_='PATTERN') and use the FACTOR procedure to rotate it:

```
DATA PAT(TYPE=FACTOR);
   _TYPE_='PATTERN';
   INPUT _NAME_ $ X Y Z;
   CARDS;
FACTOR1  .5  .7  .3
FACTOR2  .8  .2  .8
;
PROC FACTOR ROTATE=PROMAX PREROTATE=NONE;
```

If the input factors are oblique, you must also include the inter-factor correlation matrix with _TYPE_='FCORR':

```
DATA PAT(TYPE=FACTOR);
   INPUT _TYPE_ $ _NAME_ $ X Y Z;
   CARDS;
PATTERN FACTOR1  .5  .7  .3
PATTERN FACTOR2  .8  .2  .8
FCORR   FACTOR1 1.0  .2  .
FCORR   FACTOR2  .2 1.0  .
;
PROC FACTOR ROTATE=PROMAX PREROTATE=NONE;
```

Some procedures, such as PRINCOMP and CANDISC, produce TYPE=CORR data sets containing scoring coefficients (_TYPE_='SCORE'). These coefficients can be input to FACTOR and rotated by using the METHOD=SCORE option. The input data set **must** contain the correlation matrix as well as the scoring coefficients:

```
PROC PRINCOMP DATA=RAW N=2 OUTSTAT=PRIN;
PROC FACTOR DATA=PRIN METHOD=SCORE ROTATE=VARIMAX;
```

Missing Values

If the DATA= data set contains data (rather than a matrix or factor pattern), then observations with missing values for any variables in the analysis are omitted from the computations. If a correlation or covariance matrix is read, it can contain missing values as long as every pair of variables has at least one nonmissing entry. Missing values in a pattern or scoring coefficient matrix are treated as zeros.

Cautions

- The amount of time that FACTOR takes is roughly proportional to the cube of the number of variables. Factoring 100 variables therefore takes about 1000 times as long as factoring ten variables. Iterative methods (PRINIT, ALPHA, ULS, ML) may also take 100 times as long as noniterative methods (PRINCIPAL, IMAGE, HARRIS).
- No computer program is capable of reliably determining the optimal number of factors since the decision is ultimately subjective. You should not accept blindly the number of factors obtained by default. Use your own judgment to make an intelligent decision.
- Singular correlation matrices cause problems with PRIORS=SMC and METHOD=ML. Singularities may result from using a variable that is the sum of other variables, coding too many dummy variables from a classification variable, or having more variables than observations.
- If the CORR procedure is used to compute the correlation matrix, and there are missing data and the NOMISS option is not specified, then the correlation matrix may have negative eigenvalues.
- If a TYPE=CORR or TYPE=FACTOR data set is copied or modified using a DATA step, the new data set does not automatically have the same TYPE as the old data set. You must specify the TYPE= data set option in the DATA statement. If you try to analyze a data set that has lost its TYPE=CORR attribute, FACTOR prints a warning message saying that the data set contains _NAME_ and _TYPE_ variables but analyzes the data set as an ordinary SAS data set.
- For a TYPE=FACTOR data set, the default is METHOD=PATTERN, not METHOD=PRIN.
- In SAS software release 82, the OUT= option was an undocumented alias for OUTSTAT=. Now, OUT= and OUTSTAT= are separate options.

Output Data Sets

The OUT= data set contains all the data in the DATA= data set plus new variables called FACTOR1, FACTOR2, and so on, containing estimated factor scores. If more than 99 factors are requested, the new variable names are FACT1, FACT2, and so on. Each estimated factor score is computed as a linear combination of the standardized values of the variables that were factored. The coefficients are printed if the SCORE option is specified and are labeled STANDARDIZED SCORING COEFFICIENTS.

The OUTSTAT= data set is similar to the TYPE=CORR data set produced by the CORR procedure but is TYPE=FACTOR and contains many results in addition to those produced by CORR.

The output data set contains the following variables:

- the BY variables, if any
- two new character variables, _TYPE_ and _NAME_
- the variables analyzed, that is, those in the VAR statement, or, if there is no VAR statement, all numeric variables not listed in any other statement.

Each observation in the output data set contains some type of statistic as indicated by the _TYPE_ variable. The _NAME_ variable is blank except where otherwise indicated. The values of the _TYPE_ variable are as follows:

TYPE	**Contents**
MEAN	means.
STD	standard deviations.
N	sample size.
CORR	correlations. The _NAME_ variable contains the name of the variable corresponding to each row of the correlation matrix.
IMAGE	image coefficients. The _NAME_ variable contains the name of the variable corresponding to each row of the image coefficient matrix.
IMAGECOV	image covariance matrix. The _NAME_ variable contains the name of the variable corresponding to each row of the image covariance matrix.
COMMUNAL	final communality estimates.
PRIOR	prior communality estimates, or estimates from the last iteration for iterative methods.
WEIGHT	variable weights.
EIGENVAL	eigenvalues.
UNROTATE	unrotated factor pattern. The _NAME_ variable contains the name of the factor.
RESIDUAL	residual correlations. The _NAME_ variable contains the name of the variable corresponding to each row of the residual correlation matrix.
TRANSFOR	transformation matrix from rotation. The _NAME_ variable contains the name of the factor.
FCORR	inter-factor correlations. The _NAME_ variable contains the name of the factor.
PATTERN	factor pattern. The _NAME_ variable contains the name of the factor.
RCORR	reference axis correlations. The _NAME_ variable contains the name of the factor.
REFERENC	reference structure. The _NAME_ variable contains the name of the factor.
STRUCTUR	factor structure. The _NAME_ variable contains the name of the factor.
SCORE	scoring coefficients. The _NAME_ variable contains the name of the factor.

Factor Scores

Estimated factor scores can be computed directly by the FACTOR procedure if the NFACTORS= and OUT= options are specified, or indirectly using the

SCORE procedure. The latter method is preferable if you use the FACTOR procedure interactively to determine the number of factors, the rotation method, or various other aspects of the analysis. To compute factor scores for each observation using the SCORE procedure:

- Use the SCORE option in the PROC FACTOR statement.
- Create a TYPE=FACTOR output data set with the OUTSTAT= option.
- Use the SCORE procedure with both the raw data and the TYPE=FACTOR data set.
- Do **not** use the TYPE= option in the PROC SCORE statement.

For example, the following statements could be used:

```
PROC FACTOR DATA=RAW SCORE OUTSTAT=FACT;
PROC SCORE  DATA=RAW SCORE=FACT OUT=SCORES;
```

or:

```
PROC CORR   DATA=RAW OUTP=CORREL;
PROC FACTOR DATA=CORREL SCORE OUTSTAT=FACT;
PROC SCORE  DATA=RAW SCORE=FACT OUT=SCORES;
```

A component analysis (principal, image, or Harris), produces scores with mean zero and variance one. If you have done a common factor analysis, the true factor scores have mean zero and variance one, but the computed factor scores are only estimates of the true factor scores. These estimates have mean zero but variance equal to the squared multiple correlation of the factor with the variables. The estimated factor scores may have small nonzero correlations even if the true factors are uncorrelated.

Variable Weights and Variance Explained

A principal component analysis of a correlation matrix treats all variables as equally important. A principal component analysis of a covariance matrix gives more weight to variables with larger variances. A principal component analysis of a covariance matrix is equivalent to an analysis of a weighted correlation matrix, where the weight of each variable is equal to its variance. Variables with large weights tend to have larger loadings on the first component and smaller residual correlations than variables with small weights.

You may want to give weights to variables using values other than their variances. Mulaik (1972) explains how to obtain a maximally reliable component by means of a weighted principal component analysis. With the FACTOR procedure, you can indirectly give arbitrary weights to the variables by using the COV option and rescaling the variables to have variance equal to the desired weight, or directly by using the WEIGHT option and including the weights in a TYPE=CORR data set.

Arbitrary variable weights can be used with METHOD=PRINCIPAL, PRINIT, ULS, or IMAGE. Alpha and ML factor analyses compute variable weights based on the communalities (Harman 1976, 217-218). For alpha factor analysis, the weight of a variable is the reciprocal of its communality. In ML factor analysis, the weight is the reciprocal of the uniqueness. Harris component analysis uses weights equal to the reciprocal of one minus the squared multiple correlation of each variable with the other variables.

For uncorrelated factors, the variance explained by a factor can be computed with or without taking the weights into account. The usual method for computing variance accounted for by a factor is to take the sum of squares of the corresponding column of the factor pattern, yielding an unweighted result. If the square of each loading is multiplied by the weight of the variable before the sum is taken, the result is the weighted variance explained, which is equal to the corresponding eigenvalue except in image analysis. Whether the weighted or unweighted result is more important depends on the purpose of the analysis.

In the case of correlated factors, the variance explained by a factor can be computed with or without taking the other factors into account. If you want to ignore the other factors, the variance explained is given by the weighted or unweighted sum of squares of the appropriate column of the factor structure since the factor structure contains simple correlations. If you want to subtract the variance explained by the other factors from the amount explained by the factor in question (the "Type II" variance explained), you can take the weighted or unweighted sum of squares of the appropriate column of the reference structure since the reference structure contains semipartial correlations. There are other ways of measuring the variance explained. For example, given a prior ordering of the factors, by eliminating from each factor the variance explained by previous factors you could compute a "Type I" variance explained. Another method, based on direct and joint contributions, is given by Harman (1976, 268-270).

Heywood Cases and Other Anomalies

Since communalities are squared correlations, one would expect them always to lie between 0 and 1. It is a mathematical peculiarity of the common factor model, however, that final communality estimates may exceed 1. If a communality equals 1, the situation is referred to as a Heywood case, and if a communality exceeds 1, it is an ultra-Heywood case. An ultra-Heywood case implies that some unique factor has negative variance, a clear indication that something is wrong. Possible causes include:

- bad prior communality estimates
- too many common factors
- too few common factors
- not enough data to provide stable estimates
- the common factor model is not an appropriate model for the data.

Whatever the cause, an ultra-Heywood case renders a factor solution invalid. Factor analysts disagree about whether or not a factor solution with a Heywood case can be considered legitimate.

Theoretically, the communality of a variable should not exceed its reliability. Violation of this condition is called a quasi-Heywood case and should be regarded with the same suspicion as an ultra-Heywood case.

Elements of the factor structure and reference structure matrices may exceed 1 only in the presence of an ultra-Heywood case. On the other hand, an element of the factor pattern may exceed 1 in an oblique rotation.

The maximum-likelihood method is especially susceptible to (quasi- or ultra-) Heywood cases. During the iteration process, a variable with high communality is given a high weight; this tends to increase its communality, which increases its weight, and so on.

It is often stated that the squared multiple correlation of a variable with the other variables is a lower bound to its communality. This is true if the common factor model fits the data perfectly but is not generally the case with real data. A final communality estimate that is less than the squared multiple correlation may therefore indicate poor fit, possibly due to not enough factors. It is by no means as serious a problem as an ultra-Heywood case. Factor methods using the Newton-Raphson method may actually produce communalities less than 0, a result even more disastrous than an ultra-Heywood case.

The squared multiple correlation of a factor with the variables may exceed 1, even in the absence of ultra-Heywood cases. This situation is also cause for alarm.

Alpha factor analysis seems to be especially prone to this problem, but it does not occur with maximum likelihood. If a squared multiple correlation is negative, too many factors have been retained.

With data that do not fit the common factor model perfectly, you can expect some of the eigenvalues to be negative. If an iterative factor method converges properly, the sum of the eigenvalues corresponding to rejected factors should be 0; hence, some eigenvalues are positive and some negative. If a principal factor analysis fails to yield any negative eigenvalues, the prior communality estimates are probably too large. Negative eigenvalues cause the cumulative proportion of variance explained to exceed 1 for a sufficiently large number of factors. The cumulative proportion of variance explained by the retained factors should be approximately 1 for principal factor analysis and should converge to 1 for iterative methods. Occasionally, a single factor can explain more than 100% of the common variance in a principal factor analysis, indicating that the prior communality estimates are too low.

If a squared canonical correlation or a coefficient alpha is negative, too many factors have been retained.

Principal component analysis, unlike common factor analysis, has none of the above problems if the covariance or correlation matrix is computed correctly from a data set with no missing values. Various methods for missing value correlation may produce negative eigenvalues in principal components, as may severe rounding of the correlations.

Computer Resources

Let:

n = number of observations
v = number of variables
f = number of factors
i = number of iterations during factor extraction
r = number of iterations during factor rotation.

The overall time for a factor analysis is very roughly proportional to iv^3.

The time required to compute the correlation matrix is roughly proportional to nv^2.

The time required for PRIORS=SMC or ASMC is roughly proportional to v^3.

The time required for PRIORS=MAX is roughly proportional to v^2.

The time required to compute eigenvalues is roughly proportional to v^3.

The time required to compute final eigenvectors is roughly proportional to fv^2.

Each iteration in METHOD=PRINIT or ALPHA requires computation of eigenvalues and f eigenvectors.

Each iteration in METHOD=ML or ULS requires computation of eigenvalues and $v-f$ eigenvectors.

The time required for ROTATE=VARIMAX, QUARTIMAX, EQUAMAX, ORTHOMAX, PROMAX, or HK is roughly proportional to rvf^2.

ROTATE=PROCRUSTES takes time roughly proportional to vf^2.

Printed Output

FACTOR's output includes:

1. MEAN and STD DEV (standard deviation) of each variable and the number of OBSERVATIONS if SIMPLE is specified
2. CORRELATIONS if CORR is specified
3. INVERSE CORRELATION MATRIX if ALL is specified
4. PARTIAL CORRELATIONS CONTROLLING ALL OTHER VARIABLES

(negative anti-image correlations) if MSA is specified. If the data are appropriate for the common factor model, the partial correlations should be small.

5. KAISER'S MEASURE OF SAMPLING ADEQUACY (Kaiser 1970; Kaiser and Rice 1974; Cerny and Kaiser 1977) if MSA is specified, both OVERALL and for each variable. The MSA is a summary of how small the partial correlations are relative to the ordinary correlations. Values greater than .8 can be considered good. Values less than .5 require remedial action, either by deleting the offending variables or including other variables related to the offenders.
6. PRIOR COMMUNALITY ESTIMATES, unless 1.0s are used or METHOD=IMAGE, HARRIS, PATTERN, or SCORE
7. SQUARED MULTIPLE CORRELATIONS of each variable with all the other variables if METHOD=IMAGE or HARRIS
8. IMAGE COEFFICIENTS if METHOD=IMAGE
9. IMAGE COVARIANCE MATRIX if METHOD=IMAGE
10. PRELIMINARY EIGENVALUES based on the prior communalities if METHOD=PRINIT, ALPHA, ML, or ULS, including the TOTAL and the AVERAGE of the eigenvalues, the DIFFERENCE between successive eigenvalues, the PROPORTION of variation represented, and the CUMULATIVE proportion of variation
11. the number of FACTORS that WILL BE RETAINED unless METHOD=PATTERN or SCORE
12. A SCREE PLOT OF EIGENVALUES if SCREE is specified. The preliminary eigenvalues are used if METHOD=PRINIT, ALPHA, ML, or ULS.
13. the iteration history if METHOD=PRINIT, ALPHA, ML, or ULS, containing the iteration number (ITER); the CRITERION being optimized (Joreskog 1977) and the RIDGE value for the iteration if METHOD=ML or ULS; the maximum CHANGE in any communality estimate; and the COMMUNALITIES
14. SIGNIFICANCE TESTS if METHOD=ML, including CHI-SQUARED, DF, and PROB>CHI**2 for H0: NO COMMON FACTORS and H0: the factors retained ARE SUFFICIENT to explain the correlations. The variables should have an approximate multivariate normal distribution for the probability levels to be valid. Lawley and Maxwell (1921) suggest that the number of observations should exceed the number of variables by 50 or more although Geweke and Singleton (1980) claim that as few as ten observations are adequate with five variables and one common factor. Certain regularity conditions must also be satisfied for the χ^2 test to be valid (Geweke and Singleton 1980), but in practice these conditions usually are satisfied. The notation PROB>CHI**2 means "the probability under the null hypothesis of obtaining a greater χ^2 statistic than that observed."
15. AKAIKE'S INFORMATION CRITERION if METHOD=ML. Akaike's information criterion (AIC) (Akaike 1973; Akaike 1974) is a general criterion for estimating the best number of parameters to include in a model when maximum-likelihood estimation is used. The number of factors that yields the smallest value of AIC is considered best. AIC, like the chi-square test, tends to include factors that are statistically significant but inconsequential for practical purposes.
16. SCHWARZ'S BAYESIAN CRITERION if METHOD=ML. Schwarz's Bayesian criterion (SBC) (Schwarz 1978) is another criterion, similar to AIC, for determining the best number of parameters. The number of factors that yields the smallest value of SBC is considered best. SBC

seems to be less inclined to include trivial factors than either AIC or the chi-square test.

17. SQUARED CANONICAL CORRELATIONS if METHOD=ML. These are the same as the squared multiple correlations for predicting each factor from the variables.
18. COEFFICIENT ALPHA FOR EACH FACTOR if METHOD=ALPHA
19. EIGENVECTORS if EIGENVECTORS or ALL is specified, unless METHOD=PATTERN or SCORE
20. EIGENVALUES OF THE (WEIGHTED) (REDUCED) (IMAGE) CORRELATION or COVARIANCE MATRIX, unless METHOD=PATTERN or SCORE. Included are the TOTAL and the AVERAGE of the eigenvalues, the DIFFERENCE between successive eigenvalues, the PROPORTION of variation represented, and the CUMULATIVE proportion of variation.
21. the FACTOR PATTERN, which is equal to both the matrix of standardized regression coefficients for predicting variables from common factors and the matrix of correlations between variables and common factors, since the extracted factors are uncorrelated
22. VARIANCE EXPLAINED BY EACH FACTOR, both WEIGHTED and UNWEIGHTED if variable weights are used.
23. FINAL COMMUNALITY ESTIMATES, including the TOTAL communality; or FINAL COMMUNALITY ESTIMATES AND VARIABLE WEIGHTS, including the TOTAL communality, both WEIGHTED and UNWEIGHTED, if variable weights are used. Final communality estimates are the squared multiple correlations for predicting the variables from the estimated factors and can be obtained by taking the sum of squares of each row of the factor pattern, or a weighted sum of squares if variable weights are used.
24. RESIDUAL CORRELATIONS WITH UNIQUENESS ON THE DIAGONAL if RESIDUAL or ALL is specified
25. ROOT-MEAN-SQUARE OFF-DIAGONAL RESIDUALS, both OVER-ALL and for each variable, if RESIDUAL or ALL is specified
26. PARTIAL CORRELATIONS CONTROLLING FACTORS if RESIDUAL or ALL is specified
27. ROOT-MEAN-SQUARE OFF-DIAGONAL PARTIALS, both OVER-ALL and for each variable, if RESIDUAL or ALL is specified
28. a PLOT OF the FACTOR PATTERN for unrotated factors if PREPLOT is specified; the number of plots is determined by NPLOT=
29. VARIABLE WEIGHTS FOR ROTATION if NORM=WEIGHT is specified
30. FACTOR WEIGHTS FOR ROTATION if HKPOWER= is specified
31. ORTHOGONAL TRANSFORMATION MATRIX if an orthogonal rotation is requested
32. ROTATED FACTOR PATTERN if an orthogonal rotation is requested
33. VARIANCE EXPLAINED BY EACH FACTOR after rotation. If an orthogonal rotation is requested and if variable weights are used, both weighted and unweighted values are given.
34. TARGET MATRIX FOR PROCRUSTEAN TRANSFORMATION if ROTATE=PROCRUSTES or PROMAX
35. the PROCRUSTEAN TRANSFORMATION MATRIX if ROTATE=PROCRUSTES or PROMAX
36. the (NORMALIZED) OBLIQUE TRANSFORMATION MATRIX if an oblique rotation is requested, which for ROTATE=PROMAX is the product of the prerotation and the Procrustean rotation
37. INTER-FACTOR CORRELATIONS if an oblique rotation is requested
38. ROTATED FACTOR PATTERN (STD REG COEFS) if an oblique rotation is

requested, giving standardized regression coefficients for predicting the variables from the factors

39. REFERENCE AXIS CORRELATIONS if an oblique rotation is requested. These are the partial correlations between the primary factors when all factors other than the two being correlated are partialled out.
40. the REFERENCE STRUCTURE (SEMIPARTIAL CORRELATIONS) if an oblique rotation is requested. The reference structure is the matrix of semipartial correlations (Kerlinger and Pedhazur 1973) between variables and common factors, removing from each common factor the effects of other common factors. If the common factors are uncorrelated, the reference structure is equal to the factor pattern.
41. VARIANCE EXPLAINED BY EACH FACTOR ELIMINATING the effects of all OTHER FACTORS if an oblique rotation is requested. Both WEIGHTED and UNWEIGHTED values are given if variable weights are used. These variances are equal to the (weighted) sum of the squared elements of the reference structure corresponding to each factor.
42. FACTOR STRUCTURE (CORRELATIONS) if an oblique rotation is requested. The (primary) factor structure is the matrix of correlations between variables and common factors. If the common factors are uncorrelated, the factor structure is equal to the factor pattern.
43. VARIANCE EXPLAINED BY EACH FACTOR IGNORING the effects of all OTHER FACTORS if an oblique rotation is requested. Both WEIGHTED and UNWEIGHTED values are given if variable weights are used. These variances are equal to the (weighted) sum of the squared elements of the factor structure corresponding to each factor.
44. FINAL COMMUNALITY ESTIMATES for the rotated factors if ROTATE= is specified. The estimates should equal the unrotated communalities.
45. SQUARED MULTIPLE CORRELATIONS OF THE VARIABLES WITH EACH FACTOR if SCORE or ALL is specified, except for unrotated principal components
46. STANDARDIZED SCORING COEFFICIENTS if SCORE or ALL is specified
47. PLOTs OF the FACTOR PATTERN for rotated factors if PLOT is specified and an orthogonal rotation is requested. The number of plots is determined by NPLOT=
48. PLOTs OF the REFERENCE STRUCTURE for rotated factors if PLOT is specified and an oblique rotation is requested. The number of plots is determined by NPLOT=. Included are the REFERENCE AXIS CORRELATION and the ANGLE between the reference axes for each pair of factors plotted.

If ROTATE=PROMAX is used, the output includes results for both the prerotation and the Procrustean rotation.

EXAMPLES

Principal Component Analysis: Example 1

The data in the example below are five socio-economic variables for twelve census tracts in the Los Angeles Standard Metropolitan Statistical Area as given by Harman (1976).

The first analysis is a principal component analysis. Simple descriptive statistics and correlations are also printed.

```
DATA SOCECON;
   TITLE 'FIVE SOCIO-ECONOMIC VARIABLES';
```

```
   TITLE2 'SEE PAGE 14 OF HARMAN: MODERN FACTOR ANALYSIS, 3RD ED';
   INPUT POP SCHOOL EMPLOY SERVICES HOUSE;
   CARDS;
5700      12.8       2500       270        25000
1000      10.9       600        10         10000
3400      8.8        1000       10         9000
3800      13.6       1700       140        25000
4000      12.8       1600       140        25000
8200      8.3        2600       60         12000
1200      11.4       400        10         16000
9100      11.5       3300       60         14000
9900      12.5       3400       180        18000
9600      13.7       3600       390        25000
9600      9.6        3300       80         12000
9400      11.4       4000       100        13000
;
PROC FACTOR DATA=SOCECON SIMPLE CORR;
   TITLE3 'PRINCIPAL COMPONENT ANALYSIS';
```

There are two large eigenvalues, 2.873314 and 1.796660, which together account for 93.4% of the standardized variance. Thus the first two principal components provide an adequate summary of the data for most purposes. Three components, explaining 97.7% of the variation, should be sufficient for almost any application. FACTOR retains two components on the basis of the eigenvalues-greater-than-one rule since the third eigenvalue is only 0.214837.

The first component has large positive loadings for all five variables. The correlation with SERVICES (0.93239) is especially high. The second component is a contrast of POP (0.80642) and EMPLOY (0.72605) against SCHOOL (−0.54476) and HOUSE (−0.55818), with a very small loading on SERVICES (−0.10431).

The final communality estimates show that all the variables are well accounted for by two components, with final communality estimates ranging from 0.880236 for SERVICES to 0.987826 for POP.

Output 17.1 Principal Component Analysis: PROC FACTOR

```
                              FIVE SOCIO-ECONOMIC VARIABLES                                    1
                      SEE PAGE 14 OF HARMAN: MODERN FACTOR ANALYSIS, 3RD ED
                              PRINCIPAL COMPONENTS ANALYSIS

               MEANS AND STANDARD DEVIATIONS FROM             12 OBSERVATIONS

                             POP        SCHOOL       EMPLOY     SERVICES        HOUSE
❶   MEAN                 6241.67       11.4417      2333.33      120.833        17000
    STD DEV              3439.99       1.78654      1241.21      114.928      6367.53

                         ❷              CORRELATIONS

                              POP     SCHOOL     EMPLOY   SERVICES      HOUSE

               POP        1.00000    0.00975    0.97245    0.43887    0.02241
               SCHOOL     0.00975    1.00000    0.15428    0.69141    0.86307
               EMPLOY     0.97245    0.15428    1.00000    0.51472    0.12193
               SERVICES   0.43887    0.69141    0.51472    1.00000    0.77765
               HOUSE      0.02241    0.86307    0.12193    0.77765    1.00000
```

```
                    FIVE SOCIO-ECONOMIC VARIABLES                                  2
          SEE PAGE 14 OF HARMAN: MODERN FACTOR ANALYSIS, 3RD ED
                    PRINCIPAL COMPONENTS ANALYSIS

INITIAL FACTOR METHOD: PRINCIPAL COMPONENTS

   ❻         PRIOR COMMUNALITY ESTIMATES: ONE

EIGENVALUES OF THE CORRELATION MATRIX:  TOTAL =         5  AVERAGE =          1

   ⓴                       1         2         3         4         5
     EIGENVALUE     2.873314  1.796660  0.214837  0.099934  0.015255
     DIFFERENCE     1.076654  1.581823  0.114903  0.084679
     PROPORTION       0.5747    0.3593    0.0430    0.0200    0.0031
     CUMULATIVE       0.5747    0.9340    0.9770    0.9969    1.0000

   ⓫    2 FACTORS WILL BE RETAINED BY THE MINEIGEN CRITERION

              ㉑        FACTOR PATTERN

                        FACTOR1    FACTOR2

              POP       0.58096    0.80642
              SCHOOL    0.76704   -0.54476
              EMPLOY    0.67243    0.72605
              SERVICES  0.93239   -0.10431
              HOUSE     0.79116   -0.55818

              VARIANCE EXPLAINED BY EACH FACTOR
        ㉒
                    FACTOR1    FACTOR2
                    2.873314   1.796660

           FINAL COMMUNALITY ESTIMATES: TOTAL =     4.669974
   ㉓
             POP      SCHOOL    EMPLOY  SERVICES     HOUSE
        0.987826  0.885106  0.979306  0.880236  0.937500
```

Principal Factor Analysis: Example 2

The next example is a principal factor analysis using squared multiple correlations for the prior communality estimates (PRIORS=SMC). Kaiser's measure of sampling adequacy (MSA) is requested. A SCREE plot of the eigenvalues is printed. The RESIDUAL correlations and partial correlations are computed. The PREPLOT option plots the unrotated factor pattern.

Specifying ROTATE=PROMAX produces an orthogonal varimax prerotation followed by an oblique rotation. The REORDER option reorders the variables according to their largest factor loadings. The SCORE option requests scoring coefficients. The PLOT procedure produces a plot of the reference structure.

An OUTSTAT= data set is created by FACTOR and printed.

```
PROC FACTOR DATA=SOCECON PRIORS=SMC MSA SCREE RESIDUAL PREPLOT
            ROTATE=PROMAX REORDER PLOT
            OUTSTAT=FACT_ALL;
   TITLE3 'PRINCIPAL FACTOR ANALYSIS WITH PROMAX ROTATION';

PROC PRINT;
   TITLE3 'FACTOR OUTPUT DATA SET';
```

If the data are appropriate for the common factor model, the partial correlations controlling the other variables should be small compared to the original correlations. The partial correlation between SCHOOL and HOUSE, for example, is .64, slightly less than the original correlation of .86. The partial correlation between POP and SCHOOL is −.54, which is much larger than the original correlation and an indication of trouble. Kaiser's MSA is a summary, for each variable and for all variables together, of how much smaller the partial correlations are than the original correlations. Values of .8 or .9 are considered good while MSAs below .5 are unacceptable. POP, SCHOOL, and EMPLOY have very poor MSAs. Only SERVICES has a good MSA. The overall MSA of .57 is sufficiently poor that additional variables should be included in the analysis to better define the common factors. A commonly used rule-of-thumb is that there should be at least three variables per factor. It will be shown below that there seem to be two common factors in these data, so more variables are needed for a reliable analysis.

The SMCs are all fairly large; hence, the factor loadings do not differ greatly from the principal component analysis.

The eigenvalues show clearly that two common factors are present. There are two large positive eigenvalues that together account for 101.31% of the common variance, as close to 100% as one is ever likely to get without iterating. The scree plot shows a sharp bend at the third eigenvalue, reinforcing the above conclusion.

The principal factor pattern is similar to the principal component pattern. For example, SERVICES has the largest loading on the first factor, POP the smallest. POP and EMPLOY have large positive loadings on the second factor, HOUSE and SCHOOL have large negative loadings.

The final communality estimates are all fairly close to the priors, only HOUSE having increased appreciably from 0.847019 to 0.884950. Nearly 100% of the common variance is accounted for. The residual correlations are low, the largest being .03. The partial correlations are not quite as impressive since the uniqueness values are also rather small. These results indicate that the SMCs are good but not quite optimal communality estimates.

The plot of the unrotated factor pattern shows two tight clusters of variables, HOUSE and SCHOOL at the negative end of FACTOR2, EMPLOY and POP at the positive end. SERVICES is in between but closer to HOUSE and SCHOOL. A good rotation would put the reference axes through the two clusters.

The varimax rotation puts one axis through HOUSE and SCHOOL but misses POP and EMPLOY slightly. The promax rotation places an axis through POP and EMPLOY but misses HOUSE and SCHOOL. Since an independent-cluster solution would be possible if it were not for SERVICES, a Harris-Kaiser rotation weighted by the Cureton-Mulaik technique should be used.

The output data set can be used for Harris-Kaiser rotation by deleting observations with _TYPE_='PATTERN' and _TYPE_='FCORR', which are for the promax-rotated factors, and changing _TYPE_='UNROTATE' to 'PATTERN':

```
DATA FACT2(TYPE=FACTOR);
   SET;
   IF _TYPE_='PATTERN'|_TYPE_='FCORR' THEN DELETE;
   IF _TYPE_='UNROTATE' THEN _TYPE_='PATTERN';
PROC FACTOR ROTATE=HK NORM=WEIGHT REORDER PLOT;
   TITLE3 'HARRIS-KAISER ROTATION WITH CURETON-MULAIK WEIGHTS';
```

The variable SERVICES receives a small weight, and the axes are placed as desired.

Output 17.2 Principal Factor Analysis: PROC FACTOR and PROC PRINT

```
                              FIVE SOCIO-ECONOMIC VARIABLES                                         1
                    SEE PAGE 14 OF HARMAN: MODERN FACTOR ANALYSIS, 3RD ED
                        PRINCIPAL FACTOR ANALYSIS WITH PROMAX ROTATION

INITIAL FACTOR METHOD: PRINCIPAL FACTORS

                 ❹       PARTIAL CORRELATIONS CONTROLLING ALL OTHER VARIABLES

                                    POP    SCHOOL    EMPLOY  SERVICES     HOUSE

                      POP       1.00000  -0.54465   0.97083   0.09612   0.15871
                      SCHOOL   -0.54465   1.00000   0.54373   0.04996   0.64717
                      EMPLOY    0.97083   0.54373   1.00000   0.06689  -0.25572
                      SERVICES  0.09612   0.04996   0.06689   1.00000   0.59415
                      HOUSE     0.15871   0.64717  -0.25572   0.59415   1.00000

               ❺      KAISER'S MEASURE OF SAMPLING ADEQUACY: OVER-ALL MSA = 0.57536759

                                  POP    SCHOOL    EMPLOY  SERVICES     HOUSE
                             0.472079  0.551588  0.488511  0.806644  0.612814

                               PRIOR COMMUNALITY ESTIMATES: SMC

                                  POP    SCHOOL    EMPLOY  SERVICES     HOUSE
                             0.968592  0.822285  0.969181  0.785724  0.847019

          EIGENVALUES OF THE REDUCED CORRELATION MATRIX:  TOTAL =     4.3928    AVERAGE =     0.87856

                                        1         2         3         4         5
                     EIGENVALUE    2.734301  1.716069  0.039563 -0.024523 -0.072608
                     DIFFERENCE    1.018232  1.676506  0.064086  0.048084
                     PROPORTION      0.6225    0.3907    0.0090   -0.0056   -0.0165
                     CUMULATIVE      0.6225    1.0131    1.0221    1.0165    1.0000

                         2 FACTORS WILL BE RETAINED BY THE PROPORTION CRITERION
```

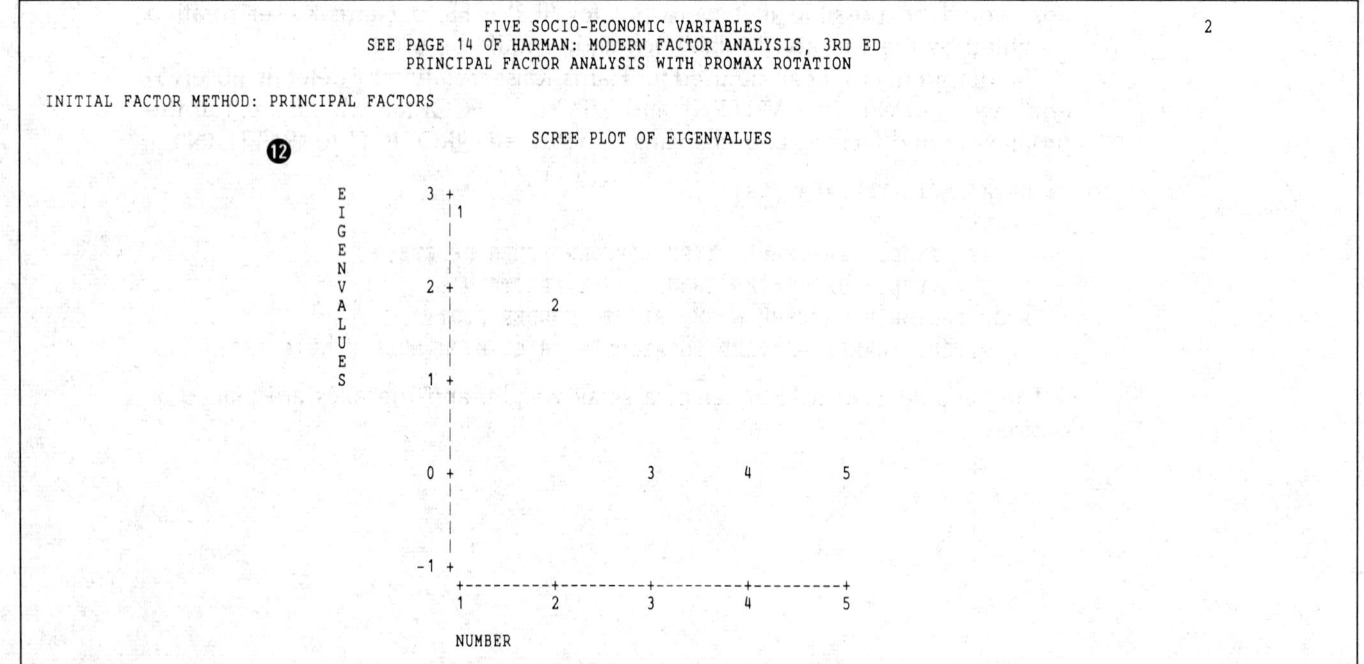

```
                        FIVE SOCIO-ECONOMIC VARIABLES                                  3
               SEE PAGE 14 OF HARMAN: MODERN FACTOR ANALYSIS, 3RD ED
                   PRINCIPAL FACTOR ANALYSIS WITH PROMAX ROTATION

INITIAL FACTOR METHOD: PRINCIPAL FACTORS

                                 FACTOR PATTERN

                                  FACTOR1   FACTOR2

                       SERVICES   0.87899  -0.15847
                       HOUSE      0.74215  -0.57806
                       EMPLOY     0.71447   0.67936
                       SCHOOL     0.71370  -0.55515
                       POP        0.62533   0.76621

                    VARIANCE EXPLAINED BY EACH FACTOR

                              FACTOR1   FACTOR2
                              2.734301  1.716069

             FINAL COMMUNALITY ESTIMATES: TOTAL =   4.450370

                  POP    SCHOOL    EMPLOY  SERVICES     HOUSE
             0.978113  0.817564  0.971999  0.797743  0.884950

(24)          RESIDUAL CORRELATIONS WITH UNIQUENESS ON THE DIAGONAL

                      POP     SCHOOL     EMPLOY  SERVICES      HOUSE

          POP         0.02189  -0.01118   0.00514   0.01063   0.00124
          SCHOOL     -0.01118   0.18244   0.02151  -0.02390   0.01248
          EMPLOY      0.00514   0.02151   0.02800  -0.00565  -0.01561
          SERVICES    0.01063  -0.02390  -0.00565   0.20226   0.03370
          HOUSE       0.00124   0.01248  -0.01561   0.03370   0.11505

(25)    ROOT MEAN SQUARE OFF-DIAGONAL RESIDUALS: OVER-ALL = 0.01693282

                  POP    SCHOOL    EMPLOY  SERVICES     HOUSE
             0.008153  0.018130  0.013828  0.021517  0.019602

(26)             PARTIAL CORRELATIONS CONTROLLING FACTORS

                      POP     SCHOOL     EMPLOY  SERVICES      HOUSE

          POP         1.00000  -0.17693   0.20752   0.15975   0.02471
          SCHOOL     -0.17693   1.00000   0.30097  -0.12443   0.08614
          EMPLOY      0.20752   0.30097   1.00000  -0.07504  -0.27509
          SERVICES    0.15975  -0.12443  -0.07504   1.00000   0.22093
          HOUSE       0.02471   0.08614  -0.27509   0.22093   1.00000

(27)    ROOT MEAN SQUARE OFF-DIAGONAL PARTIALS: OVER-ALL = 0.18550132

                  POP    SCHOOL    EMPLOY  SERVICES     HOUSE
             0.158508  0.190259  0.231818  0.154470  0.182015
```

```
                    FIVE SOCIO-ECONOMIC VARIABLES                              4
          SEE PAGE 14 OF HARMAN: MODERN FACTOR ANALYSIS, 3RD ED
             PRINCIPAL FACTOR ANALYSIS WITH PROMAX ROTATION

INITIAL FACTOR METHOD: PRINCIPAL FACTORS

   (28)      PLOT OF FACTOR PATTERN FOR FACTOR1  AND FACTOR2

                              FACTOR1
                                 1

                          D     .9

                                .8
                E
                 B              .7                C
                                                    A
                                .6

                                .5

                                .4

                                .3

                                .2
                                                            F
                                .1                          A
                                                            C
 -1 -.9-.8-.7-.6-.5-.4-.3-.2-.1  0 .1 .2 .3 .4 .5 .6 .7 .8 .9 1.0T
                                                            O
                               -.1                          R
                                                            2
                               -.2

                               -.3

                               -.4

                               -.5

                               -.6

                               -.7

                               -.8

                               -.9

                                -1

  POP     =A    SCHOOL  =B    EMPLOY  =C    SERVICES=D    HOUSE   =E
```

```
                    FIVE SOCIO-ECONOMIC VARIABLES                              5
          SEE PAGE 14 OF HARMAN: MODERN FACTOR ANALYSIS, 3RD ED
             PRINCIPAL FACTOR ANALYSIS WITH PROMAX ROTATION

PREROTATION METHOD: VARIMAX

         (31)      ORTHOGONAL TRANSFORMATION MATRIX

                                  1          2

                        1      0.78895    0.61446
                        2     -0.61446    0.78895

            (32)      ROTATED FACTOR PATTERN

                              FACTOR1    FACTOR2

                   HOUSE      0.94072   -0.00004
                   SCHOOL     0.90419    0.00055
                   SERVICES   0.79085    0.41509
                   POP        0.02255    0.98874
                   EMPLOY     0.14625    0.97499

         (33)      VARIANCE EXPLAINED BY EACH FACTOR

                          FACTOR1    FACTOR2
                          2.349857   2.100513

   (44)      FINAL COMMUNALITY ESTIMATES: TOTAL =    4.450370

                 POP     SCHOOL    EMPLOY  SERVICES     HOUSE
            0.978113   0.817564  0.971999  0.797743  0.884950
```

```
                         FIVE SOCIO-ECONOMIC VARIABLES                                   6
                SEE PAGE 14 OF HARMAN: MODERN FACTOR ANALYSIS, 3RD ED
                    PRINCIPAL FACTOR ANALYSIS WITH PROMAX ROTATION

PREROTATION METHOD: VARIMAX

         ㊼          PLOT OF FACTOR PATTERN FOR FACTOR1  AND FACTOR2

                                    FACTOR1
                                       1
                                      E
                                      .B

                                      .8         D

                                      .7

                                      .6

                                      .5

                                      .4

                                      .3

                                      .2
                                                          C  F
                                      .1                     A
                                                             C
        -1 -.9-.8-.7-.6-.5-.4-.3-.2-.1  0 .1 .2 .3 .4 .5 .6 .7 .8 .9 A.0T
                                                             O
                                     -.1                     R
                                                             2
                                     -.2

                                     -.3

                                     -.4

                                     -.5

                                     -.6

                                     -.7

                                     -.8

                                     -.9

                                      -1

        POP     =A    SCHOOL  =B    EMPLOY  =C    SERVICES=D    HOUSE   =E
```

```
                         FIVE SOCIO-ECONOMIC VARIABLES                                   7
                SEE PAGE 14 OF HARMAN: MODERN FACTOR ANALYSIS, 3RD ED
                    PRINCIPAL FACTOR ANALYSIS WITH PROMAX ROTATION

ROTATION METHOD: PROMAX

         ㉞          TARGET MATRIX FOR PROCRUSTEAN TRANSFORMATION

                                 FACTOR1   FACTOR2

                      HOUSE      1.00000  -0.00000
                      SCHOOL     1.00000   0.00000
                      SERVICES   0.69421   0.10045
                      POP        0.00001   1.00000
                      EMPLOY     0.00326   0.96793

              ㉟          PROCRUSTEAN TRANSFORMATION MATRIX

                                    1          2

                           1     1.04117   -0.09865
                           2    -0.10572    0.96303

           ㊱          NORMALIZED OBLIQUE TRANSFORMATION MATRIX

                                    1          2

                           1     0.73803    0.54202
                           2    -0.70555    0.86528
```

(continued on next page)

(continued from previous page)

```
                    ❸⑦ INTER-FACTOR CORRELATIONS

                              FACTOR1   FACTOR2

                   FACTOR1    1.00000   0.20188
                   FACTOR2    0.20188   1.00000

              ❸⑧ ROTATED FACTOR PATTERN (STD REG COEFS)

                              FACTOR1   FACTOR2

                   HOUSE      0.95558  -0.09792
                   SCHOOL     0.91842  -0.09352
                   SERVICES   0.76053   0.33932
                   POP       -0.07908   1.00192
                   EMPLOY     0.04799   0.97509

                   REFERENCE AXIS CORRELATIONS

                              FACTOR1   FACTOR2

                   FACTOR1    1.00000  -0.20188
                   FACTOR2   -0.20188   1.00000
```

```
                         FIVE SOCIO-ECONOMIC VARIABLES                          8
              SEE PAGE 14 OF HARMAN: MODERN FACTOR ANALYSIS, 3RD ED
                   PRINCIPAL FACTOR ANALYSIS WITH PROMAX ROTATION

ROTATION METHOD: PROMAX

            ❹⓪ REFERENCE STRUCTURE (SEMIPARTIAL CORRELATIONS)

                              FACTOR1   FACTOR2

                   HOUSE      0.93591  -0.09590
                   SCHOOL     0.89951  -0.09160
                   SERVICES   0.74487   0.33233
                   POP       -0.07745   0.98129
                   EMPLOY     0.04700   0.95501

     ❹① VARIANCE EXPLAINED BY EACH FACTOR ELIMINATING OTHER FACTORS

                          FACTOR1   FACTOR2
                          2.248089  2.003020

                ❹② FACTOR STRUCTURE (CORRELATIONS)

                              FACTOR1   FACTOR2

                   HOUSE      0.93582   0.09500
                   SCHOOL     0.89954   0.09189
                   SERVICES   0.82903   0.49286
                   POP        0.12319   0.98596
                   EMPLOY     0.24484   0.98478

       ❹③ VARIANCE EXPLAINED BY EACH FACTOR IGNORING OTHER FACTORS

                          FACTOR1   FACTOR2
                          2.447349  2.202280

              FINAL COMMUNALITY ESTIMATES: TOTAL =   4.450370

                   POP     SCHOOL     EMPLOY  SERVICES     HOUSE
              0.978113  0.817564  0.971999  0.797743  0.884950
```

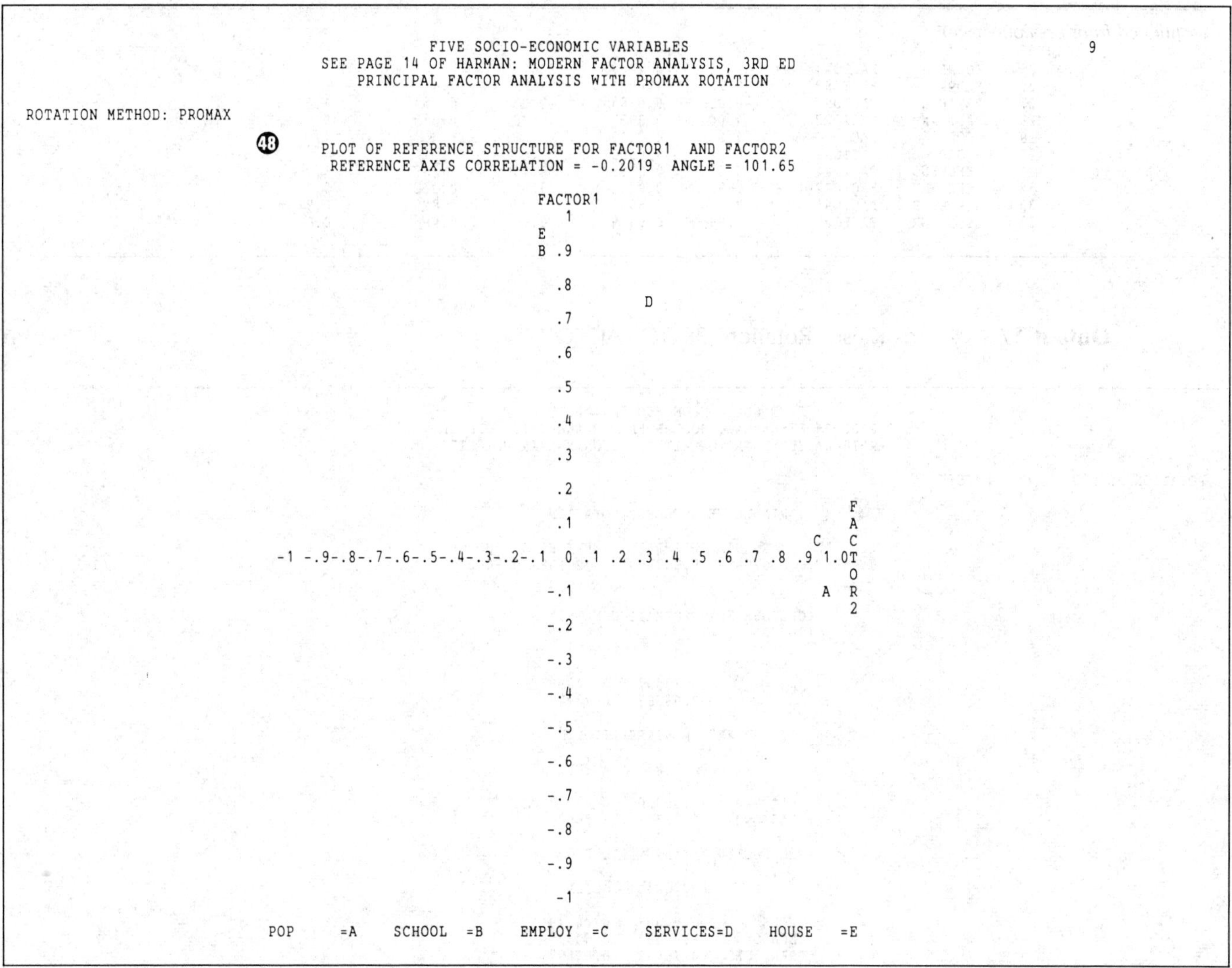

FIVE SOCIO-ECONOMIC VARIABLES 10
SEE PAGE 14 OF HARMAN: MODERN FACTOR ANALYSIS, 3RD ED
FACTOR OUTPUT DATA SET

OBS	_TYPE_	_NAME_	POP	SCHOOL	EMPLOY	SERVICES	HOUSE
1	MEAN		6241.67	11.4417	2333.33	120.833	17000.0
2	STD		3439.99	1.7865	1241.21	114.928	6367.5
3	N		12.00	12.0000	12.00	12.000	12.0
4	CORR	POP	1.00	0.0098	0.97	0.439	0.0
5	CORR	SCHOOL	0.01	1.0000	0.15	0.691	0.9
6	CORR	EMPLOY	0.97	0.1543	1.00	0.515	0.1
7	CORR	SERVICES	0.44	0.6914	0.51	1.000	0.8
8	CORR	HOUSE	0.02	0.8631	0.12	0.778	1.0
9	COMMUNAL		0.98	0.8176	0.97	0.798	0.9
10	PRIORS		0.97	0.8223	0.97	0.786	0.8
11	EIGENVAL		2.73	1.7161	0.04	-0.025	-0.1
12	UNROTATE	FACTOR1	0.63	0.7137	0.71	0.879	0.7
13	UNROTATE	FACTOR2	0.77	-0.5552	0.68	-0.158	-0.6
14	RESIDUAL	POP	0.02	-0.0112	0.01	0.011	0.0
15	RESIDUAL	SCHOOL	-0.01	0.1824	0.02	-0.024	0.0
16	RESIDUAL	EMPLOY	0.01	0.0215	0.03	-0.006	-0.0
17	RESIDUAL	SERVICES	0.01	-0.0239	-0.01	0.202	0.0
18	RESIDUAL	HOUSE	0.00	0.0125	-0.02	0.034	0.1
19	PRETRANS	FACTOR1	0.79	-0.6145	.	.	.
20	PRETRANS	FACTOR2	0.61	0.7889	.	.	.
21	PREROTAT	FACTOR1	0.02	0.9042	0.15	0.791	0.9
22	PREROTAT	FACTOR2	0.99	0.0006	0.97	0.415	-0.0
23	TRANSFOR	FACTOR1	0.74	-0.7055	.	.	.
24	TRANSFOR	FACTOR2	0.54	0.8653	.	.	.

(continued on next page)

(continued from previous page)

```
25    FCORR      FACTOR1     1.00    0.2019      .       .        .
26    FCORR      FACTOR2     0.20    1.0000      .       .        .
27    PATTERN    FACTOR1    -0.08    0.9184    0.05    0.761     1.0
28    PATTERN    FACTOR2     1.00   -0.0935    0.98    0.339    -0.1
29    RCORR      FACTOR1     1.00   -0.2019      .       .        .
30    RCORR      FACTOR2    -0.20    1.0000      .       .        .
31    REFERENC   FACTOR1    -0.08    0.8995    0.05    0.745     0.9
32    REFERENC   FACTOR2     0.98   -0.0916    0.96    0.332    -0.1
33    STRUCTUR   FACTOR1     0.12    0.8995    0.24    0.829     0.9
34    STRUCTUR   FACTOR2     0.99    0.0919    0.98    0.493     0.1
```

Output 17.3 Harris-Kaiser Rotation: PROC FACTOR

```
                              FIVE SOCIO-ECONOMIC VARIABLES                              11
                  SEE PAGE 14 OF HARMAN: MODERN FACTOR ANALYSIS, 3RD ED
                   HARRIS-KAISER ROTATION WITH CURETON-MULAIK WEIGHTS

ROTATION METHOD: HARRIS-KAISER

                   (29)    VARIABLE WEIGHTS FOR ROTATION

                       POP    SCHOOL    EMPLOY  SERVICES     HOUSE
                  0.959827  0.939454  0.997464  0.121948  0.940073


                             OBLIQUE TRANSFORMATION MATRIX

                                           1          2

                                 1      0.73537    0.61899
                                 2     -0.68283    0.78987

                               INTER-FACTOR CORRELATIONS

                                       FACTOR1    FACTOR2

                              FACTOR1   1.00000    0.08358
                              FACTOR2   0.08358    1.00000

                         ROTATED FACTOR PATTERN (STD REG COEFS)

                                       FACTOR1    FACTOR2

                              HOUSE     0.94048    0.00279
                              SCHOOL    0.90391    0.00327
                              SERVICES  0.75459    0.41892
                              POP      -0.06335    0.99227
                              EMPLOY    0.06152    0.97885

                              REFERENCE AXIS CORRELATIONS

                                       FACTOR1    FACTOR2

                              FACTOR1   1.00000   -0.08358
                              FACTOR2  -0.08358    1.00000

                     REFERENCE STRUCTURE (SEMIPARTIAL CORRELATIONS)

                                       FACTOR1    FACTOR2

                              HOUSE     0.93719    0.00278
                              SCHOOL    0.90075    0.00326
                              SERVICES  0.75195    0.41745
                              POP      -0.06312    0.98880
                              EMPLOY    0.06130    0.97543

              VARIANCE EXPLAINED BY EACH FACTOR ELIMINATING OTHER FACTORS

                                   FACTOR1   FACTOR2
                                  2.262854  2.103473
```

```
                         FIVE SOCIO-ECONOMIC VARIABLES                                  12
                 SEE PAGE 14 OF HARMAN: MODERN FACTOR ANALYSIS, 3RD ED
                  HARRIS-KAISER ROTATION WITH CURETON-MULAIK WEIGHTS

ROTATION METHOD: HARRIS-KAISER

                        FACTOR STRUCTURE (CORRELATIONS)

                                   FACTOR1   FACTOR2

                        HOUSE      0.94071   0.08139
                        SCHOOL     0.90419   0.07882
                        SERVICES   0.78960   0.48198
                        POP        0.01958   0.98698
                        EMPLOY     0.14332   0.98399

                VARIANCE EXPLAINED BY EACH FACTOR IGNORING OTHER FACTORS

                               FACTOR1   FACTOR2
                              2.346896  2.187516

                    FINAL COMMUNALITY ESTIMATES: TOTAL =    4.450370

                          POP    SCHOOL    EMPLOY  SERVICES     HOUSE
                     0.978113  0.817564  0.971999  0.797743  0.884950
```

```
                         FIVE SOCIO-ECONOMIC VARIABLES                                  13
                 SEE PAGE 14 OF HARMAN: MODERN FACTOR ANALYSIS, 3RD ED
                  HARRIS-KAISER ROTATION WITH CURETON-MULAIK WEIGHTS

ROTATION METHOD: HARRIS-KAISER

                 PLOT OF REFERENCE STRUCTURE FOR FACTOR1  AND FACTOR2
                  REFERENCE AXIS CORRELATION = -0.0836  ANGLE =  94.79

                             FACTOR1
                                1
                                E
                               .B

                               .8
                                            D
                               .7

                               .6

                               .5

                               .4

                               .3

                               .2
                                                                F
                               .1                               A
                                                             C  C
-1 -.9-.8-.7-.6-.5-.4-.3-.2-.1  0 .1 .2 .3 .4 .5 .6 .7 .8 .9 1.0T
                                                             A  O
                              -.1                               R
                                                                2
                              -.2

                              -.3

                              -.4

                              -.5

                              -.6

                              -.7

                              -.8

                              -.9

                               -1

POP     =A    SCHOOL  =B    EMPLOY  =C    SERVICES=D    HOUSE   =E
```

Maximum-Likelihood Factor Analysis: Example 3

This example uses maximum-likelihood factor analyses for one, two, and three factors. It is already apparent from the principal factor analysis that the best number of common factors is almost certainly two. The one- and three-factor ML solutions reinforce this conclusion and illustrate some of the numerical problems that can occur.

```
PROC FACTOR DATA=SOCECON METHOD=ML HEYWOOD N=1;
   TITLE3 'MAXIMUM LIKELIHOOD FACTOR ANALYSIS WITH ONE FACTOR';

PROC FACTOR DATA=SOCECON METHOD=ML HEYWOOD N=2;
   TITLE3 'MAXIMUM LIKELIHOOD FACTOR ANALYSIS WITH TWO FACTORS';

PROC FACTOR DATA=SOCECON METHOD=ML HEYWOOD N=3;
   TITLE3 'MAXIMUM LIKELIHOOD FACTOR ANALYSIS WITH THREE FACTORS';
```

With one factor, the solution on the second iteration is so close to the optimum that FACTOR cannot find a better solution even though the convergence criterion has not been met, hence the message, UNABLE TO IMPROVE CRITERION. When this message appears, you should try re-running FACTOR with some different prior communality estimates to make sure that the solution is correct. In this case, other prior estimates lead to the same solution or possibly to worse local optima, as indicated by CRITERION or CHI-SQUARE values.

The variable EMPLOY has a communality of 1.0, and therefore an infinite weight that is printed below the final communality estimate as a missing value (.). The first eigenvalue is also infinite. Infinite values are ignored in computing the total of the eigenvalues and the total final communality.

The two-factor analysis converges without incident. This time, however, the POP variable is a Heywood case.

The three-factor analysis generates the message, WARNING: TOO MANY FACTORS FOR A UNIQUE SOLUTION. The number of parameters in the model exceeds the number of elements in the correlation matrix from which they can be estimated, so an infinite number of different perfect solutions can be obtained. The CRITERION approaches zero (8.799E-08) at an improper optimum, as indicated by CONVERGED, BUT NOT TO A PROPER OPTIMUM. The degrees of freedom for the chi-square test are −2, so a probability level cannot be computed for three factors. Note also that the variable EMPLOY is a Heywood case again.

The probability levels for the chi-square test are .0001 for the hypothesis of no common factors, .0002 for one common factor, and .1382 for two common factors. Therefore the two-factor model seems to be an adequate representation. Akaike's information criterion and Schwarz's Bayesian criterion attain their minimum values at two common factors, so there is little doubt that two factors are appropriate for these data.

Output 17.4 Maximum-Likelihood Factor Analysis: PROC FACTOR

```
                              FIVE SOCIO-ECONOMIC VARIABLES                                       1
                        SEE PAGE 14 OF HARMAN: MODERN FACTOR ANALYSIS, 3RD ED
                         MAXIMUM LIKELIHOOD FACTOR ANALYSIS WITH ONE FACTOR

INITIAL FACTOR METHOD: MAXIMUM LIKELIHOOD

                           PRIOR COMMUNALITY ESTIMATES: SMC

                              POP    SCHOOL    EMPLOY  SERVICES     HOUSE
                         0.968592  0.822285  0.969181  0.785724  0.847019

                 PRELIMINARY EIGENVALUES:  TOTAL =   76.1166   AVERAGE =    15.2233

                                        1          2          3          4          5
(10)              EIGENVALUE   63.701009 13.054719  0.327639 -0.347281 -0.619501
                  DIFFERENCE   50.646289 12.727080  0.674920  0.272220
                  PROPORTION      0.8369    0.1715    0.0043   -0.0046   -0.0081
                  CUMULATIVE      0.8369    1.0084    1.0127    1.0081    1.0000

                       1 FACTORS WILL BE RETAINED BY THE NFACTOR CRITERION

             ITER CRITERION    RIDGE   CHANGE    COMMUNALITIES
(13)           1  6.542922     0.000  0.10330    0.93828 0.72227 1.00000 0.71940 0.74371
               2  3.123270     0.000  0.72885    0.94566 0.02380 1.00000 0.26493 0.01487

                               UNABLE TO IMPROVE CRITERION.
                             TRY A DIFFERENT 'PRIORS' STATEMENT.

(14)             SIGNIFICANCE TESTS BASED ON        12 OBSERVATIONS:

                     TEST OF H0: NO COMMON FACTORS.
                        VS HA: AT LEAST ONE COMMON FACTOR.

                       CHI-SQUARE =     54.252   DF =     10   PROB>CHI**2 = 0.0001

                     TEST OF H0:     1 FACTORS ARE SUFFICIENT.
                        VS HA: MORE FACTORS ARE NEEDED.

                       CHI-SQUARE =     24.466   DF =      5   PROB>CHI**2 = 0.0002

(15)             AKAIKE'S INFORMATION CRITERION =     57.47924
(16)             SCHWARZ'S BAYESIAN CRITERION =       31.16415
                 TUCKER AND LEWIS'S RELIABILITY COEFFICIENT =    0.1202314

(17)                        SQUARED CANONICAL CORRELATIONS

                                          FACTOR1
                                          1.000000

      EIGENVALUES OF THE WEIGHTED REDUCED CORRELATION MATRIX:  TOTAL =         0   AVERAGE =          0

                                        1          2          3          4          5
                  EIGENVALUE     .         1.927160 -0.228313 -0.792956 -0.905891
                  DIFFERENCE     .         2.155473  0.564643  0.112935
```

```
                              FIVE SOCIO-ECONOMIC VARIABLES                                   2
                  SEE PAGE 14 OF HARMAN: MODERN FACTOR ANALYSIS, 3RD ED
                    MAXIMUM LIKELIHOOD FACTOR ANALYSIS WITH ONE FACTOR

INITIAL FACTOR METHOD: MAXIMUM LIKELIHOOD
                                     FACTOR PATTERN

                                              FACTOR1

                                  POP          0.97245
                                  SCHOOL       0.15428
                                  EMPLOY       1.00000
                                  SERVICES     0.51472
                                  HOUSE        0.12193

                             VARIANCE EXPLAINED BY EACH FACTOR

                                               FACTOR1
                                 WEIGHTED    17.801063
                                 UNWEIGHTED   2.249260

                      FINAL COMMUNALITY ESTIMATES AND VARIABLE WEIGHTS
               TOTAL COMMUNALITY: WEIGHTED = 17.801063   UNWEIGHTED =  2.249260

                                POP    SCHOOL     EMPLOY  SERVICES     HOUSE
          COMMUNALITY   0.945656  0.023803  1.000000  0.264935  0.014866
          WEIGHT       18.401165  1.024384  .         1.360424  1.015090
```

```
                              FIVE SOCIO-ECONOMIC VARIABLES                                   3
                  SEE PAGE 14 OF HARMAN: MODERN FACTOR ANALYSIS, 3RD ED
                    MAXIMUM LIKELIHOOD FACTOR ANALYSIS WITH TWO FACTORS
INITIAL FACTOR METHOD: MAXIMUM LIKELIHOOD
                          PRIOR COMMUNALITY ESTIMATES: SMC

                         POP     SCHOOL     EMPLOY  SERVICES     HOUSE
                    0.968592  0.822285  0.969181  0.785724  0.847019

              PRELIMINARY EIGENVALUES:  TOTAL =   76.1166   AVERAGE =    15.2233

                                   1          2          3          4          5
          EIGENVALUE    63.701009 13.054719  0.327639 -0.347281 -0.619501
          DIFFERENCE    50.646289 12.727080  0.674920  0.272220
          PROPORTION       0.8369    0.1715     0.0043    -0.0046    -0.0081
          CUMULATIVE       0.8369    1.0084     1.0127     1.0081     1.0000

                     2 FACTORS WILL BE RETAINED BY THE NFACTOR CRITERION

         ITER CRITERION    RIDGE   CHANGE    COMMUNALITIES
           1   0.343122    0.000  0.04710    1.00000 0.80672 0.95058 0.79348 0.89412
           2   0.307218    0.000  0.03068    1.00000 0.80821 0.96023 0.81048 0.92480
           3   0.306786    0.000  0.00629    1.00000 0.81149 0.95948 0.81677 0.92023
           4   0.306737    0.000  0.00218    1.00000 0.80985 0.95963 0.81498 0.92241
           5   0.306732    0.000  0.00071    1.00000 0.81019 0.95955 0.81569 0.92187

                           CONVERGENCE CRITERION SATISFIED.

              SIGNIFICANCE TESTS BASED ON          12 OBSERVATIONS:

                 TEST OF H0: NO COMMON FACTORS.
                      VS HA: AT LEAST ONE COMMON FACTOR.

                    CHI-SQUARE =     54.252    DF =     10   PROB>CHI**2 = 0.0001

                 TEST OF H0:    2 FACTORS ARE SUFFICIENT.
                      VS HA: MORE FACTORS ARE NEEDED.

                    CHI-SQUARE =      2.198    DF =      1   PROB>CHI**2 = 0.1382

              AKAIKE'S INFORMATION CRITERION =      31.68079
              SCHWARZ'S BAYESIAN CRITERION =        19.23474
              TUCKER AND LEWIS'S RELIABILITY COEFFICIENT =      0.72922

                            SQUARED CANONICAL CORRELATIONS

                                   FACTOR1   FACTOR2
                                  1.000000  0.951889

   EIGENVALUES OF THE WEIGHTED REDUCED CORRELATION MATRIX:  TOTAL =   19.7853   AVERAGE =     4.94633

                                   1          2          3          4          5
          EIGENVALUE      .          19.785314  0.543185 -0.039771 -0.503412
          DIFFERENCE      .          19.242129  0.582956  0.463641
          PROPORTION        .           1.0000    0.0275    -0.0020    -0.0254
          CUMULATIVE        .           1.0000    1.0275     1.0254     1.0000
```

```
                                 FIVE SOCIO-ECONOMIC VARIABLES                                                  4
                          SEE PAGE 14 OF HARMAN: MODERN FACTOR ANALYSIS, 3RD ED
                           MAXIMUM LIKELIHOOD FACTOR ANALYSIS WITH TWO FACTORS

INITIAL FACTOR METHOD: MAXIMUM LIKELIHOOD

                                           FACTOR PATTERN

                                             FACTOR1   FACTOR2

                                  POP        1.00000   0.00000
                                  SCHOOL     0.00975   0.90003
                                  EMPLOY     0.97245   0.11797
                                  SERVICES   0.43887   0.78930
                                  HOUSE      0.02241   0.95989

                                 VARIANCE EXPLAINED BY EACH FACTOR

                                             FACTOR1   FACTOR2
                                 WEIGHTED   24.432971 19.785314
                                 UNWEIGHTED  2.138861  2.368353

                          FINAL COMMUNALITY ESTIMATES AND VARIABLE WEIGHTS
                     TOTAL COMMUNALITY: WEIGHTED = 44.218285   UNWEIGHTED =  4.507214

                                   POP     SCHOOL     EMPLOY  SERVICES      HOUSE
                    COMMUNALITY   1.000000  0.810145  0.959571  0.815603  0.921894
                    WEIGHT            .     5.268294 24.724667  5.425646 12.799679
```

```
                                 FIVE SOCIO-ECONOMIC VARIABLES                                                  5
                          SEE PAGE 14 OF HARMAN: MODERN FACTOR ANALYSIS, 3RD ED
                          MAXIMUM LIKELIHOOD FACTOR ANALYSIS WITH THREE FACTORS

INITIAL FACTOR METHOD: MAXIMUM LIKELIHOOD

                              PRIOR COMMUNALITY ESTIMATES: SMC

                                 POP    SCHOOL    EMPLOY  SERVICES     HOUSE
                            0.968592  0.822285  0.969181  0.785724  0.847019

                  PRELIMINARY EIGENVALUES:  TOTAL =    76.1166   AVERAGE =     15.2233

                                       1          2          3          4          5
                    EIGENVALUE   63.701009 13.054719  0.327639 -0.347281 -0.619501
                    DIFFERENCE   50.646289 12.727080  0.674920  0.272220
                    PROPORTION      0.8369    0.1715    0.0043   -0.0046   -0.0081
                    CUMULATIVE      0.8369    1.0084    1.0127    1.0081    1.0000

                          3 FACTORS WILL BE RETAINED BY THE NFACTOR CRITERION
                          WARNING: TOO MANY FACTORS FOR A UNIQUE SOLUTION.

               ITER CRITERION     RIDGE   CHANGE   COMMUNALITIES
                 1   0.160126     0.031  0.05102   0.96382 0.84123 1.00000 0.80346 0.89804
                 2  0.0034068     0.031  0.05878   0.98216 0.87692 1.00000 0.80295 0.95682
                 3  0.0000414     0.031  0.01013   0.98334 0.88004 1.00000 0.80507 0.96695
                 4  1.472E-06     0.031  0.00155   0.98316 0.88054 1.00000 0.80480 0.96850
                 5  8.799E-08     0.031  0.00029   0.98311 0.88065 1.00000 0.80462 0.96879

                              CONVERGED, BUT NOT TO A PROPER OPTIMUM.
                                TRY A DIFFERENT 'PRIORS' STATEMENT.

                  SIGNIFICANCE TESTS BASED ON         12 OBSERVATIONS:

                     TEST OF H0: NO COMMON FACTORS.
                          VS HA: AT LEAST ONE COMMON FACTOR.

                         CHI-SQUARE =     54.252   DF =     10   PROB>CHI**2 = 0.0001

                     TEST OF H0:     3 FACTORS ARE SUFFICIENT.
                          VS HA: MORE FACTORS ARE NEEDED.

                         CHI-SQUARE =      0.000   DF =     -2   PROB>CHI**2 = 1.0000

                  AKAIKE'S INFORMATION CRITERION =          34
                  SCHWARZ'S BAYESIAN CRITERION =       21.12171
                  TUCKER AND LEWIS'S RELIABILITY COEFFICIENT =           0

                                    SQUARED CANONICAL CORRELATIONS

                                      FACTOR1   FACTOR2   FACTOR3
                                     1.000000  0.975846  0.699066
```

```
                                FIVE SOCIO-ECONOMIC VARIABLES                                          6
                          SEE PAGE 14 OF HARMAN: MODERN FACTOR ANALYSIS, 3RD ED
                          MAXIMUM LIKELIHOOD FACTOR ANALYSIS WITH THREE FACTORS

INITIAL FACTOR METHOD: MAXIMUM LIKELIHOOD

           EIGENVALUES OF THE WEIGHTED REDUCED CORRELATION MATRIX:  TOTAL =    42.7242   AVERAGE =      10.6811

                                       1          2          3          4          5
                    EIGENVALUE    .          40.401173   2.322986   0.000319  -0.000273
                    DIFFERENCE    .          38.078186   2.322667   0.000591
                    PROPORTION        .         0.9456     0.0544     0.0000    -0.0000
                    CUMULATIVE        .         0.9456     1.0000     1.0000     1.0000

                                            FACTOR PATTERN

                                      FACTOR1   FACTOR2   FACTOR3

                               POP          0.97245  -0.11188  -0.15792
                               SCHOOL       0.15428   0.88881   0.25859
                               EMPLOY       1.00000  -0.00000   0.00000
                               SERVICES     0.51472   0.72429  -0.12272
                               HOUSE        0.12193   0.97335  -0.08071

                                 VARIANCE EXPLAINED BY EACH FACTOR

                                       FACTOR1    FACTOR2    FACTOR3
                          WEIGHTED    58.032408  40.401173   2.322986
                          UNWEIGHTED   2.249260   2.274514   0.113382

                          FINAL COMMUNALITY ESTIMATES AND VARIABLE WEIGHTS
                   TOTAL COMMUNALITY: WEIGHTED =    100.757    UNWEIGHTED =   4.637157

                                     POP      SCHOOL     EMPLOY   SERVICES      HOUSE
                    COMMUNALITY   0.983113  0.880658  1.000000  0.804594  0.968791
                    WEIGHT       59.218853  8.378825   .         5.118261  32.040674
```

REFERENCES

Akaike, H. (1973), "Information Theory and the Extension of the Maximum Likelihood Principle," in *2nd International Symposium on Information Theory*, ed. V.N. Petrov and F. Csaki, Budapest: Akailseoniai-Kiudo, 267-281.

Akaike, H. (1974), "A New Look at the Statistical Identification Model," *IEEE Transactions on Automatic Control*, 19, 716-723.

Bickel, P.J., and Doksum, K.A. (1977), *Mathematical Statistics*, San Francisco: Holden-Day.

Cattell, R.B. (1966), "The Scree Test for the Number of Factors," *Multivariate Behavioral Research*, 1, 245-276.

Cattell, R.B. (1978), *The Scientific Use of Factor Analysis*, New York: Plenum.

Cattell, R.B. and Vogelman, S. (1977), "A Comprehensive Trial of the Scree and KG Criteria for Determining the Number of Factors," *Multivariate Behavioral Research*, 12, 289-325.

Cerny, B.A. and Kaiser, H.F. (1977), "A Study of a Measure of Sampling Adequacy for Factor-Analytic Correlation Matrices," *Multivariate Behavioral Research*, 12, 43-47.

Cureton, E.E. (1968), *A Factor Analysis of Project TALENT Tests and Four Other Test Batteries*, (Interim report 4 to the U. S. Office of Education, Cooperative Research Project No. 3051.) Palo Alto: Project TALENT Office, American Institutes for Research and University of Pittsburgh.

Cureton, E.E. and Mulaik, S.A. (1975), "The Weighted Varimax Rotation and the Promax Rotation," *Psychometrika*, 40, 183-195.

Dziuban, C.D. and Harris, C.W. (1973), "On the Extraction of Components and the Applicability of the Factor Model," *American Educational Research Journal*, 10, 93-99.

Geweke, J.F. and Singleton, K.J. (1980), "Interpreting the Likelihood Ratio Statistic in Factor Models When Sample Size Is Small," *Journal of the American Statistical Association*, 75, 133-137.

Gorsuch, R.L. (1974), *Factor Analysis*, Philadelphia: W.B. Saunders Co.

Gould, S.J. (1981), *The Mismeasure of Man*, New York: W.W. Norton & Co.

Harman, H.H. (1976), *Modern Factor Analysis, Third Edition*, Chicago: University of Chicago Press.

Harris, C.W. (1962), "Some Rao-Guttman Relationships," *Psychometrika*, 27, 247-263.

Horn, J.L. and Engstrom, R. (1979), "Cattell's Scree Test in Relation to Bartlett's Chi-Square Test and Other Observations on the Number of Factors Problem," *Multivariate Behavioral Research*, 14, 283-300.

Joreskog, K.G. (1962), "On the Statistical Treatment of Residuals in Factor Analysis," *Psychometrika*, 27, 335-354.

Joreskog, K.G. (1977), "Factor Analysis by Least-Squares and Maximum Likelihood Methods," in *Statistical Methods for Digital Computers*, ed. K. Enslein, A. Ralston, and H.S. Wilf, New York: John Wiley & Sons.

Kaiser, H.F. (1963), "Image Analysis," in *Problems in Measuring Change*, ed. C.W. Harris, Madison: University of Wisconsin Press.

Kaiser, H.F. (1970), "A Second Generation Little Jiffy," *Psychometrika*, 35, 401-415.

Kaiser, H.F. and Cerny, B.A. (1979), "Factor Analysis of the Image Correlation Matrix," *Educational and Psychological Measurement*, 39, 711-714.

Kaiser, H.F. and Rice, J. (1974), "Little Jiffy, Mark IV," *Educational and Psychological Measurement*, 34, 111-117.

Kerlinger, F.N. and Pedhazur, E.J. (1973), *Multiple Regression in Behavioral Research*, New York: Holt, Rinehart & Winston.

Kim, J.O. and Mueller, C.W. (1978), *Introduction to Factor Analysis: What It Is and How To Do It*, Sage University Paper series on Quantitative Applications in the Social Sciences, series no. 07-013, Beverly Hills: Sage Publications.

Lawley, D.N. and Maxwell, A.E. (1971), *Factor Analysis as a Statistical Method*, New York: Macmillan.

Lee, H.B. and Comrey, A.L. (1979), "Distortions in a Commonly Used Factor Analytic Procedure," *Multivariate Behavioral Research*, 14, 301-321.

Mardia, K.V., Kent, J.T., and Bibby, J.M. (1979), *Multivariate Analysis*, London: Academic Press.

McDonald, R.P. (1975), "A Note on Rippe's Test of Significance in Common Factor Analysis," *Psychometrika*, 40, 117-119.

Morrison, D.F. (1976), *Multivariate Statistical Methods*, Second Edition, New York: McGraw-Hill.

Mulaik, S.A. (1972), *The Foundations of Factor Analysis*, New York: McGraw-Hill.

Rao, C.R. (1955), "Estimation and Tests of Significance in Factor Analysis," *Psychometrika*, 20, 93-111.

Schwarz, G. (1978), "Estimating the Dimension of a Model," *Annals of Statistics*, 6, 461-464.

Spearman, C. (1904), "General Intelligence Objectively Determined and Measured," *American Journal of Psychology*, 15, 201-293.

Chapter 18

The FASTCLUS Procedure

Operating systems: All

ABSTRACT

The FASTCLUS procedure is designed for disjoint clustering of very large data sets and can find good clusters with only two or three passes over the data. You specify the maximum number of clusters and, optionally, the minimum radius of the clusters. The procedure can produce an output data set containing a cluster membership variable as well as an output data set containing cluster means.

INTRODUCTION

PROC FASTCLUS performs a disjoint cluster analysis on the basis of Euclidean distances computed from one or more quantitative variables. The observations are divided into clusters such that every observation belongs to one and only one cluster (the clusters do not form a tree structure as they do in the CLUSTER procedure). If you want separate analyses for different numbers of clusters, you must run FASTCLUS once for each analysis.

The FASTCLUS procedure is intended for use with large data sets, from approximately 100 to 100,000 observations. With small data sets, the results may be highly sensitive to the order of the observations in the data set.

PROC FASTCLUS prints brief summaries of the clusters it finds. For more extensive examination of the clusters, you can request an output data set containing a cluster membership variable.

Background

The FASTCLUS procedure combines an effective method for finding initial clusters with a standard iterative algorithm for minimizing the sum of squared distances from the cluster means. The result is an efficient procedure for disjoint clustering of large data sets. FASTCLUS was directly inspired by Hartigan's *leader* algorithm (1975) and MacQueen's *k-means* algorithm (1967).

PROC FASTCLUS uses a method that Anderberg (1973) calls *nearest centroid sorting*. A set of points called *cluster seeds* is selected as a first guess of the means of the clusters. Each observation is assigned to the nearest seed to form temporary clusters. The seeds are then replaced by the means of the temporary clusters and the process is repeated until no further changes occur in the clusters. Similar techniques are described in most references on clustering (Anderberg 1973; Hartigan 1975; Everitt 1980; Spath 1980).

The FASTCLUS procedure differs from other nearest centroid sorting methods in the way the initial cluster seeds are selected. The initialization method of FASTCLUS guarantees that if there exist clusters such that all distances between observations in the same cluster are less than all distances between observations in different clusters, and if you tell FASTCLUS the correct number of clusters to find, then it always finds such a clustering without iterating. Even with clusters that are not as well separated, FASTCLUS usually finds sufficiently good initial seeds that few iterations are required. The importance of initial seed selection is demonstrated by Milligan (1980).

The initialization method used by FASTCLUS makes it sensitive to outliers. FASTCLUS can be an effective procedure for detecting outliers, since outliers often appear as clusters with only one member.

The clustering is done on the basis of Euclidean distances computed from one or more numeric variables. If there are missing values, FASTCLUS computes an adjusted distance using the nonmissing values. Observations that are very close to each other are usually assigned to the same cluster, while observations that are far apart are in different clusters.

The FASTCLUS procedure operates in four steps:

1. Observations called cluster seeds are selected.
2. Optionally, temporary clusters are formed by assigning each observation to the cluster with the nearest seed. Each time an observation is assigned, the cluster seed is updated as the current mean of the cluster.
3. Optionally, clusters are formed by assigning each observation to the nearest seed. After all observations are assigned, the cluster seeds are replaced by the cluster means. This step can be repeated until the changes in the cluster seeds become small or zero.
4. Final clusters are formed by assigning each observation to the nearest seed.

The initial cluster seeds must be observations with no missing values. You can specify the maximum number of seeds (and hence clusters) using the MAXCLUSTERS= option. You can also specify a minimum distance by which the seeds must be separated using the RADIUS= option.

PROC FASTCLUS always selects the first complete (no missing values) observation as the first seed. The next complete observation that is separated from the first seed by at least the RADIUS becomes the second seed. Later observations are selected as new seeds if they are separated from all previous seeds by at least the RADIUS, as long as the maximum number of seeds is not exceeded.

If an observation is complete but fails to qualify as a new seed, FASTCLUS considers using it to replace one of the old seeds. Two tests are made to see if the observation can qualify as a new seed.

First, an old seed is replaced if the distance between the two closest seeds is less than the distance from the observation to the nearest seed. The seed that is replaced is selected from the two seeds that are closest to each other and is the one of these two that is also closest to the observation.

If the observation fails the first test for seed replacement, a second test is made. The observation replaces the nearest seed if the smallest distance from the observation to all seeds other than the nearest one is greater than the shortest distance from the nearest seed to all other seeds. If this test is failed, FASTCLUS goes on to the next observation.

The REPLACE= option can be used to limit seed replacement. The second test for seed replacement can be omitted, causing FASTCLUS to run faster, but the seeds selected may not be as widely separated as those obtained by the default method. Seed replacement can also be suppressed entirely. In this case FASTCLUS runs much faster, but you must choose a good value for RADIUS in order to get good clusters. This method is similar to Hartigan's leader algorithm (1975, 74-78) and the *simple cluster-seeking* algorithm described by Tou and Gonzalez (1974, 90-92).

SPECIFICATIONS

You can use the following statements to invoke the FASTCLUS procedure:

PROC FASTCLUS *options;*
  VAR *variables;*
  ID *variable;*
  FREQ *variable;*
  WEIGHT *variable;*
  BY *variables;*

Usually only the VAR statement is used in addition to the PROC FASTCLUS statement.

PROC FASTCLUS Statement

PROC FASTCLUS *options;*

The following data set options can appear in the PROC statement:

DATA=*SASdataset*
: names the input data set containing observations to be clustered. If DATA= is omitted, the most recently created SAS data set is used.

SEED=*SASdataset*
: names an input data set from which initial cluster seeds are to be selected. If SEED= is not specified, initial seeds are selected from the DATA= data set.

OUT=*SASdataset*
: names an output data set to contain all the original data, plus the new variables CLUSTER and DISTANCE. If you want to create a permanent SAS data set, you must specify a two-level name. See "SAS Files" in the *SAS User's Guide: Basics* for more information on permanent data sets.

MEAN=*SASdataset*
: names an output data set to contain the cluster means and other statistics for each cluster. See "SAS Files" in the *SAS User's Guide: Basics* for more information on permanent data sets.

CLUSTER=*name*
: specifies a name for the variable in the OUT= and MEAN= data sets that indicates cluster membership. The default name for this variable is CLUSTER.

The following options control initial cluster seed selection:

MAXCLUSTERS=*n*
MAXC=*n*
: specifies the maximum number of clusters allowed. If MAXCLUSTERS= is omitted, a value of 100 is assumed.

RADIUS=*n*
: establishes the minimum distance criterion for selecting new seeds. No observation is considered as a new seed unless its minimum distance to previous seeds exceeds the value given by RADIUS=. The default value is 0. If REPLACE=RANDOM is specified, RADIUS= is ignored.

REPLACE=FULL | PART | NONE | RANDOM
: specifies how seed replacement is performed. REPLACE=FULL requests default seed replacement as described above. REPLACE=PART requests seed replacement only when the minimum distance between the observation and any current seed is greater than the minimum distance between current seeds. REPLACE=NONE suppresses seed replacement. REPLACE=RANDOM selects a simple pseudo-random sample of complete observations as initial cluster seeds.

RANDOM=*n*
: specifies a positive integer as starting value for the pseudo-random number generator for use with REPLACE=RANDOM. If RANDOM= is not specified, the time of day is used to initialize the pseudo-random number sequence.

The following options for the FASTCLUS statement control computation of final cluster seeds:

DRIFT
: executes the second of the four steps described above in the **Background** section. After initial seed selection, each observation is assigned to the cluster with the nearest seed. After an observation is processed, the seed of the cluster to which it was assigned is recalculated as the mean of the observations currently assigned to the cluster. Thus, the cluster seeds drift about rather than remaining fixed for the duration of the pass.

STRICT
STRICT=*n*
: prevents an observation from being assigned to a cluster if its distance to the nearest cluster seed exceeds the value of the STRICT= option. If STRICT is used without a numeric value, the RADIUS= option must be specified and its value is used instead. In the OUT= data set, observations that are not assigned due to the STRICT option are given a negative cluster number, the absolute value of which indicates the cluster with the nearest seed.

MAXITER=*n*
: specifies the maximum number of iterations for recomputing cluster seeds. In each iteration, each observation is assigned to the nearest seed, and the seeds are recomputed as the means of the clusters. The default value is 1.

CONVERGE=*n*
CONV=*n*
: specifies the convergence criterion. Iterations terminate when the maximum distance by which any seed has changed is less than or equal to the minimum distance between initial seeds times the CONVERGE= value. The default is 0.02. CONVERGE= is useful only if you have specified a MAXITER= value greater than 1.

DELETE=*n*
: deletes cluster seeds to which *n* or fewer observations have been assigned. Deletion occurs after processing for the DRIFT option is completed and after each iteration specified by MAXITER=. Cluster seeds are **not** deleted after the final assignment of observations to clusters, so in rare cases a final cluster may not have more than *n* members. The DELETE= option is ineffective if MAXITER=0 is specified and DRIFT is not specified. By default, no cluster seeds are deleted.

Miscellaneous options for the FASTCLUS statement:

LIST
: lists all observations, giving the value of the ID variable (if any), the number of the cluster to which the observation is assigned, and the distance between the observation and the final cluster seed.

DISTANCE
: requests that distances between the cluster means be printed.

SHORT
: suppresses printing of the initial cluster seeds, cluster means, and standard deviations.

SUMMARY
: suppresses printing of the initial cluster seeds, statistics for variables, cluster means, and standard deviations.

NOPRINT
: suppresses all printed output.

IMPUTE
: requests imputation of missing values in the OUT= data set. If an observation has a missing value for a variable used in the cluster analysis, the missing value is replaced by the corresponding value in the cluster seed to which the observation is assigned. If the observation is not assigned to a cluster, missing values are not replaced.

NOMISS
: excludes observations with missing values from the analysis. However, if the IMPUTE option is also specified, observations with missing values are included in the final cluster assignments.

VARDEF=*divisor*
: specifies the divisor to be used in the calculation of variances and covariances. Possible values for *divisor* are N, DF, WEIGHT or WGT, and WDF. VARDEF=N requests that the number of observations (*n*)

be used as the divisor. VARDEF=DF requests that the error degrees of freedom, *n-c*, be used, where *c* is the number of clusters. VARDEF=WEIGHT or WGT requests that the sum of the weights (*w*) be used. VARDEF=WDF requests that the sum of the weights minus the number of clusters *w-c* be used. The default value is DF.

VAR Statement

VAR *variables;*

The VAR statement lists the numeric variables to be used in the cluster analysis. If the VAR statement is omitted, all numeric variables not listed in other statements are used.

ID Statement

ID *variable;*

The ID variable, which can be character or numeric, is used to identify observations on the printout when the LIST option is specified.

FREQ Statement

FREQ *variable;*

The FREQ variable gives the frequency of occurrence of each observation. The values of the FREQ variable should be nonnegative integers. Each observation is treated as if it actually occurred as many times as indicated by the FREQ variable.

WEIGHT Statement

WEIGHT *variable;*

The values of the WEIGHT variable are used to compute weighted cluster means. The effect of WEIGHT is similar to that of FREQ except in determining the number of observations. The WEIGHT variable can take nonintegral values.

BY Statement

BY *variables;*

A BY statement can be used with PROC FASTCLUS to obtain separate analyses on observations in groups defined by the BY variables. When a BY statement appears, the procedure expects the DATA= data set to be sorted in order of the BY variables. If your DATA= data set is not sorted in ascending order, use the SORT procedure with a similar BY statement to sort the data, or, if appropriate, use the BY statement options NOTSORTED or DESCENDING. For more information, see the discussion of the BY statement in "Statements Used in the PROC Step" in the *SAS User's Guide: Basics.*

If SEED= is specified and the SEED= data set does not contain any of the BY variables, then the entire SEED= data set is used to obtain initial cluster seeds for each BY group in the DATA= data set.

If the SEED= data set contains some but not all of the BY variables, or if some BY variables do not have the same type or length in the SEED= data set as in the DATA= data set, then FASTCLUS prints an error message and stops.

If all the BY variables appear in the SEED= data set with the same type and length as in the DATA= data set, then each BY group in the SEED= data set is used to obtain initial cluster seeds for the corresponding BY group in the DATA=

data set. The BY groups in the SEED= data set must be in the same order as in the DATA= data set. If NOTSORTED is specified in the BY statement, there must be exactly the same BY groups in the same order in both data sets. If NOTSORTED is not specified, it is permissible for some BY groups to appear in one data set but not in the other.

DETAILS

Missing Values

Observations with all missing values are excluded from the analysis. If you specify NOMISS, observations with any missing values are excluded. Observations with missing values cannot be cluster seeds.

The distance between an observation with missing values and a cluster seed is obtained by computing the squared distance based on the nonmissing values, multiplying by the ratio of the number of variables to the number of nonmissing values, and taking the square root:

$$(n/m\ \Sigma(x_i - s_i)^2)^{1/2}$$

where

n = number of variables

m = number of nonmissing values

x_i = value of the ith variable for the observation

s_i = value of the ith variable for the seed

and the summation is taken over variables with nonmissing values.

Output Data Sets

OUT= data set The OUT= data set contains:

- the original variables.
- a new variable taking values from 1 to MAXCLUSTERS=, indicating the cluster to which each observation has been assigned. The variable name is specified by the CLUSTER= option; the default name is CLUSTER.
- a new variable DISTANCE giving the distance from the observation to its cluster seed.

If the IMPUTE option is used, the OUT= data set also contains:

- a new variable _IMPUTE_ giving the number of imputed values in each observation.

MEAN= data set The MEAN= data set contains one observation for each cluster. The variables are as follows:

- the BY variables, if any.
- a new variable giving the cluster number. The variable name is specified by the CLUSTER= option. The default name is CLUSTER.
- either the FREQ variable or a new variable called _FREQ_ giving the number of observations in the cluster.
- the WEIGHT variable, if any.
- a new variable _RMSSTD_ giving the root-mean-square standard deviation for the cluster.

- a new variable _RADIUS_ giving the maximum distance between any observation in the cluster and the cluster seed.
- a new variable _GAP_ containing the distance between the current cluster mean and the nearest other cluster mean.
- a new variable _NEAR_ specifying the cluster number of the nearest cluster.
- the VAR variables giving the cluster means.

Computational Resources

Let

n = number of observations

v = number of variables

c = number of clusters

p = number of passes over the data set.

The overall time required by FASTCLUS is roughly proportional to $nvcp$ if c is small with respect to n.

Initial seed selection requires one pass over the data set. If the observations are in random order, the time required is roughly proportional to:

$$nvc + vc^2$$

unless REPLACE=NONE is specified. In that case, a complete pass may not be necessary and the time is roughly proportional to mvc, where $c \leq m \leq n$.

The DRIFT option, each iteration, and the final assignment of cluster seeds each require one pass, with time for each pass roughly proportional to nvc.

For greatest efficiency, the variables in the VAR statement should be listed in order of decreasing variance.

Usage Notes

Before using FASTCLUS, decide whether your variables should be standardized in some way. If all variables are measured in the same units, standardization may not be necessary. Otherwise, some form of standardization is strongly recommended. The STANDARD procedure can standardize all variables to mean zero and variance one. The FACTOR or PRINCOMP procedures can compute standardized principal component scores. The ACECLUS procedure can transform the variables according to an estimated within-cluster covariance matrix.

The easiest way to use FASTCLUS is to specify the MAXCLUSTERS= and LIST options. It is usually desirable to try several values of MAXCLUSTERS=.

FASTCLUS produces relatively little printed output. In most cases you should create an output data set and use other procedures such as PRINT, PLOT, CHART, MEANS, DISCRIM, or CANDISC to study the clusters. Macros are useful for running FASTCLUS repeatedly with other procedures.

A simple application of FASTCLUS with two variables may proceed as follows:

```
PROC STANDARD MEAN=0 STD=1 OUT=STAN;
   VAR V1 V2;

PROC FASTCLUS DATA=STAN OUT=CLUST MAXCLUSTERS=2;
   VAR V1 V2;
PROC PLOT;
   PLOT V2*V1=CLUSTER;

PROC FASTCLUS DATA=STAN OUT=CLUST MAXCLUSTERS=3;
```

```
   VAR V1 V2;
PROC PLOT;
   PLOT V2*V1=CLUSTER;
```

If you have more than two variables, you can use CANDISC to compute canonical variables for plotting the clusters. For example:

```
PROC STANDARD MEAN=0 STD=1 OUT=STAN;
   VAR V1-V10;

PROC FASTCLUS DATA=STAN OUT=CLUST MAXCLUSTERS=3;
   VAR V1-V10;
PROC CANDISC OUT=CAN;
   VAR V1-V10;
   CLASS CLUSTER;
PROC PLOT;
   PLOT CAN2*CAN1=CLUSTER;
```

If the data set is not too large, it may also be helpful to use

```
PROC SORT;
   BY CLUSTER DISTANCE;
PROC PRINT;
   BY CLUSTER;
```

to list the clusters. By examining the values of DISTANCE you can determine if any observations are unusually far from their cluster seeds.

It is often advisable, especially if the data set is large or contains outliers, to make a preliminary FASTCLUS run with a large number of clusters, perhaps 20 to 100. Use MAXITER=0 and MEAN=*SASdataset*. You can save time on subsequent runs by selecting cluster seeds from this output data set using the SEED= option.

You should check the preliminary clusters for outliers, which often appear as clusters with only one member. Use a DATA step to delete outliers from the data set created by MEAN= before using it as a SEED= data set in later runs. If there are severe outliers, the subsequent FASTCLUS runs should use the STRICT option to prevent the outliers from distorting the clusters.

The MEAN= data set can be used with the PLOT procedure to plot _GAP_ by _FREQ_. An overlay of _RADIUS_ by _FREQ_ provides a baseline against which to compare the values of _GAP_. Outliers appear in the upper left area of the plot, with large values of _GAP_ and small _FREQ_ values. Good clusters appear in the upper right area, with large values of both _GAP_ and _FREQ_. Good potential cluster seeds appear in the lower right, as well as in the upper right, since large _FREQ_ values indicate high-density regions. Small _FREQ_ values in the left part of the plot indicate poor cluster seeds because the points are in low-density regions. It often helps to remove all clusters with small frequencies even though the clusters may not be remote enough to be considered outliers. Removing points in low-density regions improves cluster separation and provides visually sharper cluster outlines in scatter plots.

Printed Output

Unless SHORT or SUMMARY is specified, FASTLCLUS prints:

1. INITIAL SEEDS, initial cluster seeds
2. CHANGE IN CLUSTER SEEDS for each iteration if MAXITER= is specified.

FASTCLUS prints a CLUSTER SUMMARY, giving for each cluster:

3. CLUSTER NUMBER
4. FREQUENCY, the number of observations in the cluster

5. WEIGHT, the sum of the weights of the observations in the cluster, if a WEIGHT statement is specified
6. RMS STD DEVIATION, the root mean square across variables of the cluster standard deviations, which is equal to the root-mean-square distance between observations in the cluster
7. MAXIMUM DISTANCE FROM SEED TO OBSERVATION, the maximum distance from the cluster seed to any observation in the cluster
8. NEAREST CLUSTER, the number of the cluster with mean closest to the mean of the current cluster
9. CENTROID DISTANCE, the distance between the centroids (means) of the current cluster and the nearest other cluster.

A table of statistics for each variable is printed unless SUMMARY is specified. The table contains:

10. TOTAL STD, the total standard deviation
11. WITHIN STD, the pooled within-cluster standard deviation
12. R-SQUARED, the R^2 for predicting the variable from the cluster
13. RSQ/(1-RSQ), the ratio of between-cluster variance to within-cluster variance ($R^2/(1\text{-}R^2)$)
14. OVER-ALL, all of the above quantities pooled across variables.

FASTCLUS prints:

15. PSEUDO F STATISTIC, $(R^2/(c\text{-}1))\ /\ (1\text{-}R^2/(n\text{-}c))$, where R^2 is the observed overall R^2, c is the number of clusters, and n is the number of observations. The pseudo *F* statistic was suggested by Calinski and Harabasz (1974). See Milligan and Cooper (1983) and Cooper and Milligan (1984) regarding the use of the pseudo *F* statistic in estimating the number of clusters.

If SUMMARY is specified, FASTCLUS prints:

16. OBSERVED OVER-ALL R-SQUARED.

FASTCLUS also prints:

17. APPROXIMATE EXPECTED OVER-ALL R-SQUARED, the approximate expected value of the overall R^2 under the uniform null hypothesis assuming that the variables are uncorrelated. The value is missing if the number of clusters is greater than one-fifth the number of observations.
18. CUBIC CLUSTERING CRITERION, computed under the assumption that the variables are uncorrelated. The value is missing if the number of clusters is greater than one fifth the number of observations.

    If you are interested in the approximate expected R^2 or the cubic clustering criterion but your variables are correlated, you should cluster principal component scores from PROC PRINCOMP. Both of these statistics are described by Sarle (1983). The performance of the cubic clustering criterion in estimating the number of clusters is examined by Milligan and Cooper (1983) and Cooper and Milligan (1984).

Unless SHORT or SUMMARY is specified, FASTCLUS prints:

19. CLUSTER MEANS for each variable
20. CLUSTER STANDARD DEVIATIONS for each variable.

If DISTANCE is specified, FASTCLUS prints:

21. DISTANCES BETWEEN CLUSTER MEANS.

EXAMPLES

Fisher's Iris Data: Example 1

The iris data published by Fisher (1936) have been widely used for examples in discriminant analysis and cluster analysis. The sepal length, sepal width, petal length, and petal width were measured in millimeters on fifty iris specimens from each of three species, *Iris setosa, I. versicolor,* and *I. virginica*. Mezzich and Solomon (1980) discuss a variety of cluster analyses of the iris data.

In this example the FASTCLUS procedure is used to find two and, then, three clusters. An output data set is created and PROC FREQ is invoked to compare the clusters with the species classification. For three clusters, PROC CANDISC is used to compute canonical variables for plotting the clusters.

```
DATA IRIS;
   TITLE 'FISHER (1936) IRIS DATA';
   INPUT SEPALLEN SEPALWID PETALLEN PETALWID SPEC_NO @@;
   IF SPEC_NO=1 THEN SPECIES='SETOSA    ';
   ELSE IF SPEC_NO=2 THEN SPECIES='VERSICOLOR';
   ELSE SPECIES='VIRGINICA ';
   LABEL SEPALLEN='SEPAL LENGTH IN MM.'
         SEPALWID='SEPAL WIDTH  IN MM.'
         PETALLEN='PETAL LENGTH IN MM.'
         PETALWID='PETAL WIDTH  IN MM.';
   CARDS;
50 33 14 02 1 64 28 56 22 3 65 28 46 15 2
67 31 56 24 3 63 28 51 15 3 46 34 14 03 1
69 31 51 23 3 62 22 45 15 2 59 32 48 18 2
46 36 10 02 1 61 30 46 14 2 60 27 51 16 2
65 30 52 20 3 56 25 39 11 2 65 30 55 18 3
58 27 51 19 3 68 32 59 23 3 51 33 17 05 1
57 28 45 13 2 62 34 54 23 3 77 38 67 22 3
63 33 47 16 2 67 33 57 25 3 76 30 66 21 3
49 25 45 17 3 55 35 13 02 1 67 30 52 23 3
70 32 47 14 2 64 32 45 15 2 61 28 40 13 2
48 31 16 02 1 59 30 51 18 3 55 24 38 11 2
63 25 50 19 3 64 32 53 23 3 52 34 14 02 1
49 36 14 01 1 54 30 45 15 2 79 38 64 20 3
44 32 13 02 1 67 33 57 21 3 50 35 16 06 1
58 26 40 12 2 44 30 13 02 1 77 28 67 20 3
63 27 49 18 3 47 32 16 02 1 55 26 44 12 2
50 23 33 10 2 72 32 60 18 3 48 30 14 03 1
51 38 16 02 1 61 30 49 18 3 48 34 19 02 1
50 30 16 02 1 50 32 12 02 1 61 26 56 14 3
64 28 56 21 3 43 30 11 01 1 58 40 12 02 1
51 38 19 04 1 67 31 44 14 2 62 28 48 18 3
49 30 14 02 1 51 35 14 02 1 56 30 45 15 2
58 27 41 10 2 50 34 16 04 1 46 32 14 02 1
60 29 45 15 2 57 26 35 10 2 57 44 15 04 1
50 36 14 02 1 77 30 61 23 3 63 34 56 24 3
58 27 51 19 3 57 29 42 13 2 72 30 58 16 3
54 34 15 04 1 52 41 15 01 1 71 30 59 21 3
64 31 55 18 3 60 30 48 18 3 63 29 56 18 3
49 24 33 10 2 56 27 42 13 2 57 30 42 12 2
55 42 14 02 1 49 31 15 02 1 77 26 69 23 3
```

```
60 22 50 15 3 54 39 17 04 1 66 29 46 13 2
52 27 39 14 2 60 34 45 16 2 50 34 15 02 1
44 29 14 02 1 50 20 35 10 2 55 24 37 10 2
58 27 39 12 2 47 32 13 02 1 46 31 15 02 1
69 32 57 23 3 62 29 43 13 2 74 28 61 19 3
59 30 42 15 2 51 34 15 02 1 50 35 13 03 1
56 28 49 20 3 60 22 40 10 2 73 29 63 18 3
67 25 58 18 3 49 31 15 01 1 67 31 47 15 2
63 23 44 13 2 54 37 15 02 1 56 30 41 13 2
63 25 49 15 2 61 28 47 12 2 64 29 43 13 2
51 25 30 11 2 57 28 41 13 2 65 30 58 22 3
69 31 54 21 3 54 39 13 04 1 51 35 14 03 1
72 36 61 25 3 65 32 51 20 3 61 29 47 14 2
56 29 36 13 2 69 31 49 15 2 64 27 53 19 3
68 30 55 21 3 55 25 40 13 2 48 34 16 02 1
48 30 14 01 1 45 23 13 03 1 57 25 50 20 3
57 38 17 03 1 51 38 15 03 1 55 23 40 13 2
66 30 44 14 2 68 28 48 14 2 54 34 17 02 1
51 37 15 04 1 52 35 15 02 1 58 28 51 24 3
67 30 50 17 2 63 33 60 25 3 53 37 15 02 1
;

PROC FASTCLUS DATA=IRIS MAXC=2 MAXITER=10 OUT=CLUS;
   VAR SEPALLEN SEPALWID PETALLEN PETALWID;
PROC FREQ;
   TABLES CLUSTER*SPECIES;

PROC FASTCLUS DATA=IRIS MAXC=3 MAXITER=10 OUT=CLUS;
   VAR SEPALLEN SEPALWID PETALLEN PETALWID;
PROC FREQ;
   TABLES CLUSTER*SPECIES;

PROC CANDISC UNI OUT=CAN;
   CLASS CLUSTER;
   VAR SEPALLEN SEPALWID PETALLEN PETALWID;
   TITLE2 'CANONICAL DISCRIMINANT ANALYSIS OF IRIS CLUSTERS';
PROC PLOT;
   PLOT CAN2*CAN1=CLUSTER;
   TITLE2 'PLOT OF CANONICAL VARIABLES IDENTIFIED BY CLUSTER';
```

Output 18.1 Fisher's Iris Data: PROC FASTCLUS with MAXC=2 and PROC FREQ

```
                              FISHER (1936) IRIS DATA                                  1

                                FASTCLUS PROCEDURE

         REPLACE=FULL  RADIUS=0  MAXCLUSTERS=2  MAXITER=10  CONVERGE=0.02

                           ❶  INITIAL SEEDS

         CLUSTER        SEPALLEN        SEPALWID        PETALLEN        PETALWID
         ---------------------------------------------------------------------
         1               43.0000         30.0000         11.0000          1.0000
         2               77.0000         26.0000         69.0000         23.0000

                MINIMUM DISTANCE BETWEEN INITIAL SEEDS = 70.85196

                     ❷  ITERATION   CHANGE IN CLUSTER SEEDS
                                          1            2
                        ---------------------------------------
                               1      13.493      22.4136
                               2     4.22265      1.86994
                               3     1.23521     0.542766

                                  CLUSTER SUMMARY
  ❸            ❹             ❻                     ❼                ❽          ❾
CLUSTER                   RMS STD       MAXIMUM DISTANCE FROM     NEAREST    CENTROID
 NUMBER    FREQUENCY     DEVIATION       SEED TO OBSERVATION      CLUSTER    DISTANCE
-----------------------------------------------------------------------------------
    1            53         3.7050              21.1621                 2     39.2879
    2            97         5.6779              24.6430                 1     39.2879

                             STATISTICS FOR VARIABLES
                       ❿                                  ⓬                ⓭
      VARIABLE        TOTAL STD  ⓫  WITHIN STD           R-SQUARED         RSQ/(1-RSQ)
      ---------------------------------------------------------------------------
      SEPALLEN         8.280661       5.493128            0.562896            1.287784
      SEPALWID         4.358663       3.703931            0.282710            0.394137
      PETALLEN        17.652982       6.803310            0.852470            5.778291
      PETALWID         7.622377       3.572004            0.781868            3.584390
   ⓮ OVER-ALL        10.692237       5.072913            0.776410            3.472463

                             ⓯     PSEUDO F STATISTIC =     513.92
             ⓱ APPROXIMATE EXPECTED OVER-ALL R-SQUARED =   0.51539
               ⓲                CUBIC CLUSTERING CRITERION =    14.806
         WARNING: THE TWO ABOVE VALUES ARE INVALID FOR CORRELATED VARIABLES
```

```
                              FISHER (1936) IRIS DATA                                  2

                                FASTCLUS PROCEDURE

                            ⓳  CLUSTER MEANS

         CLUSTER        SEPALLEN        SEPALWID        PETALLEN        PETALWID
         ---------------------------------------------------------------------
         1               50.0566         33.6981         15.6038          2.9057
         2               63.0103         28.8660         49.5876         16.9588

                       ⓴  CLUSTER STANDARD DEVIATIONS

         CLUSTER        SEPALLEN        SEPALWID        PETALLEN        PETALWID
         ---------------------------------------------------------------------
         1               3.42735         4.39661         4.40428         2.10553
         2               6.33689         3.26799         7.80058         4.15561
```

```
                    FISHER (1936) IRIS DATA                                    3

                  TABLE OF CLUSTER BY SPECIES

          CLUSTER      SPECIES

          FREQUENCY|
           PERCENT |
           ROW PCT |
           COL PCT |SETOSA  |VERSICOL|VIRGINIC|
                   |        |OR      |A       |  TOTAL
          ---------+--------+--------+--------+
          1        |     50 |      3 |      0 |     53
                   |  33.33 |   2.00 |   0.00 |  35.33
                   |  94.34 |   5.66 |   0.00 |
                   | 100.00 |   6.00 |   0.00 |
          ---------+--------+--------+--------+
          2        |      0 |     47 |     50 |     97
                   |   0.00 |  31.33 |  33.33 |  64.67
                   |   0.00 |  48.45 |  51.55 |
                   |   0.00 |  94.00 | 100.00 |
          ---------+--------+--------+--------+
          TOTAL          50       50       50      150
                      33.33    33.33    33.33   100.00
```

Output 18.2 Fisher's Iris Data: PROC FASTCLUS with MAXC=3 and PROC FREQ

```
                         FISHER (1936) IRIS DATA                                4

                           FASTCLUS PROCEDURE

          REPLACE=FULL  RADIUS=0  MAXCLUSTERS=3  MAXITER=10  CONVERGE=0.02


                              INITIAL SEEDS

          CLUSTER       SEPALLEN        SEPALWID        PETALLEN        PETALWID
          ---------------------------------------------------------------------
          1              58.0000         40.0000         12.0000          2.0000
          2              77.0000         38.0000         67.0000         22.0000
          3              49.0000         25.0000         45.0000         17.0000

                 MINIMUM DISTANCE BETWEEN INITIAL SEEDS = 38.23611

                     ITERATION   CHANGE IN CLUSTER SEEDS
                                        1            2            3
                     --------------------------------------------
                             1    10.1409      12.2566      11.4148
                             2          0      1.75348      1.21228
                             3          0      0.69766     0.473303

                              CLUSTER SUMMARY

 CLUSTER                     RMS STD      MAXIMUM DISTANCE FROM     NEAREST     CENTROID
  NUMBER     FREQUENCY      DEVIATION      SEED TO OBSERVATION      CLUSTER     DISTANCE
 ----------------------------------------------------------------------------------------
     1            50          2.7803         12.4803                   3         33.5693
     2            38          4.0168         14.9736                   3         17.9718
     3            62          4.0398         16.9272                   2         17.9718


                           STATISTICS FOR VARIABLES

      VARIABLE         TOTAL STD        WITHIN STD         R-SQUARED        RSQ/(1-RSQ)
      ----------------------------------------------------------------------------------
      SEPALLEN          8.280661          4.394883          0.722096          2.598359
      SEPALWID          4.358663          3.248163          0.452102          0.825156
      PETALLEN         17.652982          4.214314          0.943773         16.784895
      PETALWID          7.622377          2.452436          0.897872          8.791618
      OVER-ALL         10.692237          3.661982          0.884275          7.641194

                                    PSEUDO F STATISTIC =    561.63
                 APPROXIMATE EXPECTED OVER-ALL R-SQUARED =   0.62728
                              CUBIC CLUSTERING CRITERION =    25.021
         WARNING: THE TWO ABOVE VALUES ARE INVALID FOR CORRELATED VARIABLES
```

```
                              FISHER (1936) IRIS DATA                                        5

                                FASTCLUS PROCEDURE

                                  CLUSTER MEANS

CLUSTER        SEPALLEN        SEPALWID         PETALLEN        PETALWID
--------------------------------------------------------------------------
1               50.0600         34.2800          14.6200          2.4600
2               68.5000         30.7368          57.4211         20.7105
3               59.0161         27.4839          43.9355         14.3387


                          CLUSTER STANDARD DEVIATIONS

CLUSTER        SEPALLEN        SEPALWID         PETALLEN        PETALWID
--------------------------------------------------------------------------
1               3.52490         3.79064          1.73664         1.05386
2               4.94155         2.90092          4.88590         2.79872
3               4.66410         2.96284          5.08895         2.97500
```

```
                              FISHER (1936) IRIS DATA                                        6

                            TABLE OF CLUSTER BY SPECIES

                     CLUSTER     SPECIES

                     FREQUENCY|
                      PERCENT |
                      ROW PCT |
                      COL PCT |SETOSA  |VERSICOL|VIRGINIC|
                              |        |OR      |A       |  TOTAL
                     ---------+--------+--------+--------+
                     1        |     50 |      0 |      0 |     50
                              |  33.33 |   0.00 |   0.00 |  33.33
                              | 100.00 |   0.00 |   0.00 |
                              | 100.00 |   0.00 |   0.00 |
                     ---------+--------+--------+--------+
                     2        |      0 |      2 |     36 |     38
                              |   0.00 |   1.33 |  24.00 |  25.33
                              |   0.00 |   5.26 |  94.74 |
                              |   0.00 |   4.00 |  72.00 |
                     ---------+--------+--------+--------+
                     3        |      0 |     48 |     14 |     62
                              |   0.00 |  32.00 |   9.33 |  41.33
                              |   0.00 |  77.42 |  22.58 |
                              |   0.00 |  96.00 |  28.00 |
                     ---------+--------+--------+--------+
                     TOTAL          50       50       50      150
                                 33.33    33.33    33.33   100.00
```

Output 18.3 Fisher's Iris Data: PROC CANDISC and PROC PLOT

```
                              FISHER (1936) IRIS DATA                                        7
                     CANONICAL DISCRIMINANT ANALYSIS OF IRIS CLUSTERS

                            CANONICAL DISCRIMINANT ANALYSIS

                     150 OBSERVATIONS          149 DF TOTAL
                       4 VARIABLES             147 DF WITHIN CLASSES
                       3 CLASSES                 2 DF BETWEEN CLASSES

                         CLUSTER  FREQUENCY    WEIGHT  PROPORTION

                               1     50            50    0.333333
                               2     38            38    0.253333
                               3     62            62    0.413333


                                 UNIVARIATE STATISTICS

VARIABLE          MEAN    TOTAL STD    WITHIN STD   BETWEEN STD    R-SQUARED  RSQ/(1-RSQ)           F    PROB > F

SEPALLEN   58.43333333   8.28066128    4.39488251    8.58925460     0.722096        2.598     190.979      0.0001
SEPALWID   30.57333333   4.35866285    3.24816253    3.57737479     0.452102        0.825      60.649      0.0001
PETALLEN   37.58000000  17.65298233    4.21431404   20.93364634     0.943773       16.785    1233.690      0.0
```

(continued on next page)

(continued from previous page)

PETALWID	11.99333333	7.62237669	2.45243581	8.81638840	0.897872	8.792	646.184	0.0001

AVERAGE R-SQUARED: UNWEIGHTED = 0.7539604 WEIGHTED BY VARIANCE = 0.8842753

CLASS MEANS

CLUSTER	SEPALLEN	SEPALWID	PETALLEN	PETALWID
1	50.06000000	34.28000000	14.62000000	2.46000000
2	68.50000000	30.73684211	57.42105263	20.71052632
3	59.01612903	27.48387097	43.93548387	14.33870968

	CANONICAL CORRELATION	ADJUSTED CANONICAL CORRELATION	APPROX STANDARD ERROR	SQUARED CANONICAL CORRELATION	EIGENVALUES OF INV(E)*H = CANRSQ/(1-CANRSQ) EIGENVALUE	DIFFERENCE	PROPORTION	CUMULATIVE
1	0.976613	0.976123	0.003787	0.953774	20.6327	20.1981	0.9794	0.9794
2	0.550384	0.543354	0.057107	0.302923	0.4346	.	0.0206	1.0000

TESTS OF H0: THE CANONICAL CORRELATION IN THE CURRENT ROW AND ALL THAT FOLLOW ARE ZERO

	LIKELIHOOD RATIO	F	NUM DF	DEN DF	PR > F
1	0.03222337	164.5474	8	288	0.0
2	0.69707749	21.0038	3	145	0.0001

FISHER (1936) IRIS DATA 8
CANONICAL DISCRIMINANT ANALYSIS OF IRIS CLUSTERS

CANONICAL DISCRIMINANT ANALYSIS

MULTIVARIATE TEST STATISTICS AND F APPROXIMATIONS
S=2 M=0.5 N=71.5

STATISTIC	VALUE	F	NUM DF	DEN DF	PR > F
WILKS' LAMBDA	0.03222337	164.547	8	288	0.0
PILLAI'S TRACE	1.256696	61.287	8	290	0.0001
HOTELLING-LAWLEY TRACE	21.06723	376.577	8	286	0.0
ROY'S GREATEST ROOT	20.63267	747.934	4	145	0.0

NOTE: F STATISTIC FOR ROY'S GREATEST ROOT IS AN UPPER BOUND
F STATISTIC FOR WILKS' LAMBDA IS EXACT

TOTAL CANONICAL STRUCTURE

	CAN1	CAN2
SEPALLEN	0.8320	0.4521
SEPALWID	-0.5151	0.8106
PETALLEN	0.9935	0.0875
PETALWID	0.9663	0.1547

BETWEEN CANONICAL STRUCTURE

	CAN1	CAN2
SEPALLEN	0.9562	0.2928
SEPALWID	-0.7481	0.6635
PETALLEN	0.9988	0.0496
PETALWID	0.9960	0.0899

WITHIN CANONICAL STRUCTURE

	CAN1	CAN2
SEPALLEN	0.3393	0.7161
SEPALWID	-0.1496	0.9144
PETALLEN	0.9008	0.3081
PETALWID	0.6501	0.4043

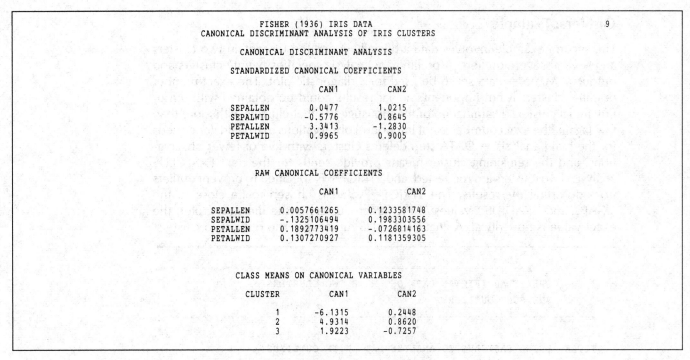

```
                         FISHER (1936) IRIS DATA                                9
                CANONICAL DISCRIMINANT ANALYSIS OF IRIS CLUSTERS

                      CANONICAL DISCRIMINANT ANALYSIS

                    STANDARDIZED CANONICAL COEFFICIENTS

                                  CAN1           CAN2

                  SEPALLEN       0.0477         1.0215
                  SEPALWID      -0.5776         0.8645
                  PETALLEN       3.3413        -1.2830
                  PETALWID       0.9965         0.9005


                       RAW CANONICAL COEFFICIENTS

                              CAN1                CAN2

              SEPALLEN     0.0057661265        0.1233581748
              SEPALWID     -.1325106494        0.1983303556
              PETALLEN     0.1892773419        -.0726814163
              PETALWID     0.1307270927        0.1181359305



                    CLASS MEANS ON CANONICAL VARIABLES

                     CLUSTER          CAN1           CAN2

                        1           -6.1315         0.2448
                        2            4.9314         0.8620
                        3            1.9223        -0.7257
```

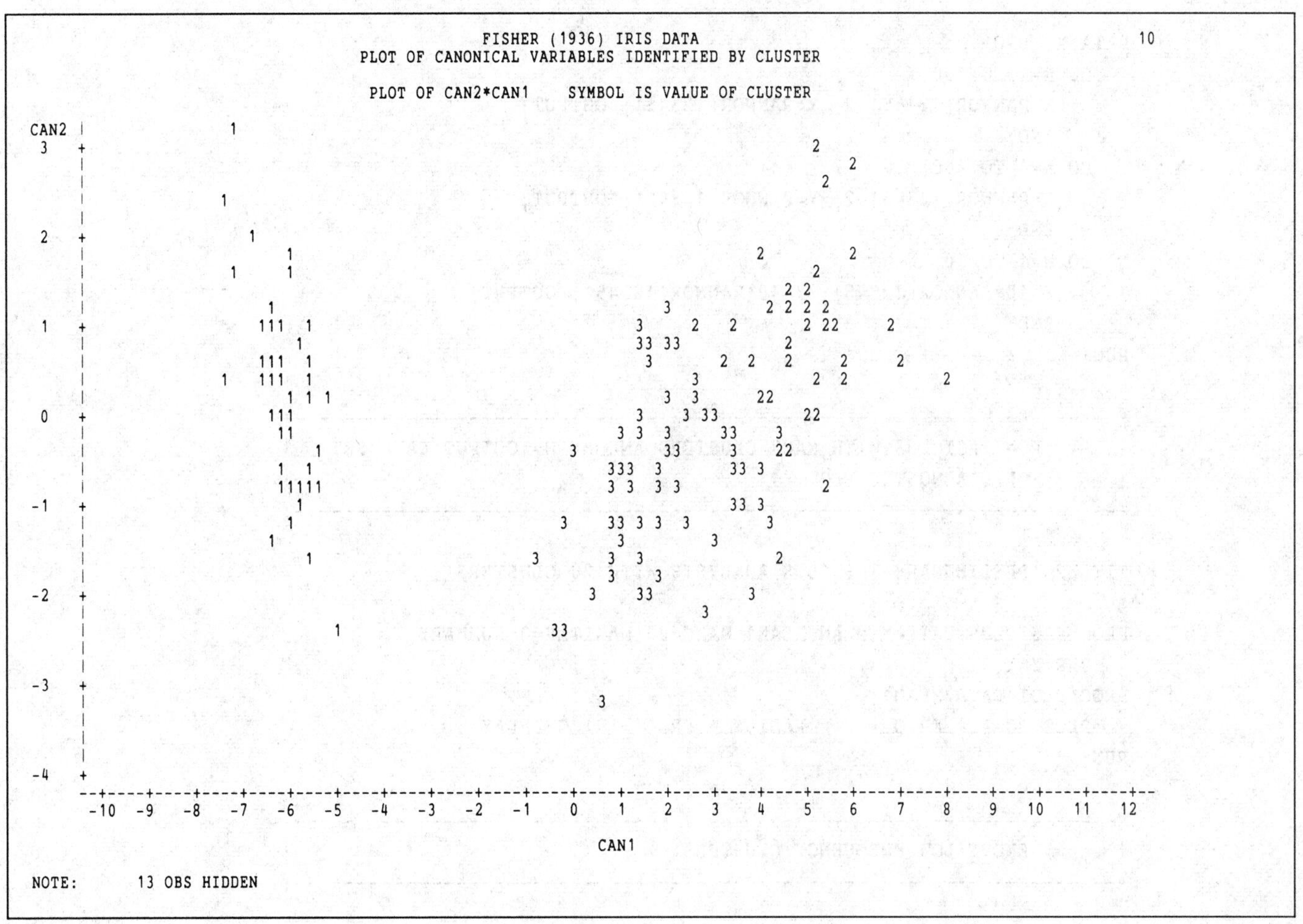

Outliers: Example 2

The second example involves data artificially generated to contain two clusters and several severe outliers. A preliminary analysis specifies twenty clusters and outputs a MEAN= data set to be used for a diagnostic plot. The exact number of initial clusters is not important; similar results could be obtained with ten or fifty initial clusters. Examination of the plot suggests that clusters with more than five (again, the exact number is not important) observations may yield good seeds for the main analysis. A DATA step deletes clusters with five or fewer observations, and the remaining cluster means provide seeds for the next FASTCLUS analysis. Two clusters are requested, and STRICT= is specified to prevent outliers from distorting the results. The STRICT= value is chosen to be close to the _GAP_ and _RADIUS_ values of the larger clusters in the diagnostic plot; the exact value is not critical. A final FASTCLUS run assigns the outliers to clusters.

```
*-------------------------------------------------------------------+
|       CREATE ARTIFICIAL DATA SET WITH TWO CLUSTERS                |
|       AND SOME OUTLIERS.                                          |
+-------------------------------------------------------------------;

TITLE 'USING FASTCLUS TO ANALYZE DATA WITH OUTLIERS';

DATA X; DROP N;
   DO N=1 TO 100;
      X=RANNOR(12345)+2; Y=RANNOR(12345); OUTPUT;
      END;
   DO N=1 TO 100;
      X=RANNOR(12345)-2; Y=RANNOR(12345); OUTPUT;
      END;
   DO N=1 TO 10;
      X=10*RANNOR(12345); Y=10*RANNOR(12345); OUTPUT;
      END;
RUN;

*-------------------------------------------------------------------+
|       RUN FASTCLUS WITH MANY CLUSTERS AND MEAN= OUTPUT DATA SET   |
|       FOR DIAGNOSTIC PLOT.                                        |
+-------------------------------------------------------------------;

TITLE2 'PRELIMINARY FASTCLUS ANALYSIS WITH 20 CLUSTERS';

PROC FASTCLUS DATA=X MEAN=MEAN1 MAXC=20 MAXITER=0 SUMMARY;
   VAR X Y;
PROC PLOT DATA=MEAN1;
   PLOT _GAP_*_FREQ_='G' _RADIUS_*_FREQ_='R'/OVERLAY;
RUN;

*-------------------------------------------------------------------+
|       REMOVE LOW-FREQUENCY CLUSTERS.                              |
+-------------------------------------------------------------------;

DATA SEED; SET MEAN1;
   IF _FREQ_>5;
RUN;
```

Output 18.4 Preliminary Analysis of Data with Outliers: PROC FASTCLUS and PROC PLOT

```
                       USING FASTCLUS TO ANALYZE DATA WITH OUTLIERS                                  1
                      PRELIMINARY FASTCLUS ANALYSIS WITH 20 CLUSTERS

                                   FASTCLUS PROCEDURE

                   REPLACE=FULL  RADIUS=0  MAXCLUSTERS=20  MAXITER=0

                                    CLUSTER SUMMARY

CLUSTER                     RMS STD        MAXIMUM DISTANCE FROM     NEAREST    CENTROID
 NUMBER    FREQUENCY       DEVIATION        SEED TO OBSERVATION      CLUSTER    DISTANCE
----------------------------------------------------------------------------------------
    1           8           0.4753               1.1924                 19        1.7205
    2           1            .                   0                       6        6.2847
    3          44           0.6252               1.6774                  5        1.4386
    4           1            .                   0                      20        5.2130
    5          38           0.5603               1.4528                  3        1.4386
    6           2           0.0542               0.1085                  2        6.2847
    7           1            .                   0                      14        2.5094
    8           2           0.6480               1.2961                  1        1.8450
    9           1            .                   0                       7        9.4534
   10           1            .                   0                      18        4.2514
   11           1            .                   0                      16        4.7582
   12          20           0.5911               1.6291                 16        1.5601
   13           5           0.6682               1.4244                  3        1.9553
   14           1            .                   0                       7        2.5094
   15           5           0.4074               1.2678                  3        1.7609
   16          22           0.4168               1.5139                 19        1.4936
   17           8           0.4031               1.4794                  5        1.5564
   18           1            .                   0                      10        4.2514
   19          45           0.6475               1.6285                 16        1.4936
   20           3           0.5719               1.3642                 15        1.8999

                                  PSEUDO F STATISTIC =    207.58
                 (16)       OBSERVED OVER-ALL R-SQUARED =   0.95404
                  APPROXIMATE EXPECTED OVER-ALL R-SQUARED =   0.96103
                             CUBIC CLUSTERING CRITERION =    -2.503
          WARNING: THE TWO ABOVE VALUES ARE INVALID FOR CORRELATED VARIABLES
```

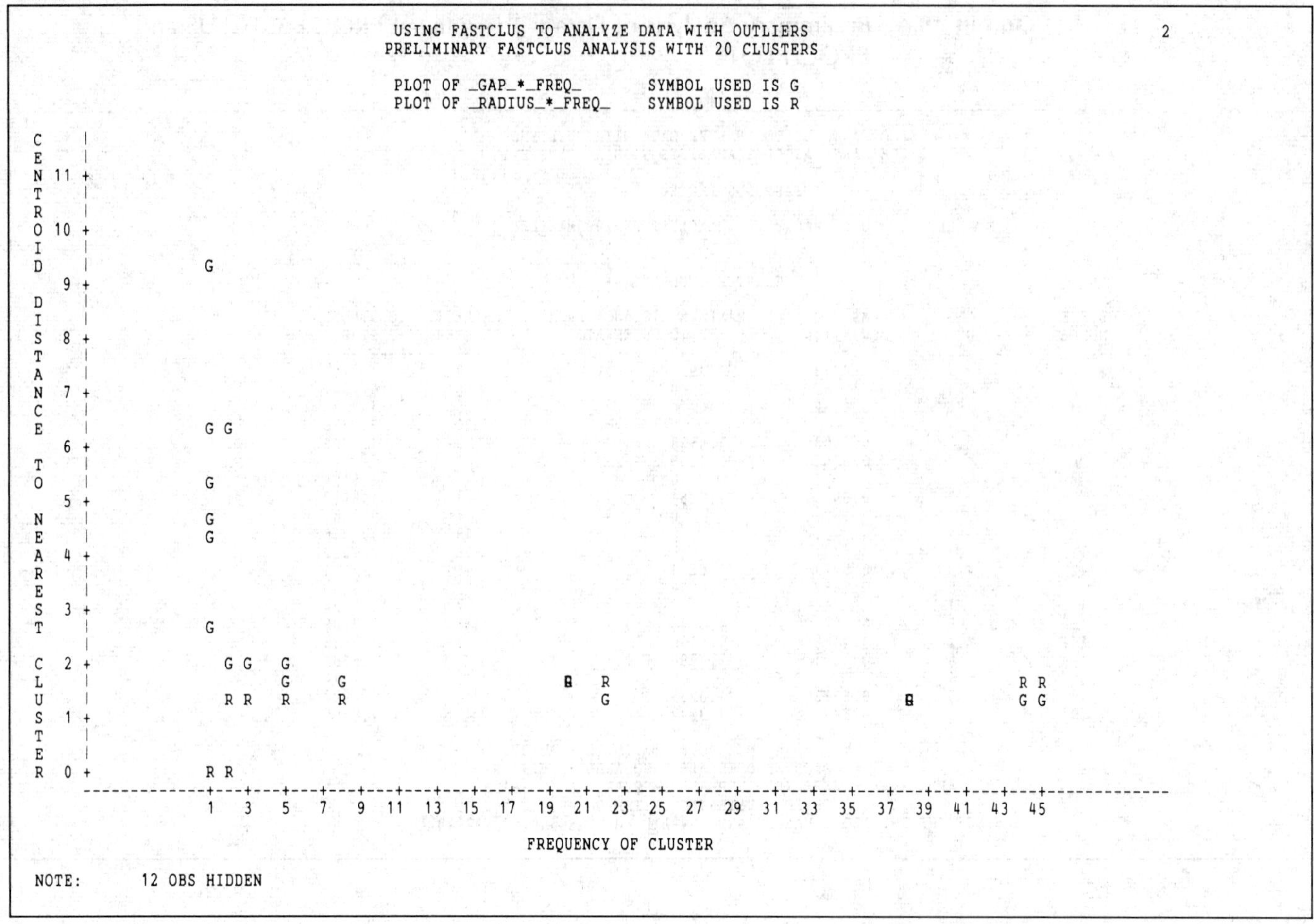


```
*------------------------------------------------------------+
|      RUN FASTCLUS AGAIN, SELECTING SEEDS FROM THE           |
|      HIGH-FREQUENCY CLUSTERS IN THE PREVIOUS ANALYSIS.      |
|      STRICT= PREVENTS OUTLIERS FROM DISTORTING THE RESULTS. |
+------------------------------------------------------------;

TITLE2 'FASTCLUS ANALYSIS USING STRICT= TO OMIT OUTLIERS';

PROC FASTCLUS DATA=X SEED=SEED MAXC=2 STRICT=3.0 OUT=OUT MEAN=MEAN2;
   VAR X Y;
PROC PLOT DATA=OUT;
   PLOT Y*X=CLUSTER;
RUN;
```

Output 18.5 Cluster Analysis with Outliers Omitted: PROC FASTCLUS and PROC PLOT

```
                      USING FASTCLUS TO ANALYZE DATA WITH OUTLIERS                              3
                    FASTCLUS ANALYSIS USING STRICT= TO OMIT OUTLIERS

                                   FASTCLUS PROCEDURE

              REPLACE=FULL  RADIUS=0  STRICT=3  MAXCLUSTERS=2  MAXITER=1


                                     INITIAL SEEDS

                          CLUSTER              X              Y
                          ----------------------------------------
                          1              2.79417       -0.06597
                          2             -2.02730       -2.05121

                                    CLUSTER SUMMARY

     CLUSTER                     RMS STD        MAXIMUM DISTANCE FROM      NEAREST    CENTROID
      NUMBER     FREQUENCY     DEVIATION          SEED TO OBSERVATION      CLUSTER    DISTANCE
     ---------------------------------------------------------------------------------------------
           1           99        0.9501          2.9589                         2       3.7666
           2           99        0.9290          2.8011                         1       3.7666

12 OBSERVATION(S) WERE NOT ASSIGNED TO A CLUSTER BECAUSE THE MINIMUM DISTANCE TO A CLUSTER SEED
                                 EXCEEDED THE STRICT= VALUE


                                STATISTICS FOR VARIABLES

         VARIABLE         TOTAL STD         WITHIN STD         R-SQUARED       RSQ/(1-RSQ)
         ------------------------------------------------------------------------------------
         X                2.0685374          0.8709773         0.8236089         4.6692189
         Y                1.0211278          1.0035198         0.0390925         0.0406829
         OVER-ALL         1.6311880          0.9395886         0.6698911         2.0293031

                                   PSEUDO F STATISTIC =    397.74
                    APPROXIMATE EXPECTED OVER-ALL R-SQUARED =  0.60615
                                CUBIC CLUSTERING CRITERION =     3.197
              WARNING: THE TWO ABOVE VALUES ARE INVALID FOR CORRELATED VARIABLES


                                     CLUSTER MEANS

                          CLUSTER              X              Y
                          ----------------------------------------
                          1              1.82511        0.14121
                          2             -1.91991       -0.26156
```

```
                      USING FASTCLUS TO ANALYZE DATA WITH OUTLIERS                              4
                    FASTCLUS ANALYSIS USING STRICT= TO OMIT OUTLIERS

                                   FASTCLUS PROCEDURE
                              CLUSTER STANDARD DEVIATIONS

                          CLUSTER              X              Y
                          ----------------------------------------
                          1              0.88955        1.00697
                          2              0.85200        1.00006
```

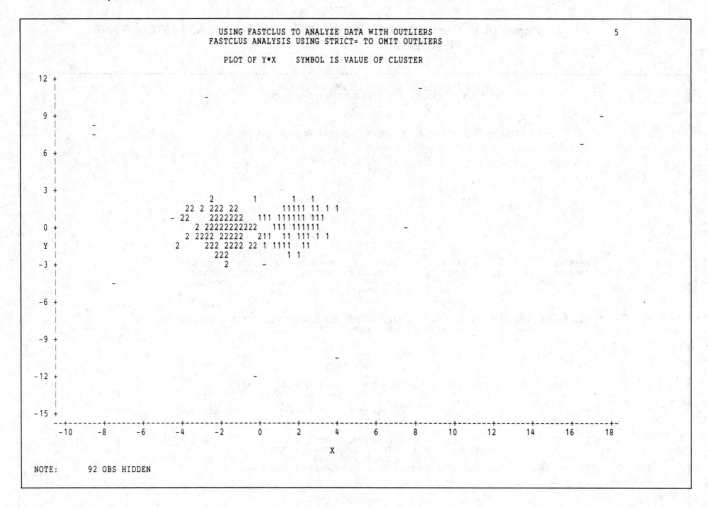

```
                              USING FASTCLUS TO ANALYZE DATA WITH OUTLIERS                                5
                             FASTCLUS ANALYSIS USING STRICT= TO OMIT OUTLIERS

                               PLOT OF Y*X     SYMBOL IS VALUE OF CLUSTER

  12 +
     |                                                                         -
     |                               -
     |
   9 +                                                                                                -
     |     -
     |     -
     |
   6 +                                                                                           -
     |
     |
     |
   3 +
     |                              2        1         1   1
     |                       22 2 222 22          11111 11 1 1
     |                    - 22     2222222    111 111111 111
   0 +                      2 22222222222    111 111111                                    -
     |                    2 2222 22222   211   11 111 1 1
   Y |                 2      222 2222 22 1 1111   11
     |                           222             1 1
  -3 +                             2        -
     |
     |         -
     |
  -6 +
     |
     |
     |
  -9 +
     |
     |                                                  -
     |
 -12 +                                       -
     |
     |
     |
 -15 +
     --+-------+-------+-------+-------+-------+-------+-------+-------+-------+-------+-------+-------+-------+-
      -10     -8      -6      -4      -2       0       2       4       6       8      10      12      14      16      18

                                                       X

NOTE:      92 OBS HIDDEN
```

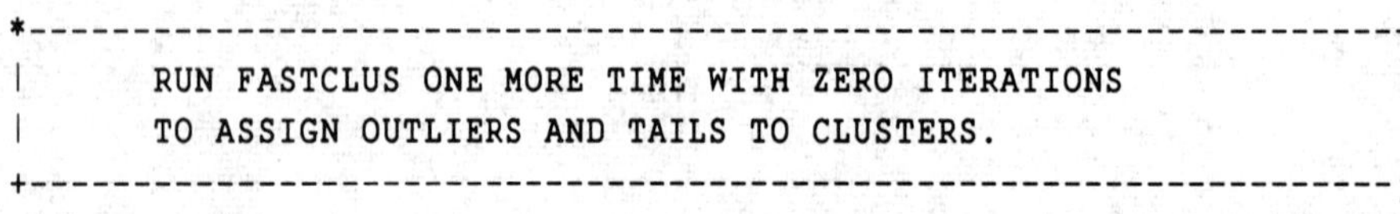

```
*----------------------------------------------------------------+
|       RUN FASTCLUS ONE MORE TIME WITH ZERO ITERATIONS          |
|       TO ASSIGN OUTLIERS AND TAILS TO CLUSTERS.                |
+----------------------------------------------------------------;

TITLE2 'FINAL FASTCLUS ANALYSIS ASSIGNING OUTLIERS TO CLUSTERS';

PROC FASTCLUS DATA=X SEED=MEAN2 MAXC=2 MAXITER=0 OUT=OUT;
   VAR X Y;
PROC PLOT DATA=OUT;
   PLOT Y*X=CLUSTER;
```

Output 18.6 Final Analysis with Outliers Assigned to Clusters: PROC FASTCLUS and PROC PLOT

```
                    USING FASTCLUS TO ANALYZE DATA WITH OUTLIERS                                   6
               FINAL FASTCLUS ANALYSIS ASSIGNING OUTLIERS TO CLUSTERS

                                 FASTCLUS PROCEDURE

                  REPLACE=FULL  RADIUS=0  MAXCLUSTERS=2  MAXITER=0


                                   INITIAL SEEDS

                        CLUSTER              X              Y
                        -----------------------------------
                        1              1.82511        0.14121
                        2             -1.91991       -0.26156

                                  CLUSTER SUMMARY

CLUSTER                  RMS STD        MAXIMUM DISTANCE FROM       NEAREST    CENTROID
 NUMBER    FREQUENCY    DEVIATION        SEED TO OBSERVATION        CLUSTER    DISTANCE
------------------------------------------------------------------------------------------
    1          103         2.2569        17.9426                          2      4.3753
    2          107         1.8371        11.7362                          1      4.3753


                             STATISTICS FOR VARIABLES

    VARIABLE         TOTAL STD        WITHIN STD          R-SQUARED       RSQ/(1-RSQ)
    ----------------------------------------------------------------------------------
    X                2.9272125         1.9552914          0.5559503         1.2520004
    Y                2.1524836         2.1475441          0.0093471         0.0094353
    OVER-ALL         2.5692176         2.0536687          0.3641188         0.5726207

                                 PSEUDO F STATISTIC =    119.11
                 APPROXIMATE EXPECTED OVER-ALL R-SQUARED =  0.49090
                              CUBIC CLUSTERING CRITERION =   -5.338
         WARNING: THE TWO ABOVE VALUES ARE INVALID FOR CORRELATED VARIABLES


                                   CLUSTER MEANS

                        CLUSTER              X              Y
                        -----------------------------------
                        1              2.28002        0.26394
                        2             -2.07555       -0.15135


                              CLUSTER STANDARD DEVIATIONS

                        CLUSTER              X              Y
                        -----------------------------------
                        1              2.41226        2.08992
                        2              1.37936        2.20157
```

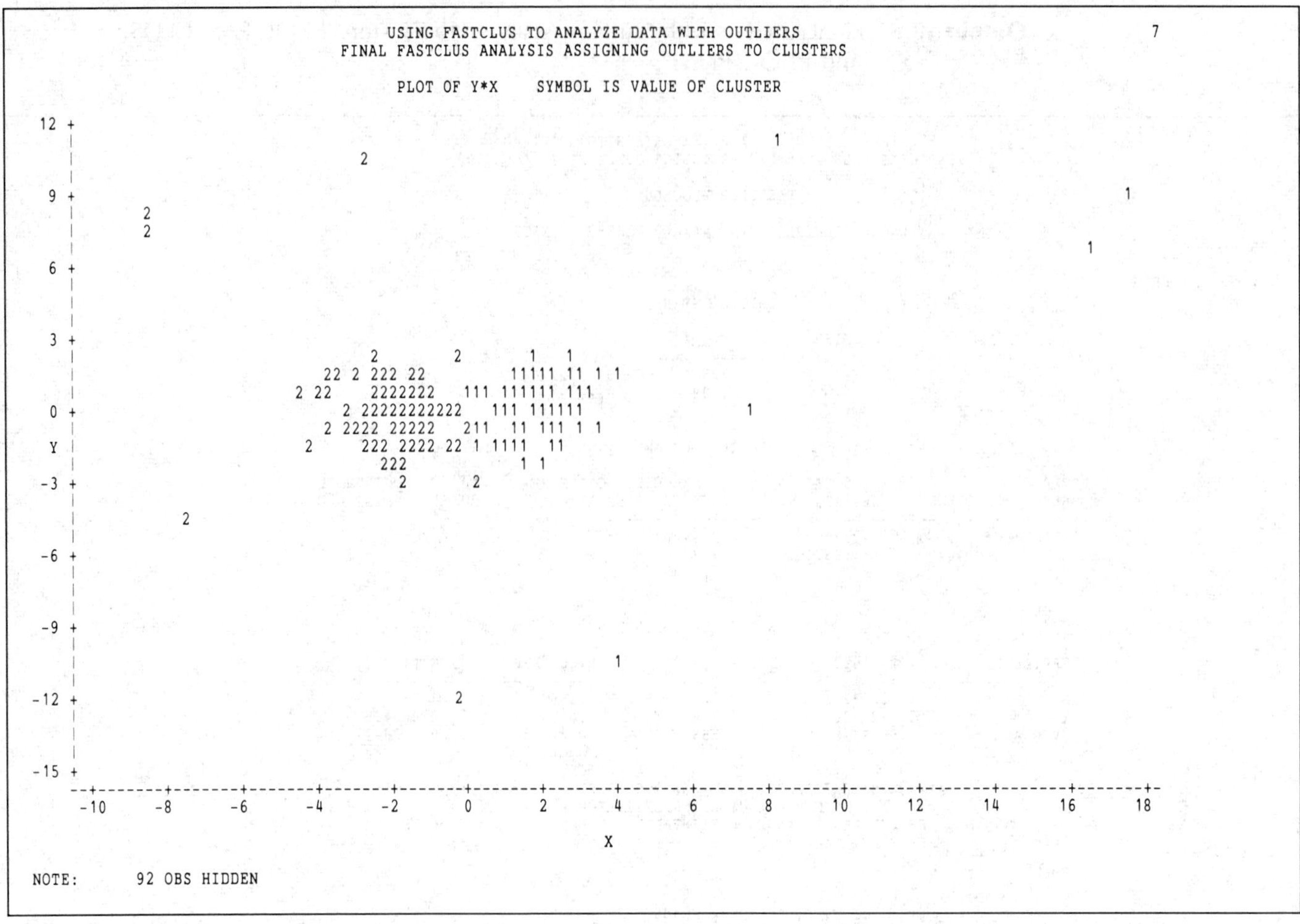

REFERENCES

Anderberg, M.R. (1973), *Cluster Analysis for Applications*, New York: Academic Press.

Calinski, T. and Harabasz, J. (1974), "A Dendrite Method for Cluster Analysis," *Communications in Statistics*, 3, 1-27.

Cooper, M.C. and Milligan, G.W. (1984), "The Effect of Error on Determining the Number of Clusters," *College of Administrative Science Working Paper Series 84-2*, Columbus: The Ohio State University.

Everitt, B.S. (1980), *Cluster Analysis*, Second Edition, London: Heineman Educational Books Ltd.

Fisher, R.A. (1936), "The Use of Multiple Measurements in Taxonomic Problems," *Annals of Eugenics*, 7, 179-188.

Hartigan, J.A. (1975), *Clustering Algorithms*, New York: John Wiley & Sons.

MacQueen, J.B. (1967), "Some Methods for Classification and Analysis of Multivariate Observations," *Proceedings of the Fifth Berkeley Symposium on Mathematical Statistics and Probability*, 1, 281-297.

Mezzich, J.E and Solomon, H. (1980), *Taxonomy and Behavioral Science*, New York: Academic Press.

Milligan, G.W. (1980), "An Examination of the Effect of Six Types of Error Perturbation on Fifteen Clustering Algorithms," *Psychometrika*, 45, 325-342.

Milligan, G.W. and Cooper, M.C. (1983), "An Examination of Procedures for Determining the Number of Clusters in a Data Set," *College of Administrative Science Working Paper Series 83-51*, Columbus: The Ohio State University.

Sarle, W.S. (1983), "The Cubic Clustering Criterion," SAS Technical Report A-108, Cary, NC: SAS Institute Inc.

Spath, H. (1980), *Cluster Analysis Algorithms*, Chichester, England: Ellis Horwood.

Tou, J.T. and Gonzalez, R.C. (1974), *Pattern Recognition Principles*, Reading, MA: Addison-Wesley Publishing Co.

Sarle, W.S. (1983), The Cubic Clustering Criterion, SAS Technical Report A-108, Cary, NC: SAS Institute Inc.

Späth, H. (1980), Cluster Analysis Algorithms, Chichester, England: Ellis Horwood.

Tou, J.T. and Gonzalez, R.C. (1974), Pattern Recognition Principles, Reading, MA: Addison-Wesley Publishing Co.

Chapter 19

The FREQ Procedure

Operating systems: All

ABSTRACT

The FREQ procedure produces one-way to *n*-way frequency and crosstabulation tables. For two-way tables, PROC FREQ computes tests and measures of association. For *n*-way tables, PROC FREQ does stratified analysis, computing statistics within as well as across strata. Frequencies can also be output to a SAS data set.

INTRODUCTION

Frequency tables show the distribution of variable values. For example, if a variable A has six possible values, a frequency table for A shows how many observations in the data set have the first value of A, how many have the second value, and so on.

Crosstabulation tables show combined frequency distributions for two or more variables. For example, a crosstabulation table for the variables SEX and EMPLOY shows the number of working females, the number of non-working females, the number of working males, and the number of non-working males.

One-Way Frequency Tables

If you want a one-way frequency table for a variable, simply name the variable in a TABLES statement. For example, the statements

```
PROC FREQ;
   TABLES A;
```

produce a one-way frequency table giving the values of A and the frequency of each value.

Two-Way Crosstabulation Tables

If you want a crosstabulation table for two variables, give their names separated by an asterisk (*). Values of the first variable form the rows of the table, and values of the second variable form the columns. For example, the statements

```
PROC FREQ;
   TABLES A*B;
```

produce a crosstabulation table with values of A down the side and values of B across the top.

For some pairs of variables, you may want information about the existence and/or the strength of any association between the variables. With respect to the existence of an association, PROC FREQ computes statistics that test the null hypothesis of no association. With respect to the strength of an association, PROC FREQ computes measures of association that tend to be close to zero when there is no association, and close to the maximum (or minimum) value when there is perfect association. You can request the computation and printing of these statistics by specifying one or more options in the TABLES statement. For information on specific statistics computed by PROC FREQ, see the section entitled **Tests and Measures of Association**.

In choosing measures of association to use in analyzing a two-way table, you should consider the study design (which indicates whether the row and column variables are dependent or independent), the measurement scale of the variables (nominal, ordinal, or interval), the type of association that each measure is designed to detect, and any assumptions required for valid interpretation of a measure. It is important to exercise care in selecting measures that are appropriate for your data. For more information to guide you in choosing measures of association for a specific set of data, see Hayes (1963) and Garson (1971). For an advanced treatment, refer to Goodman and Kruskal (1979), or Bishop, Fienberg, and Holland (1975, Chapter 11).

Similar comments apply to the choice and interpretation of the test statistics. For example, the Mantel-Haenszel chi-square statistic requires an ordinal scale for both variables, and is designed to detect a linear association. The Pearson chi-square, on the other hand, is appropriate for all variables and can detect any kind of association but it is less powerful for detecting a linear association because its power is dispersed over a greater number of degrees of freedom (except for 2 by 2 tables).

N-Way Crosstabulation Tables

If you want a three-way (or *n*-way) crosstabulation table, give the three (or *n*) variable names separated by asterisks in the TABLES statement. Values of the last variable form the columns of a contingency table; values of the next-to-last variable form the rows. Each level (or combination of levels) of the other variables form one stratum, and a separate contingency table is produced for each stratum. For example, the statements

```
PROC FREQ;
   TABLES A*B*C*D / CMH;
```

produce *k* tables, where *k* is the number of different combinations of values for the variables A and B. Each table has the values of C down the side and the values of D across the top.

The CMH option gives a stratified statistical analysis of the relationship between C and D, after controlling for A and B. The stratified analysis provides a convenient way to adjust for the possible confounding effects of A and B without being forced to estimate parameters for them. The analysis includes computation of Cochran-Mantel-Haenszel statistics, estimation of the common relative risk (case-control and cohort studies), and Breslow's test for homogeneity of the odds ratios. See the **Summary Statistics** section for details of the stratified analysis.

Note: multi-way tables can generate a great deal of printed output. For example, if the variables A, B, C, D, and E each have ten levels, five-way tables of A*B*C*D*E could generate 4000 or more pages of output.

PROC FREQ Contrasted with Other SAS Procedures

Many other procedures in SAS can collect frequency counts. PROC FREQ is distinguished by its ability to compute chi-square tests and measures of association for two-way and *n*-way tables. Other procedures to consider for counting are the following: TABULATE for more general table layouts, SUMMARY for output data sets, and CHART for bar charts and other graphical representations. PROC CATMOD can be used for general linear model analysis of categorical data.

SPECIFICATIONS

The statements available in PROC FREQ are

PROC FREQ *options;*
  TABLES *requests / options;*
  WEIGHT *variable;*
  BY *variables;*

PROC FREQ Statement

PROC FREQ *options;*

The options that can be used in the PROC FREQ statement are as follows:

DATA=*SASdataset*
: specifies the data set to be used by PROC FREQ. If the DATA= option is omitted, FREQ uses the most recently created data set.

ORDER=FREQ
ORDER=DATA
ORDER=INTERNAL
ORDER=FORMATTED

specifies the order in which the variable levels are to be reported. If ORDER=FREQ, levels are ordered by descending frequency count so that the levels with the largest frequencies come first. If ORDER=DATA, levels are put in the order in which they first occur in the input data. If ORDER=INTERNAL, then the levels are ordered by the internal value. If ORDER=FORMATTED, levels are ordered by the external formatted value. FREQ orders by the internal value if you omit ORDER= or give an unrecognized value. The ORDER= option does not apply to missing values, which are ordered first.

FORMCHAR(1,2,7)=*'string'*

defines the characters to be used for constructing the outlines and dividers for the cells of contingency tables. The string should be three characters long. The characters are used to denote (1) vertical divider, (2) horizontal divider, and (3) vertical-horizontal intersection. Any character or hexadecimal string can be used to customize table appearance. Specifying FORMCHAR(1,2,7)='   ' (3 blanks) produces tables with no outlines or dividers. If you do not specify the FORMCHAR option, FREQ uses the default FORMCHAR(1,2,7)='|−+'. See the CALENDAR and TABULATE procedures for further information.

TABLES Statement

TABLES *requests* / *options;*

For each frequency or crosstabulation table that you want, put a table request in the TABLES statement.

requests are composed of one or more variable names joined by asterisks (*). A one-way frequency is generated by a single name. Two-way crosstabulations are generated by two variables joined with an asterisk. Any number of variables can be joined for a multi-way table. A grouping syntax is also available to make the specifications of many tables easier. Several variables can be put in parentheses and joined to other effects.

For example,

TABLES A*(B C);	is equivalent to	TABLES A*B A*C;
TABLES (A B)*(C D);	is equivalent to	TABLES A*C A*D B*C B*D;
TABLES (A B C)*D;	is equivalent to	TABLES A*D B*D C*D;
TABLES (A--C);	is equivalent to	TABLES A B C;
TABLES (A--C)*D;	is equivalent to	TABLES A*D B*D C*D;
TABLES A--C*D;	is ambiguous and should not be used.	

Any number of requests can be given in one TABLES statement, and any number of TABLES statements can be included in one execution of PROC FREQ. If there is no TABLES statement, FREQ does one-way frequencies for all of the variables in the data set.

If you request a one-way table for a variable and do not specify any options, FREQ produces frequencies, cumulative frequencies, percentages of the total frequency, and cumulative percentages for each level of the variable.

If you request a two-way table and do not specify any options, FREQ produces crosstabulation tables that include cell frequencies, cell percentages of the total frequency, cell percentages of row frequencies, and cell percentages of column frequencies. Missing levels of each variable are excluded from the table, but the total frequency of missing subjects is printed below each table.

The options below can be used in the TABLES statement after a slash (/):

General options

MISSING
: requests FREQ to interpret missing values as nonmissing and to include them in calculations of percentages and other statistics.

LIST
: prints two-way to *n*-way tables in a list format rather than as crosstabulation tables. The LIST option cannot be used when statistical tests or measures of association are requested. Expected cell frequencies are not printed when LIST is specified, even if EXPECTED is specified.

OUT=*SASdataset*
: sets up an output SAS data set containing variable values and frequency counts. If more than one table request appears in the TABLES statement, the contents of the data set correspond to the last table request in the TABLES statement. For details on the output data set created by PROC FREQ, see **Output Data Set** below. If you want to create a permanent SAS data set, you must specify a two-level name. See "SAS Files" in the *SAS User's Guide: Basics* for more information on permanent SAS data sets.

Options to request statistical analysis

CHISQ
: requests a chi-square (χ^2) test of homogeneity or independence for each stratum, together with measures of association based on chi-square. The tests include Pearson chi-square, likelihood ratio chi-square, and Mantel-Haenszel chi-square. The measures include the phi coefficient, the contingency coefficient, and Cramer's V. For 2 by 2 tables, Fisher's Exact Test is also included. The formulas for these tests and measures are given in a **Details** section.

MEASURES
: requests a basic set of measures of association and their standard errors. The measures include Pearson and Spearman correlation coefficients, gamma, Kendall's tau-b, Stuart's tau-c, Somers' D, lambda (symmetric and asymmetric), uncertainty coefficients (symmetric and asymmetric), and, for 2 by 2 tables, odds ratios, risk ratios, and the corresponding confidence intervals. The formulas for these measures are given in a **Details** section.

CMH
: requests Cochran-Mantel-Haenszel statistics, which test for association between the row variable and the column variable after adjusting for all other variables in the TABLES statement. In addition, for 2 by 2 tables,

FREQ gives the estimate of the common relative risk for both case-control and cohort studies and the corresponding confidence intervals. Breslow's test for homogeneity of the odds ratios is also given for the 2 by 2 case.

ALL requests all of the tests and measures given by the CHISQ, MEASURES, and CMH options.

Options to specify details of statistical analysis

SCORES=RANK
SCORES=TABLE
SCORES=RIDIT
SCORES=MODRIDIT

specifies the type of row and column scores to be used by the Cochran-Mantel-Haenszel statistics and by the Pearson correlation. For numeric variables, TABLE scores are the values of the row headings and the column headings. For character variables, TABLE scores are defined by the row numbers and column numbers. The other scores, defined in the section below, **Summary Statistics**, yield nonparametric analyses. If no scores are specified, FREQ uses TABLE scores.

ALPHA=*p*

specifies that confidence intervals are to be 100(1-p)% confidence intervals, where $0<p<1$. If no ALPHA level is specified, FREQ uses ALPHA=.05.

Options to request additional table information

EXPECTED requests that the expected cell frequencies under the hypothesis of independence (or homogeneity) be printed.

DEVIATION requests that, for each cell, FREQ print the deviation of the cell frequency from the expected value.

CELLCHI2 requests that FREQ print each cell's contribution to the total χ^2 statistic. This is computed as *(frequency-expected)**2/expected*.

CUMCOL requests that cumulative column percentages be printed in the cells.

MISSPRINT asks FREQ to print missing value frequencies for two-way to *n*-way tables, even though the frequencies will not be used in the calculation of statistics.

SPARSE causes the procedure to write out or print information about all possible combinations of levels of the variables in the table request, even when some combinations of levels do not occur in the data. This option affects printouts under the LIST option and output data sets.

Options to suppress printing

NOFREQ suppresses printing of the cell frequencies for a crosstabulation.

NOPERCENT suppresses printing of the cell percentages for a crosstabulation.

NOROW suppresses printing of the row percentages in cells of a crosstabulation.

NOCOL suppresses printing of the column percentages in cells of a crosstabulation.

NOCUM suppresses printing of the cumulative frequencies and cumulative percentages for one-way frequencies and for frequencies in list format.

NOPRINT suppresses printing of the tables, but allows printing of the statistics specified by CHISQ, MEASURES, CMH, and ALL.

WEIGHT Statement

WEIGHT *variable;*

Normally, each observation contributes a value of 1 to the frequency counts. (In other words, each observation represents one subject.) However, when a WEIGHT statement appears, each observation contributes the weighting variable's value for that observation. (For example, a weight of 3 means that the observation represents 3 subjects.) The values must be nonnegative, but they do not have to be integers. FREQ uses double precision floating point arithmetic to accumulate the counts or weights. Values are summed and then printed with decimal places, if appropriate.

Only one WEIGHT statement can be used, and that statement applies to counts collected for all tables.

For example, suppose a data set contains variables RACE, SEX, and HRSWORK. The statements

```
PROC FREQ;
   TABLES RACE*SEX;
```

produce a table showing how many nonwhite females, nonwhite males, white females, and white males are present. The statements

```
PROC FREQ;
   TABLES RACE*SEX;
   WEIGHT HRSWORK;
```

produce a table showing the number of hours worked by nonwhite females, by nonwhite males, and so on.

BY Statement

BY *variables;*

A BY statement can be used with PROC FREQ to obtain separate analyses for the groups defined by the BY variables. When a BY statement appears, the procedure expects the input data set to be sorted in order of the BY variables. If your input data set is not sorted in ascending order, use the SORT procedure with a similar BY statement to sort the data, or, if appropriate, use the BY statement options NOTSORTED or DESCENDING. For more information, see the discussion of the BY statement in "Statements Used in the PROC Step" in the *SAS User's Guide: Basics.*

DETAILS

Missing Values

For one-way frequency tables, the missing value frequencies appear in the tables. For two-way to *n*-way tables, the missing value frequencies do not appear, but the total frequency of missing subjects is given below each table. In all cases, the statistics do not include missing values.

Missing value frequencies can be printed by specifying the MISSPRINT option in the TABLES statement; they can be included in the computation of statistics by specifying the MISSING option.

Limitations

Any number of TABLES statements can be included after the PROC FREQ statement. Since FREQ builds all the tables requested in all TABLES statements in one pass of the data, there is essentially no loss of efficiency from using multiple TABLES statements.

A TABLES statement can contain any number of table requests, and each request can include any number of variables. The maximum number of levels allowed for any one variable is 32,000. If you have a variable with more than 32,000 levels, use PROC SUMMARY and PROC PRINT or reduce the number of levels by using the FORMAT statement.

FREQ stores each combination of values in memory. When FREQ is compiling and developing multi-way tables or when some variables have many levels, you may run out of main storage. If increasing the region size is impractical, use PROC SORT to sort the data set by one or more of the variables and then use PROC FREQ with a BY statement that includes the sorted variables.

The FREQ procedure handles both internal and formatted values up to length 16 on both the printout and the output data set. Longer data values are truncated to sixteen characters, and a warning message is printed on the SAS log.

Frequency values with more than seven significant digits may be printed in scientific notation (E format), in which case only the first few significant digits of the mantissa are printed. If you need more significant digits than FREQ prints, you can specify an output data set with the OUT= option. Then use

```
PROC PRINT DATA=FREQDATA;
   FORMAT COUNT BEST32.;
```

where FREQDATA is the OUT= data set produced by PROC FREQ.

The variable COUNT, containing the frequency values, is then printed with additional significant digits.

Output Data Set

The new data set produced by PROC FREQ contains one observation for each combination of the variable values in the table request. Each observation contains these variables plus two new variables, COUNT and PERCENT, which give respectively the frequency and cell percentage for the combination of variable values.

For example, consider the statements

```
PROC FREQ;
   TABLES A A*B / OUT=D;
```

The output data set D corresponds to the rightmost table request, A*B. If A has two values (1 and 2) and B has three values (1, 2, and 3), the output data set D can have up to six observations, one for each combination of the A and B values.

In observation 1, A=1 and B=1; in observation 2, A=1 and B=2; and so on. The data set also contains the variables COUNT and PERCENT. COUNT's value in each observation is the number of subjects that have the given combination of A and B values; PERCENT's value is the percent of the total number of subjects having that A and B combination.

When FREQ collects different class values into the same formatted level, it saves the smallest internal value to output in the output data set.

Computer Resources

For each variable, PROC FREQ stores all of the levels in memory, requiring 56 bytes for each level. If FREQ runs out of memory, it stops collecting levels on the variable with the most levels and returns the memory so that counting can continue. The procedure then builds the tables that do not contain the disabled variables.

For two-way and *n*-way tables, FREQ uses a utility file to store frequencies when the number of nonzero cells exceeds sixty-three.

Grouping with Formats

When you use PROC FREQ, remember that FREQ groups the variables according to their formatted values. If you assign a format to a variable with a FORMAT statement, the variable's values are formatted for printing before FREQ divides the observations into groups for the frequency counts.

For example, say a variable X has the values 1.3, 1.7, and 2.0, among others. Each of these values appears as a level in the frequency table. If you want each value rounded to a single digit, you include the statement

```
FORMAT X 1.;
```

after the PROC FREQ statement. The frequency table levels are then 1 and 2.

Formatted character variables are treated in the same way: the formatted values are used to divide the observations into groups. For character variables, formatted or not, only the first sixteen characters are used to determine the groups.

You can also use the FORMAT statement to assign formats created by PROC FORMAT to variables. Formats created by PROC FORMAT can serve two purposes: they can define the levels, and they can label the levels. You can use the same data with different formats to collect counts on different partitions of the class values. For an example, see "PROC Step Applications" in the *SAS User's Guide: Basics*.

In frequency tables, values of both character and numeric variables appear in ascending order by the original (unformatted) values unless you specify otherwise with the ORDER= option.

Tests and Measures of Association

Definitions and notation Suppose a two-way table represents the crosstabulation of variables X and Y. Let the rows of the table be labeled by the values X_i, $i=1,2,...R$ and the columns by Y_j, $j=1,2,...C$. Let ln denote natural logarithm (base e), let the cell frequency in the ith row and the jth column be denoted n_{ij}, and define the following:

$$n_{\bullet j} = \Sigma_i n_{ij} \text{ (column totals)}$$

$$n_{i\bullet} = \Sigma_j n_{ij} \text{ (row totals)}$$

$$n = \Sigma_i \Sigma_j n_{ij} \text{ (overall total)}$$

$$A_{ij} = \Sigma_{k>i}\Sigma_{l>j}n_{kl} + \Sigma_{k<i}\Sigma_{l<j}n_{kl}$$

$$D_{ij} = \Sigma_{k>i}\Sigma_{l<j}n_{kl} + \Sigma_{k<i}\Sigma_{l>j}n_{kl}$$

$$P = \Sigma_i\Sigma_j n_{ij}A_{ij} \text{ (twice the number of concordances)}$$

$$Q = \Sigma_i\Sigma_j n_{ij}D_{ij} \text{ (twice the number of discordances)} \quad .$$

Statistics produced for each two-way table All of the test statistics in this section test the null hypothesis of no association between the row variable and the column variable. When n is large, the chi-square statistics are distributed approximately as χ^2 when the null hypothesis is true. Throughout this section, let *var* denote the variance of the most recently defined estimator.

The following subsections give the formulas that PROC FREQ uses to compute statistics for two-way tables. For further information on the formulas and on the applicability and interpretation of each statistic, consult the cited references or those listed in the **Introduction.**

Chi-square (Q_P)

The Pearson chi-square statistic involves the differences between the observed and expected frequencies. The alternative hypothesis for this statistic is one of general association. The chi-square distribution has (R-1)(C-1) degrees of freedom (df) and is determined as

$$Q_P = \Sigma_i\Sigma_j(n_{ij} - m_{ij})^2/m_{ij}$$

where

$$m_{ij} = n_{i\bullet}n_{\bullet j}/n \quad .$$

Reference: Fienberg (1977, 9).

Continuity-adjusted chi-square (Q_C)

The adjusted chi-square statistic for 2 by 2 tables is similar to the Pearson chi-square, except that it is adjusted for the continuity of the χ^2 distribution. It has (R-1) (C-1) df and is determined as

$$Q_C = \Sigma_i\Sigma_j[\max(0, |n_{ij} - m_{ij}| - .5)]^2/m_{ij} \quad .$$

Reference: Fienberg (1977, 21).

Likelihood ratio chi-square (G^2)

The likelihood ratio chi-square statistic involves the ratios between the observed and expected frequencies. The alternative hypothesis for this statistic is one of general association. The χ^2 distribution has (R-1)(C-1) df and is determined as

$$G^2 = 2\,\Sigma_i\Sigma_j n_{ij}\ln(n_{ij}/m_{ij}) \quad .$$

Reference: Fienberg (1977, 36).

Mantel-Haenszel chi-square (Q_{MH})

The Mantel-Haenszel chi-square statistic tests the alternative hypothesis that there is a linear association between the row variable and the column variable. The χ^2 distribution has 1 df and is determined as

$$Q_{MH} = (n\text{-}1)r^2$$

where r^2 is the Pearson correlation between the row variable and the column variable. Both the MH statistic and the Pearson correlation use the scores specified with the SCORES option.

References: Mantel and Haenszel (1959); Landis, Heyman, and Koch (1978).

Fisher's exact test

For 2 by 2 tables, Fisher's exact test yields the probability of observing a table that gives at least as much evidence of association as the one actually observed, given that the null hypothesis is true. With row and column margins considered fixed, the hypergeometric probability, p, of every possible table is computed, and the p-value is defined as

$$\text{PROB} = \Sigma_A\, p \quad .$$

For two-tailed tests, A=A1, the set of tables with p less than or equal to the probability of the observed table. For one-tailed tests, A is the subset of A1 which contains those tables that exhibit an association that is in the same direction as that of the observed table.

Reference: Kendall and Stuart (1979, Volume 2, 580-585).

Phi coefficient (φ)

The phi coefficient is derived from the chi-square statistic. Range: $-1 \leq \varphi \leq 1$, though the attainable upper bound may be less than 1, depending on the marginal distributions. The phi coefficient is determined as

$$\varphi = (n_{11}n_{22} - n_{12}n_{21}) / (n_{1\bullet}n_{2\bullet}n_{\bullet 1}n_{\bullet 2})^{1/2} \quad \text{for 2 by 2 tables,}$$

$$\varphi = (Q_P/n)^{1/2} \quad \text{otherwise.}$$

Reference: Fleiss (1973, 42-43).

Contingency coefficient (P)

The contingency coefficient is also derived from chi-square
though the attainable upper bound may be less than 1
ginal distributions. The contingency coefficient is

$$P = [Q_P/(Q_P + n)]^{1/2} \quad .$$

Reference: Kendall and Stuart (1979, Volume 2,

Cramer's V

A third measure of association derived from chi-square is Cramer's V, designed so that the attainable upper bound is always 1. Range: $-1 <= V <= 1$. For 2 by 2 tables, $V=\varphi$; otherwise,

$$V = [(Q_P/n)/\min(R-1,C-1)]^{1/2} \quad .$$

Reference: Kendall and Stuart (1979, Volume 2, 588).

Gamma (γ)

The estimator of gamma is based only on the number of concordant and discordant pairs of observations. It ignores tied pairs (that is, pairs of observations that have equal values of X or equal values of Y). If the two variables are independent, then the estimator of gamma will tend to be close to zero. Gamma is appropriate only when both variables lie on an ordinal scale. Range: $-1 <= \gamma <= 1$. Gamma is estimated by

$$G = (P - Q)/(P + Q)$$

with

$$\text{var} = 16 \; \Sigma n_{ij}(QA_{ij} - PD_{ij})^2/(P + Q)^4 \quad .$$

References: Goodman and Kruskal (1963, 1972).

Kendall's tau-b (τ_b)

Kendall's tau-b is similar to gamma except that tau-b uses a correction correction for ties. Tau-b is appropriate only when both variables lie on an ordinal scale. Range: $-1 \leq \text{tau}-b \leq 1$. It is estimated by

$$t_b = (P - Q)/w = (P - Q)/\,(w_r w_c)^{1/2}$$

with

$$\text{var} = [\Sigma_i \Sigma_j n_{ij}(2wd_{ij} + t_b v_{ij})^2 - n^3 t_b^2\,(w_r + w_c)^2]/w^4$$

where

$$w_r = n^2 - \Sigma_i n_{i\bullet}^2$$

$$w_c = n^2 - \Sigma_j n_{\bullet j}^2$$

$$d_{ij} = A_{ij} - D_{ij}$$

$$v_{ij} = n_{i\bullet} w_c + n_{\bullet j} w_r \quad .$$

Reference: Goodman and Kruskal (1972).

Stuart's tau-c (τ_c)

[illegible]art's tau-c makes an adjustment for table size, in addition to a correction for [illegible] Tau-c is appropriate only when both variables lie on an ordinal scale. Range: [illegible]= tau-c <= 1. It is estimated by

$$t_c = (P-Q)/[n^2(m-1)/m]$$

with

$$\text{var} = 4m^2[\Sigma_i\Sigma_j n_{ij}d_{ij}^2 - (P-Q)^2/n]/(m-1)^2n^4$$

where

$$m = \min(R,C)$$

$$d_{ij} = A_{ij} - D_{ij} \quad .$$

Reference: Brown and Benedetti (1976).

Somers' D (C | R)

Somers' D is an asymmetric modification of tau-b. C | R denotes that the row variable X is regarded as an independent variable, while the column variable Y is regarded as dependent. Somers' D differs from tau-b in that it uses a correction only for pairs that are tied on the independent variable. Somers' D is appropriate only when both variables lie on an ordinal scale. Range: $-1 \leq D \leq 1$. Formulas for Somers' D(R | C) are obtained by interchanging the indices.

$$D(C\,|\,R) = (P-Q)/w_r$$

with

$$\text{var} = 4\Sigma_i\Sigma_j n_{ij}\,[w_r d_{ij} - (P-Q)(n-n_{i\bullet})]^2/w_r^4 \quad .$$

where

$$w_r = n^2 - \Sigma_i n_{i\bullet}^2$$

$$d_{ij} = A_{ij} - D_{ij} \quad .$$

References: Somers (1962); Goodman and Kruskal (1972).

Pearson correlation coefficient (r)

The Pearson correlation coefficient is computed by using the scores specified in the SCORES option. It is appropriate only when both variables lie on an ordinal scale. Range: $-1 \leq r \leq 1$. The Pearson correlation coefficient is computed as

$$r = v/w = ss_{rc}\,/\,(ss_r ss_c)^{1/2}$$

with

$$\text{var} = \Sigma_i\Sigma_j n_{ij}\{w[r_i - m(r)][c_j - m(c)] - b_{ij}v/2w\}^2/w^4$$

where the r_i are the row scores, the c_j are the column scores, and

$$m(r) = \Sigma_i\Sigma_j n_{ij}r_i/n$$

$$m(c) = \Sigma_i\Sigma_j n_{ij}c_j/n$$

$$ss_r = \Sigma_i \Sigma_j n_{ij} [r_i - m(r)]^2$$

$$ss_c = \Sigma_i \Sigma_j n_{ij} [c_j - m(c)]^2$$

$$ss_{rc} = \Sigma_i \Sigma_j n_{ij} [r_i - m(r)][c_j - m(c)]$$

$$b_{ij} = [r_i - m(r)]^2 ss_c + [c_j - m(c)]^2 ss_r \quad .$$

References: Snedecor and Cochran (1980, 175); Brown and Benedetti (1976).

Spearman rank correlation coefficient (r_s)

The Spearman correlation coefficient is computed by using rank scores $r1_i$ and $c1_j$, defined in the **Summary Statistics** section below. The formulas are those given for the Pearson correlation coefficient, with $r_i = r1_i$ and $c_j = c1_j$. It is appropriate only when both variables lie on an ordinal scale. Range: $-1 \leq r_s \leq 1$.

References: Snedecor and Cochran (1980, 192); Brown and Benedetti (1976).

Lambda asymmetric C | R (λ(C | R))

Lambda C | R is interpreted as the probable improvement in predicting Y given that one has knowledge of X. Range: $0 \leq$ lambda ≤ 1. It is computed as

$$\lambda(C \mid R) = (\Sigma_i r_i - r)/(n - r)$$

with

$$\text{var} = (n - \Sigma_i r_i)[\Sigma_i r_i + r - 2\Sigma_i (r_i \mid l_i = l)]/(n - r)^3$$

where

$$r_i = \max_j (n_{ij})$$

$$r = \max_j (n_{\bullet j}) \quad .$$

Also,

let l_i be the unique value of j such that $r_i = n_{ij}$, and

let l be the unique value of j such that $r = n_{\bullet j}$.

Because of the uniqueness assumptions, ties in the frequencies or in the marginal totals must be broken in an arbitrary but consistent manner. In case of ties, l is defined here as the smallest value of j such that $r = n_{\bullet j}$. For a given i, if there is at least one value j such that $n_{ij} = r_i = c_j$, then l_i is defined here to be the smallest such value of j. Otherwise, if $n_{il} = r_i$, then l_i is defined to be equal to l. If neither condition is true, then l_i is taken to be the smallest value of j such that $n_{ij} = r_i$. The formulas for lambda asymmetric R | C can be obtained by interchanging the indices.

Reference: Goodman and Kruskal (1963).

Lambda symmetric (λ)

The two asymmetric lambdas are averaged to obtain the non-directional lambda. Range: $0 \leq \lambda \leq 1$. Lambda symmetric is defined as

$$\lambda = (\Sigma_i r_i + \Sigma_j c_j - r - c)/(2n - r - c) = (w - v)/w$$

with

$$\text{var} = \{wvy - 2w^2[1 - \Sigma_i\Sigma_j(n_{ij} \mid j = l_i, i = k_j)] - 2v^2(1 - n_{kl})\}/w^4$$

where

$$w = 2n - r - c$$

$$v = 2n - \Sigma_i r_i - \Sigma_j c_j$$

$$x = \Sigma_i[r_i \mid l_i = l] + \Sigma_j[c_j \mid k_j = k] + r_k + c_l$$

$$y = 8n - w - v - 2x \quad .$$

Reference: Goodman and Kruskal (1963).

Uncertainty coefficient (U(C | R))

The uncertainty coefficient, U(C | R), is the proportional reduction in the uncertainty (entropy) of Y that results from knowing the value of X. The range is: $0 \leq U(C \mid R) \leq 1$. The formulas for U(R | C) can be obtained by interchanging the indices.

$$U(C \mid R) = [H(X)+H(Y)-H(XY)]/H(Y) = v/w$$

with

$$\text{var} = \Sigma_i\Sigma_j\, n_{ij}\{\, H(Y)\ \ln(n_{ij}/n_{i\bullet}) + [H(X)-H(XY)]\ \ln(n_{\bullet j}/n)\}^2 \,/\, n^2\, w^4$$

where

$$H(X) = -\ \Sigma_i(n_{i\bullet}/n)\ \ln\ (n_{i\bullet}/n)$$

$$H(Y) = -\ \Sigma_j(n_{\bullet j}/n)\ \ln\ (n_{\bullet j}/n)$$

$$H(XY) = -\ \Sigma_i\Sigma_j(n_{ij}/n)\ \ln(n_{ij}/n) \quad .$$

References: Theil (1972, 115-120); Goodman and Kruskal (1972).

Uncertainty coefficient (U)

The uncertainty coefficient, U, is the symmetric version of the two asymmetric coefficients. Range: $0 \leq U \leq 1$. It is defined as

$$U = 2[H(X) + H(Y) - H(XY)]/[H(X) + H(Y)]$$

with

$$\text{var} = 4\ \Sigma_i\Sigma_j\ n_{ij}\ \{\ H(XY)\ \ln\ (n_{i\bullet}n_{\bullet j}/n^2)$$

$$-\ [H(X) + H(Y)]\ \ln\ (n_{ij}/n)\ \}^2/n^2[H(X) + H(Y)]^4\ .$$

Reference: Goodman and Kruskal (1972).

Relative risk estimates

For two dichotomous variables, disease(D) and exposure(E) to a risk factor, the relative risk of disease is defined as

$$RR = \text{Prob}(D = \text{yes}\,|\,E = \text{yes})/\text{Prob}(D = \text{yes}\,|\,E = \text{no})\quad .$$

Relative risk estimates are computed only for 2 by 2 tables, in which case the table is presumed to be set up with E as the row variable and D as the column variable. Throughout this section, z is the $100(1-\alpha/2)$ percent point of the Normal(0,1) distribution. The estimation of the relative risk depends on the study design:

1. Case-control studies
It is assumed that the (E=yes,D=yes) cell is on the main diagonal. The estimate of the relative risk is the odds ratio,

$$OR = n_{11}n_{22}/n_{12}n_{21}\quad .$$

The 100(1-α)% confidence interval for OR is obtained as

$$(\ OR\ \exp[\ -\ z\ v^{1/2}],\ \ OR\ \exp[z\ v^{1/2}]\ \ )$$

where

$$v = \text{var}(\ln OR) = 1/n_{11} + 1/n_{12} + 1/n_{21} + 1/n_{22}\quad .$$

If any of the four cell frequencies are zero, the estimates are not computed.

2. Cohort studies
It is assumed that (E=yes) is the first row of the contingency table. If (D=yes) is the first column, then use the estimates labeled COL1 RISK. Otherwise, use the estimates labeled COL2 RISK. Define

$$p_1 = n_{11}/n_{1\bullet}$$

$$p_2 = n_{21}/n_{2\bullet}\quad .$$

The COL1 relative risk is estimated by

$$RR = p_1/p_2$$

and the corresponding 100(1-α)% confidence interval is

$$(\ RR\ \exp[\ -\ z\ v^{1/2}],\ RR\ \exp[z\ v^{1/2}]\ )$$

where

$$v = \text{var}(\ln RR) = (1 - p_1)/n_{11} + (1 - p_2)/n_{21}\quad .$$

If either n_{11} or n_{21} is zero, the estimates are not computed.
The COL2 relative risk estimates are computed similarly.

Reference: Kleinbaum, Kupper, and Morgenstern (1982, 299).

Summary Statistics

Suppose there are q strata, indexed by h=1,2,...,q, and within each stratum is a contingency table with X as the row variable and Y as the column variable. For table h, let the cell frequency in the *i*th row and *j*th column be denoted by n_{hij}, with corresponding marginal totals denoted by $n_{hi\bullet}$ and $n_{h\bullet j}$, and with overall total N_h. The CMH summary statistics use row and column scores, for which there are several choices.

For numeric variables, TABLE scores are the values of the row headings and column headings; for character variables, they are defined as the row numbers and column numbers. TABLE scores are the same for each of the q tables, and are used by FREQ if no choice of scores is specified with the SCORES option.

RANK scores, which can be used to obtain nonparametric analyses, are defined by

$$\text{Row scores: } r1_{hi} = \Sigma_{k<i} n_{hk\bullet} + (n_{hi\bullet} + 1)/2, \quad i = 1,2,...,R$$

$$\text{Col scores: } c1_{hj} = \Sigma_{l<j} n_{h\bullet l} + (n_{h\bullet j} + 1)/2, \quad j = 1,2,...,C \quad .$$

RIDIT scores (Bross 1958; Mack and Skillings 1980) also yield nonparametric analyses, but they are standardized by the stratum sample size. RIDIT scores are derived from RANK scores as

$$r2_{hi} = r1_{hi}/N_h$$

$$c2_{hj} = c1_{hj}/N_h \quad .$$

MODified RIDIT scores (van Elteren 1960, Lehmann 1975), which also yield nonparametric analyses, represent the expected values of the within-stratum order statistics for the uniform distribution on (0,1). MODified RIDIT scores are derived from rank scores as

$$r3_{hi} = r1_{hi}/(N_h + 1)$$

$$c3_{hj} = c1_{hj}/(N_h + 1) \quad .$$

Since the formulas for the CMH statistics are more easily defined in terms of matrices, we also define the following notation. Vectors are presumed to be column vectors unless they are transposed (′):

$$\underset{(1xC)}{\mathbf{n}_{hi}'} = (n_{hi1}, n_{hi2}, \ldots, n_{hiC})$$

$$\underset{(1 \times RC)}{\mathbf{n}_h'} = (\mathbf{n}_{h1}', \mathbf{n}_{h2}', \ldots, \mathbf{n}_{hR}')$$

$$P_{hi\bullet} = n_{hi\bullet}/N_h$$

$$P_{h\bullet j} = n_{h\bullet j}/N_h$$

$$\mathbf{P}_{h*\bullet}' = (P_{h1\bullet}, P_{h2\bullet}, \ldots, P_{hR\bullet})$$

$$\mathbf{P}_{h\bullet*}' = (P_{h\bullet1}, P_{h\bullet2}, \ldots, P_{h\bullet C}) \quad .$$

Cochran-Mantel-Haenszel (CMH) statistics Assume that the strata are independent and that the marginal totals of each stratum are fixed. The null hypothesis, H_0, is that there is no association between X and Y in any of the strata. The corresponding model is the multiple hypergeometric, which implies that under H_0, the expected value and covariance matrix of the frequencies are, respectively,

$$\mathbf{m}_h = \mathbf{E}[\mathbf{n}_h \,|\, H_0] = N_h(\mathbf{P}_{h\bullet*} @ \mathbf{P}_{h*\bullet})$$

and

$$\mathbf{Var}[\mathbf{n}_h \,|\, H_0] = c[(\mathbf{D}_{\mathbf{P}_{h\bullet*}} - \mathbf{P}_{h\bullet*}\mathbf{P}_{h\bullet*}') @ (\mathbf{D}_{\mathbf{P}_{h*\bullet}} - \mathbf{P}_{h*\bullet}\mathbf{P}_{h*\bullet}')]$$

where

$$c = N_h^2/(N_h - 1) \quad .$$

@ denotes Kronecker product multiplication, and $\mathbf{D}_\mathbf{a}$ is a diagonal matrix with elements of **a** on the main diagonal.

The generalized CMH statistic (Landis, Heyman, and Koch 1978) is defined as

$$Q_{CMH} = \mathbf{G}'\mathbf{V}_G^{-1}\mathbf{G}$$

where

$$\mathbf{G} = \Sigma_h \mathbf{B}_h(\mathbf{n}_h - \mathbf{m}_h)$$

$$\mathbf{V}_G = \Sigma_h \mathbf{B}_h[\mathbf{Var}(\mathbf{n}_h \,|\, H_0)]\mathbf{B}_h'$$

and where

$$\mathbf{B}_h = \mathbf{C}_h @ \mathbf{R}_h$$

is a matrix of fixed constants based on column scores $\mathbf{C}_h$ and row scores $\mathbf{R}_h$. When the null hypothesis is true, the CMH statistic is approximately distributed as chi-square with degrees of freedom equal to the rank of $\mathbf{B}_h$.

A word of caution is necessary. CMH statistics have low power for detecting an association in which the patterns of association for some of the strata are in the opposite direction of the patterns displayed by other strata. Thus, a nonsignificant CMH statistic suggests either that there is no association, or that no pattern of association had enough strength or consistency to dominate any other pattern. FREQ computes the following types of CMH statistics:

The correlation statistic (df = 1)

The correlation statistic, with one degree of freedom, was popularized by Mantel and Haenszel (1959) and Mantel (1963) and is therefore known as the Mantel-Haenszel statistic.

The alternative hypothesis in this case is that there is a linear association between X and Y in at least one stratum. If either X or Y does not lie on an ordinal (or interval) scale, then this statistic is meaningless.

The matrix $\mathbf{C}_h$ has dimension 1xC, and the scores, one for each column, are specified in the SCORES option. Similarly, the matrix $\mathbf{R}_h$ has dimension 1xR, and these scores, one for each row, are also controlled by the SCORES option.

When there is only one stratum, this CMH statistic reduces to to $(N-1)r^2$, where r is the correlation coefficient between X and Y. When nonparametric (rank or ridit) scores are specified, then the statistic reduces to $(N-1)r_s^2$, where r_s is the Spearman rank correlation coefficient between X and Y. When there is more than one stratum, then the CMH statistic becomes a stratum-adjusted correlation statistic.

The ANOVA statistic (df=R−1)

This statistic can be used only when the column variable Y lies on an ordinal (or interval) scale, so that the mean score of Y is a meaningful notion. In that case, the mean score is computed for each row of the table, and the alternative hypothesis is that, for at least one stratum, the mean scores of the R rows are unequal. In other words, the statistic is sensitive to location differences among the R distributions of Y.

The matrix $\mathbf{C}_h$ has dimension 1xC, and the scores, one for each column, are specified in the SCORES option. The matrix $\mathbf{R}_h$ has dimension (R−1)xR, and is created internally by FREQ as

$$\mathbf{R}_h = [\ \mathbf{I}_{R-1}\ ,\ -\mathbf{J}_{R-1}\ ]$$

where $\mathbf{I}_{R-1}$ is an identity matrix of rank R−1, and $\mathbf{J}_{R-1}$ is an (R−1)x1 vector of ones. This matrix has the effect of forming R−1 independent contrasts of the R mean scores.

When there is only one stratum, this CMH statistic is essentially an analysis of variance (ANOVA) statistic in the sense that it is a function of the variance ratio F statistic that would be obtained from a one-way ANOVA on the dependent variable Y. If nonparametric scores are specified in this case, then the ANOVA statistic is a Kruskal-Wallis test.

If there is more than one stratum, then the CMH statistic corresponds to a stratum-adjusted ANOVA or Kruskal-Wallis test. In the special case where there is one subject per row and one subject per column in the contingency table of each stratum, this CMH statistic is identical to Friedman's chi-square.

The general association statistic (df=(R−1)(C−1))

This statistic is always interpretable because it does not require an ordinal scale for either X or Y. The alternative hypothesis is that, for at least one stratum, there is some kind of association between X and Y.

The matrix $\mathbf{R}_h$ is the same as the one used for the ANOVA statistic. The matrix $\mathbf{C}_h$ is defined similarly as

$$\mathbf{C}_h = [\ \mathbf{I}_{C-1}\ ,\ -\mathbf{J}_{C-1}\ ]\ .$$

Both score matrices are generated internally by FREQ.

When there is only one stratum, then the general association CMH statistic reduces to $[(N-1)/N]Q_P$, where Q_P is the Pearson chi-square statistic. When there is more than one stratum, then the CMH statistic becomes a stratum-adjusted Pearson chi-square statistic. Note that a similar adjustment can be made by summing the Pearson chi-squares across the strata. However, the latter statistic requires a large sample size in each stratum to support the resulting chi-square distribution with q(R−1)(C−1) df. The CMH statistic requires only a large overall sample size, since it has only (R−1)(C−1) df.

References: Cochran (1954); Mantel and Haenszel (1959); Mantel (1963); Birch (1965); Landis, Heyman, and Koch (1978).

Adjusted relative risk estimates We use the notation and definitions from the section **Relative Risk Estimates**, described earlier. If you would like RR estimates of E which are adjusted for confounding variables A and B, specify

```
PROC FREQ; TABLES A*B*E*D/ALL;
```

As before, E must be the row variable, D must be the column variable, and RR estimates are computed only when E and D each have two levels. Throughout this section, z is the 100(1−α/2) percent point of the Normal(0,1) distribution, and Q is the general association CMH statistic. (Note that the value of the general association statistic is independent of the scores that are specified.) Tables with a zero row or column are not included in any of the summary relative risk computations. The estimation procedure depends on the study design:

1. Case-control studies
It is assumed that the (E=yes,D=yes) cell is on the main diagonal of the matrix in each stratum. Two sets of estimators are given for case-control studies:

Mantel-Haenszel estimate and test-based confidence interval

The adjusted odds ratio estimator is given by

$$OR_{MH} = [\ \Sigma_h\ n_{h11}n_{h22}/N_h\ ]\ /[\ \Sigma_h\ n_{h12}n_{h21}/N_h\ ]$$

and is always computed unless the denominator is zero. The corresponding 100(1−α)% test-based confidence interval is given by

$$(\ OR_{MH}^{\{1\ -\ z/Q^{1/2}\}},\ OR_{MH}^{\{1\ +\ z/Q^{1/2}\}}\ )$$

if $OR_{MH}>1$. Otherwise, the lower and upper limits are reversed. The confidence interval is computed unless Q=0 or OR_{MH} is undefined.

Logit estimator with precision-based confidence interval

This odds ratio estimator (Woolf 1955) is given by

$$OR_L = \exp[(\Sigma_h w_h \ln OR_h)/\Sigma w_h]$$

and the corresponding 100(1-α)% confidence interval is

$$(OR_L \exp[\ -\ z/\ (\Sigma_h\ w_h)^{1/2}],\ OR_L \exp[z/(\Sigma_h\ w_h)^{1/2}]\ )$$

where OR_h is the odds ratio for stratum h, and

$$w_h = 1/\mathrm{var}(\ln OR_h)\quad .$$

If any cell frequency in a stratum h is zero, then 1/2 is added to each cell of the stratum before OR_h and w_h are computed (Haldane 1955), and a warning is printed.

2. Cohort studies
It is assumed that (E=yes) is the first row of the contingency tables. If (D=yes) is the first column, then use the estimates labeled COL1 RISK. Otherwise, use the estimates labeled COL2 RISK. The COL1 estimators are given in this section; the COL2 estimators have corresponding definitions. Two sets of estimators are given for cohort studies:

Mantel-Haenszel estimate and test-based confidence interval

The adjusted relative risk estimator is given by

$$RR_{MH} = [\ \Sigma_h\ n_{h11} n_{h2\bullet}/N_h\ ]\ /[\ \Sigma_h\ n_{h21} n_{h1\bullet}/N_h\ ]$$

and is always computed unless the denominator is zero. The corresponding 100(1-α)% test-based confidence interval is given by

$$(\ RR_{MH}^{\{1\ -\ z/Q^{1/2}\}},\ RR_{MH}^{\{1\ +\ z/Q^{1/2}\}})$$

if $RR_{MH}>1$. Otherwise, the lower and upper limits are reversed. The confidence interval is computed unless Q=0 or RR_{MH} is undefined.

Logit estimator with precision-based confidence interval

This relative risk estimator is given by

$$RR_L = \exp[(\Sigma_h w_h\ ln\ RR_h)/\Sigma w_h]$$

and the corresponding 100(1−α)% confidence interval is

$$(RR_L\ \exp[\ -\ z/(\Sigma_h\ w_h)^{1/2}],\ RR_L\ \exp[z/(\Sigma_h\ w_h)^{1/2}]\ )$$

where RR_h is the relative risk estimator for stratum h, and

$$w_h = 1\ /\mathrm{var}(\ln\ RR_h)\quad .$$

If n_{h11} or n_{h21} is zero, then 1/2 is added to each cell of the stratum before RR_h and w_h are computed, and a warning is printed.

Reference: Kleinbaum, Kupper, and Morgenstern (1982, Sections 17.4, 17.5).

Breslow-Day Test for Homogeneity of the odds ratios This statistic tests the hypothesis that the odds ratios from the q strata are all equal. When the hypothesis is true, the statistic is distributed approximately as chi-square with q-1 degrees of freedom. The statistic is defined as

$$Q_{BD} = \Sigma_h[n_{h11}\ -\ \mathrm{Exp}(n_{h11}\,|\,OR_{MH})]^2\ /\mathrm{Var}(n_{h11}\,|\,OR_{MH})$$

where Exp and Var denote expected value and variance, respectively. If $OR_{MH}=0$ or if it is undefined, then FREQ does not compute the statistic, and a warning message is printed. The summation does not include any tables with a zero row or column.

Reference: Breslow and Day (1980, 142).

Sample size summary The total sample size and the frequency of missing subjects are printed. The EFFECTIVE SAMPLE SIZE is the frequency of nonmissing subjects.

Printed Output

For a one-way table showing the frequency distribution of a single variable, FREQ prints these items:

1. the name of the variable and its values
2. FREQUENCY counts giving the number of subjects that have each value
3. CUMULATIVE FREQUENCY counts, giving the sum of the frequency counts of that value and all other values listed above it in the table (the total number of nonmissing subjects is the last cumulative frequency)
4. percentages, labeled PERCENT, giving the percent of the total number of subjects represented by that value
5. CUMULATIVE PERCENT values, giving the percent of the total number of subjects represented by that value and all others previously listed in the table.

   Two-way tables can be printed either as crosstabulation tables (the default) or as lists (when the LIST option is specified). Each cell of a crosstabulation table contains items 6 through 12:
6. FREQUENCY counts, giving the number of subjects that have the indicated values of the two variables
7. PERCENT, the percentage of the total frequency count represented by that cell
8. ROW PCT, or the row percentage, the percent of the total frequency count for that row represented by the cell
9. COL PCT, or column percent, the percent of the total frequency count for that column represented by the cell
10. if the EXPECTED option is specified, the expected cell frequency under the hypothesis of independence
11. if the DEVIATION option is specified, the deviation of the cell frequency from the expected value
12. if the CELLCHI2 option is specified, the cell's contribution to the total chi-square statistic.
13. if the CHISQ option is specified, the following statistics are printed for the two-way table in each stratum: Pearson chi-square, likelihood ratio chi-square, continuity-adjusted chi-square,Mantel-Haenszel chi-square, Fisher's exact test (for 2 by 2 tables), phi, the contingency coefficient, Cramer's V, the sample size, and the frequency missing. For each test statistic, its degrees of freedom (DF) and its significance probability (PROB) are also printed.
14. if the MEASURES option is specified, the following statistics are printed for the two-way table in each stratum: gamma, Kendall's tau-b, Stuart's tau-c, Somer's D, Pearson's product-moment correlation, Spearman's rank correlation, lambda (symmetric and asymmetric), the uncertainty coefficient (symmetric and asymmetric), the sample size, the frequency missing, and (for 2 by 2 tables) estimates of the relative risk for case-control and cohort studies, together with their confidence intervals.
15. if the CMH option is specified, the following statistics are printed: the total sample size, the total frequency missing, and three Cochran-Mantel-Haenszel summary statistics (the correlation statistic, the ANOVA statistic, and the general association statistic), with corresponding degrees of freedom (DF) and significance probabilities (PROB). For 2 by 2 tables, additional statistics printed are stratum-adjusted estimates (both

Mantel-Haenszel and logit estimates) of the common relative risk for case-control and cohort studies, together with their confidence intervals, and the Breslow-Day test for homogeneity of the odds ratios.

16. if the ALL option is specified, all of the statistics requested by the CHISQ, MEASURES, and CMH options are printed.
17. if two contingency tables can fit on a page, one table above the other, then the tables are printed in that manner. Similarly, a table and its corresponding statistics are printed on the same page, provided that they fit.

EXAMPLES

Evans County Study: Example 1

Data for the following example are from the Evans County cohort study of coronary heart disease. Data for the variable CAT, however, are hypothetical. The data are given in Table 17.7, and used in Examples 17.2 and 17.9 of Kleinbaum, Kupper, and Morgenstern (1982).

The purpose of the analysis is to evaluate the association between serum catecholamine (CAT) and coronary heart disease (CHD) after controlling for AGE and electrocardiogram abnormality (ECG). The summary statistics show that the association is significant (p=.04), and that subjects with high serum catecholamine are about 1.7 times more likely to develop coronary heart disease than those subjects with low serum catecholamine.

```
DATA CHD;
   INPUT AGE $ ECG $ CHD $ CAT $ WT;
   CARDS;
<55  0  YES  YES    1
<55  0  YES   NO   17
<55  0   NO  YES    7
<55  0   NO   NO  257
<55  1  YES  YES    3
<55  1  YES   NO    7
<55  1   NO  YES   14
<55  1   NO   NO   52
55+  0  YES  YES    9
55+  0  YES   NO   15
55+  0   NO  YES   30
55+  0   NO   NO  107
55+  1  YES  YES   14
55+  1  YES   NO    5
55+  1   NO  YES   44
55+  1   NO   NO   27
;
PROC FREQ ORDER=DATA;
   WEIGHT WT;
   TABLES AGE*ECG*CAT*CHD/ALL;
   TITLE 'EXAMPLE 17.9 FROM KLEINBAUM, KUPPER, AND MORGENSTERN, P. 353';
```

Output 19.1 Evans County Study of Heart Disease: PROC FREQ

```
                EXAMPLE 17.9 FROM KLEINBAUM, KUPPER, AND MORGENSTERN, P. 353                                1

                              TABLE 1 OF CAT BY CHD
                          CONTROLLING FOR AGE=<55 ECG=0

                      CAT       CHD

                 (6)  FREQUENCY|
                 (7)   PERCENT |
                 (8)   ROW PCT |
                 (9)   COL PCT |YES     |NO      |  TOTAL
                      ---------+--------+--------+
                      YES      |      1 |      7 |      8
                               |   0.35 |   2.48 |   2.84
                               |  12.50 |  87.50 |
                               |   5.56 |   2.65 |
                      ---------+--------+--------+
                      NO       |     17 |    257 |    274
                               |   6.03 |  91.13 |  97.16
                               |   6.20 |  93.80 |
                               |  94.44 |  97.35 |
                      ---------+--------+--------+
                      TOTAL          18      264      282
                                   6.38    93.62   100.00
```

```
                EXAMPLE 17.9 FROM KLEINBAUM, KUPPER, AND MORGENSTERN, P. 353                                2
                (16)
                        STATISTICS FOR TABLE 1 OF CAT BY CHD
                           CONTROLLING FOR AGE=<55 ECG=0

                  STATISTIC                         DF     VALUE        PROB
                  ------------------------------------------------------------
                  CHI-SQUARE                         1     0.516        0.473
                  LIKELIHOOD RATIO CHI-SQUARE        1     0.413        0.520
                  CONTINUITY ADJ. CHI-SQUARE         1     0.000        1.000
                  MANTEL-HAENSZEL CHI-SQUARE         1     0.514        0.474
                  FISHER'S EXACT TEST (1-TAIL)                          0.414
                                      (2-TAIL)                          0.414
                  PHI                                      0.043
                  CONTINGENCY COEFFICIENT                  0.043
                  CRAMER'S V                               0.043

                  STATISTIC                                VALUE         ASE
                  ------------------------------------------------------------
                  GAMMA                                    0.367        0.475
                  KENDALL'S TAU-B                          0.043        0.080
                  STUART'S TAU-C                           0.007        0.013

                  SOMERS' D C|R                            0.063        0.118
                  SOMERS' D R|C                            0.029        0.055

                  PEARSON CORRELATION                      0.043        0.080
                  SPEARMAN CORRELATION                     0.043        0.080

                  LAMBDA ASYMMETRIC C|R                    0.000        0.000
                  LAMBDA ASYMMETRIC R|C                    0.000        0.000
                  LAMBDA SYMMETRIC                         0.000        0.000

                  UNCERTAINTY COEFFICIENT C|R              0.003        0.011
                  UNCERTAINTY COEFFICIENT R|C              0.006        0.019
                  UNCERTAINTY COEFFICIENT SYM              0.004        0.014

                        ESTIMATES OF THE RELATIVE RISK (ROW1/ROW2)

                  TYPE OF STUDY            VALUE    95% CONFIDENCE BOUNDS
                  -------------------------------------------------------
                  CASE-CONTROL             2.160        0.251     18.578
                  COHORT (COL1 RISK)       2.015        0.304     13.340
                  COHORT (COL2 RISK)       0.933        0.717      1.214

                  SAMPLE SIZE = 282
                  WARNING:  25% OF THE CELLS HAVE EXPECTED COUNTS LESS
                            THAN 5. CHI-SQUARE MAY NOT BE A VALID TEST.

                  ASE IS THE ASYMPTOTIC STANDARD ERROR.
                  R|C MEANS ROW VARIABLE DEPENDENT ON COLUMN VARIABLE.
```

```
EXAMPLE 17.9 FROM KLEINBAUM, KUPPER, AND MORGENSTERN, P. 353                        3

                    TABLE 2 OF CAT BY CHD
                 CONTROLLING FOR AGE=<55 ECG=1

             CAT       CHD

             FREQUENCY|
              PERCENT |
              ROW PCT |
              COL PCT |YES     |NO      |  TOTAL
             ---------+--------+--------+
             YES      |      3 |     14 |     17
                      |   3.95 |  18.42 |  22.37
                      |  17.65 |  82.35 |
                      |  30.00 |  21.21 |
             ---------+--------+--------+
             NO       |      7 |     52 |     59
                      |   9.21 |  68.42 |  77.63
                      |  11.86 |  88.14 |
                      |  70.00 |  78.79 |
             ---------+--------+--------+
             TOTAL          10       66       76
                         13.16    86.84   100.00
```

```
EXAMPLE 17.9 FROM KLEINBAUM, KUPPER, AND MORGENSTERN, P. 353                        4

                 STATISTICS FOR TABLE 2 OF CAT BY CHD
                    CONTROLLING FOR AGE=<55 ECG=1

        STATISTIC                         DF       VALUE        PROB
        ------------------------------------------------------------
        CHI-SQUARE                         1       0.386       0.534
        LIKELIHOOD RATIO CHI-SQUARE        1       0.364       0.546
        CONTINUITY ADJ. CHI-SQUARE         1       0.046       0.830
        MANTEL-HAENSZEL CHI-SQUARE         1       0.381       0.537
        FISHER'S EXACT TEST (1-TAIL)                           0.394
                            (2-TAIL)                           0.684
        PHI                                        0.071
        CONTINGENCY COEFFICIENT                    0.071
        CRAMER'S V                                 0.071


        STATISTIC                                  VALUE         ASE
        ------------------------------------------------------------
        GAMMA                                      0.228       0.357
        KENDALL'S TAU-B                            0.071       0.124
        STUART'S TAU-C                             0.040       0.071

        SOMERS' D C|R                              0.058       0.102
        SOMERS' D R|C                              0.088       0.153

        PEARSON CORRELATION                        0.071       0.124
        SPEARMAN CORRELATION                       0.071       0.124

        LAMBDA ASYMMETRIC C|R                      0.000       0.000
        LAMBDA ASYMMETRIC R|C                      0.000       0.000
        LAMBDA SYMMETRIC                           0.000       0.000

        UNCERTAINTY COEFFICIENT C|R                0.006       0.021
        UNCERTAINTY COEFFICIENT R|C                0.005       0.015
        UNCERTAINTY COEFFICIENT SYM                0.005       0.018


              ESTIMATES OF THE RELATIVE RISK (ROW1/ROW2)

        TYPE OF STUDY        VALUE     95% CONFIDENCE BOUNDS
        ------------------------------------------------------------
        CASE-CONTROL         1.592        0.364       6.962
        COHORT (COL1 RISK)   1.487        0.430       5.141
        COHORT (COL2 RISK)   0.934        0.736       1.187


        SAMPLE SIZE = 76
        WARNING:  25% OF THE CELLS HAVE EXPECTED COUNTS LESS
                  THAN 5. CHI-SQUARE MAY NOT BE A VALID TEST.

        ASE IS THE ASYMPTOTIC STANDARD ERROR.
        R|C MEANS ROW VARIABLE DEPENDENT ON COLUMN VARIABLE.
```

```
EXAMPLE 17.9 FROM KLEINBAUM, KUPPER, AND MORGENSTERN, P. 353                         5

                  TABLE 3 OF CAT BY CHD
               CONTROLLING FOR AGE=55+ ECG=0

        CAT       CHD

        FREQUENCY|
         PERCENT |
        ROW PCT  |
        COL PCT  |YES     |NO      |  TOTAL
        ---------+--------+--------+
        YES      |      9 |     30 |     39
                 |   5.59 |  18.63 |  24.22
                 |  23.08 |  76.92 |
                 |  37.50 |  21.90 |
        ---------+--------+--------+
        NO       |     15 |    107 |    122
                 |   9.32 |  66.46 |  75.78
                 |  12.30 |  87.70 |
                 |  62.50 |  78.10 |
        ---------+--------+--------+
        TOTAL          24      137      161
                    14.91    85.09   100.00
```

```
EXAMPLE 17.9 FROM KLEINBAUM, KUPPER, AND MORGENSTERN, P. 353                         6

              STATISTICS FOR TABLE 3 OF CAT BY CHD
                CONTROLLING FOR AGE=55+ ECG=0

   STATISTIC                        DF       VALUE        PROB
   ------------------------------------------------------------
   CHI-SQUARE                        1       2.708        0.100
   LIKELIHOOD RATIO CHI-SQUARE       1       2.501        0.114
   CONTINUITY ADJ. CHI-SQUARE        1       1.925        0.165
   MANTEL-HAENSZEL CHI-SQUARE        1       2.692        0.101
   FISHER'S EXACT TEST (1-TAIL)                           0.086
                       (2-TAIL)                           0.122
   PHI                                       0.130
   CONTINGENCY COEFFICIENT                   0.129
   CRAMER'S V                                0.130

   STATISTIC                                 VALUE         ASE
   ------------------------------------------------------------
   GAMMA                                     0.363        0.204
   KENDALL'S TAU-B                           0.130        0.087
   STUART'S TAU-C                            0.079        0.055

   SOMERS' D C|R                             0.108        0.074
   SOMERS' D R|C                             0.156        0.105

   PEARSON CORRELATION                       0.130        0.087
   SPEARMAN CORRELATION                      0.130        0.087

   LAMBDA ASYMMETRIC C|R                     0.000        0.000
   LAMBDA ASYMMETRIC R|C                     0.000        0.000
   LAMBDA SYMMETRIC                          0.000        0.000

   UNCERTAINTY COEFFICIENT C|R               0.018        0.024
   UNCERTAINTY COEFFICIENT R|C               0.014        0.018
   UNCERTAINTY COEFFICIENT SYM               0.016        0.021

         ESTIMATES OF THE RELATIVE RISK (ROW1/ROW2)

   TYPE OF STUDY          VALUE     95% CONFIDENCE BOUNDS
   ------------------------------------------------------------
   CASE-CONTROL           2.140         0.853        5.371
   COHORT (COL1 RISK)     1.877         0.892        3.948
   COHORT (COL2 RISK)     0.877         0.729        1.055

   SAMPLE SIZE = 161

   ASE IS THE ASYMPTOTIC STANDARD ERROR.
   R|C MEANS ROW VARIABLE DEPENDENT ON COLUMN VARIABLE.
```

```
EXAMPLE 17.9 FROM KLEINBAUM, KUPPER, AND MORGENSTERN, P. 353                    7

                     TABLE 4 OF CAT BY CHD
                 CONTROLLING FOR AGE=55+ ECG=1

               CAT       CHD

               FREQUENCY|
                PERCENT |
                ROW PCT |
                COL PCT |YES     |NO      |  TOTAL
               ---------+--------+--------+
               YES      |     14 |     44 |     58
                        |  15.56 |  48.89 |  64.44
                        |  24.14 |  75.86 |
                        |  73.68 |  61.97 |
               ---------+--------+--------+
               NO       |      5 |     27 |     32
                        |   5.56 |  30.00 |  35.56
                        |  15.63 |  84.38 |
                        |  26.32 |  38.03 |
               ---------+--------+--------+
               TOTAL          19       71       90
                           21.11    78.89   100.00
```

```
EXAMPLE 17.9 FROM KLEINBAUM, KUPPER, AND MORGENSTERN, P. 353                    8

                STATISTICS FOR TABLE 4 OF CAT BY CHD
                   CONTROLLING FOR AGE=55+ ECG=1

        STATISTIC                        DF      VALUE       PROB
        ------------------------------------------------------------
        CHI-SQUARE                        1      0.897       0.343
        LIKELIHOOD RATIO CHI-SQUARE       1      0.930       0.335
        CONTINUITY ADJ. CHI-SQUARE        1      0.459       0.498
        MANTEL-HAENSZEL CHI-SQUARE        1      0.887       0.346
        FISHER'S EXACT TEST (1-TAIL)                         0.252
                            (2-TAIL)                         0.425
        PHI                                      0.100
        CONTINGENCY COEFFICIENT                  0.099
        CRAMER'S V                               0.100


        STATISTIC                                VALUE        ASE
        ------------------------------------------------------------
        GAMMA                                    0.264       0.268
        KENDALL'S TAU-B                          0.100       0.099
        STUART'S TAU-C                           0.078       0.078

        SOMERS' D C|R                            0.085       0.085
        SOMERS' D R|C                            0.117       0.116

        PEARSON CORRELATION                      0.100       0.099
        SPEARMAN CORRELATION                     0.100       0.099

        LAMBDA ASYMMETRIC C|R                    0.000       0.000
        LAMBDA ASYMMETRIC R|C                    0.000       0.000
        LAMBDA SYMMETRIC                         0.000       0.000

        UNCERTAINTY COEFFICIENT C|R              0.010       0.020
        UNCERTAINTY COEFFICIENT R|C              0.008       0.016
        UNCERTAINTY COEFFICIENT SYM              0.009       0.018

              ESTIMATES OF THE RELATIVE RISK (ROW1/ROW2)

        TYPE OF STUDY            VALUE     95% CONFIDENCE BOUNDS
        ------------------------------------------------------------
        CASE-CONTROL             1.718        0.556       5.308
        COHORT (COL1 RISK)       1.545        0.612       3.897
        COHORT (COL2 RISK)       0.899        0.730       1.107

        SAMPLE SIZE = 90

        ASE IS THE ASYMPTOTIC STANDARD ERROR.
        R|C MEANS ROW VARIABLE DEPENDENT ON COLUMN VARIABLE.
```

```
EXAMPLE 17.9 FROM KLEINBAUM, KUPPER, AND MORGENSTERN, P. 353                    9

                SUMMARY STATISTICS FOR CAT BY CHD
                   CONTROLLING FOR AGE AND ECG


 COCHRAN-MANTEL-HAENSZEL STATISTICS (BASED ON TABLE SCORES)

STATISTIC    ALTERNATIVE HYPOTHESIS    DF        VALUE      PROB
--------------------------------------------------------------
    1        NONZERO CORRELATION        1        4.153     0.042
    2        ROW MEAN SCORES DIFFER     1        4.153     0.042
    3        GENERAL ASSOCIATION        1        4.153     0.042


     ESTIMATES OF THE COMMON RELATIVE RISK (ROW1/ROW2)

                                                      95%
TYPE OF STUDY    METHOD                 VALUE    CONFIDENCE BOUNDS
--------------------------------------------------------------
CASE-CONTROL     MANTEL-HAENSZEL        1.891      1.025    3.490
  (ODDS RATIO)   LOGIT                  1.906      1.030    3.526

COHORT           MANTEL-HAENSZEL        1.696      1.020    2.818
  (COL1 RISK)    LOGIT                  1.712      1.032    2.840

COHORT           MANTEL-HAENSZEL        0.900      0.814    0.996
  (COL2 RISK)    LOGIT                  0.904      0.811    1.008

THE CONFIDENCE BOUNDS FOR THE M-H ESTIMATES ARE TEST-BASED.


     BRESLOW-DAY TEST FOR HOMOGENEITY OF THE ODDS RATIOS

CHI-SQUARE  =   0.164          DF  =   3           PROB = 0.983

TOTAL SAMPLE SIZE = 609
```

Effect of Hypnosis: Example 2

Eight subjects were asked to display certain emotions while under hypnosis (Lehmann 1975, 264). The null hypothesis is that hypnosis has the same effect on skin potential for each of the following four emotions: fear, happiness (joy), depression (sadness), and calmness. Skin potential was measured in millivolts, and the four measurements were then ranked within each subject. Since there are no tied ranks within a subject, the analysis of variance CMH statistic is Friedman's chi-square (Q=6.45, p=.09). The NOPRINT option is used to suppress printing of the contingency tables.

```
DATA HYPNOSIS;
   INPUT SUBJECT EMOTION $ RANKING @@;
   CARDS;
1 FEAR 4     1 JOY 3     1 SADNESS 1     1 CALMNESS 2
2 FEAR 4     2 JOY 2     2 SADNESS 3     2 CALMNESS 1
3 FEAR 3     3 JOY 2     3 SADNESS 4     3 CALMNESS 1
4 FEAR 4     4 JOY 1     4 SADNESS 2     4 CALMNESS 3
5 FEAR 1     5 JOY 4     5 SADNESS 3     5 CALMNESS 2
6 FEAR 4     6 JOY 3     6 SADNESS 2     6 CALMNESS 1
7 FEAR 4     7 JOY 1     7 SADNESS 2     7 CALMNESS 3
8 FEAR 3     8 JOY 4     8 SADNESS 2     8 CALMNESS 1
;
PROC FREQ;
   TABLES SUBJECT*EMOTION*RANKING/NOPRINT CMH;
   TITLE 'EFFECTIVENESS OF HYPNOSIS';
```

Output 19.2 Effect of Hypnosis: PROC FREQ

```
                              EFFECTIVENESS OF HYPNOSIS                                1

                      SUMMARY STATISTICS FOR EMOTION BY RANKING
                               CONTROLLING FOR SUBJECT


       COCHRAN-MANTEL-HAENSZEL STATISTICS (BASED ON TABLE SCORES)

     STATISTIC    ALTERNATIVE HYPOTHESIS     DF         VALUE      PROB
     --------------------------------------------------------------------
         1        NONZERO CORRELATION         1         0.240     0.624
         2        ROW MEAN SCORES DIFFER      3         6.450     0.092
         3        GENERAL ASSOCIATION         9        10.500     0.312


     TOTAL SAMPLE SIZE = 32
```

For an example using PROC FREQ with Census Data, refer to the chapter "Proc Step Applications" in the *SAS User's Guide: Basics.*

REFERENCES

Birch, M. W. (1965), "The Detection of Partial Association, II: the General Case," *Journal of the Royal Statistical Society, B, 27,* 111-124.

Bishop, Y., Fienberg, S.E., and Holland, P.W. (1975), *Discrete Multivariate Analysis: Theory and Practice,* Cambridge: The MIT Press.

Blalock, Hubert M., Jr. (1960), *Social Statistics,* New York: McGraw-Hill Book Company.

Breslow, N. E. and Day, N. E. (1980), *Statistical Methods in Cancer Research, Volume 1: The Analysis of Case-Control Studies,* Lyon, International Agency for Research on Cancer.

Bross, I. D. J. (1958), "How to Use Ridit Analysis," *Biometrics, 14,* 18-38.

Brown, Morton B. and Benedetti, Jacqueline K. (1976), "Asymptotic Standard Errors and Their Sampling Behavior for Measures of Association and Correlation in the Two-way Contingency Table," Technical Report No. 23, Health Sciences Computing Facility, University of California, Los Angeles.

Cochran, William G. (1954), "Some Methods for Strengthening the Common χ^2 Tests," *Biometrics, 10,* 417-451.

Fienberg, Stephen E.(1977), *The Analysis of Cross-Classified Data,* Cambridge: the MIT Press.

Fleiss, Joseph L.(1973), *Statistical Methods for Rates and Proportions,* New York: John Wiley & Sons.

Garson, G. David (1971), *Handbook of Political Science Methods,* Boston, MA.: Holbrook Press, Inc.

Goodman, L.A. and Kruskal, W.H. (1954, 1959, 1963, 1972), "Measures of Association for Cross-Classification I, II, III, and IV," *Journal of the American Statistical Association, 49,* 732-764; *58,* 310-364; *67,* 415-421.

Goodman, L.A. and Kruskal, W.H. (1979), *Measures of Association for Cross Classification,* New York: Springer-Verlag (reprints of JASA articles above).

Haldane, J.B.S. (1955), "The Estimation and Significance of the the Logarithm of a Ratio of Frequencies," *Annals of Human Genetics, 20,* 309-314.

Hayes, William L. (1963), *Psychological Statistics,* New York: Holt, Rinehart and Winston.

Kendall, Maurice and Stuart, Alan (1979), *The Advanced Theory of Statistics, Volume 2,* New York: Macmillan Publishing Company, Inc.

Kleinbaum, David G., Kupper, Lawrence L., and Morgenstern, Hal (1982) *Epidemiologic Research: Principles and Quantitative Methods*, Belmont, California: Wadsworth, Inc.

Landis, Richard J., Heyman, Eugene R., and Koch, Gary G. (1978), "Average Partial Association in Three-way Contingency Tables: a Review and Discussion of Alternative Tests," *International Statistical Review, 46*, 237-254.

Lehmann, E. L. (1975), *Nonparametrics: Statistical Methods Based on Ranks*, San Francisco, Holden-Day.

Mack, G. A. and Skillings, J. H. (1980), "A Friedman-Type Rank Test for Main Effects in a Two-Factor ANOVA," *Journal of the American Statistical Association, 75*, 947-951.

Mantel, N. and Haenszel, W. (1959), "Statistical Aspects of the Analysis of Data from Retrospective Studies of Disease," *Journal of the National Cancer Institute, 22*, 719-748.

Mantel, N. (1963), "Chi-square Tests with One Degree of Freedom; Extensions of the Mantel-Haenszel Procedure," *Journal of the American Statistical Association, 58*, 690-700.

Snedecor, George W. and Cochran, William G. (1980), *Statistical Methods*, Seventh Edition, Ames, Iowa: The Iowa State University Press.

Somers, Robert H. (1962), A New Asymmetric Measure of Association for Ordinal Variables," *American Sociological Review, 27*, 799-811.

Theil, Henri (1972), *Statistical Decomposition Analysis*, Amsterdam: North-Holland Publishing Company.

U.S. Bureau of the Census (1978), *County and City Data Book, 1977: A Statistical Abstract Supplement*, Washington, D.C.: U.S. Government Printing Office.

van Elteren, P. H. (1960), "On the Combination of Independent Two-Sample Tests of Wilcoxon," *Bulletin of the International Statistical Institute, 37*, 351-361.

Woolf, B. (1955), "On Estimating the Relationship between Blood Group and Disease," *Annals of Human Genetics, 19*, 251-253.

Chapter 20
The GLM Procedure

Operating systems: All

ABSTRACT

The GLM procedure uses the method of least squares to fit general linear models. Among the statistical methods available in GLM are regression, analysis of variance, analysis of covariance, multivariate analysis of variance, and partial correlation.

INTRODUCTION

PROC GLM analyzes data within the framework of **G**eneral **L**inear **M**odels, hence the name GLM. GLM handles classification variables, which have discrete levels, as well as continuous variables, which measure quantities. Thus GLM can be used for many different analyses including:

- simple regression
- multiple regression

- analysis of variance (*ANOVA*), especially for unbalanced data
- analysis of covariance
- response-surface models
- weighted regression
- polynomial regression
- partial correlation
- multivariate analysis of variance (*MANOVA*)
- repeated measures analysis of variance.

Specification of Effects

Each term in an analysis-of-variance model is an effect that is some specified combination of classification variables. Effects are specified with a special notation using variable names and operators. There are two kinds of variables: *classification* (or *class) variables* and *continuous variables*. There are two kinds of operators: *crossing* and *nesting*. A third operator, the *bar operator*, is used to simplify effect specification.

Analysis-of-variance models require independent variables that identify classification levels. In the SAS System these are called *class variables* and are declared in the CLASS statement. (They may also be called *categorical, qualitative, discrete,* or *nominal variables*.) Class variables may be either *numeric* or *character*. The values of a class variable are called *levels*.

Any independent variable used in a model that is not declared in the CLASS statement is assumed to be continuous. Continuous variables, which must be numeric, are used for response variables and covariates.

There are seven different types of effects used in GLM. In the following list assume that A, B, C, D, and E are class variables and X1, X2, and Y are continuous variables:

- Regressor effects are specified by writing continuous variables by themselves: X1 X2.
- Polynomial effects are specified by joining two or more continuous variables with asterisks: X1*X1 X1*X2.
- Main effects are specified by writing class variables by themselves: A B C.
- Crossed effects (interactions) are specified by joining class variables with asterisks: A*B B*C A*B*C.
- Nested effects are specified by placing a parenthetical field after a variable or interaction indicating the class variable within which the effect is nested:

  B(A) C(B A) D*E(C B A).

  Note: B(A) is read "B nested within A."
- Continuous-by-class effects are written by joining continuous variables with class variables: X1*A.
- Continuous-nesting effects consist of continuous variables followed by a parenthetical field of class variables: X1(A) X1*X2(A B).

One example of the general form of an effect involving seven variables is

X1*X2*A*B*C(D E) .

This example contains crossed continuous terms by crossed classification terms nested within multiple class variables. The continuous list comes first, followed by the crossed list, followed by the nested list in parentheses. Note that no asterisks appear within the nested list or before the left parenthesis. For details on how the design matrix and parameters are defined with respect to the effects specified in this section, see **Parameterization** below.

The MODEL statement and several other statements use these effects. Some examples of MODEL statements using various kinds of effects are shown below. A, B, and C represent class variables, and X1-X3 represent continuous variables.

Specification	Kind of Model
`MODEL Y = X1;`	simple regression
`MODEL Y = X1 X2;`	multiple regression
`MODEL Y = X1 X1*X1;`	polynomial regression
`MODEL Y1 Y2 = X1 X2;`	multivariate regression
`MODEL Y = A;`	one-way ANOVA
`MODEL Y = A B C;`	main-effects model
`MODEL Y = A B A*B;`	factorial model (with interaction)
`MODEL Y = A B(A) C(B A);`	nested model
`MODEL Y1 Y2 = A B;`	multivariate analysis of variance
`MODEL Y = A X1;`	analysis-of-covariance model
`MODEL Y = A X1(A);`	separate-slopes model
`MODEL Y = A X1 X1*A;`	homogeneity-of-slopes model

You can shorten the specification of a full factorial model using bar notation. For example, two ways of writing a full three-way factorial are:

```
PROC GLM;
   CLASS A B C;
   MODEL Y= A B C A*B A*C B*C A*B*C;

PROC GLM;
   CLASS A B C;
   MODEL Y=A|B|C;
```

When the bar (|) is used, the right and left sides become effects, and the cross of them becomes an effect. Multiple bars are permitted. The expressions are expanded from left to right, using rules 2-4 given in Searle (1971, p. 390):

- Multiple bars are evaluated left to right. For instance, A | B | C is {A | B} | C, which is {A B A*B} | C, which is

  A B A*B C A*C B*C A*B*C .

- Crossed and nested groups of variables are combined. For example, A(B) | C(D) generates A*C(B D), among other terms.
- Duplicate variables are removed. For example, A(C) | B(C) generates A*B(C), among other terms, and the extra C is removed.
- Effects are discarded if a variable occurs on both the crossed and nested sides of an effect. For instance, A(B) | B(D E) generates A*B(B D E), but this effect is eliminated immediately.

Other examples of the bar notation:

A | C(B)	is equivalent to A C(B) A*C(B)
A(B) | C(B)	is equivalent to A(B) C(B) A*C(B)
A(B) | B(D E)	is equivalent to A(B) B(D E)
A | B(A) | C	is equivalent to A B(A) C A*C B*C(A).

GLM for Multiple Regression

In multiple regression, the values of a dependent variable (also called a response variable) are described or predicted in terms of one or more independent or explanatory variables. The statements

```
PROC GLM;
   MODEL dependent = independents;
```

can be used to describe a multiple regression model in GLM. The REG procedure provides additional statistics for multiple regression and is often more efficient than PROC GLM for these models.

GLM for Unbalanced ANOVA

The ANOVA procedure should be used whenever possible for analysis of variance, since ANOVA processes data more efficiently than GLM. However, GLM is used in most unbalanced situations, that is, models where there are unequal numbers of observations for the different combinations of CLASS variables specified in the model statements.

Here is an example of a 2 x 2 factorial model. The data are shown in a table and then read into a SAS data set:

		A 1	A 2
B	1	12 14	20 18
B	2	11 9	17

```
DATA EXP;
   INPUT A $ B $ Y @@;
   CARDS;
A1 B1 12 A1 B1 14 A1 B2 11 A1 B2 9
A2 B1 20 A2 B1 18 A2 B2 17
;
```

Note that for the second levels of A and B there is only one value. Since one cell contains a different number of values from the other cells in the table, this is an unbalanced design, and GLM should be used. The statements needed for this two-way factorial model are:

```
PROC GLM;
   CLASS A B;
   MODEL Y=A B A*B;
```

The results from GLM are shown below:

Output 20.1 Two-Way Factorial: GLM Procedure

```
                                                                                         1

                         GENERAL LINEAR MODELS PROCEDURE
                            CLASS LEVEL INFORMATION
                          CLASS     LEVELS    VALUES
                          A              2    A1 A2
                          B              2    B1 B2

                     NUMBER OF OBSERVATIONS IN DATA SET = 7
```

```
                                                                                         2
                         GENERAL LINEAR MODELS PROCEDURE

DEPENDENT VARIABLE: Y

SOURCE            DF   SUM OF SQUARES    MEAN SQUARE   F VALUE    PR > F    R-SQUARE          C.V.
MODEL              3      91.71428571    30.57142857     15.29    0.0253    0.938596        9.8015
ERROR              3       6.00000000     2.00000000             ROOT MSE                   Y MEAN
CORRECTED TOTAL    6      97.71428571                          1.41421356              14.42857143

SOURCE            DF        TYPE I SS    F VALUE    PR > F     DF     TYPE III SS    F VALUE   PR > F
A                  1      80.04761905      40.02    0.0080      1     67.60000000      33.80   0.0101
B                  1      11.26666667       5.63    0.0982      1     10.00000000       5.00   0.1114
A*B                1       0.40000000       0.20    0.6850      1      0.40000000       0.20   0.6850
```

Four types of estimable functions of parameters are available for testing hypotheses in GLM. For data with no missing cells, the TYPE III and TYPE IV estimable functions are the same and test the same hypotheses that would be tested if the data were balanced.

The TYPE III results on this printout indicate a significant A effect but no significant B effect or A*B interaction.

GLM Features

The following list summarizes the features in PROC GLM:

- When more than one dependent variable is specified, GLM automatically groups together those variables that have the same pattern of missing values within the data set or within a BY group. This ensures that the analysis for each dependent variable brings into use all possible observations.
- GLM allows the specification of any degree of interaction (crossed effects) and nested effects. It also provides for continuous-by-continuous, continuous-by-class, and continuous-nesting effects.
- Through the concept of estimability, GLM can provide tests of hypotheses for the effects of a linear model regardless of the number of

missing cells or the extent of confounding. GLM prints not only the SS associated with each hypothesis tested, but also, upon request, the form of the estimable functions employed in the test. GLM can produce the general form of all estimable functions.

- GLM can create an output data set containing predicted and residual values from the analysis and all of the original variables.
- The MANOVA statement allows you to specify both the hypothesis effects and the error effect to use for a multivariate analysis of variance.
- The REPEATED statement lets you specify effects in the model that represent repeated measurements on the same experimental unit, and provides both univariate and multivariate tests of hypotheses.
- The RANDOM statement allows you to specify random effects in the model; expected mean squares are printed for each TYPE I, TYPE II, TYPE III, TYPE IV, and contrast mean square used in the analysis.
- You can use the ESTIMATE statement to specify an **L** vector for estimating a linear function of the parameters **L**β.
- You can use the CONTRAST statement to specify a contrast vector or matrix for testing the hypothesis that **L**β=0.

SPECIFICATIONS

Although there are numerous statements and options available in GLM, many applications use only a few of them. Often you can find the features you need by looking at an example or by quickly scanning through this section. The statements available in GLM are:

PROC GLM *options;*

Statements	Placement
CLASS *variables;*	must precede **MODEL** and **MEANS** statements
MODEL *dependents*=*independents / options;*	required statement
CONTRAST *'label'* [effect values]... / *options;* **ESTIMATE** *'name' effect values... / options;* **LSMEANS** *effects / options;* **MANOVA H**=*effects* **E**=*effect* **M**=*equations / options;* **OUTPUT OUT**=*SASdataset* *keyword*=*names...;* **RANDOM** *effects / options;* **REPEATED** *factornames / options;* **TEST H**=*effects* **E**=*effect / options;*	must follow **MODEL** statements
ABSORB *variables;* **BY** *variables;* **FREQ** *variable;* **ID** *variables;* **MEANS** *effects / options;* **WEIGHT** *variable;*	may be placed anywhere among statements

The PROC GLM and MODEL statements are required. If classification effects are used, the class variables must be declared in a CLASS statement, and the CLASS statement must appear before the MODEL statement.

The statements used with PROC GLM in addition to the PROC statement are (in alphabetical order):

ABSORB	absorbs classification effects in a model.
BY	processes BY groups.
CLASS	declares classification variables.
CONTRAST	constructs and tests linear functions of the parameters.
ESTIMATE	also constructs and tests linear functions of the parameters.
FREQ	specifies a frequency variable (similar to the WEIGHT statement).
ID	identifies observations on printed output.
LSMEANS	computes least-squares (marginal) means.
MANOVA	performs a multivariate analysis of variance.
MEANS	requests that means be printed and compared.
MODEL	defines the model to be fit.
OUTPUT	requests an output data set containing predicted values and residuals.
RANDOM	declares certain effects to be random and computes expected mean squares.
REPEATED	performs multivariate and univariate repeated measures analysis of variance.
TEST	constructs tests using the sums of squares for effects and the error term you specify.
WEIGHT	specifies a variable for weighting observations.

PROC GLM Statement

PROC GLM *options;*

Two options can be used in the PROC GLM statement:

DATA=*SASdataset*

names the SAS data set to be used by GLM. If DATA= is omitted, GLM uses the most recently created SAS data set.

ORDER=FREQ
ORDER=DATA
ORDER=INTERNAL
ORDER=FORMATTED

specifies the order in which you want the levels of the classification variables (specified on the CLASSES statement) to be sorted. This ordering determines which parameters in the model correspond to each level in the data, so the ORDER= option may be useful when you are using CONTRAST or ESTIMATE statements. If ORDER=FREQ, levels are sorted by descending frequency count so that levels with the most observations come first. If ORDER=DATA, levels are sorted in the order in which they first occur in the input data. If ORDER=INTERNAL, then the levels are sorted by the internal value. If ORDER=FORMATTED, levels are ordered by the external formatted value. If you omit ORDER=, PROC GLM orders by the formatted value.

ABSORB Statement

ABSORB *variables;*

Absorption is a computational technique that provides a large reduction in time and storage requirements for certain types of models.

For a main-effect variable with a large number of levels that does not participate in interactions, you can absorb the effect by naming it in an ABSORB statement. This means that the effect can be adjusted out prior to the construction and solution of the rest of the model.

Several variables can be specified, in which case each one is assumed to be nested in the preceding one in the ABSORB statement.

Restrictions: when the ABSORB statement is used, the data set (or each BY group) must be sorted by the variables in the ABSORB statement. GLM cannot produce predicted values or create an output data set if ABSORB is used.

See the detail section **Absorption** below for more information.

BY Statement

BY *variables;*

A BY statement can be used with PROC GLM to obtain separate analyses on observations in groups defined by the BY variables. When a BY statement appears, the procedure expects the input data set to be sorted in order of the BY variables. If your input data set is not sorted in ascending order, use the SORT procedure with a similar BY statement to sort the data, or, if appropriate, use the BY statement options NOTSORTED or DESCENDING. For more information, see the discussion of the BY statement in "Statements Used in the PROC Step" in *SAS User's Guide: Basics.*

CLASS Statement

CLASS *variables;*

The CLASS (or CLASSES) statement names the classification variables to be used in the analysis. Typical class variables are TRTMENT, SEX, RACE, GROUP, and REP.

Classification variables can be either character or numeric. Only the first sixteen characters of a character variable are used.

Class levels are determined from the formatted values of the CLASS variables. Thus you can use formats to group values into levels. See the discussion of the FORMAT procedure, the FORMAT statement, and "SAS Informats and Formats," in *SAS User's Guide: Basics.*

CONTRAST Statement

CONTRAST *'label' [effect values...] / options;*

The CONTRAST statement provides a mechanism for obtaining custom hypotheses tests. This is achieved by specifying an **L** vector or matrix for testing the univariate hypothesis $\mathbf{L}\beta=0$, or the multivariate hypothesis $\mathbf{L}\beta\mathbf{M}=0$. Thus, to use this feature you must be familiar with the details of the model parameterization which PROC GLM uses. (See the detail section **Parameterization** for more information.)

If the hypothesis is testable, in the univariate case $SS(H_0:\mathbf{L}\beta=0)$ is computed as

$$(\mathbf{Lb})'(\mathbf{L}(\mathbf{X}'\mathbf{X})^{-}\mathbf{L}')^{-1}(\mathbf{Lb})$$

where $\mathbf{b}=(\mathbf{X}'\mathbf{X})^{-}\mathbf{X}'\mathbf{y}$. This is the SS printed on the analysis-of-variance table.

For multivariate testable hypotheses, the usual multivariate tests are performed using

$$\mathbf{H} = \mathbf{M}'(\mathbf{Lb})'(\mathbf{L}(\mathbf{X}'\mathbf{X})^{-}\mathbf{L}')^{-1}(\mathbf{Lb})\mathbf{M} \; .$$

If a CONTRAST statement appears and a MANOVA or REPEATED statement is also present, appropriate tests for contrasts are carried out as part of the MANOVA or REPEATED analysis.

You can specify the effect to be used as a denominator in the *F* test for univariate tests. This effect is used as the basis of the **E** matrix when a MANOVA or REPEATED statement is present. If you use a RANDOM statement, the expected mean square of the contrast is printed. There is no limit to the number of CONTRAST statements, but they must come after the MODEL statement.

In the CONTRAST statement, '*label*' is twenty characters or less in single quotes and is used on the printout to identify the contrast. A label **must** be supplied for every contrast specified. *Effect* is the name of an effect that appears in the MODEL statement; the keyword INTERCEPT may be used as an effect when an intercept is fitted in the model. The *values* are constants that are elements of the **L** vector associated with the preceding effect. Not all effects in the MODEL statement need to be included.

Multiple-degree-of-freedom hypotheses can be specified by separating the rows of the **L** matrix with commas, as shown below.

For example, for the model

```
MODEL Y=A B;
```

with A at 5 levels and B at 2 levels, the parameter vector is

$$(\mu \;\alpha_1 \;\alpha_2 \;\alpha_3 \;\alpha_4 \;\alpha_5 \;\beta_1 \;\beta_2) \; .$$

To test the hypothesis that the pooled A linear and A quadratic effect is zero, you can use the following **L** matrix:

$$\mathrm{L} = \begin{bmatrix} 0 & -2 & -1 & 0 & 1 & 2 & 0 & 0 \\ 0 & 2 & -1 & -2 & -1 & 2 & 0 & 0 \end{bmatrix}$$

The corresponding CONTRAST statement is

```
CONTRAST 'A LINEAR & QUADRATIC'
         A -2 -1  0  1 2,
         A  2 -1 -2 -1 2;
```

If the first level of A is a control level and you want a test of control versus others, you can use this statement:

```
CONTRAST 'CONTROL VS OTHERS'  A -1 .25 .25 .25 .25;
```

The **L** matrix should be of full row rank. However, if it is not, the degrees of freedom associated with the hypotheses are reduced to the row rank of **L**. The SS computed in this situation are equivalent to the SS computed using an **L** matrix with any row deleted that is a linear combination of previous rows.

These options are available in the CONTRAST statement and are specified after a slash (/):

E

requests that the entire **L** vector be printed.

E=*effect*

specifies an effect in the model to use as an error term. If none is specified, the error MS is used.

ETYPE=*n*

specifies the type (1, 2, 3, or 4) of the E= effect. If E= is specified and ETYPE= is not, the highest type computed in the analysis is used.

SINGULAR=*number*

tunes the estimability checking. If ABS(**L**−**LH**)>C*SINGULAR for any row in the contrast, then the **L** is declared non-estimable. **H** is the **(X'X)⁻X'X** matrix, and C is ABS(**L**) except for rows where **L** is zero in which case it is 1. The default is 1E-4.

See the discussion of the ESTIMATE statement below and **Specification of ESTIMATE Expressions** for rules on specification, construction, distribution, and estimability in the CONTRAST statement.

ESTIMATE Statement

ESTIMATE *'label'* {*effect values...*} / *options;*

The ESTIMATE statement can be used to estimate linear functions of the parameters by multiplying the vector **L** by the parameter estimate vector **b** resulting in **Lb**. All of the elements of the **L** vector may be given, or if only certain portions of the **L** vector are given, the remaining elements are constructed by GLM from the context (in a manner similar to rule 4 discussed in the section **Least-Squares Means**).

The linear function is checked for estimability. The estimate **Lb**, where **b**=**(X'X)⁻X'y**, is printed along with its associated standard error, $\sqrt{(\mathbf{L}(\mathbf{X'X})^{-}\mathbf{L}'s^2)}$, and *t* test. There is no limit to the number of ESTIMATE statements, but they must come after the MODEL statement.

In the ESTIMATE statement, *'label'* is twenty characters or less in single quotes and is used on the printout to identify the estimate. A label **must** be supplied for every estimate specified. *Effect* is the name of an effect that appears in the MODEL statement; the keyword INTERCEPT may be used as an effect when an intercept is fitted in the model. The *values* are constants that are the elements of the **L** vector associated with the preceding effect. For example, with no options,

```
ESTIMATE 'A1 VS A2' A  1  -1;
```

forms an estimate which is the difference between the parameters estimated for the first and second levels of the CLASS variable A.

Not all effects in the MODEL statement need to be included.

The options below can appear in the ESTIMATE statement after a slash (/):

E

requests that the entire **L** vector be printed.

DIVISOR=*number*

specifies a value by which to divide all coefficients so that fractional coefficients can be entered as integer numerators. For example:

```
ESTIMATE '1/3(A1+A2)-2/3A3' A 1 1 -2 / DIVISOR=3;
```

instead of

```
ESTIMATE '1/3(A1+A2)-2/3A3' A .33333 .33333 -.66667;
```

SINGULAR=*number*

tunes the estimability checking. If ABS(**L**−**LH**) <C*SINGULAR, then the **L** is declared non-estimable. **H** is the **(X'X)⁻X'X** matrix, and C is ABS(**L**) except for rows where **L** is zero, in which case it is 1. The default is 1E-4.

See also **Specification of ESTIMATE Expressions** below.

FREQ Statement

FREQ *variable;*

When a FREQ statement appears, each observation in the input data set is assumed to represent *n* observations in the experiment, where *n* is the value of the variable specified in the FREQ statement.

If the value of the FREQ statement variable is less than 1, the observation is not used in the analysis. If the value is not an integer, only the integer portion is used.

The analysis produced using a FREQ statement is identical to an analysis produced using a data set that contains *n* observations in place of each observation of the input data set, where *n* is the value of the variable specified in the FREQ statement. Therefore, means and total degrees of freedom reflect the expanded number of observations.

ID Statement

ID *variables;*

When predicted values are requested as a MODEL statement option, values of the variables given in the ID statement are printed beside each observed, predicted, and residual value for identification. Although there are no restrictions on the number or length of ID variables, GLM may truncate the number of values printed in order to print on one line.

LSMEANS Statement

LSMEANS *effects / options;*

Least-squares means are computed for each effect listed in the LSMEANS statement.

Least-squares estimates of marginal means (LSMs) are to unbalanced designs as class and subclass arithmetic means are to balanced designs. LSMs are simply estimators of the class or subclass marginal means that would be expected had the design been balanced. For further information see the detail section **Least-Squares Means.**

Least-squares means can be computed for any effect involving class variables as long as the effect is in the model. Any number of LSMEANS statements can be used. They must be given after the MODEL statement.

Here is an example:

```
PROC GLM;
   CLASS A B;
   MODEL Y=A B A*B;
   LSMEANS A B A*B;
```

Least-squares means are printed for each level of the A, B, and A*B effects.

The options below can appear in the LSMEANS statement after a slash (/):

E

prints the estimable functions used to compute the LSM.

STDERR

prints the standard error of the LSM and the probability level for the hypothesis H_0:LSM=0.

PDIFF

requests that all possible probability values for the hypothesis H_0: LSM(*i*) = LSM(*j*) be printed.

E=*effect*

specifies an effect in the model to use as an error term. The mean square for the specified effect will be used when calculating standard errors (with the STDERR option) and probabilities (with the STDERR or PDIFF options). If neither STDERR nor PDIFF is specified, the E= option is ignored. If STDERR or PDIFF is specified and E= is not, the error MS is used for calculating standard errors and probabilities.

ETYPE=*n*

specifies the type (1, 2, 3, or 4) of the E= effect. If E= is specified and ETYPE= is not, the highest type computed in the analysis is used.

SINGULAR=*number*

tunes the estimability checking. If ABS(**L**−**LH**)>C*SINGULAR for any row, then the **L** is declared non-estimable. **H** is the $(\mathbf{X'X})^{-}\mathbf{X'X}$ matrix, and C is ABS(**L**) except for rows where **L** is zero, in which case it is 1. The default is 1E-4.

MANOVA Statement

MANOVA H=*effects* E=*effect* M=*equation1,equation2,...*
MNAMES=*names* PREFIX=*name* / *options;*

If the MODEL statement includes more than one dependent variable, additional multivariate statistics can be requested with the MANOVA statement.

When a MANOVA statement appears, GLM enters a multivariate mode with respect to the handling of missing values: observations with missing independent or dependent variables are excluded from the analysis. Even when you do not want multivariate statistics, use the statement

```
MANOVA;
```

to request the multivariate mode of handling missing values. The terms below are specified in the MANOVA statement:

H=*effects*

specifies effects in the preceding model to use as hypothesis matrices. For each **H** matrix (the SSCP matrix associated with that effect), the H= option prints the characteristic roots and vectors of $\mathbf{E}^{-1}\mathbf{H}$ (where **E** is the matrix associated with the error effect), Hotelling-Lawley trace, Pillai's trace, Wilks' criterion, and Roy's maximum root criterion with approximate *F* statistics. To print tests for all effects listed in the MODEL statement, use the keyword _ALL_ in place of a list of effects. For background and further details, see the detail section **Multivariate Analysis of Variance**.

E=*effect*

specifies the error effect. If E= is omitted, the error SSCP (residual) matrix from the analysis is used.

M=*equation1,equation2,...*

specifies a transformation matrix for the dependent variables listed in the MODEL statement. The equations in the M= specification are of the form

± *term* {± *term* ...}

where *term* is either *dependentvariable* or *number*dependentvariable* and brackets { } mean zero or more occurrences. Although these combinations actually represent the columns of the **M** matrix, they are printed by rows.

When an M= specification is included, the analysis requested in the MANOVA statement is carried out for the variables defined by the equations in the specification, not the original dependent variables. If M= is omitted, the analysis is performed for the original dependent variables in the MODEL statement.

If an M= specification is included without either the MNAMES= or PREFIX= option, the variables are labeled MVAR1, MVAR2, and so forth by default. Examples of the use of the M= specification are given below. For further information, see the detail section **Multivariate Analysis of Variance**.

The following two options allow you to specify labels for the transformed variables defined by the M= option:

MNAMES=*names*
provides names for the variables defined by the equations in the M= specification. Names in the list correspond to the M= equations.

PREFIX=*name*
is an alternative means of identifying the transformed variables defined by the M= specification. For example, if you specify PREFIX=DIFF, the transformed variables are labeled DIFF1, DIFF2, and so forth.

The options below can appear in the MANOVA statement after a slash (/):

PRINTH requests that the **H** matrix (the SSCP matrix) associated with each effect specified by the H parameter be printed.

PRINTE requests printing of the **E** matrix. If the **E** matrix is the error SSCP (residual) matrix from the analysis, the partial correlations of the dependent variables given the independent variables are also printed.

For example, the statement

```
MANOVA / PRINTE;
```

prints the error SSCP matrix and the partial correlation matrix computed from the error SSCP matrix.

HTYPE=*n* specifies the type (1, 2, 3, or 4) of the **H** matrix. If an HTYPE= value *n* is given, the corresponding test must have been performed in the MODEL statement, either by options SS*n*, E*n*, or the default Type I and Type III. If no HTYPE= option appears in the MANOVA statement, the HTYPE= value defaults to the highest type (largest *n*) used in the analysis.

ETYPE=*n* specifies the type (1, 2, 3, or 4) of the **E** matrix. You need this option if you use E= (rather than residual error) and you want to specify the type of SS used for the effect. See HTYPE= above for further rules.

ORTH requests that the transformation matrix in the M= specification of the MANOVA statement be orthonormalized by rows prior to the analysis.

SHORT prints the multivariate test statistics and associated *F* statistics in a condensed form.

CANONICAL requests that a canonical analysis of the **H** and **E** matrices (transformed by the **M** matrix if specified) be printed instead of the default printout of characteristic roots and vectors. This analysis is similar to that produced by PROC CANDISC.

SUMMARY produces analysis-of-variance tables for each dependent variable. When no **M** matrix is specified, a table is printed for each original dependent variable from the MODEL statement; with an **M** matrix other than the identity, a table is printed for each transformed variable defined by the **M** matrix.

Here is an example of the MANOVA statement:

```
PROC GLM;
   CLASS A B;
   MODEL Y1-Y5=A B(A);
   MANOVA H=A E=B(A) / PRINTH PRINTE HTYPE=1 ETYPE=1;
   MANOVA H=B(A) / PRINTE;
   MANOVA H=A E=B(A) M=Y1-Y2,Y2-Y3,Y3-Y4,Y4-Y5
          PREFIX=DIFF;
```

Since this MODEL statement requests no options for type, GLM uses TYPE I and TYPE III. The first MANOVA statement specifies A as the hypothesis effect and B(A) as the error effect. The PRINTH option requests that the **H** matrix associated with the A effect be printed, and the PRINTE option requests that the **E** matrix associated with the B(A) effect be printed. The HTYPE=1 option specifies that the **H** matrix be TYPE I; the ETYPE=1 option specifies that the **E** matrix be TYPE I.

The second MANOVA statement specifies B(A) as the hypothesis effect. Since no error effect is specified, GLM uses the error SSCP matrix from the analysis as the **E** matrix. The PRINTE option requests that this **E** matrix be printed. Since the **E** matrix is the error SSCP matrix from the analysis, the partial correlation matrix computed from this matrix is also printed.

The third MANOVA statement requests the same analysis as the first MANOVA statement, but the analysis is carried out for variables transformed to be successive differences between the original dependent variables. The PREFIX=DIFF option specifies that the transformed variables be labeled DIFF1, DIFF2, DIFF3, and DIFF4.

As a second example of the use of the M= specification, consider the following:

```
PROC GLM;
   CLASS GROUP;
   MODEL DOSE1-DOSE4=GROUP;
   MANOVA H=GROUP M=-3*DOSE1-DOSE2+DOSE3+3*DOSE4,
                     DOSE1-DOSE2-DOSE3+DOSE4,
                     -DOSE1+3*DOSE2-3*DOSE3+DOSE4
          MNAMES=LINEAR QUADRTIC CUBIC/ PRINTE;
```

The M= specification gives a transformation of the dependent variables DOSE1 through DOSE4 into orthogonal polynomial components, and the MNAMES= option labels the transformed variables LINEAR, QUADRTIC and CUBIC, respectively. Since the PRINTE option is specified, and the default residual matrix is used as an error term, the partial correlation matrix of the orthogonal polynomial components is also printed.

MEANS Statement

MEANS *effects* / *options;*

GLM can compute means for any effect involving CLASS variables whether or not the effect is specified in the MODEL statement. You can use any number of MEANS statements either before or after the MODEL statement.

For example:

```
PROC GLM;
    CLASS A B C;
    MODEL Y = A B C;
    MEANS A B C A*B;
```

Means are printed for each level of the variables A, B, and C and for the combined levels of A and B.

The options below can appear in the MEANS statement after a slash (/):

DEPONLY indicates that only the dependent variable means are to be printed. By default, GLM prints means for all continuous variables, including independent variables.

BON performs Bonferroni *t* tests of differences between means for all main-effect means in the MEANS statement.

DUNCAN performs Duncan's multiple-range test on all main-effect means given in the MEANS statement.

GABRIEL performs Gabriel's multiple-comparison procedure on all main-effect means in the MEANS statement.

REGWF performs the Ryan-Einot-Gabriel-Welsch multiple *F* test on all main-effect means in the MEANS statement.

REGWQ performs the Ryan-Einot-Gabriel-Welsch multiple-range test on all main-effect means in the MEANS statement.

SCHEFFE performs Scheffe's multiple-comparison procedure on all main-effect means in the MEANS statement.

SIDAK performs pairwise *t* tests on differences between means with levels adjusted according to Sidak's inequality for all main-effect means in the MEANS statement.

SMM
GT2 performs pairwise comparisons based on the studentized maximum modulus and Sidak's uncorrelated-*t* inequality, yielding Hochberg's GT2 method when sample sizes are unequal, for all main-effect means in the MEANS statement.

SNK performs the Student-Newman-Keuls multiple range test on all main-effect means in the MEANS statement.

T
LSD performs pairwise *t* tests, equivalent to Fisher's least-significant-difference test in the case of equal cell sizes, for all main-effect means in the MEANS statement.

TUKEY performs Tukey's studentized range test (HSD) on all main-effects means in the MEANS statement.

ALPHA=*p* gives the level of significance for comparisons among the means. The default ALPHA= value is .05. With the DUNCAN option, you may specify only values of .01, .05, or .1.

WALLER requests that the Waller-Duncan k-ratio *t* test be performed on all main-effect means in the MEANS statement.

KRATIO=*value* gives the type1/type2 error seriousness ratio for the Waller-Duncan test. Reasonable values for KRATIO are 50, 100, 500, which roughly correspond for the two-level case to ALPHA levels of .1, .05, and .01. If KRATIO= is omitted, the procedure uses the default value of 100.

LINES requests that the results of the BON, DUNCAN, GABRIEL, REGWF, REGWQ, SCHEFFE, SIDAK, SMM, GT2, SNK, T, LSD, TUKEY, and WALLER options be presented by listing the means in descending order and indicating nonsignificant subsets by line segments beside the corresponding means. LINES is appropriate for equal cell sizes, for which it is the default. LINES is also the default if DUNCAN, REGWF, REGWQ, SNK, or WALLER is specified, or if there are only two cells. If the cell sizes are unequal, the harmonic mean is used, which may lead to somewhat liberal tests if the cell sizes are highly disparate.

CLDIFF requests that the results of the BON, GABRIEL, SCHEFFE, SIDAK, SMM, GT2, T, LSD, and TUKEY options be presented as confidence intervals for all pairwise differences between means. CLDIFF is the default for unequal cell sizes unless DUNCAN, REGWF, REGWQ, SNK, or WALLER is specified.

NOSORT prevents the means from being sorted into descending order when CLDIFF is specified.

E=*effect* specifies the error mean square to use in the multiple comparisons. If E= is omitted, GLM uses the residual MS. The effect specified with the E= option must be a term in the model; otherwise, the procedure uses the residual MS.

ETYPE=*n* specifies the type of mean square for the error effect. When E= effect is specified, it is sometimes necessary to indicate which type (1, 2, 3, or 4) MS is to be used. The *n* value must be one of the types specified or implied by the MODEL statement. The default MS type is the highest type used in the analysis.

HTYPE=*n* gives the MS type for the hypothesis MS. The HTYPE= option is needed only when the WALLER option is specified. The default HTYPE= value is the highest type used in the model.

MODEL Statement

MODEL *dependents* = *independents* / *options;*

The MODEL statement names the dependent variables and independent effects. The syntax of effects is described in the introductory section **Specification of Effects**. If no independent effects are specified, only an intercept term is fit.

The options listed below can be specified in the MODEL statement after a slash (/):

Options for the intercept

NOINT requests that the intercept parameter not be included in the model.

INT
INTERCEPT requests that GLM print the hypothesis tests associated with the intercept as an effect in the model. By default, the intercept is included in the model, but no tests of hypotheses associated with it are printed. When the INT option is specified, these tests are printed.

Options to request printouts

NOUNI requests that no univariate statistics be printed. You typically use the NOUNI option with a multivariate or repeated measures analysis of variance when you do not need the standard univariate output printed. Note that the NOUNI option in a MODEL statement does not affect the univariate output produced by the REPEATED statement.

SOLUTION asks GLM to print a solution to the normal equations (parameter estimates). GLM always prints a solution when no CLASS statement appears.

TOLERANCE requests that the tolerances used in the SWEEP routine be printed. The tolerances are of the form D/UCSS or D/CSS, as described in the discussion of SINGULAR (under **Tuning options**, below). The tolerance value for the intercept is not divided by its uncorrected SS.

Options to control standard hypothesis tests

E asks GLM to print the general form of all estimable functions.

E1 requests that the TYPE I estimable functions for each effect in the model be printed.

E2 requests that the TYPE II estimable functions for each effect in the model be printed.

E3 requests that the TYPE III estimable functions for each effect in the model be printed.

E4 requests that the TYPE IV estimable functions for each effect in the model be printed.

SS1 asks GLM to print the SS associated with TYPE I estimable functions for each effect.

SS2 asks GLM to print the SS associated with TYPE II estimable functions for each effect.

SS3 asks GLM to print the SS associated with TYPE III estimable functions for each effect.

SS4 asks GLM to print the SS associated with TYPE IV estimable functions for each effect.

Note: if E1, E2, E3, or E4 is specified, the corresponding SS for each effect are printed. By default, the procedure prints the TYPE I and TYPE III SS for each effect.

Options for predicted values and residuals

P asks GLM to print observed, predicted, and residual values for each observation that does not contain missing values for independent variables. The Durbin-Watson statistic is also printed when P is specified. The PRESS statistic is also printed if either CLM or CLI is specified.

CLM prints confidence limits for a mean predicted value for each observation. The P option must also appear.

CLI prints confidence limits for individual predicted values for each observation. The P option must also appear. CLI should not be used with CLM; it is ignored if CLM is also specified.

ALPHA=*p* specifies the alpha level for confidence intervals. The only acceptable values for ALPHA are .01, .05, and .10. If no ALPHA level is given, GLM uses .05.

Options to print intermediate calculations

XPX prints the **X'X** crossproducts matrix.

INVERSE
I prints the inverse or the generalized inverse of the **X'X** matrix.

Tuning options

SINGULAR=*value* tunes the sensitivity of the regression routine to linear dependencies in the design. If a diagonal pivot element is less than C*SINGULAR as GLM sweeps the **X'X** matrix, the associated design column is declared to be linearly dependent with previous columns, and the associated parameter is zeroed.

The C value adjusts the check to the relative scale of the variable C, the corrected SS for the variable unless the corrected SS is 0, in which case C is 1. If NOINT is specified but the ABSORB option is not, GLM uses the uncorrected SS instead.

Note: the default value of SINGULAR, 1E-8, is perhaps too small but is necessary in order to handle the high-degree polynomials used in the literature to compare regression routines.

ZETA=*value* tunes the sensitivity of the check for estimability for Type III and Type IV functions. Any element in the estimable function basis with an absolute value less than ZETA is set to zero. The default value for ZETA is 1E-8, which suffices for all *ANOVA*-type models.

Note: although it is possible to generate data for which this absolute check can be defeated, it suffices in most practical examples. Additional research needs to be performed to make this check relative rather than absolute.

OUTPUT Statement

OUTPUT OUT=*SASdataset keyword=names...;*

The OUTPUT statement asks GLM to create a new SAS data set. Predicted and residual values as well as all the variables in the original data set are included in the new data set. If you want to create a permanent SAS data set, you must specify a two-level name (see "SAS Files" in *SAS User's Guide: Basics*, for more information on permanent SAS data sets).

The keyword options below are given in the OUTPUT statement:

OUT=*SASdataset*

gives the name of the new data set. If OUT= is omitted, the new data set is named using the DATA*n* convention.

PREDICTED | P=*variables*
RESIDUAL | R=*variables*

specifies new variable names. The names correspond to the dependent variable or variables given in the MODEL statement.

For example, the statements

```
PROC GLM;
   CLASS A B;
   MODEL Y=A B A*B;
   OUTPUT OUT=NEW P=YHAT R=RESID;
```

request an output data set named NEW. In addition to all the variables from the original data set, NEW contains the variable YHAT, whose values are predicted values of the dependent variable Y. NEW also contains the variable RESID, whose values are the residual values of Y.

Another example:

```
PROC GLM;
   BY GROUP;
   CLASS A;
   MODEL Y1-Y5=A X(A);
   OUTPUT OUT=POUT PREDICTED=PY1-PY5;
```

Data set POUT contains five new variables, PY1−PY5. PY1's values are the predicted values of Y1; PY2's values are the predicted values of Y2; and so on. The predicted value is missing for any observation with one or more missing independent variables. If an observation from the original data set is not used in the analysis, its residual value is also missing.

RANDOM Statement

RANDOM *effects / options;*

The RANDOM statement specifies which effects in the model are random. When you use a RANDOM statement, GLM prints the expected value of each TYPE I, TYPE II, TYPE III, TYPE IV, or contrast MS used in the analysis but does not make use of the information pertaining to expected mean squares in any way. Since other features in GLM assume that all effects are fixed, all tests and estimability checks are based on a fixed-effects model, even when you use a RANDOM statement.

You can use only one RANDOM statement, and it must come after the MODEL statement.

The list of effects in the RANDOM statement should contain one or more of the pure classification effects (main effects, crossed effects, or nested effects) specified in the MODEL statement. The levels of each effect specified are assumed to be normally and independently distributed with common variance. Levels in different effects are assumed independent.

The option below can appear in the RANDOM statement after a slash (/):

Q
: requests a complete printout of all quadratic forms in the fixed effects that appear in the expected mean squares.

See **Expected Mean Squares for Random Effects** below for more information on the calculation of expected mean squares.

REPEATED Statement

REPEATED *factorname levels (levelvalues) transformation [,...] / options;*

When values of the dependent variables in the MODEL statement represent repeated measurements on the same experimental unit, REPEATED allows you to test hypotheses about the measurement factors (often called *within-subject factors*) as well as the interactions of within-subject factors with independent variables in the MODEL statement (often called *between-subject factors*). The REPEATED statement provides both multivariate and univariate tests as well as hypothesis tests for a variety of single-degree-of-freedom contrasts. When more than one within-subject factor is specified, the *factornames* (and associated level and transformation information) must be separated by a comma on the REPEATED statement. There is no limit to the number of within-subject factors that can be specified.

When a REPEATED statement appears, the GLM procedure enters a multivariate mode of handling missing values. If any values for variables corresponding to each combination of the within-subject factors are missing, the observation is excluded from the analysis.

factorname
: names a factor to be associated with the dependent variables. The name should **not** be the same as any variable name that already exists in the data set being analyzed and should conform to the usual conventions of SAS variable names.

levels
: gives the number of levels associated with the factor being defined. When there is only one within-subjects factor, the number of levels is equal to the number of dependent variables. In this case, *levels* need not be specified. When more than one within-subject factor is defined, however, *levels* must be specified, and the product of the *levels* of all the factors **must** equal the number of dependent variables in the MODEL statement.

(levelvalues)
: gives values that correspond to levels of a repeated-measures factor. These values are used to label output and as spacings for constructing orthogonal polynomial contrasts. The number of level values specified must correspond to the number of levels for that

factor in the REPEATED statement. Note that the level values appear in parentheses.

The following *transformation* keywords define single-degree-of-freedom contrasts for factors specified on the REPEATED statement. Since the number of contrasts generated is always one less than the number of levels of the factor, you have some control over which contrast is omitted from the analysis by which transformation you select. If no transformation keyword is specified, REPEATED uses the CONTRAST transformation.

CONTRAST {(*ordinalreferencelevel*)}
: generates contrasts between levels of the factor and, optionally, a reference level that must appear in parentheses. The reference level corresponds to the ordinal value of the level rather than the level value specified. Without a reference level, the last level is used by default. Reference level specification must appear in parentheses.

POLYNOMIAL
: generates orthogonal polynomial contrasts. Level values, if provided, are used as spacings in the construction of the polynomials; otherwise, equal spacing is assumed.

HELMERT
: generates contrasts between each level of the factor and the mean of subsequent levels.

MEAN {(*ordinalreferencelevel*)}
: generates contrasts between levels of the factor and the mean of all other levels of the factor. Specifying a reference level eliminates the contrast between that level and the mean. Without a reference level, the contrast involving the last level is omitted. Reference level specification must appear in parentheses.

PROFILE
: generates contrasts between adjacent levels of the factor.

When specifying more than one factor, list the dependent variables in the MODEL statement so that the within-subject factors defined in the REPEATED statement are nested; that is, the first factor defined on the REPEATED statement **should be the one with values that change least frequently.** For example, assume three treatments are administered at each of four times, for a total of twelve dependent variables on each experimental unit. If the variables are listed on the MODEL statement as Y1-Y12, then the statement

```
REPEATED TRT 3, TIME 4;
```

implies the following structure:

DEP VARIABLE	Y1	Y2	Y3	Y4	Y5	Y6	Y7	Y8	Y9	Y10	Y11	Y12
value of TRT	1	1	1	1	2	2	2	2	3	3	3	3
value of TIME	1	2	3	4	1	2	3	4	1	2	3	4

REPEATED always produces a table like the one above.

The following options can appear in the REPEATED statement after a slash (/):

NOM
: prints only the results of the univariate analyses.

NOU
: prints only the results of the multivariate analyses.

PRINTM
: prints the transformation matrices that define the contrasts in the analysis.

PRINTH
: prints the **H** (SSCP) matrix associated with each multivariate test.

PRINTE
: prints the **E** matrix for each combination of within-subject factors, as well as partial correlation matrices for both the original dependent variables and the variables defined by the transformations specified in the REPEATED statement. In addition, the PRINTE option provides sphericity tests for each set of transformed variables. If the requested transformations are not orthogonal, the PRINTE option also provides a sphericity test for a set of orthogonal contrasts.

PRINTRV
: prints the characteristic roots and vectors for each multivariate test.

SHORT
: prints the multivariate test criteria and associated F statistics in a condensed form.

SUMMARY
: produces analysis-of-variance tables for each contrast defined by the within-subjects factors. Along with tests for the effects of the independent variables specified in the MODEL statement, a term labeled MEAN tests the hypothesis that the overall mean of the contrast is zero.

CANONICAL
: requests a canonical analysis of the **H** and **E** matrices corresponding to the transformed variables specified in the REPEATED statement. This analysis is similar to that produced by PROC CANDISC.

HTYPE=*n*
: specifies the type of the **H** matrix used in the multivariate tests, and the type of sums of squares used in the univariate tests. See the HTYPE= option in the specifications for the MANOVA statement for further details.

TEST Statement

TEST H=*effects* E=*effect* / *options;*

Although an *F* value is computed for all SS in the analysis using the residual MS as an error term, you may request additional *F* tests using other effects as error terms. You need a TEST statement when a non-Iσ^2 error structure (as in a split-plot) exists. However, in most unbalanced models with non-Iσ^2 error structures, most MSs are not independent and do not have equal expectations under the null hypothesis.

If you use a TEST statement, E= is required.

GLM does not check any of the assumptions underlying the *F* statistic. **When you specify a TEST statement, you assume sole responsibility for the validity of the F statistic produced.** To help validate a test, you can use the RANDOM statement and inspect the expected mean squares.

These terms are specified in the TEST statement:

H=*effects* specifies which effects in the preceding model are to be used as hypothesis (numerator) effects.

E=*effect* specifies one, and only one, effect to use as the error (denominator) term.

By default, the SS type for all hypothesis SS and error SS is the highest type computed in the model. If the hypothesis type or error type is to be another type that was computed in the model, you should specify one or both of these options after a slash (/):

HTYPE=*n* specifies the type of SS to use for the hypothesis. The type must be a type computed in the model (n = 1, 2, 3, or 4).

ETYPE=*n* specifies the type of SS to use for the error term. The type must be a type computed in the model (n = 1, 2, 3, or 4).

This example illustrates the TEST statement with a balanced split-plot model:

```
PROC GLM;
   CLASS A B C;
   MODEL Y=A  B(A) C A*C B*C(A);
   TEST H=A E=B(A)/ HTYPE=1 ETYPE=1;
   TEST H=C A*C E=B*C(A) / HTYPE=1 ETYPE=1;
```

WEIGHT Statement

WEIGHT *variable;*

When a WEIGHT statement is used, a weighted residual sum of squares

$$\Sigma w(y\text{-}\hat{y})^2$$

is minimized, where w is the value of the variable specified in the WEIGHT statement.

The observation is used in the analysis only if the value of the WEIGHT statement variable is greater than zero.

Means and total degrees of freedom are unaffected by the presence of a WEIGHT statement. The normal equations used when a WEIGHT statement is present are:

$$\beta = (\mathbf{X'WX})^{-}\mathbf{X'W\ Y}$$

where **W** is a diagonal matrix consisting of the values of the variable specified in the WEIGHT statement.

If the weights for the observations are proportional to the reciprocals of the error variances, then the weighted least-squares estimates are B.L.U.E. (best linear unbiased estimators).

DETAILS

Missing Values

For an analysis involving one dependent variable, GLM uses an observation if values are present for that dependent variable and all the variables used in independent effects.

For an analysis involving multiple dependent variables without the MANOVA or REPEATED statement, a missing value in one dependent variable does not eliminate the observation from the analysis of other nonmissing dependent variables. For an analysis with the MANOVA or REPEATED statement, GLM requires values for all dependent variables to be present for an observation to be used for any.

During processing, GLM groups the dependent variables on their missing values across observations so that sums and crossproducts can be collected in the most efficient manner.

Output Data Set

The OUTPUT statement produces an output data set that contains:

- all original data from the SAS data set input to GLM
- the PREDICTED= variables named in the OUTPUT statement to contain predicted values
- the RESIDUAL= variables named in the OUTPUT statement to contain the residual values.

With multiple dependent variables, a name can be specified for predicted and residual values for each of the dependent variables in the order they occur in the MODEL statement.

For example, suppose the input data set A contains the variables Y1, Y2, Y3, X1, and X2. Then you can code:

```
PROC GLM DATA=A;
   MODEL Y1 Y2 Y3 = X1;
   OUTPUT P=Y1HAT Y2HAT Y3HAT R=Y1RESID;
```

The output data set contains Y1, Y2, Y3, X1, X2, Y1HAT, Y2HAT, Y3HAT, and Y1RESID. X2 is output even though it was not used by GLM. Although predicted variables are generated for all three dependent variables, residuals are output for only the first dependent variable.

On the output data set the predicted values are missing when any independent variable in the analysis is missing. The residuals are missing if either an independent variable in the analysis or the dependent variable is missing.

Computer Resources

Memory For large problems, most of the memory resources are required for holding the **X'X** matrix of the sums and crossproducts. The section on **Parameterization of GLM Models** describes how columns of the **X** matrix are allocated for various types of effects. For each level that occurs in the data for a combination of class variables in a given effect, a row and column for **X'X** is needed.

An example illustrates the calculation. Suppose A has 20 levels, B has 4, and C has 3. Then consider the model:

```
PROC GLM;
   CLASS A B C;
   MODEL Y1 Y2 Y3 = A B A*B C A*C B*C A*B*C X1 X2;
```

The **X'X** matrix (bordered by **X'Y** and **Y'Y**) can have as many as 425 rows and columns:

1 for the intercept term
20 for A
4 for B
80 for A*B

3 for C
60 for A*C
12 for B*C
240 for A*B*C
2 for X1 and X2 (continuous variables)
3 for Y1, Y2, and Y3 (dependent variables).

The matrix has 425 rows and columns only if all combinations of levels occurred for each effect in the model. For m rows and columns, 8 x $m^2/2$ bytes are needed for crossproducts. In this case, 8 x $425^2/2$ is 722500 bytes. To convert to K units, divide by 1024.

For this example, the analysis requires 706K of memory for **X'X** and 200K or more memory for SAS and the GLM program; so at least 900K should be requested. Since system configurations vary so widely, it is difficult to determine the amount of memory for SAS and the GLM program; one way to do so is to run a job consisting of only the following statements:

```
PROC GLM;
RUN;
```

and noting the amount of memory used as indicated on the SAS log.

The required memory grows as the square of the number of columns of **X** and **X'X**; most is for the A*B*C interaction. Without A*B*C, we have 185 columns and need only 134K for **X'X**. Without A*B we only need 43K. If A is recoded to have ten levels, then even the full model has only 220 columns and requires only 189K.

The second time that a large amount of memory is needed is when Type III or IV or contrast sums of squares are being calculated. This memory requirement is a function of the number of degrees of freedom of the model being analyzed, and the maximum degrees of freedom for any single source. Let RANK equal the sum of the model degrees of freedom, MAXDF be the maximum number of degrees of freedom for any single source, and NY be the number of dependent variables in the model. Then the memory requirement is

8*(RANK*(RANK + 1)/2 + NY*RANK +
MAXDF*(MAXDF + 1)/2 + NY*MAXDF) bytes .

Unfortunately, these quantities are not available when the **X'X** matrix is being constructed, so GLM may occasionally request additional memory even after you have increased the memory allocation available to the program.

If you have a very large model that will not fit the region or would be too expensive to run, these are your options:

- cut out terms, especially high-level interactions
- cut down the number of levels for variables with many levels
- use ABSORB for parts of the model that are large
- use PROC ANOVA or PROC REG rather than PROC GLM, if your design allows.

CPU time For large problems, two operations consume a lot of CPU time: the collection of sums and crossproducts and the solution of the normal equations.

The time required for collecting sums and crossproducts is difficult to calculate since it is a complicated function of the model. For a model with m columns and n rows (observations) in X, the worst case occurs if all columns are continuous variables, involving n x $m^2/2$ multiplications and additions. If the columns are levels of a classification, then only m sums may be needed, but a significant amount of time may be spent in lookup operations. Solving the normal equations requires time for approximately $m^3/2$ multiplications and additions.

If you know that Type IV sums of squares will be appropriate for the model you are analyzing (for example, if your design has no missing cells), you may achieve a savings in CPU time by requesting the Type IV sums of squares instead of the more computationally burdensome Type III sums of squares by specifying the SS4 option in your MODEL statement. This will prove to be especially useful if you have a factor in your model with many levels which is involved in several interactions.

Parameterization of GLM Models

GLM constructs a linear model according to the specifications in the MODEL statement. Each effect generates one or more columns in a design matrix **X**. This section shows precisely how **X** is built.

Intercept All models automatically include a column of 1s to estimate an intercept parameter μ. You can use the NOINT option to suppress the intercept.

Regression effects Regression effects (covariates) have the values of the variables copied into the design matrix directly. Polynomial terms are multiplied out and then installed in **X**.

Main effects If a class variable has *m* levels, GLM generates *m* columns in the design matrix for its main effect. Each column is an indicator variable for a given level. The order of the columns is the sort order of the values of their levels and can be controlled with the ORDER= option of the PROC GLM statement. For example:

data		int	A		B		
A	B	μ	A1	A2	B1	B2	B3
1	1	1	1	0	1	0	0
1	2	1	1	0	0	1	0
1	3	1	1	0	0	0	1
2	1	1	0	1	1	0	0
2	2	1	0	1	0	1	0
2	3	1	0	1	0	0	1

There are more columns for these effects than there are degrees of freedom for them; in other words, GLM is using an over-parameterized model.

Crossed effects First, GLM reorders the terms to correspond to the order of the variables in the CLASS statement; thus B*A becomes A*B if A precedes B in the CLASS statement. Then GLM generates columns for all combinations of levels that occur in the data. The order of the columns is such that the rightmost variables in the cross index faster than the leftmost variables. Empty columns (that would contain all zeros) are not generated.

data		int	A		B			A*B					
A	B	μ	A1	A2	B1	B2	B3	A1B1	A1B2	A1B3	A2B1	A2B2	A2B3
1	1	1	1	0	1	0	0	1	0	0	0	0	0
1	2	1	1	0	0	1	0	0	1	0	0	0	0
1	3	1	1	0	0	0	1	0	0	1	0	0	0
2	1	1	0	1	1	0	0	0	0	0	1	0	0
2	2	1	0	1	0	1	0	0	0	0	0	1	0
2	3	1	0	1	0	0	1	0	0	0	0	0	1

In the above matrix, main-effects columns are not linearly independent of crossed-effect columns; in fact, the column space for the crossed effects contains the space of the main effect.

Nested effects Nested effects are generated in the same manner as crossed effects. Hence the design columns generated by the following statements are the same (but the ordering of the columns is different):

```
MODEL Y=A B(A)
```

(B nested within A)

and

```
MODEL =A A*B;
```

(omitted main effect for B).

The nesting operator in GLM is more a notational convenience than an operation distinct from crossing. Nested effects are characterized by the property that the nested variables never appear as main effects. The order of the variables within nesting parentheses is made to correspond to the order of these variables in the CLASS statement. The order of the columns is such that variables outside the parentheses index faster than those inside the parentheses, and the rightmost nested variables index faster than the leftmost ones.

data		int	A		B(A)					
A	B	μ	A1	A2	B1A1	B2A1	B3A1	B1A2	B2A2	B3A2
1	1	1	1	0	1	0	0	0	0	0
1	2	1	1	0	0	1	0	0	0	0
1	3	1	1	0	0	0	1	0	0	0
2	1	1	0	1	0	0	0	1	0	0
2	2	1	0	1	0	0	0	0	1	0
2	3	1	0	1	0	0	0	0	0	1

Continuous-nesting-class effects When a continuous variable nests with a class variable, the design columns are constructed by multiplying the continuous values into the design columns for the class effect.

data		int	A		X(A)	
X	A	μ	A1	A2	X(A1)	X(A2)
21	1	1	1	0	21	0
24	1	1	1	0	24	0
22	1	1	1	0	22	0
28	2	1	0	1	0	28
19	2	1	0	1	0	19
23	2	1	0	1	0	23

This model estimates a separate slope for **X** within each level of A.

Continuous-by-class effects Continuous-by-class effects generate the same design columns as continuous-nesting class effects. The two models are made different by the presence of the continuous variable as a regressor by itself as well as a contributor to a compound effect.

data			X	A		X*A	
X	A	μ	X	A1	A2	X*A1	X*A2
21	1	1	21	1	0	21	0
24	1	1	24	1	0	24	0
22	1	1	22	1	0	22	0
28	2	1	28	0	1	0	28
19	2	1	19	0	1	0	19
23	2	1	23	0	1	0	23

Continuous-by-class effects are used to test the homogeneity of slopes. If the continuous-by-class effect is nonsignificant, the effect can be removed so that the response with respect to **X** is the same for all levels of the class variables.

General effects An example that combines all the effects is:

X1*X2*A*B*C(D E) .

The continuous list comes first, followed by the crossed list, followed by the nested list in parentheses.

The sequencing of parameters is not important to learn unless you contemplate using the CONTRAST or ESTIMATE statements to compute some function of the parameter estimates.

Effects may be retitled by GLM to correspond to ordering rules. For example, B*A(E D) might be retitled A*B(D E) to satisfy the following:

- class variables that occur outside parentheses (crossed effects) are sorted in the order they appear in the CLASS statement
- variables within parentheses (nested effects) are sorted in the order they appear in a CLASS statement.

The sequencing of the parameters generated by an effect can be described by which variables have their levels indexed faster:

- variables in the crossed part index faster than variables in the nested list
- within a crossed or nested list, variables to the right index faster than variables to the left.

For example, suppose a model includes four effects—A, B, C, and D—each having two levels, 1 and 2. If the CLASS statement is

```
CLASS A B C D;
```

then the order of the parameters for the effect B*A(C D), which is retitled A*B(C D), is:

$$A_1B_1C_1D_1 \rightarrow A_1B_2C_1D_1 \rightarrow A_2B_1C_1D_1 \rightarrow A_2B_2C_1D_1 \rightarrow A_1B_1C_1D_2 \rightarrow$$

$$A_1B_2C_1D_2 \rightarrow A_2B_1C_1D_2 \rightarrow A_2B_2C_1D_2 \rightarrow A_1B_1C_2D_1 \rightarrow A_1B_2C_2D_1 \rightarrow$$

$$A_2B_1C_1D_2 \rightarrow A_2B_2C_2D_1 \rightarrow A_1B_1C_2D_2 \rightarrow A_1B_2C_2D_2 \rightarrow A_2B_1C_2D_2 \rightarrow$$

$$A_2B_2C_2D_2 \quad .$$

Note that first the crossed effects B and A are sorted in the order that they appear in the CLASS statement so that A precedes B in the parameter list. Then, for each combination of the nested effects in turn, combinations of A and B appear. B moves fastest since it is rightmost in the cross list. Then A moves next fastest. D moves next fastest. C is the slowest, since it is leftmost in the nested list.

When numeric levels are used, levels are sorted by their character format, which may not correspond to their numeric sort sequence. Therefore, it is advisable to include a format for numeric levels, or to use the ORDER=INTERNAL option in the PROC GLM statement to insure that levels are sorted by their internal values.

Degrees of freedom For models with class variables, there are more design columns constructed than there are degrees of freedom for the effect. There are thus linear dependencies among the columns. In this event, the parameters are not estimable; there will be an infinite number of least-squares solutions. GLM uses a generalized (G2) inverse to obtain values for the estimates. The solution values are not even printed unless the SOLUTION option is specified. The solution has the characteristic that estimates are zero whenever the design column for that parameter is a linear combination of previous columns. (Strictly termed, the solution values should not even be called estimates.) With this full parameterization, hypothesis tests are constructed to test linear functions of the parameters that are estimable.

Other programs (such as PROC CATMOD) reparameterize models to full rank using certain restrictions on the parameters. GLM does not reparameterize, making the hypotheses that are commonly tested more understandable. See Goodnight (1978) for additional reasons for not reparameterizing.

GLM does not actually construct the design matrix **X**; rather, the procedure constructs directly the crossproduct matrix **X′X**, which is made up of counts, sums, and crossproducts.

Hypothesis Testing in GLM

A complete discussion of the four standard types of hypothesis tests appears in "The Four Types of Estimable Functions."

Example To illustrate the four types of tests and the principles upon which they are based, consider a two-way design with interaction based on these data:

		B 1	B 2
A	1	23.5 23.7	28.7
A	2	8.9	5.6 8.9
A	3	10.3 12.5	13.6 14.6

Invoke GLM and ask for all the estimable functions options to examine what GLM can test. The code below is followed by the summary *ANOVA* table from the printout.

```
DATA EXAMPLE;
   INPUT A B Y @@;
   CARDS;
1 1 23.5  1 1 23.7  1 2 28.7  2 1  8.9  2 2  5.6
2 2  8.9  3 1 10.3  3 1 12.5  3 2 13.6  3 2 14.6
;
PROC GLM;
   CLASS A B;
   MODEL Y= A B A*B / E E1 E2 E3 E4;
```

Output 20.2 Summary ANOVA Table: PROC GLM

```
                                                                                                   1
                                   GENERAL LINEAR MODELS PROCEDURE

DEPENDENT VARIABLE: Y

SOURCE                  DF      SUM OF SQUARES        MEAN SQUARE     F VALUE       PR > F     R-SQUARE          C.V.

MODEL                    5        520.47600000       104.09520000       49.66       0.0011     0.984145        9.6330

ERROR                    4          8.38500000         2.09625000                  ROOT MSE                    Y MEAN

CORRECTED TOTAL          9        528.86100000                                    1.44784322               15.03000000
```

The following sections show the general form of estimable functions and discuss the four standard tests, their properties, and abbreviated printouts for our two-way crossed example.

Estimability The first printout is the general form of estimable functions. In order to be testable, a hypothesis must be able to fit within the framework printed here.

Output 20.3 General Form of Estimable Functions: PROC GLM

```
                                                                                                    2

                                      GENERAL LINEAR MODELS PROCEDURE

DEPENDENT VARIABLE: Y

GENERAL FORM OF ESTIMABLE FUNCTIONS

EFFECT                  COEFFICIENTS

INTERCEPT               L1

A                  1    L2
                   2    L3
                   3    L1-L2-L3

B                  1    L5
                   2    L1-L5

A*B               1 1   L7
                  1 2   L2-L7
                  2 1   L9
                  2 2   L3-L9
                  3 1   L5-L7-L9
                  3 2   L1-L2-L3-L5+L7+L9
```

If a hypothesis is estimable, the Ls in the above scheme can be set to values that match the hypothesis. All the standard tests in GLM can be shown in the format above, with some of the Ls zeroed, some set to functions of other Ls.

The following sections show how many of the hypotheses can be tested by comparing the model sum-of-squares regression from one model to a submodel. The notation used is

$$SS(\mathit{Beffects} \mid \mathit{Aeffects}) = SS(\mathit{Beffects},\mathit{Aeffects}) - SS(\mathit{Aeffects})$$

where SS(*Aeffects*) denotes the regression model sum of squares for the model consisting of *Aeffects*. This notation is equivalent to the "reduction" notation defined by Searle (1971).

Type I tests Type I sums of squares, also called *sequential sums of squares,* are the incremental improvement in error SS as each effect is added to the model. They can be computed by fitting the model in steps and recording the difference in SSE at each step.

Source	Type I SS
A	$SS(A \mid \mu)$
B	$SS(B \mid \mu,A)$
A*B	$SS(A{*}B \mid \mu,A,B)$

Type I SS are printed out by default since they are easy to obtain and can be used in various hand calculations to produce SS values for a series of different models.

The Type I hypotheses have these properties:

- Type I SS for all effects add up to the model SS. None of the other SS types have this property, except in special cases.
- Type I hypotheses can be derived from rows of the forward Dolittle transformation of **X′X**.
- Type I SS are statistically independent from each other if the residual errors are independent and identically distributed normal.
- Type I hypotheses depend on the order in which effects are specified in the MODEL.
- Type I hypotheses are uncontaminated by effects preceding the effect being tested; however, the hypotheses usually involve parameters for effects following the tested effect in the model. For example, in the model

  ```
  Y=A B;
  ```

  the Type I hypothesis for B does not involve A parameters, but the Type I hypothesis for A does involve B parameters.
- Type I hypotheses are functions of the cell counts for unbalanced data; the hypotheses are not usually the same hypotheses that are tested if the data are balanced.
- Type I SS are useful for polynomial models where you want to know the contribution of a term as though it had been made orthogonal to preceding effects. Thus, Type I SS correspond to tests of the orthogonalized polynomials.

Output 20.4 Type I Estimable Functions and Associated Tests: PROC GLM

```
                                                                                                              3

                                              GENERAL LINEAR MODELS PROCEDURE

DEPENDENT VARIABLE: Y

TYPE I ESTIMABLE FUNCTIONS FOR: A         FUNCTIONS FOR: B        FUNCTIONS FOR: A*B

EFFECT                COEFFICIENTS        COEFFICIENTS            COEFFICIENTS

INTERCEPT             0                   0                       0

A               1     L2                  0                       0
                2     L3                  0                       0
                3     -L2-L3              0                       0

B               1     0.1667*L2-0.1667*L3     L5                  0
                2     -0.1667*L2+0.1667*L3    -L5                 0

A*B             1 1   0.6667*L2           0.2857*L5               L7
                1 2   0.3333*L2           -0.2857*L5              -L7
                2 1   0.3333*L3           0.2857*L5               L9
                2 2   0.6667*L3           -0.2857*L5              -L9
                3 1   -0.5*L2-0.5*L3      0.4286*L5               -L7-L9
                3 2   -0.5*L2-0.5*L3      -0.4286*L5              L7+L9


SOURCE                   DF        TYPE I SS     F VALUE    PR > F

A                         2     494.03100000      117.84    0.0003
B                         1      10.71428571        5.11    0.0866
A*B                       2      15.73071429        3.75    0.1209
```

Type II tests The Type II tests can also be calculated by comparing the error SS for subset models. The Type II SS are the reduction in error SS due to adding the term after all other terms have been added to the model except terms that contain the effect being tested. An effect is contained in another effect if it can be derived by deleting terms in the effect. For example, A and B are both contained in A*B. For this model:

Source	Type II SS
A	SS(A | μ,B)
B	SS(B | μ,A)
A*B	SS(A*B | μ,A,B)

Type II SS have these properties:

- Type II SS do not necessarily add to the model SS.
- The hypothesis for an effect does not involve parameters of other effects except for containing effects (which it must involve to be estimable).
- Type II SS are invariant to the ordering of effects in the model.
- For unbalanced designs, Type II hypotheses for effects that are contained in other effects are not usually the same hypotheses that are tested if the data are balanced. The hypotheses are generally functions of the cell counts.

Output 20.5 Type II Estimable Functions and Associated Tests: PROC GLM

```
                                                                                        4

                                   GENERAL LINEAR MODELS PROCEDURE

DEPENDENT VARIABLE: Y

TYPE II ESTIMABLE FUNCTIONS FOR: A        FUNCTIONS FOR: B       FUNCTIONS FOR: A*B

EFFECT              COEFFICIENTS          COEFFICIENTS           COEFFICIENTS

INTERCEPT           0                     0                      0

A             1     L2                    0                      0
              2     L3                    0                      0
              3     -L2-L3                0                      0

B             1     0                     L5                     0
              2     0                     -L5                    0

A*B           1 1   0.619*L2+0.0476*L3    0.2857*L5              L7
              1 2   0.381*L2-0.0476*L3    -0.2857*L5             -L7
              2 1   -0.0476*L2+0.381*L3   0.2857*L5              L9
              2 2   0.0476*L2+0.619*L3    -0.2857*L5             -L9
              3 1   -0.5714*L2-0.4286*L3  0.4286*L5              -L7-L9
              3 2   -0.4286*L2-0.5714*L3  -0.4286*L5             L7+L9


SOURCE                 DF        TYPE II SS     F VALUE     PR > F

A                       2      499.12028571      119.05     0.0003
B                       1       10.71428571        5.11     0.0866
A*B                     2       15.73071429        3.75     0.1209
```

Type III and Type IV tests Type III and Type IV SS, sometimes referred to as *partial sums of squares*, are considered by many to be the most desirable. These SS cannot in general be computed by comparing model SS from several models using GLM's parameterization. (However, they can sometimes be computed by "reduction" for methods that reparameterize to full rank.) In GLM they are computed by constructing an estimated hypothesis matrix **L** and then computing the SS associated with the hypothesis $\mathbf{L}\beta=0$. As long as there are no missing cells in the design, Type III and Type IV SS are the same.

These are properties of Type III and Type IV SS:

- The hypothesis for an effect does not involve parameters of other effects except for containing effects (which it must involve to be estimable).
- The hypotheses to be tested are invariant to the ordering of effects in the model.
- The hypotheses are the same hypotheses that are tested if there are no missing cells. They are not functions of cell counts.
- The SS do not normally add up to the model SS.

They are constructed from the general form of estimable functions. Type III and Type IV tests are only different if the design has missing cells. In this case the Type III tests have an orthogonality property, while the Type IV tests have a balancing property. These properties are discussed in "The Four Types of Estimable Functions." For this example, Type IV tests are identical to the Type III tests that are shown.

Output 20.6 Type III Estimable Functions and Associated Tests: PROC GLM

```
                                                                                                              5

                                      GENERAL LINEAR MODELS PROCEDURE

DEPENDENT VARIABLE: Y

TYPE III ESTIMABLE FUNCTIONS FOR: A     FUNCTIONS FOR: B       FUNCTIONS FOR: A*B

EFFECT               COEFFICIENTS       COEFFICIENTS           COEFFICIENTS

INTERCEPT            0                  0                      0

A              1     L2                 0                      0
               2     L3                 0                      0
               3     -L2-L3             0                      0

B              1     0                  L5                     0
               2     0                  -L5                    0

A*B            1 1   0.5*L2             0.3333*L5              L7
               1 2   0.5*L2             -0.3333*L5             -L7
               2 1   0.5*L3             0.3333*L5              L9
               2 2   0.5*L3             -0.3333*L5             -L9
               3 1   -0.5*L2-0.5*L3     0.3333*L5              -L7-L9
               3 2   -0.5*L2-0.5*L3     -0.3333*L5             L7+L9


SOURCE                  DF      TYPE III SS    F VALUE    PR > F        DF      TYPE IV SS    F VALUE    PR > F

A                        2     479.10785714     114.28    0.0003         2    479.10785714     114.28    0.0003
B                        1       9.45562500       4.51    0.1009         1      9.45562500       4.51    0.1009
A*B                      2      15.73071429       3.75    0.1209         2     15.73071429       3.75    0.1209
```

Computational Method

Let **X** represent the $n \times p$ design matrix. (When effects containing only class variables are involved, the columns of **X** corresponding to these effects contain only 0s and 1s. No reparameterization is made.) Let **Y** represent the $n \times 1$ vector of dependent variables.

The normal equations $\mathbf{X'X}\beta=\mathbf{X'Y}$ are solved using a modified sweep routine that produces a generalized (g2) inverse $(\mathbf{X'X})^{-}$ and a solution $b=(\mathbf{X'X})^{-}\mathbf{X'y}$ (Pringle and Raynor 1971).

For each effect in the model, a matrix **L** is computed such that the rows of **L** are estimable. Tests of the hypothesis $\mathbf{L}\beta=0$ are then made by first computing

$$SS(\mathbf{L}\beta = 0) = (\mathbf{Lb})'\ (\mathbf{L}(\mathbf{X}'\mathbf{X})^{-}\mathbf{L}')^{-1}\ (\mathbf{Lb})$$

then computing the associated *F* value using the mean squared error.

Absorption

Absorption is a computational technique used to reduce computing resource needs in certain cases. The classic use of absorption occurs when a blocking factor with a large number of levels is a term in the model.

For example, the statements

```
PROC GLM;
   ABSORB HERD;
   CLASS A B;
   MODEL Y=A B A*B;
```

are equivalent to

```
PROC GLM;
   CLASS HERD A B;
   MODEL Y= HERD A B A*B;
```

with the exception that the TYPE II, TYPE III, or TYPE IV SS for HERD are not computed when HERD is absorbed.

Several effects may be absorbed at one time. For example, these statements

```
PROC GLM;
   ABSORB HERD COW;
   CLASS A B;
   MODEL Y=A B A*B;
```

are equivalent to

```
PROC GLM;
   CLASS HERD COW A B;
   MODEL Y=HERD COW(HERD) A B A*B;
```

When you use absorption, the size of the **X'X** matrix is a function only of the effects in the MODEL statement. The effects being absorbed do not contribute to the size of the **X'X** matrix.

For the example above, A and B could be absorbed:

```
PROC GLM;
   ABSORB A B;
   CLASS HERD COW;
   MODEL Y=HERD COW(HERD);
```

Although the sources of variation in the results are listed as

```
A B(A) HERD COW(HERD)
```

all types of estimable functions for HERD and COW(HERD) are free of A, B, and A*B parameters.

To illustrate the savings in computing using ABSORB, we ran GLM on general data with 1276 degrees of freedom in the model with these statements:

```
DATA A;
   LENGTH HERD COW TRTMENT 2;
   DO HERD=1 TO 40;
```

```
      N=1+UNIFORM(1234567)*60;
      DO COW=1 TO N;
         DO TRTMENT=1 TO 3;
            DO REP=1 TO 2;
               Y=HERD/5+COW/10+TRTMENT+NORMAL(1234567);
               OUTPUT;
               END;
            END;
         END;
      END;
   DROP N;
```

This analysis would have required over 6 megabytes of memory for the **X′X** matrix had GLM solved it directly. However, GLM only needed a 4 x 4 matrix for intercept and treatment, since the other effects were absorbed.

```
PROC GLM;
   ABSORB HERD COW;
   CLASS TRTMENT;
   MODEL Y=TRTMENT;
```

Output 20.7 Absorption Technique: PROC GLM

```
                                                                                              1

                              GENERAL LINEAR MODELS PROCEDURE

                                  CLASS LEVEL INFORMATION

                                CLASS      LEVELS    VALUES

                                TRTMENT         3    1 2 3

                         NUMBER OF OBSERVATIONS IN DATA SET = 7650
```

```
                                                                                              2

                              GENERAL LINEAR MODELS PROCEDURE

DEPENDENT VARIABLE: Y

SOURCE                DF    SUM OF SQUARES      MEAN SQUARE    F VALUE     PR > F     R-SQUARE       C.V.

MODEL               1276    62208.68496838      48.75288791      48.14     0.0001     0.905997    12.4013

ERROR               6373     6454.52506857       1.01279226               ROOT MSE                 Y MEAN

CORRECTED TOTAL     7649    68663.21003694                                1.00637580            8.11507114

SOURCE                DF       TYPE I SS    F VALUE    PR > F     DF      TYPE III SS    F VALUE    PR > F

HERD                  39  44824.52687244    1134.83    0.0001
COW(HERD)           1235  12224.34481401       9.77    0.0001
TRTMENT                2   5159.81328193    2547.32    0.0001      2    5159.81328193    2547.32    0.0001
```

Expected Mean Squares for Random Effects

The RANDOM statement in GLM declares one or more effects in the model to be random rather than fixed components. GLM does not estimate variance components, nor does it determine what tests are appropriate. However, GLM does print the coefficients of the expected mean squares. From this printout you can form variance component estimates and determine proper tests by yourself.

The expected mean squares are computed as follows. Consider the model

$$Y = X_0\beta_0 + X_1\beta_1 + X_2\beta_2 ... + X_k\beta_k + \varepsilon$$

where β_0 represents the fixed effects, and β_1, β_2..., ε represent the random effects normally and independently distributed. For any **L** in the row space of

$$\mathbf{X} = (X_0 \,|\, X_1 \,|\, X_2 \,|\, ... \,|\, X_k)$$

then

$$E(SS_L) = \beta_0'C_0'C_0\beta_0 + SSQ(C_1)\sigma_1^2 + SSQ(C_2)\sigma_2^2 ... + SSQ(C_k)\sigma_k^2 + \text{rank}(\mathbf{L})\sigma_\varepsilon^2$$

where **C** is of the same dimensions as **L** and partitioned as the **X** matrix. In other words,

$$\mathbf{C} = (C_0 \,|\, C_1 \,|\, ... \,|\, C_k) \quad .$$

Furthermore, **C=ML** where **M** is the inverse of the lower triangular Cholesky decomposition matrix of **L(X'X)⁻L'**. SSQ(**A**) is defined as tr(**A'A**).

For the model in this MODEL statement

```
MODEL Y=A B(A) C A*C;
```

with B(A) declared as random, the expected mean square of each effect is printed as

```
VAR(ERROR) + constant*VAR(B(A)) + Q(A,C,A*C)   .
```

If any fixed effects appear in the expected mean square of an effect, the letter Q followed by the list of fixed effects in the expected value is printed. The actual numeric values of the quadratic form (**Q** matrix) may be printed using the Q option.

See Goodnight and Speed (1978) for further theoretical discussion.

Comparisons of Means

When comparing more than two means, an *ANOVA F* test tells you if the means are significantly different from each other, but it does not tell you which means differ from which other means. Multiple comparison methods (also called *mean separation tests*) give you more detailed information about the differences among the means. A variety of multiple comparison methods are available with the MEANS statement in the ANOVA and GLM procedures.

By *multiple comparisons* we mean **more than one comparison among three or more means**. There is a serious lack of standardized terminology in the literature on comparison of means. Einot and Gabriel (1975), for example, use the term *multiple comparison procedure* to mean what we define below as a *step-down multiple-stage test*. Some methods for multiple comparisons have not yet been given names, such as those referred to below as REGWQ and REGWF. When reading the literature, you may need to determine what methods are being discussed based on the formulas and references given.

When you interpret multiple comparisons, it is important to remember that failure to reject the hypothesis that two or more means are equal should not lead to the conclusion that the population means are in fact equal. Failure to reject the null hypothesis implies only that the difference between population means, if any, is not large enough to be detected with the given sample size. A related point is that nonsignificance is nontransitive: given three sample means, the largest and smallest may be significantly different from each other, while neither is significantly different from the middle one. Nontransitive results of this type occur frequently in multiple comparisons.

Multiple comparisons can also lead to counter-intuitive results when the cell sizes are unequal. Consider four cells labeled A, B, C, and D, with sample means in the order A > B > C > D. If A and D each have two observations, and B and C each have 10,000 observations, then the difference between B and C may be significant while the difference between A and D is not.

Confidence intervals may be more useful than significance tests in multiple comparisons. Confidence intervals show the degree of uncertainty in each comparison in an easily interpretable way; they make it easier to assess the practical significance of a difference as well as the statistical significance; and they are less likely to lead non-statisticians to the invalid conclusion that nonsignificantly different sample means imply equal population means.

The simplest approach to multiple comparisons is to do a *t* test on every pair of means (the T option in the MEANS statement). For the *i*th and *j*th means you can reject the null hypothesis that the population means are equal if

$$|\bar{y}_i - \bar{y}_j| / s(1/n_i + 1/n_j)^{1/2} \geq t(\alpha;\nu)$$

where $\bar{y}_i$ and $\bar{y}_j$ are the means, n_i and n_j are the number of observations in the two cells, s is the root mean square error based on ν degrees of freedom, α is the significance level, and $t(\alpha;\nu)$ is the two-tailed critical value from a Student's *t* distribution. If the cell sizes are all equal to, say, n, the above formula can be rearranged to give

$$|\bar{y}_i - \bar{y}_j| \geq t(\alpha;\nu)s(2/n)^{1/2}$$

the value of the right-hand side being Fisher's least significant difference (LSD).

There is a problem with repeated *t* tests, however. Suppose there are ten means and each *t* test is performed at the .05 level. There are $10(10-1)/2 = 45$ pairs of means to compare, each with a .05 probability of a type 1 error (a false rejection of the null hypothesis). The chance of making at least one type 1 error is much higher than .05. It is difficult to calculate the exact probability, but you can derive a pessimistic approximation by assuming the comparisons are independent, giving an upper bound to the probability of making at least one type 1 error (the experimentwise error rate) of

$$1-(1-.05)^{45} = .90 \quad .$$

The actual probability is somewhat less than .90, but as the number of means increases, the chance of making at least one type 1 error approaches 1.

It is up to you to decide whether to control the comparisonwise error rate or the experimentwise error rate, but there are many situations in which the experimentwise error rate should be held to a small value. Statistical methods for making two or more inferences while controlling the probability of making at least one type 1 error are called *simultaneous inference methods* (Miller 1981), although Einot and Gabriel (1975) use the term *simultaneous test procedure* in a much more restrictive sense.

It has been suggested that the experimentwise error rate can be held to the α level by performing the overall *ANOVA F* test at the α level and making further comparisons only if the *F* test is significant, as in Fisher's protected LSD. This assertion is false if there are more than three means (Einot and Gabriel 1975). Consider again the situation with ten means. Suppose that one population mean differs from the others by a sufficiently large amount that the power (probability of correctly rejecting the null hypothesis) of the *F* test is near 1, but that all the other population means are equal to each other. There will be $9(9-1)/2 = 36$ *t* tests of true null hypotheses, with an upper limit of .84 on the probability of at least one type 1 error. Thus you must distinguish between the experimentwise error rate under the complete null hypothesis, in which all population means are equal, and the experimentwise error rate under a partial null hypothesis, in which some means are equal but others differ. The following abbreviations are used in the discussion below:

CER	comparisonwise error rate
EERC	experimentwise error rate under the complete null hypothesis
EERP	experimentwise error rate under a partial null hypothesis
MEER	maximum experimentwise error rate under any complete or partial null hypothesis.

A preliminary *F* test controls the EERC but not the EERP or the MEER.

The MEER can be controlled at the α level by setting the CER to a sufficiently small value. The Bonferroni inequality (Miller 1981) has been widely used for this purpose. If

$$\text{CER} = \alpha/c$$

where c is the total number of comparisons, then the MEER is less than α. Bonferroni *t* tests (the BON option) with MEER < α declare two means to be significantly different if

$$|\bar{y}_i - \bar{y}_j| / s(1/n_i + 1/n_j)^{1/2} \geq t(\varepsilon;\nu)$$

where $\varepsilon = \alpha/(k(k-1)/2)$ for comparison of *k* means. If the cell sizes are equal, the test simplifies to

$$|\bar{y}_i - \bar{y}_j| \geq t(\varepsilon;\nu)s(2/n)^{1/2} \quad .$$

Sidak (1967) has provided a tighter bound, showing that

$$\text{CER} = 1-(1-\alpha)^{1/c}$$

also insures MEER ≤ α for any set of *c* comparisons. A Sidak *t* test (Games 1977), provided by the SIDAK option, is thus given by

$$|\bar{y}_i - \bar{y}_j| / s(1/n_i + 1/n_j)^{1/2} \geq t(\varepsilon;\nu)$$

where $\varepsilon = 1-(1-\alpha)^{1/(k(k-1)/2)}$ for comparison of *k* means. If the sample sizes are equal, the test simplifies to

$$|\bar{y}_i - \bar{y}_j| \geq t(\varepsilon;\nu)s(2/n)^{1/2} \quad .$$

The Bonferroni additive inequality and the Sidak multiplicative inequality can be used to control the MEER for any set of contrasts or other hypothesis tests, not just pairwise comparisons. The Bonferroni inequality can provide simultaneous inferences in any statistical application requiring tests of more than one hypothesis. Other methods discussed below for pairwise comparisons can also be adapted for general contrasts (Miller 1981).

Scheffe (1953, 1959) proposed another method to control the MEER for any set of contrasts or other linear hypotheses in the analysis of linear models, including pairwise comparisons, obtained with the SCHEFFE option. Two means are declared significantly different if

$$|\bar{y}_i - \bar{y}_j| / s(1/n_i + 1/n_j)^{1/2} \geq ((k-1)F(\alpha;k-1,\nu))^{1/2},$$

or, for equal cell sizes,

$$|\bar{y}_i - \bar{y}_j| \geq ((k-1)F(\alpha;k-1,\nu)s(2/n))^{1/2},$$

where $F(\alpha;k-1,\nu)$ is the α-level critical value of an F distribution with k-1 numerator degrees of freedom and ν denominator degrees of freedom.

Scheffe's test is compatible with the overall *ANOVA* F test in that Scheffe's method never declares a contrast significant if the overall F test is nonsignificant. Most other multiple comparison methods are capable of finding significant contrasts when the overall F is nonsignificant and will therefore suffer a loss of power when used with a preliminary F test.

Scheffe's method may be more powerful than the Bonferroni or Sidak methods if the number of comparisons is large relative to the number of means. For pairwise comparisons, Sidak *t* tests are generally more powerful.

Tukey (1952, 1953) proposed a test designed specifically for pairwise comparisons based on the studentized range, sometimes called the "honestly significant difference" test, that controls the MEER when the sample sizes are equal. Tukey (1953) and Kramer (1956) independently proposed a modification for unequal cell sizes. The Tukey or Tukey-Kramer method is provided by the TUKEY option. There is not yet a general proof that the Tukey-Kramer procedure controls the MEER but the method has fared extremely well in Monte Carlo studies (Dunnett 1980). The Tukey-Kramer method is more powerful than the Bonferroni, Sidak, or Scheffe methods for pairwise comparisons. Two means are considered significantly different by the Tukey-Kramer criterion if

$$|\bar{y}_i - \bar{y}_j| / s((1/n_i + 1/n_j)/2)^{1/2} \geq q(\alpha;k,\nu)$$

where $q(\alpha;k,\nu)$ is the α-level critical value of a studentized range distribution of k independent normal random variables with ν degrees of freedom. For equal cell sizes, Tukey's method rejects the null hypothesis of equal population means if

$$|\bar{y}_i - \bar{y}_j| \geq q(\alpha;k,\nu)s/n^{1/2} .$$

Hochberg (1974) devised a method (the GT2 or SMM option) similar to Tukey's but using the studentized maximum modulus instead of the studentized range and employing Sidak's (1967) uncorrelated-*t* inequality. It was proved to hold the MEER at a level not exceeding α with unequal sample sizes. It is generally less powerful than the Tukey-Kramer method and always less powerful than Tukey's test for equal cell sizes. Two means are declared significantly different if

$$|\bar{y}_i - \bar{y}_j| / s(1/n_i + 1/n_j)^{1/2} \geq m(\alpha;c,\nu)$$

where $m(\alpha;c,\nu)$ is the α-level critical value of the studentized maximum modulus distribution of c independent normal random variables with ν degrees of freedom and $c = k(k-1)/2$. For equal cell sizes, the test simplifies to

$$|\bar{y}_i - \bar{y}_j| \geq m(\alpha;c,\nu)s(2/n)^{1/2} \quad .$$

Gabriel (1978) proposed another method (the GABRIEL option) based on the studentized maximum modulus for unequal cell sizes that rejects if

$$|\bar{y}_i - \bar{y}_j| / s((2n_i)^{-1/2} + (2n_j)^{-1/2}) \geq m(\alpha;k,\nu) \quad .$$

For equal cell sizes, Gabriel's test is equivalent to Hochberg's GT2 method. For unequal cell sizes, Gabriel's method is more powerful than GT2 but may become liberal with highly disparate cell sizes (see also Dunnett 1980). Gabriel's test is the only method for unequal sample sizes that lends itself to a convenient graphical representation. Assuming $\bar{y}_i > \bar{y}_j$, the above inequality can be rewritten as

$$\bar{y}_i - m(\alpha;k,\nu)s/(2n_i)^{1/2} \geq \bar{y}_j + m(\alpha;k,\nu)s\ /(2n_j)^{1/2} \quad .$$

The expression on the left does not depend on j, nor does the expression on the right depend on i. Hence one can form what Gabriel calls an *(l,u)*-interval around each sample mean and declare two means to be significantly different if their *(l,u)* -intervals do not overlap.

All of the methods discussed so far can be used to obtain simultaneous confidence intervals (Miller 1981). By sacrificing the facility for simultaneous estimation, it is possible to obtain simultaneous tests with greater power using multiple-stage tests (MSTs). MSTs come in both step-up and step-down varieties (Welsch 1977). The step-down methods, which have been more widely used, are available in SAS.

Step-down MSTs first test the homogeneity of all of the means at a level γ_k. If the test results in a rejection, then each subset of k-1 means is tested at level γ_{k-1}; otherwise, the procedure stops. In general, if the hypothesis of homogeneity of a set of p means is rejected at the γ_p level, then each subset of $p-1$ means is tested at the γ_{p-1} level; otherwise, the set of p means is considered not to differ significantly and none of its subsets are tested. The many varieties of MSTs that have been proposed differ in the levels γ_p and the statistics on which the subset tests are based. Clearly, the EERC of a step-down MST is not greater than γ_k, and the CER is not greater than γ_2, but the MEER is a complicated function of γ_p, $p = 2,\ldots,k$.

MSTs can be used with unequal cell sizes but the resulting operating characteristics are undesirable, so only the balanced case will be considered here. With equal sample sizes, the means can be arranged in ascending or descending order, and only contiguous subsets need be tested. It is common practice to report the results of an MST by writing the means in such an order and drawing lines parallel to the list of means spanning the homogeneous subsets. This form of presentation is also convenient for pairwise comparisons with equal cell sizes.

The best known MSTs are the Duncan (the DUNCAN option) and Student-Newman-Keuls (the SNK option) methods (Miller 1981). Both use the studentized range statistic and hence are called *multiple range tests*. Duncan's method is often called the "new" multiple range test despite the fact that it is one of the oldest MSTs in current use. The Duncan and SNK methods differ in the γ_p values used. For Duncan's method they are

$$\gamma_p = 1-(1-\alpha)^{p-1}$$

whereas the SNK method uses

$$\gamma_p = \alpha \quad .$$

Duncan's method controls the CER at the α level. Its operating characteristics appear similar to those of Fisher's unprotected LSD or repeated *t* tests at level α (Petrinovich and Hardyck 1969). Since repeated *t* tests are easier to compute, easier to explain, and applicable to unequal sample sizes, Duncan's method is not recommended. Several published studies (for example, Carmer and Swanson 1973) have claimed that Duncan's method is superior to Tukey's because of greater power without considering that the greater power of Duncan's method is due to its higher type 1 error rate (Einot and Gabriel 1975).

The SNK method holds the EERC to the α level but does not control the EERP (Einot and Gabriel 1975). Consider ten population means that occur in five pairs such that means within a pair are equal, but there are large differences between pairs. Making the usual sampling assumptions and also assuming that the sample sizes are very large, all subset homogeneity hypotheses for three or more means are rejected. The SNK method then comes down to five independent tests, one for each pair, each at the α level. Letting α be .05, the probability of at least one false rejection is

$$1-(1-.05)^5 = .23 \quad .$$

As the number of means increases, the MEER approaches 1. Therefore, the SNK method cannot be recommended.

A variety of MSTs that control the MEER have been proposed, but these methods are not as well known as those of Duncan and SNK. An approach developed by Ryan (1959, 1960), Einot and Gabriel (1975), and Welsch (1977) sets

$$\gamma_p = 1-(1-\alpha)^{p/k} \text{ for } p < k-1$$
$$= \alpha \text{ for } p \geq k-1 \quad .$$

Either range or *F* statistics can be used, leading to what we call the REGWQ and REGWF methods, respectively, after the authors' initials. Assuming the sample means have been arranged in descending order from $\bar{y}_1$ through $\bar{y}_k$, the homogeneity of means $\bar{y}_i,...,\bar{y}_j$, $i<j$, is rejected by REGWQ if

$$\bar{y}_i-\bar{y}_j \geq q(\gamma_p;p,\nu)s/n^{1/2},$$

or by REGWF if

$$n(\Sigma\bar{y}_u{}^2-(\Sigma\bar{y}_u)^2/k)/(p-1)s^2 \geq F(\gamma_p;p-1,\nu)$$

where $p=j-i+1$ and the summations are over $u = i,...,j$ (Einot and Gabriel 1975).

REGWQ and REGWF appear to be the most powerful step-down MSTs in the current literature (for example, Ramsey 1978). REGWF has the advantage of being compatible with the overall *ANOVA F* test in that REGWF rejects the complete null hypothesis if and only if the overall *F* test does so, since the latter is identical to the first step in REGWF. Use of a preliminary *F* test decreases the power of all the other multiple comparison methods discussed above except for Scheffe's test.

Other multiple comparison methods proposed by Peritz (Marcus, Peritz, and Gabriel 1976; Begun and Gabriel 1981) and Welsch (1977) are still more powerful than the REGW procedures. These methods have not yet been implemented in SAS.

Waller and Duncan (1969) and Duncan (1975) take an approach to multiple comparisons that differs from all the methods discussed above in minimizing the Bayes risk under additive loss rather than controlling type 1 error rates. For each pair of population means $\mu_i$and μ_j, null (H_0^{ij}) and alternative (H_a^{ij}) hypotheses are defined:

$$H_0^{ij}\text{: } \mu_i - \mu_j \leq 0$$

$$H_a^{ij}\text{: } \mu_i - \mu_j > 0 \quad .$$

For any i,j pair let d_0 indicate a decision in favor of H_0^{ij} and d_a indicate a decision in favor of H_a^{ij}, and let $\delta = \mu_i - \mu_j$. The loss function for the decision on the i,j pair is

$$\begin{aligned} L(d_0 \mid \delta) &= 0 \text{ if } \delta \leq 0 \\ &= \delta \text{ if } \delta > 0 \end{aligned}$$

$$\begin{aligned} L(d_a \mid \delta) &= -k\delta \text{ if } \delta \leq 0 \\ &= 0 \text{ if } \delta > 0 \end{aligned}$$

where k represents a constant that you specify rather than the number of means. The loss for the joint decision involving all pairs of means is the sum of the losses for each individual decision. The population means are assumed to have a normal prior distribution with unknown variance, the logarithm of the variance of the means having a uniform prior distribution. For the i,j pair, the null hypothesis is rejected if

$$\bar{y}_i - \bar{y}_j \geq t_B s (2/n)^{1/2}$$

where t_B is the Bayesian t value (Waller and Kemp 1975) depending on k, the F statistic for the one-way *ANOVA*, and the degrees of freedom for F. The value of t_B is a decreasing function of F, so the Waller-Duncan test becomes more liberal as F increases.

In summary, if you want to control the CER, the recommended methods are repeated t tests or Fisher's unprotected LSD (the T or LSD option). If you want to control the MEER, do not need confidence intervals, and have equal cell sizes, then the REGWF and REGWQ methods are recommended. If you want to control the MEER and need confidence intervals or have unequal cell sizes, then use the Tukey or Tukey-Kramer methods (the TUKEY option). If you agree with the Bayesian approach and Waller and Duncan's assumptions, you should use the Waller-Duncan test (the WALLER option).

Multivariate Analysis of Variance

If you fit several dependent variables to the same effects, you may want to make tests jointly involving parameters of several dependent variables. Suppose you have p dependent variables, k parameters for each dependent variable, and n observations. The models can be collected into one equation:

$$\mathbf{Y} = \mathbf{X}\beta + \varepsilon$$

where $\mathbf{Y}$ is $n \times p$, $\mathbf{X}$ is $n \times k$, β is $k \times p$, and ε is $n \times p$. Each of the p models can be estimated and tested separately. However, you may also want to consider the joint distribution. With p dependent variables, there are $n \times p$ errors that are independent across observations, but not across dependent variables. Assume:

$$\text{vec}(\varepsilon) \sim N(0, I_n \otimes \Sigma)$$

where vec(ε) strings ε out by rows, and Σ is $p \times p$. Σ can be estimated by:

$$\mathbf{S} = (\mathbf{e}'\mathbf{e})/(n-r) = (\mathbf{Y}-\mathbf{Xb})'(\mathbf{Y}-\mathbf{Xb})/(n-r)$$

where $\mathbf{b}=(\mathbf{X}'\mathbf{X})^{-}\mathbf{X}'\mathbf{Y}$, r is the rank of the **X** matrix, and **e** is the vector of residuals.

If **S** is scaled to unit diagonals, the values in **S** are called *partial correlations of the Ys adjusting for the Xs*. This matrix can be printed by GLM if PRINTE is specified as a MANOVA option.

You can form hypotheses for linear combinations across columns as well as across rows of β. The multivariate general linear hypothesis is written:

$$\mathbf{L}\beta\mathbf{M} = 0 .$$

The MANOVA statement of the GLM procedure tests special cases where **L** is for Type I, Type II, Type III, or Type IV tests and **M** is the $p \times p$ identity matrix. These tests are joint tests that the Type I, Type II, Type III, or Type IV hypothesis holds for all dependent variables in the model, and will often be sufficient to test all hypotheses of interest.

When these special cases are not appropriate, you can specify your own **L** and **M** matrices through use of the CONTRAST statement (which is used by MANOVA whenever it is present) and the M= option of the MANOVA statement, respectively. Another alternative may be to use a REPEATED statement, which automatically generates a variety of **M** matrices useful in repeated measures analysis of variance. See the discussion of the REPEATED statement, and the detail section **Repeated Measures Analysis of Variance** for more information.

One useful way to think of a MANOVA analysis with an **M** matrix other than the identity is as an analysis of a set of transformed variables defined by the columns of the **M** matrix. You should note, however, that GLM always prints the **M** matrix so that the transformed variables are defined by the **rows** of the **M** matrix on the printout.

All multivariate tests carried out by GLM first construct the matrices **H** and **E** that correspond to the numerator and denominator of a univariate F test.

$$\mathbf{H} = \mathbf{M}'(\mathbf{Lb})'(\mathbf{L}(\mathbf{X}'\mathbf{X})^{-}\mathbf{L}')^{-1}(\mathbf{Lb})\mathbf{M}$$

$$\mathbf{E} = \mathbf{M}'(\mathbf{Y}'\mathbf{Y}-\mathbf{b}'(\mathbf{X}'\mathbf{X})\mathbf{b})\mathbf{M} .$$

The diagonal elements of **H** and **E** correspond to the hypothesis and error SS for univariate tests. When the **M** matrix is the identity matrix (the default), these tests are those for the original dependent variables on the left hand side of the MODEL statement; when an **M** matrix other than the identity is specified, the tests are for transformed variables defined by the columns of the **M** matrix. (The **M** matrix is always printed when the M= option is specified on the MANOVA statement.) These tests can be studied by requesting the SUMMARY option, which produces univariate analyses for each original or transformed variable.

Four test statistics, all functions of the eigenvalues of $\mathbf{E}^{-1}\mathbf{H}$ (or $(\mathbf{E}+\mathbf{H})^{-1}\mathbf{H}$) are constructed:

- Wilks' lambda = $\det(\mathbf{E})/\det(\mathbf{H}+\mathbf{E})$
- Pillai's trace = $\mathrm{trace}(\mathbf{H}(\mathbf{H}+\mathbf{E})^{-1})$
- Hotelling-Lawley trace = $\mathrm{trace}(\mathbf{E}^{-1}\mathbf{H})$
- Roy's maximum root = λ, largest eigenvalue of $\mathbf{E}^{-1}\mathbf{H}$.

All four are reported with F approximations. For further details on these four statistics, see the section **Multivariate Tests** in the REG procedure description.

Repeated Measures Analysis of Variance

When several measurements are taken on the same experimental unit (person, plant, machine, and so on), the measurements tend to be correlated with each other. When the measurements represent qualitatively different things, such as weight, length and width, this correlation is taken into account by use of multivariate methods, such as multivariate analysis of variance. When the measurements can be thought of as responses to levels of an experimental factor of interest, such as time, treatment, or dose, the correlation may be taken into account by performing a repeated measures analysis of variance.

PROC GLM provides both univariate and multivariate tests for repeated measures. For an overall reference on univariate repeated measures, see Winer (1971). The mutivariate approach is covered in Cole and Grizzle (1966). For a discussion of the relative merits of the two approaches, see LaTour and Miniard (1983).

The multivariate tests for interactions of within-subjects (repeated measures) factors and between-subjects factors are produced by testing the hypothesis $\mathbf{L}\beta\mathbf{M} = 0$, where the **L** matrix is the usual matrix corresponding to Type I, Type II, Type III or Type IV hypotheses tests, and the **M** matrix is one of several matrices that you can specify in the REPEATED statement. When the design specifies more than one repeated measures factor, GLM computes the **M** matrix for a given effect as the direct (Kronecker) product of the **M** matrices defined by the REPEATED statement if the factor is involved in the effect or a vector of 1s if the factor is not involved. The test for the main effect of a repeated-measures factor is constructed using an **L** matrix which corresponds to a test that the mean of the observation is zero. Thus, the main effect test for repeated measures is a test that the means of the variables defined by the **M** matrix are all equal to zero, while interactions involving repeated-measures effects are tests that the between-subjects factors involved in the interaction have no effect on the means of the transformed variables defined by the **M** matrix. In addition, you can specify other **L** matrices to test hypotheses of interest through the use of the CONTRAST statement, which is used by REPEATED whenever it is present. To see which combinations of the original variables the transformed variables represent, you can specify the PRINTM option in the REPEATED statement. The tests produced are the same for any choice of transformation (**M**) matrix specified in the REPEATED statement; however, depending on the nature of the repeated measurements being studied, a particular choice of transformation matrix, coupled with the CANONICAL or SUMMARY options, can provide additional insight into the data being studied.

The univariate sums of squares for hypotheses involving repeated measures effects can be easily calculated from the **H** and **E** matrices corresponding to the multivariate tests described above. If the **M** matrix is orthogonal, the univariate sums of squares is calculated as the trace (sum of diagonal elements) of the appropriate **H** matrix; if it is not orthogonal, GLM calculates the trace of of the **H** matrix which would result from an orthogonal **M** matrix transformation. The appropriate error term for the univariate F-tests is constructed in a similar way from the error SSCP matrix and is labeled ERROR(*factorname*), where *factorname* indicates the **M** matrix which was used in the transformation.

The tests formed from these sums of squares are **not** adjusted for the correlation which is inherent in repeated measures analyses. For certain correlation patterns, known as Type H covariances (Huynh and Feldt 1970), the usual F-tests are exact. This condition can be tested by applying a sphericity test (Anderson 1958) to any set of variables defined by an orthogonal contrast transformation. Such a set of variables is known as a set of orthogonal components. When you use the PRINTE option of the REPEATED statement, this sphericity test is applied both to the transformed variables defined by the REPEATED statement, and to a set of orthogonal components, if the specified transformation was not orthogonal. It is the test applied to the orthogonal components which is important in determining if your data have Type H covariance structure.

If your data do not satisfy the assumption of Type H covariance, an adjustment to numerator and denominator degrees of freedom can be used to help ensure that the protection levels of the univariate F tests are close to their nominal values. Two such adjustments, based on a degrees of freedom adjustment factor known as ε (epsilon) (Box 1954), are provided in PROC GLM. The first, initially proposed for use in data analysis by Greenhouse and Geisser (1959), is labeled "G-G" and represents the maximum likelihood estimate of Box's ε factor. Huynh and Feldt (1976) have shown that this estimate tends to be biased downward (that is, too conservative), especially for small samples, and have proposed an alternative estimator that is constructed using unbiased estimators of the numerator and denominator of Box's ε. Although ε must be in the range of 0 to 1, Huynh and Feldt's estimator, labeled "H-F" in the GLM printout, can be outside this range. When the H-F estimator is greater than 1, a value of 1 is used in all calculations.

For tests that involve only between subjects factors, both the multivariate and univariate approaches give rise to the same tests. These tests are equivalent to an analysis of variance on the sum of the dependent variables which represent the repeated measures factor. In other words, these tests are tests of the hypothesis $\mathbf{L}\boldsymbol{\beta}\mathbf{M} = 0$, where $\mathbf{M}$ is simply a vector of 1s. These tests are provided for all effects in the MODEL statement, as well as for any CONTRASTs specified. The ANOVA table for these tests is labeled "Tests of Hypotheses for Between Subjects Effects" in the GLM printout.

Organization of data for repeated measures analysis In order to deal efficiently with the correlation of repeated measures, GLM uses the multivariate method of specifying the model, even if only a univariate analysis is desired. In some cases, data may already be entered in the univariate mode, that is, each repeated measure listed as a separate observation, along with a variable that represents the experimental unit (subject) on which measurement was taken. Consider the following data set OLD:

```
SUBJ   GROUP   TIME    Y
  1      1       1    15
  1      1       2    19
  1      1       3    25
  2      1       1    21
  2      1       2    18
  2      1       3    17
  1      2       1    14
  1      2       2    12
  1      2       3    16
  2      2       1    11
  2      2       2    20
  2      2       3    21
  .      .       .     .
  .      .       .     .
  .      .       .     .
 10      3       1    14
 10      3       2    18
 10      3       3    16
```

These data could be analyzed using the following statements:

```
PROC GLM DATA=OLD;
   CLASSES GROUP SUBJ TIME;
   MODEL Y=GROUP SUBJ(GROUP) TIME GROUP*TIME;
   TEST H=GROUP E=SUBJ(GROUP);
```

However, a more complete and efficient repeated measures analysis could be performed using data set NEW:

GROUP	Y1	Y2	Y3
1	15	19	25
1	21	18	17
2	14	12	16
2	11	20	21
.	.	.	.
.	.	.	.
.	.	.	.
3	14	18	16

In this case, the statements for a repeated measures analysis (assuming default options) would be:

```
PROC GLM DATA=NEW;
   CLASS GROUP;
   MODEL Y1-Y3=GROUP/NOUNI;
   REPEATED TIME;
```

To convert the univariate form of repeated measures data to the multivariate form, you can use a program like the following:

```
PROC SORT DATA=OLD;
   BY GROUP SUBJ;

DATA NEW(KEEP=Y1-Y3 GROUP);
   ARRAY YY {3} Y1-Y3;
   DO I=1 TO 3;
      SET OLD;
      BY GROUP SUBJ;
      YY{TIME}=Y;
      IF LAST.SUBJ THEN RETURN;
      END;
```

Alternatively, you could use PROC TRANSPOSE to achieve the same results with a program like this one:

```
PROC SORT DATA=OLD;
   BY GROUP SUBJ;

PROC TRANSPOSE OUT=NEW(RENAME=(_1=Y1 _2=Y2 _3=Y3));
   BY GROUP SUBJ;
   ID TIME;
```

See the *SAS User's Guide: Basics* and the *SAS Applications Guide* for more information on rearrangement of data sets.

Transformations used in repeated measures analysis of variance As mentioned in the specifications of the REPEATED statement, several different **M** matrices can be generated automatically, based on the transformation that you specify in the REPEATED statement. It is important to remember that both the univariate and multivariate tests that GLM performs are unaffected by the choice of transformation; the choice of transformation is only important when you are trying to study the nature of a repeated measures effect, particularly with the CANONICAL and SUMMARY options. If one of these matrices does not meet your needs for a particular analysis, you may want to use the M= option of the MANOVA statement to perform the tests of interest.

The following sections describe the transformations available in REPEATED, provide an example of the **M** matrix that is produced, and give guidelines for the use of the transformation.

CONTRAST transformation This is the default used by REPEATED, and is useful when one level of the repeated measures effect can be thought of as a control level, against which the others are compared. For example, if five drugs are administered to each of several animals, and the first drug is a control or placebo, the statements

```
PROC GLM;
   MODEL D1-D5 = /NOUNI;
   REPEATED DRUG 5 CONTRAST(1)/SUMMARY;
```

produce the following **M** matrix:

$$\mathbf{M} = \begin{bmatrix} -1 & 1 & 0 & 0 & 0 \\ -1 & 0 & 1 & 0 & 0 \\ -1 & 0 & 0 & 1 & 0 \\ -1 & 0 & 0 & 0 & 1 \end{bmatrix}$$

Examination of the analysis of variance tables produced by the SUMMARY option allows you to tell which of the drugs differed significantly from the placebo.

POLYNOMIAL transformation This transformation is useful when the levels of the repeated measure represent quantitative values of a treatment, such as dose or time. If the levels are unequally spaced, *level values* can be specified in parentheses after the number of levels in the REPEATED statement. For example, if five levels of a drug corresponding to 1, 2, 5, 10 and 20 milligrams are administered to different treatment groups, represented by GROUP, the statements

```
PROC GLM;
   CLASS GROUP;
   MODEL R1-R5=GROUP /NOUNI;
   REPEATED DOSE 5 (1 2 5 10 20) POLYNOMIAL/SUMMARY;
```

produce the following **M** matrix:

$$\mathbf{M} = \begin{bmatrix} -0.4250 & -0.3606 & -0.1674 & 0.1545 & 0.7984 \\ 0.4349 & 0.2073 & -0.3252 & -0.7116 & 0.3946 \\ -0.4331 & 0.1366 & 0.7253 & -0.5108 & 0.0821 \\ 0.4926 & -0.7800 & 0.3743 & -0.0936 & 0.0066 \end{bmatrix}$$

The SUMMARY option in this example provides univariate ANOVAs for the variables defined by the rows of the above **M** matrix. In this case they represent the linear, quadratic, cubic, and quartic trends for dose, and are labeled DOSE.1, DOSE.2, DOSE.3, and DOSE.4, respectively.

HELMERT transformation Since the Helmert transformation compares a level of a repeated measure to the mean of subsequent levels, it is useful when interest lies in the point at which responses cease to change. For example, if four levels of a repeated measures factor represent responses to treatments administered over time to males and females, the statements

```
PROC GLM;
   CLASS SEX;
   MODEL RESP1-RESP4 = SEX / NOUNI;
   REPEATED TRTMNT 4 HELMERT/ CANON;
```

produce the following **M** matrix:

$$\mathbf{M} = \begin{bmatrix} 1 & -0.33333 & -0.33333 & -0.33333 \\ 0 & 1 & -0.50000 & -0.50000 \\ 0 & 0 & 1 & -1 \end{bmatrix}$$

To determine the point at which the treatment effect reaches a plateau, you can examine the canonical coefficients based on the **H** and **E** matrices corresponding to the main effect of TRTMNT, and conclude that the plateau was reached when these coefficients became small.

MEAN transformation This transformation can be useful in the same types of situations that the CONTRAST transformation is useful. For the statements in the CONTRAST section above, if you substitute

```
REPEATED DRUG 5 MEAN;
```

for the REPEATED statement in that example, the following **M** matrix is produced:

$$\mathbf{M} = \begin{bmatrix} 1 & -0.25 & -0.25 & -0.25 & -0.25 \\ -0.25 & 1 & -0.25 & -0.25 & -0.25 \\ -0.25 & -0.25 & 1 & -0.25 & -0.25 \\ -0.25 & -0.25 & -0.25 & 1 & -0.25 \end{bmatrix}$$

As with the CONTRAST transformation, if you want to omit a level other than the last, you can specify it in parentheses after the keyword MEAN in the REPEATED statement.

PROFILE transformation When a repeated measure represents a series of factors administered over time, but a polynomial response is unreasonable, a profile transformation may prove useful. As an example, consider a training program in which four different methods are employed to teach students at several different schools. The repeated measure is the score on tests administered after each of the methods is completed. The statements

```
PROC GLM;
   CLASS SCHOOL;
   MODEL T1-T4 = SCHOOL / NOUNI;
   REPEATED METHOD 4 PROFILE/SUMMARY NOM;
```

produce the following **M** matrix:

$$\mathbf{M} = \begin{bmatrix} 1 & -1 & 0 & 0 \\ 0 & 1 & -1 & 0 \\ 0 & 0 & 1 & -1 \end{bmatrix}$$

To determine at which point an improvement in test scores takes place, the analyses of variance for the transformed variables representing the differences between adjacent tests can be examined. These analyses are requested by the SUMMARY option in the REPEATED statement, and the variables are labeled METHOD.1, METHOD.2, and METHOD.3.

Least-Squares Means

Simply put, least-squares means, or *population marginal means,* are the expected value of class or subclass means that you would expect for a balanced design involving the class variable with all covariates at their mean value. This informal concept is explained further in Searle, Speed, and Milliken (1980).

To construct a least-squares mean (LSM) for a given level of a given effect, construct a set of Xs according to the following rules and use them in the linear model with the parameter estimates to yield the value of the LSM.

1. Hold all covariates (continuous variables) to their mean value.
2. Consider effects contained by the given effect. Give the Xs for levels associated with the given level a value of 1. Make the other Xs equal to 0.
3. Consider the given effect. Make the **X** associated with the given level equal to 1. Set the Xs for the other levels to 0.
4. Consider the effects that contain the given effect. If these effects are not nested within the given effect, then for the columns associated with the given level, use $1/k$ where k is the number of such columns. If these effects are nested within the given effect, then for the columns associated with the given level, use $1/k_1k_2$, where k_1 is the number of nested levels within this combination of nested effects, and k_2 is the number of such combinations. For the other columns use 0.
5. Consider the other effects not yet considered. If there are no nested factors, then use $1/j$ where j is the number of levels in the effect. If there are nested factors, use $1/j_1j_2$, where j_1 is the number of nested levels within a given combination of nested effects, and j_2 is the number of such combinations.

The consequence of these rules is that the sum of the Xs within any classification effect is 1. This set of Xs forms a linear combination of the parameters that is checked for estimability before it is evaluated.

For example, consider the model:

```
PROC GLM;
   CLASS A B C;
   MODEL Y=A B A*B C X;
   LSMEANS A B A*B C;
```

Assume A has 3 levels, B has 2, and C has 2, and assume that every combination of levels of A and B exists in the data. Assume also that the average of **X** is 12.5. Then the least-squares means are computed by the following linear combinations of the parameter estimates:

		A			B		A*B						C		X
	μ	1	2	3	1	2	11	21	31	12	22	32	1	2	.
LSM( )	1	1/3	1/3	1/3	1/2	1/2	1/6	1/6	1/6	1/6	1/6	1/6	1/2	1/2	12.5
LSM(A1)	1	1	0	0	1/2	1/2	1/2	0	0	1/2	0	0	1/2	1/2	12.5
LSM(A2)	1	0	1	0	1/2	1/2	0	1/2	0	0	1/2	0	1/2	1/2	12.5
LSM(A3)	1	0	0	1	1/2	1/2	0	0	1/2	0	0	1/2	1/2	1/2	12.5
LSM(B1)	1	1/3	1/3	1/3	1	0	1/3	1/3	1/3	0	0	0	1/2	1/2	12.5
LSM(B2)	1	1/3	1/3	1/3	0	1	0	0	0	1/3	1/3	1/3	1/2	1/2	12.5
LSM(AB11)	1	1	0	0	1	0	1	0	0	0	0	0	1/2	1/2	12.5
LSM(AB21)	1	0	1	0	1	0	0	1	0	0	0	0	1/2	1/2	12.5
LSM(AB31)	1	0	0	1	1	0	0	0	1	0	0	0	1/2	1/2	12.5
LSM(AB12)	1	1	0	0	0	1	0	0	0	1	0	0	1/2	1/2	12.5
LSM(AB22)	1	0	1	0	0	1	0	0	0	0	1	0	1/2	1/2	12.5
LSM(AB32)	1	0	0	1	0	1	0	0	0	0	0	1	1/2	1/2	12.5
LSM(C1)	1	1/3	1/3	1/3	1/2	1/2	1/6	1/6	1/6	1/6	1/6	1/6	1	0	12.5
LSM(C2)	1	1/3	1/3	1/3	1/2	1/2	1/6	1/6	1/6	1/6	1/6	1/6	0	1	12.5

Specification of ESTIMATE Expressions

For this example of the regression model:

```
MODEL Y=X1 X2 X3;
```

the associated parameters are β_0, β_1, β_2, and β_3 (where β_0 represents the intercept). To estimate $3\beta_1 + 2\beta_2$, you need the following **L** vector:

$$L = (0\ 3\ 2\ 0)\ .$$

The corresponding ESTIMATE statement is

```
ESTIMATE '3B1+2B2'  X1 3  X2 2;
```

To estimate $\beta_0+\beta_1-2\beta_3$ you need this **L** vector:

$$L = (1\ 1\ 0\ -2)\ .$$

The corresponding ESTIMATE statement is

```
ESTIMATE 'B0+B1-2B3' INTERCEPT 1 X1 1 X3 -2;
```

Now consider models involving class variables such as

```
MODEL Y=A B A*B;
```

with the associated parameters:

$$(\mu\ \alpha_1\ \alpha_2\ \alpha_3\ \beta_1\beta_2\ \alpha\beta_{11}\ \alpha\beta_{12}\ \alpha\beta_{21}\alpha\beta_{22}\ \alpha\beta_{31}\ \alpha\beta_{32})\ .$$

To estimate the least-squares mean for α_1, you need the following **L** vector:

$$L = (1\ |1\ 0\ 0\ |\ .5\ .5\ |\ .5\ .5\ 0\ 0\ 0\ 0)$$

and you could use this ESTIMATE statement:

```
ESTIMATE 'LSM(A1)' INTERCEPT 1 A 1 B .5. 5. A*B .5 .5;
```

Note in the above statement that only one element of **L** is specified following the A effect, even though A has three levels. Whenever the list of constants following an effect name is shorter than the effect's number of levels, zeros are used as the remaining constants. In the event that the list of constants is longer than the number of levels for the effect, the extra constants are ignored.

To estimate the A linear effect in the model above, assuming equally spaced levels for A, the following **L** can be used:

$$L = (0\ |\ -1\ 0\ 1\ |\ 0\ 0\ |\ -.5\ -.5\ 0\ 0\ .5\ .5)\ .$$

The ESTIMATE statement for the above **L** is written as

```
ESTIMATE 'A LINEAR' A -1 0 1;
```

If the elements of **L** are not specified for an effect that contains a specified effect, then the elements of the specified effect are equitably distributed over the levels of the higher-order effect. In addition, if the intercept is specified in an ESTIMATE or CONTRAST statement, it is distributed over all classification effects which are not contained by any other specified effect. The distribution of lower-order coefficients to higher-order effect coefficients follows the same general rules as in the LSMEANS statement and is similar to that used to construct TYPE IV **L**s. In the previous example, the -1 associated with α_1 is divided by the number of $\alpha\beta_{1j}$parameters; then each $\alpha\beta_{1j}$ coefficient is set to $-1/(\text{number of } \alpha\beta_{1j})$. The 1 associated with α_3 is distributed among the $\alpha\beta_{3j}$ parameters in a similar fashion. In the event that an unspecified effect contains several specified effects, only that specified effect with the most factors in common with the unspecified effect is used for distribution of coefficients to the higher-order effect.

Note: numerous syntactical expressions for the ESTIMATE statement were considered, including many that involved specifying the effect and level information associated with each coefficient. For models involving higher-level effects, the requirement of specifying level information would lead to very bulky specifications. Consequently, the simpler form of the ESTIMATE statement described above was implemented. The syntax of this ESTIMATE statement puts a burden on you to know *a priori* the order of the parameter list associated with each effect. The ORDER= option of the PROC GLM statement can be used to ensure that the levels of the classification effects are sorted appropriately. When you first begin to use this statement, use the E option to make sure that the actual **L** constructed is the one you envisioned.

A note on estimability Each **L** is checked for estimability using the relationship: $\mathbf{L}=\mathbf{LH}$ where $\mathbf{H}=(\mathbf{X'X})^{-}\ \mathbf{X'X}$. The **L** vector is declared non-estimable, if for any *i*

$$\text{ABS}(\mathbf{L}_i-(\mathbf{LH})_i) > \begin{cases} 1\text{E}-4 \text{ if } \mathbf{L}_i = 0 \text{ or} \\ 1\text{E}-4*\text{ABS}(\mathbf{L}_i) \text{ otherwise} \end{cases}$$

Continued fractions (like 1/3) should be specified to at least six decimal places, or the DIVISOR parameter should be used.

Printed Output

The GLM procedure produces the following printed output by default:

1. The overall analysis-of-variance table breaks down the CORRECTED TOTAL sum of squares for the dependent variable
2. into the portion attributed to the MODEL
3. and the portion attributed to ERROR.
4. The MEAN SQUARE term is the
5. SUM OF SQUARES divided by the
6. DEGREES OF FREEDOM (DF).
7. The MEAN SQUARE for ERROR, (MS(ERROR)), is an estimate of σ^2, the variance of the true errors.
8. The F VALUE is the ratio produced by dividing MS(MODEL) by MS(ERROR). It tests how well the model as a whole (adjusted for the mean) accounts for the dependent variable's behavior. An *F* test is a joint test that all parameters except the intercept are zero.
9. A small significance probability, PR>F, indicates that some linear function of the parameters is significantly different from zero.
10. R-SQUARE, R^2, measures how much variation in the dependent variable can be accounted for by the model. R^2, which can range from 0 to 1, is the ratio of the sum of squares for the model divided by the sum of squares for the corrected total. In general, the larger the value of R^2, the better the model's fit.
11. C.V., the coefficient of variation, which describes the amount of variation in the population, is 100 times the standard deviation estimate of the dependent variable, ROOT MSE, divided by the MEAN. The coefficient of variation is often a preferred measure because it is unitless.
12. ROOT MSE estimates the standard deviation of the dependent variable (or equivalently, the error term) and equals the square root of MS(ERROR).
13. MEAN is the sample mean of the dependent variable.

These tests are used primarily in analysis-of-variance applications:

14. The TYPE I SS measures incremental sums of squares for the model as each variable is added.
15. The TYPE III SS is the sum of squares that results when that variable is added last to the model.
16. The F VALUE and PR>F values for TYPE III tests in this section of the output.
17. This section of the output gives the ESTIMATES for the model PARAMETERs—the intercept and the coefficients.
18. T FOR H_0: PARAMETER=0 is the Student's *t* value for testing the null hypothesis that the parameter (if it is estimable) equals zero.
19. The significance level, PR> |T|, is the probability of getting a larger value of *t* if the parameter is truly equal to zero. A very small value for this probability leads to the conclusion that the independent variable contributes significantly to the model.

20. The STD ERROR OF ESTIMATE is the standard error of the estimate of the true value of the parameter.

EXAMPLES

Balanced Data from Randomized Complete Block with Means Comparisons and Contrasts: Example 1

Since these data are balanced, you can obtain the same answer more efficiently using the ANOVA procedure; however, GLM presents the results in a slightly different way. Notice that since the data are balanced, the Type I and Type III SS are the same and will equal the ANOVA SS.

First, the standard analysis is shown followed by a run that uses the SOLUTION option and includes MEANS and CONTRAST statements. The ORDER=DATA option in the PROC GLM statement is used so that the ordering of coefficients in the contrast statement can correspond to the ordering in the input data. The SOLUTION option requests a printout of the parameter estimates, which are only printed by default if there are no CLASS variables. A MEANS statement is used to request a printout of the means with two of the multiple comparisons procedures requested. In experiments with well understood treatment levels, CONTRAST statements are preferable to a blanket means comparison method.

```
*---------------SNAPDRAGON EXPERIMENT---------------*
| AS REPORTED BY STENSTROM, 1940, AN EXPERIMENT WAS |
| UNDERTAKEN TO INVESTIGATE HOW SNAPDRAGONS GREW IN |
| VARIOUS SOILS. EACH SOIL TYPE WAS USED IN THREE   |
| BLOCKS.                                           |
*---------------------------------------------------*;

DATA PLANTS;
   INPUT TYPE $ @;
   DO BLOCK=1 TO 3;
      INPUT STEMLENG @;
      OUTPUT;
      END;
   CARDS;
CLARION  32.7 32.3 31.5
CLINTON  32.1 29.7 29.1
KNOX     35.7 35.9 33.1
O'NEILL  36.0 34.2 31.2
COMPOST  31.8 28.0 29.2
WABASH   38.2 37.8 31.9
WEBSTER  32.5 31.1 29.7
;
PROC GLM;
   CLASS TYPE BLOCK;
   MODEL STEMLENG = TYPE BLOCK;
PROC GLM ORDER = DATA;
   CLASS TYPE BLOCK;
   MODEL STEMLENG = TYPE BLOCK / SOLUTION;
   MEANS TYPE / WALLER REGWQ;
```

```
*-TYPE-ORDER----------------------CLRN-CLTN-KNOX-ONEL-CPST-WBSH-WSTR;
  CONTRAST 'COMPOST VS OTHERS'  TYPE -1   -1   -1   -1    6   -1   -1;
  CONTRAST 'RIVER SOILS VS.NON' TYPE -1   -1   -1   -1    0    5   -1,
                                TYPE -1    4   -1   -1    0    0   -1;
  CONTRAST 'GLACIAL VS DRIFT'   TYPE -1    0    1    1    0    0   -1;
  CONTRAST 'CLARION VS WEBSTER' TYPE -1    0    0    0    0    0    1;
  CONTRAST 'KNOX VS ONEILL'     TYPE  0    0    1   -1    0    0    0;
```

Output 20.8 Standard Analysis for Randomized Complete Block: PROC GLM

```
                                                                         1

                       GENERAL LINEAR MODELS PROCEDURE

                          CLASS LEVEL INFORMATION

            CLASS     LEVELS    VALUES

            TYPE           7    CLARION CLINTON COMPOST KNOX O'NEILL WABASH WEBSTER

            BLOCK          3    1 2 3

                    NUMBER OF OBSERVATIONS IN DATA SET = 21
```

```
                                                                         2

                       GENERAL LINEAR MODELS PROCEDURE

DEPENDENT VARIABLE: STEMLENG
                      ❻            ❺               ❹              ❽            ❾           ❿            ⓫
SOURCE               DF       SUM OF SQUARES      MEAN SQUARE     F VALUE      PR > F     R-SQUARE       C.V.

MODEL                 8   ❷ 142.18857143       17.77357143       10.80       0.0002     0.878079      3.9397

ERROR                12   ❸  19.74285714    ❼  1.64523810               ⓬ ROOT MSE            STEMLENG MEAN⓭

CORRECTED TOTAL      20   ❶ 161.93142857                                 1.28266835             32.55714286
                                  ⓮                                              ⓯               ⓰
SOURCE               DF          TYPE I SS    F VALUE    PR > F       DF       TYPE III SS    F VALUE    PR > F

TYPE                  6       103.15142857      10.45    0.0004        6      103.15142857      10.45    0.0004
BLOCK                 2        39.03714286      11.86    0.0014        2       39.03714286      11.86    0.0014
```

Output 20.9 Randomized Complete Block with Means Comparisons and Contrasts: PROC GLM

```
                                                                         3

                       GENERAL LINEAR MODELS PROCEDURE

                          CLASS LEVEL INFORMATION

            CLASS     LEVELS    VALUES

            TYPE           7    CLARION CLINTON KNOX O'NEILL COMPOST WABASH WEBSTER

            BLOCK          3    1 2 3
```

```
                              NUMBER OF OBSERVATIONS IN DATA SET = 21
                                                                                                    4

                                  GENERAL LINEAR MODELS PROCEDURE

DEPENDENT VARIABLE: STEMLENG

SOURCE                  DF       SUM OF SQUARES        MEAN SQUARE      F VALUE        PR > F      R-SQUARE          C.V.

MODEL                    8         142.18857143        17.77357143        10.80        0.0002      0.878079        3.9397

ERROR                   12          19.74285714         1.64523810                   ROOT MSE                STEMLENG MEAN

CORRECTED TOTAL         20         161.93142857                                    1.28266835                  32.55714286


SOURCE                  DF            TYPE I SS    F VALUE     PR > F         DF         TYPE III SS     F VALUE     PR > F

TYPE                     6         103.15142857      10.45     0.0004          6        103.15142857       10.45     0.0004
BLOCK                    2          39.03714286      11.86     0.0014          2         39.03714286       11.86     0.0014


CONTRAST                DF                   SS    F VALUE     PR > F

COMPOST VS OTHERS        1          29.24198413      17.77     0.0012
RIVER SOILS VS.NON       2          48.24694444      14.66     0.0006
GLACIAL VS DRIFT         1          22.14083333      13.46     0.0032
CLARION VS WEBSTER       1           1.70666667       1.04     0.3285
KNOX VS ONEILL           1           1.81500000       1.10     0.3143

                                                (18)          (19)              (20)
                                             T FOR H0:      PR > |T|         STD ERROR OF
PARAMETER    (17)               ESTIMATE    PARAMETER=0                        ESTIMATE

INTERCEPT                  29.35714286 B          34.96       0.0001        0.83970354
TYPE         CLARION        1.06666667 B           1.02       0.3285        1.04729432
             CLINTON       -0.80000000 B          -0.76       0.4597        1.04729432
             KNOX           3.80000000 B           3.63       0.0035        1.04729432
             O'NEILL        2.70000000 B           2.58       0.0242        1.04729432
             COMPOST       -1.43333333 B          -1.37       0.1962        1.04729432
             WABASH         4.86666667 B           4.65       0.0006        1.04729432
             WEBSTER        0.00000000 B            .          .             .
BLOCK        1              3.32857143 B           4.85       0.0004        0.68561507
             2              1.90000000 B           2.77       0.0169        0.68561507
             3              0.00000000 B            .          .             .

NOTE: THE X'X MATRIX HAS BEEN DEEMED SINGULAR AND A GENERALIZED INVERSE HAS BEEN EMPLOYED TO SOLVE THE NORMAL EQUATIONS.
      THE ABOVE ESTIMATES REPRESENT ONLY ONE OF MANY POSSIBLE SOLUTIONS TO THE NORMAL EQUATIONS. ESTIMATES FOLLOWED BY
      THE LETTER B ARE BIASED AND DO NOT ESTIMATE THE PARAMETER BUT ARE BLUE FOR SOME LINEAR COMBINATION OF PARAMETERS
      (OR ARE ZERO). THE EXPECTED VALUE OF THE BIASED ESTIMATORS MAY BE OBTAINED FROM THE GENERAL FORM OF ESTIMABLE
      FUNCTIONS. FOR THE BIASED ESTIMATORS, THE STD ERR IS THAT OF THE BIASED ESTIMATOR AND THE T VALUE TESTS
      H0: E(BIASED ESTIMATOR) = 0. ESTIMATES NOT FOLLOWED BY THE LETTER B ARE BLUE FOR THE PARAMETER.
```

```
                                                                                                    5
                                  GENERAL LINEAR MODELS PROCEDURE

                      WALLER-DUNCAN K-RATIO T TEST FOR VARIABLE: STEMLENG
                      NOTE: THIS TEST MINIMIZES THE BAYES RISK UNDER ADDITIVE LOSS
                            AND CERTAIN OTHER ASSUMPTIONS

                               KRATIO=100  DF=12  MSE=1.64524  F=10.4495
                               CRITICAL VALUE OF T=2.12
                               MINIMUM SIGNIFICANT DIFFERENCE=2.2206

                      MEANS WITH THE SAME LETTER ARE NOT SIGNIFICANTLY DIFFERENT.

                            WALLER  GROUPING             MEAN       N  TYPE

                                            A          35.967       3  WABASH
                                            A
                                            A          34.900       3  KNOX
                                            A
                                    B       A          33.800       3  O'NEILL
                                    B
                                    B       C          32.167       3  CLARION
                                            C
                                    D       C          31.100       3  WEBSTER
                                    D       C
                                    D       C          30.300       3  CLINTON
                                    D
                                    D                  29.667       3  COMPOST
```

```
                                                                                                    6

                              GENERAL LINEAR MODELS PROCEDURE

                 RYAN-EINOT-GABRIEL-WELSCH MULTIPLE RANGE TEST FOR VARIABLE: STEMLENG
                 NOTE: THIS TEST CONTROLS THE TYPE I EXPERIMENTWISE ERROR RATE

                              ALPHA=0.05  DF=12  MSE=1.64524

             NUMBER OF MEANS         2          3          4          5          6          7
             CRITICAL RANGE    2.98765    3.28384    3.43963    3.54025    3.51781    3.66539

                 MEANS WITH THE SAME LETTER ARE NOT SIGNIFICANTLY DIFFERENT.

                       REGWQ     GROUPING              MEAN       N  TYPE

                                      A              35.967       3  WABASH
                                      A
                             B        A              34.900       3  KNOX
                             B        A
                             B        A    C         33.800       3  O'NEILL
                             B             C
                             B        D    C         32.167       3  CLARION
                                      D    C
                                      D    C         31.100       3  WEBSTER
                                      D
                                      D              30.300       3  CLINTON
                                      D
                                      D              29.667       3  COMPOST
```

Regression with Mileage Data: Example 2

A car is tested for gas mileage at various speeds to determine at what speed the car achieves the greatest gas mileage. A quadratic response surface is fit to the experimental data.

```
*-----------GASOLINE MILEAGE EXPERIMENT-------------;

DATA MILEAGE;
   INPUT MPH MPG @@;
   CARDS;
20 15.4 30 20.2 40 25.7 50 26.2 50 26.6 50 27.4 55  . 60 24.8
;
PROC GLM;
   MODEL MPG=MPH MPH*MPH / P CLM;
   OUTPUT OUT=PP P=MPGPRED R=RESID;
PROC PLOT DATA=PP;
   PLOT MPG*MPH='A' MPGPRED*MPH='P' / OVERLAY;
```

Output 20.10 Regression: PROC GLM

```
                                                                                                    1

                              GENERAL LINEAR MODELS PROCEDURE

                               DEPENDENT VARIABLE INFORMATION

                          NUMBER OF OBSERVATIONS IN DATA SET = 8

NOTE: ALL DEPENDENT VARIABLES ARE CONSISTENT WITH RESPECT TO THE PRESENCE OR ABSENCE OF MISSING VALUES. HOWEVER,
      ONLY       7 OBSERVATIONS CAN BE USED IN THIS ANALYSIS.
```

```
                                                                                                              2
                                          GENERAL LINEAR MODELS PROCEDURE

DEPENDENT VARIABLE: MPG

SOURCE                  DF     SUM OF SQUARES        MEAN SQUARE      F VALUE         PR > F      R-SQUARE          C.V.

MODEL                    2       111.80861827        55.90430913        77.96         0.0006      0.974986        3.5646

ERROR                    4         2.86852459         0.71713115                    ROOT MSE                    MPG MEAN

CORRECTED TOTAL          6       114.67714286                                     0.84683596                 23.75714286


SOURCE                  DF          TYPE I SS    F VALUE    PR > F          DF        TYPE III SS    F VALUE    PR > F

MPH                      1        85.64464286     119.43    0.0004           1        41.01171219      57.19    0.0016
MPH*MPH                  1        26.16397541      36.48    0.0038           1        26.16397541      36.48    0.0038


                                  T FOR H0:       PR > |T|          STD ERROR OF
PARAMETER             ESTIMATE   PARAMETER=0                          ESTIMATE

INTERCEPT          -5.98524590         -1.88        0.1334            3.18522249
MPH                 1.30524590          7.56        0.0016            0.17259876
MPH*MPH            -0.01309836         -6.04        0.0038            0.00216852


OBSERVATION           OBSERVED            PREDICTED              RESIDUAL         LOWER 95% CL        UPPER 95% CL
                         VALUE                VALUE                                  FOR MEAN            FOR MEAN

      1            15.40000000          14.88032787            0.51967213          12.69704271         17.06361303
      2            20.20000000          21.38360656           -1.18360656          20.01729041         22.74992270
      3            25.70000000          25.26721311            0.43278689          23.87461925         26.65980698
      4            26.20000000          26.53114754           -0.33114754          25.44574892         27.61654616
      5            26.60000000          26.53114754            0.06885246          25.44574892         27.61654616
      6            27.40000000          26.53114754            0.86885246          25.44574892         27.61654616
      7 *                    .          26.18073770                     .          24.88681059         27.47466482
      8            24.80000000          25.17540984           -0.37540984          23.05957840         27.29124127

* OBSERVATION WAS NOT USED IN THIS ANALYSIS

           SUM OF RESIDUALS                                 0.00000000
           SUM OF SQUARED RESIDUALS                         2.86852459
           SUM OF SQUARED RESIDUALS - ERROR SS             -0.00000000
           PRESS STATISTIC                                 23.18107335
           FIRST ORDER AUTOCORRELATION                     -0.54376613
           DURBIN-WATSON D                                  2.94425592
```

Output 20.11 Plot of Mileage Data

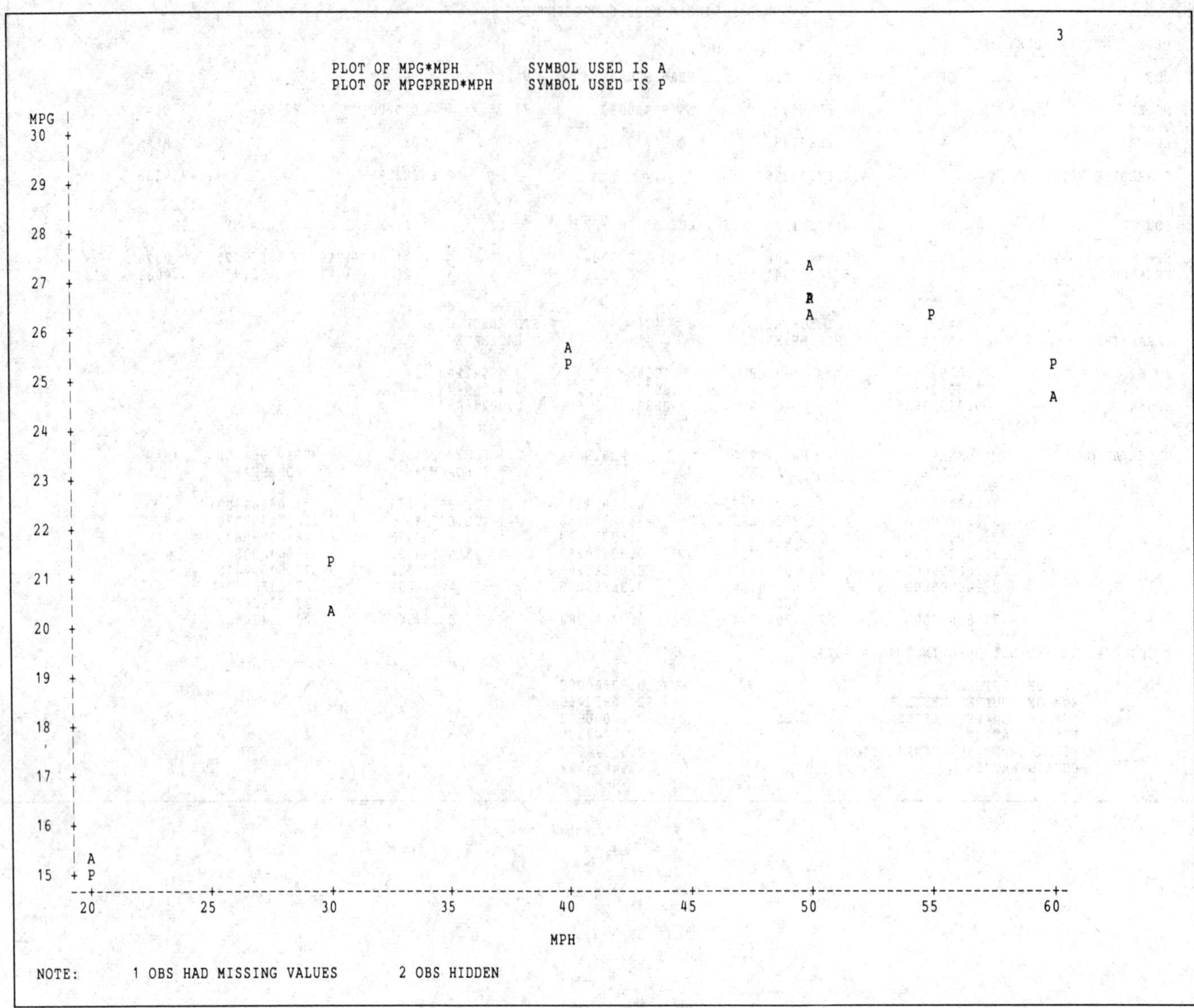

Unbalanced ANOVA for Two-Way Design with Interaction: Example 3

This example uses data from Kutner (1974) to illustrate a two-way analysis of variance. The original data source is Afifi and Azen (1972).

```
*-----------------------------------------------------------------*
| A TWO-WAY ANALYSIS OF VARIANCE EXAMPLE USING THE DATA FROM:     |
| KUTNER, MICHAEL H., THE AMERICAN STATISTICIAN, AUG.74, P.98.    |
| ORIGINAL DATA SOURCE: AFIFI AND AZEN(1972), STATISTICAL ANALYSIS:|
| A COMPUTER-ORIENTED APPROACH. ACADEMIC PRESS, NY, P.166.        |
*---------------------------------------------------------------- *;

DATA A;
   INPUT DRUG DISEASE @;
```

```
    DO I=1 TO 6;
       INPUT Y @;
       OUTPUT;
       END;
CARDS;
1 1 42 44 36 13 19 22
1 2 33  . 26  . 33 21
1 3 31 -3  . 25 25 24
2 1 28  . 23 34 42 13   KUTNER'S 24 CHANGED TO 34
2 2  . 34 33 31  . 36
2 3  3 26 28 32  4 16
3 1  .  .  1 29  . 19
3 2  . 11  9  7  1 -6
3 3 21  1  .  9  3  .
4 1 24  .  9 22 -2 15
4 2 27 12 12 -5 16 15
4 3 22  7 25  5 12  .
PROC GLM;
   CLASS DRUG DISEASE;
   MODEL Y=DRUG DISEASE DRUG*DISEASE /SS1 SS2 SS3 SS4 ;
```

Output 20.12 Unbalanced ANOVA for Two-Way Design with Interaction: PROC GLM

```
                                                                                                   1

                                    GENERAL LINEAR MODELS PROCEDURE

                                        CLASS LEVEL INFORMATION

                                      CLASS      LEVELS     VALUES

                                      DRUG            4     1 2 3 4

                                      DISEASE         3     1 2 3

                                  NUMBER OF OBSERVATIONS IN DATA SET = 72

NOTE: ALL DEPENDENT VARIABLES ARE CONSISTENT WITH RESPECT TO THE PRESENCE OR ABSENCE OF MISSING VALUES. HOWEVER,
      ONLY     58 OBSERVATIONS CAN BE USED IN THIS ANALYSIS.
```

```
                                                                                                   2

                                    GENERAL LINEAR MODELS PROCEDURE

DEPENDENT VARIABLE: Y

SOURCE                   DF       SUM OF SQUARES        MEAN SQUARE       F VALUE        PR > F     R-SQUARE          C.V.

MODEL                    11        4259.33850575       387.21259143          3.51        0.0013     0.456024       55.6675

ERROR                    46        5080.81666667       110.45253623                    ROOT MSE                     Y MEAN

CORRECTED TOTAL          57        9340.15517241                                    10.50964016                18.87931034


SOURCE                   DF          TYPE I SS    F VALUE     PR > F         DF         TYPE II SS     F VALUE     PR > F

DRUG                      3      3133.23850575       9.46     0.0001          3      3063.43286350        9.25     0.0001
DISEASE                   2       418.83374069       1.90     0.1617          2       418.83374069        1.90     0.1617
DRUG*DISEASE              6       707.26625931       1.07     0.3958          6       707.26625931        1.07     0.3958
```

(continued on next page)

(continued from previous page)

SOURCE	DF	TYPE III SS	F VALUE	PR > F	DF	TYPE IV SS	F VALUE	PR > F
DRUG	3	2997.47186048	9.05	0.0001	3	2997.47186048	9.05	0.0001
DISEASE	2	415.87304632	1.88	0.1637	2	415.87304632	1.88	0.1637
DRUG*DISEASE	6	707.26625931	1.07	0.3958	6	707.26625931	1.07	0.3958

Analysis of Covariance: Example 4

Analysis of covariance combines some of the features of regression and analysis of variance. Typically, a continuous variable (the covariate) is introduced into the model of an analysis-of-variance experiment.

Data in the following example were selected from a larger experiment on the use of drugs in the treatment of leprosy (Snedecor and Cochran 1967, p. 422).

Variables in the study are

DRUG	two antibiotics (A and D) and a control (F)
X	a pre-treatment score of leprosy bacilli
Y	a post-treatment score of leprosy bacilli.

Ten patients were selected for each treatment (DRUG), and six sites on each patient were measured for leprosy bacilli.

The covariate (a pre-treatment score) is included in the model for increased precision in determining the effect of drug treatments on the post-treatment count of bacilli.

The code for creating the data set and invoking GLM is

```
* FROM SNEDECOR AND COCHRAN (1967), STATISTICAL METHODS, P. 422.;

DATA DRUGTEST;
   INPUT DRUG $ X Y @@;
   CARDS;
A 11  6  A  8  0  A  5  2  A 14  8  A 19 11
A  6  4  A 10 13  A  6  1  A 11  8  A  3  0
D  6  0  D  6  2  D  7  3  D  8  1  D 18 18
D  8  4  D 19 14  D  8  9  D  5  1  D 15  9
F 16 13  F 13 10  F 11 18  F  9  5  F 21 23
F 16 12  F 12  5  F 12 16  F  7  1  F 12 20
;
PROC GLM;
   CLASS DRUG;
   MODEL Y=DRUG X / SOLUTION;
   LSMEANS DRUG / STDERR PDIFF;
```

Output 20.13 Analysis of Covariance: PROC GLM

```
                                                                                        1

                              GENERAL LINEAR MODELS PROCEDURE

                                  CLASS LEVEL INFORMATION

                                 CLASS      LEVELS     VALUES

                                 DRUG          3       A D F
```

```
                          NUMBER OF OBSERVATIONS IN DATA SET = 30
                                                                                        2

                              GENERAL LINEAR MODELS PROCEDURE

DEPENDENT VARIABLE: Y

SOURCE                  DF      SUM OF SQUARES        MEAN SQUARE      F VALUE       PR > F      R-SQUARE          C.V.

MODEL                    3        871.49740304       290.49913435        18.10       0.0001      0.676261       50.7060

ERROR                   26        417.20259696        16.04625373                   ROOT MSE                      Y MEAN

CORRECTED TOTAL         29       1288.70000000                                   4.00577754                   7.90000000

SOURCE                  DF      (1) TYPE I SS    F VALUE    PR > F         DF     (2) TYPE III SS    F VALUE     PR > F

DRUG                     2        293.60000000      9.15    0.0010          2         68.55371060       2.14     0.1384
X                        1        577.89740304     36.01    0.0001          1        577.89740304      36.01     0.0001

                                           T FOR H0:        PR > |T|          STD ERROR OF
PARAMETER                    ESTIMATE      PARAMETER=0                         ESTIMATE

INTERCEPT               -0.43467116 B          -0.18          0.8617           2.47135356
DRUG            A       -3.44613828 B          -1.83          0.0793           1.88678065
                D       -3.33716695 B          -1.80          0.0835           1.85386642
                F        0.00000000 B            .              .                .
X                        0.98718381             6.00          0.0001           0.16449757

NOTE: THE X'X MATRIX HAS BEEN DEEMED SINGULAR AND A GENERALIZED INVERSE HAS BEEN EMPLOYED TO SOLVE THE NORMAL EQUATIONS.
      THE ABOVE ESTIMATES REPRESENT ONLY ONE OF MANY POSSIBLE SOLUTIONS TO THE NORMAL EQUATIONS. ESTIMATES FOLLOWED BY
      THE LETTER B ARE BIASED AND DO NOT ESTIMATE THE PARAMETER BUT ARE BLUE FOR SOME LINEAR COMBINATION OF PARAMETERS
      (OR ARE ZERO). THE EXPECTED VALUE OF THE BIASED ESTIMATORS MAY BE OBTAINED FROM THE GENERAL FORM OF ESTIMABLE
      FUNCTIONS. FOR THE BIASED ESTIMATORS, THE STD ERR IS THAT OF THE BIASED ESTIMATOR AND THE T VALUE TESTS
      H0: E(BIASED ESTIMATOR) = 0. ESTIMATES NOT FOLLOWED BY THE LETTER B ARE BLUE FOR THE PARAMETER.
```

```
                                                                                        3

                              GENERAL LINEAR MODELS PROCEDURE

                                   LEAST SQUARES MEANS
          (3)                               (4)                           (5)
          DRUG              Y          STD ERR     PROB > |T|     PROB > |T| H0: LSMEAN(I)=LSMEAN(J)
                       LSMEAN           LSMEAN    H0:LSMEAN=0     I/J      1        2        3

          A         6.7149635        1.2884943         0.0001     1        .     0.9521   0.0793
          D         6.8239348        1.2724690         0.0001     2   0.9521       .      0.0835
          F        10.1611017        1.3159234         0.0001     3   0.0793   0.0835      .

NOTE: TO ENSURE OVERALL PROTECTION LEVEL, ONLY PROBABILITIES ASSOCIATED WITH PRE-PLANNED COMPARISONS SHOULD BE USED.
```

The numbers on the printout correspond to the numbered descriptions that follow:

1. The TYPE I SS for DRUG gives the between-drug sums of squares that would be obtained for the analysis-of-variance model Y=DRUG.
2. TYPE III SS for DRUG gives the DRUG SS "adjusted" for the covariate.

3. The LSMEANS printed are the same as adjusted means (means adjusted for the covariate).
4. The STDERR option on the LSMEANS statement causes the standard error of the least-squares means and the probability of getting a larger $|t|$ value under the hypothesis H_0:LSM=0 to be printed.
5. Specifying the PDIFF option causes all probability values for the hypothesis H_0: LSM(I)=LSM(J) to be printed.

Three-Way Analysis of Variance with Contrasts: Example 5

This example uses data from Cochran and Cox (1957, p. 176) to illustrate a three-way factorial design with replication and two uses of the CONTRAST statement. The object of the study is to determine the effects of electric current on denervated muscle.

The variables are

REP	the replicate number, 1 or 2
TIME	the length of time the current was applied to the muscle, ranging from 1 to 4
CURRENT	the level of electric current applied, ranging from 1 to 4
NUMBER	the number of treatments per day, ranging from 1 to 3
Y	the weight of the denervated muscle.

The code for creating the data set and invoking PROC GLM follows:

```
DATA ONE;
   DO REP=1 TO 2;
      DO TIME=1 TO 4;
         DO CURRENT = 1 TO 4;
            DO NUMBER = 1 TO 3;
               INPUT Y @@;
               OUTPUT;
               END;
            END;
         END;
      END;
   CARDS;
72 74 69 61 61 65 62 65 70 85 76 61
67 52 62 60 55 59 64 65 64 67 72 60
57 66 72 72 43 43 63 66 72 56 75 92
57 56 78 60 63 58 61 79 68 73 86 71
46 74 58 60 64 52 71 64 71 53 65 66
44 58 54 57 55 51 62 61 79 60 78 82
53 50 61 56 57 56 56 56 71 56 58 69
46 55 64 56 55 57 64 66 62 59 58 88
PROC GLM;
   CLASS REP CURRENT TIME NUMBER;
   MODEL Y =  REP CURRENT|TIME|NUMBER;
   CONTRAST 'TIME IN CURRENT 3'
   TIME 1 0 0 -1 CURRENT*TIME 0 0 0 0 0 0 0 0 1 0 0 -1,
   TIME 0 1 0 -1 CURRENT*TIME 0 0 0 0 0 0 0 0 0 1 0 -1,
   TIME 0 0 1 -1 CURRENT*TIME 0 0 0 0 0 0 0 0 0 0 1 -1;
   CONTRAST 'CURR 1 VS. CURR 2' CURRENT 1 -1;
```

The first contrast statement examines the effects of TIME within level 3 of CURRENT. Note that since there are three degrees of freedom, it is necessary to specify three rows in the CONTRAST statement, separated by commas. Since the parameterization that PROC GLM uses is determined in part by the ordering of the variables in the CLASS statement, CURRENT was specified before TIME so that the TIME parameters would be nested within the CURRENT*TIME parameters; thus the CURRENT*TIME parameters in each row are simply the TIME parameters of that row within the appropriate level of CURRENT.

The second CONTRAST statement isolates a single degree of freedom effect corresponding to the difference between the first two levels of CURRENT. Such a contrast can be useful in a large experiment where certain pre-planned comparisons are important, but it is desired to take advantage of the additional error degrees of freedom available when all levels of the factors are considered.

Output 20.14 Three-Way Analysis of Variance with Contrasts: PROC GLM

```
                                                                                                    1

                                  GENERAL LINEAR MODELS PROCEDURE

                                     CLASS LEVEL INFORMATION

                                   CLASS       LEVELS    VALUES

                                   REP              2    1 2

                                   CURRENT          4    1 2 3 4

                                   TIME             4    1 2 3 4

                                   NUMBER           3    1 2 3

                               NUMBER OF OBSERVATIONS IN DATA SET = 96
```

```
                                                                                                    2

                                  GENERAL LINEAR MODELS PROCEDURE

DEPENDENT VARIABLE: Y

SOURCE                  DF      SUM OF SQUARES        MEAN SQUARE       F VALUE        PR > F      R-SQUARE          C.V.

MODEL                   48       5782.91666667       120.47743056          1.77        0.0261      0.643805       13.0511

ERROR                   47       3199.48958333        68.07424645                   ROOT MSE                       Y MEAN

CORRECTED TOTAL         95       8982.40625000                                     8.25071188                  63.21875000


SOURCE                  DF         TYPE I SS    F VALUE    PR > F          DF       TYPE III SS    F VALUE      PR > F

REP                      1      605.01041667       8.89    0.0045           1      605.01041667       8.89      0.0045
CURRENT                  3     2145.44791667      10.51    0.0001           3     2145.44791667      10.51      0.0001
TIME                     3      223.11458333       1.09    0.3616           3      223.11458333       1.09      0.3616
CURRENT*TIME             9      298.67708333       0.49    0.8756           9      298.67708333       0.49      0.8756
NUMBER                   2      447.43750000       3.29    0.0461           2      447.43750000       3.29      0.0461
CURRENT*NUMBER           6      644.39583333       1.58    0.1747           6      644.39583333       1.58      0.1747
TIME*NUMBER              6      367.97916667       0.90    0.5023           6      367.97916667       0.90      0.5023
CURRENT*TIME*NUMBER     18     1050.85416667       0.86    0.6276          18     1050.85416667       0.86      0.6276


CONTRAST                DF                SS    F VALUE    PR > F

TIME IN CURRENT 3        3       34.83333333       0.17    0.9157
CURR 1 VS. CURR 2        1       99.18750000       1.46    0.2334
```

Multivariate Analysis of Variance: Example 6

Using data from A. Anderson, Oregon State University, this example performs a multivariate analysis of variance.

```
*---------MULTIVARIATE ANALYSIS OF VARIANCE-------*
| DATA FROM A. ANDERSON, OREGON STATE UNIVERSITY. |
| FOUR DIFFERENT RESPONSE VARIABLES ARE MEASURED. |
| THE HYPOTHESIS THAT WE WANT TO TEST IS THAT SEX |
| DOES NOT AFFECT ANY OF THE FOUR RESPONSES.      |
*-------------------------------------------------*;

DATA SKULL;
   INPUT SEX $ LENGTH BASILAR ZYGOMAT POSTORB @@;
   CARDS;
M 6460 4962 3286 1100 M 6252 4773 3239 1061 M 5772 4480 3200 1097
M 6264 4806 3179 1054 M 6622 5113 3365 1071 M 6656 5100 3326 1012
M 6441 4918 3153 1061 M 6281 4821 3133 1071 M 6606 5060 3227 1064
M 6573 4977 3392 1110 M 6563 5025 3234 1090 M 6552 5086 3292 1010
M 6535 4939 3261 1065 M 6573 4962 3320 1091 M 6537 4990 3309 1059
M 6302 4761 3204 1135 M 6449 4921 3256 1068 M 6481 4887 3233 1124
M 6368 4824 3258 1130 M 6372 4844 3306 1137 M 6592 5007 3284 1148
M 6229 4746 3257 1153 M 6391 4834 3244 1169 M 6560 4981 3341 1038
M 6787 5181 3334 1104 M 6384 4834 3195 1064 M 6282 4757 3180 1179
M 6340 4791 3300 1110 M 6394 4879 3272 1241 M 6153 4557 3214 1039
M 6348 4886 3160  991 M 6534 4990 3310 1028 M 6509 4951 3282 1104
F 6287 4845 3218  996 F 6583 4992 3300 1107 F 6518 5023 3246 1035
F 6432 4790 3249 1117 F 6450 4888 3259 1060 F 6379 4844 3266 1115
F 6424 4855 3322 1065 F 6615 5088 3280 1179 F 6760 5206 3337 1219
F 6521 5011 3208  989 F 6416 4889 3200 1001 F 6511 4910 3230 1100
F 6540 4997 3320 1078 F 6780 5259 3358 1174 F 6336 4781 3165 1126
F 6472 4954 3125 1178 F 6476 4896 3148 1066 F 6276 4709 3150 1134
F 6693 5177 3236 1131 F 6328 4792 3214 1018 F 6661 5104 3395 1141
F 6266 4721 3257 1031 F 6660 5146 3374 1069 F 6624 5032 3384 1154
F 6331 4819 3278 1008 F 6298 4683 3270 1150
;
PROC GLM;
   CLASS SEX;
   MODEL LENGTH BASILAR ZYGOMAT POSTORB = SEX;
   MANOVA H=SEX / PRINTE PRINTH;
   TITLE 'MULTIVARIATE ANALYSIS OF VARIANCE';
```

Output 20.15 Multivariate Analysis of Variance: PROC GLM

```
                    MULTIVARIATE ANALYSIS OF VARIANCE                        1

                     GENERAL LINEAR MODELS PROCEDURE

                       CLASS LEVEL INFORMATION

                       CLASS     LEVELS    VALUES

                       SEX            2    F M


                 NUMBER OF OBSERVATIONS IN DATA SET = 59
```

```
                              MULTIVARIATE ANALYSIS OF VARIANCE                                           2
                               GENERAL LINEAR MODELS PROCEDURE
DEPENDENT VARIABLE: LENGTH
SOURCE                   DF        SUM OF SQUARES        MEAN SQUARE        F VALUE        PR > F      R-SQUARE          C.V.
MODEL                     1        47060.93163052     47060.93163052           1.59        0.2119      0.027201        2.6624
ERROR                    57      1683039.20396301     29527.00357830                     ROOT MSE                 LENGTH MEAN
CORRECTED TOTAL          58      1730100.13559353                                    171.83423285               6454.22033898

SOURCE                   DF           TYPE I SS    F VALUE    PR > F           DF       TYPE III SS    F VALUE    PR > F
SEX                       1      47060.93163052       1.59    0.2119            1    47060.93163052       1.59    0.2119
```

```
                              MULTIVARIATE ANALYSIS OF VARIANCE                                           3
                               GENERAL LINEAR MODELS PROCEDURE
DEPENDENT VARIABLE: BASILAR
SOURCE                   DF        SUM OF SQUARES        MEAN SQUARE        F VALUE        PR > F      R-SQUARE          C.V.
MODEL                     1        23985.10578405     23985.10578405           1.02        0.3174      0.017539        3.1229
ERROR                    57      1343555.19930095     23571.14384739                     ROOT MSE                BASILAR MEAN
CORRECTED TOTAL          58      1367540.30508500                                    153.52896745               4916.16949153

SOURCE                   DF           TYPE I SS    F VALUE    PR > F           DF       TYPE III SS    F VALUE    PR > F
SEX                       1      23985.10578405       1.02    0.3174            1    23985.10578405       1.02    0.3174
```

```
                              MULTIVARIATE ANALYSIS OF VARIANCE                                           4
                               GENERAL LINEAR MODELS PROCEDURE
DEPENDENT VARIABLE: ZYGOMAT
SOURCE                   DF        SUM OF SQUARES        MEAN SQUARE        F VALUE        PR > F      R-SQUARE          C.V.
MODEL                     1           66.95272806        66.95272806           0.01        0.9045      0.000255        2.0823
ERROR                    57       262647.62354317      4607.85304462                     ROOT MSE                ZYGOMAT MEAN
CORRECTED TOTAL          58       262714.57627124                                     67.88116856               3259.91525424

SOURCE                   DF           TYPE I SS    F VALUE    PR > F           DF       TYPE III SS    F VALUE    PR > F
SEX                       1         66.95272806       0.01    0.9045            1       66.95272806       0.01    0.9045
```

```
                              MULTIVARIATE ANALYSIS OF VARIANCE                                           5
                               GENERAL LINEAR MODELS PROCEDURE
DEPENDENT VARIABLE: POSTORB
SOURCE                   DF        SUM OF SQUARES        MEAN SQUARE        F VALUE        PR > F      R-SQUARE          C.V.
MODEL                     1          192.91266643       192.91266643           0.06        0.8132      0.000987        5.3592
ERROR                    57       195162.71445222      3423.90727109                     ROOT MSE                POSTORB MEAN
CORRECTED TOTAL          58       195355.62711865                                     58.51416300               1091.84745763

SOURCE                   DF           TYPE I SS    F VALUE    PR > F           DF       TYPE III SS    F VALUE    PR > F
SEX                       1        192.91266643       0.06    0.8132            1      192.91266643       0.06    0.8132
```

MULTIVARIATE ANALYSIS OF VARIANCE 6

GENERAL LINEAR MODELS PROCEDURE

E = ERROR SS&CP MATRIX

DF=57	LENGTH	BASILAR	ZYGOMAT	POSTORB
LENGTH	1683039.20396301	1430839.75174861	386107.03613056	74382.90326344
BASILAR	1430839.75174861	1343555.19930095	324249.61888114	38106.47202801
ZYGOMAT	386107.03613056	324249.61888114	262647.62354317	33070.58857810
POSTORB	74382.90326344	38106.47202801	33070.58857810	195162.71445222

PARTIAL CORRELATION COEFFICIENTS FROM THE ERROR SS&CP MATRIX / PROB > |R|

DF=56	LENGTH	BASILAR	ZYGOMAT	POSTORB
LENGTH	1.000000	0.951516	0.580729	0.129786
	0.0000	0.0001	0.0001	0.3315
BASILAR	0.951516	1.000000	0.545840	0.074417
	0.0001	0.0000	0.0001	0.5788
ZYGOMAT	0.580729	0.545840	1.000000	0.146069
	0.0001	0.0001	0.0000	0.2739
POSTORB	0.129786	0.074417	0.146069	1.000000
	0.3315	0.5788	0.2739	0.0000

MULTIVARIATE ANALYSIS OF VARIANCE 7

GENERAL LINEAR MODELS PROCEDURE

H = TYPE III SS&CP MATRIX FOR: SEX

DF=1	LENGTH	BASILAR	ZYGOMAT	POSTORB
LENGTH	47060.93163052	33597.04486192	1775.06556438	3013.07978744
BASILAR	33597.04486192	23985.10578405	1267.22857651	2151.05339576
ZYGOMAT	1775.06556438	1267.22857651	66.95272806	113.64871005
POSTORB	3013.07978744	2151.05339576	113.64871005	192.91266643

CHARACTERISTIC ROOTS AND VECTORS OF: E INVERSE * H, WHERE H = TYPE III SS&CP MATRIX FOR: SEX E = ERROR SS&CP MATRIX

CHARACTERISTIC ROOT	PERCENT	CHARACTERISTIC VECTOR V'EV=1 LENGTH	BASILAR	ZYGOMAT	POSTORB
0.04525085	100.00	-0.00181900	0.00111840	0.00115382	-0.00005517
0.00000000	0.00	0.00020100	-0.00039597	0.00209834	0.00003958
0.00000000	0.00	0.00011655	-0.00035160	-0.00016657	0.00219820
0.00000000	0.00	-0.00186772	0.00255844	-0.00016772	0.00074290

MULTIVARIATE ANALYSIS OF VARIANCE 8

GENERAL LINEAR MODELS PROCEDURE

MANOVA TEST CRITERIA FOR THE HYPOTHESIS OF NO OVERALL SEX EFFECT

```
H = TYPE III SS&CP MATRIX FOR: SEX
E = ERROR SS&CP MATRIX
P = RANK OF (H+E)      =     4
Q = HYPOTHESIS DF      =     1
NE= DF OF E            =    57
S = MIN(P,Q)           =     1
M = .5(ABS(P-Q)-1)     =   1.0
N = .5(NE-P)           =  26.5
```

```
WILKS' CRITERION      L = DET(E)/DET(H+E) =      0.95670815     (SEE RAO 1973 P 555)

        EXACT F = (1-L)/L*(NE+Q-P)/P                          WITH P AND NE+Q-P DF

              F(4,54) =      0.61      PROB > F = 0.6566
```

(continued on next page)

(continued from previous page)

```
---------------------------------------------------------------------------------------------

PILLAI'S TRACE          V = TR(H*INV(H+E)) =          0.04329185      (SEE PILLAI'S TABLE #2)

        F APPROXIMATION = (2N+S)/(2M+S+1) * V/(S-V)               WITH S(2M+S+1) AND S(2N+S) DF

              F(4,54) =      0.61      PROB > F = 0.6566
---------------------------------------------------------------------------------------------

HOTELLING-LAWLEY TRACE = TR(E**-1*H) =               0.04525085      (SEE PILLAI'S TABLE #3)

        F APPROXIMATION = (2S*N-S+2)*TR(E**-1*H)/(S*S*(2M+S+1)) WITH S(2M+S+1) AND 2S*N-S+2 DF

              F(4,54) =      0.61      PROB > F = 0.6566

---------------------------------------------------------------------------------------------

ROY'S MAXIMUM ROOT CRITERION =                       0.04525085      (SEE AMS VOL 31 P 625)

        FIRST CANONICAL VARIABLE YIELDS AN F UPPER BOUND

              F(4,54) =      0.61      PROB > F = 0.6566

---------------------------------------------------------------------------------------------
```

Repeated Measures Analysis of Variance: Example 7

This example uses data from Cole and Grizzle (1966) to illustrate a commonly occurring repeated measures ANOVA design. Sixteen dogs were randomly assigned to four groups. (One animal is removed from the analysis due to a missing value for one dependent variable.) Dogs in each group received either morphine or trimethaphan (variable DRUG) and had either depleted or intact histamine levels (variable DEPL) before receiving the drugs. The dependent variable is the blood concentration of histamine at 0, 1, 3 and 5 minutes after injection of the drug. Logarithms were applied to these concentrations to minimize correlation between the mean and the variance of the data.

The SAS statements to produce the data set and perform both univariate and multivariate repeated measures analyses are as follows:

```
DATA DOGS;
   INPUT DRUG $ DEPL $ HISTO HIST1 HIST3 HIST5;
   LHISTO = LOG(HISTO); LHIST1 = LOG(HIST1);
   LHIST3 = LOG(HIST3); LHIST5 = LOG(HIST5);
   CARDS;
MORPHINE N  .04  .20  .10  .08
MORPHINE N  .02  .06  .02  .02
MORPHINE N  .07 1.40  .48  .24
MORPHINE N  .17  .57  .35  .24
MORPHINE Y  .10  .09  .13  .14
MORPHINE Y  .12  .11  .10   .
MORPHINE Y  .07  .07  .06  .07
MORPHINE Y  .05  .07  .06  .07
TRIMETH  N  .03  .62  .31  .22
TRIMETH  N  .03 1.05  .73  .60
TRIMETH  N  .07  .83 1.07  .80
TRIMETH  N  .09 3.13 2.06 1.23
TRIMETH  Y  .10  .09  .09  .08
TRIMETH  Y  .08  .09  .09  .10
TRIMETH  Y  .13  .10  .12  .12
TRIMETH  Y  .06  .05  .05  .05
;
```

```
PROC GLM;
   CLASS DRUG DEPL;
   MODEL LHIST0--LHIST5 = DRUG DEPL DRUG*DEPL/NOUNI;
   REPEATED TIME 4 (0 1 3 5) POLYNOMIAL/SHORT SUMMARY;
```

The NOUNI option in the MODEL statement suppresses the individual ANOVAs for the original dependent variables. These analyses are usually of no interest in a repeated measures analysis. The POLYNOMIAL option in the REPEATED statement indicates that the transformation used to implement the repeated measures analysis is an orthogonal polynomial transformation, and the SUMMARY option requests that the univariate analyses for the orthogonal polynomial contrast variables be printed. The parenthetical numbers (0 1 3 5) determine the spacing of the orthogonal polynomials used in the analysis.

Output 20.16 Repeated Measures Analysis of Variance: PROC GLM

```
                                                                                              1

                              GENERAL LINEAR MODELS PROCEDURE

                                  CLASS LEVEL INFORMATION

                             CLASS      LEVELS      VALUES

                             DRUG           2       MORPHINE TRIMETH

                             DEPL           2       N Y

                            NUMBER OF OBSERVATIONS IN DATA SET = 16

NOTE: WHEN A REPEATED STATEMENT IS SPECIFIED, NO OBSERVATIONS
      WITH MISSING VALUES ARE USED. THUS, ONLY       15
      OBSERVATIONS CAN BE USED IN THIS ANALYSIS.
```

```
                                                                                              2

                              GENERAL LINEAR MODELS PROCEDURE

                            REPEATED MEASURES ANALYSIS OF VARIANCE

                              REPEATED MEASURES LEVEL INFORMATION

                   DEPENDENT VARIABLE      LHIST0    LHIST1    LHIST3    LHIST5

                        LEVEL OF TIME           0         1         3         5

         MANOVA TEST CRITERIA AND EXACT F STATISTICS FOR THE HYPOTHESIS OF NO TIME EFFECT;
                    H = TYPE III SS&CP MATRIX FOR: TIME    E = ERROR SS&CP MATRIX

                                     S=1     M=0.5     N=4

     STATISTIC                      VALUE              F           NUM DF         DEN DF      PR > F

     WILKS' LAMBDA              0.1109771         24.033                3              9      0.0001
     PILLAI'S TRACE             0.8890229         24.033                3              9      0.0001
     HOTELLING-LAWLEY TRACE      8.010871         24.033                3              9      0.0001
     ROY'S GREATEST ROOT         8.010871         24.033                3              9      0.0001
```

(continued on next page)

(continued from previous page)

MANOVA TEST CRITERIA AND EXACT F STATISTICS FOR THE HYPOTHESIS OF NO TIME*DRUG EFFECT;
H = TYPE III SS&CP MATRIX FOR: TIME*DRUG E = ERROR SS&CP MATRIX

S=1 M=0.5 N=4

STATISTIC	VALUE	F	NUM DF	DEN DF	PR > F
WILKS' LAMBDA	0.3415598	5.783	3	9	0.0175
PILLAI'S TRACE	0.6584402	5.783	3	9	0.0175
HOTELLING-LAWLEY TRACE	1.927745	5.783	3	9	0.0175
ROY'S GREATEST ROOT	1.927745	5.783	3	9	0.0175

MANOVA TEST CRITERIA AND EXACT F STATISTICS FOR THE HYPOTHESIS OF NO TIME*DEPL EFFECT;
H = TYPE III SS&CP MATRIX FOR: TIME*DEPL E = ERROR SS&CP MATRIX

S=1 M=0.5 N=4

STATISTIC	VALUE	F	NUM DF	DEN DF	PR > F
WILKS' LAMBDA	0.1233999	21.311	3	9	0.0002
PILLAI'S TRACE	0.8766001	21.311	3	9	0.0002
HOTELLING-LAWLEY TRACE	7.103736	21.311	3	9	0.0002
ROY'S GREATEST ROOT	7.103736	21.311	3	9	0.0002

3

MANOVA TEST CRITERIA AND EXACT F STATISTICS FOR THE HYPOTHESIS OF NO TIME*DRUG*DEPL EFFECT;
H = TYPE III SS&CP MATRIX FOR: TIME*DRUG*DEPL E = ERROR SS&CP MATRIX

S=1 M=0.5 N=4

STATISTIC	VALUE	F	NUM DF	DEN DF	PR > F
WILKS' LAMBDA	0.1938301	12.477	3	9	0.0015
PILLAI'S TRACE	0.8061699	12.477	3	9	0.0015
HOTELLING-LAWLEY TRACE	4.159157	12.477	3	9	0.0015
ROY'S GREATEST ROOT	4.159157	12.477	3	9	0.0015

4

GENERAL LINEAR MODELS PROCEDURE

TESTS OF HYPOTHESES FOR BETWEEN SUBJECTS EFFECTS

SOURCE	DF	TYPE III SS	MEAN SQUARE	F VALUE	PR > F
DRUG	1	5.99336243	5.99336243	2.71	0.1281
DEPL	1	15.44840703	15.44840703	6.98	0.0229
DRUG*DEPL	1	4.69087508	4.69087508	2.12	0.1734
ERROR	11	24.34683348	2.21334850		

5

GENERAL LINEAR MODELS PROCEDURE

UNIVARIATE TESTS OF HYPOTHESES FOR WITHIN SUBJECT EFFECTS

SOURCE	DF	TYPE III SS	MEAN SQUARE	F VALUE	PR > F	ADJ PR > F G - G	ADJ PR > F H - F
TIME	3	12.05898677	4.01966226	53.44	0.0001	0.0001	0.0001
TIME*DRUG	3	1.84429514	0.61476505	8.17	0.0003	0.0039	0.0008
TIME*DEPL	3	12.08978557	4.02992852	53.57	0.0001	0.0001	0.0001
TIME*DRUG*DEPL	3	2.93077939	0.97692646	12.99	0.0001	0.0005	0.0001
ERROR(TIME)	33	2.48238887	0.07522391				

GREENHOUSE-GEISSER EPSILON = 0.5694
HUYNH-FELDT EPSILON = 0.8475

6

ANALYSIS OF VARIANCE OF CONTRAST VARIABLES

TIME.N REPRESENTS THE NTH DEGREE POLYNOMIAL CONTRAST FOR TIME

CONTRAST VARIABLE: TIME.1

SOURCE	DF	TYPE III SS	MEAN SQUARE	F VALUE	PR > F
MEAN	1	2.00963483	2.00963483	34.99	0.0001
DRUG	1	1.18069076	1.18069076	20.56	0.0009
DEPL	1	1.36172504	1.36172504	23.71	0.0005
DRUG*DEPL	1	2.04346848	2.04346848	35.58	0.0001
ERROR	11	0.63171161	0.05742833		

CONTRAST VARIABLE: TIME.2

SOURCE	DF	TYPE III SS	MEAN SQUARE	F VALUE	PR > F
MEAN	1	5.40988418	5.40988418	57.15	0.0001
DRUG	1	0.59173192	0.59173192	6.25	0.0295
DEPL	1	5.94945506	5.94945506	62.86	0.0001
DRUG*DEPL	1	0.67031587	0.67031587	7.08	0.0221
ERROR	11	1.04118707	0.09465337		

CONTRAST VARIABLE: TIME.3

SOURCE	DF	TYPE III SS	MEAN SQUARE	F VALUE	PR > F
MEAN	1	4.63946776	4.63946776	63.04	0.0001
DRUG	1	0.07187246	0.07187246	0.98	0.3443
DEPL	1	4.77860547	4.77860547	64.94	0.0001
DRUG*DEPL	1	0.21699504	0.21699504	2.95	0.1139
ERROR	11	0.80949018	0.07359002		

REFERENCES

Afifi, A.A. and Azen, S.P. (1972), *Statistical Analysis: A Computer-Oriented Approach*, New York: Academic Press.

Anderson, T.W. (1952), *An Introduction to Multivariate Statistical Analysis*, New York: John Wiley & Sons.

Anderson, T.W. (1958), *An Introduction to Multivariate Statistical Analysis*, New York: John Wiley & Sons.

Begun, J.M. and Gabriel, K.R. (1981), "Closure of the Newman-Keuls Multiple Comparisons Procedure," *Journal of the American Statistical Association*, 76, 374.

Box, G.E.P. (1954), "Some Theorems on Quadratic Forms Applied in the Study of Analysis of Variance Problems," II, Effects of Inequality of Variance and of Correlation Between Errors in the Two-Way Classification, *Annals of Mathematical Statistics, 25*, 484-498.

Carmer, S.G. and Swanson, M.R. (1973), "Evaluation of Ten Pairwise Multiple Comparison Procedures by Monte-Carlo Methods," *Journal of the American Statistical Association*, 68, 66-74.

Cole, I.W.L and Grizzle, I.E. (1966), "Applications of Multivariate Analysis of Variance to Repeated Measures Experiments," *Biometrics*, 22, 810-828.

Draper, N.R. and Smith, H. (1966), *Applied Regression Analysis*, New York: John Wiley & Sons.

Duncan, D.B. (1975), "*t*-Tests and Intervals for Comparisons Suggested by the Data," *Biometrics*, 31, 339-359.

Dunnett, C.W. (1980), "Pairwise Multiple Comparisons in the Homogeneous Variance, Unequal Sample Size Case," *Journal of the American Statistical Association*, 75, 372.

Einot, I. and Gabriel, K.R. (1975), "A Study of the Powers of Several Methods of Multiple Comparisons," *Journal of the American Statistical Association*, 70, 351.

Freund, R.J. and Littell, R. (1981), *SAS For Linear Models*, Cary, NC: SAS Institute Inc.

Gabriel, K.R. (1978), "A Simple Method of Multiple Comparisons of Means," *Journal of the American Statistical Association*, 73, 364.

Games, P.A. (1977), "An Improved *t* Table for Simultaneous Control on g Contrasts," *Journal of the American Statistical Association*, 72, 359.

Goodnight, J.H. (1976), "The New General Linear Models Procedure," *Proceedings of the First International SAS Users' Meeting*, Cary, NC: SAS Institute Inc.

Goodnight, J.H. (1978), *Tests of Hypothesis in Fixed Effects Linear Models*, SAS Technical Report R-101, Cary, NC: SAS Institute Inc.

Goodnight, J.H. (1979), "A Tutorial on the Sweep Operator," *American Statistician*, 33, 149-158. (Also available as SAS Technical Report R-106.)

Goodnight, J.H. and Harvey, W.R. (1978), *Least Squares Means in the Fixed Effects General Linear Model*, SAS Technical Report R-103, Cary, NC: SAS Institute Inc.

Goodnight, J.H. and Speed, F.M. (1978), *Computing Expected Mean Squares*, SAS Technical Report R-102, Cary, NC: SAS Institute Inc.

Graybill, F.A. (1961), *An Introduction to Linear Statistical Models, Volume I*, New York: McGraw-Hill.

Greenhouse, S.W. and Geisser, S. (1959), "On Methods in the Analysis of Profile Data," *Psychometrika*, 32(3), 95-112.

Harvey, Walter R. (1975), *Least-squares Analysis of Data with Unequal Subclass Numbers*, USDA Report ARS H-4.

Heck, D.L. (1960), "Charts of Some Upper Percentage Points of the Distribution of the Largest Characteristic Root," *Annals of Mathematical Statistics*, 31, 625-642.

Hochburg, Y. (1974), "Some Conservative Generalizations of the T-Method in Simultaneous Inference," *Journal of Multivariate Analysis*, 4, 224-234.

Hocking, R.R. (1976), "The Analysis and Selection of Variables in a Linear Regression," *Biometrics*, 32, 1-50.

Huynh, H. and Feldt, L. S. (1970), "Conditions under Which Mean Square Ratios in Repeated Measurements Designs Have Exact F-Distributions," *Journal of the American Statistical Association*, 65, 1582-1589.

Huynh, H. and Feldt, L.S. (1976), "Estimation of the Box Correction for Degrees of Freedom from Sample Data in the Randomized Block and Split Plot Designs," *Journal of Educational Statistics*, 1, 69-82.

Kennedy, W.J., Jr. and Gentle, J.E. (1980), *Statistical Computing*, Chapter 9, New York: Marcel Dekker.

Kramer, C.Y. (1956), "Extension of Multiple Range Tests to Group Means with Unequal Numbers of Replications," *Biometrics*, 12, 307-310.

Kutner, M.H. (1974), "Hypothesis Testing in Linear Models (Eisenhart Model)," *American Statistician*, 28, 98-100.

LaTour, S.A. and Miniard, P.W. (1983), "The Misuse of Repeated Measures Analysis in Marketing Research," *Journal of Marketing Research*, XX, 45-57.

Marcus, R., Peritz, E., and Gabriel, K.R. (1976), "On Closed Testing Procedures with Special Reference to Ordered Analysis of Variance," *Biometrika*, 63, 655-660.

Miller, R.G., Jr. (1981), *Simultaneous Statistical Inference*, New York: Springer-Verlag.

Morrison, D. F. (1970), *Multivariate Statistical Methods*, Second Edition, New York: McGraw Hill.

Morrison, D.F. (1976), *Multivariate Statistical Methods*, Second Edition, New York: McGraw-Hill.

Petrinovich, L.F. and Hardyck, C.D. (1969), "Error Rates for Multiple Comparison Methods: Some Evidence Concerning the Frequency of Erroneous Conclusions," *Psychological Bulletin*, 71, 43-54.

Pillai, K.C.S. (1960), *Statistical Tables for Tests of Multivariate Hypotheses*, Manila: The Statistical Center, University of the Philippines.

Pringle, R.M. and Raynor, A.A. (1971), *Generalized Inverse Matrices with Applications to Statistics*, New York: Hafner Publishing Company.

Ramsey, P.H. (1978), "Power Differences Between Pairwise Multiple Comparisons," *Journal of the American Statistical Association*, 73, 363.

Rao, C.R. (1965), *Linear Statistical Inference and Its Applications*, New York: John Wiley & Sons.

Ryan, T.A. (1959), "Multiple Comparisons in Psychological Research," *Psychological Bulletin*, 56, 26-47.

Ryan, T.A. (1960), "Significance Tests for Multiple Comparison of Proportions, Variances, and Other Statistics," *Psychological Bulleting*, 57, 318-328.

Schatzoff, M. (1966), "Exact Distributions of Wilks' Likelihood Ratio Criterion," *Biometrika*, 53, 347-358.

Scheffe, H. (1953), "A Method for Judging All Contrasts in the Analysis of Variance," *Biometrika*, 40, 87-104.

Scheffe, H. (1959), *The Analysis of Variance*, New York: John Wiley & Sons.

Searle, S.R. (1971), *Linear Models*, New York: John Wiley & Sons.

Searle, S.R., Speed, F.M., and Milliken, G.A. (1980), "Populations Marginal Means in the Linear Model: An Alternative to Least Squares Means," *The American Statistican*, 34, 216-221.

Sidak, Z. (1967), "Rectangular Confidence Regions for the Means of Multivariate Normal Distributions," *Journal of the American Statistical Association*, 62, 626-633.

Steel, R.G.D. and Torrie, J.H. (1960), *Principles and Procedures of Statistics*, New York: McGraw-Hill.

Tukey, J.W. (1952), "Allowances for Various Types of Error Rates," Unpublished IMS address, Chicago, Illinois.

Tukey, J.W. (1953), "The Problem of Multiple Comparisons," Unpublished manuscript.

Waller, R.A. and Duncan, D.B. (1969), "A Bayes Rule for the Symmetric Multiple Comparison Problem," *Journal of the American Statistical Association*, 64, 1484-1499, and (1972) Corrigenda, 67, 253-255.

Waller, R.A. and Kemp, K.E. (1976), "Computations of Bayesian t-Values for Multiple Comparisons," *Journal of Statistical Computation and Simulation*, 75, 169-172.

Welsch, R.E. (1977), "Stepwise Multiple Comparison Procedures," *Journal of the American Statistical Association*, 72, 359.

Winer, B. J. (1971), *Statistical Principles in Experimental Design*, Second Edition, New York: McGraw Hill.

Chapter 21

The LIFEREG Procedure

Operating systems: All

ABSTRACT

The LIFEREG procedure fits parametric models to failure-time data that may be right censored. The class of models includes exponential, Weibull, log normal and log logistic models.

The model assumed for the response failure times is

$$\mathbf{y} = \mathbf{X}\boldsymbol{\beta} + \sigma\boldsymbol{\varepsilon}$$

where **y** is usually the log of the failure time, **X** is a matrix of covariates or independent variables, **β** is a vector of unknown regression parameters, σ is a scale parameter and **ε** is a vector of errors from an assumed distribution. In general, the distribution may depend on additional shape parameters. These models are often called accelerated failure-time models since the effect of the covariates is to scale a baseline distribution of failure times.

The parameters are estimated by maximum likelihood using a Newton-Raphson algorithm. The estimates of the standard errors of the parameter estimates are computed from the inverse of the observed information matrix.

INTRODUCTION

The accelerated failure time model assumes that the effect of independent variables on an event-time distribution is multiplicative on the event time. Usually, the scale function is $\exp(\mathbf{x}'\boldsymbol{\beta})$, where $\mathbf{x}$ is the vector of covariate values and $\boldsymbol{\beta}$ is a vector of unknown parameters. Thus, if T_0 is an event time from a baseline distribution with values corresponding to zero for the covariates, then a unit with a vector of covariates $\mathbf{x}$ will have an event time $T=\exp(\mathbf{x}'\beta)T_0$. If $y=\log(T)$ and $y_0=\log(T_0)$ then

$$y = \mathbf{x}'\boldsymbol{\beta} + y_0 \quad .$$

This is a log-linear model with y_0 playing the role of an error term. Usually, an intercept parameter and a scale parameter are allowed in the above model. In terms of the orginal event times the effects of the intercept term and the scale term are to scale the event time and power the event time respectively. That is, if $y=\mu+\sigma y_0$ then $T=\exp(\mu)T_0^{\sigma}$.

In terms of survival probabilities this model is

$$\text{Prob}(T>t\,|\,\mathbf{x}) = \text{Prob}(T_0>\exp(-\mathbf{x}'\beta)t)$$

where the left-hand side is evaluated assuming the value $\mathbf{x}$ for the covariates and the right-hand side is computed using the baseline probability distribution, but at a scaled value of the argument. The right-hand side of the equation represents the value of the baseline *Survival Distribution Function* evaluated at $\exp(-\mathbf{x}'\beta)t$.

Although it is possible to fit these models to the original response variable using the NOLOG option, it is more common to model the log of the response variable. Because of this log transformation, zero values for the observed failure times are not allowed. Similarly, small values for the observed failure times lead to large negative values for the transformed response. The fitted model for the normal distribution is sensitive to any such values, and care must be taken that the fitted model is not unduly influenced by such values. Likewise, values that are extremely large even after the log transformation will have a strong influence in fitting the normal and extreme value (Weibull) distributions. You should examine the residuals and check the effects on the model parameters of removing observations with large residuals or extreme values of covariates.

The standard errors of the parameter estimates are computed from large sample normal approximations using the observed information matrix. In small samples, these may be poor approximations. See Lawless (1982) for more discussion and further references. Better confidence intervals can sometimes be constructed by transforming the parameters. For example, it is often the case that the large sample theory is more accurate for $\log(\sigma)$ than σ. Therefore, confidence intervals can be constructed for $\log(\sigma)$ and transformed into confidence intervals for σ. The parameter estimates and their estimated covariance matrix are available in an output SAS data set and can be used to transform the parameters and their standard errors. Additionally, tests of parameters may be based on log-likelihood ratios. See Cox and Oakes (1984) for a discussion of the merits of some possible test methods including score, Wald, and likelihood ratio tests. It is believed that log likelihood ratio tests are generally more reliable in small samples than tests based on the information matrix.

The log-likelihood function is computed using the log of the failure time as a response. This log likelihood differs from the log likelihood obtained using the failure time as the response by an additive term of $\Sigma\log(t_i)$ where the sum is over the noncensored failure times. This term does not depend on the unknown parameters and will not affect parameter or standard error estimates. However, many published values of log likelihoods use the failure time as the basic response variable and hence will differ by the above additive term from the value computed by the LIFEREG procedure.

SPECIFICATIONS

The following statements can be used with PROC LIFEREG:

PROC LIFEREG *options;*
CLASS *variables;*
[*label*]:**MODEL** *response=variables / options;*
OUTPUT OUT=*SASdataset options;*
BY *variables;*

The MODEL statement is required. The PROC LIFEREG statement invokes the procedure. The CLASS statement specifies which variables are to be treated as discrete. However, only main effects may be specified in the MODEL statements. The MODEL statement specifies what variables are to be used in the regression part of the model and what distribution is to be assumed for the failure time. Initial values can be specified on the model statement. If no initial values are specified, the starting estimates are obtained by ordinary least squares. The OUTPUT statement is used to request an output data set containing predicted values and residuals.

PROC LIFEREG Statement

PROC LIFEREG *options;*

The options that can appear in the PROC LIFEREG statement are listed below:

DATA=*SASdataset*
specifies the input SAS data set. If DATA= is omitted, the most recently created SAS data set is used.

OUTEST=*SASdataset*
requests that a SAS data set be created containing the parameter estimates, the maximized log likelihood and (optionally) the estimated covariance matrix. See the section **Output Data Sets** for a detailed description of the contents of the OUTEST= data set. This data set will **not** be created if class variables are used.

COVOUT
requests that the OUTEST= SAS data set contain the estimated variance matrix as well as the parameter estimates.

NOPRINT
requests that the procedure not produce any printed results.

CLASS Statement

CLASS *variables;*

Any variables that are to be treated as classification variables instead of continuous numeric variables **must** be listed in the CLASS statement. If a variable listed in the CLASS statement is used as an independent variable in a MODEL statement then indicator variables are generated for the levels taken on by the CLASS variable. Using a CLASS statement precludes the ability to output parameter estimates to a SAS data set.

MODEL Statement

[label]: MODEL *variable* [* *censor(number list)*] =*variables* /*options*;

Multiple MODEL statements can be used with one invocation of the LIFEREG procedure. The optional *label* field is used to label the model estimates in the output SAS data set and in the printed output. The first variable is the response variable, which can be right censored. If the response is censored then a second variable, labeled *censor* above, must appear after the response variable together with a list of parenthesized values separated by commas or blanks that indicate censoring. That is, if the *censor* variable takes on a value given in the list that follows, the response is a right censored value; otherwise, it is a failure time.

The variables following the equal sign (=) are the covariates in the model. No higher order effects, such as interactions, are allowed in the covariables list; only variable names are allowed to appear in this list. However, a class variable can be used as a main effect, and indicator variables will be generated for the class levels.

An example of a valid MODEL statement is

```
A:MODEL TIME*FLAG(1,3)=TEMP TRTMENT;
```

This statement indicates that the response is contained in a variable named TIME and that if the variable FLAG takes on the values 1 or 3 the observation is right censored. The independent variables are TEMP and TRTMENT, either of which could be a class variable.

The following options can appear in the MODEL statement:

DISTRIBUTION=WEIBULL | EXPONENTIAL | LNORMAL | LLOGISTIC | GAMMA
DIST=WEIBULL | EXPONENTIAL | LNORMAL | LLOGISTIC | GAMMA
D=WEIBULL | EXPONENTIAL | LNORMAL | LLOGISTIC | GAMMA

specifies the distribution type assumed for the failure time. The EXPONENTIAL distribution is treated as a WEIBULL distribution with the scale parameter restricted to the value 1. The default is WEIBULL.

NOLOG

requests that no log of the response variable be taken. The default is to model the log of the indicated response variable.

COVB

requests that the inverse observed information matrix be printed as an estimate of the covariance matrix of the parameters.

CORRB

requests that the estimated correlation matrix of the parameter estimates be printed.

NOINT

requests that the intercept term be held fixed. If no inital intercept value is given, the intercept is set at the value zero. Because of the usual log transformation of the response, the intercept parameter is usually a scale parameter for the untransformed response.

INTERCPT=*number*
INTERCEPT=*number*

requests that the intercept term be intialized at this value. If NOINT is also specified, the intercept is fixed at this value.

NOSCALE

requests that the scale parameter be held fixed. If no value is specified with the SCALE= option, the scale parameter is fixed at the value 1. Because of the usual log transformation, this parameter usually represents a power transformation of the orginal response.

SCALE=*number*
requests that the scale parameter be initialized at this value. Note that the exponential model is the same as a Weibull model with the scale parameter fixed at the value 1.

NOSHAPE1
requests that the first shape parameter be held fixed. If no value is specified with the SHAPE1= option, this parameter is fixed at a value which depends on the DISTRIBUTION type.

SHAPE1=*number*
requests that the first shape parameter be initialized to this value. If the specified distribution does not depend on this parameter then the option has no effect. See the section **Distributions Allowed** for descriptions of the parameterizations of the distributions.

INITIAL=*numbers*
sets initial values for the regression parameters in the case of convergence difficulty. The values listed are used to initialize the regression coefficients for the covariates specified in the MODEL statement. The intercept parameter is initialized with the INTERCPT= option and is not included here. The values are assigned to the variables in the MODEL statement in the same order as listed in the MODEL statement. Note that a class variable requires *k−1* values when the class variable takes on *k* different levels. The order of the class levels is determined by the order in which you enter them in the data. If there is no intercept term, the first class variable requires *k* initial values. If a BY statement is used, all class variables must take on the same number of levels in each BY group or no meaningful initial values can be specified.

MAXIT=*number*
gives the maximum allowed iterations which will be attempted. The default is 50.

ITPRINT
requests that the iterations history and the final evaluations of the gradient and the second derivative matrix or Hessian be printed.

CONVERGE=*number*
gives the convergence criterion. The iterations are considered to have converged when the maximum change in the parameter estimates between Newton-Raphson steps is less than the number specified. The change is a relative change if the parameter is greater than .01 in absolute value or an absolute change otherwise. The default is .001.

SINGULAR=*number*
gives the tolerance for testing singularity of the information matrix and the crossproducts matrix for the initial least squares estimates. Roughly, the test requires that a pivot be at least this number times the original diagonal value. The default is 1E−12.

OUTPUT Statement

OUTPUT OUT=*SASdataset keyword=name* ... ;

The OUTPUT statement requests that fitted values and estimated quantiles be written to a SAS data set. Each OUTPUT statement applies to the preceding MODEL statement.

The following options can be specified in the OUTPUT statement:

OUT=*SASdataset*
: names the output SAS data set. If you want to create a permanent SAS data set, you must specify a two-level name (see "SAS Files" in the *SAS User's Guide: Basics* for more information on permanent data sets). If OUT= is omitted, the SAS System names the new data set using the DATA*n* naming convention.

QUANTILES= *values*
QUANTILE= *values*
Q= *values*
: specifies a list of values separated by blanks for which quantiles are to be calculated. The values must be between 0 and 1 noninclusive. For each value a corresponding quantile is estimated. The default is *Q=.5.*

CONTROL=*variable*
: specifies a variable in the input data set that controls the estimation of quantiles. For each observation in the input data set, if *variable* has the value of 1, estimates for all the values listed in the QUANTILE= list are computed; otherwise, no estimates are computed. If no CONTROL= variable is specified, all quantiles are estimated for all observations.

PREDICTED=*name*
P=*name*
: specifies the name of the variable to contain the quantile estimates.

XBETA=*name*
: specifies the name of a variable to contain the computed value of **x'b** where **x** is the covariate vector and **b** is the vector of parameter estimates.

STD_ERR=*name*
STD=*name*
: specifies the name of a variable to contain the estimates of the standard errors of the estimated quantiles. These estimates can be used to compute confidence intervals for the quantiles. However, if the model is fit to the log of the event time, better confidence intervals can usually be computed by transforming the estimated quantiles. See **Example 1** for such a tranformation.

SURVIVAL=*name*
: specifies the name of a variable to contain the estimates of the survival distribution evaluated at the observed response. See **Predicted Values** for more information.

CENSORED=*name*
: specifies the name of an indicator variable that is created to signal censoring. The variable takes on the value 1 if the observation was right censored and 0 otherwise.

In addition to the above optional variables, all other variables in the input data set are added to the OUTPUT data set. The following variable is always added to the OUTPUT data set:

PROB

a numeric variable giving the probability value for the quantile estimates. These values are taken from the QUANTILES= list above and are given as a fraction between 0 and 1 and not as a value between 0 and 100.

BY Statement

BY *variables;*

A BY statement can be used with PROC LIFEREG to obtain separate analyses on observations in groups defined by the BY variables. When a BY statement appears, the procedure expects the input data set to be sorted in order of the BY variables. If your input data set is not sorted in ascending order, use the SORT procedure with a similar BY statement to sort the data, or, if appropriate, use the BY statement options NOTSORTED or DESCENDING. For more information, see the discussion of the BY statement in "Statements Used in the PROC Step" in the *SAS User's Guide: Basics.*

DETAILS

Missing Values

Any observation with missing values for the dependent variable, the independent variables, or the censoring variable is not used in the model estimation. For any observation to be useful in the estimation of a model, only the variables used in that model need to be nonmissing. Predicted values are computed for all observations with no missing independent variable values. If the censoring variable is missing, the CENSORED= variable on the OUTPUT= SAS data set is also missing.

Main Effects

Unlike the GLM procedure, only main effect terms are allowed in the model specification. For numeric variables, this is a linear term equal to the value of the variable unless the variable appears in the CLASS statement. For variables listed in the CLASS statement, PROC LIFEREG creates indicator variables (variables taking the values zero or one) for every level of the variable except the last level. The levels are ordered according to the order that they are encountered in the input data set. If there is no intercept term, the first class variable has indicator variables created for all levels including the last level.

Computational Method

An initial ordinary least squares calculation is performed to compute the starting values for the parameter estimates and also to estimate the rank of the design matrix **X**. Columns of **X** that are judged linearly dependent on other columns have the corresponding parameters set to zero. The test for linear dependence is controlled by the SINGULAR= option in the MODEL statement. The variables are included in the model in the order listed in the MODEL statement **except** that the non-class variables are included in the model before any class variables.

Class variables have a composite chi-square test statistic computed for testing whether there is any effect from any of the levels of the variable. This statistic is computed as a quadratic form in the appropriate parameter estimates using the corresponding submatrix of the asymptotic covariance matrix estimate. The asymptotic covariance matrix is computed as the inverse of the observed information matrix. Note that if the NOINT option is specified, the first class variable will contain a contribution from an intercept term. The log likelihood function is maximized by means of a ridge stabilized Newton-Raphson algorithm. Unless initial values are specified for the parameters, the initial values of the regression parameters are computed using ordinary least squares with both censored and noncensored responses, ignoring the censoring variable.

Suppose there are n observations from the model $\mathbf{y}=\mathbf{X}\boldsymbol{\beta}+\sigma\boldsymbol{\varepsilon}$, where $\mathbf{X}$ is an $n \times k$ matrix of covariate values, $\mathbf{y}$ is a vector of responses and and $\boldsymbol{\varepsilon}$ is a vector of errors with survival distribution $S(.)$, and probability density function $f(.)$. That is, $S(e)=PROB(\varepsilon>e)$ and $f(e)=-\partial S(e)/\partial e$. Also, let δ_i be an indicator variable that takes on the value 1 if the observation is not censored, and 0 if the observation is right- censored. Then, following the notation and treatment of Kalbfleisch and Prentice (1980), the log-likelihood L as a function of the parameters σ and $\boldsymbol{\beta}$ is written

$$L = \Sigma_{i=1}^{n} \delta_i \log(f(w_i)/\sigma) + (1-\delta_i)\log(S(w_i))$$

where $w_i=(y_i-\mathbf{x}_i'\boldsymbol{\beta})/\sigma$. The terms of the gradient are given by

$$\partial L/\partial\beta_j = -\Sigma_{i=1}^{n}(\delta_i f'(w_i)/f(w_i) - (1-\delta_i)f(w_i)/S(w_i))X_{ij}/\sigma$$

$$\partial L/\partial\sigma = -\Sigma_{i=1}^{n}(\delta_i f'(w_i)/f(w_i) - (1-\delta_i)f(w_i)/S(w_i))w_i/\sigma - m/\sigma$$

where m is the number of noncensored observations. The terms of the second derivative matrix, or the Hessian, are given by

$$\partial^2 L/\partial\beta_j\partial\beta_k = -\Sigma_{i=1}^{n} A_i X_{ij} X_{ik}/\sigma^2$$

$$\partial^2 L/\partial\beta_j\partial\sigma = -\Sigma_{i=1}^{n} A_i w_i X_{ij}/\sigma^2 - (\partial L/\partial\beta_j)/\sigma$$

$$\partial^2 L/\partial\sigma^2 = -\Sigma_{i=1}^{n} A_i w_i^2/\sigma^2 - m/\sigma^2 - 2(\partial L/\partial\sigma)/\sigma$$

where $A_i=-\delta_i\partial^2 log(f(w_i))/\partial w_i^2-(1-\delta_i)\partial^2 log(S(w_i))/\partial w_i^2$. If the distribution includes shape parameters, there are additional derivative terms with respect to the shape parameters, and mixed derivatives with respect to the shape parameters and the covariate parameters.

The covariance matrix of the final parameter estimates is computed as the inverse of the negative of the second derivative matrix. The negative of the second derivative matrix is denoted **I** and called the observed information matrix. If **I** is not positive definite, a positive definite submatrix of **I** is inverted and the remaining rows and columns of the inverse are set to zero. If some of the parameters such as the scale and intercept are restricted, the corresponding elements of the estimated covariance matrix are set to zero.

For restrictions placed on the intercept, scale, and shape parameters, one-degree-of-freedom Lagrange Multiplier test statistics are computed. These statistics are computed as

$$\chi^2 = g^2/V$$

where g is the derivative of the log likelihood with respect to the restricted parameter at the restricted maximum and

$$V = (\mathbf{I}_{11} - \mathbf{I}_{12}\mathbf{I}_{22}^{-1}\mathbf{I}_{21})^{-1}$$

where the *1* subscripts refer to the restricted parameter and the *2* subscripts refer to the unrestricted parameters. The information matrix is evaluated at the restricted maximum. Under the null hypothesis the restrictions are valid, provided that some regularity conditions hold. These statistics are asymptotically distributed as chi squares with one degree of freedom. See Rao (1973, 418) for a more complete discussion. It is possible for these statistics to be missing if the observed information matrix is not positive definite. Higher degree-of-freedom tests for multiple restrictions are not currently computed.

In the second example below, a Weibull model and an exponential model are both fit to the same data. The exponential distribution is equivalent to a Weibull distribution with the scale parameter constrained to one. A Lagrange multiplier test statistic is computed to test this constraint. Notice that this test statistic is comparable to the Wald test statistic computed from the Weibull model. This statistic is the result of squaring the difference of the estimate of the scale parameter from 1 and dividing this by the square of its estimated standard error.

Distributions Allowed

The baseline distributions allowed are listed below. For each distribution the baseline survival function (F) and the probability density function (f) for the response, *t* and for the log response, *w* (G and g) are given. The chosen baseline functions serve to define the meaning of the intercept, scale and shape parameters. Notice that for the Weibull distribution, the accelerated failure time model is also a proportional-hazards model, but the parameterization for the covariates differs by a multiple of the scale parameter from the parameterization commonly used for the proportional hazards model.

Exponential

$$F(t) = \exp(-\alpha t)$$
$$f(t) = \alpha\exp(-\alpha t)$$

$$G(w) = \exp(-\exp(w-\mu))$$
$$g(w) = \exp(w-\mu)\exp(-\exp(w-\mu))$$

where $\exp(-\mu)=\alpha$.

Weibull

$$F(t) = \exp(-\alpha t^{\gamma})$$
$$f(t) = \gamma\alpha t^{\gamma-1}\exp(-\alpha t^{\gamma})$$

$$G(w) = \exp(-\exp((w-\mu)/\sigma))$$
$$g(w) = \exp((w-\mu)/\sigma)\exp(-\exp((w-\mu)/\sigma))/\sigma$$

where $\sigma=1/\gamma$ and $\alpha=\exp(-\mu/\sigma)$.

Lognormal

$$F(t) = 1-\Phi((\log(t)-\mu)/\sigma)$$
$$f(t) = \exp(-(\log(t)-\mu)^2/2\sigma^2)/(\sqrt{(2\pi)}\sigma t)$$

$$G(w) = 1-\Phi((w-\mu)/\sigma)$$
$$g(w) = \exp(-(w-\mu)^2/2\sigma^2)/(\sqrt{(2\pi)}\sigma)$$

where Φ is the cumulative distribution function for the normal distribution.

Loglogistic

$$F(t) = 1/(1 + \alpha t^{\gamma})$$
$$f(t) = \alpha\gamma t^{\gamma-1}/(1 + \alpha t^{\gamma})^2$$

$$G(w) = 1/(1 + \exp((w-\mu)/\sigma))$$
$$g(w) = \exp((w-\mu)/\sigma)/(1 + \exp((w-\mu)/\sigma))^2\sigma$$

where $\gamma=1/\sigma$ and $\alpha=\exp(-\mu/\sigma)$.

Gamma (with $\mu=0$, $\sigma=1$)

$$F(t) = \Gamma(1/\lambda^2, t^{\lambda}/\lambda^2)/\Gamma(1/\lambda^2) \quad \text{if } \lambda>0$$
$$F(t) = 1-\Gamma(1/\lambda^2, t^{\lambda}/\lambda^2)/\Gamma(1/\lambda^2) \quad \text{if } \lambda<0$$
$$f(t) = |\lambda|(t^{\lambda}/\lambda^2)^{(1/\lambda^2)}\exp(-t^{\lambda}/\lambda^2)/(t\Gamma(1/\lambda^2))$$
$$G(w) = \Gamma(1/\lambda^2, \exp(\lambda w)/\lambda^2)/\Gamma(1/\lambda^2) \quad \text{if } \lambda>0$$
$$G(w) = 1-\Gamma(1/\lambda^2, \exp(\lambda w)/\lambda^2)/\Gamma(1/\lambda^2) \quad \text{if } \lambda<0$$
$$g(w) = |\lambda|(\exp(\lambda w)/\lambda^2)^{(1/\lambda^2)}\exp(-\exp(\lambda w)/\lambda^2)/\Gamma(1/\lambda^2)$$

where $\Gamma(z)$ denotes the complete gamma function, $\Gamma(a,z)$ denotes the incomplete gamma function, and λ is a free shape parameter. The λ parameter is referred to as SHAPE1 by the program.

Note that the expected value of the baseline log response is, in general, not zero and that the distributions are not symmetric in all cases. Thus for a given set of covariates, **x**, the expected value of the log response is not always $\mathbf{x}'\boldsymbol{\beta}$.

Some relations among the distributions are as follows:

- The gamma with SHAPE1=1 is a Weibull distribution
- The gamma with SHAPE1=0 is a log normal distribution
- The Weibull with SCALE=1 is an exponential distribution.

Predicted Values

For a given set of covariates, **x**, the *p*th quantile of the log response, y_p, is given by

$$y_p = \mathbf{x}'\boldsymbol{\beta} + \sigma w_p$$

where w_p is the *p*th quantile of the baseline distribution. The estimated quantile is computed with replacing the unknown parameters by their estimates, including any shape parameters on which the baseline distribution might depend. The estimated quantile of the original response is obtained by taking the exponential of the estimated log quantile unless the NOLOG option was specified in the preceding MODEL statement. The standard errors of the quantile estimates are computed using the estimated covariance matrix of the parameter estimates and a Taylor series expansion of the quantile estimate. The standard error is computed as

$$\text{STD} = (\mathbf{z}'\mathbf{V}\mathbf{z})^{1/2}$$

where **V** is the estimated covariance matrix and **z** is the vector

$$\mathbf{z} = \begin{pmatrix} \mathbf{x} \\ \hat{w}_p \\ \hat{\sigma}\ \partial\hat{w}_p/\partial\alpha \end{pmatrix}$$

where α is a vector of the shape parameters. Unless the NOLOG option is specified, this standard error estimate is converted into a standard error estimate for $\exp(y_p)$ as $\exp(\hat{y}_p)STD$. It may be desirable to compute confidence limits on the log response and convert them back to the orginal response variable. See **Example 1** for a 90% confidence interval of the response constructed by exponentiating a confidence interval for the log response.

The survival variable, S, is computed as

$$S = G((y - \mathbf{x'b})/\hat{\sigma})$$

where G is the baseline distribution function.

Output Data Set

The OUTEST= data set contains parameter estimates and the log likelihood for the specified models. A set of observations is created for each MODEL statement specified. You can use a *label* field on the MODEL statement to distinguish between the estimates for different MODEL statements. If the COVOUT option is specified, the OUTEST= data set also contains the estimated covariance matrix of the parameter estimates.

The OUTEST= data set is not created if there are any CLASS variables in any models. If created, this data set contains each variable used as a dependent or independent variable in any MODEL statement. One observation consists of parameter values for the model with the dependent variable having the value −1. If the COVOUT option is specified, there are additional observations containing the rows of the estimated covariance matrix. For these observations the dependent variable contains the parameter estimate for the corresponding row variable. The variables listed below are also added to the data set:

MODEL	a character variable of length 8 containing the label of the MODEL statement if present or blank otherwise
NAME	a character variable of length 8 containing the name of the dependent variable for the parameter estimates observations or the name of the row for the covariance matrix estimates
TYPE	a character variable of length 8 containing the type of the observation, either PARM for parameter estimates or COV for covariance estimates
DIST	a character variable of length 8 containing the name of the distribution modeled
LNLIKE	a numeric variable containing the last computed value of the log likelihood
INTERCEP	a numeric variable containing the intercept parameter values and covariances
SCALE	a numeric variable containing the scale parameter values and covariances
SHAPE1	a numeric variable containing the first shape parameter values and covariances if the specified distribution has additional shape parameters.

Any BY variables specified are also added to the OUTEST= data set.

Printed Output

For each model PROC LIFEREG prints:

1. the number of LEVELS and their VALUES for any class variables
2. the name of the DATA SET
3. the name of the DEPENDENT VARIABLE
4. the name of the CENSORING VARIABLE
5. the VALUE(S) of the CENSORING VARIABLE that indicate a censored observation
6. the number of NONCENSORED and CENSORED VALUES
7. the final estimate of the maximized LOGLIKELIHOOD
8. the iteration history and the LAST EVALUATION OF THE GRADIENT AND HESSIAN if the ITPRINT option was specified.

For each independent variable in the model the LIFEREG procedure prints:

9. the name of the VARIABLE
10. the degrees of freedom (DF) associated with the variable in the model
11. the ESTIMATE of the parameter
12. the standard error (STD ERR) estimate for the observed information matrix
13. an approximate CHISQUARE statistic for testing that the parameter is zero (the class variables also have an overall chi-square test statistic computed which precedes the individual level parameters)
14. the probability of a larger chi-square value (PR>CHI)
15. the LABEL of the variable or, if the variable is a class level, the VALUE of the class variable.

If there were constrained parameters in the model, such as the scale or intercept, then LIFEREG prints:

16. a LAGRANGE MULTIPLIER test for the constraint.

EXAMPLES

Motorette Failure: Example 1

This example fits a Weibull model and a log normal model to the example given in Kalbfleisch and Prentice (1980, 5). An output data set called MODEL is specified to contain the parameter estimates. Since the Weibull and log normal distributions do not contain any shape parameters, the variable SHAPE1 is missing. An additional output data set is requested that contains the predicted quantiles and their standard errors for values of the covariate corresponding to TEMP=130 and 150. This is done with the CONTROL variable, which is set to 1 for only two observations. Using the standard error estimates obtained from the output data set, approximate 90% confidence limits are then created in a subsequent DATA step for the log response. These confidence limits are then converted back to the orginal scale by the exponential function.

```
TITLE 'MOTORETTE FAILURES WITH OPERATING TEMPERATURE AS A COVARIATE';
DATA;
   INPUT TIME CENSOR TEMP @@;
   IF _N_=1 THEN DO;
   TEMP=130; TIME=.; CONTROL=1; Z=1000/(273.2+TEMP);
```

```
   OUTPUT;
   TEMP=150; TIME=.; CONTROL=1; Z=1000/(273.2+TEMP);
   OUTPUT;
   END;
   IF TEMP>150;
   CONTROL=0;
   Z=1000/(273.2+TEMP);
   OUTPUT;
   CARDS;
8064 0 150 8064 0 150 8064 0 150 8064 0 150 8064 0 150
8064 0 150 8064 0 150 8064 0 150 8064 0 150 8064 0 150
1764 1 170 2772 1 170 3444 1 170 3542 1 170 3780 1 170
4860 1 170 5196 1 170 5448 0 170 5448 0 170 5448 0 170
 408 1 190  408 1 190 1344 1 190 1344 1 190 1440 1 190
1680 0 190 1680 0 190 1680 0 190 1680 0 190 1680 0 190
 408 1 220  408 1 220  504 1 220  504 1 220  504 1 220
 528 0 220  528 0 220  528 0 220  528 0 220  528 0 220
;

PROC LIFEREG OUTEST=MODELS COVOUT;
   A:MODEL TIME*CENSOR(0)=Z;
   B:MODEL TIME*CENSOR(0)=Z/DIST=LNORMAL;
   OUTPUT OUT=OUT QUANTILES=.1 .5 .9 STD_ERR=STD P=PREDTIME
          CONTROL=CONTROL;

PROC PRINT DATA=MODELS;
   ID _MODEL_;
   TITLE 'FITTED MODELS';

DATA;        /* 90% CONFIDENCE INTERVAL FOR THE RESPONSE */
   SET OUT;
   LTIME=LOG(PREDTIME);
   STDE=STD/PREDTIME;
   UPPER=EXP(LTIME+1.64*STDE);
   LOWER=EXP(LTIME-1.64*STDE);

PROC PRINT;
   ID TEMP;
   TITLE 'QUANTILE ESTIMATES AND CONFIDENCE LIMITS';
```

Output 21.1 Motorette Failure: PROC LIFEREG

```
              MOTORETTE FAILURES WITH OPERATING TEMPERATURE AS A COVARIATE                    1

                                 L I F E R E G   P R O C E D U R E

❷  DATA SET          =WORK.DATA1
   DEPENDENT VARIABLE=TIME      ❸
❹  CENSORING VARIABLE=CENSOR
   CENSORING VALUE(S)=    0     ❺
❻  NONCENSORED VALUES=   17  CENSORED VALUES=   13
   OBSERVATIONS WITH MISSING VALUES=   2
```

(continued on next page)

(continued from previous page)

```
(7)  LOGLIKELIHOOD FOR WEIBULL      -22.9514831
                                (12)        (13)    (14)      (15)
 (9) VARIABLE (10)DF (11)ESTIMATE STD ERR CHISQUARE  PR>CHI LABEL/VALUE

     INTERCPT     1    -11.8912  1.96402  36.6574  0.0001 INTERCEPT
     Z            1     9.03834 0.905334  99.6689  0.0001
     SCALE        1    0.361281 .0794401                  EXTREME VALUE SCALE PARAMETER
```

```
                  MOTORETTE FAILURES WITH OPERATING TEMPERATURE AS A COVARIATE                    2
                                  L I F E R E G   P R O C E D U R E

     DATA SET            =WORK.DATA1
     DEPENDENT VARIABLE=TIME
     CENSORING VARIABLE=CENSOR
     CENSORING VALUE(S)=      0
     NONCENSORED VALUES=   17  CENSORED VALUES=   13
     OBSERVATIONS WITH MISSING VALUES=     2

     LOGLIKELIHOOD FOR LNORMAL      -24.4738103

     VARIABLE   DF    ESTIMATE STD ERR CHISQUARE  PR>CHI LABEL/VALUE

     INTERCPT    1    -10.4706  2.77037  14.2845  0.0002 INTERCEPT
     Z           1     8.32208  1.28341  42.0468  0.0001
     SCALE       1    0.604034 0.110588                  LOG NORMAL SCALE PARAMETER
```

```
                                          FITTED MODELS                                               3

_MODEL_   _NAME_    _TYPE_   _DIST_    _LNLIKE_   INTERCEP     TIME         Z      _SCALE_    _SHAPE1_

   A      TIME      PARMS    WEIBULL   -22.951    -11.891     -1.000     9.0383   0.361281       .
   A      INTERCPT  COV      WEIBULL   -22.951      3.857    -11.891    -1.7761   0.034332       .
   A      Z         COV      WEIBULL   -22.951     -1.776      9.038     0.8196  -0.014818       .
   A      SCALE     COV      WEIBULL   -22.951      0.034      0.361    -0.0148   0.006311       .
   B      TIME      PARMS    LNORMAL   -24.474    -10.471     -1.000     8.3221   0.604034       .
   B      INTERCPT  COV      LNORMAL   -24.474      7.675    -10.471    -3.5517   0.032562       .
   B      Z         COV      LNORMAL   -24.474     -3.552      8.322     1.6471  -0.012807       .
   B      SCALE     COV      LNORMAL   -24.474      0.033      0.604    -0.0128   0.012230       .
```

```
                              QUANTILE ESTIMATES AND CONFIDENCE LIMITS                                4

TEMP   _PROB_   PREDTIME       STD   TIME  CENSOR   CONTROL      Z       LTIME     STDE      UPPER    LOWER

130    0.1     12033.2     5479.0    .      0         1     2.48016    9.3954  0.455326    25391   5702.7
130    0.5     26095.7    11353.3    .      0         1     2.48016   10.1695  0.435065    53265  12784.9
130    0.9     56592.2    26020.9    .      0         1     2.48016   10.9436  0.459797   120294  26623.8
150    0.1      4536.9     1442.2    .      0         1     2.36295    8.4200  0.317875     7641   2693.7
150    0.5      9838.9     2899.6    .      0         1     2.36295    9.1941  0.294706    15953   6068.0
150    0.9     21337.0     7167.1    .      0         1     2.36295    9.9682  0.335903    37015  12299.5
```

VA Lung Cancer Data: Example 2

This example uses the data presented in Appendix I of Kalbfeisch and Prentice (1980). The response is the survival time in days of a group of lung cancer patients. The covariates are type of cancer cell (CELL), type of therapy (THERAPY), prior therapy (PRIOR), age in years (AGE), time in months from diagnosis to entry into the trial (DIAGTIME), and a measure of the overall status of the patient at entry into the trial (KPS). The first three variables are taken to be class variables although only CELL has more than two levels. The censored values are given as negative, and censoring indicator (CENSOR) is created. Before beginning any modeling, it is a good idea to do preliminary investigations of the data with graphic and other descriptive methods. However, we are concentrating here only on the use of the LIFEREG procedure and the following does not comprise a complete analysis of the data.

First, a model is fit assuming an underlying Weibull distribution. A classification variable, CELLTHPY, is created for the interaction of CELL and THERAPY, and a model with all the covariates is fit. Models are also fit with only CELL and KPS as covariates and using the Weibull, exponential, log normal, and log logistic distributions. An output data set containing predicted values from the reduced Weibull model is also created. The OUTPUT statement must immediately follow the desired MODEL statement.

```
DATA VALUNG;
   DROP CHECK X4 M;
   RETAIN THERAPY CELL;
   INFILE CARDS COLUMN=COLUMN;
   LENGTH PRIOR $ 3 CHECK $ 1;
   LABEL T        = 'Failure or Censoring Time'
         KPS      = 'Karnofsky Performance Status'
         DIAGTIME = 'Months Till Randomization'
         AGE      = 'Age in Years'
         PRIOR    = 'Prior Treatment?'
         CELL     = 'Cell Type'
         THERAPY  = 'Type of Treatment'
         CELLTHPY = 'Cell by Treatment';

   M=COLUMN;
   INPUT CHECK $ @@;

   IF M>COLUMN THEN M=1;

   IF CHECK='S'|CHECK='T' THEN INPUT @M THERAPY $ CELL $ ;
      ELSE INPUT @M T KPS DIAGTIME AGE X4 @@;

   IF T>.;
      CENSOR=(T<0); T=ABS(T);

   IF X4=10 THEN PRIOR='YES';
            ELSE PRIOR='NO';
   CELLTHPY=THERAPY||CELL;

   CARDS;
 STANDARD SQUAMOUS
  72 60  7 69  0  411 70  5 64 10  228 60  3 38  0
 126 60  9 63 10  118 70 11 65 10   10 20  5 49  0
  82 40 10 69 10  110 80 29 68  0  314 50 18 43  0
-100 70  6 70  0   42 60  4 81  0    8 40 58 63 10
 144 30  4 63  0  -25 80  9 52 10   11 70 11 48 10
 STANDARD SMALL
  30 60  3 61  0  384 60  9 42  0    4 40  2 35  0
  54 80  4 63 10   13 60  4 56  0 -123 40  3 55  0
 -97 60  5 67  0  153 60 14 63 10   59 30  2 65  0
 117 80  3 46  0   16 30  4 53 10  151 50 12 69  0
  22 60  4 68  0   56 80 12 43 10   21 40  2 55 10
  18 20 15 42  0  139 80  2 64  0   20 30  5 65  0
  31 75  3 65  0   52 70  2 55  0  287 60 25 66 10
  18 30  4 60  0   51 60  1 67  0  122 80 28 53  0
  27 60  8 62  0   54 70  1 67  0    7 50  7 72  0
  63 50 11 48  0  392 40  4 68  0   10 40 23 67 10
```

```
 STANDARD ADENO
   8 20 19 61 10   92 70 10 60  0   35 40  6 62  0
 117 80  2 38  0  132 80  5 50  0   12 50  4 63 10
 162 80  5 64  0    3 30  3 43  0   95 80  4 34  0
 STANDARD LARGE
 177 50 16 66 10  162 80  5 62  0  216 50 15 52  0
 553 70  2 47  0  278 60 12 63  0   12 40 12 68 10
 260 80  5 45  0  200 80 12 41 10  156 70  2 66  0
-182 90  2 62  0  143 90  8 60  0  105 80 11 66  0
 103 80  5 38  0  250 70  8 53 10  100 60 13 37 10
 TEST SQUAMOUS
 999 90 12 54 10  112 80  6 60  0  -87 80  3 48  0
-231 50  8 52 10  242 50  1 70  0  991 70  7 50 10
 111 70  3 62  0    1 20 21 65 10  587 60  3 58  0
 389 90  2 62  0   33 30  6 64  0   25 20 36 63  0
 357 70 13 58  0  467 90  2 64  0  201 80 28 52 10
   1 50  7 35  0   30 70 11 63  0   44 60 13 70 10
 283 90  2 51  0   15 50 13 40 10
 TEST SMALL
  25 30  2 69  0 -103 70 22 36 10   21 20  4 71  0
  13 30  2 62  0   87 60  2 60  0    2 40 36 44 10
  20 30  9 54 10    7 20 11 66  0   24 60  8 49  0
  99 70  3 72  0    8 80  2 68  0   99 85  4 62  0
  61 70  2 71  0   25 70  2 70  0   95 70  1 61  0
  80 50 17 71  0   51 30 87 59 10   29 40  8 67  0
 TEST ADENO
  24 40  2 60  0   18 40  5 69 10  -83 99  3 57  0
  31 80  3 39  0   51 60  5 62  0   90 60 22 50 10
  52 60  3 43  0   73 60  3 70  0    8 50  5 66  0
  36 70  8 61  0   48 10  4 81  0    7 40  4 58  0
 140 70  3 63  0  186 90  3 60  0   84 80  4 62 10
  19 50 10 42  0   45 40  3 69  0   80 40  4 63  0
 TEST LARGE
  52 60  4 45  0  164 70 15 68 10   19 30  4 39 10
  53 60 12 66  0   15 30  5 63  0   43 60 11 49 10
 340 80 10 64 10  133 75  1 65  0  111 60  5 64  0
 231 70 18 67 10  378 80  4 65  0   49 30  3 37  0
;
  TITLE 'VA LUNG CANCER DATA FROM APPENDIX I of K&P';

PROC LIFEREG;
   CLASS PRIOR THERAPY CELL CELLTHPY;

   MODEL T*CENSOR(1)=KPS AGE DIAGTIME PRIOR CELL THERAPY CELLTHPY/
                  DIST=WEIBULL;
   MODEL T*CENSOR(1)=KPS CELL/D=WEIBULL;
   OUTPUT OUT=OUT SURVIVAL=S P=PRED CENSORED=FLAG;
   MODEL T*CENSOR(1)=KPS CELL/D=EXPONENTIAL;
   MODEL T*CENSOR(1)=KPS CELL/D=LNORMAL;
   MODEL T*CENSOR(1)=KPS CELL/D=LLOGISTIC;

PROC PRINT;
```

Output 21.2 VA Lung Cancer Data: PROC LIFEREG

```
                         VA lung cancer data from Appendix I of K&P                        1

                              L I F E R E G   P R O C E D U R E

                                  CLASS LEVEL INFORMATION

CLASS   LEVELS  VALUES

PRIOR       2   NO  YES
CELL        4   ADENO     LARGE     SMALL     SQUAMOUS
THERAPY     2   STANDARD TEST
CELLTHPY    8   STANDARDADENO     STANDARDLARGE     STANDARDSMALL     STANDARDSQUAMOUS TEST     ADENO     TEST     LARGE
                TEST     SMALL     TEST     SQUAMOUS
```

```
                         VA lung cancer data from Appendix I of K&P                        2

                              L I F E R E G   P R O C E D U R E

          DATA SET          =WORK.VALUNG
          DEPENDENT VARIABLE=T             Failure or Censoring Time
          CENSORING VARIABLE=CENSOR
          CENSORING VALUE(S)=      1
          NONCENSORED VALUES= 128  CENSORED VALUES=    9

          LOGLIKELIHOOD FOR WEIBULL    -192.5961885

          VARIABLE   DF   ESTIMATE STD ERR CHISQUARE  PR>CHI LABEL/VALUE

          INTERCPT    1    2.46895 0.708977   12.1272  0.0005 INTERCEPT
          KPS         1  0.0295675 .0047287   39.0968  0.0001 Karnofsky Performance Status
          AGE         1 0.00554711 .0080173   0.47871  0.4890 Age in Years
          DIAGTIME    1  0.0036495 .0080119  0.207489  0.6487 Months Till Randomization

          PRIOR       1                      0.198419  0.6560 Prior Treatment?
                      1  0.0910715 0.204452 0.198419  0.6560 NO
                      0          0        0        .       .  YES


          CELL        3                       21.6933  0.0001 Cell Type
                      1   0.736766 0.332432  4.91194  0.0267 ADENO
                      1  -0.657318 0.349708  3.53297  0.0602 LARGE
                      1   -0.47555 0.344763  1.90262  0.1678 SMALL
                      0          0        0        .       .  SQUAMOUS


          THERAPY     1                       1.66766  0.1966 Type of Treatment
                      1   0.457216 0.354052   1.66766  0.1966 STANDARD
                      0          0        0        .       .  TEST


          CELLTHPY    3                       7.93321  0.0474 Cell by Treatment
                      1  -0.776979 0.482371  2.59451  0.1072 STANDARDADENO
                      1   0.283976 0.451407 0.395756  0.5293 STANDARDLARGE
                      1  -0.667089 0.511373  1.70173  0.1921 STANDARDSMALL
                      0          0        0        .       .  STANDARDSQUAMOUS
                      0          0        0        .       .  TEST     ADENO
                      0          0        0        .       .  TEST     LARGE
                      0          0        0        .       .  TEST     SMALL
                      0          0        0        .       .  TEST     SQUAMOUS

          SCALE       1   0.885819 .0606402                   EXTREME VALUE SCALE PARAMETER
```

```
                         VA lung cancer data from Appendix I of K&P                        3

                              L I F E R E G   P R O C E D U R E

                                  CLASS LEVEL INFORMATION

                         CLASS   LEVELS  VALUES

                         CELL         4  ADENO     LARGE     SMALL     SQUAMOUS
```

```
                        VA lung cancer data from Appendix I of K&P                              4

                              L I F E R E G   P R O C E D U R E

        DATA SET          =WORK.VALUNG
        DEPENDENT VARIABLE=T            Failure or Censoring Time
        CENSORING VARIABLE=CENSOR
        CENSORING VALUE(S)=     1
        NONCENSORED VALUES= 128  CENSORED VALUES=   9

        LOGLIKELIHOOD FOR WEIBULL   -197.1021854

        VARIABLE   DF   ESTIMATE STD ERR CHISQUARE  PR>CHI LABEL/VALUE

        INTERCPT    1    3.15863 0.358031  77.8316  0.0001 INTERCEPT
        KPS         1  0.0291758 .0046234  39.8221  0.0001 Karnofsky Performance Status

        CELL        3                      21.3582  0.0001 Cell Type
                    1   0.322002 0.250015  1.65876  0.1978 ADENO
                    1  -0.386153 0.241822  2.54992  0.1103 LARGE
                    1  -0.786488 0.265086  8.80261  0.0030 SMALL
                    0          0        0        .       . SQUAMOUS

        SCALE       1   0.937816 .0618609                  EXTREME VALUE SCALE PARAMETER
```

```
                        VA lung cancer data from Appendix I of K&P                              5

                              L I F E R E G   P R O C E D U R E

                                   CLASS LEVEL INFORMATION

                         CLASS  LEVELS  VALUES

                         CELL        4  ADENO    LARGE    SMALL    SQUAMOUS
```

```
                        VA lung cancer data from Appendix I of K&P                              6

                              L I F E R E G   P R O C E D U R E

        DATA SET          =WORK.VALUNG
        DEPENDENT VARIABLE=T            Failure or Censoring Time
        CENSORING VARIABLE=CENSOR
        CENSORING VALUE(S)=     1
        NONCENSORED VALUES= 128  CENSORED VALUES=   9

        LOGLIKELIHOOD FOR WEIBULL   -197.5593560

        VARIABLE   DF   ESTIMATE STD ERR CHISQUARE  PR>CHI LABEL/VALUE

        INTERCPT    1    3.11091 0.375894  68.4925  0.0001 INTERCEPT
        KPS         1  0.0297103 .0048627  37.3304  0.0001 Karnofsky Performance Status

        CELL        3                      18.5784  0.0003 Cell Type
                    1   0.311275 0.266348  1.36581  0.2425 ADENO
                    1  -0.398919 0.257023  2.40894  0.1206 LARGE
                    1  -0.782054 0.282344  7.67211  0.0056 SMALL
                    0          0        0        .       . SQUAMOUS

        SCALE       0          1        0                  EXTREME VALUE SCALE PARAMETER
        LAGRANGE MULTIPLIER CHI-SQUARE FOR SCALE     1.017548 PR>CHI .3131
```

```
                        VA lung cancer data from Appendix I of K&P                              7

                              L I F E R E G   P R O C E D U R E

                                   CLASS LEVEL INFORMATION

                         CLASS  LEVELS  VALUES

                         CELL        4  ADENO    LARGE    SMALL    SQUAMOUS
```

```
                    VA lung cancer data from Appendix I of K&P                    8

                         L I F E R E G   P R O C E D U R E

DATA SET          =WORK.VALUNG
DEPENDENT VARIABLE=T              Failure or Censoring Time
CENSORING VARIABLE=CENSOR
CENSORING VALUE(S)=     1
NONCENSORED VALUES= 128  CENSORED VALUES=    9

LOGLIKELIHOOD FOR LNORMAL    -196.7494809

VARIABLE    DF    ESTIMATE STD ERR CHISQUARE  PR>CHI LABEL/VALUE

INTERCPT     1     2.37395 0.373221   40.4585  0.0001 INTERCEPT
KPS          1   0.0374235 .0047975   60.8507  0.0001 Karnofsky Performance Status

CELL         3                        11.2432  0.0105 Cell Type
             1   -0.112633  0.28082  0.160871  0.6884 ADENO
             1   -0.645984 0.265792   5.90688  0.0151 LARGE
             1   -0.766983 0.297116   6.66378  0.0098 SMALL
             0           0        0         .       . SQUAMOUS

SCALE        1     1.07324 .0671607                   LOG NORMAL SCALE PARAMETER
```

```
                    VA lung cancer data from Appendix I of K&P                    9

                         L I F E R E G   P R O C E D U R E

                              CLASS LEVEL INFORMATION

                    CLASS  LEVELS  VALUES

                    CELL        4  ADENO    LARGE    SMALL    SQUAMOUS
```

```
                    VA lung cancer data from Appendix I of K&P                    10

                         L I F E R E G   P R O C E D U R E

DATA SET          =WORK.VALUNG
DEPENDENT VARIABLE=T              Failure or Censoring Time
CENSORING VARIABLE=CENSOR
CENSORING VALUE(S)=     1
NONCENSORED VALUES= 128  CENSORED VALUES=    9

LOGLIKELIHOOD FOR LLOGISTC   -193.1813512

VARIABLE    DF    ESTIMATE STD ERR CHISQUARE  PR>CHI LABEL/VALUE

INTERCPT     1     2.45119 0.343523   50.9146  0.0001 INTERCEPT
KPS          1    0.036061 .0044092   66.8899  0.0001 Karnofsky Performance Status

CELL         3                        16.0463  0.0011 Cell Type
             1   0.0289734 0.263535  .0120871  0.9125 ADENO
             1   -0.660811 0.240251   7.56529  0.0060 LARGE
             1   -0.749366 0.261417   8.21717  0.0041 SMALL
             0           0        0         .       . SQUAMOUS

SCALE        1       0.581 0.043102                   LOG LOGISTIC SCALE PARAMETER
```

VA lung cancer data from Appendix I of K&P 11

OBS	PRED	S	FLAG	THERAPY	CELL	PRIOR	T	KPS	DIAGTIME	AGE	CELLTHPY	CENSOR
1	132.616	0.303290	0	STANDARD	SQUAMOUS	NO	72	60	7	69	STANDARDSQUAMOUS	0
2	177.544	0.816661	0	STANDARD	SQUAMOUS	YES	411	70	5	64	STANDARDSQUAMOUS	0
3	132.616	0.709249	0	STANDARD	SQUAMOUS	NO	228	60	3	38	STANDARDSQUAMOUS	0
4	132.616	0.481251	0	STANDARD	SQUAMOUS	YES	126	60	9	63	STANDARDSQUAMOUS	0
5	177.544	0.361332	0	STANDARD	SQUAMOUS	YES	118	70	11	65	STANDARDSQUAMOUS	0
6	41.282	0.141732	0	STANDARD	SQUAMOUS	NO	10	20	5	49	STANDARDSQUAMOUS	0
7	73.991	0.538572	0	STANDARD	SQUAMOUS	YES	82	40	10	69	STANDARDSQUAMOUS	0
8	237.692	0.262729	0	STANDARD	SQUAMOUS	NO	110	80	29	68	STANDARDSQUAMOUS	0
9	99.058	0.906694	0	STANDARD	SQUAMOUS	NO	314	50	18	43	STANDARDSQUAMOUS	0
10	177.544	0.313279	1	STANDARD	SQUAMOUS	NO	100	70	6	70	STANDARDSQUAMOUS	1
11	132.616	0.184055	0	STANDARD	SQUAMOUS	NO	42	60	4	81	STANDARDSQUAMOUS	0
12	73.991	0.062620	0	STANDARD	SQUAMOUS	YES	8	40	58	63	STANDARDSQUAMOUS	0

(continued on next page)

(continued from previous page)

OBS	PRED	S	FLAG	THERAPY	CELL	PRIOR	T	KPS	DIAGTIME	AGE	CELLTHPY	CENSOR
13	55.268	0.854036	0	STANDARD	SQUAMOUS	NO	144	30	4	63	STANDARDSQUAMOUS	0
14	237.692	0.060860	1	STANDARD	SQUAMOUS	YES	25	80	9	52	STANDARDSQUAMOUS	1
15	177.544	0.035082	0	STANDARD	SQUAMOUS	YES	11	70	11	48	STANDARDSQUAMOUS	0
16	65.320	0.260911	0	STANDARD	SMALL	NO	30	60	3	61	STANDARDSMALL	0
17	65.320	0.989772	0	STANDARD	SMALL	NO	384	60	9	42	STANDARDSMALL	0
18	36.444	0.063597	0	STANDARD	SMALL	NO	4	40	2	35	STANDARDSMALL	0
19	117.076	0.261930	0	STANDARD	SMALL	YES	54	80	4	63	STANDARDSMALL	0
20	65.320	0.116572	0	STANDARD	SMALL	NO	13	60	4	56	STANDARDSMALL	0
21	36.444	0.920808	1	STANDARD	SMALL	NO	123	40	3	55	STANDARDSMALL	1
22	65.320	0.652384	1	STANDARD	SMALL	NO	97	60	5	67	STANDARDSMALL	1
23	65.320	0.820543	0	STANDARD	SMALL	YES	153	60	14	63	STANDARDSMALL	0
24	27.222	0.794304	0	STANDARD	SMALL	NO	59	30	2	65	STANDARDSMALL	0
25	117.076	0.499761	0	STANDARD	SMALL	NO	117	80	3	46	STANDARDSMALL	0
26	27.222	0.325171	0	STANDARD	SMALL	YES	16	30	4	53	STANDARDSMALL	0
27	48.791	0.900941	0	STANDARD	SMALL	NO	151	50	12	69	STANDARDSMALL	0
28	65.320	0.195231	0	STANDARD	SMALL	NO	22	60	4	68	STANDARDSMALL	0
29	117.076	0.270740	0	STANDARD	SMALL	YES	56	80	12	43	STANDARDSMALL	0
30	36.444	0.319596	0	STANDARD	SMALL	YES	21	40	2	55	STANDARDSMALL	0
31	20.334	0.455920	0	STANDARD	SMALL	NO	18	20	15	42	STANDARDSMALL	0
32	117.076	0.564983	0	STANDARD	SMALL	NO	139	80	2	64	STANDARDSMALL	0
33	27.222	0.392831	0	STANDARD	SMALL	NO	20	30	5	65	STANDARDSMALL	0
34	101.184	0.178267	0	STANDARD	SMALL	NO	31	75	3	65	STANDARDSMALL	0
35	87.450	0.328472	0	STANDARD	SMALL	NO	52	70	2	55	STANDARDSMALL	0
36	65.320	0.965250	0	STANDARD	SMALL	YES	287	60	25	66	STANDARDSMALL	0
37	27.222	0.359769	0	STANDARD	SMALL	NO	18	30	4	60	STANDARDSMALL	0
38	65.320	0.412793	0	STANDARD	SMALL	NO	51	60	1	67	STANDARDSMALL	0
39	117.076	0.515325	0	STANDARD	SMALL	NO	122	80	28	53	STANDARDSMALL	0
40	65.320	0.236780	0	STANDARD	SMALL	NO	27	60	8	62	STANDARDSMALL	0
41	87.450	0.339364	0	STANDARD	SMALL	NO	54	70	1	67	STANDARDSMALL	0
42	48.791	0.083719	0	STANDARD	SMALL	NO	7	50	7	72	STANDARDSMALL	0
43	48.791	0.597598	0	STANDARD	SMALL	NO	63	50	11	48	STANDARDSMALL	0
44	36.444	0.999838	0	STANDARD	SMALL	NO	392	40	4	68	STANDARDSMALL	0
45	36.444	0.160177	0	STANDARD	SMALL	YES	10	40	23	67	STANDARDSMALL	0
46	13.625	0.324873	0	STANDARD	ADENO	YES	8	20	19	61	STANDARDADENO	0
47	58.600	0.674132	0	STANDARD	ADENO	NO	92	70	10	60	STANDARDADENO	0
48	24.421	0.638464	0	STANDARD	ADENO	NO	35	40	6	62	STANDARDADENO	0
49	78.452	0.654061	0	STANDARD	ADENO	NO	117	80	2	38	STANDARDADENO	0
50	78.452	0.700966	0	STANDARD	ADENO	NO	132	80	5	50	STANDARDADENO	0
51	32.695	0.211836	0	STANDARD	ADENO	YES	12	50	4	63	STANDARDADENO	0
52	78.452	0.777275	0	STANDARD	ADENO	NO	162	80	5	64	STANDARDADENO	0
53	18.241	0.096190	0	STANDARD	ADENO	NO	3	30	3	43	STANDARDADENO	0
54	78.452	0.572617	0	STANDARD	ADENO	NO	95	80	4	34	STANDARDADENO	0

VA lung cancer data from Appendix I of K&P 12

OBS	PRED	S	FLAG	THERAPY	CELL	PRIOR	T	KPS	DIAGTIME	AGE	CELLTHPY	CENSOR
55	71.787	0.837071	0	STANDARD	LARGE	YES	177	50	16	66	STANDARDLARGE	0
56	172.255	0.477555	0	STANDARD	LARGE	NO	162	80	5	62	STANDARDLARGE	0
57	71.787	0.893930	0	STANDARD	LARGE	NO	216	50	15	52	STANDARDLARGE	0
58	128.666	0.962430	0	STANDARD	LARGE	NO	553	70	2	47	STANDARDLARGE	0
59	96.107	0.883669	0	STANDARD	LARGE	NO	278	60	12	63	STANDARDLARGE	0
60	53.621	0.131044	0	STANDARD	LARGE	YES	12	40	12	68	STANDARDLARGE	0
61	172.255	0.658766	0	STANDARD	LARGE	NO	260	80	5	45	STANDARDLARGE	0
62	172.255	0.556387	0	STANDARD	LARGE	YES	200	80	12	41	STANDARDLARGE	0
63	128.666	0.573101	0	STANDARD	LARGE	NO	156	70	2	66	STANDARDLARGE	0
64	230.611	0.416387	1	STANDARD	LARGE	NO	182	90	2	62	STANDARDLARGE	1
65	230.611	0.340589	0	STANDARD	LARGE	NO	143	90	8	60	STANDARDLARGE	0
66	172.255	0.335602	0	STANDARD	LARGE	NO	105	80	11	66	STANDARDLARGE	0
67	172.255	0.330065	0	STANDARD	LARGE	NO	103	80	5	38	STANDARDLARGE	0
68	128.666	0.755232	0	STANDARD	LARGE	YES	250	70	8	53	STANDARDLARGE	0
69	96.107	0.514768	0	STANDARD	LARGE	YES	100	60	13	37	STANDARDLARGE	0
70	318.217	0.904395	0	TEST	SQUAMOUS	YES	999	90	12	54	TEST SQUAMOUS	0
71	237.692	0.267076	0	TEST	SQUAMOUS	NO	112	80	6	60	TEST SQUAMOUS	0
72	237.692	0.211284	1	TEST	SQUAMOUS	NO	87	80	3	48	TEST SQUAMOUS	1
73	99.058	0.819089	1	TEST	SQUAMOUS	YES	231	50	8	52	TEST SQUAMOUS	1
74	99.058	0.834155	0	TEST	SQUAMOUS	NO	242	50	1	70	TEST SQUAMOUS	0
75	177.544	0.986914	0	TEST	SQUAMOUS	YES	991	70	7	50	TEST SQUAMOUS	0
76	177.544	0.342996	0	TEST	SQUAMOUS	NO	111	70	3	62	TEST SQUAMOUS	0
77	41.282	0.013034	0	TEST	SQUAMOUS	YES	1	20	21	65	TEST SQUAMOUS	0
78	132.616	0.966161	0	TEST	SQUAMOUS	NO	587	60	3	58	TEST SQUAMOUS	0
79	318.217	0.576282	0	TEST	SQUAMOUS	NO	389	90	2	62	TEST SQUAMOUS	0
80	55.268	0.329655	0	TEST	SQUAMOUS	NO	33	30	6	64	TEST SQUAMOUS	0
81	41.282	0.333712	0	TEST	SQUAMOUS	NO	25	20	36	63	TEST SQUAMOUS	0
82	177.544	0.767725	0	TEST	SQUAMOUS	NO	357	70	13	58	TEST SQUAMOUS	0
83	318.217	0.647757	0	TEST	SQUAMOUS	NO	467	90	2	64	TEST SQUAMOUS	0
84	237.692	0.439915	0	TEST	SQUAMOUS	YES	201	80	28	52	TEST SQUAMOUS	0
85	99.058	0.005146	0	TEST	SQUAMOUS	NO	1	50	7	35	TEST SQUAMOUS	0
86	177.544	0.098862	0	TEST	SQUAMOUS	NO	30	70	11	63	TEST SQUAMOUS	0
87	132.616	0.192451	0	TEST	SQUAMOUS	YES	44	60	13	70	TEST SQUAMOUS	0
88	318.217	0.457551	0	TEST	SQUAMOUS	NO	283	90	2	51	TEST SQUAMOUS	0
89	99.058	0.088453	0	TEST	SQUAMOUS	YES	15	50	13	40	TEST SQUAMOUS	0

(continued on next page)

(continued from previous page)

OBS	PRED	S	FLAG	THERAPY	CELL	PRIOR	T	KPS	DIAGTIME	AGE	CELLTHPY	CENSOR
90	27.222	0.468994	0	TEST	SMALL	NO	25	30	2	69	TEST SMALL	0
91	87.450	0.561901	1	TEST	SMALL	YES	103	70	22	36	TEST SMALL	1
92	20.334	0.511979	0	TEST	SMALL	NO	21	20	4	71	TEST SMALL	0
93	27.222	0.270345	0	TEST	SMALL	NO	13	30	2	62	TEST SMALL	0
94	65.320	0.609728	0	TEST	SMALL	NO	87	60	2	60	TEST SMALL	0
95	36.444	0.030892	0	TEST	SMALL	YES	2	40	36	44	TEST SMALL	0
96	27.222	0.392831	0	TEST	SMALL	YES	20	30	9	54	TEST SMALL	0
97	20.334	0.199351	0	TEST	SMALL	NO	7	20	11	66	TEST SMALL	0
98	65.320	0.212047	0	TEST	SMALL	NO	24	60	8	49	TEST SMALL	0
99	87.450	0.546690	0	TEST	SMALL	NO	99	70	3	72	TEST SMALL	0
100	117.076	0.038868	0	TEST	SMALL	NO	8	80	2	68	TEST SMALL	0
101	135.463	0.391127	0	TEST	SMALL	NO	99	85	4	62	TEST SMALL	0
102	87.450	0.376303	0	TEST	SMALL	NO	61	70	2	71	TEST SMALL	0
103	87.450	0.166705	0	TEST	SMALL	NO	25	70	2	70	TEST SMALL	0
104	87.450	0.530994	0	TEST	SMALL	NO	95	70	1	61	TEST SMALL	0
105	48.791	0.690995	0	TEST	SMALL	NO	80	50	17	71	TEST SMALL	0
106	27.222	0.741741	0	TEST	SMALL	YES	51	30	87	59	TEST SMALL	0
107	36.444	0.419152	0	TEST	SMALL	NO	29	40	8	67	TEST SMALL	0
108	24.421	0.493588	0	TEST	ADENO	NO	24	40	2	60	TEST ADENO	0

VA lung cancer data from Appendix I of K&P 13

OBS	PRED	S	FLAG	THERAPY	CELL	PRIOR	T	KPS	DIAGTIME	AGE	CELLTHPY	CENSOR
109	24.421	0.393871	0	TEST	ADENO	YES	18	40	5	69	TEST ADENO	0
110	136.569	0.334741	1	TEST	ADENO	NO	83	99	3	57	TEST ADENO	1
111	78.452	0.227050	0	TEST	ADENO	NO	31	80	3	39	TEST ADENO	0
112	43.771	0.557738	0	TEST	ADENO	NO	51	60	5	62	TEST ADENO	0
113	43.771	0.775750	0	TEST	ADENO	YES	90	60	22	50	TEST ADENO	0
114	43.771	0.565223	0	TEST	ADENO	NO	52	60	3	43	TEST ADENO	0
115	43.771	0.697566	0	TEST	ADENO	NO	73	60	3	70	TEST ADENO	0
116	32.695	0.143147	0	TEST	ADENO	NO	8	50	5	66	TEST ADENO	0
117	58.600	0.337868	0	TEST	ADENO	NO	36	70	8	61	TEST ADENO	0
118	10.178	0.973302	0	TEST	ADENO	NO	48	10	4	81	TEST ADENO	0
119	24.421	0.167134	0	TEST	ADENO	NO	7	40	4	58	TEST ADENO	0
120	58.600	0.826996	0	TEST	ADENO	NO	140	70	3	63	TEST ADENO	0
121	105.030	0.720547	0	TEST	ADENO	NO	186	90	3	60	TEST ADENO	0
122	78.452	0.525520	0	TEST	ADENO	YES	84	80	4	62	TEST ADENO	0
123	32.695	0.321976	0	TEST	ADENO	NO	19	50	10	42	TEST ADENO	0
124	24.421	0.735538	0	TEST	ADENO	NO	45	40	3	69	TEST ADENO	0
125	24.421	0.914266	0	TEST	ADENO	NO	80	40	4	63	TEST ADENO	0
126	96.107	0.302373	0	TEST	LARGE	NO	52	60	4	45	TEST LARGE	0
127	128.666	0.592548	0	TEST	LARGE	YES	164	70	15	68	TEST LARGE	0
128	40.052	0.268715	0	TEST	LARGE	YES	19	30	4	39	TEST LARGE	0
129	96.107	0.307508	0	TEST	LARGE	NO	53	60	12	66	TEST LARGE	0
130	40.052	0.215905	0	TEST	LARGE	NO	15	30	5	63	TEST LARGE	0
131	96.107	0.254740	0	TEST	LARGE	YES	43	60	11	49	TEST LARGE	0
132	172.255	0.760989	0	TEST	LARGE	YES	340	80	10	64	TEST LARGE	0
133	148.873	0.459159	0	TEST	LARGE	NO	133	75	1	65	TEST LARGE	0
134	96.107	0.554361	0	TEST	LARGE	NO	111	60	5	64	TEST LARGE	0
135	128.666	0.725741	0	TEST	LARGE	YES	231	70	18	67	TEST LARGE	0
136	172.255	0.798593	0	TEST	LARGE	NO	378	80	4	65	TEST LARGE	0
137	40.052	0.576589	0	TEST	LARGE	NO	49	30	3	37	TEST LARGE	0

REFERENCES

Cox, D.R. (1972), "Regression Models and Life Tables (with discussion)," *Journal of the Royal Statistical Society*, B34, 187-220.

Cox, D.R. and Oakes, D. (1984), *Analysis of Survival Data*, London: Chapman and Hall.

Elandt-Johnson, R.C. and Johnson, N.L. (1980), *Survival Models and Data Analysis*, New York: John Wiley & Sons.

Gross, A.J. and Clark, V.A. (1975), *Survival Distributions: Reliability Applications in the Biomedical Sciences*, New York: John Wiley & Sons.

Kalbfleisch, J.D. and Prentice, R.L. (1980), *The Statistical Analysis of Failure Time Data*, New York: John Wiley & Sons.

Lawless, J.E. (1982), *Statistical Models and Methods for Lifetime Data*, New York: John Wiley & Sons.

Lee, E.T. (1980), *Statistical Methods for Survival Data Analysis*, Belmont, CA: Lifetime Learning Publications.

Rao, C.R. (1973), *Linear Statistical Inference and Its Applications*, New York: John Wiley & Sons.

Chapter 22

The LIFETEST Procedure

Operating systems: All

ABSTRACT

The LIFETEST procedure can be used with data that may be right censored to compute nonparametric estimates of the survival distribution and to compute rank tests for association of the response variable with other variables. The survival estimates are computed within defined strata levels, and the rank tests are pooled over the strata. Additionally, statistics testing homogeneity over strata are computed.

INTRODUCTION

A common feature of lifetime or survival data is the presence of right-censored observations due either to withdrawal of experimental units or termination of the experiment. For such observations it is only known that the lifetime exceeded the given value. The exact lifetime remains unknown. Such data cannot be analyzed by ignoring the censored observations since, among other considerations, the longer-lived units are generally more likely to be censored. The analysis methodology must correctly utilize the censored observations as well as the noncensored observations.

Usually, a first step in the analysis of such data is the estimation of the distribution of the failure times. The survival distribution function (SDF) is used to describe the lifetimes of the population of interest. The SDF evaluated at *t* is the probability that an experimental unit from the population will have a lifetime exceeding *t*, that is

$$S(t)=\text{Prob}(T>t)$$

where S(*t*) denotes the survival function and T is the lifetime of a randomly selected experimental unit. The LIFETEST procedure can compute estimates of the survival distribution function either by the product limit method or the life table method. See **Computational Formulas** for a brief description of the estimators or see one of the books listed in the references for a more complete description of these methods.

Some functions closely related to the SDF are the cumulative distribution function (CDF), the probability density function (PDF), and the hazard function. The CDF denoted F(*t*) is defined as 1-S(*t*) and is the probability that a lifetime is smaller than *t*. The PDF denoted *f(t)* is defined as the derivative of F(*t*), and the hazard function denoted *h(t)* is defined as *f*(*t*)/S(*t*). If the life table method is chosen, the estimates of the probability density function and the hazard function can also be computed. Printer plots of these estimates can be produced as well as SAS data sets containing the estimates. The output SAS data set can be used to produce graphical plots of the estimates.

Consider the example program given below. The data are taken from Kalbfleisch and Prentice (1980, 2) and represent the lifetimes in days of a group of rats following exposure to a carcinogen. The right-censored observations are indicated by giving the censoring times as negative.

From the plot of the survival estimates it appears that the two treatment groups differ primarily at larger survival times. The rank tests for homogeneity also indicate a difference at larger survival times since the log rank test, which places more weight on larger survival times, is marginally significant while the Wilcoxon test, which places more weight on early survival times, is not significant.

```
TITLE 'LIFETIMES OF RATS EXPOSED TO DMBA';
DATA VAGCAN;
   LABEL DAYS ='DAYS FROM EXPOSURE TO DEATH'
         GROUP='TREATMENT GROUP';
   INPUT DAYS @@;
   CENSOR=(DAYS<0);
   DAYS=ABS(DAYS);
   GROUP=(_N_>19);
   CARDS;
143 164 188 188 190 192 206 209 213 216
220 227 230 234 246 265 304  -216  -244
142 156 163 198 205 232 232 233 233 233 233 239
240 261 280 280 296 296 323 -204 -344
;

PROC LIFETEST PLOTS=(S,LLS);
   TIME DAYS*CENSOR(1);
   STRATA GROUP;
```

Output 22.1 Lifetime in Days of Rats Exposed to a Carcinogen: PROC LIFETEST

```
                        Lifetimes of rats exposed to DMBA                                 1

                         PRODUCT LIMIT SURVIVAL ESTIMATES
                                     GROUP=0

                                                 STANDARD        NUM.         NUM.
    DAYS         SURVIVAL        FAILURE          ERROR         EVENT         LEFT

   0.000          1.0000          0.0000          0.0000          0           19
 143.000          0.9474          0.0526          0.0512          1           18
 164.000          0.8947          0.1053          0.0704          2           17
 188.000            .               .               .             3           16
 188.000          0.7895          0.2105          0.0935          4           15
 190.000          0.7368          0.2632          0.1010          5           14
 192.000          0.6842          0.3158          0.1066          6           13
 206.000          0.6316          0.3684          0.1107          7           12
 209.000          0.5789          0.4211          0.1133          8           11
 213.000          0.5263          0.4737          0.1145          9           10
 216.000          0.4737          0.5263          0.1145         10            9
 216.000*           .               .               .            10            8
 220.000          0.4145          0.5855          0.1145         11            7
 227.000          0.3553          0.6447          0.1124         12            6
 230.000          0.2961          0.7039          0.1082         13            5
 234.000          0.2368          0.7632          0.1015         14            4
 244.000*           .               .               .            14            3
 246.000          0.1579          0.8421          0.0934         15            2
 265.000          0.0789          0.9211          0.0728         16            1
 304.000          0.0000          1.0000          0.0000         17            0
                          * CENSORED OBSERVATION


                      QUANTILES
                     75%   234.000   MEAN              218.757
                     50%   216.000   STANDARD ERROR      9.403
                     25%   190.000
```

```
                        Lifetimes of rats exposed to DMBA                                 2

                         PRODUCT LIMIT SURVIVAL ESTIMATES
                                     GROUP=1

                                                 STANDARD        NUM.         NUM.
    DAYS         SURVIVAL        FAILURE          ERROR         EVENT         LEFT

   0.000          1.0000          0.0000          0.0000          0           21
 142.000          0.9524          0.0476          0.0465          1           20
 156.000          0.9048          0.0952          0.0641          2           19
 163.000          0.8571          0.1429          0.0764          3           18
 198.000          0.8095          0.1905          0.0857          4           17
 204.000*           .               .               .             4           16
 205.000          0.7589          0.2411          0.0941          5           15
 232.000            .               .               .             6           14
 232.000          0.6577          0.3423          0.1053          7           13
 233.000            .               .               .             8           12
 233.000            .               .               .             9           11
 233.000            .               .               .            10           10
 233.000          0.4554          0.5446          0.1114         11            9
 239.000          0.4048          0.5952          0.1099         12            8
 240.000          0.3542          0.6458          0.1072         13            7
 261.000          0.3036          0.6964          0.1031         14            6
 280.000            .               .               .            15            5
 280.000          0.2024          0.7976          0.0902         16            4
 296.000            .               .               .            17            3
 296.000          0.1012          0.8988          0.0678         18            2
 323.000          0.0506          0.9494          0.0493         19            1
 344.000*           .               .               .            19            0
                          * CENSORED OBSERVATION


                      QUANTILES
                     75%   280.000   MEAN              240.795
                     50%   233.000   STANDARD ERROR     11.206
                     25%   232.000


                 EVENTS CENSORED     TOTAL %CENSORED STRATA
                    17         2        19   10.5263            0
                    19         2        21    9.5238            1
                 ======    ======   ======   =======
                    36         4        40   10.0000 TOTAL
```

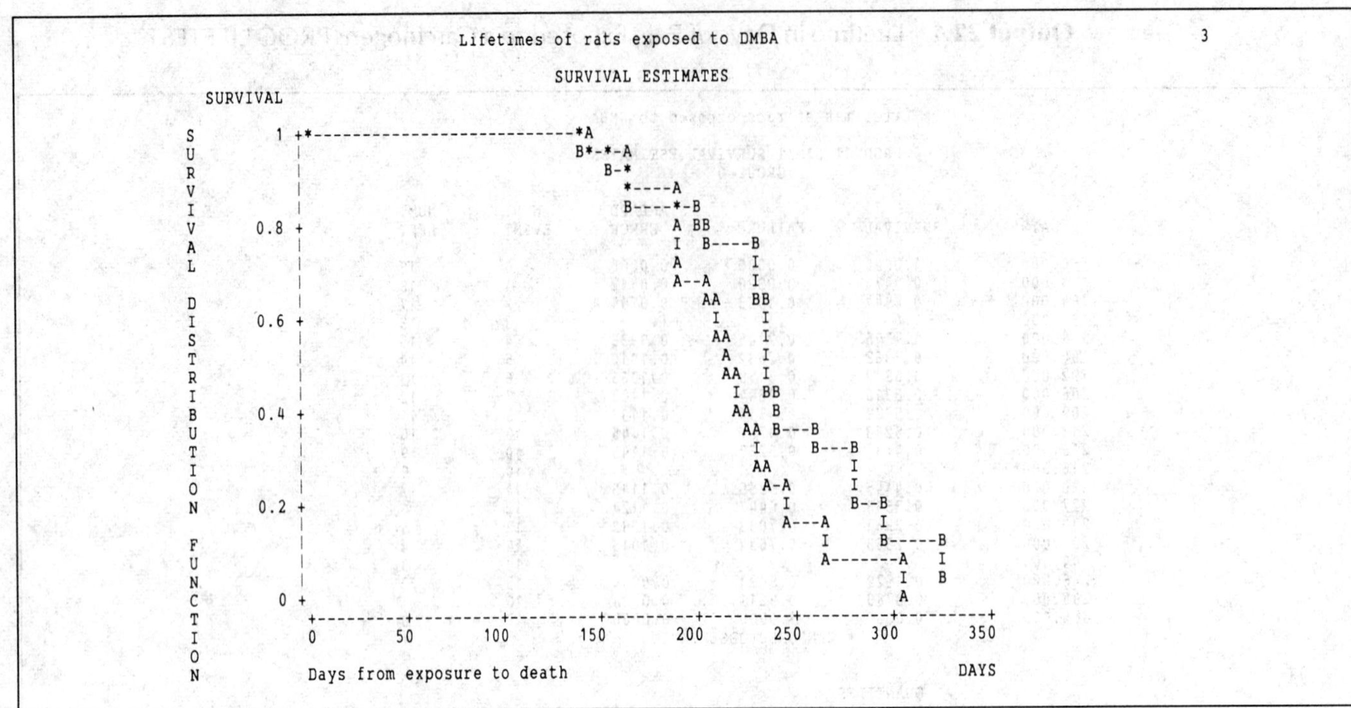

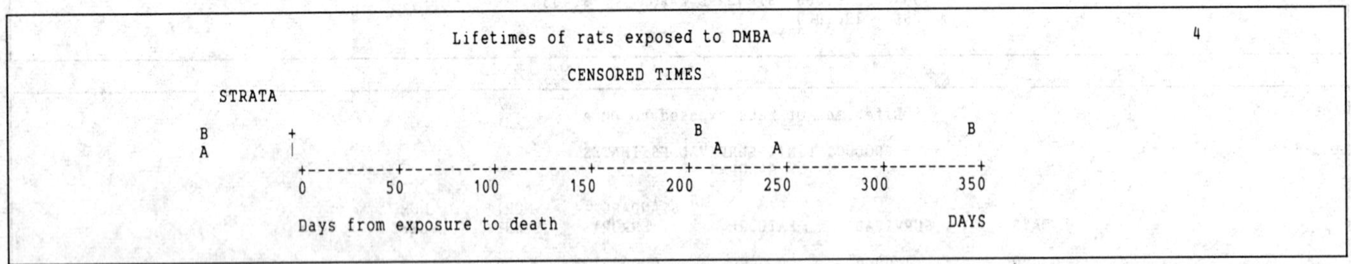

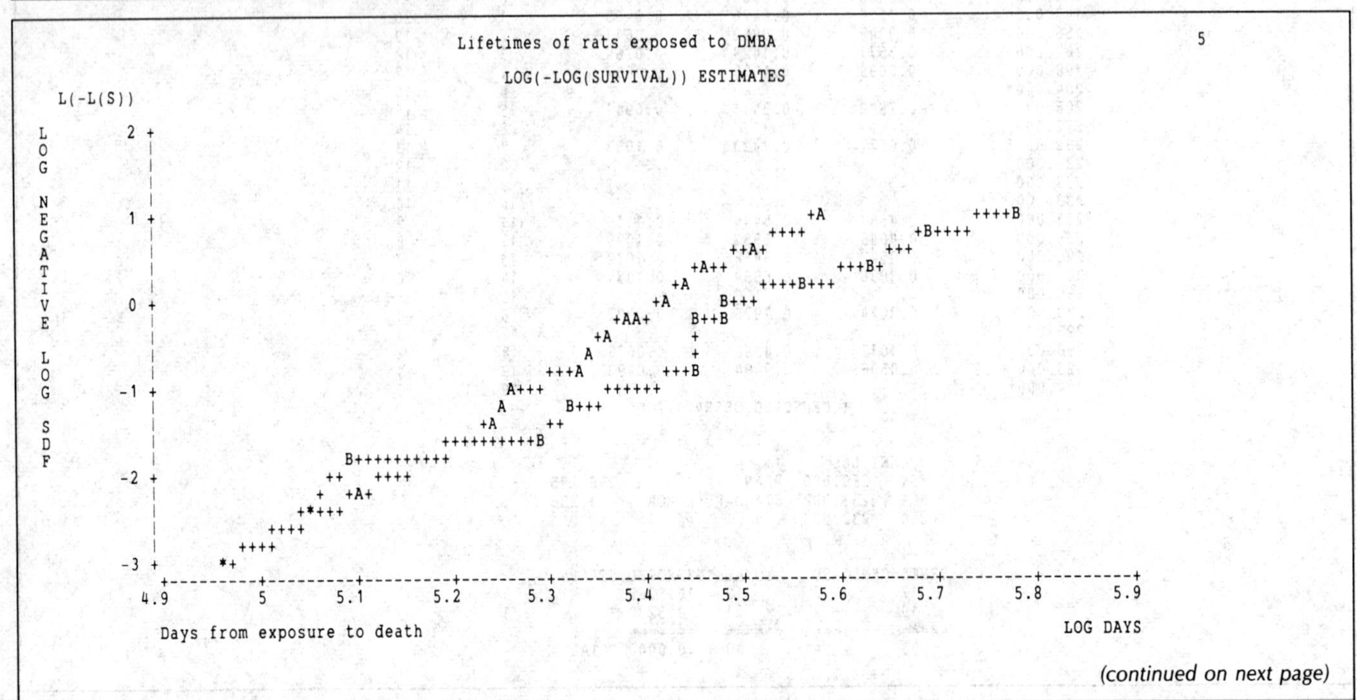

(continued on next page)

(continued from previous page)

```
                                                              LEGEND FOR STRATA SYMBOLS
                  GROUP              GROUP
            A=                 0 B=                1


                       LOG RANK TESTS
LOG RANK                   A                  B

A                    7.26327          -7.26327         4.76247
B                   -7.26327           7.26327        -4.76247
                     4.76247          -4.76247         0.00000
```

```
                 Lifetimes of rats exposed to DMBA                                          6

                        WILCOXON RANK TESTS

WILCOXON                   A                  B

A                    4902.22          -4902.22         114.000
B                   -4902.22           4902.22        -114.000
                      114.00           -114.00           0.000


                                                              LEGEND FOR STRATA SYMBOLS
                  GROUP              GROUP
            A=                 0 B=                1
           TESTS OF EQUALITY OVER STRATA

       TEST         CHI-SQUARE     DF   APPROX P-VALUE
       LOGRANK        3.122712      1           0.0772
       WILCOXON       2.651042      1           0.1035
       -2*LN(L)       0.077498      1           0.7807
```

The PROC LIFETEST statement requests a plot of estimated survival against time and a plot of the log of the negative log of the estimated survival against log time. The estimates are by default product limit estimates. The TIME statement indicates that the time variable is DAYS and that if the variable CENSOR has the value 1 the observation is right censored. The STRATA statement indicates that the data are to be divided into strata based on the values of the GROUP variable. The SDF estimates are thus computed within strata, but the plots are superimposed on one plot. Additionally, two rank tests and a likelihood ratio test are computed to test equality of the SDF between the treatment groups

Often there are additional variables called covariates that may be related to the failure time. These variables can either be used to define strata and the resulting SDF estimates visually compared, or they can be used to construct statistics which test for association between the covariate and the lifetime variable. The LIFETEST procedure will compute two such test statistics, the log rank test and a variation of the Wilcoxon rank test modified for censoring. These tests are computed by pooling over any defined strata thus adjusting for the strata variables. Except for a difference in the treatment of ties these two rank tests are the same as those used to test for homogeneity.

Consider the following set of data presented in Cox and Oakes (1984, 9). The data consist of the failure times in weeks and white blood cell counts for two groups of leukemia patients. The following example computes tests for the relation of the log of the white blood cell count to failure time pooled over the two groups. A test for homogeneity of the two samples is also computed.

```
TITLE 'RELATION OF LOG WHITE BLOOD COUNT AND LIFETIME':
DATA WBC;
   INPUT WBC T @@;
   GROUP=(_N_<18);
   LWBC=LOG(WBC);
```

```
   CARDS;
  2.3  65    .75 156    4.3 100   2.6 134    6.0   16 10.5 108
 10.0 121   17.0    4    5.4   39  7.0 143    9.4   56 32.0   26
 35.0  22  100.0    1  100.0    1  52.0    5 100.0   65

  4.4  56    3.0   65    4.0   17   1.5    7    9.0   16   5.3   22
 10.0   3   19.0    4   27.0    2  28.0    3   31.0    8  26.0    4
 21.0   3   79.0   30  100.0    4 100.0  43
;
PROC LIFETEST;
   STRATA GROUP;
   TIME T;
   TEST LWBC;
```

Output 22.2 White Blood Cell Counts for Leukemia Patients: PROC LIFETEST

```
                         Relation of White Blood Count and Lifetime                                1

                               PRODUCT LIMIT SURVIVAL ESTIMATES
                                           GROUP=0

                                                     STANDARD        NUM.        NUM.
                 T          SURVIVAL      FAILURE       ERROR       EVENT        LEFT

             0.000            1.0000       0.0000      0.0000           0          16
             2.000            0.9375       0.0625      0.0605           1          15
             3.000             .            .           .               2          14
             3.000             .            .           .               3          13
             3.000            0.7500       0.2500      0.1083           4          12
             4.000             .            .           .               5          11
             4.000             .            .           .               6          10
             4.000            0.5625       0.4375      0.1240           7           9
             7.000            0.5000       0.5000      0.1250           8           8
             8.000            0.4375       0.5625      0.1240           9           7
            16.000            0.3750       0.6250      0.1210          10           6
            17.000            0.3125       0.6875      0.1159          11           5
            22.000            0.2500       0.7500      0.1083          12           4
            30.000            0.1875       0.8125      0.0976          13           3
            43.000            0.1250       0.8750      0.0827          14           2
            56.000            0.0625       0.9375      0.0605          15           1
            65.000            0.0000       1.0000      0.0000          16           0

                              QUANTILES
                              75%     26.000  MEAN                 17.938
                              50%      7.500  STANDARD ERROR        5.076
                              25%      3.500
```

```
                         Relation of White Blood Count and Lifetime                                2

                               PRODUCT LIMIT SURVIVAL ESTIMATES
                                           GROUP=1

                                                     STANDARD        NUM.        NUM.
                 T          SURVIVAL      FAILURE       ERROR       EVENT        LEFT

             0.000            1.0000       0.0000      0.0000           0          17
             1.000             .            .           .               1          16
             1.000            0.8824       0.1176      0.0781           2          15
             4.000            0.8235       0.1765      0.0925           3          14
             5.000            0.7647       0.2353      0.1029           4          13
            16.000            0.7059       0.2941      0.1105           5          12
            22.000            0.6471       0.3529      0.1159           6          11
            26.000            0.5882       0.4118      0.1194           7          10
            39.000            0.5294       0.4706      0.1211           8           9
            56.000            0.4706       0.5294      0.1211           9           8
            65.000             .            .           .              10           7
            65.000            0.3529       0.6471      0.1159          11           6
           100.000            0.2941       0.7059      0.1105          12           5
```

(continued on next page)

(continued from previous page)

```
       108.000          0.2353        0.7647        0.1029          13          4
       121.000          0.1765        0.8235        0.0925          14          3
       134.000          0.1176        0.8824        0.0781          15          2
       143.000          0.0588        0.9412        0.0571          16          1
       156.000          0.0000        1.0000        0.0000          17          0


                     QUANTILES
                     75%    108.000  MEAN               62.471
                     50%     56.000  STANDARD ERROR     13.183
                     25%     16.000


                 EVENTS CENSORED    TOTAL %CENSORED STRATA
                   16        0         16   0.0000           0
                   17        0         17   0.0000           1
                 ======  ======    ======   =======
                   33        0         33   0.0000 TOTAL


                                 LOG RANK TESTS

             LOG RANK                A                 B

             A                 5.31858          -5.31858          6.70336
             B                -5.31858           5.31858         -6.70336
                               6.70336          -6.70336          0.00000


                               WILCOXON RANK TESTS

             WILCOXON                A                 B
             A                 2927.69          -2927.69          128.000
             B                -2927.69           2927.69         -128.000
                                128.00           -128.00            0.000
```

```
                      Relation of White Blood Count and Lifetime                       3
                                                                  LEGEND FOR STRATA SYMBOLS
                            GROUP             GROUP
                          A=        0 B=        1
                          TESTS OF EQUALITY OVER STRATA
                          TEST        CHI-SQUARE    DF  APPROX P-VALUE
                          LOGRANK       8.448691     1        0.0037
                          WILCOXON      5.596216     1        0.0180
                          -2*LN(L)     11.940094     1        0.0005


                             UNIVARIATE CHISQUARES FOR WILCOXON
                                   TEST
        VARIABLE           STATISTIC        VARIANCE        CHISQUARE        PROB>CHI

        LWBC                -11.7337         15.8531           8.6848          0.0032


                                 VARIANCE MATRIX FOR WILCOXON

                              WILCOXON         LWBC

                              LWBC          15.8531


                  FORWARD STEPWISE SEQUENCE OF CHISQUARES FOR WILCOXON
    VARIABLE        DF       CHISQUARE        PROB>CHI        CHISQ INCR        PROB>CHI

    LWBC             1          8.6848          0.0032            8.6848          0.0032

                             UNIVARIATE CHISQUARES FOR LOG RANK
                                   TEST
        VARIABLE           STATISTIC        VARIANCE        CHISQUARE        PROB>CHI

        LWBC                 19.4051         50.7236           7.4237          0.0064
```

(continued on next page)

(continued from previous page)

```
                         VARIANCE MATRIX FOR LOG RANK

                           LOG RANK          LWBC

                           LWBC           50.7236


                  FORWARD STEPWISE SEQUENCE OF CHISQUARES FOR LOG RANK
VARIABLE           DF      CHISQUARE     PROB>CHI     CHISQ INCR      PROB>CHI

LWBC                1         7.4237       0.0064          7.4237        0.0064
```

SPECIFICATIONS

The following statements can be used with the LIFETEST procedure:

PROC LIFETEST *options*;
  TIME *time specification*;
  STRATA *variable(ranges) ...* ;
  TEST *variables*;
  ID *variables*;
  FREQ *variables*;
  BY *variables*;

The PROC LIFETEST statement invokes the procedure. The TIME statement is used to specify the variables defining the survival times and censoring indicator. The STRATA statement specifies how a set of variables defines the strata for the analysis. The TEST statement gives a list of numeric covariates to be tested for their association with the response survival time. Each variable is tested individually, and a joint test statistic is also computed. The ID statement provides a list of variables whose values are used to identify observations on the printout of the product-limit estimates of the survival distribution function. All statements but the TIME statement are optional. When only the TIME statement appears, no strata are defined, and no tests are performed.

There is no required order for the statements following the PROC LIFETEST statement, but only one TIME statement is allowed.

PROC LIFETEST Statement

PROC LIFETEST *options;*

The options that can appear in the PROC LIFETEST statement are given below. If no options are given, LIFETEST computes and prints product-limit estimates of the survival distribution within each stratum and tests of equality of the distribution over the strata.

DATA=*SASdataset*
: names the SAS data set to be used by PROC LIFETEST. If it is omitted, the most recently created SAS data set is used.

METHOD=PL | KM | LT | LIFE | ACT
: specifies the method used to compute the survival distribution function estimates. Product-limit or Kaplan-Meier estimates will be computed if PL or KM is specified. Life table estimates will be computed if LT, LIFE, or ACT is specified. The default is to compute product-limit estimates.

NOPRINT
: requests that the procedure not produce any printed results.

NOTABLE
: requests that the procedure not print any survival function estimates. Only plots and test results will be printed.

MISSING
: requests that missing values for numeric variables and blank values for character variables be allowed as valid stratum levels. The default is not to use observations with missing values for any stratum variables.

OUTSURV=*SASdataset*
OUTS=*SASdataset*
: requests that a SAS data set of the given name be created containing the estimates of the survival distribution function and corresponding confidence limits. See **Output Data Sets** for more information on the contents of the OUTS= SAS data set.

OUTTEST=*SASdataset*
OUTT=*SASdataset*
: requests that a SAS data set of the given name be created containing the values of the rank test statistics, their estimated covariances and the overall chi-square test statistic. See **Output Data Sets** for more information on the contents of the OUTT= SAS data set.

PLOTS=(*list of plots*)
: requests that the specified printer plots of the estimates against time be produced. The valid list entries are: SURVIVAL (or S) for a plot of the estimated survival function, LOGSURV (or LS) for a plot of the -*log*(SDF), LOGLOGS (or LLS) for a plot of the log(-log(*SDF*)), HAZARD (or H) for a plot of the estimated hazard function and PDF (or P) for a plot of the estimated probability density function. The HAZARD and PDF plots will only be produced if the life table method is specified.

MAXTIME=*number*
: gives the maximum value of the time variable allowed on the printer plots so that outlying points do not determine the scale of the time axis of the plots. This parameter only affects the printed output and has no effect on the calculations.

INTERVALS=*numberlist*
: specifies the interval endpoints for the life table calculations and the printing intervals for the product-limit estimates. The interval endpoints must all be nonnegative numbers. The initial interval is assumed to start at zero whether zero is specified in the list or not.

NINTERVAL=*number*
: gives the number of intervals to be used to compute the life table estimates of the survival distribution function. This parameter is overriden by the WIDTH or the INTERVALS= parameters. The default is 10.

WIDTH=*number*
: specifies the width of the intervals to be used in the life table calculation of the survival distribution function. This parameter is overriden by the INTERVALS= parameter.

ALPHA=*number*
: specifies a number between .0001 and .9999 which sets the confidence level to be used for the confidence intervals for the distribution function estimates. The confidence level for the interval

is 1−ALPHA. For example, ALPHA=.05 requests a 95% confidence interval for the SDF at each time point. The default is ALPHA=.05.

SINGULAR=*number*

specifies a tolerance for the singularity check when computing rank test statistics. When sweeping a covariance matrix if the pivot becomes less that this number times a norm of the matrix, the pivot is deemed zero. The default is 1E−12.

TIME Statement

The TIME statement is **required** and is used to indicate the failure time variable and an optional censoring variable. The form of the statement is

TIME *timevariable* < * *censor(value,...)* >;

where *time* is the name of the failure time variable that can be optionally followed by an asterisk (*), the name of the censoring variable, and a parenthetical list of numerical values that correspond to right-hand censorship. For example the statement

```
TIME T*FLAG(1,2);
```

specifies that the variable T contains the values of the failure or censoring time and that if the variable FLAG is 1 or 2 the value is a right-censored value and not an observed failure time.

STRATA Statement

The STRATA statement indicates which variables determine strata levels for the computations. The strata are formed according to the nonmissing values of the designated stratum variables. The MISSING option can be used to allow any values for the stratum variables. The form of the STRATA statement is

STRATA *variable* < *(interval list)* > ... ;

where *variable* is a variable whose values are to determine the strata levels and *interval list* is a list of cutpoints for a numeric variable. If the variable is character or if the variable is numeric and no interval list appears then the strata are defined by the unique values of the strata variable. More than one variable can be specified in the list and each numeric variable may be followed by an interval list. The corresponding strata are formed by the combination of levels. If a variable is numeric and is followed by an interval list then the levels for that variable correspond to the intervals defined by the list. For example the specification

```
STRATA  AGE(5,10 to 70 by 10) SEX;
```

indicates that the levels of the AGE variable are to be: less than 5, 5-10, 10-20, 20-30, ... , 60-70, greater than 70 and that the strata are these age groups for males and these age groups for females. In this example there would be 9 age groups by 2 sex groups totaling 18 strata.

The specification of several variables, for example, A B C, is equivalent to the A*B*C... syntax of the FREQ procedure TABLE statement. The number of strata levels usually grows **very** rapidly with the number of strata variables, so you must be cautious when specifying the STRATA list.

TEST Statement

TEST *variables;*

The TEST statement is used to give a list of numeric covariables that are tested for association with the failure time.

Two sets of rank statistics using logrank scores and Wilcoxon scores are computed. These rank statistics and their variances are pooled over any strata that may have been defined. Marginal test statistics are computed and printed for each of the covariates.

Additionally, a sequence of test statistics for joint effects of covariates is computed and printed. The first element of the sequence is the largest marginal test statistic. Other variables are then added on the basis of the largest increase in the joint test statistic. The process is continued until all the variables have been added or the remaining variables are linearly dependent on the previously added variables. More detail is given in **Computational Formulas**.

FREQ Statement

FREQ *variable*;

If one variable in your input data set represents the frequency of occurrence for values of the other variables in the observation, include the variable's name in a FREQ statement. LIFETEST then treats the data set as if each observation appeared *n* times, where *n* is the value of the FREQ variable for the observation. The FREQ statement is useful for producing life tables when the data are already in the form of a summary data set. If not an integer, the frequency value is truncated to an integer. If the frequency value is less than one, the observation is not used.

ID Statement

ID *variables;*

The ID variable values are used to label the observations of the product limit survival function estimates. They are not used for any other purpose.

BY Statement

BY *variables;*

A BY statement can be used with the LIFETEST procedure to obtain separate analyses on observations in groups defined by the BY variables. For large data sets it is more efficient to use the BY statement than the STRATA statement to define your strata groups. However, if the BY statement is used to define strata, no pooling is done over strata and no tests of homogeneity are computed. When a BY statement appears, the procedure expects the input data set to be sorted in order of the BY variables. If your input data set is not sorted in ascending order, use the SORT procedure with a similar BY statement to sort the data, or, if appropriate, use the BY statement options NOTSORTED or DESCENDING. For more information, see the discussion of the BY statement in "Statements Used in the the PROC Step," in the *SAS User's Guide: Basics.*

DETAILS

Missing Values

Any observation with a missing value for the failure time or the censoring variable, if a censoring variable is listed, is not used in the analysis. If a stratum variable is missing, survival function estimates are computed for the strata labeled by the missing value, but these data are not used in any rank tests. However, the MISSING option can be used to request that missing values be treated as valid stratum values. If any variable specified in the TEST statement has a missing value, that observation is not used in the calculation of the rank statistics.

Computational Formulas

Let $i=1,2,\ldots,k$ label the distinct failure times t_i and let n_i be the number of surviving units, the size of the risk set, just prior to t_i. Let d_i be the number of units that fail at t_i and let $s_i=n_i-d_i$. Then the product limit estimate of the SDF at t_i is the cumulative product

$$S(t_i) = \Pi_{j=1}^{i}(1-d_j/n_j) \quad .$$

Notice that the estimator is defined to be right continuous; that is, the events at t_i are included in the estimate of $S(t_i)$. The estimated variance of $S(t_i)$ is computed using Greenwood's formula as $\sigma_i^2 S^2(t_i)$ where

$$\sigma_i^2=\Sigma_{j=1}^{i} d_j/(n_j s_j) \quad .$$

The standard error estimate is the square root of the estimated variance. The confidence limits for the survival estimate contained in the output data set are computed as

$$S^+(t_i)=S(t_i)(1+z_{\alpha/2}\sigma_i)$$
$$S^-(tsbi)=S(t_i)(1-z_{\alpha/2}\sigma_i)$$

where $z_{\alpha/2}$ is the critical value for the normal distribution. That is, $\Phi(-z_{\alpha/2})=\alpha/2$, where Φ is the CDF for the normal distribution. The value of α can be specified with the ALPHA option.

The estimated mean of the survival distribution is computed as

$$\hat{\mu}=\Sigma_{i=1}^{k} S(t_i)(t_i-t_{i-1})$$

where t_0 is defined to be zero. If the last observation is censored, this sum underestimates the mean. The variance of $\hat{\mu}$ is estimated as

$$\hat{\sigma}_{\hat{\mu}}^2 = \Sigma_{i=1}^{k-1} A_i^2/(n_i S_i)$$

where

$$A_i=\Sigma_{j=i}^{k-1} S(t_j)(t_{j+1}-t_j) \quad .$$

The life table estimates are computed by counting the number of events and censored observations which fall into each of the time intervals $[t_{i-1},t_i)$, $i=1,2,\ldots k+1$ where $t_0=0$ and $t_{k+1}=\infty$. Let n_i be the number of units entering the interval $[t_{i-1},t_i)$, $n'_i=n_i-w_i/2$ where w_i is the number of units censored in the interval, and $b_i=t_i-t_{i-1}$. Then the estimates and their variances are computed as:

Survival function, $S(t_i)$

$$\Pi_{j=1}^{i}(1-d_j/n'_j)$$

Variance of $S(t_i)$

$$S^2(t_i)\Sigma_{j=1}^{i} d_j/(n'_j(n'_j-d_j))$$

Conditional probability of an event in the ith interval, q_i

$$d_i/n'_i$$

Variance of q_i

$$q_i p_i/n'_i \text{ where } p_i=1-q_i$$

PDF at the middle of the ith interval, $f(t_{mi})$

$S(t_{i-1})q_i/b_i$

Variance of PDF where t_{mi} is the midpoint of the ith interval

$f^2(t_{mi})\ (\Sigma_{j=1}^{i-1} d_j/(n'_j(n'_j-d_j)\ +\ p_i/(n'_iq_i)\ )$

Hazard at the middle of the ith interval, $h(t_{mi})$

$2q_i/(b_i(1+p_i))$

Variance of hazard

$h^2(t_{mi})(1-(b_ih(t_{mi})/2)^2)/(n'_iq_i)$

Median residual lifetime, M_i

$S^{-1}(S(t_i)/2)-t_i$

Variance of M_i

$S^2(t_i)/(4n'_if^2(t_{mJ}))$ where J labels the interval that contains the median of the residual survival function.

The upper and lower endpoints of the confidence intervals for the statistics added to the output data set are computed as

$$\text{Upper}=S+z_{\alpha/2}V$$
$$\text{Lower}=S-z_{\alpha/2}V$$

where S is the statistic value, V is the square root of the estimated variance.

The rank statistics used to test homogeneity between the strata are computed as $\mathbf{v'V^-v}$ where $\mathbf{v}$ is a $cx1$ vector $(v_1,v_2,...,v_c)'$ with

$$v_j=\Sigma_{i=1}^{k} w_i(d_{ij}-n_{ij}d_i/n_i)$$

where c is the number of strata and $\mathbf{V}$, the covariance matrix, is estimated as

$$V_{jl}=\Sigma_{i=1}^{k} w^2_i(n_in_{il}\delta_{jl}-n_{ij}n_{il})d_is_i/(n^2_i(n_i-1))$$

where i labels the distinct failure times, δ_{jl} is 1 if $j=l$ and 0 otherwise, n_{ij} is the size of the risk set in the jth strata at the ith failure time, d_{ij} is the number of events in the jth strata at the ith time, $n_i=\Sigma_{j=1}^{c} n_{ij}$, $d_i=\ \Sigma_{j=1}^{c} d_{ij}$ and $s_i=n_i-d_i$. The weight w_i is 1 for the log rank test and n_i for the Wilcoxon test. The overall test statistic for homogeneity is $\mathbf{v'V^-v}$ where $(^-)$ denotes generalized inverse. This statistic is treated as a chi-square with degrees of freedom equal the rank of $\mathbf{V}$ for the purposes of computing an approximate probability level.

The likelihood ratio test statistic for homogeneity assumes that the data in the various strata are exponentially distributed and tests that the scale parameters are equal. The test statistic is computed as

$$Z=2(N\ \log(T/N)-\Sigma_{j=1}^{c} N_j\log(T_j/N_j))$$

where N_j is the total number of events in the jth stratum, $N=\Sigma_{j=1}^{c} N_j$, $T_j=\Sigma_{i=1}^{m_j} t_{ij}$ is the total time on test in the jth stratum where m_j is the total number of observations in the jth stratum, and $T=\Sigma_{j=1}^{c} T_j$. The approximate probability value is computed by treating Z as distributed chi-square with $c-1$ degrees of freedom.

The rank tests for the association of covariates are more general cases of the rank tests for homogeneity. A good discussion of these tests can be found in Kalbfleisch and Prentice (1980, chapter 6). In this section the index α will be used to label all observations, $\alpha=1,2,...,n$ and the indices i,j will range only over the observations which correspond to events, $i,j=1,2,...,k$. The ordered event times will be denoted as $t_{(i)}$, the corresponding vectors of covariates will be denoted $\mathbf{z}_{(i)}$, and the ordered times, both censored and event times, will be denoted t_α.

The rank test statistics have the form

$$\mathbf{v}=\Sigma_{\alpha=1}^{n} c_{\alpha,\delta_\alpha}\mathbf{z}_\alpha$$

where n is the total number of observations, δ_α is 1 if the observation is an event and 0 if the observation is censored, and $\mathbf{z}_\alpha$ is the vector of covariates from the TEST statement for the αth observation. The observations are assumed ordered by increasing event and censoring times with events coming before censored observations in the case of ties. Notice that the scores, c_{α,δ_α}, depend on the censoring pattern and that the summation is over all observations.

The logrank scores are

$$c_{\alpha,\delta_\alpha}=\Sigma_{(j:t_{(j)}<=t_\alpha)}(1/n_j)-\delta_\alpha$$

and the Wilcoxon scores are

$$c_{\alpha,\delta_\alpha}=1-(1+\delta_\alpha)\Pi_{(j:t_{(j)}<=t_\alpha)}n_j/(n_j+1) \quad .$$

The estimates used for the covariance matrix of the logrank statistics are

$$\mathbf{V}=\Sigma_{i=1}^{k}\mathbf{V}_i/n_i$$

where $\mathbf{V}_i$ is the corrected sum of squares and crossproducts matrix for the risk set at time $t_{(i)}$, that is,

$$\mathbf{V}_i=\Sigma_{(\alpha:t_\alpha>=t_{(i)})}(\mathbf{z}_\alpha-\bar{\mathbf{z}}_i)'(\mathbf{z}_\alpha-\bar{\mathbf{z}}_i) \quad .$$

where

$$\bar{\mathbf{z}}_i=\Sigma_{(\alpha:t_\alpha>=t_{(i)})}\mathbf{z}_\alpha/n_i \quad .$$

The estimate used for the covariance matrix of the Wilcoxon statistics is

$$\mathbf{V}=\Sigma_{i=1}^{k}(a_i(1-a^*_i)(2\mathbf{z}_{(i)}\mathbf{z}'_{(i)}+\mathbf{S}_i)-(a^*_i-a_i)(a_i\mathbf{x}_i\mathbf{x}'_i+\Sigma_{j=i+1}^{k}a_j(\mathbf{x}_i\mathbf{x}'_j+\mathbf{x}_j\mathbf{x}'_i)))$$

where

$$a_i=\Pi_{j=1}^{i}n_j/(n_j+1)$$

$$a^*_i=\Pi_{j=1}^{i}(n_j+1)/(n_j+2)$$

$$\mathbf{S}_i=\Sigma_{(\alpha:t_{(i+1)}>t_\alpha>t(i))}\mathbf{z}_\alpha\mathbf{z}'_\alpha$$

$$\mathbf{s}_i=\Sigma_{(\alpha:t_{(i+1)}>t_\alpha>t(i))}/\mathbf{z}_\alpha$$

$$\mathbf{x}_i=2\mathbf{z}_{(i)}+\mathbf{s}_i \quad .$$

In the case of tied failure times, the statistics $\mathbf{v}$ are computed as averaged over the possible orderings of the tied failure times. The variance matrices are also averaged over the tied failure times. Averaging the variance matrices over the tied orderings gives functions with appropriate symmetries for the tied observations; however, the actual variances of the $\mathbf{v}$ statistics will probably be smaller than the above estimates. Unless the proportion of ties is large, it is unlikely that this will be a problem.

The marginal tests for each covariate are formed from each component of **v** and the corresponding diagonal element of **V** as v^2_i/V_{ii}. These statistics are treated as coming from a χ^2_1 distribution for calculation of probability values.

The statistic **v'V⁻v** is computed by sweeping each pivot of the **V** matrix in the order of greatest increase to the statistic. The corresponding sequence of partial statistics is included in the printout unless the NOPRINT option is specified.

If desired for data screening purposes, the output data set requested by the OUTTEST= option can be treated as a sum of squares and crossproducts matrix and processed by the RSQUARE procedure. Then the sets of variables of a given size can be found that give the largest test statistics. **Example 1** illustrates this process.

Output Data Sets

The output data set containing the survival estimates is requested and named with the OUTSURV= option in the LIFETEST statement. The output data set contains:

- any BY variables specified
- any STRATA variables specified, their values coming from either the first values encountered in a stratum or the midpoints of the stratum intervals if cutpoints are used to define strata (semi-infinite intervals are labeled by their finite endpoint)
- _STRTNO_, a numeric variable that numbers the strata
- the time variable with the same name as on the TIME statement
- SURVIVAL, a variable containing the survival estimates
- SDF_LCL, a variable containing the lower endpoint of the α-level survival confidence interval
- SDF_UCL, a variable containing the upper endpoint of the α-level survival confidence interval.

If the estimation uses the life table method, then the data set also contains:

- MIDPOINT, a variable containing the value of the midpoint of the time interval
- PDF, a variable containing the PDF estimates
- PDF_LCL, a variable containing the lower endpoint of the PDF confidence interval
- PDF_UCL, a variable containing the upper endpoint of the PDF confidence interval
- HAZARD, a variable containing the hazard estimates
- HAZ_LCL, a variable containing the lower endpoint of the hazard confidence interval
- HAZ_UCL, a variable containing the upper endpoint of the hazard confidence interval.

Each survival curve contains an initial observation with a value 1 for the SDF and a value 0 for the time. Otherwise, the output data set contains an observation for each unique failure time if the product limit method was used or an observation for each time interval if the life table method was used. The product limit survival estimates are defined so as to be right continuous; that is, the estimates at a given time include the factor for the failure events that occurred at that time.

The output data set containing the rank statistics includes the following variables:

- any BY variables

- _NAME_, a character variable of length 8 that labels the rows of the covariance matrix and the test statistics
- _TYPE_, a character variable of length 8 that labels the type of rank test, either "LOG RANK" or "WILCOXON"
- the time variable, containing the overall test statistic in the observation that has _NAME_ equal to the name of the time variable
- all variables listed in the TEST statement.

If the value of the _NAME_ variable is the name of a variable in the TEST list, the observation contains a row of the covariance matrix in the variables from the TEST list and the value of the rank statistic in the time variable. If the value of the _NAME_ variable is the name of the time variable then the observation contains the values of the rank statistics in the variables from the TEST list and the value of the overall "chi-square" test statistic in the time variable. Thus, the output is in the form of a symmetric matrix formed by the covariance matrix bordered by the rank statistics and the chi-square statistic.

Two complete sets of statistics labeled by the _TYPE_ variable are output, one for log rank scores and one for Wilcoxon scores.

Printed Output

For each stratum, the LIFETEST procedure prints:

1. the values of the strata variables
2. the survival estimates, product limit or life table
3. the values of the ID variables
4. the estimated mean of the survival times
5. the estimated standard error of the estimated mean
6. the sample quartiles.

Then summarized over all strata are printed:

7. the number of censored and noncensored values
8. a Wilcoxon test for homogeneity over strata
9. a logrank test for homogeneity over strata
10. a likelihood ratio test for homogeneity based on the exponential distribution.

If the plots were requested, then printer plots are generated for:

11. the estimated SURVIVAL FUNCTION against FAILURE TIME
12. the -log(SDF) against FAILURE TIME
13. the log(-log(SDF)) against log(FAILURE TIME)

and if the life table estimation method was requested

14. the estimated PDF against FAILURE TIME
15. the estimated HAZARD against FAILURE TIME

If a TEST statement was specified then the following statistics are printed:

16. the covariance matrix for the logrank statistics
17. the logrank statistics
18. the marginal approximate chi-square statistics
19. the approximate probability values
20. the covariance matrix for the Wilcoxon statistics
21. the Wilcoxon statistics
22. the marginal approximate chi-square statistics
23. the approximate probability values.

Computer Resources

The data are first read and sorted into strata. If the data were originally sorted by failure time and censoring state, with smaller failure times coming first and censored values preceding noncensored values in cases of ties, the data can be processed by strata without additional sorting. Otherwise, the data are read into core by strata and sorted. If sufficient memory is not available to sort the data in memory, the procedure will terminate.

EXAMPLES

Product Limit Estimates and Tests of Association: Example 1

This example uses the data presented in Appendix I of Kalbfeisch and Prentice (1980). The response is the survival time in days of a group of lung cancer patients. The covariates are type of cancer cell (CELL), type of therapy (THERAPY), prior therapy (PRIOR), age in years (AGE), time in months from diagnosis to entry into the trial (DIAGTIME) and a measure of the overall status of the patient at entry into the trial (KPS). An indicator variable for therapy type (TREAT) is created in the program. This data set is given in the **Examples** section of the LIFEREG procedure and is not reproduced here.

Because of a few large survival times, a MAXTIME of 600 is used to set the scale of the time axis. An output data set named TEST containing the rank test matrices is requested. The rank tests using the log rank scores are then passed to the RSQUARE procedure to find the sets of variables that yield the largest chi-square test statistics. For example, KPS generates the largest marginal test statistic, KPS and TREAT generate a larger test statistic than any other pair, and so on. Based on the rank tests, the stratification variable CELL and the variable KPS appear to be related to the survival time, but the other variables do not exhibit much relationship.

```
* DATA FROM KALBFLEISCH AND PRENTICE (1980, 223);


DATA VALUNG;
   DROP CHECK M;
   RETAIN THERAPY CELL;
   INFILE CARDS COLUMN=COLUMN;
   LENGTH CHECK $ 1;
   LABEL T        = 'Failure or Censoring Time'
      KPS         = 'Karnofsky Index'
      DIAGTIME    = 'Months Till Randomization'
      AGE         = 'Age in Years'
      PRIOR       = 'Prior Treatment?'
      CELL        = 'Cell Type'
      THERAPY     = 'Type of Treatment'
      TREAT       = 'Treatment indicator';

   M=COLUMN;
   INPUT CHECK $ @@;

   IF M>COLUMN THEN M=1;

   IF CHECK='S'|CHECK='T' THEN INPUT @M THERAPY $ CELL $ ;
    ELSE INPUT @M T KPS DIAGTIME AGE PRIOR @@;
```

```
    IF T>.;
    CENSOR=(T<0); T=ABS(T);

    TREAT=(THERAPY='TEST');

    CARDS;
data lines
    TITLE 'VA lung cancer data from Appendix I of K&P';

PROC LIFETEST PLOTS=(S,LS,LLS) OUTTEST=TEST MAXTIME=600;
    TIME T*CENSOR(1);
    ID THERAPY;
    STRATA CELL;
    TEST AGE PRIOR DIAGTIME KPS TREAT;

DATA RSQ; SET TEST;
    IF _TYPE_='LOG RANK';
    _TYPE_='COV';

PROC RSQUARE DATA=RSQ(TYPE=COV);
    MODEL T=AGE PRIOR DIAGTIME KPS TREAT/SIGMA=1;
```

Output. 22.3 Product Limit Estimates and Tests of Association

VA lung cancer data from Appendix I of K&P 1

PRODUCT LIMIT SURVIVAL ESTIMATES
CELL=ADENO

❶ T	❷ SURVIVAL	FAILURE	STANDARD ERROR	NUM. EVENT	NUM. LEFT	❸ THERAPY
0.000	1.0000	0.0000	0.0000	0	27	
3.000	0.9630	0.0370	0.0363	1	26	STANDARD
7.000	0.9259	0.0741	0.0504	2	25	TEST
8.000	.	.	.	3	24	STANDARD
8.000	0.8519	0.1481	0.0684	4	23	TEST
12.000	0.8148	0.1852	0.0748	5	22	STANDARD
18.000	0.7778	0.2222	0.0800	6	21	TEST
19.000	0.7407	0.2593	0.0843	7	20	TEST
24.000	0.7037	0.2963	0.0879	8	19	TEST
31.000	0.6667	0.3333	0.0907	9	18	TEST
35.000	0.6296	0.3704	0.0929	10	17	STANDARD
36.000	0.5926	0.4074	0.0946	11	16	TEST
45.000	0.5556	0.4444	0.0956	12	15	TEST
48.000	0.5185	0.4815	0.0962	13	14	TEST
51.000	0.4815	0.5185	0.0962	14	13	TEST
52.000	0.4444	0.5556	0.0956	15	12	TEST
73.000	0.4074	0.5926	0.0946	16	11	TEST
80.000	0.3704	0.6296	0.0929	17	10	TEST
83.000*	.	.	.	17	9	TEST
84.000	0.3292	0.6708	0.0913	18	8	TEST
90.000	0.2881	0.7119	0.0887	19	7	TEST
92.000	0.2469	0.7531	0.0850	20	6	STANDARD
95.000	0.2058	0.7942	0.0802	21	5	STANDARD
117.000	0.1646	0.8354	0.0740	22	4	STANDARD
132.000	0.1235	0.8765	0.0659	23	3	STANDARD
140.000	0.0823	0.9177	0.0553	24	2	TEST
162.000	0.0412	0.9588	0.0401	25	1	STANDARD
186.000	0.0000	1.0000	0.0000	26	0	TEST

* CENSORED OBSERVATION

❻ QUANTILES

75%	92.000	MEAN	65.556	❹
50%	51.000	STANDARD ERROR	10.127	❺
25%	19.000			

VA lung cancer data from Appendix I of K&P 2

PRODUCT LIMIT SURVIVAL ESTIMATES
CELL=LARGE

T	SURVIVAL	FAILURE	STANDARD ERROR	NUM. EVENT	NUM. LEFT	THERAPY
0.000	1.0000	0.0000	0.0000	0	27	
12.000	0.9630	0.0370	0.0363	1	26	STANDARD
15.000	0.9259	0.0741	0.0504	2	25	TEST
19.000	0.8889	0.1111	0.0605	3	24	TEST
43.000	0.8519	0.1481	0.0684	4	23	TEST
49.000	0.8148	0.1852	0.0748	5	22	TEST
52.000	0.7778	0.2222	0.0800	6	21	TEST
53.000	0.7407	0.2593	0.0843	7	20	TEST
100.000	0.7037	0.2963	0.0879	8	19	STANDARD
103.000	0.6667	0.3333	0.0907	9	18	STANDARD
105.000	0.6296	0.3704	0.0929	10	17	STANDARD
111.000	0.5926	0.4074	0.0946	11	16	TEST
133.000	0.5556	0.4444	0.0956	12	15	TEST
143.000	0.5185	0.4815	0.0962	13	14	STANDARD
156.000	0.4815	0.5185	0.0962	14	13	STANDARD
162.000	0.4444	0.5556	0.0956	15	12	STANDARD
164.000	0.4074	0.5926	0.0946	16	11	TEST
177.000	0.3704	0.6296	0.0929	17	10	STANDARD
182.000*	.	.	.	17	9	STANDARD
200.000	0.3292	0.6708	0.0913	18	8	STANDARD
216.000	0.2881	0.7119	0.0887	19	7	STANDARD
231.000	0.2469	0.7531	0.0850	20	6	TEST
250.000	0.2058	0.7942	0.0802	21	5	STANDARD
260.000	0.1646	0.8354	0.0740	22	4	STANDARD
278.000	0.1235	0.8765	0.0659	23	3	STANDARD
340.000	0.0823	0.9177	0.0553	24	2	TEST
378.000	0.0412	0.9588	0.0401	25	1	TEST
553.000	0.0000	1.0000	0.0000	26	0	STANDARD

* CENSORED OBSERVATION

QUANTILES

75%	231.000	MEAN	170.506
50%	156.000	STANDARD ERROR	25.098
25%	53.000		

VA lung cancer data from Appendix I of K&P 3

PRODUCT LIMIT SURVIVAL ESTIMATES
CELL=SMALL

T	SURVIVAL	FAILURE	STANDARD ERROR	NUM. EVENT	NUM. LEFT	THERAPY
0.000	1.0000	0.0000	0.0000	0	48	
2.000	0.9792	0.0208	0.0206	1	47	TEST
4.000	0.9583	0.0417	0.0288	2	46	STANDARD
7.000	.	.	.	3	45	STANDARD
7.000	0.9167	0.0833	0.0399	4	44	TEST
8.000	0.8958	0.1042	0.0441	5	43	TEST
10.000	0.8750	0.1250	0.0477	6	42	STANDARD
13.000	.	.	.	7	41	STANDARD
13.000	0.8333	0.1667	0.0538	8	40	TEST
16.000	0.8125	0.1875	0.0563	9	39	STANDARD
18.000	.	.	.	10	38	STANDARD
18.000	0.7708	0.2292	0.0607	11	37	STANDARD
20.000	.	.	.	12	36	STANDARD
20.000	0.7292	0.2708	0.0641	13	35	TEST
21.000	.	.	.	14	34	STANDARD
21.000	0.6875	0.3125	0.0669	15	33	TEST
22.000	0.6667	0.3333	0.0680	16	32	STANDARD
24.000	0.6458	0.3542	0.0690	17	31	TEST
25.000	.	.	.	18	30	TEST
25.000	0.6042	0.3958	0.0706	19	29	TEST
27.000	0.5833	0.4167	0.0712	20	28	STANDARD
29.000	0.5625	0.4375	0.0716	21	27	TEST
30.000	0.5417	0.4583	0.0719	22	26	STANDARD
31.000	0.5208	0.4792	0.0721	23	25	STANDARD
51.000	.	.	.	24	24	STANDARD
51.000	0.4792	0.5208	0.0721	25	23	TEST
52.000	0.4583	0.5417	0.0719	26	22	STANDARD
54.000	.	.	.	27	21	STANDARD
54.000	0.4167	0.5833	0.0712	28	20	STANDARD
56.000	0.3958	0.6042	0.0706	29	19	STANDARD
59.000	0.3750	0.6250	0.0699	30	18	STANDARD
61.000	0.3542	0.6458	0.0690	31	17	TEST

(continued on next page)

(continued from previous page)

T	SURVIVAL	FAILURE	STANDARD ERROR	NUM. EVENT	NUM. LEFT	THERAPY
63.000	0.3333	0.6667	0.0680	32	16	STANDARD
80.000	0.3125	0.6875	0.0669	33	15	TEST
87.000	0.2917	0.7083	0.0656	34	14	TEST
95.000	0.2708	0.7292	0.0641	35	13	TEST
97.000*	.	.	.	35	12	STANDARD
99.000	.	.	.	36	11	TEST
99.000	0.2257	0.7743	0.0609	37	10	TEST
103.000*	.	.	.	37	9	TEST
117.000	0.2006	0.7994	0.0591	38	8	STANDARD
122.000	0.1755	0.8245	0.0567	39	7	STANDARD
123.000*	.	.	.	39	6	STANDARD
139.000	0.1463	0.8537	0.0543	40	5	STANDARD
151.000	0.1170	0.8830	0.0507	41	4	STANDARD
153.000	0.0878	0.9122	0.0457	42	3	STANDARD
287.000	0.0585	0.9415	0.0387	43	2	STANDARD
384.000	0.0293	0.9707	0.0283	44	1	STANDARD
392.000	0.0000	1.0000	0.0000	45	0	STANDARD

* CENSORED OBSERVATION

VA lung cancer data from Appendix I of K&P 4

QUANTILES

75%	99.000	MEAN	78.981
50%	51.000	STANDARD ERROR	14.837
25%	20.000		

VA lung cancer data from Appendix I of K&P 5

PRODUCT LIMIT SURVIVAL ESTIMATES
CELL=SQUAMOUS

T	SURVIVAL	FAILURE	STANDARD ERROR	NUM. EVENT	NUM. LEFT	THERAPY
0.000	1.0000	0.0000	0.0000	0	35	
1.000	.	.	.	1	34	TEST
1.000	0.9429	0.0571	0.0392	2	33	TEST
8.000	0.9143	0.0857	0.0473	3	32	STANDARD
10.000	0.8857	0.1143	0.0538	4	31	STANDARD
11.000	0.8571	0.1429	0.0591	5	30	STANDARD
15.000	0.8286	0.1714	0.0637	6	29	TEST
25.000	0.8000	0.2000	0.0676	7	28	TEST
25.000*	.	.	.	7	27	STANDARD
30.000	0.7704	0.2296	0.0713	8	26	TEST
33.000	0.7407	0.2593	0.0745	9	25	TEST
42.000	0.7111	0.2889	0.0772	10	24	STANDARD
44.000	0.6815	0.3185	0.0794	11	23	TEST
72.000	0.6519	0.3481	0.0813	12	22	STANDARD
82.000	0.6222	0.3778	0.0828	13	21	STANDARD
87.000*	.	.	.	13	20	TEST
100.000*	.	.	.	13	19	STANDARD
110.000	0.5895	0.4105	0.0847	14	18	STANDARD
111.000	0.5567	0.4433	0.0861	15	17	TEST
112.000	0.5240	0.4760	0.0870	16	16	TEST
118.000	0.4912	0.5088	0.0875	17	15	STANDARD
126.000	0.4585	0.5415	0.0876	18	14	STANDARD
144.000	0.4257	0.5743	0.0873	19	13	STANDARD
201.000	0.3930	0.6070	0.0865	20	12	TEST
228.000	0.3602	0.6398	0.0852	21	11	STANDARD
231.000*	.	.	.	21	10	TEST
242.000	0.3242	0.6758	0.0840	22	9	TEST
283.000	0.2882	0.7118	0.0820	23	8	TEST
314.000	0.2522	0.7478	0.0793	24	7	STANDARD
357.000	0.2161	0.7839	0.0757	25	6	TEST
389.000	0.1801	0.8199	0.0711	26	5	TEST
411.000	0.1441	0.8559	0.0654	27	4	STANDARD
467.000	0.1081	0.8919	0.0581	28	3	TEST
587.000	0.0720	0.9280	0.0487	29	2	TEST
991.000	0.0360	0.9640	0.0352	30	1	TEST
999.000	0.0000	1.0000	0.0000	31	0	TEST

* CENSORED OBSERVATION

QUANTILES

75%	357.000	MEAN	230.225
50%	118.000	STANDARD ERROR	48.475
25%	33.000		

(continued on next page)

(continued from previous page)

❼

EVENTS	CENSORED	TOTAL	%CENSORED	STRATA
26	1	27	3.7037	ADENO
26	1	27	3.7037	LARGE
45	3	48	6.2500	SMALL
31	4	35	11.4286	SQUAMOUS
======	======	======	=======	
128	9	137	6.5693	TOTAL

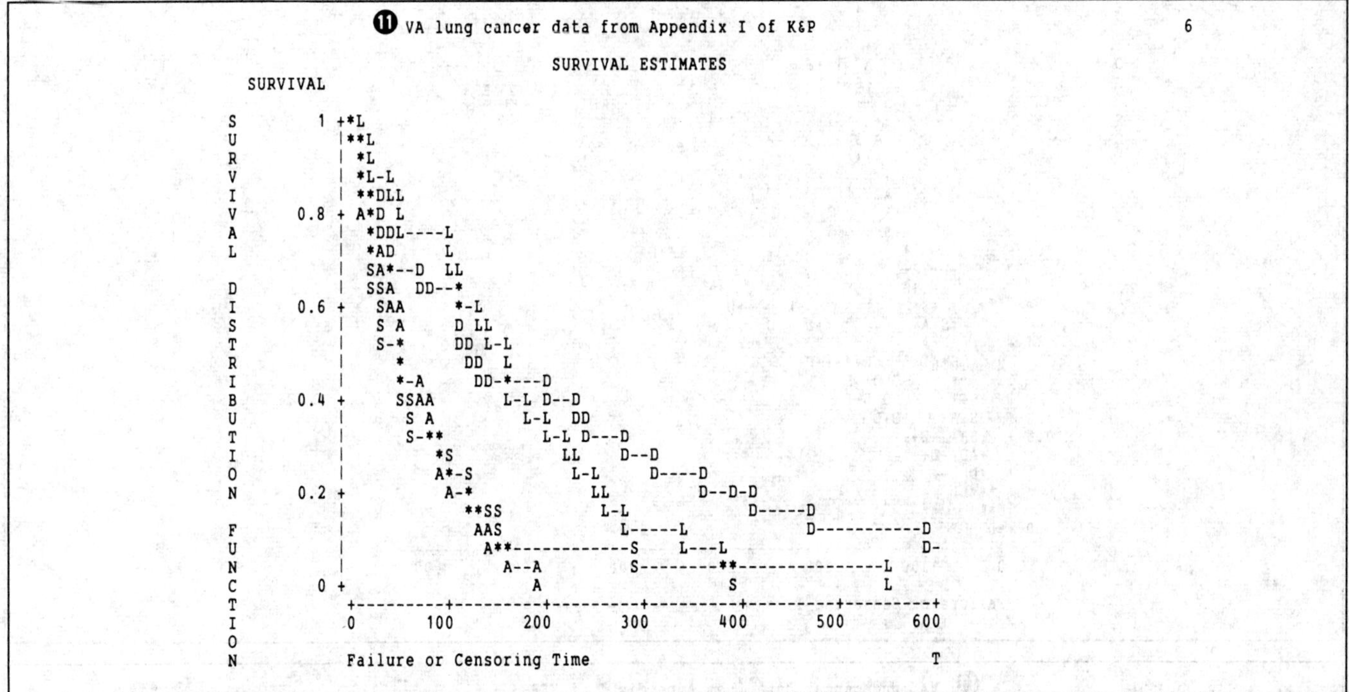

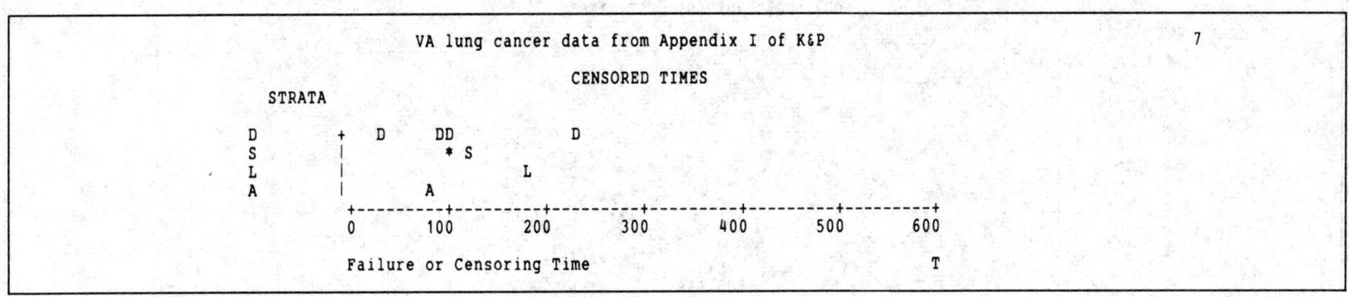

```
12  VA lung cancer data from Appendix I of K&P                              8

                         -LOG(SURVIVAL) ESTIMATES
    -LOG SDF

N   3.5 +                                      S
E       |                                     +
G       |                                    ++
A       |                A                  +  L
T       |                +                 +   +
I     3 +                +               ++    +                         +
V       |                +              +     +                          +
E       |                +             +S     +                          +
        |                +         ++++      +                           +
L       |               +      +++           +                          +D
O   2.5 +               A  ++++            L                         +++
G       |               +S+               ++                      +++
        |               ++               +                     +++
S       |              + +              ++                  +D+
D       |              A S             L                  ++
F     2 +              + +            +                 ++
        |             + S             +               D
        |             A+             L               +
        |            +S              +              D
        |           A+S             L             ++
    1.5 +           *              +            ++D
        |          A+              L          D++
        |          +S              +        ++
        |        +S*             +L    ++D
        |       S A            +L    D+
      1 +       S A          +L    +D
        |      S*A        D+*+++D+
        |      *          D  L
        |    S+*         D L+L
        |    S A       D+L
    0.5 +    SA    D++*
        |  *AD++D++L
        |  *DDL++
        | ***LL
        |D*L
      0 +*L
        +---------+---------+---------+---------+---------+---------+
        0        100       200       300       400       500       600

        Failure or Censoring Time                                     T
```

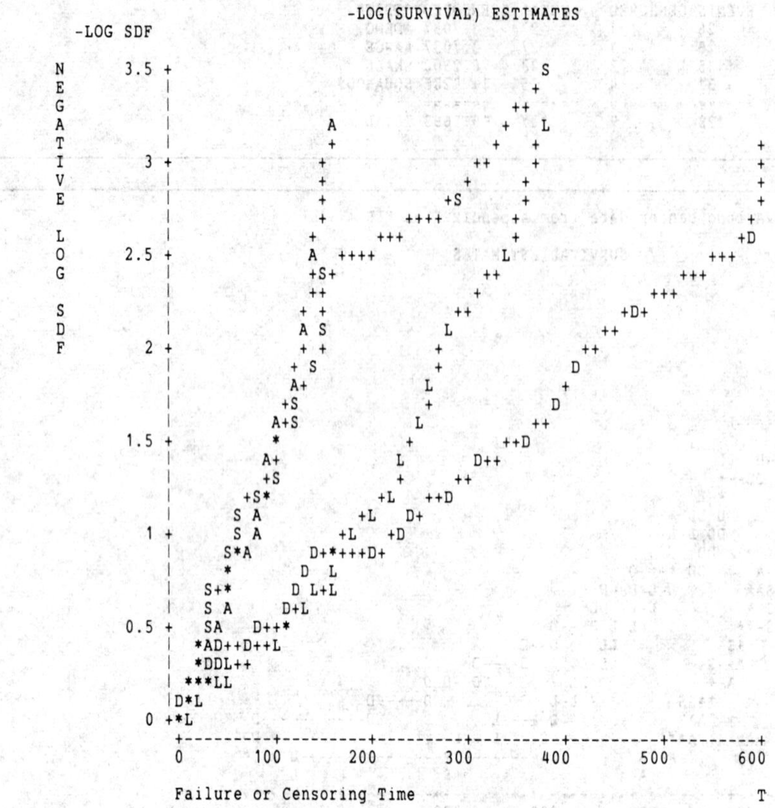

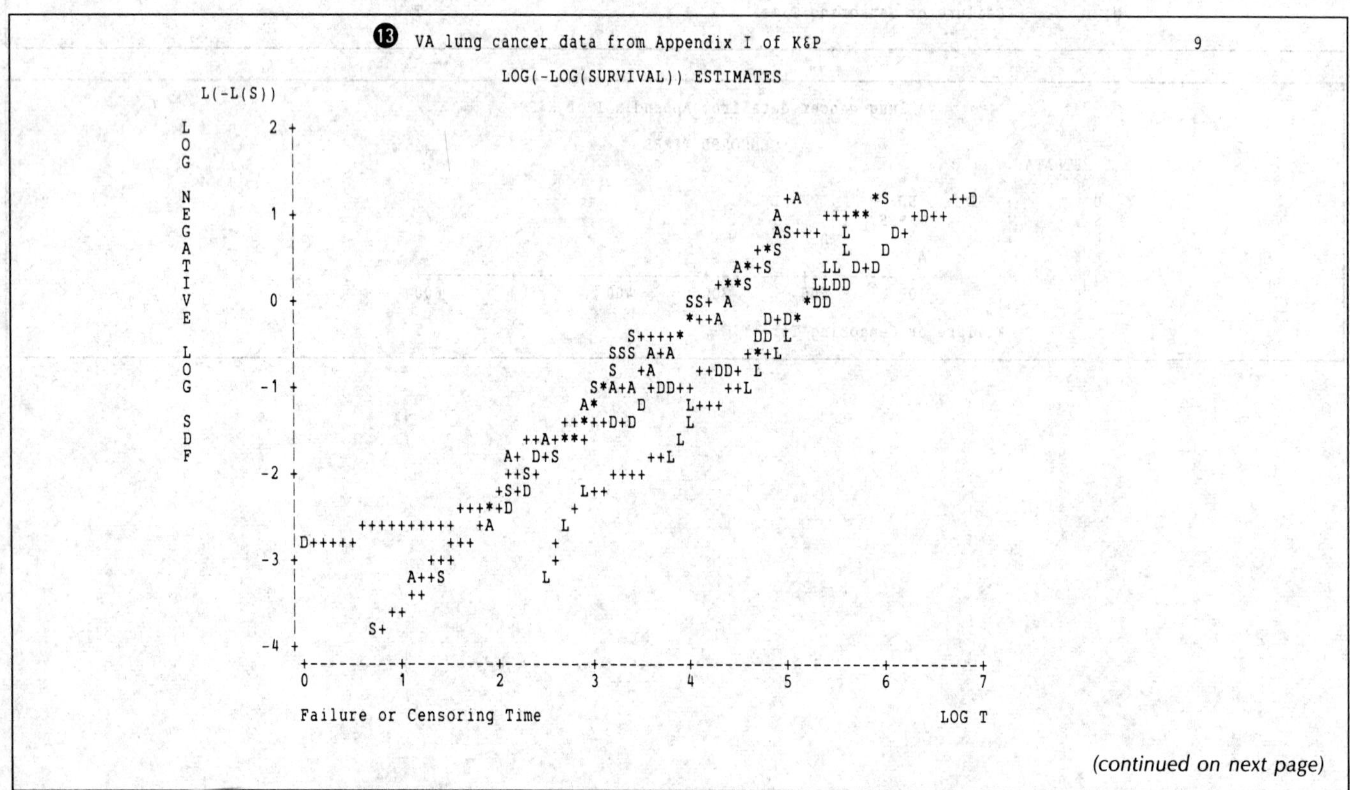

(continued on next page)

(continued from previous page)

```
                                                                 LEGEND FOR STRATA SYMBOLS
                                CELL        CELL        CELL        CELL
                             A=ADENO     L=LARGE     S=SMALL     D=SQUAMOUS


                                          LOG RANK TESTS

              LOG RANK              A              L              S              D

              A               12.9662        -4.0701        -4.4087        -4.4873        10.3062
              L               -4.0701        24.1990        -7.8117       -12.3172        -8.5495
              S               -4.4087        -7.8117        21.7543        -9.5339        14.8979
              D               -4.4873       -12.3172        -9.5339        26.3384       -16.6547
                              10.3062        -8.5495        14.8979       -16.6547         0.0000
```

```
                              VA lung cancer data from Appendix I of K&P                                  10

                                          WILCOXON RANK TESTS

              WILCOXON              A              L              S              D

              A                121188         -34718         -46639         -39831         697.00
              L                -34718         151241         -59948         -56576       -1085.00
              S                -46639         -59948         175590         -69002        1278.00
              D                -39831         -56576         -69002         165410        -890.00
                                  697          -1085           1278           -890           0.00

                                                                 LEGEND FOR STRATA SYMBOLS
                                CELL        CELL        CELL        CELL
                             A=ADENO     L=LARGE     S=SMALL     D=SQUAMOUS
                                     TESTS OF EQUALITY OVER STRATA

                          (9) TEST        CHI-SQUARE    DF  APPROX P-VALUE
                          (8)   LOGRANK     25.403700     3          0.0001
                          (10)  WILCOXON    19.433126     3          0.0002
                                -2*LN(L)    33.934346     3          0.0001


                                    UNIVARIATE CHISQUARES FOR WILCOXON
                            TEST
      VARIABLE         STATISTIC         VARIANCE       CHISQUARE        PROB>CHI       LABEL

      AGE          (21)  14.4158           4456.9     (22) 0.0466     (23) 0.8290       Age in Years
      PRIOR             -26.3997            836.1          0.8336          0.3612       Prior Treatment?
      DIAGTIME          -82.5069           5185.7          1.3127          0.2519       Months Till Randomization
      KPS                  856.0          14113.4         51.9159          0.0001       Karnofsky Index
      TREAT              -3.1952          10.1822          1.0027          0.3167       Treatment indicator


                                    (20)   VARIANCE MATRIX FOR WILCOXON

              WILCOXON            AGE          PRIOR       DIAGTIME            KPS          TREAT

              AGE             4456.87       -214.674        -343.81        -1153.9        31.9756
              PRIOR           -214.67        836.077         777.59         -197.1        -4.1379
              DIAGTIME        -343.81        777.589        5185.69        -1548.2        15.8733
              KPS            -1153.92       -197.131       -1548.22        14113.4       -24.5202
              TREAT             31.98         -4.138          15.87          -24.5        10.1822


                             FORWARD STEPWISE SEQUENCE OF CHISQUARES FOR WILCOXON
 VARIABLE        DF      CHISQUARE        PROB>CHI       CHISQ INCR        PROB>CHI       LABEL

 KPS              1        51.9159          0.0001          51.9159          0.0001       Karnofsky Index
 AGE              2        53.5489          0.0001           1.6329          0.2013       Age in Years
 TREAT            3        54.0758          0.0001           0.5269          0.4679       Treatment indicator
 PRIOR            4        54.2139          0.0001           0.1381          0.7101       Prior Treatment?
 DIAGTIME         5        54.4814          0.0001           0.2674          0.6051       Months Till Randomization
```

VA lung cancer data from Appendix I of K&P 11

UNIVARIATE CHISQUARES FOR LOG RANK

VARIABLE	TEST STATISTIC ⑰	VARIANCE	CHISQUARE ⑱	PROB>CHI ⑲	LABEL
AGE	40.7383	11175.4	0.1485	0.7000	Age in Years
PRIOR	19.9435	2207.5	0.1802	0.6712	Prior Treatment?
DIAGTIME	115.9	9578.7	1.4013	0.2365	Months Till Randomization
KPS	-1123.1	29015.6	43.4747	0.0001	Karnofsky Index
TREAT	4.2076	25.4090	0.6967	0.4039	Treatment indicator

⑯ VARIANCE MATRIX FOR LOG RANK

LOG RANK	AGE	PRIOR	DIAGTIME	KPS	TREAT
AGE	11175.4	-301.23	-892.24	-2948.4	119.297
PRIOR	-301.2	2207.46	2010.85	78.6	13.875
DIAGTIME	-892.2	2010.85	9578.69	-2295.3	21.859
KPS	-2948.4	78.64	-2295.32	29015.6	61.945
TREAT	119.3	13.87	21.86	61.9	25.409

FORWARD STEPWISE SEQUENCE OF CHISQUARES FOR LOG RANK

VARIABLE	DF	CHISQUARE	PROB>CHI	CHISQ INCR	PROB>CHI	LABEL
KPS	1	43.4747	0.0001	43.4747	0.0001	Karnofsky Index
TREAT	2	45.2008	0.0001	1.7261	0.1889	Treatment indicator
AGE	3	46.3012	0.0001	1.1004	0.2942	Age in Years
PRIOR	4	46.4134	0.0001	0.1122	0.7377	Prior Treatment?
DIAGTIME	5	46.4200	0.0001	.0066517	0.9350	Months Till Randomization

VA lung cancer data from Appendix I of K&P 12

N=10000 REGRESSION MODELS FOR DEPENDENT VARIABLE: T MODEL: MODEL1

NUMBER IN MODEL	R-SQUARE	VARIABLES IN MODEL
1	0.00319916	AGE
1	0.00388154	PRIOR
1	0.01500948	TREAT
1	0.03018749	DIAGTIME
1	0.93655158	KPS
2	0.00753586	AGE PRIOR
2	0.01590303	AGE TREAT
2	0.01805867	PRIOR TREAT
2	0.03041878	PRIOR DIAGTIME
2	0.03534445	AGE DIAGTIME
2	0.04339589	DIAGTIME TREAT
2	0.93822385	DIAGTIME KPS
2	0.94170901	PRIOR KPS
2	0.94722032	AGE KPS
2	0.97373615	KPS TREAT
3	0.01922675	AGE PRIOR TREAT
3	0.03552332	AGE PRIOR DIAGTIME
3	0.04380568	PRIOR DIAGTIME TREAT
3	0.04558237	AGE DIAGTIME TREAT
3	0.94181173	PRIOR DIAGTIME KPS
3	0.94809518	AGE DIAGTIME KPS
3	0.95154354	AGE PRIOR KPS
3	0.97465738	DIAGTIME KPS TREAT
3	0.97742399	PRIOR KPS TREAT
3	0.99744050	AGE KPS TREAT
4	0.04592628	AGE PRIOR DIAGTIME TREAT
4	0.95154408	AGE PRIOR DIAGTIME KPS
4	0.97743976	PRIOR DIAGTIME KPS TREAT
4	0.99755435	AGE DIAGTIME KPS TREAT
4	0.99985671	AGE PRIOR KPS TREAT
5	1.00000000	AGE PRIOR DIAGTIME KPS TREAT

Life Table Estimates: Example 2

The data in this example come from Lee (1980, 93) and represent the survival rate of males with angina pectoris. The data are read as number of events and number of withdrawals in each time interval. Life table estimates of the survival curve are requested. Plots of the survival, -log(survival), log(-log(survival)), hazard and probability density estimates are also printed.

```
/* DATA FROM LEE: STATISTICAL METHODS FOR SURVIVAL DATA ANALYSIS */
/*                        PAGE 90-98                             */

DATA; KEEP FREQ TIME C;
   RETAIN TIME -.5;
   INPUT FAIL WITHDRAW @@;
   TIME=TIME+1;
   C=0; T=TIME; FREQ=FAIL;      OUTPUT;
   C=1;         FREQ=WITHDRAW; OUTPUT;
   CARDS;
 456   0 226  39 152  22 171  23 135 24 125 107
  83 133  74 102  51  68  42  64  43 45  34  53
  18  33   9  27   6  23   0   0   0 30
;

PROC LIFETEST PLOTS=(S,LS,LLS,H,P) INTERVALS=(0 TO 15) METHOD=ACT;
   TIME TIME*C(1);
   FREQ FREQ;
```

Output 22.4 Life Table Estimates

1

LIFE TABLE SURVIVAL ESTIMATES

INTERVAL	MIDPOINT	EVENTS	WITHDRAWALS	EFFECTIVE SIZE	CONDITIONAL PROBABILITY	PROBABLITY STD ERROR	SURVIVAL	FAILURE
0	0.5	456	0	2418.0	0.18859	0.00796	1.0000	0.0000
1	1.5	226	39	1942.5	0.11634	0.00728	0.8114	0.1886
2	2.5	152	22	1686.0	0.09015	0.00698	0.7170	0.2830
3	3.5	171	23	1511.5	0.11313	0.00815	0.6524	0.3476
4	4.5	135	24	1317.0	0.10251	0.00836	0.5786	0.4214
5	5.5	125	107	1116.5	0.11196	0.00944	0.5193	0.4807
6	6.5	83	133	871.5	0.09524	0.00994	0.4611	0.5389
7	7.5	74	102	671.0	0.11028	0.01209	0.4172	0.5828
8	8.5	51	68	512.0	0.09961	0.01324	0.3712	0.6288
9	9.5	42	64	395.0	0.10633	0.01551	0.3342	0.6658
10	10.5	43	45	298.5	0.14405	0.02032	0.2987	0.7013
11	11.5	34	53	206.5	0.16465	0.02581	0.2557	0.7443
12	12.5	18	33	129.5	0.13900	0.03040	0.2136	0.7864
13	13.5	9	27	81.5	0.11043	0.03472	0.1839	0.8161
14	14.5	6	23	47.5	0.12632	0.04820	0.1636	0.8364
15	.	0	30	15.0	0.00000	.	0.1429	0.8571

(continued on next page)

(continued from previous page)

		SURVIVAL STD ERROR	PDF	PDF STD ERROR	HAZARD	HAZARD STD ERROR	CONDITIONAL MEDIAN	MEDIAN STD ERROR
0	0.5	0.0000	0.1886	.0079551	0.2082	.0096978	5.33127	0.174907
1	1.5	0.0080	0.0944	.0059752	0.1235	.0082015	6.24994	0.200065
2	2.5	0.0092	0.0646	.0050692	0.0944	.0076491	6.34324	0.236136
3	3.5	0.0097	0.0738	0.005428	0.1199	.0091537	6.22616	0.236087
4	4.5	0.0101	0.0593	0.004946	0.1080	.0092853	6.21851	0.185265
5	5.5	0.0103	0.0581	0.005034	0.1186	0.0106	5.9077	0.180588
6	6.5	0.0104	0.0439	.0046905	0.1000	0.0110	5.59619	0.185539
7	7.5	0.0105	0.0460	.0051751	0.1167	0.0135	5.1671	0.271288
8	8.5	0.0106	0.0370	.0050246	0.1048	0.0147	4.9421	0.276317
9	9.5	0.0107	0.0355	.0053076	0.1123	0.0173	4.8258	0.414084
10	10.5	0.0109	0.0430	0.00627	0.1552	0.0236	4.68878	0.418349
11	11.5	0.0111	0.0421	.0068475	0.1794	0.0306	.	.
12	12.5	0.0114	0.0297	.0066827	0.1494	0.0351	.	.
13	13.5	0.0118	0.0203	.0065148	0.1169	0.0389	.	.
14	14.5	0.0123	0.0207	.0080351	0.1348	0.0549	.	.
15	.	0.0133	.	.	.	.	.	.

EVENTS	CENSORED	TOTAL	%CENSORED
1625	793	2418	32.7957

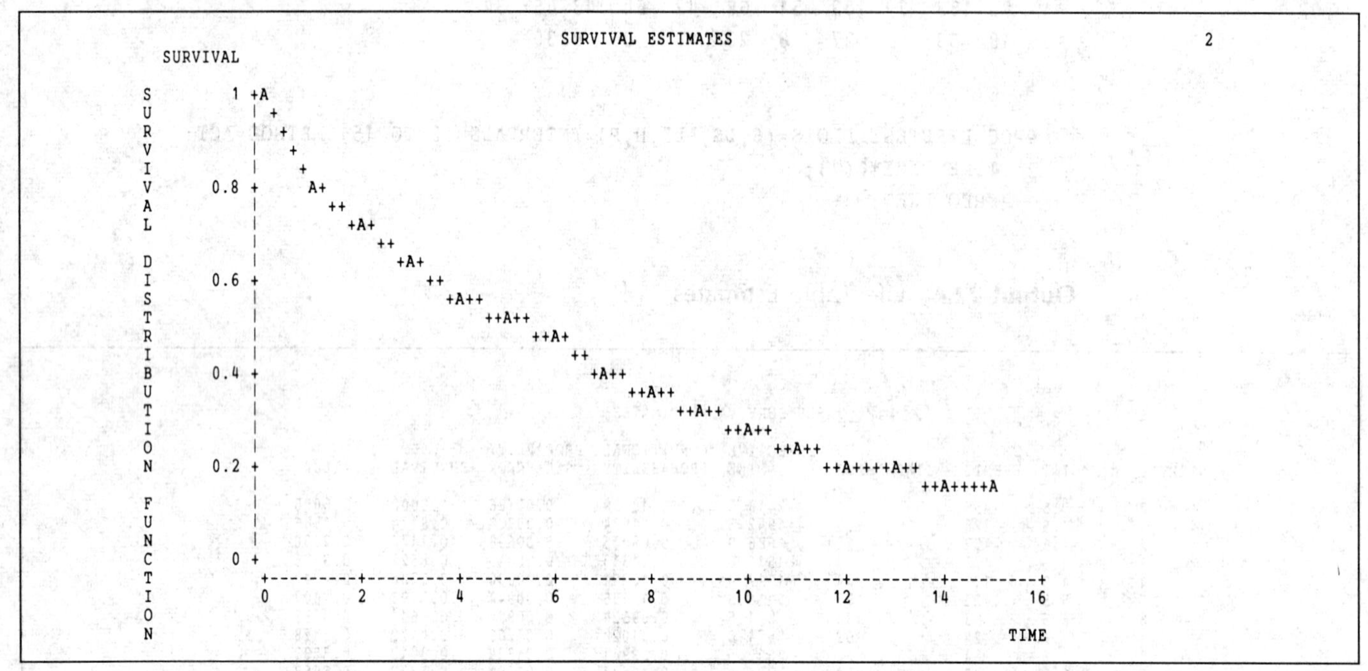

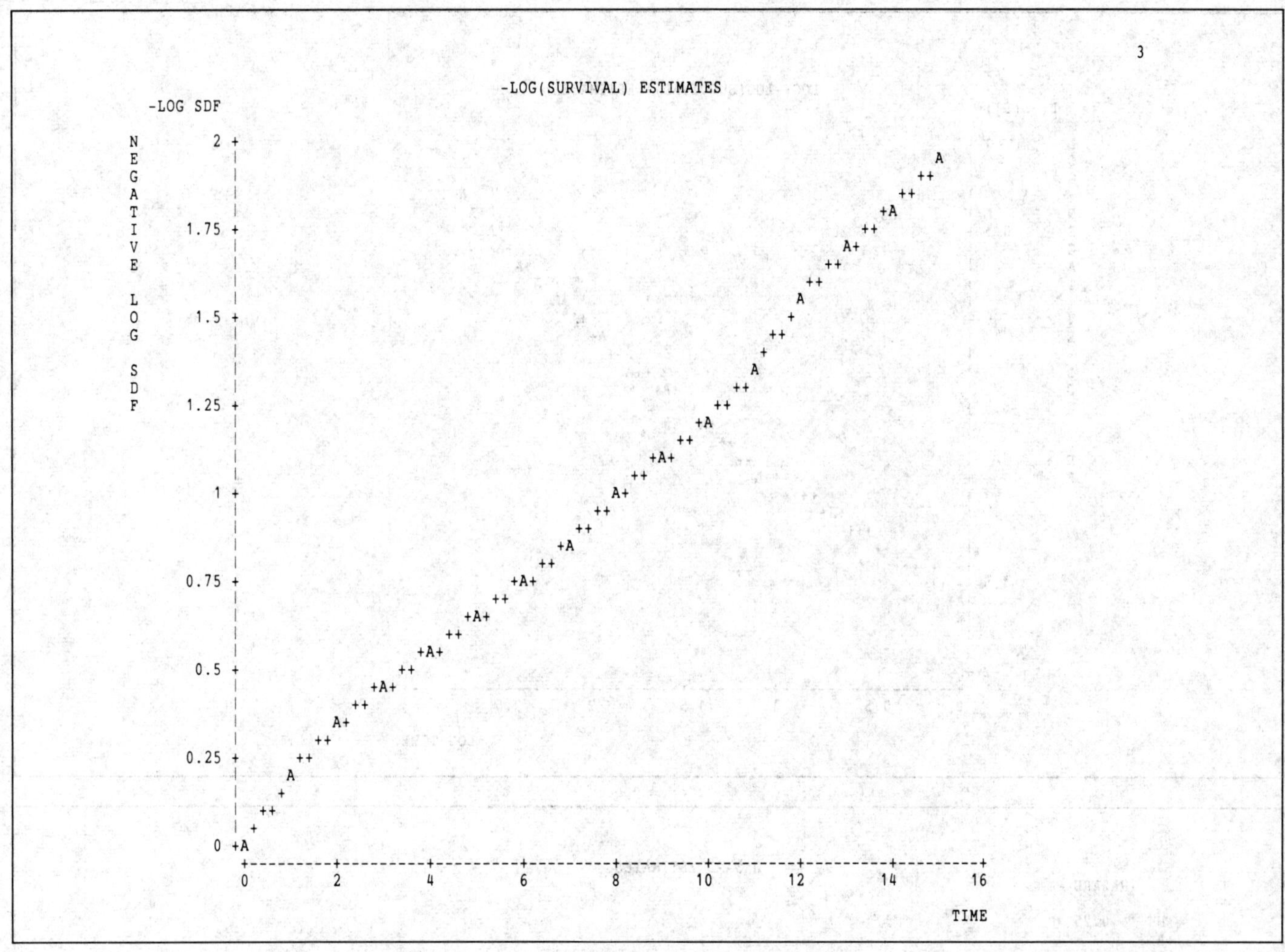
3
-LOG(SURVIVAL) ESTIMATES
-LOG SDF
NEGATIVE LOG SDF
2
1.75
1.5
1.25
1
0.75
0.5
0.25
0
0
2
4
6
8
10
12
14
16
TIME

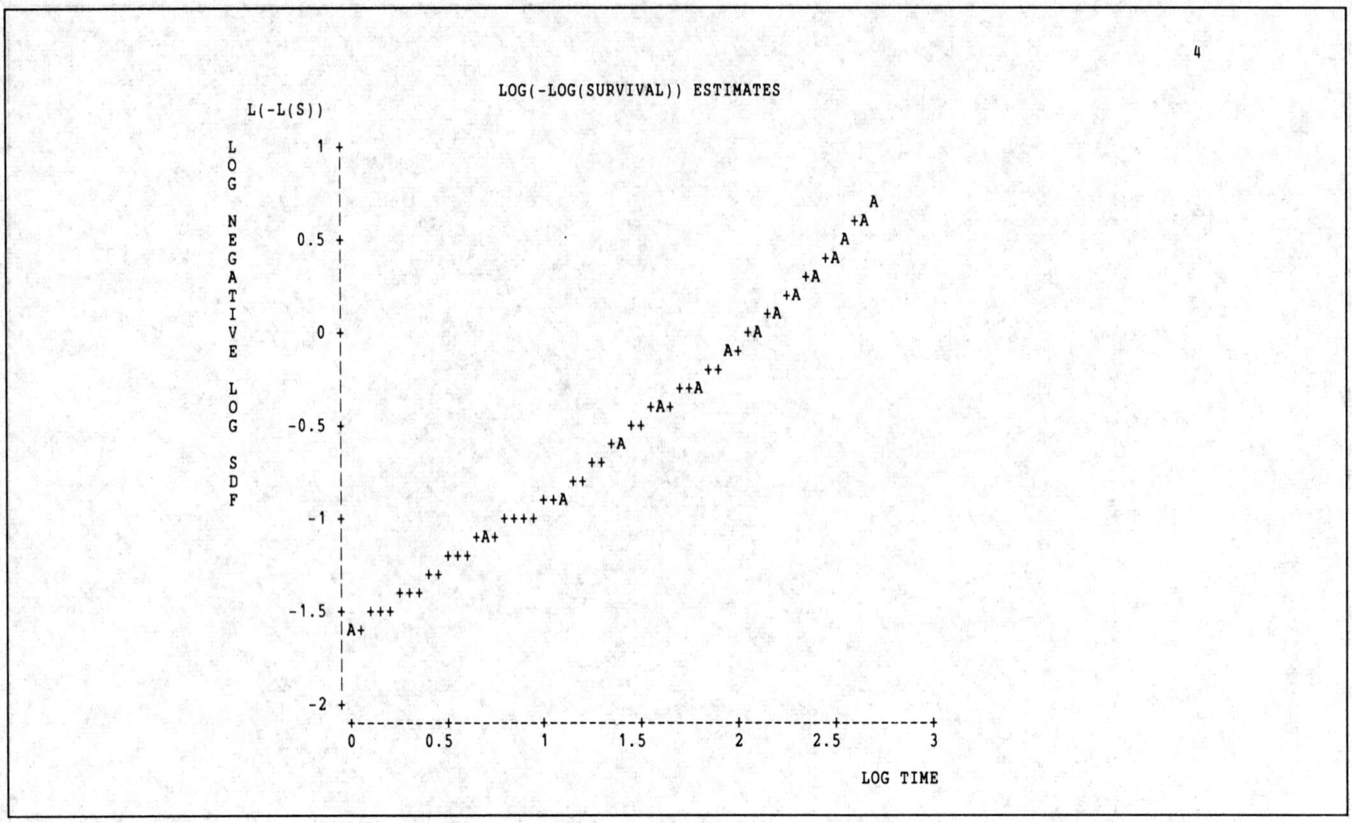

```
                                                                                                    4

                            LOG(-LOG(SURVIVAL)) ESTIMATES
  L(-L(S))
L        1 +
O          |
G          |
           |                                                      A
N          |                                                    +A
E      0.5 +                                                   A
G          |                                                 +A
A          |                                               +A
T          |                                             +A
I          |                                           +A
V        0 +                                         +A
E          |                                       A+
           |                                     ++
L          |                                  ++A
O          |                               +A+
G     -0.5 +                             ++
           |                           +A
S          |                         ++
D          |                       ++
F          |                    ++A
        -1 +                ++++
           |             +A+
           |          +++
           |        ++
           |     +++
      -1.5 +  +++
           |A+
           |
           |
           |
        -2 +
            +---------+---------+---------+---------+---------+---------+
            0        0.5        1        1.5        2        2.5        3

                                                                 LOG TIME
```

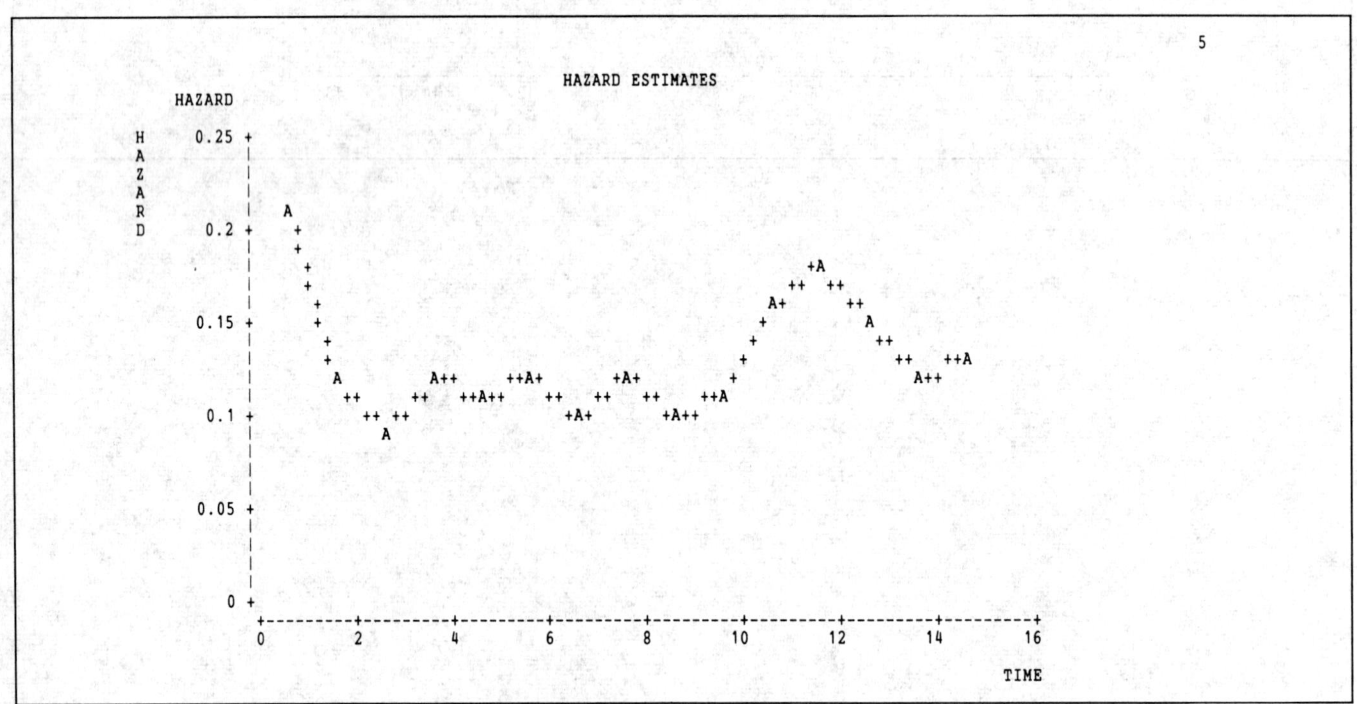

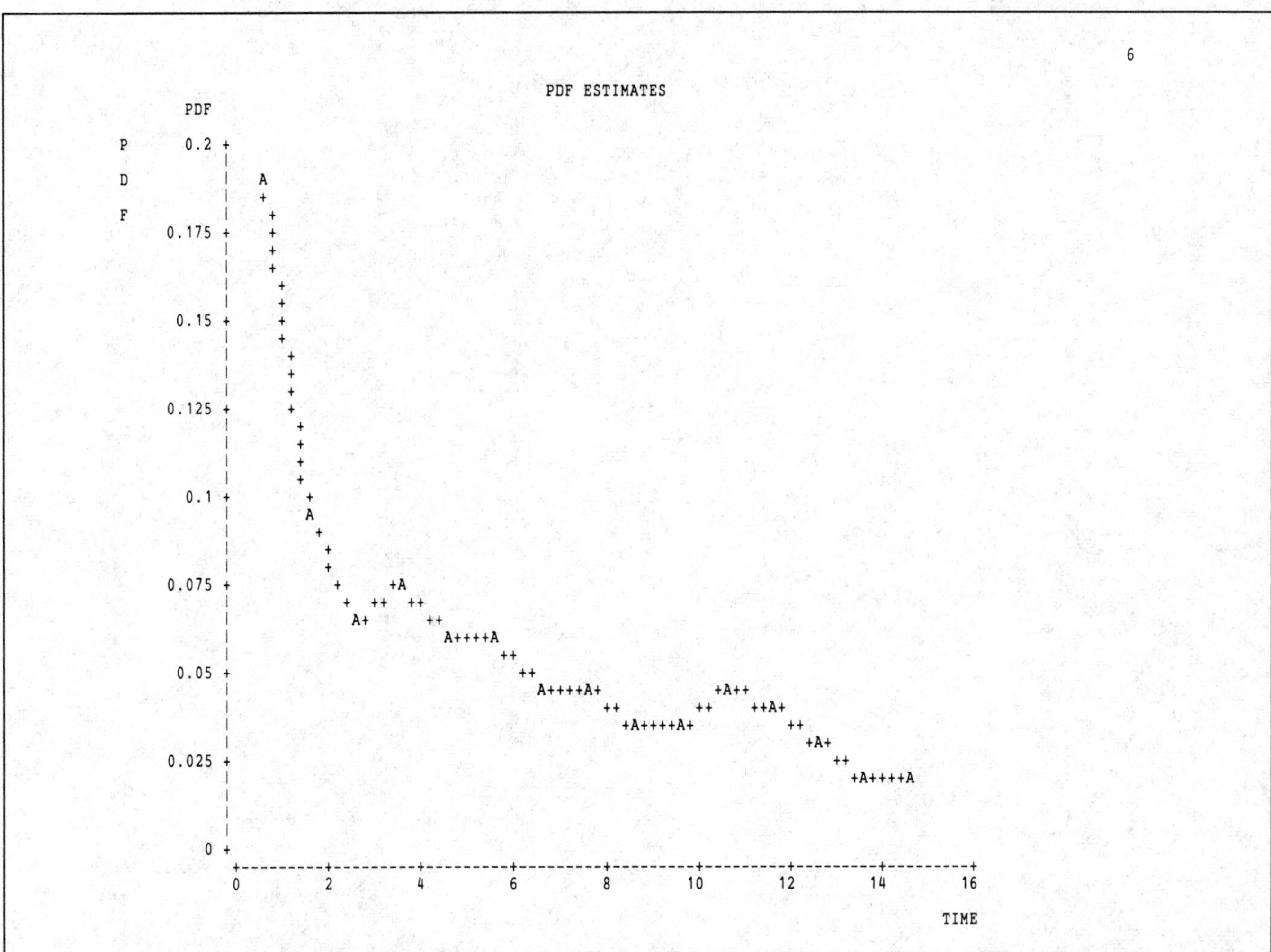

REFERENCES

Cox, D.R. and Oakes, D. (1984), *Analysis of Survival Data*, London: Chapman and Hall.

Elandt-Johnson, R.C. and Johnson, N.L. (1980), *Survival Models and Data Analysis*, New York: John Wiley & Sons.

Kalbfleisch, J.D. and Prentice, R.L. (1980), *The Statistical Analysis of Failure Time Data*, New York: John Wiley & Sons.

Lawless, J.E. (1982), *Statistical Models and Methods for Lifetime Data*, New York: John Wiley & Sons.

Lee, E.T. (1980), *Statistical Methods for Survival Data Analysis*, Belmont, CA: Lifetime Learning Publications.

Chapter 23

The NEIGHBOR Procedure

Operating systems: AOS/VS, CMS, OS, VM/PC, VMS, and VSE

ABSTRACT

PROC NEIGHBOR performs a nearest neighbor discriminant analysis, classifying observations into groups according to either the nearest neighbor rule or the *k*-nearest-neighbor rule.

INTRODUCTION

PROC NEIGHBOR can be used to classify observations when the classes do not have multivariate normal distributions. Given an observation to classify, NEIGHBOR looks at the *k* observations closest to it, that is, the *k* nearest neighbors. Either Mahalanobis distance, based on the total covariance matrix, or Euclidean distance can be used to determine proximity. The observation is placed in the class containing the highest proportion of the *k* nearest neighbors. Optionally, classification can be based on the proportion of nearest neighbors multiplied by a prior probability for each class.

Background

Nearest neighbor discriminant analysis is a nonparametric method for classifying observations into one of several classes on the basis of one or more quantitative variables.

Letting $\mathbf{x}_1$ and $\mathbf{x}_2$ represent two observation vectors, NEIGHBOR computes the Mahalanobis distance between $\mathbf{x}_1$ and $\mathbf{x}_2$ based on the total-sample covariance matrix **T**:

$$d^2(\mathbf{x}_1, \mathbf{x}_2) = (\mathbf{x}_1 - \mathbf{x}_2)'\mathbf{T}^{-1}(\mathbf{x}_1 - \mathbf{x}_2)$$

or optionally the Euclidean distance:

$$d^2(\mathbf{x}_1, \mathbf{x}_2) = (\mathbf{x}_1 - \mathbf{x}_2)'(\mathbf{x}_1 - \mathbf{x}_2) \quad .$$

Using the nearest neighbor rule, $\mathbf{x}_2$ is classified into the group corresponding to the $\mathbf{x}_1$ point that yields the smallest $d^2(\mathbf{x}_1,\mathbf{x}_2)$. Using the *k*-nearest-neighbor rule, the *k* smallest distances are saved. Of these *k* distances, let n_i represent the number of distances that correspond to group *i*. The posterior probability of membership in group *i* is

$$P_i = \frac{n_i \text{ prior}_i}{\Sigma\, n_j \text{ prior}_j}$$

Then $\mathbf{x}_2$ is assigned to the group for which P_i is a maximum, unless there is a tie for largest or unless this maximum probability is less than the threshold specified. In these cases, $\mathbf{x}_2$ is classified into group OTHER.

SPECIFICATIONS

The following statements are used with NEIGHBOR:

PROC NEIGHBOR *options;*
CLASS *variable;*
VAR *variables;*
ID *variable;*
PRIORS *probabilities;*
TESTCLASS *variable;*
TESTID *variable;*
BY *variables;*

The CLASS statement is required.

PROC NEIGHBOR Statement

PROC NEIGHBOR *options;*

The options below can appear in the PROC NEIGHBOR statement:

K=*k*
: specifies a *k* value for the *k*-nearest-neighbor rule. If K= is not specified, the default *k* value is 1, producing nearest neighbor classification.

IDENTITY
: specifies use of Euclidean distances. If IDENTITY is not specified, Mahalanobis distances are used.

THRESHOLD=*p*
: specifies the minimum acceptable posterior probability for classification. If the posterior probability associated with the smallest distance is less than the THRESHOLD value, the observation is classified into group OTHER. If THRESHOLD= is omitted, no

observations are classified into group OTHER unless there is a tie for the largest posterior probability.

LIST

prints the classification results for each observation.

LISTERR

prints only misclassified observations.

DATA=*SASdataset*

names the SAS data set to be analyzed. If DATA= is not specified, NEIGHBOR uses the most recently created SAS data set.

TESTDATA=*SASdataset*

names a SAS data set to be classified by the classification criterion developed by NEIGHBOR using the DATA= data set. The variable names in the TESTDATA= data set must match those in the DATA= data set.

TESTLIST

lists all the observations in the TESTDATA= data set.

TESTLISTERR

lists only misclassified observations in the TESTDATA= data set.

CLASS Statement

CLASS *variable;*

The CLASS statement gives the name of a *variable* to define the classes. Class levels are determined by the unformatted values of the class variable. A CLASS statement must accompany the PROC NEIGHBOR statement.

VAR Statement

VAR *variables;*

List the *variables* to be included in the analysis in the VAR statement. If the VAR statement is omitted, all numeric variables that are not specified in other statements are included in the analysis.

ID Statement

ID *variable;*

When you use an ID statement and also specify the LIST or LISTERR option, NEIGHBOR prints the value of the identification *variable* to identify observations in the classification results, rather than the observation number.

PRIORS Statement

PRIORS *probabilities;*

If you do not want NEIGHBOR to assume that the prior probabilities are equal, use a PRIORS statement. If you want NEIGHBOR to set the prior probabilities proportional to the sample sizes, use the statement:

```
PRIORS PROPORTIONAL;
```

The keyword PROPORTIONAL can be abbreviated PROP. If you want other than equal or proportional priors, give the prior probability for each level of the classification variable. Each class level can be written as a numeric constant, a SAS name, or a quoted string, and must be followed by an equal sign and a numeric constant between zero and one. For example, if the classification variable GRADE has the four values A, B, C, and D, you can write the PRIORS statement:

```
PRIORS A=.1  B=.3  C=.5  D=.1;
```

If GRADE is a numeric variable with values of 1, 2, and 3, you can write:

```
PRIORS 1=.3  2=.6  3=.1;
```

The prior probabilities specified in the PRIORS statement should sum to one.

TESTCLASS Statement

TESTCLASS *variable*;

The TESTCLASS statement names the *variable* in the TESTDATA= data set to use in determining whether an observation in the TESTDATA= data set is misclassified. The TESTCLASS variable should have the same type (character or numeric) and length as the variable given in the CLASS statement. NEIGHBOR considers an observation misclassified when the TESTCLASS variable's value does not match the group into which the TESTDATA= observation is classified.

TESTID Statement

TESTID *variable*;

When the TESTID statement appears and the TESTLIST or TESTLISTERR options are specified, NEIGHBOR uses the value of the TESTID variable, instead of the observation number, to identify each observation in the classification results for the TESTDATA= data set. The variable given in the TESTID statement must be in the TESTDATA= data set.

BY Statement

BY *variables*;

A BY statement can be used with PROC NEIGHBOR to obtain separate analyses on observations in groups defined by the BY variables. When a BY statement appears, the procedure expects the DATA= data set to be sorted in order of the BY variables. If your DATA= data set is not sorted in ascending order, use the SORT procedure with a similar BY statement to sort the data, or, if appropriate, use the BY statement options NOTSORTED or DESCENDING. For more information, see the discussion of the BY statement "Statements Used in the PROC Step" in the *SAS User's Guide: Basics*.

If TESTDATA= is specified and the TESTDATA= data set does not contain any of the BY variables, then the entire TESTDATA= data set is classified according to the discriminant functions computed in each BY group in the DATA= data set.

If the TESTDATA= data set contains some but not all of the BY variables, or if some BY variables do not have the same type or length in the TESTDATA= data set as in the DATA= data set, then NEIGHBOR prints an error message and stops.

If all the BY variables appear in the TESTDATA= data set with the same type and length as in the DATA= data set, then each BY group in the TESTDATA= data set is classified by the discriminant function from the corresponding BY group in the DATA= data set. The BY groups in the TESTDATA= data set must be in the same order as in the DATA= data set. If NOTSORTED is specified on the BY statement, there must be exactly the same BY groups in the same order in both data sets. If NOTSORTED is not specified, it is permissible for some BY groups to appear in one data set but not in the other.

DETAILS

Missing Values

When an observation contains a missing value for a variable needed in the analysis, that observation is excluded from the development of the classification criterion. If the classification value for an observation is missing, but no other variables in that observation have missing values, the observation is classified according to the classification criterion.

Computer Resources

In the following discussion, let:

n=number of observations in the DATA= data set
t=number of observations in the TESTDATA= data set
v=number of variables.

NEIGHBOR stores the data and the covariance matrix in core, requiring:

$$120v + 4v(v + 1) + n(8v + 16)$$

bytes of array storage. The time required to classify the observations is roughly proportional to:

$$(n + t)nv$$

if IDENTITY is specified; otherwise:

$$(n + t)nv^2 \quad .$$

Printed Output

PROC NEIGHBOR produces printed output that includes:

1. values of the classification variable, and the FREQUENCY and PRIOR PROBABILITY for each group.
   Optionally, the classification results for each observation are printed, including:
2. the observation number, or if an ID statement is included, the values of the ID variable are substituted for the observation number
3. the actual group for the observation
4. the group into which the developed criterion classifies it
5. the POSTERIOR PROBABILITY OF its MEMBERSHIP IN each group
6. CLASSIFICATION SUMMARY FOR CALIBRATION DATA, a summary of the performance of the classification criterion when LIST or LISTERR is specified in the PROC NEIGHBOR statement.

EXAMPLE

Nearest Neighbor Discriminant Analysis of Five Crops

In the example below, observations are grouped into five crops: clover, corn, cotton, soybeans, and sugar beets. Four measures, X1−X4, make up the descriptive variables. The classification variable is CROP. Specifying K=4 in the PROC NEIGHBOR statement requests a *k*-nearest-neighbor discriminant analysis, with a *k* value of 4. The LIST option prints the classification results for each observation.

The TESTDATA= and TESTLIST options classify the observations in the data set TEST using the classification function based on the data set CROPS. Since the ID statement is included, values of the variable XVALUES identify the observations on the output. Note that the values of the identification variable, XVALUES, are obtained by rereading the X1-X4 fields in the data lines as one character variable.

```
DATA CROPS;
   TITLE 'REMOTE SENSING DATA ON FIVE CROPS';
   INPUT CROP $ 1-10 X1-X4 XVALUES $ 11-21;
   CARDS;
CORN        16 27 31 33
CORN        15 23 30 30
CORN        16 27 27 26
CORN        18 20 25 23
CORN        15 15 31 32
CORN        15 32 32 15
CORN        12 15 16 73
SOYBEANS    20 23 23 25
SOYBEANS    24 24 25 32
SOYBEANS    21 25 23 24
SOYBEANS    27 45 24 12
SOYBEANS    12 13 15 42
SOYBEANS    22 32 31 43
COTTON      31 32 33 34
COTTON      29 24 26 28
COTTON      34 32 28 45
COTTON      26 25 23 24
COTTON      53 48 75 26
COTTON      34 35 25 78
SUGARBEETS22 23 25 42
SUGARBEETS25 25 24 26
SUGARBEETS34 25 16 52
SUGARBEETS54 23 21 54
SUGARBEETS25 43 32 15
SUGARBEETS26 54  2 54
CLOVER      12 45 32 54
CLOVER      24 58 25 34
CLOVER      87 54 61 21
CLOVER      51 31 31 16
CLOVER      96 48 54 62
CLOVER      31 31 11 11
CLOVER      56 13 13 71
CLOVER      32 13 27 32
CLOVER      36 26 54 32
CLOVER      53 08 06 54
CLOVER      32 32 62 16
;
DATA TEST;
   INPUT CROP $ 1-10 X1-X4 XVALUES $ 11-21;
   CARDS;
CORN        16 27 31 33
SOYBEANS    21 25 23 24
COTTON      29 24 26 28
SUGARBEETS54 23 21 54
```

```
CLOVER    32 32 62 16
;
PROC NEIGHBOR DATA=CROPS TESTDATA=TEST K=4 LIST TESTLIST;
   CLASS CROP;
   ID XVALUES;
   TESTCLASS CROP;
   TESTID XVALUES;
   VAR X1-X4;
```

Output 23.1 Discriminant Analysis of Five Crops: PROC NEIGHBOR

```
                              REMOTE SENSING DATA ON FIVE CROPS                                    1
                   ❶
                           NEAREST 4 NEIGHBORS DISCRIMINANT ANALYSIS

                   CROP                FREQUENCY      PRIOR PROBABILITY

                   CLOVER                  11            0.20000000

                   CORN                     7            0.20000000

                   COTTON                   6            0.20000000

                   SOYBEANS                 6            0.20000000

                   SUGARBEETS               6            0.20000000
                   -----                   --            ----------
                   TOTAL                   36            1.00000000
```

```
                              REMOTE SENSING DATA ON FIVE CROPS                                    2
     NEAREST 4 NEIGHBORS DISCRIMINANT ANALYSIS     CLASSIFICATION RESULTS FOR CALIBRATION DATA: WORK.CROPS

                                            2                    -1
                         DISTANCE FUNCTION:  D (X,Y) = (X-Y)' COV  (X-Y)
                                                                         ❺
                                                    POSTERIOR PROBABILITY OF MEMBERSHIP IN CROP:
 ❷                   ❸           ❹
 XVALUES             FROM        CLASSIFIED         CLOVER       CORN      COTTON    SOYBEANS  SUGARBEETS
                     CROP        INTO CROP

 16 27 31 33         CORN        CORN               0.0000      0.5000     0.0000     0.2500     0.2500
 15 23 30 30         CORN        CORN               0.0000      0.7500     0.0000     0.2500     0.0000
 16 27 27 26         CORN        SOYBEANS   *       0.0000      0.2500     0.0000     0.7500     0.0000
 18 20 25 23         CORN        SOYBEANS   *       0.0000      0.0000     0.0000     0.7500     0.2500
 15 15 31 32         CORN        CORN               0.0000      0.7500     0.0000     0.0000     0.2500
 15 32 32 15         CORN        SOYBEANS   *       0.0000      0.2500     0.0000     0.5000     0.2500
 12 15 16 73         CORN        SOYBEANS   *       0.0000      0.0000     0.2500     0.5000     0.2500
 20 23 23 25         SOYBEANS    OTHER      @       0.0000      0.2500     0.2500     0.2500     0.2500
 24 24 25 32         SOYBEANS    SOYBEANS           0.0000      0.0000     0.2500     0.5000     0.2500
 21 25 23 24         SOYBEANS    COTTON     *       0.0000      0.0000     0.5000     0.2500     0.2500
 27 45 24 12         SOYBEANS    OTHER      @       0.2500      0.2500     0.2500     0.0000     0.2500
 12 13 15 42         SOYBEANS    CORN       *       0.0000      0.5000     0.0000     0.2500     0.2500
 22 32 31 43         SOYBEANS    COTTON     *       0.0000      0.2500     0.5000     0.0000     0.2500
 31 32 33 34         COTTON      SOYBEANS   *       0.0000      0.2500     0.2500     0.5000     0.0000
 29 24 26 28         COTTON      SOYBEANS   *       0.0000      0.0000     0.2500     0.5000     0.2500
 34 32 28 45         COTTON      SUGARBEETS *       0.0000      0.0000     0.2500     0.2500     0.5000
 26 25 23 24         COTTON      SOYBEANS   *       0.0000      0.0000     0.2500     0.5000     0.2500
 53 48 75 26         COTTON      CLOVER     *       0.5000      0.0000     0.2500     0.2500     0.0000
 34 35 25 78         COTTON      OTHER      @       0.2500      0.2500     0.2500     0.2500     0.0000
 22 23 25 42         SUGARBEETS  OTHER      @       0.0000      0.5000     0.0000     0.5000     0.0000
 25 25 24 26         SUGARBEETS  OTHER      @       0.0000      0.0000     0.5000     0.5000     0.0000
 34 25 16 52         SUGARBEETS  SUGARBEETS         0.0000      0.0000     0.2500     0.2500     0.5000
 54 23 21 54         SUGARBEETS  CLOVER     *       0.5000      0.0000     0.2500     0.0000     0.2500
 25 43 32 15         SUGARBEETS  OTHER      @       0.0000      0.5000     0.0000     0.5000     0.0000
 26 54  2 54         SUGARBEETS  CLOVER     *       0.5000      0.0000     0.0000     0.2500     0.2500
 12 45 32 54         CLOVER      COTTON     *       0.0000      0.2500     0.5000     0.2500     0.0000
 24 58 25 34         CLOVER      SUGARBEETS *       0.2500      0.0000     0.0000     0.2500     0.5000
 87 54 61 21         CLOVER      OTHER      @       0.5000      0.0000     0.5000     0.0000     0.0000
 51 31 31 16         CLOVER      COTTON     *       0.2500      0.0000     0.5000     0.0000     0.2500
 96 48 54 62         CLOVER      CLOVER             0.5000      0.0000     0.2500     0.0000     0.2500
 31 31 11 11         CLOVER      SOYBEANS   *       0.2500      0.0000     0.2500     0.5000     0.0000
 56 13 13 71         CLOVER      OTHER      @       0.5000      0.0000     0.0000     0.0000     0.5000
```

(continued on next page)

(continued from previous page)

```
32 13 27 32          CLOVER      CORN      *     0.0000      0.5000      0.2500      0.2500      0.0000
36 26 54 32          CLOVER      CORN      *     0.2500      0.7500      0.0000      0.0000      0.0000
53 08 06 54          CLOVER      OTHER     @     0.5000      0.0000      0.0000      0.0000      0.5000
32 32 62 16          CLOVER      CORN      *     0.2500      0.5000      0.2500      0.0000      0.0000

                   * MISCLASSIFIED OBSERVATION     @ THRESHOLD PROBABILITY NOT MET
```

```
                                 REMOTE SENSING DATA ON FIVE CROPS                                      3

          NEAREST 4 NEIGHBORS DISCRIMINANT ANALYSIS      CLASSIFICATION SUMMARY FOR CALIBRATION DATA: WORK.CROPS

                                                  2                -1
  ❻                             DISTANCE FUNCTION:  D (X,Y) = (X-Y)' COV  (X-Y)

                           NUMBER OF OBSERVATIONS AND PERCENTS CLASSIFIED INTO CROP:
  FROM
  CROP              CLOVER        CORN      COTTON    SOYBEANS  SUGARBEETS       OTHER       TOTAL

  CLOVER                 1           3           2           1           1           3          11
                      9.09       27.27       18.18        9.09        9.09       27.27      100.00

  CORN                   0           3           0           4           0           0           7
                      0.00       42.86        0.00       57.14        0.00        0.00      100.00

  COTTON                 1           0           0           3           1           1           6
                     16.67        0.00        0.00       50.00       16.67       16.67      100.00

  SOYBEANS               0           1           2           1           0           2           6
                      0.00       16.67       33.33       16.67        0.00       33.33      100.00

  SUGARBEETS             2           0           0           0           1           3           6
                     33.33        0.00        0.00        0.00       16.67       50.00      100.00

  TOTAL                  4           7           4           9           3           9          36
  PERCENT            11.11       19.44       11.11       25.00        8.33       25.00      100.00

  PRIORS            0.2000      0.2000      0.2000      0.2000      0.2000
```

```
                                 REMOTE SENSING DATA ON FIVE CROPS                                      4

          NEAREST 4 NEIGHBORS DISCRIMINANT ANALYSIS      CLASSIFICATION RESULTS FOR TEST DATA: WORK.TEST

                                                  2                -1
                                DISTANCE FUNCTION:  D (X,Y) = (X-Y)' COV  (X-Y)

                                               POSTERIOR PROBABILITY OF MEMBERSHIP IN CROP:

XVALUES              FROM        CLASSIFIED          CLOVER        CORN      COTTON    SOYBEANS  SUGARBEETS
                     CROP        INTO CROP

16 27 31 33          CORN        CORN                0.0000      0.7500      0.0000      0.0000      0.2500
21 25 23 24          SOYBEANS    SOYBEANS            0.0000      0.0000      0.2500      0.5000      0.2500
29 24 26 28          COTTON      COTTON              0.0000      0.0000      0.5000      0.2500      0.2500
54 23 21 54          SUGARBEETS  OTHER       @       0.5000      0.0000      0.0000      0.0000      0.5000
32 32 62 16          CLOVER      CLOVER              0.5000      0.2500      0.2500      0.0000      0.0000

                   * MISCLASSIFIED OBSERVATION     @ THRESHOLD PROBABILITY NOT MET

  FROM
  CROP              CLOVER        CORN      COTTON    SOYBEANS  SUGARBEETS       OTHER       TOTAL

  CLOVER                 1           0           0           0           0           0           1
                    100.00        0.00        0.00        0.00        0.00        0.00      100.00

  CORN                   0           1           0           0           0           0           1
                      0.00      100.00        0.00        0.00        0.00        0.00      100.00

  COTTON                 0           0           1           0           0           0           1
                      0.00        0.00      100.00        0.00        0.00        0.00      100.00

  SOYBEANS               0           0           0           1           0           0           1
                      0.00        0.00        0.00      100.00        0.00        0.00      100.00

  SUGARBEETS             0           0           0           0           0           1           1
                      0.00        0.00        0.00        0.00        0.00      100.00      100.00

  TOTAL                  1           1           1           1           0           1           5
  PERCENT            20.00       20.00       20.00       20.00        0.00       20.00      100.00
```

(continued on next page)

(continued from previous page)

```
            PRIORS            0.2000      0.2000      0.2000      0.2000      0.2000
```

REFERENCES

Cover, T.M. and Hart, P.E. (1967), "Nearest Neighbor Pattern Classification," *IEEE Transactions on Information Theory*, IT-13, 21-27.

Fix, Evelyn and Hodges, J.L., Jr. (1959), "Discriminatory Analysis: Nonparametric Discrimination: Consistency Properties," *Report No. 4, Project No. 21-49-004, School of Aviation Medicine*, Randolph Air Force Base, Texas.

Hand, D.J. (1981), *Discrimination and Classification*, New York: John Wiley & Sons.

Chapter 24
The NESTED Procedure

Operating systems: All

ABSTRACT

The NESTED procedure performs analysis of variance and analysis of covariance for data from an experiment with a nested (hierarchical) structure. Each effect is assumed to be a random effect.[1]

INTRODUCTION

Although both the GLM and VARCOMP procedures provide similar analyses, NESTED is more efficient for this special type of design, especially for designs involving large numbers of levels and observations.

The data set that NESTED uses must first be sorted by the classification or CLASS variables defining the effects.

The CLASS variables in PROC NESTED are assumed to form a nested set of effects. For example, these statements for PROC NESTED

```
CLASS A B C;
   VAR Y;
```

form a design specification that is specified in the GLM, ANOVA, or VARCOMP procedures as:

```
CLASS A B C;
   MODEL Y=A B(A) C(A B);
```

SPECIFICATIONS

The NESTED procedure is specified by the following statements:

PROC NESTED *option;*
CLASS *variables;*
VAR *variables;*
BY *variables;*

The CLASS statement is required.

PROC NESTED Statement

PROC NESTED *options;*

The options below can appear in the PROC NESTED statement:

DATA=*SASdataset* names the SAS data set to be used by PROC NESTED. If DATA= is omitted, the most recently created SAS data set is used.

AOV suppresses the analysis of covariance statistics if you only want statistics for the analysis of variance.

CLASS Statement

CLASS *variables;*

A CLASS statement specifying the classification variables for the analysis **must** be included. The data set must be sorted by the classification variables in the order that they are given in the CLASS statement. Use PROC SORT to sort the data if they are not already sorted.

Values of a variable in the CLASS statement denote the levels of an effect. The name of that variable is also the name of the corresponding effect.

The second effect is assumed to be nested within the first effect, the third effect is assumed to be nested within the second effect, and so on.

VAR Statement

VAR *variables;*

List the dependent variables for the analysis in the VAR statement. If the VAR statement is omitted, NESTED performs an analysis of variance for all numeric variables in the data set, except those in the CLASS statement.

BY Statement

BY *variables;*

A BY statement can be used with PROC NESTED to obtain separate analyses on observations in groups defined by the BY variables. The input data set must be sorted in order of the BY variables. If your data set is not sorted in ascending order, use the SORT procedure with a similar BY statement to sort the data, or if appropriate, use the BY statement options NOTSORTED or DESCENDING. For more information, see the discussion of the BY statement in "Statements Used in the PROC Step" in the *SAS User's Guide: Basics.*

DETAILS

Missing Values

An observation with missing values for any of the variables used by NESTED is omitted from the analysis. Blank values of CLASS variables are treated as missing values.

Printed Output

For each effect in the model, NESTED prints

1. COEFFICIENTS OF EXPECTED MEAN SQUARES, the coefficients of the variance components making up the expected mean square.

   For every dependent variable, NESTED prints an analysis-of-variance table containing the following items:
2. VARIANCE SOURCE, sources of variation
3. D.F., degrees of freedom
4. SUM OF SQUARES
5. MEAN SQUARES
6. VARIANCE COMPONENT, estimates of variance components
7. PERCENT, the percentage associated with a source of variance. The value is 100 times the ratio of that source's estimated variance component to the total variance component.

   The following statistics are printed below each analysis-of-variance table:
8. MEAN, the overall mean
9. STANDARD DEVIATION
10. COEFFICIENT OF VARIATION of the response variable, based on the error mean square.

    For each pair of dependent variables, NESTED prints an analysis-of-covariance table (unless AOV is specified). For each source of variation, this table includes
11. D.F., the degrees of freedom
12. SUM OF PRODUCTS
13. MEAN PRODUCTS
14. COVARIANCE COMPONENT, the estimate of the covariance component
15. VARIANCE COMPONENT CORRELATION, the covariance component correlation
16. MEAN SQUARE CORRELATION.

EXAMPLE

Variability of Calcium Concentration in Turnip Greens

In the following example from Snedecor and Cochran (1967), an experiment is conducted to determine the variability of calcium concentration in turnip greens. Four plants are selected at random, then three leaves are randomly selected from each plant. Two 100-mg samples are taken from each leaf. The amount of calcium is determined by microchemical methods.

Since the data are read in sorted order, it is not necessary to use PROC SORT on the class variables. LEAF is nested in PLANT; SAMPLE is nested in LEAF and is left for the residual term. All the effects are random effects.

```
TITLE 'CALCIUM CONCENTRATION IN TURNIP LEAVES -- NESTED RANDOM MODEL';
TITLE2 'SNEDECOR AND COCHRAN, STATISTICAL METHODS, 1967, P. 286';

DATA TURNIP;
   DO PLANT=1 TO 4;
      DO LEAF=1 TO 3;
         DO SAMPLE=1 TO 2;
            INPUT CALCIUM @@;
            OUTPUT;
            END;
         END;
      END;
   CARDS;
3.28 3.09 3.52 3.48 2.88 2.80
2.46 2.44 1.87 1.92 2.19 2.19
2.77 2.66 3.74 3.44 2.55 2.55
3.78 3.87 4.07 4.12 3.31 3.31
;
PROC NESTED;
   CLASSES PLANT LEAF;
   VAR CALCIUM;
```

Output 24.1 Analysis of Calcium Concentration in Turnip Greens Using PROC NESTED

```
                    CALCIUM CONCENTRATION IN TURNIP LEAVES -- NESTED RANDOM MODEL                         1
                       SNEDECOR AND COCHRAN, STATISTICAL METHODS, 1967, P. 286

                       ❶          COEFFICIENTS OF EXPECTED MEAN SQUARES

                        SOURCE              PLANT               LEAF              ERROR

                        PLANT                   6                  2                  1
                        LEAF                    0                  2                  1
                        ERROR                   0                  0                  1
```

```
                    CALCIUM CONCENTRATION IN TURNIP LEAVES -- NESTED RANDOM MODEL                         2
                       SNEDECOR AND COCHRAN, STATISTICAL METHODS, 1967, P. 286

                              ANALYSIS OF VARIANCE CALCIUM
❷              ❸            ❹              ❺            ❻              ❼
VARIANCE                  SUM OF           MEAN         VARIANCE
SOURCE         D.F.       SQUARES          SQUARES      COMPONENT      PERCENT

TOTAL            23      10.270396      0.44653895    0.53293796         100

PLANT             3      7.5603458       2.5201153    0.36522338     68.5302

LEAF              8         2.6302        0.328775    0.16106042     30.2212

ERROR            12        0.07985 0.0066541667 0.0066541667     1.24858

❽ MEAN                                3.01208333
❾ STANDARD DEVIATION                  0.0815730756
❿ COEFFICIENT OF VARIATION            2.70819452
```

REFERENCES

Snedecor, G.W. and Cochran, W.G. (1967), *Statistical Methods*, Ames, Iowa: The Iowa State University Press.

Steel, R.G.D. and Torrie, J.H. (1980), *Principles and Procedures of Statistics*, New York: McGraw-Hill Book Company.

NOTE

1. NESTED is modeled after the General Purpose Nested Analysis of Variance program of the Dairy Cattle Research Branch of the United States Department of Agriculture. That program was originally written by Merrill R. Swanson, Statistical Reporting Service, United States Department of Agriculture.

Chapter 25

The NLIN Procedure

Operating systems: All

ABSTRACT

The NLIN (NonLINear regression) procedure produces least-squares or weighted least-squares estimates of the parameters of a nonlinear model.

INTRODUCTION

PROC NLIN fits nonlinear regression models by least squares. Nonlinear models are more difficult to specify and estimate than linear models. Instead of simply listing regressor variables, you must write the regression expression, declare parameter names, guess starting values for them, and possibly specify derivatives of the model with respect to the parameters. Some models are difficult to fit, and there is no guarantee that the procedure will be able to fit the model successfully.

The NLIN procedure first examines the starting value specifications of the parameters. If a grid of values is specified, NLIN evaluates the residual sum of squares at each combination of values to determine the best set of values to start the iterative algorithm. Then NLIN uses one of these four iterative methods:

- modified Gauss-Newton method
- Marquardt method
- gradient or steepest-descent method
- multivariate secant or false position (DUD).

The Gauss-Newton and Marquardt iterative methods regress the residuals onto the partial derivatives of the model with respect to the parameters until the iterations converge.

For each nonlinear model to be analyzed, you must specify:

- the names and starting values of the parameters to be estimated
- the model (using a single dependent variable)
- partial derivatives of the model with respect to each parameter (except for METHOD=DUD).

You can also:

- confine the estimation procedure to a certain range of values of the parameters by imposing bounds on the estimates
- adjust the convergence criterion
- produce new SAS data sets containing predicted values, residuals, estimates of parameters, and the residual sum of squares
- define your own objective function to be minimized.

The NLIN procedure can be used for segmented models (see **Example 4**). It can also be used to compute maximum-likelihood estimates for certain models (see Jennrich and Moore 1975; Charnes et al. 1976).

SPECIFICATIONS

You can use the following statements to invoke PROC NLIN:

PROC NLIN *options;*
PARAMETERS (PARMS) *parameter=values ...;*
BOUNDS *expressions ...;*
other programming statements
MODEL *dependent=expression;*
DER.*parameter=expression;*

OUTPUT OUT=*SASdataset keyword*=*variables*;
ID *variables*;

The PARMS and MODEL statements are required.

PROC NLIN Statement

PROC NLIN *options*;

The options below can appear in the PROC NLIN statement:

DATA=*SASdataset*
: names the SAS data set containing the data to be analyzed by PROC NLIN. If DATA= is omitted, the most recently created SAS data set is used.

OUTEST=*SASdataset*
: names the SAS data set to contain the parameter estimates produced by PROC NLIN. See the **OUTPUT Statement** below for details. If you want to create a permanent SAS data set, you must specify a two-level name. See "SAS Files" in the *SAS User's Guide: Basics* for more information on permanent SAS data sets.

Grid search options

BEST=*n*
: requests that PROC NLIN print the residual sums of squares only for the best *n* combinations of possible starting values from the grid. When BEST= is not specified, NLIN prints the residual sum of squares for every combination of possible parameter starting values.

PLOT
: requests that PROC NLIN print a contour plot of the residual sums of squares. The two axes of the plot represent a grid of starting values for the two parameters. The PLOT option is appropriate only when the PARMS statement includes exactly two parameters, each with a grid of values.

Method options

METHOD=GAUSS
METHOD=MARQUARDT
METHOD=GRADIENT
METHOD=DUD
: specifies the iterative method NLIN uses. METHOD=GAUSS is the default if DER statements are present; otherwise, METHOD=DUD is the default. See the section **Computational Methods** for details.

NOHALVE
: turns off the step halving during iteration. This is used with some types of weighted regression problems.

SIGSQ=*value*
: specifies a value to replace the mean square error for computing the standard errors of the estimates. SIGSQ= is used with maximum-likelihood estimation.

G4
: specifies that a G4 or Moore-Penrose inverse be used in parameter estimation.

G4SINGULAR
: specifies that a G4 or Moore-Penrose inverse be used in parameter estimation if the Jacobian matrix is of less than maximum rank.

TAU=*value*

specifies a value to use in controlling the step-size search. See the section **Computational Methods** for more details.

RHO=*value*

specifies a value to use in controlling the step-size search. See the section **Computational Methods** for more details.

Tuning options

EFORMAT

requests that NLIN print all numeric values in scientific E-notation. This is useful if your parameters have very different scales.

MAXITER=*i*

places a limit on the number of iterations NLIN performs before it gives up trying to converge. The *i* value must be a positive integer. The default is 50.

CONVERGE=c

specifies the relative convergence criterion. The iterations are said to have converged if

$$(SSE_{i-1} - SSE_i)/(SSE_i + 10^{-6}) < c \quad .$$

The default is 10^{-8}. The constant c should be a small positive number.

Programming statements with PROC NLIN Any number of SAS programming statements can be used after the PROC NLIN statement. These statements should follow the PARMS statement and precede the MODEL statement.

PROC NLIN can execute assignment statements, explicitly subscripted ARRAY statements, explicitly subscripted array references, IF statements, and program control statements. You can use program statements to create new SAS variables for the duration of the procedure (these variables are not permanently included in the data set to which NLIN is applied). Program statements can include variables in the DATA= data set, parameter names, and variables created by preceding program statements within PROC NLIN.

LAG and DIF are the only SAS functions that do not operate in PROC NLIN as they do in a DATA step. In PROC NLIN, the LAG and DIF functions operate correctly across observations but are not reset at the beginning of a new iteration.

The DO OVER statement is no longer supported. Instead, you can use a DO loop with explicit array indexing.

Consult the section **Special Variables** for information on special variables available to the NLIN procedure.

PARAMETERS Statement

PARAMETERS *parameter=values ...;*
PARMS *parameter=values ...;*

A PARAMETERS (or PARMS) statement must follow the PROC NLIN statement. Several parameter names and values can appear. The parameter names must all be valid SAS names and must not duplicate the names of any variables in the data set to which the NLIN procedure is applied.

In each *parameter=values* specification, the parameter name identifies a parameter to be estimated, both in subsequent procedure statements and in NLIN's printed output. The *values* specify the possible starting values of the parameter.

Usually, only one value is specified for each parameter. If you specify several values for each parameter, NLIN evaluates the model at each point on the grid. The value specifications can take any of several forms:

m	a single value
*m*1,*m*2,...,*mn*	several values
m TO *n*	a sequence: starting, ending, increment=1
m TO *n* BY *i*	a sequence: starting, ending, increment
*m*1, *m*2 TO *m*3	mixed values and sequences.

This PARMS statement names five parameters and sets their possible starting values as shown:

```
PARMS B0=0
      B1=4 TO 8
      B2=0 TO .6 BY .2
      B3=1, 10, 100
      B4=0, .5, 1 TO 4;
```

possible starting values	B0	B1	B2	B3	B4
	0	4	0	1	0
		5	.2	10	.5
		6	.4	100	1
		7	.6		2
		8			3
					4

Residual sums of squares are calculated for each of the 1x5x4x3x6=360 combinations of possible starting values. (This can be expensive.)

See the section **Special Variables** for information on programming parameter starting values.

BOUNDS Statement

BOUNDS *expressions...*;

The BOUNDS statement restrains the parameter estimates within specified bounds. In each BOUNDS statement, you can specify a series of bounds separated by commas. Each bound contains an expression consisting of a parameter name, an inequality comparison operator, and a value. Double-bounded expressions are also permitted. For example:

```
BOUNDS A<=20, 0<=B<=10, 20>C;
```

If you need to restrict an expression involving several parameters, for example, A+B<1, you can reparameterize the model so that the expression becomes a parameter.

If the iteration procedure sticks at the boundary of a constrained parameter, the computational method used does not guarantee that the other parameter estimates finally obtained will produce the restricted minimum residual sum of squares (Jennrich and Sampson 1968).

MODEL Statement

MODEL *dependent*=*expression*;

The MODEL statement defines the prediction equation by declaring the dependent variable and defining an expression that evaluates predicted values. The expression can be any valid SAS expression yielding a numeric result. NLIN uses the CMP compiler, so any operators or functions defined there are available here. The expression can include parameter names, variables in the data set, and variables created by program statements.

A statement such as

```
MODEL Y=expression;
```

is translated into the form

```
MODEL.Y=expression;
```

using the compound variable name MODEL.Y to hold the predicted value. You can use this assignment as an alternative to the MODEL statement. Either a MODEL statement or an assignment to the compound variable MODEL.Y must appear.

DER Statements

DER.*parameter*=*expression*;

For most of the computational methods, you must include a DER statement for each parameter to be estimated. The expression must be an algebraic representation of the partial derivative of the expression in the MODEL statement with respect to the parameter whose name immediately follows DER. The expression in the DER statement must conform to the rules for a valid SAS expression and can include any quantities that the MODEL statement expression contains.

The set of statements below specifies that a model

$$Y=\beta_0(1-e^{-\beta_1 x})$$

be fitted by the modified Gauss-Newton method, where observed values of the dependent and independent variables are contained in the SAS variables Y and X, respectively.

```
PROC NLIN;
   PARMS B0=0 TO 10
         B1=.01 TO .09 BY .005;
   MODEL Y=B0*(1-EXP(-B1*X));
   DER.B0=1-EXP(-B1*X);
   DER.B1=B0*X*EXP(-B1*X);
```

Replacing the last three statements above with the statements

```
TEMP=EXP(-B1*X);
MODEL Y=B0*(1-TEMP);
DER.B0=1-TEMP;
DER.B1=B0*X*TEMP;
```

saves computer time, since the expression EXP(−B1*X) is evaluated only once per program execution rather than three times, as in the earlier example. If necessary, numerical rather than analytical derivatives can be used.

Weighted Regression

WEIGHT=*expression*;

To get weighted least-squares estimates of parameters, the _WEIGHT_ variable can be given a value in an assignment statement. When it is included, the expression is evaluated for each observation in the data set to be analyzed, and the values obtained are taken as inverse elements of the diagonal variance-covariance matrix of the dependent variable. When a variable name is given after the equal sign, the values of the variable are taken as the inverse elements of the variance-covariance matrix. The larger the _WEIGHT_ value, the more importance the observation is given.

OUTPUT Statement

OUTPUT OUT=*SASdataset keyword*=*variables*...;

The OUTPUT statement specifies an output data set to contain statistics calculated for each observation. For each statistic, specify the keyword, an equal sign, and a variable name for the statistic in the output data set.

The options below can appear in the OUTPUT statement:

OUT=*SASdataset*
: names the SAS data set to be created by PROC NLIN when an OUTPUT statement is included. The new data set includes all the variables in the data set to which NLIN is applied, plus new variables whose names are given in the OUTPUT statement. If you want to create a permanent SAS data set, you must specify a two-level name. See "SAS Files" in the *SAS User's Guide: Basics* for more information on permanent SAS data sets.

  All of the names appearing in the OUTPUT statement must be valid SAS names, and none of the new variable names may match a variable already existing in the data set to which NLIN is applied.

PREDICTED=*variable*
P=*variable*
: names a variable in the output data set to contain the predicted values of the dependent variable.

RESIDUAL=*variable*
R=*variable*
: names a variable in the output data set to contain the residuals (actual values minus predicted values).

L95M=*variable*
: names a variable to contain the lower bound of a 95% confidence interval for the expected value (mean).

U95M=*variable*
: names a variable to contain the upper bound of a 95% confidence interval for the expected value (mean).

L95=*variable*
: names a variable to contain the lower bound of a 95% confidence interval for an individual prediction. This includes the variance of the error as well as the variance of the parameter estimates.

U95=*variable*
: names a variable to contain the upper bound of a 95% confidence interval for an individual prediction.

STDP=*variable*
: names a variable to contain the standard error of the mean predicted value.

STDR=*variable*
names a variable to contain the standard error of the residual.

STUDENT=*variable*
names a variable to contain the studentized residuals, each residual divided by its standard error.

H=*variable*
names a variable to contain the leverage, $x_i(\mathbf{X'X})^{-1}x_i'$, where $\mathbf{X}=\partial\mathbf{F}/\partial\beta$.

PARMS=*variables*
names variables in the output data set to contain parameter estimates. These are normally the same variable names as listed in the PARAMETERS statement; however, you can choose new names for the parameters identified in the sequence from the PARAMETERS statement. Note that for each of these new variables, the values are the same for every observation in the new data set.

SSE=*variable*
ESS=*variable*
names a variable to include in the new data set. The values for the variable are the residual sums of squares finally determined by the procedure. The values of the variable are the same for every observation in the new data set.

The data set produced by the OUTEST= option in the PROC NLIN statement contains the parameter estimates on each iteration including the grid search. The variable _ITER_ contains the iteration number. The variable _TYPE_ denotes whether the observation contains iteration parameter estimates (ITER), final parameter estimates (FINAL), or covariance estimates (COVB). The variable _NAME_ contains the parameter name for covariances, and the variable _SSE_ contains the objective function value for the parameter estimates.

ID Statement

ID *variables;*

The ID statement specifies additional variables to place in the output data set. Any variable on the left-hand side of any assignment statement is eligible. Also the special underscore variables can be specified.

DETAILS

Missing Values

If the value of any one of the SAS variables involved in the model is missing from an observation, that observation is omitted from the analysis. If only the value of the dependent variable is missing, that observation has a predicted value calculated for it when you use an OUTPUT statement and specify the PREDICTED= option.

If an observation includes a missing value for one of the independent variables, both the predicted value and the residual value are missing for that observation. If the iterations fail to converge, all the values of all the variables named in the OUTPUT statement are missing values.

Troubleshooting

This section describes a number of problems that can occur in your analysis with PROC NLIN.

Time exceeded If you specify a grid of starting values that contains many points, the job may run out of time since the procedure must go through the entire data set for each point on the grid. The job may also run out of time if your problem takes many iterations to converge since each iteration requires as much time as a linear regression with predicted values and residuals calculated.

Dependencies The matrix of partial derivatives may be singular, possibly indicating an over-parameterized model. For example, if B0 starts at zero in the following model, the derivatives for B1 are all zero for the first iteration.

```
PARMS B0=0 B1=.022;
MODEL POP=B0*EXP(B1*(YEAR-1790));
DER.B0=EXP(B1*(YEAR-1790));
DER.B1=(YEAR-1790)*B0*EXP(B1*(YEAR-1790));
```

The first iteration changes a subset of the parameters; then the procedure can make progress in succeeding iterations. This singularity problem is local. The next example shows a global problem.

You may have an add-factor B2 in the exponential that is nonidentifiable since it trades roles with B0.

```
PARMS B0=3.9 B1=.022 B2=0;
MODEL POP=B0*EXP(B1*(YEAR-1790)+B2);
DER.B0=EXP(B1*(YEAR-1790)+B2);
DER.B1=(YEAR-1790)*B0*EXP(B1*(YEAR-1790)+B2);
DER.B2=B0*EXP(B1*(YEAR-1790)+B2);
```

Unable to improve The method may lead to steps that do not improve the estimates, even after a series of step halvings. If this happens, the procedure issues a message stating that it was unable to make further progress, but it then prints the message "CONVERGENCE ASSUMED," and prints out the results. This often means that you have not converged at all. You should check the derivatives very closely and check the sum-of-squares error surface before proceeding. If you have not converged, try a different set of starting values, a different METHOD= specification, or the G4 option.

Divergence The iterative process may diverge, resulting in overflows in computations. It is also possible that parameters will enter a space where arguments to such functions as LOG and SQRT become illegal. For example, consider the model:

```
PARMS B=0;
MODEL Y=X/B;
```

Suppose that Y happens to be all zero and X is nonzero. There is no least-squares estimate for B since the SSE declines as B approaches infinity or minus infinity. The same model could be parameterized with no problem into Y=A*X.

If you actually run the model, the procedure claims to converge after awhile since it measures convergence with respect to changes in the sum-of-squares error rather than to the parameter estimates. If you have divergence problems, try reparameterizing, selecting different starting values, or including a BOUNDS statement.

Local minimum The program may converge very nicely to a local rather than a global minimum. For example, consider the model:

```
PARMS A=1 B=-1;
MODEL Y=(1-A*X)*(1-B*X);
```

```
DER.A=-X*(1-B*X);
DER.B=-X*(1-A*X);
```

Once a solution is found, an equivalent solution with the same SSE is to switch the values between A and B.

Discontinuities The computational methods assume that the model is a continuous and smooth function of the parameters. If this is not true, the method does not work. For example, the following models will not work:

```
MODEL Y=A+INT(B*X);

MODEL Y=A+B*X+4*(Z>C);
```

Responding to trouble NLIN does not necessarily produce a good solution the first time. Much depends on specifying good initial values for the parameters. You can specify a grid of values in the PARMS statement to search for good starting values. While most practical models should give you no trouble, other models may require switching to a different iteration method or inverse computation method. METHOD=MARQUARDT sometimes works when the default method (Gauss-Newton) does not work.

Computational Methods

For the nonlinear model,

$$\mathbf{Y} = \mathbf{F}(\beta_0,\beta_1,\ldots,\beta_k,\mathbf{X}_1,\mathbf{X}_2,\ldots,\mathbf{X}_n) + \varepsilon = \mathbf{F}(\beta) + \varepsilon$$

the nonlinear "normal" equations are

$$\mathbf{X}'\mathbf{F}(\beta) = \mathbf{X}'\mathbf{y}$$

where $\mathbf{X} = \partial\mathbf{F}/\partial\beta$.

In the nonlinear situation, both $\mathbf{X}$ and $\mathbf{F}(\beta)$ are functions of β and a closed-form solution generally does not exist. Thus NLIN uses an iterative process: a starting value for β is chosen and continually improved until the error sum of squares $\varepsilon'\varepsilon$ (SSE) is minimized.

The iterative techniques NLIN uses are similar to a series of linear regressions involving the matrix $\mathbf{X}$ evaluated for the current values of β and $\mathbf{e}=\mathbf{Y}-\hat{\mathbf{Y}}$, where

$$\hat{\mathbf{Y}} = \mathbf{F}(\beta)$$

are the predicted values evaluated for the current values of β .

The iterative process begins at some point β_0. Then $\mathbf{X}$ and $\mathbf{Y}$ are employed to compute a $\boldsymbol{\Delta}$ such that

$$\mathrm{SSE}(\beta_0+\mathbf{k}\boldsymbol{\Delta}) < \mathrm{SSE}(\beta_0) \quad .$$

The three methods differ in how $\boldsymbol{\Delta}$ is computed to change the vector of parameters.

Steepest descent	$\boldsymbol{\Delta}=\mathbf{X}'\mathbf{y}$ (direction)
Gauss-Newton	$\boldsymbol{\Delta}=(\mathbf{X}'\mathbf{X})^{-}\mathbf{X}'\mathbf{y}$ (direction and distance)
Marquardt	$\boldsymbol{\Delta}=(\mathbf{X}'\mathbf{X}+\lambda\mathbf{I})^{-}(\mathbf{X}'\mathbf{y})$ (direction and distance)

The default method used to compute $(\mathbf{X}'\mathbf{X})^{-}$ is the sweep operator producing a G2 inverse. In some cases it would be preferable to use a G4 or Moore-Penrose inverse. If the G4 option is specified in the PROC NLIN statement, a G4 inverse is used to calculate $\mathbf{\Delta}$; also the eigenvalues and eigenvectors are printed on each iteration. If the G4SINGULAR option is specified, a G4 inverse is used to calculate $\mathbf{\Delta}$ when $(\mathbf{X'X})$ is singular.

The default method of finding the step size *k* is step halving. If $SSE(\beta_0+\mathbf{\Delta})>SSE(\beta_0)$, compute $SSE(\beta_0+.5\mathbf{\Delta})$, $SSE(\beta_0+.25\mathbf{\Delta})$,..., until a smaller SSE is found. If either of the PROC NLIN parameters TAU or RHO is specified, the step size *k* is determined by a golden section search. TAU determines the length of the initial interval to be searched, with the interval having length TAU or 2*TAU, depending on $SSE(\beta_0+\Delta)$. The RHO parameter specifies how fine the search is to be. The SSE at each endpoint of the interval is evaluated, and a new subinterval is chosen. The size of the interval is reduced until its length is less than RHO. One pass through the data is required each time the interval is reduced. Hence, if RHO is very small relative to TAU, a large amount of time can be spent determining a step size. If neither TAU nor RHO is specified, step halving is used when the NOHALVE option has not been specified. The default value for TAU is 1 and for RHO is .1. For more information on the golden search, see Kennedy and Gentle (1980).

Steepest descent (gradient) The steepest descent method is based on the gradient of $\varepsilon'\varepsilon$:

$$.5\ \partial\varepsilon'\varepsilon/\partial\beta \ = \ -\mathbf{X'Y} + \mathbf{X'F}(\beta) \ = \ -\mathbf{X'e} \quad .$$

The quantity $-\mathbf{X'e}$ is the gradient along which $\varepsilon'\varepsilon$ increases. Thus $\mathbf{\Delta}=\mathbf{X'e}$ is the direction of steepest descent.

Using the method of steepest descent, let

$$\beta_{i+1} \ = \ \beta_i+\mathbf{k\Delta}$$

where the scalar $\mathbf{k}$ is chosen such that

$$SSE(\beta_i+\mathbf{k\Delta}) \ < \ SSE(\beta_i) \quad .$$

Note: the steepest descent method converges very slowly and is therefore not recommended.

Gauss-Newton The Gauss-Newton method uses the Taylor series

$$\mathbf{F}(\beta) \ = \ \mathbf{F}(\beta_0) \ + \ \mathbf{X}(\beta-\beta_0) \ + \ ...$$

where $\mathbf{X} \ = \ \partial\mathbf{F}/\partial\beta$ is evaluated at $\beta=\beta_0$.

Substituting the first two terms of this series into the "normal" equations:

$$\mathbf{X'F}(\beta)=\mathbf{X'Y}$$

$$\mathbf{X'}(\mathbf{F}(\beta_0)+\mathbf{X}(\beta-\beta_0))=\mathbf{X'Y}$$

$$\mathbf{X'F}(\beta_0)+\mathbf{X'X}(\beta-\beta_0)=\mathbf{X'Y}$$

$$(\mathbf{X'X})(\beta\text{-}\beta_0)=\mathbf{X'Y}-\mathbf{X'F}(\beta_0)$$

$$(\mathbf{X'X})\mathbf{\Delta}=\mathbf{X'e}$$

and therefore

$$\Delta=(\mathbf{X}'\mathbf{X})^{-1}\mathbf{X}'\mathbf{e}\quad .$$

Marquardt The Marquardt updating formula is as follows:

$$\Delta = (\mathbf{X}'\mathbf{X}+\lambda\text{diag}(\mathbf{X}'\mathbf{X}))^{-1}\mathbf{X}'\mathbf{e}\quad .$$

The Marquardt method is a compromise between Gauss-Newton and steepest descent (Marquardt 1963). As $\lambda\rightarrow 0$, the direction approaches Gauss-Newton. As $\lambda\rightarrow\infty$, the direction approaches steepest descent.

Marquardt's studies indicate that the average angle between Gauss-Newton and steepest descent directions is about 90º. A choice of λ between 0 and ∞ produces a compromise direction.

By default NLIN chooses $\lambda=10^{-3}$ to start and computes a Δ. If $SSE(\beta_0+\Delta)<SSE(\beta_0)$, then $\lambda=\lambda/10$ for the next iteration. Each time $SSE(\beta+\Delta)>SSE(\beta_0)$, then $\lambda=\lambda x10$.

If G4 is specified in the PROC NLIN statement, λ is determined using the eigenvalues of (**X'X**). If the smallest eigenvalue is nonpositive, λ is the absolute value of the smallest eigenvalue plus .00001. Otherwise, λ is zero. This method tries to pick the smallest value of λ such that $(\mathbf{X}'\mathbf{X}+\lambda\text{diag}(\mathbf{X}'\mathbf{X}))$ is positive definite. If TAU or RHO is specified, a step-size search is conducted.

If TAU or RHO is specifed but G4 is not, NLIN chooses λ=TAU to start and computes a Δ. If $SSE(\beta_0+\Delta)<SSE(\beta_0)$, then $\lambda=\lambda$/RHO for the next iteration. Each time $SSE(\beta+\Delta)>SSE(\beta_0)$, then $\lambda=\lambda$xRHO. In the Marquardt method the default value for TAU is .01 and for RHO is 10.

Note: if the SSE improves on each iteration, then $\lambda\rightarrow 0$, and you are essentially using Gauss-Newton. If SSE does not improve, then λ is increased until you are moving in the steepest descent direction.

Marquardt's method is equivalent to performing a series of ridge regressions and is most useful when the parameter estimates are highly correlated.

Secant method (DUD) The multivariate secant method is like Gauss-Newton, except that the derivatives are estimated from the history of iterations rather than being supplied analytically. The method is also called the *method of false position*, or the DUD method (Ralston and Jennrich 1979). If only one parameter is being estimated, the derivative for iteration $i+1$ can be estimated from the previous two iterations:

$$der_{i+1} = (\hat{\mathbf{Y}}_i-\hat{\mathbf{Y}}_{i-1})/(b_i-b_{i-1})\quad .$$

When k parameters are to be estimated, the method uses the last $k+1$ iterations to estimate the derivatives.

Special Variables

Several special variables are created automatically and can be used in PROC NLIN program statements. The values of these special variables are set by NLIN and **should not** be reset to a different value by programming statements.

_N_	indicates the number of times the program has been entered. It is never reset for successive passes through the data set.
ERROR	is set to 1 if a numerical error or invalid argument to a function occurs during the current execution of the program. It is reset to 0 before each new execution.

OBS indicates the observation number in the data set for the current program execution. It is reset to 1 to start each pass through the data set (unlike _N_).

ITER represents the current iteration number. The variable _ITER_ is set to −1 during the grid search phase.

MODEL is set to 1 for passes through the data when only the predicted values are needed, not the derivatives. It is 0 when both predicted values and derivatives are needed. If your derivative calculations consume a lot of time, you can save resources by coding

```
IF _MODEL_ THEN RETURN;
```

after your MODEL statement but before your derivative calculations.

SSE has the error sum of squares of the last iteration. During the grid search phase _SSE_ is set to 0; it is set to a large value for iteration 0.

The special variables _HALVE_ and _LOSS_ are to be used by the programmer to determine convergence criteria.

HALVE is a new automatic variable that is checked to control step halving during execution. The value of _HALVE_ is the maximum number of step halvings that will be done during an iteration before a nonconvergence message is printed and execution terminates.

LOSS is used to determine the criterion function for convergence and step shortening. PROC NLIN looks for the variable _LOSS_ in the program statements and, if it is defined, uses the (weighted) sum of this value instead of residual sum of squares to determine the criterion function for convergence and step shortening. This feature is useful in certain types of maximum-likelihood estimation where the residual sum of squares is not the basic criterion.

For the derivative methods (GAUSS, MARQUARDT, and GRADIENT), the parameter values in the procedure are updated after the first observation of iteration 0. If you want to supply starting parameter values in your program (rather than using the values in the PARMS statement), follow this example:

```
PROC NLIN;
   PARMS B0=1 B1=1;
   IF _ITER_=0 THEN IF _N_=1 THEN DO;
      B0=B0START;
      B1=B1START;
      END;
   MODEL Y=expression;
   DER.B0=expression;
   DER.B1=expression;
```

where B0START and B1START are in the input data set or calculated with program statements.

Printed Output

In addition to the output data sets, NLIN also produces the items below:

1. the estimates of the parameters and the residual sums of squares determined in each iteration
2. a list of the residual sums of squares associated with all or some of the combinations of possible starting values of parameters
3. for two-parameter models, a contour plot of residual sums of squares associated with possible starting values of parameters.

If the convergence criterion is met, NLIN prints:

4. an analysis-of-variance table including as sources of variation REGRESSION, RESIDUAL, UNCORRECTED TOTAL, and CORRECTED TOTAL
5. parameter estimates
6. an asymptotically valid standard error of the estimate, ASYMPTOTIC STD. ERROR
7. an ASYMPTOTIC 95% CONFIDENCE INTERVAL for the estimate of the parameter
8. an ASYMPTOTIC CORRELATION MATRIX OF THE PARAMETERS.

EXAMPLES

Negative Exponential Growth Curve: Example 1

This example demonstrates typical NLIN specifications for Marquardt's method and a grid of starting values. The predicted values and residuals are output for plotting.

```
TITLE 'NEGATIVE EXPONENTIAL: Y=B0*(1-EXP(-B1*X))';

DATA A;
   INPUT X Y @@;
   CARDS;
020 0.57 030 0.72 040 0.81 050 0.87 060 0.91 070 0.94
080 0.95 090 0.97 100 0.98 110 0.99 120 1.00 130 0.99
140 0.99 150 1.00 160 1.00 170 0.99 180 1.00 190 1.00
200 0.99 210 1.00
;
PROC NLIN BEST=10 PLOT METHOD=MARQUARDT;
   PARMS B0=0 TO 2 BY .5  B1=.01 TO .09 BY .01;
   MODEL Y=B0*(1-EXP(-B1*X));
   DER.B0=1-EXP(-B1*X);
   DER.B1=B0*X*EXP(-B1*X);
   OUTPUT OUT=B P=YHAT R=YRESID;
PROC PLOT DATA=B;
   PLOT Y*X='A' YHAT*X='P' /OVERLAY VPOS=25;
   PLOT YRESID*X / VREF=0 VPOS=25;
```

Output 25.1 Negative Exponential Growth Function: PROC NLIN, METHOD=MARQUARDT and PROC PLOT

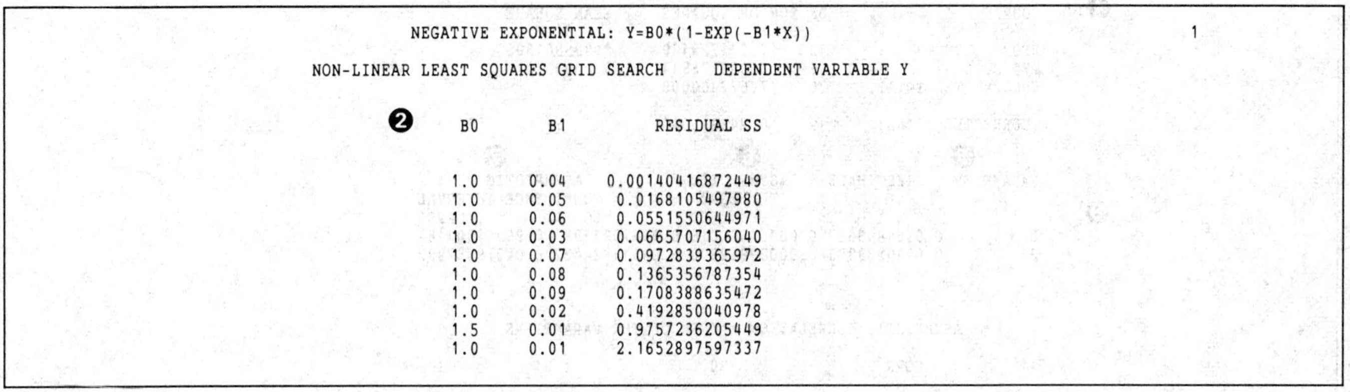

```
                    NEGATIVE EXPONENTIAL: Y=B0*(1-EXP(-B1*X))                      1

          NON-LINEAR LEAST SQUARES GRID SEARCH     DEPENDENT VARIABLE Y

                 ❷      B0        B1          RESIDUAL SS

                        1.0      0.04     0.0014041687 2449
                        1.0      0.05     0.0168105497980
                        1.0      0.06     0.0551550644971
                        1.0      0.03     0.0665707156040
                        1.0      0.07     0.0972839365972
                        1.0      0.08     0.1365356787354
                        1.0      0.09     0.1708388635472
                        1.0      0.02     0.4192850040978
                        1.5      0.01     0.9757236205449
                        1.0      0.01     2.1652897597337
```

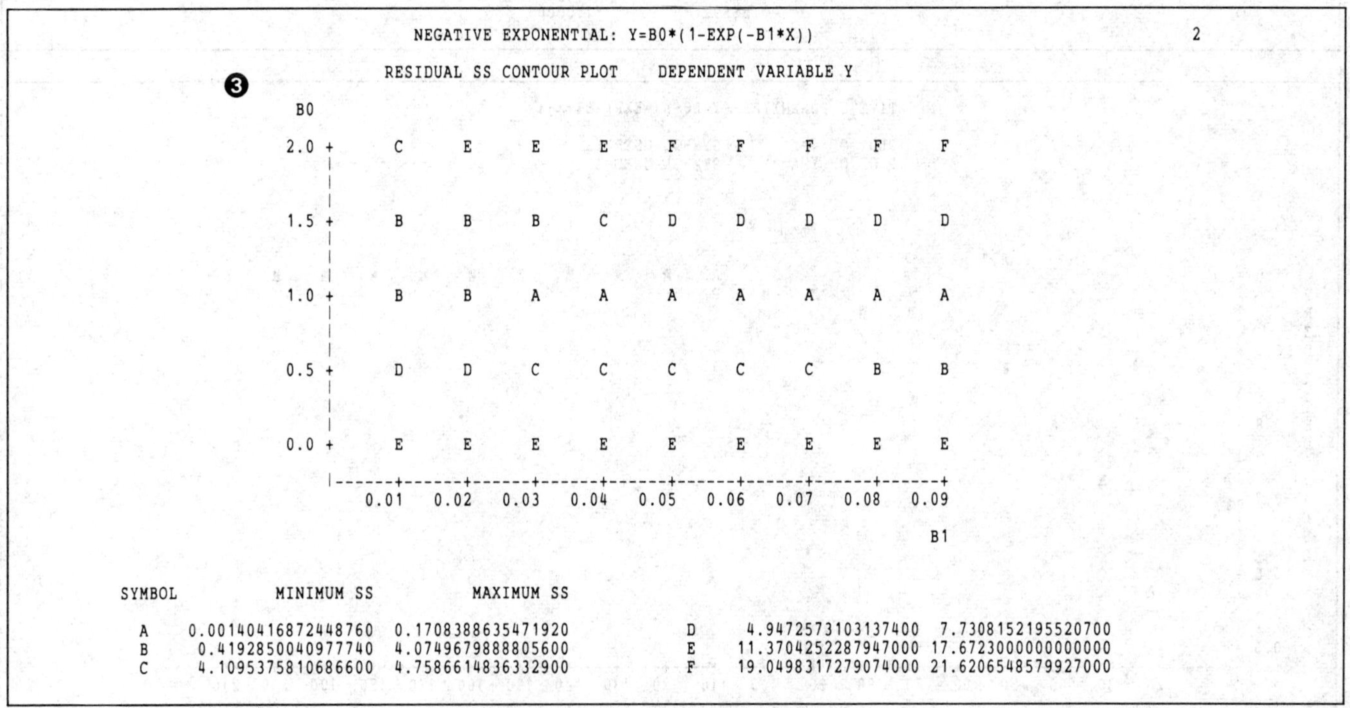

```
                    NEGATIVE EXPONENTIAL: Y=B0*(1-EXP(-B1*X))                      2

                    RESIDUAL SS CONTOUR PLOT    DEPENDENT VARIABLE Y
           ❸
         B0

     2.0 +      C      E      E      E      F      F      F      F      F
         |
         |
     1.5 +      B      B      B      C      D      D      D      D      D
         |
         |
     1.0 +      B      B      A      A      A      A      A      A      A
         |
         |
     0.5 +      D      D      C      C      C      C      C      B      B
         |
         |
     0.0 +      E      E      E      E      E      E      E      E      E
         |
         ------+------+------+------+------+------+------+------+------+
             0.01   0.02   0.03   0.04   0.05   0.06   0.07   0.08   0.09

                                                                       B1

SYMBOL          MINIMUM SS              MAXIMUM SS

  A     0.0014041687244876O  0.1708388635471920          D      4.9472573103137400   7.7308152195520700
  B     0.4192850040977740  4.0749679888805600          E     11.3704252287947000  17.6723000000000000
  C     4.1095375810686600  4.7586614836332900          F     19.0498317279074000  21.6206548579927000
```

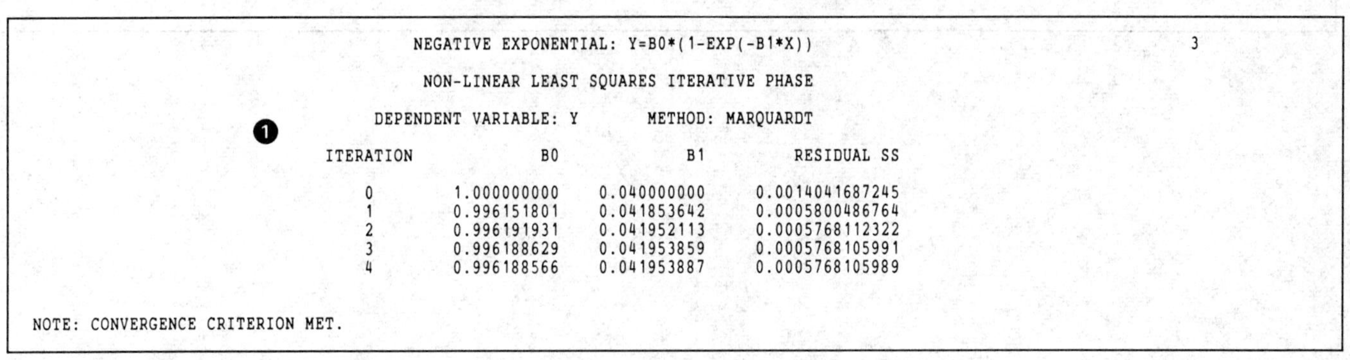

```
                    NEGATIVE EXPONENTIAL: Y=B0*(1-EXP(-B1*X))                      3

                    NON-LINEAR LEAST SQUARES ITERATIVE PHASE

               DEPENDENT VARIABLE: Y        METHOD: MARQUARDT
        ❶
          ITERATION           B0              B1             RESIDUAL SS

              0          1.000000000     0.040000000     0.0014041687245
              1          0.996151801     0.041853642     0.0005800486764
              2          0.996191931     0.041952113     0.0005768112322
              3          0.996188629     0.041953859     0.0005768105991
              4          0.996188566     0.041953887     0.0005768105989

NOTE: CONVERGENCE CRITERION MET.
```

```
              NEGATIVE EXPONENTIAL: Y=B0*(1-EXP(-B1*X))                                    4

      NON-LINEAR LEAST SQUARES SUMMARY STATISTICS     DEPENDENT VARIABLE Y

❹       SOURCE                 DF SUM OF SQUARES     MEAN SQUARE

        REGRESSION              2   17.671723189     8.835861595
        RESIDUAL               18    0.000576811     0.000032045
        UNCORRECTED TOTAL      20   17.672300000

        (CORRECTED TOTAL)      19    0.243855000
                  ❺                      ❻                        ❼
        PARAMETER     ESTIMATE     ASYMPTOTIC             ASYMPTOTIC 95 %
                                   STD. ERROR          CONFIDENCE INTERVAL
❽                                                      LOWER            UPPER
        B0        0.9961885657 0.00161380016 0.99279811981 0.99957901164
        B1        0.0419538868 0.00039822900 0.04111724422 0.04279052932


                ASYMPTOTIC CORRELATION MATRIX OF THE PARAMETERS

                    CORR               B0               B1

                    B0             1.0000          -0.5559
                    B1            -0.5559           1.0000
```

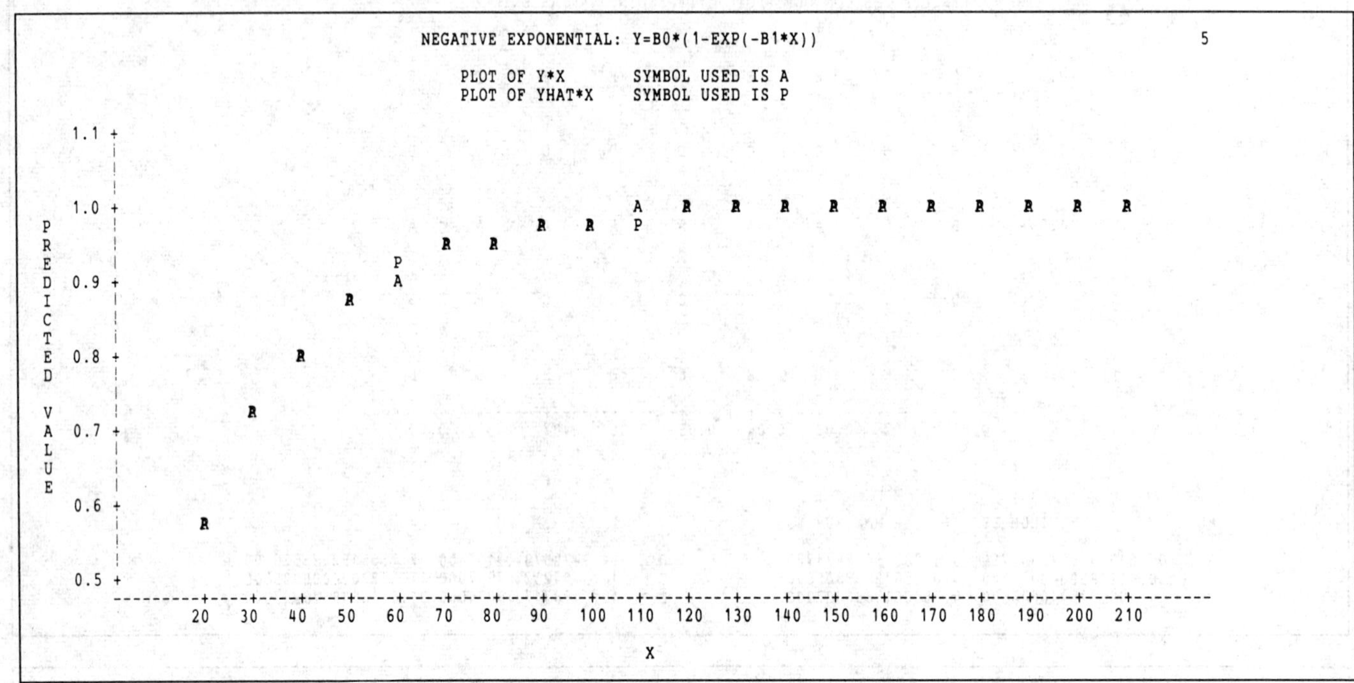

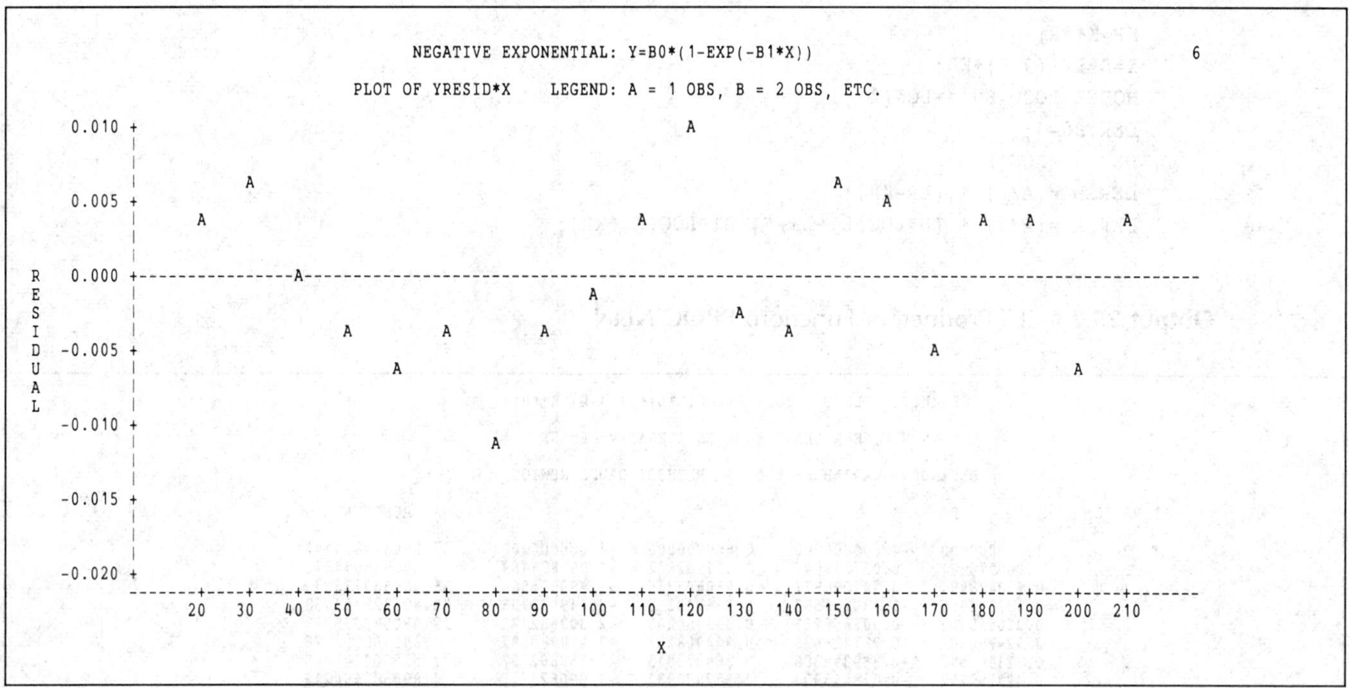

CES Production Function: Example 2

The CES production function in economics models the quantity produced as a function of inputs such as capital, K, and labor, L. Arrow, Chenery, Minhas, and Solow developed the CES production function and named it for its property of constant elasticity of substitution. A is the efficiency parameter, D is the distribution or factor share parameter, and R is the substitution parameter. This example was described by Lutkepohl in the encyclopedic work by Judge et al. (1980).

```
TITLE 'CES MODEL: LOGQ = B0 + A*LOG(D*L**R+(1-D)*K**R)';

DATA CES;
   INPUT L K LOGQ @@;
   CARDS;
.228 .802 -1.359  .258 .249 -1.695
.821 .771   .193  .767 .511  -.649
.495 .758  -.165  .487 .425  -.270
.678 .452  -.473  .748 .817   .031
.727 .845  -.563  .695 .958  -.125
.458 .084 -2.218  .981 .021 -3.633
.002 .295 -5.586  .429 .277  -.773
.231 .546 -1.315  .664 .129 -1.678
.631 .017 -3.879  .059 .906 -2.301
.811 .223 -1.377  .758 .145 -2.270
.050 .161 -2.539  .823 .006 -5.150
.483 .836  -.324  .682 .521  -.253
.116 .930 -1.530  .440 .495  -.614
.456 .185 -1.151  .342 .092 -2.089
.358 .485  -.951  .162 .934 -1.275
;
PROC NLIN DATA=CES;
   PARMS B0=1 A=-1 D=.5 R=-1;
   LR=L**R;
```

```
KR=K**R;
Z=D*LR+(1-D)*KR;
MODEL LOGQ=B0+A*LOG(Z);
DER.B0=1;
DER.A =LOG(Z);
DER.D =(A/Z) * (LR-KR);
DER.R =(A/Z) * (D*LOG(L)*LR+(1-D)*LOG(K)*KR);
```

Output 25.2 CES Production Function: PROC NLIN

```
                         CES MODEL: LOGQ = B0 + A*LOG(D*L**R+(1-D)*K**R)                         1

                             NON-LINEAR LEAST SQUARES ITERATIVE PHASE

                        DEPENDENT VARIABLE: LOGQ     METHOD: GAUSS-NEWTON

      ITERATION             B0             A              D              R           RESIDUAL SS

          0         1.000000000   -1.000000000    0.500000000   -1.000000000    37.096511851144
          .         0.066976981    0.037818047    0.401202632   -1.999871169     158.975034575
          1         0.533488491   -0.481090977    0.450601316   -1.499935584    35.486563732231
          .         0.107542675   -0.134221553    0.315719213   -3.119428706    49.495829161488
          2         0.320515583   -0.307656265    0.383160265   -2.309682145    22.690597039249
          3         0.124790207   -0.287428475    0.301408287   -3.418180692     1.845468008476
          .         0.121805577   -0.369399386    0.364373615   -2.562862757     2.535561544446
          .         0.123297892   -0.328413931    0.332890951   -2.990521725     1.890582664219
          4         0.124044050   -0.307921203    0.317149619   -3.204351209     1.833362091801
          5         0.122933169   -0.355632218    0.349729665   -2.800352380     1.820337056943
          6         0.125085173   -0.324294836    0.330214118   -3.089113046     1.774003551871
          7         0.124010536   -0.342504988    0.340529715   -2.951604091     1.762107877512
          8         0.124712600   -0.332753787    0.334595899   -3.038982646     1.761176529159
          9         0.124346408   -0.338243620    0.337848828   -2.993734677     1.761056980675
         10         0.124562521   -0.335197406    0.336024211   -3.020170602     1.761042687446
         11         0.124446177   -0.336890038    0.337035327   -3.005869885     1.761040136390
         12         0.124512365   -0.335946730    0.336471495   -3.013965821     1.761039527866
         13         0.124476009   -0.336470840    0.336784884   -3.009505499     1.761039360388
         14         0.124496399   -0.336178902    0.336610395   -3.012001935     1.761039309684
         15         0.124485105   -0.336341238    0.336707458   -3.010617415     1.761039294257

NOTE: CONVERGENCE CRITERION MET.
```

```
                         CES MODEL: LOGQ = B0 + A*LOG(D*L**R+(1-D)*K**R)                         2

               NON-LINEAR LEAST SQUARES SUMMARY STATISTICS      DEPENDENT VARIABLE LOGQ

                   SOURCE                DF SUM OF SQUARES      MEAN SQUARE

                   REGRESSION             4   130.00369371      32.50092343
                   RESIDUAL              26     1.76103929       0.06773228
                   UNCORRECTED TOTAL     30   131.76473300

                   (CORRECTED TOTAL)     29    61.28965430

                   PARAMETER      ESTIMATE    ASYMPTOTIC            ASYMPTOTIC 95 %
                                              STD. ERROR          CONFIDENCE INTERVAL
                                                                LOWER             UPPER
                   B0          0.124485105  0.0783429642 -0.0365498914  0.2855201005
                   A          -0.336341238  0.2721800618 -0.8958109440  0.2231284680
                   D           0.336707458  0.1360850556  0.0569828319  0.6164320846
                   R          -3.010617415  2.3229032585 -7.7853756933  1.7641408635


                           ASYMPTOTIC CORRELATION MATRIX OF THE PARAMETERS

                CORR                  B0                  A                   D                   R

                B0                1.0000             0.2965             -0.1765             -0.3267
                A                 0.2965             1.0000             -0.7836             -0.9991
                D                -0.1765            -0.7836              1.0000              0.7834
                R                -0.3267            -0.9991              0.7834              1.0000
```

Probit Model with Numerical Derivatives: Example 3

This example fits the population of the U.S. across time to the inverse of the cumulative normal distribution function. Numerical derivatives are coded since the analytic derivatives are messy.

The C parameter is the upper population limit. The A and B parameters scale time.

```
TITLE 'U.S. POPULATION GROWTH';
TITLE2 'PROBIT MODEL WITH NUMERICAL DERIVATIVES';

DATA USPOP;
   INPUT POP :6.3 @@;
   RETAIN YEAR 1780;
   YEAR=YEAR+10;
   YEARSQ=YEAR*YEAR;
   CARDS;
3929 5308 7239 9638 12866 17069 23191 31443 39818 50155
62947 75994 91972 105710 122775 131669 151325 179323 203211
;

PROC NLIN DATA=USPOP;
   PARMS A=-2.4 B=.012 C=400;
   DELTA=.0001;
   X=YEAR-1790;
   POPHAT=C*PROBNORM(A+B*X);
   MODEL POP=POPHAT;
   DER.A=(POPHAT-C*PROBNORM((A-DELTA)+B*X))/DELTA;
   DER.B=(POPHAT-C*PROBNORM(A+(B-DELTA)*X))/DELTA;
   DER.C=POPHAT/C;
   OUTPUT OUT=P P=PREDICT;
PROC PLOT DATA=P;
   PLOT POP*YEAR PREDICT*YEAR='P' /OVERLAY VPOS=30;
RUN;
```

Output 25.3 Probit Model with Numerical Derivatives: PROC NLIN

```
                               U.S. POPULATION GROWTH                                         1
                        PROBIT MODEL WITH NUMERICAL DERIVATIVES

                        NON-LINEAR LEAST SQUARES ITERATIVE PHASE

                    DEPENDENT VARIABLE: POP      METHOD: GAUSS-NEWTON

         ITERATION               A              B               C             RESIDUAL SS

             0          -2.400000000    0.012000000     400.000000       7174.590805091
             1          -2.271908363    0.012622923     399.066499        209.327927092
             2          -2.302425176    0.012660783     404.804742        177.392064067
             3          -2.302787592    0.012628220     407.072751        177.370043910
             4          -2.302818505    0.012628562     407.079801        177.369803522
             5          -2.302818263    0.012628514     407.082668        177.369803042

NOTE: CONVERGENCE CRITERION MET.
```

```
                              U.S. POPULATION GROWTH                                   2
                        PROBIT MODEL WITH NUMERICAL DERIVATIVES

      NON-LINEAR LEAST SQUARES SUMMARY STATISTICS      DEPENDENT VARIABLE POP

         SOURCE                  DF SUM OF SQUARES      MEAN SQUARE

         REGRESSION               3   164227.89925      54742.63308
         RESIDUAL                16      177.36980         11.08561
         UNCORRECTED TOTAL       19   164405.26906

         (CORRECTED TOTAL)       18    71922.76175

         PARAMETER      ESTIMATE    ASYMPTOTIC            ASYMPTOTIC 95 %
                                    STD. ERROR         CONFIDENCE INTERVAL
                                                       LOWER          UPPER
         A            -2.3028183   0.032832711   -2.37242015    -2.23321637
         B             0.0126285   0.000956986    0.01059980     0.01465722
         C           407.0826677  61.784898470  276.10518493   538.06015048


                 ASYMPTOTIC CORRELATION MATRIX OF THE PARAMETERS

            CORR                 A                  B                  C

            A               1.0000            -0.0079            -0.2198
            B              -0.0079             1.0000            -0.9723
            C              -0.2198            -0.9723             1.0000
```

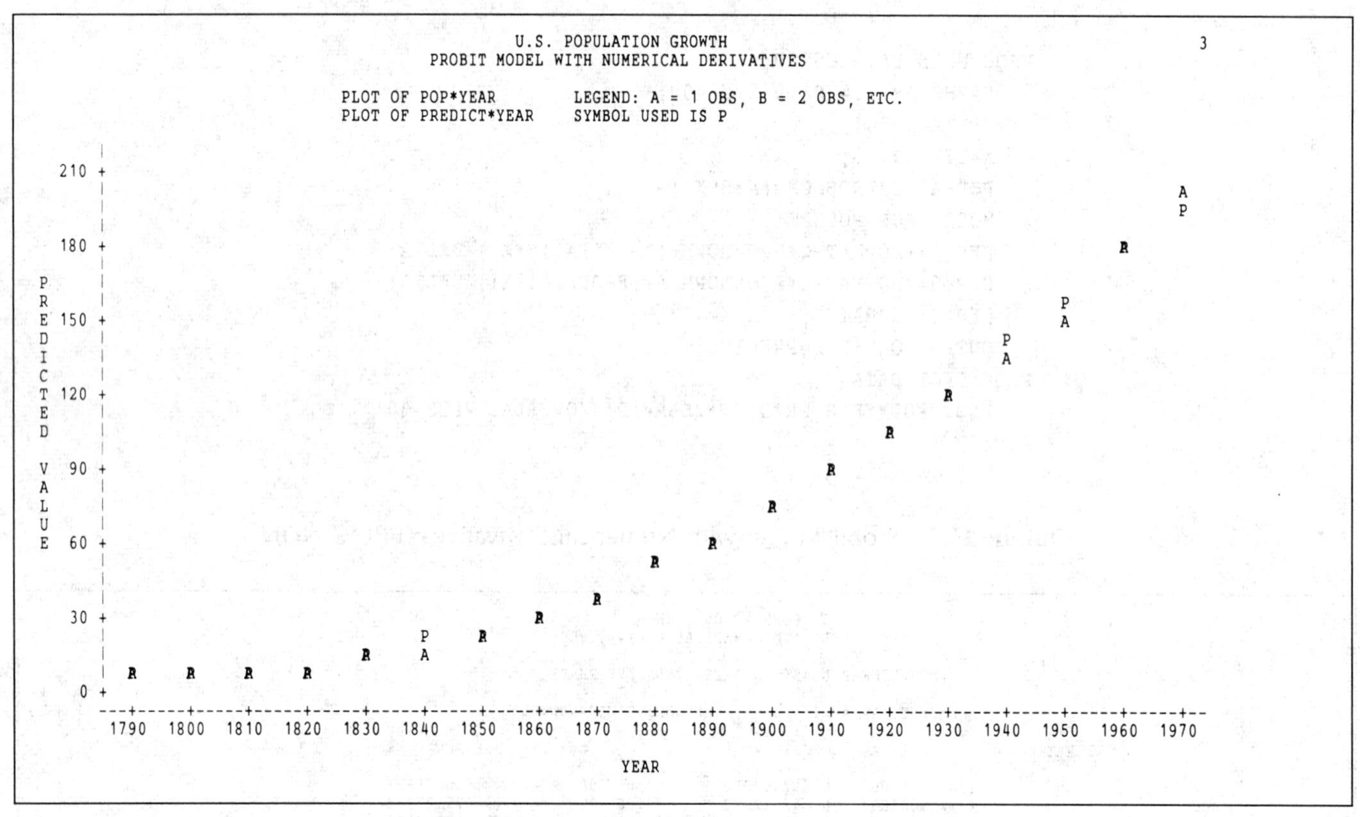

Segmented Model: Example 4

From theoretical considerations we can hypothesize that

$$y = a+bx+cx2 \quad \text{if } x<x_0$$

$$y = p \quad \text{if } x>x_0 \quad .$$

That is, for values of x less than x_0, the equation relating y and x is quadratic (a parabola) and, for values of x greater than x_0, the equation is constant (a horizontal line). PROC NLIN can fit such a segmented model even when the joint point, x_0, is unknown.

The curve must be continuous (the two sections must meet at x_0), and the curve must be smooth (the first derivatives with respect to x are the same at x_0).

These conditions imply that

$$x_0 = -b/2c$$

$$p = a-b^2/4c \quad .$$

The segmented equation includes only three parameters; however, the equation is nonlinear with respect to these parameters.

You can write program statements with PROC NLIN to conditionally execute different sections of code for the two parts of the model, depending on whether x is less than x_0.

A PUT statement is used to print the constrained parameters every time the program is executed for the first observation (where x=1).

```
*---------FITTING A SEGMENTED MODEL USING NLIN-----*
|        |                                         |
|    Y   | QUADRATIC            PLATEAU            |
|        | Y=A+B*X+C*X*X        Y=P                |
|        |                    .....................|
|        |          .         :                    |
|        |       .            :                    |
|        |     .              :                    |
|        |   .                :                    |
|        |  .                 :                    |
|        +----------------------------------------X |
|                             X0                    |
|                                                  |
| CONTINUITY RESTRICTION: P=A+B*X0+C*X0**2         |
| SMOOTHNESS RESTRICTION: 0=B+2*C*X0 SO X0=-B/(2*C)|
*-------------------------------------------------*;

TITLE 'QUADRATIC MODEL WITH PLATEAU';

DATA A;
   INPUT Y X @@;
   CARDS;
.46 1  .47  2 .57  3 .61  4 .62  5 .68  6 .69  7
.78 8  .70  9 .74 10 .77 11 .78 12 .74 13 .80 13
.80 15 .78 16
;
PROC NLIN;
   PARMS A=.45 B=.05 C=-.0025;
   X0=-.5*B/C;                        * ESTIMATE JOIN POINT;
   DB=-.5/C;                          * DERIV OF X0 WRT B;
   DC=.5*B/C**2;                      * DERIV OF X0 WRT C;
   IF X<X0 THEN DO;                   * QUADRATIC PART OF MODEL;
      MODEL Y = A + B*X + C*X*X;
      DER.A = 1;
      DER.B = X;
```

```
         DER.C = X*X;
         END;
      ELSE DO;                    * PLATEAU PART OF MODEL;
         MODEL Y = A +B*X0 +C*X0*X0;
         DER.A = 1;
         DER.B = X0 + B*DB +      2*C*X0*DB;
         DER.C =      B*DC + X0*X0 + 2*C*X0*DC;
         END;
      IF _OBS_=1 & _MODEL_=1 THEN DO; * PRINT OUT IF 1ST OBS;
         PLATEAU = A +B*X0 +C*X0*X0;
         PUT X0= PLATEAU=;
         END;
      OUTPUT OUT=B PREDICTED=YP;
   PROC PLOT;
      PLOT Y*X YP*X='*' / OVERLAY VPOS=35;
```

Output 25.4 Segmented Model: PROC NLIN and PROC PLOT

```
                                  QUADRATIC MODEL WITH PLATEAU                                        1

                               NON-LINEAR LEAST SQUARES ITERATIVE PHASE

                            DEPENDENT VARIABLE: Y      METHOD: GAUSS-NEWTON

                  ITERATION              A                B              C              RESIDUAL SS

                          0       0.450000000     0.050000000  -0.0025000000       0.056231250000
X0=13.165937 PLATEAU=0.79366217
                          1       0.388117761     0.061605095  -0.0023395636       0.011764344892
X0=12.822301 PLATEAU=0.77805058
                          2       0.393040389     0.060053213  -0.0023417487       0.010068402089
X0=12.755625 PLATEAU=0.77755307
                          3       0.392216429     0.060418310  -0.0023683007       0.010066017755
X0=12.748464 PLATEAU=0.77750259
                          4       0.392125787     0.060458545  -0.0023712089       0.010065990812
X0=12.747742 PLATEAU=0.77749789
                          5       0.392116319     0.060462721  -0.0023715072       0.010065990540
X0=12.747669 PLATEAU=0.77749743
                          6       0.392115366     0.060463141  -0.0023715371       0.010065990537

NOTE: CONVERGENCE CRITERION MET.
```

```
                                  QUADRATIC MODEL WITH PLATEAU                                        2

                     NON-LINEAR LEAST SQUARES SUMMARY STATISTICS     DEPENDENT VARIABLE Y

                        SOURCE                 DF SUM OF SQUARES     MEAN SQUARE

                        REGRESSION              3   7.7256340095     2.5752113365
                        RESIDUAL               13   0.0100659905     0.0007743070
                        UNCORRECTED TOTAL      16   7.7357000000

                        (CORRECTED TOTAL)      15   0.1869437500

                        PARAMETER      ESTIMATE      ASYMPTOTIC            ASYMPTOTIC 95 %
                                                     STD. ERROR          CONFIDENCE INTERVAL
                                                                         LOWER          UPPER
                        A          0.3921153660 0.02667414696 0.33448940946 0.44974132253
                        B          0.0604631414 0.00842304248 0.04226627534 0.07866000749
                        C          -.0023715371 0.00055131779 -.00356258609 -.00118048817
```

(continued on next page)

(continued from previous page)

```
                         ASYMPTOTIC CORRELATION MATRIX OF THE PARAMETERS

                    CORR              A               B              C

                    A            1.0000         -0.9020         0.8124
                    B           -0.9020          1.0000        -0.9788
                    C            0.8124         -0.9788         1.0000
X0=12.747669 PLATEAU=0.77749743
```

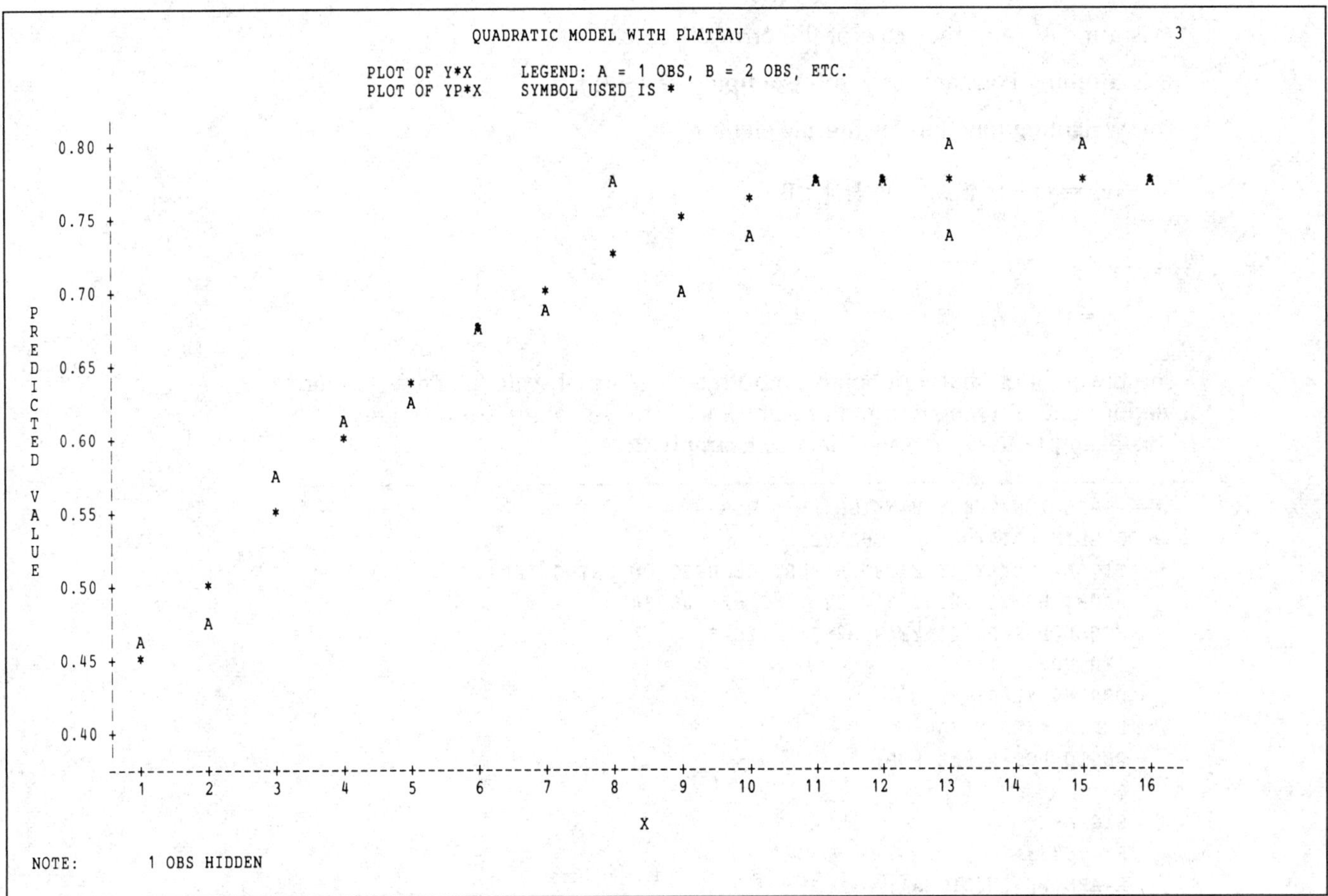

Iteratively Reweighted Least Squares: Example 5

The NLIN procedure is suited to methods that make the weight a function of the parameters in each iteration since the _WEIGHT_ variable can be computed with program statements. The NOHALVE option is used because we are modifying the SSE definition at each iteration and are thus circumventing the step-shortening criteria.

Iteratively reweighted least squares (IRLS) can produce estimates for many of the robust regression criteria suggested in the literature. These methods act like automatic outlier rejectors since large residual values lead to very small weights. Holland and Welsch (1977) outline several of these robust methods. For example, the biweight criterion suggested by Beaton and Tukey (1974) tries to minimize

$$S_{\text{biweight}} = \Sigma\ \rho(r)$$

where

$$\rho(r)=(B^2/2)(1-(1-(r/B)^2)^3) \quad \text{if } |r| \leq B$$

or otherwise

$$\rho(r)=(B^2/2)$$

where

r is abs(residual)/σ

σ is a measure of the scale of the error

B is a tuning constant (uses the example B=4.685).

The weighting function for the biweight is

$$w_i = (1-(r_i/B)^2)^2 \quad \text{if } |r_i| \leq B$$

or

$$w_i=0 \text{ if } |r_i|>B \quad .$$

The biweight estimator depends on both a measure of scale (like the standard deviation) and a tuning constant; results vary if these values are changed.

This example uses the same data as **Example 3**:

```
*-----BEATON/TUKEY BIWEIGHT BY IRLS-----;
PROC NLIN DATA=USPOP NOHALVE;
   TITLE 'TUKEY BIWEIGHT ROBUST REGRESSION USING IRLS';
   PARMS B0=20450.43 B1=-22.7806 B2=.0063456;
   MODEL POP=B0+B1*YEAR+B2*YEAR*YEAR;
   DER.B0=1;
   DER.B1=YEAR;
   DER.B2=YEAR*YEAR;
   RESID=POP-MODEL.POP;

   SIGMA=2;
   B=4.685;
   R=ABS(RESID/SIGMA);
   IF R<=B THEN _WEIGHT_=(1-(R/B)**2)**2;
   ELSE _WEIGHT_=0;
   OUTPUT OUT=C R=RBI;
DATA C;
SET C;
   SIGMA=2;
   B=4.685;
   R=ABS(RBI/SIGMA);
   IF R<=B THEN _WEIGHT_=(1-(R/B)**2)**2;
   ELSE _WEIGHT_=0;
PROC PRINT;
```

Output 25.5 Iteratively Reweighted Least Squares: PROC NLIN and PROC PRINT

```
                    TUKEY BIWEIGHT ROBUST REGRESSION USING IRLS                                1

                     NON-LINEAR LEAST SQUARES ITERATIVE PHASE

                  DEPENDENT VARIABLE: POP       METHOD: GAUSS-NEWTON

ITERATION           B0               B1               B2  WEIGHTED RESIDUAL SS

    0      20450.430000  -22.780600000  0.0063456000      57.264816854552600
    1      20711.580896  -23.068940135  0.0064251417      31.316348293700600
    2      20889.771438  -23.263967641  0.0064784893      19.794508672249800
    3      20950.186052  -23.330291552  0.0064966865      16.754875447765400
    4      20966.814401  -23.348568238  0.0065017070      16.057279212896600
    5      20970.962721  -23.353128506  0.0065029598      15.895347692801800
    6      20971.960688  -23.354225563  0.0065032612      15.857197932231900
    7      20972.198207  -23.354486663  0.0065033330      15.848167401796400
    8      20972.254576  -23.354548627  0.0065033500      15.846027181309300
    9      20972.267943  -23.354563321  0.0065033540      15.845519805343800
   10      20972.271113  -23.354566805  0.0065033550      15.845399514837000
   11      20972.271864  -23.354567631  0.0065033552      15.845370995463000
   12      20972.272042  -23.354567827  0.0065033553      15.845364233858800
   13      20972.272084  -23.354567874  0.0065033553      15.845362630789900
   14      20972.272094  -23.354567885  0.0065033553      15.845362250676500
   15      20972.272097  -23.354567887  0.0065033553      15.845362160594100

NOTE: CONVERGENCE CRITERION MET.
```

```
                    TUKEY BIWEIGHT ROBUST REGRESSION USING IRLS                                2

        NON-LINEAR LEAST SQUARES SUMMARY STATISTICS      DEPENDENT VARIABLE POP

          SOURCE                  DF    WEIGHTED SS      WEIGHTED MS

          REGRESSION               3   122571.96279     40857.32093
          RESIDUAL                16       15.84536         0.99034
          UNCORRECTED TOTAL       19   122587.80815

          (CORRECTED TOTAL)       18    59465.92678

          PARAMETER      ESTIMATE    ASYMPTOTIC           ASYMPTOTIC 95 %
                                     STD. ERROR       CONFIDENCE INTERVAL
                                                      LOWER          UPPER
          B0          20972.27210  309.61766713  20315.915225  21628.628968
          B1            -23.35457    0.32987833    -24.053875    -22.655261
          B2              0.00650    0.00008781      0.006317      0.006690


                  ASYMPTOTIC CORRELATION MATRIX OF THE PARAMETERS

             CORR                B0                 B1                B2

             B0              1.0000            -0.9999            0.9996
             B1             -0.9999             1.0000           -0.9999
             B2              0.9996            -0.9999            1.0000
```

```
                    TUKEY BIWEIGHT ROBUST REGRESSION USING IRLS                                3

OBS       POP    YEAR    YEARSQ        RBI      SIGMA      B          R       _WEIGHT_

  1     3.929    1790   3204100    -1.0673       2       4.685    0.53364    0.974220
  2     5.308    1800   3240000     0.3869       2       4.685    0.19347    0.996592
  3     7.239    1810   3276100     1.0925       2       4.685    0.54625    0.972996
  4     9.638    1820   3312400     0.9654       2       4.685    0.48269    0.978883
  5    12.866    1830   3348900     0.3666       2       4.685    0.18330    0.996941
  6    17.069    1840   3385600    -0.5579       2       4.685    0.27894    0.992923
  7    23.191    1850   3422500    -0.8640       2       4.685    0.43200    0.983067
  8    31.443    1860   3459600    -0.3408       2       4.685    0.17040    0.997356
  9    39.818    1870   3496900    -0.9953       2       4.685    0.49764    0.977562
 10    50.155    1880   3534400    -0.9884       2       4.685    0.49421    0.977868
 11    62.947    1890   3572100     0.1728       2       4.685    0.08638    0.999320
 12    75.994    1900   3610000     0.2883       2       4.685    0.14414    0.998108
 13    91.972    1910   3648100     2.0341       2       4.685    1.01706    0.907966
 14   105.710    1920   3686400     0.2393       2       4.685    0.11964    0.998696
```

(continued on next page)

(continued from previous page)

```
  15    122.775    1930    3724900     0.4708     2     4.685    0.23539    0.994957
  16    131.669    1940    3763600    -8.7694     2     4.685    4.38469    0.015399
  17    151.325    1950    3802500    -8.5482     2     4.685    4.27411    0.028128
  18    179.323    1960    3841600    -1.2857     2     4.685    0.64287    0.962697
  19    203.211    1970    3880900     0.5661     2     4.685    0.28304    0.992714
```

The printout of the computed weights shows that the observations for 1940 and 1950 are highly discounted because of their large residuals.

The printout contains a note that missing values were propagated in thirty-two places. This happens when the last observation with a missing value for POP is handled. Since there are fifteen iterations plus an initial iteration and the program is executed twice for each iteration (for each observation), these propagations occurred thirty-two times.

Maximum Likelihood for Binary Data: Example 6

It is also possible to fit binary data models as described by Nelder and Wedderburn (1972). Maximum-likelihood estimates can be computed by iteratively reweighted least squares, where the weights are the reciprocals of the variances. In this case you maximize the binomial likelihood with a probit link function.

```
%MACRO BINOMIAL(DATA=_LAST_,RESPONSE=,NUMBER=,VARS=);

/*------------------------------------------------------------*/
/* VARIABLE     FUNCTION                                       */
/* --------     --------                                       */
/*                                                             */
/* DATA         INPUT DATA SET                                 */
/* RESPONSE     VARIABLE CONTAINING THE NUMBER OF RESPONDANTS */
/* NUMBER       VARIABLE CONTAINING THE NUMBER IN GROUP       */
/* VARS         LIST OF INDEPENDENT VARIABLES                  */
/* P            RESPONSE PROB AS FUNCTION OF Z (=XB)          */
/* PHI          DERIVATIVE OF P AS A FUNCTION OF Z AND/OR P   */
/*                                                             */
/*------------------------------------------------------------*/
/* RESPONSE~Bin(NUMBER,P)                                      */
/* E(RESPONSE)=NUMBER*P                                        */
/* Z=XB                                                        */
/* LOGIT  LINK FUNCTION  P=1/[1+EXP[-Z]]                       */
/* PROBIT LINK FUNCTION  P=PROBNORM[Z]                         */
/* PHI=DERIVATIVE  P/WRT(Z)                                    */
/* FOR LOGIT  LINK PHI=NUMBER*P*[1-P]                          */
/* FOR PROBIT LINK PHI=NUMBER*EXP[-Z*Z/2]/SQRT(8*ATAN(1))     */
/* VAR(RESPONSE)=NUMBER*P*(1-P)                                */
/* MODEL RESPONSE=NUMBER*P                                     */
/* _WEIGHT_=1/VAR(RESPONSE)=1/(NUMBER*P*(1-P))                */
/* _LOSS_= (-RESPONSE*LOG(P)-(NUMBER-RESPONSE)*LOG(1-P))      */
/*              /_WEIGHT_                                      */
/* DER.B=PHI*DER(Z)/WRT(B)                                     */
/*                                                             */
/*------------------------------------------------------------*/
   %LET N=0;          /* SPLIT OUT INDIVIDUAL NAMES */
   %LET OLD=;
```

```
   %DO %WHILE(%SCAN(&VARS,&N+1)¬=);
      %LET N=%EVAL(&N+1);
      %LET VAR&N=%SCAN(&VARS,&N);
      %LET OLD=&OLD _OLD&N;
   %END;

   /* DO MLE WITH NONLINEAR LEAST SQUARES */

PROC NLIN DATA=&DATA(RENAME=(
   %DO I=1 %TO &N;
      &&VAR&I=_OLD&I
   %END; )) ;

   RETAIN LOGLIKE 0;

   /* START INITIAL VALUES AT ZERO */
   PARMS
      INTERCPT=0
      %DO I=1 %TO &N; &&VAR&I=0 %END; ;

   /* COMPUTE INNER PRODUCT */
   Z=INTERCPT %DO I=1 %TO &N; + &&VAR&I*_OLD&I %END; ;

   /* MODEL RESPONSE PROBABILITY: CHANGE THIS FOR DIFFERENT MODEL */
   P=PROBNORM(Z);      /*PROBIT REGRESSION*/
   *P=1/(1+EXP(-Z));  /*LOGIT  REGRESSION*/
   IF _MODEL_=1 THEN DO;
      IF _OBS_=1 THEN DO; PUT LOGLIKE=; LOGLIKE=0; END;
      LOGLIKE= LOGLIKE +
           &RESPONSE*LOG(P)+(&NUMBER-&RESPONSE)*LOG(1-P);
   END;

   MODEL &RESPONSE=&NUMBER*P;

   _WEIGHT_=1/(&NUMBER*P*(1-P));

   _LOSS_=(-&RESPONSE*LOG(P)-(&NUMBER-&RESPONSE)*LOG(1-P))/_WEIGHT_;


   /* CHANGE THIS FOR DIFFERENT PROBABILITY MODEL */
   PHI=&NUMBER*EXP(-Z*Z/2)/SQRT(8*ATAN(1));  /* PROBIT REGRESSION */
   *PHI=&NUMBER * P * (1-P);                 /* LOGIT  REGRESSION */

   DER.INTERCPT=PHI;
   %DO I=1 %TO &N;
      DER.&&VAR&I=PHI*_OLD&I;
   %END;
%MEND;


   /* RESPONSE DATA FROM                                   */
   /* FINNEY, D.J., PROBIT ANALYSIS, 3RD EDITION PAGE 104 */

DATA;
   INPUT X N R GROUP;
```

```
   G1=0; G2=0; G3=0; GX1=0; GX2=0; GX3=0;
   /* INDICATOR VARIABLES FOR GROUP */
        IF GROUP=1 THEN DO; G1=1; GX1=X; END;
   ELSE IF GROUP=2 THEN DO; G2=1; GX2=X; END;
   ELSE IF GROUP=3 THEN DO; G3=1; GX3=X; END;
   CARDS;
.18 103 19 1
.48 120 53 1
.78 123 83 1
.18  60 14 2
.48 110 54 2
.78 100 81 2
-.12 90 31 3
.18  80 54 3
.48  90 80 3
.70  60 13 4
.88  85 27 4
1.0  60 32 4
1.18 90 55 4
1.30 60 44 4
;

TITLE 'MLE ESTIMATES OF A PROBIT MODEL';
%BINOMIAL(RESPONSE=R,NUMBER=N,VARS=%STR(G1 G2 G3 X GX1 GX2 GX3));
%BINOMIAL(DATA=DATA1,RESPONSE=R,NUMBER=N,VARS=%STR(G1 G2 G3 X));
*-------------------INGOT DATA-----------------------------*
| INGOTS ARE TESTED FOR READINESS TO ROLL AFTER DIFFERENT  |
| TREATMENTS OF HEATING TIME AND SOAKING TIME.             |
| FROM COX (1970, pp. 67-68).                              |
*----------------------------------------------------------* ;
DATA INGOTS;
   INPUT HEAT SOAK NREADY NTOTAL @@;
   CARDS;
7 1.0  0 10   14 1.0  0 31   27 1.0  1 56   51 1.0  3 13
7 1.7  0 17   14 1.7  0 43   27 1.7  4 44   51 1.7  0  1
7 2.2  0  7   14 2.2  2 33   27 2.2  0 21   51 2.2  0  1
7 2.8  0 12   14 2.8  0 31   27 2.8  1 22
7 4.0  0  9   14 4.0  0 19   27 4.0  1 16   51 4.0  0  1
;
%BINOMIAL(RESPONSE=NREADY,NUMBER=NTOTAL,VARS=%STR(HEAT SOAK));
```

Output 25.6 Regression Analysis of Finney Data for Full Model: PROC NLIN and %BINOMIAL Macro

```
                              MLE ESTIMATES OF A PROBIT MODEL                                    1

                           NON-LINEAR LEAST SQUARES ITERATIVE PHASE

                        DEPENDENT VARIABLE: R        METHOD: GAUSS-NEWTON

      ITERATION        INTERCPT              G1              G2              G3               X          SUM OF LOSS
                   GX1            GX2             GX3

            0               0               0               0               0               0     853.264179269292
                            0               0               0

LOGLIKE=0
            1    -2.291054531     1.143410841     1.143308008     2.219069309     2.207842867     730.241254304598
                 -0.162483685     0.228487339     0.066690197

LOGLIKE=-730.24125
            2    -2.454065133     1.192682206     1.184645930     2.390270660     2.360510465     728.563960242655
                 -0.132281555     0.341141542     0.316392870

LOGLIKE=-728.56396
            3    -2.456341817     1.191415916     1.183427542     2.393833305     2.362557396     728.555294109034
                 -0.128990471     0.347622103     0.352295267

LOGLIKE=-728.55529
            4    -2.456342881     1.191396006     1.183431127     2.393848179     2.362557854     728.555293791452
                 -0.128960540     0.347642576     0.352512678


NOTE: CONVERGENCE CRITERION MET.
```

```
                              MLE ESTIMATES OF A PROBIT MODEL                                    2

                    NON-LINEAR LEAST SQUARES SUMMARY STATISTICS     DEPENDENT VARIABLE R

                     SOURCE                 DF     WEIGHTED SS      WEIGHTED MS

                     REGRESSION              8    2293.8098604      286.7262325
                     RESIDUAL                6       2.4899710        0.4149952
                     UNCORRECTED TOTAL      14    2296.2998313

                     (CORRECTED TOTAL)      13     566.9510536
                     SUM OF LOSS                   728.5552938

                     PARAMETER      ESTIMATE     ASYMPTOTIC           ASYMPTOTIC 95 %
                                                 STD. ERROR         CONFIDENCE INTERVAL
                                                                   LOWER          UPPER
                     INTERCPT  -2.456342881 0.23544554578 -3.0324577936 -1.8802279694
                     G1         1.191396006 0.26028055306  0.5545119761  1.8282800353
                     G2         1.183431127 0.27241817098  0.5168473950  1.8500148593
                     G3         2.393848179 0.24388724950  1.7970771473  2.9906192110
                     X          2.362557854 0.22607136385  1.8093807551  2.9157349524
                     GX1       -0.128960540 0.29959638837 -0.8620470222  0.6041259426
                     GX2        0.347642576 0.33301559124 -0.4672178091  1.1625029608
                     GX3        0.352512678 0.32697943346 -0.4475777498  1.1526031067


                         ASYMPTOTIC CORRELATION MATRIX OF THE PARAMETERS

CORR          INTERCPT            G1            G2            G3             X           GX1           GX2           GX3

INTERCPT        1.0000       -0.9046       -0.8643       -0.9654       -0.9818        0.7409        0.6665        0.6788
G1             -0.9046        1.0000        0.7818        0.8733        0.8881       -0.9249       -0.6029       -0.6141
G2             -0.8643        0.7818        1.0000        0.8344        0.8486       -0.6403       -0.9170       -0.5867
G3             -0.9654        0.8733        0.8344        1.0000        0.9478       -0.7152       -0.6435       -0.7466
X              -0.9818        0.8881        0.8486        0.9478        1.0000       -0.7546       -0.6789       -0.6914
GX1             0.7409       -0.9249       -0.6403       -0.7152       -0.7546        1.0000        0.5123        0.5217
GX2             0.6665       -0.6029       -0.9170       -0.6435       -0.6789        0.5123        1.0000        0.4694
GX3             0.6788       -0.6141       -0.5867       -0.7466       -0.6914        0.5217        0.4694        1.0000
```

Output 25.7 Regression Analysis of Finney Data for Restricted Model: PROC NLIN and %BINOMIAL Macro

```
                              MLE ESTIMATES OF A PROBIT MODEL                                         3

                           NON-LINEAR LEAST SQUARES ITERATIVE PHASE

                        DEPENDENT VARIABLE: R        METHOD: GAUSS-NEWTON

    ITERATION        INTERCPT             G1              G2              G3               X          SUM OF LOSS

         0                  0              0               0               0               0        853.264179269292
LOGLIKE=0
         1       -2.306052169    1.070263704     1.270399861     2.243416475     2.222591236        730.788241408382
LOGLIKE=-730.78824
         2       -2.561204918    1.177738449     1.413792367     2.527749660     2.465363082        729.330438473991
LOGLIKE=-729.33044
         3       -2.571850373    1.182176518     1.420036160     2.541111384     2.475475859        729.327397379903
LOGLIKE=-729.3274
         4       -2.571896252    1.182203043     1.420079950     2.541201896     2.475519350        729.327397137794

NOTE: CONVERGENCE CRITERION MET.
```

```
                              MLE ESTIMATES OF A PROBIT MODEL                                         4

                  NON-LINEAR LEAST SQUARES SUMMARY STATISTICS     DEPENDENT VARIABLE R

                   SOURCE                 DF    WEIGHTED SS     WEIGHTED MS

                   REGRESSION              5   2197.9366418    439.5873284
                   RESIDUAL                9      4.0310449      0.4478939
                   UNCORRECTED TOTAL      14   2201.9676867

                   (CORRECTED TOTAL)      13    547.1912375
                   SUM OF LOSS                  729.3273971

                   PARAMETER     ESTIMATE     ASYMPTOTIC             ASYMPTOTIC 95 %
                                              STD. ERROR          CONFIDENCE INTERVAL
                                                                  LOWER           UPPER
                   INTERCPT  -2.571896252 0.12738015242 -2.8600526281 -2.2837398761
                   G1         1.182203043 0.08913326103  0.9805678823  1.3838382033
                   G2         1.420079950 0.09239180462  1.2110733893  1.6290865112
                   G3         2.541201896 0.12651919645  2.2549931541  2.8274106374
                   X          2.475519350 0.11589308720  2.2133487422  2.7376899582


                        ASYMPTOTIC CORRELATION MATRIX OF THE PARAMETERS

         CORR              INTERCPT              G1                 G2                 G3                 X

         INTERCPT            1.0000         -0.8045            -0.7745            -0.8914           -0.9307
         G1                 -0.8045          1.0000             0.6814             0.7282            0.6588
         G2                 -0.7745          0.6814             1.0000             0.7012            0.6339
         G3                 -0.8914          0.7282             0.7012             1.0000            0.8130
         X                  -0.9307          0.6588             0.6339             0.8130            1.0000
```

Output 25.8 Regression Analysis of Ingot Data: PROC NLIN and %BINOMIAL Macro

```
                                MLE ESTIMATES OF A PROBIT MODEL                                     5

                           NON-LINEAR LEAST SQUARES ITERATIVE PHASE

                      DEPENDENT VARIABLE: NREADY   METHOD: GAUSS-NEWTON

               ITERATION       INTERCPT            HEAT            SOAK           SUM OF LOSS

                       0              0               0               0      268.247958876699
LOGLIKE=0
                       1   -1.353207100    0.0086970174    0.0023391251      71.710426318718900
LOGLIKE=-71.710426
                       2   -2.053504353     0.020273912    0.0073888189      51.641218525235200
LOGLIKE=-51.641219
                       3   -2.581302262     0.032625961     0.018503009      47.889468278503500
LOGLIKE=-47.889468
                       4   -2.838938311     0.038762504     0.030909943      47.489235733455900
LOGLIKE=-47.489236
                       5   -2.890129492     0.039889431     0.035650705      47.479966984354000
LOGLIKE=-47.479967
                       6   -2.893270346     0.039952862     0.036216612      47.479945369063100
LOGLIKE=-47.479945
                       7   -2.893408210     0.039955339     0.036251825      47.479945327430300

NOTE: CONVERGENCE CRITERION MET.
```

```
                                MLE ESTIMATES OF A PROBIT MODEL                                     6

            NON-LINEAR LEAST SQUARES SUMMARY STATISTICS        DEPENDENT VARIABLE NREADY

                SOURCE                    DF     WEIGHTED SS       WEIGHTED MS

                REGRESSION                 3     13.011673421      4.337224474
                RESIDUAL                  16     13.850931733      0.865683233
                UNCORRECTED TOTAL         19     26.862605154

                (CORRECTED TOTAL)         18     25.730010271
                SUM OF LOSS                      47.479945327

                PARAMETER      ESTIMATE     ASYMPTOTIC              ASYMPTOTIC 95 %
                                            STD. ERROR            CONFIDENCE INTERVAL
                                                                  LOWER          UPPER
                INTERCPT  -2.893408210 0.46576916971 -3.8807898343 -1.9060265860
                HEAT       0.039955339 0.01102232149  0.0165891777  0.0633215009
                SOAK       0.036251825 0.13653295992 -0.2531836817  0.3256873321


                        ASYMPTOTIC CORRELATION MATRIX OF THE PARAMETERS

                 CORR                  INTERCPT                 HEAT                 SOAK

                 INTERCPT                1.0000              -0.7951              -0.7538
                 HEAT                   -0.7951               1.0000               0.2959
                 SOAK                   -0.7538               0.2959               1.0000
```

REFERENCES

Bard, Jonathan (1970), "Comparison of Gradient Methods for the Solution of the Nonlinear Parameter Estimation Problem," *SIAM Journal of Numerical Analysis*, 7, 157-186.

Bard, Jonathan (1974), *Nonlinear Parameter Estimation*, New York: Academic Press.

Charnes, A., Frome, E.L., and Yu, P.L. (1976). "The Equivalence of Generalized Least Squares and Maximum Likelihood Estimation in the Exponential Family," *Journal of the American Statistical Association*, 71, 169-172.

Cox, D.R. (1970), *Analysis of Binary Data*, London: Chapman and Hall.

Gallant, A.R. (1975), "Nonlinear Regression," *American Statistician*, 29, 73-81.

Hartley, H.O. (1961), "The Modified Gauss-Newton Method for the Fitting of Non-Linear Regression Functions by Least Squares," *Technometrics*, 3, 269-280.

Hartley, H.O. (1961), "Least Squares Estimators," *Annals of Mathematical Statistics*, 40, 633-643.

Holland, Paul H. and Welsch, Roy E. (1977), "Robust Regression Using Iteratively Reweighted Least-Squares," *Communications Statistics: Theory and Methods*, 6, 813-827.

Jennrich, R.I. and Moore, R.H. (1975), "Maximum Likelihood Estimation by Means of Nonlinear Least Squares," American Statistical Association, *1975 Proceedings of the Statistical Computing Section*, 57-65.

Jennrich, R.I. and Sampson, P.F. (1968), "Application of Stepwise Regression to Non-Linear Estimation," *Technometrics*, 10, 63-72.

Judge, George G., Griffiths, William E., Hill, R. Carter, and Lee, Tsoung-Chao (1980), *The Theory and Practice of Econometrics*, New York: John Wiley & Sons.

Kennedy, William J., Gentle, James E. (1980), *Statistical Computing*, New York: Marcel Dekker, Inc.

Marquardt, Donald W. (1963), "An Algorithm for Least-Squares Estimation of Nonlinear Parameters," *Journal for the Society of Industrial and Applied Mathematics*, 11, 431-441.

Ralston, M.L. and Jennrich, R.I. (1979), "DUD, A Derivative-Free Algorithm for Nonlinear Least Squares," *Technometrics*, 1, 7-14.

Chapter 26
The NPAR1WAY Procedure

Operating systems: All

ABSTRACT

The NPAR1WAY procedure performs analysis of variance on ranks and certain rank scores of a response variable across a one-way classification. NPAR1WAY is a nonparametric procedure for testing that the distribution of a variable has the same location parameter across different groups.

INTRODUCTION

Most nonparametric tests are derived by examining the distribution of rank scores of the response variable. The rank scores are simply functions of the ranks of the response variable, where the values are ranked from low to high. Statistics defined as linear combinations of these rank scores are called *linear rank statistics*. The NPAR1WAY procedure calculates these four scores:

- **Wilcoxon scores** are the ranks

  $$z_i = R_i$$

  and are locally most powerful for location shifts of a logistic distribution.
- **Median scores** are 1 for points above the median, 0 otherwise:

  $$z_i = (R_i > (n + 1)/2)$$

  and are locally most powerful for double exponential distributions.

- **van der Waerden scores** are approximations to the expected values of the order statistics for a normal distribution

  $$z_i = \Phi^{-1}(R_i/(n + 1))$$

  where Φ is the distribution function for the normal distribution. These scores are powerful for normal distributions.
- **Savage scores** are expected values minus 1 of order statistics for the exponential distribution

  $$z_i = \Sigma_{j=1}^{Ri} 1/(n - j + 1) - 1$$

  and are powerful for comparing scale differences in exponential distributions (Hajek 1969, 83). NPAR1WAY subtracts 1 to center the scores around 0.

The statistics computed by PROC NPAR1WAY can also be computed by calculating the rank scores using PROC RANK and analyzing these rank scores with PROC ANOVA. **Table 26.1** shows the correspondence between PROC NPAR1WAY scores and various nonparametric tests.

Table 26.1 Comparison of NPAR1WAY with Nonparametric Tests

NPAR1WAY scores...	correspond to these tests if data are classified in two levels...*	correspond to these tests for a one-way layout or k-sample location test...**
Wilcoxon	Wilcoxon rank sum test Mann-Whitney U test	Kruskal-Wallis test
Median	median test for two samples	K-sample median test (Brown-Mood)
van der Waerden	van der Waerden Test	k-sample van der Waerden test
Savage	Savage test	k-sample Savage test

SPECIFICATIONS

The following statements are used to control NPAR1WAY:

PROC NPAR1WAY *options;*
  VAR *variables;*
  CLASS *variable;*
  BY *variables;*

The CLASS statement is required.

* The tests are two-tailed. For a one tailed test transform the significance probability by p/2 or (1-p/2).

** NPAR1WAY provides a chi-square approximate test.

PROC NPAR1WAY Statement

PROC NPAR1WAY *options;*

The options below can be used in the PROC NPAR1WAY statement:

DATA=*SASdataset*
: names the SAS data set containing the data to be analyzed. If DATA= is omitted, the most recently created SAS data set is used.

These options can be specified in the PROC NPAR1WAY statement. If none is specified, then all five analyses are performed by default.

ANOVA
: requests a standard analysis of variance.

WILCOXON
: requests an analysis of the ranks of the data, or the Wilcoxon scores. For two levels, this is the same as a Wilcoxon rank-sum test. For any number of levels, this is a Kruskal-Wallis test.

MEDIAN
: requests an analysis of the median scores. The median score is 1 for points above the median, 0 otherwise. For two samples, this produces a median test; for any number of levels, this is the Brown-Mood test.

VW
: requests that van der Waerden scores be analyzed. These are approximate normal scores derived by applying the inverse normal distribution function to the fractional ranks:

$$\Phi^{-1}(R_i/(n + 1)) \quad .$$

For two levels, this is the standard van der Waerden test.

SAVAGE
: requests that Savage scores be analyzed. These are expected order statistics for the exponential minus 1. This test is appropriate for comparing groups of data with exponential distributions.

VAR Statement

VAR *variables;*

This statement names the response or dependent variables to be analyzed. If the VAR statement is omitted, all numeric variables in the data set are analyzed.

CLASS Statement

CLASS *variable;*

The CLASS statement, which is required, names one and only one classification variable.

BY Statement

BY *variables;*

A BY statement can be used with PROC NPAR1WAY to obtain separate analyses on observations in groups defined by the BY variables. When a BY statement appears, the procedure expects the input data set to be sorted in order of the

BY variables. If your input data set is not sorted in ascending order, use the SORT procedure with a similar BY statement to sort the data, or, if appropriate, use the BY statement options NOTSORTED or DESCENDING. For more information, see the discussion of the BY statement in "Statements Used in the PROC Step," in the *SAS User's Guide: Basics*.

DETAILS

Missing Values

If an observation has a missing value for a response variable or the classification variable, that observation is excluded from the analysis.

Limitations

The procedure must have 20**n* bytes of memory available to store the data, where *n* is the number of nonmissing observations.

Resolution of Tied Values

Although the nonparametric tests were developed for continuous distributions, tied values do occur in practice. Ties are handled in all methods by assigning the average score for the different ranks corresponding to the tied values. Adjustments to variance estimates are performed in the manner described by Hajek (1969, Chapter 7).

Printed Output

NPAR1WAY produces the printed output described below.

If the ANOVA option is specified, NPAR1WAY prints

1. the traditional ANALYSIS OF VARIANCE table
2. the effect mean square reported as AMONG MS
3. the error mean square reported as WITHIN MS.

(These are the same values that would result from using a procedure such as ANOVA or GLM.)

NPAR1WAY produces a table for each rank score and includes the following for each level in the classification:

4. the LEVEL
5. the number of observations in the level (N)
6. the SUM OF SCORES
7. the EXPECTED sum of scores UNDER H0, the null hypothesis
8. STD DEV, the standard deviation estimate of the sum of scores, and
9. the MEAN SCORE.

For two or more levels, NPAR1WAY prints

10. a chi-square statistic (CHISQ)
11. its degrees of freedom (DF)
12. PROB>CHISQ, the significance probability.

If there are only two levels, NPAR1WAY reports

13. the smallest sum of scores as S
14. the ratio (S-expected)/std as Z, which is approximately normally distributed under the null hypothesis
15. PROB>|Z|, the probability of a greater observed Z value
16. T-TEST APPROX, the significance level for the the *t*-test approximation.

EXAMPLE

Weight Gains Data

The data are read in with a variable number of observations per record. In this example, NPAR1WAY first performs all five analyses on five levels of the class variable DOSE. Then the two lowest levels are output to a second data set to illustrate the two-sample tests.

```
TITLE 'WEIGHT GAINS WITH GOSSYPOL ADDITIVE';
TITLE3 'HALVERSON AND SHERWOOD - 1932';
DATA G;
   INPUT DOSE N;
   DO I=1 TO N;
      INPUT GAIN @@;
      OUTPUT;
      END;
   CARDS;
  0 16
    228 229 218 216 224 208 235 229 233 219 224 220 232 200 208 232
.04 11
    186 229 220 208 228 198 222 273 216 198 213
.07 12
    179 193 183 180 143 204 114 188 178 134 208 196
.10 17
    130  87 135 116 118 165 151  59 126  64  78  94 150 160 122 110 178
.13 11
    154 130 130 118 118 104 112 134  98 100 104
;
PROC NPAR1WAY;
   CLASS DOSE;
   VAR GAIN;
DATA G2;
   SET G;
   IF DOSE<=.04;
PROC NPAR1WAY;
   CLASS DOSE;
   VAR GAIN;
   TITLE4 'DOSES<=.04';
```

Output 26.1 Two Separate Runs of PROC NPAR1WAY: All CLASS Levels and Two Levels Only.

```
                    WEIGHT GAINS WITH GOSSYPOL ADDITIVE                          1

                      HALVERSON AND SHERWOOD - 1932

            ANALYSIS FOR VARIABLE GAIN CLASSIFIED BY VARIABLE  DOSE

                      AVERAGE SCORES WERE USED FOR TIES


                    ❶      ANALYSIS OF VARIANCE
                                                       ❷         ❸
       LEVEL              N        MEAN                AMONG MS  WITHIN MS
                                                        35020.7    627.452
           0     16     222.19
        0.04     11     217.36                          F VALUE     PROB>F
        0.07     12     175.00                            55.81     0.0001
         0.1     17     120.18
        0.13     11     118.36


                          WILCOXON SCORES (RANK SUMS)
      ❹                 ❺     ❻          ❼          ❽             ❾
                                SUM OF    EXPECTED     STD DEV          MEAN
       LEVEL             N      SCORES    UNDER H0    UNDER H0          SCORE

           0     16     890.50      544.00       67.98          55.66
        0.04     11     555.00      374.00       59.06          50.45
        0.07     12     395.50      408.00       61.14          32.96
         0.1     17     275.50      578.00       69.38          16.21
        0.13     11     161.50      374.00       59.06          14.68

             KRUSKAL-WALLIS TEST (CHI-SQUARE APPROXIMATION)
             CHISQ=  52.67       DF=  4     PROB > CHISQ=0.0001
            ❿                  ⓫          ⓬

                   MEDIAN SCORES (NUMBER POINTS ABOVE MEDIAN)

                                SUM OF    EXPECTED     STD DEV          MEAN
       LEVEL             N      SCORES    UNDER H0    UNDER H0          SCORE

           0     16      16.00        7.88        1.76           1.00
        0.04     11      11.00        5.42        1.53           1.00
        0.07     12       6.00        5.91        1.58           0.50
         0.1     17       0.00        8.37        1.79           0.00
        0.13     11       0.00        5.42        1.53           0.00

             MEDIAN 1-WAY ANALYSIS (CHI-SQUARE APPROXIMATION)
             CHISQ=  54.18       DF=  4     PROB > CHISQ=0.0001
```

```
                    WEIGHT GAINS WITH GOSSYPOL ADDITIVE                          2

                      HALVERSON AND SHERWOOD - 1932

            ANALYSIS FOR VARIABLE GAIN CLASSIFIED BY VARIABLE  DOSE

                      VAN DER WAERDEN SCORES (NORMAL)

                                SUM OF    EXPECTED     STD DEV          MEAN
       LEVEL             N      SCORES    UNDER H0    UNDER H0          SCORE

           0     16      16.12        0.00        3.33           1.01
        0.04     11       8.34        0.00        2.89           0.76
        0.07     12      -0.58        0.00        2.99          -0.05
         0.1     17     -14.69        0.00        3.39          -0.86
        0.13     11      -9.19        0.00        2.89          -0.84

             VAN DER WAERDEN 1-WAY (CHI-SQUARE APPROXIMATION)
             CHISQ=  47.30       DF=  4     PROB > CHISQ=0.0001
```

(continued on next page)

(continued from previous page)

```
                         SAVAGE SCORES (EXPONENTIAL)

                               SUM OF    EXPECTED     STD DEV        MEAN
LEVEL                  N       SCORES    UNDER H0    UNDER H0       SCORE

            0         16        16.07        0.00        3.39        1.00
         0.04         11         7.69        0.00        2.94        0.70
         0.07         12        -3.58        0.00        3.04       -0.30
          0.1         17       -11.98        0.00        3.46       -0.70
         0.13         11        -8.20        0.00        2.94       -0.75

              SAVAGE 1-WAY (CHI-SQUARE APPROXIMATION
              CHISQ=  39.49      DF=  4     PROB > CHISQ=0.0001
```

```
                       WEIGHT GAINS WITH GOSSYPOL ADDITIVE                              3

                          HALVERSON AND SHERWOOD - 1932
                                    DOSES<=.04

 ANALYSIS FOR VARIABLE GAIN CLASSIFIED BY VARIABLE  DOSE

                        AVERAGE SCORES WERE USED FOR TIES


                               ANALYSIS OF VARIANCE

LEVEL                  N         MEAN                   AMONG MS  WITHIN MS
                                                         151.684    271.479
            0         16       222.19
         0.04         11       217.36                    F VALUE     PROB>F
                                                            0.56     0.4617


                          WILCOXON SCORES (RANK SUMS)

                               SUM OF    EXPECTED     STD DEV        MEAN
LEVEL                  N       SCORES    UNDER H0    UNDER H0       SCORE

            0         16       253.50      224.00       20.22       15.84
         0.04         11       124.50      154.00       20.22       11.32

              WILCOXON 2-SAMPLE TEST (NORMAL APPROXIMATION)
              (WITH CONTINUITY CORRECTION OF .5)
(13)          S=  124.50 (14) Z=-1.4341  (15) PROB >|Z|=0.1515

(16)          T-TEST APPROX. SIGNIFICANCE=0.1635

              KRUSKAL-WALLIS TEST (CHI-SQUARE APPROXIMATION)
              CHISQ=   2.13      DF=  1     PROB > CHISQ=0.1446


                    MEDIAN SCORES (NUMBER POINTS ABOVE MEDIAN)

                               SUM OF    EXPECTED     STD DEV        MEAN
LEVEL                  N       SCORES    UNDER H0    UNDER H0       SCORE

            0         16         9.00        7.70        1.30        0.56
         0.04         11         4.00        5.30        1.30        0.36

              MEDIAN 2-SAMPLE TEST (NORMAL APPROXIMATION)
              S=    4.00      Z=-0.9972      PROB >|Z|=0.3187

              MEDIAN 1-WAY ANALYSIS (CHI-SQUARE APPROXIMATION)
              CHISQ=   0.99      DF=  1     PROB > CHISQ=0.3187
```

```
                WEIGHT GAINS WITH GOSSYPOL ADDITIVE                                  4

                   HALVERSON AND SHERWOOD - 1932
                             DOSES<=.04

   ANALYSIS FOR VARIABLE GAIN CLASSIFIED BY VARIABLE  DOSE

                VAN DER WAERDEN SCORES (NORMAL)

                                 SUM OF    EXPECTED     STD DEV         MEAN
LEVEL                    N       SCORES    UNDER H0    UNDER H0        SCORE

                0       16         3.35        0.00        2.32         0.21
             0.04       11        -3.35        0.00        2.32        -0.30

         VAN DER WAERDEN 2-SAMPLE TEST  (NORMAL APPROXIMATION)

         S=    -3.35      Z=-1.4423         PROB >|Z|=0.1492

         VAN DER WAERDEN 1-WAY (CHI-SQUARE APPROXIMATION)
         CHISQ=    2.08       DF=  1     PROB > CHISQ=0.1492


                SAVAGE SCORES (EXPONENTIAL)

                                 SUM OF    EXPECTED     STD DEV         MEAN
LEVEL                    N       SCORES    UNDER H0    UNDER H0        SCORE

                0       16         1.83        0.00        2.40         0.11
             0.04       11        -1.83        0.00        2.40        -0.17

         SAVAGE 2-SAMPLE TEST (NORMAL APPROXIMATION)
         S=    -1.83      Z=-0.7638        PROB >|Z|=0.4450

         SAVAGE 1-WAY (CHI-SQUARE APPROXIMATION
         CHISQ=    0.58       DF=  1     PROB > CHISQ=0.4450
```

REFERENCES

Conover, W.J. (1980), *Practical Nonparametric Statistics*, Second Edition, New York: John Wiley & Sons.

Hajek, J. (1969), *A Course in Nonparametric Statistics*, San Francisco: Holden-Day.

Lehmann, E.L. (1975), *Nonparametrics: Statistical Methods Based on Ranks*, San Francisco: Holden-Day.

Quade, D. (1966), "On Analysis of Variance for the *k*-Sample Problem," *Annals of Mathematical Statistics*, 37, 1747-1758.

Chapter 27
The PLAN Procedure

Operating systems: All

ABSTRACT

The PLAN procedure generates randomized plans for experiments. These plans are represented as groups of random permutations of positive integers.

INTRODUCTION

One or more random permutations can be generated for each item in another random permutation; there is no limit to the depth to which the random permutations can be nested. Any number of randomized plans can be generated.

The random permutations are selected from uniform pseudo-random variates generated as in the RANUNI function (see the *SAS User's Guide: Basics*).

SPECIFICATIONS

The PLAN procedure is controlled by two statements:

PROC PLAN *option;*
  FACTORS *requests;*

You include a FACTORS statement for each plan you want. Several FACTORS statements are permitted.

PROC PLAN Statement

PROC PLAN *option;*

Since the PLAN procedure does not require input data, the DATA= option is never used.

The option below can appear in the PROC PLAN statement:

SEED=*number*

specifies a 5-, 6-, or 7-digit odd integer for PLAN to use to generate the first random permutation. If SEED= *number* is omitted, the first random permutation is generated from a reading of the time of day from the computer's clock.

FACTORS Statement

FACTORS *requests;*

request

specifies the randomized plan to be provided by PLAN. The form of a *request* is

```
name=[m OF ]n [ORDERED] ...
```

where brackets ([ ]) denote an optional specification. More than one request can appear in the same FACTORS statement. The names in a request must be valid SAS names. *N* or *m* values must be positive integers.

A positive integer *n* appearing alone after an equal sign produces a random permutation of the integers 1, 2, ..., *n*.

A positive integer *n* followed by the word ORDERED generates the list of integers 1, 2, ..., *n*, in that order.

The specification *m* OF *n* tells PLAN to pick a random sample of *m* integers (without replacement) from the set of integers 1, 2, ..., *n* and to arrange the sample randomly.

For every integer generated for the first name specified, a permutation is generated for the second name according to the specifications following the second equal sign; for each of the integers generated, a permutation is generated for the second name, the third name, and so forth. For example,

```
PROC PLAN;
  FACTORS ONE=4 TWO=3;
```

You can think of a factor TWO as being nested within factor ONE, where the levels of factor ONE are to be randomly assigned to 4 units.

Six random permutations of the numbers 1, 2, 3, for instance, can be generated simply by specifying

```
FACTORS A=6 ORDERED B=3;
```

DETAILS

Printed Output

The PLAN procedure prints for each factor:

1. the initial random number
2. the number of levels of nesting in the plan
3. the random permutations making up each plan.

EXAMPLES

A Completely Random Design: Example 1

This first plan is appropriate for a completely random design with twelve experimental units and several treatments. The FACTORS statement requests a permutation of the integers 1, 2, ..., 12. If there are two treatments, the experimenter might then assign treatment 1 to the units corresponding to the first six integers in the permutations and treatment 2 to the other units.

```
PROC PLAN SEED=27371;
   TITLE 'COMPLETELY RANDOMIZED DESIGN';
   FACTORS U=12;
```

Output 27.1 A Completely Random Design

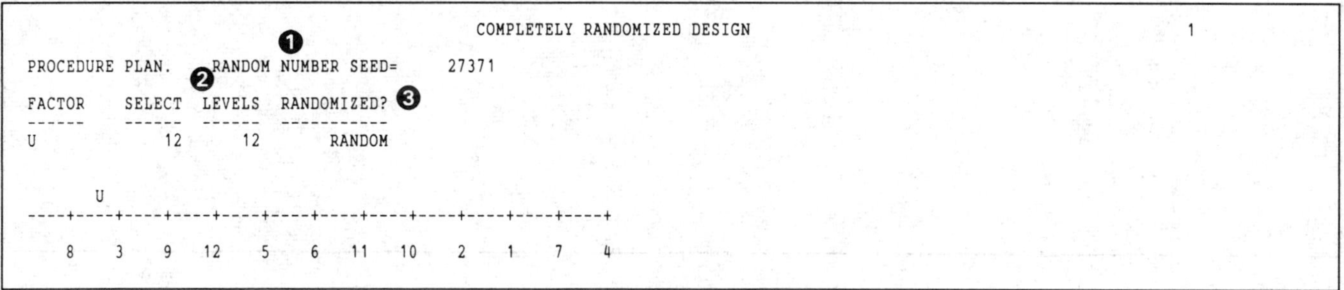

```
                              COMPLETELY RANDOMIZED DESIGN                              1

PROCEDURE PLAN.    RANDOM NUMBER SEED=    27371

FACTOR     SELECT  LEVELS  RANDOMIZED?
------     ------  ------  -----------
U              12      12       RANDOM

      U
----+----+----+----+----+----+----+----+----+----+----+----+

    8    3    9   12    5    6   11   10    2    1    7    4
```

A Split-Plot Design: Example 2

The second plan is appropriate for a split-plot design with main plots forming a randomized complete blocks design. For instance, if there are three blocks, four main plots per block, and two subplots per main plot, then three random permutations (one for each of the blocks) of the integers 1, 2, 3, and 4 are produced. The four integers correspond to the four levels of factor A; the permutation determines how the levels of A are assigned to the main plots within a block. For each of those twelve numbers, a random permutation of the integers 1 and 2 is produced. Each two-integer permutation determines the assignment of the two levels of factor B to the subplots within a main plot. See **Output 27.2**.

```
PROC PLAN SEED=37277;
   TITLE 'SPLIT PLOT DESIGN';
   FACTORS BLOCK=3 ORDERED A=4 B=2;
```

A Hierarchical Design: Example 3

The third plan is appropriate for a hierarchical design. The FACTORS statement requests a random permutation of the numbers 1, 2, and 3; a random permutation of the numbers 1, 2, 3, and 4 for each of those first three numbers; and a random permutation of 1, 2, and 3 for each of the twelve integers in the second set of permutations. See **Output 27.3**.

```
PROC PLAN SEED=17431;
   TITLE 'HIERARCHICAL DESIGN';
   FACTORS HOUSES=3 POTS=4 PLANTS=3;
```

Output 27.2 A Split-Plot Design

```
PROCEDURE PLAN.     RANDOM NUMBER SEED=      37277                                          1

FACTOR     SELECT  LEVELS  RANDOMIZED?
------     ------  ------  -----------
BLOCK           3       3      ORDERED
A               4       4       RANDOM
B               2       2       RANDOM


   BLOCK       A          B
-------- -------- ----+----+

       1        2    1    2

                3    1    2

                1    2    1

                4    1    2

       2        2    2    1

                3    1    2

                4    2    1

                1    1    2

       3        4    1    2

                2    1    2

                3    1    2

                1    1    2
```

Output 27.3 A Hierarchical Design

```
PROCEDURE PLAN.     RANDOM NUMBER SEED=      17431                                          1

FACTOR     SELECT  LEVELS  RANDOMIZED?
------     ------  ------  -----------
HOUSES          3       3       RANDOM
POTS            4       4       RANDOM
PLANTS          3       3       RANDOM


  HOUSES      POTS   PLANTS
-------- -------- ----+----+----+

       2        2    3    1    2

                3    1    2    3

                4    1    3    2

                1    1    3    2

       3        2    1    3    2

                4    1    3    2

                3    1    2    3

                1    2    1    3

       1        2    1    2    3

                3    2    3    1

                1    1    3    2

                4    3    2    1
```

REFERENCES

Cochran, W.G. and Cox, G.M. (1957), *Experimental Designs*, Second Edition, New York: John Wiley & Sons.

Fishman, G.S. and Moore, L.R. (1982), "A Statistical Evaluation of Multiplicative Congruential Generators with Modulus (2^{31}-1)," *Journal of the American Statistical Association*, 77, 129-136.

Chapter 28

The PRINCOMP Procedure

Operating systems: All

ABSTRACT

The PRINCOMP procedure performs principal component analysis. As input you can use raw data, a correlation matrix, or a covariance matrix; either the correlation matrix or the covariance matrix can be analyzed. Output data sets containing eigenvalues, eigenvectors, and standardized or unstandardized principal component scores can be created.

INTRODUCTION

Principal component analysis is a multivariate technique for examining relationships among several quantitative variables. It is used for summarizing data and detecting linear relationships. Plots of principal components are especially valuable tools in exploratory data analysis. Principal components can be used to reduce the number of variables in regression, clustering, and so on.

Background

Principal component analysis was originated by Pearson (1901) and later developed by Hotelling (1933). The application of principal components is discussed by Rao (1964), Cooley and Lohnes (1971), and Gnanadesikan (1977). Excellent statistical treatments of principal components are found in Kshirsagar (1972), Morrison (1976), and Mardia, Kent, and Bibby (1979).

Given a data set with *p* numeric variables, *p* principal components can be computed. Each principal component is a linear combination of the original variables, with coefficients equal to the eigenvectors of the correlation or covariance matrix. The eigenvectors are customarily taken with unit-norm. The principal components are sorted by descending order of the eigenvalues, which are equal to the variances of the components.

Principal components have a variety of useful properties (Rao 1964; Kshirsagar 1972).

- The eigenvectors are orthogonal, so the principal components represent jointly perpendicular directions through the space of the original variables.
- The principal component scores are jointly uncorrelated. Note that this property is quite distinct from the previous one.
- The first principal component has the largest variance of any unit-length linear combination of the observed variables. The *j*th principal component has the largest variance of any unit-length linear combination orthogonal to the first $j-1$ principal components. The last principal component has the smallest variance of any linear combination of the original variables.
- The scores on the first *j* principal components have the highest possible generalized variance of any set of unit-norm linear combinations of the original variables.
- The first *j* principal components give a least-squares solution to the model

  $$\mathbf{Y}=\mathbf{XB}+\mathbf{E}$$

  where **Y** is an *n* by *p* matrix of the centered observed variables; **X** is the *n* by *j* matrix of scores on the first *j* principal components; **B** is the *j* by *p* matrix of eigenvectors; **E** is an *n* by *p* matrix of residuals; and it is desired to minimize trace (**E′E**), the sum of all the squared elements in **E**. In other words, the first *j* principal components are the best linear predictors of the original variables among all possible sets of *j* variables, although any non-singular linear transformation of the first *j* principal components would provide equally good prediction. The same result is obtained if you want to minimize the determinant or the Euclidean (Schur, Frobenious) norm of **E′E** rather than the trace.
- In geometric terms, the *j*-dimensional linear subspace spanned by the first *j* principal components gives the best possible fit to the data points as measured by the sum of squared perpendicular distances from each data point to the subspace.

Principal component analysis can also be used for exploring polynomial relationships and for multivariate outlier detection (Gnanadesikan 1977) and is related to factor analysis, correspondence analysis, allometry, and biased regression techniques (Mardia, Kent, and Bibby 1979).

SPECIFICATIONS

The PRINCOMP procedure is invoked by the following statements:

PROC PRINCOMP *options;*
  VAR *variables;*
  PARTIAL *variables;*
  FREQ *variable;*
  WEIGHT *variable;*
  BY *variables;*

Usually only the VAR statement is used in addition to the PROC PRINCOMP statement.

PROC PRINCOMP Statement

PROC PRINCOMP *options;*

The following options can appear in the PROC statement:

DATA=*SASdataset*
: names the SAS data set to be analyzed. The data set can be an ordinary SAS data set or a TYPE=CORR or TYPE=COV data set. If DATA= is omitted, the most recently created SAS data set is used.

OUT=*SASdataset*
: names an output SAS data set that contains all the original data as well as the principal component scores. If you want to create a permanent SAS data set, you must specify a two-level name (see "SAS Files" in the *SAS User's Guide: Basics* for information on permanent SAS data sets).

OUTSTAT=*SASdataset*
: names an output SAS data set that contains means, standard deviations, number of observations, correlations or covariances, eigenvalues, and eigenvectors. If the COV option is specified, the data set is TYPE=COV and contains covariances; otherwise, it is TYPE=CORR and contains correlations. If you want to create a permanent SAS data set, you must specify a two-level name (see "SAS Files" in the *SAS User's Guide: Basics* for information on permanent SAS data sets).

NOINT
: requests that the covariance or correlation matrix not be corrected for the mean, that is, that no intercept be used in the model.

COVARIANCE
COV
: requests that the principal components be computed from the covariance matrix. If COV is not specified, the correlation matrix is analyzed.

N=*n*
: specifies the number of principal components to be computed.

STANDARD
STD
: requests that the principal component scores in the OUT= data set be standardized to unit variance. If STANDARD is not specified, the scores have variance equal to the corresponding eigenvalue.

PREFIX=*name*

specifies a prefix for naming the principal components. By default the names are PRIN1, PRIN2,...,PRIN*n*. If PREFIX=ABC is specified, the components are named ABC1, ABC2, ABC3, and so on. The number of characters in the prefix plus the number of digits required to designate the components should not exceed eight.

NOPRINT

suppresses the printout.

VAR Statement

VAR *variables;*

The VAR statement lists the numeric variables to be analyzed. If the VAR statement is omitted, all numeric variables not specified in other statements are analyzed.

PARTIAL Statement

PARTIAL *variables;*

If you want to analyze a partial correlation or covariance matrix, specify the names of the numeric variables to be partialled out in the PARTIAL statement.

FREQ Statement

FREQ *variable;*

If a variable in your data set represents the frequency of occurrence for the other values in the observation, include the variable's name in a FREQ statement. The procedure then treats the data set as if each observation appears *n* times, where *n* is the value of the FREQ variable for the observation. The total number of observations is considered equal to the sum of the FREQ variable when the procedure determines degrees of freedom for significance probabilities.

The WEIGHT and FREQ statements have a similar effect except in the calculation of degrees of freedom.

WEIGHT Statement

WEIGHT *variable;*

If you want to use relative weights for each observation in the input data set, place the weights in a variable in the data set and specify the name in a WEIGHT statement. This is often done when the variance associated with each observation is different and the values of the weight variable are proportional to the reciprocals of the variances.

BY Statement

BY *variables;*

You can use a BY statement with PROC PRINCOMP to obtain separate analyses on observations in groups defined by the BY variables. When a BY statement appears, the procedure expects the input data set to be sorted in order of the BY variables. If your input data set is not sorted in ascending order, use the SORT procedure with a similar BY statement to sort the data, or, if appropriate, use the BY statement options NOTSORTED or DESCENDING. For more information, see the discussion of the BY statement in "Statements Used in the PROC Step" in the *SAS User's Guide: Basics.*

DETAILS

Missing Values

Observations with missing values are omitted from the analysis and are given missing values for principal component scores in the OUT= data set.

Output Data Sets

OUT= data set The OUT= data set contains all the variables in the original data set plus new variables containing the principal component scores. The N= option determines the number of new variables. The names of the new variables are formed by concatenating the value given by the PREFIX= option (or PRIN if PREFIX= is omitted) and the numbers 1, 2, 3, and so on. The new variables have mean 0 and variance equal to the corresponding eigenvalue, unless the STANDARD option is specified to standardize the scores to unit variance.

An OUT= data set cannot be created if the DATA= data set is TYPE=CORR or TYPE=COV or if a PARTIAL statement is used.

OUTSTAT= data set The OUTSTAT= data set is similar to the TYPE=CORR data set produced by the CORR procedure. The OUTSTAT= data set is TYPE=CORR unless the COV option is specified, in which case it is TYPE=COV.

The new data set contains the following variables:

- the BY variables, if any
- two new character variables, _TYPE_ and _NAME_
- the variables analyzed, that is, those in the VAR statement, or, if there is no VAR statement, all numeric variables not listed in any other statement.

Each observation in the new data set contains some type of statistic as indicated by the _TYPE_ variable. The values of the _TYPE_ variable are as follows:

TYPE	**Contents**
MEAN	mean of each variable.
STD	standard deviations. This observation is omitted if the COV option is specified so the SCORE procedure does not standardize the variables before computing scores.
N	number of observations on which the analysis is based. This value is the same for each variable.
CORR	correlations between each variable and the variable named by the _NAME_ variable. The number of observations with _TYPE_='CORR' is equal to the number of variables being analyzed. If the COV option is specified, no _TYPE_='CORR' observations are produced.
COV	covariances between each variable and the variable named by the _NAME_ variable. _TYPE_='COV' observations are produced only if the COV option is specified.
EIGENVAL	eigenvalues. If the N= option requested fewer than the maximum number of principal components, only the specified number of eigenvalues are produced, with missing values filling out the observation.
SCORE	eigenvectors. The _NAME_ variable contains the name of the corresponding principal component as

constructed from the PREFIX= option. The number of observations with _TYPE_='SCORE' equals the number of principal components computed.

The data set can be used with the SCORE procedure to compute principal component scores, or it can be used as input to the FACTOR procedure specifying METHOD=SCORE to rotate the components.

Computational Resources

Let:

n = number of observations

v = number of variables

c = number of components.

The time required to compute the correlation matrix is roughly proportional to nv^2.

The time required to compute eigenvalues is roughly proportional to v^3.

The time required to compute eigenvectors is roughly proportional to cv^2.

Printed Output

The PRINCOMP procedure prints

1. SIMPLE STATISTICS, including the MEAN and ST DEV (standard deviation) for each variable, if the DATA= data set is neither TYPE=CORR nor TYPE=COV
2. the CORRELATIONS or COVARIANCES among the variables if the DATA= data set is neither TYPE=CORR nor TYPE=COV
3. the TOTAL VARIANCE if the COV option is used
4. EIGENVALUES of the correlation or covariance matrix, as well as the DIFFERENCE between successive eigenvalues, the PROPORTION of variance explained by each eigenvalue, and the CUMULATIVE proportion of variance explained
5. the EIGENVECTORS.

EXAMPLES

January and July Temperatures: Example 1

The first example analyzes mean daily temperatures in selected cities in January and July. Both the raw data and the principal components are plotted to illustrate how principal components are orthogonal rotations of the original variables.

Note that since the COV option is used and JANUARY has a higher standard deviation than JULY, JANUARY receives a higher loading on the first component.

```
DATA TEMPERAT;
   TITLE 'MEAN TEMPERATURE IN JANUARY AND JULY FOR SELECTED CITIES';
   INPUT CITY $1-15 JANUARY JULY;
   CARDS;
MOBILE          51.2 81.6
PHOENIX         51.2 91.2
LITTLE ROCK     39.5 81.4
SACRAMENTO      45.1 75.2
DENVER          29.9 73.0
HARTFORD        24.8 72.7
```

```
WILMINGTON      32.0 75.8
WASHINGTON DC   35.6 78.7
JACKSONVILLE    54.6 81.0
MIAMI           67.2 82.3
ATLANTA         42.4 78.0
BOISE           29.0 74.5
CHICAGO         22.9 71.9
PEORIA          23.8 75.1
INDIANAPOLIS    27.9 75.0
DES MOINES      19.4 75.1
WICHITA         31.3 80.7
LOUISVILLE      33.3 76.9
NEW ORLEANS     52.9 81.9
PORTLAND, MAINE 21.5 68.0
BALTIMORE       33.4 76.6
BOSTON          29.2 73.3
DETROIT         25.5 73.3
SAULT STE MARIE 14.2 63.8
DULUTH           8.5 65.6
MINNEAPOLIS     12.2 71.9
JACKSON         47.1 81.7
KANSAS CITY     27.8 78.8
ST LOUIS        31.3 78.6
GREAT FALLS     20.5 69.3
OMAHA           22.6 77.2
RENO            31.9 69.3
CONCORD         20.6 69.7
ATLANTIC CITY   32.7 75.1
ALBUQUERQUE     35.2 78.7
ALBANY          21.5 72.0
BUFFALO         23.7 70.1
NEW YORK        32.2 76.6
CHARLOTTE       42.1 78.5
RALEIGH         40.5 77.5
BISMARCK         8.2 70.8
CINCINNATI      31.1 75.6
CLEVELAND       26.9 71.4
COLUMBUS        28.4 73.6
OKLAHOMA CITY   36.8 81.5
PORTLAND, OREG  38.1 67.1
PHILADELPHIA    32.3 76.8
PITTSBURGH      28.1 71.9
PROVIDENCE      28.4 72.1
COLUMBIA        45.4 81.2
SIOUX FALLS     14.2 73.3
MEMPHIS         40.5 79.6
NASHVILLE       38.3 79.6
DALLAS          44.8 84.8
EL PASO         43.6 82.3
HOUSTON         52.1 83.3
SALT LAKE CITY  28.0 76.7
BURLINGTON      16.8 69.8
NORFOLK         40.5 78.3
RICHMOND        37.5 77.9
SPOKANE         25.4 69.7
CHARLESTON, WV  34.5 75.0
MILWAUKEE       19.4 69.9
CHEYENNE        26.6 69.1
;
PROC PLOT;
```

```
   PLOT JULY*JANUARY=CITY/VPOS=36;
PROC PRINCOMP COV OUT=PRIN;
   VAR JULY JANUARY;
PROC PLOT;
   PLOT PRIN2*PRIN1=CITY/VPOS=26;
   TITLE2 'PLOT OF PRINCIPAL COMPONENTS';
```

Output 28.1 Plot of Raw Data: PROC PLOT

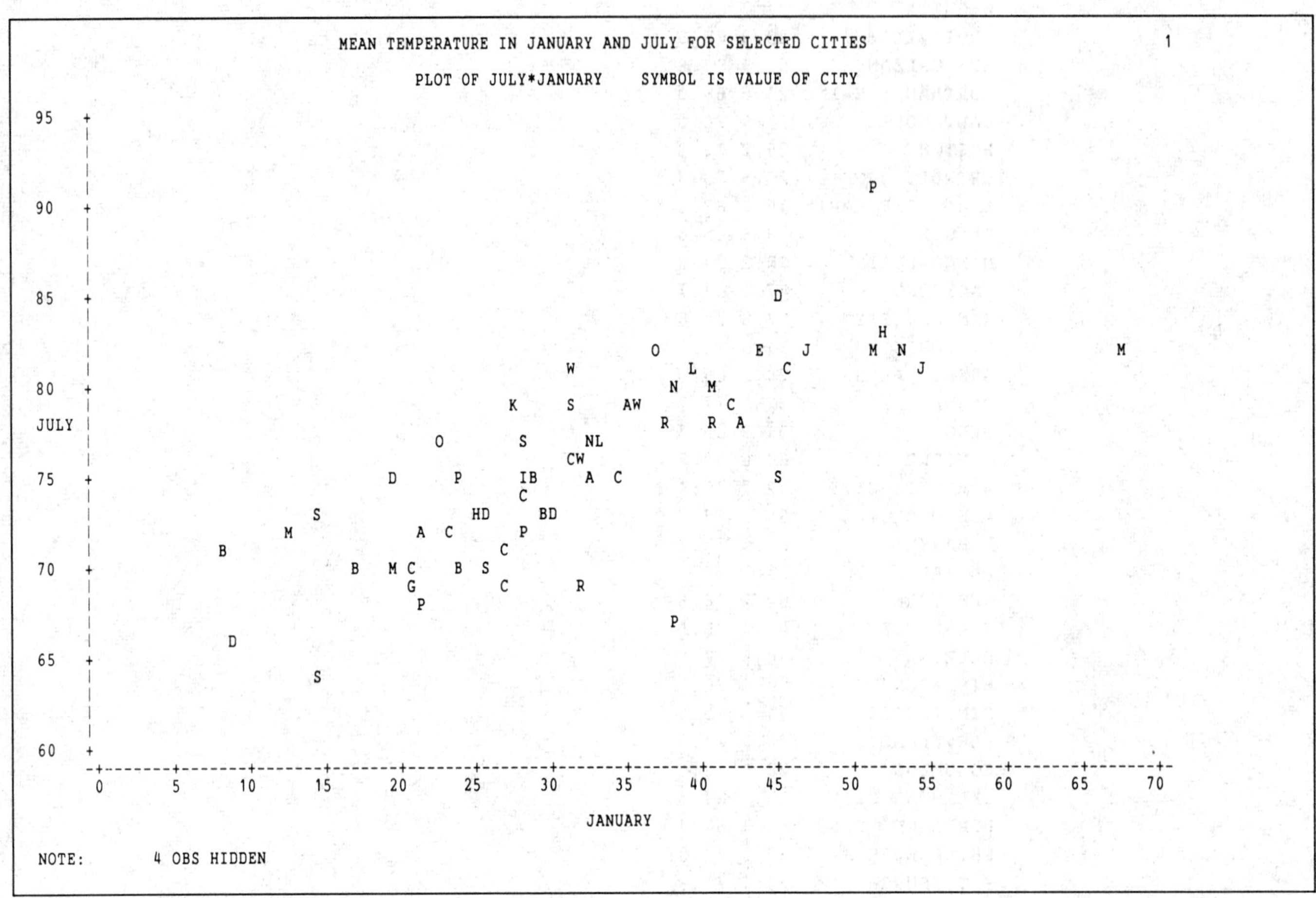

Output 28.2 Results of Principal Component Analysis: PROC PRINCOMP

```
                    MEAN TEMPERATURE IN JANUARY AND JULY FOR SELECTED CITIES                    2

                                  PRINCIPAL COMPONENT ANALYSIS

64 OBSERVATIONS
 2 VARIABLES


                                       ❶
                                       SIMPLE STATISTICS

                                               JULY         JANUARY

                               MEAN         75.6078         32.0953
                               ST DEV        5.1276         11.7124

                                          ❷
                                          COVARIANCES

                                               JULY              JANUARY

                          JULY              26.29248            46.82829
                          JANUARY           46.82829            137.1811
                             ❸        TOTAL VARIANCE=163.4736


                        ❹
                        EIGENVALUE       DIFFERENCE       PROPORTION        CUMULATIVE

            PRIN1         154.311          145.148          0.943948           0.94395
            PRIN2           9.163                .          0.056052           1.00000

                                          ❺
                                          EIGENVECTORS

                                              PRIN1          PRIN2

                               JULY        0.343532       0.939141
                               JANUARY     0.939141       -.343532
```

Output 28.3 Plot of Principal Components: PROC PLOT

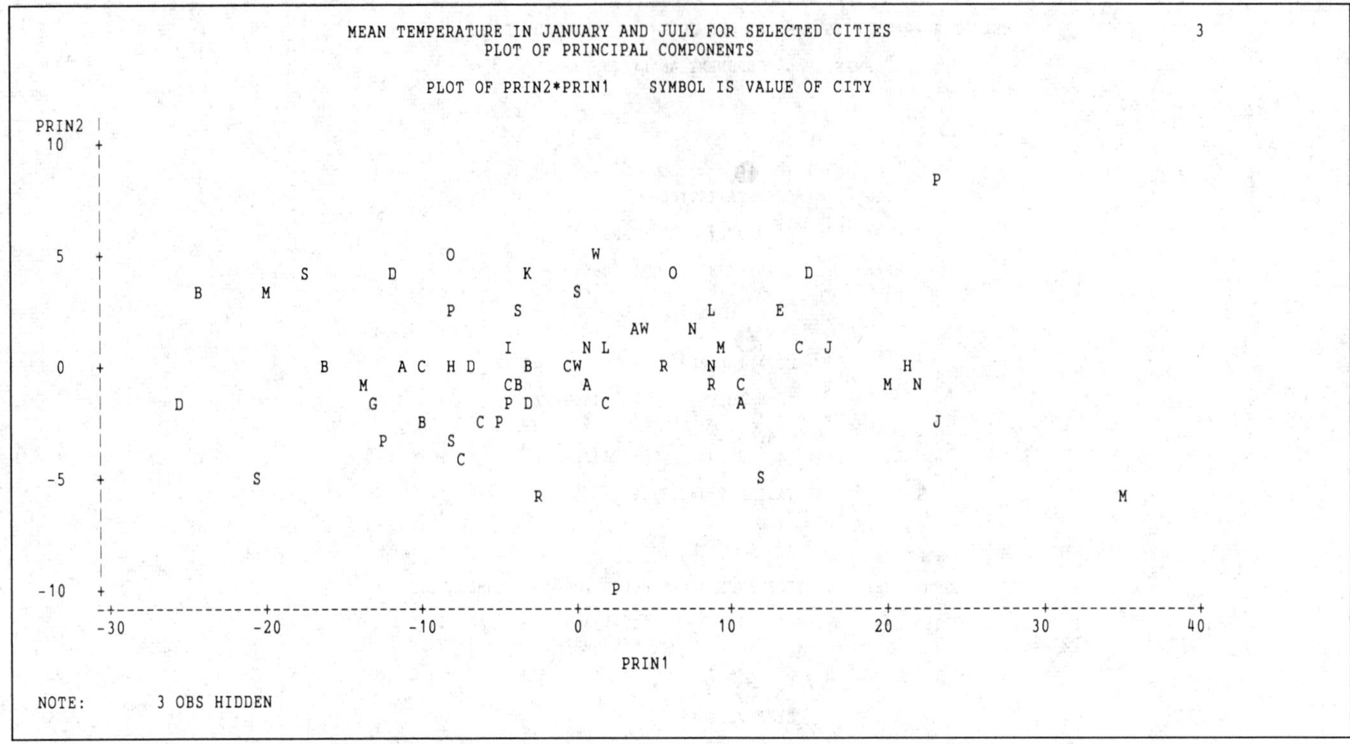

Crime Rates: Example 2

The data below give crime rates per 100,000 people in seven categories for each of the fifty states. Since there are seven variables, it is impossible to plot all the variables simultaneously. Principal components can be used to summarize the data in two or three dimensions and help to visualize the data.

```
DATA CRIME;
   TITLE 'CRIME RATES PER 100,000 POPULATION BY STATE';
   INPUT STATE $1-15 MURDER RAPE ROBBERY ASSAULT BURGLARY LARCENY AUTO;
   CARDS;
ALABAMA         14.2 25.2  96.8 278.3 1135.5 1881.9 280.7
ALASKA          10.8 51.6  96.8 284.0 1331.7 3369.8 753.3
ARIZONA          9.5 34.2 138.2 312.3 2346.1 4467.4 439.5
ARKANSAS         8.8 27.6  83.2 203.4  972.6 1862.1 183.4
CALIFORNIA      11.5 49.4 287.0 358.0 2139.4 3499.8 663.5
COLORADO         6.3 42.0 170.7 292.9 1935.2 3903.2 477.1
CONNECTICUT      4.2 16.8 129.5 131.8 1346.0 2620.7 593.2
DELAWARE         6.0 24.9 157.0 194.2 1682.6 3678.4 467.0
FLORIDA         10.2 39.6 187.9 449.1 1859.9 3840.5 351.4
GEORGIA         11.7 31.1 140.5 256.5 1351.1 2170.2 297.9
HAWAII           7.2 25.5 128.0  64.1 1911.5 3920.4 489.4
IDAHO            5.5 19.4  39.6 172.5 1050.8 2599.6 237.6
ILLINOIS         9.9 21.8 211.3 209.0 1085.0 2828.5 528.6
INDIANA          7.4 26.5 123.2 153.5 1086.2 2498.7 377.4
IOWA             2.3 10.6  41.2  89.8  812.5 2685.1 219.9
KANSAS           6.6 22.0 100.7 180.5 1270.4 2739.3 244.3
KENTUCKY        10.1 19.1  81.1 123.3  872.2 1662.1 245.4
LOUISIANA       15.5 30.9 142.9 335.5 1165.5 2469.9 337.7
```

```
MAINE           2.4 13.5  38.7 170.0 1253.1 2350.7 246.9
MARYLAND        8.0 34.8 292.1 358.9 1400.0 3177.7 428.5
MASSACHUSETTS   3.1 20.8 169.1 231.6 1532.2 2311.3 1140.1
MICHIGAN        9.3 38.9 261.9 274.6 1522.7 3159.0 545.5
MINNESOTA       2.7 19.5  85.9  85.8 1134.7 2559.3 343.1
MISSISSIPPI    14.3 19.6  65.7 189.1  915.6 1239.9 144.4
MISSOURI        9.6 28.3 189.0 233.5 1318.3 2424.2 378.4
MONTANA         5.4 16.7  39.2 156.8  804.9 2773.2 309.2
NEBRASKA        3.9 18.1  64.7 112.7  760.0 2316.1 249.1
NEVADA         15.8 49.1 323.1 355.0 2453.1 4212.6 559.2
NEW HAMPSHIRE   3.2 10.7  23.2  76.0 1041.7 2343.9 293.4
NEW JERSEY      5.6 21.0 180.4 185.1 1435.8 2774.5 511.5
NEW MEXICO      8.8 39.1 109.6 343.4 1418.7 3008.6 259.5
NEW YORK       10.7 29.4 472.6 319.1 1728.0 2782.0 745.8
NORTH CAROLINA 10.6 17.0  61.3 318.3 1154.1 2037.8 192.1
NORTH DAKOTA    0.9  9.0  13.3  43.8  446.1 1843.0 144.7
OHIO            7.8 27.3 190.5 181.1 1216.0 2696.8 400.4
OKLAHOMA        8.6 29.2  73.8 205.0 1288.2 2228.1 326.8
OREGON          4.9 39.9 124.1 286.9 1636.4 3506.1 388.9
PENNSYLVANIA    5.6 19.0 130.3 128.0  877.5 1624.1 333.2
RHODE ISLAND    3.6 10.5  86.5 201.0 1489.5 2844.1 791.4
SOUTH CAROLINA 11.9 33.0 105.9 485.3 1613.6 2342.4 245.1
SOUTH DAKOTA    2.0 13.5  17.9 155.7  570.5 1704.4 147.5
TENNESSEE      10.1 29.7 145.8 203.9 1259.7 1776.5 314.0
TEXAS          13.3 33.8 152.4 208.2 1603.1 2988.7 397.6
UTAH            3.5 20.3  68.8 147.3 1171.6 3004.6 334.5
VERMONT         1.4 15.9  30.8 101.2 1348.2 2201.0 265.2
VIRGINIA        9.0 23.3  92.1 165.7  986.2 2521.2 226.7
WASHINGTON      4.3 39.6 106.2 224.8 1605.6 3386.9 360.3
WEST VIRGINIA   6.0 13.2  42.2  90.9  597.4 1341.7 163.3
WISCONSIN       2.8 12.9  52.2  63.7  846.9 2614.2 220.7
WYOMING         5.4 21.9  39.7 173.9  811.6 2772.2 282.0
;
PROC PRINCOMP OUT=CRIMCOMP;
```

Output 28.4 Results of Principal Component Analysis: PROC PRINCOMP

CRIME RATES PER 100,000 POPULATION BY STATE 1

PRINCIPAL COMPONENT ANALYSIS

50 OBSERVATIONS
7 VARIABLES

SIMPLE STATISTICS

	MURDER	RAPE	ROBBERY	ASSAULT	BURGLARY	LARCENY	AUTO
MEAN	7.44400	25.7340	124.092	211.300	1291.90	2671.29	377.526
ST DEV	3.86677	10.7596	88.349	100.253	432.46	725.91	193.394

CORRELATIONS

	MURDER	RAPE	ROBBERY	ASSAULT	BURGLARY	LARCENY	AUTO
MURDER	1.0000	0.6012	0.4837	0.6486	0.3858	0.1019	0.0688
RAPE	0.6012	1.0000	0.5919	0.7403	0.7121	0.6140	0.3489
ROBBERY	0.4837	0.5919	1.0000	0.5571	0.6372	0.4467	0.5907
ASSAULT	0.6486	0.7403	0.5571	1.0000	0.6229	0.4044	0.2758
BURGLARY	0.3858	0.7121	0.6372	0.6229	1.0000	0.7921	0.5580
LARCENY	0.1019	0.6140	0.4467	0.4044	0.7921	1.0000	0.4442
AUTO	0.0688	0.3489	0.5907	0.2758	0.5580	0.4442	1.0000

	EIGENVALUE	DIFFERENCE	PROPORTION	CUMULATIVE
PRIN1	4.11496	2.87624	0.587851	0.58785
PRIN2	1.23872	0.51291	0.176960	0.76481
PRIN3	0.72582	0.40938	0.103688	0.86850
PRIN4	0.31643	0.05846	0.045205	0.91370
PRIN5	0.25797	0.03593	0.036853	0.95056
PRIN6	0.22204	0.09798	0.031720	0.98228
PRIN7	0.12406	.	0.017722	1.00000

EIGENVECTORS

	PRIN1	PRIN2	PRIN3	PRIN4	PRIN5	PRIN6	PRIN7
MURDER	0.300279	-.629174	0.178245	-.232114	0.538123	0.259117	0.267593
RAPE	0.431759	-.169435	-.244198	0.062216	0.188471	-.773271	-.296485
ROBBERY	0.396875	0.042247	0.495861	-.557989	-.519977	-.114385	-.003903
ASSAULT	0.396652	-.343528	-.069510	0.629804	-.506651	0.172363	0.191745
BURGLARY	0.440157	0.203341	-.209895	-.057555	0.101033	0.535987	-.648117
LARCENY	0.357360	0.402319	-.539231	-.234890	0.030099	0.039406	0.601690
AUTO	0.295177	0.502421	0.568384	0.419238	0.369753	-.057298	0.147046

The eigenvalues indicate that two or three components provide a good summary of the data, two components accounting for 76% of the standardized variance and three components explaining 87%. Subsequent components contribute less than 5% each.

The first component is a measure of overall crime rate. The first eigenvector shows approximately equal loadings on all variables. The second eigenvector has high positive loadings on AUTO and LARCENY, and high negative loadings on MURDER and ASSAULT. There is also a small positive loading on BURGLARY and a small negative loading on RAPE. This component seems to measure the preponderance of property crime over violent crime. The interpretation of the third component is not obvious.

A simple way to examine the principal components in more detail is to print the output data set sorted by each of the large components.

```
PROC SORT;
   BY PRIN1;
```

```
PROC PRINT;
   ID STATE;
   VAR PRIN1 PRIN2 MURDER RAPE ROBBERY ASSAULT BURGLARY LARCENY AUTO;
   TITLE2 'STATES LISTED IN ORDER OF OVERALL CRIME RATE';
   TITLE3 'AS DETERMINED BY THE FIRST PRINCIPAL COMPONENT';
PROC SORT;
   BY PRIN2;
PROC PRINT;
   ID STATE;
   VAR PRIN1 PRIN2 MURDER RAPE ROBBERY ASSAULT BURGLARY LARCENY AUTO;
   TITLE2 'STATES LISTED IN ORDER OF PROPERTY VS. VIOLENT CRIME';
   TITLE3 'AS DETERMINED BY THE SECOND PRINCIPAL COMPONENT';
```

Output 28.5 The OUT= Data Set Sorted by Principal Components: PROC PRINT

CRIME RATES PER 100,000 POPULATION BY STATE
STATES LISTED IN ORDER OF OVERALL CRIME RATE
AS DETERMINED BY THE FIRST PRINCIPAL COMPONENT

2

STATE	PRIN1	PRIN2	MURDER	RAPE	ROBBERY	ASSAULT	BURGLARY	LARCENY	AUTO
NORTH DAKOTA	-3.9641	0.3877	0.9	9.0	13.3	43.8	446.1	1843.0	144.7
SOUTH DAKOTA	-3.1720	-0.2545	2.0	13.5	17.9	155.7	570.5	1704.4	147.5
WEST VIRGINIA	-3.1477	-0.8143	6.0	13.2	42.2	90.9	597.4	1341.7	163.3
IOWA	-2.5816	0.8248	2.3	10.6	41.2	89.8	812.5	2685.1	219.9
WISCONSIN	-2.5030	0.7808	2.8	12.9	52.2	63.7	846.9	2614.2	220.7
NEW HAMPSHIRE	-2.4656	0.8250	3.2	10.7	23.2	76.0	1041.7	2343.9	293.4
NEBRASKA	-2.1507	0.2257	3.9	18.1	64.7	112.7	760.0	2316.1	249.1
VERMONT	-2.0643	0.9450	1.4	15.9	30.8	101.2	1348.2	2201.0	265.2
MAINE	-1.8263	0.5788	2.4	13.5	38.7	170.0	1253.1	2350.7	246.9
KENTUCKY	-1.7269	-1.1466	10.1	19.1	81.1	123.3	872.2	1662.1	245.4
PENNSYLVANIA	-1.7201	-0.1959	5.6	19.0	130.3	128.0	877.5	1624.1	333.2
MONTANA	-1.6680	0.2710	5.4	16.7	39.2	156.8	804.9	2773.2	309.2
MINNESOTA	-1.5543	1.0564	2.7	19.5	85.9	85.8	1134.7	2559.3	343.1
MISSISSIPPI	-1.5074	-2.5467	14.3	19.6	65.7	189.1	915.6	1239.9	144.4
IDAHO	-1.4325	-0.0080	5.5	19.4	39.6	172.5	1050.8	2599.6	237.6
WYOMING	-1.4246	0.0627	5.4	21.9	39.7	173.9	811.6	2772.2	282.0
ARKANSAS	-1.0544	-1.3454	8.8	27.6	83.2	203.4	972.6	1862.1	183.4
UTAH	-1.0500	0.9366	3.5	20.3	68.8	147.3	1171.6	3004.6	334.5
VIRGINIA	-0.9162	-0.6927	9.0	23.3	92.1	165.7	986.2	2521.2	226.7
NORTH CAROLINA	-0.6993	-1.6703	10.6	17.0	61.3	318.3	1154.1	2037.8	192.1
KANSAS	-0.6341	-0.0280	6.6	22.0	100.7	180.5	1270.4	2739.3	244.3
CONNECTICUT	-0.5413	1.5012	4.2	16.8	129.5	131.8	1346.0	2620.7	593.2
INDIANA	-0.4999	0.0000	7.4	26.5	123.2	153.5	1086.2	2498.7	377.4
OKLAHOMA	-0.3214	-0.6243	8.6	29.2	73.8	205.0	1288.2	2228.1	326.8
RHODE ISLAND	-0.2016	2.1466	3.6	10.5	86.5	201.0	1489.5	2844.1	791.4
TENNESSEE	-0.1366	-1.1350	10.1	29.7	145.8	203.9	1259.7	1776.5	314.0
ALABAMA	-0.0499	-2.0961	14.2	25.2	96.8	278.3	1135.5	1881.9	280.7
NEW JERSEY	0.2179	0.9642	5.6	21.0	180.4	185.1	1435.8	2774.5	511.5
OHIO	0.2395	0.0905	7.8	27.3	190.5	181.1	1216.0	2696.8	400.4
GEORGIA	0.4904	-1.3808	11.7	31.1	140.5	256.5	1351.1	2170.2	297.9
ILLINOIS	0.5129	0.0942	9.9	21.8	211.3	209.0	1085.0	2828.5	528.6
MISSOURI	0.5564	-0.5585	9.6	28.3	189.0	233.5	1318.3	2424.2	378.4
HAWAII	0.8231	1.8239	7.2	25.5	128.0	64.1	1911.5	3920.4	489.4
WASHINGTON	0.9306	0.7378	4.3	39.6	106.2	224.8	1605.6	3386.9	360.3
DELAWARE	0.9646	1.2967	6.0	24.9	157.0	194.2	1682.6	3678.4	467.0
MASSACHUSETTS	0.9784	2.6311	3.1	20.8	169.1	231.6	1532.2	2311.3	1140.1
LOUISIANA	1.1202	-2.0833	15.5	30.9	142.9	335.5	1165.5	2469.9	337.7
NEW MEXICO	1.2142	-0.9508	8.8	39.1	109.6	343.4	1418.7	3008.6	259.5
TEXAS	1.3970	-0.6813	13.3	33.8	152.4	208.2	1603.1	2988.7	397.6
OREGON	1.4490	0.5860	4.9	39.9	124.1	286.9	1636.4	3506.1	388.9
SOUTH CAROLINA	1.6034	-2.1621	11.9	33.0	105.9	485.3	1613.6	2342.4	245.1
MARYLAND	2.1828	-0.1947	8.0	34.8	292.1	358.9	1400.0	3177.7	428.5
MICHIGAN	2.2733	0.1549	9.3	38.9	261.9	274.6	1522.7	3159.0	545.5
ALASKA	2.4215	0.1665	10.8	51.6	96.8	284.0	1331.7	3369.8	753.3
COLORADO	2.5093	0.9166	6.3	42.0	170.7	292.9	1935.2	3903.2	477.1
ARIZONA	3.0141	0.8449	9.5	34.2	138.2	312.3	2346.1	4467.4	439.5
FLORIDA	3.1118	-0.6039	10.2	39.6	187.9	449.1	1859.9	3840.5	351.4
NEW YORK	3.4525	0.4329	10.7	29.4	472.6	319.1	1728.0	2782.0	745.8
CALIFORNIA	4.2838	0.1432	11.5	49.4	287.0	358.0	2139.4	3499.8	663.5
NEVADA	5.2670	-0.2526	15.8	49.1	323.1	355.0	2453.1	4212.6	559.2

CRIME RATES PER 100,000 POPULATION BY STATE 3
STATES LISTED IN ORDER OF PROPERTY VS. VIOLENT CRIME
AS DETERMINED BY THE SECOND PRINCIPAL COMPONENT

STATE	PRIN1	PRIN2	MURDER	RAPE	ROBBERY	ASSAULT	BURGLARY	LARCENY	AUTO
MISSISSIPPI	-1.5074	-2.5467	14.3	19.6	65.7	189.1	915.6	1239.9	144.4
SOUTH CAROLINA	1.6034	-2.1621	11.9	33.0	105.9	485.3	1613.6	2342.4	245.1
ALABAMA	-0.0499	-2.0961	14.2	25.2	96.8	278.3	1135.5	1881.9	280.7
LOUISIANA	1.1202	-2.0833	15.5	30.9	142.9	335.5	1165.5	2469.9	337.7
NORTH CAROLINA	-0.6993	-1.6703	10.6	17.0	61.3	318.3	1154.1	2037.8	192.1
GEORGIA	0.4904	-1.3808	11.7	31.1	140.5	256.5	1351.1	2170.2	297.9
ARKANSAS	-1.0544	-1.3454	8.8	27.6	83.2	203.4	972.6	1862.1	183.4
KENTUCKY	-1.7269	-1.1466	10.1	19.1	81.1	123.3	872.2	1662.1	245.4
TENNESSEE	-0.1366	-1.1350	10.1	29.7	145.8	203.9	1259.7	1776.5	314.0
NEW MEXICO	1.2142	-0.9508	8.8	39.1	109.6	343.4	1418.7	3008.6	259.5
WEST VIRGINIA	-3.1477	-0.8143	6.0	13.2	42.2	90.9	597.4	1341.7	163.3
VIRGINIA	-0.9162	-0.6927	9.0	23.3	92.1	165.7	986.2	2521.2	226.7
TEXAS	1.3970	-0.6813	13.3	33.8	152.4	208.2	1603.1	2988.7	397.6
OKLAHOMA	-0.3214	-0.6243	8.6	29.2	73.8	205.0	1288.2	2228.1	326.8
FLORIDA	3.1118	-0.6039	10.2	39.6	187.9	449.1	1859.9	3840.5	351.4
MISSOURI	0.5564	-0.5585	9.6	28.3	189.0	233.5	1318.3	2424.2	378.4
SOUTH DAKOTA	-3.1720	-0.2545	2.0	13.5	17.9	155.7	570.5	1704.4	147.5
NEVADA	5.2670	-0.2526	15.8	49.1	323.1	355.0	2453.1	4212.6	559.2
PENNSYLVANIA	-1.7201	-0.1959	5.6	19.0	130.3	128.0	877.5	1624.1	333.2
MARYLAND	2.1828	-0.1947	8.0	34.8	292.1	358.9	1400.0	3177.7	428.5
KANSAS	-0.6341	-0.0280	6.6	22.0	100.7	180.5	1270.4	2739.3	244.3
IDAHO	-1.4325	-0.0080	5.5	19.4	39.6	172.5	1050.8	2599.6	237.6
INDIANA	-0.4999	0.0000	7.4	26.5	123.2	153.5	1086.2	2498.7	377.4
WYOMING	-1.4246	0.0627	5.4	21.9	39.7	173.9	811.6	2772.2	282.0
OHIO	0.2395	0.0905	7.8	27.3	190.5	181.1	1216.0	2696.8	400.4
ILLINOIS	0.5129	0.0942	9.9	21.8	211.3	209.0	1085.0	2828.5	528.6
CALIFORNIA	4.2838	0.1432	11.5	49.4	287.0	358.0	2139.4	3499.8	663.5
MICHIGAN	2.2733	0.1549	9.3	38.9	261.9	274.6	1522.7	3159.0	545.5
ALASKA	2.4215	0.1665	10.8	51.6	96.8	284.0	1331.7	3369.8	753.3
NEBRASKA	-2.1507	0.2257	3.9	18.1	64.7	112.7	760.0	2316.1	249.1
MONTANA	-1.6680	0.2710	5.4	16.7	39.2	156.8	804.9	2773.2	309.2
NORTH DAKOTA	-3.9641	0.3877	0.9	9.0	13.3	43.8	446.1	1843.0	144.7
NEW YORK	3.4525	0.4329	10.7	29.4	472.6	319.1	1728.0	2782.0	745.8
MAINE	-1.8263	0.5788	2.4	13.5	38.7	170.0	1253.1	2350.7	246.9
OREGON	1.4490	0.5860	4.9	39.9	124.1	286.9	1636.4	3506.1	388.9
WASHINGTON	0.9306	0.7378	4.3	39.6	106.2	224.8	1605.6	3386.9	360.3
WISCONSIN	-2.5030	0.7808	2.8	12.9	52.2	63.7	846.9	2614.2	220.7
IOWA	-2.5816	0.8248	2.3	10.6	41.2	89.8	812.5	2685.1	219.9
NEW HAMPSHIRE	-2.4656	0.8250	3.2	10.7	23.2	76.0	1041.7	2343.9	293.4
ARIZONA	3.0141	0.8449	9.5	34.2	138.2	312.3	2346.1	4467.4	439.5
COLORADO	2.5093	0.9166	6.3	42.0	170.7	292.9	1935.2	3903.2	477.1
UTAH	-1.0500	0.9366	3.5	20.3	68.8	147.3	1171.6	3004.6	334.5
VERMONT	-2.0643	0.9450	1.4	15.9	30.8	101.2	1348.2	2201.0	265.2
NEW JERSEY	0.2179	0.9642	5.6	21.0	180.4	185.1	1435.8	2774.5	511.5
MINNESOTA	-1.5543	1.0564	2.7	19.5	85.9	85.8	1134.7	2559.3	343.1
DELAWARE	0.9646	1.2967	6.0	24.9	157.0	194.2	1682.6	3678.4	467.0
CONNECTICUT	-0.5413	1.5012	4.2	16.8	129.5	131.8	1346.0	2620.7	593.2
HAWAII	0.8231	1.8239	7.2	25.5	128.0	64.1	1911.5	3920.4	489.4
RHODE ISLAND	-0.2016	2.1466	3.6	10.5	86.5	201.0	1489.5	2844.1	791.4
MASSACHUSETTS	0.9784	2.6311	3.1	20.8	169.1	231.6	1532.2	2311.3	1140.1

Another recommended procedure is to make scatter plots of the first few components. The sorted listings help to identify observations on the plots.

```
PROC PLOT;
   PLOT PRIN2*PRIN1=STATE;
   TITLE2 'PLOT OF THE FIRST TWO PRINCIPAL COMPONENTS';
PROC PLOT;
   PLOT PRIN3*PRIN1=STATE;
   TITLE2 'PLOT OF THE FIRST AND THIRD PRINCIPAL COMPONENTS';
```

Output 28.6 Plots of Principal Components: PROC PLOT

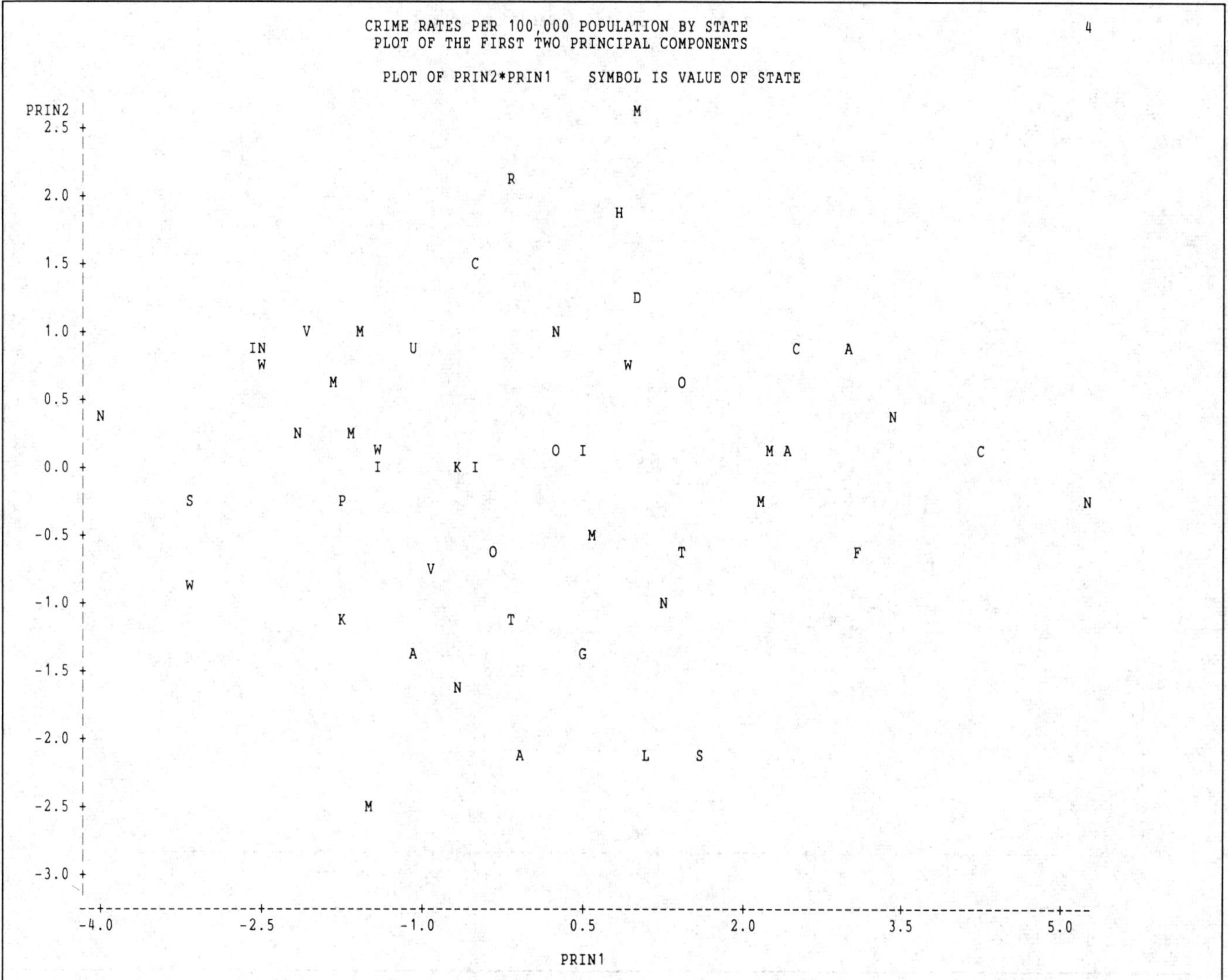

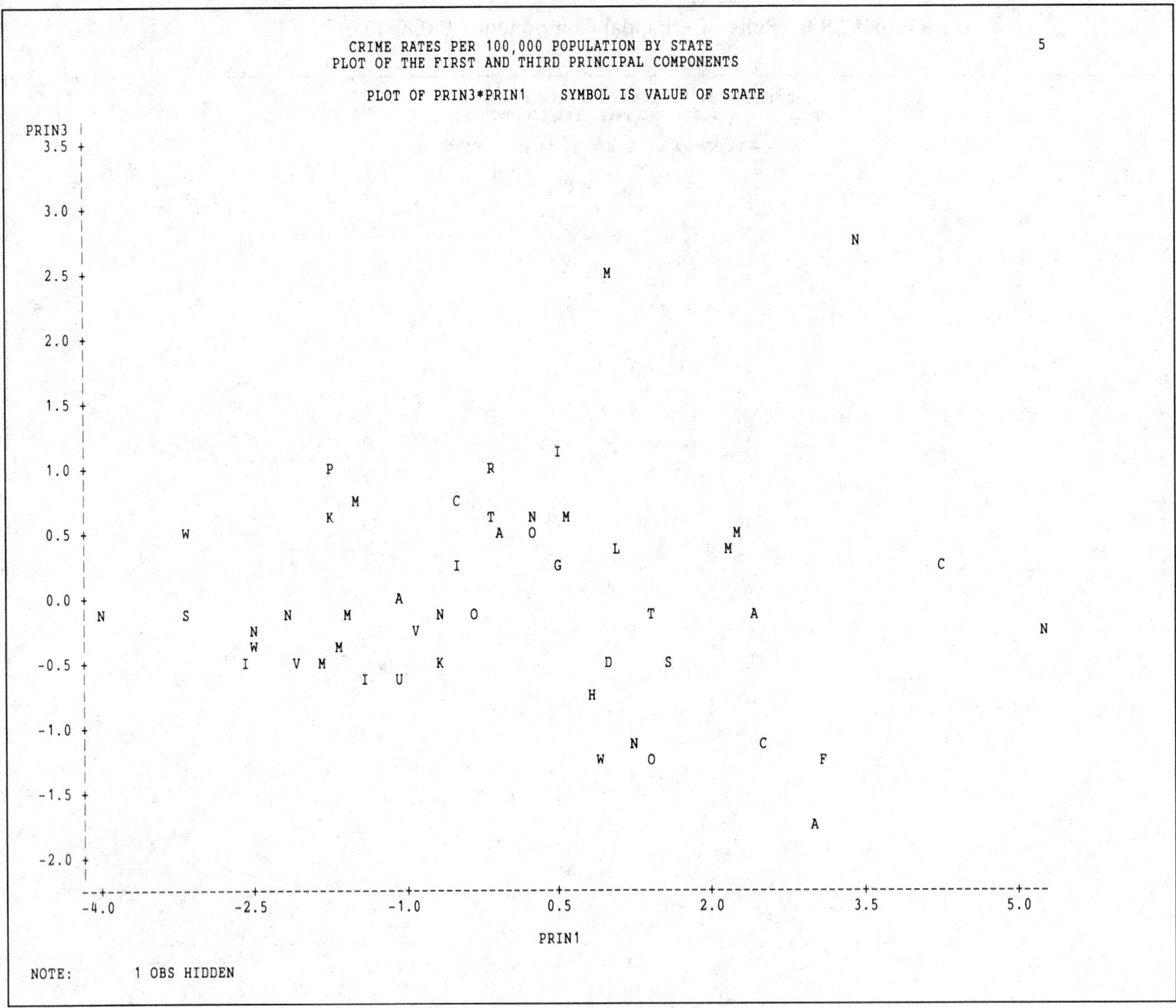

It is possible to identify regional trends on the plot of the first two components. Nevada and California are at the extreme right, with high overall crime rates but an average ratio of property crime to violent crime. North and South Dakota are on the extreme left with low overall crime rates. Southeastern states tend to be in the bottom of the plot, with a higher-than-average ratio of violent crime to property crime. New England states tend to be in the upper part of the plot, with a greater-than-average ratio of property crime to violent crime.

The most striking feature of the plot of the first and third principal components is that Massachusetts and New York are outliers on the third component.

REFERENCES

Cooley, W.W. and Lohnes, P.R. (1971), *Multivariate Data Analysis*, New York: John Wiley & Sons.

Gnanadesikan, R. (1977), *Methods for Statistical Data Analysis of Multivariate Observations*, New York: John Wiley & Sons.

Hotelling, H. (1933), "Analysis of a Complex of Statistical Variables into Principal Components," *Journal of Educational Psychology*, 24, 417-441, 498-520.

Kshirsagar, A.M. (1972), *Multivariate Analysis*, New York: Marcel Dekker.

Mardia, K.V., Kent, J.T., and Bibby, J.M. (1979), *Multivariate Analysis*, London: Academic Press.

Morrison, D.F. (1976), *Multivariate Statistical Methods*, Second Edition, New York: McGraw-Hill.

Pearson, K. (1901), "On Lines and Planes of Closest Fit to Systems of Points in Space," *Philosophical Magazine*, 6, (2), 559-572.

Rao, C.R. (1964), "The Use and Interpretation of Principal Component Analysis in Applied Research," *Sankya A*, 26, 329-358.

Chapter 29
The PROBIT Procedure

Operating systems: All

ABSTRACT

The PROBIT procedure calculates maximum-likelihood estimates of the intercept, slope, and natural (threshold) response rate for biological assay data.

INTRODUCTION

The maximum-likelihood estimates are calculated for the parameters A, B>0, and 1>C>=0 in the probit equation

$$\Phi^{-1}((y-C)/(1-C))+5 = A + Bx$$

where

Φ	is the cumulative distribution function of the standard normal distribution.
x	is the level of the dose.
y	is the probability of a response.

Optionally, the threshold parameter C can be set to a constant value and not estimated. The default value for C is 0.

A modified Gauss-Newton algorithm is used to compute the estimates. You can request that the natural (threshold) response rate C be estimated. If you have an initial estimate of C from a control group, it can be specified.

The data set used by PROBIT must include

- a variable specifying the dose (level of the stimulus)
- a variable giving the number of subjects tested at that dose

- a variable giving the number of subjects responding to the dose.

For small goodness-of-fit chi-square values, the fiducial limits are computed using a *t* value of 1.96. In the case of large chi-squares, variances and covariances are multiplied by the heterogeneity factor, which is the goodness-of-fit chi-square divided by its degrees of freedom, and the usual *t* value is used to compute the fiducial limits. The *p* value used for the chi-square test can be set with the HPROB= option. The default *p* value is .10.

SPECIFICATIONS

These statements are used to control PROC PROBIT:

PROC PROBIT *options;*
  VAR *dose subjects response;*
  BY *variables;*

The VAR statement is required.

PROC PROBIT Statement

PROC PROBIT *options;*

The following options can appear in the PROC PROBIT statement:

DATA=*SASdataset*
: names the SAS data set to be used by PROBIT. If DATA= is omitted, the most recently created SAS data set is used.

OPTC
C=*rate*
: control how the threshold response is handled. Specify OPTC to request that the estimation of the natural (threshold) response rate C be optimized. Specify C=*rate* for the threshold rate or initial estimate of threshold rate. The threshold rate value must be a number between 0 and 1.

  If neither OPTC nor C= is specified, a threshold rate of 0 is assumed.

  If you specify both OPTC and C=, then C= should be a reasonable initial estimate of the threshold rate, for example, the ratio of the number of responses to the number of subjects in a control group.

  If you specify C= but not OPTC, then C= specifies a constant threshold rate.

  If you specify OPTC but not C=, PROBIT's action depends on the response variable. If you specify the LN or LOG10 option and some observations have *dose* values less than or equal to zero, then the initial estimate of C= is the ratio of the number of responses to the number of subjects in these groups. Otherwise when all the responses are greater than 0, the initial estimate of threshold rate is the smallest ratio of response value to subject value in the experiment. When one or more of the responses is zero, the initial estimate of threshold rate is the reciprocal of twice the largest number of subjects in any *dose* group in the experiment.

HPROB=*p*
: specifies a probability level other than .10 to indicate a good fit. For chi-square values with probability greater than the HPROB= value, the fiducial limits are computed using *t*=1.96.

LOG
LN

requests that PROC PROBIT analyze the data using the natural (Naperian) logarithm of the *dose* value. In addition to the usual output, the estimated *dose* values and 95% fiducial limits for *dose* are also printed. If you specify OPTC, any observations with a *dose* value less than or equal to zero are used in the estimation as a control group. LOG and LN have the same effect.

LOG10

specifies an analysis like that of LN or LOG above except that the common logarithm (log to the base 10) of the *dose* value is used rather than the natural logarithm.

VAR Statement

VAR *dose subjects response;*

A VAR statement must accompany the PROC PROBIT statement. The three variables representing the level of stimulus (*dose*), the number of subjects (*subjects*), and the number of subjects responding to that dose (*response*) must appear in that order in the VAR statement.

BY Statement

BY *variables;*

A BY statement can be used with PROC PROBIT to obtain separate analyses on observations in groups defined by the BY variables. When a BY statement appears, the procedure expects the input data set to be sorted in order of the BY variables. If your input data set is not sorted in ascending order, use the SORT procedure with a similar BY statement to sort the data, or, if appropriate, use the BY statement options NOTSORTED or DESCENDING. For more information, see the discussion of the BY statement in "Statements Used in the PROC Step" in the *SAS User's Guide: Basics.*

DETAILS

Missing Values

PROBIT does not include any observations having missing values for either the dose or the number of subjects. If the number of responses is missing, it is assumed to be 0.

Tolerance Distribution

The probit model can be justified on the basis of a normal population with mean μ and standard deviation σ of tolerances for the subjects. Then, given a dose x, the probability, P, of observing a response in a particular subject is the probability that the subject's tolerance is less than the dose or

$$P = \Phi((x-\mu)/\sigma) \quad .$$

Thus the previously defined parameters A and B are related to μ and σ by

$$B = 1/\sigma$$

and

$$A = 5 - \mu/\sigma \quad .$$

Printed Output

For each iteration, PROBIT prints

1. the current estimate of the parameter A, called INTERCEPT
2. the current estimate of the parameter B, called SLOPE
3. for a threshold model, the current estimate of the parameter C (not shown in this example)
4. the mean MU of the stimulus tolerance
5. the standard deviation SIGMA of the stimulus tolerance.

PROBIT also prints

6. the estimated dose along with the 95% fiducial limits for probability levels .01-.10, .15, .20, .25, .85, and .90-.99
7. the covariance matrix for INTERCEPT and SLOPE
8. the covariance matrix for MU and SIGMA.

PROBIT also produces these two plots:

9. a plot of the empirical probit at each level of stimulus (dose) superimposed on the probit line
10. a plot of points computed as the raw probability at each level of stimulus superimposed on the normal probability sigmoid curve.

EXAMPLE

Dosage Levels

DOSE in this example is the variable representing the level of the stimulus, N represents the number of subjects tested at each level of the stimulus, and RESPONSE is the number of subjects responding to that level of the stimulus.

```
DATA A;
   INPUT DOSE N RESPONSE;
   CARDS;
1 10 1
2 12 2
3 10 4
4 10 5
5 12 8
6 10 8
7 10 10
;
PROC PROBIT LOG10;
   VAR DOSE N RESPONSE;
   TITLE 'OUTPUT FROM PROBIT PROCEDURE';
```

Output 29.1 Dosage Levels: PROC PROBIT

```
                              OUTPUT FROM PROBIT PROCEDURE                                      1

                             PROBIT ANALYSIS ON LOG10(DOSE)

     ITERATION           INTERCEPT              SLOPE                  MU                  SIGMA

             0          3.49590967         2.72791853          0.55136923          0.36657986
             1          3.21396434         3.36710678          0.53043630          0.29699088
             2          3.18748146         3.41779512          0.53031808          0.29258629
             3          3.18729497         3.41811802          0.53032254          0.29255865
             4          3.18729496         3.41811804          0.53032254          0.29255865


COVARIANCE MATRIX                                          COVARIANCE MATRIX
                  INTERCEPT             SLOPE                                     MU              SIGMA

INTERCEPT        0.20190710       -0.31111112              MU            0.00241827        -0.00040909
SLOPE           -0.31111112        0.55583899              SIGMA        -0.00040909         0.00407193

                  CHI-SQ =       3.6497 WITH        5 DF  PROB > CHI-SQ = 0.6009

NOTE: SINCE THE CHI-SQUARE IS SMALL (P > 0.10), FIDUCIAL LIMITS WILL BE COMPUTED USING A T VALUE OF 1.96 .
```

```
                              OUTPUT FROM PROBIT PROCEDURE                                      2
```

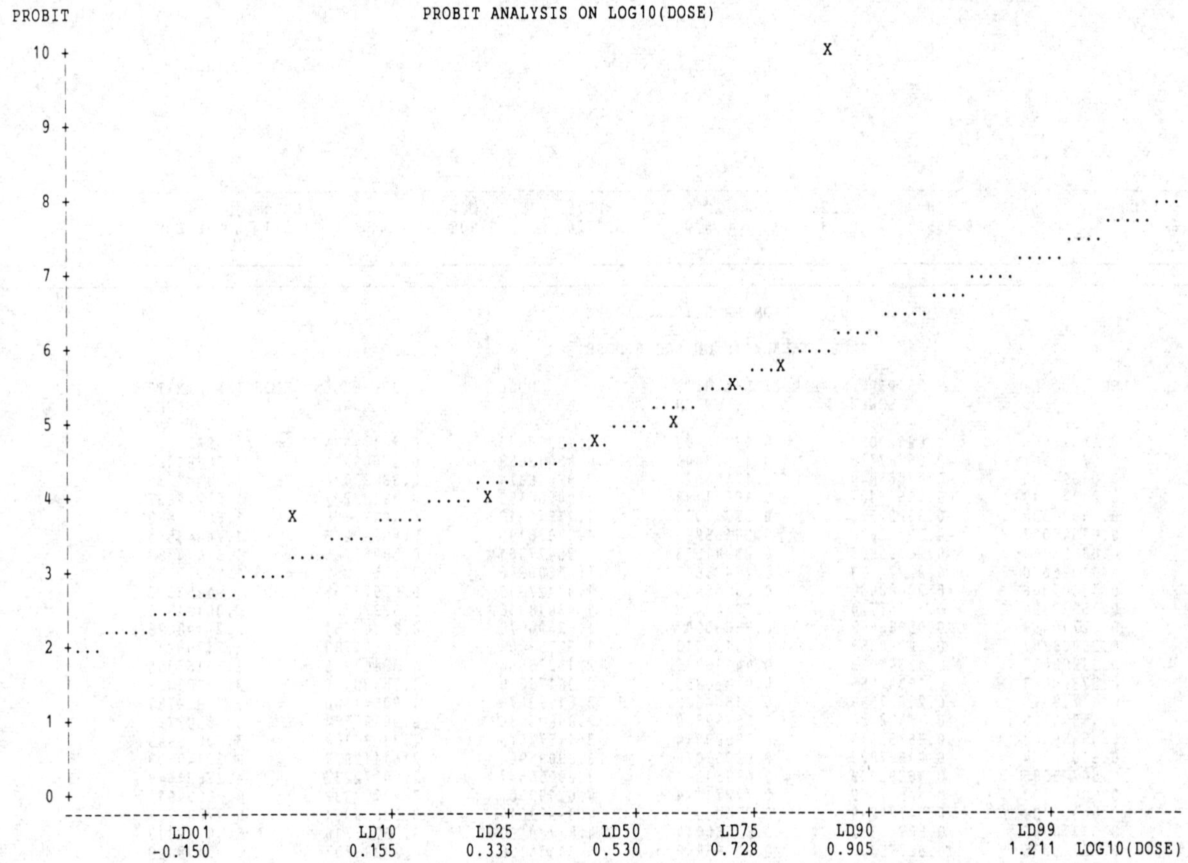

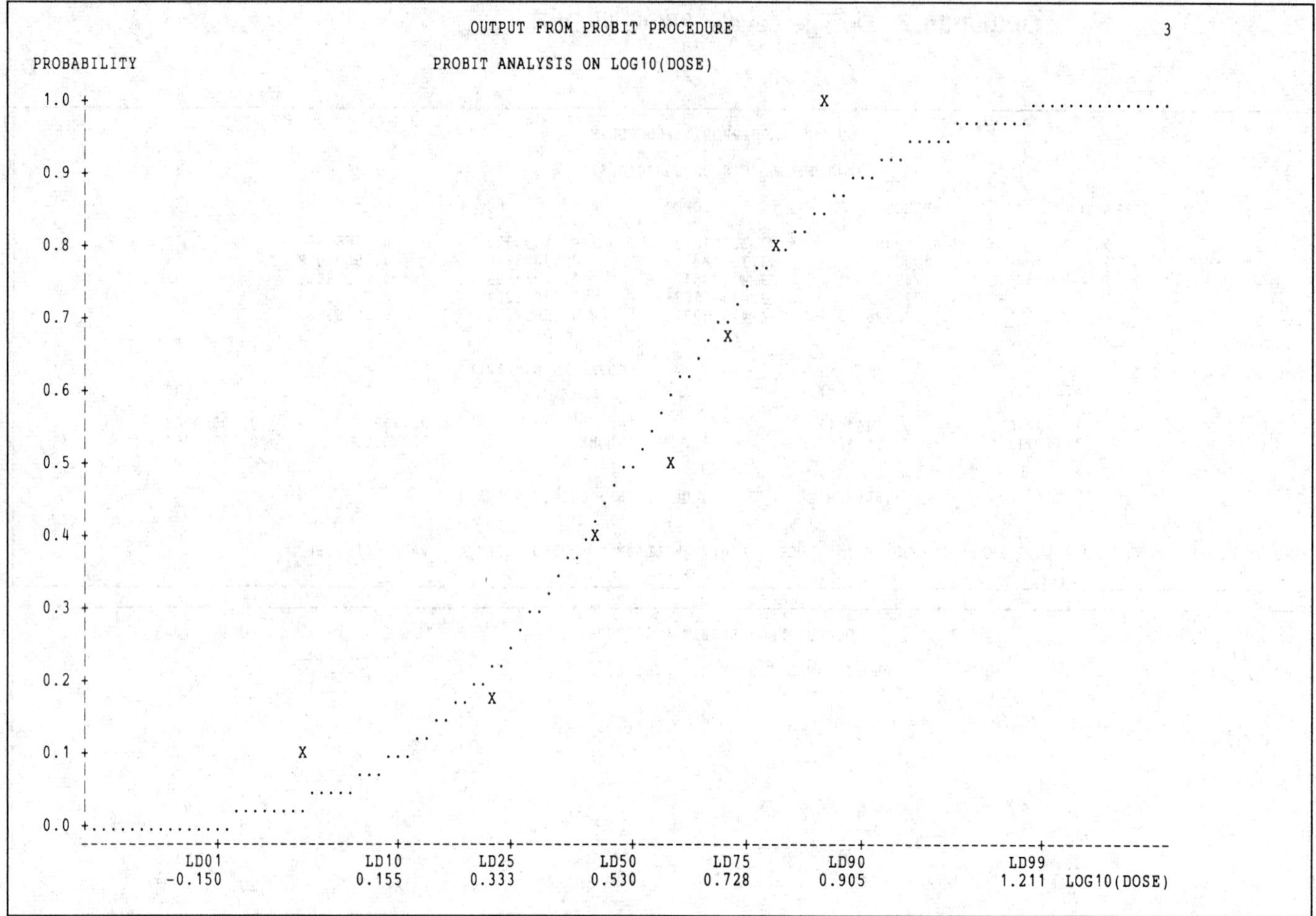

OUTPUT FROM PROBIT PROCEDURE 4

PROBIT ANALYSIS ON LOG10(DOSE)

PROBABILITY	LOG10(DOSE)	95 PERCENT FIDUCIAL LIMITS LOWER	UPPER	DOSE	95 PERCENT FIDUCIAL LIMITS LOWER	UPPER
0.01	-0.15027066	-0.69520058	0.07710499	0.70750473	0.20174344	1.19427677
0.02	-0.07051947	-0.55767746	0.13475446	0.85012058	0.27689974	1.36381184
0.03	-0.01991990	-0.47065849	0.17156624	0.95516874	0.33833078	1.48445229
0.04	0.01814419	-0.40535107	0.19941188	1.04266353	0.39323207	1.58274837
0.05	0.04910638	-0.35234570	0.22217933	1.11971213	0.44427748	1.66793582
0.06	0.07546007	-0.30732670	0.24165490	1.18976195	0.49280295	1.74443545
0.07	0.09856711	-0.26793800	0.25881533	1.25477861	0.53958765	1.81474383
0.08	0.11925670	-0.23274573	0.27425605	1.31600246	0.58513257	1.88042516
0.09	0.13807306	-0.20080938	0.28836839	1.37427313	0.62978255	1.94253292
0.10	0.15539354	-0.17147720	0.30142410	1.43018936	0.67378726	2.00181575
0.15	0.22710499	-0.05086498	0.35630907	1.68696078	0.88947761	2.27148078
0.20	0.28409897	0.04368359	0.40124010	1.92353001	1.10581783	2.51906919
0.25	0.33299473	0.12342032	0.44116445	2.15275560	1.32867975	2.76162335
0.30	0.37690463	0.19347555	0.47856856	2.38179639	1.56126115	3.01001428
0.35	0.41759370	0.25657599	0.51504522	2.61573476	1.80541060	3.27374781
0.40	0.45620365	0.31428484	0.55182530	2.85893086	2.06198184	3.56307777
0.45	0.49355923	0.36753513	0.58999414	3.11572576	2.33096167	3.89039893
0.50	0.53032254	0.41692823	0.63057076	3.39095900	2.61172972	4.27140503
0.55	0.56708585	0.46295509	0.67451361	3.69050547	2.90372237	4.72621649
0.60	0.60444143	0.50617659	0.72271124	4.02199407	3.20757332	5.28094011
0.65	0.64305138	0.54734298	0.77603379	4.39593614	3.52649261	5.97081734
0.70	0.68374045	0.58744572	0.83550814	4.82770190	3.86763716	6.84712313
0.75	0.72765035	0.62775880	0.90265440	5.34134156	4.24383807	7.99198029
0.80	0.77654611	0.66998827	0.98008602	5.97786512	4.67722508	9.55181750
0.85	0.83354009	0.71675292	1.07280097	6.81616497	5.20898273	11.82499507
0.90	0.90525154	0.77312953	1.19192154	8.03991645	5.93102198	15.55684549
0.91	0.92257202	0.78645406	1.22098490	8.36704342	6.11581111	16.63354807
0.92	0.94138838	0.80082817	1.25265947	8.73752394	6.32161688	17.89202405
0.93	0.96207797	0.81652514	1.28759550	9.16384998	6.55428229	19.39078981

(continued on next page)

(continued from previous page)

0.94	0.98518500	0.83393814	1.32673162	9.66462492	6.82241517	21.21932777
0.95	1.01153870	0.85366509	1.37149925	10.26924929	7.13945542	23.52335446
0.96	1.04250089	0.87668630	1.42425086	11.02810503	7.52811591	26.56139405
0.97	1.08056498	0.90479395	1.48929626	12.03829493	8.03144984	30.85291940
0.98	1.13116455	0.94188765	1.57603332	13.52584944	8.74757449	37.67327033
0.99	1.21091573	0.99987059	1.71322298	16.25233381	9.99702055	51.66815855

REFERENCE

Finney, D.J. (1971), *Probit Analysis*, Third Edition, London: Cambridge University Press.

REFERENCE

Chapter 30

The RANK Procedure

Operating systems: All

ABSTRACT

The RANK procedure computes ranks for one or more numeric variables across the observations of a SAS data set. The ranks are output to a new SAS data set. Alternatively, PROC RANK produces normal scores or other rank scores.

INTRODUCTION

The RANK procedure ranks values from smallest to largest, assigning the rank 1 to the smallest number, 2 to the next largest, and so on up to rank n, the number of nonmissing observations. Tied values are given averaged ranks. Several options are available to request other ranking and tie-handling rules.

Many nonparametric statistical methods use ranks rather than the original values of a variable. For example, a set of data may be passed through PROC RANK to obtain the ranks for a response variable that could then be fit to an analysis-of-variance model using the ANOVA or GLM procedures.

Ranks are also useful for investigating the distribution of values for a variable. The ranks divided by n or $n+1$ form values in the range 0 to 1, and they estimate the cumulative distribution function. Inverse cumulative distribution functions can be applied to these fractional ranks to obtain probability quantile scores, which can be compared to the original values to judge the fit to the distribution. For example, if a set of data has a normal distribution, the normal scores should be a linear function of the original values, and a plot of scores versus original values should be a straight line.

PROC RANK is also useful for grouping continuous data into ranges. The GROUPS= option can break a population into approximately equal-sized groups.

SPECIFICATIONS

The following statements can be specified to invoke PROC RANK:

PROC RANK *options;*
VAR *variables;*
RANKS *names;*
BY *variables;*

PROC RANK Statement

PROC RANK *options;*

The options below can appear in the PROC RANK statement:

DATA=*SASdataset*
names the SAS data set to be used by PROC RANK. If DATA= is omitted, the most recently created SAS data set is used.

TIES=MEAN
TIES=HIGH
TIES=LOW
specifies which rank to report for tied values. TIES=MEAN requests that tied values receive the mean of the corresponding ranks (mid-ranks). The specification TIES=HIGH requests that the largest of the corresponding ranks be used. TIES=LOW requests that the smallest of the corresponding ranks be used. The default method is TIES=MEAN.

To illustrate the three options available for handling tied values, consider the values of the variable WEIGHT and the ranks that are assigned for each TIES value:

Table 30.1 Options Available for Handling Tied Values

WEIGHT	TIES=MEAN	TIES=HIGH	TIES=LOW
107	1	1	1
110	2.5	3	2
110	2.5	3	2
121	4	4	4
125	6	7	5
125	6	7	5
125	6	7	5
132	8	8	8

DESCENDING
reverses the ranking from largest to smallest. The largest value is given a rank of 1, the next smallest a rank of 2, and so on. When DESCENDING is omitted, values are ranked from smallest to largest.

GROUPS=*n*
requests grouping scores, where *n* is the number of groups. The scores are the integers 0 to (*n*−1). The groups have equal or nearly

equal numbers of observations. The lowest values are in the first group; the highest values are in the last group. The following are common GROUP values: 100 produces percentile ranks, 10 produces deciles, and 4 produces quartiles.

For example, if you want quartile ranks, you specify GROUPS=4. RANK then separates the values of the ranking variable into four groups according to size. The values in the group containing the smallest values receive a quartile value of 0, the values in the next group receive a value of 1, the values in the next group receive a value of 2, and the largest values receive the value 3.

The formula used to calculate the quantile rank of a value is

FLOOR (*rank***k*/(*n* + 1))

where *rank* is the value's rank, *k* is the number of groups specified with the GROUPS= option, and *n* is the number of observations having nonmissing values of the ranking variable.

FRACTION
F

requests fractional ranks. RANK divides each rank by the number of observations having nonmissing values of the ranking variable and expresses the ranks as fractions. If the TIES= option is omitted or if TIES=HIGH is specified, these fractional ranks can be considered values of a right-continuous empirical cumulative distribution function.

PERCENT
P

asks RANK to divide each rank by the number of observations having nonmissing values of the ranking variable and then to multiply the result by 100 to get percentages. Like the FRACTION option, the PERCENT option implies TIES=HIGH unless another TIES= value is specified.

Note: the PERCENT option does not give what are usually called *percentile ranks*. These are produced by specifying GROUPS=100.

NORMAL=BLOM
NORMAL=TUKEY
NORMAL=VW

requests normal scores to be computed from the ranks. The resulting variables appear normally distributed. If NORMAL= is specified, either BLOM, TUKEY, or VW must be given. The formulas are as follows:

BLOM $y_i = \Psi(r_i - 3/8)/(n + 1/4)$

TUKEY $y_i = \Psi(r_i - 1/3)/(n + 1/3)$

VW $y_i = \Psi(r_i)/(n + 1)$

where Ψ is the inverse cumulative normal (PROBIT) function, r_i is the rank, and n is the number of nonmissing observations for the ranking variable. VW stands for van der Waerden, whose scores are used for a nonparametric location test.

These normal scores are approximations to the exact expected order statistics for the normal distribution, also called *normal scores*. The BLOM version appears to fit slightly better than the others (Blom 1958, 145; Tukey 1962, 22).

SAVAGE
requests Savage (or exponential) scores to be computed from the ranks. The scores are computed by this formula (Lehman 1975):

$$y_i = \left[\sum_{j=n-r_i+1}^{n} (1/j) \right] - 1$$

OUT=*SASdataset*
names the output data set created by PROC RANK to contain the resulting ranks. If you do not specify OUT=, the default name is OUT=_DATA_, which produces a name such as DATA*n*. If you want to create a permanent SAS data set, you must specify a two-level name (see "SAS Files" in the *SAS User's Guide: Basics* for more information on permanent SAS data sets). For details on the data set created by RANK, see **Output Data Set** below.

VAR Statement

VAR *variables;*

RANK computes ranks for the variables given in the VAR statement. These variables must be numeric. If the VAR statement is omitted, ranks are computed for all numeric variables in the data set. The VAR statement must be included if a RANKS statement (below) is used.

RANKS Statement

RANKS *names;*

If you want the original variables included in the output data set in addition to the ranks, use the RANKS statement to assign variable names to the ranks. First, name the rank corresponding to the first variable in the VAR statement, next name the rank that corresponds to the second variable in the VAR statement, and so on.

BY Statement

BY *variables;*

A BY statement can be used with PROC RANK to obtain separate analyses on observations in groups defined by the BY variables. When a BY statement appears, the procedure expects the input data set to be sorted in order of the BY variables. If your input data set is not sorted in ascending order, use the SORT procedure with a similar BY statement to sort the data, or, if appropriate, use the BY statement options NOTSORTED or DESCENDING. For more information, see the discussion of the BY statement in "Statements Used in the PROC Step" in the *SAS User's Guide: Basics.*

DETAILS

Missing Values

Missing values are not ranked and are left missing when ranks or rank scores replace the other values of the ranking variable.

Output Data Set

RANK creates a new SAS data set containing the ranks or rank scores but no printed output.

The new output data set contains all the variables from the input data set plus the variables named in the RANKS statement if one is specified. If a RANKS statement is used, a VAR statement must also be included. If no RANKS statement is given, then the procedure stores the ranks in the output data set in the original variables that were ranked. If no VAR statement is included, the procedure ranks all numeric variables.

Nonparametric Statistics

Many nonparametric methods are based on taking the ranks of a variable and analyzing these ranks instead of the original values.

- A two-sample *t* test applied to the ranks is equivalent to a Wilcoxon rank sum test using the *t* approximation for the significance level. If the *t* test is applied to the normal scores rather than to the ranks, the test becomes equivalent to the van der Waerden test. If the *t* test is applied to median scores (GROUPS=2), the test becomes the median test.
- A one-way analysis of variance applied to ranks is equivalent to the Kruskal-Wallis *k*-sample test; the F test generated by the parametric procedure applied to the ranks is often better than the χ^2 approximation used by Kruskal-Wallis. This test can be extended to other rank scores (Quade 1966).
- Friedman's two-way analysis for block designs can be obtained by ranking within blocks (using a BY statement with PROC RANK) and then performing a main-effects analysis of variance on these ranks (Conover 1980).
- Regression relationships can be investigated using rank transformations with a method described by Iman and Conover (1979).

EXAMPLE

Ranking of Gain Values

This example uses PROC RANK to get the ranks of the variable GAIN. The RANKS statement assigns the name RANKGAIN to the variable containing the ranks in the output data set. Since OUT= is not specified, RANK creates a new data set using the DATA*n* naming rules. The PRINT procedure prints the contents of the output data set. The second execution of PROC RANK uses a BY variable.

```
DATA A;
   INPUT LOCATION GAIN;
   CARDS;
1 7.2
1 7.9
1 7.6
1 6.3
1 8.4
1 8.1
2 8.1
2 7.3
2 7.7
2 7.7
```

```
;
PROC RANK;
   VAR GAIN;
   RANKS RANKGAIN;
PROC PRINT;
   TITLE 'RANK THE GAIN VALUES';
PROC RANK DATA=A OUT=B;
   BY LOCATION;
   RANKS RGAIN;
   VAR GAIN;
PROC PRINT;
   BY LOCATION;
   TITLE 'RANKINGS WITHIN LOCATIONS';
```

Output 30.1 Data Sets Generated with PROC RANK and Reproduced Using PROC PRINT

```
                              RANK THE GAIN VALUES                                1

                      OBS   LOCATION   GAIN   RANKGAIN

                        1       1       7.2      2.0
                        2       1       7.9      7.0
                        3       1       7.6      4.0
                        4       1       6.3      1.0
                        5       1       8.4     10.0
                        6       1       8.1      8.5
                        7       2       8.1      8.5
                        8       2       7.3      3.0
                        9       2       7.7      5.5
                       10       2       7.7      5.5
```

```
                          RANKINGS WITHIN LOCATIONS                               2

----------------------------------------LOCATION=1----------------------------------------

                            OBS    GAIN    RGAIN

                              1     7.2      2
                              2     7.9      4
                              3     7.6      3
                              4     6.3      1
                              5     8.4      6
                              6     8.1      5

----------------------------------------LOCATION=2----------------------------------------

                            OBS    GAIN    RGAIN

                              7     8.1     4.0
                              8     7.3     1.0
                              9     7.7     2.5
                             10     7.7     2.5
```

REFERENCES

Blom, G. (1958), *Statistical Estimates and Transformed Beta Variables*, New York: John Wiley & Sons.

Conover, W.J. (1980), *Practical Nonparametric Statistics*, Second Edition, New York: John Wiley & Sons.

Conover, W.J. and Iman, R.L. (1976), "On Some Alternative Procedures Using Ranks for the Analysis of Experimental Designs," *Communications in Statistics*, A5, 14, 1348-1368.

Conover, W.J. and Iman, R.L. (1981) "Rank Transformations as a Bridge between Parametric and Nonparametric Statistics," *The American Statistician*, 35, 124-129.

Iman, R.L. and Conover, W.J. (1979), "The Use of the Rank Transform in Regression," *Technometrics*, 21, 499-509.

Lehman, E.L. (1975), *Nonparametrics: Statistical Methods Based on Ranks*, San Francisco: Holden-Day.

Quade, D. (1966), "On Analysis of Variance for the *k*-Sample Problem," *Annals of Mathematical Statistics*, 37, 1747-1758.

Tukey, John W. (1962), "The Future of Data Analysis," *Annals of Mathematical Statistics*, 33, 22.

Chapter 31
The REG Procedure

Operating systems: All

ABSTRACT

The REG procedure fits least-squares estimates to linear regression models.

INTRODUCTION

Suppose that a response variable Y can be predicted by a linear combination of some regressor variables X1 and X2. You can fit the β parameters in the equation

$$Y_i = \beta_0 + \beta_1 X1_i + \beta_2 X2_i + \varepsilon_i$$

for the observations $i=1...n$. To fit this model with the REG procedure, specify:

```
PROC REG;
   MODEL Y = X1 X2;
```

REG uses the principle of least squares to produce estimates that are the best linear unbiased estimates (BLUE) under classical statistical assumptions (Gauss 1809, Markov 1900).

For example, we can apply regression techniques to the behavior of gross investment in General Electric as a linear function of lagged capital stock and the value of outstanding shares (Grunfeld 1958). We use PROC REG to fit the model

$$I = \beta_0 + \beta_1 C + \beta_2 F + \varepsilon \ .$$

The SAS statements that read the data and perform the regression are

```
TITLE 'GRUNFELD''S INVESTMENT MODEL';
DATA GRUNFELD;
   INPUT YEAR I F C @@;
   LABEL I='GROSS INVESTMENT GE'
         C='CAPITAL STOCK LAGGED GE'
         F='VALUE OF SHARES GE LAGGED';
   CARDS;
1935  33.1  1170.6  97.8   1936  45.0  2015.8 104.4
1937  77.2  2803.3 118.0   1938  44.6  2039.7 156.2
1939  48.1  2256.2 172.6   1940  74.4  2132.2 186.6
1941 113.0  1834.1 220.9   1942  91.9  1588.0 287.8
1943  61.3  1749.4 319.9   1944  56.8  1687.2 321.3
1945  93.6  2007.7 319.6   1946 159.9  2208.3 346.0
1947 147.2  1656.7 456.4   1948 146.3  1604.4 543.4
1949  98.3  1431.8 618.3   1950  93.5  1610.5 647.4
1951 135.2  1819.4 671.3   1952 157.3  2079.7 726.1
1953 179.5  2371.6 800.3   1954 189.6  2759.9 888.9
;
PROC REG;
   MODEL I = F C ;
```

The results are shown in **Output 31.1**.

Output 31.1 Regression of Investment Data: REG Procedure

```
                                GRUNFELD'S INVESTMENT MODEL                                         1

DEP VARIABLE: I          GROSS INVESTMENT GE
                                      ANALYSIS OF VARIANCE

                                      SUM OF           MEAN
                    SOURCE    DF     SQUARES         SQUARE       F VALUE        PROB>F

                    MODEL      2  31632.03023    15816.01511        20.344        0.0001
                    ERROR     17  13216.58777      777.44634
                    C TOTAL   19  44848.61800

                       ROOT MSE      27.88272       R-SQUARE       0.7053
                       DEP MEAN        102.29       ADJ R-SQ       0.6706
                       C.V.           27.2585

                                      PARAMETER ESTIMATES

                          PARAMETER         STANDARD      T FOR H0:                    VARIABLE
       VARIABLE  DF        ESTIMATE            ERROR    PARAMETER=0    PROB > |T|         LABEL

       INTERCEP   1     -9.95630645      31.37424914         -0.317        0.7548     INTERCEPT
       F          1      0.02655119       0.01556610          1.706        0.1063     VALUE OF SHARES GE LAGGED
       C          1      0.15169387       0.02570408          5.902        0.0001     CAPITAL STOCK LAGGED GE
```

PROC REG is one of many regression procedures in the SAS System. REG is a general-purpose procedure for regression, while other SAS regression procedures have more specialized applications. GLM is designed to handle classification effects that occur in analysis-of-variance problems. STEPWISE and RSQUARE choose variables for building regression models. NLIN handles nonlinear models. SAS/ETS procedures are specialized for applications in time-series or simultaneous systems. Other SAS regression procedures are discussed in the chapter "SAS Regression Procedures."

PROC REG

- handles multiple MODEL statements
- can use either correlations or crossproducts for input
- prints predicted values, residuals, studentized residuals, and confidence limits, and can output these items to an output SAS data set
- prints special influence statistics
- produces partial regression leverage plots
- estimates parameters subject to linear restrictions
- tests linear hypotheses
- tests multivariate hypotheses
- writes estimates to an output data set
- writes the crossproducts matrix to an output SAS data set
- computes special collinearity diagnostics.

SPECIFICATIONS

The following statements are used with the REG procedure:

PROC REG *options*;
label: **MODEL** *dependents=regressors / options*;
  VAR *variables*;
  FREQ *variable*;
  WEIGHT *variable*;
  ID *variable*;
  OUTPUT OUT=*SASdataset keyword=names...*;
  RESTRICT *equation1,...,equation k*;

TEST *equation1,...,equationk/options;*
MTEST *equation1,...,equationk/options;*
BY *variables;*

The PROC REG statement is always accompanied by one or more MODEL statements to specify regression models. One OUTPUT statement can follow each MODEL statement. Several RESTRICT, TEST, and MTEST statements can follow each MODEL statement. WEIGHT, FREQ, and ID statements are optionally specified once for the entire PROC step. The purposes of the statements are as follows:

- The MODEL statement specifies the dependent and independent variables in the regression model.
- The OUTPUT statement requests an output data set and names the variables to contain predicted values, residuals, and other output values.
- The RESTRICT statement places linear restrictions on the parameter estimates.
- The TEST statement composes an *F* test on linear functions of the parameters.
- The MTEST statement composes multivariate tests across multiple dependent variables.
- The ID statement names a variable to identify observations in the printout.
- The WEIGHT and FREQ statements declare variables to weight observations.
- The VAR statement, rarely used with REG, lists variables for which crossproducts are to be computed.
- The BY statement specifies variables to define subgroups for the analysis.

PROC REG Statement

PROC REG *options;*

These options can be specified in the PROC REG statement:

DATA=*SASdataset*
: names the SAS data set to be used by PROC REG. If DATA= is not specified, REG uses the most recently created SAS data set.

OUTEST=*SASdataset*
: requests that parameter estimates be output to this data set. See **Output Data Sets** later in this chapter for details. If you want to create a permanent SAS data set, you must specify a two-level name (see "SAS Files" in *SAS User's Guide: Basics* for more information on permanent SAS data sets).

OUTSSCP=*SASdataset*
: requests that the sums of squares and crossproducts matrix be output to this TYPE=SSCP data set. See **Output Data Sets** for details. If you want to create a permanent SAS data set, you must specify a two-level name (see "SAS Files" in *SAS User's Guide: Basics* for more information on permanent SAS data sets).

NOPRINT
: suppresses the normal printed output. Using this option on the PROC REG statement is equivalent to specifying NOPRINT on each MODEL statement.

SIMPLE
: prints the "simple" descriptive statistics for each variable used in REG.

USSCP

prints the (uncorrected) sums-of-squares and crossproducts matrix for all variables used in the procedure.

ALL

requests many different printouts. Using ALL on the PROC REG statement is equivalent to specifying ALL on every MODEL statement. ALL also implies SIMPLE and USSCP.

COVOUT

outputs the covariance matrices for the parameter estimates to the OUTEST= data set. This option is valid only if OUTEST= is also specified. See **Output Data Sets** later in this chapter.

SINGULAR=*n*

tunes the mechanism used to check for singularities. The default value is 1E-8. This option is rarely needed. Singularity checking is described in **Computational Methods**.

MODEL Statement

label: MODEL *dependents*=*regressors* / *options*;

After the keyword MODEL, the dependent (response) variables are specified, followed by an equal sign and the regressor variables. Variables specified in the MODEL statement must be variables in the data set being analyzed. The label is optional.

General options

NOPRINT suppresses the normal printout of regression results.

NOINT suppresses the intercept term that is normally included in the model automatically.

ALL requests all the features of these options: XPX, SS1, SS2, STB, TOL, COVB, CORRB, SEQB, P, R, CLI, CLM, SPEC, ACOV, PCORR1, PCORR2, SCORR1, SCORR2.

Options to request regression calculations

XPX prints the **X'X** crossproducts matrix for the model. The crossproducts matrix is bordered with the **X'Y** and **Y'Y** matrices.

I prints the $(\mathbf{X'X})^{-1}$ matrix. The inverse of the crossproducts matrix is bordered with the parameter estimates and SSE matrices.

Options for details on the estimates

SS1 prints the sequential sums of squares (Type I SS) along with the parameter estimates for each term in the model.

SS2 prints the partial sums of squares (Type II SS) along with the parameter estimates for each term in the model.

STB prints standardized regression coefficients. A standardized regression coefficient is computed by dividing a parameter estimate by the ratio of the sample standard deviation of the dependent variable to the sample standard deviation of the regressor.

TOL prints tolerance values for the estimates. Tolerance is defined as $1-R^2$ for a variable with respect to all other regressor variables in the model.

VIF prints variance inflation factors with the parameter estimates. Variance inflation is the reciprocal of tolerance.

COVB prints the estimated covariance matrix of the estimates. This matrix is $(\mathbf{X'X})^{-1}S^2$ where S^2 is the mean squared error.

CORRB prints the correlation matrix of the estimates. This is the $(\mathbf{X'X})^{-1}$ matrix scaled to unit diagonals.

SEQB prints a sequence of parameter estimates as each variable is entered into the model. This is printed as a lower triangular matrix where each row is a set of parameter estimates.

COLLIN requests a detailed analysis of collinearity among the regressors. This includes eigenvalues, condition indices, and decomposition of the variances of the estimates with respect to each eigenvalue. (See **Collinearity Diagnostics** below.)

COLLINOINT requests the same analysis as the COLLIN option with the intercept variable adjusted out rather than included in the diagnostics. (Also see **Parameter Estimates and Associated Statistics** later in this chapter.)

ACOV prints the estimated asymptotic covariance matrix of the estimates under the hypothesis of heteroskedasticity. This matrix is

$$(\mathbf{X'X}/n)^{-1}(\mathbf{X'diag(e^2_{\mathit{i}})X}/n)\ (\mathbf{X'X}/n)^{-1}$$

where

$$e_i = y_i - X_i\beta \quad .$$

See the section **Model Specification Testing** for more information.

SPEC performs a test that the first and second moments of the model are correctly specified. See the section **Model Specification Testing** for more information.

PCORR1 prints the partial correlation coefficients using Type I sums of squares.

PCORR2 prints the partial correlation coefficients using Type II sums of squares.

SCORR1 prints the semi-partial correlation coefficients using Type I sums of squares.

SCORR2 prints the semi-partial correlation coefficients using Type II sums of squares.

Options for predicted values and residuals

P calculates predicted values from the input data and the estimated model. The printout includes the observation number, the first ID variable if specified, the actual and predicted values, and the residual.

R requests that the residual be analyzed. The printed output includes everything requested by the P option plus the standard errors of the predicted and residual values, the studentized residual, and Cook's D statistic to measure the influence of each observation on the parameter estimates.

CLM prints the 95% upper- and lower-confidence limits for the expected value of the dependent variable (mean) for each observation. This is not a prediction interval (see the CLI option) because it takes into account only the variation in the parameter estimates, not the variation in the error term.

CLI requests the 95% upper- and lower-confidence limits for an individual predicted value. The confidence limits reflect variation in the error, as well as variation in the parameter estimates.

DW calculates a Durbin-Watson statistic to test whether or not the errors have first-order autocorrelation. (This test is only appropriate for time-series data.) The sample autocorrelation of the residuals is also printed. (See **Autocorrelation in Time-Series Data**.)

INFLUENCE requests a detailed analysis of the influence of each observation on the estimates and the predicted values. (See **Influence Diagnostics**.)

PARTIAL requests partial regression leverage plots for each regressor. (See the sections **Influence Diagnostics** and **Predicted Values and Residuals**.)

VAR Statement

VAR *variables;*

The VAR statement is used to include variables in the crossproducts matrix that are not specified in any MODEL statement. This statement is rarely used with REG and then only with the OUTSSCP= feature.

FREQ Statement

FREQ *variable;*

If a variable in your data set represents the frequency of occurrence for the other values in the observation, include the variable's name in a FREQ statement. The procedure then treats the data set as if each observation appears *n* times, where *n* is the value of the FREQ variable for the observation. The total number of observations is considered equal to the sum of the FREQ variable when the procedure determines degrees of freedom for significance probabilities.

The WEIGHT and FREQ statements have similar effects except in the calculation of degrees of freedom.

WEIGHT Statement

WEIGHT *variable;*

A WEIGHT statement names a variable on the input data set whose values are relative weights for a weighted least-squares fit. If the weight value is proportional to the reciprocal of the variance for each observation, then the weighted estimates are the best linear unbiased estimates (BLUE). A more complete description of the WEIGHT statement can be found in "The GLM Procedure."

ID Statement

ID *variable;*

The ID statement specifies one variable identifying observations as output from the MODEL options P, R, CLM, CLI, and INFLUENCE.

OUTPUT Statement

The OUTPUT statement specifies an output data set containing statistics calculated for each observation. For each statistic, specify the keyword, an equal sign, and a variable name for the statistic in the output data set. If the MODEL has several dependent variables, then a list of output variable names can be specified after each keyword to correspond to the list of dependent variables.

OUTPUT OUT=*SASdataset*
PREDICTED=*names* or P=*names*
RESIDUAL=*names* or R=*names*
L95M=*names*
U95M=*names*
L95=*names*
U95=*names*
STDP=*names*
STDR=*names*
STDI=*names*
STUDENT=*names*
COOKD=*names*
H=*names*
PRESS=*names*
RSTUDENT=*names*
DFFITS=*names*
COVRATIO=*names;*

The output data set named with OUT= contains all the variables in the input data set, including any BY variables, any ID variables, and variables named in the OUTPUT statement that contain statistics.

For example, the SAS statements

```
PROC REG DATA=A;
   MODEL Y Z=X1 X2;
   OUTPUT OUT=B
      P=YHAT ZHAT
      R=YRESID ZRESID;
```

create an output data set named B. In addition to the variables on the input data set, B contains the variable YHAT, whose values are predicted values of the dependent variable Y; ZHAT, whose values are predicted values of the dependent variable Z; YRESID, whose values are the residual values of Y; and ZRESID, whose values are the residual values of Z.

These statistics can be output to the new data set:

PREDICTED= P=	predicted values.
RESIDUAL= R=	residuals, calculated as ACTUAL minus PREDICTED.
L95M=	lower bound of a 95% confidence interval for the expected value (mean) of the dependent variable.
U95M=	upper bound of a 95% confidence interval for the expected value (mean) of the dependent variable.
L95=	lower bound of a 95% confidence interval for an individual prediction. This includes the variance of the error, as well as the variance of the parameter estimates.
U95=	upper bound of a 95% confidence interval for an individual prediction.
STDP=	standard error of the mean predicted value.
STDR=	standard error of the residual.
STDI=	standard error of the individual predicted value.
STUDENT=	studentized residuals, the residual divided by its standard error.
COOKD=	Cook's D influence statistic.
H=	leverage, $x_i(\mathbf{X'X})^{-1}x_i'$.
PRESS=	residual for estimates dropping this observation, which is the residual divided by (1-*h*) where *h* is leverage above.
RSTUDENT=	a studentized residual with the current observation deleted.
DFFITS=	standard influence of observation on predicted value.
COVRATIO=	standard influence of observation on covariance of betas, as discussed with INFLUENCE option.

(See **Predicted Values and Residuals** and **Influence Diagnostics** for details.)

RESTRICT Statement

RESTRICT *equation1=equation2=equation3,*
equation4,
.
.
.
equationk;

A RESTRICT statement is used to place restrictions on the parameter estimates in the MODEL preceding it. If the restrictions are not equal, they should be separated by commas. The statement

```
RESTRICT equation1=equation2=equation3;
```

is equivalent to imposing the two restrictions

```
equation1=equation2
```

and

equation2=equation3

Each restriction is written as a linear equation. The form of an equation is

$\underline{+}term\{\underline{+}term...\}\ \{=\underline{+}term\{\underline{+}term...\}\}$

where *term* is a *variable* | *number* | *number*variable* and brackets { } mean zero or more.

When no equal sign appears, the linear combination is set equal to zero. Each variable name mentioned must be a variable in the MODEL statement to which the RESTRICT statement refers. The keyword INTERCEPT can also be used as a variable name and refers to the intercept parameter in the regression model.

Note that the parameters associated with the variables are restricted, not the variables themselves. Restrictions should be consistent and not redundant.

Examples of valid RESTRICT statements:

```
RESTRICT A+B=1;
RESTRICT A=B=C; or RESTRICT A=B, B=C;
RESTRICT 2*F=G+H, INTERCEPT+F=0;
RESTRICT F=G=H=INTERCEPT;
```

You cannot specify

```
RESTRICT F-G=0,
         F-INTERCEPT=0,
         G-INTERCEPT=1;
```

because the three restrictions are not consistent. If these restrictions are included in a RESTRICT statement, one of the restrict parameters is zero and has zero degrees of freedom, indicating that REG is unable to apply a restriction.

The restrictions usually operate even if the model is not of full rank. Check to ensure that DF=−1 for each restriction.

The parameter estimates are those that minimize the quadratic criterion (SSE) subject to the restrictions. If a restriction cannot be applied, its parameter value and degrees of freedom are listed as zero.

The method used for restricting the parameter estimates is to introduce a Lagrangian parameter for each restriction (Pringle and Raynor 1971). The estimates of these parameters are printed with test statistics. The Lagrangian parameter λ measures the sensitivity of the SSE to the restriction constant. If the restriction constant is changed by a small amount ε, the SSE is changed by $2\lambda\varepsilon$. The *t* ratio tests the significance of the restrictions. If λ is zero, the restricted estimates are the same as the unrestricted estimates, and a change in the restriction constant in either direction increases the SSE.

TEST Statement

label: TEST *equation1*,
equation2,
.
.
.
equationk;

label: TEST *equation1,..., equationk / options;*

The TEST statement, which has the same syntax as the RESTRICT statement except for options, tests hypotheses about the parameters estimated in the preceding MODEL statement. Each equation specifies a linear hypothesis to be tested. The rows of the hypothesis are separated by commas. The syntax of a hypothesis is identical to the form of a restriction in a RESTRICT statement. Variable names must correspond to regressors, and each variable name represents the coefficient of the corresponding variable in the model. An optional label is useful in identifying each test with a name. Again, INTERCEPT can be used instead of a variable name to refer to the model's intercept.

REG performs an F test for the joint hypotheses specified in a single TEST statement. More than one TEST statement can accompany a MODEL statement. The numerator is the usual quadratic form of the estimates; the denominator is the mean squared error. If hypotheses can be represented by

$$\mathbf{L}\boldsymbol{\beta}=\mathbf{c},$$

then the numerator of the F test is

$$\mathbf{Q}=(\mathbf{Lb}-\mathbf{c})'(\mathbf{L}(\mathbf{X'X})^{-}\mathbf{L'})^{-1}(\mathbf{Lb}-\mathbf{c})$$

divided by degrees of freedom, where **b** is the estimate of β.

For example,

```
        MODEL Y = A1 A2 B1 B2;
APLUS:  TEST A1+A2=1;
B1:     TEST B1=0, B2=0;
B2:     TEST B1, B2;
```

The last two tests are equivalent; since no constant is specified, zero is assumed.

One option can be specified in the TEST statement after a slash (/):

PRINT prints intermediate calculations. This includes $\mathbf{L}(\mathbf{X'X})^{-}\mathbf{L'}$ bordered by **Lb-c**, and $(\mathbf{L}(\mathbf{X'X})^{-}\mathbf{L'})^{-1}$ bordered by $(\mathbf{L}(\mathbf{X'X})^{-}\mathbf{L'})^{-1}$ **(Lb-c)**.

MTEST Statement

The MTEST statement is used to test hypotheses in multivariate regression models where there are several dependent variables fit to the same regressors. The hypotheses that can be estimated are of the form

$$(\mathbf{L}\boldsymbol{\beta}-\mathbf{cj})\mathbf{M}=0$$

where **L** is a linear function on the regressor side, β is a matrix of parameters, **c** is a column vector of constants, **j** is a row vector of ones, and **M** is a linear function on the dependent side. The special case where the constants are zero is

$$\mathbf{L}\boldsymbol{\beta}\mathbf{M}=0\ .$$

(See **Multivariate Tests** later in this chapter.)

The MTEST statement has the same syntax as the TEST and RESTRICT statements

label: MTEST *equation1*,
equation2,
.
.
.
equationk;

label: MTEST *equation1*,..., *equationk* / *options*;

where the equations are linear functions composed of coefficients and variable names.

Each linear function extends across either the regressor variables or the dependent variables. If the equation is across the dependent variables, then the constant term, if specified, must be zero. The equations for the regressor variables form the **L** matrix and **c** vector in the above formula; the equations for dependent variables form the **M** matrix. If no equations for the dependent variables are given, REG uses an identity matrix for **M**, testing the same hypothesis across all dependent variables. If no equations for the regressor variables are given, REG forms a linear function that tests all nonintercept parameters.

For example,

```
MODEL Y1 Y2 = X1 X2 X3;
```

The statement

```
MTEST X1,X2;
```

tests the hypothesis that the X1 and X2 parameters are zero in both Y1 and Y2. The statement

```
MTEST Y1-Y2, X1;
```

tests the hypothesis that the X1 parameter is the same for both dependent variables.

The statement

```
MTEST Y1-Y2;
```

tests the hypothesis that all parameters except the intercept are the same for both dependent variables.

The statement

```
MTEST;
```

tests the hypothesis that all nonintercept parameters for all dependent variables are zero.

These options are available on the MTEST statement:

PRINT prints the **H** and **E** matrices.

CANPRINT prints the canonical correlations for the hypothesis combinations and the dependent variable combinations. If you specify

```
MTEST / CANPRINT;
```

the canonical correlations between the regressors and the dependent variables are printed. See CANCORR for a description of the statistics printed.

DETAILS prints the **M** matrix and various intermediate calculations.

BY Statement

BY *variables;*

A BY statement can be used with PROC REG to obtain separate analyses on observations in groups defined by the BY variables. When a BY statement appears, the procedure expects the input data set to be sorted in order of the BY variables. If your input data set is not sorted in ascending order, use the SORT procedure with a similar BY statement to sort the data, or, if appropriate, use the

BY statement options NOTSORTED or DESCENDING. For more information, see the discussion of the BY statement in "Statements Used in the PROC Step" in *SAS User's Guide: Basics.*

DETAILS

Missing Values

REG constructs only one crossproducts matrix for the variables in all regressions. If any variable needed for any regression is missing, the observation is excluded from all estimates.

Input Data Set

The input data set for most applications of PROC REG contains standard rectangular data, but special TYPE=CORR or TYPE=SSCP data sets can also be used. TYPE=CORR data sets created by PROC CORR contain means, standard deviations, and correlations. TYPE=SSCP data sets created in previous runs of PROC REG contain the sums of squares and crossproducts of the variables. See "SAS Files" in *SAS User's Guide: Basics* for more information on special SAS data sets.

Here is an example using PROC CORR. The fitness data for this analysis can be found in **Example 2** at the end of this chapter.

```
PROC CORR DATA=FITNESS OUTP=R;
   VAR  OXY RUNTIME AGE WEIGHT RUNPULSE MAXPULSE RSTPULSE;
PROC PRINT DATA=R;
PROC REG  DATA=R;
   MODEL OXY=RUNTIME AGE WEIGHT;
```

The data set containing the correlation matrix is printed by the PRINT procedure, as shown in **Output 31.2**.

Output 31.2 Output Created by PROC CORR

1

VARIABLE	N	MEAN	STD DEV	SUM	MINIMUM	MAXIMUM
OXY	31	47.37580645	5.32723050	1468.65000000	37.38800000	60.05500000
RUNTIME	31	10.58612903	1.38741409	328.17000000	8.17000000	14.03000000
AGE	31	47.67741935	5.21144316	1478.00000000	38.00000000	57.00000000
WEIGHT	31	77.44451613	8.32856764	2400.78000000	59.08000000	91.63000000
RUNPULSE	31	169.64516129	10.25198643	5259.00000000	146.00000000	186.00000000
MAXPULSE	31	173.77419355	9.16409544	5387.00000000	155.00000000	192.00000000
RSTPULSE	31	53.45161290	7.61944315	1657.00000000	40.00000000	70.00000000

PEARSON CORRELATION COEFFICIENTS / PROB > |R| UNDER H0:RHO=0 / N = 31

	OXY	RUNTIME	AGE	WEIGHT	RUNPULSE	MAXPULSE	RSTPULSE
OXY	1.00000	-0.86219	-0.30459	-0.16275	-0.39797	-0.23674	-0.39936
	0.0000	0.0001	0.0957	0.3817	0.0266	0.1997	0.0260
RUNTIME	-0.86219	1.00000	0.18875	0.14351	0.31365	0.22610	0.45038
	0.0001	0.0000	0.3092	0.4412	0.0858	0.2213	0.0110
AGE	-0.30459	0.18875	1.00000	-0.23354	-0.33787	-0.43292	-0.16410
	0.0957	0.3092	0.0000	0.2061	0.0630	0.0150	0.3777

(continued on next page)

(continued from previous page)

```
WEIGHT   -0.16275  0.14351 -0.23354  1.00000  0.18152  0.24938  0.04397
           0.3817   0.4412   0.2061   0.0000   0.3284   0.1761   0.8143

RUNPULSE -0.39797  0.31365 -0.33787  0.18152  1.00000  0.92975  0.35246
           0.0266   0.0858   0.0630   0.3284   0.0000   0.0001   0.0518

MAXPULSE -0.23674  0.22610 -0.43292  0.24938  0.92975  1.00000  0.30512
           0.1997   0.2213   0.0150   0.1761   0.0001   0.0000   0.0951

RSTPULSE -0.39936  0.45038 -0.16410  0.04397  0.35246  0.30512  1.00000
           0.0260   0.0110   0.3777   0.8143   0.0518   0.0951   0.0000
```

2

OBS	_TYPE_	_NAME_	OXY	RUNTIME	AGE	WEIGHT	RUNPULSE	MAXPULSE	RSTPULSE
1	MEAN		47.3758	10.5861	47.6774	77.4445	169.645	173.774	53.4516
2	STD		5.32723	1.38741	5.21144	8.32857	10.252	9.1641	7.61944
3	N		31	31	31	31	31	31	31
4	CORR	OXY	1	-.862195	-.304592	-.162753	-.397974	-0.23674	-.399356
5	CORR	RUNTIME	-.862195	1	0.188745	0.143508	0.313648	0.226103	0.450383
6	CORR	AGE	-.304592	0.188745	1	-.233539	-0.33787	-.432916	-0.1641
7	CORR	WEIGHT	-.162753	0.143508	-.233539	1	0.181516	0.249381	.0439742
8	CORR	RUNPULSE	-.397974	0.313648	-0.33787	0.181516	1	0.929754	0.352461
9	CORR	MAXPULSE	-0.23674	0.226103	-.432916	0.249381	0.929754	1	0.305124
10	CORR	RSTPULSE	-.399356	0.450383	-0.1641	.0439742	0.352461	0.305124	1

Output 31.3 Regression of Data Created by PROC CORR

```
                                                                                        1
DEP VARIABLE: OXY
                                   ANALYSIS OF VARIANCE

                               SUM OF         MEAN
          SOURCE     DF       SQUARES        SQUARE      F VALUE       PROB>F

          MODEL       3     656.27095     218.75698       30.272       0.0001
          ERROR      27     195.11060    7.22631835
          C TOTAL    30     851.38154

              ROOT MSE       2.688181      R-SQUARE       0.7708
              DEP MEAN       47.37581      ADJ R-SQ       0.7454
              C.V.           5.674165

                                   PARAMETER ESTIMATES

                           PARAMETER       STANDARD      T FOR H0:
          VARIABLE  DF      ESTIMATE          ERROR    PARAMETER=0     PROB > |T|

          INTERCEP   1   93.12615008     7.55915630         12.320         0.0001
          RUNTIME    1   -3.14038657     0.36737984         -8.548         0.0001
          AGE        1   -0.17387679     0.09954587         -1.747         0.0921
          WEIGHT     1   -0.05443652     0.06180913         -0.881         0.3862
```

The following is an example using the saved crossproducts matrix:

```
PROC REG DATA=FITNESS OUTSSCP=SSCP;
   MODEL OXY=RUNTIME AGE WEIGHT RUNPULSE MAXPULSE RSTPULSE;
PROC PRINT DATA=SSCP;
PROC REG DATA=SSCP;
   MODEL OXY=RUNTIME AGE WEIGHT;
```

The SSCP printout from PROC PRINT is shown in **Output 31.4**.

Output 31.4 Regression Using Saved SSCP Matrix

1

DEP VARIABLE: OXY

ANALYSIS OF VARIANCE

SOURCE	DF	SUM OF SQUARES	MEAN SQUARE	F VALUE	PROB>F
MODEL	6	722.54361	120.42393	22.433	0.0001
ERROR	24	128.83794	5.36824741		
C TOTAL	30	851.38154			

ROOT MSE	2.316948	R-SQUARE	0.8487
DEP MEAN	47.37581	ADJ R-SQ	0.8108
C.V.	4.890572		

PARAMETER ESTIMATES

VARIABLE	DF	PARAMETER ESTIMATE	STANDARD ERROR	T FOR H0: PARAMETER=0	PROB > |T|
INTERCEP	1	102.93448	12.40325810	8.299	0.0001
RUNTIME	1	-2.62865282	0.38456220	-6.835	0.0001
AGE	1	-0.22697380	0.09983747	-2.273	0.0322
WEIGHT	1	-0.07417741	0.05459316	-1.359	0.1869
RUNPULSE	1	-0.36962776	0.11985294	-3.084	0.0051
MAXPULSE	1	0.30321713	0.13649519	2.221	0.0360
RSTPULSE	1	-0.02153364	0.06605428	-0.326	0.7473

2

OBS	_NAME_	_TYPE_	INTERCEP	OXY	RUNTIME	AGE	WEIGHT	RUNPULSE	MAXPULSE	RSTPULSE
1	INTERCEP	SSCP	31.00	1469	328.2	1478	2401	5259	5387	1657
2	OXY	SSCP	1468.65	70430	15356.1	69768	113522	248497	254867	78015
3	RUNTIME	SSCP	328.17	15356	3531.8	15687	25465	55806	57114	17684
4	AGE	SSCP	1478.00	69768	15687.2	71282	114159	250194	256218	78806
5	WEIGHT	SSCP	2400.78	113522	25464.7	114159	188008	407746	417765	128409
6	RUNPULSE	SSCP	5259.00	248497	55806.3	250194	407746	895317	916499	281928
7	MAXPULSE	SSCP	5387.00	254867	57113.7	256218	417765	916499	938641	288583
8	RSTPULSE	SSCP	1657.00	78015	17684.0	78806	128409	281928	288583	90311
9		N	31.00	31	31.0	31	31	31	31	31

3

DEP VARIABLE: OXY

ANALYSIS OF VARIANCE

SOURCE	DF	SUM OF SQUARES	MEAN SQUARE	F VALUE	PROB>F
MODEL	3	656.27095	218.75698	30.272	0.0001
ERROR	27	195.11060	7.22631835		
C TOTAL	30	851.38154			

ROOT MSE	2.688181	R-SQUARE	0.7708
DEP MEAN	47.37581	ADJ R-SQ	0.7454
C.V.	5.674165		

PARAMETER ESTIMATES

VARIABLE	DF	PARAMETER ESTIMATE	STANDARD ERROR	T FOR H0: PARAMETER=0	PROB > |T|
INTERCEP	1	93.12615008	7.55915630	12.320	0.0001
RUNTIME	1	-3.14038657	0.36737984	-8.548	0.0001
AGE	1	-0.17387679	0.09954587	-1.747	0.0921
WEIGHT	1	-0.05443652	0.06180913	-0.881	0.3862

These summary files save CPU time. It takes nk^2 operations (n=number of observations, k=number of variables) to calculate crossproducts; the regressions are of the order k^3. When n is in the thousands and k in units, you can save 99% of the CPU time by reusing the SSCP matrix rather than recomputing it.

When special SAS data sets are used, REG must be informed by the data set TYPE parameter. PROC CORR and PROC REG automatically set the type for output data sets; however, if you create the data set by some other means, you have to specify its type with the data set option TYPE= and include an observation in the data set with the value of the _TYPE_ variable as *n*, the number of observations.

```
PROC REG DATA=A(TYPE=CORR);
```

When data sets of TYPE=CORR or TYPE=SSCP are used with REG, options that require predicted values or residuals have no effect. The OUTPUT statement and the MODEL options P, R, CLM, CLI, DW, INFLUENCE, and PARTIAL are disabled.

REG does not compute new values for regressors. For example, if you need a lagged variable, you should create it when you prepare the input data.

Parameter Estimates and Associated Statistics

The following example shows the parameter estimates using all optional features.

```
PROC REG DATA=FITNESS;
   MODEL OXY=RUNTIME AGE WEIGHT RUNPULSE MAXPULSE RSTPULSE
      / SS1 SS2 STB TOL VIF COVB CORRB;
```

For further discussion of the parameters and statistics, see "SAS Regression Procedures" and the **Printed Output** section.

Output 31.5 Regression Using All Options

1

DEP VARIABLE: OXY

ANALYSIS OF VARIANCE

SOURCE	DF	SUM OF SQUARES	MEAN SQUARE	F VALUE	PROB>F
MODEL	6	722.54361	120.42393	22.433	0.0001
ERROR	24	128.83794	5.36824741		
C TOTAL	30	851.38154			

ROOT MSE	2.316948	R-SQUARE	0.8487
DEP MEAN	47.37581	ADJ R-SQ	0.8108
C.V.	4.890572		

PARAMETER ESTIMATES

VARIABLE	DF	PARAMETER ESTIMATE	STANDARD ERROR	T FOR H0: PARAMETER=0	PROB > |T|	TYPE I SS	TYPE II SS	STANDARDIZED ESTIMATE	TOLERANCE
INTERCEP	1	102.93448	12.40325810	8.299	0.0001	69578.47815	369.72831	0	.
RUNTIME	1	-2.62865282	0.38456220	-6.835	0.0001	632.90010	250.82210	-0.68460149	0.62858771
AGE	1	-0.22697380	0.09983747	-2.273	0.0322	17.76563252	27.74577148	-0.22204052	0.66101010
WEIGHT	1	-0.07417741	0.05459316	-1.359	0.1869	5.60521700	9.91058836	-0.11596863	0.86555401
RUNPULSE	1	-0.36962776	0.11985294	-3.084	0.0051	38.87574195	51.05805832	-0.71132998	0.11852169
MAXPULSE	1	0.30321713	0.13649519	2.221	0.0360	26.82640270	26.49142405	0.52160512	0.11436612
RSTPULSE	1	-0.02153364	0.06605428	-0.326	0.7473	0.57051299	0.57051299	-0.03079918	0.70641990

VARIABLE	DF	VARIANCE INFLATION
INTERCEP	1	0
RUNTIME	1	1.59086788
AGE	1	1.51283618
WEIGHT	1	1.15532940
RUNPULSE	1	8.43727418
MAXPULSE	1	8.74384843
RSTPULSE	1	1.41558865

(continued on next page)

(continued from previous page)

COVARIANCE OF ESTIMATES

COVB	INTERCEP	RUNTIME	AGE	WEIGHT	RUNPULSE	MAXPULSE	RSTPULSE
INTERCEP	153.8408	0.7678374	-0.902049	-0.178238	0.2807965	-0.832762	-0.147955
RUNTIME	0.7678374	0.1478881	-0.0141917	-0.00441767	-0.00904778	0.00462495	-0.0109152
AGE	-0.902049	-0.0141917	0.009967521	0.00102191	-0.00120391	0.003582384	0.001489753
WEIGHT	-0.178238	-0.00441767	0.00102191	0.002980413	0.0009644683	-0.00137224	0.0003799295
RUNPULSE	0.2807965	-0.00904778	-0.00120391	0.0009644683	0.01436473	-0.0149525	-0.000764507
MAXPULSE	-0.832762	0.00462495	0.003582384	-0.00137224	-0.0149525	0.01863094	0.0003425724
RSTPULSE	-0.147955	-0.0109152	0.001489753	0.0003799295	-0.000764507	0.0003425724	0.004363167

2

CORRELATION OF ESTIMATES

CORRB	INTERCEP	RUNTIME	AGE	WEIGHT	RUNPULSE	MAXPULSE	RSTPULSE
INTERCEP	1.0000	0.1610	-0.7285	-0.2632	0.1889	-0.4919	-0.1806
RUNTIME	0.1610	1.0000	-0.3696	-0.2104	-0.1963	0.0881	-0.4297
AGE	-0.7285	-0.3696	1.0000	0.1875	-0.1006	0.2629	0.2259
WEIGHT	-0.2632	-0.2104	0.1875	1.0000	0.1474	-0.1842	0.1054
RUNPULSE	0.1889	-0.1963	-0.1006	0.1474	1.0000	-0.9140	-0.0966
MAXPULSE	-0.4919	0.0881	0.2629	-0.1842	-0.9140	1.0000	0.0380
RSTPULSE	-0.1806	-0.4297	0.2259	0.1054	-0.0966	0.0380	1.0000

If the model is not full rank, there are an infinite number of least-squares solutions for the estimates. REG chooses a nonzero solution for all variables that are linearly independent of previous variables and a zero solution for other variables. This solution corresponds to using a generalized inverse in the normal equations, and the expected values of the estimates are the HERMITE NORMAL FORM of **X** times the true parameters:

$$E(\mathbf{b}) = (\mathbf{X'X})^{-}(\mathbf{X'X})\beta \ .$$

Degrees of freedom for the zeroed estimates are reported as zero. The hypotheses that are not testable have *t* tests printed as missing. The message that the model is not full rank includes a printout of the relations that exist in the matrix.

In this example, we introduce another term DIF=RUNPULSE−RSTPULSE into the model to show how this problem is diagnosed.

```
DATA FIT2;
   SET FITNESS;
   DIF=RUNPULSE-RSTPULSE;
PROC REG DATA=FIT2;
   MODEL OXY=RUNTIME AGE WEIGHT RUNPULSE MAXPULSE RSTPULSE DIF;
```

Output 31.6 Model That is Not Full Rank: REG Procedure

```
                                                                                                            1
DEP VARIABLE: OXY
                                          ANALYSIS OF VARIANCE

                                   SUM OF          MEAN
                 SOURCE     DF    SQUARES        SQUARE      F VALUE       PROB>F

                 MODEL       6  722.54361     120.42393       22.433       0.0001
                 ERROR      24  128.83794    5.36824741
                 C TOTAL    30  851.38154

                    ROOT MSE     2.316948      R-SQUARE       0.8487
                    DEP MEAN     47.37581      ADJ R-SQ       0.8108
                    C.V.         4.890572

NOTE: MODEL IS NOT FULL RANK. LEAST SQUARES SOLUTIONS FOR THE
      PARAMETERS ARE NOT UNIQUE. SOME STATISTICS WILL BE
      MISLEADING. A REPORTED DF OF 0 OR B MEANS THAT THE
      ESTIMATE IS BIASED. THE FOLLOWING PARAMETERS HAVE BEEN
      SET TO 0, SINCE THE VARIABLES ARE A LINEAR COMBINATION
      OF OTHER VARIABLES AS SHOWN.
DIF        =+1*RUNPULSE-1*RSTPULSE

                                          PARAMETER ESTIMATES

                              PARAMETER        STANDARD      T FOR H0:
             VARIABLE  DF      ESTIMATE           ERROR    PARAMETER=0     PROB > |T|

             INTERCEP   1     102.93448     12.40325810          8.299         0.0001
             RUNTIME    1   -2.62865282      0.38456220         -6.835         0.0001
             AGE        1   -0.22697380      0.09983747         -2.273         0.0322
             WEIGHT     1   -0.07417741      0.05459316         -1.359         0.1869
             RUNPULSE   B   -0.36962776      0.11985294         -3.084         0.0051
             MAXPULSE   1    0.30321713      0.13649519          2.221         0.0360
             RSTPULSE   B   -0.02153364      0.06605428         -0.326         0.7473
             DIF        0             0               .              .              .
```

Collinearity Diagnostics

When a regressor is nearly a linear combination of other regressors in the model, the affected estimates are unstable and have high standard errors. This problem is called *collinearity* or *multicollinearity*. It is a good idea to find out which variables are nearly collinear with which other variables. The approach in PROC REG follows that of Belsley, Kuh, and Welsch (1980).

The COLLIN option in the MODEL statement requests that a collinearity analysis be done. First, **X'X** is scaled to have 1s on the diagonal. If COLLINOINT is specified, the intercept variable is adjusted out first. Then the eigenvalues and eigenvectors are extracted. The analysis in REG is reported with eigenvalues of **X'X** rather than singular values of **X**. The eigenvalues of **X'X** are the squares of the singular values of **X**.

The condition indices are the square roots of the ratio of the largest eigenvalue to each individual eigenvalue. The largest condition index is the condition number of the scaled **X** matrix. When this number is large, the problem is said to be ill-conditioned. When this number is extremely large, the estimates may have a fair amount of numerical error (although the statistical standard error almost always is much greater than the numerical error).

For each variable, REG prints the proportion of the variance of the estimate accounted for by each principal component. A collinearity problem occurs when a component associated with a high condition index contributes strongly to the variance of two or more variables.

Here is an example using the COLLIN option on the fitness data found in **Example 2**:

```
PROC REG DATA=FITNESS;
   MODEL OXY=RUNTIME AGE WEIGHT RUNPULSE MAXPULSE RSTPULSE
      / TOL VIF COLLIN;
```

Output 31.7 Regression Using TOL, VIF, and COLLIN Options

```
                                                                                                    1
DEP VARIABLE: OXY
                                           ANALYSIS OF VARIANCE

                                  SUM OF           MEAN
              SOURCE     DF      SQUARES         SQUARE       F VALUE        PROB>F

              MODEL       6    722.54361      120.42393        22.433        0.0001
              ERROR      24    128.83794     5.36824741
              C TOTAL    30    851.38154

                 ROOT MSE      2.316948      R-SQUARE        0.8487
                 DEP MEAN      47.37581      ADJ R-SQ        0.8108
                 C.V.          4.890572

                                           PARAMETER ESTIMATES

                   PARAMETER        STANDARD      T FOR H0:                                     VARIANCE
 VARIABLE  DF       ESTIMATE           ERROR    PARAMETER=0     PROB > |T|      TOLERANCE      INFLATION

 INTERCEP   1      102.93448     12.40325810          8.299         0.0001              .              0
 RUNTIME    1    -2.62865282      0.38456220         -6.835         0.0001     0.62858771     1.59086788
 AGE        1    -0.22697380      0.09983747         -2.273         0.0322     0.66101010     1.51283618
 WEIGHT     1    -0.07417741      0.05459316         -1.359         0.1869     0.86555401     1.15532940
 RUNPULSE   1    -0.36962776      0.11985294         -3.084         0.0051     0.11852169     8.43727418
 MAXPULSE   1     0.30321713      0.13649519          2.221         0.0360     0.11436612     8.74384843
 RSTPULSE   1    -0.02153364      0.06605428         -0.326         0.7473     0.70641990     1.41558865

                                        COLLINEARITY DIAGNOSTICS

                            CONDITION   VAR PROP   VAR PROP   VAR PROP   VAR PROP   VAR PROP   VAR PROP   VAR PROP
NUMBER      EIGENVALUE         NUMBER   INTERCEP   RUNTIME    AGE        WEIGHT     RUNPULSE   MAXPULSE   RSTPULSE

     1        6.949911       1.000000     0.0000     0.0002     0.0002     0.0002     0.0000     0.0000     0.0003
     2        0.018676      19.290870     0.0022     0.0252     0.1463     0.0104     0.0000     0.0000     0.3906
     3        0.015034      21.500719     0.0006     0.1286     0.1501     0.2357     0.0012     0.0012     0.0281
     4       0.0091095      27.621151     0.0064     0.6090     0.0319     0.1831     0.0015     0.0012     0.1903
     5       0.0060729      33.829179     0.0013     0.1250     0.1128     0.4444     0.0151     0.0083     0.3648
     6       0.0010177      82.637571     0.7997     0.0975     0.4966     0.1033     0.0695     0.0056     0.0203
     7       0.0001795        196.786     0.1898     0.0146     0.0621     0.0228     0.9128     0.9836     0.0057
```

Predicted Values and Residuals

The printout of the predicted values and residuals is controlled by the P, R, CLM, and CLI options. The P option causes REG to print out the observation number, the ID value (if an ID statement is used), the actual value, the predicted value, and the residual. The R, CLI, and CLM options also produce the items under the P option. Thus, P is unnecessary if you use one of the other options.

The R option requests more detail, especially about the residuals. The standard errors of the predicted value and the residual are printed. The studentized residual, which is the residual divided by its standard error, is both printed and plotted. A measure of influence, Cook's D, is printed. Cook's D measures the change to the estimates that results from deleting each observation. See Cook (1977, 1979). (This statistic is very similar to DFFITS.)

The CLM option requests that REG print the 95% lower and upper confidence limits for the predicted values. This accounts for the variation due to estimating the parameters only. If you want a 95% confidence interval for observed values, then you would use the CLI option, which adds in the variability of the error term.

Here is an example using U.S. population data found in **Example 1** below:

```
PROC REG DATA=USPOP;
   ID YEAR;
   MODEL POP=YEAR YEARSQ / P R CLI CLM;
   OUTPUT OUT=C P=PRED L95=L95 U95=U95 R=RESID COOKD=COOKD;
PROC PLOT DATA=C;
   PLOT POP*YEAR='A' PRED*YEAR='P' U95*YEAR='U' L95*YEAR='L'
      / OVERLAY VPOS=32 HPOS=80;
   PLOT RESID*YEAR / VREF=0 VPOS=18 HPOS=60;
   PLOT COOKD*YEAR / VREF=0 VPOS=18 HPOS=60;
```

Output 31.8 Regression Using P, R, CLI, and CLM Options

1

DEP VARIABLE: POP

ANALYSIS OF VARIANCE

SOURCE	DF	SUM OF SQUARES	MEAN SQUARE	F VALUE	PROB>F
MODEL	2	71799.01619	35899.50810	4641.719	0.0001
ERROR	16	123.74556	7.73409771		
C TOTAL	18	71922.76175			

ROOT MSE	2.781025	R-SQUARE	0.9983
DEP MEAN	69.76747	ADJ R-SQ	0.9981
C.V.	3.986133		

PARAMETER ESTIMATES

VARIABLE	DF	PARAMETER ESTIMATE	STANDARD ERROR	T FOR H0: PARAMETER=0	PROB > |T|
INTERCEP	1	20450.43359	843.47532	24.245	0.0001
YEAR	1	-22.78060612	0.89784903	-25.372	0.0001
YEARSQ	1	0.006345585	0.000238770	26.576	0.0001

OBS	ID	ACTUAL	PREDICT VALUE	STD ERR PREDICT	LOWER95% MEAN	UPPER95% MEAN	LOWER95% PREDICT	UPPER95% PREDICT	RESIDUAL	STD ERR RESIDUAL
1	1790	3.9290	5.0384	1.7289	1.3734	8.7035	-1.9034	11.9803	-1.1094	2.1783
2	1800	5.3080	5.0389	1.3909	2.0904	7.9874	-1.5528	11.6306	0.2691	2.4082
3	1810	7.2390	6.3085	1.1304	3.9122	8.7047	-0.0554	12.6723	0.9305	2.5409
4	1820	9.6380	8.8472	0.9571	6.8182	10.8761	2.6123	15.0820	0.7908	2.6111
5	1830	12.8660	12.6550	0.8721	10.8062	14.5037	6.4764	18.8335	0.2110	2.6408
6	1840	17.0690	17.7319	0.8578	15.9133	19.5504	11.5623	23.9015	-0.6629	2.6454
7	1850	23.1910	24.0779	0.8835	22.2050	25.9509	17.8921	30.2637	-0.8869	2.6369
8	1860	31.4430	31.6931	0.9202	29.7424	33.6437	25.4832	37.9029	-0.2501	2.6244
9	1870	39.8180	40.5773	0.9487	38.5661	42.5885	34.3482	46.8064	-0.7593	2.6142
10	1880	50.1550	50.7307	0.9592	48.6972	52.7642	44.4944	56.9670	-0.5757	2.6104
11	1890	62.9470	62.1532	0.9487	60.1420	64.1644	55.9241	68.3823	0.7938	2.6142
12	1900	75.9940	74.8448	0.9202	72.8942	76.7955	68.6350	81.0547	1.1492	2.6244
13	1910	91.9720	88.8056	0.8835	86.9326	90.6785	82.6197	94.9914	3.1664	2.6369
14	1920	105.7	104.0	0.8578	102.2	105.9	97.8659	110.2	1.6746	2.6454
15	1930	122.8	120.5	0.8721	118.7	122.4	114.4	126.7	2.2406	2.6408
16	1940	131.7	138.3	0.9571	136.3	140.3	132.1	144.5	-6.6335	2.6111
17	1950	151.3	157.3	1.1304	154.9	159.7	151.0	163.7	-6.0147	2.5409
18	1960	179.3	177.6	1.3909	174.7	180.6	171.1	184.2	1.6770	2.4082
19	1970	203.2	199.2	1.7289	195.6	202.9	192.3	206.2	3.9895	2.1783
20	1980	.	222.1	2.1348	217.5	226.6	214.6	229.5	.	.
21	1990	.	246.2	2.6019	240.7	251.7	238.1	254.3	.	.
22	2000	.	271.6	3.1257	264.9	278.2	262.7	280.4	.	.

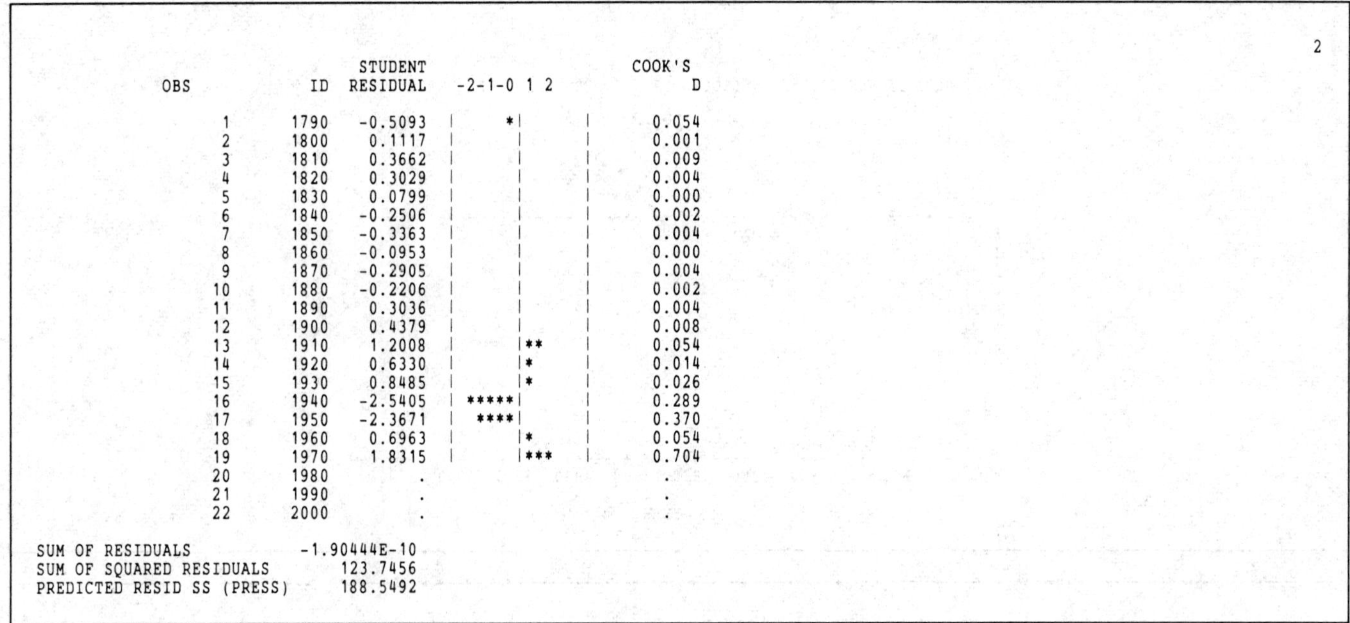

2

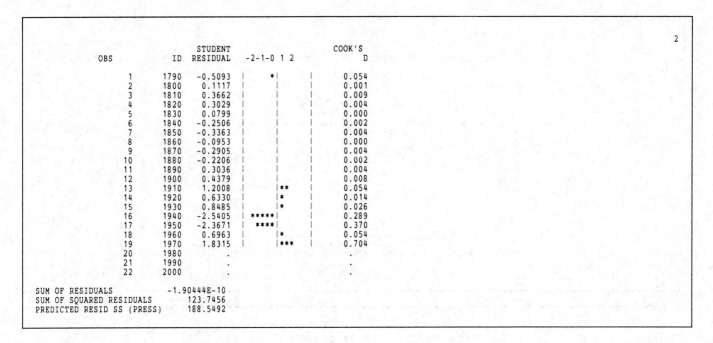

OBS	ID	STUDENT RESIDUAL	-2-1-0 1 2	COOK'S D
1	1790	-0.5093	| *| |	0.054
2	1800	0.1117	| | |	0.001
3	1810	0.3662	| | |	0.009
4	1820	0.3029	| | |	0.004
5	1830	0.0799	| | |	0.000
6	1840	-0.2506	| | |	0.002
7	1850	-0.3363	| | |	0.004
8	1860	-0.0953	| | |	0.000
9	1870	-0.2905	| | |	0.004
10	1880	-0.2206	| | |	0.002
11	1890	0.3036	| | |	0.004
12	1900	0.4379	| | |	0.008
13	1910	1.2008	| |** |	0.054
14	1920	0.6330	| |* |	0.014
15	1930	0.8485	| |* |	0.026
16	1940	-2.5405	| *****| |	0.289
17	1950	-2.3671	| ****| |	0.370
18	1960	0.6963	| |* |	0.054
19	1970	1.8315	| |*** |	0.704
20	1980	.		.
21	1990	.		.
22	2000	.		.

SUM OF RESIDUALS -1.90444E-10
SUM OF SQUARED RESIDUALS 123.7456
PREDICTED RESID SS (PRESS) 188.5492

Output 31.9 Plots of Population Data: PLOT Procedure

```
                                                                                      1
                          PLOT OF POP*YEAR      SYMBOL USED IS A
                          PLOT OF PRED*YEAR     SYMBOL USED IS P
                          PLOT OF U95*YEAR      SYMBOL USED IS U
                          PLOT OF L95*YEAR      SYMBOL USED IS L

       |
       |
       |
   210 +
       |                                                                           R
       |                                                                           L
       |                                                                       U
   180 +                                                                       R
P      |                                                                       L
R      |                                                                   U
E      |                                                                   P
D  150 +                                                                   R
I      |                                                               U
C      |                                                               R
T      |                                                           U
E  120 +                                                           R
D      |                                                       U   L
       |                                                       R
V      |                                                   U   L
A   90 +                                                   R
L      |                                               U   L
U      |                                               R
E      |                                           U   L
    60 +                                       U   R
       |                                       R   L
       |                                   U   L
       |                               U   R
    30 +                           U   R
       |                   U   U   R   L
       |   U   U   U   U   R   R   L
       |   R   R   R   R   L
     0 +   L   L   L   L
       ---+-------+-------+-------+-------+-------+-------+-------+-------+-------+---
        1790    1810    1830    1850    1870    1890    1910    1930    1950    1970

                                         YEAR
```

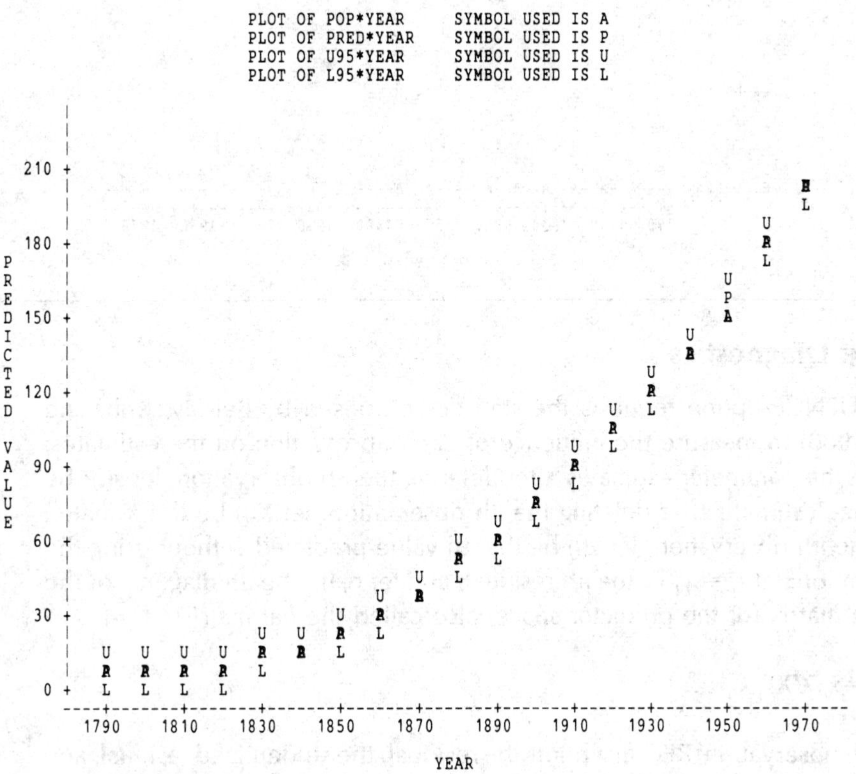

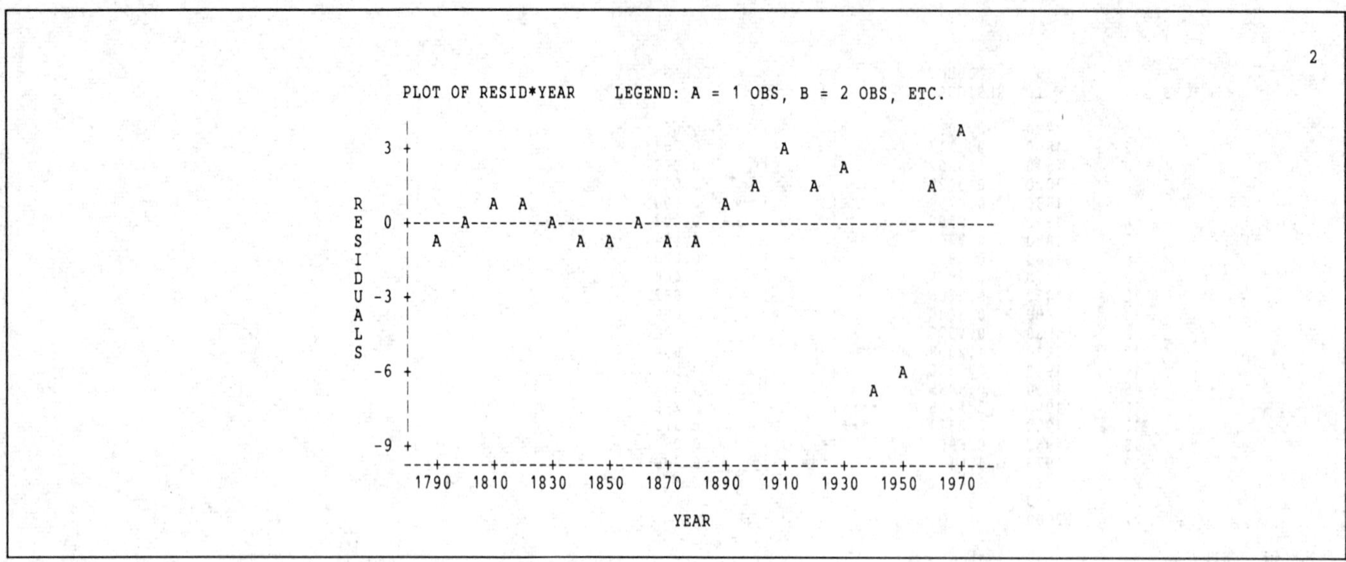

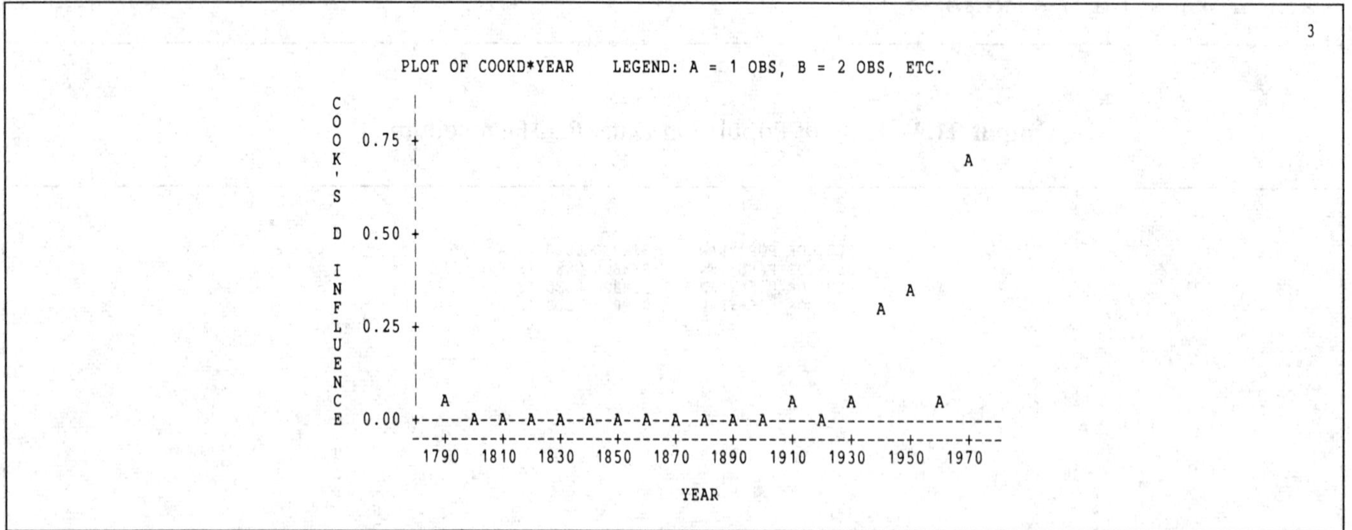

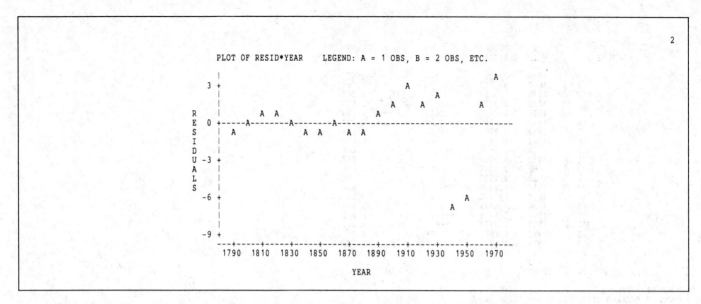

Influence Diagnostics

The INFLUENCE option requests the statistics proposed by Belsley, Kuh, and Welsch (1980) to measure the influence of each observation on the estimates. Let **b**(i) be the parameter estimates after deleting the ith observation; let $s(i)^2$ be the variance estimate after deleting the ith observation; let **X**(i) be the **X** matrix without the ith observation; let $\hat{y}(i)$ be the ith value predicted without using the ith observation; let $r_i = y_i - \hat{y}_i$, the ith residual; and let $\mathbf{h}_i$ be the ith diagonal of the projection matrix for the predictor space, also called the *hat matrix*:

$$\mathbf{h}_i = \mathbf{x}_i(\mathbf{X}'\mathbf{X})^{-1}\mathbf{x}'_i \quad .$$

For each observation, REG first prints the residual, the studentized residual, and the $\mathbf{h}_i$. The studentized residual differs slightly from that in the previous section since the error variance is estimated by $\mathbf{s}(i)^2$ without the ith observation, not by $\mathbf{s}^2$:

$$\text{RSTUDENT} = \mathbf{r}_i / (\mathbf{s}(i)\sqrt{(1-\mathbf{h}_i)}) \quad .$$

The COVRATIO statistic measures the change in the determinant of the covariance matrix of the estimates by deleting the ith observation:

$$\text{COVRATIO} = \det(\mathbf{s}^2(i)(\mathbf{X}(i)'\mathbf{X}(i))^{-1})/\det(\mathbf{s}^2(\mathbf{X}'\mathbf{X})^{-1}) \quad .$$

The DFFITS statistic is a scaled measure of the change in the predicted value for the ith observation and is calculated by deleting the ith observation. A large value indicates that the observation is very influential in its neighborhood of the **X** space.

$$\text{DFFITS} = (\hat{y}_i - \hat{y}(i))/(\mathbf{s}(i)\sqrt{(\mathbf{h}(i))}) \quad .$$

DFFITS is very similar to Cook's D, defined in the previous section.

DFBETAS are the scaled measures of the change in each parameter estimate and are calculated by deleting the ith observation:

$$\text{DFBETAS}_j = (b_j - b_j(i))/(s(i)\sqrt{((X'X)^{jj})})$$

where

$$(\mathbf{X'X})^{jj} \text{ is the } (j,j)\text{th element of } (\mathbf{X'X})^{-1} \quad .$$

Output 31.10 is produced when the INFLUENCE option is used with the population example:

```
PROC REG DATA=USPOP;
   MODEL POP=YEAR YEARSQ / INFLUENCE;
```

Output 31.10 Regression Using INFLUENCE Option

```
                                                                                                1
DEP VARIABLE: POP
                                     ANALYSIS OF VARIANCE

                                SUM OF          MEAN
             SOURCE     DF     SQUARES        SQUARE        F VALUE      PROB>F

             MODEL       2  71799.01619   35899.50810      4641.719      0.0001
             ERROR      16    123.74556    7.73409771
             C TOTAL    18  71922.76175

                ROOT MSE     2.781025      R-SQUARE      0.9983
                DEP MEAN     69.76747      ADJ R-SQ      0.9981
                C.V.         3.986133

                                     PARAMETER ESTIMATES

                              PARAMETER        STANDARD       T FOR H0:
        VARIABLE  DF           ESTIMATE           ERROR     PARAMETER=0     PROB > |T|

        INTERCEP   1        20450.43359       843.47532          24.245         0.0001
        YEAR       1       -22.78060612      0.89784903         -25.372         0.0001
        YEARSQ     1        0.006345585     0.000238770          26.576         0.0001


                                        HAT DIAG       COV                  INTERCEP      YEAR       YEARSQ
 OBS        RESIDUAL     RSTUDENT            H        RATIO      DFFITS     DFBETAS     DFBETAS     DFBETAS

   1         -1.1094      -0.4972       0.3865       1.8834     -0.3946     -0.2842      0.2810     -0.2779
   2          0.2691       0.1082       0.2501       1.6147      0.0625      0.0376     -0.0370      0.0365
   3          0.9305       0.3561       0.1652       1.4176      0.1584      0.0666     -0.0651      0.0636
```

(continued on next page)

(continued from previous page)

4	0.7908	0.2941	0.1184	1.3531	0.1078	0.0182	-0.0172	0.0161
5	0.2110	0.0774	0.0983	1.3444	0.0256	-0.0030	0.0033	-0.0035
6	-0.6629	-0.2431	0.0951	1.3255	-0.0788	0.0296	-0.0302	0.0307
7	-0.8869	-0.3268	0.1009	1.3214	-0.1095	0.0609	-0.0616	0.0621
8	-0.2501	-0.0923	0.1095	1.3605	-0.0324	0.0216	-0.0217	0.0218
9	-0.7593	-0.2820	0.1164	1.3519	-0.1023	0.0743	-0.0745	0.0747
10	-0.5757	-0.2139	0.1190	1.3650	-0.0786	0.0586	-0.0587	0.0587
11	0.7938	0.2949	0.1164	1.3499	0.1070	-0.0784	0.0783	-0.0781
12	1.1492	0.4265	0.1095	1.3144	0.1496	-0.1018	0.1014	-0.1009
13	3.1664	1.2189	0.1009	1.0168	0.4084	-0.2357	0.2338	-0.2318
14	1.6746	0.6207	0.0951	1.2430	0.2013	-0.0811	0.0798	-0.0784
15	2.2406	0.8407	0.0983	1.1724	0.2776	-0.0427	0.0404	-0.0380
16	-6.6335	-3.1845	0.1184	0.2924	-1.1673	-0.1531	0.1636	-0.1747
17	-6.0147	-2.8433	0.1652	0.3989	-1.2649	-0.4843	0.4958	-0.5076
18	1.6770	0.6847	0.2501	1.4757	0.3954	0.2240	-0.2274	0.2308
19	3.9895	1.9947	0.3865	0.9766	1.5831	1.0902	-1.1025	1.1151
20	.	.	.	.	.	.	.	.
21	.	.	.	.	.	.	.	.
22	.	.	.	.	.	.	.	.

The PARTIAL option produces partial regression leverage plots. One plot is printed for each regressor. For a given regressor, the partial regression leverage plot is the plot of the dependent variable and the regressor after they have been made orthogonal to the other regressors in the model. These can be obtained by plotting the residuals of the dependent variable omitting the selected regressor against the residuals of the selected regressor on all the other regressors. A line fit to the points has a slope equal to the parameter estimate in the full model. In the plot, each observation is represented by a plus sign (+) or up to 8 characters of the ID value. For overlapping points, an asterisk (*) is printed. If the points go outside the plot, a greater than (>) or less than (<) sign is printed on the side. The following statements use the fitness data in **Example 2** with the PARTIAL option:

```
PROC REG DATA=FITNESS;
   MODEL OXY=RUNTIME WEIGHT AGE / PARTIAL;
```

Output 31.11 Regression Using PARTIAL Option

1

DEP VARIABLE: OXY

ANALYSIS OF VARIANCE

SOURCE	DF	SUM OF SQUARES	MEAN SQUARE	F VALUE	PROB>F
MODEL	3	656.27095	218.75698	30.272	0.0001
ERROR	27	195.11060	7.22631835		
C TOTAL	30	851.38154			

ROOT MSE	2.688181	R-SQUARE	0.7708
DEP MEAN	47.37581	ADJ R-SQ	0.7454
C.V.	5.674165		

PARAMETER ESTIMATES

VARIABLE	DF	PARAMETER ESTIMATE	STANDARD ERROR	T FOR H0: PARAMETER=0	PROB > |T|
INTERCEP	1	93.12615008	7.55915630	12.320	0.0001
RUNTIME	1	-3.14038657	0.36737984	-8.548	0.0001
WEIGHT	1	-0.05443652	0.06180913	-0.881	0.3862
AGE	1	-0.17387679	0.09954587	-1.747	0.0921

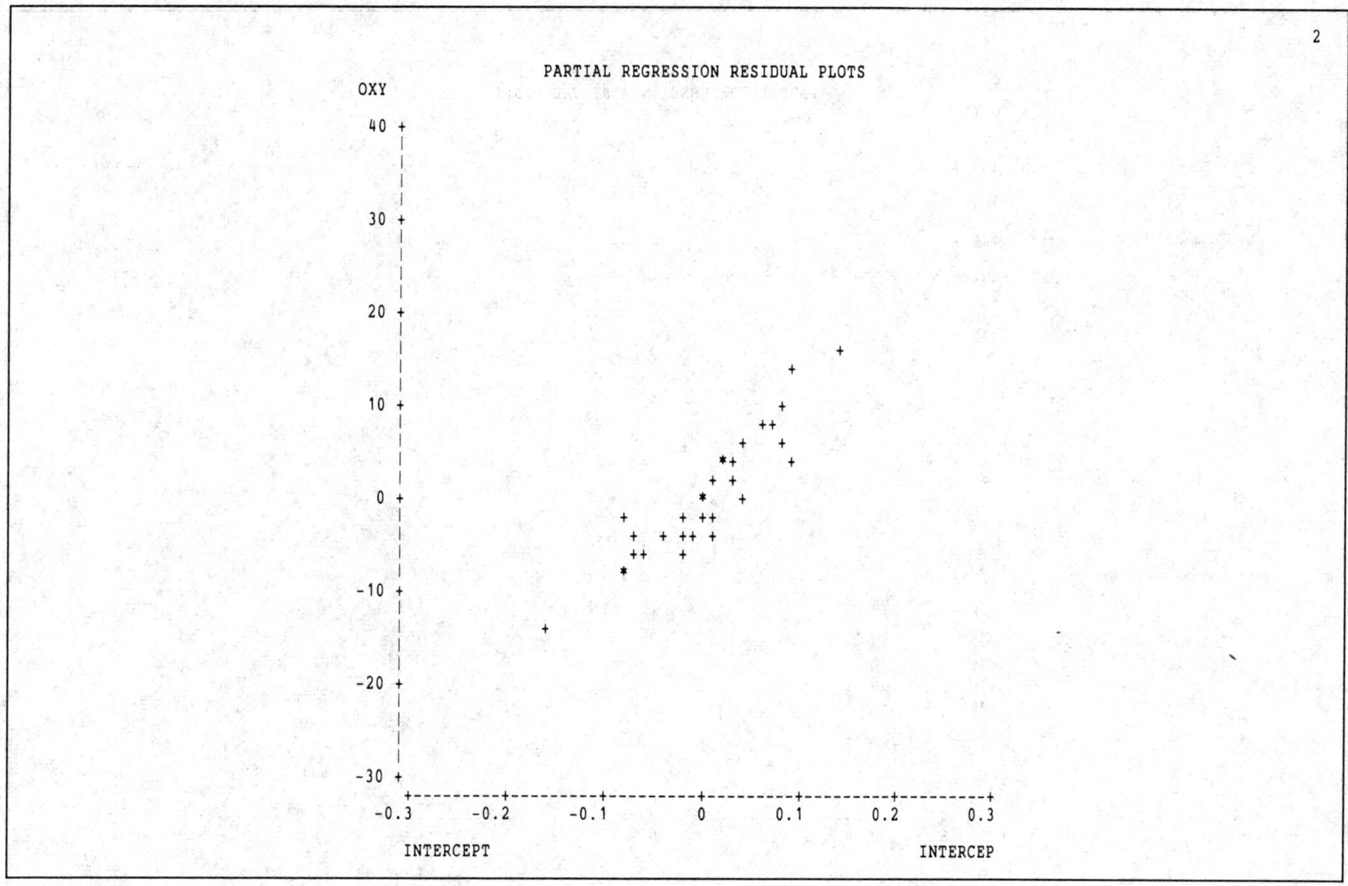
2
PARTIAL REGRESSION RESIDUAL PLOTS
OXY
40
30
20
10
0
-10
-20
-30
-0.3
-0.2
-0.1
0
0.1
0.2
0.3
INTERCEPT
INTERCEP

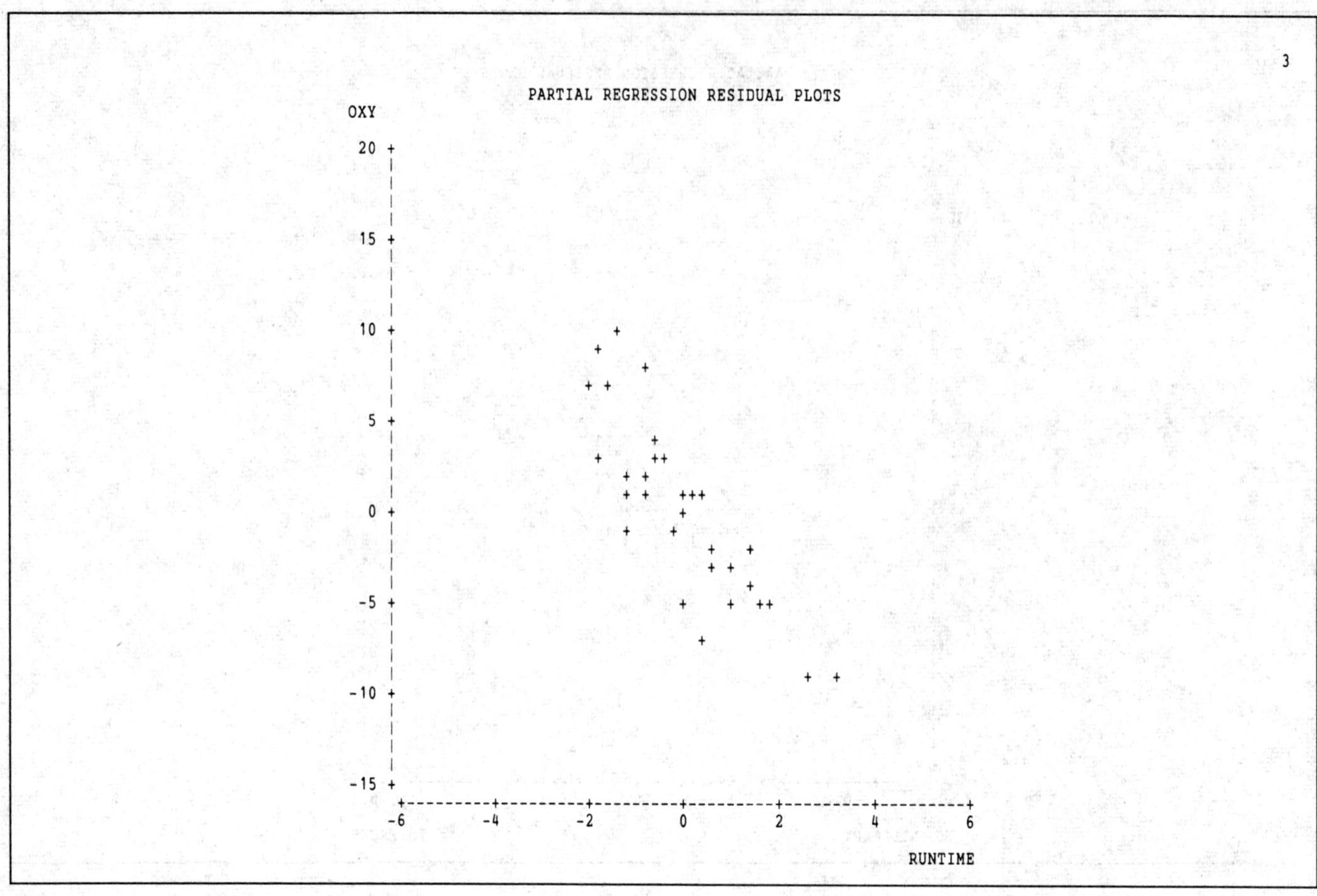
3
PARTIAL REGRESSION RESIDUAL PLOTS
OXY
20
15
10
5
0
-5
-10
-15
-6
-4
-2
0
2
4
6
RUNTIME

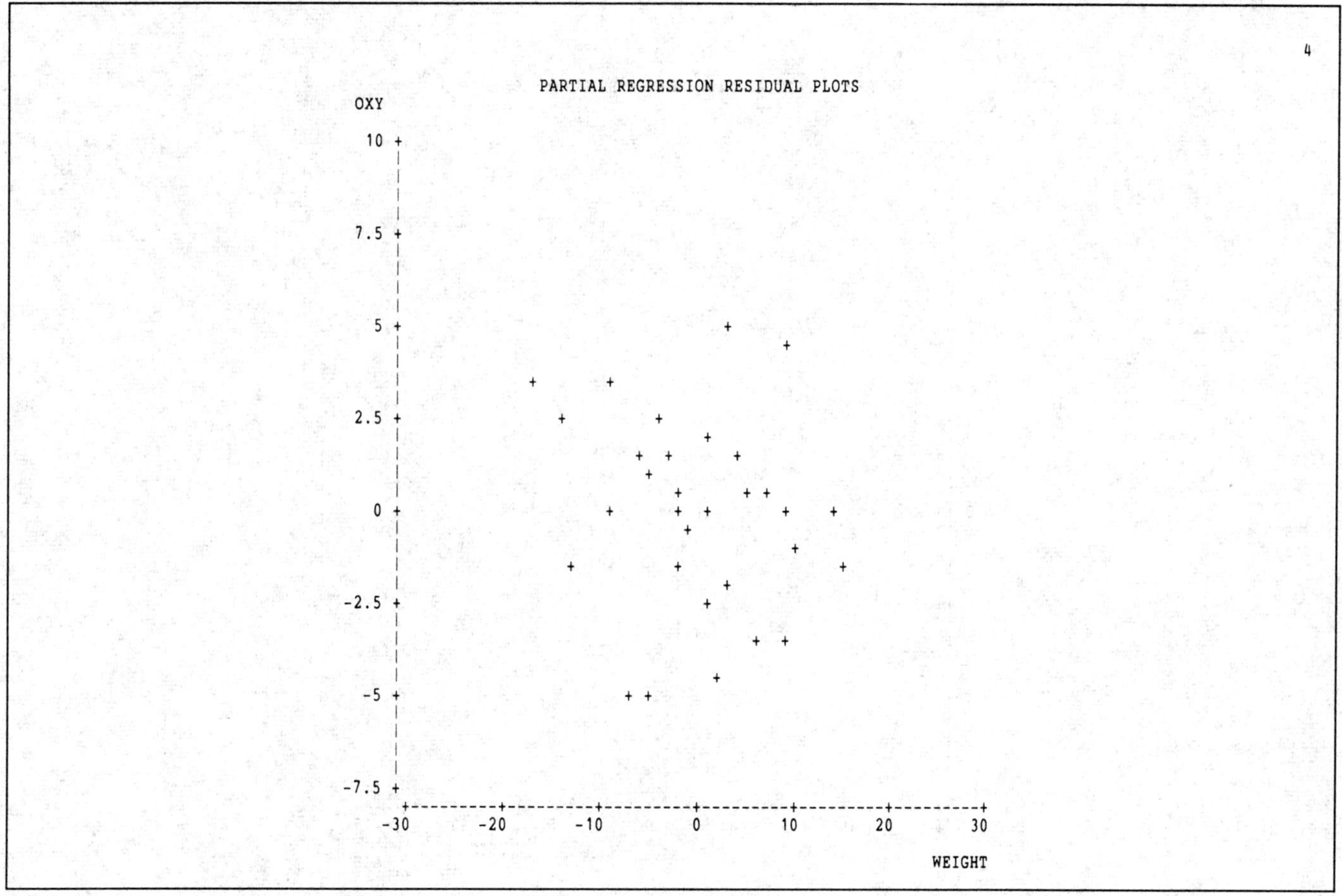
4
PARTIAL REGRESSION RESIDUAL PLOTS
OXY
10
7.5
5
2.5
0
-2.5
-5
-7.5
-30
-20
-10
0
10
20
30
WEIGHT

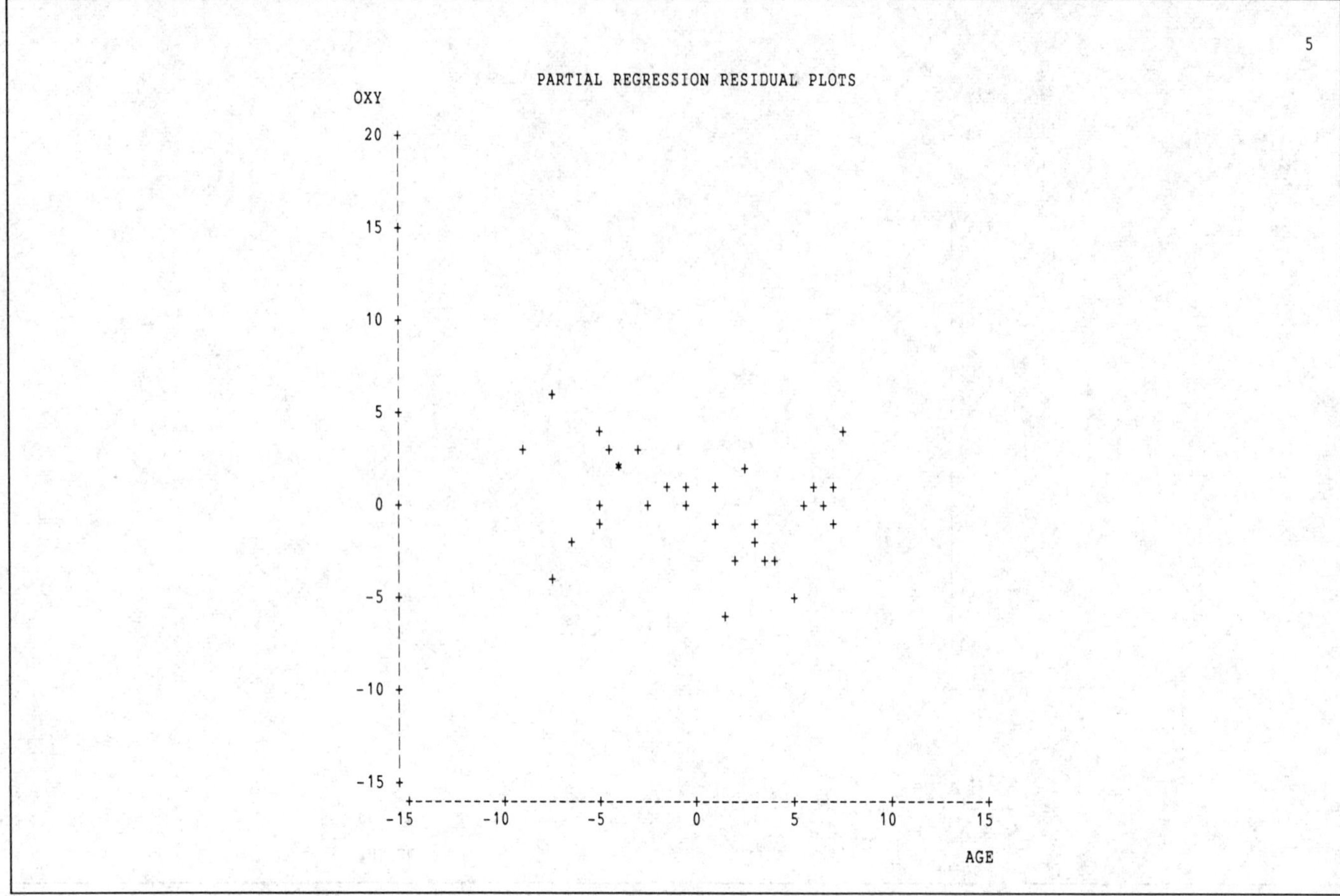

Model Specification Testing

The regression model is specified as $Y_i = X_i\beta + \varepsilon_i$, where ε_is are identically and independently distributed: $E(\varepsilon)=0$ and $E(\varepsilon'\varepsilon)=\sigma^2 I$. If the ε_i are not independent or their variances are not constant, the parameter estimates are unbiased, but the estimate of the covariance matrix is inconsistent. In the case of heteroskedasticity, the ACOV option provides a consistent estimate of the covariance matrix. If the regression data is from a simple random sample, the ACOV option produces the correct covariance matrix.

The SPEC option performs a test for heteroskedasticity. When the SPEC option has been specified, it performs test statements with both the usual covariance matrix and the heteroskedasticity consistent covariance matrix. Tests performed with the consistent covariance matrix are asymptotic. For more information see White (1980).

Autocorrelation in Time-Series Data

When regression is done on time-series data, the errors may not be independent. Often errors are autocorrelated; in other words, each error is correlated with the error immediately before it. Autocorrelation is also a symptom of systematic lack of fit. The DW option provides the Durbin-Watson *d* statistic to test that the autocorrelation is zero:

$$d = \Sigma_2^n (e_i - e_{i-1})^2 \;/\; \Sigma e_i^2 \;.$$

The value of *d* is close to 2 if the errors are uncorrelated. The distribution of *d* is reported by Durbin and Watson (1950, 1951). Tables of the distribution are found in most econometrics textbooks, such as Johnston (1972) and Pindyck and Rubinfeld (1976).

The sample autocorrelation estimate is shown after the Durbin-Watson statistic on the printout. The sample is computed as

$$r = \Sigma e_i e_{i-1} / \Sigma e_i^2 \quad .$$

This autocorrelation of the residuals may not be a very good estimate of the autocorrelation of the true errors, especially if there are few observations and the independent variables have certain patterns.

If there are missing observations in the regression, these measures cannot be computed strictly by the formula. When PROC REG encounters missing data, the statistics are calculated based on all adjacent nonmissing pairs of observations.

If autocorrelation is present, the residual error estimate is inflated, and tests on the parameters are less able to reject the null hypothesis. There are several better estimation methods available in this case. (Consult the *SAS/ETS User's Guide*.)

The following SAS statements request the DW option for the population data:

```
PROC REG DATA=USPOP;
   MODEL POP=YEAR YEARSQ / DW;
```

Output 31.12 Regression Using DW Option

```
                                                                                                    1
DEP VARIABLE: POP
                                              ANALYSIS OF VARIANCE

                                              SUM OF             MEAN
                         SOURCE      DF      SQUARES            SQUARE       F VALUE         PROB>F

                         MODEL        2  71799.01619    35899.50810         4641.719         0.0001
                         ERROR       16    123.74556     7.73409771
                         C TOTAL     18  71922.76175

                              ROOT MSE     2.781025      R-SQUARE         0.9983
                              DEP MEAN     69.76747      ADJ R-SQ         0.9981
                              C.V.         3.986133

                                              PARAMETER ESTIMATES

                                        PARAMETER        STANDARD      T FOR H0:
                    VARIABLE  DF         ESTIMATE           ERROR    PARAMETER=0       PROB > |T|

                    INTERCEP   1      20450.43359       843.47532         24.245           0.0001
                    YEAR       1     -22.78060612      0.89784903        -25.372           0.0001
                    YEARSQ     1      0.006345585     0.000238770         26.576           0.0001

DURBIN-WATSON D              1.264
(FOR NUMBER OF OBS.)            19
1ST ORDER AUTOCORRELATION    0.299
```

Multivariate Tests

The MTEST statement described above can test hypotheses involving several dependent variables in the form

$$(\mathbf{L}\beta - \mathbf{cj})\mathbf{M} = 0$$

where **L** is a linear function on the regressor side, β is a matrix of parameters, **c** is a column vector of constants, **j** is a row vector of ones, and **M** is a linear function on the dependent side. The special case where the constants are zero is

$$\mathbf{L\beta M} = 0 \ .$$

To test this hypothesis, REG constructs two matrices called **H** and **E** that correspond to the numerator and denominator of a univariate F test:

$$\mathbf{H} = \mathbf{M}'(\mathbf{LB}-\mathbf{cj})'(\mathbf{L}(\mathbf{X}'\mathbf{X})^{-}\mathbf{L}')^{-1}(\mathbf{LB}-\mathbf{cj})\mathbf{M}$$

$$\mathbf{E} = \mathbf{M}'(\mathbf{Y}'\mathbf{Y}-\mathbf{B}'(\mathbf{X}'\mathbf{X})\mathbf{B})\mathbf{M} \ .$$

These matrices are printed for each MTEST statement if the PRINT option is specified.

Four test statistics, based on the eigenvalues of $\mathbf{E}^{-1}\mathbf{H}$ or $(\mathbf{E}+\mathbf{H})^{-1}\mathbf{H}$, are formed. These are Wilks' Lambda, Pillai's Trace, the Hotelling-Lawley Trace, and Roy's maximum root. These are discussed in "SAS Regression Procedures."

Here is an example of a multivariate analysis of variance:

```
* MANOVA DATA FROM MORRISON'S MULTIVARIATE TEXT, 2ND EDITION, PAGE 190;
DATA A;
   INPUT SEX $ DRUG $ @;
   DO REP=1 TO 4;
   INPUT Y1 Y2 @;
   OUTPUT;
   END;
   CARDS;
M A  5  6  5  4  9  9  7  6
M B  7  6  7  7  9 12  6  8
M C 21 15 14 11 17 12 12 10
F A  7 10  6  6  9  7  8 10
F B 10 13  8  7  7  6  6  9
F C 16 12 14  9 14  8 10  5
;
DATA B;
   SET A;
   SEXCODE=(SEX='M')-(SEX='F');
   DRUG1=(DRUG='A')-(DRUG='C');
   DRUG2=(DRUG='B')-(DRUG='C');
   SEXDRUG1=SEXCODE*DRUG1;
   SEXDRUG2=SEXCODE*DRUG2;
PROC REG;
   MODEL Y1 Y2=SEXCODE DRUG1 DRUG2 SEXDRUG1 SEXDRUG2;
SEX:       MTEST SEXCODE;
DRUG:      MTEST DRUG1,DRUG2;
SEXDRUG:   MTEST SEXDRUG1,SEXDRUG2;
Y1MY2:     MTEST Y1-Y2;
Y1Y2DRUG:  MTEST Y1=Y2, DRUG1,DRUG2;
DRUGSHOW:  MTEST DRUG1, DRUG2 /PRINT CANPRINT;
```

Output 31.13 Multivariate Analysis of Variance: REG Procedure

```
                                                                                                    1
DEP VARIABLE: Y1
                                         ANALYSIS OF VARIANCE

                                         SUM OF          MEAN
                    SOURCE     DF       SQUARES        SQUARE        F VALUE        PROB>F

                    MODEL       5     316.00000   63.20000000         12.038        0.0001
                    ERROR      18   94.50000000    5.25000000
                    C TOTAL    23     410.50000

                       ROOT MSE        2.291288      R-SQUARE         0.7698
                       DEP MEAN            9.75      ADJ R-SQ         0.7058
                       C.V.            23.50039

                                         PARAMETER ESTIMATES

                                   PARAMETER        STANDARD       T FOR H0:
                 VARIABLE  DF       ESTIMATE           ERROR     PARAMETER=0        PROB > |T|

                 INTERCEP   1     9.75000000      0.46770717          20.846            0.0001
                 SEXCODE    1     0.16666667      0.46770717           0.356            0.7257
                 DRUG1      1    -2.75000000      0.66143783          -4.158            0.0006
                 DRUG2      1    -2.25000000      0.66143783          -3.402            0.0032
                 SEXDRUG1   1    -0.66666667      0.66143783          -1.008            0.3269
                 SEXDRUG2   1    -0.41666667      0.66143783          -0.630            0.5366
```

```
                                                                                                    2
DEP VARIABLE: Y2
                                         ANALYSIS OF VARIANCE

                                         SUM OF          MEAN
                    SOURCE     DF       SQUARES        SQUARE        F VALUE        PROB>F

                    MODEL       5   69.33333333   13.86666667          2.189        0.1008
                    ERROR      18     114.00000    6.33333333
                    C TOTAL    23     183.33333

                       ROOT MSE        2.516611      R-SQUARE         0.3782
                       DEP MEAN        8.666667      ADJ R-SQ         0.2055
                       C.V.            29.03782

                                         PARAMETER ESTIMATES

                                   PARAMETER        STANDARD       T FOR H0:
                 VARIABLE  DF       ESTIMATE           ERROR     PARAMETER=0        PROB > |T|

                 INTERCEP   1     8.66666667      0.51370117          16.871            0.0001
                 SEXCODE    1     0.16666667      0.51370117           0.324            0.7493
                 DRUG1      1    -1.41666667      0.72648316          -1.950            0.0669
                 DRUG2      1    -0.16666667      0.72648316          -0.229            0.8211
                 SEXDRUG1   1    -1.16666667      0.72648316          -1.606            0.1257
                 SEXDRUG2   1    -0.41666667      0.72648316          -0.574            0.5734
```

```
                                                                                                    3
MULTIVARIATE TEST: SEX


                          MULTIVARIATE TEST STATISTICS AND EXACT F STATISTICS
                                        S=1     M=0      N=8

          STATISTIC                          VALUE           F          NUM DF        DEN DF      PR > F

          WILKS' LAMBDA                  0.9925369       0.064               2            17      0.9383
          PILLAI'S TRACE               0.007463063       0.064               2            17      0.9383
          HOTELLING-LAWLEY TRACE       0.007519179       0.064               2            17      0.9383
          ROY'S GREATEST ROOT          0.007519179       0.064               2            17      0.9383
```

(continued on next page)

(continued from previous page)

MULTIVARIATE TEST: DRUG

MULTIVARIATE TEST STATISTICS AND F APPROXIMATIONS
S=2 M=-0.5 N=8

STATISTIC	VALUE	F	NUM DF	DEN DF	PR > F
WILKS' LAMBDA	0.1686295	12.199	4	34	0.0001
PILLAI'S TRACE	0.8803781	7.077	4	36	0.0003
HOTELLING-LAWLEY TRACE	4.639537	18.558	4	32	0.0001
ROY'S GREATEST ROOT	4.576027	41.184	2	18	0.0001

NOTE: F STATISTIC FOR ROY'S GREATEST ROOT IS AN UPPER BOUND
F STATISTIC FOR WILKS' LAMBDA IS EXACT

MULTIVARIATE TEST: SEXDRUG

MULTIVARIATE TEST STATISTICS AND F APPROXIMATIONS
S=2 M=-0.5 N=8

STATISTIC	VALUE	F	NUM DF	DEN DF	PR > F
WILKS' LAMBDA	0.7743623	1.159	4	34	0.3459
PILLAI'S TRACE	0.2269491	1.152	4	36	0.3481
HOTELLING-LAWLEY TRACE	0.2896916	1.159	4	32	0.3473
ROY'S GREATEST ROOT	0.2837227	2.554	2	18	0.1056

NOTE: F STATISTIC FOR ROY'S GREATEST ROOT IS AN UPPER BOUND
F STATISTIC FOR WILKS' LAMBDA IS EXACT

MULTIVARIATE TEST: Y1MY2

MULTIVARIATE TEST STATISTICS AND EXACT F STATISTICS
S=1 M=1.5 N=8.5

STATISTIC	VALUE	F	NUM DF	DEN DF	PR > F
WILKS' LAMBDA	0.2749794	9.492	5	18	0.0001
PILLAI'S TRACE	0.7250206	9.492	5	18	0.0001
HOTELLING-LAWLEY TRACE	2.636637	9.492	5	18	0.0001
ROY'S GREATEST ROOT	2.636637	9.492	5	18	0.0001

4

MULTIVARIATE TEST: Y1Y2DRUG

MULTIVARIATE TEST STATISTICS AND EXACT F STATISTICS
S=1 M=0 N=8.5

STATISTIC	VALUE	F	NUM DF	DEN DF	PR > F
WILKS' LAMBDA	0.2805392	23.081	2	18	0.0001
PILLAI'S TRACE	0.7194608	23.081	2	18	0.0001
HOTELLING-LAWLEY TRACE	2.564565	23.081	2	18	0.0001
ROY'S GREATEST ROOT	2.564565	23.081	2	18	0.0001

(continued on next page)

(continued from previous page)

```
MULTIVARIATE TEST: DRUGSHOW


                                          E, THE ERROR MATRIX


                                          94.5              76.5
                                          76.5               114


                                       H, THE HYPOTHESIS MATRIX


                                           301              97.5
                                          97.5          36.33333

                                                                    EIGENVALUES OF INV(E)*H
                       ADJUSTED      APPROX        SQUARED                    = CANRSQ/(1-CANRSQ)
         CANONICAL     CANONICAL     STANDARD      CANONICAL
         CORRELATION   CORRELATION   ERROR         CORRELATION  EIGENVALUE  DIFFERENCE  PROPORTION  CUMULATIVE

     1   0.905903      0.899927      0.040101      0.820661         4.5760      4.5125      0.9863      0.9863
     2   0.244371          .         0.210254      0.059717         0.0635         .        0.0137      1.0000

            TESTS OF H0: THE CANONICAL CORRELATION IN THE CURRENT ROW AND ALL THAT FOLLOW ARE ZERO

                               LIKELIHOOD
                                  RATIO          F        NUM DF     DEN DF  PR > F

                             1  0.16862952    12.1991         4         34  0.0001
                             2  0.94028273     1.1432         1         18  0.2991
```

```
                                                                                                      5

                                             EIGENVECTORS


                                           0.06261          -0.03258
                                          -0.03510           0.11177


                             MULTIVARIATE TEST STATISTICS AND F APPROXIMATIONS
                                          S=2    M=-0.5     N=8

         STATISTIC                        VALUE          F          NUM DF       DEN DF       PR > F

         WILKS' LAMBDA                 0.1686295      12.199           4           34         0.0001
         PILLAI'S TRACE                0.8803781       7.077           4           36         0.0003
         HOTELLING-LAWLEY TRACE         4.639537      18.558           4           32         0.0001
         ROY'S GREATEST ROOT            4.576027      41.184           2           18         0.0001

                       NOTE: F STATISTIC FOR ROY'S GREATEST ROOT IS AN UPPER BOUND
                             F STATISTIC FOR WILKS' LAMBDA IS EXACT
```

Output Data Sets

Estimates The OUTEST= specification produces a TYPE=EST output SAS data set containing estimates from the regression models. For each BY group on each dependent variable occurring in each MODEL statement, REG outputs an observation to the OUTEST= data set. The parameter estimates are stored under the names of the variables associated with the estimates. A special variable, INTERCEP, is created for the intercept parameter. The dependent variable is coded as −1. Variables not in the model are coded missing. A special variable, _SIGMA_, stores the root mean squared error, the estimate of the standard deviation of the error term. The name of the dependent variable is stored in a special variable, _DEPVAR_. If the model is identified with a label, the label is stored in a special variable, _MODEL_, for the observation containing the parameter estimates. If the COVOUT option is used, the covariance matrix of the estimates is output after the estimates; the names of the rows are identified by a special variable, _MODEL_.

Here is an example with a printout of the OUTEST= data set:

```
PROC REG DATA=USPOP OUTEST=EST;
M1:  MODEL POP=YEAR;
M2:  MODEL POP=YEAR YEARSQ;
PROC PRINT DATA=EST;
```

Output 31.14 Regression with Printout of OUTEST= Data Set

```
                                                                                      1
MODEL: M1
DEP VARIABLE: POP
                              ANALYSIS OF VARIANCE

                              SUM OF          MEAN
          SOURCE      DF     SQUARES        SQUARE      F VALUE      PROB>F

          MODEL        1  66336.46923  66336.46923      201.873      0.0001
          ERROR       17   5586.29253    328.60544
          C TOTAL     18  71922.76175

             ROOT MSE       18.12748      R-SQUARE       0.9223
             DEP MEAN       69.76747      ADJ R-SQ       0.9178
             C.V.           25.98271

                              PARAMETER ESTIMATES

                         PARAMETER        STANDARD      T FOR H0:
      VARIABLE  DF        ESTIMATE           ERROR    PARAMETER=0    PROB > |T|

      INTERCEP   1     -1958.36630       142.80455        -13.714        0.0001
      YEAR       1      1.07879456      0.07592765         14.208        0.0001
```

```
                                                                                      2
MODEL: M2
DEP VARIABLE: POP
                              ANALYSIS OF VARIANCE

                              SUM OF          MEAN
          SOURCE      DF     SQUARES        SQUARE      F VALUE      PROB>F

          MODEL        2  71799.01619  35899.50810     4641.719      0.0001
          ERROR       16    123.74556   7.73409771
          C TOTAL     18  71922.76175

             ROOT MSE       2.781025      R-SQUARE       0.9983
             DEP MEAN       69.76747      ADJ R-SQ       0.9981
             C.V.           3.986133

                              PARAMETER ESTIMATES

                         PARAMETER        STANDARD      T FOR H0:
      VARIABLE  DF        ESTIMATE           ERROR    PARAMETER=0    PROB > |T|

      INTERCEP   1     20450.43359       843.47532         24.245        0.0001
      YEAR       1    -22.78060612      0.89784903        -25.372        0.0001
      YEARSQ     1     0.006345585     0.000238770         26.576        0.0001
```

```
                                                                                      3

 OBS  _TYPE_  _MODEL_  _DEPVAR_  _SIGMA_  POP     YEAR      YEARSQ    INTERCEP

  1    OLS      M1       POP     18.1275   -1    1.079          .       -1958.4
  2    OLS      M2       POP      2.7810   -1  -22.781   0.00634559    20450.4
```

Sums of squares and crossproducts The OUTSSCP= option produces a TYPE=SSCP output SAS data set containing sums of squares and crossproducts.

A special row (observation) and column (variable) of the matrix called INTERCEP contain the number of observations and sums. Observations are identified by the 8-byte character variable, _NAME_. The data set contains all variables used in MODEL statements. You specify additional variables that you want included in the crossproducts matrix with a VAR statement.

The SSCP data set is used when a large number of observations are explored in many different runs. The SSCP data set can be saved and used for subsequent runs, which are much less expensive since REG never reads the original data again. In the step that creates the SSCP data set, you should include in the regression all the variables that you need.

Here is an example of the OUTSSCP= option used with the exercise data:

```
PROC REG DATA=FITNESS OUTSSCP=SSCP;
   VAR OXY RUNTIME AGE WEIGHT RSTPULSE RUNPULSE MAXPULSE;
PROC PRINT DATA=SSCP;
```

Output 31.15 SSCP Data Set Created with OUTSSCP= Option: REG Procedure

1

OBS	_NAME_	_TYPE_	INTERCEP	OXY	RUNTIME	AGE	WEIGHT	RSTPULSE	RUNPULSE	MAXPULSE
1	INTERCEP	SSCP	31.00	1469	328.2	1478	2401	1657	5259	5387
2	OXY	SSCP	1468.65	70430	15356.1	69768	113522	78015	248497	254867
3	RUNTIME	SSCP	328.17	15356	3531.8	15687	25465	17684	55806	57114
4	AGE	SSCP	1478.00	69768	15687.2	71282	114159	78806	250194	256218
5	WEIGHT	SSCP	2400.78	113522	25464.7	114159	188008	128409	407746	417765
6	RSTPULSE	SSCP	1657.00	78015	17684.0	78806	128409	90311	281928	288583
7	RUNPULSE	SSCP	5259.00	248497	55806.3	250194	407746	281928	895317	916499
8	MAXPULSE	SSCP	5387.00	254867	57113.7	256218	417765	288583	916499	938641
9		N	31.00	31	31.0	31	31	31	31	31

Computational Methods

The REG procedure first composes a crossproducts matrix. The matrix can be calculated from input data, reformed from an input correlation matrix, or read in from an SSCP data set. For each model, the procedure selects the appropriate crossproducts from the main matrix. The normal equations formed from the crossproducts are solved using a sweep algorithm (Goodnight 1979). The method is accurate for data that are reasonably scaled and not too collinear.

The mechanism PROC REG uses to check for singularity involves the diagonal (pivot) elements of **X′X** as it is being swept. If a pivot is less than SINGULAR*CSS, then a singularity is declared, and the pivot is not swept (where CSS is the corrected sum of squares for the regressor, and SINGULAR is 1E-8 or reset in the PROC statement).

Computer Resources

The REG procedure is efficient for ordinary regression; however, requests for optional features can multiply the costs several times.

The major computational expense is the collection of the crossproducts matrix. For p variables and n observations, the time required is proportional to np^2. For each model run, REG needs time roughly proportional to k^3, where k is the number of regressors in the model. Add an additional nk^2 for one of the R, CLM, or CLI options, and another nk^2 for the INFLUENCE option.

Most of the memory REG needs to solve large problems is used for crossproducts matrices. PROC REG requires $4p^2$ bytes for the main crossproducts matrix plus $4k^2$ bytes for the largest model. If several output data sets are requested, memory is needed for buffers also.

Printed Output

Many of the more specialized printouts are described in detail in the sections above. Most of the formulas for the statistics are in "SAS Regression Procedures."

The analysis-of-variance table is always printed and includes

1. the SOURCE of the variation, MODEL for the fitted regression, ERROR for the residual error, and C TOTAL for the total variation after correcting for the mean.
2. the degrees of freedom (DF) associated with the source.
3. the SUM OF SQUARES for the term.
4. the MEAN SQUARE, the sum of squares divided by the degrees of freedom.
5. the F VALUE for testing the hypothesis that all parameters are zero except for the intercept. This is formed by dividing the mean square for MODEL by the mean square for ERROR.
6. the PROB>F, the probability of getting a greater F statistic than that observed if the hypothesis is true. This is the significance probability.

Other statistics are printed:

7. ROOT MSE is an estimate of the standard deviation of the error term. It is calculated as the square root of the mean square error.
8. DEP MEAN is the sample mean of the dependent variable.
9. C.V. is the coefficient of variation, computed as 100 times ROOT MSE divided by DEP MEAN. This expresses the variation in unitless values.
10. R-SQUARE is a measure between 0 and 1 that indicates the portion of the (corrected) total variation that is attributed to the fit rather than left to residual error. It is calculated as SS(MODEL) divided by SS(TOTAL). It is also called the *coefficient of determination*. It is the square of the multiple correlation, in other words, the square of the correlation between the dependent variable and the predicted values.
11. ADJ R-SQ, the adjusted R^2, is a version of R^2 that has been adjusted for degrees of freedom. It is calculated

$$\bar{R}^2 = 1 - (1 - R^2)(n-1)/dfe$$

where *dfe* is the degrees of freedom for error.

The parameter estimates and associated statistics are then printed, and they include:

12. the VARIABLE used as the regressor, including the name INTERCEP to estimate the intercept parameter.
13. the degree of freedom (DF) for the variable. There is one degree of freedom unless the model is not full rank.
14. the PARAMETER ESTIMATE.
15. the STANDARD ERROR, the estimate of the standard deviation of the parameter estimate.
16. T FOR H0: PARAMETER=0, the *t* test that the parameter is zero. This is computed as PARAMETER ESTIMATE divided by the STANDARD ERROR.
17. the PROB>|T|, the probability that a *t* statistic would obtain a greater absolute value than that observed given that the true parameter is zero. This is the two-tailed significance probability.

EXAMPLES

Population Growth Trends: Example 1

In the following example, the population of the United States from 1790 to 1970 is fit to linear and quadratic functions of time. The statements request influence diagnostic options and plots of the output data set.

```
DATA USPOP;
   INPUT POP @@;
   RETAIN YEAR 1780;
   YEAR=YEAR+10;
   YEARSQ=YEAR*YEAR;
   POP=POP/1000;
   CARDS;
3929 5308 7239 9638 12866 17069 23191 31443 39818 50155
62947 75994 91972 105710 122775 131669 151325 179323 203211
. . .
;
PROC REG DATA=USPOP;
   MODEL POP=YEAR / R CLI CLM INFLUENCE DW;
   MODEL POP=YEAR YEARSQ / R CLI CLM INFLUENCE DW;
   OUTPUT OUT=C P=PRED L95=L95 U95=U95 R=RESID COOKD=COOKD;
PROC PLOT DATA=C;
   PLOT POP*YEAR='A' PRED*YEAR='P' U95*YEAR='U' L95*YEAR='L'
      / OVERLAY VPOS=40 HPOS=80;
   PLOT RESID*YEAR / VREF=0 VPOS=30 HPOS=80;
   PLOT COOKD*YEAR / VREF=0 VPOS=30 HPOS=80;
```

Output 31.16 Population Growth Trends: PROC REG

```
                                                                                                          1
DEP VARIABLE: POP
                                            ANALYSIS OF VARIANCE
                                    (3)
                (1)        (2)        SUM OF        (4) MEAN       (5)           (6)
               SOURCE      DF        SQUARES          SQUARE      F VALUE        PROB>F

               MODEL        1    66336.46923     66336.46923     201.873        0.0001
               ERROR       17     5586.29253       328.60544
               C TOTAL     18    71922.76175

           (7) ROOT MSE          18.12748   (10) R-SQUARE      0.9223
           (8) DEP MEAN          69.76747   (11) ADJ R-SQ      0.9178
           (9) C.V.              25.98271

                                            PARAMETER ESTIMATES
                                  (14)                                (16)
          (12)       (13)        PARAMETER      (15) STANDARD        T FOR H0:          (17)
          VARIABLE    DF          ESTIMATE            ERROR        PARAMETER=0       PROB > |T|

          INTERCEP     1       -1958.36630        142.80455            -13.714           0.0001
          YEAR         1        1.07879456       0.07592765             14.208           0.0001


                    PREDICT   STD ERR  LOWER95%  UPPER95%  LOWER95%  UPPER95%             STD ERR   STUDENT                COOK'S
OBS       ACTUAL      VALUE   PREDICT      MEAN      MEAN   PREDICT   PREDICT  RESIDUAL  RESIDUAL  RESIDUAL  -2-1-0 1 2       D

   1      3.9290   -27.3240    7.9995  -44.2014  -10.4467  -69.1278   14.4797   31.2530   16.2670    1.9213  |      |***  | 0.446
   2      5.3080   -16.5361    7.3615  -32.0673   -1.0049  -57.8148   24.7426   21.8441   16.5655    1.3187  |      |**   | 0.172
   3      7.2390    -5.7481    6.7486  -19.9864    8.4901  -46.5579   35.0616   12.9871   16.8244    0.7719  |      |*    | 0.048
```

(continued on next page)

(continued from previous page)

4	9.6380	5.0398	6.1684	-7.9743	18.0539	-35.3592	45.4388	4.5982	17.0457	0.2698			0.005
5	12.8660	15.8277	5.6309	3.9476	27.7079	-24.2204	55.8758	-2.9617	17.2307	-0.1719			0.002
6	17.0690	26.6157	5.1497	15.7509	37.4805	-13.1430	66.3744	-9.5467	17.3806	-0.5493	*		0.013
7	23.1910	37.4036	4.7417	27.3996	47.4076	-2.1285	76.9358	-14.2126	17.4963	-0.8123	*		0.024
8	31.4430	48.1916	4.4273	38.8508	57.5323	8.8220	87.5611	-16.7486	17.5785	-0.9528	*		0.029
9	39.8180	58.9795	4.2275	50.0604	67.8987	19.7079	98.2512	-19.1615	17.6276	-1.0870	**		0.034
10	50.1550	69.7675	4.1587	60.9934	78.5416	30.5285	109.0	-19.6125	17.6440	-1.1116	**		0.034
11	62.9470	80.5554	4.2275	71.6363	89.4746	41.2838	119.8	-17.6084	17.6276	-0.9989	*		0.029
12	75.9940	91.3434	4.4273	82.0026	100.7	51.9738	130.7	-15.3494	17.5785	-0.8732	*		0.024
13	91.9720	102.1	4.7417	92.1273	112.1	62.5992	141.7	-10.1593	17.4963	-0.5807	*		0.012
14	105.7	112.9	5.1497	102.1	123.8	73.1606	152.7	-7.2093	17.3806	-0.4148			0.008
15	122.8	123.7	5.6309	111.8	135.6	83.6591	163.8	-0.9322	17.2307	-0.0541			0.000
16	131.7	134.5	6.1684	121.5	147.5	94.0962	174.9	-2.8261	17.0457	-0.1658			0.002
17	151.3	145.3	6.7486	131.0	159.5	104.5	186.1	6.0419	16.8244	0.3591			0.010
18	179.3	156.1	7.3615	140.5	171.6	114.8	197.3	23.2520	16.5655	1.4036		**	0.195
19	203.2	166.9	7.9995	150.0	183.7	125.1	208.7	36.3520	16.2670	2.2347		****	0.604
20	.	177.6	8.6571	159.4	195.9	135.3	220.0	.	.	.			.
21	.	188.4	9.3301	168.8	208.1	145.4	231.4	.	.	.			.
22	.	199.2	10.0155	178.1	220.4	155.5	242.9	.	.	.			.

SUM OF RESIDUALS -9.91207E-13
SUM OF SQUARED RESIDUALS 5586.293
PREDICTED RESID SS (PRESS) 7619.904

2

OBS	RESIDUAL	RSTUDENT	HAT DIAG H	COV RATIO	DFFITS	INTERCEP DFBETAS	YEAR DFBETAS
1	31.2530	2.1066	0.1947	0.8592	1.0359	0.9002	-0.8849
2	21.8441	1.3502	0.1649	1.0894	0.6000	0.5048	-0.4951
3	12.9871	0.7624	0.1386	1.2203	0.3058	0.2462	-0.2408
4	4.5982	0.2623	0.1158	1.2658	0.0949	0.0719	-0.0701
5	-2.9617	-0.1669	0.0965	1.2451	-0.0545	-0.0379	0.0368
6	-9.5467	-0.5377	0.0807	1.1848	-0.1593	-0.0977	0.0940
7	-14.2126	-0.8038	0.0684	1.1196	-0.2178	-0.1102	0.1046
8	-16.7486	-0.9501	0.0596	1.0757	-0.2393	-0.0886	0.0821
9	-19.1615	-1.0932	0.0544	1.0336	-0.2622	-0.0546	0.0471
10	-19.6125	-1.1198	0.0526	1.0247	-0.2639	-0.0077	-0.0000
11	-17.6084	-0.9988	0.0544	1.0578	-0.2395	0.0361	-0.0430
12	-15.3494	-0.8668	0.0596	1.0952	-0.2183	0.0689	-0.0749
13	-10.1593	-0.5690	0.0684	1.1642	-0.1542	0.0701	-0.0741
14	-7.2093	-0.4045	0.0807	1.2033	-0.1198	0.0678	-0.0707
15	-0.9322	-0.0525	0.0965	1.2490	-0.0172	0.0112	-0.0116
16	-2.8261	-0.1610	0.1158	1.2726	-0.0583	0.0419	-0.0430
17	6.0419	0.3497	0.1386	1.2907	0.1403	-0.1079	0.1105
18	23.2520	1.4482	0.1649	1.0567	0.6436	-0.5202	0.5310
19	36.3520	2.5798	0.1947	0.6992	1.2686	-1.0641	1.0837
20	.	.	.	.	.	.	.
21	.	.	.	.	.	.	.
22	.	.	.	.	.	.	.

DURBIN-WATSON D 0.180
(FOR NUMBER OF OBS.) 19
1ST ORDER AUTOCORRELATION 0.704

3

DEP VARIABLE: POP

ANALYSIS OF VARIANCE

SOURCE	DF	SUM OF SQUARES	MEAN SQUARE	F VALUE	PROB>F
MODEL	2	71799.01619	35899.50810	4641.719	0.0001
ERROR	16	123.74556	7.73409771		
C TOTAL	18	71922.76175			

ROOT MSE	2.781025	R-SQUARE	0.9983
DEP MEAN	69.76747	ADJ R-SQ	0.9981
C.V.	3.986133		

PARAMETER ESTIMATES

VARIABLE	DF	PARAMETER ESTIMATE	STANDARD ERROR	T FOR H0: PARAMETER=0	PROB > |T|
INTERCEP	1	20450.43359	843.47532	24.245	0.0001
YEAR	1	-22.78060612	0.89784903	-25.372	0.0001

(continued on next page)

(continued from previous page)

YEARSQ	1	0.006345585	0.000238770	26.576	0.0001

OBS	ACTUAL	PREDICT VALUE	STD ERR PREDICT	LOWER95% MEAN	UPPER95% MEAN	LOWER95% PREDICT	UPPER95% PREDICT	RESIDUAL	STD ERR RESIDUAL	STUDENT RESIDUAL	-2-1-0 1 2	COOK'S D
1	3.9290	5.0384	1.7289	1.3734	8.7035	-1.9034	11.9803	-1.1094	2.1783	-0.5093	| *| |	0.054
2	5.3080	5.0389	1.3909	2.0904	7.9874	-1.5528	11.6306	0.2691	2.4082	0.1117	| | |	0.001
3	7.2390	6.3085	1.1304	3.9122	8.7047	-0.0554	12.6723	0.9305	2.5409	0.3662	| | |	0.009
4	9.6380	8.8472	0.9571	6.8182	10.8761	2.6123	15.0820	0.7908	2.6111	0.3029	| | |	0.004
5	12.8660	12.6550	0.8721	10.8062	14.5037	6.4764	18.8335	0.2110	2.6408	0.0799	| | |	0.000
6	17.0690	17.7319	0.8578	15.9133	19.5504	11.5623	23.9015	-0.6629	2.6454	-0.2506	| | |	0.002
7	23.1910	24.0779	0.8835	22.2050	25.9509	17.8921	30.2637	-0.8869	2.6369	-0.3363	| | |	0.004
8	31.4430	31.6931	0.9202	29.7424	33.6437	25.4832	37.9029	-0.2501	2.6244	-0.0953	| | |	0.000
9	39.8180	40.5773	0.9487	38.5661	42.5885	34.3482	46.8064	-0.7593	2.6142	-0.2905	| | |	0.004
10	50.1550	50.7307	0.9592	48.6972	52.7642	44.4944	56.9670	-0.5757	2.6104	-0.2206	| | |	0.002
11	62.9470	62.1532	0.9487	60.1420	64.1644	55.9241	68.3823	0.7938	2.6142	0.3036	| | |	0.004
12	75.9940	74.8448	0.9202	72.8942	76.7955	68.6350	81.0547	1.1492	2.6244	0.4379	| | |	0.008
13	91.9720	88.8056	0.8835	86.9326	90.6785	82.6197	94.9914	3.1664	2.6369	1.2008	| |** |	0.054
14	105.7	104.0	0.8578	102.2	105.9	97.8659	110.2	1.6746	2.6454	0.6330	| |* |	0.014
15	122.8	120.5	0.8721	118.7	122.4	114.4	126.7	2.2406	2.6408	0.8485	| |* |	0.026
16	131.7	138.3	0.9571	136.3	140.3	132.1	144.5	-6.6335	2.6111	-2.5405	|*****| |	0.289
17	151.3	157.3	1.1304	154.9	159.7	151.0	163.7	-6.0147	2.5409	-2.3671	| ****| |	0.370
18	179.3	177.6	1.3909	174.7	180.6	171.1	184.2	1.6770	2.4082	0.6963	| |* |	0.054
19	203.2	199.2	1.7289	195.6	202.9	192.3	206.2	3.9895	2.1783	1.8315	| |*** |	0.704
20	.	222.1	2.1348	217.5	226.6	214.6	229.5	.	.	.		.
21	.	246.2	2.6019	240.7	251.7	238.1	254.3	.	.	.		.
22	.	271.6	3.1257	264.9	278.2	262.7	280.4	.	.	.		.

```
SUM OF RESIDUALS               -1.90444E-10
SUM OF SQUARED RESIDUALS           123.7456
PREDICTED RESID SS (PRESS)         188.5492
```

OBS	RESIDUAL	RSTUDENT	HAT DIAG H	COV RATIO	DFFITS	INTERCEP DFBETAS	YEAR DFBETAS	YEARSQ DFBETAS
1	-1.1094	-0.4972	0.3865	1.8834	-0.3946	-0.2842	0.2810	-0.2779
2	0.2691	0.1082	0.2501	1.6147	0.0625	0.0376	-0.0370	0.0365
3	0.9305	0.3561	0.1652	1.4176	0.1584	0.0666	-0.0651	0.0636
4	0.7908	0.2941	0.1184	1.3531	0.1078	0.0182	-0.0172	0.0161
5	0.2110	0.0774	0.0983	1.3444	0.0256	-0.0030	0.0033	-0.0035
6	-0.6629	-0.2431	0.0951	1.3255	-0.0788	0.0296	-0.0302	0.0307
7	-0.8869	-0.3268	0.1009	1.3214	-0.1095	0.0609	-0.0616	0.0621
8	-0.2501	-0.0923	0.1095	1.3605	-0.0324	0.0216	-0.0217	0.0218
9	-0.7593	-0.2820	0.1164	1.3519	-0.1023	0.0743	-0.0745	0.0747
10	-0.5757	-0.2139	0.1190	1.3650	-0.0786	0.0586	-0.0587	0.0587
11	0.7938	0.2949	0.1164	1.3499	0.1070	-0.0784	0.0783	-0.0781
12	1.1492	0.4265	0.1095	1.3144	0.1496	-0.1018	0.1014	-0.1009
13	3.1664	1.2189	0.1009	1.0168	0.4084	-0.2357	0.2338	-0.2318
14	1.6746	0.6207	0.0951	1.2430	0.2013	-0.0811	0.0798	-0.0784
15	2.2406	0.8407	0.0983	1.1724	0.2776	-0.0427	0.0404	-0.0380
16	-6.6335	-3.1845	0.1184	0.2924	-1.1673	-0.1531	0.1636	-0.1747
17	-6.0147	-2.8433	0.1652	0.3989	-1.2649	-0.4843	0.4958	-0.5076
18	1.6770	0.6847	0.2501	1.4757	0.3954	0.2240	-0.2274	0.2308
19	3.9895	1.9947	0.3865	0.9766	1.5831	1.0902	-1.1025	1.1151
20	.	.	.	.	.	.	.	.
21	.	.	.	.	.	.	.	.
22	.	.	.	.	.	.	.	.

```
DURBIN-WATSON D              1.264
(FOR NUMBER OF OBS.)            19
1ST ORDER AUTOCORRELATION    0.299
```

Output 31.17 Plots of Population Data: PROC PLOT

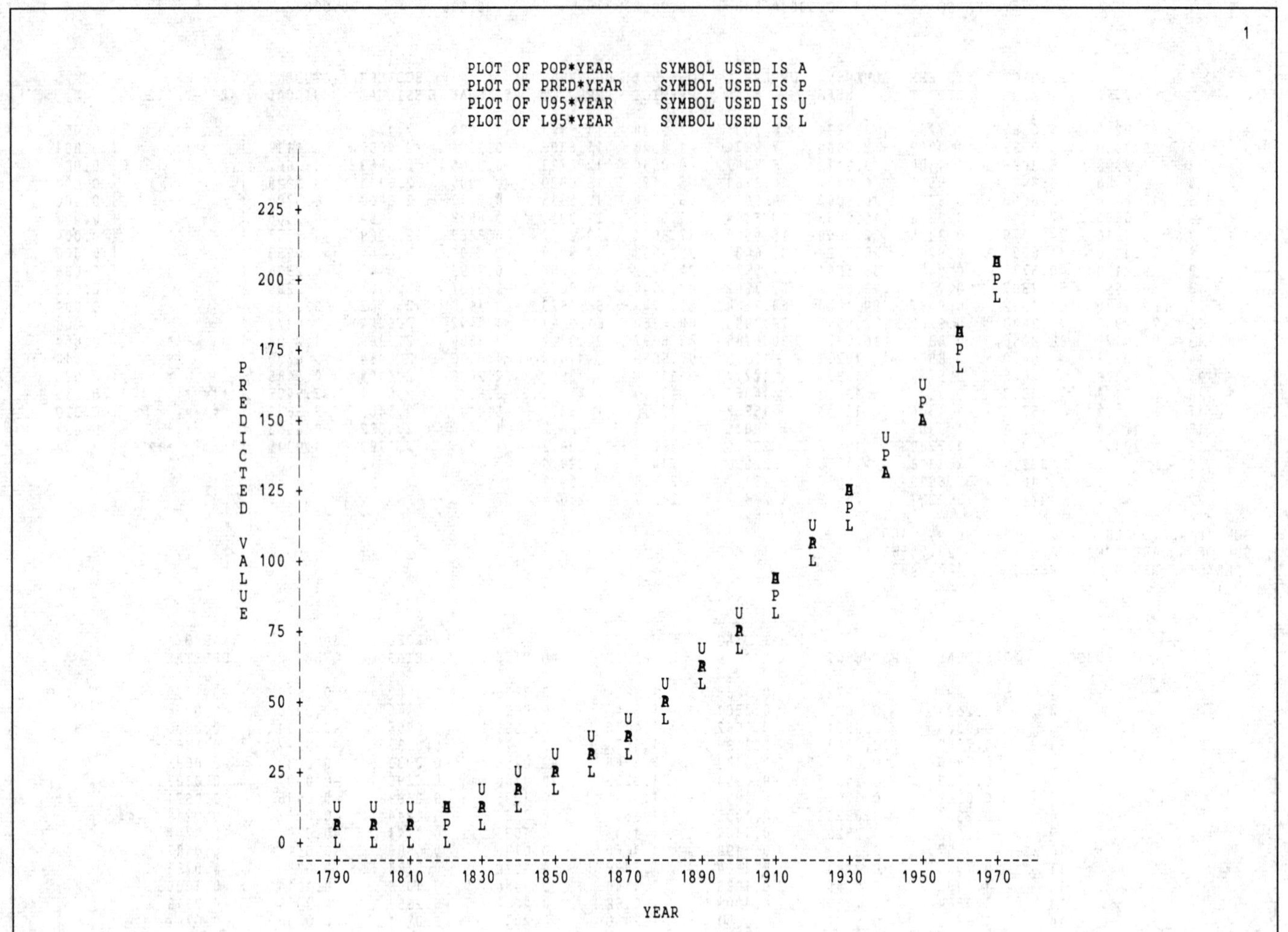

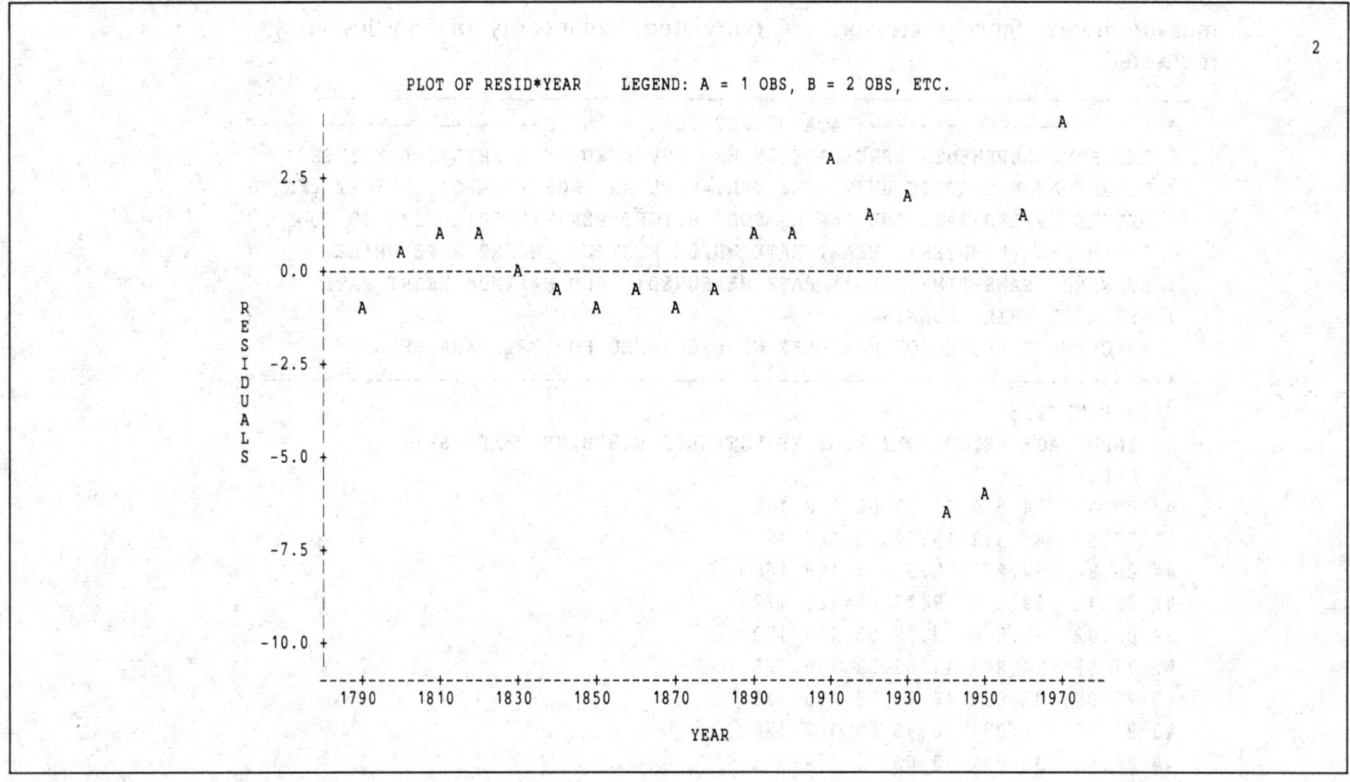

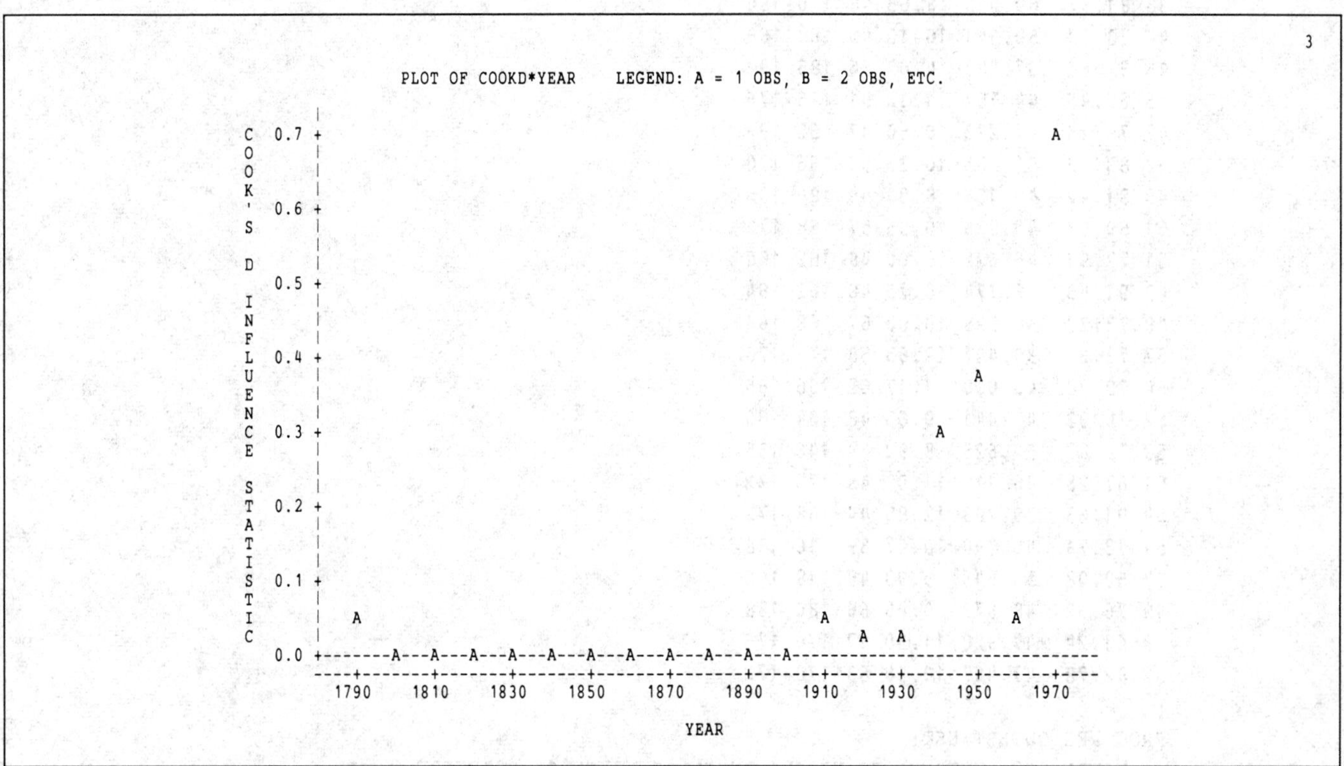

Aerobic Fitness Prediction: Example 2

Aerobic fitness (measured by the ability to consume oxygen) is fit to some simple exercise tests. The goal is to develop an equation to predict fitness based on the exercise tests rather than on expensive and cumbersome oxygen consumption measurements. Since regressors are correlated, collinearity diagnostics are requested.

```
*-------------------------DATA ON PHYSICAL FITNESS-----------------------*
| THESE MEASUREMENTS WERE MADE ON MEN INVOLVED IN A PHYSICAL FITNESS    |
| COURSE AT N.C.STATE UNIV. THE VARIABLES ARE AGE (YEARS), WEIGHT (KG),|
| OXYGEN UPTAKE RATE (ML PER KG BODY WEIGHT PER MINUTE), TIME TO RUN    |
| 1.5 MILES (MINUTES), HEART RATE WHILE RESTING, HEART RATE WHILE       |
| RUNNING (SAME TIME OXYGEN RATE MEASURED), AND MAXIMUM HEART RATE      |
| RECORDED WHILE RUNNING.                                               |
| ***CERTAIN VALUES OF MAXPULSE WERE CHANGED FOR THIS ANALYSIS          |
*-----------------------------------------------------------------------*;
DATA FITNESS;
   INPUT AGE WEIGHT OXY RUNTIME RSTPULSE RUNPULSE MAXPULSE;
   CARDS;
44 89.47  44.609 11.37 62 178 182
40 75.07  45.313 10.07 62 185 185
44 85.84  54.297  8.65 45 156 168
42 68.15  59.571  8.17 40 166 172
38 89.02  49.874  9.22 55 178 180
47 77.45  44.811 11.63 58 176 176
40 75.98  45.681 11.95 70 176 180
43 81.19  49.091 10.85 64 162 170
44 81.42  39.442 13.08 63 174 176
38 81.87  60.055  8.63 48 170 186
44 73.03  50.541 10.13 45 168 168
45 87.66  37.388 14.03 56 186 192
45 66.45  44.754 11.12 51 176 176
47 79.15  47.273 10.60 47 162 164
54 83.12  51.855 10.33 50 166 170
49 81.42  49.156  8.95 44 180 185
51 69.63  40.836 10.95 57 168 172
51 77.91  46.672 10.00 48 162 168
48 91.63  46.774 10.25 48 162 164
49 73.37  50.388 10.08 67 168 168
57 73.37  39.407 12.63 58 174 176
54 79.38  46.080 11.17 62 156 165
52 76.32  45.441  9.63 48 164 166
50 70.87  54.625  8.92 48 146 155
51 67.25  45.118 11.08 48 172 172
54 91.63  39.203 12.88 44 168 172
51 73.71  45.790 10.47 59 186 188
57 59.08  50.545  9.93 49 148 155
49 76.32  48.673  9.40 56 186 188
48 61.24  47.920 11.50 52 170 176
52 82.78  47.467 10.50 53 170 172
;
PROC REG OUTEST=EST;
   MODEL OXY=RUNTIME AGE WEIGHT RUNPULSE MAXPULSE RSTPULSE
      /PARTIAL COLLIN;
```

Output 31.18 Aerobic Fitness Prediction: PROC REG

1

DEP VARIABLE: OXY

ANALYSIS OF VARIANCE

SOURCE	DF	SUM OF SQUARES	MEAN SQUARE	F VALUE	PROB>F
MODEL	6	722.54361	120.42393	22.433	0.0001
ERROR	24	128.83794	5.36824741		
C TOTAL	30	851.38154			

ROOT MSE	2.316948	R-SQUARE	0.8487
DEP MEAN	47.37581	ADJ R-SQ	0.8108
C.V.	4.890572		

PARAMETER ESTIMATES

VARIABLE	DF	PARAMETER ESTIMATE	STANDARD ERROR	T FOR H0: PARAMETER=0	PROB > |T|
INTERCEP	1	102.93448	12.40325810	8.299	0.0001
RUNTIME	1	-2.62865282	0.38456220	-6.835	0.0001
AGE	1	-0.22697380	0.09983747	-2.273	0.0322
WEIGHT	1	-0.07417741	0.05459316	-1.359	0.1869
RUNPULSE	1	-0.36962776	0.11985294	-3.084	0.0051
MAXPULSE	1	0.30321713	0.13649519	2.221	0.0360
RSTPULSE	1	-0.02153364	0.06605428	-0.326	0.7473

COLLINEARITY DIAGNOSTICS

NUMBER	EIGENVALUE	CONDITION NUMBER	VAR PROP INTERCEP	VAR PROP RUNTIME	VAR PROP AGE	VAR PROP WEIGHT	VAR PROP RUNPULSE	VAR PROP MAXPULSE	VAR PROP RSTPULSE
1	6.949911	1.000000	0.0000	0.0002	0.0002	0.0002	0.0000	0.0000	0.0003
2	0.018676	19.290870	0.0022	0.0252	0.1463	0.0104	0.0000	0.0000	0.3906
3	0.015034	21.500719	0.0006	0.1286	0.1501	0.2357	0.0012	0.0012	0.0281
4	0.0091095	27.621151	0.0064	0.6090	0.0319	0.1831	0.0015	0.0012	0.1903
5	0.0060729	33.829179	0.0013	0.1250	0.1128	0.4444	0.0151	0.0083	0.3648
6	0.0010177	82.637571	0.7997	0.0975	0.4966	0.1033	0.0695	0.0056	0.0203
7	0.0001795	196.786	0.1898	0.0146	0.0621	0.0228	0.9128	0.9836	0.0057

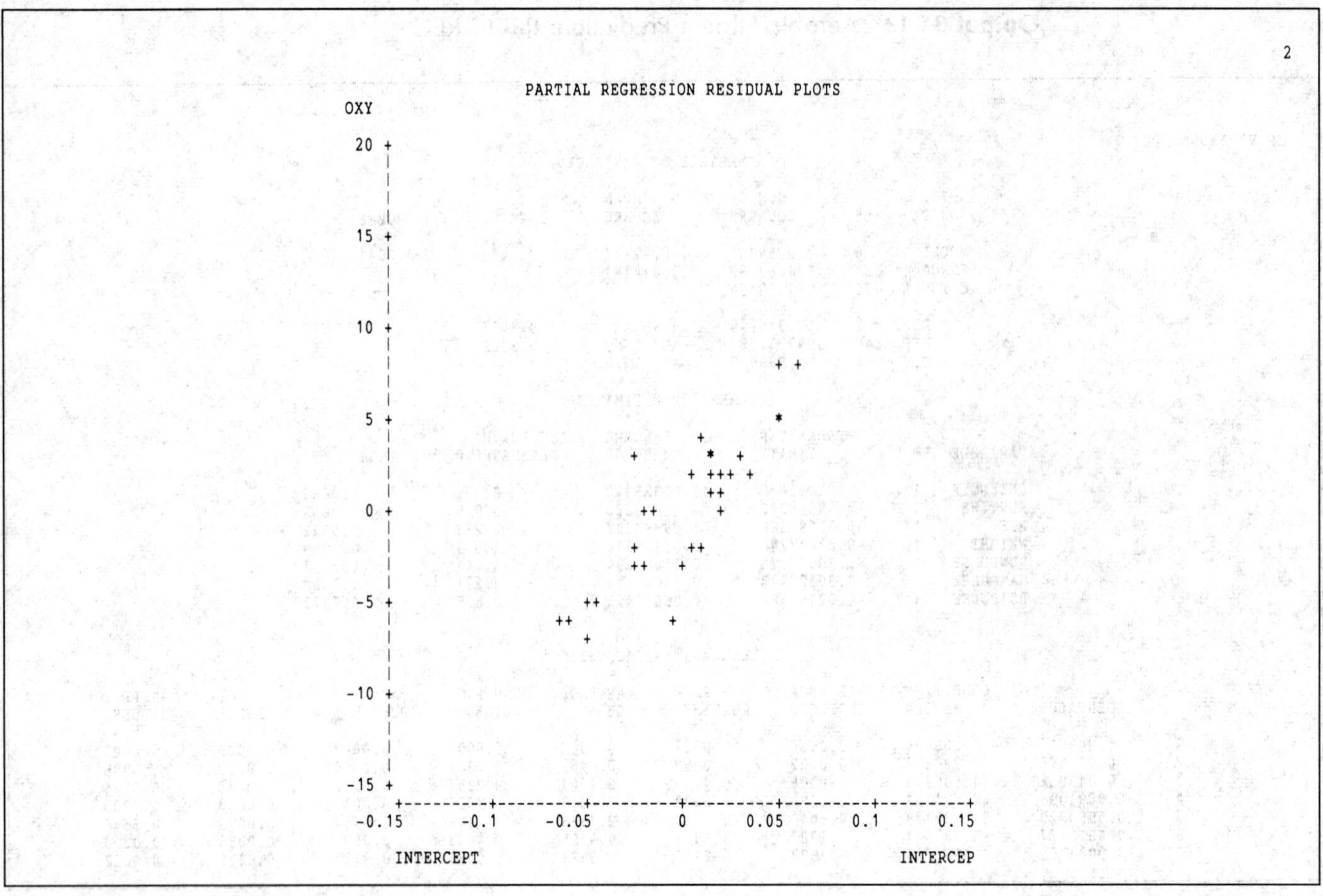
2
PARTIAL REGRESSION RESIDUAL PLOTS
OXY
20
15
10
5
0
-5
-10
-15
-0.15
-0.1
-0.05
0
0.05
0.1
0.15
INTERCEPT
INTERCEP

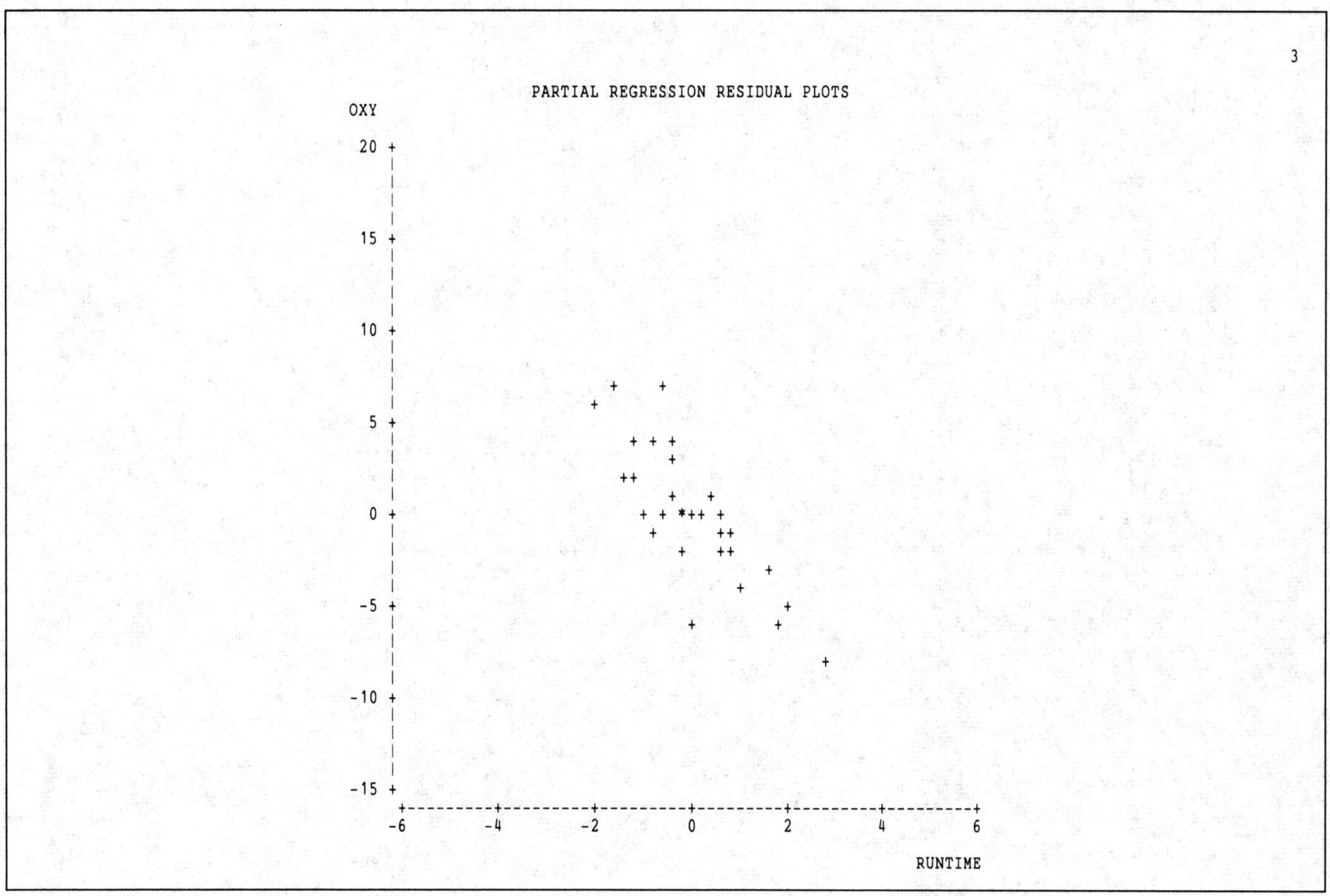
3
PARTIAL REGRESSION RESIDUAL PLOTS
OXY
20
15
10
5
0
-5
-10
-15
-6
-4
-2
0
2
4
6
RUNTIME

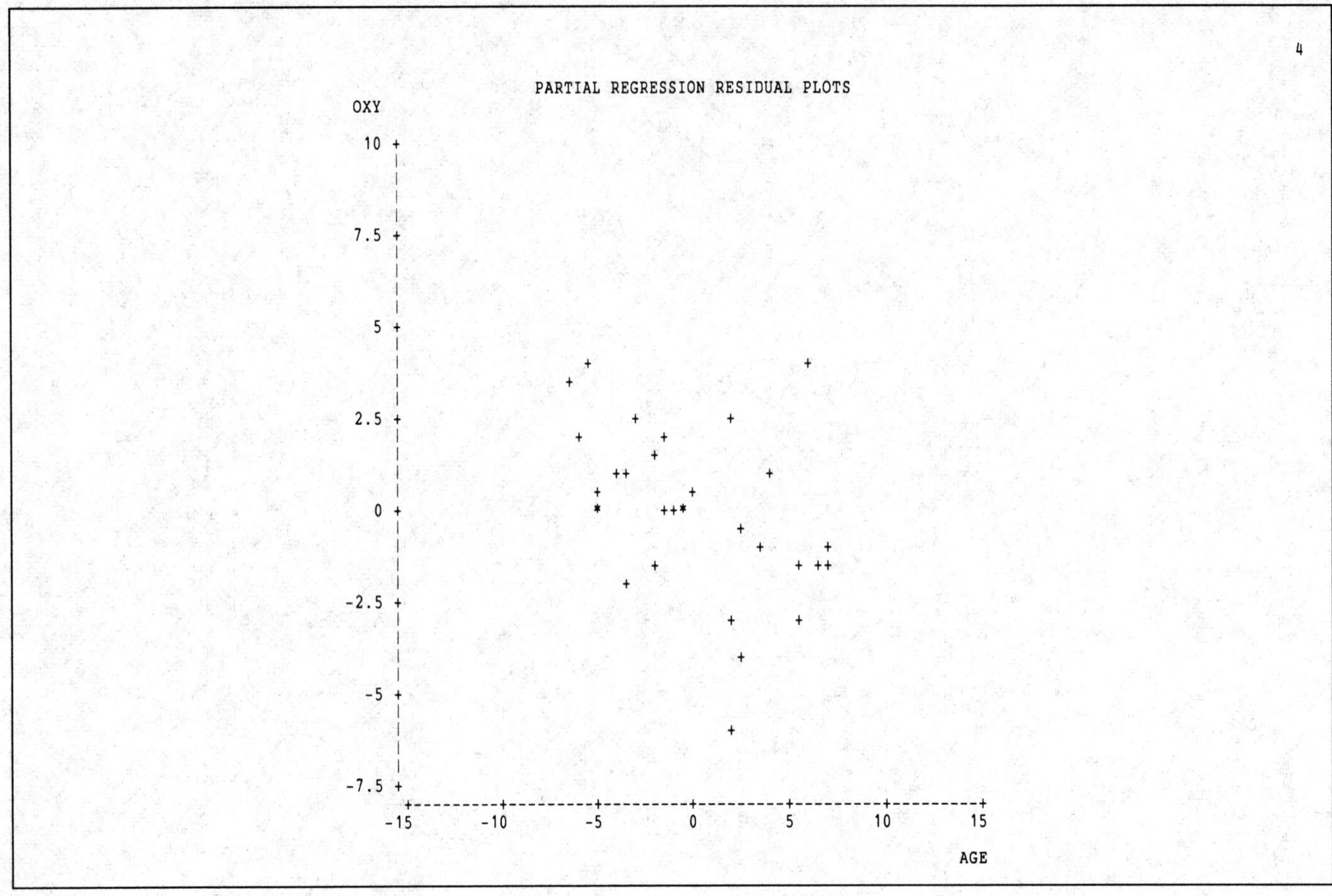
4
PARTIAL REGRESSION RESIDUAL PLOTS
OXY
10
7.5
5
2.5
0
-2.5
-5
-7.5
-15
-10
-5
0
5
10
15
AGE

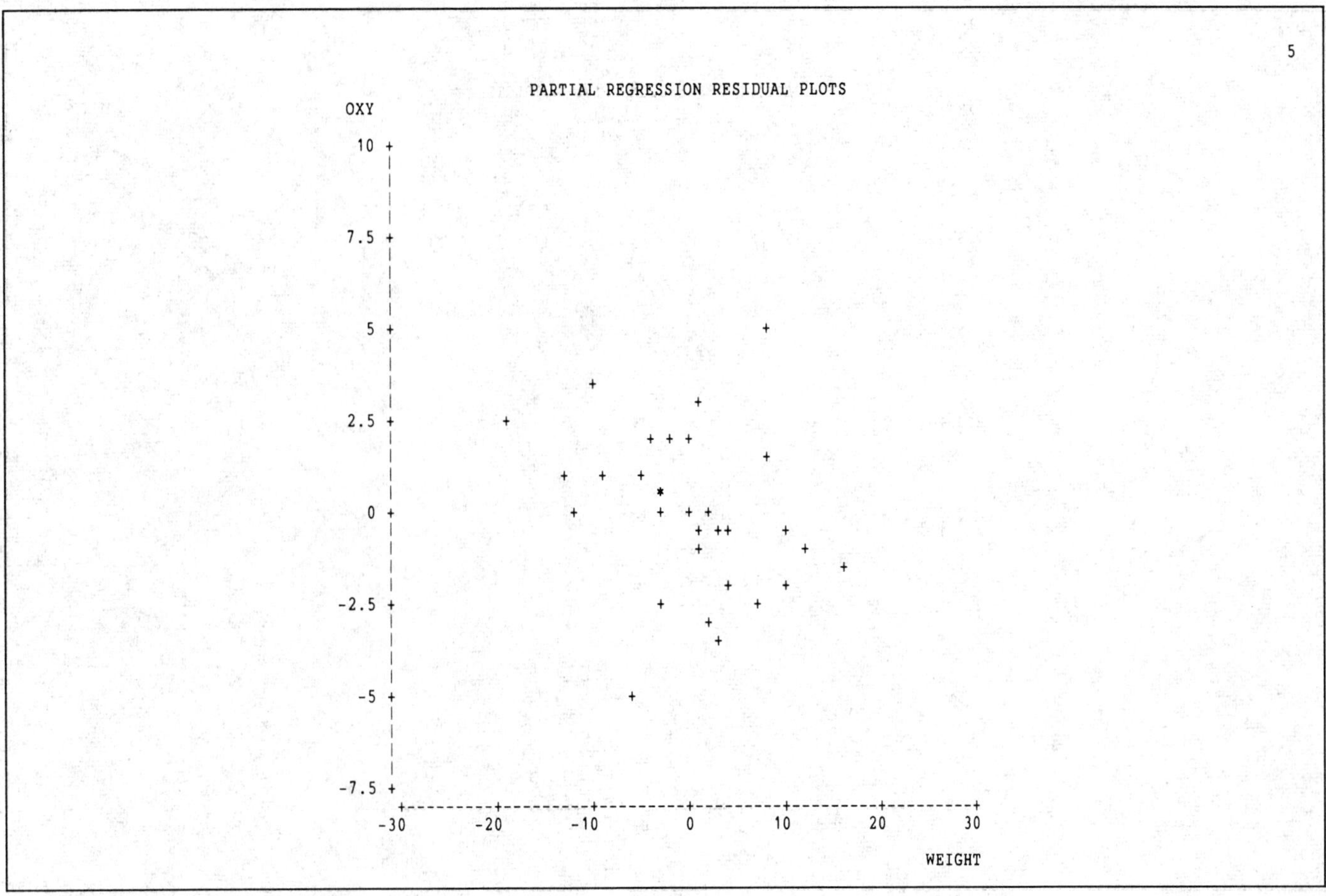
5
PARTIAL REGRESSION RESIDUAL PLOTS
OXY
10
7.5
5
2.5
0
-2.5
-5
-7.5
-30
-20
-10
0
10
20
30
WEIGHT

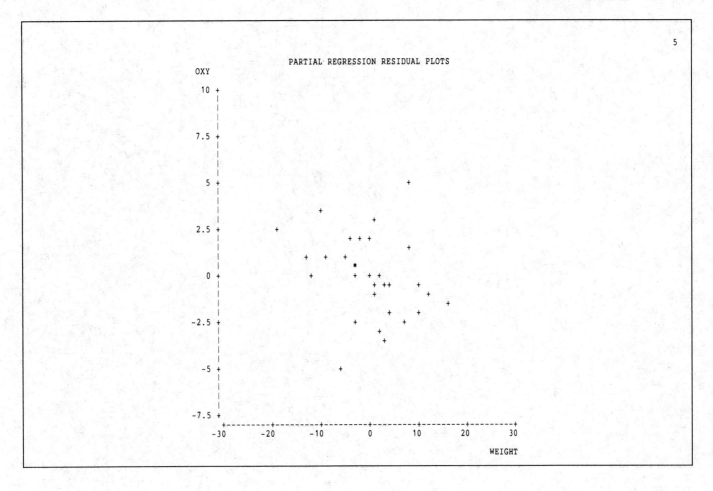

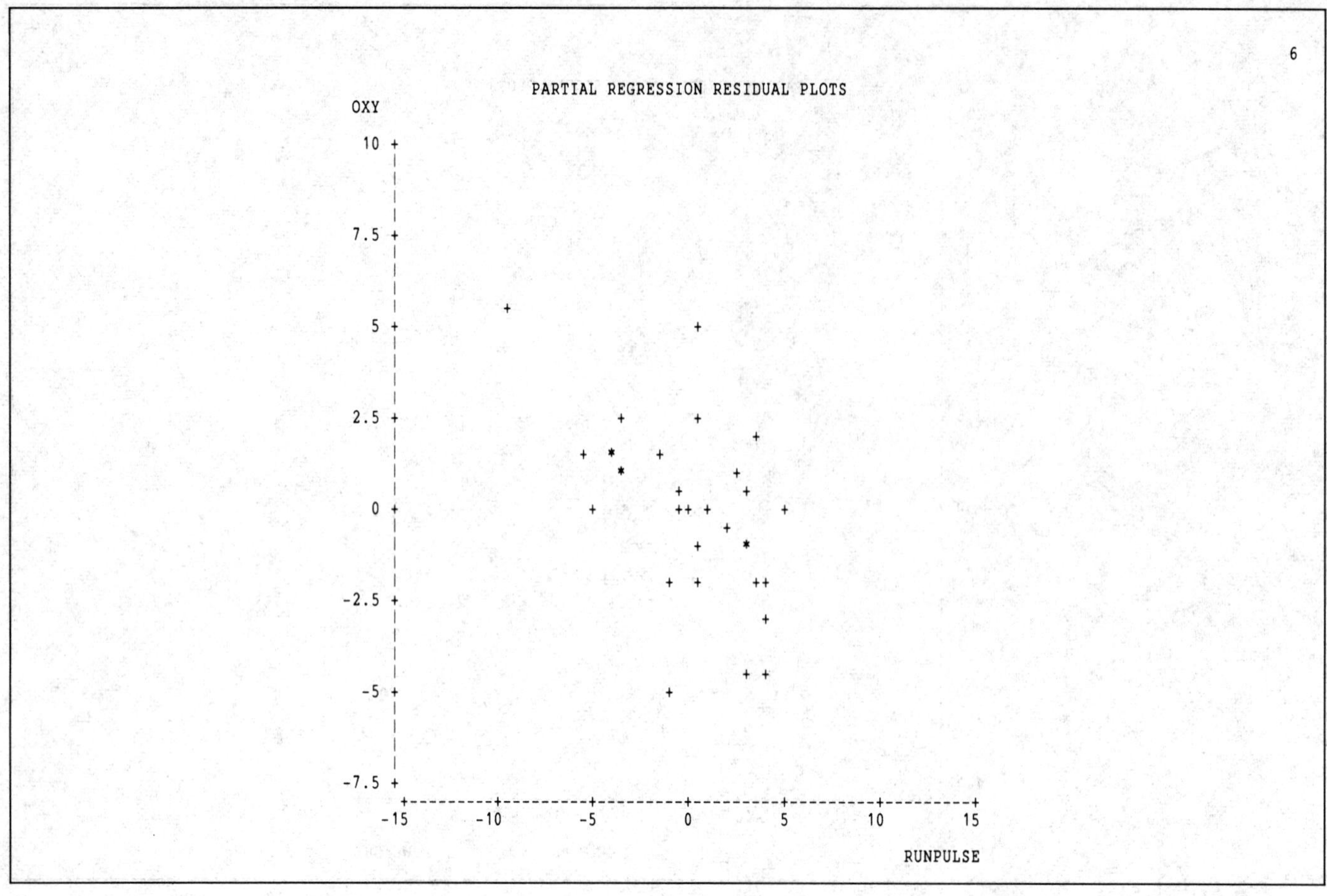
6
PARTIAL REGRESSION RESIDUAL PLOTS
OXY
10
7.5
5
2.5
0
-2.5
-5
-7.5
-15
-10
-5
0
5
10
15
RUNPULSE

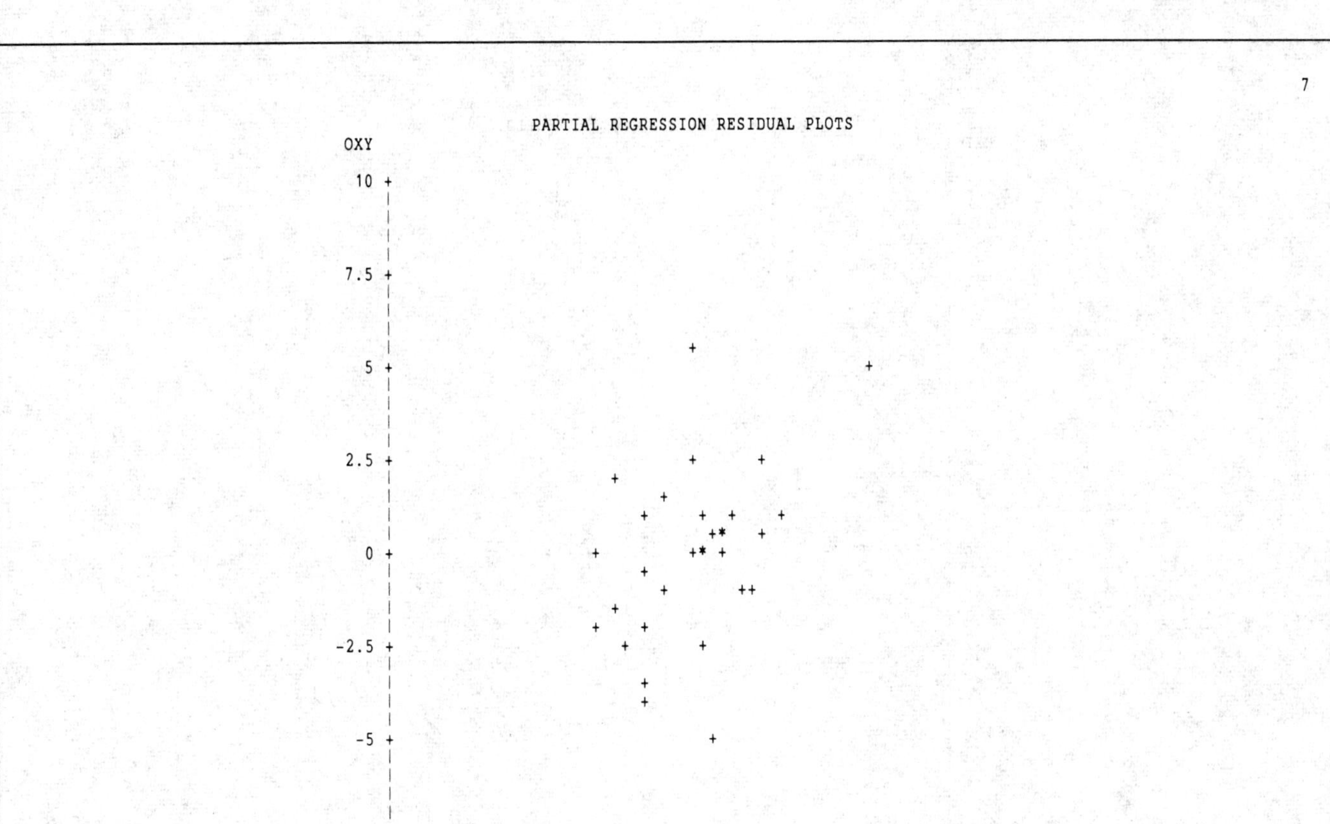
7
PARTIAL REGRESSION RESIDUAL PLOTS
OXY
10
7.5
5
2.5
0
-2.5
-5
-7.5
-15
-10
-5
0
5
10
15
MAXPULSE

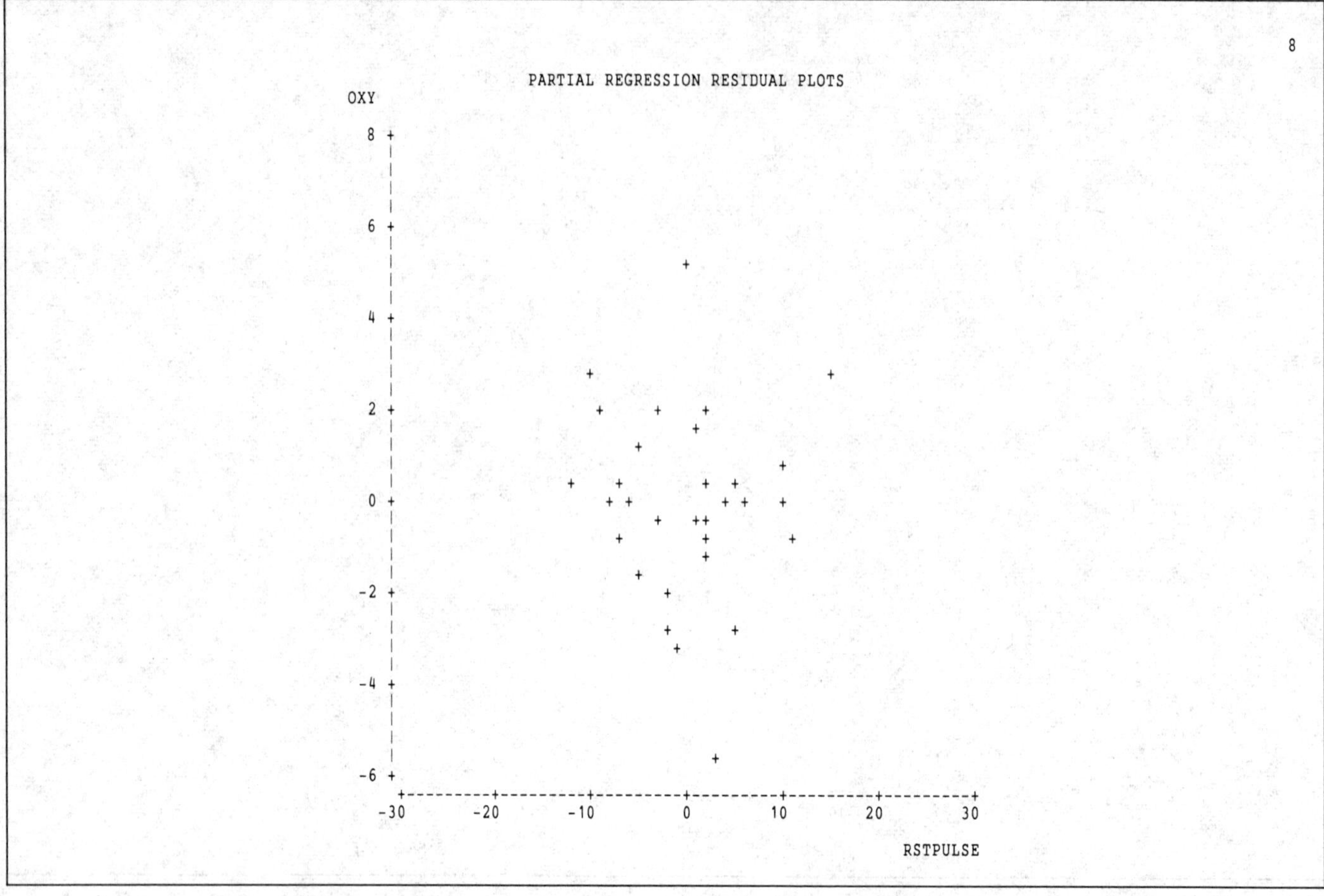

Predicting Weight by Height and Age: Example 3

To illustrate multiple MODEL statements, BY groups, and the OUTEST= and OUTSSCP= options, a prediction is given for WEIGHT by HEIGHT and AGE in this group of students.

```
*---------------DATA ON AGE, WEIGHT, AND HEIGHT OF CHILDREN----------*
|AGE (MONTHS), HEIGHT (INCHES), AND WEIGHT (POUNDS) WERE RECORDED FOR|
|A GROUP OF SCHOOLCHILDREN.                                          |
|FROM T. LEWIS & L.R. TAYLOR, "INTRODUCTION TO EXPERIMENTAL ECOLOGY."|
*--------------------------------------------------------------------*;

DATA HTWT;
   INPUT SEX $ AGE :3.1 HEIGHT WEIGHT @@;
   CARDS;
F 143 56.3  85.0 F 155 62.3 105.0 F 153 63.3 108.0 F 161 59.0  92.0
F 191 62.5 112.5 F 171 62.5 112.0 F 185 59.0 104.0 F 142 56.5  69.0
F 160 62.0  94.5 F 140 53.8  68.5 F 139 61.5 104.0 F 178 61.5 103.5
F 157 64.5 123.5 F 149 58.3  93.0 F 143 51.3  50.5 F 145 58.8  89.0
F 191 65.3 107.0 F 150 59.5  78.5 F 147 61.3 115.0 F 180 63.3 114.0
F 141 61.8  85.0 F 140 53.5  81.0 F 164 58.0  83.5 F 176 61.3 112.0
F 185 63.3 101.0 F 166 61.5 103.5 F 175 60.8  93.5 F 180 59.0 112.0
F 210 65.5 140.0 F 146 56.3  83.5 F 170 64.3  90.0 F 162 58.0  84.0
F 149 64.3 110.5 F 139 57.5  96.0 F 186 57.8  95.0 F 197 61.5 121.0
F 169 62.3  99.5 F 177 61.8 142.5 F 185 65.3 118.0 F 182 58.3 104.5
F 173 62.8 102.5 F 166 59.3  89.5 F 168 61.5  95.0 F 169 62.0  98.5
```

```
F 150 61.3  94.0 F 184 62.3 108.0 F 139 52.8  63.5 F 147 59.8  84.5
F 144 59.5  93.5 F 177 61.3 112.0 F 178 63.5 148.5 F 197 64.8 112.0
F 146 60.0 109.0 F 145 59.0  91.5 F 147 55.8  75.0 F 145 57.8  84.0
F 155 61.3 107.0 F 167 62.3  92.5 F 183 64.3 109.5 F 143 55.5  84.0
F 183 64.5 102.5 F 185 60.0 106.0 F 148 56.3  77.0 F 147 58.3 111.5
F 154 60.0 114.0 F 156 54.5  75.0 F 144 55.8  73.5 F 154 62.8  93.5
F 152 60.5 105.0 F 191 63.3 113.5 F 190 66.8 140.0 F 140 60.0  77.0
F 148 60.5  84.5 F 189 64.3 113.5 F 143 58.3  77.5 F 178 66.5 117.5
F 164 65.3  98.0 F 157 60.5 112.0 F 147 59.5 101.0 F 148 59.0  95.0
F 177 61.3  81.0 F 171 61.5  91.0 F 172 64.8 142.0 F 190 56.8  98.5
F 183 66.5 112.0 F 143 61.5 116.5 F 179 63.0  98.5 F 186 57.0  83.5
F 182 65.5 133.0 F 182 62.0  91.5 F 142 56.0  72.5 F 165 61.3 106.5
F 165 55.5  67.0 F 154 61.0 122.5 F 150 54.5  74.0 F 155 66.0 144.5
F 163 56.5  84.0 F 141 56.0  72.5 F 147 51.5  64.0 F 210 62.0 116.0
F 171 63.0  84.0 F 167 61.0  93.5 F 182 64.0 111.5 F 144 61.0  92.0
F 193 59.8 115.0 F 141 61.3  85.0 F 164 63.3 108.0 F 186 63.5 108.0
F 169 61.5  85.0 F 175 60.3  86.0 F 180 61.3 110.5 M 165 64.8  98.0
M 157 60.5 105.0 M 144 57.3  76.5 M 150 59.5  84.0 M 150 60.8 128.0
M 139 60.5  87.0 M 189 67.0 128.0 M 183 64.8 111.0 M 147 50.5  79.0
M 146 57.5  90.0 M 160 60.5  84.0 M 156 61.8 112.0 M 173 61.3  93.0
M 151 66.3 117.0 M 141 53.3  84.0 M 150 59.0  99.5 M 164 57.8  95.0
M 153 60.0  84.0 M 206 68.3 134.0 M 250 67.5 171.5 M 176 63.8  98.5
M 176 65.0 118.5 M 140 59.5  94.5 M 185 66.0 105.0 M 180 61.8 104.0
M 146 57.3  83.0 M 183 66.0 105.5 M 140 56.5  84.0 M 151 58.3  86.0
M 151 61.0  81.0 M 144 62.8  94.0 M 160 59.3  78.5 M 178 67.3 119.5
M 193 66.3 133.0 M 162 64.5 119.0 M 164 60.5  95.0 M 186 66.0 112.0
M 143 57.5  75.0 M 175 64.0  92.0 M 175 68.0 112.0 M 175 63.5  98.5
M 173 69.0 112.5 M 170 63.8 112.5 M 174 66.0 108.0 M 164 63.5 108.0
M 144 59.5  88.0 M 156 66.3 106.0 M 149 57.0  92.0 M 144 60.0 117.5
M 147 57.0  84.0 M 188 67.3 112.0 M 169 62.0 100.0 M 172 65.0 112.0
M 150 59.5  84.0 M 193 67.8 127.5 M 157 58.0  80.5 M 168 60.0  93.5
M 140 58.5  86.5 M 156 58.3  92.5 M 156 61.5 108.5 M 158 65.0 121.0
M 184 66.5 112.0 M 156 68.5 114.0 M 144 57.0  84.0 M 176 61.5  81.0
M 168 66.5 111.5 M 149 52.5  81.0 M 142 55.0  70.0 M 188 71.0 140.0
M 203 66.5 117.0 M 142 58.8  84.0 M 189 66.3 112.0 M 188 65.8 150.5
M 200 71.0 147.0 M 152 59.5 105.0 M 174 69.8 119.5 M 166 62.5  84.0
M 145 56.5  91.0 M 143 57.5 101.0 M 163 65.3 117.5 M 166 67.3 121.0
M 182 67.0 133.0 M 173 66.0 112.0 M 155 61.8  91.5 M 162 60.0 105.0
M 177 63.0 111.0 M 177 60.5 112.0 M 175 65.5 114.0 M 166 62.0  91.0
M 150 59.0  98.0 M 150 61.8 118.0 M 188 63.3 115.5 M 163 66.0 112.0
M 171 61.8 112.0 M 162 63.0  91.0 M 141 57.5  85.0 M 174 63.0 112.0
M 142 56.0  87.5 M 148 60.5 118.0 M 140 56.8  83.5 M 160 64.0 116.0
M 144 60.0  89.0 M 206 69.5 171.5 M 159 63.3 112.0 M 149 56.3  72.0
M 193 72.0 150.0 M 194 65.3 134.5 M 152 60.8  97.0 M 146 55.0  71.5
M 139 55.0  73.5 M 186 66.5 112.0 M 161 56.8  75.0 M 153 64.8 128.0
M 196 64.5  98.0 M 164 58.0  84.0 M 159 62.8  99.0 M 178 63.8 112.0
M 153 57.8  79.5 M 155 57.3  80.5 M 178 63.5 102.5 M 142 55.0  76.0
M 164 66.5 112.0 M 189 65.0 114.0 M 164 61.5 140.0 M 167 62.0 107.5
M 151 59.3  87.0
;

TITLE '-------- DATA ON AGE, WEIGHT, AND HEIGHT OF CHILDREN ---------';
PROC REG OUTEST=EST1 OUTSSCP=SSCP1;
   BY SEX;
   EQ1: MODEL  WEIGHT=HEIGHT;
```

```
   EQ2: MODEL  WEIGHT=HEIGHT AGE;
PROC PRINT DATA=SSCP1;
   TITLE2 'SSCP TYPE DATA SET';
PROC PRINT DATA=EST1;
   TITLE2 'EST TYPE DATA SET';
```

Output 31.19 Height and Weight Data: PROC REG

```
                   -------- DATA ON AGE, WEIGHT, AND HEIGHT OF CHILDREN ---------                       1

                                              SEX=F

MODEL: EQ1
DEP VARIABLE: WEIGHT
                                        ANALYSIS OF VARIANCE

                                    SUM OF         MEAN
                  SOURCE     DF     SQUARES        SQUARE       F VALUE       PROB>F

                  MODEL       1  21506.52309  21506.52309       141.094       0.0001
                  ERROR     109  16614.58502    152.42739
                  C TOTAL   110  38121.10811

                      ROOT MSE     12.34615      R-SQUARE       0.5642
                      DEP MEAN     98.87838      ADJ R-SQ       0.5602
                      C.V.          12.4862

                                        PARAMETER ESTIMATES

                                PARAMETER       STANDARD       T FOR H0:
              VARIABLE  DF       ESTIMATE          ERROR     PARAMETER=0      PROB > |T|

              INTERCEP   1     -153.12891    21.24814273          -7.207          0.0001
              HEIGHT     1     4.16361173     0.35052308          11.878          0.0001
```

```
                   -------- DATA ON AGE, WEIGHT, AND HEIGHT OF CHILDREN ---------                       2

                                              SEX=F

MODEL: EQ2
DEP VARIABLE: WEIGHT
                                        ANALYSIS OF VARIANCE

                                    SUM OF         MEAN
                  SOURCE     DF     SQUARES        SQUARE       F VALUE       PROB>F

                  MODEL       2  22432.27243  11216.13621        77.210       0.0001
                  ERROR     108  15688.83568    145.26700
                  C TOTAL   110  38121.10811

                      ROOT MSE     12.05268      R-SQUARE       0.5884
                      DEP MEAN     98.87838      ADJ R-SQ       0.5808
                      C.V.         12.18939

                                        PARAMETER ESTIMATES

                                PARAMETER       STANDARD       T FOR H0:
              VARIABLE  DF       ESTIMATE          ERROR     PARAMETER=0      PROB > |T|

              INTERCEP   1     -150.59698    20.76729993          -7.252          0.0001
              HEIGHT     1     3.60377969     0.40776801           8.838          0.0001
              AGE        1     1.90702588     0.75542849           2.524          0.0130
```

```
                  -------- DATA ON AGE, WEIGHT, AND HEIGHT OF CHILDREN ---------                              3
                                              SEX=M

MODEL: EQ1
DEP VARIABLE: WEIGHT
                                        ANALYSIS OF VARIANCE

                                     SUM OF          MEAN
                 SOURCE      DF     SQUARES        SQUARE        F VALUE        PROB>F

                 MODEL        1  31126.05991   31126.05991      206.239         0.0001
                 ERROR      124  18714.35477     150.92222
                 C TOTAL    125  49840.41468

                      ROOT MSE       12.28504     R-SQUARE        0.6245
                      DEP MEAN       103.4484     ADJ R-SQ        0.6215
                      C.V.           11.87552

                                        PARAMETER ESTIMATES

                              PARAMETER        STANDARD        T FOR H0:
           VARIABLE  DF        ESTIMATE           ERROR      PARAMETER=0        PROB > |T|

           INTERCEP   1      -125.69807     15.99362486           -7.859            0.0001
           HEIGHT     1      3.68977077      0.25692946           14.361            0.0001
```

```
                  -------- DATA ON AGE, WEIGHT, AND HEIGHT OF CHILDREN ---------                              4
                                              SEX=M

MODEL: EQ2
DEP VARIABLE: WEIGHT
                                        ANALYSIS OF VARIANCE

                                     SUM OF          MEAN
                 SOURCE      DF     SQUARES        SQUARE        F VALUE        PROB>F

                 MODEL        2  32974.75022   16487.37511      120.241         0.0001
                 ERROR      123  16865.66447     137.11922
                 C TOTAL    125  49840.41468

                      ROOT MSE       11.70979     R-SQUARE        0.6616
                      DEP MEAN       103.4484     ADJ R-SQ        0.6561
                      C.V.           11.31945

                                        PARAMETER ESTIMATES

                              PARAMETER        STANDARD        T FOR H0:
           VARIABLE  DF        ESTIMATE           ERROR      PARAMETER=0        PROB > |T|

           INTERCEP   1      -113.71346     15.59021361           -7.294            0.0001
           HEIGHT     1      2.68074932      0.36809058            7.283            0.0001
           AGE        1      3.08167226      0.83927355            3.672            0.0004
```

```
                  -------- DATA ON AGE, WEIGHT, AND HEIGHT OF CHILDREN ---------                              5
                                       SSCP TYPE DATA SET

           OBS    SEX    _NAME_       _TYPE_     INTERCEP      WEIGHT      HEIGHT       AGE

             1     F     INTERCEP     SSCP          111.0       10976        6718      1825
             2     F     WEIGHT       SSCP        10975.5     1123361      669470    182445
             3     F     HEIGHT       SSCP         6718.4      669470      407879    110818
             4     F     AGE          SSCP         1824.9      182445      110818     30364
             5     F                  N             111.0         111         111       111
             6     M     INTERCEP     SSCP          126.0       13035        7825      2072
             7     M     WEIGHT       SSCP        13034.5     1398239      817920    217717
             8     M     HEIGHT       SSCP         7825.0      817920      488244    129433
             9     M     AGE          SSCP         2072.1      217717      129433     34516
            10     M                  N             126.0         126         126       126
```

-------- DATA ON AGE, WEIGHT, AND HEIGHT OF CHILDREN --------- 6
EST TYPE DATA SET

OBS	SEX	_TYPE_	_MODEL_	_DEPVAR_	_SIGMA_	WEIGHT	HEIGHT	AGE	INTERCEP
1	F	OLS	EQ1	WEIGHT	12.3461	-1	4.16361	.	-153.13
2	F	OLS	EQ2	WEIGHT	12.0527	-1	3.60378	1.90703	-150.60
3	M	OLS	EQ1	WEIGHT	12.2850	-1	3.68977	.	-125.70
4	M	OLS	EQ2	WEIGHT	11.7098	-1	2.68075	3.08167	-113.71

REFERENCES

Allen, D.M. (1971), "Mean Square Error of Prediction as a Criterion for Selecting Variables," *Technometrics*, 13, 469-475.

Allen, D.M. and Cady, F.B. (1982), *Analyzing Experimental Data by Regression*, Belmont, CA: Lifetime Learning Publications.

Belsley, D.A., Kuh, E., and Welsch, R.E. (1980), *Regression Diagnostics*, New York: John Wiley & Sons.

Bock, R.D. (1975), *Multivariate Statistical Methods in Behavioral Research*, New York: McGraw-Hill.

Box, G.E.P. (1966), "The Use and Abuse of Regression," *Technometrics*, 8, 625-629.

Cook, R.D. (1977), "Detection of Influential Observations in Linear Regression," *Technometrics*, 19, 15-18.

Cook, R.D. (1979), "Influential Observations in Linear Regression," *Journal of the American Statistical Association*, 74, 169-174.

Daniel, C. and Wood, F. (1980), *Fitting Equations to Data*, Revised Edition, New York: John Wiley & Sons.

Draper, N. and Smith, H. (1981), *Applied Regression Analysis*, Second Edition, New York: John Wiley & Sons.

Durbin, J. and Watson, G.S. (1951), "Testing for Serial Correlation in Least Squares Regression," *Biometrika*, 37, 409-428.

Gauss, K.F. (1809), *Werke*, 4, 1-93.

Goodnight, J.H. (1979), "A Tutorial on the SWEEP Operator," *The American Statistician*, 33, 149-158.

Grunfeld, Y. (1958), "The Determinants of Corporate Investment," Unpublished Thesis, Chicago discussed in Boot, J.C.G. (1960), "Investment Demand: An Empirical Contribution to the Aggregation Problem," *International Economic Review*, 1, 3-30.

Johnston, J. (1972), *Econometric Methods*, New York: McGraw-Hill.

Kennedy, W.J. and Gentle, J.E. (1980), *Statistical Computing*, New York: Marcel Dekker.

Lewis, T. and Taylor, L.R. (1967), *Introduction to Experimental Ecology*, New York: Academic Press.

Mallows, C.L. (1973), "Some Comments on Cp," *Technometrics*, 15, 661-675.

Mardia, K.V., Kent, J.T., and Bibby, J.M. (1979), *Multivariate Analysis*, London: Academic Press.

Markov, A.A. (1900), *Wahrscheinlichkeitscrechnung*, Tebrer, Leipzig.

Morrison, D.F. (1976), *Multivariate Statistical Methods*, Second Edition, New York: McGraw-Hill.

Mosteller, F. and Tukey, J.W. (1977), *Data Analysis and Regression*, Reading, MA: Addison-Wesley.

Neter, J. and Wasserman, W. (1974), *Applied Linear Statistical Models*, Homewood, IL: Irwin.

Pillai, K.C.S. (1960), *Statistical Table for Tests of Multivariate Hypotheses*, Manila: The Statistical Center, University of Philippines.

Pindyck, R.S. and Rubinfeld, D.L. (1981), *Econometric Models and Econometric Forecasts*, Second Edition, New York: McGraw-Hill.

Pringle, R.M. and Raynor, A.A. (1971), *Generalized Inverse Matrices with Applications to Statistics*, New York: Hafner Publishing Company.

Rao, C.R. (1973), *Linear Statistical Inference and Its Applications*, Second Edition, New York: John Wiley & Sons.

Sall, J.P. (1981), "SAS Regression Applications," Revised Edition, SAS Technical Report A-102, Cary, NC: SAS Institute Inc.

Timm, N.H. (1975), *Multivariate Analysis with Applications in Education and Psychology*, Monterey, CA: Brooks/Cole.

Weisberg, S. (1980), *Applied Linear Regression*, New York: John Wiley & Sons.

White, Halbert (1980), "A Heteroskedasticity-Consistent Covariance Matrix Estimator and a Direct Test for Heteroskedasticity," *Econometrics*, 48, 817-838.

Chapter 32

The RSQUARE Procedure

Operating systems: All

ABSTRACT

The RSQUARE procedure selects optimal subsets of independent variables in a multiple regression analysis. Regression coefficients and a variety of statistics useful for model selection can be printed or output to a SAS data set.

INTRODUCTION

The RSQUARE procedure finds subsets of independent variables that best predict a dependent variable by linear regression in the given sample. You can specify the largest and smallest number of independent variables to appear in a subset and the number of subsets of each size to be selected. The R^2 statistic is the criterion for selecting subsets. PROC RSQUARE can also efficiently perform all possible subset regressions and print the models in decreasing order of R^2 magnitude within each subset size. Other statistics are available for comparing subsets of different sizes. These statistics, as well as estimated regression coefficients, can be printed or output to a SAS data set.

The subset models selected by PROC RSQUARE are optimal in terms of R^2 for the given sample, but they are not necessarily optimal for the population from which the sample was drawn or for any other sample in which you may want to make predictions. If a subset model is selected on the basis of a large R^2 value or any other criterion commonly used for model selection, then all regression statistics computed for that model under the assumption that the model is given *a priori*, including all statistics computed by RSQUARE, are biased.

While RSQUARE is a useful tool for exploratory model building, no statistical method can be relied on to identify the "true" model. Effective model building requires substantive theory to suggest relevant predictors and plausible functional forms for the model.

Reviews of model selection methods are given by Hocking (1976) and Judge et al. (1980).

SPECIFICATIONS

The following statements control the RSQUARE procedure:

PROC RSQUARE *options;*
MODEL *dependents=independents/options;*
FREQ *variable;*
WEIGHT *variable;*
BY *variables;*

There must be one or more MODEL statements. The FREQ, WEIGHT, and BY statements can appear only once. The MODEL, FREQ, WEIGHT, and BY statements can appear in any order.

PROC RSQUARE Statement

PROC RSQUARE *options;*

The following options can be specified in the PROC statement:

DATA=*SASdataset*
: names the SAS data set to be used. The data set can be an ordinary SAS data set or a TYPE=CORR, COV, or SSCP data set. If the DATA= option is omitted, RSQUARE uses the most recently created SAS data set.

SIMPLE
S
: prints means and standard deviations for every variable listed in a MODEL statement.

CORR
C
: prints the correlation matrix for all variables in the analysis.

NOINT
: suppresses the intercept term from all models.

NOPRINT
: suppresses the regression printout.

OUTEST=*SASdataset*
: creates a TYPE=EST data set containing model-selection statistics and parameter estimates for the selected models.

The options listed in the **MODEL Statement** section can also be used in the PROC RSQUARE statement. Any option specified in the PROC statement applies to every MODEL statement except those in which you specify a different value of the option. Optional statistics will appear in the OUTEST= data set only if the corresponding options are specified in the PROC statement.

MODEL Statement

label: MODEL *dependents=independents/options;*

The MODEL statement specifies the variables to use for one or more subset regression analyses. On the left side of the equal sign list one or more dependent variables; on the right side of the equal sign list one or more independent variables (regressors). The label is optional.

When more than one dependent variable is used, RSQUARE performs a separate analysis for each dependent variable. No multivariate analyses are performed.

Any number of MODEL statements can follow the PROC RSQUARE statement.

The following options can appear in either the PROC RSQUARE statement or any MODEL statement after the slash (/):

SELECT=*n* specifies the maximum number of subset models of each size to be printed or output to the OUTEST= data set. If SELECT= is used without the B option, the variables in each MODEL are listed in order of inclusion instead of the order in which they appear in the MODEL statement. If SELECT= is omitted and the number of regressors is less than 11, all possible subsets are evaluated. If SELECT= is omitted and the number of regressors is greater than 10, the number of subsets selected is at most equal to the number of regressors. A small value of SELECT= greatly reduces the CPU time required for large problems.

INCLUDE=*i* requests that the first *i* variables after the equal sign in the MODEL statement be included in every regression model. By default, no variables are required to appear in every model.

START=*n* specifies the smallest number of regressors to be reported in a subset model. The default value is one more than the value specified by the INCLUDE= option, or one if INCLUDE= is omitted.

STOP=*n* specifies the largest number of regressors to be reported in a subset model. The default is the number of regressors listed in the MODEL statement.

SIGMA=*n* specifies the true standard deviation of the error term to be used in computing CP and BIC (see below). If SIGMA= is not specified, an estimate from the full model is used.

ADJRSQ computes R^2 adjusted for degrees of freedom (Darlington 1968; Judge et al. 1980) for each model selected.

AIC computes Akaike's information criterion (Akaike 1969; Judge et al. 1980) for each model selected.

BIC computes Sawa's Bayesian information criterion (Sawa 1978; Judge et al. 1980) for each model selected.

CP computes Mallows' C_p statistic (Mallows 1973; Hocking 1976) for each model selected.

GMSEP computes the estimated mean square error of prediction assuming that both independent and dependent variables are multivariate normal (Stein 1960; Darlington 1969). Hocking's formula (1976, eq. 4.20) contains a misprint: "*n*-1" should read "*n*-2".

JP computes J_p, the estimated mean square error of prediction for each model selected assuming that the values of the regressors are fixed and that the model is correct. The J_p statistic is also called the final prediction error (FPE) by Akaike (Nicholson 1948; Lord 1950; Mallows 1967; Darlington 1968; Rothman 1968; Akaike 1969; Hocking 1976; Judge et al. 1980).

MSE computes the mean square error (Darlington 1968) for each model selected.

PC computes Amemiya's prediction criterion (Amemiya 1976; Judge et al. 1980) for each model selected.

RMSE prints the root mean square error for each model selected.

SBC computes the SBC statistic (Schwarz 1978; Judge et al. 1980) for each model selected.

SP computes the S_p statistic (Hocking, 1976) for each model selected.

SSE computes the error sum of squares for each model selected.

B computes estimated regression coefficients for each model selected.

FREQ Statement

FREQ *variable;*

If a variable in your data set represents the frequency of occurrence for the other values in the observation, include the variable's name in a FREQ statement. The procedure then treats the data set as if each observation appears *n* times, where *n* is the value of the FREQ variable for the observation. The total number of observations will be considered equal to the sum of the FREQ variable when the procedure determines degrees of freedom for significance probabilities.

WEIGHT Statement

WEIGHT *variable;*

A WEIGHT statement names a variable in the input data set whose values are relative weights for a weighted least-squares fit. If the weight value is proportional to the reciprocal of the variance for each observation, then the weighted estimates are the best linear unbiased estimates (BLUE).

The WEIGHT and FREQ statements have similar effects, except in the calculation of degrees of freedom.

BY Statement

BY *variables;*

A BY statement can be used with PROC RSQUARE to obtain separate analyses on observations in groups defined by the BY variables. When a BY statement appears, the procedure expects the input data set to be sorted in order of the BY variables. If your input data set is not sorted in ascending order, use the SORT procedure with a similar BY statement to sort the data, or, if appropriate, use the BY statement options NOTSORTED or DESCENDING. For more information, see the discussion of the BY statement in "Statements Used in the PROC Step" in the *SAS User's Guide: Basics*.

DETAILS

Limitations

There is no built-in limit on the number of independent variables, but the calculations for a large number of independent variables can be lengthy. In the worst case, adding one more variable to the list from which regressors are selected approximately doubles the CPU time. Therefore, we recommend that no more than about 20 independent variables be used for a single analysis. The time required for the analysis is highly dependent on the data and on the values of the SELECT=, START=, and STOP= options. Using the B option can also increase the CPU time substantially.

If the INCLUDE= option is used to include certain variables in all the models, the recommended limit on the number of independent variables is $20+i$, where i is the INCLUDE= value.

Missing Values

The data are read only once. Observations with missing values for any variable used by the procedure are omitted from the entire analysis.

Definitions

n	is the number of observations.
p	is the number of parameters including intercept, if any.
i	is equal to 1 if there is an intercept, 0 otherwise.
$\hat{\sigma}^2$	is the estimate of pure error variance from the SIGMA= option or from fitting the full model.
TSS_0	is the uncorrected total sum of squares for the dependent variable.
TSS_1	is the total sum of squares corrected for the mean for the dependent variable.
SSE	is the error sum of squares.
MSE	is equal to $SSE/(n-p)$.
RMSE	is equal to $\sqrt{MSE}$.
R^2	is equal to $1-SSE/TSS_i$.
adjusted R^2	is equal to $1-(n-i)(1-R^2)/(n-p)$.
J_p	is equal to $(n+p)MSE/n$.
PC	is equal to $(1-R^2)((n+p)/(n-p)) = J_p(n/TSS_i)$.
C_p	is equal to $(SSE/\hat{\sigma}^2)+2p-n$.
S_p	is equal to $MSE/(n-p-1)$.
GMSEP	is equal to $MSE(n+1)(n-2)/(n(n-p-1)) = S_p(n+1)(n-2)/n$.
AIC	is equal to $(n)\ln(SSE/n)+2p$.

SBC is equal to $(n)\ln(SSE/n) + (p)\ln(n)$.

BIC is equal to $(n)\ln(SSE/n) + 2(p + 2)q - 2q^2$ where $q = \hat{\sigma}^2/(SSE/n)$.

OUTEST= Data Set

The OUTEST= data set contains one observation for each subset model selected. For optional statistics to appear in the OUTEST= data set, the appropriate options must be specified in the PROC statement, not the MODEL statement(s). The variables are as follows:

- the BY variables, if any
- _MODEL_, a character variable containing the label of the corresponding MODEL statement, or MODEL*n* if no label was specified, where *n* is 1 for the first MODEL statement, 2 for the second model statement, and so on
- _TYPE_, a character variable with the value B for every observation
- _DEPVAR_, the name of the dependent variable
- _IN_, the number of regressors in the model not including the intercept
- _P_, the number of parameters in the model including the intercept, if any
- _EDF_, the error degrees of freedom
- _SSE_, the error sum of squares, if the SSE option is specified
- _MSE_, the mean squared error, if the MSE option is specified
- _RMSE_, the root mean squared error or standard error of estimate
- _RSQ_, the R^2 statistic
- _ADJRSQ_, the adjusted R^2, if the ADJRSQ option is specified
- _CP_, the C_p statistic, if the CP option is specified
- _SP_, the S_p statistic, if the SP option is specified
- _JP_, the J_p statistic, if the JP option is specified
- _PC_, the PC statistic, if the PC option is specified
- _GMSEP_, the GMSEP statistic, if the GMSEP option is specified
- _AIC_, the AIC statistic, if the AIC option is specified
- _BIC_, the BIC statistic, if the BIC option is specified
- _SBC_, the SBC statistic, if the SBC option is specified
- INTERCEP, the estimated intercept, unless NOINT is specified
- all the variables listed in any MODEL statement containing the estimated regression coefficients for the model. A variable that does not appear in the model corresponding to a given observation has a missing value in that observation. The dependent variable in each model is given a value of −1.

Printed Output

PROC RSQUARE prints its results beginning with the model containing the fewest independent variables and producing the smallest R^2. Results for other models with the same number of variables are then printed in order of increasing R^2, and so on for models with larger numbers of variables.

For each model considered, RSQUARE prints:

1. NUMBER IN MODEL or IN, the number of independent variables used in each model
2. R-SQUARE or RSQ, the squared multiple correlation coefficient

RSQUARE prints the following statistics for each model if requested:

3. ADJUSTED R-SQUARE or ADJ RSQ, R^2 adjusted for degrees of freedom

4. PC, Amemiya's prediction criterion
5. SSE, the error sum of squares
6. ROOT MSE, the root mean square error or standard error of estimate
7. MSE, the mean square error
8. J(P), the J_p statistic
9. GMSEP, the estimated mean square error of prediction assuming that both independent and dependent variables are multivariate normal
10. S(P), the S_p statistic
11. AIC, Akaike's information criterion
12. SBC, Schwarz's Bayesian criterion
13. BIC, Sawa's Bayesian information criterion
14. C(P), Mallows' C_p statistic

If the B option is specified, RSQUARE prints:

15. PARAMETER ESTIMATES, the estimated regression coefficients

If the B option is not specified, RSQUARE prints:

16. VARIABLES IN MODEL, the names of the independent variables included in the model.

EXAMPLES

Physical Fitness Data—All Models: Example 1

The example below requests R^2 and C_p statistics for all possible combinations of the six independent variables.

```
*------------------------DATA ON PHYSICAL FITNESS----------------------*
| THESE MEASUREMENTS WERE MADE ON MEN INVOLVED IN A PHYSICAL FITNESS  |
| COURSE AT N.C. STATE UNIV. THE VARIABLES ARE AGE(YEARS), WEIGHT(KG),|
| OXYGEN UPTAKE RATE(ML PER KG BODY WEIGHT PER MINUTE), TIME TO RUN   |
| 1.5 MILES(MINUTES), HEART RATE WHILE RESTING, HEART RATE WHILE      |
| RUNNING (SAME TIME OXYGEN RATE MEASURED), AND MAXIMUM HEART RATE    |
| RECORDED WHILE RUNNING. CERTAIN VALUES OF MAXPULSE WERE MODIFIED    |
| FOR CONSISTENCY.         DATA COURTESY DR. A.C. LINNERUD            |
*---------------------------------------------------------------------*;
DATA FITNESS;
   TITLE 'PHYSICAL FITNESS DATA: ALL MODELS';
   INPUT AGE WEIGHT OXY RUNTIME RSTPULSE RUNPULSE MAXPULSE @@;
   CARDS;
44 89.47  44.609 11.37 62 178 182    40 75.07  45.313 10.07 62 185 185
44 85.84  54.297  8.65 45 156 168    42 68.15  59.571  8.17 40 166 172
38 89.02  49.874  9.22 55 178 180    47 77.45  44.811 11.63 58 176 176
40 75.98  45.681 11.95 70 176 180    43 81.19  49.091 10.85 64 162 170
44 81.42  39.442 13.08 63 174 176    38 81.87  60.055  8.63 48 170 186
44 73.03  50.541 10.13 45 168 168    45 87.66  37.388 14.03 56 186 192
45 66.45  44.754 11.12 51 176 176    47 79.15  47.273 10.60 47 162 164
54 83.12  51.855 10.33 50 166 170    49 81.42  49.156  8.95 44 180 185
51 69.63  40.836 10.95 57 168 172    51 77.91  46.672 10.00 48 162 168
48 91.63  46.774 10.25 48 162 164    49 73.37  50.388 10.08 67 168 168
57 73.37  39.407 12.63 58 174 176    54 79.38  46.080 11.17 62 156 165
52 76.32  45.441  9.63 48 164 166    50 70.87  54.625  8.92 48 146 155
51 67.25  45.118 11.08 48 172 172    54 91.63  39.203 12.88 44 168 172
51 73.71  45.790 10.47 59 186 188    57 59.08  50.545  9.93 49 148 155
```

```
49 76.32  48.673  9.40 56 186 188     48 61.24  47.920 11.50 52 170 176
52 82.78  47.467 10.50 53 170 172
;
PROC RSQUARE CP;
   MODEL OXY=AGE WEIGHT RUNTIME RUNPULSE RSTPULSE MAXPULSE;
```

Output 32.1 Physical Fitness Data—All Models: PROC RSQUARE

```
                              PHYSICAL FITNESS DATA: ALL MODELS                                1

 N=31              REGRESSION MODELS FOR DEPENDENT VARIABLE: OXY  MODEL: MODEL1
 ❶                 ❷           ⓮            ⓰
 NUMBER IN        R-SQUARE         C(P)      VARIABLES IN MODEL
   MODEL

     1          0.02648849      127.395      WEIGHT
     1          0.05604592      122.707      MAXPULSE
     1          0.09277653      116.882      AGE
     1          0.15838344      106.477      RUNPULSE
     1          0.15948531      106.302      RSTPULSE
     1          0.74338010    13.698840      RUNTIME
 ------------------------------------------------------
     2          0.06751590      122.888      WEIGHT MAXPULSE
     2          0.15063534      109.706      AGE WEIGHT
     2          0.16685536      107.133      WEIGHT RUNPULSE
     2          0.17403933      105.994      RSTPULSE MAXPULSE
     2          0.18060672      104.952      WEIGHT RSTPULSE
     2          0.23503072    96.320923      RUNPULSE RSTPULSE
     2          0.25998174    92.363796      AGE MAXPULSE
     2          0.28941948    87.695093      RUNPULSE MAXPULSE
     2          0.30027026    85.974204      AGE RSTPULSE
     2          0.37599543    73.964510      AGE RUNPULSE
     2          0.74353296    15.674598      RUNTIME RSTPULSE
     2          0.74493479    15.452274      WEIGHT RUNTIME
     2          0.74522106    15.406872      RUNTIME MAXPULSE
     2          0.76142381    12.837184      RUNTIME RUNPULSE
     2          0.76424693    12.389449      AGE RUNTIME
 ----------------------------------------------------------
     3          0.18823207      105.743      WEIGHT RSTPULSE MAXPULSE
     3          0.24465116    96.795160      WEIGHT RUNPULSE RSTPULSE
     3          0.29021246    89.569330      AGE WEIGHT MAXPULSE
     3          0.32077932    84.721553      WEIGHT RUNPULSE MAXPULSE
     3          0.35377183    79.489080      RUNPULSE RSTPULSE MAXPULSE
     3          0.35684729    79.001324      AGE WEIGHT RSTPULSE
     3          0.39000680    73.742365      AGE RSTPULSE MAXPULSE
     3          0.40912553    70.710215      AGE WEIGHT RUNPULSE
     3          0.42227346    68.625008      AGE RUNPULSE MAXPULSE
     3          0.46664844    61.587323      AGE RUNPULSE RSTPULSE
     3          0.74511138    17.424267      WEIGHT RUNTIME RSTPULSE
     3          0.74522683    17.405958      RUNTIME RSTPULSE MAXPULSE
     3          0.74615485    17.258776      WEIGHT RUNTIME MAXPULSE
     3          0.76182904    14.772916      WEIGHT RUNTIME RUNPULSE
     3          0.76189848    14.761903      RUNTIME RUNPULSE RSTPULSE
     3          0.76734943    13.897406      AGE RUNTIME RSTPULSE
     3          0.77083060    13.345306      AGE WEIGHT RUNTIME
     3          0.78173017    11.616680      AGE RUNTIME MAXPULSE
     3          0.80998844     7.135037      RUNTIME RUNPULSE MAXPULSE
     3          0.81109446     6.959627      AGE RUNTIME RUNPULSE
 ----------------------------------------------------------
     4          0.38579687    76.410043      WEIGHT RUNPULSE RSTPULSE MAXPULSE
     4          0.42560710    70.096306      AGE WEIGHT RSTPULSE MAXPULSE
     4          0.47171966    62.783048      AGE WEIGHT RUNPULSE MAXPULSE
     4          0.50245083    57.909213      AGE RUNPULSE RSTPULSE MAXPULSE
     4          0.50339774    57.759038      AGE WEIGHT RUNPULSE RSTPULSE
     4          0.74617854    19.255019      WEIGHT RUNTIME RSTPULSE MAXPULSE
     4          0.76225238    16.705777      WEIGHT RUNTIME RUNPULSE RSTPULSE
     4          0.77503285    14.678848      AGE WEIGHT RUNTIME RSTPULSE
```

```
                              PHYSICAL FITNESS DATA: ALL MODELS                                2

 NUMBER IN        R-SQUARE         C(P)      VARIABLES IN MODEL
   MODEL

     4          0.78343214    13.346755      AGE RUNTIME RSTPULSE MAXPULSE
     4          0.78622430    12.903931      AGE WEIGHT RUNTIME MAXPULSE
     4          0.81040041     9.069700      RUNTIME RUNPULSE RSTPULSE MAXPULSE
```

(continued on next page)

(continued from previous page)

```
      4         0.81167015        8.868324        AGE RUNTIME RUNPULSE RSTPULSE
      4         0.81584902        8.205573        WEIGHT RUNTIME RUNPULSE MAXPULSE
      4         0.81649255        8.103512        AGE WEIGHT RUNTIME RUNPULSE
      4         0.83681815        4.879958        AGE RUNTIME RUNPULSE MAXPULSE
-------------------------------------------------------------------------------
      5         0.55406593       51.723275        AGE WEIGHT RUNPULSE RSTPULSE MAXPULSE
      5         0.78870109       14.511122        AGE WEIGHT RUNTIME RSTPULSE MAXPULSE
      5         0.81608280       10.168497        WEIGHT RUNTIME RUNPULSE RSTPULSE MAXPULSE
      5         0.81755611        9.934837        AGE WEIGHT RUNTIME RUNPULSE RSTPULSE
      5         0.83703132        6.846150        AGE RUNTIME RUNPULSE RSTPULSE MAXPULSE
      5         0.84800181        5.106275        AGE WEIGHT RUNTIME RUNPULSE MAXPULSE
-------------------------------------------------------------------------------
      6         0.84867192        7.000000        AGE WEIGHT RUNTIME RUNPULSE RSTPULSE MAXPULSE
-------------------------------------------------------------------------------------------
```

Physical Fitness Data—Best Models: Example 2

This example requests only the best model for each subset size but asks for a variety of model selection statistics, as well as the estimated regression coefficients. An OUTEST= data set is created, printed, and used to plot several statistics.

```
PROC RSQUARE DATA=FITNESS OUTEST=EST
             MSE JP GMSEP CP AIC BIC SBC B SELECT=1;
   MODEL OXY=AGE WEIGHT RUNTIME RUNPULSE RSTPULSE MAXPULSE;

PROC PRINT DATA=EST;

PROC PLOT;
   PLOT _CP_*_P_='C' _P_*_P_='P' / OVERLAY;
   PLOT _MSE_*_P_='M' _JP_*_P_='J' _GMSEP_*_P_='G' / OVERLAY;
   PLOT _AIC_*_P_='A' _BIC_*_P_='B' _SBC_*_P_='S' / OVERLAY;
   TITLE 'PHYSICAL FITNESS DATA: BEST MODELS';
```

Output 32.2 Physical Fitness Data—Best Models: PROC RSQUARE

PHYSICAL FITNESS DATA: BEST MODELS 1

N=31 REGRESSION MODELS FOR DEPENDENT VARIABLE: OXY MODEL: MODEL1

IN	RSQ	MSE (7)	J(P) (8)	GMSEP (9)	AIC (11)	SBC (12)	BIC (13)	C(P)	PARAMETER ESTIMATES (15) INTERCEPT	AGE	WEIGHT	RUNTIME	RUNPULSE	RSTPULSE	MAXPULSE
1	0.7434	7.53	8.02	8.05	64.534	67.402	65.467	13.699	82.4218	.	.	-3.31056	.	.	.
2	0.7642	7.17	7.86	7.95	63.905	68.207	64.821	12.389	88.4623	-0.15037	.	-3.20395	.	.	.
3	0.8111	5.96	6.73	6.86	59.037	64.773	61.313	6.9596	111.7	-0.25640	.	-2.82538	-.130909	.	.
4	0.8368	5.34	6.21	6.40	56.499	63.669	60.4	4.88	98.1479	-0.19773	.	-2.76758	-.348108	.	0.270513
5	0.8480	5.18	6.18	6.46	56.299	64.903	61.567	5.1063	102.2	-0.21962	-.072302	-2.68252	-.373401	.	0.304908
6	0.8487	5.37	6.58	6.99	58.162	68.2	64.075	7	102.9	-0.22697	-.074177	-2.62865	-.369628	-.021534	0.303217

Output 32.3 Physical Fitness Data—OUTEST= Data Set: PROC PRINT

PHYSICAL FITNESS DATA: BEST MODELS 2

OBS	_MODEL_	_TYPE_	_DEPVAR_	_IN_	_P_	_EDF_	_MSE_	_RMSE_	_RSQ_	_CP_	_JP_	_GMSEP_
1	MODEL1	B	OXY	1	2	29	7.53384	2.74478	0.743380	13.6988	8.01990	8.05462
2	MODEL1	B	OXY	2	3	28	7.16842	2.67739	0.764247	12.3894	7.86214	7.94778
3	MODEL1	B	OXY	3	4	27	5.95669	2.44063	0.811094	6.9596	6.72530	6.85833
4	MODEL1	B	OXY	4	5	26	5.34346	2.31159	0.836818	4.8800	6.20531	6.39837
5	MODEL1	B	OXY	5	6	25	5.17634	2.27516	0.848002	5.1063	6.17821	6.45651
6	MODEL1	B	OXY	6	7	24	5.36825	2.31695	0.848672	7.0000	6.58043	6.98700

OBS	_AIC_	_BIC_	_SBC_	INTERCEP	OXY	AGE	WEIGHT	RUNTIME	RUNPULSE	RSTPULSE	MAXPULSE
1	64.5341	65.4673	67.4021	82.422	-1	.	.	-3.3106	.	.	.
2	63.9050	64.8212	68.2069	88.462	-1	-0.15037	.	-3.2040	.	.	.
3	59.0373	61.3127	64.7733	111.718	-1	-0.25640	.	-2.8254	-0.13091	.	.
4	56.4995	60.3996	63.6694	98.148	-1	-0.19773	.	-2.7676	-0.34811	.	0.270513
5	56.2986	61.5667	64.9025	102.204	-1	-0.21962	-0.072302	-2.6825	-0.37340	.	0.304908
6	58.1616	64.0748	68.1995	102.934	-1	-0.22697	-0.074177	-2.6287	-0.36963	-0.021534	0.303217

Output 32.4 Physical Fitness Data—Best Models: PROC PLOT

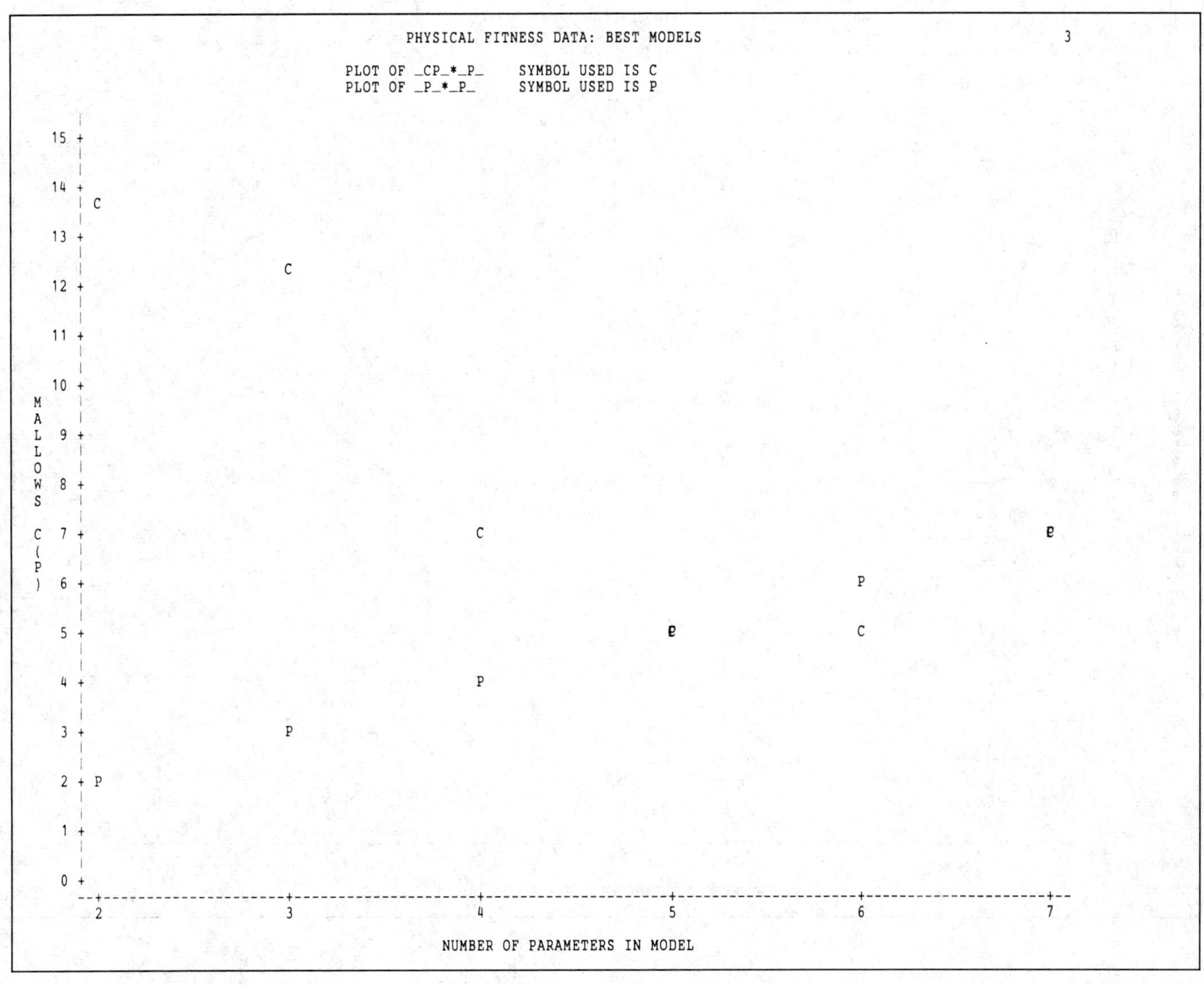

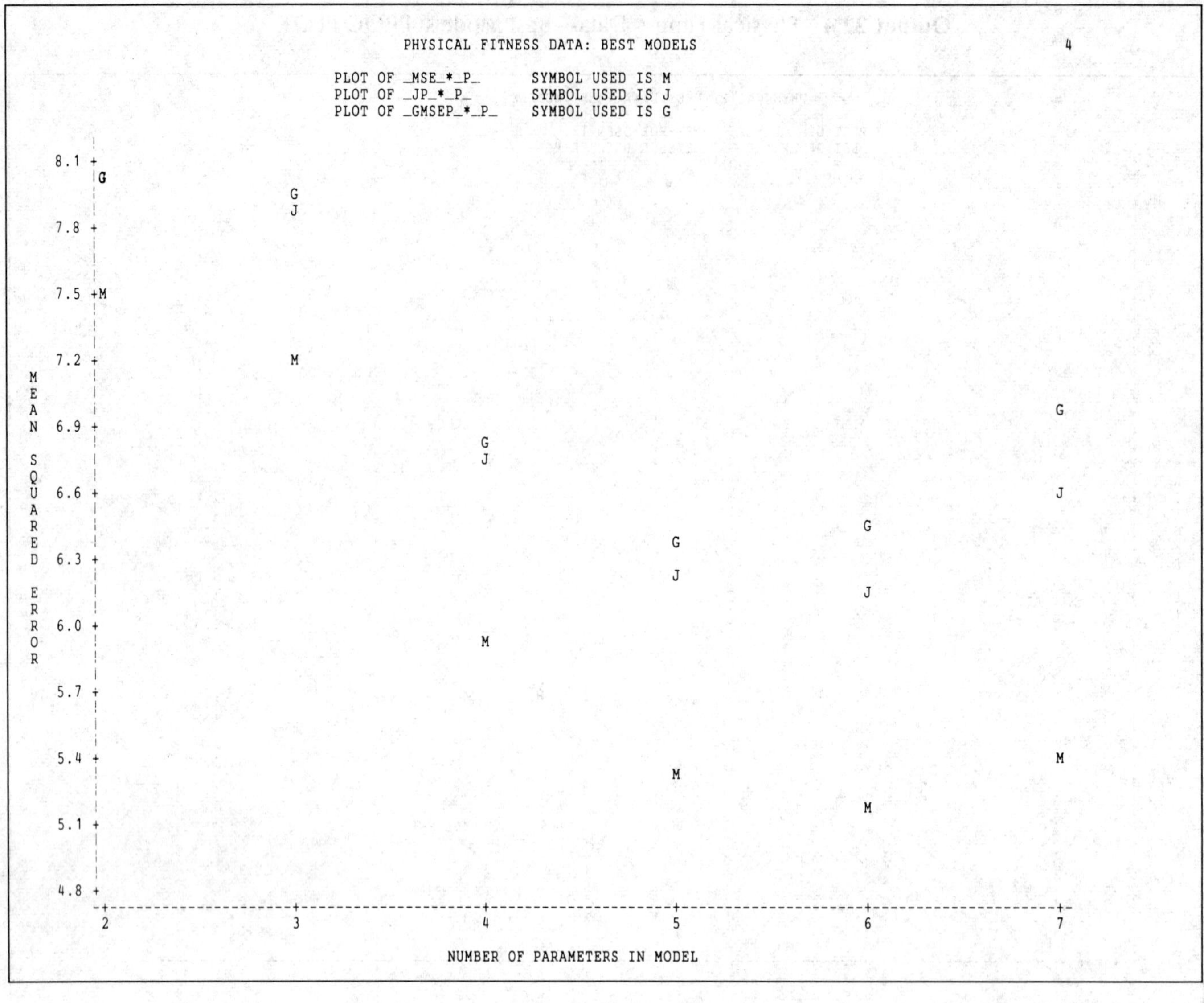
PHYSICAL FITNESS DATA: BEST MODELS
4
PLOT OF _MSE_*_P_ SYMBOL USED IS M
PLOT OF _JP_*_P_ SYMBOL USED IS J
PLOT OF _GMSEP_*_P_ SYMBOL USED IS G
MEAN SQUARED ERROR
8.1
7.8
7.5
7.2
6.9
6.6
6.3
6.0
5.7
5.4
5.1
4.8
2
3
4
5
6
7
NUMBER OF PARAMETERS IN MODEL

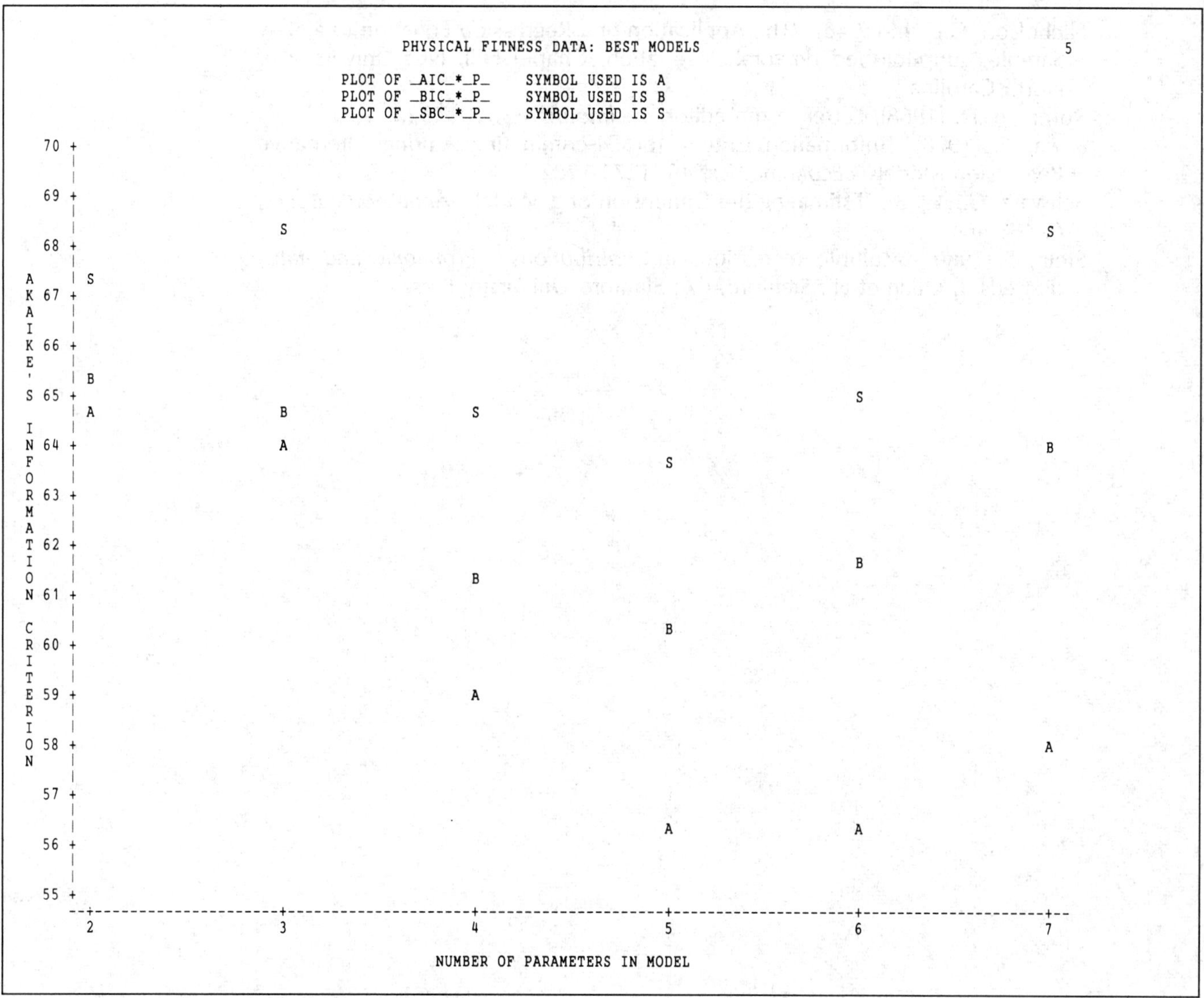

REFERENCES

Akaike, H. (1969), "Fitting Autoregressive Models for Prediction," *Annals of the Institute of Statistical Mathematics*, 21, 243-247.

Amemiya, T. (1976), "Selection of Regressors," Technical Report No. 225, Stanford, CA: Stanford University.

Darlington, R.B. (1968), "Multiple Regression in Psychological Research and Practice," *Psychological Bulletin*, 69, 161-182.

Hocking, R.R. (1976), "The Analysis and Selection of Variables in a Linear Regression," *Biometrics*, 32, 1-50.

Judge, G.G., Griffiths, W.E., Hill, R.C., and Lee, T. (1980), *The Theory and Practice of Econometrics*, New York: John Wiley & Sons.

Lord, F.M. (1950), "Efficiency of Prediction when a Progression Equation from One Sample is Used in a New Sample," Research Bulletin No. 50-40, Princeton, NJ: Educational Testing Service.

Mallows, C.L. (1967), "Choosing a Subset Regression," Bell Telephone Laboratories, unpublished report.

Mallows, C.L. (1973), "Some Comments on C(p)," *Technometrics*, 15, 661-675.

Nicholson, G.E., Jr. (1948), "The Application of a Regression Equation to a New Sample," unpublished doctoral dissertation, Chapel Hill, NC: University of North Carolina.

Rothman, D. (1968), Letter to the editor, *Technometrics*, 10, 432.

Sawa, T. (1978), "Information Criteria for Discriminating Among Alternative Regression Models," *Econometrica*, 46, 1273-1282.

Schwarz, G. (1978), "Estimating the Dimension of a Model," *Annals of Statistics*, 6, 461-464.

Stein, C. (1960), "Multiple Regression," in *Contributions to Probability and Statistics*, eds. I. Olkin et al., Stanford, CA: Stanford University Press.

Chapter 33

The RSREG Procedure

Operating systems: All

ABSTRACT

The RSREG procedure fits the parameters of a complete quadratic response surface and then determines critical values to optimize the response with respect to the factors in the model.

INTRODUCTION

Many industrial experiments are conducted to discover which factor values optimize a response. If each factor variable is measured at three or more values, a quadratic response surface can be estimated by least-squares regression. The predicted optimal value can be found from the estimated surface if the surface is shaped appropriately.

Suppose that a response variable y is measured at combinations of values of two factor variables, x_1 and x_2. The quadratic response-surface model for this variable is written:

$$y = \beta_0 + \beta_1 x_1 + \beta_2 x_2 + \beta_3 x_1^2 + \beta_4 x_2^2 + \beta_5 x_1 x_2 + \varepsilon \quad .$$

The parameters in the model are estimated by least-squares regression using the statements

```
PROC RSREG;
   MODEL Y = X1 X2;
```

The results from PROC RSREG can answer these questions:

1. How much does each type of effect contribute to the statistical fit? (The types are linear, quadratic, and cross product.)
2. Is part of the residual error due to lack-of-fit? Does the quadratic response model adequately represent the true response surface?
3. How much does each factor variable contribute to the statistical fit? Can the response be predicted as well if the variable is removed?
4. What combination of factor values yields the maximum or minimum response? Where is the optimum?
5. Is the surface shaped like a hill, a valley, a saddle-surface, or a flat surface?
6. For a grid of factor values, what are the predicted responses? Use them for plotting or selecting purposes.

Other procedures in the SAS System can be used for these response-surface problems, but PROC RSREG is more specialized. The RSREG MODEL statement

```
MODEL Y = X1 X2 X3;
```

is more compact than the MODEL statement for other regression procedures in the SAS System. For example, GLM's MODEL statement appears below:

```
MODEL Y = X1 X1*X1
          X2 X1*X2 X2*X2
          X3 X1*X3 X2*X3 X3*X3;
```

Variables are used according to the following conventions:

factor variables
: the factor variables for which the quadratic response surface is constructed. Variables must be numeric. For the necessary parameters to be estimated, each variable should have at least three distinct values in the data.

response variables
: the response (or dependent) variables must be numeric.

covariates
: additional independent variables to be included in the regression but not considered in the response surface.

WEIGHT variable
: a numeric variable for weighting the observations in the regression.

ID variables
: variables not in the above list that you want transferred to an output data set.

SPECIFICATIONS

The RSREG procedure allows one of each of the following statements:

PROC RSREG *options;*
  MODEL *response=independents / options;*

WEIGHT *variable;*
ID *variables;*
BY *variables;*

PROC RSREG Statement

PROC RSREG *options;*

The PROC RSREG statement can have the following options:

DATA=*SASdataset* specifies the input SAS data set that contains the data to be analyzed. If not specified, PROC RSREG uses the most recently created SAS data set.

OUT=*SASdataset* names an output SAS data set to contain the BY variables, ID variables, WEIGHT variable, and variables in the MODEL statement. If you want to create a permanent SAS data set, you must specify a two-level name (see "SAS Data Sets" in the *SAS User's Guide: Basics* for more information on permanent SAS data sets). For details on the data set created by PROC RSREG, see **Output Data Set** below.

NOPRINT suppresses the printed results when you want an output data set only.

MODEL Statement

The MODEL statement has the following form:

MODEL *response*=*independents* / *options;*

where any of the following options can be specified:

LACKFIT specifies that a lack-of-fit test is to be performed. If you specify LACKFIT, you must first sort your data on the independent variables so that observations repeating the same values are grouped together.

NOOPTIMAL
NOOPT suppresses the feature that finds the critical values for the quadratic response surface.

COVAR=*n* declares that the first *n* variables on the independent side of the model are simple regressors (covariates) rather than factors in the quadratic response surface. If you do not specify COVAR=, then PROC RSREG forms quadratic and cross product effects for all regressor variables in the MODEL statement.

Output options The following options control which types of statistics are output to the OUT= data set. The option keywords become values of the special variable _TYPE_ in the output data set.

ACTUAL the actual values from the input data set

PREDICT the values predicted by the model

RESIDUAL residual = actual - predicted

U95M upper 95% confidence limit for mean

L95M lower 95% confidence limit for mean

U95 upper 95% confidence limit for prediction

L95	lower 95% confidence limit for prediction
D	Cook's *D* influence statistic

BYOUT requests that only the first BY group be used to estimate the model. Subsequent BY groups have scoring statistics computed in the output data set only. BYOUT is used only when a BY statement is specified.

WEIGHT Statement

WEIGHT *variable;*

The WEIGHT statement names a numeric variable in the input data set. The values are to be used as relative weights on the observations to produce weighted least-squares estimates.

ID Statement

ID *variables;*

The ID statement names variables that you want to transfer to the output data set in addition to variables mentioned in other statements.

BY Statement

BY *variables;*

A BY statement can be used with PROC RSREG to obtain separate analyses on observations in groups defined by the BY variables. When a BY statement appears, the procedure expects the input data set to be sorted in order of the BY variables. If your input data set is not sorted in ascending order, use the SORT procedure with a similar BY statement to sort the data, or, if appropriate, use the BY statement options NOTSORTED or DESCENDING. For more information, see the discussion of the BY statement in "Statements Used in the PROC Step" in the *SAS User's Guide: Basics.*

DETAILS

Missing Values

If an observation has missing data for any of the variables used by the procedure, then that observation is not used in the estimation process. If one or more response variables are missing, but no factor or covariate variables are missing, then predicted values and confidence limits are computed for the output data set, but the residual and *D* statistic are missing.

Output Data Set

An output data set is created whenever the OUT= option is specified in the PROC RSREG statement. The data set contains the following variables:

- the BY variables.
- the ID variables.
- the WEIGHT variable.
- the independent variables in the MODEL statement.
- the variable _TYPE_, which identifies the observation type in the output data set. _TYPE_ is a character variable with a length of eight, and it

takes on the values ACTUAL, PREDICT, RESIDUAL, U95M, L95M, U95, L95, and D.

- the response variables containing special output values identified by the _TYPE_ variable.

All confidence limits use the two-tailed Student's *t* value.

Lack-of-Fit Test

If the LACKFIT option is specified, the data should be sorted so that repeated observations appear together. If the data are not sorted, the procedure cannot find these repeats. Since all other test statistics for the model are tested by total error rather than pure error, you may want to hand-calculate the tests with respect to pure error if the lack-of-fit is significant.

Plotting the Surface

You can generate predicted values for a grid of points to be plotted with the PREDICT option (see the example later in this chapter). Contour plots are possible for only two factor variables at a time, with other factor variables held to constant values. First, form a grid of points in the input data set using DO loops after the end-of-file. Response variables should be set to missing so that the grid data do not affect the estimates. The OUT= feature and PREDICT option create the output data set from PROC RSREG. The data set is then subset and used with the PLOT procedure to plot the contours in the grid (see the example later in this chapter).

Searching for Multiple Response Conditions

Suppose you want to find the factor setting that produces responses in a certain region. For example, you want to find the values of x_1 and x_2 that maximize y_1 subject to $y_2<2$ and $y_3<y_2+y_1$. The exact answer is not easy to obtain analytically, but brute force can be applied. Approach the problem by checking conditions across a grid of values in the range of interest.

```
DATA B; SET A END=EOF; OUTPUT;
   IF EOF THEN DO; Y1=.; Y2=.; Y3=.;
      DO X1=1 TO 5 BY .1;
         DO X2=1 TO 5 BY .1;
            OUTPUT;
            END;
         END;
      END;
PROC RSREG DATA=B OUT=C;
   MODEL Y1 Y2 Y3 = X1 X2 / PREDICT;
DATA D; SET C;
   IF Y2<2; IF Y3<Y2+Y1;
PROC SORT DATA=D; BY DESCENDING Y1;
PROC PRINT;
```

Computational Method

The model can be written in the form:

$$y_i = x_i'\mathbf{A}x_i + \mathbf{b}'x_i + \mathbf{c}'z_i + \varepsilon_i$$

where

y_i	is the i th observation on the response variable
x_i	$= (x_{i1}, x_{i2}, \ldots, x_{ik})$ are the k factor variables for the ith observation
z_i	$= (z_{i1}, z_{i2} \ldots, z_{iL})$ are the L covariate variables including the intercept term
A	is the k by k matrix of quadratic parameters
b	is the k by 1 vector of linear parameters
c	is the L by 1 vector of covariate parameters.

The parameters in **A**, **b**, and **c** are estimated by least squares. To optimize y with respect to x, take partial derivatives, set them to zero, and solve. Making **A** symmetric, this equation is written:

$$\partial y / \partial x = 2x'\mathbf{A} + \mathbf{b}' = 0$$
$$x = -.5A^{-1}\mathbf{b} \; .$$

To determine if the solution of critical values is a maximum or minimum, find out if **A** is negative or positive definite by looking at the eigenvalues of **A**.

if eigenvalues	then solution is
are all negative	maximum
are all positive	minimum
have mixed signs	saddle-point
contain zeros	in a flat area

The eigenvectors are also printed. The eigenvector for the largest eigenvalue gives the direction of steepest ascent, if positive, or steepest descent, if negative. The eigenvectors corresponding to small or zero eigenvalues point in directions of relative flatness.

Printed Output

All estimates and hypothesis tests depend on the correctness of the model and the error distributed according to classical statistical assumptions.

The individual items in the output from RSREG are

1. RESPONSE MEAN is the mean of the response variable in the sample.
2. ROOT MSE estimates the standard deviation of the response variable by the square root of the TOTAL ERROR mean square.
3. R-SQUARE is R^2, or the coefficient of determination. R^2 measures the portion of the variation in the response that is attributed to the model rather than to random error.
4. COEF OF VARIATION is the coefficient of variation, which is equal to 100*rootmse/mean for the response variable.
5. Terms are brought into the regression in four steps: (1) INTERCEPT and COVARIATES (not shown), (2) LINEAR terms like X1 AND X2, (3)

QUADRATIC terms like X1*X1 or X2*X2, and (4) CROSSPRODUCT terms like X1*X2.

6. DF indicates degrees of freedom and should be the same as the number of parameters unless one or more of the parameters are not estimable.
7. TYPE I SS, also called the sequential sums of squares, measure the reduction in the error sum of squares as terms are added to the model individually (LINEAR, QUADRATIC, and so forth).
8. These R-SQUAREs measure the portion of total R^2 contributed as each set of terms (LINEAR, QUADRATIC, and so forth) is added to the model.
9. Each F-RATIO tests the hypothesis that all parameters in the term are zero using the TOTAL ERROR mean square as the denominator. This item is a test of a TYPE I hypothesis, containing the usual F test numerator, conditional on the effects of subsequent variables not being in the model.
10. PROB is the significance value or probability of obtaining at least as great an *F* ratio given that the hypothesis is true. When PROB$<$.05, the effect is usually termed significant.
11. The TOTAL ERROR sum of squares can be partitioned into LACK OF FIT and PURE ERROR. When LACK OF FIT is significantly different from PURE ERROR, then there is variation in the model not accounted for by random error.
12. The TOTAL ERROR MEAN SQUARE estimates σ^2, the variance.
13. If an effect is a linear combination of previous effects, the parameter for it is not estimable. When this happens, the DF is zero, the parameter estimate is set to zero, and the estimates and tests on other parameters are conditional on this parameter being zero (not shown).
14. The ESTIMATE column contains the parameter estimates.
15. The STD DEV column contains the estimated standard deviations of the parameter estimates.
16. The T-RATIO column contains *t* values of a test of the hypothesis that the true parameter is zero.
17. PROB gives the significance value or probability of a greater absolute *t* ratio given that the hypothesis is true.
18. The test on a factor, say X1, is a joint test on all the parameters involving that factor. For example, the test for X1 tests the hypothesis that the parameters for X1, X1*X1, and X1*X2 are all zero.
19. The CRITICAL VALUEs for the factor variables are solved to find the factor combinations that yield the optimum response. The critical values can be at a minimum, maximum, or saddle point.
20. The EIGENVALUES and EIGENVECTORS are from the matrix of quadratic parameter estimates that determine the curvature of the response surface.

EXAMPLE

A Three-Factor Quadratic Model

The following example uses the three-factor quadratic model discussed in John (1971). The objective is to minimize the unpleasant odor of a chemical.

```
*-------------------RESPONSE SURFACE EXPERIMENT--------------------*
| SCHNEIDER AND STOCKETT (1963) PERFORMED AN EXPERIMENT AIMED AT   |
| REDUCING THE UNPLEASANT ODOR OF A CHEMICAL PRODUCT WITH SEVERAL  |
| FACTORS. FROM PETER W. M. JOHN, STATISTICAL DESIGN AND ANALYSIS  |
| OF EXPERIMENTS, MACMILLAN 1971.                                  |
*------------------------------------------------------------------*;

   DATA A;
      INPUT Y X1-X3 @@;
      LABEL Y=ODOR
          X1=TEMPERATURE
          X2=GAS-LIQUID RATIO
          X3=PACKING HEIGHT;
      CARDS;
   66 -1 -1  0     39  1 -1  0     43 -1  1  0     49  1  1  0
   58 -1  0 -1     17  1  0 -1     -5 -1  0  1    -40  1  0  1
   65  0 -1 -1      7  0  1 -1     43  0 -1  1    -22  0  1  1
   -31 0  0  0    -35  0  0  0    -26  0  0  0
   ;
   PROC SORT; BY X1-X3;
   PROC RSREG;
      MODEL Y=X1-X3 /LACKFIT;
```

Output 33.1 A Three-Factor Quadratic Model using the LACKFIT Option

```
                                                                         1
RESPONSE SURFACE FOR VARIABLE Y

        (1) RESPONSE MEAN              15.2
        (2) ROOT MSE               22.47851
        (3) R-SQUARE              0.8819895
        (4) COEF OF VARIATION      1.478849

        (5) REGRESSION      (6) DF (7) TYPE I SS (8) R-SQUARE (9) F-RATIO (10) PROB

            LINEAR              3   7143.25000     0.3337      4.71  0.0641
            QUADRATIC           3  11445.23333     0.5346      7.55  0.0264
            CROSSPRODUCT        3    293.50000     0.0137      0.19  0.8965
            TOTAL REGRESS       9  18881.98333     0.8820      4.15  0.0657

            RESIDUAL           DF           SS  MEAN SQUARE   F-RATIO    PROB

            LACK OF FIT         3   2485.75000    828.58333    40.750  0.0240
            PURE ERROR          2  40.66666667  20.33333333
       (11) TOTAL ERROR         5   2526.41667    505.28333 (12)

                                  (14)           (15)         (16)      (17)
            PARAMETER          DF     ESTIMATE      STD DEV   T-RATIO    PROB

            INTERCEPT           1 -30.66666667  12.97797279     -2.36  0.0645
            X1                  1 -12.12500000   7.94735281     -1.53  0.1876
            X2                  1 -17.00000000   7.94735281     -2.14  0.0854
            X3                  1 -21.37500000   7.94735281     -2.69  0.0433
            X1*X1               1  32.08333333  11.69818659      2.74  0.0407
            X2*X1               1   8.25000000  11.23925413      0.73  0.4959
            X2*X2               1  47.83333333  11.69818659      4.09  0.0095
            X3*X1               1   1.50000000  11.23925413      0.13  0.8990
            X3*X2               1  -1.75000000  11.23925413     -0.16  0.8824
            X3*X3               1   6.08333333  11.69818659      0.52  0.6252
```

(continued on next page)

(continued from previous page)

```
                    FACTOR              DF            SS  MEAN SQUARE   F-RATIO     PROB
                                                                                      ⓳
                    X1                   4      5258.016     1314.504      2.60  0.1613 TEMPERATURE
                    X2                   4       11044.6     2761.151      5.46  0.0454 GAS-LIQUID RATIO
                 ⓲  X3                   4      3813.016      953.254      1.89  0.2510 PACKING HEIGHT
```

```
                                                                                                   2

SOLUTION FOR OPTIMUM RESPONSE

            FACTOR CRITICAL VALUE

            X1          0.12191255
            X2          0.19957464
            X3          1.77052494

PREDICTED VALUE AT OPTIMUM        -52.0246


EIGENVALUES    EIGENVECTORS
                         X1            X2            X3
    48.85881      0.2380908     0.9711161    -0.0156903
    31.10346      0.9706958     -0.237384    0.03739919
    6.037732     -0.0325943    0.02413488     0.9991772

SOLUTION WAS A MINIMUM
```

To plot the response surface with respect to two of the dimensions, we fix X3 at the optimum and generate a grid of points for X1 and X2. PROC RSREG computes the predicted values, which are output and plotted using the CONTOUR feature of PROC PLOT.

```
DATA B;
   *-----THE ACTUAL VALUES-----;
   SET A END=EOF;
   OUTPUT;
   *-----FOLLOWED BY AN X1*X2 GRID FOR PLOTTING-----;
   IF EOF THEN DO; Y=.; X3=1.77;
      DO X1=-1.5 TO 1.5 BY .1;
         DO X2=-2 TO 2 BY .1;
            OUTPUT;
            END;
         END;
      END;
PROC RSREG DATA=B OUT=C NOPRINT;
   MODEL Y=X1-X3 / PREDICT NOPRINT;
DATA D; SET C; IF X3=1.77;
PROC PLOT DATA=D;
PLOT X1*X2=Y /CONTOUR=6 HPOS=50 VPOS=36;
```

Output 33.2 A Plot of the Response Surface using the PREDICT Option

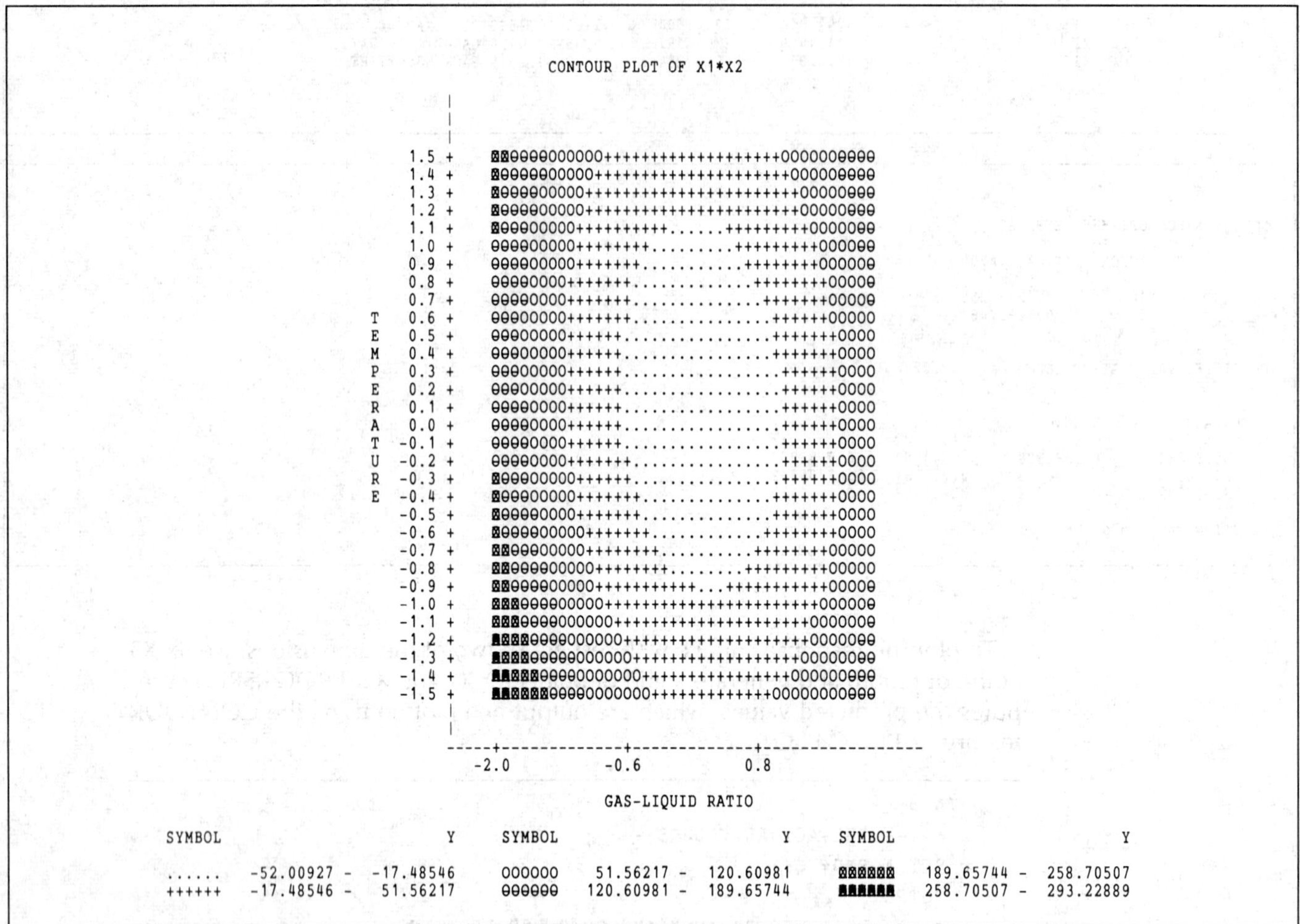

REFERENCES

Box, G.E.P. and Hunter, J.S. (1957), "Multifactor Experimental Designs for Exploring Response Surfaces," *Annuals of Mathematical Statistics*, 28, 195-242.

Box, G.E.P. and Wilson, K.J. (1951), "On the Experimental Attainment of Optimum Conditions," *Journal of the Royal Statistical Society*, Ser. B, 13, 1-45.

Cochran, W.G. and Cox, G.M. (1957), *Experimental Designs*, (2nd ed.), New York: John Wiley & Sons.

John, P.W.M. (1971), *Statistical Design and Analysis of Experiments*, New York: Macmillan.

Myers, Raymond H. (1976), *Response Surface Methodology*, Blacksburg, Virginia: Virginia Polytechnic Institute and State University.

Chapter 34

The SCORE Procedure

Operating systems: All

ABSTRACT

The SCORE procedure multiplies values from two SAS data sets, one containing coefficients (for example, factor-scoring coefficients or regression coefficients) and the other containing data to be scored using the coefficients. The result of this multiplication is an output SAS data set containing the linear combinations of the coefficients and the original data values.

INTRODUCTION

Many statistical procedures output coefficients that PROC SCORE can apply to raw data to produce scores. The new score variable is formed as a linear combination of old variables, where the linear combination uses the scoring coefficients. In other words, SCORE crossmultiplies part of one data set with another.

The data set containing scoring coefficients must also have two special variables: the _TYPE_ variable identifies the observations that contain scoring coefficients; the _NAME_ or _MODEL_ variable contains a SAS name that can be used to name the new variables output from PROC SCORE.

For example, PROC FACTOR produces an output data set that contains factor scoring coefficients. These scoring coefficients are identified on the data set output from FACTOR by _TYPE_='SCORE', which is the TYPE that PROC SCORE searches for unless the TYPE= option in the PROC SCORE statement specifies otherwise. The _NAME_ variable in the data set from FACTOR gives each score a name like FACTOR1, FACTOR2, and so forth. The data set output from PROC FACTOR also has _TYPE_=MEAN and _TYPE_=STD records, which PROC SCORE uses to standardize the data before scores are calculated. Thus, with the FACTOR procedure you do not produce factor scores directly, but rather you invoke PROC SCORE using the FACTOR output data set to obtain scores.

Several other multivariate procedures in base SAS software involve methods for forming linear combinations of variables and produce coefficients in a form convenient for PROC SCORE to use. Consult the descriptions of the PRINCOMP, CANCORR, CANDISC, and VARCLUS procedures.

Some regression procedures, such as REG, can send the parameter estimates to an output data set specified by the OUTEST= option. The _TYPE_ variable is given a value such as OLS, which corresponds to the estimation method. The _MODEL_ variable contains the label of the MODEL statement. When PROC SCORE is invoked using the TYPE=OLS option, the procedure first reads in the parameter estimates, then multiplies them into the original data to produce scores. Since the dependent variable is coded with coefficient −1, the scores are the negative residuals. If SCORE is told to ignore the −1 coefficient (PREDICT option), the scores are predicted values.

When the data set containing the coefficients also includes observations containing means and standard deviations (_TYPE_='MEAN' and _TYPE_='STD'), the data are standardized before scoring.

SPECIFICATIONS

You can invoke PROC SCORE with the following statements:

PROC SCORE *options*;
  VAR *variables*;

Since the SCORE procedure has not been programmed to synchronize BY groups across two input data sets, the BY statement **cannot** be used with PROC SCORE.

PROC SCORE Statement

PROC SCORE *options*;

The options below can appear in the PROC SCORE statement:

DATA=*SASdataset*
: names the input SAS data set containing the raw data to score. This specification is **required**.

SCORE=*SASdataset*
: names the data set containing the scoring coefficients. If SCORE= is omitted, the most recently created SAS data set is used. This data set must have two special variables: _TYPE_ and either _NAME_ or _MODEL_.

OUT=*SASdataset*
: names the output SAS data set to be created by SCORE. This data set has all the variables from the DATA= data set, plus score variables named from the _NAME_ or _MODEL_ values in the SCORE= data set. If you want to create a permanent SAS data set, you must specify a two-level name. (See "SAS Files" in the *SAS User's Guide: Basics* for more information on permanent SAS data sets.)

TYPE=*value*
: specifies the observations in the SCORE= data set that have scoring coefficients. The TYPE procedure option is unrelated to the data set parameter that has the same name. The procedure examines the values of the special variable _TYPE_ in the SCORE= data set. When the value matches the TYPE= value, the observation is used to score a new variable. The default is TYPE=SCORE, which selects scoring coefficients for which the variable _TYPE_ has the value of

SCORE. Since this is what is desired from data sets produced by FACTOR, you need not specify TYPE= for factor scoring. When regression coefficients are used, TYPE= is specified as a regression method, usually TYPE=OLS.

PREDICT
: specifies that PROC SCORE should treat coefficients of −1 in the SCORE= data set as 0. In regression applications, the dependent variable is coded with a coefficient of −1. Applied directly to regression results, PROC SCORE produces (negative) residuals; the PREDICT option changes this so that predicted values are produced instead.

NOSTD
: suppresses centering and scaling the raw data. Ordinarily, if SCORE finds MEAN and STD observations in the SCORE= data set, the procedure uses these to standardize the data before scoring.

VAR Statement

VAR *variables;*

The VAR statement specifies the variables to be used in computing a score. These variables must be in both the DATA= and SCORE= input data sets. If no VAR statement is given, the procedure uses all numeric variables in the SCORE= data set. You should almost always use a VAR statement with PROC SCORE since you rarely want to score all the numeric variables.

DETAILS

Missing Values

If one of the original variables has a missing value for an observation, all the scores have missing values for that observation. The exception to this is if the PREDICT option is specified, the variable with a coefficient of −1 can tolerate a missing value and still produce a prediction score.

Output Data Set

PROC SCORE produces an output data set but no printed output.

EXAMPLE

Three Kinds of Scoring

First, PROC FACTOR produces an output data set containing scoring coefficients in observations identified by _TYPE_='SCORE'. These data, together with the original data set FITNESS, are supplied to PROC SCORE, resulting in a data set containing scores FACTOR1 and FACTOR2. (See the chapters on the CANCORR, CANDISC, PRINCOMP, and VARCLUS procedures for more examples.)

```
* THIS DATA SET CONTAINS ONLY THE FIRST 12 OBSERVATIONS FROM;
* THE FULL DATA SET USED IN THE REGRESSION CHAPTERS.        ;
DATA FITNESS;
   INPUT AGE WEIGHT OXY RUNTIME RSTPULSE RUNPULSE @@;
   CARDS;
```

```
44 89.47  44.609 11.37 62 178      40 75.07  45.313 10.07 62 185
44 85.84  54.297  8.65 45 156      42 68.15  59.571  8.17 40 166
38 89.02  49.874  9.22 55 178      47 77.45  44.811 11.63 58 176
40 75.98  45.681 11.95 70 176      43 81.19  49.091 10.85 64 162
44 81.42  39.442 13.08 63 174      38 81.87  60.055  8.63 48 170
44 73.03  50.541 10.13 45 168      45 87.66  37.388 14.03 56 186
;
PROC FACTOR DATA=FITNESS OUTSTAT=FACTOUT
        METHOD=PRIN ROTATE=VARIMAX SCORE;
   VAR AGE WEIGHT RUNTIME RUNPULSE RSTPULSE;
   TITLE 'FACTOR SCORING EXAMPLE';
PROC PRINT DATA=FACTOUT;
   TITLE2 'DATA SET FROM PROC FACTOR';

PROC SCORE DATA=FITNESS SCORE=FACTOUT OUT=FSCORE;
   VAR AGE WEIGHT RUNTIME RUNPULSE RSTPULSE;
PROC PRINT DATA=FSCORE;
   TITLE2 'DATA SET FROM PROC SCORE';
```

Output 34.1 Creating an OUTSTAT= Data Set with PROC FACTOR

```
                                        FACTOR SCORING EXAMPLE                                                        1
INITIAL FACTOR METHOD: PRINCIPAL COMPONENTS

                                  PRIOR COMMUNALITY ESTIMATES: ONE

              EIGENVALUES OF THE CORRELATION MATRIX:  TOTAL =          5   AVERAGE =           1

                                     1          2          3          4          5
                   EIGENVALUE    2.309306   1.192200   0.882227   0.502567   0.113700
                   DIFFERENCE    1.117107   0.309972   0.379660   0.388867
                   PROPORTION      0.4619     0.2384     0.1764     0.1005     0.0227
                   CUMULATIVE      0.4619     0.7003     0.8767     0.9773     1.0000

                          2 FACTORS WILL BE RETAINED BY THE MINEIGEN CRITERION
                                           FACTOR PATTERN

                                          FACTOR1    FACTOR2

                             AGE          0.29795    0.93675
                             WEIGHT       0.43282   -0.17750
                             RUNTIME      0.91983    0.28782
                             RUNPULSE     0.72671   -0.38191
                             RSTPULSE     0.81179   -0.23344
                                  VARIANCE EXPLAINED BY EACH FACTOR

                                        FACTOR1    FACTOR2
                                       2.309306   1.192200

                         FINAL COMMUNALITY ESTIMATES: TOTAL =    3.501506
                               AGE     WEIGHT    RUNTIME   RUNPULSE   RSTPULSE
                          0.966284   0.218834   0.928933   0.673962   0.713493
```

```
                         FACTOR SCORING EXAMPLE                                   2

ROTATION METHOD: VARIMAX

                      ORTHOGONAL TRANSFORMATION MATRIX

                                     1         2

                         1     0.92536   0.37908
                         2    -0.37908   0.92536

                         ROTATED FACTOR PATTERN

                                FACTOR1   FACTOR2

                    AGE        -0.07939   0.97979
                    WEIGHT      0.46780  -0.00018
                    RUNTIME     0.74207   0.61503
                    RUNPULSE    0.81725  -0.07792
                    RSTPULSE    0.83969   0.09172

                      VARIANCE EXPLAINED BY EACH FACTOR

                            FACTOR1   FACTOR2
                           2.148775  1.352731

              FINAL COMMUNALITY ESTIMATES: TOTAL =    3.501506

                    AGE    WEIGHT   RUNTIME  RUNPULSE  RSTPULSE
               0.966284  0.218834  0.928933  0.673962  0.713493

                   SCORING COEFFICIENTS ESTIMATED BY REGRESSION

          SQUARED MULTIPLE CORRELATIONS OF THE VARIABLES WITH EACH FACTOR

                            FACTOR1   FACTOR2
                           1.000000  1.000000

                      STANDARDIZED SCORING COEFFICIENTS

                                FACTOR1   FACTOR2

                    AGE        -0.17846   0.77600
                    WEIGHT      0.22987  -0.06672
                    RUNTIME     0.27707   0.37440
                    RUNPULSE    0.41263  -0.17714
                    RSTPULSE    0.39952  -0.04793
```

Output 34.2 OUTEST= Data Set from PROC FACTOR Reproduced with PROC PRINT

```
                          FACTOR SCORING EXAMPLE                                  3
                          DATA SET FROM PROC FACTOR

 OBS   _TYPE_     _NAME_        AGE     WEIGHT    RUNTIME    RUNPULSE   RSTPULSE

   1   MEAN                  42.4167   80.5125    10.6483    172.917    55.6667
   2   STD                    2.8431    6.7660     1.8444      8.918     9.2769
   3   N                     12.0000   12.0000    12.0000     12.000    12.0000
   4   CORR       AGE         1.0000    0.0128     0.5005     -0.095    -0.0080
   5   CORR       WEIGHT      0.0128    1.0000     0.2637      0.173     0.2396
   6   CORR       RUNTIME     0.5005    0.2637     1.0000      0.556     0.6620
   7   CORR       RUNPULSE   -0.0953    0.1731     0.5555      1.000     0.4853
   8   CORR       RSTPULSE   -0.0080    0.2396     0.6620      0.485     1.0000
   9   COMMUNAL               0.9663    0.2188     0.9289      0.674     0.7135
  10   PRIORS                 1.0000    1.0000     1.0000      1.000     1.0000
  11   EIGENVAL               2.3093    1.1922     0.8822      0.503     0.1137
  12   UNROTATE   FACTOR1     0.2980    0.4328     0.9198      0.727     0.8118
  13   UNROTATE   FACTOR2     0.9368   -0.1775     0.2878     -0.382    -0.2334
  14   TRANSFOR   FACTOR1     0.9254   -0.3791      .           .          .
  15   TRANSFOR   FACTOR2     0.3791    0.9254      .           .          .
  16   PATTERN    FACTOR1    -0.0794    0.4678     0.7421      0.817     0.8397
  17   PATTERN    FACTOR2     0.9798   -0.0002     0.6150     -0.078     0.0917
  18   SCORE      FACTOR1    -0.1785    0.2299     0.2771      0.413     0.3995
  19   SCORE      FACTOR2     0.7760   -0.0667     0.3744     -0.177    -0.0479
```

Output 34.3 OUT= Data Set from PROC SCORE Reproduced with PROC PRINT

```
                              FACTOR SCORING EXAMPLE                                          4
                              DATA SET FROM PROC SCORE

OBS   AGE   WEIGHT     OXY     RUNTIME   RSTPULSE   RUNPULSE   FACTOR1    FACTOR2

  1    44    89.47   44.609    11.37        62         178       0.8213    0.3566
  2    40    75.07   45.313    10.07        62         185       0.7117   -0.9961
  3    44    85.84   54.297     8.65        45         156      -1.4606    0.3651
  4    42    68.15   59.571     8.17        40         166      -1.7609   -0.2766
  5    38    89.02   49.874     9.22        55         178       0.5582   -1.6768
  6    47    77.45   44.811    11.63        58         176      -0.0011    1.4071
  7    40    75.98   45.681    11.95        70         176       0.9532   -0.4860
  8    43    81.19   49.091    10.85        64         162      -0.1295    0.3672
  9    44    81.42   39.442    13.08        63         174       0.6627    0.8574
 10    38    81.87   60.055     8.63        48         170      -0.4450   -1.5310
 11    44    73.03   50.541    10.13        45         168      -1.1183    0.5535
 12    45    87.66   37.388    14.03        56         186       1.2084    1.0595
```

In the next part of the example, regression coefficients are output by the REG procedure. The TYPE= specification is OLS, and the names of the variables are found in the variable _MODEL_, which gets its values from the label of a model. If the scoring variables include only the independent variables, the resulting score variable contains predicted values. If the dependent variable is included (with a score coefficient of −1), the resulting scores are negative residuals. You can also use the PREDICT option to ignore a scoring coefficient of −1.

```
PROC REG DATA=FITNESS OUTEST=REGOUT;
   OXYHAT: MODEL OXY=AGE WEIGHT RUNTIME RUNPULSE RSTPULSE;
   TITLE 'REGRESSION SCORING EXAMPLE';
PROC PRINT DATA=REGOUT;
   TITLE2 'OUTEST= DATA SET FROM PROC REG';
PROC SCORE DATA=FITNESS SCORE=REGOUT OUT=RSCOREP TYPE=OLS;
   VAR AGE WEIGHT RUNTIME RUNPULSE RSTPULSE;
PROC PRINT DATA=RSCOREP;
   TITLE2 'PREDICTED SCORES FOR REGRESSION';

PROC SCORE DATA=FITNESS SCORE=REGOUT OUT=RSCORER TYPE=OLS;
   VAR OXY AGE WEIGHT RUNTIME RUNPULSE RSTPULSE;
PROC PRINT DATA=RSCORER;
   TITLE2 'RESIDUAL SCORES FOR REGRESSION';
```

Output 34.4 Creating an OUTEST= Data Set with PROC REG

```
                                 REGRESSION SCORING EXAMPLE                                   5
MODEL: OXYHAT
DEP VARIABLE: OXY
                                    ANALYSIS OF VARIANCE

                                  SUM OF         MEAN
              SOURCE      DF     SQUARES        SQUARE      F VALUE      PROB>F

              MODEL        5   509.62201     101.92440       15.802      0.0021
              ERROR        6  38.70060343   6.45010057
              C TOTAL     11   548.32261
```

(continued on next page)

(continued from previous page)

ROOT MSE	2.539705	R-SQUARE	0.9294
DEP MEAN	48.38942	ADJ R-SQ	0.8706
C.V.	5.248472		

PARAMETER ESTIMATES

VARIABLE	DF	PARAMETER ESTIMATE	STANDARD ERROR	T FOR H0: PARAMETER=0	PROB > |T|
INTERCEP	1	151.91550	31.04737619	4.893	0.0027
AGE	1	-0.63044969	0.42502668	-1.483	0.1885
WEIGHT	1	-0.10586234	0.11868838	-0.892	0.4068
RUNTIME	1	-1.75697762	0.93844085	-1.872	0.1103
RUNPULSE	1	-0.22891008	0.12168627	-1.881	0.1090
RSTPULSE	1	-0.17910210	0.13005008	-1.377	0.2176

Output 34.5 OUTEST= Data Set from PROC REG Reproduced with PROC PRINT

REGRESSION SCORING EXAMPLE 6
OUTEST= DATA SET FROM PROC REG

OBS	_TYPE_	_MODEL_	_DEPVAR_	_SIGMA_	OXY	AGE	WEIGHT	RUNTIME	RUNPULSE	RSTPULSE	INTERCEP
1	OLS	OXYHAT	OXY	2.5397	-1	-0.63045	-0.10586	-1.757	-0.22891	-0.1791	151.916

Output 34.6 Predicted and Residual Scores from the OUT= Data Set Created by PROC SCORE: Reproduced Using PROC PRINT

REGRESSION SCORING EXAMPLE 7
PREDICTED SCORES FOR REGRESSION

OBS	AGE	WEIGHT	OXY	RUNTIME	RSTPULSE	RUNPULSE	OXYHAT
1	44	89.47	44.609	11.37	62	178	42.8771
2	40	75.07	45.313	10.07	62	185	47.6050
3	44	85.84	54.297	8.65	45	156	56.1211
4	42	68.15	59.571	8.17	40	166	58.7044
5	38	89.02	49.874	9.22	55	178	51.7386
6	47	77.45	44.811	11.63	58	176	42.9756
7	40	75.98	45.681	11.95	70	176	44.8329
8	43	81.19	49.091	10.85	64	162	48.6020
9	44	81.42	39.442	13.08	63	174	41.4613
10	38	81.87	60.055	8.63	48	170	56.6171
11	44	73.03	50.541	10.13	45	168	52.1299
12	45	87.66	37.388	14.03	56	186	37.0080

REGRESSION SCORING EXAMPLE 8
RESIDUAL SCORES FOR REGRESSION

OBS	AGE	WEIGHT	OXY	RUNTIME	RSTPULSE	RUNPULSE	OXYHAT
1	44	89.47	44.609	11.37	62	178	-1.7319
2	40	75.07	45.313	10.07	62	185	2.2920
3	44	85.84	54.297	8.65	45	156	1.8241
4	42	68.15	59.571	8.17	40	166	-0.8666
5	38	89.02	49.874	9.22	55	178	1.8646
6	47	77.45	44.811	11.63	58	176	-1.8354
7	40	75.98	45.681	11.95	70	176	-0.8481
8	43	81.19	49.091	10.85	64	162	-0.4890
9	44	81.42	39.442	13.08	63	174	2.0193
10	38	81.87	60.055	8.63	48	170	-3.4379
11	44	73.03	50.541	10.13	45	168	1.5889
12	45	87.66	37.388	14.03	56	186	-0.3800

The final part of the example uses a specially created custom scoring data set. The first scoring coefficient creates a variable that is AGE−WEIGHT; the second evaluates RUNPULSE−RSTPULSE; and the third totals all six variables.

```
DATA A;
   INPUT _TYPE_ $ _NAME_ $
         AGE WEIGHT RUNTIME RUNPULSE RSTPULSE;
   CARDS;
SCORE  AGE_WGT  1 -1  0  0  0
SCORE  RUN_RST  0  0  0  1 -1
SCORE  TOTAL    1  1  1  1  1
;
PROC PRINT DATA=A;
   TITLE 'CONSTRUCTED SCORING EXAMPLE';
   TITLE2 'SCORING COEFFICIENTS';
PROC SCORE DATA=FITNESS SCORE=A OUT=B;
   VAR AGE WEIGHT RUNTIME RUNPULSE RSTPULSE;
PROC PRINT DATA=B;
   TITLE2 'SCORED DATA';
```

Output 34.7 Custom Scoring Data Set and Scored Fitness Data: PROC PRINT

CONSTRUCTED SCORING EXAMPLE 9
SCORING COEFFICIENTS

OBS	_TYPE_	_NAME_	AGE	WEIGHT	RUNTIME	RUNPULSE	RSTPULSE
1	SCORE	AGE_WGT	1	-1	0	0	0
2	SCORE	RUN_RST	0	0	0	1	-1
3	SCORE	TOTAL	1	1	1	1	1

CONSTRUCTED SCORING EXAMPLE 10
SCORED DATA

OBS	AGE	WEIGHT	OXY	RUNTIME	RSTPULSE	RUNPULSE	AGE_WGT	RUN_RST	TOTAL
1	44	89.47	44.609	11.37	62	178	-45.47	116	384.84
2	40	75.07	45.313	10.07	62	185	-35.07	123	372.14
3	44	85.84	54.297	8.65	45	156	-41.84	111	339.49
4	42	68.15	59.571	8.17	40	166	-26.15	126	324.32
5	38	89.02	49.874	9.22	55	178	-51.02	123	369.24
6	47	77.45	44.811	11.63	58	176	-30.45	118	370.08
7	40	75.98	45.681	11.95	70	176	-35.98	106	373.93
8	43	81.19	49.091	10.85	64	162	-38.19	98	361.04
9	44	81.42	39.442	13.08	63	174	-37.42	111	375.50
10	38	81.87	60.055	8.63	48	170	-43.87	122	346.50
11	44	73.03	50.541	10.13	45	168	-29.03	123	340.16
12	45	87.66	37.388	14.03	56	186	-42.66	130	388.69

Chapter 35
The STANDARD Procedure

Operating systems: All

ABSTRACT

The STANDARD procedure standardizes some or all of the variables in a SAS data set to a given mean and standard deviation and produces a new SAS data set to contain the standardized values.

INTRODUCTION

Standardizing is a technique for removing location and scale attributes from a set of data. Sometimes you need to center the values on a variable to a mean of 0 and a standard deviation of 1. Some statistical techniques begin the analysis by standardizing the data in this way. If your data are normally distributed, standardizing is also studentizing since the result has a Student's *t* distribution.

SPECIFICATIONS

The statements that control PROC STANDARD are

PROC STANDARD *options;*
  VAR *variables;*
  FREQ *variable;*
  WEIGHT *variable;*
  BY *variables;*

PROC STANDARD Statement

PROC STANDARD *options;*

The options below can appear in the PROC STANDARD statement. At least one of the last three options must be specified to prevent your output SAS data set from becoming an exact copy of the input data set.

DATA=*SASdataset*

gives the name of the data set to be used by PROC STANDARD. If it is omitted, STANDARD uses the most recently created SAS data set.

OUT=*SASdataset*

gives the name of the new SAS data set to contain the standardized variables. If OUT= is omitted, SAS names the new data set using the DATA*n* convention. The OUT= data set contains all the variables from the input data set, including those not standardized. If you want to create a permanent SAS data set, you must supply a two-level name. (See "SAS Files" in the *SAS User's Guide: Basics* for more information on permanent SAS data sets.)

VARDEF=DF
VARDEF=WEIGHT | WGT
VARDEF=N
VARDEF=WDF

specifies the divisor to be used in the calculation of the variance. DF requests the degrees of freedom (N-1) be used as the divisor. WGT or WEIGHT requests the sum of the weights; N requests the number of observations (N); and WDF requests the sum of the weights minus one. The default divisor is DF.

MEAN=*m*
M=*m*

requests that all the variables in the VAR statement (or all the numeric variables if the VAR statement is omitted) be standardized to a mean of *m*. Without the MEAN option, the mean of the output values is the same as the mean of the input values.

STD=*s*
S=*s*

requests that all the variables in the VAR statement (or all the numeric variables if the VAR statement is omitted) be standardized to a standard deviation of *s*. Without the STD option, the standard deviation of the output values is the same as the standard deviation of the input values. The REPLACE option, below, does not affect STD's action.

REPLACE

requests that all missing values be replaced with the variable mean. If MEAN=*m* is also specified, missing values are set instead to *m*.

VAR Statement

VAR *variables;*

The VAR statement allows you to list the variables you want standardized. If the VAR statement is omitted, all the numeric variables in the data set are standardized.

FREQ Statement

FREQ *variable;*

The FREQ statement specifies a numeric variable on the input SAS data set. If a FREQ statement is used, each observation in the input data set is assumed to represent *n* observations, where *n* is the value of the FREQ variable. If the value is not an integer, it is truncated to the integer portion. An observation is skipped for the calculation of the mean and standard deviation if the FREQ value is less than one or is missing. However, the variables to be standardized for the observation are still adjusted.

WEIGHT Statement

WEIGHT *variable;*

The WEIGHT statement specifies a numeric variable on the input SAS data set the values of which are used to weight each observation. Only one variable can be specified. The WEIGHT variable values can be nonintegers and are used to calculate a weighted mean and a weighted variance. If the value of the WEIGHT variable is less than zero or missing, a value of zero is assumed. Both FREQ and WEIGHT statements can be used.

BY Statement

BY *variables;*

A BY statement can be used with PROC STANDARD to obtain separate analyses on observations in groups defined by the BY variables. When a BY statement appears, the procedure expects the input data set to be sorted in order of the BY variables. If your input data set is not sorted in ascending order, use the SORT procedure with a similar BY statement to sort the data, or, if appropriate, use the BY statement options NOTSORTED or DESCENDING. For more information, see the discussion of the BY statement in "Statements Used in the PROC Step" in the *SAS User's Guide: Basics*.

DETAILS

Missing Values

Missing values are excluded from the standardization process. Unless the REPLACE option is specified, missing values are left as missing in the output data set. When REPLACE is specified, missing values are replaced with the variable mean or with the mean specified by the MEAN option in the PROC STANDARD statement.

Output Data Set

The STANDARD procedure produces an output SAS data set to contain the standardized variables but no printed output.

EXAMPLE

Standardizing Test Scores

The data in the example below consist of three test scores for students in two sections of a course. For each section, you want to standardize all three test scores to a mean of 80 and a standard deviation of 5. To keep the original test scores with the standardized scores in the same SAS data set, create the three variables STEST1-STEST3 to contain the test scores.

The PROC STANDARD statement includes the MEAN and STD options and gives the name NEW to the new SAS data set containing the standardized values. Since only STEST1-STEST3 appear in the VAR statement, they are the only variables standardized; the original variables TEST1-TEST3 are not standardized. The BY statement asks that the standardization be done for each section of the course separately. The PROC PRINT statement prints the new data set, and the PROC MEANS output shows that STEST1-STEST3 in both sections have (1) means of 80 and (2) standard deviations of 5.

```
DATA A;
   INPUT STUDENT SECTION TEST1-TEST3;
   STEST1=TEST1;
   STEST2=TEST2;
   STEST3=TEST3;
   CARDS;
238900545 1 94 91 87
254701167 1 95 96 97
238806445 2 91 86 94
999002527 2 80 76 78
263924860 1 92 40 85
459700886 2 75 76 80
416724915 2 66 69 72
999001230 1 82 84 80
242760674 1 75 76 70
990001252 2 51 66 91
;
PROC SORT;
   BY SECTION;
PROC STANDARD MEAN=80 STD=5 OUT=NEW;
   BY SECTION;
   VAR STEST1-STEST3;
PROC PRINT DATA=NEW;
   BY SECTION;
   TITLE 'STANDARDIZED TEST SCORES';
PROC MEANS DATA=NEW(DROP=STUDENT) MAXDEC=2 N MEAN STD;
   BY SECTION;
```

Output 35.1 Standardizing Test Scores: PROC STANDARD

```
                              STANDARDIZED TEST SCORES                                                  1

----------------------------------------------------SECTION=1----------------------------------------------------

              OBS     STUDENT      TEST1     TEST2     TEST3     STEST1      STEST2      STEST3

                1    238900545      94        91        87       83.6634     83.0601     81.6187
                2    254701167      95        96        97       84.2358     84.1851     86.6772
                3    263924860      92        40        85       82.5186     71.5848     80.6070
                4    999001230      82        84        80       76.7945     81.4850     78.0778
                5    242760674      75        76        70       72.7876     79.6850     73.0193

----------------------------------------------------SECTION=2----------------------------------------------------

              OBS     STUDENT      TEST1     TEST2     TEST3     STEST1      STEST2      STEST3

                6    238806445      91        86        94       86.1022     87.3710     85.9656
                7    999002527      80        76        78       82.4542     80.9052     77.2884
                8    459700886      75        76        80       80.7959     80.9052     78.3730
                9    416724915      66        69        72       77.8112     76.3792     74.0344
               10    990001252      51        66        91       72.8365     74.4394     84.3386
```

```
                              STANDARDIZED TEST SCORES                                                  2

                     VARIABLE            N          MEAN          STANDARD
                                                                  DEVIATION

                     ------------------ SECTION=1 --------------------

                     TEST1               5          87.60            8.73
                     TEST2               5          77.40           22.22
                     TEST3               5          83.80            9.88
                     STEST1              5          80.00            5.00
                     STEST2              5          80.00            5.00
                     STEST3              5          80.00            5.00

                     ------------------ SECTION=2 --------------------

                     TEST1               5          72.60           15.08
                     TEST2               5          74.60            7.73
                     TEST3               5          83.00            9.22
                     STEST1              5          80.00            5.00
                     STEST2              5          80.00            5.00
                     STEST3              5          80.00            5.00
```

Chapter 36

The STEPDISC Procedure

Operating systems: All

ABSTRACT

The STEPDISC procedure performs a stepwise discriminant analysis by forward selection, backward elimination, or stepwise selection of variables that can be useful for discriminating among several classes.

INTRODUCTION

The STEPDISC procedure selects a subset of quantitative variables to produce a good discrimination model using forward selection, backward elimination, or stepwise selection (Klecka 1980). The classes are assumed to be multivariate normal with a common covariance matrix.

Variables are chosen to enter or leave the model according to one of two criteria:

1. the significance level of an F test from an analysis of covariance, where the variables already chosen act as covariates and the variable under consideration is the dependent variable, or
2. the squared partial correlation for predicting the variable under consideration from the CLASS variable, controlling for the effects of the variables already selected for the model.

It is important to remember that when many significance tests are performed, each at a level of, for example, 5%, the overall probability of rejecting at least one true null hypothesis is much larger than 5%. If you want to guard against including any variables that do not contribute to the discriminatory power of the model in the population, you should specify a very small significance level. In most applications, all variables considered have some discriminatory power, however small. If you want to choose the model that provides the best discrimination using the sample estimates, you need only guard against estimating more parameters than can be reliably estimated with the given sample size. In this case you should use a moderate significance level, perhaps in the range of 10% to 25% (Costanza and Afifi, 1979).

The significance level and the squared partial correlation criteria select variables in the same order, although they may select different numbers of variables. Increasing the sample size tends to increase the number of variables selected when you use significance levels, but has little effect on the number selected using squared partial correlations.

Forward selection begins with no variables in the model. At each step the variable is entered that contributes most to the discriminatory power of the model as measured by Wilks' *lambda*, the likelihood ratio criterion. When none of the unselected variables meet the entry criterion, the forward selection process stops.

Backward elimination begins with all variables in the model except those that are linearly dependent with previous variables in the VAR statement. At each step the variable that contributes least to the discriminatory power of the model as measured by Wilks' *lambda* is removed. When all remaining variables meet the criterion to stay in the model, the backward elimination process stops.

Stepwise selection begins with no variables in the model. At each step, if the variable in the model that contributes least to the discriminatory power of the model as measured by Wilks' *lambda* fails to meet the criterion to stay, then that variable is removed. Otherwise, the variable not in the model that contributes most to the discriminatory power of the model is entered. When all variables in the model meet the criterion to stay, and none of the other variables meet the criterion to enter, the stepwise selection process stops.

The models selected by STEPDISC are not necessarily the best possible models and Wilks' *lambda* may not be the best measure of discriminatory power for your application. However, if STEPDISC is used carefully, in combination with your knowledge of the data and careful cross-validation, it can be a valuable aid in selecting a discrimination model.

SPECIFICATIONS

The following statements are used with STEPDISC:

PROC STEPDISC *options;*
VAR *variables;*
CLASS *variable;*
PROB *variables;*
FREQ *variable;*
WEIGHT *variable;*
BY *variables;*

Either a CLASS statement or a PROB statement must appear, but not both.

PROC STEPDISC Statement

PROC STEPDISC *options;*

The following options can appear in the PROC statement:

DATA=*SASdataset*
: names the data set to be analyzed. The data set can be an ordinary SAS data set, or a TYPE=CORR or TYPE=COV data set produced by either the CANDISC procedure with the OUTSTAT= option or the CORR procedure using a BY statement. If DATA= is omitted, the most recently created SAS data set is used.

STEPWISE
SW
: requests stepwise selection, which is the default if neither FORWARD nor BACKWARD is requested.

FORWARD
FW
: requests forward selection.

BACKWARD
BW
: requests backward elimination.

SLENTRY=*p*
SLE=*p*
: specifies the significance level to enter, where 0<=*p*<=1. The default is .15.

SLSTAY=*p*
SLS=*p*
: specifies the significance level to stay, where 0<=*p*<=1. The default is .15.

PR2ENTRY=*p*
PR2E=*p*
: specifies the partial R^2 to enter, where *p*<=1.

PR2STAY=*p*
PR2S=*p*
: specifies the partial R^2 to stay, where *p*<=1.

SINGULAR=*p*
SING=*p*
: specifies the singularity criterion for entering variables, where 0<*p*<1. STEPDISC refuses to enter a variable if the R^2 for predicting that variable from the variables already in the model exceeds 1-*p*. The default is SINGULAR=1E-8.

INCLUDE=*n*
: requests that the first *n* variables in the VAR statement be included in every model.

MAXSTEP=*n*
: specifies the maximum number of steps.

SIMPLE
: prints means and standard deviations.

STDMEAN
: prints within- and total-standardized class means.

TCORR
: prints total sample correlations.

WCORR
: prints within-group correlations.

SHORT
: prints the summary table only.

VAR Statement

VAR *variables;*

The VAR statement specifies the numeric variables eligible for selection. The default is all numeric variables not mentioned in other statements.

CLASS Statement

CLASS *variable;*

The CLASS statement specifies the name of one numeric or character variable defining the groups in the discriminant analysis. Class levels are determined by the formatted values of the class variable.

PROB Statement

PROB *variables;*

A PROB statement can be used instead of a CLASS statement. Each variable in the PROB statement defines a class. The variables must be numeric, with values summing to one for each observation. There are at least two situations in which the PROB statement can be used:

- when some observations are repeated many times. The FREQ variable (see below) gives the total number of times each observation occurs, while the PROB statement gives the proportion belonging to each class.
- when you do not know with certainty the class to which each observation belongs. The PROB variables give the probabilities of the observations coming from each class. The standard errors and significance levels printed by STEPDISC are not valid in this case.

FREQ Statement

FREQ *variable;*

If a variable in your data set represents the frequency of occurrence for the other values in the observation, include the variable's name in a FREQ statement. The procedure then treats the data set as if each observation appears *n* times, where *n* is the value of the FREQ variable for the observation. The total number of observations is considered to be equal to the sum of the FREQ variable when the procedure determines degrees of freedom for significance probabilities.

The WEIGHT and FREQ statements have a similar effect except in the calculation of degrees of freedom.

WEIGHT Statement

WEIGHT *variable;*

If you want to use relative weights for each observation in the input data set, place the weights in a variable in the data set and specify the name in a WEIGHT statement. This is often done when the variance associated with each observation is different and the values of the weight variable are proportional to the reciprocals of the variances.

BY Statement

BY *variables;*

A BY statement can be used with PROC STEPDISC to obtain separate analyses on observations in groups defined by the BY variables. When a BY statement appears, the procedure expects the input data set to be sorted in order of the BY variables. If your input data set is not sorted in ascending order, use the SORT procedure with a similar BY statement to sort the data, or, if appropriate, use the BY statement options NOTSORTED or DESCENDING. For more information, see the discussion of the BY statement in "Statements Used in the PROC Step" in the *SAS User's Guide: Basics.*

DETAILS

Missing Values

Observations containing missing values are omitted from the analysis.

Printed Output

STEPDISC prints:

1. CLASS LEVEL INFORMATION, including the values of the classification variable, the FREQUENCY of each value, and its PROPORTION in the total sample.

Optional output includes:

2. CLASS MEANS
3. STANDARD DEVIATIONS, both for the TOTAL SAMPLE and pooled WITHIN CLASS
4. WITHIN-STANDARDIZED CLASS MEANS, obtained by subtracting the grand mean from each class mean and dividing by the pooled within-class standard deviation
5. TOTAL-STANDARDIZED CLASS MEANS, obtained by subtracting the grand mean from each class mean and dividing by the total sample standard deviation
6. TOTAL SAMPLE CORRELATIONS
7. POOLED WITHIN CLASS CORRELATIONS.

At each step the following statistics are printed:

8. for each variable considered for entry or removal: (PARTIAL) R**2, the squared (partial) correlation, the F statistic, and PROB>F, the probability level, from a one-way analysis covariance.
9. the TOLERANCE for each variable being considered for entry. Tolerance is one minus the squared multiple correlation of the variable with the other variables already in the model.

   A variable is entered only if its tolerance is greater than the value specified in the SINGULAR= option. The TOLERANCE is computed using the total sample correlation matrix. It is customary to compute tolerance using the within-group correlation matrix (Jennrich 1977), but it is possible for a variable with excellent discriminatory power to have a high total-sample tolerance and a low within-group tolerance. For example, STEPDISC enters a variable that yields perfect discrimination (that is, produces a canonical correlation of one) but a program using within-group tolerance does not.
10. the variable LABEL, if any.
11. the name of the variable chosen.
12. the variable(s) already selected or removed.
13. WILKS' LAMBDA and the associated F approximation with degrees of

freedom and PROB<F, the associated probability level after the selected variable has been entered or removed. Wilks' *lambda* is the likelihood ratio statistic for testing the hypothesis that the means of the classes on the selected variables are equal in the population. See **Multivariate Tests** in "SAS Regression Procedures." Lambda is close to 0 if any two groups are well separated.

14. PILLAI'S TRACE and the associated F approximation with degrees of freedom and PROB<F, the associated probability level after the selected variable has been entered or removed. Pillai's trace is a multivariate statistic for testing the hypothesis that the means of the classes on the selected variables are equal in the population. See **Multivariate Tests** in "SAS Regression Procedures."
15. AVERAGE SQUARED CANONICAL CORRELATION (ASCC). The ASCC is Pillai's trace divided by the number of groups minus 1. The ASCC is close to 1 if all groups are well separated and if all or most directions in the discriminant space show good separation for at least two groups.

A summary table is printed giving statistics associated with the variable chosen at each step.

The summary table includes:

- STEP number
- VARIABLE ENTERED or REMOVED
- NUMBER of variables IN the model
- PARTIAL R**2
- F STATISTIC for entering or removing the variable
- PROB>F, the probability level for the previous F statistic
- WILKS' LAMBDA
- PROB<LAMBDA based on the F approximation to Wilks' lambda
- AVERAGE SQUARED CANONICAL CORRELATION
- PROB>ASCC based on the F approximation to Pillai's trace
- the variable LABEL, if any.

EXAMPLE

Performing a Stepwise Discriminant Analysis

The iris data published by Fisher (1936) have been widely used for examples in discriminant analysis and cluster analysis. The sepal length, sepal width, petal length, and petal width were measured in millimeters on fifty iris specimens from each of three species, *Iris setosa, I. versicolor,* and *I. virginica*. A stepwise discriminant analysis is performed using stepwise selection.

```
DATA IRIS;
   TITLE 'FISHER (1936) IRIS DATA';
   INPUT SEPALLEN SEPALWID PETALLEN PETALWID SPEC_NO @@;
   IF SPEC_NO=1 THEN SPECIES='SETOSA    ';
   ELSE IF SPEC_NO=2 THEN SPECIES='VERSICOLOR';
   ELSE SPECIES='VIRGINICA ';
   LABEL SEPALLEN='SEPAL LENGTH IN MM.'
         SEPALWID='SEPAL WIDTH  IN MM.'
         PETALLEN='PETAL LENGTH IN MM.'
         PETALWID='PETAL WIDTH  IN MM.';
   CARDS;
 50 33 14 02 1 64 28 56 22 3 65 28 46 15 2
```

```
67 31 56 24 3 63 28 51 15 3 46 34 14 03 1
69 31 51 23 3 62 22 45 15 2 59 32 48 18 2
46 36 10 02 1 61 30 46 14 2 60 27 51 16 2
65 30 52 20 3 56 25 39 11 2 65 30 55 18 3
58 27 51 19 3 68 32 59 23 3 51 33 17 05 1
57 28 45 13 2 62 34 54 23 3 77 38 67 22 3
63 33 47 16 2 67 33 57 25 3 76 30 66 21 3
49 25 45 17 3 55 35 13 02 1 67 30 52 23 3
70 32 47 14 2 64 32 45 15 2 61 28 40 13 2
48 31 16 02 1 59 30 51 18 3 55 24 38 11 2
63 25 50 19 3 64 32 53 23 3 52 34 14 02 1
49 36 14 01 1 54 30 45 15 2 79 38 64 20 3
44 32 13 02 1 67 33 57 21 3 50 35 16 06 1
58 26 40 12 2 44 30 13 02 1 77 28 67 20 3
63 27 49 18 3 47 32 16 02 1 55 26 44 12 2
50 23 33 10 2 72 32 60 18 3 48 30 14 03 1
51 38 16 02 1 61 30 49 18 3 48 34 19 02 1
50 30 16 02 1 50 32 12 02 1 61 26 56 14 3
64 28 56 21 3 43 30 11 01 1 58 40 12 02 1
51 38 19 04 1 67 31 44 14 2 62 28 48 18 3
49 30 14 02 1 51 35 14 02 1 56 30 45 15 2
58 27 41 10 2 50 34 16 04 1 46 32 14 02 1
60 29 45 15 2 57 26 35 10 2 57 44 15 04 1
50 36 14 02 1 77 30 61 23 3 63 34 56 24 3
58 27 51 19 3 57 29 42 13 2 72 30 58 16 3
54 34 15 04 1 52 41 15 01 1 71 30 59 21 3
64 31 55 18 3 60 30 48 18 3 63 29 56 18 3
49 24 33 10 2 56 27 42 13 2 57 30 42 12 2
55 42 14 02 1 49 31 15 02 1 77 26 69 23 3
60 22 50 15 3 54 39 17 04 1 66 29 46 13 2
52 27 39 14 2 60 34 45 16 2 50 34 15 02 1
44 29 14 02 1 50 20 35 10 2 55 24 37 10 2
58 27 39 12 2 47 32 13 02 1 46 31 15 02 1
69 32 57 23 3 62 29 43 13 2 74 28 61 19 3
59 30 42 15 2 51 34 15 02 1 50 35 13 03 1
56 28 49 20 3 60 22 40 10 2 73 29 63 18 3
67 25 58 18 3 49 31 15 01 1 67 31 47 15 2
63 23 44 13 2 54 37 15 02 1 56 30 41 13 2
63 25 49 15 2 61 28 47 12 2 64 29 43 13 2
51 25 30 11 2 57 28 41 13 2 65 30 58 22 3
69 31 54 21 3 54 39 13 04 1 51 35 14 03 1
72 36 61 25 3 65 32 51 20 3 61 29 47 14 2
56 29 36 13 2 69 31 49 15 2 64 27 53 19 3
68 30 55 21 3 55 25 40 13 2 48 34 16 02 1
48 30 14 01 1 45 23 13 03 1 57 25 50 20 3
57 38 17 03 1 51 38 15 03 1 55 23 40 13 2
66 30 44 14 2 68 28 48 14 2 54 34 17 02 1
51 37 15 04 1 52 35 15 02 1 58 28 51 24 3
67 30 50 17 2 63 33 60 25 3 53 37 15 02 1
;
PROC STEPDISC STEPWISE SIMPLE STDMEAN TCORR WCORR;
   CLASS SPECIES;
   VAR SEPALLEN SEPALWID PETALLEN PETALWID;
```

Output 36.1 Iris Data: PROC STEPDISC

```
                         FISHER (1936) IRIS DATA                               1

                      STEPWISE DISCRIMINANT ANALYSIS

           150 OBSERVATIONS       4 VARIABLE(S) IN THE ANALYSIS
             3 CLASS LEVELS       0 VARIABLE(S) WILL BE INCLUDED

              THE METHOD(S) FOR SELECTING VARIABLES WILL BE:
                                 STEPWISE

                  SIGNIFICANCE LEVEL TO ENTER =   0.1500
                  SIGNIFICANCE LEVEL TO STAY  =   0.1500

  ❶                      CLASS LEVEL INFORMATION

                  SPECIES        FREQUENCY   PROPORTION

                  SETOSA              50       0.333333
                  VERSICOLOR          50       0.333333
                  VIRGINICA           50       0.333333


                               CLASS MEANS
  ❷
VARIABLE         SETOSA      VERSICOLOR        VIRGINICA

SEPALLEN        50.0600         59.3600          65.8800      SEPAL LENGTH IN MM.
SEPALWID        34.2800         27.7000          29.7400      SEPAL WIDTH  IN MM.
PETALLEN        14.6200         42.6000          55.5200      PETAL LENGTH IN MM.
PETALWID         2.4600         13.2600          20.2600      PETAL WIDTH  IN MM.


                          STANDARD DEVIATIONS
  ❸
    VARIABLE      TOTAL SAMPLE      WITHIN CLASS

    SEPALLEN            8.2807            5.1479      SEPAL LENGTH IN MM.
    SEPALWID            4.3587            3.3969      SEPAL WIDTH  IN MM.
    PETALLEN           17.6530            4.3033      PETAL LENGTH IN MM.
    PETALWID            7.6224            2.0465      PETAL WIDTH  IN MM.


                      WITHIN-STANDARDIZED CLASS MEANS
  ❹
VARIABLE         SETOSA      VERSICOLOR        VIRGINICA

SEPALLEN       -1.62656         0.18001          1.44655      SEPAL LENGTH IN MM.
SEPALWID        1.09120        -0.84587         -0.24532      SEPAL WIDTH  IN MM.
PETALLEN       -5.33538         1.16653          4.16885      PETAL LENGTH IN MM.
PETALWID       -4.65836         0.61894          4.03942      PETAL WIDTH  IN MM.
```

```
                         FISHER (1936) IRIS DATA                               2

                      STEPWISE DISCRIMINANT ANALYSIS
  ❺
                      TOTAL-STANDARDIZED CLASS MEANS

VARIABLE         SETOSA      VERSICOLOR        VIRGINICA

SEPALLEN       -1.01119         0.11191          0.89928      SEPAL LENGTH IN MM.
SEPALWID        0.85041        -0.65922         -0.19119      SEPAL WIDTH  IN MM.
PETALLEN       -1.30063         0.28437          1.01626      PETAL LENGTH IN MM.
PETALWID       -1.25070         0.16618          1.08453      PETAL WIDTH  IN MM.


                        TOTAL SAMPLE CORRELATIONS
  ❻
                SEPALLEN        SEPALWID         PETALLEN        PETALWID

    SEPALLEN       1.000          -0.118            0.872           0.818
    SEPALWID      -0.118           1.000           -0.428          -0.366
    PETALLEN       0.872          -0.428            1.000           0.963
    PETALWID       0.818          -0.366            0.963           1.000
```

(continued on next page)

(continued from previous page)

```
❼                  POOLED WITHIN CLASS CORRELATIONS

                   SEPALLEN      SEPALWID      PETALLEN      PETALWID

     SEPALLEN        1.000         0.530         0.756         0.365
     SEPALWID        0.530         1.000         0.378         0.471
     PETALLEN        0.756         0.378         1.000         0.484
     PETALWID        0.365         0.471         0.484         1.000
```

```
                              FISHER (1936) IRIS DATA                                    3

STEPWISE SELECTION:  STEP   1

                         STATISTICS FOR ENTRY, DF = 2, 147
                               ❽                    ❾      ❿
           VARIABLE     R**2          F      PROB > F  TOLERANCE  LABEL

           SEPALLEN   0.6187     119.265    0.0001      1.0000  SEPAL LENGTH IN MM.
           SEPALWID   0.4008      49.160    0.0001      1.0000  SEPAL WIDTH  IN MM.
           PETALLEN   0.9414    1180.161    0.0001      1.0000  PETAL LENGTH IN MM.
           PETALWID   0.9289     960.007    0.0001      1.0000  PETAL WIDTH  IN MM.

              ⓫          VARIABLE PETALLEN WILL BE ENTERED

                    THE FOLLOWING VARIABLE(S) HAVE BEEN ENTERED:
                         ⓬           PETALLEN

                              MULTIVARIATE STATISTICS

      ⓭    WILKS' LAMBDA  = 0.05862828    F(2,147) = 1180.161          PROB > F = 0.0
      ⓮    PILLAI'S TRACE =   0.941372    F(2,147) = 1180.161          PROB > F = 0.0

             ⓯      AVERAGE SQUARED CANONICAL CORRELATION = 0.47068586

--------------------------------------------------------------------------------------------------

STEPWISE SELECTION:  STEP   2

                        STATISTICS FOR REMOVAL,  DF = 2, 147

              VARIABLE      R**2          F     PROB > F  LABEL

              PETALLEN    0.9414    1180.161    0.0001  PETAL LENGTH IN MM.

                            NO VARIABLES CAN BE REMOVED

                            ---------------------------

                         STATISTICS FOR ENTRY, DF = 2, 146

                      PARTIAL
           VARIABLE     R**2          F      PROB > F  TOLERANCE  LABEL

           SEPALLEN   0.3198      34.323    0.0001      0.2400  SEPAL LENGTH IN MM.
           SEPALWID   0.3709      43.035    0.0001      0.8164  SEPAL WIDTH  IN MM.
           PETALWID   0.2533      24.766    0.0001      0.0729  PETAL WIDTH  IN MM.

                         VARIABLE SEPALWID WILL BE ENTERED

                    THE FOLLOWING VARIABLE(S) HAVE BEEN ENTERED:
                                 SEPALWID PETALLEN
```

```
                              FISHER (1936) IRIS DATA                                    4

STEPWISE SELECTION:  STEP   2

                              MULTIVARIATE STATISTICS

           WILKS' LAMBDA  = 0.03688411    F(4,292) = 307.105          PROB > F = 0.0
           PILLAI'S TRACE =   1.119908    F(4,294) = 93.528           PROB > F = 0.0001

                    AVERAGE SQUARED CANONICAL CORRELATION = 0.55995394

--------------------------------------------------------------------------------------------------
```

(continued on next page)

(continued from previous page)

```
STEPWISE SELECTION:  STEP   3

                                        STATISTICS FOR REMOVAL,  DF = 2, 146

                                      PARTIAL
                       VARIABLE        R**2          F      PROB > F  LABEL

                       SEPALWID     0.3709       43.035     0.0001  SEPAL WIDTH   IN MM.
                       PETALLEN     0.9384     1112.954     0.0001  PETAL LENGTH IN MM.

                                           NO VARIABLES CAN BE REMOVED

                                           ---------------------------

                                         STATISTICS FOR ENTRY, DF = 2, 145

                               PARTIAL
                 VARIABLE        R**2          F       PROB > F  TOLERANCE  LABEL

                 SEPALLEN     0.1447       12.268     0.0001     0.1323  SEPAL LENGTH IN MM.
                 PETALWID     0.3229       34.569     0.0001     0.0662  PETAL WIDTH  IN MM.

                                         VARIABLE PETALWID WILL BE ENTERED

                                    THE FOLLOWING VARIABLE(S) HAVE BEEN ENTERED:
                                              SEPALWID PETALLEN PETALWID

                                              MULTIVARIATE STATISTICS

                WILKS' LAMBDA  = 0.02497554     F(6,290) = 257.503            PROB > F = 0.0
                PILLAI'S TRACE =   1.189914     F(6,292) = 71.485             PROB > F = 0.0001

                           AVERAGE SQUARED CANONICAL CORRELATION = 0.59495691
```

```
                                              FISHER (1936) IRIS DATA                                           5

STEPWISE SELECTION:  STEP   4

                                        STATISTICS FOR REMOVAL,  DF = 2, 145

                                      PARTIAL
                       VARIABLE        R**2          F      PROB > F  LABEL

                       SEPALWID     0.4295       54.577     0.0001  SEPAL WIDTH   IN MM.
                       PETALLEN     0.3482       38.724     0.0001  PETAL LENGTH IN MM.
                       PETALWID     0.3229       34.569     0.0001  PETAL WIDTH   IN MM.

                                           NO VARIABLES CAN BE REMOVED

                                           ---------------------------

                                         STATISTICS FOR ENTRY, DF = 2, 144

                               PARTIAL
                 VARIABLE        R**2          F       PROB > F  TOLERANCE  LABEL

                 SEPALLEN     0.0615        4.721     0.0103     0.0320  SEPAL LENGTH IN MM.

                                         VARIABLE SEPALLEN WILL BE ENTERED

                                           ALL VARIABLES HAVE BEEN ENTERED

                                              MULTIVARIATE STATISTICS

                WILKS' LAMBDA  = 0.02343863     F(8,288) = 199.145            PROB > F = 0.0
                PILLAI'S TRACE =   1.191899     F(8,290) = 53.466             PROB > F = 0.0001

                           AVERAGE SQUARED CANONICAL CORRELATION = 0.59594941
-----------------------------------------------------------------------------------------------------------------
```

(continued on next page)

(continued from previous page)

```
STEPWISE SELECTION:  STEP   5

                                   STATISTICS FOR REMOVAL,  DF = 2, 144

                                     PARTIAL
                          VARIABLE     R**2          F      PROB > F  LABEL

                          SEPALLEN   0.0615        4.721     0.0103  SEPAL LENGTH IN MM.
                          SEPALWID   0.2335       21.936     0.0001  SEPAL WIDTH  IN MM.
                          PETALLEN   0.3308       35.590     0.0001  PETAL LENGTH IN MM.
                          PETALWID   0.2570       24.904     0.0001  PETAL WIDTH  IN MM.

                                       NO VARIABLES CAN BE REMOVED

NO FURTHER STEPS ARE POSSIBLE
```

```
                                          FISHER (1936) IRIS DATA                                                6

STEPWISE SELECTION:  SUMMARY

                                                                                                  AVERAGE
                                                                                                  SQUARED
           VARIABLE          NUMBER    PARTIAL         F          PROB >       WILKS'     PROB <    CANONICAL     PROB >
 STEP   ENTERED   REMOVED      IN       R**2       STATISTIC        F          LAMBDA     LAMBDA   CORRELATION     ASCC
---------------------------------------------------------------------------------------------------------------------------
    1   PETALLEN                1      0.9414      1180.161     0.0001    0.05862828    0.0       0.47068586    0.0
    2   SEPALWID                2      0.3709        43.035     0.0001    0.03688411    0.0       0.55995394    0.0001
    3   PETALWID                3      0.3229        34.569     0.0001    0.02497554    0.0       0.59495691    0.0001
    4   SEPALLEN                4      0.0615         4.721     0.0103    0.02343863    0.0       0.59594941    0.0001
```

```
                                          FISHER (1936) IRIS DATA                                                7

STEPWISE SELECTION:  STEP   1

                                    STATISTICS FOR ENTRY, DF = 2, 147

                    VARIABLE     R**2          F       PROB > F  TOLERANCE  LABEL

                    SEPALLEN    0.6187     119.265    0.0001      1.0000  SEPAL LENGTH IN MM.
                    SEPALWID    0.4008      49.160    0.0001      1.0000  SEPAL WIDTH  IN MM.
                    PETALLEN    0.9414    1180.161    0.0001      1.0000  PETAL LENGTH IN MM.
                    PETALWID    0.9289     960.007    0.0001      1.0000  PETAL WIDTH  IN MM.
                                    VARIABLE PETALLEN WILL BE ENTERED

                               THE FOLLOWING VARIABLE(S) HAVE BEEN ENTERED:
                                                 PETALLEN

                                          MULTIVARIATE STATISTICS

                   WILKS' LAMBDA  = 0.05862828     F(2,147) = 1180.161          PROB > F = 0.0
                   PILLAI'S TRACE =   0.941372     F(2,147) = 1180.161          PROB > F = 0.0

                               AVERAGE SQUARED CANONICAL CORRELATION = 0.47068586

---------------------------------------------------------------------------------------------------------------------------
```

(continued on next page)

(continued from previous page)

```
STEPWISE SELECTION:  STEP   2

                              STATISTICS FOR REMOVAL,  DF = 2, 147

               VARIABLE     R**2         F     PROB > F  LABEL

               PETALLEN   0.9414   1180.161    0.0001  PETAL LENGTH IN MM.

                                NO VARIABLES CAN BE REMOVED
                                ---------------------------

                               STATISTICS FOR ENTRY, DF = 2, 146

                         PARTIAL
                VARIABLE    R**2        F       PROB > F  TOLERANCE  LABEL

                SEPALLEN    0.3198     34.323    0.0001      0.2400  SEPAL LENGTH IN MM.
                SEPALWID    0.3709     43.035    0.0001      0.8164  SEPAL WIDTH  IN MM.
                PETALWID    0.2533     24.766    0.0001      0.0729  PETAL WIDTH  IN MM.

                               VARIABLE SEPALWID WILL BE ENTERED

                           THE FOLLOWING VARIABLE(S) HAVE BEEN ENTERED:
                                      SEPALWID PETALLEN
```

```
                                   FISHER (1936) IRIS DATA                                        8
STEPWISE SELECTION:  STEP   2

                                   MULTIVARIATE STATISTICS

              WILKS' LAMBDA  = 0.03688411    F(4,292) = 307.105         PROB > F = 0.0
              PILLAI'S TRACE =   1.119908    F(4,294) = 93.528          PROB > F = 0.0001

                         AVERAGE SQUARED CANONICAL CORRELATION = 0.55995394

--------------------------------------------------------------------------------------------------

STEPWISE SELECTION:  STEP   3

                              STATISTICS FOR REMOVAL,  DF = 2, 146
                             PARTIAL
               VARIABLE     R**2         F     PROB > F  LABEL

               SEPALWID    0.3709      43.035    0.0001  SEPAL WIDTH  IN MM.
               PETALLEN    0.9384    1112.954    0.0001  PETAL LENGTH IN MM.

                                NO VARIABLES CAN BE REMOVED
                                ---------------------------

                               STATISTICS FOR ENTRY, DF = 2, 145
                         PARTIAL
                VARIABLE    R**2        F       PROB > F  TOLERANCE  LABEL

                SEPALLEN    0.1447     12.268    0.0001      0.1323  SEPAL LENGTH IN MM.
                PETALWID    0.3229     34.569    0.0001      0.0662  PETAL WIDTH  IN MM.

                               VARIABLE PETALWID WILL BE ENTERED

                           THE FOLLOWING VARIABLE(S) HAVE BEEN ENTERED:
                                  SEPALWID PETALLEN PETALWID

                                   MULTIVARIATE STATISTICS

              WILKS' LAMBDA  = 0.02497554    F(6,290) = 257.503         PROB > F = 0.0
              PILLAI'S TRACE =   1.189914    F(6,292) = 71.485          PROB > F = 0.0001

                         AVERAGE SQUARED CANONICAL CORRELATION = 0.59495691
```

```
                                        FISHER (1936) IRIS DATA                                                    9

STEPWISE SELECTION:  STEP   4

                                    STATISTICS FOR REMOVAL,  DF = 2, 145

                                  PARTIAL
                        VARIABLE     R**2          F     PROB > F  LABEL

                        SEPALWID   0.4295      54.577     0.0001  SEPAL WIDTH  IN MM.
                        PETALLEN   0.3482      38.724     0.0001  PETAL LENGTH IN MM.
                        PETALWID   0.3229      34.569     0.0001  PETAL WIDTH  IN MM.

                                        NO VARIABLES CAN BE REMOVED
                                        ---------------------------

                                     STATISTICS FOR ENTRY, DF = 2, 144

                            PARTIAL
                  VARIABLE     R**2          F      PROB > F  TOLERANCE  LABEL

                  SEPALLEN    0.0615        4.721     0.0103      0.0320  SEPAL LENGTH IN MM.

                                     VARIABLE SEPALLEN WILL BE ENTERED

                                      ALL VARIABLES HAVE BEEN ENTERED

                                          MULTIVARIATE STATISTICS

                 WILKS' LAMBDA  = 0.02343863     F(8,288) = 199.145           PROB > F = 0.0
                 PILLAI'S TRACE =    1.191899    F(8,290) = 53.466            PROB > F = 0.0001

                              AVERAGE SQUARED CANONICAL CORRELATION = 0.59594941
-----------------------------------------------------------------------------------------------------------------

STEPWISE SELECTION:  STEP   5

                                    STATISTICS FOR REMOVAL,  DF = 2, 144

                                  PARTIAL
                        VARIABLE     R**2          F     PROB > F  LABEL

                        SEPALLEN   0.0615       4.721     0.0103  SEPAL LENGTH IN MM.
                        SEPALWID   0.2335      21.936     0.0001  SEPAL WIDTH  IN MM.
                        PETALLEN   0.3308      35.590     0.0001  PETAL LENGTH IN MM.
                        PETALWID   0.2570      24.904     0.0001  PETAL WIDTH  IN MM.

                                        NO VARIABLES CAN BE REMOVED

NO FURTHER STEPS ARE POSSIBLE
```

```
                                        FISHER (1936) IRIS DATA                                                   10

STEPWISE SELECTION:  SUMMARY

                                                                                             AVERAGE
                                                                                             SQUARED
            VARIABLE          NUMBER    PARTIAL         F        PROB >       WILKS'    PROB <   CANONICAL     PROB >
STEP    ENTERED   REMOVED       IN        R**2      STATISTIC      F         LAMBDA    LAMBDA  CORRELATION     ASCC
-----------------------------------------------------------------------------------------------------------------------
   1    PETALLEN                 1       0.9414     1180.161    0.0001    0.05862828   0.0      0.47068586   0.0
   2    SEPALWID                 2       0.3709       43.035    0.0001    0.03688411   0.0      0.55995394   0.0001
   3    PETALWID                 3       0.3229       34.569    0.0001    0.02497554   0.0      0.59495691   0.0001
   4    SEPALLEN                 4       0.0615        4.721    0.0103    0.02343863   0.0      0.59594941   0.0001
```

REFERENCES

Costanza, M.C. and Afifi, A.A. (1979), "Comparison of Stopping Rules in Forward Stepwise Discriminant Analysis," *Journal of the American Statistical Association*, 74, 777-785.

Jennrich, R.I. (1977), "Stepwise Discriminant Analysis," in *Statistical Methods for Digital Computers*, eds. K. Enslein, A. Ralston, and H. Wilf, New York: John Wiley & Sons.

Klecka, W.R. (1980), *Discriminant Analysis*, Sage University Paper series on Quantitative Applications in the Social Sciences, series no. 07-019, Beverly Hills: Sage Publications.

Chapter 37

The STEPWISE Procedure

Operating systems: All

ABSTRACT

The STEPWISE procedure provides five methods for stepwise regression. PROC STEPWISE is useful when you have many independent variables and want to find which of the variables should be included in a regression model.

INTRODUCTION

PROC STEPWISE is most helpful for exploratory analysis because it can give you insight into the relationships between the independent variables and the dependent or response variable. However, PROC STEPWISE is not guaranteed to give you the "best" model for your data, or even the model with the largest R^2. And no model developed by these means can be guaranteed to represent real-world processes accurately.

STEPWISE and Other Model-building Procedures

PROC STEPWISE differs from PROC RSQUARE, which is used for exploratory model analysis. PROC RSQUARE finds the R^2 value for all possible combinations of the independent variables. Therefore, PROC RSQUARE always identifies the model with the largest R^2 for each number of variables considered. PROC STEPWISE uses the selection strategies described below in choosing the variables for the models it considers, and it is not guaranteed to find the model with the largest R^2. PROC RSQUARE requires much more computer time than PROC STEPWISE, so PROC STEPWISE is a good choice when there are independent variables to consider.

Model-Selection Methods

The five methods of model selection implemented in PROC STEPWISE are

FORWARD	forward selection
BACKWARD	backward elimination
STEPWISE	stepwise regression, forward and backward
MAXR	forward selection with pair switching
MINR	forward selection with pair searching.

A survey article by Hocking (1976) describes these and other variable-selection methods. The five methods are described below with the keyword value of the METHOD= option to request each method.

Forward selection (FORWARD) The forward-selection technique begins with no variables in the model. For each of the independent variables, FORWARD calculates F statistics reflecting the variable's contribution to the model if it is included. These F statistics are compared to the SLENTRY= value that is specified in the MODEL statement (or to .50 if SLENTRY= is omitted). If no F statistic has a significance level greater than the SLENTRY= value, FORWARD stops. Otherwise, FORWARD adds the variable that has the largest F statistic to the model. FORWARD then calculates F statistics again for the variables still remaining outside the model, and the evaluation process is repeated. Thus, variables are added one by one to the model until no remaining variable produces a significant F statistic. Once a variable is in the model, it stays.

Backward elimination (BACKWARD) The backward elimination technique begins by calculating statistics for a model, including all of the independent variables. Then the variables are deleted from the model one by one until all the variables remaining in the model produce F statistics significant at the SLSTAY= level specified in the MODEL statement (or at the .10 level, if SLSTAY= is omitted). At each step, the variable showing the smallest contribution to the model is deleted.

Stepwise (STEPWISE) The stepwise method is a modification of the forward-selection technique and differs in that variables already in the model do not necessarily stay there. As in the forward-selection method, variables are added one by one to the model, and the F statistic for a variable to be added must be significant at the SLENTRY= level. After a variable is added, however, the stepwise method looks at all the variables already included in the model and deletes any variable that does not produce an F statistic significant at the SLSTAY= level. Only after this check is made and the necessary deletions accomplished can another variable be added to the model. The stepwise process ends when none of the variables outside the model has an F statistic significant at the SLENTRY=

level and every variable in the model is significant at the SLSTAY= level or when the variable to be added to the model is one just deleted from it.

Maximum R^2 improvement (MAXR) The maximum R^2 improvement technique developed by James Goodnight is considered superior to the stepwise technique and almost as good as all possible regressions. Unlike the three techniques above, this method does not settle on a single model. Instead, it tries to find the best one-variable model, the best two-variable model, and so forth, although it is not guaranteed to find the model with the largest R^2 for each size.

The MAXR method begins by finding the one-variable model producing the highest R^2. Then another variable, the one that yields the greatest increase in R^2, is added. Once the two-variable model is obtained, each of the variables in the model is compared to each variable not in the model. For each comparison, MAXR determines if removing one variable and replacing it with the other variable increases R^2. After comparing all possible switches, MAXR makes the switch that produces the largest increase in R^2. Comparisons begin again, and the process continues until MAXR finds that no switch could increase R^2. Thus, the two-variable model achieved is considered the "best" two-variable model the technique can find. Another variable is then added to the model, and the comparing-and-switching process is repeated to find the "best" three-variable model, and so forth.

The difference between the stepwise technique and the maximum R^2 improvement method is that all switches are evaluated before any switch is made in the MAXR method. In the stepwise method, the "worst" variable may be removed without considering what adding the "best" remaining variable might accomplish. The MAXR method may require much more computer time than the STEPWISE method.

Minimum R^2 improvement (MINR) The MINR method closely resembles MAXR, but the switch chosen is the one that produces the smallest increase in R^2. For a given number of variables in the model, MAXR and MINR usually produce the same "best" model, but MINR considers more models of each size.

Significance Levels

When many significance tests are performed, each at a level of, say 5%, the overall probability of rejecting at least one true null hypothesis is much larger than 5%. If you want to guard against including any variables that do not contribute to the predictive power of the model in the population, you should specify a very small significance level. In most applications many variables considered have some predictive power, however small. If you want to choose the model that provides the best prediction using the sample estimates, you need only guard against estimating more parameters than can be reliably estimated with the given sample size, so you should use a moderate significance level, perhaps in the range of 10% to 25%.

C_p Statistic

C_p was proposed by Mallows as a criterion for selecting a model. C_p is a measure of total squared error defined as:

$$C_p = \frac{\text{SSE}_p}{s^2} - (N-2p)$$

where s^2 is the MSE for the full model and SSE_p is the sum-of-squares error for a model with p variables plus the intercept. If C_p is graphed with p, Mallows recommends the model where C_p first approaches p. When the right model is chosen, the parameter estimates are unbiased, and this reflects in C_p near p. For further discussion, see Daniel and Wood (1980).

SPECIFICATIONS

The statements used to control PROC STEPWISE are

PROC STEPWISE *options;*
  MODEL *dependents = independents /options;*
  WEIGHT *variable;*
  BY *variables;*

STEPWISE needs at least one MODEL statement. The BY and WEIGHT statements can be placed anywhere.

PROC STEPWISE Statement

PROC STEPWISE *options;*

Only one option is used on the PROC statement:

DATA=*SASdataset*
: names the SAS data set containing the data for the regression. If it is omitted, the most recently created data set is used.

MODEL Statement

MODEL *dependents = independents / options;*

In the MODEL statement, list the dependent variables on the left side of the equal sign and the independent variables on the right side of the equal sign.

For each dependent variable given, PROC STEPWISE goes through the model-building process using the independent variables listed. Any number of MODEL statements can be included. The options below may be specified in the MODEL statement after a slash (/):

NOINT
: prevents the procedure from automatically including an intercept term in the model.

FORWARD
F
: requests the forward-selection technique.

BACKWARD
B
: requests the backward-elimination technique.

STEPWISE
: requests the stepwise technique, the default.

MAXR
: requests the maximum R^2 improvement technique.

MINR
: requests the minimum R^2 improvement technique.

SLENTRY=*value*
SLE=*value*

specifies the significance level for entry into the model used in the forward-selection and stepwise techniques. If SLENTRY= is omitted, STEPWISE uses the SLENTRY= value .50 for forward selection, .15 for stepwise.

SLSTAY=*value*
SLS=*value*

specifies the significance level for staying in the model for the backward elimination and stepwise techniques. If it is omitted, STEPWISE uses the SLSTAY= value .10 for backward elimination, .15 for stepwise.

INCLUDE=*n*

forces the first *n* independent variables always to be included in the model. The selection techniques are performed on the other variables in the MODEL statement.

START=*s*

is used to begin the comparing-and-switching process for a model containing the first *s* independent variables in the MODEL statement, where *s* is the START value. Consequently, no model is evaluated that contains fewer than *s* variables. This applies only to the MAXR, MINR, and STEPWISE methods.

STOP=*s*

causes STEPWISE to stop when it has found the "best" *s*-variable model, where *s* is the STOP value. This applies only to the MAXR or MINR methods.

DETAILS

produces a table of statistics for entry and removal for each variable at each step in the model-building process. These statistics include the tolerance, R^2, and F statistic that result if each variable is added to the model, or the partial and model R^2 that results if the variable is deleted from the model. This applies only to the FORWARD, BACKWARD, and STEPWISE methods.

WEIGHT Statement

WEIGHT *variable;*

The WEIGHT statement is used to specify a variable on the data set containing weights for the observations. Only observations with positive values of the WEIGHT variable are used in the analysis.

BY Statement

BY *variables;*

A BY statement can be used with PROC STEPWISE to obtain separate analyses on observations in groups defined by the BY variables. When a BY statement appears, the procedure expects the input data set to be sorted in order of the BY variables. If your input data set is not sorted in ascending order, use the SORT procedure with a similar BY statement to sort the data, or, if appropriate, use the BY statement options NOTSORTED or DESCENDING. For more information, see the discussion of the BY statement in "Statements Used in the PROC Step" in the *SAS User's Guide: Basics.*

DETAILS

Missing Values

The STEPWISE procedure omits observations from the calculations for a given model if the observation has missing values for any of the variables in the model. The observation is included for any models that do not include the variables with missing values.

Limitations

Any number of dependent variables can be included in a MODEL statement. Although there is no built-in limit on the number of independent variables, the calculations for a model with many variables are lengthy. For the MAXR or MINR technique, a reasonable maximum for the number of independent variables in a single MODEL statement is about twenty.

Printed Output

For each model of a given size, PROC STEPWISE prints an analysis-of-variance table, the regression coefficients, and related statistics.

The analysis-of-variance table includes

1. the source of variation REGRESSION, which is the variation that is attributed to the independent variables in the model
2. the source of variation ERROR, which is the residual variation that is not accounted for by the model
3. the source of variation TOTAL, which is corrected for the mean of y if an intercept is included in the model, uncorrected if an intercept is not included
4. DF, degrees of freedom
5. SUMS OF SQUARES for REGRESSION, ERROR, and TOTAL
6. MEAN SQUARES for REGRESSION and ERROR
7. the F value, which is the ratio of the REGRESSION mean square to the ERROR mean square
8. PROB > F, the significance probability of the F value
9. R SQUARE or R^2, the square of the multiple correlation coefficient
10. C(P) statistic proposed by Mallows.

Below the analysis-of-variance table are printed

11. the names of the independent variables included in the model
12. B VALUES, the corresponding estimated regression coefficients
13. STD ERROR of the estimates
14. TYPE II SS (sum of squares) for each variable, which is the SS that is added to the error SS if that one variable is removed from the model
15. F values and PROB>F associated with the Type II sums of squares
16. bounds on the condition number of the correlation matrix for the variables in the model (Berk 1977).

After statistics for the final model have been printed, when the method chosen is FORWARD, BACKWARD, or STEPWISE, the following is printed

17. A summary table listing step number, variable entered or removed, partial and model R^2, and C(P) and F statistics.

EXAMPLE

Three Selection Methods: PROC STEPWISE

The example below asks for the FORWARD, BACKWARD, and MAXR methods:

```
*-----------------------DATA ON PHYSICAL FITNESS---------------------*
| THESE MEASUREMENTS WERE MADE ON MEN INVOLVED IN A PHYSICAL FITNESS  |
| COURSE AT N.C.STATE UNIV. THE VARIABLES ARE AGE(YEARS), WEIGHT(KG), |
| OXYGEN UPTAKE RATE(ML PER KG BODY WEIGHT PER MINUTE), TIME TO RUN   |
| 1.5 MILES(MINUTES), HEART RATE WHILE RESTING, HEART RATE WHILE      |
| RUNNING (SAME TIME OXYGEN RATE MEASURED), AND MAXIMUM HEART RATE    |
| RECORDED WHILE RUNNING. CERTAIN VALUES OF MAXPULSE WERE MODIFIED    |
| FOR CONSISTENCY.          DATA COURTESY DR. A. C. LINNERUD          |
*---------------------------------------------------------------------*;
DATA FITNESS;
   INPUT AGE WEIGHT OXY RUNTIME RSTPULSE RUNPULSE MAXPULSE @@;
   CARDS;
44 89.47  44.609 11.37 62 178 182    40 75.07  45.313 10.07 62 185 185
44 85.84  54.297  8.65 45 156 168    42 68.15  59.571  8.17 40 166 172
38 89.02  49.874  9.22 55 178 180    47 77.45  44.811 11.63 58 176 176
40 75.98  45.681 11.95 70 176 180    43 81.19  49.091 10.85 64 162 170
44 81.42  39.442 13.08 63 174 176    38 81.87  60.055  8.63 48 170 186
44 73.03  50.541 10.13 45 168 168    45 87.66  37.388 14.03 56 186 192
45 66.45  44.754 11.12 51 176 176    47 79.15  47.273 10.60 47 162 164
54 83.12  51.855 10.33 50 166 170    49 81.42  49.156  8.95 44 180 185
51 69.63  40.836 10.95 57 168 172    51 77.91  46.672 10.00 48 162 168
48 91.63  46.774 10.25 48 162 164    49 73.37  50.388 10.08 67 168 168
57 73.37  39.407 12.63 58 174 176    54 79.38  46.080 11.17 62 156 165
52 76.32  45.441  9.63 48 164 166    50 70.87  54.625  8.92 48 146 155
51 67.25  45.118 11.08 48 172 172    54 91.63  39.203 12.88 44 168 172
51 73.71  45.790 10.47 59 186 188    57 59.08  50.545  9.93 49 148 155
49 76.32  48.673  9.40 56 186 188    48 61.24  47.920 11.50 52 170 176
52 82.78  47.467 10.50 53 170 172
;
PROC STEPWISE;
   MODEL OXY=AGE WEIGHT RUNTIME RUNPULSE RSTPULSE MAXPULSE
         / FORWARD BACKWARD MAXR;
```

Output 37.1 Forward Selection Procedure: PROC STEPWISE

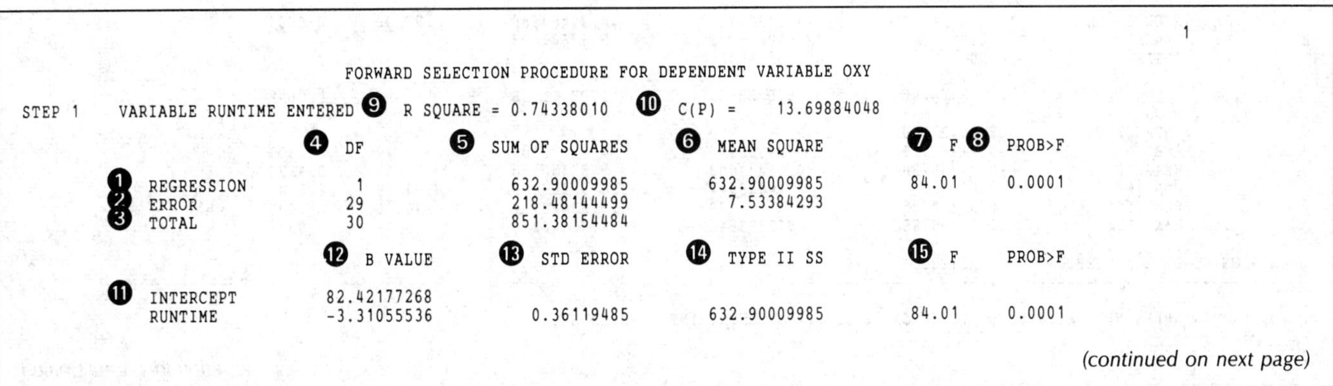

```
                                                                              1

                 FORWARD SELECTION PROCEDURE FOR DEPENDENT VARIABLE OXY

STEP 1    VARIABLE RUNTIME ENTERED ❾ R SQUARE = 0.74338010  ❿ C(P) =    13.69884048

                        ❹ DF        ❺ SUM OF SQUARES   ❻ MEAN SQUARE     ❼ F ❽ PROB>F

       ❶ REGRESSION        1         632.90009985      632.90009985     84.01    0.0001
       ❷ ERROR            29         218.48144499        7.53384293
       ❸ TOTAL            30         851.38154484

                       ⓬ B VALUE     ⓭ STD ERROR      ⓮ TYPE II SS     ⓯ F     PROB>F

       ⓫ INTERCEPT    82.42177268
         RUNTIME      -3.31055536      0.36119485      632.90009985     84.01    0.0001
```

(continued on next page)

(continued from previous page)

```
BOUNDS ON CONDITION NUMBER:              1,        2
------------------------------------------------------------------------------------------------------------------------

STEP 2    VARIABLE AGE ENTERED       R SQUARE = 0.76424693       C(P) =     12.38944895

                                DF             SUM OF SQUARES         MEAN SQUARE              F        PROB>F

            REGRESSION           2             650.66573237        325.33286618            45.38        0.0001
            ERROR               28             200.71581247          7.16842187
            TOTAL               30             851.38154484

                                  B VALUE            STD ERROR         TYPE II SS              F        PROB>F

            INTERCEPT        88.46228749
            AGE              -0.15036567           0.09551468        17.76563252              2.48        0.1267
            RUNTIME          -3.20395056           0.35877488       571.67750579             79.75        0.0001

BOUNDS ON CONDITION NUMBER:      1.036941,      8.295526
------------------------------------------------------------------------------------------------------------------------

STEP 3    VARIABLE RUNPULSE ENTERED  R SQUARE = 0.81109446       C(P) =      6.95962673

                                DF             SUM OF SQUARES         MEAN SQUARE              F        PROB>F

            REGRESSION           3             690.55085627        230.18361876            38.64        0.0001
            ERROR               27             160.83068857          5.95669217
            TOTAL               30             851.38154484

                                  B VALUE            STD ERROR         TYPE II SS              F        PROB>F

            INTERCEPT       111.71806443
            AGE              -0.25639826           0.09622892        42.28867438              7.10        0.0129
            RUNTIME          -2.82537867           0.35828041       370.43528607             62.19        0.0001
            RUNPULSE         -0.13090870           0.05059011        39.88512390              6.70        0.0154

BOUNDS ON CONDITION NUMBER:      1.354763,      23.19489
------------------------------------------------------------------------------------------------------------------------
```

```
                                                                                                                      2

                            FORWARD SELECTION PROCEDURE FOR DEPENDENT VARIABLE OXY

STEP 4    VARIABLE MAXPULSE ENTERED  R SQUARE = 0.83681815       C(P) =      4.87995808

                                DF             SUM OF SQUARES         MEAN SQUARE              F        PROB>F

            REGRESSION           4             712.45152692        178.11288173            33.33        0.0001
            ERROR               26             138.93001792          5.34346223
            TOTAL               30             851.38154484

                                  B VALUE            STD ERROR         TYPE II SS              F        PROB>F

            INTERCEPT        98.14788797
            AGE              -0.19773470           0.09563662        22.84231496              4.27        0.0488
            RUNTIME          -2.76757879           0.34053643       352.93569605             66.05        0.0001
            RUNPULSE         -0.34810795           0.11749917        46.90088674              8.78        0.0064
            MAXPULSE          0.27051297           0.13361978        21.90067065              4.10        0.0533

BOUNDS ON CONDITION NUMBER:        8.4182,      153.7027
------------------------------------------------------------------------------------------------------------------------

STEP 5    VARIABLE WEIGHT ENTERED    R SQUARE = 0.84800181       C(P) =      5.10627546

                                DF             SUM OF SQUARES         MEAN SQUARE              F        PROB>F

            REGRESSION           5             721.97309402        144.39461880            27.90        0.0001
            ERROR               25             129.40845082          5.17633803
            TOTAL               30             851.38154484

                                  B VALUE            STD ERROR         TYPE II SS              F        PROB>F

            INTERCEPT       102.20427520
            AGE              -0.21962138           0.09550245        27.37429100              5.29        0.0301
            WEIGHT           -0.07230234           0.05331009         9.52156710              1.84        0.1871
            RUNTIME          -2.68252297           0.34098544       320.35967836             61.89        0.0001
            RUNPULSE         -0.37340085           0.11714109        52.59623720             10.16        0.0038
            MAXPULSE          0.30490783           0.13393642        26.82640270              5.18        0.0316

BOUNDS ON CONDITION NUMBER:      8.731225,      209.6508
------------------------------------------------------------------------------------------------------------------------

NO OTHER VARIABLES MET THE 0.5000 SIGNIFICANCE LEVEL FOR ENTRY INTO THE MODEL.
```

(continued on next page)

(continued from previous page)

⓱ SUMMARY OF FORWARD SELECTION PROCEDURE FOR DEPENDENT VARIABLE OXY

STEP	VARIABLE ENTERED	NUMBER IN	PARTIAL R**2	MODEL R**2	C(P)	F	PROB>F
1	RUNTIME	1	0.7434	0.7434	13.6988	84.0076	0.0001
2	AGE	2	0.0209	0.7642	12.3894	2.4783	0.1267
3	RUNPULSE	3	0.0468	0.8111	6.9596	6.6959	0.0154
4	MAXPULSE	4	0.0257	0.8368	4.8800	4.0986	0.0533
5	WEIGHT	5	0.0112	0.8480	5.1063	1.8394	0.1871

Output 37.2 Backward Selection Procedure: PROC STEPWISE

```
                                                                                                   1

                          BACKWARD ELIMINATION PROCEDURE FOR DEPENDENT VARIABLE OXY

STEP 0    ALL VARIABLES ENTERED        R SQUARE = 0.84867192        C(P) =      7.00000000

                              DF              SUM OF SQUARES         MEAN SQUARE            F      PROB>F

          REGRESSION           6                722.54360701        120.42393450        22.43      0.0001
          ERROR               24                128.83793783          5.36824741
          TOTAL               30                851.38154484

                                B VALUE            STD ERROR         TYPE II SS            F      PROB>F

          INTERCEPT        102.93447948
          AGE               -0.22697380           0.09983747        27.74577148         5.17      0.0322
          WEIGHT            -0.07417741           0.05459316         9.91058836         1.85      0.1869
          RUNTIME           -2.62865282           0.38456220       250.82210090        46.72      0.0001
          RUNPULSE          -0.36962776           0.11985294        51.05805832         9.51      0.0051
          RSTPULSE          -0.02153364           0.06605428         0.57051299         0.11      0.7473
          MAXPULSE           0.30321713           0.13649519        26.49142405         4.93      0.0360

BOUNDS ON CONDITION NUMBER:      8.743848,       274.2689
-------------------------------------------------------------------------------------------------------

STEP 1    VARIABLE RSTPULSE REMOVED    R SQUARE = 0.84800181        C(P) =      5.10627546

                              DF              SUM OF SQUARES         MEAN SQUARE            F      PROB>F

          REGRESSION           5                721.97309402        144.39461880        27.90      0.0001
          ERROR               25                129.40845082          5.17633803
          TOTAL               30                851.38154484

                                B VALUE            STD ERROR         TYPE II SS            F      PROB>F

          INTERCEPT        102.20427520
          AGE               -0.21962138           0.09550245        27.37429100         5.29      0.0301
          WEIGHT            -0.07230234           0.05331009         9.52156710         1.84      0.1871
          RUNTIME           -2.68252297           0.34098544       320.35967836        61.89      0.0001
          RUNPULSE          -0.37340085           0.11714109        52.59623720        10.16      0.0038
          MAXPULSE           0.30490783           0.13393642        26.82640270         5.18      0.0316

BOUNDS ON CONDITION NUMBER:      8.731225,       209.6508
-------------------------------------------------------------------------------------------------------
```

```
                                                                                                   2

                          BACKWARD ELIMINATION PROCEDURE FOR DEPENDENT VARIABLE OXY

STEP 2    VARIABLE WEIGHT REMOVED      R SQUARE = 0.83681815        C(P) =      4.87995808

                              DF              SUM OF SQUARES         MEAN SQUARE            F      PROB>F

          REGRESSION           4                712.45152692        178.11288173        33.33      0.0001
          ERROR               26                138.93001792          5.34346223
          TOTAL               30                851.38154484

                                B VALUE            STD ERROR         TYPE II SS            F      PROB>F

          INTERCEPT         98.14788797
          AGE               -0.19773470           0.09563662        22.84231496         4.27      0.0488
```

(continued on next page)

(continued from previous page)

```
          RUNTIME            -2.76757879          0.34053643        352.93569605         66.05       0.0001
          RUNPULSE           -0.34810795          0.11749917         46.90088674          8.78       0.0064
          MAXPULSE            0.27051297          0.13361978         21.90067065          4.10       0.0533

BOUNDS ON CONDITION NUMBER:        8.4182,      153.7027
--------------------------------------------------------------------------------------------------------------

ALL VARIABLES IN THE MODEL ARE SIGNIFICANT AT THE 0.1000 LEVEL.

                          SUMMARY OF BACKWARD ELIMINATION PROCEDURE FOR DEPENDENT VARIABLE OXY

                         VARIABLE    NUMBER    PARTIAL      MODEL
                 STEP    REMOVED         IN       R**2       R**2          C(P)            F        PROB>F

                    1    RSTPULSE         5     0.0007     0.8480        5.1063       0.1063        0.7473
                    2    WEIGHT           4     0.0112     0.8368        4.8800       1.8394        0.1871
```

Output 37.3 Maximum R-Square Improvement Selection Procedure: PROC STEPWISE

```
                                                                                                            1

                                   MAXIMUM R-SQUARE IMPROVEMENT FOR DEPENDENT VARIABLE OXY

STEP 1     VARIABLE RUNTIME ENTERED            R SQUARE = 0.74338010         C(P) =      13.69884048

                                     DF              SUM OF SQUARES          MEAN SQUARE             F       PROB>F

          REGRESSION                  1                632.90009985         632.90009985         84.01       0.0001
          ERROR                      29                218.48144499           7.53384293
          TOTAL                      30                851.38154484

                                B VALUE                  STD ERROR           TYPE II SS             F       PROB>F

          INTERCEPT         82.42177268
          RUNTIME           -3.31055536                 0.36119485         632.90009985         84.01       0.0001

BOUNDS ON CONDITION NUMBER:               1,            2
--------------------------------------------------------------------------------------------------------------

THE ABOVE MODEL IS THE BEST  1 VARIABLE MODEL FOUND.

STEP 2     VARIABLE AGE ENTERED                R SQUARE = 0.76424693         C(P) =      12.38944895

                                     DF              SUM OF SQUARES          MEAN SQUARE             F       PROB>F

          REGRESSION                  2                650.66573237         325.33286618         45.38       0.0001
          ERROR                      28                200.71581247           7.16842187
          TOTAL                      30                851.38154484

                                B VALUE                  STD ERROR           TYPE II SS             F       PROB>F

          INTERCEPT         88.46228749
          AGE               -0.15036567                 0.09551468          17.76563252          2.48       0.1267
          RUNTIME           -3.20395056                 0.35877488         571.67750579         79.75       0.0001

BOUNDS ON CONDITION NUMBER:     1.036941,      8.295526
--------------------------------------------------------------------------------------------------------------

THE ABOVE MODEL IS THE BEST  2 VARIABLE MODEL FOUND.
```

(continued on next page)

(continued from previous page)

```
STEP 3     VARIABLE RUNPULSE ENTERED        R SQUARE = 0.81109446        C(P) =      6.95962673

                              DF              SUM OF SQUARES          MEAN SQUARE             F        PROB>F

           REGRESSION          3                690.55085627         230.18361876         38.64        0.0001
           ERROR              27                160.83068857           5.95669217
           TOTAL              30                851.38154484

                                 B VALUE             STD ERROR          TYPE II SS             F        PROB>F

           INTERCEPT      111.71806443
           AGE             -0.25639826            0.09622892         42.28867438          7.10        0.0129
           RUNTIME         -2.82537867            0.35828041        370.43528607         62.19        0.0001
           RUNPULSE        -0.13090870            0.05059011         39.88512390          6.70        0.0154

BOUNDS ON CONDITION NUMBER:       1.354763,       23.19489
------------------------------------------------------------------------------------------------------------------

THE ABOVE MODEL IS THE BEST  3 VARIABLE MODEL FOUND.
```

```
                                                                                                                    2

                                 MAXIMUM R-SQUARE IMPROVEMENT FOR DEPENDENT VARIABLE OXY

STEP 4     VARIABLE MAXPULSE ENTERED        R SQUARE = 0.83681815        C(P) =      4.87995808

                              DF              SUM OF SQUARES          MEAN SQUARE             F        PROB>F

           REGRESSION          4                712.45152692         178.11288173         33.33        0.0001
           ERROR              26                138.93001792           5.34346223
           TOTAL              30                851.38154484

                                 B VALUE             STD ERROR          TYPE II SS             F        PROB>F

           INTERCEPT       98.14788797
           AGE             -0.19773470            0.09563662         22.84231496          4.27        0.0488
           RUNTIME         -2.76757879            0.34053643        352.93569605         66.05        0.0001
           RUNPULSE        -0.34810795            0.11749917         46.90088674          8.78        0.0064
           MAXPULSE         0.27051297            0.13361978         21.90067065          4.10        0.0533

BOUNDS ON CONDITION NUMBER:         8.4182,       153.7027
------------------------------------------------------------------------------------------------------------------

THE ABOVE MODEL IS THE BEST  4 VARIABLE MODEL FOUND.

STEP 5     VARIABLE WEIGHT ENTERED          R SQUARE = 0.84800181        C(P) =      5.10627546

                              DF              SUM OF SQUARES          MEAN SQUARE             F        PROB>F

           REGRESSION          5                721.97309402         144.39461880         27.90        0.0001
           ERROR              25                129.40845082           5.17633803
           TOTAL              30                851.38154484
                                 B VALUE             STD ERROR          TYPE II SS             F        PROB>F

           INTERCEPT      102.20427520
           AGE             -0.21962138            0.09550245         27.37429100          5.29        0.0301
           WEIGHT          -0.07230234            0.05331009          9.52156710          1.84        0.1871
           RUNTIME         -2.68252297            0.34098544        320.35967836         61.89        0.0001
           RUNPULSE        -0.37340085            0.11714109         52.59623720         10.16        0.0038
           MAXPULSE         0.30490783            0.13393642         26.82640270          5.18        0.0316

BOUNDS ON CONDITION NUMBER:       8.731225,       209.6508
------------------------------------------------------------------------------------------------------------------

THE ABOVE MODEL IS THE BEST  5 VARIABLE MODEL FOUND.
```

```
                                                                                                                    3

                                 MAXIMUM R-SQUARE IMPROVEMENT FOR DEPENDENT VARIABLE OXY

STEP 6     VARIABLE RSTPULSE ENTERED        R SQUARE = 0.84867192        C(P) =      7.00000000

                              DF              SUM OF SQUARES          MEAN SQUARE             F        PROB>F

           REGRESSION          6                722.54360701         120.42393450         22.43        0.0001
           ERROR              24                128.83793783           5.36824741
           TOTAL              30                851.38154484
```

(continued on next page)

(continued from previous page)

```
                     B VALUE            STD ERROR           TYPE II SS            F      PROB>F

INTERCEPT        102.93447948
AGE               -0.22697380          0.09983747          27.74577148          5.17     0.0322
WEIGHT            -0.07417741          0.05459316           9.91058836          1.85     0.1869
RUNTIME           -2.62865282          0.38456220         250.82210090         46.72     0.0001
RUNPULSE          -0.36962776          0.11985294          51.05805832          9.51     0.0051
RSTPULSE          -0.02153364          0.06605428           0.57051299          0.11     0.7473
MAXPULSE           0.30321713          0.13649519          26.49142405          4.93     0.0360

BOUNDS ON CONDITION NUMBER:     8.743848,      274.2689
------------------------------------------------------------------------------------------------------------

THE ABOVE MODEL IS THE BEST  6 VARIABLE MODEL FOUND.
```

REFERENCES

Berk, Kenneth N. (1977), "Tolerance and Condition in Regression Computations," *Journal of the American Statistical Association*, 72, 863-866.

Daniel, Cuthbert and Wood, Fred S. (1980), *Fitting Equations to Data*, Second Edition, New York: John Wiley & Sons.

Draper, N.R. and Smith, H. (1981), *Applied Regression Analysis*, Second Edition, New York: John Wiley & Sons.

Hocking, R.R. (1976), "The Analysis and Selection of Variables in Linear Regression," *Biometrics*, 32, 1-50.

Mallows, C.L. (1964), "Some Comments on C_p," *Technometrics*, 15, 661-675.

Sall, J. (1981), *SAS Regression Applications*, Technical Report A-102, Cary, N.C.: SAS Institute Inc.

Chapter 38

The TREE Procedure

Operating systems: All

ABSTRACT

The TREE procedure prints a tree diagram, also known as a dendrogram or phenogram, using a data set created by the CLUSTER or VARCLUS procedure. PROC TREE can also create an output data set identifying disjoint clusters at a specified level in the tree.

INTRODUCTION

The CLUSTER and VARCLUS procedures create output data sets giving the results of hierarchical clustering as a tree structure. The TREE procedure uses the output data set to print a diagram of the tree structure in the style of Johnson (1967) with the root at the top. Any numeric variable in the output data set can be used to specify the heights of the clusters. PROC TREE can also create an output data set containing a variable to indicate the disjoint clusters at a specified level in the tree.

Trees are discussed in the context of cluster analysis by Duran and Odell (1974), Hartigan (1975), and Everitt (1980). Knuth (1973) provides a general treatment of trees in computer programming.

The literature on trees contains a mixture of botanical and genealogical terminology. The objects that are clustered are *leaves*. The cluster containing all objects is the *root*. A cluster containing at least two objects but not all of them is a *branch*.

The general term for leaves, branches, and roots is *node*. If a cluster *A* is the union of clusters *B* and *C*, then *A* is the *parent* of *B* and *C*, and *B* and *C* are *children* of *A*. A leaf is thus a node with no children, and a root is a node with no parent. If every cluster has at most two children, the tree is a *binary* tree. The CLUSTER procedure always produces binary trees. The VARCLUS procedure can produce trees with clusters that have many children.

SPECIFICATIONS

The TREE procedure is invoked by the following statements:

PROC TREE *options;*
  NAME *variable;*
  PARENT *variable;*
  HEIGHT *variable;*
  ID *variable;*
  COPY *variables;*
  FREQ *variable;*
  BY *variables;*

If the input data set has been created by CLUSTER or VARCLUS, the only statement required is the PROC TREE statement.

PROC TREE Statement

PROC TREE *options;*

The following options can appear in the PROC TREE statement:

DATA=*SASdataset*
: names the input data set defining the tree. If DATA= is omitted, the most recently created SAS data set is used.

OUT=*SASdataset*
: names an output data set that contains one observation for each object in the tree or subtree being processed and variables called CLUSTER and CLUSNAME showing cluster membership at any specified level in the tree. If OUT= is used, then either NCLUSTERS= or LEVEL= must be specified to define the output partition level. If you want to create a permanent SAS data set you must specify a two-level name (see "SAS Files" in *SAS User's Guide: Basics*).

HEIGHT | H=NCL | N
HEIGHT | H=HEIGHT | H
HEIGHT | H=MODE | M
HEIGHT | H=RSQ | R
HEIGHT | H=LENGTH | L
: specifies certain conventional variables to be used for the height axis of the tree diagram. A value of NCL or N specifies the _NCL_ variable. A value of HEIGHT or H specifies the _HEIGHT_ variable. A value of MODE or M specifies the _MODE_ variable. A value of RSQ or R specifies the _RSQ_ variable. A value of LENGTH or L causes the height of each node to be defined as its path length from the root, that is, the number of ancestors of the node. See also the HEIGHT statement, which can specify any variable in the input data set to be used for the height axis.

SIMILAR
SIM

implies that the values of the HEIGHT variable are similarities, that is, a large height value means that the clusters are very similar or close together.

DISSIMILAR
DIS

implies that the values of the HEIGHT variable are dissimilarities, that is, a large height value means that the clusters are very dissimilar or far apart.

If neither SIMILAR nor DISSIMILAR is specified, TREE attempts to infer from the data whether the height values are similarities or dissimilarities. If TREE cannot tell this from the data, it issues an error message and does not print a tree diagram.

LEVEL=*n*

causes only clusters between the root and a height of *n* to be printed and specifies the level of the tree defining disjoint clusters in the OUT= data set. The clusters in the output data set are those that exist at a height of *n* on the tree diagram. For example, if the HEIGHT variable is _NCL_ (number of clusters) and LEVEL=5 is specified, then the OUT= data set contains 5 disjoint clusters. If the HEIGHT variable is _RSQ_ (R^2) and LEVEL=.9 is specified, then the OUT= data set contains the smallest number of clusters that yields an R^2 of at least .9.

NCLUSTERS=*n*
NCL=*n*
N=*n*

specifies the number of clusters desired in the OUT= data set. The number of clusters obtained may not equal the number specified if: 1) there are fewer than *n* leaves in the tree, 2) there are more than *n* unconnected trees in the data set, 3) a multi-way tree does not contain a level with the specified number of clusters, or 4) the DOCK= option eliminates too many clusters. The NCLUSTERS= option uses the _NCL_ variable to determine the order in which the clusters were formed. If there is no _NCL_ variable, the height variable (as determined by the HEIGHT statement or HEIGHT= option) is used instead.

DOCK=*n*

causes observations assigned to output clusters with a frequency of *n* or less to be given missing values for the output variables CLUSTER and CLUSNAME. If NCLUSTERS= is specified, DOCK= also prevents clusters with a frequency of *n* or less from being counted toward the number of clusters requested by NCLUSTERS=. The default is DOCK=0.

ROOT='*name*'

specifies the value of the NAME variable for the root of a subtree to be printed if you do not wish to print the entire tree. If OUT= is also specified, the output data set contains only objects belonging to the subtree specified by ROOT=.

SORT

sorts the children of each node by the HEIGHT variable, in the order of cluster formation.

DESCENDING
reverses the sorting order for the SORT option.

MINHEIGHT=*n*
MINH=*n*
specifies the minimum value printed on the height axis.

MAXHEIGHT=*n*
MAXH=*n*
specifies the maximum value printed on the height axis.

SPACES=*s*
S=*s*
specifies the number of spaces between objects on the printout. The default depends on the number of objects and the line size used.

PAGES=*n*
specifies the number of pages over which the tree (from root to leaves) is to extend. The default is chosen to make the tree diagram approximately square.

POS=*n*
specifies the number of print positions on the height axis. The default depends on the value of the PAGES= option.

TICKPOS=*n*
specifies the number of print positions per tick interval on the height axis. The default value is usually between 5 and 10, although a different value may be used for consistency with other options.

NTICK=*n*
specifies the number of tick intervals on the height axis. The default depends on the values of other options.

INC=*n*
specifies the increment between tick values on the height axis. If the HEIGHT variable is _NCL_, the default is usually 1, although a different value may be used for consistency with other options. For any other HEIGHT variable, the default is some power of 10 times 1, 2, 2.5, or 5.

LEAFCHAR='*c*'
LC='*c*'
specifies a character to represent clusters containing only one object. The character should be enclosed in single quotes. The default is a period.

TREECHAR='*c*'
TC='*c*'
specifies a character to represent clusters containing more than one object. The character should be enclosed in single quotes. The default is X.

JOINCHAR='*c*'
JC='*c*'
specifies the character to print between leaves that have been joined into a cluster. The character should be enclosed in single quotes. The default is X.

FILLCHAR='*c*'
FC='*c*'
specifies the character to print between leaves that have not been joined into a cluster. The character should be enclosed in single quotes. The default is a blank.

LIST

lists all the nodes in the tree, printing the height, parent, and children of each node.

NOPRINT

suppresses printing the tree if you only want to create an OUT= data set.

NAME Statement

NAME *variable;*

The NAME statement specifies a character variable identifying the node represented by each observation. The NAME variable and PARENT variable jointly define the tree structure. If the NAME statement is omitted, TREE looks for a variable called _NAME_. If the _NAME_ variable is not found in the data set, TREE issues an error message and stops.

PARENT Statement

PARENT *variable;*

The PARENT statement specifies a character variable identifying the node in the tree that is the parent of each observation. The PARENT variable must be the same length as the NAME variable. If the PARENT statement is omitted, TREE looks for a variable called _PARENT_. If the _PARENT_ variable is not found in the data set, TREE issues an error message and stops.

HEIGHT Statement

HEIGHT *variable;*

The HEIGHT statement specifies the name of a numeric variable to define the height of each node (cluster) in the tree. The height variable can also be specified by the HEIGHT= option in the PROC TREE statement. If both the HEIGHT statement and the HEIGHT= option are omitted, TREE looks for a variable called _HEIGHT_. If the data set does not contain _HEIGHT_, TREE looks for a variable called _NCL_. If _NCL_ is not found either, the height of each node is defined to be its path length from the root.

ID Statement

ID *variable;*

The ID variable is used to identify the objects (leaves) in the tree on the printout. The ID variable can be a character or numeric variable of any length. If the ID statement is omitted, the variable in the NAME statement is used instead. If both ID and NAME are omitted, TREE looks for a variable called _NAME_. If the _NAME_ variable is not found in the data set, TREE issues an error message and stops.

COPY Statement

COPY *variables;*

The COPY statement lists one or more character or numeric variables to be copied to the OUT= data set.

FREQ Statement

FREQ *variable;*

The FREQ statement lists one numeric variable that tells how many objects belong to the cluster represented by each observation. If the FREQ statement is omitted, TREE looks for a variable called _FREQ_ to specify the number of observations per cluster. If neither the FREQ statement nor the _FREQ_ variable is present, each leaf is assumed to represent one object, and the frequency for each internal node is found by summing the frequencies of its children.

If an observation has a zero or negative frequency, it is omitted from the tree and is given missing values for the variables CLUSTER and CLUSNAME in the OUT= data set.

BY Statement

BY *variables;*

A BY statement can be used with PROC TREE to obtain separate analyses on observations in groups defined by the BY variables. When a BY statement appears, the procedure expects the input data set to be sorted in order of the BY variables. If your input data set is not sorted in ascending order, use the SORT procedure with a similar BY statement to sort the data, or, if appropriate, use the BY statement options NOTSORTED or DESCENDING. For more information, see the discussion of the BY statement in "Statements Used in the PROC Step" in the *SAS User's Guide: Basics.*

DETAILS

Missing Values

An observation with a missing value for the NAME variable is omitted from processing. If the PARENT variable has a missing value but the NAME variable is present, the observation is treated as the root of a tree. A data set can contain several roots, hence several trees.

Missing values of the HEIGHT variable are set to upper or lower bounds determined from the nonmissing values under the assumption that the heights are monotonic with respect to the tree structure.

Missing values of the FREQ variable are inferred from nonmissing values where possible and otherwise treated as 0.

Output Data Set

The OUT= data set contains one observation for each object in the tree or subtree being processed. The variables are

- the BY variables, if any.
- the ID variable, or the NAME variable if the ID statement is not used.
- the COPY variables.
- a numeric variable CLUSTER taking values from 1 to *c*, where *c* is the number of disjoint clusters. The cluster to which the first observation

belongs is given the number 1, the cluster to which the next observation belongs that does not belong to cluster 1 is given the number 2, and so on.

- a character variable CLUSNAME giving the value of the NAME variable of the cluster to which the observation belongs.

The CLUSTER and CLUSNAME variables are missing if the corresponding leaf has a nonpositive frequency.

Printed Output

The printed output from the TREE procedure includes:

1. the names of the objects in the tree printed along the top of the tree diagram
2. the height axis printed along the left edge of the tree diagram
3. the tree diagram. The root (the cluster containing all the objects) is at the top, indicated by a solid line of the character specified by TREECHAR= (the default character is X). At each horizontal level in the tree, clusters are shown by unbroken lines of the TREECHAR= symbol with the FILLCHAR= symbol (the default is a blank) separating the clusters. The LEAFCHAR= symbol (the default character is a period) represents single-member clusters.

EXAMPLES

Mammals' Teeth: Example 1

The data below give the numbers of different kinds of teeth for a variety of mammals. The mammals are clustered by average linkage using CLUSTER. The first PROC TREE uses the average-linkage distance as the height axis, which is the default. The second PROC TREE sorts the clusters at each branch in order of formation and uses the number of clusters for the height axis. The third PROC TREE produces no printed output but creates an output data set indicating the cluster to which each observation belongs at the 6-cluster level in the tree; this data set is reproduced by PROC PRINT.

```
DATA TEETH;
   TITLE 'MAMMALS'' TEETH';
   INPUT MAMMAL $ 1-16 @21 (V1-V8) (1.);
   LABEL V1=TOP INCISORS
         V2=BOTTOM INCISORS
         V3=TOP CANINES
         V4=BOTTOM CANINES
         V5=TOP PREMOLARS
         V6=BOTTOM PREMOLARS
         V7=TOP MOLARS
         V8=BOTTOM MOLARS;
   CARDS;
BROWN BAT           23113333
MOLE                32103333
SILVER HAIR BAT     23112333
PIGMY BAT           23112233
HOUSE BAT           23111233
RED BAT             13112233
PIKA                21002233
```

```
RABBIT              21003233
BEAVER              11002133
GROUNDHOG           11002133
GRAY SQUIRREL       11001133
HOUSE MOUSE         11000033
PORCUPINE           11001133
WOLF                33114423
BEAR                33114423
RACCOON             33114432
MARTEN              33114412
WEASEL              33113312
WOLVERINE           33114412
BADGER              33113312
RIVER OTTER         33114312
SEA OTTER           32113312
JAGUAR              33113211
COUGAR              33113211
FUR SEAL            32114411
SEA LION            32114411
GREY SEAL           32113322
ELEPHANT SEAL       21114411
REINDEER            04103333
ELK                 04103333
DEER                04003333
MOOSE               04003333
;

PROC CLUSTER METHOD=AVERAGE STD PSEUDO NOEIGEN OUTTREE=TREE;
   ID MAMMAL;
   VAR V1-V8;
PROC TREE;
PROC TREE SORT HEIGHT=N;
PROC TREE NOPRINT OUT=PART NCLUSTERS=6;
   ID MAMMAL;
   COPY V1-V8;
PROC SORT;
   BY CLUSTER;
PROC PRINT UNIFORM;
   ID MAMMAL;
   VAR V1-V8;
   FORMAT V1-V8 1.;
   BY CLUSTER;
```

Output 38.1 Clustering of Mammals: PROC CLUSTER

MAMMALS' TEETH 1

AVERAGE LINKAGE CLUSTER ANALYSIS

ROOT-MEAN-SQUARE TOTAL-SAMPLE STANDARD DEVIATION = 1
ROOT-MEAN-SQUARE DISTANCE BETWEEN OBSERVATIONS = 4

NUMBER OF CLUSTERS	CLUSTERS JOINED		FREQUENCY OF NEW CLUSTER	PSEUDO F	PSEUDO T**2	NORMALIZED RMS DISTANCE
31	DEER	MOOSE	2	.	.	0.000000
30	REINDEER	ELK	2	.	.	0.000000
29	FUR SEAL	SEA LION	2	.	.	0.000000
28	JAGUAR	COUGAR	2	.	.	0.000000
27	WEASEL	BADGER	2	.	.	0.000000
26	MARTEN	WOLVERINE	2	.	.	0.000000
25	WOLF	BEAR	2	.	.	0.000000
24	GRAY SQUIRREL	PORCUPINE	2	.	.	0.000000
23	BEAVER	GROUNDHOG	2	.	.	0.000000
22	PIGMY BAT	RED BAT	2	281.19	.	0.228930
21	CL26	RIVER OTTER	3	138.67	.	0.229221
20	PIKA	RABBIT	2	109.35	.	0.235702
19	BROWN BAT	SILVER HAIR BAT	2	95.13	.	0.235702
18	CL23	CL24	4	73.24	.	0.235702
17	CL27	SEA OTTER	3	67.37	.	0.246183
16	CL22	HOUSE BAT	3	62.89	1.75	0.285937
15	CL21	CL17	6	47.42	6.81	0.332845
14	CL29	ELEPHANT SEAL	3	45.04	.	0.336177
13	CL19	CL16	5	40.83	3.50	0.367188
12	CL15	GREY SEAL	7	38.90	2.78	0.407838
11	CL25	RACCOON	3	38.02	.	0.422997
10	CL20	CL18	6	34.51	10.27	0.433918
9	CL12	CL28	9	30.01	7.27	0.507122
8	CL30	CL31	4	28.69	.	0.547281
7	CL9	CL14	12	25.74	6.99	0.566841
6	CL10	HOUSE MOUSE	7	28.32	4.12	0.579239
5	CL11	CL7	15	26.83	6.87	0.662106
4	CL13	MOLE	6	31.93	7.23	0.715610
3	CL4	CL8	10	30.98	12.67	0.879851
2	CL3	CL6	17	27.83	16.12	1.031622
1	CL2	CL5	32	.	27.83	1.193815

Output 38.2 Clustering of Mammals: PROC TREE

```
                                               MAMMALS' TEETH                                              2

                                        AVERAGE LINKAGE CLUSTER ANALYSIS

                                             NAME OF OBSERVATION OR CLUSTER

                 S
                 I
                 L                                      G                                                  E
                 V                                      R                                                  L
                 E                                      A     H                 R                          E
                 R                                      Y     O                 I                          P
              B     P     H                          G     P  U              W  V        S  G              H
              R  H  I     O     R                    R  S  O  S              O  E        E  R        F  S  A
              O  A  G  R  U     E                    O  Q  R  E        R     L  R        A  E        U  E  N
              W  I  M  E  S     I              R  B  U  U  C           A  M  V     W  B     Y  J  C  R  A  T
              N  R  Y  D  E     N        M     A  E  N  I  U  M        C  A  E  O  E  A  O     A  O
                             M  D     D  O  P  B  A  D  R  P  O  W  B  C  R  R  T  A  D  T  S  G  U  S  L  S
              B  B  B  B  B  O  E  E  E  O  I  B  V  H  R  I  U  O  E  O  T  I  T  S  G  T  E  U  G  E  I  E
              A  A  A  A  A  L  E  L  E  S  K  I  E  O  E  N  S  L  A  O  E  N  E  E  E  E  A  A  A  A  O  A
              T  T  T  T  T  E  R  K  R  E  A  T  R  G  L  E  E  F  R  N  N  E  R  L  R  R  L  R  R  L  N  L
         1.2 +XXXXXXXXXXXXXXXXXXXXXXXXXXXXXXXXXXXXXXXXXXXXXXXXXXXXXXXXXXXXXXXXXXXXXXXXXXXXXXXXXXXXXXXXXXXXXX
             |XXXXXXXXXXXXXXXXXXXXXXXXXXXXXXXXXXXXXXXXXXXXXXXXX  XXXXXXXXXXXXXXXXXXXXXXXXXXXXXXXXXXXXXXXXXXX
A            |XXXXXXXXXXXXXXXXXXXXXXXXXXXXXXXXXXXXXXXXXXXXXXXXX  XXXXXXXXXXXXXXXXXXXXXXXXXXXXXXXXXXXXXXXXXXX
V            |XXXXXXXXXXXXXXXXXXXXXXXXXXXXXXXXXXXXXXXXXXXXXXXXX  XXXXXXXXXXXXXXXXXXXXXXXXXXXXXXXXXXXXXXXXXXX
E            |XXXXXXXXXXXXXXXXXXXXXXXXXXXXXXXXXXXXXXXXXXXXXXXXX  XXXXXXXXXXXXXXXXXXXXXXXXXXXXXXXXXXXXXXXXXXX
R            |XXXXXXXXXXXXXXXXXXXXXXXXXXXXXXXXXXXXXXXXXXXXXXXXX  XXXXXXXXXXXXXXXXXXXXXXXXXXXXXXXXXXXXXXXXXXX
A          1 +XXXXXXXXXXXXXXXXXXXXXXXXXXXX  XXXXXXXXXXXXXXXXXXX  XXXXXXXXXXXXXXXXXXXXXXXXXXXXXXXXXXXXXXXXXXX
G            |XXXXXXXXXXXXXXXXXXXXXXXXXXXX  XXXXXXXXXXXXXXXXXXX  XXXXXXXXXXXXXXXXXXXXXXXXXXXXXXXXXXXXXXXXXXX
E            |XXXXXXXXXXXXXXXXXXXXXXXXXXXX  XXXXXXXXXXXXXXXXXXX  XXXXXXXXXXXXXXXXXXXXXXXXXXXXXXXXXXXXXXXXXXX
             |XXXXXXXXXXXXXXXXXXXXXXXXXXXX  XXXXXXXXXXXXXXXXXXX  XXXXXXXXXXXXXXXXXXXXXXXXXXXXXXXXXXXXXXXXXXX
D            |XXXXXXXXXXXXXXXXXXXXXXXXXXXX  XXXXXXXXXXXXXXXXXXX  XXXXXXXXXXXXXXXXXXXXXXXXXXXXXXXXXXXXXXXXXXX
I            |XXXXXXXXXXXXXXXX  XXXXXXXXXX  XXXXXXXXXXXXXXXXXXX  XXXXXXXXXXXXXXXXXXXXXXXXXXXXXXXXXXXXXXXXXXX
S        0.8 +XXXXXXXXXXXXXXXX  XXXXXXXXXX  XXXXXXXXXXXXXXXXXXX  XXXXXXXXXXXXXXXXXXXXXXXXXXXXXXXXXXXXXXXXXXX
T            |XXXXXXXXXXXXXXXX  XXXXXXXXXX  XXXXXXXXXXXXXXXXXXX  XXXXXXXXXXXXXXXXXXXXXXXXXXXXXXXXXXXXXXXXXXX
A            |XXXXXXXXXXXXXXXX  XXXXXXXXXX  XXXXXXXXXXXXXXXXXXX  XXXXXXXXXXXXXXXXXXXXXXXXXXXXXXXXXXXXXXXXXXX
N            |XXXXXXXXXXXXXXXX  XXXXXXXXXX  XXXXXXXXXXXXXXXXXXX  XXXXXXXXXXXXXXXXXXXXXXXXXXXXXXXXXXXXXXXXXXX
C            |XXXXXXXXXXXXX  .  XXXXXXXXXX  XXXXXXXXXXXXXXXXXXX  XXXXXXXXXXXXXXXXXXXXXXXXXXXXXXXXXXXXXXXXXXX
E            |XXXXXXXXXXXXX  .  XXXXXXXXXX  XXXXXXXXXXXXXXXXXXX  XXXXXXX  XXXXXXXXXXXXXXXXXXXXXXXXXXXXXXXXXX
         0.6 +XXXXXXXXXXXXX  .  XXXXXXXXXX  XXXXXXXXXXXXXXXXXXX  XXXXXXX  XXXXXXXXXXXXXXXXXXXXXXXXXXXXXXXXXX
B            |XXXXXXXXXXXXX  .  XXXXXXXXXX  XXXXXXXXXXXXXXXXXXX  XXXXXXX  XXXXXXXXXXXXXXXXXXXXXXXXXXXXXXXXXX
E            |XXXXXXXXXXXXX  .  XXXXXXXXXX  XXXXXXXXXXXXXXXX  .  XXXXXXX  XXXXXXXXXXXXXXXXXXXXXXXXX  XXXXXXX
T            |XXXXXXXXXXXXX  .  XXXX  XXXX  XXXXXXXXXXXXXXXX  .  XXXXXXX  XXXXXXXXXXXXXXXXXXXXXXXXX  XXXXXXX
W            |XXXXXXXXXXXXX  .  XXXX  XXXX  XXXXXXXXXXXXXXXX  .  XXXXXXX  XXXXXXXXXXXXXXXXXXX  XXXX  XXXXXXX
E            |XXXXXXXXXXXXX  .  XXXX  XXXX  XXXXXXXXXXXXXXXX  .  XXXXXXX  XXXXXXXXXXXXXXXXXXX  XXXX  XXXXXXX
E        0.4 +XXXXXXXXXXXXX  .  XXXX  XXXX  XXXX  XXXXXXXXXX  .  XXXX  .  XXXXXXXXXXXXXXXXXXX  XXXX  XXXXXXX
N            |XXXXXXXXXXXXX  .  XXXX  XXXX  XXXX  XXXXXXXXXX  .  XXXX  .  XXXXXXXXXXXXXXXX  .  XXXX  XXXXXXX
             |XXXX  XXXXXXX  .  XXXX  XXXX  XXXX  XXXXXXXXXX  .  XXXX  .  XXXXXXXXXXXXXXXX  .  XXXX  XXXXXXX
C            |XXXX  XXXXXXX  .  XXXX  XXXX  XXXX  XXXXXXXXXX  .  XXXX  .  XXXXXXX  XXXXXXX  .  XXXX  XXXX  .
L            |XXXX  XXXX  .  .  XXXX  XXXX  XXXX  XXXXXXXXXX  .  XXXX  .  XXXXXXX  XXXXXXX  .  XXXX  XXXX  .
U            |XXXX  XXXX  .  .  XXXX  XXXX  XXXX  XXXXXXXXXX  .  XXXX  .  XXXXXXX  XXXXXXX  .  XXXX  XXXX  .
S        0.2 +.  .  .  .  .  .  XXXX  XXXX  .  .  XXXX  XXXX  .  XXXX  .  XXXX  .  XXXX  .  .  XXXX  XXXX  .
T            |.  .  .  .  .  .  XXXX  XXXX  .  .  XXXX  XXXX  .  XXXX  .  XXXX  .  XXXX  .  .  XXXX  XXXX  .
E            |.  .  .  .  .  .  XXXX  XXXX  .  .  XXXX  XXXX  .  XXXX  .  XXXX  .  XXXX  .  .  XXXX  XXXX  .
R            |.  .  .  .  .  .  XXXX  XXXX  .  .  XXXX  XXXX  .  XXXX  .  XXXX  .  XXXX  .  .  XXXX  XXXX  .
S            |.  .  .  .  .  .  XXXX  XXXX  .  .  XXXX  XXXX  .  XXXX  .  XXXX  .  XXXX  .  .  XXXX  XXXX  .
             |.  .  .  .  .  .  XXXX  XXXX  .  .  XXXX  XXXX  .  XXXX  .  XXXX  .  XXXX  .  .  XXXX  XXXX  .
           0 +.  .  .  .  .  .  XXXX  XXXX  .  .  XXXX  XXXX  .  XXXX  .  XXXX  .  XXXX  .  .  XXXX  XXXX  .
```

Output 38.3 Clustering of Mammals: PROC TREE Specifying the SORT and HEIGHT= Options

```
                                       MAMMALS' TEETH                                         3

                                AVERAGE LINKAGE CLUSTER ANALYSIS

                                     NAME OF OBSERVATION OR CLUSTER

                                                                                           S
                                                                                           I
                E                                            G                             L
                L                                            R                             V
                E                 R                 H        A                             E
                P                 I                 O        Y                             R
                H              G  V     W  S        U           P     G                 B     H  P
                A  F  S        R  E     O  E        S        S  O     R        R        R  H  O  I
       R        N  U  E        E  R     L  A        E        Q  R     O        E        O  A  U  G  R
       A        T  R  A  J  C  Y     M  V     W  B        R  U  C  B  U        I        W  I  S  M  E
       C                 A  O     O  A  E  O  E  A  M     A  I  U  E  N     M  N        N  R  E  Y  D
       C  W  B  S  S  L  G  U  S  T  R  R  T  A  D  O  P  B  R  P  A  D  D  O  D     M
       O  O  E  E  E  I  U  G  E  T  T  I  T  S  G  U  I  B  R  I  V  H  E  O  E  E  O  B  B  B  B  B
       O  L  A  A  A  O  A  A  A  E  E  N  E  E  E  S  K  I  E  N  E  O  E  S  E  L  L  A  A  A  A  A
       N  F  R  L  L  N  R  R  L  R  N  E  R  L  R  E  A  T  L  E  R  G  R  E  R  K  E  T  T  T  T  T
    1 +XXXXXXXXXXXXXXXXXXXXXXXXXXXXXXXXXXXXXXXXXXXXXXXXXXXXXXXXXXXXXXXXXXXXXXXXXXXXXXXXXXXXXXXXXXXXXXX
    2 +XXXXXXXXXXXXXXXXXXXXXXXXXXXXXXXXXXXXXXXXXXX  XXXXXXXXXXXXXXXXXXXXXXXXXXXXXXXXXXXXXXXXXXXXXXXXX
    3 +XXXXXXXXXXXXXXXXXXXXXXXXXXXXXXXXXXXXXXXXXXX  XXXXXXXXXXXXXXXXXXX  XXXXXXXXXXXXXXXXXXXXXXXXXXXX
    4 +XXXXXXXXXXXXXXXXXXXXXXXXXXXXXXXXXXXXXXXXXXX  XXXXXXXXXXXXXXXXXXX  XXXXXXXXXX  XXXXXXXXXXXXXXXX
    5 +XXXXXXXXXXXXXXXXXXXXXXXXXXXXXXXXXXXXXXXXXXX  XXXXXXXXXXXXXXXXXXX  XXXXXXXXXX  .  XXXXXXXXXXXXX
    6 +XXXXXXX  XXXXXXXXXXXXXXXXXXXXXXXXXXXXXXXXXX  XXXXXXXXXXXXXXXXXXX  XXXXXXXXXX  .  XXXXXXXXXXXXX
    7 +XXXXXXX  XXXXXXXXXXXXXXXXXXXXXXXXXXXXXXXXXX  .  XXXXXXXXXXXXXXXX  XXXXXXXXXX  .  XXXXXXXXXXXXX
N   8 +XXXXXXX  XXXXXXX  XXXXXXXXXXXXXXXXXXXXXXXXX  .  XXXXXXXXXXXXXXXX  XXXXXXXXXX  .  XXXXXXXXXXXXX
U   9 +XXXXXXX  XXXXXXX  XXXXXXXXXXXXXXXXXXXXXXXXX  .  XXXXXXXXXXXXXXXX  XXXX  XXXX  .  XXXXXXXXXXXXX
M  10 +XXXXXXX  XXXXXXX  XXXX  XXXXXXXXXXXXXXXXXXX  .  XXXXXXXXXXXXXXXX  XXXX  XXXX  .  XXXXXXXXXXXXX
B  11 +XXXXXXX  XXXXXXX  XXXX  XXXXXXXXXXXXXXXXXXX  .  XXXX  XXXXXXXXXX  XXXX  XXXX  .  XXXXXXXXXXXXX
E  12 +.  XXXX  XXXXXXX  XXXX  XXXXXXXXXXXXXXXXXXX  .  XXXX  XXXXXXXXXX  XXXX  XXXX  .  XXXXXXXXXXXXX
R  13 +.  XXXX  XXXXXXX  XXXX  .  XXXXXXXXXXXXXXXX  .  XXXX  XXXXXXXXXX  XXXX  XXXX  .  XXXXXXXXXXXXX
   14 +.  XXXX  XXXXXXX  XXXX  .  XXXXXXXXXXXXXXXX  .  XXXX  XXXXXXXXXX  XXXX  XXXX  .  XXXX  XXXXXXX
O  15 +.  XXXX  .  XXXX  XXXX  .  XXXXXXXXXXXXXXXX  .  XXXX  XXXXXXXXXX  XXXX  XXXX  .  XXXX  XXXXXXX
F  16 +.  XXXX  .  XXXX  XXXX  .  XXXXXXX  XXXXXXX  .  XXXX  XXXXXXXXXX  XXXX  XXXX  .  XXXX  XXXXXXX
   17 +.  XXXX  .  XXXX  XXXX  .  XXXXXXX  XXXXXXX  .  XXXX  XXXXXXXXXX  XXXX  XXXX  .  XXXX  .  XXXX
C  18 +.  XXXX  .  XXXX  XXXX  .  XXXXXXX  .  XXXX  .  XXXX  XXXXXXXXXX  XXXX  XXXX  .  XXXX  .  XXXX
L  19 +.  XXXX  .  XXXX  XXXX  .  XXXXXXX  .  XXXX  .  XXXX  XXXX  XXXX  XXXX  XXXX  .  XXXX  .  XXXX
U  20 +.  XXXX  .  XXXX  XXXX  .  XXXXXXX  .  XXXX  .  XXXX  XXXX  XXXX  XXXX  XXXX  .  .  .  .  XXXX
S  21 +.  XXXX  .  XXXX  XXXX  .  XXXXXXX  .  XXXX  .  .  .  XXXX  XXXX  XXXX  XXXX  .  .  .  .  XXXX
T  22 +.  XXXX  .  XXXX  XXXX  .  .  XXXX  .  XXXX  .  .  .  XXXX  XXXX  XXXX  XXXX  .  .  .  .  XXXX
E  23 +.  XXXX  .  XXXX  XXXX  .  .  XXXX  .  XXXX  .  .  .  XXXX  XXXX  XXXX  XXXX  .  .  .  .  .  .
R  24 +.  XXXX  .  XXXX  XXXX  .  .  XXXX  .  XXXX  .  .  .  XXXX  .  .  XXXX  XXXX  .  .  .  .  .  .
S  25 +.  XXXX  .  XXXX  XXXX  .  .  XXXX  .  XXXX  .  .  .  .  .  .  .  XXXX  XXXX  .  .  .  .  .  .
   26 +.  .  .  .  XXXX  XXXX  .  .  XXXX  .  XXXX  .  .  .  .  .  .  .  XXXX  XXXX  .  .  .  .  .  .
   27 +.  .  .  .  XXXX  XXXX  .  .  .  .  .  XXXX  .  .  .  .  .  .  .  XXXX  XXXX  .  .  .  .  .  .
   28 +.  .  .  .  XXXX  XXXX  .  .  .  .  .  .  .  .  .  .  .  .  .  .  XXXX  XXXX  .  .  .  .  .  .
   29 +.  .  .  .  XXXX  .  .  .  .  .  .  .  .  .  .  .  .  .  .  .  .  XXXX  XXXX  .  .  .  .  .  .
   30 +.  .  .  .  .  .  .  .  .  .  .  .  .  .  .  .  .  .  .  .  .  .  XXXX  XXXX  .  .  .  .  .  .
   31 +.  .  .  .  .  .  .  .  .  .  .  .  .  .  .  .  .  .  .  .  .  .  XXXX  .  .  .  .  .  .  .  .
   32 +.  .  .  .  .  .  .  .  .  .  .  .  .  .  .  .  .  .  .  .  .  .  .  .  .  .  .  .  .  .  .  .
```

Output 38.4 Clustering of Mammals: PROC PRINT

```
                                        MAMMALS' TEETH                                        4
---------------------------------------------CLUSTER=1---------------------------------------------

                  MAMMAL              V1    V2    V3    V4    V5    V6    V7    V8

                  DEER                 0     4     0     0     3     3     3     3
                  MOOSE                0     4     0     0     3     3     3     3
                  REINDEER             0     4     1     0     3     3     3     3
                  ELK                  0     4     1     0     3     3     3     3

---------------------------------------------CLUSTER=2---------------------------------------------

                  MAMMAL              V1    V2    V3    V4    V5    V6    V7    V8

                  FUR SEAL             3     2     1     1     4     4     1     1
                  SEA LION             3     2     1     1     4     4     1     1
                  JAGUAR               3     3     1     1     3     2     1     1
```

(continued on next page)

(continued from previous page)

```
                   COUGAR               3     3     1     1     3     2     1     1
                   WEASEL               3     3     1     1     3     3     1     2
                   BADGER               3     3     1     1     3     3     1     2
                   MARTEN               3     3     1     1     4     4     1     2
                   WOLVERINE            3     3     1     1     4     4     1     2
                   RIVER OTTER          3     3     1     1     4     3     1     2
                   SEA OTTER            3     2     1     1     3     3     1     2
                   ELEPHANT SEAL        2     1     1     1     4     4     1     1
                   GREY SEAL            3     2     1     1     3     3     2     2

------------------------------------------------------CLUSTER=3------------------------------------------------------

                   MAMMAL              V1    V2    V3    V4    V5    V6    V7    V8

                   WOLF                 3     3     1     1     4     4     2     3
                   BEAR                 3     3     1     1     4     4     2     3
                   RACCOON              3     3     1     1     4     4     3     2

------------------------------------------------------CLUSTER=4------------------------------------------------------

                   MAMMAL              V1    V2    V3    V4    V5    V6    V7    V8

                   GRAY SQUIRREL        1     1     0     0     1     1     3     3
                   PORCUPINE            1     1     0     0     1     1     3     3
                   BEAVER               1     1     0     0     2     1     3     3
                   GROUNDHOG            1     1     0     0     2     1     3     3
                   PIKA                 2     1     0     0     2     2     3     3
                   RABBIT               2     1     0     0     3     2     3     3
                   HOUSE MOUSE          1     1     0     0     0     0     3     3

------------------------------------------------------CLUSTER=5------------------------------------------------------

                   MAMMAL              V1    V2    V3    V4    V5    V6    V7    V8

                   PIGMY BAT            2     3     1     1     2     2     3     3
                   RED BAT              1     3     1     1     2     2     3     3
                   BROWN BAT            2     3     1     1     3     3     3     3
                   SILVER HAIR BAT      2     3     1     1     2     3     3     3
```

```
                                              MAMMALS' TEETH                                              5
------------------------------------------------------CLUSTER=5------------------------------------------------------

                   MAMMAL              V1    V2    V3    V4    V5    V6    V7    V8

                   HOUSE BAT            2     3     1     1     1     2     3     3

------------------------------------------------------CLUSTER=6------------------------------------------------------

                   MAMMAL              V1    V2    V3    V4    V5    V6    V7    V8

                   MOLE                 3     2     1     0     3     3     3     3
```

To see how the first tree diagram is interpreted, consider the level at the tick mark labeled 0.6. The five BATs are in a cluster indicated by an unbroken line of Xs. The next cluster is represented by a period (.) because it contains only one mammal, MOLE. REINDEER, ELK, DEER, and MOOSE form the next cluster, indicated by Xs again. The mammals PIKA through HOUSE MOUSE are in the fourth cluster. WOLF, BEAR, and RACCOON form the fifth cluster, while the last cluster contains MARTEN through ELEPHANT SEAL. The same clusters can be seen at the 6-cluster level of the second tree diagram, although they appear in a different order.

Iris Data: Example 2

Fisher's (1936) iris data are clustered by *k*th-nearest-neighbor density linkage using the CLUSTER procedure with K=8. Observations are identified by species in the tree diagram.

```
DATA IRIS;
   TITLE 'FISHER''S IRIS DATA';
   INPUT SEPALLEN SEPALWID PETALLEN PETALWID SPEC_NO @@;
   IF SPEC_NO=1 THEN SPECIES='SETOSA    ';
   ELSE IF SPEC_NO=2 THEN SPECIES='VERSICOLOR';
   ELSE IF SPEC_NO=3 THEN SPECIES='VIRGINICA ';
   CARDS;
50 33 14 02 1 64 28 56 22 3 65 28 46 15 2 67 31 56 24 3
63 28 51 15 3 46 34 14 03 1 69 31 51 23 3 62 22 45 15 2
59 32 48 18 2 46 36 10 02 1 61 30 46 14 2 60 27 51 16 2
65 30 52 20 3 56 25 39 11 2 65 30 55 18 3 58 27 51 19 3
68 32 59 23 3 51 33 17 05 1 57 28 45 13 2 62 34 54 23 3
77 38 67 22 3 63 33 47 16 2 67 33 57 25 3 76 30 66 21 3
49 25 45 17 3 55 35 13 02 1 67 30 52 23 3 70 32 47 14 2
64 32 45 15 2 61 28 40 13 2 48 31 16 02 1 59 30 51 18 3
55 24 38 11 2 63 25 50 19 3 64 32 53 23 3 52 34 14 02 1
49 36 14 01 1 54 30 45 15 2 79 38 64 20 3 44 32 13 02 1
67 33 57 21 3 50 35 16 06 1 58 26 40 12 2 44 30 13 02 1
77 28 67 20 3 63 27 49 18 3 47 32 16 02 1 55 26 44 12 2
50 23 33 10 2 72 32 60 18 3 48 30 14 03 1 51 38 16 02 1
61 30 49 18 3 48 34 19 02 1 50 30 16 02 1 50 32 12 02 1
61 26 56 14 3 64 28 56 21 3 43 30 11 01 1 58 40 12 02 1
51 38 19 04 1 67 31 44 14 2 62 28 48 18 3 49 30 14 02 1
51 35 14 02 1 56 30 45 15 2 58 27 41 10 2 50 34 16 04 1
46 32 14 02 1 60 29 45 15 2 57 26 35 10 2 57 44 15 04 1
50 36 14 02 1 77 30 61 23 3 63 34 56 24 3 58 27 51 19 3
57 29 42 13 2 72 30 58 16 3 54 34 15 04 1 52 41 15 01 1
71 30 59 21 3 64 31 55 18 3 60 30 48 18 3 63 29 56 18 3
49 24 33 10 2 56 27 42 13 2 57 30 42 12 2 55 42 14 02 1
49 31 15 02 1 77 26 69 23 3 60 22 50 15 3 54 39 17 04 1
66 29 46 13 2 52 27 39 14 2 60 34 45 16 2 50 34 15 02 1
44 29 14 02 1 50 20 35 10 2 55 24 37 10 2 58 27 39 12 2
47 32 13 02 1 46 31 15 02 1 69 32 57 23 3 62 29 43 13 2
74 28 61 19 3 59 30 42 15 2 51 34 15 02 1 50 35 13 03 1
56 28 49 20 3 60 22 40 10 2 73 29 63 18 3 67 25 58 18 3
49 31 15 01 1 67 31 47 15 2 63 23 44 13 2 54 37 15 02 1
56 30 41 13 2 63 25 49 15 2 61 28 47 12 2 64 29 43 13 2
51 25 30 11 2 57 28 41 13 2 65 30 58 22 3 69 31 54 21 3
54 39 13 04 1 51 35 14 03 1 72 36 61 25 3 65 32 51 20 3
61 29 47 14 2 56 29 36 13 2 69 31 49 15 2 64 27 53 19 3
68 30 55 21 3 55 25 40 13 2 48 34 16 02 1 48 30 14 01 1
45 23 13 03 1 57 25 50 20 3 57 38 17 03 1 51 38 15 03 1
55 23 40 13 2 66 30 44 14 2 68 28 48 14 2 54 34 17 02 1
51 37 15 04 1 52 35 15 02 1 58 28 51 24 3 67 30 50 17 2
63 33 60 25 3 53 37 15 02 1
;
PROC CLUSTER DATA=IRIS METHOD=DENSITY K=8 NOEIGEN;
   VAR SEPALLEN SEPALWID PETALLEN PETALWID;
   COPY SPECIES;
PROC TREE PAGES=1;
   ID SPECIES;
```

Output 38.5 Fisher's Iris Data: PROC CLUSTER with METHOD=DENSITY

FISHER'S IRIS DATA 1

DENSITY LINKAGE CLUSTER ANALYSIS

K = 8

ROOT-MEAN-SQUARE TOTAL-SAMPLE STANDARD DEVIATION = 10.6922

NUMBER OF CLUSTERS	CLUSTERS JOINED		FREQUENCY OF NEW CLUSTER	NORMALIZED FUSION DENSITY	MAXIMUM DENSITY IN EACH CLUSTER	
					LESSER	GREATER
149	OB65	OB126	2	0.1297	0.1013	0.1801
148	CL149	OB96	3	0.1118	0.0811	0.1801
147	CL148	OB1	4	0.0791	0.0507	0.1801
146	CL147	OB107	5	0.0791	0.0507	0.1801
145	CL146	OB73	6	0.0721	0.0450	0.1801
144	CL145	OB146	7	0.0721	0.0450	0.1801
143	CL144	OB108	8	0.0617	0.0372	0.1801
142	CL143	OB36	9	0.0559	0.0331	0.1801
141	CL142	OB89	10	0.0507	0.0507	0.1801
140	CL141	OB31	11	0.0507	0.0507	0.1801
139	CL140	OB113	12	0.0429	0.0372	0.1801
138	CL139	OB136	13	0.0400	0.0331	0.1801
137	CL138	OB51	14	0.0400	0.0331	0.1801
136	CL137	OB145	15	0.0360	0.0200	0.1801
135	CL136	OB102	16	0.0357	0.0275	0.1801
134	CL135	OB69	17	0.0335	0.0250	0.1801
133	CL134	OB101	18	0.0335	0.0250	0.1801
132	CL133	OB68	19	0.0334	0.0200	0.1801
131	CL132	OB135	20	0.0321	0.0200	0.1801
130	CL131	OB64	21	0.0312	0.0225	0.1801
129	CL130	OB37	22	0.0297	0.0162	0.1801
128	CL129	OB150	23	0.0297	0.0162	0.1801
127	CL128	OB47	24	0.0287	0.0200	0.1801
126	CL127	OB140	25	0.0278	0.0151	0.1801
125	CL126	OB40	26	0.0204	0.0162	0.1801
124	CL125	OB56	27	0.0184	0.0113	0.1801
123	CL124	OB52	28	0.0180	0.0113	0.1801
122	CL123	OB116	29	0.0180	0.0113	0.1801
121	CL122	OB55	30	0.0178	0.0108	0.1801
120	CL121	OB79	31	0.0175	.0095925	0.1801
119	OB86	OB122	2	0.0142	0.0134	0.0151
118	CL119	OB77	3	0.0120	0.009907	0.0151
117	CL120	OB26	32	0.0109	0.005629	0.1801
116	CL118	OB43	4	0.0107	.0082711	0.0151
115	CL116	OB134	5	0.0105	.0081057	0.0151
114	CL115	OB100	6	0.0105	.0081057	0.0151
113	CL114	OB67	7	.0097496	.0072051	0.0151
112	CL113	OB87	8	.0097496	.0072051	0.0151
111	CL117	OB44	33	0.009621	0.005629	0.1801
110	CL111	OB18	34	.0095361	.0050035	0.1801
109	CL110	OB6	35	.0093193	.0056095	0.1801
108	CL109	OB144	36	.0091075	.0050035	0.1801
107	CL108	OB92	37	.0091075	.0063326	0.1801
106	CL112	OB19	9	.0089182	.0063326	0.0151
105	CL106	OB14	10	0.008883	.0095925	0.0151
104	CL107	OB97	38	.0086924	.0050035	0.1801
103	CL104	OB42	39	.0086002	.0044907	0.1801

FISHER'S IRIS DATA 2

DENSITY LINKAGE CLUSTER ANALYSIS

NUMBER OF CLUSTERS	CLUSTERS JOINED		FREQUENCY OF NEW CLUSTER	NORMALIZED FUSION DENSITY	MAXIMUM DENSITY IN EACH CLUSTER		
					LESSER	GREATER	
102	CL105	OB106	11	.0086002	.0063326	0.0151	
101	OB29	OB114	2	.0072893	0.005629	0.0103	
100	CL103	OB125	40	.0068547	.0041356	0.1801	
99	CL101	OB3	3	.0067435	.0050035	0.0103	
98	CL99	OB93	4	.0067435	.0050035	0.0103	
97	CL102	OB117	12	0.006388	.0040528	0.0151	
96	CL98	OB62	5	.0062616	.0044907	0.0103	
95	CL96	OB142	6	.0062616	.0044907	0.0103	
94	CL97	OB30	13	.0062232	.0040528	0.0151	
93	CL100	OB80	41	.0059931	.0036761	0.1801	
92	OB4	OB103	2	.0059491	.0056095	.0063326	
91	CL94	OB70	14	.0059491	.0056095	0.0151	
90	CL92	OB41	3	.0059491	.0056095	.0063326	
89	CL91	OB66	15	.0057524	.0040528	0.0151	
88	CL89	OB33	16	.0056982	.0040528	0.0151	
87	CL90	OB133	4	.0056203	0.005052	.0063326	
86	CL88	OB104	17	.0056203	0.005052	0.0151	
85	CL87	OB13	5	.0053162	.0056095	.0063326	
84	OB12	OB46	2	.0052978	.0050035	0.005629	
83	CL85	OB27	6	.0052892	.0050035	.0063326	
82	CL84	OB53	3	.0050597	.0045951	0.005629	
81	CL93	OB54	42	.0050268	.0025938	0.1801	
80	CL82	OB63	4	.0049958	.0044907	0.005629	
79	CL95	OB120	7	.0049958	.0044907	0.0103	
78	CL83	OB132	7	.0049881	.0044907	.0063326	
77	CL86	OB129	18	.0049881	.0044907	0.0151	
76	CL77	OB83	19	.0049881	.0044907	0.0151	
75	CL76	CL79	26	.0047548	0.0103	0.0151	
74	CL75	OB48	27	.0047433	.0028145	0.0151	
73	CL78	CL80	11	.0047333	0.005629	.0063326	
72	CL74	CL73	38	.0047333	.0063326	0.0151	*
71	CL72	OB22	39	.0047277	.0030645	0.0151	
70	CL71	OB11	40	.0047126	.0040528	0.0151	
69	CL70	OB32	41	.0044476	.0036761	0.0151	
68	CL69	OB143	42	.0044245	.0028145	0.0151	
67	CL68	OB124	43	.0043815	.0033495	0.0151	
66	CL67	OB123	44	.0043815	.0033495	0.0151	
65	CL81	OB61	43	.0042831	.0023981	0.1801	
64	CL66	OB58	45	.0042556	.0036761	0.0151	
63	CL64	OB5	46	.0041998	.0033495	0.0151	
62	CL63	OB118	47	.0041998	.0033495	0.0151	
61	CL62	OB2	48	.0041944	.0033495	0.0151	
60	CL61	OB15	49	.0041944	.0033495	0.0151	
59	CL60	OB141	50	.0041379	.0023981	0.0151	
58	CL59	OB16	51	.0039685	.0030645	0.0151	
57	CL58	OB76	52	.0039685	.0030645	0.0151	
56	CL57	OB82	53	.0039073	.0029977	0.0151	
55	CL56	OB17	54	0.003897	.0028145	0.0151	
54	CL55	OB38	55	.0038757	.0022238	0.0151	
53	CL54	OB99	56	0.003837	.0023981	0.0151	
52	CL53	OB23	57	.0036802	.0025938	0.0151	

FISHER'S IRIS DATA 3
DENSITY LINKAGE CLUSTER ANALYSIS

NUMBER OF CLUSTERS	CLUSTERS JOINED		FREQUENCY OF NEW CLUSTER	NORMALIZED FUSION DENSITY	MAXIMUM DENSITY IN EACH CLUSTER	
					LESSER	GREATER
51	CL52	OB148	58	.0036603	.0022238	0.0151
50	CL65	OB88	44	.0036025	.0020264	0.1801
49	CL50	OB139	45	.0036025	.0020264	0.1801
48	CL51	OB84	59	.0035473	.0025938	0.0151
47	CL48	OB119	60	.0034788	.0023981	0.0151
46	CL47	OB35	61	.0033599	.0023981	0.0151
45	CL46	OB128	62	.0033599	.0023981	0.0151
44	CL45	OB9	63	.0032887	.0023263	0.0151
43	CL44	OB94	64	0.003218	.0018013	0.0151
42	CL43	OB130	65	.0031756	.0018013	0.0151
41	CL49	OB10	46	.0030588	.0015831	0.1801
40	CL42	OB75	66	.0030217	.0020678	0.0151
39	CL40	OB34	67	0.00298	.0020264	0.0151
38	CL39	OB81	68	.0029556	.0019276	0.0151
37	CL38	OB95	69	.0029556	.0019276	0.0151
36	CL37	OB28	70	.0029006	.0016869	0.0151
35	CL36	OB7	71	.0027269	.0018013	0.0151
34	CL41	OB59	47	.0026907	.0014024	0.1801
33	CL35	OB109	72	.0025712	.0018013	0.0151
32	CL33	OB131	73	.0024697	.0014024	0.0151
31	CL32	OB110	74	.0023259	.0013234	0.0151
30	CL31	OB71	75	.0020101	.0011227	0.0151
29	CL30	OB20	76	.0019758	.0011991	0.0151
28	CL29	OB138	77	.0019567	.0011842	0.0151
27	CL28	OB115	78	.0017603	.0010658	0.0151
26	CL34	OB60	48	.0016636	8.8E-04	0.1801
25	CL27	OB91	79	.0016369	9.6E-04	0.0151
24	CL25	OB149	80	.0015793	9.2E-04	0.0151
23	CL24	OB50	81	.0014791	8.4E-04	0.0151
22	CL23	OB112	82	.0013821	8.0E-04	0.0151
21	CL22	OB8	83	.0011085	6.2E-04	0.0151
20	CL21	OB105	84	.0010965	7.7E-04	0.0151
19	CL20	OB111	85	.0010965	7.7E-04	0.0151
18	CL19	OB147	86	.0010255	5.8E-04	0.0151
17	CL18	OB57	87	.0010119	5.6E-04	0.0151
16	CL17	OB78	88	.0010017	5.6E-04	0.0151
15	CL26	OB72	49	8.1E-04	4.2E-04	0.1801
14	CL16	OB127	89	7.0E-04	3.7E-04	0.0151
13	CL15	OB137	50	6.6E-04	3.3E-04	0.1801
12	CL14	OB74	90	6.4E-04	3.8E-04	0.0151
11	CL12	OB49	91	5.8E-04	3.1E-04	0.0151
10	CL11	OB85	92	5.8E-04	3.1E-04	0.0151
9	CL10	OB98	93	5.2E-04	2.7E-04	0.0151
8	CL9	OB24	94	5.0E-04	3.6E-04	0.0151
7	CL8	OB25	95	4.9E-04	2.5E-04	0.0151
6	CL7	OB121	96	4.7E-04	2.5E-04	0.0151
5	CL6	OB45	97	2.5E-04	1.5E-04	0.0151
4	CL5	OB39	98	1.9E-04	1.1E-04	0.0151
3	CL4	OB21	99	1.7E-04	9.7E-05	0.0151
2	CL3	OB90	100	1.3E-04	6.7E-05	0.0151

FISHER'S IRIS DATA 4
DENSITY LINKAGE CLUSTER ANALYSIS
* INDICATES FUSION OF TWO MODAL CLUSTERS

3 MODAL CLUSTERS WERE FORMED

Output 38.6 Fisher's Iris Data: PROC TREE

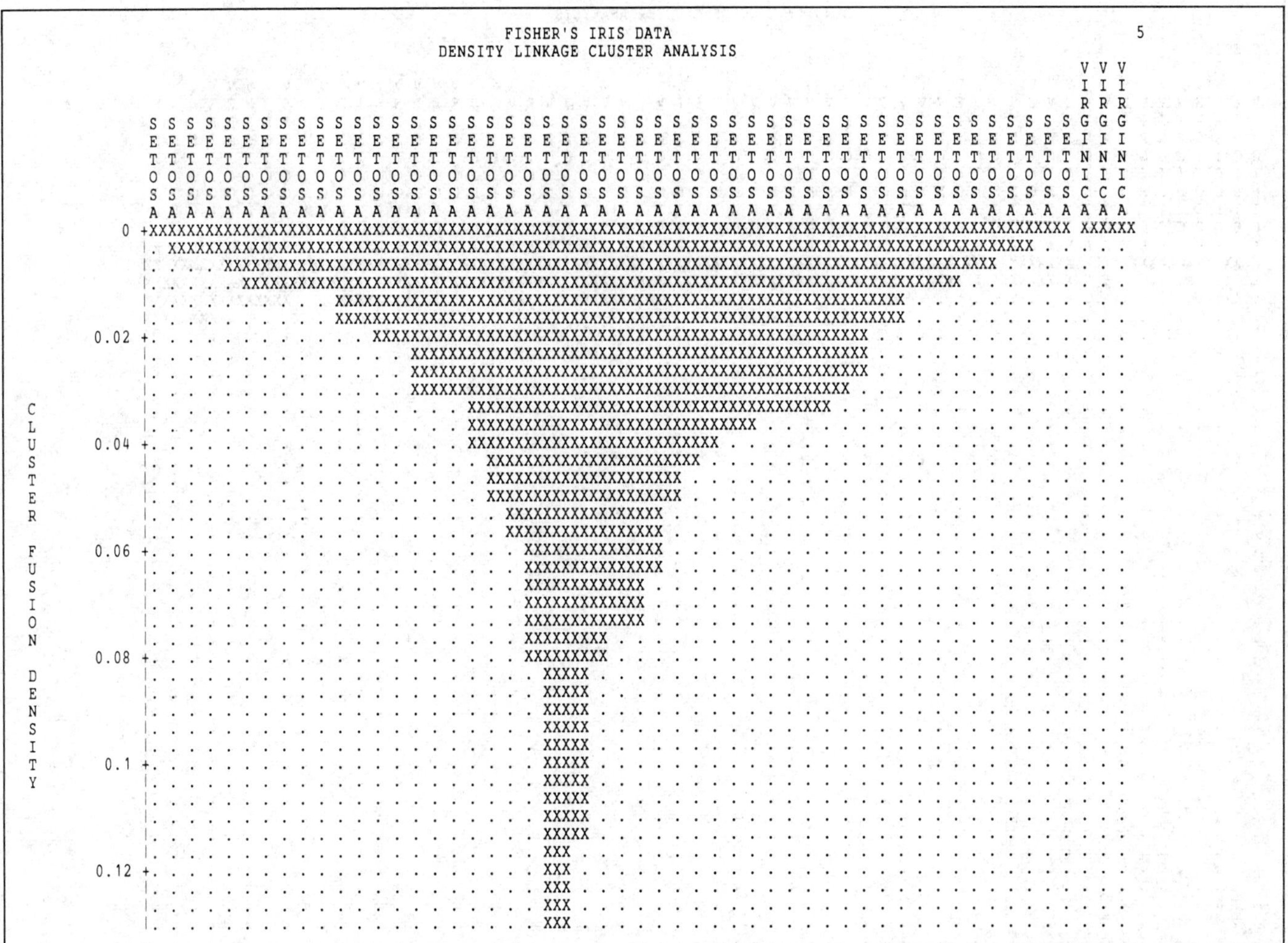

```
                                                  FISHER'S IRIS DATA                                                    6

                                           DENSITY LINKAGE CLUSTER ANALYSIS

SPECIES

    V V       V     V   V       V       V                   V V               V       V V V V V V V V   V V V V V V V V
V V E E V V V E V V E V E V V V E V V V E V V V V V V V V V E E V V V V V V V E V V V E E E E E E E E V E E E E E E E E
I I R R I I I R I I R I R I I I R I I I R I I I I I I I I I R R I I I I I I I R I I I R R R R R R R R I R R R R R R R R
R R S S R R R S R R S R S R R R S R R R S R R R R R R R R R S S R R R R R R R S R R R S S S S S S S S R S S S S S S S S
G G I I G G G I G G I G I G G G I G G G I G G G G G G G G G I I G G G G G G G I G G G I I I I I I I I G I I I I I I I I
I I C C I I I C I I C I C I I I C I I I C I I I I I I I I I C C I I I I I I I C I I I C C C C C C C C I C C C C C C C C
N N O O N N N O N N O N O N N N O N N N O N N N N N N N N N O O N N N N N N N O N N N O O O O O O O O N O O O O O O O O
I I L L I I I L I I L I L I I I L I I I L I I I I I I I I I L L I I I I I I I L I I I L L L L L L L L I L L L L L L L L
C C O O C C C O C C O C O C C C O C C C O C C C C C C C C C O O C C C C C C C O C C C O O O O O O O O C O O O O O O O O
A A R R A A A R A A R A R A A A R A A A R A A A A A A A A A R R A A A A A A A R A A A R R R R R R R R A R R R R R R R R
XXXXXXXXXXXXXXXXXXXXXXXXXXXXXXXXXXXXXXXXXXXXXXXXXXXXXXXXXXXXXXXXXXXXXXXXXXXXXXXXXXXXXXXXXXXXXXXXXXXXXXXXXXXXXXXXXXXXXXXX
. . . . . . . . . XXXXXXXXXXXXXXXXXXXXXXXXXXXXXXXXXXXXXXXXXXXXXXXXXXXXXXXXXXXXXXXXXXXXXXXXXXXXXXXXXXXXXXXXXXXXXXXXXXXXXX
. . . . . . . . . . . . . . . . . . . . . . . . . . . . . . . . XXXXXXXXXXX . XXXXX . . XXXXXXXXXXX . . XXXXXXXXXXXXXXXX
. . . . . . . . . . . . . . . . . . . . . . . . . . . . . . . . . . . . . . . . . . . . . . . . . . . . . . . XXXXXXXX
. . . . . . . . . . . . . . . . . . . . . . . . . . . . . . . . . . . . . . . . . . . . . . . . . . . . . . . . . . . .
. . . . . . . . . . . . . . . . . . . . . . . . . . . . . . . . . . . . . . . . . . . . . . . . . . . . . . . . . . . .
. . . . . . . . . . . . . . . . . . . . . . . . . . . . . . . . . . . . . . . . . . . . . . . . . . . . . . . . . . . .
. . . . . . . . . . . . . . . . . . . . . . . . . . . . . . . . . . . . . . . . . . . . . . . . . . . . . . . . . . . .
. . . . . . . . . . . . . . . . . . . . . . . . . . . . . . . . . . . . . . . . . . . . . . . . . . . . . . . . . . . .
. . . . . . . . . . . . . . . . . . . . . . . . . . . . . . . . . . . . . . . . . . . . . . . . . . . . . . . . . . . .
. . . . . . . . . . . . . . . . . . . . . . . . . . . . . . . . . . . . . . . . . . . . . . . . . . . . . . . . . . . .
. . . . . . . . . . . . . . . . . . . . . . . . . . . . . . . . . . . . . . . . . . . . . . . . . . . . . . . . . . . .
. . . . . . . . . . . . . . . . . . . . . . . . . . . . . . . . . . . . . . . . . . . . . . . . . . . . . . . . . . . .
. . . . . . . . . . . . . . . . . . . . . . . . . . . . . . . . . . . . . . . . . . . . . . . . . . . . . . . . . . . .
. . . . . . . . . . . . . . . . . . . . . . . . . . . . . . . . . . . . . . . . . . . . . . . . . . . . . . . . . . . .
. . . . . . . . . . . . . . . . . . . . . . . . . . . . . . . . . . . . . . . . . . . . . . . . . . . . . . . . . . . .
. . . . . . . . . . . . . . . . . . . . . . . . . . . . . . . . . . . . . . . . . . . . . . . . . . . . . . . . . . . .
. . . . . . . . . . . . . . . . . . . . . . . . . . . . . . . . . . . . . . . . . . . . . . . . . . . . . . . . . . . .
. . . . . . . . . . . . . . . . . . . . . . . . . . . . . . . . . . . . . . . . . . . . . . . . . . . . . . . . . . . .
. . . . . . . . . . . . . . . . . . . . . . . . . . . . . . . . . . . . . . . . . . . . . . . . . . . . . . . . . . . .
. . . . . . . . . . . . . . . . . . . . . . . . . . . . . . . . . . . . . . . . . . . . . . . . . . . . . . . . . . . .
. . . . . . . . . . . . . . . . . . . . . . . . . . . . . . . . . . . . . . . . . . . . . . . . . . . . . . . . . . . .
. . . . . . . . . . . . . . . . . . . . . . . . . . . . . . . . . . . . . . . . . . . . . . . . . . . . . . . . . . . .
. . . . . . . . . . . . . . . . . . . . . . . . . . . . . . . . . . . . . . . . . . . . . . . . . . . . . . . . . . . .
. . . . . . . . . . . . . . . . . . . . . . . . . . . . . . . . . . . . . . . . . . . . . . . . . . . . . . . . . . . .
. . . . . . . . . . . . . . . . . . . . . . . . . . . . . . . . . . . . . . . . . . . . . . . . . . . . . . . . . . . .
. . . . . . . . . . . . . . . . . . . . . . . . . . . . . . . . . . . . . . . . . . . . . . . . . . . . . . . . . . . .
. . . . . . . . . . . . . . . . . . . . . . . . . . . . . . . . . . . . . . . . . . . . . . . . . . . . . . . . . . . .
. . . . . . . . . . . . . . . . . . . . . . . . . . . . . . . . . . . . . . . . . . . . . . . . . . . . . . . . . . . .
. . . . . . . . . . . . . . . . . . . . . . . . . . . . . . . . . . . . . . . . . . . . . . . . . . . . . . . . . . . .
. . . . . . . . . . . . . . . . . . . . . . . . . . . . . . . . . . . . . . . . . . . . . . . . . . . . . . . . . . . .
. . . . . . . . . . . . . . . . . . . . . . . . . . . . . . . . . . . . . . . . . . . . . . . . . . . . . . . . . . . .
. . . . . . . . . . . . . . . . . . . . . . . . . . . . . . . . . . . . . . . . . . . . . . . . . . . . . . . . . . . .
. . . . . . . . . . . . . . . . . . . . . . . . . . . . . . . . . . . . . . . . . . . . . . . . . . . . . . . . . . . .
. . . . . . . . . . . . . . . . . . . . . . . . . . . . . . . . . . . . . . . . . . . . . . . . . . . . . . . . . . . .
. . . . . . . . . . . . . . . . . . . . . . . . . . . . . . . . . . . . . . . . . . . . . . . . . . . . . . . . . . . .
. . . . . . . . . . . . . . . . . . . . . . . . . . . . . . . . . . . . . . . . . . . . . . . . . . . . . . . . . . . .
. . . . . . . . . . . . . . . . . . . . . . . . . . . . . . . . . . . . . . . . . . . . . . . . . . . . . . . . . . . .
. . . . . . . . . . . . . . . . . . . . . . . . . . . . . . . . . . . . . . . . . . . . . . . . . . . . . . . . . . . .
. . . . . . . . . . . . . . . . . . . . . . . . . . . . . . . . . . . . . . . . . . . . . . . . . . . . . . . . . . . .
```

```
                                   FISHER'S IRIS DATA                                          7

                              DENSITY LINKAGE CLUSTER ANALYSIS

SPECIES

V V V V V V V V V V V     V V V V V   V V V   V V   V               V V
E E E E E E E E E E E V V E E E E E V E E E V E E V E V V V V V V V E E V
R R R R R R R R R R R I I R R R R R I R R R I R R I R I I I I I I I R R I
S S S S S S S S S S S R R S S S S S R S S S R S S R S R R R R R R R S S R
I I I I I I I I I I I G G I I I I I G I I I G I I G I G G G G G G G I I G
C C C C C C C C C C C I I C C C C C I C C C I C C I C I I I I I I I C C I
O O O O O O O O O O O N N O O O O O N O O O N O O N O N N N N N N N O O N
L L L L L L L L L L L I I L L L L L I L L L I L L I L I I I I I I I L L I
O O O O O O O O O O O C C O O O O O C O O O C O O C O C C C C C C C O O C
R R R R R R R R R R R A A R R R R R A R R R A R R A R A A A A A A A R R A
XXXXXXXXXXXXXXXXXXXXXXXXXXXXXXXXXXXXXXXXXXXXXXXXXXXXXXXXXXXXXXXXXXXXXXXXX
XXXXXXXXXXXXXXXXXXXXXXXXXXXXXXXXXXXXXXXXXXXXXXXXXXXXX . . . . . . . . . .
XXXXXXXXXXXXXXXXX . . . . . . . . . . . . . . . . . . . . . . . . . . . .
XXXXXXXXXXXXX . . . . . . . . . . . . . . . . . . . . . . . . . . . . . .
XXXXX . . . . . . . . . . . . . . . . . . . . . . . . . . . . . . . . . .
. . . . . . . . . . . . . . . . . . . . . . . . . . . . . . . . . . . . .
. . . . . . . . . . . . . . . . . . . . . . . . . . . . . . . . . . . . .
. . . . . . . . . . . . . . . . . . . . . . . . . . . . . . . . . . . . .
. . . . . . . . . . . . . . . . . . . . . . . . . . . . . . . . . . . . .
. . . . . . . . . . . . . . . . . . . . . . . . . . . . . . . . . . . . .
. . . . . . . . . . . . . . . . . . . . . . . . . . . . . . . . . . . . .
. . . . . . . . . . . . . . . . . . . . . . . . . . . . . . . . . . . . .
. . . . . . . . . . . . . . . . . . . . . . . . . . . . . . . . . . . . .
. . . . . . . . . . . . . . . . . . . . . . . . . . . . . . . . . . . . .
. . . . . . . . . . . . . . . . . . . . . . . . . . . . . . . . . . . . .
. . . . . . . . . . . . . . . . . . . . . . . . . . . . . . . . . . . . .
. . . . . . . . . . . . . . . . . . . . . . . . . . . . . . . . . . . . .
. . . . . . . . . . . . . . . . . . . . . . . . . . . . . . . . . . . . .
. . . . . . . . . . . . . . . . . . . . . . . . . . . . . . . . . . . . .
. . . . . . . . . . . . . . . . . . . . . . . . . . . . . . . . . . . . .
. . . . . . . . . . . . . . . . . . . . . . . . . . . . . . . . . . . . .
. . . . . . . . . . . . . . . . . . . . . . . . . . . . . . . . . . . . .
. . . . . . . . . . . . . . . . . . . . . . . . . . . . . . . . . . . . .
. . . . . . . . . . . . . . . . . . . . . . . . . . . . . . . . . . . . .
. . . . . . . . . . . . . . . . . . . . . . . . . . . . . . . . . . . . .
. . . . . . . . . . . . . . . . . . . . . . . . . . . . . . . . . . . . .
. . . . . . . . . . . . . . . . . . . . . . . . . . . . . . . . . . . . .
. . . . . . . . . . . . . . . . . . . . . . . . . . . . . . . . . . . . .
. . . . . . . . . . . . . . . . . . . . . . . . . . . . . . . . . . . . .
. . . . . . . . . . . . . . . . . . . . . . . . . . . . . . . . . . . . .
. . . . . . . . . . . . . . . . . . . . . . . . . . . . . . . . . . . . .
. . . . . . . . . . . . . . . . . . . . . . . . . . . . . . . . . . . . .
. . . . . . . . . . . . . . . . . . . . . . . . . . . . . . . . . . . . .
. . . . . . . . . . . . . . . . . . . . . . . . . . . . . . . . . . . . .
. . . . . . . . . . . . . . . . . . . . . . . . . . . . . . . . . . . . .
. . . . . . . . . . . . . . . . . . . . . . . . . . . . . . . . . . . . .
. . . . . . . . . . . . . . . . . . . . . . . . . . . . . . . . . . . . .
. . . . . . . . . . . . . . . . . . . . . . . . . . . . . . . . . . . . .
. . . . . . . . . . . . . . . . . . . . . . . . . . . . . . . . . . . . .
```

REFERENCES

Duran, B.S. and Odell, P.L. (1974), *Cluster Analysis*, New York: Springer-Verlag.

Everitt, B.S. (1980), *Cluster Analysis,* Second Edition, London: Heineman Educational Books Ltd.

Fisher, R.A. (1936), "The Use of Multiple Measurements in Taxonomic Problems," *Annals of Eugenics*, 7, 179-188.

Hartigan, J.A. (1975), *Clustering Algorithms*, New York: John Wiley & Sons.

Johnson, S.C. (1967), "Hierarchical Clustering Schemes," *Psychometrika*, 32, 241-254.

Knuth, D.E. (1973), *The Art of Computer Programming, Volume 1, Fundamental Algorithms*, Reading, Massachusetts: Addison-Wesley.

Chapter 39

The TTEST Procedure

Operating systems: All

ABSTRACT

The TTEST procedure computes a *t* statistic for testing the hypothesis that the means of two groups of observations in a SAS data set are equal.

INTRODUCTION

Means for a variable are computed for each of the two groups of observations identified by values of a classification or CLASS variable. The *t* test tests the hypothesis that the true means are the same. This can be considered as a special case of a one-way analysis of variance with two levels of classification.

TTEST computes the *t* statistic based on the assumption that the variances of the two groups are equal and also computes an approximate *t* based on the assumption that the variances are unequal. For each *t*, the degrees of freedom and probability level are given; Satterthwaite's (1946) approximation is used to compute the degrees of freedom associated with the approximate *t*. An *F'* (folded) statistic is computed to test for equality of the two variances (Steel and Torrie 1980).

The TTEST procedure was not designed for paired comparisons. See **Examples** below for a method of using the MEANS procedure to get a paired-comparisons *t* test.

Note that the underlying assumption of the *t* test computed by the TTEST procedure is that the variables are normally and independently distributed within each group.

SPECIFICATIONS

The statements used to control the procedure are

PROC TTEST *option;*
CLASS *variables;*
VAR *variables;*
BY *variables;*

No statement may be used more than once. There is no restriction on the order of the statements after the PROC statement. The CLASS statement is required.

PROC TTEST Statement

PROC TTEST *option;*

The following option can appear in the PROC TTEST statement:

DATA=*SASdataset*
names the SAS data set for the procedure to use. If DATA= is not given, PROC TTEST uses the most recently created SAS data set.

CLASS Statement

CLASS *variable;*

A CLASS statement giving the name of the grouping variable must accompany the PROC TTEST statement. The grouping variable must have two, and only two, values. PROC TTEST divides the observations into the two groups for the *t* test using the values of this variable.

You can use either a numeric or a character variable in the CLASS statement. If you use a character variable longer than 16 characters, the value is truncated and a warning message is issued.

VAR Statement

VAR *variables;*

The VAR statement gives the names of the dependent variables whose means are to be compared. If the VAR statement is omitted, all numeric variables in the input data set (except a numeric variable appearing in the CLASS statement) are included in the analysis.

BY Statement

BY *variables;*

A BY statement can be used with PROC TTEST to obtain separate analyses on observations in groups defined by the BY variables. When a BY statement appears, the procedure expects the input data set to be sorted in order of the BY variables. If your input data set is not sorted in ascending order, use the SORT procedure with a similar BY statement to sort the data, or, if appropriate, use the BY statement options NOTSORTED or DESCENDING. For more information see the discussion of the BY statement in "Statements Used in the PROC Step" in the *SAS User's Guide: Basics.*

DETAILS

Missing Values

An observation is always omitted from the calculations if it has a missing value for either the CLASS variable or for the variable to be tested.

Computational Method

The usual t statistic for testing the equality of means $\bar{x}_1$ and $\bar{x}_2$ from two independent samples with n_1 and n_2 observations is

$$t = (\bar{x}_1 - \bar{x}_2)/\sqrt{s^2(1/n_1 + 1/n_2)}$$

where s^2 is the pooled variance

$$s^2 = \{(n_1 - 1)s_1^2 + (n_2 - 1)s_2^2\} / (n_1 + n_2 - 2)$$

and where s_1^2 and s_2^2 are the sample variances of the two groups. The use of this t statistic depends on the assumption that $\sigma_1^2 = \sigma_2^2$, where σ_1^2 and σ_2^2 are the population variances of the two groups.

You can use the folded form of the F statistic, F', to test the assumption that the variances are equal, where

$$F' = (\text{larger of } s_1^2, s_2^2) / (\text{smaller of } s_1^2, s_2^2) \ .$$

A test of F' is a two-tailed F test since we do not specify which variance we expect to be larger. The printout value of PROB > F gives the probability of a greater F value under the null hypothesis that $\sigma_1^2 = \sigma_2^2$.

Under the assumption of equal variances, the t statistic is computed with the formula given above, using the pooled variance estimate s^2.

Under the assumption of unequal variances, the approximate t is computed as

$$t = (\bar{x}_1 - \bar{x}_2) / \sqrt{(s_1^2/n_1 + s_2^2/n_2)} \ .$$

The formula for Satterthwaite's (1946) approximation for the degrees of freedom is as follows:

$$df = \frac{(s_1^2/n_1 + s_2^2/n_2)^2}{(s_1^2/n_1)^2 / (n_1 - 1) + (s_2^2/n_2)^2/(n_2 - 1)}$$

Refer to Steel and Torrie (1980) and *SAS for Linear Models* (Freund and Littell 1981) for more information.

Printed Output

For each dependent variable included in the analysis, the TTEST procedure prints the following statistics for each group

1. the name of the dependent variable
2. the levels of the classification variable
3. N, the number of nonmissing values
4. the MEAN or average
5. STD DEV, the standard deviation
6. STD ERROR, the standard error

7. the MINIMUM value
8. the MAXIMUM value.

Under the assumption of unequal variances, the TTEST procedure prints

9. T, an approximate *t* statistic for testing the null hypothesis that the means of the two groups are equal
10. DF, Satterthwaite's approximation for the degrees of freedom
11. PROB > |T|, the probability of a greater absolute value of *t* under the null hypothesis. This is the two-tailed significance probability.

Under the assumption of equal variances, the TTEST procedure prints

12. T, the *t* statistic for testing the null hypothesis that the means of the two groups are equal
13. DF, the degrees of freedom
14. PROB > |T|, the probability of a greater absolute value of *t* under the null hypothesis. This is the two-tailed significance probability.

PROC TTEST then gives the results of the test of equality of variances:

15. the F' (folded) statistic (see the **Details** section above)
16. the degrees of freedom, DF, in each group
17. PROB > F', the probability of a greater F value.

EXAMPLES

Comparing Group Means: Example 1

The data for this example consist of golf scores for a physical education class. We want to use a *t* test to determine if the mean golf score for the males in the class differs significantly from the mean score for the females.

The grouping variable is SEX, and it appears in the CLASS statement.

The numbers on the sample output correspond to the statistics described above.

```
DATA SCORES;
   INPUT SEX $ SCORE @@;
   CARDS;
F 75  F 76  F 80  F 77  F 80  F 77  F 73
M 82  M 80  M 85  M 85  M 78  M 87  M 82
;
PROC TTEST;
   CLASS SEX;
   VAR SCORE;
   TITLE 'GOLF SCORES';
```

Output 39.1 Comparing Group Means with PROC TTEST

```
                                             GOLF SCORES                                                        1

                                           TTEST PROCEDURE
              ❶
VARIABLE: SCORE
                            ❹              ❺              ❻              ❼              ❽
SEX ❷     N ❸         MEAN          STD DEV      STD ERROR         MINIMUM         MAXIMUM     VARIANCES          T        DF   PROB > |T|

F          7  76.85714286    2.54483604    0.96185761   73.00000000   80.00000000     UNEQUAL❾  -3.8288 ❿  11.5  ⓫   0.0026
M          7  82.71428571    3.14718317    1.18952343   78.00000000   87.00000000     EQUAL  ⓬  -3.8288 ⓭  12.0  ⓮   0.0024
                                      ⓯              ⓰              ⓱
FOR H0: VARIANCES ARE EQUAL, F'=     1.53 WITH 6 AND 6 DF     PROB > F'= 0.6189
```

Paired Comparisons Using PROC MEANS: Example 2

For paired comparisons, use PROC MEANS rather than PROC TTEST. You can create a new variable containing the differences between the paired variables and use the T and PRT options of PROC MEANS to test whether the mean difference is significantly different from zero.

This is useful if you have a PRETEST and POSTTEST value for each observation in a data set and you want to test whether there is a significant difference between the two sets of scores.

Following the INPUT statement in the DATA step is an assignment statement to create a new variable DIFF by subtracting PRETEST from POSTTEST. Then, you use PROC MEANS with the T and PRT options to get a *t* statistic and a probability value for the null hypothesis that DIFF's mean is equal to zero.

```
DATA A;
   INPUT ID PRETEST POSTTEST;
   DIFF=POSTTEST-PRETEST;
   CARDS;
1   80   82
2   73   71
3   70   95
4   60   69
5   88  100
6   84   71
7   65   75
8   37   60
9   91   95
10  98   99
11  52   65
12  78   83
13  40   60
14  79   86
15  59   62
;
PROC MEANS MEAN STDERR T PRT;
   VAR DIFF;
   TITLE 'PAIRED-COMPARISONS T TEST';
```

Output 39.2 Making Paired Comparisons with PROC MEANS

```
                         PAIRED-COMPARISONS T TEST                                  1

          VARIABLE        MEAN          STD ERROR        T      PR>|T|
                                         OF MEAN

          DIFF        7.93333333     2.56434651        3.09    0.0079
```

REFERENCES

Freund, R.J. and Littell, R.C. (1981), *SAS for Linear Models: A Guide to the ANOVA and GLM Procedures*, Cary, NC: SAS Institute Inc.

Satterthwaite, F.W. (1946), "An Approximate Distribution of Estimates of Variance Components," *Biometrics Bulletin*, 2, 110-114.

Steel, R.G.D. and Torrie, J.H. (1980), *Principles and Procedures of Statistics*, Second Edition, New York: McGraw-Hill Book Company.

Chapter 40

The VARCLUS Procedure

Operating systems: All

ABSTRACT

The VARCLUS procedure performs either disjoint or hierarchical clustering of variables based on a correlation or covariance matrix. The clusters are chosen to maximize the variation accounted for by either the first principal component or the centroid component of each cluster. An output data set containing the results of the analysis can be created and used with the SCORE procedure to compute cluster component scores.

INTRODUCTION

The VARCLUS procedure divides a set of numeric variables into either disjoint or hierarchical clusters. Associated with each cluster is a linear combination of the variables in the cluster, which may be either the first principal component or the centroid component. PROC VARCLUS tries to maximize the sum across clusters of the variance of the original variables that is explained by the cluster components.

Either the correlation or the covariance matrix can be analyzed. If correlations are used, all variables are treated as equally important. If covariances are used, variables with larger variances have more importance in the analysis.

PROC VARCLUS creates an output data set that can be used with the SCORE procedure to compute component scores for each cluster. A second output data set can be used by the TREE procedure to draw a tree diagram of hierarchical clusters.

Background

The VARCLUS procedure attempts to divide a set of variables into non-overlapping clusters in such a way that each cluster can be interpreted as essentially unidimensional. For each cluster, VARCLUS computes a component that can be either the first principal component or the centroid component, and tries to maximize the sum across clusters of the variation accounted for by the cluster components. VARCLUS is a type of oblique component analysis related to multiple group factor analysis (Harman 1976).

VARCLUS can be used as a variable-reduction method. A large set of variables can often be replaced by the set of cluster components with little loss of information. A given number of cluster components does not generally explain as much variance as the same number of principal components, but the cluster components are usually easier to interpret than the principal components, even if the latter are rotated.

For example, an educational test might contain fifty items. VARCLUS could be used to divide the items into, say, five clusters. Each cluster could be treated as a subtest, and the subtest scores would be given by the cluster components. If the cluster components were centroid components of the covariance matrix, each subtest score would simply be the sum of the item scores for that cluster.

By default, VARCLUS begins with all variables in a single cluster. It then repeats the following steps:

1. A cluster is chosen for splitting. The selected cluster has either the smallest percentage of variation explained by its cluster component or the largest second eigenvalue.
2. The chosen cluster is split into two clusters by finding the first two principal components, performing an orthoblique rotation (raw quartimax rotation on the eigenvectors), and assigning each variable to the rotated component with which it has the higher squared correlation.
3. Variables are iteratively reassigned to clusters to maximize the variance accounted for by the cluster components. The reassignment may be required to maintain a hierarchical structure.

The procedure stops when each cluster satisfies a user-specified criterion involving either the percentage of variation accounted for or the second eigenvalue of each cluster. By default, VARCLUS stops when each cluster has only a single eigenvalue greater than one, thus satisfying the most popular criterion for determining the sufficiency of a single underlying factor dimension.

The iterative reassignment of variables to clusters proceeds in two phases. The first is a nearest component sorting (NCS) phase, similar in principle to the nearest centroid sorting algorithms described by Anderberg (1973). In each iteration the cluster components are computed, and each variable is assigned to the component with which it has the highest squared correlation. The second phase involves a search algorithm in which each variable in turn is tested to see if assigning it to a different cluster increases the amount of variance explained. If a variable is reassigned during the search phase, the components of the two clusters involved are recomputed before the next variable is tested. The NCS phase is much faster than the search phase but is more likely to be trapped by a local optimum.

If principal components are used, the NCS phase is an alternating least-squares method and converges rapidly. The search phase is very time consuming for a large number of variables and is omitted by default. If the default initialization method is used, the search phase is rarely able to improve the results of the NCS phase. If random initialization is used, the NCS phase may be trapped by a local optimum from which the search phase can escape.

If centroid components are used, the NCS phase may not increase the amount of variance explained. It is therefore limited to one iteration by default.

SPECIFICATIONS

The VARCLUS procedure is invoked by the following statements:

PROC VARCLUS *options;*
VAR *variables;*
SEED (or SEEDS) *variables;*
PARTIAL *variables;*
WEIGHT *variable;*
FREQ *variable;*
BY *variables;*

Usually only the VAR statement is used in addition to the PROC VARCLUS statement.

PROC VARCLUS Statement

PROC VARCLUS *options;*

The following data set options can appear in the PROC statement:

DATA=*SASdataset*
names the input data set to be analyzed. The data set can be an ordinary SAS data set or TYPE=CORR, COV, or FACTOR. If DATA= is omitted, the most recently created SAS data set is used.

OUTSTAT=*SASdataset*
names an output data set to contain statistics including means, standard deviations, correlations, cluster scoring coefficients, and the cluster structure. If you want to create a permanent SAS data set, you must specify a two-level name. See "SAS Files" in the *SAS User's Guide: Basics* for more information on permanent SAS data sets.

OUTTREE=*SASdataset*
names an output data set to contain information on the tree structure that can be used by the TREE procedure to print a tree diagram. The OUTTREE= option implies the HIERARCHY option. If you want to create a permanent SAS data set, you must specify a two-level name. See "SAS Files" in the *SAS User's Guide: Basics* for more information on permanent SAS data sets.

These options allow printing of descriptive statistics:

SIMPLE
S
prints means and standard deviations.

CORR
C
prints the correlation matrix.

The following options control the number of clusters:

MINCLUSTERS=*n*
MINC=*n*

specifies the smallest number of clusters desired. The default value is 2 if INITIAL=RANDOM or INITIAL=SEED; otherwise the procedure begins with one cluster and tries to split it in accordance with the PROPORTION= or MAXEIGEN= options.

MAXCLUSTERS=*n*
MAXC=*n*

specifies the largest number of clusters desired. The default value is the number of variables.

PROPORTION=*n*
PERCENT=*n*

gives the proportion or percentage of variation that must be explained by the cluster component. Since PROPORTION=0.75 and PERCENT=75 are equivalent, you need specify only one. If the CENTROID option (see below) is specified, the default value is 0.75; otherwise, the default value is 0.

MAXEIGEN=*n*

specifies the largest permissible value of the second eigenvalue in each cluster. If neither PROPORTION= nor MAXCLUSTERS= is specified, the default value is 1 if the correlation matrix is analyzed, or the average variance of the variables if the covariance matrix is analyzed. Otherwise the default is 0. MAXEIGEN= cannot be used with the CENTROID option.

The following options control the method of cluster formation:

COVARIANCE
COV

analyzes the covariance matrix rather than the correlation matrix.

INITIAL=*method*

specifies the method for initializing the clusters. Values for INITIAL= can be RANDOM, SEED, INPUT, or GROUP. If INITIAL= is omitted and MINCLUSTERS= is greater than 1, the initial cluster components are obtained by extracting the required number of principal components and performing an orthoblique rotation.

INITIAL=RANDOM

assigns variables randomly to clusters. If INITIAL=RANDOM is used without the CENTROID option, it is recommended that MAXSEARCH=5 be specified, although the CPU time required is substantially increased.

INITIAL=SEED

assigns to clusters variables named in the SEED statement. Each variable listed in the SEED statement becomes the sole member of a cluster, and the other variables remain unassigned. If the SEED statement is omitted, the first MINCLUSTERS= variables in the VAR statement are used as seeds.

INITIAL=INPUT

can be used if the input data set is a TYPE=CORR, COV, or FACTOR data set, in which case scoring coefficients are read from the data set. Scoring coefficients from the FACTOR procedure or a previous run of VARCLUS can be used, or you can enter other coefficients in a DATA step.

INITIAL=GROUP
can be used if the input data set is a TYPE=CORR, COV, or FACTOR data set. The cluster membership of each variable is obtained from an observation with _TYPE_='GROUP', which contains an integer for each variable ranging from one to the number of clusters. You can use a data set created either by a previous run of VARCLUS or in a DATA step.

CENTROID
uses centroid components rather than principal components. Centroid components should be used if you want the cluster components to be (unweighted) averages of the standardized variables (the default) or the unstandardized variables (if you specify the COV option). It is possible to obtain locally optimal clusterings in which a variable is not assigned to the cluster component with which it has the highest squared correlation.

MAXITER=*n*
specifies the maximum number of iterations during the alternating least-squares phase. The default value is 1 if CENTROID is specified, 10 otherwise.

MAXSEARCH=*n*
specifies the maximum number of iterations during the search phase. The default is 10 if CENTROID is specified, 0 otherwise.

HIERARCHY
HI
requires the clusters at different levels to maintain a hierarchical structure.

MULTIPLEGROUP
MG
performs a multiple group component analysis. The input data set must be TYPE=CORR, COV, or FACTOR and must contain an observation with _TYPE_='GROUP' defining the variable groups. Specifying MULTIPLEGROUP is equivalent to specifying all of the following options:

```
MINC=1  MAXITER=0  MAXSEARCH=0  MAXEIGEN=0
PROPORTION=0  INITIAL=GROUP
```

These options control the amount of printed ouput:

SHORT
suppresses printing of the cluster structure, scoring coefficient, and inter-cluster correlation matrices.

SUMMARY
suppresses all default printout except the final summary table.

NOPRINT
suppresses the printout.

TRACE
lists the cluster to which each variable is assigned during the iterations.

VAR Statement

VAR *variables;*

The VAR statement specifies the variables to be clustered. If the VAR statement is omitted, all numeric variables not listed in other statements (except the SEED statement) are processed.

SEED Statement

SEEDS *variables;*
SEED *variables;*

The SEED statement specifies variables to be used as seeds to initialize the clusters. It is not necessary to use INITIAL=SEED if the SEED statement is present, but if any other INITIAL= option is specified, the SEED statement is ignored.

PARTIAL Statement

PARTIAL *variables;*

If you want to base the clustering on partial correlations, list the variables to be partialled out in the PARTIAL statement.

WEIGHT Statement

WEIGHT *variable;*

If you want to use relative weights for each observation in the input data set, place the weights in a variable in the data set and specify the name in a WEIGHT statement. This is often done when the variance associated with each observation is different and the values of the weight variable are proportional to the reciprocals of the variances.

FREQ Statement

FREQ *variable;*

If a variable in your data set represents the frequency of occurrence for the other values in the observation, include the variable's name in a FREQ statement. The procedure then treats the data set as if each observation appears *n* times, where *n* is the value of the FREQ variable for the observation. The total number of observations is considered equal to the sum of the FREQ variable.

BY Statement

BY *variables;*

A BY statement can be used with PROC VARCLUS to obtain separate analyses on observations in groups defined by the BY variables. When a BY statement appears, the procedure expects the input data set to be sorted in order of the BY variables. If your input data set is not sorted in ascending order, use the SORT procedure with a similar BY statement to sort the data, or, if appropriate, use the BY statement options NOTSORTED or DESCENDING. For more information, see the discussion of the BY statement in "Statements Used in the PROC Step" in the *SAS User's Guide: Basics.*

DETAILS

Missing Values

Observations containing missing values are omitted from the analysis.

Usage Notes

Default options for VARCLUS often provide satisfactory results. If you want to change the final number of clusters, use the MAXCLUSTERS=, MAXEIGEN=, or PROPORTION= options. The MAXEIGEN= and PROPORTION= options usually produce similar results but occasionally cause different clusters to be selected for splitting. MAXEIGEN= tends to choose clusters with a large number of variables, while PROPORTION= is more likely to select a cluster with a small number of variables.

VARCLUS usually requires more computer time than principal factor analysis but can be faster than some of the iterative factoring methods. If you have more than thirty variables you may want to reduce execution time by one or more of the following methods:

- Use the MINCLUSTERS= and MAXCLUSTERS= options if you know how many clusters you want.
- Use the HIERARCHY option.
- Use the SEED statement if you have some prior knowledge of what clusters to expect.

If you have sufficient computer time, you may want to try one of the following methods to obtain a better solution:

- Use the MAXSEARCH= option with principal components and specify a value of 5 or 10.
- Try several factoring and rotation methods with FACTOR to use as input to VARCLUS.
- Run VARCLUS several times specifying INITIAL=RANDOM.

Computational Resources

The time required for VARCLUS to analyze a given data set varies greatly depending on the number of clusters requested, the number of iterations in both the alternating least-squares and search phases, and whether centroid or principal components are used.

Let

n = number of observations
v = number of variables
c = number of clusters.

It is assumed that at each stage of clustering, the clusters all contain the same number of variables.

The time required to compute the correlation matrix is roughly proportional to nv^2.

Default cluster initialization requires time roughly proportional to v^3. Any other method of initialization requires time roughly proportional to cv^2.

In the alternating least-squares phase, each iteration requires time roughly proportional to cv^2 if centroid components are used, or

$$(c + 5v/c^2)v^2$$

if principal components are used.

In the search phase, each iteration requires time roughly proportional to v^3/c if centroid components are used, or v^4/c^2 if principal components are used. The HIERARCHY option speeds up each iteration after the first split by as much as c/2.

Interpreting VARCLUS Output

Since VARCLUS is a type of oblique component analysis, its output is similar to the output from PROC FACTOR for oblique rotations. The scoring coefficients have the same meaning in both VARCLUS and FACTOR; they are coefficients applied to the standardized variables to compute component scores. The cluster structure is analogous to the factor structure, containing the correlations between each variable and each cluster component. A cluster pattern is not printed because it would be the same as the cluster structure, except that zeros would appear in the same places that zeros appear in the scoring coefficients. The inter-cluster correlations are analogous to inter-factor correlations; they are the correlations among cluster components.

VARCLUS also has a cluster summary and a cluster listing. The cluster summary gives the number of variables in each cluster and the variation explained by the cluster component. The latter is similar to the variation explained by a factor but includes contributions from only the variables in that cluster rather than from all variables, as in FACTOR. The PROPORTIONs value is obtained by dividing the variance explained by the total variance of variables in the cluster. If the cluster contains two or more variables and the CENTROID option is not used, the second largest eigenvalue of the cluster is also printed.

The cluster listing gives the variables in each cluster. Two squared correlations are printed for each cluster. The column labeled OWN CLUSTER gives the squared correlation of the variable with its own cluster component. This value should be higher than the squared correlation with any other cluster unless an iteration limit has been exceeded or the CENTROID option has been used. The larger the squared correlation is, the better. The column labeled NEXT CLOSEST contains the next highest squared correlation of the variable with a cluster component. This value is low if the clusters are well-separated. The column headed 1−R**2 RATIO gives the ratio of one minus the OWN CLUSTER R^2 to one minus the NEXT CLOSEST R^2. A small 1−R**2 RATIO indicates a good clustering.

Output Data Sets

OUTSTAT= data set The OUTSTAT= data set is of TYPE=CORR and can be used as input to the SCORE procedure or a subsequent run of VARCLUS. The variables it contains are

- BY variables
- _NCL_, a numeric variable giving the number of clusters
- _TYPE_, a character variable indicating the type of statistic the observation contains
- _NAME_, a character variable containing a variable name or a cluster name
- the variables that were clustered.

The values of _TYPE_ are listed here:

TYPE	**Contents**
MEAN	means
STD	standard deviations

N	number of observations
CORR	correlations
MEMBERS	number of members in each cluster
VAREXP	variance explained by each cluster
PROPOR	proportion of variance explained by each cluster
GROUP	number of the cluster to which each variable belongs
RSQUARED	squared multiple correlation of each variable with its cluster component
SCORE	standardized scoring coefficients
STRUCTUR	cluster structure
CCORR	correlations between cluster components.

The observations with _TYPE_='MEAN', 'STD', 'N', and 'CORR' have missing values for _NCL_. All other values of _TYPE_ are repeated for each cluster solution, with different solutions distinguished by the value of _NCL_. If you want to use the OUTSTAT= data set with the SCORE procedure, you must use a DATA step to select observations with _NCL_ missing or equal to the desired number of clusters.

OUTTREE= data set The OUTTREE= data set contains one observation for each variable clustered plus one observation for each cluster of two or more variables; that is, one observation for each node of the cluster tree. The total number of output observations is between *n* and 2*n*-1, where *n* is the number of variables clustered.

The variables in the OUTTREE= data set are

- the BY variables, if any.
- _NAME_, a character variable giving the name of the node. If the node is a cluster, the name is CL*n* where *n* is the number of the cluster. If the node is a single variable, the variable name is used.
- _PARENT_, a character variable giving the value of _NAME_ of the parent of the node.
- _NCL_, the number of clusters.
- _VAREXP_, the total variance explained by the clusters at the current level of the tree.
- _PROPOR_, the total proportion of variance explained by the clusters at the current level of the tree.

Printed Output

The items described below are printed for each cluster solution unless NOPRINT or SUMMARY is specified. The CLUSTER SUMMARY table includes:

1. the CLUSTER number.
2. MEMBERS, the number of members in the cluster.
3. CLUSTER VARIATION of the variables in the cluster.
4. VARIATION EXPLAINED by the cluster component. This statistic is based only on the variables in the cluster rather than all variables.
5. PROPORTION EXPLAINED, the result of dividing the variation explained by the cluster variation.
6. SECOND EIGENVALUE, the second largest eigenvalue of the cluster. This is printed if the cluster contains more than one variable and the CENTROID option is not specified.

VARCLUS also prints:

7. TOTAL VARIATION EXPLAINED, the sum across clusters of the variation explained by each cluster.
8. PROPORTION, the total explained variation divided by the total variation of all the variables.

The cluster listing includes:

9. VARIABLE, the variables in each cluster.
10. R-SQUARED WITH OWN CLUSTER, the squared correlation of the variable with its own cluster component; and R-SQUARED WITH NEXT CLOSEST, the next highest squared correlation of the variable with a cluster component. OWN CLUSTER values should be higher than the R^2 with any other cluster unless an iteration limit has been exceeded or the CENTROID option was used. NEXT HIGHEST should be a low value if the clusters are well-separated.
11. 1−R**2 RATIO, the ratio of one minus the value in the OWN CLUSTER column to one minus the value in the NEXT CLOSEST column. The occurrence of low ratios indicates well-separated clusters.

If SHORT is not specified, VARCLUS also prints:

12. STANDARDIZED SCORING COEFFICIENTS, standardized regression coefficients for predicting clusters from variables
13. CLUSTER STRUCTURE, the correlations between each variable and each cluster component
14. INTER-CLUSTER CORRELATIONS, the correlations between the cluster components.

If the analysis includes partitions for two or more numbers of clusters, a final summary table is printed. Each row of the table corresponds to one partition. The columns include:

15. NUMBER OF CLUSTERS
16. TOTAL VARIATION EXPLAINED BY CLUSTERS
17. PROPORTION OF VARIATION EXPLAINED BY CLUSTERS
18. MINIMUM PROPORTION of variation EXPLAINED BY A CLUSTER
19. MAXIMUM SECOND EIGENVALUE IN A CLUSTER
20. MINIMUM R-SQUARED FOR A VARIABLE
21. MAXIMUM 1−R**2 RATIO FOR A VARIABLE.

EXAMPLE

Correlations among Physical Variables

The data are correlations among eight physical variables as given by Harman (1976). The first VARCLUS run uses principal cluster components, the second uses centroid cluster components. The third analysis is hierarchical, and the TREE procedure is used to print a tree diagram.

```
DATA PHYS8(TYPE=CORR);
   TITLE 'EIGHT PHYSICAL VARIABLES MEASURED ON 305 SCHOOL GIRLS';
   TITLE2 'SEE PAGE 22 OF HARMAN: MODERN FACTOR ANALYSIS, 3RD ED';
   LABEL HEIGHT='HEIGHT'
         ARM_SPAN='ARM SPAN'
         FOREARM='LENGTH OF FOREARM'
         LOW_LEG='LENGTH OF LOWER LEG'
```

```
          WEIGHT='WEIGHT'
          BIT_DIAM='BITROCHANTERIC DIAMETER'
          GIRTH='CHEST GIRTH'
          WIDTH='CHEST WIDTH';
   INPUT _NAME_ $ 1-8
          (HEIGHT ARM_SPAN FOREARM LOW_LEG WEIGHT BIT_DIAM GIRTH WIDTH)
          (8.);
   _TYPE_ = 'CORR';
   CARDS;
HEIGHT  1.0     .846    .805    .859    .473    .398    .301    .382
ARM_SPAN.846    1.0     .881    .826    .376    .326    .277    .415
FOREARM .805    .881    1.0     .801    .380    .319    .237    .345
LOW_LEG .859    .826    .801    1.0     .436    .329    .327    .365
WEIGHT  .473    .376    .380    .436    1.0     .762    .730    .629
BIT_DIAM.398    .326    .319    .329    .762    1.0     .583    .577
GIRTH   .301    .277    .237    .327    .730    .583    1.0     .539
WIDTH   .382    .415    .345    .365    .629    .577    .539    1.0
;
PROC VARCLUS DATA=PHYS8;
PROC VARCLUS DATA=PHYS8 CENTROID;
PROC VARCLUS DATA=PHYS8 MAXC=8 SUMMARY OUTTREE=TREE;
PROC TREE;
   HEIGHT _PROPOR_;
```

Output 40.1 Principal Cluster Components: PROC VARCLUS

```
                    EIGHT PHYSICAL VARIABLES MEASURED ON 305 SCHOOL GIRLS                      1
                    SEE PAGE 22 OF HARMAN: MODERN FACTOR ANALYSIS, 3RD ED

                         OBLIQUE PRINCIPAL COMPONENT CLUSTER ANALYSIS

                       10000 OBSERVATIONS        PROPORTION  = 0.000000
                           8 VARIABLES           MAXEIGEN    =        1


                                  CLUSTER SUMMARY FOR    1 CLUSTER
                      ❶       ❷         ❸             ❹          ❺             ❻
                                       CLUSTER    VARIATION  PROPORTION      SECOND
                   CLUSTER MEMBERS    VARIATION   EXPLAINED   EXPLAINED    EIGENVALUE
                   ----------------------------------------------------------------
                        1       8       8.00000     4.67288     0.5841        1.77098
                                                                  ❽
                ❼  TOTAL VARIATION EXPLAINED =      4.67288    PROPORTION = 0.584110

CLUSTER     1 WILL BE SPLIT
```

```
                    EIGHT PHYSICAL VARIABLES MEASURED ON 305 SCHOOL GIRLS                      2
                    SEE PAGE 22 OF HARMAN: MODERN FACTOR ANALYSIS, 3RD ED

                         OBLIQUE PRINCIPAL COMPONENT CLUSTER ANALYSIS

                              CLUSTER SUMMARY FOR    2 CLUSTERS

                                       CLUSTER    VARIATION  PROPORTION      SECOND
                   CLUSTER MEMBERS    VARIATION   EXPLAINED   EXPLAINED    EIGENVALUE
                   ----------------------------------------------------------------
                        1       4       4.00000     3.50922     0.8773        0.23614
                        2       4       4.00000     2.91728     0.7293        0.47642

                   TOTAL VARIATION EXPLAINED =       6.4265    PROPORTION = 0.803313
```

(continued on next page)

(continued from previous page)

```
                  ⑩   R-SQUARED WITH
                      ----------------    ⑪
          ⑨              OWN      NEXT     1-R**2
          VARIABLE    CLUSTER  CLOSEST     RATIO
CLUSTER   1--------------------------------------
          HEIGHT       0.8777   0.2088    0.1545    HEIGHT
          ARM_SPAN     0.9002   0.1658    0.1196    ARM SPAN
          FOREARM      0.8661   0.1413    0.1560    LENGTH OF FOREARM
          LOW_LEG      0.8652   0.1829    0.1650    LENGTH OF LOWER LEG
CLUSTER   2--------------------------------------
          WEIGHT       0.8477   0.1974    0.1898    WEIGHT
          BIT_DIAM     0.7386   0.1341    0.3019    BITROCHANTERIC DIAMETER
          GIRTH        0.6981   0.0929    0.3328    CHEST GIRTH
          WIDTH        0.6329   0.1619    0.4380    CHEST WIDTH


          ⑫   STANDARDIZED SCORING COEFFICIENTS

CLUSTER                 1             2
------------------------------------------
HEIGHT           0.266977      0.000000      HEIGHT
ARM_SPAN         0.270377      0.000000      ARM SPAN
FOREARM          0.265194      0.000000      LENGTH OF FOREARM
LOW_LEG          0.265057      0.000000      LENGTH OF LOWER LEG
WEIGHT           0.000000      0.315597      WEIGHT
BIT_DIAM         0.000000      0.294591      BITROCHANTERIC DIAMETER
GIRTH            0.000000      0.286407      CHEST GIRTH
WIDTH            0.000000      0.272710      CHEST WIDTH


                ⑬   CLUSTER STRUCTURE

CLUSTER                 1             2
------------------------------------------
HEIGHT           0.936881      0.456908      HEIGHT
ARM_SPAN         0.948813      0.407210      ARM SPAN
FOREARM          0.930624      0.375865      LENGTH OF FOREARM
LOW_LEG          0.930142      0.427715      LENGTH OF LOWER LEG
WEIGHT           0.444281      0.920686      WEIGHT
BIT_DIAM         0.366201      0.859404      BITROCHANTERIC DIAMETER
GIRTH            0.304779      0.835529      CHEST GIRTH
WIDTH            0.402430      0.795572      CHEST WIDTH
```

```
                  EIGHT PHYSICAL VARIABLES MEASURED ON 305 SCHOOL GIRLS                 3
                  SEE PAGE 22 OF HARMAN: MODERN FACTOR ANALYSIS, 3RD ED

                      OBLIQUE PRINCIPAL COMPONENT CLUSTER ANALYSIS

                     ⑭    INTER-CLUSTER CORRELATIONS

                        CLUSTER              1              2

                        1              1.00000        0.44513
                        2              0.44513        1.00000

NO CLUSTER MEETS THE CRITERION FOR SPLITTING
```

```
                  EIGHT PHYSICAL VARIABLES MEASURED ON 305 SCHOOL GIRLS                 4
                  SEE PAGE 22 OF HARMAN: MODERN FACTOR ANALYSIS, 3RD ED

                      OBLIQUE PRINCIPAL COMPONENT CLUSTER ANALYSIS
   ⑮           ⑯              ⑰              ⑱              ⑲            ⑳              ㉑
                     TOTAL      PROPORTION        MINIMUM         MAXIMUM      MINIMUM         MAXIMUM
  NUMBER         VARIATION    OF VARIATION     PROPORTION          SECOND    R-SQUARED    1-R**2 RATIO
    OF           EXPLAINED       EXPLAINED       EXPLAINED      EIGENVALUE        FOR A           FOR A
 CLUSTERS      BY CLUSTERS     BY CLUSTERS    BY A CLUSTER    IN A CLUSTER     VARIABLE        VARIABLE
-------------------------------------------------------------------------------------------------------
     1            4.672880          0.5841          0.5841        1.770983       0.3810               .
     2            6.426502          0.8033          0.7293        0.476418       0.6329          0.4380
```

```
                    EIGHT PHYSICAL VARIABLES MEASURED ON 305 SCHOOL GIRLS                    5
                    SEE PAGE 22 OF HARMAN: MODERN FACTOR ANALYSIS, 3RD ED

                       OBLIQUE CENTROID COMPONENT CLUSTER ANALYSIS

                     10000 OBSERVATIONS       PROPORTION  = 0.750000
                         8 VARIABLES          MAXEIGEN    =        0


                            CLUSTER SUMMARY FOR    1 CLUSTER

                           CLUSTER    VARIATION PROPORTION     SECOND
                 CLUSTER MEMBERS  VARIATION   EXPLAINED  EXPLAINED   EIGENVALUE
                 ----------------------------------------------------------------
                       1      8       8.00000     4.63100     0.5789

                 TOTAL VARIATION EXPLAINED =        4.631    PROPORTION = 0.578875

CLUSTER    1 WILL BE SPLIT
```

Output 40.2 Centroid Cluster Components: PROC VARCLUS

```
                    EIGHT PHYSICAL VARIABLES MEASURED ON 305 SCHOOL GIRLS                    6
                    SEE PAGE 22 OF HARMAN: MODERN FACTOR ANALYSIS, 3RD ED

                       OBLIQUE CENTROID COMPONENT CLUSTER ANALYSIS

                           CLUSTER SUMMARY FOR    2 CLUSTERS

                           CLUSTER    VARIATION PROPORTION     SECOND
                 CLUSTER MEMBERS  VARIATION   EXPLAINED  EXPLAINED   EIGENVALUE
                 ----------------------------------------------------------------
                       1      4       4.00000     3.50900     0.8772
                       2      4       4.00000     2.91000     0.7275

                 TOTAL VARIATION EXPLAINED =        6.419    PROPORTION = 0.802375

                            R-SQUARED WITH
                            ----------------
                              OWN      NEXT      1-R**2
                   VARIABLE CLUSTER  CLOSEST     RATIO
           CLUSTER    1-------------------------------------
                   HEIGHT     0.8778   0.2075    0.1543      HEIGHT
                   ARM_SPAN   0.8994   0.1669    0.1208      ARM SPAN
                   FOREARM    0.8663   0.1410    0.1557      LENGTH OF FOREARM
                   LOW_LEG    0.8658   0.1824    0.1641      LENGTH OF LOWER LEG
           CLUSTER    2-------------------------------------
                   WEIGHT     0.8368   0.1975    0.2033      WEIGHT
                   BIT_DIAM   0.7335   0.1341    0.3078      BITROCHANTERIC DIAMETER
                   GIRTH      0.6988   0.0929    0.3321      CHEST GIRTH
                   WIDTH      0.6473   0.1618    0.4207      CHEST WIDTH


                          STANDARDIZED SCORING COEFFICIENTS

               CLUSTER                1              2
               ------------------------------------------
               HEIGHT         0.266918       0.000000       HEIGHT
               ARM_SPAN       0.266918       0.000000       ARM SPAN
               FOREARM        0.266918       0.000000       LENGTH OF FOREARM
               LOW_LEG        0.266918       0.000000       LENGTH OF LOWER LEG
               WEIGHT         0.000000       0.293105       WEIGHT
               BIT_DIAM       0.000000       0.293105       BITROCHANTERIC DIAMETER
               GIRTH          0.000000       0.293105       CHEST GIRTH
               WIDTH          0.000000       0.293105       CHEST WIDTH
```

(continued on next page)

(continued from previous page)

```
                         CLUSTER STRUCTURE

CLUSTER                 1              2
--------------------------------------------
HEIGHT         0.936883       0.455485        HEIGHT
ARM_SPAN       0.948361       0.408589        ARM SPAN
FOREARM        0.930744       0.375468        LENGTH OF FOREARM
LOW_LEG        0.930477       0.427054        LENGTH OF LOWER LEG
WEIGHT         0.444419       0.914781        WEIGHT
BIT_DIAM       0.366212       0.856453        BITROCHANTERIC DIAMETER
GIRTH          0.304821       0.835936        CHEST GIRTH
WIDTH          0.402246       0.804574        CHEST WIDTH
```

```
          EIGHT PHYSICAL VARIABLES MEASURED ON 305 SCHOOL GIRLS                 7
          SEE PAGE 22 OF HARMAN: MODERN FACTOR ANALYSIS, 3RD ED

               OBLIQUE CENTROID COMPONENT CLUSTER ANALYSIS

                        INTER-CLUSTER CORRELATIONS

                    CLUSTER             1             2

                       1          1.00000       0.44484
                       2          0.44484       1.00000

CLUSTER    2 WILL BE SPLIT
```

```
          EIGHT PHYSICAL VARIABLES MEASURED ON 305 SCHOOL GIRLS                 8
          SEE PAGE 22 OF HARMAN: MODERN FACTOR ANALYSIS, 3RD ED

               OBLIQUE CENTROID COMPONENT CLUSTER ANALYSIS

                    CLUSTER SUMMARY FOR    3 CLUSTERS

                       CLUSTER    VARIATION PROPORTION     SECOND
CLUSTER MEMBERS      VARIATION    EXPLAINED  EXPLAINED   EIGENVALUE
--------------------------------------------------------------------
      1       4        4.00000      3.50900     0.8772
      2       3        3.00000      2.38333     0.7944
      3       1        1.00000      1.00000     1.0000

TOTAL VARIATION EXPLAINED =         6.89233   PROPORTION = 0.861542

                        R-SQUARED WITH
                        ---------------
                          OWN     NEXT    1-R**2
                VARIABLE CLUSTER CLOSEST   RATIO
      CLUSTER  1------------------------------------
                HEIGHT    0.8778  0.1921  0.1513     HEIGHT
                ARM_SPAN  0.8994  0.1722  0.1215     ARM SPAN
                FOREARM   0.8663  0.1225  0.1524     LENGTH OF FOREARM
                LOW_LEG   0.8658  0.1668  0.1611     LENGTH OF LOWER LEG
      CLUSTER  2------------------------------------
                WEIGHT    0.8685  0.3956  0.2175     WEIGHT
                BIT_DIAM  0.7691  0.3329  0.3461     BITROCHANTERIC DIAMETER
                GIRTH     0.7482  0.2905  0.3548     CHEST GIRTH
      CLUSTER  3------------------------------------
                WIDTH     1.0000  0.4259  0.0000     CHEST WIDTH


                     STANDARDIZED SCORING COEFFICIENTS

CLUSTER                1              2              3
------------------------------------------------------------
HEIGHT           0.26692        0.00000        0.00000        HEIGHT
ARM_SPAN         0.26692        0.00000        0.00000        ARM SPAN
FOREARM          0.26692        0.00000        0.00000        LENGTH OF FOREARM
LOW_LEG          0.26692        0.00000        0.00000        LENGTH OF LOWER LEG
WEIGHT           0.00000        0.37398        0.00000        WEIGHT
BIT_DIAM         0.00000        0.37398        0.00000        BITROCHANTERIC DIAMETER
GIRTH            0.00000        0.37398        0.00000        CHEST GIRTH
WIDTH            0.00000        0.00000        1.00000        CHEST WIDTH
```

```
                     EIGHT PHYSICAL VARIABLES MEASURED ON 305 SCHOOL GIRLS                        9
                     SEE PAGE 22 OF HARMAN: MODERN FACTOR ANALYSIS, 3RD ED

                          OBLIQUE CENTROID COMPONENT CLUSTER ANALYSIS

                                      CLUSTER STRUCTURE

              CLUSTER              1              2              3
              ---------------------------------------------------------
              HEIGHT         0.93688        0.43830        0.38200        HEIGHT
              ARM_SPAN       0.94836        0.36613        0.41500        ARM SPAN
              FOREARM        0.93074        0.35004        0.34500        LENGTH OF FOREARM
              LOW_LEG        0.93048        0.40838        0.36500        LENGTH OF LOWER LEG
              WEIGHT         0.44442        0.93196        0.62900        WEIGHT
              BIT_DIAM       0.36621        0.87698        0.57700        BITROCHANTERIC DIAMETER
              GIRTH          0.30482        0.86501        0.53900        CHEST GIRTH
              WIDTH          0.40225        0.65259        1.00000        CHEST WIDTH


                                 INTER-CLUSTER CORRELATIONS

                     CLUSTER              1              2              3

                     1              1.00000        0.41716        0.40225
                     2              0.41716        1.00000        0.65259
                     3              0.40225        0.65259        1.00000

NO CLUSTER MEETS THE CRITERION FOR SPLITTING
```

```
                     EIGHT PHYSICAL VARIABLES MEASURED ON 305 SCHOOL GIRLS                        10
                     SEE PAGE 22 OF HARMAN: MODERN FACTOR ANALYSIS, 3RD ED

                          OBLIQUE CENTROID COMPONENT CLUSTER ANALYSIS

                          TOTAL      PROPORTION         MINIMUM        MINIMUM          MAXIMUM
             NUMBER     VARIATION   OF VARIATION       PROPORTION      R-SQUARED      1-R**2 RATIO
               OF       EXPLAINED     EXPLAINED         EXPLAINED        FOR A            FOR A
            CLUSTERS   BY CLUSTERS   BY CLUSTERS       BY A CLUSTER     VARIABLE        VARIABLE
            ---------------------------------------------------------------------------------------
                1       4.631000       0.5789            0.5789          0.4306             .
                2       6.419000       0.8024            0.7275          0.6473           0.4207
                3       6.892333       0.8615            0.7944          0.7482           0.3548
```

Output 40.3 Hierarchical Clusters: PROC VARCLUS Specifying the SUMMARY Option

```
                     EIGHT PHYSICAL VARIABLES MEASURED ON 305 SCHOOL GIRLS                        11
                     SEE PAGE 22 OF HARMAN: MODERN FACTOR ANALYSIS, 3RD ED

                          OBLIQUE PRINCIPAL COMPONENT CLUSTER ANALYSIS

                         10000 OBSERVATIONS        PROPORTION  = 1.000000
                             8 VARIABLES           MAXEIGEN    =        0


                  TOTAL      PROPORTION        MINIMUM           MAXIMUM        MINIMUM         MAXIMUM
   NUMBER       VARIATION   OF VARIATION      PROPORTION          SECOND       R-SQUARED     1-R**2 RATIO
     OF         EXPLAINED     EXPLAINED        EXPLAINED        EIGENVALUE       FOR A           FOR A
  CLUSTERS     BY CLUSTERS   BY CLUSTERS      BY A CLUSTER      IN A CLUSTER     VARIABLE        VARIABLE
  --------------------------------------------------------------------------------------------------------
      1         4.672880       0.5841           0.5841          1.770983         0.3810             .
      2         6.426502       0.8033           0.7293          0.476418         0.6329          0.4380
      3         6.895347       0.8619           0.7954          0.418369         0.7421          0.3634
      4         7.271218       0.9089           0.8773          0.238000         0.8652          0.2548
      5         7.509218       0.9387           0.8773          0.238000         0.8652          0.1665
      6         7.740000       0.9675           0.9295          0.238000         0.9295          0.2560
      7         7.881000       0.9851           0.9405          0.238000         0.9405          0.2093
      8         8.000000       1.0000           1.0000          0.238000         1.0000          0.0000
```

Output 40.4 TREE Diagram: PROC TREE

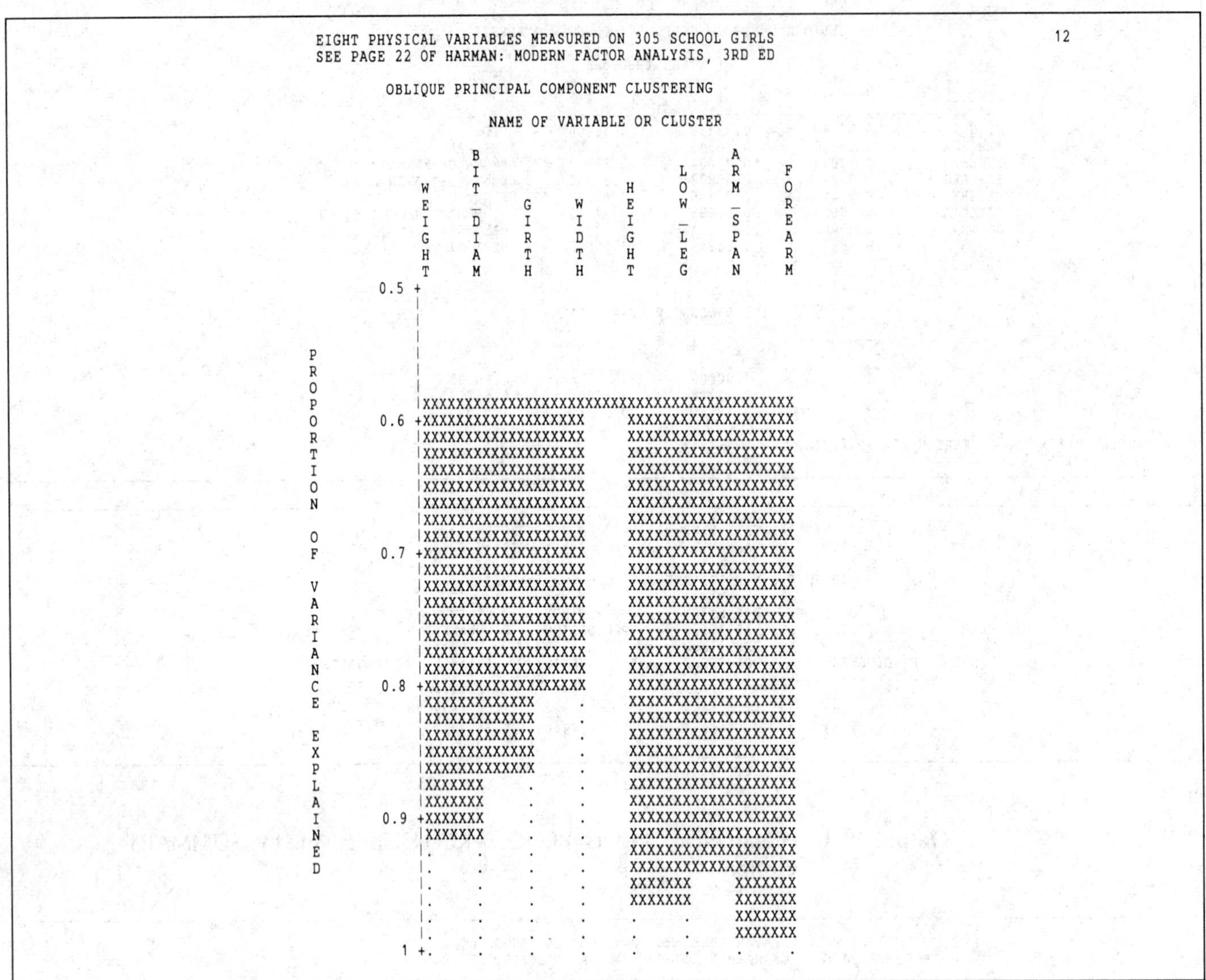

REFERENCES

Anderberg, M.R. (1973), *Cluster Analysis for Applications*, New York: Academic Press.

Harman, H.H. (1976), *Modern Factor Analysis*, Third Edition, Chicago: University of Chicago Press.

Chapter 41
The VARCOMP Procedure

Operating systems: All

ABSTRACT

The VARCOMP procedure computes estimates of the variance components in a general linear model.

INTRODUCTION

VARCOMP is designed to handle models that have random effects. Random effects are classification effects where the levels of the effect are assumed to be randomly selected from an infinite population of normally distributed levels. The goal of VARCOMP is to estimate the variances of each one of these populations.

A single MODEL statement specifies the dependent variables and the effects: main effects, interactions, and nested effects. The effects must be composed of class variables; no continuous variables are allowed on the right-hand side of the equal sign.

You can specify certain effects as fixed (non-random) by putting them first in the MODEL statement and indicating the number of fixed effects with the FIXED option. An intercept is always fitted and assumed fixed. Except the effects specified as fixed, all other effects are assumed to be normally and independently distributed.

The dependent variables are grouped based on the similarity of their missing values. Each group of dependent variables is then analyzed separately. The columns of the design matrix **X** are formed in the same order as the effects are specified in the MODEL statement. No reparameterization is done. Thus, the columns of **X** contain only 0s and 1s.

Four methods of estimation are available, and each one is described below.

The Type I method This method (METHOD=TYPE1) computes the Type I sum of squares for each effect, equates each mean square involving only random effects to its expected value, and solves the resulting system of equations (Gaylor, Lucas, and Anderson 1970). The **X'X | X'Y** matrix is computed and adjusted in segments whenever memory is not sufficient to hold the entire matrix.

The MIVQUE0 method Based on the technique suggested by Hartley, Rao, and LaMotte (1978), the MIVQUE0 method produces estimates that are invariant with respect to the fixed effects of the model and are locally best quadratic unbiased estimates given that the true ratio of each component to the residual error component is zero. The technique is similar to TYPE1 except that the random effects are adjusted only for the fixed effects. This affords a considerable timing advantage over the TYPE1 method; thus, MIVQUE0 is the default method used in VARCOMP. The **X'X | X'Y** matrix is computed and adjusted in segments whenever memory is not sufficient to hold the entire matrix. For more information, refer to Rao (1971, 1972).

The maximum-likelihood method The ML method (METHOD=ML) computes maximum-likelihood estimates of the variance components using the W-transformation developed by Hemmerle and Hartley (1973). Initial estimates of the components are computed using MIVQUE0. The procedure then iterates until the log-likelihood objective function converges.

The restricted maximum-likelihood method Similar to the maximum-likelihood method is the REML method (METHOD=REML), but it first separates the likelihood into two parts; one that contains the fixed effects, and one that does not (Patterson and Thompson 1971). Initial estimates are obtained using MIVQUE0, and the procedure iterates until convergence is reached for the log-likelihood objective function of the portion of the likelihood that does not contain the fixed effects.

SPECIFICATIONS

The statements used in VARCOMP are

PROC VARCOMP *options;*
  CLASS *variables;*
  MODEL *dependents = effects / options;*
  BY *variables;*

PROC VARCOMP Statement

PROC VARCOMP *options;*

The options below can appear in the PROC VARCOMP statement:

METHOD=TYPE1
METHOD=MIVQUE0
METHOD=ML
METHOD=REML

specifies which of the four methods (TYPE1, MIVQUE0, ML, or REML) the VARCOMP procedure should use. If METHOD= is omitted, MIVQUE0 is the default.

MAXITER=*number*

specifies the maximum number of iterations for METHOD=ML or REML. If a value for MAXITER= is omitted, its value is set to 50.

EPSILON=*number*

specifies the convergence value of the objective function for METHOD=ML or REML. If EPSILON= is omitted, its value is 1E-8.

DATA=*SASdataset*

names the SAS data set to be used by VARCOMP. If DATA= is omitted, VARCOMP uses the most recently created SAS data set.

CLASS Statement

CLASS *variables;*

The CLASS statement specifies the classification variables to be used in the analysis. Class variables may be either numeric or character; if character, their lengths must be sixteen or less.

Numeric class variables are not restricted to integers since a variable's format determines the levels. For more information, see the FORMAT statement in the *SAS User's Guide: Basics.*

MODEL Statement

MODEL *dependents = effects / options;*

The MODEL statement gives the dependent variables and independent effects. If more than one dependent variable is specified, a separate analysis is performed for each one. The independent effects are limited to main effects, interactions, and nested effects; no continuous effects are allowed. Effects are specified in VARCOMP in the same way as described for the ANOVA procedure. Only one MODEL statement is allowed.

Only one option is available on the MODEL statement:

FIXED=*n* specifies to VARCOMP that the first *n* effects in the MODEL statement are fixed effects; the remaining effects are assumed to be random.

BY Statement

BY *variables;*

A BY statement can be used with PROC VARCOMP to obtain separate analyses on observations in groups defined by the BY variables. When a BY statement appears, the procedure expects the input data set to be sorted in order of the BY variables. If your input data set is not sorted in ascending order, use the SORT procedure with a similar BY statement to sort the data, or, if appropriate, use the BY statement options NOTSORTED or DESCENDING. For more information, see the discussion of the BY statement in the chapter "Statements Used in the PROC Step," in the *SAS User's Guide: Basics.*

DETAILS

Missing Values

The dependent variables are grouped based on the similarity of their missing values. This feature is similar to the way GLM treats missing values.

Printed Output

VARCOMP prints the following items:

1. CLASS LEVEL INFORMATION for verifying the levels and number of observations in your data
2. for METHOD=TYPE1, an analysis-of-variance table with SOURCE, DF, TYPE I SS, TYPE I MS, and EXPECTED MEAN SQUARE
3. for METHOD=MIVQUE0, the SSQ MATRIX containing sums of squares of partitions of the **X'X** cross-products matrix adjusted for the fixed effects. Each element (i,j) of this matrix is computed:

   $$SSQ(X_i'MX_j)$$

   where

   $$M = I - X_0(X_0'X_0)^{-1}X_0'$$

   $\mathbf{X}_0$ is part of the design matrix for the fixed effects,
   $\mathbf{X}_i$ is part of the design matrix for one of the random effects, and
   SSQ is an operator that takes the sum of squares of the elements.
4. for METHOD=ML and METHOD=REML, the iteration history, including the OBJECTIVE function, as well as variance component estimates
5. for METHOD=ML and METHOD=REML, the estimated asymptotic covariance matrix of the variance components.

EXAMPLE

PROC VARCOMP for Four Estimation Methods

In this example, A and B are classification variables and Y is the dependent variable. A is declared fixed, and B and A*B are random. VARCOMP is invoked four times, one for each of the estimation methods. The data are from Hemmerle and Hartley (1973).

```
DATA A;
   INPUT A B Y @@;
   CARDS;
1 1 237 1 1 254 1 1 246 1 2 178 1 2 179 2 1 208
2 1 178 2 1 187 2 2 146 2 2 145 2 2 141 3 1 186
3 1 183 3 2 142 3 2 125 3 2 136
;

PROC VARCOMP METHOD=TYPE1;
   CLASS A B;
   MODEL Y=A|B / FIXED=1;

PROC VARCOMP METHOD=MIVQUE0;
   CLASS A B;
```

```
   MODEL Y=A|B / FIXED=1;

PROC VARCOMP METHOD=ML;
   CLASS A B;
   MODEL Y=A|B / FIXED=1;

PROC VARCOMP METHOD=REML;
   CLASS A B;
   MODEL Y=A|B / FIXED=1;
```

Output 41.1 VARCOMP Procedure Invoked Once for Each Estimation Method

```
                                                                                1
           ❶      VARIANCE COMPONENT ESTIMATION PROCEDURE

                        CLASS LEVEL INFORMATION

                       CLASS      LEVELS     VALUES

                       A               3      1 2 3

                       B               2      1 2

                  NUMBER OF OBSERVATIONS IN DATA SET = 16
```

```
                                                                                2
           ❷      VARIANCE COMPONENT ESTIMATION PROCEDURE

DEPENDENT VARIABLE: Y

SOURCE               DF        TYPE I SS        TYPE I MS      EXPECTED MEAN SQUARE

A                     2   11736.43750000    5868.21875000      VAR(ERROR) + 2.725 VAR(A*B) + 0.1 VAR(B) + Q(A)

B                     1   11448.12564103   11448.12564103      VAR(ERROR) + 2.63076923 VAR(A*B) + 7.8 VAR(B)

A*B                   2     299.04102564     149.52051282      VAR(ERROR) + 2.58461538 VAR(A*B)

ERROR                10     786.33333333      78.63333333      VAR(ERROR)

CORRECTED TOTAL      15   24269.93750000


VARIANCE COMPONENT                ESTIMATE

VAR(B)                       1448.37683150

VAR(A*B)                       27.42658730

VAR(ERROR)                     78.63333333
```

```
                                                                                3
                  VARIANCE COMPONENT ESTIMATION PROCEDURE

                        CLASS LEVEL INFORMATION

                       CLASS      LEVELS     VALUES

                       A               3      1 2 3

                       B               2      1 2

                  NUMBER OF OBSERVATIONS IN DATA SET = 16
```

4

❸ MIVQUE(0) VARIANCE COMPONENT ESTIMATION PROCEDURE

SSQ MATRIX

SOURCE	B	A*B	ERROR	Y
B	60.84000000	20.52000000	7.80000000	89295.38000000
A*B	20.52000000	20.52000000	7.80000000	30181.30000000
ERROR	7.80000000	7.80000000	13.00000000	12533.50000000

VARIANCE COMPONENT	ESTIMATE Y
VAR(B)	1466.12301587
VAR(A*B)	-35.49170274
VAR(ERROR)	105.73659674

5

VARIANCE COMPONENT ESTIMATION PROCEDURE

CLASS LEVEL INFORMATION

CLASS	LEVELS	VALUES
A	3	1 2 3
B	2	1 2

NUMBER OF OBSERVATIONS IN DATA SET = 16

6

❹ MAXIMUM LIKELIHOOD VARIANCE COMPONENT ESTIMATION PROCEDURE

DEPENDENT VARIABLE: Y

ITERATION	OBJECTIVE	VAR(B)	VAR(A*B)	VAR(ERROR)
0	78.38503712	1031.49069751	0.00000074	74.39097179
1	78.27509393	803.16016856	0.00000000	76.46378992
2	78.26354795	723.03651500	0.00000000	77.53998860
3	78.26354713	723.58608059	0.00000000	77.53169511
4	78.26354712	723.65578949	0.00000000	77.53064414
5	78.26354712	723.66456063	0.00000000	77.53051192

CONVERGENCE CRITERION MET

❺ ASYMPTOTIC COVARIANCE MATRIX OF ESTIMATES

	VAR(B)	VAR(A*B)	VAR(ERROR)
VAR(B)	537822.408	0.000	-107.325
VAR(A*B)	0.000	0.000	0.000
VAR(ERROR)	-107.325	0.000	858.711

7

VARIANCE COMPONENT ESTIMATION PROCEDURE

CLASS LEVEL INFORMATION

CLASS	LEVELS	VALUES
A	3	1 2 3
B	2	1 2

NUMBER OF OBSERVATIONS IN DATA SET = 16

8

RESTRICTED MAXIMUM LIKELIHOOD VARIANCE COMPONENT ESTIMATION PROCEDURE

DEPENDENT VARIABLE: Y

ITERATION	OBJECTIVE	VAR(B)	VAR(A*B)	VAR(ERROR)
0	63.19653900	1204.93525180	8.68997700	86.89976996
1	64.84803833	1162.77184351	279.34207242	68.78245514
2	63.88623682	1521.83227699	134.83280638	69.42595882
3	67.02954536	1621.74262131	953.93349024	64.93143329
4	65.62472542	1450.34333796	446.96962311	66.52873464
5	64.46892860	1469.91496765	213.85899747	68.10602900
6	63.65864246	1507.78034719	108.75650645	70.35561998
7	63.18826611	1616.11496909	55.82862443	73.44082580
8	63.04004056	1570.08491597	22.34487489	79.61050851
9	63.03132294	1445.28075491	26.38872409	79.07890958
10	63.03113760	1460.68840357	26.80128863	78.89947386
11	63.03112713	1463.53401192	26.92087555	78.85586243
12	63.03112655	1464.17236132	26.94990196	78.84555646
13	63.03112651	1464.32154830	26.95674970	78.84313341
14	63.03112651	1464.35654217	26.95835893	78.84256439

CONVERGENCE CRITERION MET

ASYMPTOTIC COVARIANCE MATRIX OF ESTIMATES

	VAR(B)	VAR(A*B)	VAR(ERROR)
VAR(B)	4401575.70	1.23	-273.23
VAR(A*B)	1.23	3559.01	-502.85
VAR(ERROR)	-273.23	-502.85	1249.70

REFERENCES

Gaylor, D.W., Lucas, H.L., and Anderson, R.L. (1970), "Calculations of Expected Mean Squares by the Abbreviated Doolittle and Square Root Method," *Biometrics*, 26, 641-655.

Goodnight, J.H. (1978), "Computing MIVQUE0 Estimates of Variance Components," SAS Technical Report R-105. Cary, NC: SAS Institute Inc.

Goodnight, J.H. and Hemmerle, W.J. (1979), "A Simplified Algorithm for the W-Transformation in Variance Component Estimation," *Technometrics*, 21, 265-268.

Hartley, H.O., Rao, J.N.K., and LaMotte, Lynn (1978), "A Simple Synthesis-Based Method of Variance Component Estimation," *Biometrics*, 34, 233-242.

Hemmerle, W.J. and Hartley, H.O. (1973), "Computing Maximum Likelihood Estimates for the Mixed AOV Model Using the W-Transformation," *Technometrics*, 15, 819-831.

Patterson, H.D. and Thompson, R. (1971), "Recovery of Inter-Block Information When Block Sizes Are Unequal," *Biometrika*, 58, 545-554.

Rao, C.R. (1971), "Minimum Variance Quadratic Unbiased Estimation of Variance Components," *Journal of Multivariate Analysis*, 1, 445-456.

Rao, C.R. (1972), "Estimation of Variance and Covariance Components in Linear Models," *Journal of the American Statistical Association*, 57, 112-15.

APPENDICES

Special SAS® Data Sets

Version 5 Changes and Enhancements to Base SAS® Software: Statistics

Operating System Notes

Full-Screen Editing

SAS® Display Manager

Appendix 1
Special SAS® Data Sets

In addition to standard SAS data sets and transport-format SAS data sets, there are several specially structured SAS data sets that are used by some SAS statistical procedures. These SAS data sets are in standard format, but they contain special variables and observations. These special data sets are usually created by SAS statistical procedures, but you can also use a DATA step to create a special SAS data set in the proper format. If created by a DATA step, you use the TYPE= data set option to indicate the data set's type to SAS.

TYPE=CORR Data Sets

A TYPE=CORR data set contains a correlation matrix along with the variable means, standard deviations, the number of observations in the original SAS data set from which the correlation matrix was computed, and possibly other statistics (depending on which procedure created the SAS data set).

Using PROC CORR with an output data set specification automatically produces a TYPE=CORR data set. You can also create a TYPE=CORR data set from input data that contain a correlation matrix (see the example below). In this case, TYPE=CORR must be specified as a data set option.

TYPE=CORR data sets can be used as input for PROC FACTOR, PROC REG, and other procedures.

Variables in a TYPE=CORR data set When a BY statement is used with PROC CORR, the BY variable(s) appears first in the data set. Next come two special character variables, each eight characters long. The first is named _TYPE_, and its values identify the type of each observation in the TYPE=CORR data set (MEAN, STD, N, CORR). The second special variable is named _NAME_, and its values identify the variable with which a given row of the correlation matrix is associated. The variables from the original data set that were analyzed by PROC CORR come next.

Observations in a TYPE=CORR data set For the first observation, which contains the variable mean, the _TYPE_ variable's value is 'MEAN'; for the second observation, containing standard deviations, _TYPE_'s value is 'STD'; for the third observation, containing the number of observations, _TYPE_'s value is 'N'. The _NAME_ variable's value is blank for these first three observations.

The first three observations are produced when PROC CORR creates the TYPE=CORR data set. However, if you create the TYPE=CORR data set, the data set need not contain these three observations. Any procedure that uses the data set uses 0 for all the variable means, 1 for all the standard deviations, and 100 for the number of observations, with the exception of CANCORR, CANDISC, FACTOR, PRINCOMP, RSQUARE, STEPDISC, and VARCLUS, which use 10,000 for the number of observations.

Following the first three observations are the observations containing the correlation matrix; one for each row of the matrix. _TYPE_'s value for each of these observations is 'CORR'. _NAME_'s value for each observation is the variable name associated with that observation (row).

A TYPE=CORR data set: example 1 See **Output A1.1** for an example of a TYPE=CORR data set containing a 2-variable correlation matrix. In the output, 12.2 and -4.5 are the means of X and Y; 3.2 and 1.1 are the standard deviations of X and Y; 5 is the number of observations containing X and Y; and .7 is the correlation between X and Y.

Output A1.1 A TYPE=CORR SAS Data Set with Two-variable Matrix

OBS	_TYPE_	_NAME_	X	Y
1	MEAN		12.2	-4.5
2	STD		3.2	1.1
3	N		5.0	5.0
4	CORR	X	1.0	0.7
5	CORR	Y	0.7	1.0

Using BY variables: example 2 **Output A1.2** shows an example of a TYPE=CORR data set created with PROC CORR and a BY statement:

```
PROC CORR DATA=MEASURE OUTP=CORMAT;
   BY SEX;
   VAR A B C;
PROC PRINT;
```

Output A1.2 A TYPE=CORR SAS Data Set with BY Variables

OBS	SEX	_TYPE_	_NAME_	A	B	C
1	F	MEAN		14.7	29.6	9.6
2	F	STD		1.2	3.1	0.7
3	F	N		23.0	22.0	23.0
4	F	CORR	A	1.0	0.8	0.3
5	F	CORR	B	0.8	1.0	0.6
6	F	CORR	C	0.3	0.6	1.0
7	M	MEAN		12.3	33.4	7.6
8	M	STD		1.1	2.9	0.9
9	M	N		31.0	33.0	32.0
10	M	CORR	A	1.0	0.4	0.8
11	M	CORR	B	0.4	1.0	0.3
12	M	CORR	C	0.8	0.3	1.0

Creating a TYPE=CORR data set in a DATA step: example 3 This example creates a TYPE=CORR data set by reading an input correlation matrix in a DATA step. The matrix is for three variables. **Output A1.3** shows the new data set.

```
DATA CORRMATR(TYPE=CORR);
   INPUT (A B C) (10.7);
   _TYPE_='CORR';
   LENGTH _NAME_ $ 8.;
   IF_N_=1 THEN _NAME_='A';
   IF_N_=2 THEN _NAME_='B';
   IF_N_=3 THEN _NAME_='C';
   CARDS;
1.0000000 0.6198688 0.5297345
0.6198688 1.0000000 0.4292545
0.5297345 0.4292545 1.0000000
;
PROC PRINT;
TITLE 'TYPE=CORR Data Set';
```

Output A1.3 A TYPE=CORR SAS Data Set Created By a DATA Step

TYPE=CORR Data Set 1

OBS	A	B	C	_TYPE_	_NAME_
1	1.00000	0.61987	0.52973	CORR	A
2	0.61987	1.00000	0.42925	CORR	B
3	0.52973	0.42925	1.00000	CORR	C

TYPE=COV Data Sets

A TYPE=COV data set is similar to a TYPE=CORR data set, except that it has _TYPE_='COV' observations rather than _TYPE_='CORR' observations, and it contains a covariance matrix rather than a correlation matrix. COV data sets are created by PROC PRINCOMP if the COV option is specified. PROC CORR produces COV data sets if the COV and NOCORR options are specified and the OUT= data set is assigned TYPE=COV with the TYPE= data set option. For example:

```
PROC CORR COV NOCORR OUT=CVMTRX(TYPE=COV);
```

TYPE=COV data sets are used by these procedures: CANCORR, CANDISC, FACTOR, PRINCOMP, and VARCLUS.

TYPE=SSCP Data Sets

TYPE=SSCP data sets are used to store the uncorrected sums of squares and crossproducts for variables. TYPE=SSCP data sets are produced automatically by PROC REG when OUTSSCP= is specified in the PROC REG statement. You can also create TYPE=SSCP data sets in a DATA step, and in this case TYPE=SSCP must be specified as a data set option.

Variables in a TYPE=SSCP data set If a BY statement is used with PROC REG, the BY variable(s) is first in the TYPE=SSCP data set. The next variable is a special character variable, _NAME_, eight characters long, whose values are the variable names in the original data set from which the SSCP matrix was computed. The next variable is INTERCEP, whose values are the variable sums. Finally come the variables from the original data set that appear in the VAR statement or a MODEL statement.

Observations in a TYPE=SSCP data set For the first observation in the TYPE=SSCP data set, the _NAME_ variable's value is 'INTERCEP'. The value of the INTERCEP variable for this first observation is the number of observations in the original data set. The values of the remaining variables for the INTERCEP observation are the sums of the variables. For the second and following observations in the TYPE=SSCP data set, the _NAME_ variable's value is the name of the corresponding variable in the original data set. The INTERCEP variable's values contain the variable sums. The other variables' values are the sums of the products for the variables.

Using REG with a BY statement: example 4 Output A1.4 shows a TYPE=SSCP data set created when PROC REG was used with a BY statement. The variables were X and Y.

Output A1.4 A TYPE=SSCP SAS Data Set with BY Variable

OBS	STATE	_NAME_	INTERCEP	X	Y
1	NC	INTERCEP	7.0	350.6	126.6
2	NC	X	350.6	17722.8	6416.9
3	NC	Y	126.6	6416.9	2334.5
4	VA	INTERCEP	8.0	413.1	114.3
5	VA	X	413.1	21484.9	6058.8
6	VA	Y	114.3	6058.8	1811.1

As you can see in the output, for STATE='NC', 7 is the number of observations, 350.6 and 126.6 are the sums of X and Y respectively; 17722.8 and 2334.5 are the sums of X2 and Y2; and 6416.9 is the sum of the crossproducts of X and Y. If a WEIGHT statement is used with PROC REG (for weighted least squares analyses), then the sum of the weights replaces the number of observations in the TYPE=SSCP data set, and all sums of products are weighted.

TYPE=FACTOR Data Sets

TYPE=FACTOR data sets, created automatically by PROC FACTOR when an output data set is specified, contain information about factor analyses. PROC FACTOR and PROC SCORE use TYPE=FACTOR data sets as input.

Variables in a TYPE=FACTOR data set The variables in a TYPE=FACTOR data set correspond to those in a TYPE=CORR data set: BY variables, if any; _TYPE_; _NAME_; and the names of the variables used by PROC FACTOR.

Observations in a TYPE=FACTOR data set Each observation in the output data set contains some type of statistic as indicated by the _TYPE_ variable. The _NAME_ variable is blank except where otherwise indicated. The values of the _TYPE_ variable are as follows:

TYPE	**Contents**
MEAN	means.
STD	standard deviations.
N	sample size.
CORR	correlations. The _NAME_ variable contains the name of the variable corresponding to each row of the correlation matrix.
IMAGE	image coefficients. The _NAME_ variable contains the name of the variable corresponding to each row of the image coefficient matrix.
IMAGECOV	image covariance matrix. The _NAME_ variable contains the name of the variable corresponding to each row of the image covariance matrix.
COMMUNAL	final communality estimates.
PRIOR	prior communality estimates, or estimates from the last iteration for iterative methods.
WEIGHT	variable weights.
EIGENVAL	eigenvalues.
UNROTATE	unrotated factor pattern. The _NAME_ variable contains the name of the factor.
RESIDUAL	residual correlations. The _NAME_ variable contains the name of the variable corresponding to each row of the residual correlation matrix.
TRANSFOR	transformation matrix from rotation. The _NAME_ variable contains the name of the factor.
TCORR	inter-factor correlations. The _NAME_ variable contains the name of the factor.
PATTERN	factor pattern. The _NAME_ variable contains the name of the factor.
RCORR	reference axis correlations. The _NAME_ variable contains the name of the factor.
REFERENC	reference structure. The _NAME_ variable contains the name of the factor.
STRUCTUR	factor structure. The _NAME_ variable contains the name of the factor.

SCORE scoring coefficients. The _NAME_ variable contains the name of the factor.

For an example of a TYPE=FACTOR data set, see the description of PROC FACTOR.

TYPE=EST Data Sets

TYPE=EST data sets, produced by PROC REG when the OUTEST= option is specified, store the coefficients of linear models.

Variables in a TYPE=EST data set If a BY statement is used with PROC REG, the BY variables appear first in the TYPE=EST data set. Next comes the character variable _TYPE_, eight characters long, which indicates the source of the coefficients (identity, OLS, 2SLS). The variable _MODEL_ is next, and it contains the label that is associated with the MODEL statement in PROC REG. _DEPVAR_ contains the name of the dependent variable. Next is the variable _SIGMA_, which contains the standard deviation for the error term. The regression coefficients of the variables in the model appear next in the order they first appear in a MODEL statement. The last variable in the data set is INTERCEP, which contains the equation constant.

If the COVOUT option is used in PROC REG, the covariance matrix of the estimates is output after the parameter estimates. The value of the _TYPE_ variable for these observations is COVB, and the rows are identified by the value of the _MODEL_ variable.

Observations in a TYPE=EST data set The TYPE=EST data set has one observation for each dependent variable on the left-hand side of a MODEL statement specified with PROC REG.

Creating a TYPE=EST data set: example 5 **Output A1.5** shows the TYPE=EST data set produced by the PROC REG step below.

```
PROC REG OUTEST=B;
   L1: MODEL Y=X W;
   L2: MODEL W=Z;
PROC PRINT;
TITLE 'TYPE=EST Data Set';
```

Output A1.5 A TYPE=EST SAS Data Set

TYPE=EST Data Set 1

OBS	_TYPE_	_MODEL_	_DEPVAR_	_SIGMA_	Y	X	W	Z	INTERCEP
1	OLS	L1	Y	0.567	-1	0.234	0.045	.	4.3338
2	OLS	L2	W	0.400	.	.	-1.000	0.309	2.9877

TYPE=DISCAL Data Sets

The TYPE=DISCAL data set contains calibration information developed PROC DISCRIM. TYPE=DISCAL data sets can be used by PROC DISCRIM to classify observations in other data sets.

Variables in a TYPE=DISCAL data set The first variable in a TYPE=DISCAL data set is the _TYPE_ variable; its values identify the type of each observation in the data set. The second variable is the variable specified in the CLASS statement of PROC DISCRIM. _LNDET_ is the third variable; it contains the log determinant of the covariance matrix. The next variable is _PRIOR_, the prior probability of classification membership. The remaining variables are those specified in the VAR statement of PROC DISCRIM.

Observations in a TYPE=DISCAL data set The first observation has one of four values for _TYPE_: PLEQ, PLPR, NOEQ, or NOPR. These values indicate whether the analysis is based on the pooled (PL) or within-group (NO) covariance matrix, and whether the prior probabilities are equal (EQ) or proportional (PR). The next observation contains the means for all variables listed in the VAR statement (_TYPE_='MEAN'). If POOL=YES, all _TYPE_='MEAN' observations are printed before the remaining observation types. The next observation contains the standard deviation (_TYPE_='STD'). There is one _TYPE_='STD' observation if POOL=YES; if POOL=NO there are as many STD observations as levels of the CLASS variable. The remaining observations are _TYPE_='RINV'; one for each row of each correlation inverse matrix. There is one matrix if POOL=YES. If POOL=NO, there is a matrix for each level of the CLASS variable.

A DISCAL data set with POOL=NO: example 6 **Output A1.6** shows a TYPE=DISCAL data set produced by PROC DISCRIM with POOL=NO.

Output A1.6 A TYPE=DISCAL SAS Data Set with POOL=NO

REMOTE SENSING DATA ON FIVE CROPS
CLASSIFICATION OF CROP DATA

OBS	_TYPE_	CROP	_LNDET_	_PRIOR_	X1	X2	X3	X4
1	NOEQ		5.0000	.	.	.	.	.
2	MEAN	CLOVER	23.6462	0.2	46.364	32.636	34.182	36.636
3	STD	CLOVER	23.6462	0.2	25.905	17.078	20.517	20.568
4	RINV	CLOVER	23.6462	0.2	1.294	-0.002	-0.557	-0.450
5	RINV	CLOVER	23.6462	0.2	-0.002	1.346	-0.653	0.091
6	RINV	CLOVER	23.6462	0.2	-0.557	-0.653	1.633	0.435
7	RINV	CLOVER	23.6462	0.2	-0.450	0.091	0.435	1.238
8	MEAN	CORN	11.1347	0.2	15.286	22.714	27.429	33.143
9	STD	CORN	11.1347	0.2	1.799	6.448	5.623	18.632
10	RINV	CORN	11.1347	0.2	3.768	1.063	1.815	5.153
11	RINV	CORN	11.1347	0.2	1.063	2.055	0.372	2.486
12	RINV	CORN	11.1347	0.2	1.815	0.372	4.146	5.115
13	RINV	CORN	11.1347	0.2	5.153	2.486	5.115	10.915
14	MEAN	COTTON	13.2357	0.2	34.500	32.667	35.000	39.167
15	STD	COTTON	13.2357	0.2	9.566	8.664	19.890	20.478
16	RINV	COTTON	13.2357	0.2	49.877	1.466	-53.645	-14.7044
17	RINV	COTTON	13.2357	0.2	1.466	36.516	-39.363	-16.9000
18	RINV	COTTON	13.2357	0.2	-53.645	-39.363	97.963	33.239
19	RINV	COTTON	13.2357	0.2	-14.704	-16.900	33.239	12.888
20	MEAN	SOYBEANS	12.4526	0.2	21.000	27.000	23.500	29.667
21	STD	SOYBEANS	12.4526	0.2	5.060	10.714	5.128	11.843
22	RINV	SOYBEANS	12.4526	0.2	10.861	-2.052	-6.386	5.558
23	RINV	SOYBEANS	12.4526	0.2	-2.052	4.287	-1.082	1.377
24	RINV	SOYBEANS	12.4526	0.2	-6.386	-1.082	6.097	-4.675
25	RINV	SOYBEANS	12.4526	0.2	5.558	1.377	-4.675	5.355
26	MEAN	SUGARBEETS	17.7629	0.2	31.000	32.167	20.000	40.500
27	STD	SUGARBEETS	17.7629	0.2	11.967	13.152	10.257	16.489
28	RINV	SUGARBEETS	17.7629	0.2	2.020	-0.454	-2.003	-2.569
29	RINV	SUGARBEETS	17.7629	0.2	-0.454	3.091	4.098	3.572
30	RINV	SUGARBEETS	17.7629	0.2	-2.003	4.098	8.702	7.895
31	RINV	SUGARBEETS	17.7629	0.2	-2.569	3.572	7.895	8.534

A DISCAL data set with POOL=YES: example 7 **Output A1.7** shows a TYPE=DISCAL data set produced by PROC DISCRIM using the same original data set, but with POOL=YES.

Output A1.7 A TYPE=DISCAL SAS Data Set with POOL=YES

```
                    REMOTE SENSING DATA ON FIVE
                    CLASSIFICATION OF CROP DATA

OBS _TYPE_  CROP        _LNDET_   _PRIOR_   X1        X2        X3        X4

  1  PLEQ                  5        .        .         .         .         .
  2  MEAN   CLOVER         .       0.2    46.3636   32.6364   34.1818   36.6364
  3  MEAN   CORN           .       0.2    15.2857   22.7143   27.4286   33.1429
  4  MEAN   COTTON         .       0.2    34.5000   32.6667   35.0000   39.1667
  5  MEAN   SOYBEANS       .       0.2    21.0000   27.0000   23.5000   29.6667
  6  MEAN   SUGARBEETS     .       0.2    31.0000   32.1667   20.0000   40.5000
  7  STD                   .        .     16.0960   12.6748   15.0642   18.3787
  8  RINV                  .        .      1.2881   -0.0463   -0.5969   -0.4027
  9  RINV                  .        .     -0.0463    1.2270   -0.4620    0.1129
 10  RINV                  .        .     -0.5969   -0.4620    1.6007    0.5365
 11  RINV                  .        .     -0.4027    0.1129    0.5365    1.2672
```

Appendix 2
Version 5 Changes and Enhancements to Base SAS® Software: Statistics

ACECLUS Procedure
ANOVA Procedure
CANCORR Procedure
CANDISC Procedure
CATMOD Procedure
CLUSTER Procedure
FACTOR Procedure
FASTCLUS Procedure
FREQ Procedure
GLM Procedure
LIFEREG Procedure
LIFETEST Procedure
NLIN Procedure
RANK Procedure
REG Procedure
RSQUARE Procedure
STANDARD Procedure
  FREQ Statement
  WEIGHT Statement
STEPDISC Procedure
TREE Procedure
VARCLUS Procedure
VARCOMP Procedure
  The restricted maximum-likelihood method

ACECLUS Procedure

ACECLUS (Approximate Covariance Estimation for CLUStering) is a new procedure that obtains approximate estimates of the pooled within-cluster covariance matrix when the clusters can be assumed multivariate normal with equal covariance matrices. Neither cluster membership nor the number of clusters need be known. ACECLUS is useful for preprocessing data to be subsequently clustered by CLUSTER or FASTCLUS. ACECLUS can produce output data sets containing the approximate within-cluster covariance estimate, eigenvalues and eigenvectors from a canonical analysis, and canonical variable scores. The method is a variation on an algorithm developed by Art, Gnanadesikan, and Kettenring (1982).

ANOVA Procedure

There are several important enhancements to the ANOVA procedure. The ANOVA procedure is now better equipped to handle repeated measures designs. The REPEATED statement allows you to specify effects in the model that represent repeated measurements on the same experimental unit and provides both univariate and multivariate tests of hypotheses.

The following *transformation* keywords define single-degree-of-freedom contrasts for factors specified on the REPEATED statement.

CONTRAST {(*ordinalreferencelevel*)}
: generates contrasts between levels of the factor and, optionally, a reference level that corresponds to the ordinal value of the level.

POLYNOMIAL
: generates orthogonal polynomial contrasts.

HELMERT
: generates contrasts between each level of the factor and the mean of subsequent levels.

MEAN {(*ordinalreferencelevel*)}
: generates contrasts between levels of the factor and the mean of all other levels of the factor.

PROFILE
: generates contrasts between adjacent levels of the factor.

The following options can appear in the REPEATED statement after a slash (/):

NOM
: prints only the results of the univariate analyses.

NOU
: prints only the results of the multivariate analyses.

PRINTM
: prints the transformation matrices that define the contrasts in the analysis.

PRINTH
: prints the **H** (SSCP) matrix associated with each multivariate test.

PRINTE
: prints the **E** matrix for each combination of within-subject factors, as well as partial correlation matrices for both the original dependent variables and the variables defined by the transformations specified in the REPEATED statement. In addition, the PRINTE option provides sphericity tests for each set of transformed variables. If the requested transformations are not orthogonal, the PRINTE option also provides a sphericity test for a set of orthogonal contrasts.

PRINTRV
: prints the characteristic roots and vectors for each multivariate test.

SHORT
: prints the multivariate test criteria and associated F statistics in a condensed form.

SUMMARY
: produces analysis-of-variance tables for each contrast defined by the within-subjects factors.

CANONICAL
: requests a canonical analysis of the **H** and **E** matrices corresponding to the transformed variables specified in the REPEATED statement.

The term below is now specified in the MANOVA statement:

M=*equation1,equation2,...*
: specifies a transformation matrix for the dependent variables listed in the MODEL statement.

The following two options allow you to specify labels for the transformed variables defined by the M= option:

MNAMES=*names*
: provides names for the variables defined by the equations in the M= specification. Names in the list correspond to the M= equations.

PREFIX=*name*
: is an alternative means of identifying the transformed variables defined by the M= specification. For example, if you specify PREFIX=DIFF, the transformed variables are labeled DIFF1, DIFF2, and so forth.

Four new options are now available for use in the MANOVA statement:

ORTH
: requests that the transformation matrix in the M= specification of the MANOVA statement be orthonormalized by rows prior to the analysis.

SHORT
: prints the multivariate test statistics and associated *F* statistics in a condensed form.

CANONICAL
: requests that a canonical analysis of the **H** and **E** matrices (transformed by the **M** matrix if specified) be printed instead of the default printout of characteristic roots and vectors.

SUMMARY
: produces analysis-of-variance tables for each dependent variable.

A new option can now be specified in the MODEL statement. The INTERCEPT (or INT) option requests that GLM print the hypothesis tests associated with the intercept as an effect in the model.

CANCORR Procedure

The CANCORR procedure has changed the options for printing output. Skewness and kurtosis are no longer printed, and an option is available to suppress printed output.

CANDISC Procedure

The CANDISC procedure now has new options available to produce printed output, such as the total SSCP matrix.

CATMOD Procedure

The CATMOD procedure replaces PROC FUNCAT, which appeared in previous versions of base SAS software. The major enhancements contained in the CATMOD procedure are features that facilitate repeated measurement analysis and log-linear modeling. Moreover, there are numerous design features that make the CATMOD procedure more flexible and more informative than FUNCAT. CATMOD fits linear models to functions of response frequencies, and it can be used for linear modeling, log-linear modeling, logistic regression, and repeated measurement analysis.

CLUSTER Procedure

You can now use either distances or coordinates as input to the CLUSTER procedure. If the input data set is TYPE=DISTANCE, the data are interpreted as a distance matrix. If the data set is not TYPE=DISTANCE, the data are interpreted as coordinates in a Euclidean space.

There are eight additional clustering methods now available:

- complete linkage, in which the distance between two clusters is the maximum distance between an observation in one cluster and an observation in the other cluster
- density linkage, a class of clustering methods using nonparametric probability density estimation
- EML, maximum-likelihood hierarchical clustering for mixtures of spherical multivariate normal distributions with equal variances but possibly unequal mixing proportions
- the Lance-Williams flexible-beta method
- McQuitty's similarity analysis
- Gower's median method
- single linkage, in which the distance between two clusters is the minimum distance between an observation in one cluster and an observation in the other cluster
- two-stage density linkage, a modification of density linkage that ensures that all points are assigned to modal clusters before the modal clusters are allowed to join.

If you request an analysis that requires density estimation, you must specify one of three new options: K=, R=, or HYBRID.

Three more new options (NOSQUARE, TRIM=, and DIM=) affect data processing before the actual clustering.

There are other new options affecting the printout of the cluster history. If the data are coordinates or if you specify METHOD=AVERAGE, CENTROID, or WARD, you can request the following: the root-mean-square standard deviation of each cluster; the cubic clustering criterion and expected R^2 under the uniform null hypothesis; and the pseudo *F* and t^2 statistics. The R^2 and semipartial R^2 statistics are always printed if METHOD=WARD, and they can be requested if the data are coordinates or METHOD=AVERAGE or CENTROID. You can also suppress printing of ID values at each generation of cluster history. With most methods, you can prevent distances from being normalized to unit mean or unit root mean square.

FACTOR Procedure

There are two new options available in the PROC FACTOR statement. OUT=, an alias of OUTSTAT= in SAS Release 82, is now a separate data set option. The OUT= data set contains all the data from the DATA= data set plus variables containing estimated factor scores. The other new option, PRIORS=, can be used instead of the PRIORS statement. With the PRIORS= option, you can specify values between 0.0 and 1.0 for the prior communality estimates for each variable.

The SINGULAR= option replaces the TOLERANCE= option.

These are additional differences in PROC FACTOR:

- When two or more eigenvalues are nearly equal, the corresponding eigenvectors may be different on different machines, but the eigenvectors still span the same subspace.
- When ROTATE=HK is specified, the rotated factors may appear in different orders on different machines.
- The scaling of the axes in the scree plot may differ between SAS Release 82 and Version 5 of the SAS System.

FASTCLUS Procedure

You can no longer use MAXGROUPS= or MAXG= as aliases for MAXCLUSTERS=.

The new CLUSTER= option allows you to specify a name other than CLUSTER for the variable in the OUT= and MEAN= data sets that indicates cluster membership.

If you specify REPLACE=RANDOM, you can also use RANDOM= to specify a positive integer as the starting value for the pseudo-random number generator.

There are two new options to control computation of final cluster seeds:

- the STRICT= option prevents an observation from being assigned to a cluster if its distance to the nearest cluster seed exceeds the specified value
- the DELETE= option deletes cluster seeds with too few observations.

Three new options affect the printed output: DISTANCE, SUMMARY, and NOPRINT.

Also, PROC FASTCLUS has a new option, IMPUTE, that requests imputation of missing values in the OUT= data set.

FASTCLUS now supports the VARDEF= option that allows you to specify the divisor when calculating variances and covariances.

FREQ Procedure

The FREQ procedure has many new tests and measures of association for two-way tables available. The MEASURES option requests a basic set of measures of association and their errors. The CMH option requests stratified analysis on *n*-way tables. The ALL option now specifies all MEASURES and CMH tests and measures.

GLM Procedure

There are several important enhancements to the GLM procedure: The GLM procedure is now better equipped to handle repeated measures designs. The REPEATED statement allows you to specify effects in the model that represent repeated measurements on the same experimental unit and provides both univariate and multivariate tests of hypotheses.

The following *transformation* keywords define single-degree-of-freedom contrasts for factors specified on the REPEATED statement:

CONTRAST {(*ordinalreferencelevel*)}
generates contrasts between levels of the factor and, optionally, a reference level that corresponds to the ordinal value of the level.

POLYNOMIAL
generates orthogonal polynomial contrasts.

HELMERT
generates contrasts between each level of the factor and the mean of subsequent levels.

MEAN {(*ordinalreferencelevel*)}
generates contrasts between levels of the factor and the mean of all other levels of the factor.

PROFILE
generates contrasts between adjacent levels of the factor.

The following options can appear in the REPEATED statement after a slash (/):

NOM
prints only the results of the univariate analyses.

NOU
prints only the results of the multivariate analyses.

PRINTM
prints the transformation matrices that define the contrasts in the analysis.

PRINTH
prints the **H** (SSCP) matrix associated with each multivariate test.

PRINTE
prints the **E** matrix for each combination of within-subject factors, as well as partial correlation matrices for both the original dependent variables and the variables defined by the transformations specified in the REPEATED statement. In addition, the PRINTE option provides sphericity tests for each set of transformed variables. If the requested transformations are not orthogonal, the PRINTE option also provides a sphericity test for a set of orthogonal contrasts.

PRINTRV
prints the characteristic roots and vectors for each multivariate test.

SHORT
prints the multivariate test criteria and associated F statistics in a condensed form.

SUMMARY
produces analysis-of-variance tables for each contrast defined by the within-subjects factors.

CANONICAL
requests a canonical analysis of the **H** and **E** matrices corresponding to the transformed variables specified in the REPEATED statement.

HTYPE=*n*
specifies the type of the **H** matrix used in the multivariate tests and the type of sums of squares used in the univariate tests.

You can now specify the order in which you want the levels of the classification variables (specified on the CLASSES statement) to be sorted by including the ORDER= option on the PROC GLM statement. If ORDER=FREQ is specified, levels are sorted by descending frequency count so that levels with the most observations come first. If ORDER=DATA is used, levels are sorted in the order in which they first occur in the input data. If ORDER=INTERNAL, then the levels are sorted by the internal value. If ORDER=FORMATTED, levels are ordered by the external formatted value. If you omit ORDER=, PROC GLM orders by the formatted value.

The tuning option SINGULAR= replaces the EPSILON= option. SINGULAR= is included on the CONTRAST, ESTIMATE, or LSMEANS statement and tunes the estimability checking. If ABS(**L**-**LH**)<CSINGULAR for any row, then the **L** is declared non-estimable. **H** is the **(X'X)⁻X'X** matrix, and **C** is ABS(**L**) except for rows where **L** is zero in which case it is 1. The default is 1E-4.

Besides the SINGULAR= option, the following options can be used on the LSMEANS statement:

E=*effect*
: specifies an effect in the model to use as an error term.

ETYPE=*n*
: specifies the type (1, 2, 3, or 4) of the E= effect.

The term below is now specified in the MANOVA statement:

M=*equation1,equation2,...*
: specifies a transformation matrix for the dependent variables listed in the MODEL statement.

The following two options allow you to specify labels for the transformed variables defined by the M= option:

MNAMES=*names*
: provides names for the variables defined by the equations in the M= specification. Names in the list correspond to the M= equations.

PREFIX=*name*
: is an alternative means of identifying the transformed variables defined by the M= specification. For example, if you specify PREFIX=DIFF, the transformed variables are labeled DIFF1, DIFF2, and so forth.

Four new options are now available for use in the MANOVA statement:

ORTH
: requests that the transformation matrix in the M= specification of the MANOVA statement be orthonormalized by rows prior to the analysis.

SHORT
: prints the multivariate test statistics and associated F statistics in a condensed form.

CANONICAL
: requests that a canonical analysis of the **H** and **E** matrices (transformed by the **M** matrix if specified) be printed instead of the default printout of characteristic roots and vectors.

SUMMARY
: produces analysis-of-variance tables for each dependent variable.

A new option can now be specified on the MODEL statement. The INTERCEPT (or INT) option requests that GLM print the hypothesis tests associated with the intercept as an effect in the model.

LIFEREG Procedure

LIFEREG is a new procedure that fits parametric models to failure-time data that may be right censored. The class of models includes exponential, Weibull, lognormal and log-logistic models. A common feature of lifetime or survival data is the presence of right-censored observations, due either to withdrawal of experimental units or termination of the experiment.

LIFETEST Procedure

LIFETEST is a new procedure that can be used with data that may be right censored to compute nonparametric estimates of the survival distribution and to compute rank tests for the association of the response variable with other variables.

NLIN Procedure

The NLIN procedure still does not support the DO OVER programming statement but does now support explicitly subscripted ARRAY statements and explicitly subscripted array references.

NLIN now supports all DATA step functions. However, in NLIN the LAG and DIF functions are not reset at the beginning of a new iteration although they operate correctly across observations.

NLIN now supports the RETAIN statement and some forms of the PUT statement but does not support INPUT, FILE, INFILE, SET, or MERGE statements.

A new data set option, OUTEST=, allows you to output parameter estimates, including those from the grid search and the iterative search.

The new G4 and G4SINGULAR options allow you to specify the inverse to use in parameter estimation; and two other options, TAU= and RHO=, let you control the step-size search.

New OUTPUT statement options enable you to have these additional statistics put in the OUT= data set:

- upper and lower 95% confidence limits for the expected values and individual predictions
- the standard error of the mean predicted value
- the standard error of the residual
- studentized residuals
- the leverage.

The ID statement is now supported by NLIN. With the ID statement, you can specify additional variables to include in the output data set, such as, the new special variables _HALVE_ and _LOSS_.

In addition to the features mentioned above, the current PROC NLIN version differs from previous releases in the following respects:

- Statements of the form

  MODEL Y=*expression;*

  are translated into the form

  MODEL.Y=*expression;*

  using the compound variable name MODEL.Y to hold the predicted value. You can use this assignment as an alternative to the MODEL statement.
- NLIN no longer requires all data to be in memory for DUD.

- NLIN no longer holds all data in memory even if it can. It passes through the data for every observation in every iteration.
- The dependent variable need not be in the input data set.
- In the past, NLIN with the DUD method depended on the property that actual values of the dependent variable did not change from iteration to iteration. The dependency has been eliminated so that NLIN can handle certain types of maximum-likelihood estimation that do change the dependent values.

RANK Procedure

The upper limit of 32767 has been removed. Now the maximum number of observations that can be ranked is (2^{31})-1. Numbers longer than seven digits can now be distinguished.

REG Procedure

The following options for regression calculations were added to PROC REG:

ACOV
: prints the estimated asymptotic covariance matrix of the estimates under the hypothesis of heteroskedasticity. This matrix is

$$(\mathbf{X'X}/n)^{-1}(\mathbf{X'diag(e^2{}_i)X}/n)(\mathbf{X'X}/n)^{-1}$$

where $e_i = y_i - X_i\beta$.

SPEC
: performs a test that the first and second moments of the model are correctly specified.

PCORR1
: prints the partial correlation coefficients using Type I sums of squares.

PCORR2
: prints the partial correlation coefficients using Type II sums of squares.

SCORR1
: prints the semi-partial correlation coefficients using Type I sums of squares.

SCORR2
: prints the semi-partial correlation coefficients using Type II sums of squares.

The following statistic can now be specified in the OUTPUT statement to be included in an output data set:

STDI=
: standard error of the individual predicted value.

RSQUARE Procedure

The FREQ and WEIGHT statements are now available in PROC RSQUARE.

New PROC statement options affect the printed output:

- SIMPLE prints the means and standard deviations.
- CORR prints the correlation matrix for all variables in the analysis.
- NOPRINT suppresses the regression output.

You can now input matrices as well as ordinary data, and an OUTEST= option allows you to output parameter estimates for selected models. The NOINT option can now be specified only in the PROC statement.

At least one MODEL statement must be specified. Options that can appear in the MODEL statement after a slash (/) can also appear in the PROC statement. However, the NOINT option is no longer available in the MODEL statement. One new MODEL statement option, SELECT=, allows you to specify the maximum number of subset models of each size to be printed or output. Fifteen more new options affect the computation and printing of statistics.

Previously, observations with missing values were used for models that did not contain the affected variables. This is no longer the case. The data are read only once, and observations with missing values for any variable used by the procedure are omitted from the entire analysis.

More efficient algorithms are used. If you specify PRINT=1, RSQUARE can be used for as many as twenty regressors. The amount of CPU time required is highly data dependent.

STANDARD Procedure

The option below can appear in the PROC STANDARD statement:

VARDEF=DF | WEIGHT | N | WDF

specifies the divisor to be used in the calculation of the variance. DF requests the degrees of freedom (N-1) be used as the divisor. WGT or WEIGHT requests the sum of the weights; N requests the number of observations (N); and WDF requests the sum of the weights minus one. The default divisor is DF.

Two new statements can now be used with PROC STANDARD:

FREQ Statement The FREQ statement specifies a numeric variable on the input SAS data set. If a FREQ statement is used, each observation in the input data set is assumed to represent *n* observations, where *n* is the value of the FREQ variable.

WEIGHT Statement The WEIGHT statement specifies a numeric variable on the input SAS data set, the values of which are used to weight each observation. The WEIGHT variable values can be nonintegers and are used to calculate a weighted mean and a weighted variance.

STEPDISC Procedure

The STEPDISC procedure has added PROB, FREQ, and WEIGHT statements. The input data can be TYPE=COV or TYPE=CORR produced by either the CANDISC procedure with the OUTSTAT= option or the CORR procedure using a BY statement.

TREE Procedure

The PRUNE= option is no longer in effect.

A new option, HEIGHT= can be used instead of the HEIGHT statement. With this option, you can make the height axis equal to one of the special variables _NCL_, _HEIGHT_, _MODEL_, or _RSQ_; or you can cause the height of each node to be defined as its path length from the root. Values of the height variable can be further specified using the new SIMILAR and DISSIMILAR options. MINHEIGHT= and MAXHEIGHT= allow you to specify minimum and maximum values to be printed on the height axis.

Other new options allow you to specify the character to print between clusters.

Using NCLUSTERS= and DOCK=, you can determine the number of clusters to be included in the output data set while preventing the inclusion of clusters whose frequency of occurrence is less than or equal to a specified value.

VARCLUS Procedure

The VAR statement is no longer necessary when the SEED statement is used.

You can suppress all or part of the printed output with NOPRINT and SUMMARY options.

If solutions are obtained for two or more different numbers of clusters, a summary table is printed at the end of the printout.

VARCOMP Procedure

An additional method of estimation is now available:

The restricted maximum-likelihood method Similar to the maximum-likelihood method is the REML method (METHOD=REML), but it first separates the likelihood into two parts; one that contains the fixed effects and one that does not (Patterson and Thompson 1971). Initial estimates are obtained using MIVQUE0, and the procedure iterates until convergence is reached for the log-likelihood objective function of the portion of the likelihood that does not contain the fixed effects.

Appendix 3

Operating System Notes

INTRODUCTION

This appendix provides a general description of the basic functions of an operating system and how the operating system and the SAS System interact to execute your SAS program. You will also learn about SAS features that relate to file access.

A detailed section for each operating system includes examples to illustrate these features.

To use SAS software products, you do not need to be an expert on operating systems; however, as you learn more about your operating system, you will be able to do more with SAS. After reading this material, you should have a better idea of how the operating system and the SAS System work together and where to find more information.

THE OPERATING SYSTEM

Your SAS programs execute in an environment controlled by a set of powerful programs called an *operating system*. The operating system controls all work done by the computer, such as allocating computer resources to run programs and storing data. Because an operating system oversees activities of the computer, it is sometimes called the *host environment*.

There are different operating systems for different types of computers. However, all operating systems are designed to handle certain basic tasks:

- accept jobs for execution
- store and retrieve data files
- manage terminal sessions
- allocate resources, such as internal memory, time, and disk space, to individual jobs
- control the action of peripheral equipment, such as printers, plotters, and disk and tape drives.

In the same way that you communicate with the SAS System using the SAS language, you communicate with an operating system using the operating system's language. We refer to operating system languages generally as *control languages*. **Table A3.1** lists the types of computers and operating systems under which the SAS System runs, and it gives the commonly used names of their control languages.

INTERACTIONS BETWEEN THE OPERATING SYSTEM AND THE SAS USER

Each time a SAS program executes, many interactions between the SAS System and the operating system occur. The amount of interaction that you need to be aware of depends on your program.

Consider the following example:

```
DATA WEATHER;
   INPUT TEMP PRECIP SUNHRS;
   CARDS;
85.5 0.00 12.33
84.2 0.09 12.31
79.5 0.10 12.30
;
PROC PRINT DATA=WEATHER;
   TITLE 'WEATHER INFORMATION';
```

Table A3.1 Computers, Operating Systems, and Control Languages

Computers	Operating Systems	Control Language Name
Data General ECLIPSE MV	AOS/VS	Command Line interpreter (CLI)
Digital VAX	VMS	Digital Command Language (DCL)
IBM and compatible mainframes*	OS	Job Control Language (JCL)
	TSO (OS interactive)	TSO Command Language
	CMS	CMS and CP Command Language
	VM/PC	CMS and CP Command Language
	VSE	Job Control Language (JCL)
	ICCF (VSE interactive)	ICCF Command Language
PRIME	PRIMOS	Command Procedure Language (CPL)

*The 370, 308X, and 4300 series are examples of IBM mainframes. Amdahl 470 V6 is an example of an IBM-compatible mainframe.

Even in the simplest SAS execution, like this one, you need to be aware of two interactions:

1. *Invoking SAS*. You make a request to the operating system to use the SAS software.
2. *Receiving output*. The output from a SAS program is printed, displayed on a terminal, or written to a file.

Many of the SAS programs you write may involve no more interaction than our example. However, you need to be aware of two fairly common situations in SAS programming that require you to specify information to the operating system:

1. *Defining permanent files*. You can define a file when you want to read or write data that are stored independently from your SAS program.
2. *Rerouting output*. You can send output from a SAS program to the destination of your choice rather than to its default destination.

The following pages discuss each of these common situations in more detail.

Invoking the SAS System

In order to run a SAS program, you must issue a request to the operating system to use the SAS System. The request is made using the operating system's control language, for example, with the SAS command:

```
SAS
```

When the request is received, the operating system executes a set of instructions that makes all the components of the SAS System (such as statements, procedures, formats, and functions) available to your SAS job. The operating system also provides space in the computer's main memory in which to execute the SAS program.

You can invoke SAS to execute in *batch mode*, *noninteractive mode*, or *interactive mode*. The mode determines how your program executes, as described below:

Batch Mode
: Submit a group of control language statements and SAS statements to the operating system. The control language and SAS statements may be stored in a file or may be in a stack of cards. When you submit the job, the operating system schedules (enqueues) the job for execution. Once execution begins, you cannot alter the job or the execution process.

Noninteractive Mode
: Create a file containing your SAS program only (with no control language). When you enter the command to invoke SAS from your terminal, you also enter the name of the file containing your SAS program. The operating system invokes SAS, locates the file, and executes the program. This mode is similar to batch in that once execution begins, you cannot alter the execution process. However, execution does proceed immediately; the job is not enqueued.

Interactive Mode
: (also called *conversational* mode) Issue a command to invoke SAS from your terminal. One of two things happens:

- You will begin a *line-prompt session* in which SAS prompts you, usually with a line number and question mark, to enter your SAS program line by line. Your program executes one step at a time as you enter the statements.
- You will begin a *display manager session* in which you enter the SAS program on the program editor screen and issue the SUBMIT command to submit the code to SAS.

Whether your session is in line-prompt or display manager mode depends on the setting of the SAS system option DMS | NODMS and the kind of terminal you have. To use display manager, you must have a full-screen terminal and DMS must be in effect. Line-prompt mode occurs when your terminal is not full screen or when NODMS is in effect.

The **Details** section for your operating system illustrates how to invoke SAS. Also see the "SAS Display Manager" appendix of this book for information on executing SAS programs in a display manager session.

Receiving the Output

The set of instructions that the operating system executes when you invoke SAS includes requests telling the operating system where to send the output from the SAS job. This is called the *default destination*. SAS output consists of two main parts: 1) the SAS log, which contains the SAS statements used in the job, notes, and error messages; and 2) the SAS procedure output. All SAS jobs output a SAS log; however, not all SAS jobs produce procedure output.

The default destination of the SAS output depends on the execution mode:

- For a batch job the default destination is often a printer or a disk file.
- In noninteractive mode the SAS log and procedure output are displayed on the screen after the entire job executes.

- In interactive line-prompt mode, the SAS log and procedure output are displayed on the terminal screen as each step of your program executes instead of after the entire job executes.
- In interactive display manager mode, lines written to the SAS log appear on the SAS log screen; procedure output displays on the procedure output screen.

You can change the default destination for SAS output by using proper control language and SAS system options. (See **Re-routing SAS Output**, below). For more information on SAS output, refer to the chapter "Log and Procedure Output" in the *SAS User's Guide: Basics*.

Defining Files

In many SAS programs you will want to read or write a *permanent file* (a file that is stored for later use.) For example, you may want a SAS program to read a file of data that are stored on tape in order to create a SAS data set that can be printed by PROC PRINT, or you may want to enter new data after a CARDS statement and then store the data in a permanent disk file for later use.

A permanent file resides in a storage location managed by the operating system. Thus, the SAS System must interact with the operating system to access a permanent file. You allow this interaction to take place by *defining* the permanent file(s) needed by your program.

SAS programs use two general kinds of files: *SAS files* and *external files*. SAS files are specially structured files that can be created and processed only by the SAS System. SAS data sets are the most commonly used of the SAS files. External files can be created and processed by other programming languages, as well as by SAS. For the most part, SAS procedures use SAS files.

Following is a general description of how to define permanent SAS and external files. Refer to **Details** for your operating system for examples that illustrate how to define files for programs that read and create external files and SAS files.

External files To define a permanent external file, associate a fileref (short for "file reference") with the complete name of the external file. You then specify the fileref in SAS statements to refer to the external file. For example, if you are reading an external file, specify the fileref in the INFILE statement. If you are creating an external file, specify the fileref in the FILE statement.

In most cases you must explicitly associate the fileref with the complete name of the external file. The method used to associate the fileref with the file's name differs for each operating system, so be sure to see the **Details** section for your operating system.

SAS files To define a permanent SAS file, associate a *libref* (short for "library reference") with a permanent library of SAS files, called a *SAS data library*. The **Details** section for your operating system includes complete instructions on how to associate a libref with a SAS data library in your environment.

After the file is defined, you use the libref as the first-level name of the SAS file's complete two-level name in any SAS statement that requests the file. For example, the name could be specified in a PROC, DATA, or SET statement.

Once defined, a libref can be used repeatedly in SAS statements in that job or session to refer to any existing SAS file in the library or to add SAS files to the library.

In most cases librefs and filerefs must follow the rules for SAS names. Exceptions, if any, are given in **Details** for your operating system. For a general discussion of SAS files, their names, and SAS data libraries, see the chapter "SAS Files" in the *SAS User's Guide: Basics*.

SAS statements used to request files The following list contains a brief description of the SAS statements that are used to request files. If you use one of these statements to request a permanent file, the file must also be defined. See the next section for a list of SAS statements used to define permanent files. All of these statements are fully described in the *SAS User's Guide: Basics*:

DATA	initiates the DATA step and allows you to create a SAS data set. If the data set is permanent, you must define the SAS library in which to store it unless your operating system is one that defines it for you (see **Details**).
FILE	specifies a fileref that refers to an external file. Subsequent PUT statements write to this file. Refer to **Details** for your operating system for information on how to define an external file.
%INCLUDE	specifies a fileref that refers to an external file containing SAS statements that you want to execute. Refer to **Details** for your operating system for information on how to define an external file.
INFILE	specifies a fileref that refers to an external file to be read by the SAS program. Refer to **Details** for your operating system for information on how to define an external file.
PROC	uses an option to refer to a SAS library or an external file that is to be read or created. For those procedures that can read and create files in the same execution, more than one option can be specified to refer to the appropriate SAS library or external file. When the procedure uses an entire SAS library, the value of the option is a libref. The value is a two-level permanent SAS file name when the procedure uses a SAS file within the library. If the procedure reads from or writes to an external file, the value of the option is a fileref.
SET MERGE UPDATE	read and manipulate observations in SAS data sets. If a data set being accessed by one of these statements is permanent, you must define the SAS library in which it is stored unless your operating system is one that defines the library for you (see **Details**).

SAS statements used to define files The following list contains a brief description of the SAS statements that are used to define permanent files. Note that under some operating systems, only control language can be used to define a file, not SAS statements. Be sure to read the **Details** section for your operating system. All of these statements are fully described in the *SAS User's Guide: Basics*:

FILENAME	specifies a fileref with a complete file name, which includes a directory name and the name of a specific file in the directory. If the FILENAME statement does not precede a SAS statement that specifies a fileref, the SAS System uses a file in the current default directory.
LIBNAME	associates a libref with a directory name. This statement must precede a SAS statement that specifies the libref.

LIBSEARCH establishes a search list of directories by specifying a list of librefs. Each libref listed must be associated with a directory in a LIBNAME statement. LIBSEARCH must follow LIBNAME statements that define the directories.

X allows you to issue operating system commands from within your SAS program if executing in interactive or noninteractive mode. If the X statement is used to issue an operating system command to define a permanent file, it must precede the statement that refers to that file (see **Details**).

Re-routing SAS Output

As discussed above, the default destination of SAS output is determined by the mode of execution. You can change the default destination with the proper control language or with SAS options. For example, if you are executing SAS in display manager mode, by default the SAS log appears on the log screen, and the procedure output appears on the output screen. You can copy the SAS log and procedure output with the PRINT command of display manager.

When you re-route output, you must override default output handling. This endeavor is both operating system- and site-specific. The method you use will also depend on what you want to do. For example, you can route your output to a particular printer or terminal, or you can even route it to a permanent file. Use the following sources of information to learn how to route output:

- *SAS User's Guide: Basics.* Look for SAS system options used to re-route output on your operating system.
- SAS Companion or Technical Report for your operating system. Look for options and control language used to re-route output.
- The SAS consultant at your site.

DETAILS FOR THE AOS/VS OPERATING SYSTEM

The SAS System running under the AOS/VS operating system is documented in "Changes and Enhancements in the Base SAS and SAS/GRAPH Products under AOS/VS," SAS Technical Report P-129.

Invoking the SAS System

Enter the SAS command after you receive the) prompt:

```
) SAS
```

or

```
) SAS/options
```

or

```
) SAS filename
```

If you enter *SAS* you will invoke the SAS System in interactive mode. Use the second method to specify valid *options* when you invoke SAS. For example, you can specify *SAS/FSDEVICE=devicename* to invoke SAS in display manager mode. With the third method, you can specify *SAS filename* to give the name of a file containing the SAS program to be executed. This method is called *noninteractive mode*.

Note that the SAS command is a CLI macro file that contains a set of control language instructions to invoke the SAS System.

Read more about the SAS command in SAS Technical Report P-129. For information on executing SAS in batch mode see P-129 and the *AOS/VS CLI User's Manual*.

Defining Files

How you define a file depends on whether the file is a SAS or non-SAS (external) file. The method that you use allows the SAS System to distinguish between SAS files and external files.

External files You can define an external file in one of the following two ways:

- with the CREATE/LINK command of the CLI control language before you invoke the SAS System
- in the FILENAME statement within your SAS program.

With either method you associate a *fileref* with a complete file name. The complete file name includes the directory name and the name of a specific file within the directory. You can also issue the CREATE/LINK command in the X statement, a SAS statement that allows you to enter CLI commands in your SAS program.

The fileref is then used in SAS statements, such as FILE and INFILE, to refer to the external file. If you specify a fileref in a SAS statement before you define the external file, the SAS System reads or creates a file in the current default directory with the following name:

```
:UDD:currentdefaultdirectory:fileref
```

where *fileref* is specified in the INFILE statement to give the name of the file that is read from the current default directory or where *fileref* is specified in the FILE statement to give the name of the file being created in the current default directory.

SAS files If you want to read or create a SAS file, you must define the appropriate directory with the LIBNAME statement. In the LIBNAME statement you associate a *libref* with a directory name only. The libref is then specified in SAS statements, such as DATA, SET, MERGE, and so on, to refer to the directory. Once you have defined a directory in the LIBNAME statement, you can use the associated libref to refer to any file in that directory.

If you do not specify the LIBNAME statement before you use the libref in a SAS statement, you will receive an error message that the directory to which you are referring cannot be found.

Note: discussion of SAS files in the following examples is limited to the most commonly used type, a **SAS data set.** A SAS data set is a SAS file containing observations and variables.

Methods for defining SAS data sets and external files are illustrated in the following sections.

Reading an External File

The following program reads an external file and includes a FILENAME statement to define the external file:

```
) SAS (invoke the SAS System)
SAS messages
1? FILENAME DAILY ':UDD:YOURDIR1:YOUR.RAW.DATA';
2? DATA WEATHER;
3?    INFILE DAILY;
more SAS statements
```

```
7? ENDSAS;
```

The FILENAME statement associates the fileref DAILY with the complete file name, and DAILY is then specified in the INFILE statement. Note that the complete file name includes a directory named YOURDIR1 and the file YOUR.RAW. DATA within the directory.

You can also use the CREATE/LINK to define the external file before you invoke the SAS System. For example:

```
CREATE/LINK DAILY :UDD:YOURDIR1:YOUR.RAW.DATA
```

If you use the CREATE/LINK command, you do not need the FILENAME statement. If you chose to define the file by issuing the CREATE/LINK command with the X statement, you can simply replace the FILENAME statement in the above program with the following SAS statement:

```
X 'CREATE/LINK DAILY :UDD:YOURDIR1:YOUR.RAW.DATA';
```

Since the X statement is a SAS statement, be sure to put a semicolon at the end.

If you do not define the external file, the SAS System will read (or attempt to read) a file from the current default directory with the following name:

```
:UDD:currentdefaultdirectory:DAILY
```

Reading a SAS Data Set

Use the LIBNAME statement to define the directory containing the SAS data set to be read, as shown in the following program:

```
) SAS (invoke the SAS System)
SAS messages
1? LIBNAME REPORT ':UDD:DIR2';
2? PROC PRINT DATA=REPORT.STATION;
3?    VAR A B C;
more SAS messages
4? ENDSAS;
```

The LIBNAME statement associates the libref REPORT with the directory :UDD:DIR2. REPORT is then used as the first level of the permanent SAS data set name REPORT.STATION in the PROC PRINT statement. When this program executes, the SAS System reads a SAS data set named STATION from the directory named :UDD:DIR2 and prints the values for variables A, B, and C.

If the LIBNAME statement is omitted or does not precede the PROC PRINT statement, you will receive an error message stating that the directory cannot be found.

Creating a SAS Data Set

Use the LIBNAME statement to define a directory in which to store a newly created SAS data set. The following program creates a SAS data set using an external file as input:

```
) SAS (invoke the SAS System)
SAS messages
1? FILENAME DAILY ':UDD:YOURDIR1:YOUR.RAW.DATA';
2? LIBNAME MAP ':UDD:YOURDIR2';
3? DATA MAP.WEATHER;
4?    INFILE DAILY;
more SAS statements and messages
```

```
5? ENDSAS;
```

The LIBNAME statement associates the libref MAP with YOURDIR2, the directory in which the SAS data set WEATHER is stored. MAP is then used as the first level of the permanent SAS data set name in the DATA statement. The FILENAME statement associates DAILY with the directory YOURDIR1 and the file YOUR.RAW.DATA, the input file.

If the LIBNAME statement is omitted, you will receive an error message stating that the directory cannot be found. If you do not specify the FILENAME statement, the SAS System will search the current default directory for a file named DAILY.

Creating an External File

Since the following program creates an external file, use the FILENAME statement to associate the fileref with the complete file name. The complete file name includes the directory name and the name of the file that is created within that directory. Since the following program uses a SAS data set as input, you must use a LIBNAME statement to define the appropriate directory:

```
) SAS (invoke the SAS System)
(SAS messages)
1? LIBNAME MAP ':UDD:DIR2'
2? FILENAME FREEZE ':UDD:DIR3:COLD.RAW.DATA';
3? DATA _NULL_;
4?    SET MAP.WEATHER;
5?    FILE FREEZE;
6?    IF TEMP < 32 THEN PUT TEMP;
more SAS statements and messages
9? ENDSAS;
```

The FILENAME statement associates FREEZE with the complete file name :UDD:DIR3:COLD.RAW.DATA. FREEZE is then specified in the FILE statement. You can also issue the CREATE/LINK command (before you invoke the SAS System or in the X statement) to define the external file.

If you do not define the external file for the above program, the SAS System will create a file in the current default directory with the following name:

```
:UDD:currentdefaultdirectory:FREEZE
```

DETAILS FOR THE CMS OPERATING SYSTEM

The SAS System running under the CMS operating System is documented in the *SAS Companion for the VM/CMS Operating System.*

Invoking the SAS System

Enter the SAS command after you receive the READY or R; prompt:

```
SAS filename (options)
```

If your SAS program is stored in a file, specify the *filename* after the SAS command. File characteristics must be fixed-length, 80-character line. Invoking the SAS System to execute in this way is called *noninteractive mode.* If you want to invoke SAS in interactive mode do not specify a filename. If you want to specify any of the valid *options* for the SAS command, enter a right parenthesis, followed by the options. The DMS | NODMS option and the type of terminal you are using determine whether you enter a line-prompt or display manager session. If you have a full-screen terminal and DMS is in effect, you enter display manager. If your terminal is not full screen or NODMS is in effect, you enter a line-prompt interactive session.

Note that the SAS command is a CMS command created by the SAS Institute that contains a set of control language instructions to invoke the SAS System.

Read more about the SAS command in the *SAS Companion for the VM/CMS Operating System*. To learn about running a SAS job in a CMS batch machine, refer to the *IBM Virtual/System Product: CMS User's Guide*.

Defining Files

The CMS command FILEDEF is used to define files for use in SAS programs. The FILEDEF command associates a *libref* with a SAS file or a *fileref* with an external (non-SAS) file. The libref or fileref is called a *DDname* in CMS terminology. The form of the FILEDEF command is

```
FILEDEF DDname device filename filetype filemode(options)
```

where

- *DDname* serves as a SAS file's libref or an external file's fileref
- *device* indicates the file's storage medium (usually DISK or TAPE)
- *filename* and *filetype* are the names by which CMS knows the file
- *filemode* is a letter (or letter/number combination) indicating the minidisk on which the file is stored (for disk files only)
- *options* are any of a number of CMS options for the FILEDEF command.

In most cases, you do not have to issue the FILEDEF explicitly to define a SAS file because the SAS System issues the FILEDEF automatically. You must explicitly issue the FILEDEF for an external file.

A FILEDEF can be issued before the SAS System is invoked or after SAS is invoked in an X or CMS statement. In any case, the FILEDEF must be issued before the SAS statement that references the file.

Special Naming Conventions

Although the SAS System allows you to use an underscore (_) in SAS names, CMS does not. Therefore, do not use an underscore character in a libref or a fileref.

Reading an External File

Issue a FILEDEF command to associate a fileref with the external file to be read. Then, use the fileref in the INFILE statement of your SAS program. For example, suppose you write a DATA step that reads the external disk file CLIMATE DATA, which is stored on your A-disk, and you want to use DAILY as the fileref:

```
R;
FILEDEF DAILY DISK CLIMATE DATA A
R;
SAS (invoke the SAS System)
(SAS messages)
1?
DATA WEATHER;
2?
INFILE DAILY;
3?
INPUT TEMP PRECIP SUNHRS;
```

```
4?
more SAS statements
```

The fileref DAILY points to the CMS file CLIMATE DATA A.

Reading a SAS Data Set

Under most circumstances you do not need to define a libref explicitly for a SAS file because SAS makes the association automatically. To access an existing SAS file on any minidisk, just use the file's two-level name in the appropriate SAS statement. SAS searches all accessed minidisks for the file you have specified and issues the appropriate FILEDEF when it finds the file. For example, suppose the SAS data set FOOD.PRICES is stored on your B-disk. When SAS reads this statement:

```
SET FOOD.PRICES;
```

it searches all accessed minidisks for a data set with filename PRICES and filetype FOOD. When it finds PRICES FOOD B, this FILEDEF is automatically issued:

```
FILEDEF FOOD DISK PRICES FOOD B
```

Note: if you have multiple SAS files with the same filename and filetype on different minidisks, SAS will find only the file on the minidisk that is first in the search order. For example, if you have a PRICES FOOD A and a PRICES FOOD B, SAS will find PRICES FOOD A. You must issue a FILEDEF for PRICES FOOD B explicitly if you want to access it.

Creating a SAS Data Set

Under most circumstances, you do not need to define a libref explicitly to create a SAS file because SAS makes the association automatically. When you are creating a new SAS file and you specify a two-level SAS name, SAS automatically issues a FILEDEF using the libref (first-level name) for the DDname parameter **and** for the filetype unless a FILEDEF with that DDname is already in effect. By default, the data set will be written to your A-disk. For example, suppose you are creating a SAS data set called FOOD.PRICES:

```
DATA FOOD.PRICES;
  INPUT ... ;
more SAS statements
```

When SAS reads the name FOOD.PRICES, it checks to see if a FILEDEF with DDname FOOD has been issued. If there is no such FILEDEF, SAS issues one automatically, using FOOD for both the DDname and filetype, PRICES as the filename, and A as the filemode:

```
FILEDEF FOOD DISK PRICES FOOD A
```

Note: do not use the same filetype for SAS files and external (non-SAS) files.

If you want a new SAS data set to be stored on a disk other than your A-disk, you must issue the appropriate FILEDEF explicitly. Specify the appropriate values for the DDname and filemode parameters. You can specify any value for filename and filetype; SAS will substitute the libref (first-level name) and data set name (second-level name) for filetype and filename, respectively. For example, if you want to store FOOD.PRICES on a B-disk, your FILEDEF could be:

```
FILEDEF FOOD DISK DUMMY DUMMY B
```

Notice that CMS and SAS identify the file by the same two names, but the order is reversed. For example, SAS calls the data set FOOD.PRICES, and CMS calls it PRICES FOOD.

Creating an External File

To create an external file in a SAS program, first issue a FILEDEF command to associate a fileref with the name of the external file to be created. Then use the fileref in the FILE statement of your SAS program. For example, suppose you write a DATA step that reads the external disk file CLIMATE DATA, (which is stored on your A-disk) and creates a second external file called COLD TEMPS A. You use the filerefs DAILY and FREEZE to reference the files:

```
R;
FILEDEF DAILY DISK CLIMATE DATA A
R;
FILEDEF FREEZE DISK COLD TEMPS A
R;
SAS
1?
DATA _NULL_;
2?
INFILE DAILY;
3?
INPUT TEMP PRECIP SUNHRS;
4?
FILE FREEZE;
5?
more SAS statements
```

DETAILS FOR THE OS OPERATING SYSTEM AND TSO

The SAS System running under the OS operating system is documented in the *SAS Companion for the OS Operating System and TSO.*

OS Batch

Invoking the SAS System Use the EXEC statement in your JCL:

```
// EXEC SAS,OPTIONS='options'
```

In this case, the OS cataloged procedure named *SAS* contains all the job control language instructions to invoke the SAS System in batch mode. The *OPTIONS=* parameter can be used to specify valid SAS system options.

Read more about the SAS cataloged procedure in the *SAS Companion for OS Operating System and TSO.*

Defining files Use the DD (Data Definition) statement to define permanent files, both SAS and external files. The DD statement associates a *fileref* with a permanent external file or a *libref* with a permanent library of SAS files. In OS terminology the fileref or the libref is called a *DDname.*

The external file can be an OS sequential data set or a partitioned data set (PDS). A sequential data set contains records stored in a sequence under a unique name. If the external file is a sequential data set, you associate a fileref with the sequential data set name in the DD statement, as follows:

```
//fileref DD DSN=external.file.name,DISP=disposition
```

The *fileref* is then specified in SAS statements, such as INFILE and FILE, to refer to the external file. For example,

```
INFILE fileref;
```

A PDS contains a group of data sets called members. The PDS has a name that identifies the group. Each member within the PDS has a unique name. You can identify one member by enclosing the member name in parentheses and including it as the last level of the PDS name. For example, if you want to define an external file that is a member of a PDS, you must specify the DD statement as follows:

```
//fileref DD DSN=external.file.name(member),DISP=disposition
```

In this case you only have access to the member specified. Then, you use the fileref in SAS statements, such as INFILE and FILE, to refer to that member.

To have access to all members of the PDS, use the PDS name only (without a member name) in the DD statement, as follows:

```
//fileref DD DSN=external.file.name,DISP=disposition
```

When you define the PDS in this way, you include the member name in parentheses after the fileref to refer to the specific member in the PDS. For example,

```
INFILE fileref(member1);
FILE fileref(member2);
```

The above statements refer to two members of the same PDS.

If you use a fileref in a SAS statement that is not associated with an external file in the DD statement, you will receive an error message indicating that the file to which you are referring has not been defined.

A group of SAS files is called a *SAS data library*. Once defined, all SAS files within the library are accessible. For example,

```
//libref DD DSN=SAS.library.name,DISP=disposition
```

Then use the *libref* in SAS statements, such as DATA, SET, and MERGE, to refer to the SAS library. You refer to a specific file within the library by including the SAS file name after the libref. The libref and the SAS file name are always separated by a period. For example,

```
DATA libref.SASname;
```

In some SAS statements, such as certain PROC statements, you use only the libref to refer to the entire SAS library. The utility procedure DATASETS is a good example:

```
PROC DATASETS LIBRARY=libref;
```

All of the SAS files in the library referred to by the libref are available to be processed by the DATASETS procedure.

A SAS library can contain several different types of SAS files. The discussion of SAS files in this section is limited to the most commonly used type, a **SAS data set.** A SAS data set is a SAS file that contains observations and variables.

If you use a libref in a SAS statement that is not associated with a SAS library in the DD statement, you will receive an error message indicating that the file to which you are referring has not been defined.

The DISP= parameter Each of the DD statement examples includes a DISP= parameter. DISP= specifies a disposition (status) for the file at the beginning and end of the job. The disposition also implies an access method. (Refer to the *SAS Companion for OS Operating Systems and TSO* for details on specifying the DISP= parameter in the DD statement.) All of the examples in the following sections use existing files and, therefore, specify either DISP=OLD to obtain exclusive access to an existing file or DISP=SHR to obtain shared access to an existing file.

If your SAS program writes to an existing SAS library, you must specify DISP=OLD in the DD statement because you are updating the library. You must have exclusive access to a SAS library to update it. The need to specify DISP=OLD is noted for the following examples, where appropriate.

Methods for defining SAS libraries and external files are illustrated in the following sections.

Reading an external file To read an external file you must include a DD statement in the JCL used to invoke the SAS System. In the following job:

```
//jobname JOB accountinginformation
// EXEC SAS
//DAILY DD DSN=YOUR.RAW.DATA(MON),DISP=SHR
//SYSIN  DD  *
DATA WEATHER;
   INFILE DAILY;
   INPUT TEMP PRECIP SUNHRS;
more SAS statements
```

the DD statement associates the fileref DAILY with the external file YOUR.RAW. DATA(MON). Notice that the external file is a PDS and the member MON is specified. DAILY is then used in the INFILE statement to refer to the external file.

Reading a SAS data set You also use the DD statement to define a permanent SAS library. The DD statement in the following job associates the libref REPORT with the SAS library named YOUR.SAS.LIB. REPORT is then specified as the first level of a permanent SAS data set name in the PROC PRINT statement.

```
//jobname JOB accountinginformation
// EXEC SAS
//REPORT DD DSN=YOUR.SAS.LIB,DISP=SHR
//SYSIN DD *
PROC PRINT DATA=REPORT.STATION;
   VAR A B C;
```

The association is necessary to allow the SAS System to read a SAS data set named STATION from the SAS library YOUR.SAS.LIB. When the program executes, PROC PRINT locates STATION and prints the values of the variables A, B, and C.

Note: in the DD statement YOUR.SAS.LIB is an existing SAS library defined with DISP=SHR to allow for shared use of the SAS library that is being read.

Creating a SAS data set The following program creates a SAS data set using an external file as input. Use the DD statement to define the existing SAS library in which to store the SAS data set created by this program. You must also define the external file in a DD statement:

```
//jobname JOB accountinginformation
// EXEC SAS
//DAILY DD DSN=YOUR.RAW.DATA(MON),DISP=SHR
//MAP DD DSN=YOUR.SAS.LIB,DISP=OLD
//SYSIN DD *
DATA MAP.WEATHER;
   INFILE DAILY;
more SAS statements
```

The first DD statement associates the fileref DAILY with the permanent external file named YOUR.RAW.DATA(MON). Notice that you again refer to a specific member of a PDS. The second DD statement associates the libref MAP with the existing SAS library named YOUR.SAS.LIB. MAP is then used as the first level of the permanent SAS data set name in the DATA statement. The SAS data set WEATHER created by this program is stored in YOUR.SAS.LIB.

Note: in contrast to the previous example, the SAS library must be defined with DISP=OLD because it is existing and because the SAS System will not allow you to write to a SAS library defined with shared access (DISP=SHR). Remember, if your program updates a SAS library, you must have exclusive access to the library.

Creating an external file If your SAS program creates an external file, you must use a DD statement to define the file. The following program creates an external file using a SAS data set as input; therefore, you must include two DD statements in the JCL used to invoke the SAS System:

```
//jobname JOB accountinginformation
// EXEC SAS
//MAP DD DSN=YOUR.SAS.LIB,DISP=SHR
//FREEZE DD DSN=COLD.RAW.DATA,DISP=OLD
//SYSIN  DD  *
DATA _NULL_;
   SET MAP.WEATHER;
   FILE FREEZE(JAN);
   IF TEMP < 32 THEN PUT TEMP;
more SAS statements
```

In this case the libref MAP refers to a file named YOUR.SAS.LIB, and MAP is then used as the first level of the permanent SAS data set name in the SET statement. The fileref FREEZE refers to a PDS named COLD.RAW.DATA. The member of the PDS (JAN) created by this program is specified in the FILE statement. FREEZE is then used in the FILE statement. When this program executes, the PUT statement writes all TEMP values less than 32 to the external file COLD.RAW.DATA(JAN).

TSO (OS Interactive)

Invoking the SAS System Enter the TSO command after you receive the READY prompt:

```
SAS OPTIONS('options')
```

or

```
SAS INPUT('''filename''')
```

Enter *SAS OPTIONS('options')* to invoke SAS in interactive mode and specify valid SAS *options*. The DMS | NODMS option and the type of terminal you use determine whether you enter a line-prompt or display manager session. If you use a full-screen terminal and if DMS is in effect, you enter a display manager session. If your terminal is not full screen or if NODMS is in effect, you enter a line-prompt session.

Enter *SAS INPUT('''filename''')* to invoke SAS in noninteractive mode and specify *filename* to give the name of the file containing the SAS program to be executed. File characteristics must be RECFM=F or FB and LRECL=80.

The SAS command is a TSO CLIST (Command LIST) that contains a set of control language instructions to invoke the SAS System.

Defining files Use the ALLOCATE command of TSO to define permanent files—SAS files and external files. The ALLOCATE command associates a *fileref* with a permanent external file or a *libref* with a permanent library of SAS files. In TSO terminology a libref or fileref is called a *DDname*.

The external file can be an OS sequential data set or a partitioned data set (PDS). A sequential data set contains records stored in a sequence under a unique name. If the external file to be defined is a sequential data set, you associate a fileref with the sequential data set name in the ALLOCATE command, as follows:

```
ALLOCATE FILE(fileref) DATASET('external.file.name') disposition
```

The *fileref* is then specified in SAS statements, such as INFILE and FILE, to refer to the external file. For example,

```
INFILE fileref;
```

A PDS contains a group of data sets called members. The PDS has a name that identifies the group. Each member within the PDS has a unique name. You can identify one member by enclosing the member name in parentheses and including it as the last level of the PDS name. For example, if you want to define an external file that is a member of a PDS, you must specify the ALLOCATE command as follows:

```
ALLOCATE FILE(fileref)DATASET('external.file.name.(member)') disposition
```

In this case you only have access to the member specified. Then you use the fileref in SAS statements, such as INFILE and FILE, to refer to that member.

To have access to all members, give the PDS name only (without a member name) in the ALLOCATE command, as follows:

```
ALLOCATE FILE(fileref) DATASET('external.file.name') disposition
```

When you use the fileref in SAS statements, such as INFILE and FILE, you include the member name in parentheses after the fileref to refer to a specific member in the PDS. For example,

```
INFILE fileref(member1);
FILE fileref(member2);
```

The above statements refer to two members of the same PDS.

If you use a fileref in a SAS statement that is not associated with an external file in the ALLOCATE command, you will receive an error message indicating that the file to which you are referring has not been defined.

A group of SAS files is called a *SAS data library*. Once defined, all SAS files within the library can be accessed. For example,

```
ALLOCATE FILE(libref) DATASET('SAS.library.name')disposition
```

Then use the *libref* in SAS statements, such as DATA, SET, and MERGE, to refer to the SAS library. You refer to a specific file within the library by including the SAS file name after the libref. The libref and the SAS file name are always separated by a period. For example,

```
DATA libref.SASname;
```

In some SAS statements, such as certain PROC statements, you use only the libref to refer to the entire SAS library. The utility procedure DATASETS is a good example:

```
PROC DATASETS LIBRARY=libref;
```

All of the SAS files in the library referred to by the libref are available to be processed by the DATASETS procedure.

A SAS library can contain several different types of SAS files. The discussion of SAS files in this section is limited to one type, **SAS data sets**. A SAS data set is a SAS file that contains observations and variables.

If you use a libref in a SAS statement that is not associated with a SAS library in the ALLOCATE command, you will receive an error message indicating that the file to which you are referring has not been defined.

The disposition operand Each ALLOCATE command example includes a disposition operand. *Disposition* specifies the status of the file at the beginning and end of the job and also implies an access method. (Refer to the *SAS Companion for OS Operating Systems and TSO* for details on specifying the disposition operand.) All of the examples in this section use existing files and, therefore, specify either OLD to obtain exclusive access to an existing file or SHR to obtain shared access to an existing file.

If your SAS program writes to an existing SAS library, you must specify a disposition of OLD in the ALLOCATE command because you are updating the library. You must have exclusive access to a SAS library to update it. The need to specify OLD is noted for the following examples, where appropriate.

If your TSO CLIST invokes the SASCP command, you can also issue the ALLOCATE command from within your SAS program with the X or TSO statement. If you use the X or TSO statement, be sure to include it before the SAS statement that requests the file. For example, the X statement that issues an ALLOCATE command to define an input file must be specified before the INFILE statement.

If you do not define the permanent files requested by your SAS program, you will receive an error message.

Methods for defining SAS libraries and external files are illustrated in the following sections.

Reading an external file You can enter the ALLOCATE command before you invoke the SAS System to define the file to be read by the following program:

```
ALLOCATE FILE(DAILY) DATASET('YOUR.RAW.DATA(MON)') SHR
SAS  (invoke the SAS System)
SAS messages
1? DATA WEATHER;
2?    INFILE DAILY;
more SAS statements
6? ENDSAS;
```

The ALLOCATE command associates the fileref DAILY with the permanent external file YOUR.RAW.DATA(MON). Notice that you are defining a specific member of a PDS. DAILY is then specified in the INFILE statement. You can also define the file by issuing the ALLOCATE command in the X statement, as follows:

```
X ALLOCATE FILE(DAILY) DATASET('YOUR.RAW.DATA(MON)') SHR;
```

The X statement must precede the INFILE statement in the above program; otherwise, you will receive an error message indicating that you are referring to a file that has not been defined.

Reading a SAS data set Use the ALLOCATE statement to define a permanent SAS library to be used as input. In the following example the ALLOCATE command associates the libref REPORT with the SAS library named YOUR.SAS.LIB. REPORT is then used as the first level of the permanent SAS data set name in the PROC PRINT statement:

```
SAS  (invoke the SAS System)
SAS messages
```

```
1? TSO ALLOCATE FILE(REPORT) DATASET('YOUR.SAS.LIB') SHR;
2? PROC PRINT DATA=REPORT.STATION;
3?     VAR A B C;
SAS messages
4? ENDSAS;
```

In this case, the TSO statement (the equivalent of the X statement under TSO) is used to issue the ALLOCATE command. When this program executes, PROC PRINT locates the data set named STATION and prints the values of the variables A, B, and C.

Creating a SAS data set The following program creates a SAS data set using a permanent external file as input. Therefore, you must issue the ALLOCATE command twice: once to define the external file to be used as input, and once to define the SAS library in which to store WEATHER, the SAS data set created by this program:

```
ALLOCATE FILE(DAILY) DATASET('YOUR.RAW.DATA(MON)') SHR
ALLOCATE FILE(MAP) DATASET('YOUR.SAS.LIB') OLD
SAS  (invoke the SAS System)
SAS messages
1? DATA MAP.WEATHER;
2?    INFILE DAILY;
3?    INPUT TEMP PRECIP SUNHRS;
more SAS statements and messages
6? ENDSAS;
```

The first ALLOCATE command associates the fileref DAILY with the external file YOUR.RAW.DATA(MON), a specific PDS member. DAILY is then used in the INFILE statement. The second ALLOCATE command associates the libref MAP with the SAS library YOUR.SAS.LIB. MAP is then used as the first level of the permanent SAS data set name in the DATA statement. When this program executes, the permanent SAS data set WEATHER contains observations with variables TEMP, PRECIP, and SUNHRS.

Note: this program creates a new SAS data set in the SAS library YOUR.SAS.LIB and thereby updates the library. Notice that the YOUR.SAS.LIB is defined in the ALLOCATE command with a disposition of OLD.

Creating an external file The following program creates an external file using a SAS data set as input. As before, you must issue the ALLOCATE command twice: once to define the permanent external file created by the program and once to define the permanent SAS library that is used as input:

```
ALLOCATE FILE(MAP) DATASET('YOUR.SAS.LIB') SHR
ALLOCATE FILE(FREEZE) DATASET('COLD.RAW.DATA') OLD
SAS  (invoke the SAS System)
SAS messages
1? DATA _NULL_;
2?    SET MAP.WEATHER;
3?    FILE FREEZE(JAN);
4?    IF TEMP < 32 THEN PUT TEMP;
more SAS statements
8? ENDSAS;
```

The first ALLOCATE command associates the libref MAP with the SAS library named YOUR.SAS.LIB. MAP is then used in the SET statement as the first level in the permanent SAS data set name MAP.WEATHER. The second ALLOCATE command associates the fileref FREEZE with a PDS named COLD.RAW.DATA.

FREEZE is then used in the FILE statement along with the PDS member JAN that is created by this program. When the program executes, the SAS data set WEATHER is read from the SAS library YOUR.SAS.LIB and all TEMP values less than 32 are written to the external file COLD.RAW.DATA(JAN).

DETAILS FOR THE PRIMOS OPERATING SYSTEM

The SAS System running under the PRIMOS operating system is documented in "Changes and Enhancements in the Base SAS and SAS/GRAPH Products under PRIMOS," SAS Technical Report P-130.

Invoking the SAS System

Enter the SAS command after you receive the OK, prompt:

```
OK, SAS
```

or

```
OK, SAS -options
```

or

```
OK, SAS filename
```

If you enter *SAS* you will invoke the SAS System in interactive mode. Use the second method to specify valid *options* when you invoke SAS. For example, you can specify *SAS -FSDEVICE=devicename* to invoke SAS in display manager mode. With the third method, you can specify *filename* to give the name of a file containing the SAS program to be executed. This method is called *noninteractive mode*.

Read more about the SAS command in SAS Technical Report P-130.

For information on executing SAS in batch mode, refer to P-130 and *PRIMOS Command Reference Guide*.

Defining Files

How you define a file depends on whether the file is a SAS or non-SAS (external) file. The method that you use allows the SAS System to distinguish between SAS files and external files.

External files Use the FILENAME statement to define an external file. In the FILENAME statement you associate the *fileref* with a complete file name, which includes the directory name and a specific file within the directory. The FILENAME statement must be included in the SAS program before a SAS statement that refers to the permanent external file. For example, if your program uses an external file as input, the FILENAME statement that defines the file must precede the INFILE statement.

If you do not define the external file to be read or created by your program, the SAS System reads or creates a file in the current directory with the following name:

```
<masterfiledirectory>currentdirectory>fileref
```

where *fileref* is specified in the INFILE statement to give the name of the file that is read from the current default directory or where *fileref* is specified in the FILE statement to give the name of the file being created in the current default directory.

SAS files If you want to read or create a permanent SAS file, you must define the appropriate directory with the LIBNAME statement. In the LIBNAME statement you associate a *libref* with a directory name only. The libref is then used in SAS statements, such as DATA, SET, MERGE, and so on, to refer to the directory. Once you have defined a directory in the LIBNAME statement, you can use the associated libref to refer to any file in that directory.

The LIBNAME statement must precede a SAS statement that refers to the SAS files (that is, a statement that specifies the libref); otherwise, you will get an error message stating that the directory to which you are referring cannot be found.

Note: when you specify the directory name in the LIBNAME statement or the complete file name (directory name and specific file in the directory) in the FILENAME statement, consider including the master file directory name in the specification. For example,

```
LIBNAME libref '<MASTERDIR>YOURDIR';
FILENAME fileref '<MASTERDIR>YOURDIR2>INPUT.STUFF';
```

Although PRIMOS does not require this level of specification, including the name of the master file directory in a directory specification will ensure that you get the file you want.

Note: discussion of SAS files in the following examples is limited to the most commonly used type, a **SAS data set**. A SAS data set is a SAS file containing observations and variables.

Methods for defining SAS data sets and external files are illustrated in the following sections.

Reading an External File

Use the FILENAME statement in the SAS program to define the file to be read. The FILENAME statement associates the fileref DAILY with the complete file name <MFD>YOURDIR1>YOUR.RAW.DATA:

```
OK, SAS (invoke the SAS System)
SAS messages
1? FILENAME DAILY '<MFD>YOURDIR1>YOUR.RAW.DATA';
2? DATA WEATHER;
3?     INFILE DAILY;
more SAS statements
7? ENDSAS;
```

DAILY is then used in the INFILE statement. If you do not specify the FILENAME statement, the SAS System searches the current directory for the following file:

```
<masterfiledirectory>currentdirectory>DAILY
```

Reading a SAS data set

Use the LIBNAME statement to define the directory containing the SAS data set to be read:

```
OK, SAS (invoke the SAS System)
SAS messages
1? LIBNAME REPORT '<MFD>DIR2';
2? PROC PRINT DATA=REPORT.STATION;
3?     VAR A B C;
more SAS messages
4? ENDSAS;
```

In the above program the LIBNAME statement associates the libref REPORT with the directory named <MFD>DIR2. REPORT is then used as the first level of the permanent SAS data set name REPORT.STATION in the PROC PRINT statement. This association is necessary to allow PROC PRINT to locate a SAS data set named STATION in this directory and print the values of variables A, B, and C.

If the LIBNAME statement is omitted or is not included before the SAS statement that specifies the libref, the SAS System will issue an error message that the directory cannot be found.

Creating a SAS Data Set

The following program creates a permanent SAS data set named WEATHER. You must use the LIBNAME statement to define the directory in which to store WEATHER. This program also uses a external file as input:

```
OK, SAS (invoke the SAS System)
SAS messages
1? FILENAME DAILY '<MFD>YOURDIR1>YOUR.RAW.DATA';
2? LIBNAME MAP '<MFD>YOURDIR2';
3? DATA MAP.WEATHER;
4?    INFILE DAILY;
more SAS statements and messages
5? ENDSAS;
```

In this case LIBNAME associates the libref MAP with the directory <MFD>YOURDIR2. MAP is then used as the first level of the SAS data set name in the DATA statement.

If the LIBNAME statement is omitted, you will receive an error message stating that the directory cannot be found. If you do not specify the FILENAME statement, the SAS System will search the current directory for a file named DAILY.

Creating an External File

The following program creates an external file using a SAS data set as input. Use the FILENAME statement to associate the fileref with the complete file name. The complete file name will include the directory name and the name of a file to be created in that directory. Use a LIBNAME statement to define the directory containing the SAS data set to be read:

```
OK, SAS (invoke the SAS System)
SAS messages
1? LIBNAME MAP '<MFD>YOURDIR2'
2? FILENAME FREEZE '<MFD>DIR3>COLD.RAW.DATA';
3? DATA _NULL_;
4?    SET MAP.WEATHER;
5?    FILE FREEZE;
6?    IF TEMP < 32 THEN PUT TEMP;
more SAS statements and messages
9? ENDSAS;
```

The LIBNAME statement associates the libref MAP with <MFD>YOURDIR2, the directory containing the SAS data set WEATHER. MAP is then used as the first level of a permanent SAS data set name in the SET statement.

When this program executes, all TEMP values less than 32 in the SAS data set WEATHER are written to an external file named COLD.RAW.DATA. This file is located in the directory <MFD>DIR3. If the FILENAME statement is omitted, the SAS System writes the values to a file in the current directory with the following name:

```
<masterfiledirectory>currentdirectory>FREEZE
```

DETAILS FOR THE VM/PC OPERATING SYSTEM

The SAS System running under the VM/PC operating system is documented in the *SAS Companion for the VM/CMS Operating System*.

Invoking the SAS System

Enter the SAS command after you receive the READY or R; prompt:

```
R;    (or READY)
SAS filename (options)
```

If your SAS program is stored in a file, specify the *filename* after the SAS command. Invoking the SAS System to execute in this way is called *noninteractive mode*. If you want to invoke SAS in interactive mode do not specify a filename. If you want to specify any of the valid *options* for the SAS command, enter a right parenthesis, followed by the options. The DMS | NODMS option and the type of terminal you are using determine whether you enter a line-prompt or display manager session. If you are using a full-screen terminal and DMS is in effect, you enter a display manager session. If your terminal is not full screen or if NODMS is in effect, you enter a line-prompt session.

Note that the SAS command is a CMS command created by SAS Institute that contains a set of control language instructions to invoke the SAS System.

Read more about the SAS command in the *SAS Companion for the VM/CMS Operating System*.

Defining Files

The CMS command FILEDEF is used to define files for use in SAS programs. The FILEDEF command associates a *libref* with a SAS file or a *fileref* with an external (non-SAS) file. The libref or fileref is called a *DDname* in CMS terminology. The form of the FILEDEF command is

```
FILEDEF DDname device filename filetype filemode(options
```

where

- *DDname* serves as a SAS file's libref or an external file's fileref
- *device* indicates the file's storage medium (usually DISK)
- *filename* and *filetype* are the names by which CMS knows the file
- *filemode* is a letter (or letter/number combination) indicating the minidisk on which the file is stored (for disk files only)
- *options* are any of a number of CMS options for the FILEDEF command.

In most cases, you do not have to issue the FILEDEF explicitly to define a SAS file because the SAS System issues the FILEDEF automatically. You do have to issue the FILEDEF explicitly for an external file.

A FILEDEF can be issued before the SAS System is invoked or after SAS is invoked in an X or CMS statement. In any case, the FILEDEF must be issued before the SAS statement that references the file.

Special Naming Conventions

Although the SAS System allows you to use an underscore (_) in SAS names, VM/PC does not. Therefore, do no use an underscore character in a libref or a fileref.

Reading an External File

Issue a FILEDEF command to associate a fileref with the external file to be read. Then use the fileref in the INFILE statement of your SAS program. For example, suppose you write a DATA step that reads the external disk file CLIMATE DATA, which is stored on your A-disk, and you want to use DAILY as the fileref:

```
R;
FILEDEF DAILY DISK CLIMATE DATA A
R;
SAS (invoke the SAS System)
(SAS messages)
1?
DATA WEATHER;
2?
INFILE DAILY;
3?
INPUT TEMP PRECIP SUNHRS;
4?
more SAS statements
```

The fileref DAILY points to the CMS file CLIMATE DATA A.

Reading a SAS Data Set

Under most circumstances, you do not need to define a libref explicitly for a SAS file because SAS makes the association automatically. To access an existing SAS file on any minidisk, just use the file's two-level name in the appropriate SAS statement. SAS searches all accessed minidisks for the file you have specified and issues the appropriate FILEDEF when it finds the file. For example, suppose the SAS data set FOOD.PRICES is stored on your B-disk. When SAS reads this statement,

```
SET FOOD.PRICES;
```

it searches all accessed minidisks for a data set with filename PRICES and filetype FOOD. When it finds PRICES FOOD B, this FILEDEF is automatically issued:

```
FILEDEF FOOD DISK PRICES FOOD B
```

Note: if you have multiple SAS files with the same filename and filetype on different minidisks, SAS will find only the file on the minidisk that is first in the search order. For example, if you have a PRICES FOOD A and a PRICES FOOD B, SAS will find PRICES FOOD A. You must issue a FILEDEF for PRICES FOOD B explicitly if you want to access it.

Creating a SAS Data Set

Under most circumstances, you do not need to define a libref explicitly to create a SAS file because SAS makes the association automatically. When you are creating a new SAS file and you specify a two-level SAS name, SAS automatically issues a FILEDEF using the libref (first-level name) for the DDname parameter **and** for the filetype unless a FILEDEF with that DDname is already in effect. By default, the data set will be written to your A-disk. For example, suppose you are creating a SAS data set called FOOD.PRICES:

```
DATA FOOD.PRICES;
  INPUT ... ;
more SAS statements
```

When SAS reads the name FOOD.PRICES, it checks to see if a FILEDEF with DDname FOOD has been issued. If there is no such FILEDEF, SAS issues one automatically, using FOOD for both the DDname and filetype, PRICES as the filename, and A as the filemode:

```
FILEDEF FOOD DISK PRICES FOOD A
```

Note: do not use the same filetype for SAS files and external (non-SAS) files. If you want a new SAS data set to be stored on a disk other than your A-disk, you must issue the appropriate FILEDEF explicitly. Specify the appropriate values for the DDname and filemode parameters. You can specify any value for filename and filetype; SAS will substitute the libref (first-level name) and data set name (second-level name) for filetype and filename, respectively. For example, if you want to store FOOD.PRICES on a B-disk, your FILEDEF could be:

```
FILEDEF FOOD DISK DUMMY DUMMY B
```

Notice that CMS and SAS identify the file by the same two names, but the order is reversed. For example, SAS calls the data set FOOD.PRICES, and CMS calls it PRICES FOOD.

Creating an External File

To create an external file in a SAS program, first issue a FILEDEF command to associate a fileref with the name of the external file to be created. Then use the fileref in the FILE statement of your SAS program. For example, suppose you write a DATA step that reads the external disk file CLIMATE DATA (which is stored on your A-disk) and creates a second external file called COLD TEMPS A. You use the filerefs DAILY and FREEZE to reference the files:

```
R;
FILEDEF DAILY DISK CLIMATE DATA A
R;
FILEDEF FREEZE DISK COLD TEMPS A
R;
SAS
1?
DATA _NULL_;
2?
INFILE DAILY;
3?
INPUT TEMP PRECIP SUNHRS;
4?
FILE FREEZE;
5?
more SAS statements
```

DETAILS FOR THE VMS OPERATING SYSTEM

The SAS System running under the VMS operating system is documented in "Changes and Enhancements in the Base SAS and SAS/GRAPH Products under VMS," SAS Technical Report P-128.

Invoking the SAS System

Enter the SAS command after you receive the $ prompt:

```
$ SAS
```

or

```
$ SAS/options
```

or

```
$ SAS filename
```

If you enter *SAS* you will invoke the SAS System in line-prompt mode. Use the second method to specify valid *options* when you invoke SAS. For example, you can specify *FSDEVICE=devicename* to invoke SAS in display manager mode. With the third method, you can specify *filename* to give the name of a file containing the SAS program to be executed. This method is called *noninteractive mode*.

Read more about the SAS command and how to execute SAS in batch mode in Technical Report P-128.

Defining Files

The method that you use to define a file depends on whether the file is a SAS or non-SAS (external) file. The method that you use allows the SAS System to distinguish between SAS files and external files.

External files You can define an external file in one of the following two ways:

- with the ASSIGN command of the DCL control language before you invoke the SAS System
- in the FILENAME statement within you SAS program.

With either method you associate the *fileref* with a complete file name, which includes the directory name and the name of a specific file within the directory. You can also issue the ASSIGN command in the X statement, a SAS statement that allows you to enter DCL commands in your SAS program.

The fileref is then used in SAS statements, such as INFILE and FILE, to refer to external files. If you specify a fileref in a SAS statement before you define the external file, the SAS System reads or creates a file in the current default directory with the following name:

```
[currentdefaultdirectory]fileref.extension
```

where *fileref* is specified in the INFILE statement to give the name of the file that is read from the current default directory or where *fileref* is specified in the FILE statement to give the name of the file being created in the current default directory.

Extension is a part of the file name that indicates the type of information a file contains. You must include the extension in the complete file name when you define an external file. (Refer to SAS Technical Report P-128 for more information on extension names.)

SAS files If you want to read or create a permanent SAS file, you must define the appropriate directory with the LIBNAME statement. In the LIBNAME statement you associate a *libref* with a directory name only. The libref is then used in SAS statements, such as DATA, SET, MERGE, and so on, to refer to the directory. Once you have defined a directory in the LIBNAME statement, you can use the associated libref to refer to any file in that directory.

If you do not include the LIBNAME statement in your program before a SAS statement that specifies the libref, you will get and error message stating that the directory to which you are referring cannot be found.

Note: discussion of SAS files in the following examples is limited to the most commonly used type, a **SAS data set**. A SAS data set is a SAS file containing observations and variables.

Methods for defining SAS data sets and external files are illustrated in the following sections.

Special Naming Conventions

Although the SAS System allows you to use an underscore (_) in SAS names, VMS does not. Therefore, do not use the underscore character in a libref or a fileref.

Reading an External File

You can use the FILENAME statement to define an external file. In the following program the FILENAME statement associates a fileref with a complete file name:

```
SAS (invoke the SAS System)
SAS messages
1? FILENAME DAILY '[YOURDIR1]YOURRAW.DAT';
2? DATA WEATHER;
3?    INFILE DAILY;
4?    INPUT TEMP PRECIP SUNHRS;
more SAS statements and messages
7? ENDSAS;
```

The FILENAME statement associates the fileref DAILY with the complete file name [YOURDIR1]YOURRAW.DAT. DAILY is then specified in the INFILE statement. Notice that the file name includes the directory name YOURDIR1 and the file YOURRAW within the directory DAT is the extension name.

You can also use the ASSIGN command to define the permanent external file before you invoke SAS. For example,

```
ASSIGN [YOURDIR1]YOURAW.DAT DAILY
```

Notice that the fileref DAILY is specified after the complete file name in the ASSIGN statement, which is opposite from the way you specify the FILENAME statement. If you chose to define the file by issuing the ASSIGN command with the X statement, you can simply replace the FILENAME statement in the above program with the following SAS statement:

```
X 'ASSIGN [YOURDIR1]YOURRAW.DAT DAILY';
```

Since the X statement is a SAS statement, be sure to put a semicolon at the end.

If you do not define the external file to be read by the above program, the SAS System will read (or attempt to read) a file from the current default directory with the following name:

```
[currentdefaultdirectory]DAILY.DAT
```

Reading a SAS Data Set

Use the LIBNAME statement to define the directory containing the SAS data set to be read, as shown in the following program:

```
SAS (invoke the SAS System)
(SAS messages)
1? LIBNAME REPORT '[DIR2]';
2? PROC PRINT DATA=REPORT.STATION;
3?    VAR A B C;
```

```
more SAS messages
4? ENDSAS;
```

The LIBNAME statement associates the libref REPORT with the directory [DIR2]. REPORT is then used as the first level of the permanent SAS data set name in the PROC PRINT statement. When this program executes, the SAS System reads a SAS data set named STATION from the directory named [DIR2], and PROC PRINT prints the values for the variables A, B, and C.

If you specify a libref that has not been associated with a directory in the LIBNAME statement, you will receive an error message that the directory cannot be found.

Creating a SAS Data Set

The following program creates a SAS data set using an external file as input. You must use the LIBNAME statement to define the directory in which to store the SAS data set. You must also use the FILENAME statement to associate a fileref with the complete file name [YOURDIR1]YOURRAW.DAT.

```
SAS (invoke the SAS System)
SAS messages
1? FILENAME DAILY '[YOURDIR1]YOURRAW.DAT';
2? LIBNAME MAP '[YOURDIR2]';
3? DATA MAP.WEATHER;
4?     INFILE DAILY;
more SAS statements and messages
5? ENDSAS;
```

The LIBNAME statement associates the libref MAP with the directory [YOURDIR2], the directory in which WEATHER is stored. MAP is then specified as the first-level name of the SAS data set in the DATA statement.

If the LIBNAME statement is not specified before a statement that specifies the libref, you will receive an error message that the directory cannot be found. If you do not specify the FILENAME statement, the SAS System will search the current default directory for a file named DAILY.DAT.

Creating an External File

When you are creating an external file, you can use the FILENAME statement or the ASSIGN command to define the complete file name. The following program uses a SAS data set as input to create an external file:

```
SAS (invoke the SAS System)
SAS messages
1? FILENAME FREEZE '[DIR3]COLDRAW.DAT';
2? LIBNAME MAP '[YOURDIR2]';
3? DATA _NULL_;
4?     SET MAP.WEATHER;
5?     FILE FREEZE;
6?     IF TEMP < 32 THEN PUT TEMP;
more SAS statements and messages
9? ENDSAS;
```

The FILENAME statement associates the fileref FREEZE with the complete file name [DIR3]COLDRAW.DAT, and the LIBNAME statement associates the libref MAP with the directory containing WEATHER, the SAS data set being used as input.

When this program executes, all TEMP values less than 32 are written to an external file named COLDRAW.DAT. This file is located in the directory [DIR3]. If you do not specify the FILENAME statement, the SAS System writes the values in a file in the current default directory. The file has the following name:

```
[currentdefaultdirectory]FREEZE.DAT
```

DETAILS FOR THE VSE OPERATING SYSTEM AND ICCF

The *SAS Companion for the VSE Operating System* and "Enhancements and Updates for the VSE Operating System," SAS Technical Report P-132, give complete information on using the SAS System with the VSE operating system and ICCF.

The examples in this section use the word SAS to invoke the SAS System.

VSE Batch

Invoking the SAS System Use the EXEC statement in your JCL:

```
// EXEC PROC=SAS
```

In this case, a VSE batch procedure named *SAS* contains all the standard job control language required to invoke the SAS System in batch mode. Refer to the *SAS Companion for the VSE Operating System* for information on how to specify options at SAS invocation.

If your installation does not support a batch procedure to invoke the SAS System, your SAS consultant can tell you how to invoke SAS.

Defining files To define files stored on disk use the following set of JCL statements: DLBL, EXTENT, and ASSGN. You must issue this set of statements for each disk file needed—SAS and non-SAS. (In this context non-SAS means an external file—a file that is not a SAS file.)

The DLBL statement associates a *fileref* with an external file or a *libref* with a library of SAS files. In VSE terminology the fileref or the libref is called a *filename*. The EXTENT statement provides information about disk space occupied by the file, names a disk volume, and assigns a logical unit. The ASSGN statement associates the logical unit with the disk volume.

For example, the following statements define an external file stored on disk:

```
// DLBL fileref,'external.file.name',expiry
// EXTENT logicalunit,volumeserial,type,seq,begin,trks/blks
// ASSGN logicalunit,DISK,VOL=volumeserial,disposition
```

Use the following statements to define a library of SAS files stored on disk:

```
// DLBL libref,'SAS.library.name',expiry
// EXTENT logicalunit,volumeserial,type,seq,begin,trks/blks
// ASSGN logicalunit,DISK,VOL=volumeserial,disposition
```

The *fileref* is then used in SAS statements, such as FILE and INFILE, to refer to a permanent external file, and the *libref* is then used in SAS statements, such as DATA, SET, MERGE, and so on, to refer to a permanent SAS library. Once defined the libref can be used repeatedly in SAS statements to read or create SAS files in the library.

These three statements must be specified in the order shown above. Notice that both DLBL statements show how to specify an expiration date (expiry), and the EXTENT statements show how to specify full extent information (type,seq, begin,trks | blks). These specifications are required when you are creating either a new SAS library or an external file, but they are not necessary for existing files. Example programs in the following sections use existing files.

Note: a SAS library can contain several different types of files. This discussion of SAS files is limited to one type, **SAS data sets**. A SAS data set is a SAS file containing observations and variables.

To define files stored on tape, use the TLBL, ASSGN, PAUSE, MTC, and UPSI statements. These statements are explained in the *SAS Companion for the VSE Operating System*, along with more detailed information on how to define tape and disk files.

If you use a libref or fileref in a SAS statement without having defined the file to which you are referring, you will receive an error message.

Special naming conventions The following information concerning fileref and libref naming conventions is summarized from the *SAS Companion for the VSE Operating System*:

- **Filerefs** or **librefs** specified in DLBL and TLBL statements must not exceed seven characters, although most SAS documentation states that as many as eight characters are allowed.
- The first letter of the **libref** specifies how the SAS library is accessed, that is, how the file is opened and whether you can write to it. Use one of the following letters as the first letter in a libref to indicate the appropriate access mode:

  W — to specify a work library assumed to be a temporary file.

  O — to create a new SAS library, not to be confused with writing a newly created SAS data set to an existing SAS library. The EXTENT statement must contain full extent information, as shown above.

  I or S — to read a SAS file from a SAS library; the file can be used for input only.

  U — (or any letter except W, O, S, or I) to specify read and write access to a SAS library.
- To access a permanent external file or SAS library stored on tape, you must use a libref or fileref ending with a 1-, 2-, or 3-digit number that matches the logical unit number specified in the control language.

These naming conventions are reflected in the following examples where appropriate. For more information on VSE naming conventions, please refer to the *SAS Companion for the VSE Operating System* and "Enhancements and Updates in SAS82.4 under VSE," SAS Technical Report P-132.

Methods for defining SAS libraries and external files are illustrated in the following sections.

Reading an external file In the following example, you must use the DLBL, EXTENT, and ASSGN statements to define the external file to be read:

```
* $$ JNM=jobname ...
* $$ LST LST= ...
* $$ LST LST= ...
// JOB jobname ...
// DLBL DAILY,'YOUR.RAW.DATA'
// EXTENT SYS050,VSE123
// ASSGN SYS050,DISK,VOL=VSE123,SHR
```

```
// EXEC  PROC=SAS
DATA WEATHER;
   INFILE DAILY RECFM=FB BLKSIZE=192 LRECL=1920;
   INPUT TEMP PRECIP SUNHRS;
more SAS statements
```

The DLBL statement associates the fileref DAILY with the file named YOUR. RAW.DATA. DAILY is then used in the INFILE statement

Note: the INFILE statement, in addition to giving fileref DAILY, must also supply the record format and block size. You must specify these two file characteristics for any file that you are reading by using the SAS options RECFM= and BLKSIZE=. You must also give the logical record length (LRECL=) if the file's record format is FB (fixed blocked) or VB (variable blocked).

Reading a SAS data set Use DLBL, EXTENT, and ASSGN statements to define a SAS library. In the following job, the DLBL statement associates the libref REPORT with a SAS library named YOUR.SAS.LIB. REPORT is then used in the PROC PRINT statement as the first level of the permanent SAS data set name:

```
* $$ JNM=jobname ...
* $$ LST LST= ...
* $$ LST LST= ...
// JOB jobname ...
// DLBL REPORT,'YOUR.SAS.LIB'
// EXTENT SYS050,VSE123
// ASSGN SYS050,DISK,VOL=VSE123,SHR
// EXEC  PROC=SAS
PROC PRINT DATA=REPORT.STATION;
   VAR A B C;
more SAS statements
```

When this program executes, the SAS data set named STATION is read from the SAS library YOUR.SAS.LIB, and PROC PRINT prints all the values for variables A, B, and C.

Note: if you specify a libref beginning with the letter I or S in this example, you have read-only access to the SAS library. For example, if YOUR.SAS.LIB is protected and allows only read access, you must specify IREPORT instead of REPORT. Remember that a libref beginning with a letter other than W, I, S, or O requests read and write access.

Creating a SAS data set The following program creates a permanent SAS data set using an external file as input. Therefore, you must use two sets of DLBL, EXTENT, and ASSGN statements: one set to define the SAS library that will store the newly created SAS data set and one to define the external file to be read.

```
* $$ JNM=jobname ...
* $$ LST LST= ...
* $$ LST LST= ...
// JOB jobname ...
// DLBL DAILY,'YOUR.RAW.DATA'
// EXTENT SYS050,VSE123
// ASSGN SYS050,DISK,VOL=VSE123,SHR
// DLBL MAP,'YOUR.SAS.LIB'
// EXTENT SYS067,ABC321
// ASSGN SYS067,DISK,VOL=ABC321,SHR
// EXEC  PROC=SAS
DATA MAP.WEATHER;
```

```
    INFILE DAILY RECFM=recfmBLKSIZE=blksizeLRECL=lrecl;
    INPUT TEMP PRECIP SUNHRS;
more SAS statements
```

The first DLBL statement associates the fileref DAILY with the permanent external file YOUR.RAW.DATA. DAILY is then used in the INFILE statement. The second DLBL statement associates the libref MAP with the SAS library YOUR.SAS.LIB. MAP is then used as the first level of the permanent SAS data set name in the DATA statement. When this program executes the new SAS data set WEATHER is stored in YOUR.SAS.LIB. Observations in WEATHER will contain the variables TEMP, PRECIP, and SUNHRS.

Creating an external file The following program creates an external file using a SAS data set as input. Again, you must include one set of JCL statements to define the SAS library to be used as input and one set to define the external file that is created by this program.

```
* $$ JNM=jobname ...
* $$ LST LST= ...
* $$ LST LST= ...
// JOB jobname ...
// DLBL MAP,'YOUR.SAS.LIB'
// EXTENT SYS051,VSE123
// ASSGN SYS051,DISK,VOL=VSE123,SHR
// DLBL FREEZE,'COLD.RAW.DATA',99/365
// EXTENT SYS050,VSE123,1,0,5280,300
// ASSGN SYS050,DISK,VOL=VSE123,SHR
// EXEC  PROC=SAS
DATA _NULL_;
    SET MAP.WEATHER;
    FILE FREEZE;
    IF TEMP < 32 THEN PUT TEMP;
    more SAS statements
```

The first DLBL statement associates the libref MAP with the SAS library YOUR.SAS.LIB. MAP is then used in the SET statement as the first level of the permanent SAS data set name. The second DLBL statement associates the fileref FREEZE with the permanent external file COLD.RAW.DATA. FREEZE is then used in the FILE statement. When this program executes, all TEMP values less then 32 that are read from the SAS data set WEATHER are written to the file COLD.RAW.DATA. These values replace existing information in the file.

ICCF (VSE Interactive)

Invoking the SAS System Enter the ICCF proc (short for procedure) after you receive the *READY prompt:

```
*READY
SAS
```

The ICCF proc (named *SAS,* in this case) contains the standard job control language used to invoke the SAS System. If you are using a full-screen terminal, display manager mode is default; otherwise, line-prompt mode is the default. Refer to the *SAS Companion for the VSE Operating System* for information on how to specify options at SAS invocation.

If your installation does not support a proc to invoke the SAS System, your SAS consultant can tell you how to invoke SAS.

Defining files In the ICCF proc that is used to invoke the SAS System, you must include a /FILE statement to define each permanent file—SAS and non-SAS. In this context non-SAS means an external file—any file that is not a SAS file.

In the /FILE statement you associate a *fileref* with a permanent external file and a *libref* with a library of SAS files. In ICCF terminology the fileref or the libref is called a *filename*. For example, to define an external file include the /FILE statement in the ICCF proc:

```
/FILE NAME=fileref,ID'external.file.name',UNITS=logicalunit,
/  SERIAL=volumeserial,DATE=expiry,LOC=begin,trks|blks
```

The *fileref* is then used in SAS statements, such as FILE and INFILE, to refer to the external file.

To define a SAS data library, include the following /FILE statement in the ICCF proc:

```
/FILE NAME=libref,ID'SAS.library.name',UNITS=logicalunit,
/  SERIAL=volumeserial,DATE=expiry,LOC=begin,trks|blks
```

The *libref* is then used in SAS statements, such as DATA, SET, MERGE, and so on, to refer to the library of SAS files.

The /FILE statements shown above include parameters for specifying an expiration date (DATE=expiry), beginning tracks, and number of tracks or blocks used (LOC=begin,trks | blks). This information is required if you are creating a new SAS library or a new external file, but it is not necessary if you are using an existing library.

Note: UNITS must specify a logical unit that was assigned to the disk volume *volumeserial* in the ICCF start-up JCL. See your systems personnel for more information on logical units.

You cannot use tape files with the SAS System running under ICCF.

If you use a libref or fileref in a SAS statement without having defined the file to which you are referring, you will receive an error message.

Note: a SAS library can contain several different types of files. This discussion of SAS files is limited the most commmonly used type, a **SAS data set**. A SAS data set is a SAS file containing observations and variables.

Special naming conventions The following information concerning fileref and libref naming conventions is summarized from the *SAS Companion for the VSE Operating System*:

- Filerefs or librefs specified in /FILE statements must not exceed seven characters, although most SAS documentation states that as many as eight characters are allowed.
- The first letter of the **libref** specifies how the SAS library is accessed, that is, how the file is opened and whether you can write to it. Use the following letters as the first letter in a libref to indicate the appropriate access mode:

  W to specify a work library assumed to be a temporary file.

  O to create a new SAS library, not to be confused with writing a newly created SAS data set to an existing SAS library. Remember to include the DATE= and LOC= parameters in the /FILE statement, as shown above.

  I or S to read a SAS file from a SAS library; the file is used for input only.

U (or any letter except W, O, S, or I) to specify read and write access to a SAS library.

These naming conventions are reflected in the following examples where appropriate. For more information on VSE naming conventions, please refer to the *SAS Companion for the VSE Operating System* and "Enhancements and Updates in SAS82.4 under VSE," SAS Technical Report P-132.

Methods for defining SAS libraries and external files are illustrated in the following sections.

Reading an external file If your SAS program reads an external file, you must define that file by including the /FILE statement in the ICCF proc. Assume that the file to be read is an existing file named YOUR.RAW.DATA. Include the following statement:

```
/FILE NAME=DAILY,ID'YOUR.RAW.DATA',UNITS=SYS050,SERIAL=VSE123
```

The /FILE statement associates the fileref DAILY with the external file YOUR. RAW.DATA, an existing file.

Now, invoke the SAS System and enter your program. You will use the fileref DAILY in the INFILE statement to refer to the external file:

```
SAS (invoke the SAS System)
SAS messages
*ENTER DATA?
DATA WEATHER;
*ENTER DATA?
INFILE DAILY RECFM=recfm BLKSIZE=blksize LRECL=lrecl;
*ENTER DATA?
INPUT TEMP PRECIP SUNHRS;
more SAS statements and messages
*ENTER DATA?
ENDSAS;
```

Note: the INFILE statement, in addition to fileref DAILY, must also supply the record format and block size. You must specify these two file characteristics for any file that you are reading by using the SAS options RECFM= and BLKSIZE=. You must also give the logical record length (LRECL=) if the file's record format is FB (fixed blocked) or VB (variable blocked).

Reading a SAS data set The following program reads a SAS data set from an existing SAS library. You must define the library by including a /FILE statement in the ICCF proc:

```
/FILE NAME=REPORT,ID'YOUR.SAS.LIB',UNITS=SYS050,SERIAL=VSE123
```

The /FILE statement associates the libref REPORT with the SAS library named YOUR.SAS.LIB.

You are now ready to invoke the SAS System and enter the program:

```
SAS (invoke the SAS System)
SAS messages
*ENTER DATA?
PROC PRINT DATA=REPORT.STATION;
*ENTER DATA?
VAR A B C;
      more SAS messages
*ENTER DATA?
ENDSAS;
```

The libref REPORT is used in the PROC PRINT statement as the first level of the permanent SAS data set name. When this program executes the SAS data set named STATION is read from the SAS library YOUR.SAS.LIB, and PROC PRINT prints all values for variables A, B, and C.

Note: if you specify a libref beginning with the letter I or S, you have read-only access to the SAS library. For example, if you specify IREPORT instead of REPORT in this example, you have read-only access to YOUR.SAS.LIB. Remember that a libref beginning with a letter other than W, I, S, or O requests read and write access.

Creating a SAS data set The following program creates a SAS data set using an external file as input. Therefore, you include two /FILE statements in the ICCF proc: one to define the SAS library that will store the newly created SAS data set and one to define the external file to be used as input:

```
/FILE NAME=DAILY,ID'YOUR.RAW.DATA',UNITS=SYS050,SERIAL=VSE123
/FILE NAME=MAP,ID'YOUR.SAS.LIB',UNITS=SYS067,SERIAL=ABC321
```

The first /FILE statement associates the fileref DAILY with the permanent external file YOUR.RAW.DATA. The second /FILE statement associates the fileref MAP with the permanent SAS data library YOUR.SAS.LIB, an existing SAS library.

You are now ready to invoke the SAS System and enter the program statements:

```
SAS (invoke the SAS System)
SAS messages
*ENTER DATA?
DATA MAP.WEATHER;
*ENTER DATA?
INFILE DAILY RECFM=recfm BLKSIZE=blksize LRECL=lrecl;
*ENTER DATA?
INPUT TEMP PRECIP SUNHRS;
more SAS statements and messages
*ENTER DATA?
ENDSAS;
```

DAILY is used in the INFILE statement to refer to the external file. MAP is used as the first level of the permanent SAS data set name in the DATA statement. When this program executes, it creates the new SAS data set WEATHER in YOUR.SAS.LIB. Observations in WEATHER will contain the variables TEMP, PRECIP, and SUNHRS.

Creating an external file The following program creates an external file using a SAS data set as input. Again, in the ICCF proc you must include one /FILE statement to define the SAS library to be used as input and another /FILE statement to define the external file that is created by this program:

```
/FILE NAME=MAP,ID'YOUR.SAS.LIB',UNITS=SAS051,SERIAL=VSE123
/FILE NAME=FREEZE,ID'COLD.RAW.DATA',UNITS=SYS050,SERIAL=VSE789
```

The first /FILE statement associates the libref MAP with an existing SAS library, YOUR.SAS.LIB. The second /FILE statement associates the fileref FREEZE with the external file COLD.RAW.DATA, also existing.

You are now ready to invoke the SAS System and enter the program:

```
SAS (invoke the SAS System)
SAS messages
*ENTER DATA?
DATA _NULL_;
*ENTER DATA?
```

```
SET MAP.WEATHER;
*ENTER DATA?
FILE FREEZE;
*ENTER DATA?
IF TEMP < 32 THEN PUT TEMP;
more SAS statements and messages
*ENTER DATA?
8? ENDSAS;
```

The libref MAP is used as the first level of the permanent SAS data set name in the SET statement. The fileref FREEZE is used in the FILE statement. When this program executes, all TEMP values less then 32 that are read from the SAS data set WEATHER are written to the file COLD.RAW.DATA. These values replace existing information in the external file.

NOTES

1. **AOS/VS, PRIMOS, VMS**: If you do not define the external file to be read or created by your SAS program, the SAS System uses a file in the current default directory with the following name:

```
AOS/VS   :UDD:currentdefaultdirectory:fileref
PRIMOS   <masterdirectory>currentdirectory>fileref
VMS      [currentdefaultdirectory]fileref.DAT
```

2. **AOS/VS, PRIMOS, VMS**: A SAS data library is a logical concept, not a physical entity. All permanent SAS files in a directory belong to the same SAS data library.

CMS, VM/PC: A SAS data library is a logical concept, not a physical entity. All SAS files with the same filetype and filemode make up a logical SAS data library.

OS, VSE: A SAS data library is a physical data set— an OS or VSE data set that contains one or more SAS files.

3. **AOS/VS, PRIMOS, VMS**: The LIBNAME statement is available if you are running the SAS System under one of these operating systems.

4. **AOS/VS, PRIMOS, VMS**: The LIBSEARCH statement is available if you are running the SAS System under one of these operating systems.

5. **CMS, OS**: Under TSO you can use the SAS TSO statement to issue TSO commands from within your SAS program. Under CMS you can use the SAS CMS statement to issue CMS commands from within your SAS program. The X statement is used like a CMS statement under CMS and like a TSO statement under TSO.

Appendix 4

Full-Screen Editing

INTRODUCTION

This appendix shows you how to enter information if you are using the SAS System with a full-screen terminal. Use the editing features described here with the SAS Display Manager System for entering SAS program statements. These editing features can also be used to enter text in other full-screen SAS software products, for example, to enter FSLETTER text in the SAS/FSP software product or to compose screen applications with the SAS/AF software product. You can also set your terminal keys to convenient functions with the SAS user profile facility.

The display manager examples below illustrate full-screen editing capabilities that are available wherever you need them in the SAS System.

```
Command ===>                                          SAS Log  00:00







----------------------------------------------------------------------
Command ===>                                          Program Editor

00001    PROC PRINT DATA=A;
00002    RUN;
00003
00004 /* MOVING TEXT AROUND ON THE SCREEN
00005 IS EASY.  IF YOU ARE ENTERING A SAS PROGRAM,
00006 FIRST TYPE YOUR STATEMENTS ON THE
00007 NUMBERED LINES LIKE THIS: */
00008
```

Screen A4.1 Entering Text

```
Command ===>                                          SAS Log  00:00







----------------------------------------------------------------------
Command ===>                                          Program Editor

I0001    PROC PRINT DATA=A;
00002    _
00003    RUN;
00004
00005 /* TO ENTER ANOTHER LINE BETWEEN THE TWO LINES OF
00006 YOUR PROGRAM, YOU CAN ENTER THE CHARACTER I ON
00007 ONE OF THE LINE NUMBERS ON THE LEFT AND PRESS
00008 THE ENTER KEY.  I (INSERT) IS CALLED A LINE COMMAND.
00009 LINE COMMANDS USUALLY AFFECT ONLY ONE LINE OR A BLOCK
00010 OF SPECIFIED LINES. */
```

Screen A4.2 Inserting Lines with a Line Command

```
Command ===>                                              SAS Log  00:00




------------------------------------------------------------------------
Command ===> CAPS ON                                      Program Editor
   PROC PRINT DATA=A;
      TITLE 'RESEARCH FUNDS ACCOUNT BALANCE';
   RUN;

/* TO CAUSE ALL TEXT ENTERED OR ALTERED AFTER THE
COMMAND IS EXECUTED TO BE TRANSLATED INTO UPPERCASE,
YOU CAN TYPE A CAPS ON COMMAND ON THE COMMAND LINE
IN THE AREA FOLLOWING THE ARROW AND PRESS THE ENTER
KEY. THIS IS CALLED A COMMAND-LINE COMMAND.  COMMAND-
LINE COMMANDS APPLY TO THE ENTIRE FILE. */
```

Screen A4.3 Translating Text into Uppercase with a Command-Line Command

```
Command ===>                                              SAS Log  00:00




------------------------------------------------------------------------
Command ===>                                              Program Editor

   PROC PRINT DATA=A;
      TITLE 'RESEARCH FUNDS ACCOUNT BALANCE';
   RUN;

/* IF YOU WANT TO CHANGE THE WORD 'FUNDS' TO 'FUND'
IN THE TITLE STATEMENT, YOU WILL NEED TO USE THE
DELETE KEY.  THIS IS ONE OF DISPLAY MANAGER'S EDITING
KEYS. THESE ARE THE EDITING KEYS THAT THE SAS SYSTEM
SETS FOR YOUR CONVENIENCE.  IF YOU ALSO NEED TO USE
YOUR TERMINAL'S OWN EDITING KEYS, YOU NEED TO REFER
TO THE MANUAL THAT CAME WITH THE TERMINAL. */
```

Screen A4.4 Deleting Characters with an Editing Key

```
Command ===>                                              SAS Log  00:00

----------------------------------------------------------------------
Command ===> SUBMIT                                     Program Editor

   PROC PRINT DATA=A;
      TITLE 'RESEARCH FUND ACCOUNT BALANCE';
   RUN;
/* WHEN YOU ARE READY TO RUN YOUR PROGRAM, YOU
CAN TYPE THE SUBMIT COMMAND ON THE COMMAND LINE
AND PRESS THE ENTER KEY. */
```

Screen A4.5 Submitting SAS Program Statements

```
Command ===>                                              SAS Log  00:00

----------------------------------------------------------------------
Command ===> KEYS                                       Program Editor
/* THE EXAMPLES SO FAR HAVE SHOWN YOU HOW TO USE LINE
COMMANDS, COMMAND-LINE COMMANDS, AND THE EDITING
KEYS.  YOU CAN ALSO SET EACH FUNCTION
KEY ON YOUR TERMINAL TO ANY OF THE SAS FULL-SCREEN
LINE OR COMMAND-LINE COMMANDS VALID IN THE DISPLAY
MANAGER OR FULL-SCREEN PROCEDURE SCREEN YOU ARE USING.
TO FIND OUT THE CURRENT SETTINGS, TYPE THE WORD
KEYS ON THE COMMAND LINE AND PRESS THE ENTER KEY. */
```

Screen A4.6 Function Key Settings

The result of the KEYS command is shown below. These are the default function key settings for the program editor screen that SAS Institute provides to your site; yours may be different from those shown.

```
                FUNCTION KEY DEFINITIONS
Command ===>
KEY     COMMAND
01      help
02      split
03      submit
04      recall
05      rfind
06      rchange
07      backward
08      forward
09      output
10      left
11      right
12      cursor
13      help
14      split
15      submit
16      recall
17      rfind
18      rchange
19      backward
20      forward
21      output
22      left
23      right
24      cursor
```

Screen A4.7 Function Key Definition Screen

Notice that one of the function keys is set to execute the SUBMIT command. Instead of typing the word SUBMIT on the command line and pressing ENTER as you did above to submit your program statements, simply press the function key set to execute the SUBMIT command.

EDITING KEYS

The editing keys you can use with display manager and the procedures that allow full-screen editing are shown below. You can use these same keys when editing text on data lines and commands on command lines. In general, you use an editing key to make a change to one character or one line of an unprotected field and a function key to search or scroll an entire file. The editing keys you can use in full-screen editing are listed and defined in **Figure A4.1**.

Note: the words or symbols on the editing keys described in **Figure A4.1** may not be the same as those on the terminal you are using.[1]

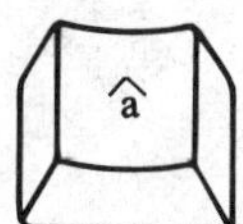

The INSERT key allows you to insert characters within a line. Press the key and position the cursor where you want to insert text. Characters are shifted to the right to make room for new text. *

* **IBM users**: On a 3270 series terminal, press the RESET key to discontinue the insert.
Minicomputer users: Press the INSERT key again to discontinue the INSERT.

The DELETE key erases the character either preceding the cursor position or in the current cursor position, depending on the terminal keyboard you are using.

The ERASE EOF (End-of-Field) key deletes or erases all the characters from the cursor position to the end of either a data entry line or, on some screens, the end of a field.

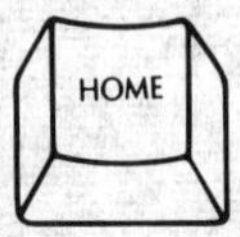

The HOME key moves the cursor to the first column of the first unprotected field on the screen, the entry area of the command line on most screens. *

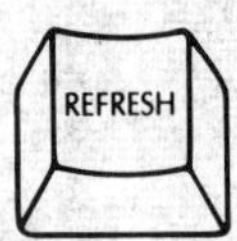

The REFRESH key redisplays the contents of the screen line-by-line. It removes messages from the operating system and is especially useful for removing unwanted characters input since the last time you pressed ENTER or a function key. **

The NEW LINE key moves the cursor to the first unprotected field of the next line. Use the NEXT FIELD key to move the cursor from the line number to the data entry area.

The PRIOR FIELD key moves the cursor to the previous unprotected field.

The NEXT FIELD key moves the cursor to the next unprotected field.

The ENTER key executes commands entered on a command line or on a line number.

Figure A4.1 Editing Keys

---

* **IBM users**: Press the ALT and Home keys.

** **CMS, OS, and VM/PC**: Press ALT PA2.
VSE: Press ALT CLEAR.

COMMANDS

Command Conventions

SAS full-screen editing commands follow these conventions:

COMMAND OPTION | *option* [| **OPTION** | *option* | ...]

where

bold CAPS
: indicates a **KEYWORD**; use exactly the same spelling and form as shown.

lowercase italic
: indicates you supply the actual value.

vertical bar |
: means *or* use only one of the terms separated by vertical bars.

brackets [ ]
: indicate optional information or keywords.

three periods (...)
: mean that more than one of the terms preceding ... can be optionally specified.

For example, in the FIND command

FIND *characterstring* [**PREFIX** | **SUFFIX** | **WORD**]

FIND
: is the command **KEYWORD**.

characterstring
: is a user-defined option. You supply the value of the string of characters you want to locate. It is not in brackets so you know you are required to specify a character string.

[**PREFIX** | **SUFFIX** | **WORD**]
: are three system-defined option **KEYWORDS** that appear in bold uppercase letters, enclosed by brackets [ ], separated by vertical bars |; the bold uppercase letters indicate that each is entered exactly as written; the brackets indicate that these options are allowed but not required; the vertical bars indicate that you can specify only one of the three.

Line Commands

You can use line commands to perform such tasks as moving, copying, inserting, and deleting lines or blocks of lines, and designating target locations for moved, copied, and inserted lines. As an example, a list of line commands that you can use for full-screen editing in the text editor in SAS software products follows. See "SAS Display Manager" appendix for the line commands available in the display manager program editor.

SINGLE COMMANDS:

A,B target position, A (after) or B (before), of an M, MM, C, CC, or COPY command.

C copy a line to the location indicated either by an A (after) or B (before) line command. To copy more than one line, see the CC line command below.

D[*n*] delete one or more lines.

I[*n* | A[*n*] | B[*n*]] insert one or more lines immediately following or preceding an I command.

M move a line to the location indicated either by an A or B line command. To move more than one line, see the MM line command below.

MASK enter the mask to be used for newly inserted lines.

O a target position command that overlays the contents of one or more lines with moved or copied lines.

R[*n*] repeat a line *n* times immediately following that line.

TF[*n*] flow lines of text, deleting trailing blanks. You can follow TF with some number *n* to specify the right margin.

TS[*n*] insert one or more blank lines within a line of text.

BLOCK COMMANDS:

CC copy block of lines designated by CC on the first and last lines.

DD delete block of lines designated by DD on the first and last lines.

MM move block of lines designated by MM on the first and last lines.

RR repeat block of lines designated by RR on the first and last lines.

SPECIAL SHIFT COMMANDS:

>*n* shift data *n* columns to the right.

<*n* shift data *n* columns to the left.

>>*n* shift data on block of lines *n* columns to the right.

<<*n* shift data on block of lines *n* columns to the left.

Command-Line Commands

You can use command-line commands to perform many editing and file management tasks. As an example, the command-line commands that you can use in the SAS text editor are listed below by function:

Scrolling Commands

AUTOADD LEFT
BACKWARD *n*
FORWARD RIGHT
TOP HSCROLL
BOTTOM VSCROLL

File Management Commands

COPY	END	INCLUDE

General Editing Commands

CHANGE	CAPS
RCHANGE	CPRO
DES	CUNPRO
FILL	CURSOR
FIND	NULLS
RFIND	NUMS
BOUNDS	PREVCMD
CANCEL	RESET

Help, Function Keys, and Host-level Commands

HELP	KEYS	X command

Many of these commands can also be used in other screens in SAS full-screen procedures, as well as in display manager. See "SAS Display Manager" appendix for a list and glossary of display manager commands.

USING COMMANDS: MORE EXAMPLES

Entering Commands Directly

Both command-line commands and line commands can be entered directly or executed with function keys. To execute a command with a function key, you need to know the function key settings. In some procedures you can alter function key settings and then permanently store the new settings. See the **Function Keys** section for a discussion of executing commands with function keys.

Entering command-line commands directly To enter a command-line command directly, type the command on the command line and press the ENTER key. For example, to scroll backward the default vertical scroll amount, type

```
BAC
```

on the command line and press ENTER. The BAC command is an example of the most basic kind of command to enter; it requires only that you type a keyword and press ENTER. The examples below include commands that allow options and commands that require cursor placement.

Command-line commands with options The BAC command allows options to be specified. For example, to scroll backward the maximum amount, type

```
BAC MAX
```

on the command line and press ENTER.

Entering line commands directly To enter a line command directly, type the command over a line number and press the ENTER key. In the text editor screens of most full-screen procedures, unlike the program editor screen in display manager, the numbering facility is OFF by default. To number the data entry lines, use the NUMS ON command-line command. Type NUMS ON on the command line and press ENTER.

Examples below include single line commands, line commands with options, line commands requiring target commands and positioning of the cursor, and block commands. Note the underscore (_) marking the cursor position in several of the examples.

Single line command As an example, to insert a new line for entering text, type I, the insert line command, on any part of a line number

```
00I001 data line one
000002 data line two
000003 data line three
```

and press ENTER. One new line, the default, is inserted between the first and second lines.

```
000001 data line one
000002 _
000003 data line two
000004 data line three
```

Line command with option Some line commands, the I line command, for example, allow you to specify an option for which you supply the value, such as some number *n*. To specify how many lines to insert, follow the I line command with some number *n*, such as 3, and a blank space

```
I3 001 data line one
000002 data line two
000003 data line three
```

and press ENTER. Three new lines are inserted between the first and second lines.

```
000001 data line one
000002 _
000003
000004
000005 data line two
000006 data line three
```

Line command requiring cursor position The TS (text split) line command requires that you enter the command, then position the cursor before pressing ENTER. Enter the TS command on a line number, position the cursor,

```
TS0001 Split this line after the semicolon;_then add new copy
```

and then press ENTER. A new line is inserted:

```
000001 Split this line after the semicolon;_
000002
000003                                          then add new copy.
```

Line command requiring a target command The following example shows how to use the M (move) and A (after) line commands:

```
M00001 Move this line
A00002 after the second line
000003 with the M (move) and A (after) line commands.
```

The first line becomes the second line:

```
000001 after the second line
000002 Move this line
000003 with the M (move) and A (after) line commands.
```

Block line command You can also use line commands to affect blocks of lines. For example,

```
MM0001 Move the first two lines
MM0002 after the third line
A00003 with the M (move) and A (after) line commands.

000001 with the M (move) and A (after) line commands.
000002 Move the first two lines
000003 after the third line
```

See **Command Conventions** earlier in this appendix for a description of command conventions.

Executing line commands without line numbers If your data lines are not numbered, you can still execute line commands without having to use the NUMS ON command to display line numbers. Type the line command, preceded by a colon (:), on the command line, position the cursor on the line you want to be affected by the line command, and press ENTER. For example, to execute the TS (text split) line command from the command line, type :TS on the command line, position the cursor, and press ENTER.

You can also execute a line command with a function key even when line numbers are not displayed. Position the cursor where you want the command to take effect, and press a function key set to execute that line command. See **Altering Settings: the Function Key Definition Screen** for setting a function key to execute a line command.

Entering Multiple Commands

You can enter a series of commands on the command line by separating the commands with semicolons. For example, you can type the BACKWARD MAX scroll command and the FIND command on the command line, separate them with a semicolon,

```
BACKWARD MAX; FIND 'DATA ONE'
```

and execute both by pressing the ENTER key once.

FUNCTION KEYS

Executing Commands with Function Keys

To execute a command with a function key can be as simple as pressing the function key instead of typing a command on the command line and pressing ENTER. To use a function key to execute a command with an option, you can either assign that function key the command with the option, such as BACKWARD MAX, or you can type the option MAX on the command line and press the BACKWARD function key. You can execute a command that requires cursor placement, such as SPLIT, by positioning the cursor before pressing the SPLIT function key.

Function keys and multiple commands You can also combine the use of function keys and the submission of multiple commands. For example, if you set a function key to execute the command and option BACKWARD MAX followed by a semicolon,

```
BACKWARD MAX;
```

then you can enter

```
FIND 'DATA ONE'
```

on the command line and execute both by pressing the key you set to execute BACKWARD MAX; . The procedure executes the BACKWARD MAX command first and then the FIND command.

Altering Settings: the Function Key Definition Screen

You can alter the function key settings to execute any commands that are valid for the particular screen in the SAS full-screen software product that you are using. Use the KEYS command to display the function key definition screen for the screen you are currently using. Twenty-four function keys with settings are listed although some terminals may have only twelve function keys.

You can assign any valid command-line command or line command to any function key on your terminal. Precede line commands with a colon (:). You can use editing keys such as EOF and DELETE, or simply type over a function key setting to alter it. On the function key definition screen, you can use the following commands:

```
BACKWARD
CANCEL
FORWARD
END
```

You can use any of these commands by pressing a function key set to execute it or by typing it on the command line and pressing the ENTER key. You can scroll backward and forward to view the entire list of key settings; you can cancel any changes made; you can use the END command, or a key assigned to execute the END command, to save your altered settings and return to the screen on which you executed the KEYS command. Altered function key settings remain in effect until you exit from the procedure or until you alter the settings again. The next time you enter the procedure, the original default settings will be in effect again.

To keep your altered function key settings from one session to another, you must store them in your own user profile catalog. At the beginning of each SAS session, use the appropriate operating system commands to make your user profile catalog available. See the sections **User Profile** and **Access to Your PROFILE Catalog**.

SAS USER PROFILE

Installation Profile

Each installation of the SAS System receives a special SAS data library that contains information used by SAS software to control various aspects of your SAS session. For example, in base SAS software, a catalog in the installation profile library contains the default function key settings for the SAS Display Manager System and PROC DATASETS; similiar information for additional SAS software products is contained in other catalogs within that same library. In some cases, these default settings can be tailored to your site by your SAS installation representative.

Keep in mind that any changes made to the installation profile library are universal for your site. That is, the default settings stored in the catalogs in this library are for everyone using the SAS System at your installation. If these default settings are not suitable for your own applications, you can set up your own user profile. See **User Profile** below.

User Profile

A user profile catalog is available for customizing default function key settings to meet individual needs and preferences. When looking for current function key settings, for example, the SAS System searches the user profile for function key settings stored under the appropriate names before it looks in a catalog in the installation profile library.

Your own user profile information is stored in either a permanent catalog named SASUSER.PROFILE or a temporary catalog named WORK.PROFILE.[2] SASUSER is a reserved libref and PROFILE is a reserved SAS catalog name. The PROFILE catalog stores the function key settings for a particular screen or procedure each time you enter the function key definition screen and save the settings. You create a function key definition screen in your user profile catalog each time you use the KEYS command to display a function key definition screen and then save that screen by exiting it with the END command. By default, any function key definition screen that you create in this way is automatically stored under the appropriate name in the PROFILE catalog. For example, in base SAS software, you can have different function key settings for each display manager screen and PROC DATASETS because the system assigns a reserved name to each function key definition screen when it stores it in the user profile catalog. When you are using a particular display manager screen or full-screen procedure, the system looks for your function key setting information stored under a particular name for that screen or procedure only.

The user profile catalog is intended to be a personal catalog and cannot be accessed by more than one SAS user. Normally, an individual's profile is associated with an individual's user id.[3] It should not be stored in a SAS data library that is shared by a number of users.

Access to Your PROFILE Catalog

The individual user profile information is stored in a catalog named PROFILE in a SAS data library.[4] You should have access to your own user profile. In some cases, the reserved libref and catalog name SASUSER.PROFILE is used in a command procedure and automatically accessed when you invoke the SAS System at your site. In other cases, you may need to make the catalog SASUSER.PROFILE available to your session each time you execute the SAS System.

If you do not make the catalog SASUSER.PROFILE available to your session, WORK.PROFILE is opened and any function key definition screens you create are stored there. As with SAS data sets placed in temporary storage, your function key definition screens placed in the catalog WORK.PROFILE are available only for that session.

The library referenced by SASUSER, unlike the library containing the profile information for the entire installation, does not exist until you create it. (You can, however, reference an existing SAS data library using the libref SASUSER.) You must use a host operating system command to create a file or data set to contain a SAS data library that is associated with the reserved libref SASUSER. The system creates a PROFILE catalog automatically the first time you make a library referenced by SASUSER available to your session. Note that you must have write access to this SAS data library.

NOTES

1. If you are using one of the terminals listed below, use **Table A4.1** to determine the keys that have been assigned special editing functions in SAS full-screen procedures and display manager. See **Figure A4.1** for a description of the functions of these editing keys. If you are using a terminal other than one of those listed below that does not have keys matching the words or symbols shown in **Figure A4.1**, consult your SAS representative. If you are using an IBM terminal in the 3270-series, you can disregard this section.

Table A4.1 Full-Screen Editing Functions Assigned to Terminal Keys

Full-Screen Editing Key	PT45 Key	PST100 Key	PT25 Key
â (INSERT)	ichar or shift/del	insert or backspace	shift/del
a̸ (DELETE)	dchar or backspace	delete or del	backspace
ERASE EOF	line feed	erase	shift/f8
HOME	home	home	home
REFRESH	control/ clear	pf10	control/erase
NEW LINE	return or enter	return or enter	new line or enter
NEXT FIELD	f13	f2	shift/f5
PRIOR FIELD	f14	f3	shift/f6
ENTER	f3 or f15	f1 or pf13	f3 or shift/f7
MOVE CURSOR UP	↑	↑	↑
MOVE CURSOR DOWN	↓	↓	(not available)
MOVE CURSOR LEFT	←	←	←
MOVE CURSOR RIGHT	→	→	→

continued on next page

Table A4.1 *continued*

Full-Screen Editing Key	TEK4105 Key	VT100 Key	DASHER Key
â (INSERT)	backspace	backspace	C1
a̸ (DELETE)	rub out	delete	DEL
ERASE EOF	line feed	line feed	erase EOL
HOME	- (minus sign on numeric keypad)	- (minus sign on numeric keypad)	home
REFRESH	, (on numeric keypad)	, (on numeric keypad)	erase page
NEW LINE	return	return	new line or enter
NEXT FIELD	. (on numeric keypad)	. (on numeric keypad)	C4
PRIOR FIELD	0 (on numeric keypad)	0 (on numeric keypad)	C3
ENTER	enter	enter	CR
MOVE CURSOR UP	F1	↑	↑
MOVE CURSOR DOWN	F2	↓	↓
MOVE CURSOR LEFT	F3	←	←
MOVE CURSOR RIGHT	F4	→	→

2. **CMS and VM/PC**: The SAS System automatically creates SASUSER.PROFILE for you on your A-disk the first time you enter display manager or a SAS full-screen procedure. The SASUSER.PROFILE catalog remains on your A-disk for use in different SAS sessions. Disregard all references to explicitly making SASUSER .PROFILE available to your session.

3. **CMS and VM/PC**: The SASUSER.PROFILE catalog is stored on your own A-disk. This catalog is created automatically by the SAS System. You need not issue any CMS commands to use it.

4. **CMS and VM/PC**: Skip the section **Access to Your PROFILE Catalog**.

Appendix 5

SAS® Display Manager

INTRODUCTION

The SAS Display Manager System is a full-screen facility that allows you to interact with all parts of your SAS job—program statements, log, and procedure output. It provides you with a full-screen editor for inputting and preparing your SAS statements and data, displays the SAS log created when you run a SAS job, and displays the output produced by your SAS program statements. Display manager has three primary screens:

- the program editor screen where you input, edit, and save SAS source files and submit SAS program statements
- the log screen where you can browse the SAS log
- the output screen where you can browse output from your SAS jobs.

You also have access to special screens, such as the function key definition screen, and to SAS HELP, an on-line help facility where you can browse information about the entire SAS System.

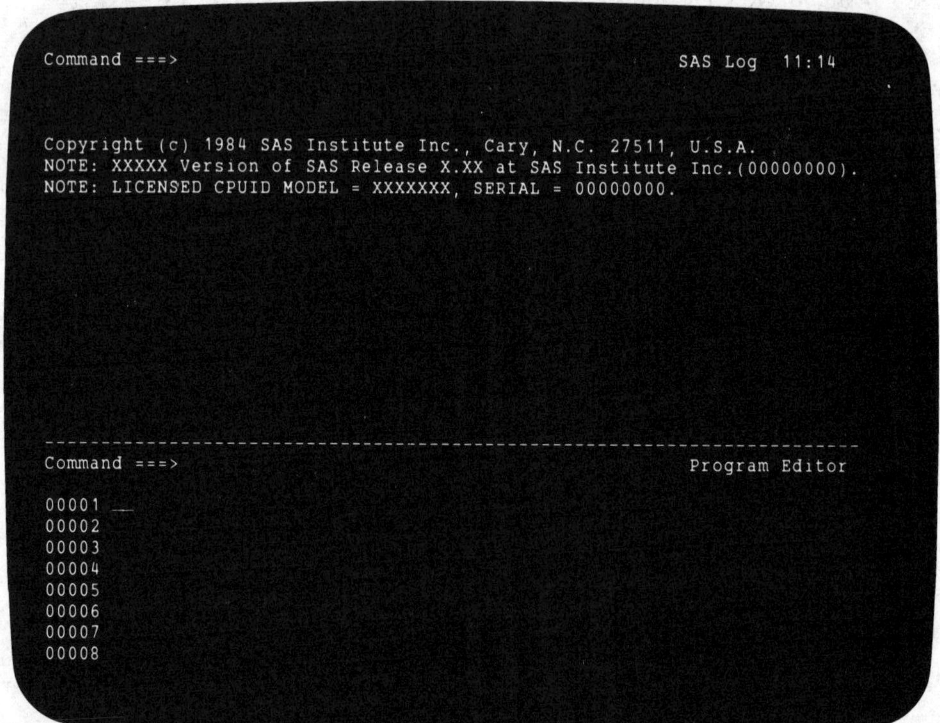

Screen A5.1 Program Editor/Log Screen

The display manager first shows you the screen shown in **Screen A5.1**. The bottom half is a program entry and edit area for your SAS statements; the top half of this split screen displays the SAS log.

Program Editor Screen

You type SAS statements in the program editor, review, make changes, and submit the statements for execution. In a SAS line-prompt session your program statements are submitted to the SAS System each time you enter a line; in a display manager session, you can delete and insert lines, enter, edit, and re-edit your SAS program statements and then submit them to SAS all at one time.

Log Screen

The top half of **Screen A5.1** is the log screen. Statements submitted to the SAS System from the program editor produce the SAS log that, together with any notes or error messages, is displayed in the display manager log screen. Except for entering commands on the command line, you cannot alter any text displayed in the log screen. As statements and messages build up in the SAS log, lines scroll off the top of the screen. Scrolling commands, which can be executed from the command line as well as with function keys, are available for browsing text in the log screen.

Output Screen

When you submit SAS program statements containing a PROC step that produces printed output, you can view that output in the output screen. The display manager displays the first page of the output and then allows you to see the rest of the output, one page at a time, or to skip to the last page of output. After the last page of requested output has been displayed, you can choose to return to the program editor/log screen or to browse the output in page-browse or line-browse mode. You can use function keys to scroll in page-browse mode; you can use function keys and execute command-line commands in line-browse mode.

TERMINALS, KEYS, AND COMMANDS

Function Keys

The SAS Display Manager System defines function keys for you to use to prepare your SAS program statements, to scroll information displayed on each screen, and to move from one screen to another. Some keys on your terminal keyboard, therefore, take on new meanings when you enter display manager. The default function key settings for display manager that were provided to your SAS site are described in this appendix. To set your own function keys, see the appendix on "Full-Screen Editing" for a discussion of the user profile facility.

Function keys on each screen The set of function keys that is available to you depends on the display manager screen with which you are working. In addition to entering commands directly on the command line or on line numbers, you can use function keys to execute commands. See the appendix on "Full-Screen Editing" for a discussion of

- using function keys to execute commands
- viewing the default settings
- altering the settings

• storing your altered settings.

Editing Keys

You can continue using some of your terminal's own editing keys with display manager, such as enter, insert, delete, and cursor movement keys. Ask someone knowledgeable at your site if you need help getting started with these keys.

The editing keys you use with display manager are shown below. You can use these same keys when editing program statements in the program editor or when entering commands on the command line of the program editor, log, or output screens. You can use these keys in all **unprotected fields**. In general, you choose an editing key to make a change to one character or one line of an unprotected field on the screen, whereas you choose a function key to search or scroll an entire file.

Note: the words or symbols on the editing keys described in **Figure A5.1** may not be the same as those on the terminal you are using.[1]

Press the INSERT key once to turn it on, and position the cursor where you want to insert a character. The next key you press inserts its character before the cursor position, shifting characters to the right to make room.*

The DELETE key erases the character either preceding the cursor position or in the current cursor position, depending on the terminal you are using.

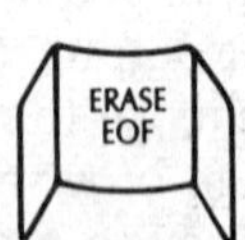

The ERASE EOF (End-of-Field) key deletes or erases all the characters from the cursor position to the end of either a data entry line or, on some screens, the end of a field.

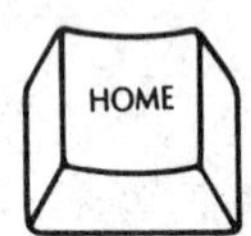

The HOME key moves the cursor to the first column of the first unprotected field on the screen, the entry area of the command line on most screens.**

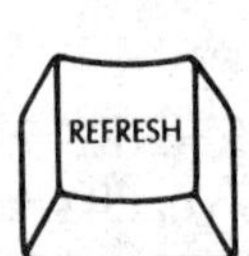

The REFRESH key redisplays the contents of the screen line-by-line. It removes messages from the operating system and is especially useful for removing unwanted characters input since the last time you pressed ENTER or a function key.***

The NEW LINE key moves the cursor to the first unprotected field of the next line. Use the NEXT FIELD key to move the cursor from the line number to the data entry area.

---

* **IBM users:** On a 3270 series terminal, press the RESET key to discontinue the INSERT.
Minicomputer users: Press the INSERT key again to discontinue the INSERT.

** **IBM users:** Press the ALT and Home keys.

*** **CMS, OS and VM/PC:** Press ALT PA2.
VSE: Press ALT CLEAR.

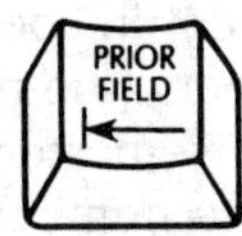

The PRIOR FIELD key moves the cursor to the previous unprotected field.

The NEXT FIELD key moves the cursor to the next unprotected field.

The ENTER key executes a command entered on a command line or on a line number. Do not confuse the ENTER key with the SUBMIT key. This key executes commands; the SUBMIT key submits SAS statements to the SAS System from the data lines of the program editor screen.

Figure A5.1 Editing Keys

Commands

Most of the commands you use with display manager are *command-line commands* entered on the command line of each screen. Notice in **Screen A5.1** that both screens in the program editor/log screen have a command line in the top left corner. You can also add a command line to the output screen.

Another type of command, called a *line command*, is used for editing SAS program statements and is available only in the program editor screen. See the appendix on "Full-Screen Editing" for a discussion of both kinds of commands, their execution, and command definitions. Commands you can use in display manager are listed according to screen in the sections that follow. Command definitions appear at the end of this appendix.

A COMPLETE EXAMPLE

This section uses an education example to go through a SAS display manager session step-by-step. This example illustrates a simple SAS program that you can use display manager to execute. You can enter your DATA and PROC statements in the program editor screen, use the log screen to view your SAS log, and use the output screen to view your output.

Suppose your company encourages employees to continue their education by taking night courses at a local college, weekend seminars, and so on. You have available for each person in your department:

- his or her name
- the number of credit hours he or she completed in the past year at the college
- the number of hours he or she spends in other educational activities
- the number of years he or she has been in your department.

You want to find out whether people who have been in your department for a short time participate more in continuing education than those with several years' seniority. You can:

1. create a data set, giving it a two-level name if you want to store it
2. identify your variables, the employee's name, the number of education

hours spent in regular courses, the number of hours spent in special educational activities, the total number of education hours (the regular course hours multiplied by the number of weeks in the semester plus the hours spent in special educational activities), and the number of years employed
3. enter your data
4. print a chart showing employee names, educational activities, and the number of years employed
5. print a graph to examine the relationship between the hours spent in educational activities and the number of years employed.

To begin, log on to your system, and, after receiving the operating system prompt, invoke the SAS System by executing the command

```
SAS
```

Under some operating systems, you are required to identify the type of terminal you are using when you execute the SAS command.[2]

If the cursor is on the command line press the NEXT FIELD key twice to move the cursor to the data entry area. You are now ready to enter the SAS statements and data lines.[3]

Enter the statements and data lines for the DATA step. Remember that SAS statements can begin in any column and that you can split a statement between two lines or enter several statements on one line. You may find your programs easier to read if you follow our convention of beginning DATA, PROC, and global statements in column 1 and indenting other statements. **Screen A5.2** shows the program editor after you have filled in all the lines.

When you have filled in the last line on the program editor, press the FORWARD function key to scroll more lines into view. To control the forward and backward scroll amount, enter

```
VSCROLL n
```

(where *n* is the number of lines) on the command line of the program editor and press the ENTER key. You can also set the vertical scroll amount to HALF or PAGE for scrolling a half or a whole page at a time. HALF is the default vertical scroll amount.

Scroll forward each time you fill in the lines in the program editor screen until you have entered all statements and data lines (see **Screen A5.3**).

You can scroll back through the example to check for errors. When you are ready to run the DATA step, use the SUBMIT command or function key.

Screen A5.4 displays messages indicating completion of the DATA step in the log screen.[4] Move the cursor to the log screen with the UP or DOWN cursor key or the HOME key, and press the FORWARD or BACKWARD function key to scroll through the log. You can alter the vertical scroll amount by entering the command VSCROLL and the scroll amount on the command line of the log screen, just as you did in the program editor.

The program editor is now empty so you can enter more statements in **Screen A5.5**. To see the statements you entered before, browse the log. To rerun those statements, first return the cursor to the program screen and use the RECALL command or function key; the previously submitted lines are displayed in the program editor. Use the SUBMIT command or function key to submit these program statements to the SAS System for execution again.

Now enter the PROC PRINT and PROC PLOT steps in the program editor. Precede the PROC PRINT statement with the OPTIONS statement specifying the DATE and NUMBER options if you want the date and page number to appear at the top of your output.

```
Command ===>                                                    SAS Log  11:14


Copyright (c) 1984 SAS Institute Inc., Cary, N.C. 27511, U.S.A.
NOTE: XXXXX Version of SAS Release X.XX at SAS Institute Inc.(00000000).
NOTE: LICENSED CPUID MODEL = XXXXXX, SERIAL = 00000000.













------------------------------------------------------------------------
Command ===>                                              Program Editor

00001 data educatn;
00002    input name $ credhrs othered yrsexp;
00003    toted=(credhrs*16)+othered;
00004    cards;
00005 aiken 0 16 3
00006 barker 2 0 3
00007 faulkner 3 8 2
00008 house 3 16 2 _
```

Screen A5.2 Entering Your Program Statements

```
Command ===>                                                    SAS Log  11:14


Copyright (c) 1984 SAS Institute Inc., Cary, N.C. 27511, U.S.A.
NOTE: XXXXX Version of SAS Release X.XX at SAS Institute Inc.(00000000).
NOTE: LICENSED CPUID MODEL = XXXXXX, SERIAL = 00000000.







------------------------------------------------------------------------
Command ===>                                              Program Editor

00009 mailer 0 16 4
00010 noble 0 0 5
00011 parker 2 0 2
00012 radner 3 4 1
00013 restin 3 0 3
00014 rusk 3 4 2
00015 silver 0 8 5
00016 smith 0 0 4
00017 tate 3 8 2
00018 tucker 0 0 4
00019 volker 0 8 5
00020 ;
00021 run;
```

Screen A5.3 Scrolling to Enter More Program Statements

```
Command ===>                                                    SAS Log  11:14

NOTE: THE DATA SET WORK.EDUCATN HAS 15 OBSERVATIONS AND 5 VARIABLES.
   20 ;

-------------------------------------------------------------------------------
Command ===>                                                    Program Editor

_
```

Screen A5.4 Messages in the Log Screen

```
Command ===>                                                    SAS Log  11:14

NOTE: THE DATA SET WORK.EDUCATN HAS 15 OBSERVATIONS AND 5 VARIABLES.
   20 ;

-------------------------------------------------------------------------------
Command ===>                                                    Program Editor

options date number;
proc print;
run;
proc plot;
   plot yrsexp*toted;
run;
```

Screen A5.5 Entering More Program Statements

When you use the SUBMIT command or function key, the SAS System executes your program statements. Because these statements contain PROC steps that produce printed output, the program editor/log screen is removed, and the output screen appears, displaying the results of the PRINT procedure.

Output A5.1 PRINT Procedure Output

```
                                   11:44 FRIDAY, JANUARY 18, 1985   1

OBS      NAME      CREDHRS    OTHERED    YRSEXP    TOTED

  1      AIKEN        0          16         3        16
  2      BARKER       2           0         3        32
  3      FAULKNER     3           8         2        56
  4      HOUSE        3          16         2        64
  5      MAILER       0          16         4        16
  6      NOBLE        0           0         5         0
  7      PARKER       2           0         2        32
  8      RADNER       3           4         1        52
  9      RESTIN       3           0         3        48
 10      RUSK         3           4         2        52
 11      SILVER       0           8         5         8
 12      SMITH        0           0         4         0
 13      TATE         3           8         2        56
 14      TUCKER       0           0         4         0
 15      VOLKER       0           8         5         8
```

When the PRINT procedure produces only one page of output, as in this example, you will hear a beep from the terminal when that one page has been displayed. Press the END function key to view the output of the PLOT procedure. (By default, function keys number 3 and 15 on the output screen are set to execute the END command.)

Output A5.2 PLOT Procedure Output

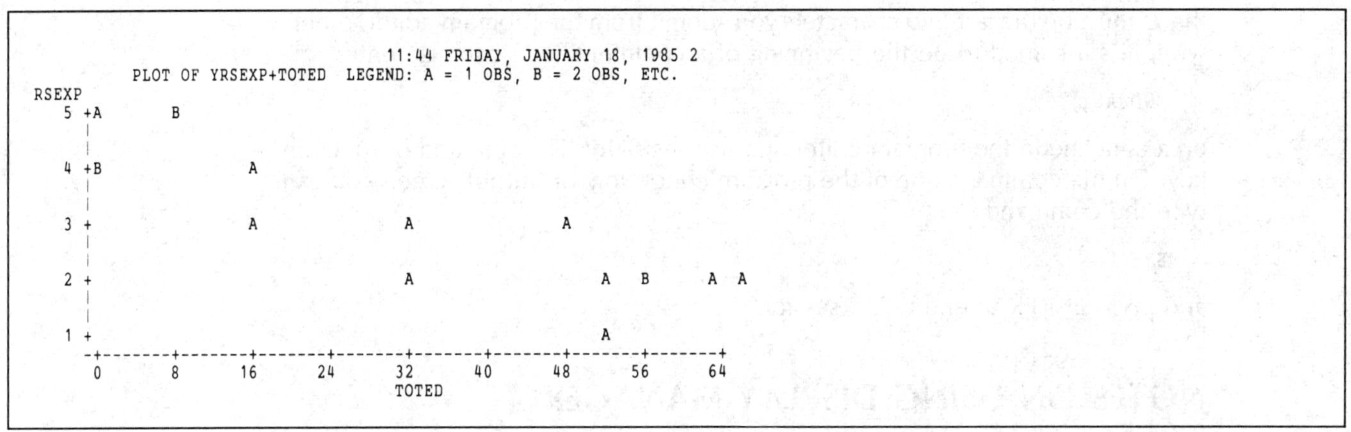

```
                                   11:44 FRIDAY, JANUARY 18, 1985 2
          PLOT OF YRSEXP*TOTED  LEGEND: A = 1 OBS, B = 2 OBS, ETC.
RSEXP
  5 +A       B
    I
    I
  4 +B           A
    I
    I
  3 +            A       A       A
    I
    I
  2 +                    A           A   B   A  A
    I
    I
  1 +                                A
    -+-------+-------+-------+-------+-------+-------+-------+-------+
     0       8      16      24      32      40      48      56      64
                                   TOTED
```

You will hear another beep from the terminal, signifying that all output produced by the PLOT procedure has been displayed. You can then browse the output in page-browse mode, enter line-browse mode, or return to the program editor/log screen. Press the COMMAND function key to enter line-browse mode. (By default, function keys number 2 and 14 are set to execute the COMMAND command.) A command line then appears at the top of the output screen. Use the END command or function key to return to the program editor/log screen.

When you return to the program editor/log screen, you see the most recent SAS statements and messages about your job (**Screen A5.6**). You can view the earlier statements by scrolling backward.

```
Command ===>                                              SAS Log  11:14

      24    PLOT YRSEXP*TOTED;
      25 RUN;

------------------------------------------------------------------------
Command ===> _                                           Program Editor

00001
00002
00003
00004
00005
00006
00007
00008
```

Screen A5.6 SAS Statements and Messages in the Log Screen

You can leave your SAS session in one of several ways. Enter /* in the first two columns of a data line and use the SUBMIT command or function key. Note that the /* must be the last two characters you submit from the program editor; otherwise, it is assumed to be the beginning of a comment. You can also enter

```
ENDSAS;
```

on a data line in the program editor and use the SUBMIT command or function key. On the command line of the program editor, log, or output screen you can type the command

```
BYE
```

and press ENTER to end a SAS session.

NOTES ON USING DISPLAY MANAGER

Active Screen

On the program editor/log screen, only one screen is active at a time. The active screen is defined by display manager as the screen that the cursor is on. When you press ENTER or a function key, only the screen active at that time is affected.

Protected and Unprotected Areas

In display manager screens, protected areas are areas of the display that you are allowed to view but not alter in any way. Unprotected areas are those in which you are allowed to enter and alter text. For example, in the program editor screen, you can type commands in the entry area of the command line, line commands over the line numbers, and data in the data entry area that follows the line numbers; most of the program editor screen is unprotected. On the other hand, the log and output screens and the help facility are browsing screens. Most of the areas on these screens are protected; you are not allowed to enter or alter any text. The only area on these screens that is unprotected is the entry area of the command line. You can type and edit commands on the command lines of these screens.

The boxed areas in **Screen A5.7** mark the unprotected areas of the program editor/log screen.

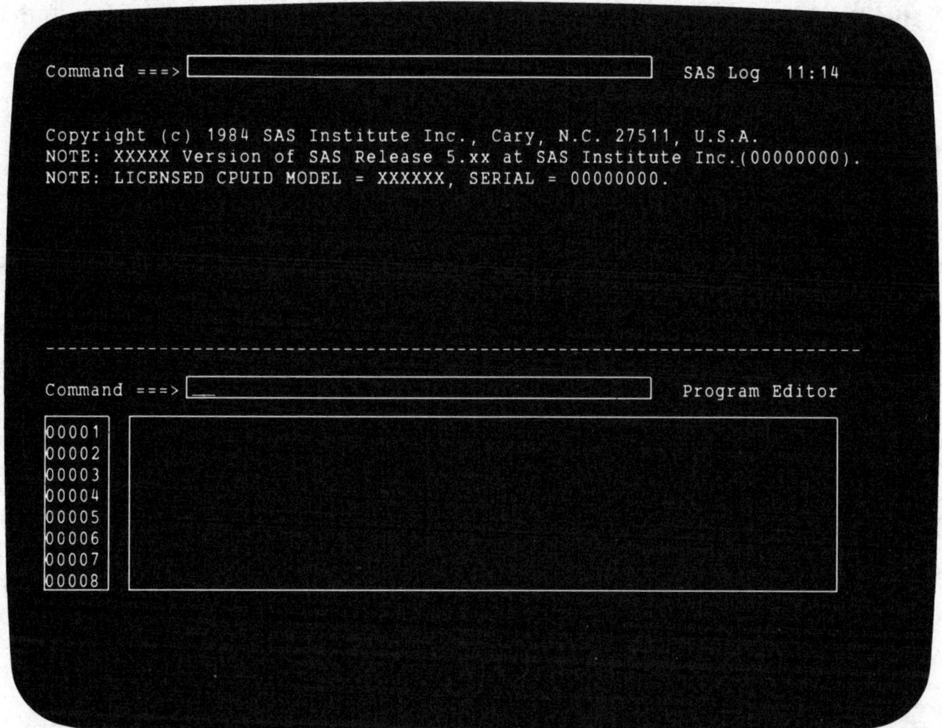

Screen A5.7 Unprotected Areas of the Program Editor/Log Screen

Color and Highlighting Attributes

If you are using a color terminal that has extended color and highlighting attributes in an environment that supports them, you can use the following display manager commands to set and change colors and highlighting:

CBANNER	to change the color or highlighting of the border, the line numbers, and screen description.
CPROT	to change the color or highlighting of all protected areas other than the banner. See CBANNER above.
CSOURCE	to change the color or highlighting of SAS source lines in the log screen.
CUNPROT	to change the color or highlighting of unprotected areas.

The colors and highlighting you can use are determined by the features of your terminal. See the *SAS/GRAPH User's Guide* and the *SAS/GRAPH Guide to Hardware Interfaces* for the colors available for your terminal.

Color Use the following abbreviations to specify color attributes in display manager commands:

B blue
R red
P pink
G green
C cyan
Y yellow
W white

Highlighting Use the following abbreviations to specify highlighting attributes in display manager commands:

H highlight
U underline
R reverse video
B blinking

Setting both color and highlighting You can assign an appropriate highlighting attribute at the same time you set a color attribute. Follow the color code with a highlighting code. For example, to set the color attribute of unprotected fields to yellow and the highlighting attribute to underline, use the command

```
CUNPROT Y U
```

To turn off the highlighting attribute, reissue the same color command and specify only a color code. For example, execute

```
CUNPROT Y
```

to allow the color of the unprotected areas of the screen to remain yellow but to remove the underlining.

Function Key Definition Screen

You can display the function key definition screen for the screen you are currently using by executing the KEYS command. You can view the current function key settings, or you can alter a key setting by typing the name of another valid command over the current one. On the function key definition screen you can use the following commands or function keys set to execute these commands:

BACKWARD
CANCEL
FORWARD
END

You can scroll backward and forward to view the entire list of key settings; you can cancel any changes made; you can use the END command, or a function key assigned to execute the END command, to save your altered settings and return to the screen on which you executed the KEYS command.

Note that the function key settings displayed on the screen are those currently active. If you want to execute a command that a function key is not currently set to execute, you must enter the command on the command line. For example, on the program editor and log screens there is no END function key by default because there is no END command for these screens. Execute the END command from the command line to save your settings and exit the function key definition screens of the program editor and log screens.

Entering Multiple Commands

You can enter a series of commands on the command line by separating the commands with semicolons. For example, you can type the BACKWARD MAX scroll command and the FIND command on the command line, separating them with a semicolon, and execute them in order by pressing the ENTER key once.

```
BACKWARD MAX; FIND 'DATA ONE'
```

Function keys and multiple commands You can also combine the use of function keys and the submission of multiple commands. For example, if you set a function key to the command and option BACKWARD MAX followed by a semicolon,

```
BACKWARD MAX;
```

then you can enter

```
FIND 'DATA ONE'
```

on the command line and execute them in order by pressing the key you set to execute BACKWARD MAX; . The procedure executes the BACKWARD MAX command first and then the FIND command.

As a general rule, when you assign commands that do not allow any options to a function key, you may want to follow that command keyword with a semicolon. On the function key definition screen of the program editor screen, for example, you may want to place semicolons after the following commands:

```
BOTTOM;
RECALL;
SPLIT;
TOP;
```

Executing Display Manager Commands Stored in External Files

Executing command list at initialization time You can execute a list of display manager commands stored in an external file automatically at initialization time. When you enter display manager, the system looks for a file, a sequential data set, or a member of a partitioned data set assigned the reserved fileref SASEXEC. If you have assigned SASEXEC to an external file containing a list of display manager commands, those commands are automatically executed. If the system finds no such file, no action is taken, and all default settings are used when you enter display manager.

By executing a series of commands stored in an external file, you can save time and decrease the possibility of errors. Suppose there is a series of commands you want executed each time you enter display manager. You can:

- alter the default active screen
- alter the default colors of protected and unprotected areas of the screen
- execute host-level commands that make SAS data libraries, external files, or data sets available to your session
- copy and submit SAS statements that take you directly into a full-screen procedure.

Using the AUTOEXEC command You can execute a list of display manager commands stored in an external file at any time during your display manager session by executing the AUTOEXEC command. You can follow the AUTOEXEC command with any fileref assigned to a file or data set containing a list of display manager commands. If you do not specify a fileref, the system looks for a file assigned the fileref SASEXEC by default. Because you can specify a fileref other than SASEXEC, you can use the AUTOEXEC command to execute more than one file of display manager commands during your session. The syntax and definitions of the AUTOEXEC and AUTOSHOW commands are shown below.

When you execute the AUTOEXEC command and specify the fileref of a file containing a list of display manager commands, the first command is then executed from the command line of the active screen, which is the screen from which you executed the AUTOEXEC command. You can send commands to all of the display manager screens, one at a time, by including commands that change the active screen. For example, if you issue the AUTOEXEC command from the program editor, the first command is sent to that command line to be executed. Use the LOG command to make the log screen active; all following commands are executed on the log screen. Similarly, you can use the OUTPUT command to make the output screen active and the PROGRAM command for the program editor.

An invalid command If an invalid command is encountered during the execution of your file of commands, an error message is displayed, and the AUTOEXEC processing stops.

Display of executing commands By default these commands are not displayed as they are executed. The command AUTOSHOW ON causes each command to be displayed on the appropriate command line just before execution. AUTOSHOW OFF turns off the display of the AUTOEXEC commands as they are being executed.

The AUTOEXEC and AUTOSHOW commands Enter the AUTOEXEC command to send a list of commands stored in an external file to one or more command lines in display manager. The list of commands is sent to the command line of the screen from which you enter the AUTOEXEC command.

You are not required to specify SASEXEC to execute commands stored in a file associated with the fileref SASEXEC; SASEXEC is the default. If you specify another fileref, the display manager commands stored in the file assigned that fileref are then executed.[5]

Use the AUTOSHOW command with the OFF or ON option to specify whether the commands are to be displayed on the command line as they are executed. AUTOSHOW OFF is the default.

Creating your file of display manager commands The commands you want to be executed from a display manager command line, whether at initialization time or with the AUTOEXEC command, must be stored in an external file, **not** a SAS data set. You can store them in a file, a sequential data set, or a member of a partitioned data set.

Here are some general rules to follow when entering a list of commands to be executed at initialization time or with the AUTOEXEC command:

1. Enter only one command on each line and follow each command with a semicolon. Note: when you are working in display manager and entering commands on the command line directly, one at a time, you do not need to end a command with a semicolon.
2. Do not type beyond the 80th column.[6]
3. You can send commands to each display manager screen one at a time. Use the commands PROGRAM, LOG, OUTPUT, and HELP to designate which screen you want to be active and, therefore, the one on which the following commands will be executed.[7]

4. After you designate the active screen, list only commands that are valid on that screen.
5. The file in which the list of commands is stored **must** be assigned the reserved fileref SASEXEC if you want it to be executed automatically when you enter display manager.[8]

A sample list of stored commands Below is a sample list of commands that you can store in an external file and execute with the AUTOEXEC command or at initialization time:

```
PROGRAM;
INCLUDE MYFILE;
SUBMIT;
CBA G;
LOG;
CURSOR 5;
SPLIT;
CSO B;
VSCROLL PAGE;
OUTPUT;
CPRO;
PROGRAM;
OUTPUT OFF;
VSCROLL PAGE;
```

These commands are explained in detail below:

PROGRAM designates that the active screen is the program editor; therefore, all commands that follow this command are sent to the command line of the program editor screen to be executed **until** you specify that another screen is active. In a file executed at initialization time, you are not required to specify PROGRAM because the program editor is the active screen by default.

INCLUDE MYFILE brings the contents of the external file identified by the fileref MYFILE to the data lines of the program editor screen.[5] This file contains a series of SAS program statements that you want submitted from the program editor to the SAS System. It could, for example, make some SAS data sets available to your session by containing X statements that make fileref assignments through host-level commands; it may also be used to enter an OPTIONS statement.

SUBMIT submits the program statements that you brought into the data lines of the program editor with the INCLUDE command.

CBA G sets the color of the banner on the program editor screen to green.

LOG activates the log screen. All commands that follow the LOG command are sent to the command line of the log screen to be executed **until** you make another screen active.

CURSOR 5 positions the cursor five lines below its default position, the command line of the log screen. This command positions the cursor in preparation for the execution of the next command.

SPLIT	tells the screen to split at the cursor location. Because you just positioned the cursor five lines below the command line of the log screen, you have altered the default location of the split between the program editor and log screens.
CSO G	sets the color of the source lines on the log screen. CSO G sets the color of the source lines to green.
VSCROLL PAGE	alters the vertical scroll amount of the log screen and sets it to the full depth of the log screen. HALF is the default.
OUTPUT	activates the output screen in page-browse mode. All commands that follow are now sent to the output screen.
CPRO B	sets the color of the protected text in the output screen. CPRO B sets the color of the protected text to blue.
PROGRAM	activates the program editor screen. All commands that follow are now sent to the command line of the program editor screen.
OUTPUT OFF	indicates that you do not want output produced during your session automatically displayed in the output screen.
VSCROLL PAGE	alters the vertical scroll amount of the program editor screen and sets it to the full depth of the screen. The default is HALF.

This list is just a sample of the kind of commands you may want to store and execute from an external file.

PROGRAM EDITOR SCREEN

Notes on Using the Program Editor Screen

Submitting SAS source lines from the program editor You can think of the program editor as being entirely separate from the SAS System since SAS does not see the lines entered until you are ready to submit your job with the SUBMIT command or function key. After the job has executed, you can resume working in the program editor, entering commands, using editing keys and functions keys, and entering and editing program statements or data.

Program editor screen line length When you submit SAS program statements for execution from the program editor screen, the data lines are broken into lengths of 80 columns. It is recommended that you not submit source lines longer than 80 columns. If you do submit longer source lines, do not continue a word from the 80th to the 81st column; it will be divided when submitted.[9]

Executing line commands without line numbers You can execute line commands even if you have set NUMS OFF. You can position the cursor where you want the line command to be executed and then press a function key set to execute a line command. For example, you can position the cursor where you want a line to split and then press a function key set to execute :TS (the text split line command preceded by a colon). You can also execute a line command from the command line by preceding it with a colon, just as you do when you set a function key. You can type :TS on the command line, position the cursor, and then press the ENTER key.

Line Commands

The line commands available in the program editor screen of display manager are listed below. You can use line commands to move, copy, repeat, insert, and delete lines or blocks of lines; and to designate target locations for moved, copied, and inserted lines. In display manager you can use line commands only on the program editor screen. The log screen, whether you are using it to view the SAS log or SAS HELP, and the output screen are browsing screens; therefore, you cannot use line commands to alter text. Below is a list of line commands. Complete definitions appear at the end of this appendix.

Single commands

A[*n*],B[*n*]
C[*n*]
COLS
D[*n*]
I[*n* | A[*n*] | B[*n*]]
M[*n*]
MASK
O[*n*]
P[*n*]
R[*n*]
TF
TS

Block commands

CC
DD
MM
OO
PP
RR[*n*]

Special shift commands

>[*n*]
<[*n*]
>>[*n*]
<<[*n*]
)[*n*]
([*n*]
))[*n*]
(([*n*]

Command-Line Commands

You can use the command-line commands listed below on the command line of the program editor screen. Definitions of all commands you can use with display manager appear at the end of this appendix.

ASSIGN*
AUTOADD*
AUTOEXEC
AUTOSHOW
BACKWARD
BOTTOM
BYE
CAPS
CBANNER
CHANGE
CPRO(T)
CUNPRO(T)
CURSOR
FIND
FORWARD
HELP
HSCROLL
INCLUDE
KEYS
LEFT
LINESIZE
LOC
LOG
NODMS**
NULLS
NUMBER
OUTPUT
PRINT
PROGRAM
RCHANGE
RECALL
RESET
RFIND
RIGHT
RULE*
SAVE
SCREEN*
SPLIT
SUBMIT
TOP
VSCROLL
X***

LOG SCREEN

Notes on Using the Log Screen

Line length The length of data lines on the log screen is sensitive to the value of certain line size options that you can specify with the OPTIONS statement.[10] You can scroll RIGHT to view data lines longer than the line length of your terminal screen.

---

* not in IBM versions.
** not in IBM versions.
*** not available under VSE.

Command-Line Commands

You can use the command-line commands listed below on the command line of the log screen. Definitions of all commands you can use with display manager appear at the end of this appendix.

ASSIGN*
AUTOEXEC
AUTOSHOW
BACKWARD
BOTTOM
BYE
CAPS
CBANNER
CPROT
CSOURCE
CUNPROT
CURSOR
FIND
FORWARD
HELP
HSCROLL
KEYS
LEFT
LOC
OUTPUT
PRINT
PROGRAM
RFIND
RIGHT
RULE*
SAVE*
SCREEN*
SPLIT
TOP
VSCROLL
X**

OUTPUT SCREEN

Notes on Using the Output Screen

When the output screen displays output resulting from any procedures you have executed, the procedure displays the first page of output and then waits for your prompt to go to the next page. To display each succeeding page of output, press the ENTER key or any function key **except** the END key.

If you have many pages of output and do not want to wait for the procedure to display them all, one by one, you can press the END key to cause the display manager to skip over all the intervening pages and display only the last page of output. All output is produced whether or not you choose to view each page. The terminal emits a beep when the last page of output is displayed.

When the last page of output is displayed and you receive the audible signal from the terminal, you are in page-browse mode. Now that you have entered page-browse mode, you have three choices; you can:

---

* not in IBM versions.

** not available under VSE.

1. use the function keys operable in page-browse mode to browse the output
2. return to the program editor/log screen by pressing the END key
3. enter line-browse mode by pressing the COMMAND function key. A command line then appears at the top of the screen, and you can either use function keys or enter commands that are operable in line-browse mode.

Browsing more than one set of output If your submitted statements included more than one PROC step that produced output, you cannot return to the program editor/log screen from the last page of the first set of output by pressing the END key. You must reach the last page of the last set of output produced before you can exit the output screen.

When you reach the last page of the first set of output, you can press the COMMAND key to put a command line on the screen and to take you into line-browse mode for browsing that set of output; or you can proceed to the first page of the next set of output by pressing the END key. If you enter line-browse mode, pressing the END key also takes you to the first page of the next set of output. If you do not want to view all pages of a set of output, press the END key again to display the last page of that set of output. At this point, you have the same choices described above. You can browse the output in page-browse mode, browse it in line-browse mode by pressing the COMMAND key, or press the END key to return you to the program editor/log screen.

Using function keys in page-browse mode Because there is no command line available to you in page-browse mode of the output screen, you must use function keys to execute commands. The same function key settings apply to the output screen in both page-browse and line-browse mode. You cannot view the function key definition screen from page-browse mode unless you have a function key for the output screen defined to execute the KEYS command. Use the COMMAND function key to create a command line to take you into line-browse mode where you can execute the KEYS command to view the function key settings for the output screen. (By default function keys number 2 and 14 are set to execute the COMMAND command.) Use the END function key to take you to the next procedure's output or to exit the output screen. (By default function keys number 3 and 15 are set to execute the END command.)

You can also view the function key settings of the output screen by executing the following commands in sequence from the command line of the program editor or the log screen:

```
OUTPUT; KEYS
```

The OUTPUT command takes you to the OUTPUT screen; the KEYS command then displays the function key definition screen of the output screen.

Linesize on output screen The maximum line length depends on the operating system under which you are using the SAS System.[11]

Command-Line Commands in Line-Browse Mode

When viewing the output screen, you must enter line-browse mode to be able to enter commands directly. After hearing a beep from the terminal, which signifies that all of the output has been displayed and that you have entered page-browse mode, press the COMMAND function key to create a command line on the output screen and to enter line-browse mode. Then you can use the command-line commands listed below. Definitions of all commands you can use with display manager appear at the end of this appendix.

ASSIGN*
AUTOEXEC
AUTOSHOW
BACKWARD
BOTTOM
BYE
CAPS
CBANNER
COMMAND
CPROT
CUNPROT
CURSOR
END
FIND
FORWARD
HELP
HSCROLL
KEYS
LEFT
LOC
LOG
OUTPUT
PRINT
PROGRAM
RFIND
RIGHT
RULE**
SAVE*
SCREEN*
SPLIT*
TOP
VSCROLL
X***

COMMAND GLOSSARY

Line Commands

A[*n*],**B**[*n*] A line command that marks the target position of a *source* line(s), a line or lines being moved or copied with a C, M, P, CC, MM, PP, or INCLUDE command. Indicate an A (after) on the line number of the line you want the source line(s) to follow. Use a B (before) to mark the line you want the source line(s) to precede. After the A or B, you can specify the number of times you want the source line or lines to be duplicated. Follow A or B with some number *n* and a blank space. **CMS, OS, VM/PC, and VSE**: You cannot use the target commands with the INCLUDE command.

C[*n*] A line command that copies one or more lines to another location in the file, indicated by a target line

* not in IBM versions.
** not in IBM versions.
*** not available under VSE.

command. Indicate C on the line number of the line to be copied. Then indicate an A on the number of the line you want the copied line to follow, a B on the number of the line you want it to precede, or an O or OO on the line or lines you want it to overlay. You can also specify *n* number of lines to be copied. Follow C with some number *n* and a blank space.

CC A line command that copies a block of lines to another location in the file, indicated by a target line command. Indicate CC on the line numbers of the first and last lines of the block of lines to be copied.

COLS A line command that creates a special line indicating the column numbers across your display screen. The column indicator line appears above the line on which you execute the COLS command. The COLS line is a special line that is not submitted when you submit program statements from the program editor. Use the RESET key or command or delete the line to remove the COLS line.

D[*n*] A line command that deletes one or more lines. Indicate D on the line number of the line to be deleted. By default, one line is deleted. To delete more than one line, follow D with some number *n* and a blank space.

DD A line command that deletes a block of lines. Indicate DD on the line numbers of the block of lines to be deleted.

I[*n*] This line command is used to insert one or more new lines. By default one line is inserted after the line on which you execute the I command. To insert more than one line, follow I with some number *n* and a blank space. See also the IA and IB commands below. See the MASK command to insert lines with a defined content other than a blank line. See the TS (text split) command to insert space within a line of text.

IA[*n*] Use this line command to insert one or more lines after the line on which you enter the IA (insert after) command. By default only one line is inserted. See also the I and IB commands.

IB[*n*] Use this line command to insert one or more lines before the line on which you enter the IB (insert before) command. By default only one line is inserted. See also the I and IA commands.

M[*n*] A line command that moves one or more lines to another location in the file, indicated by a target line command. Indicate M on the line number of the line to be moved. If you move more than one line, follow M with some number *n* and a blank space. Then specify an A on the line number of the line you want the moved line to follow, a B on the line you want it to precede, or an O on the line you want the moved line or lines to overlay.

MASK A line command that defines the initial contents of a new line. Type MASK on any line number and press ENTER. Then type on that line whatever characters you want to be repeated and press ENTER again. After you define a MASK, a line with the contents of the MASK line is inserted when you use the I (insert) line command.

The MASK remains in effect throughout the session. To redefine it, simply repeat the steps described above. To return to the default, a blank line, use the same process and leave the line blank.

MM A line command that moves a block of lines to another location in the file, indicated by a target line command. Indicate the block to be moved with an MM line command on the first and last line numbers of the block.

> [*n*] A line command that shifts data one or more spaces to the right. Indicate > or > followed by some number *n* and a blank space on the line number of the line to be shifted. Note that a **data** shift command allows no loss of data. The default is one space.

< [*n*] A line command that shifts data one or more spaces to the left. Indicate < or < followed by some number *n* and a blank space on the line number of the line to be shifted. Note that a **data** shift command allows no loss of data. The default is one space.

> > [*n*] A line command that shifts a block of lines one or more spaces to the right. Indicate >> or >> followed by some number *n* and a blank space on the line number of the first line of the block to be shifted and another >> or >>*n* on the last line number of the block. Note that a **data** shift command allows no loss of data. The default is one space.

< < [*n*] A line command that shifts a block of lines one or more spaces to the left. Indicate << or << followed by some number *n* and a blank space on the line number of the first line of the block to be shifted and another << or <<*n* on the last line number of the block. Note that a **data** shift command allows no loss of data. The default is one space.

)[*n*] A line command that shifts columns of data one or more columns to the right. Indicate) or) followed by some number *n* and a blank space on the line number of the line to be shifted. Note that a **column** shift command, unlike a **data** shift command, can cause loss of data. The default is one column.

([*n*] A line command that shifts columns of data one or more columns to the left. Indicate (or (followed by some number *n* and a blank space on the line number of the line to be shifted. Note that a **column** shift command, unlike a **data** shift command, can cause loss of data. The default is one column.

))[*n*] The column shift line command shifts a block of lines one or more columns to the right. Indicate)) or)) followed by some number *n* and a blank space on the line number of the first line of the block to be shifted and another)) or))*n* on the last line number of the block. Note that a **column** shift command, unlike a **data** shift command, can cause loss of data. The default is one column.

(([*n*] A line command that shifts a block of lines one or more columns to the left. Indicate ((or ((followed by some number *n* and a blank space on the line number of the first line of the block to be shifted and another ((or ((*n* on the last line number of the block. Note that a **column** shift command, unlike a **data** shift command, can cause loss of data. The default is one space.

O[*n*] A line command that marks the target position of a C, M, P, CC, MM, or PP line command. Indicate the O (overlay) line command on the line number of the line you want the contents of the *source line*, the moved or copied line, to overlay. Characters from the source line overlay blank or null spaces on the *target line*, the line marked with the O line command. After the O line command you can specify the number of target lines you want the source line or lines to overlay. Follow O with some number *n* and a blank space.

If any characters occupy the same positions on the source and target lines, the characters on the target line remain, and characters from the source line do not appear. If you are executing the M (move) command, you receive an error message, and the line intended to be moved remains in its original position.

OO A line command that marks a block of lines, identified by an OO on the line numbers of the first and last lines of the block, as the target position of source lines, lines marked with the C, M, P, CC, MM, or PP line commands. See the O line command.

P[*n*] A line command that copies or overlays one or more lines to another location in the file, indicated by a target line command. The P (pattern) line command is similiar to the C (copy) line command; the difference is that the system remembers the line marked with the P line command and copies it to the new location each time you enter a target line command until you remove the P line command. You can remove it with the RESET key or command or by using any of the editing keys you normally use to erase or remove characters, such as the EOF key, the character delete key, or the space bar. Indicate P on the line number of the source line, the line you want to copy. Then indicate an A on the number of the line you want the source line to follow, a B on the number of the line you want it to precede, or an O or OO on the line or lines you want it to overlay. You can also specify *n* number of lines to be copied. Follow P with some number *n* and a blank space.

PP A line command that copies a block of lines to another location in the file, indicated by a target line command. The PP (pattern block) command is similiar to the CC line command; the difference is that the system remembers the block of lines marked with the PP line command and copies it to the new location each time you enter a target line command until you remove the PP line command. You can remove it with the RESET key or command or by using any of the editing keys you normally use to erase or remove characters, such as the EOF key, the character delete key, or the space bar. Indicate PP on the first and last line numbers of the block of lines you want to designate as the source lines, the lines you want to copy. Then indicate an A on the number of the line you want the source lines to follow, a B on the number of the line you want them to precede, an O or OO on the first and last lines of the block you want the source lines to overlay.

R[*n*] A line command that repeats a line one or more times immediately following. Indicate R on the line number of the line to be repeated. To repeat a line more than once, follow R with some number *n* and a blank space.

RR[*n*] A line command that repeats a block of lines immediately following that block. Indicate RR on the line numbers of the first and last lines of the block of lines to be repeated. You can also specify how many times you want the block of lines repeated; follow RR with some number *n* and a blank space. You can specify *n* on the first or last RR command or on both.

TF A line command that flows a paragraph or an indicated block of text by removing trailing blanks from each line. You can use the TF (text flow) line command to move text into wasted space left at ends of lines, especially after performing insertions and deletions.

TS A line command that inserts a blank line for inserting new text. Either type TS (text split) on a line number, position the cursor where you want the text to split, and press ENTER, or position the cursor and press the :TS function key. See the I (insert) command for inserting space between lines rather than within the text of a line.

Command-Line Commands

Command-line commands that are available in display manager screens are defined below:

ASSIGN *'filename' fileref*

AOS/VS, PRIMOS, and VMS only: Use the ASSIGN command to assign a fileref to an external file. You can specify a fully qualified file name, according to the requirements of the operating system you are using, or just an individual file name (and type under VMS) if it is in a directory to which you currently have access. For example, to assign the fileref PROG1 to an AOS/VS, PRIMOS, or VMS fully-qualified file name, you can execute the ASSIGN command in the form

```
ASSIGN ':UDD:youruserdir:PROG.SAS' PROG1

ASSIGN '[yourdir]PROG.SAS' PROG1

ASSIGN '<masterfiledirectory>userfiledirectory>PROG.SAS' PROG1
```

See the INCLUDE and SAVE commands.

CMS, OS, and VM/PC: You can execute host-level commands before entering display manager or after entering display manager with the X command or statement.

VSE: You can place a /FILE statement, an ICCF control language statement, in the ICCF procedure that invokes the SAS System. You cannot use the X command or statement in the ICCF environment. See the INCLUDE and SAVE commands.

AUTOADD [ON | OFF]

AOS/VS, PRIMOS, and VMS only: The AUTOADD ON command adds data entry lines to the bottom of the screen each time you scroll forward so that you do not have to use an INSERT command to insert new lines for entering new data or text. If line numbers are on (NUMS ON), these lines are numbered each time you scroll forward. If you execute AUTOADD OFF, the editor does not add new lines for data entry each time you scroll forward.

AUTOEXEC [SASEXEC | *fileref***]**

Enter the AUTOEXEC command to send a list of commands stored in an external file to one or more command lines in display manager. The first command in the list is sent to the command line of the screen from which you enter the AUTOEXEC command.

If you do not specify a fileref that you assigned to an external file through a host-level command, the procedure looks for a file assigned the fileref SASEXEC by default. If you specify another fileref, the display manager commands stored in file associated with that fileref are then executed.

AUTOSHOW OFF | ON

Use the AUTOSHOW command with the OFF or ON option to specify whether commands being executed from an external file are to be displayed on the command line as they are executed. AUTOSHOW OFF is the default.

BACKWARD [*n* | MAX]

In addition to using a function key, you can scroll toward the top of the screen with the BAC command. The amount of scroll is controlled by the VSCROLL command.

You can specify a particular number of lines to scroll backward by entering BAC *n* (*n* being the number of lines you want to scroll backward). You can scroll the maximum amount by entering BAC MAX or BAC M. The scroll value specified with the BAC command, either *n* or MAX, is operative only for that scroll; it temporarily overrides but does not alter the default scroll value or the one set by the VSCROLL command.

BOTTOM

Use the BOTTOM or BOT command to scroll the last line of text to the bottom of the screen.

BYE

You can use the BYE command to end a SAS session. You can execute the BYE command from the command line of the log or program editor screen.

CAPS OFF | ON

When you execute CAPS ON, all text entered, as well as text on lines that have been modified, is translated into uppercase letters when you press ENTER or a function key. All text is left as entered when CAPS OFF is in effect. The CAPS command affects only the screen on which it is entered and is in effect for the remainder of the SAS session or until changed by another CAPS command. The default is CAPS ON in minicomputer versions and CAPS OFF in IBM versions.

CBANNER *color* [*highlight*]

The CBA command changes the color or color and highlighting attributes of the banner lines. These lines are the borders, line numbers if any, and command line. Specifying CBA affects only the screen on which the command is entered and is in effect for the remainder of the SAS session or until changed by another CBA command.

CHANGE *string1 string2* [**NEXT | FIRST | LAST | PREV | ALL**]
[**WORD | SUFFIX | PREFIX**]

Use the CHANGE command to change one or more occurrences of *string1* to *string2*. Follow the CHANGE command with string of characters to be changed, a space, and then the new string, or type the strings on the command line and press the CHANGE function key.

You can specify on the CHANGE command that the system search for and alter the NEXT occurrence of the specified string after the current cursor location; the FIRST occurrence of the string in the file, regardless of your current cursor location; the LAST occurrence of the string in the file; or the PREVious occurrence. If you specify ALL, you receive a message that reports how many times the string occurs in the entire file, and each occurrence is changed. By default, the CHANGE command searches for and changes the NEXT occurrence of the specified string after the current cursor location.

You can also specify one of the following options: PREFIX, SUFFIX, or WORD. If you do not specify one of these, *string1* is changed to *string2*, regardless of context.

In the CHANGE command, as in the FIND command, a WORD is one or more symbols preceded and followed by a delimiter. A delimiter is any symbol other than an uppercase letter, a lowercase letter, a digit, or an underscore.

Remember to use single quotes to enclose strings with special characters or embedded blanks. Single word strings require no quotation marks. For example,

```
C YOUR MY
C 'YOUR DATA SET' 'MY DATA SET'
```

Also enclose your string in single quotes if CAPS are ON and you do not want lowercase letters in the string translated into uppercase letters.

If your string contains a single quotation mark, such as

```
C "Bob's" "Bill's"
```

enclose it in double quotation marks.

You can combine the use of the CHANGE command and RFIND function key (or command). For example, after you enter a CHANGE command, you can press the RFIND function key to locate the next occurrence of *string1* before pressing RCHANGE to change it to *string2*.

Also see the RCHANGE, FIND, and RFIND commands.

COMMAND

Use the CMD command, assigned to a function key, in page-browse mode of the procedure output screen to put a command line at the top of the screen, taking you into line-browse mode. Execute the command again to remove the command line and return you to page-browse mode.

CPROT *color* [*highlight*]

The CPROT command changes the color or color and highlighting attributes of protected fields on the log or output screen to those specified for the remainder of the SAS session or until changed by another CPROT command. This color or color and highlighting attributes become the default for the protected fields only for the screen on which you enter the command.

The CPROT command has no effect on the program editor screen since its protected areas are governed by the CBANNER command.

CSOURCE *color* [*highlight*]

The CSO command changes the color or color and highlighting attributes of SAS source line on the log screen to those specified. The CSO command is in effect for the remainder of the SAS session or until changed by another CSO command.

CUNPROT *color* [*highlight*]

The CUN command changes the color or color and highlighting attributes of unprotected fields to those specified for the remainder of the SAS session or until changed by another CUN command. This color or color and highlighting attributes become the default for all unprotected fields that are not otherwise defined by color or highlighting attribute commands. Note: the CUNPROT command affects the unprotected fields only for the screen on which it is executed.

CURSOR [*rownumber*] | [*rownumber colnumber*]

The CURSOR command, without any options specified, is designed to be executed with a function key. Press the CURSOR key to return the cursor to the command line of whatever screen you are currently using.

Specifying options with the CURSOR command is especially useful when executing a list of commands stored in an external file. (See the AUTOEXEC command.) You can use the CURSOR command to position the cursor in preparation for the execution of a following command. For example, if you execute

```
CURSOR 10
```

on the command line of the log screen and then execute the SPLIT command, you can alter the location of the split between the program editor and the log screens. Note: do not move the cursor outside the boundaries of the screen from which you want the next command to be executed.

END

In line-browse mode of the procedure output screen, the END command either returns you to the program editor/log screen or takes you to the first page of the next procedure's output. In page-browse mode, it takes you to the next page of output or, if you are already viewing the last page, returns you to the program editor/log screen.

FIND *characterstring* [**NEXT | FIRST | LAST | PREV | ALL**] [**PREFIX | SUFFIX | WORD**]

Use the FIND command to search for a specified string of characters. Remember to enclose the string in single quotes if it contains embedded blanks or special characters. You can execute the FIND command by entering it directly or by typing the character string on the command line and pressing the FIND function key.

You can specify in the FIND command that the system search for the NEXT occurrence of the specified string after the current cursor location; the FIRST occurrence of the string in the file, regardless of your current cursor location; the LAST occurrence of the string in the file; or the PREVious occurrence. If you specify ALL, you receive a message that reports how many times the string occurs in the entire file. By default, the FIND command searches for the NEXT occurrence of the specified string after the current cursor location.

You can also specify one of the following options: PREFIX, SUFFIX, or WORD. If you do not specify one of these options, the system searches for each occurrence of the string, regardless of context.

In the FIND command, a WORD is one or more symbols preceded and followed by a delimiter. A delimiter is any symbol other than an uppercase letter, a lowercase letter, a digit, or an underscore. For example,

```
ABC123
```

is a WORD, but

```
ABC$123
```

is two WORDs separated by the delimiter $. A PREFIX or SUFFIX is treated just as its grammatical definition. In the first example, ABC123, you could specify ABC as a PREFIX and 123 as a SUFFIX. In the second example, ABC$123, ABC and 123 are WORDs, not a PREFIX and a SUFFIX.

Remember to use single quotes to enclose strings with special characters or embedded blanks. For example,

```
F YOUR
F 'YOUR DATA SET'
```

Also enclose your string in single quotes if CAPS are ON and you do not want lowercase letters in the string translated into uppercase letters.

If your string contains a single quotation mark, such as

```
F "Bob's"
```

enclose it in double quotation marks.

See also the CHANGE, RCHANGE, and RFIND commands.

FORWARD [*n* | **MAX**]

In addition to using a function key, you can scroll toward the bottom of the screen with the FOR *n* command. The amount of scroll is controlled by the VSCROLL command.

You can specify a particular number of lines to scroll forward by entering FOR *n* (*n* being the number of lines you want to scroll foward). You can scroll the maximum amount by entering FOR MAX or FOR M. The scroll value specified with the FOR command, either *n* or MAX, is operative only for that scroll; it temporarily overrides but does not alter the default scroll value or the one set by the VSCROLL command.

HELP [*topic*]

When you enter the HELP command, SAS HELP, an on-line help facility, appears on your display screen. You can specify a topic at the same time that you execute the HELP command. If you do not specify a topic, a list of allowed topics is displayed.

CMS, OS, VM/PC, and VSE: You can execute HELP from any of the three display manager screens. SAS HELP is then displayed, occupying the entire display area. Use the END command or function key to return display manager to the screen.

AOS/VS, PRIMOS, and VMS: You can execute HELP from any of the three display manager command lines, but SAS HELP is always displayed in the upper portion of the program editor/log screen. You can browse help information by using the same commands and function keys that are available in the log screen. If you execute HELP from the output screen, you must return to the program editor/log screen to view the help information. After viewing the help information, you can return the SAS log to the log screen by entering the LOG command or submitting at least one statement from the program editor.

HSCROLL HALF | PAGE | *n*

The HSCROLL command sets the horizontal scroll amount, the amount the active screen scrolls when you press the LEFT or RIGHT scrolling keys. If you specify PAGE, the scroll amount is equal to the entire width of the display area. If you specify HALF, the scroll amount is one-half of the display area. HALF is the default.

INCLUDE *fileref* | *fileref(membername)*
INCLUDE *fileref* | *'filename'*
INCLUDE *singlelinenumber* | *firstline lastline*

The INCLUDE command allows either an entire external file or lines from the log screen to be displayed in the program editor screen. When including lines from the log screen, you can specify particular lines. The included lines are inserted at the bottom of the list of SAS source statement lines or wherever you specify with the A, B, or O line command. When specifying lines on the log screen, you can optionally use a hyphen or a colon between your first and last line specifications.

CMS, OS, and VM/PC: If you are working with an external file, you should use a host-operating system command to assign it a fileref. You can execute it before invoking SAS or from display manager with an X command.

AOS/VS and VMS: You can bring an external file to the program editor screen with the INCLUDE command in one of four ways. The *filename* can be a fully qualified filename, according to the conventions of the operating system you are using, or the name (and type under VMS) of a file in a directory to which you currently have access.

1. Assign a fileref to a file name with a host-level command either before invoking SAS or from display manager with an X command.
2. Assign a fileref to a file name with the display manager ASSIGN command.
3. Specify an actual file name by enclosing it in single quote. In AOS/VS, the file name specified must be in your current working directory; in VMS, it must be specified in your home directory. Under VMS, you must include the file type.
4. Specify an unassigned fileref; the system then assigns that specified fileref to an existing file of the name *fileref*.SAS in your current working directory.

PRIMOS: See the note above for AOS/VS and VMS. You can use all but the first method listed.

VSE: You can place a /FILE statement, an ICCF control language statement, in the ICCF procedure that invokes the SAS System. You cannot use the X command or statement in the ICCF environment. If the file referred to is a sequential file, you must use a /FILE statement in the ICCF procedure. If it is a member of an ICCF library, you are not allowed to use a /FILE statement in the ICCF procedure. Instead, specify the actual ICCF member name.

KEYS

Use the KEYS command to display the function key definition screen. You can view the current settings or alter them and store your new ones. You can scroll forward and backward on the function key definition screen; use the END command or function key to return to the previous screen.

LEFT [*n* | **MAX**]

This command scrolls the screen *n* spaces to the left. By default the screen scrolls half of its width. To override the scroll amount temporarily, enter LEFT and the number of spaces you want the screen to scroll. Enter LEFT MAX to scroll the screen to the left boundary.

LINESIZE *n*

Use the LINESIZE command to alter the line length of data lines on the program editor screen; *n* can be any number between the width of your screen minus 1 and 256. The LINESIZE command allows you to use the INCLUDE command to display files of long data lines in the program editor for editing, for example, saved SAS output files. Note: if you specify a LINESIZE shorter than your current line length, your data lines will be truncated.

AOS/VS, PRIMOS, and VMS: The maximum line length of the program editor is 256 columns.

CMS, OS, VM/PC, and VSE: The maximum line length of the program editor is 80 columns.

LOC *n*

Use the LOC or LOCATE command, followed by some line number *n*, to scroll that line to the top of the display screen.

LOG

The LOG command moves the cursor to the command line of the log screen and makes it the active screen.

AOS/VS, PRIMOS, and VMS only: You can also use the LOG command to return the SAS log to the upper portion of the program editor/log screen, replacing the output screen or help information.

NODMS

AOS/VS, PRIMOS, and VMS only: The NODMS command takes you from display manager to line mode and turns off the SOURCE option. The screen is cleared, and you receive the SAS prompt. The SAS System is then ready to receive your next SAS statement. Leaving display manager does not close the file that is currently open or end your SAS session. When you leave display manager and enter line mode, all of your current WORK data sets are still available to you.

NULLS ON | OFF

When you execute NULLS ON, all data lines are padded with nulls instead of blanks. Turning NULLS ON allows you to use the INSERT editing key to insert characters between text already entered on a line.

If you execute NULLS OFF, the data lines are padded with blanks. To use the INSERT editing key, you must first use the EOF editing key to turn those blanks into nulls.

The effect of the NULLS command on how a file is saved with the SAVE command depends on the host operating system you are using.

AOS/VS, PRIMOS, and VMS: If NULLS are ON when you save the file, the file is saved with no trailing blanks. If NULLS are OFF, trailing blanks are saved.

CMS, OS, VM/PC, and VSE: If you are saving a file in a sequential or partitioned data set with a fixed block record format, the setting of the NULLS command has no effect. If you are saving to a data set with a variable block record format, NULLS ON causes no trailing blanks to be saved, and NULLS OFF causes the trailing blanks to be saved.

NUMBER ON | OFF
NUMS ON | OFF

AOS/VS, PRIMOS, and VMS: Use the NUMS ON command to create line numbers for data lines on your screen. If your screen already contains text, all data are shifted to the right, and the line numbers appear on the left. Execute NUMS OFF to remove line numbers and shift text back to the left. NUMS ON is the default on the display manager program editor screen.

If the data line numbers are displayed, you can type line commands directly over line numbers. If you set NUMS OFF, you can still execute line commands by entering them from the command line or by using a function key. Precede the line command with a colon when executing it on the command line rather than on a line number. For example, type :TS (text split) or :I (insert) on the command line, position the cursor, and then press ENTER. When using a function key, position the cursor, and then press the function key set to execute :TS.

OUTPUT
OUTPUT [ON | OFF]
OUTPUT [TOP]

The OUTPUT command, executed with no option specified, replaces the program editor/log screen with the output screen.

The OUTPUT command followed by ON or OFF specifies whether procedure output is displayed in the output screen immediately while the procedure is executing (ON) or held for later viewing (OFF). If OUTPUT OFF is in effect, specify OUTPUT to view your output. The default is OUTPUT ON.

AOS/VS, PRIMOS, and VMS only: The OUTPUT TOP command replaces the log screen in the upper portion of the program editor/log screen with the output screen.

PRINT [**PROGRAM | RECALL | LOG | OUTPUT**]
[*fileref* | *fileref(membername)*]

CMS, OS, VM/PC and **VSE only:** You can use the PRINT command to print the entire information stream of a display manager screen, not just what is currently displayed.

You can print the stream of information in the program editor by specifying the PROGRAM option; print all statements previously submitted from the program editor with the RECALL option; the stream of information in the log screen with the LOG option; and all procedure output with the OUTPUT option.

Under OS and VSE, the information is sent to the default system printer unless you specify a fileref. Under CMS and VM/PC, assign a fileref to a printer, and then specify it with the PRINT command.

You can also send the contents to an external file by specifying its previously assigned fileref or fileref followed by a member name.

PRINT [**ALL**]

AOS/VS, PRIMOS, and VMS only: With the PRINT command, you can print what is currently showing in the screen on the default system printer. By specifying ALL, you can print the entire contents of the current screen, not just what is visible at the time you enter the PRINT command.

PROGRAM
PGM

The PROGRAM command moves the cursor to the command line of the program editor screen and makes it the active screen.

RCHANGE

Use the RCHANGE or RC command to continue to FIND and CHANGE a string of characters previously specified in a FIND or CHANGE command.

See also the CHANGE, FIND, and RFIND commands.

RECALL

Use the RECALL command to bring back to the program editor screen any lines you have submitted to SAS since you entered display manager. The system adds the recalled lines to the top of the program editor screen in front of any other nonblank lines already entered. After you have used the RECALL command to recall the most recently submitted block of statements, you can enter it again to recall the next most recent block.

RESET

You can use the RESET command on the program editor screen to remove any pending line commands, any conflicting line commands, and the COLS and MASK lines.

RFIND

Use the RFIND or RF command to continue the search for a string of characters previously specified in a FIND or CHANGE command.

See also the FIND, CHANGE, and RCHANGE commands.

RIGHT [*n* | **MAX**]

This command scrolls the screen *n* spaces to the right. By default the screen scrolls half of its width. To override the scroll amount temporarily, enter RIGHT and the number of spaces you want the screen to scroll. Enter RIGHT MAX to scroll the screen to the right boundary.

RULE OFF | ON

AOS/VS, PRIMOS, and VMS only: You can use the RULE ON command to display a ruler on the message line beneath the command line. The ruler marks vertical columns and moves with the data lines as you scroll right and left.

The ruler is temporarily overridden by any message that SAS displays on the message line, but the ruler returns when the message is removed. The default is RULE OFF.

SAVE *fileref* | *fileref(membername)*

CMS, OS, and VM/PC: The SAVE command writes all program lines in the program editor screen into a file that you designate with a fileref (DDname).

See also the NULLS command.

VSE: The SAVE command writes all program lines in the program editor screen into a file that you designate with a fileref (DDname).[5]

SAVE *fileref* | *'filename'*

AOS/VS, PRIMOS, and VMS: The SAVE command writes the entire information stream of the display manager screen from which you execute the SAVE command into a file that you designate with a fileref or an actual file name. You can use a host operating system command to assign a fileref to a sequential file **before** you enter display manager (except under PRIMOS), or you can use the SAS display manager command ASSIGN once you have entered display manager. If you specify an unassigned fileref, the system writes the information stream into a file named *fileref*.SAS in your current working directory. If you specify an actual file name, enclose it in single quotes. The *filename* can be either a fully qualified file name, according to the conventions of the operating system you are using, or just the name (and type under VMS) of a file in a directory to which you currently have access.

See also the NULLS command.

SCREEN OFF | ON

AOS/VS, PRIMOS, and VMS only: You can use the SCREEN command to store the contents of the display manager screen in an external file, **not** a SAS data set or catalog. After you have entered the SCREEN ON command, a file is immediately created with the exact contents of what is displayed on the physical screen. Each time you press ENTER, SUBMIT, or any function key thereafter, another file is created. Each external file containing the contents of a screen is given a file name in the form *SCRNnnnn.SCR*. The first file created is given the name SCRN0001, and each file is given the extension SCR. The screen file is stored in your current working directory.

Each time you begin a SAS session, the system begins numbering screen files with SCRN0001.SCR. If SCRN0001.SCR already exists, the newly created one is written over the existing one.

Enter the SCREEN OFF command when you no longer want the contents of the screen copied to external data files. The default is SCREEN OFF.

SPLIT

You can indicate where you want the screen to split between the log and program editor screens with the SPLIT command. Enter SPLIT on the command line, position the cursor where you want the split to occur, and press ENTER; or position the cursor and press the SPLIT function key. Note: you **must** position the cursor within the boundaries of the screen on which you entered the SPLIT command. Moving the cursor into the area of another screen activates the command line of that screen.

SUBMIT [*'SAS statement;'*]

Use the SUBMIT key or command with no option specified to submit SAS program statements from the data lines of the program editor screen

Optionally, you can submit a SAS program statement directly from the command line with the SUBMIT command. You can type the command, one or more SAS statements, each followed by a semicolon, on the command line and press ENTER, or you can type just the statements with semicolons on the command line and press the SUBMIT function key.

TOP

Use the TOP command to scroll the first line of text to the top of the screen.

VSCROLL HALF | PAGE | *n*

The VSCROLL command sets the vertical scroll amount, the amount the active screen scrolls when you press the FORWARD or BACKWARD scrolling function keys. If you specify PAGE, the scroll amount is the number of data lines currently displayed. If you specify HALF, the scroll amount is one-half of the display area. If you specify *n*, the scroll amount is *n* lines. HALF is the default.

X *hostcommand*
X *'hostcommand'*

You can issue many host commands by entering an X on the command line followed by one or more host commands. Note that in minicomputer environments, the host command or string of commands **must** be enclosed in single quotation marks if it contains special characters; in IBM environments you are not allowed to enclose the host command in single quotes.

See the documentation available for SAS under the operating system you are using for any restrictions on the execution of host operating system commands.

VSE: The X command is not currently supported.

NOTES

1. If you are using one of the terminals listed below in **Table A5.1**, use the following charts to determine the keys that have been assigned special editing functions in SAS full-screen procedures and display manager. See **Figure A5.1** for a description of the functions of these editing keys. If you are using a terminal other than one of those listed below that does not have keys matching the words

or symbols shown in **Figure A5.1**, consult your SAS representative. If you are using an IBM terminal in the 3270-series, you can disregard this section.

Table A5.1 Full-Screen Editing Functions Assigned to Terminal Keys

Display Manager Editing Key	PT45 Key	PST100 Key	PT25 Key
â (INSERT)	ichar or shift/del	insert or backspace	shift/del
a̷ (DELETE)	dchar or backspace	delete or del	backspace
ERASE EOF*	line feed	erase	shift/f8
HOME	home	home	home
REFRESH	control/ clear	pf10	control/erase
NEW LINE	return or enter	return or enter	new line or enter
NEXT FIELD	f13	f2	shift/f5
PRIOR FIELD	f14	f3	shift/f6
ENTER	f3 or f15	f1 or pf13	f3 or shift/f7
MOVE CURSOR UP	↑	↑	↑
MOVE CURSOR DOWN	↓	↓	(not available)
MOVE CURSOR LEFT	←	←	←
MOVE CURSOR RIGHT	→	→	→

Continued on next page

* The PRIME computer does not accept the LINEFEED key. When using any of the terminals above under PRIMOS, use the TAB key to execute the display manager function ERASE EOF.

Table A5.1 *Continued*

Display Manager Editing Key	TEK4105 Key	VT100 Key	DASHER Key
⇬ (INSERT)	backspace	backspace	C1
✗ (DELETE)	rub out	delete	DEL
ERASE EOF*	line feed	line feed	erase EOL
HOME	- (minus sign on numeric keypad)	- (minus sign on numeric keypad)	home
REFRESH	, (on numeric keypad)	, (on numeric keypad)	erase page
NEW LINE	return	return	new line or enter
NEXT FIELD	. (on numeric keypad)	. (on numeric keypad)	C4
PRIOR FIELD	0 (on numeric keypad)	0 (on numeric keypad)	C3
ENTER	enter	enter	CR
MOVE CURSOR UP	F1	↑	↑
MOVE CURSOR DOWN	F2	↓	↓
MOVE CURSOR LEFT	F3	←	←
MOVE CURSOR RIGHT	F4	→	→

2. If you are using one of the terminals listed in **Table A5.1**, you must identify it to the SAS System. If you have already invoked the SAS System, you can use the statement

```
OPTIONS DMS;
```

and then receive a prompt, asking you to identify the devicename. When invoking the SAS System, you can specify the devicename with the FSDEVICE= (FSD=) option. For example

AOS/VS	SAS/FSD=D1
PRIMOS	SAS -FSD=PT25
VMS	SAS/FSD=VT100

Table A5.2 Devices to Be Identified with the FSDEVICE= Option

TERMINALS: Manufacturer	Model No.	Devicename
Data General	6052	DG6052 D1 (alias)
	6053	DG6053 D2 (alias)
	6093	DG6093 D3 (alias)
	D100	D100
	D200	D200
	D210	D210
	D211	D211
	D400	D400
	D410	D410
	D450	D450
	D460	D460
	D470C	D470C
	G300	G300
	G500	G500
Note: devicename DG605X is an alias for all Data General terminals.		
Digital Equipment	VT52	VT52
	VT100	VT100
	VT125	VT125
	VT131	VT131
	VT132	VT132
	VT220	VT220
	VT240	VT240
	VT241	VT241
Prime Computer (PRIME)	PT25	PT25
	PT45	PT45
	PST100	PST100
Tektronix	4105	TEK4105

3. **AOS/VS, PRIMOS, and VMS:** By default the program editor translates all characters into uppercase. If you want to prevent the translation, execute the

CAPS OFF command on the program editor screen either from the command line or with a function key before entering program statements.

CMS, OS, VM/PC, and VSE: By default the program editor does not translate all characters into uppercase. Execute the CAPS ON command if you want text entered or lines altered after you execute the command to be translated into uppercase.

4. **AOS/VS, PRIMOS, and VMS:** A message indicating the use of computer resources is also displayed in the log screen unless you previously specified the NOSTIMER option.

5. **VSE:** If the file referred to is a sequential file, you must use a /FILE statement in the ICCF procedure. If it is a member of an ICCF library, you are not allowed to use a /FILE statement in the ICCF procedure. Instead, specify the actual ICCF member name.

6. **AOS/VS, PRIMOS, and VMS:** The display manager editor breaks information into 80-column lengths; a command that exceeds 80 columns is divided and may not be properly executed.

CMS, OS, VM/PC, and VSE: Any characters typed beyond the 80th column are truncated.

7. **CMS, OS, VM/PC, and VSE:** You can specify only PROGRAM, LOG, and OUTPUT to indicate an active screen.

8. **AOS/VS, PRIMOS, and VMS:** SASEXEC.SAS can be the actual file name and file type. As long as you have access to the directory in which SASEXEC.SAS is stored, you do not have to assign it a fileref. **Do not** give another file the name SASEXEC.

9. **CMS, OS, VM/PC, and VSE:** 80 columns is the maximum line length in the program editor.

AOS/VS, PRIMOS, and VMS: 256 columns is the maximum line length in the program editor.

10. **AOS/VS, PRIMOS, and VMS:** The length of the data line on the log screen is sensitive to the value of the LINESIZE= option in the OPTIONS statement. The maximum line length on the log screen is 256 columns.

CMS, OS, VM/PC, and VSE: The length of the data line on the log screen is sensitive to the value of the TLS= option in the OPTIONS statement. The maximum line length on the log screen is 132 columns.

11. **AOS/VS, PRIMOS, and VMS:** The maximum line length on the output screen is 256 columns.

CMS, OS, VM/PC, and VSE: The maximum line length on the output screen is 132 columns.

Index

A

B

D

G

H

I

J

K

L

M

N

O

P

S

T

U

SAS® User's Guide: Statistics, Version 5 Edition

Stephenie P. Joyner edited the *SAS® User's Guide: Statistics, Version 5 Edition.*

Writers	Regina Luginbuhl Mary Ann Kaufman Larry Crum
Contributing Editors	John P. Sall Alice T. Allen

Editorial Services Copyeditors, proofreaders, and coders provided editorial support under the direction of **Judith K. Whatley**.

Copyeditors	David D. Baggett Betty Fried
Proofreaders	Gigi Hassan James K. Hart Frances A. Kienzle
Manuals Composition Coders	Gail C. Freeman Blanche Weatherspoon Amy G. Power
Administrative Services	Barbara D. Johnson Toni P. Sherrill June F. Zglinski

Graphic Arts provided the text composition and production under the direction of **Carol M. Thompson**.

Programmers	Craig R. Sampson Pamela A. Troutman
Compositors	Arlene B. Drezek Sarah M. Richardson
Artist	Michael J. Pezzoni

Your Turn

If you have comments about SAS software or the *SAS User's Guide: Statistics, Version 5 Edition*, please let us know by writing your ideas in the space below. If you include your name and address, we will reply to you.

Please return this sheet to the Publications Division, SAS Institute Inc., SAS Circle, Box 8000, Cary, NC 27511-8000.